POSTCARDS FROM

@Frommer's®

California 2002

D1244003

A surfer braves the waves at Huntington Beach, site of the U.S. Open of Surfing every August. See chapter 14. © Sunstar/Instock

Few sights are more breathtaking than a view of San Francisco from the Golden Gate Bridge, which you can cross by foot. See chapter 4. © Jose Fuste Raga/The Stock Market

◄ *This view from Alamo Square offers a fantastic juxtaposition of San Francisco architecture—sharp-edged Financial District skyscrapers behind a row of Victorian "Painted Ladies." See chapter 4.* © Alan Kearney/Viesti Collection, Inc.

Learn about the wonderful world of winemaking in Napa Valley. See chapter 6.
© Catherine Karnow Photography

Emerald Bay is one of Lake Tahoe's prettiest little inlets. See chapter 8.
© Robert Holmes Photography

The Merced River is just one of many of the awe-inspiring treasures you'll find in Yosemite National Park. See chapter 9. © Christopher Talbot Frank Photography

You can gape at the majestic sequoias, the world's largest trees, in Mariposa Grove at Yosemite National Park. See chapter 9. © Jose Fuste Raga/The Stock Market

A view of Big Sur at dusk, one of the most romantic and relaxing places on earth. See chapter 11. © David D. Keaton/The Stock Market

Palm trees mix with skyscrapers in a view from the steps of the Central Library in downtown Los Angeles. See chapter 13. © Richard Cummins Photography

Skateboarders, surfers, cyclists, and roller skaters are all in on the action at Venice Beach. See chapter 13. © Stephen Wilkes/The Image Bank

Glorious or grotesque? Form your own opinions about the unique Joshua trees at Joshua Tree National Park, a popular place for climbing, biking, and hiking. See chapter 15.
© Photophile

Spectacular sand dunes in the Mojave National Preserve are famous for "booming." See chapter 15 for details. © Christopher Talbot Frank Photography

A New Star-Rating System & Other Exciting News from Frommer's!

In our continuing effort to publish the savviest, most up-to-date, and most appealing travel guides available, we've added some great new features.

Frommer's guides now include a new **star-rating system.** Every hotel, restaurant, and attraction is rated from 0 to 3 stars to help you set priorities and organize your time.

We've also added **seven brand-new features** that point you to the great deals, in-the-know advice, and unique experiences that separate travelers from tourists. Throughout the guide look for:

Finds	Special finds—those places only insiders know about
Fun Fact	Fun facts—details that make travelers more informed and their trips more fun
Kids	Best bets for kids—advice for the whole family
Moments	Special moments—those experiences that memories are made of
Overrated	Places or experiences not worth your time or money
Tips	Insider tips—some great ways to save time and money
Value	Great values—where to get the best deals

We've also added a **"What's New"** section in every guide—a timely crash course in what's hot and what's not in every destination we cover.

Other Great Guides for Your Trip:

Frommer's Great Outdoor Guide to Northern California

Frommer's Los Angeles

Frommer's Portable Disneyland

Frommer's San Diego

Frommer's San Francisco

Frommer's Yosemite & Sequoia/Kings Canyon National Parks

California

12th Edition

by Erika Lenkert, Mary Anne Moore, Matthew R. Poole & Stephanie Avnet Yates

Here's what the critics say about Frommer's:

"Amazingly easy to use. Very portable, very complete."

—*Booklist*

"The only mainstream guide to list specific prices. The Walter Cronkite of guidebooks—with all that implies."

—*Travel & Leisure*

"Complete, concise, and filled with useful information."

—*New York Daily News*

"Hotel information is close to encyclopedic."

—*Des Moines Sunday Register*

Hungry Minds™

Best-Selling Books • Digital Downloads • e-Books • Answer Networks
e-Newsletters • Branded Web Sites • e-Learning

New York, NY • Cleveland, OH • Indianapolis, IN

About the Authors

Native San Franciscan **Erika Lenkert** spent the past four years seeking adventure, great food, and great accommodations throughout California while celebrating a delightfully wild three-year stint in Hollywood. She has a restaurant column in *San Francisco* magazine and hopes to find time to continue contributing to *Los Angeles, InStyle, Travel & Leisure,* and *Bon Appétit.*

Mary Anne Moore is co-author of the *Unofficial Guide to Bed & Breakfasts in California* and has contributed to numerous other travel books. In her non-writing life, Mary Anne is a legislative consultant in the California State Capitol, spending her off hours traveling the globe in search of places even more wonderful than California. So far she hasn't found any.

Combining the only three things he's good at—eating, sleeping, and criticizing— **Matthew R. Poole** has written and co-authored more than 20 travel guides to California and Hawaii, including *Frommer's San Francisco* and *Frommer's Portable California Wine Country.* A native Californian, he currently lives in San Francisco.

A native of Los Angeles and an avid traveler, antiques hound, and pop-history enthusiast, **Stephanie Avnet Yates** believes that California is best seen from behind the wheel of a little red convertible. Stephanie has authored *Frommer's Los Angeles, Frommer's San Diego,* and *Frommer's Wonderful Weekends from Los Angeles,* in addition to contributing to several other regional guidebooks and websites.

Published by:

Hungry Minds, Inc.

909 Third Ave.
New York, NY 10022

ISBN 0-7645-8287-9
ISSN 1044-2146

Editor: Myka Carroll
Production Editor: Jennifer Connolly
Photo Editor: Richard Fox
Cartographer: John Decamillis
Production by Hungry Minds Indianapolis Production Services
Front cover photo: Cathedral Rocks, Yosemite National Park

Special Sales

For general information on Hungry Minds' products and services please contact our Customer Care department; within the U.S. at 800-762-2974, outside the U.S. at 317-572-3993 or fax 317-572-4002. For sales inquiries and reseller information, including discounts, bulk sales, customized editions, and premium sales, please contact our Customer Care department at 800-434-3422.

Manufactured in the United States of America

5 4 3 2 1

Contents

5   The San Francisco Bay Area   133

6   The Wine Country   155

7   The Northern Coast   193

8   The Far North: Lake Tahoe, the Shasta Cascades & Lassen Volcanic National Park   233

List of Maps

An Invitation to the Reader

In researching this book, we discovered many wonderful places—hotels, restaurants, shops, and more. We're sure you'll find others. Please tell us about them, so we can share the information with your fellow travelers in upcoming editions. If you were disappointed with a recommendation, we'd love to know that, too. Please write to:

Frommer's California, 12th Edition
Hungry Minds, Inc. • 909 Third Avenue • New York, NY 10022

An Additional Note

Please be advised that travel information is subject to change at any time—and this is especially true of prices. We therefore suggest that you write or call ahead for confirmation when making your travel plans. The authors, editors, and publisher cannot be held responsible for the experiences of readers while traveling. Your safety is important to us, however, so we encourage you to stay alert and be aware of your surroundings. Keep a close eye on cameras, purses, and wallets, all favorite targets of thieves and pickpockets.

New! Frommer's Star Ratings & Icons

Every hotel, restaurant, and attraction listing in this guide has been ranked for quality, value, service, amenities, and special features using a star-rating scale. In country, state, and regional guides, we also rate towns and regions to help you narrow down your choices and budget your time accordingly. Hotels and restaurants in the Very Expensive and Expensive categories are rated on a scale of one (highly recommended) to three stars (exceptional). Those in the Moderate and Inexpensive categories rate from zero (recommended) to two stars (very highly recommended). Attractions, towns, and regions are rated according to the following scale: zero stars (recommended), one star (highly recommended), two stars (very highly recommended), and three stars (must-see).

In addition to the rating system, we also use seven icons to highlight insider information, useful tips, special bargains, hidden gems, memorable experiences, kid-friendly venues, places to avoid, and other useful information:

| Finds | Fun Fact | Kids | Moments | Overrated | Tips | Value |

The following abbreviations are used for credit cards:

AE American Express	DISC Discover	V Visa
DC Diners Club	MC MasterCard	

FROMMERS.COM

Now that you have the guidebook to a great trip, visit our website at **www.frommers.com** for travel information on nearly 2,000 destinations. With features updated regularly, we give you instant access to the most current trip-planning information available. At Frommers.com, you'll also find the best prices on airfares, accommodations, and car rentals—and you can even book travel online through our travel booking partners. At Frommers.com you'll also find the following:

- Daily Newsletter highlighting the best travel deals
- Hot Spot of the Month/Vacation Sweepstakes & Travel Photo Contest
- More than 200 Travel Message Boards
- Outspoken Newsletters and Feature Articles on travel bargains, vacation ideas, tips & resources, and more!

What's New in California

From sumptuously renovated hotels in San Francisco to the recent opening of Disneyland's California Adventure in Anaheim, California will leave you spoilt for choice with new accommodation, dining, and sightseeing options. Here are the highlights of what you can look forward to during your trip.

SAN FRANCISCO Accommodations San Francisco's never had enough rooms to accommodate its annual visitors, but new hotel openings in recent years have proven there's an effort underway. After a $10 million renovation, **Campton Place Hotel,** 340 Stockton St. (© 800/235-4300), actually has fewer rooms, but man oh man are they posh. In July 2001, Ian Schrager debuted his revamp of historic **Clift Hotel,** 495 Geary St. (© 800/652-5438). **The Juliana Hotel,** 590 Bush St. (© 800/328-3880) barely had time to get scuffed after its 1996 overhaul before its latest renovation, which closed the hotel until mid-2001 and produced an even better boutique hotel. Already bargain-beautiful, **The Clarion Bedford Hotel,** 761 Post St. (© 800/252-7466 or 415/673-6040) spruced up half its rooms in 2001.

Other hotels that recently received facelifts include the fabulous **Fairmont Hotel & Tower,** 950 Mason St. (© 800/527-4727 or 415/772-5000), which gussied up to the tune of $85 million; and chic home-away-from-home **The Huntington Hotel,** 1075 California St. (© 800/227-4683 or 415/474-5400), which now beckons with a full spa. **Hotel Del Sol,** 3100 Webster St. (© 877/433-5765 or 415/921-5520), is one of the Marina's newer and cheerier motels. **The Hotel Majestic,** 1500 Sutter St. (© 800/869-8966 or 415/441-1100) revamped its tranquil restaurant, Perlot. For complete hotel listings, see "Accommodations" in chapter 4.

Dining Food is still the focus in the city surrounded on all sides by edible wonders from the land, sea, and vineyards. New additions include Vietnamese oasis **Ana Mandara,** 891 Beach St. (© 415/771-6800), which gives even locals a reason to head to the Fisherman's Wharf area. **Ella's,** 500 Presidio Ave. (© 415/441-5669), encourages breakfast lovers to venture lower Pacific Heights. **Bacar,** 448 Brannan St. (© 415/904-4100), the hottest new restaurant of 2001, pours on the charm with industrial-chic surroundings and the ultimate wine-drinking experience. For complete details, see "Dining" in chapter 4.

After Dark Despite all the changes in San Francisco, few of them have to do with nightlife beyond the restaurant scene. One especially noteworthy exception is **The Top of the Mark** in the Mark Hopkins Intercontinental Hotel, 1 Nob Hill (© 800/327-0200 or 415/392-3434). The famous cocktail lounge underwent renovation and added dinner service a few days per week. For details, see "San Francisco After Dark" in chapter 4.

THE FAR NORTH   After 10 years of planning, the community of **South Lake Tahoe** is shedding its decades-long accumulation of ugly, haphazard strip mall properties and replacing them with open spaces and environmentally friendly, attractive new accommodations. The area's $1 billion redevelopment is well underway with the centerpiece state-of-the-art ski gondola completed and construction in progress on a 91,000 square foot convention center, 1000 additional hotel rooms, a theater complex, and, of course, shopping areas. A 2-acre replica of Lake Tahoe will serve as an environmental learning center and outdoor recreation center. Completion of the project is slated for 2003. See "Lake Tahoe" in chapter 8 for further details.

THE HIGH SIERRA   Always in the shadow of their glamorous neighbor, Yosemite, California's lesser known gems, **Sequoia and Kings Canyon National Parks**, remain relatively undiscovered, at least in comparison to the throngs next door. Long the playground of no-nonsense hikers and backpackers, the parks' accommodations have not attracted the kind of vacationer whose idea of a good time may be to admire Mother Nature awhile and then retire to a good dining room and some fine, silky sheets. Enter the new **Shoshone Inn,** 40387 Sierra Drive (© **559/561-8000**), right smack at the doorstep of Sequoia in the pretty town of Three Rivers. On the banks of the Kaweah River, the inn has a 3-foot-thick white mission-style walls, gorgeous tiles and furnishings, and sits on 14 lush acres. The inn's two new restaurants, the Menachi Café, and Le Provencal, are open for business and 60 lodging units will be finished next year. See "En Route to Sequoia & Kings Canyon" in chapter 9 for more details.

SACRAMENTO, THE GOLD COUNTRY & THE CENTRAL VALLEY Accommodations   It's hard to feel good about yourself when your closest sister-city is the much adored and pampered San Francisco, but Sacramento tries. One of the capital city's chief attributes (besides its trees, its riverside bike trail, and the Sacramento Kings) is a long-time commitment to, and heavy investment in, good public art. The new downtown, 504-room **Grand Sacramento Hotel,** 1230 J St. (© **800/325-3535**), adjacent to the Sacramento Convention Center, opened its doors in 2001 in a building that encompasses an historic public market building designed by Julia Morgan of Hearst Castle fame. The design of the hotel is intended to remain true to the theme and spirit of Morgan's original design. The hotel is also the site of major new artworks by four internationally renowned contemporary artists. Boasting two new restaurants, an appealing street-level bar, and a 10,000 square foot ballroom, the new hotel is expected to be a hot commodity in River City, as the locals call it. For details, see chapter 10, "Sacramento: Where to Stay."

Dining   Nevada City is everybody's favorite gold rush town because it's so darned cute. Blessed with a super-abundance of first-rate bed-and-breakfast establishments, the town is now blessed with two new first-rate restaurants as well. **Citronée,** 320 Broad St. (© **530/265-5697**), touted by no less than the *New York Times,* serves all the delicious things you'd expect to find in a San Francisco restaurant, but at half the price, and you can find a place to park your car, too. Try a Maui onion stuffed with sautéed wild mushrooms on a bed of polenta. There's a five-course surprise menu each night, and *Wine Spectator* magazine bestowed the restaurant with an award of excellence.

All of us who remember the Nevada City classic restaurant called Potager de Selaya, and who went into mourning when it closed, were overjoyed to find that Peter Selaya has a new restaurant, the **New Moon,** 203 York Street (© 530/265-6399). Using things that Californians love, like free-range creatures, house-made pastas using organic flours and grains, and local organic vegetables, the guy's packing them in again. Who could resist line-caught fresh salmon with freshly plucked vegetables, and perhaps a fresh strawberry Napolean for dessert, madame? You betcha. For details, see chapter 10, "The Gold Country: Where to Dine."

LOS ANGELES   For years they promised it, and finally they delivered. While L.A.'s "subway" will never be like New York's or San Francisco's, the **Metro Red Line** from downtown now carries riders to Hollywood Boulevard destinations and beyond. Take the train into the Valley, where the Universal City station is just a shuttle-ride away from Universal Studios Hollywood—no traffic, no parking, no problem! For more information, call the **Metropolitan Transit Authority** (© 213/626-4455; www.mta.net).

Hollywood Boulevard welcomes the long-awaited **Hollywood & Vine** entertainment complex, the center-piece of the once-seedy (OK, still a little seedy) historic boulevard's ongoing rejuvenation. Named for the prime street corner it dominates, the project includes shops and restaurants, a luxurious new Radisson high-rise hotel, and a grand theater designed to be the permanent home of the Academy Awards Oscar presentation gala each year. See "Neighborhoods in Brief" in chapter 13 for details.

SIDE TRIPS FROM LOS ANGELES
The buzz in Southern California this year is all about Disney's new theme park, **California Adventure** (© 714/781-4565), a spirited tribute to the Golden State. Surrounding Anaheim has joined in with freeway improvements and newly landscaped boulevards to complement the innovative new park and Disney's other additions: the lavish Grand Californian Hotel, and lively Downtown Disney entertainment district. See "Disneyland & Other Anaheim-Area Attractions" in chapter 14 for full details.

THE SOUTHERN CALIFORNIA DESERT   Accommodations Interest in the Golden Age of Palm Springs continues to rise, as fans of mid-century modern design welcome a flock of stylish new boutique hotels that showcase the architecture, furnishings, and lifestyle of the 1940s to 1960s. The frontrunner is **Ballantines Original,** 1420 N. Indian Cyn. Dr., Palm Springs (© 800/780-3464), who were already renovating their second fabulous property, **Ballantine's Movie Colony,** 726 N. Indian Cyn. Dr. (same phone number), before anyone else got started. But it wasn't long before the ultra-cool **Orbit In,** 562 W. Arenas Rd. (© 877-99-ORBIT), got into the act in the prime "Tennis Club" part of town. Poolside twilight cocktails are *de rigueur* at all three! See "The Palm Springs Desert Resorts" in chapter 15 for complete listings.

Sightseeing   Avid desert rats—and students of Native American lore—thrilled in 2001 to the reopening of mystical and picturesque **Tahquitz Canyon** (© 760/416-7044) in Palm Springs. Closed for 30 years to prevent vandalism and accidents, the Cahuilla sacred place now features a state-of-the-art visitor center and ranger-led hikes into the oft-admired and sometimes-feared canyon (Indian legend maintains evil spirits dwell in Tahquitz). See "The Palm Springs Desert Resorts" in chapter 15 for complete information.

SAN DIEGO & ENVIRONS No one visits San Diego without experiencing one of the city's fantastic family-attraction animal parks, and each has something new to crow about. At Balboa Park's **San Diego Zoo,** 2920 Zoo Dr. (© **619/234-3153;** www. sandiegozoo.org), a state-of-the-art naturalistic forest habitat houses douc langurs, one of the rarest monkeys in the world. The colorful Southeast Asian primate is seriously endangered; the Zoo's douc langurs are the only ones in the United States.

At the **San Diego Wild Animal Park,** 15500 San Pasqual Valley Rd., Escondido (© **760/747-8702;** www. wildanimalpark.org), they've been rescuing and breeding endangered California condors for years. Now, for the first time, visitors can see these eerily impressive birds along the mountain trails of **Condor Ridge,** a habitat created for some of California's critically endangered species; along with condors, you'll see thick-billed parrots, black-footed ferrets, hawks, owls, and bighorn sheep.

Meanwhile, a new adventure awaits at **SeaWorld,** 500 Sea World Dr. (© **619/226-3901;** www.seaworld. com), which recently welcomed *Pirates,* a wacky "4-D" movie and attraction written by *Monty Python*'s Eric Idle. Prepare for some unexpected interactive effects as you join Idle and funnyman Leslie Nielsen as hapless, pratfall-prone pirates. For details about all three parks, see "The Main Attractions: The Zoo, SeaWorld & the Wild Animal Park" in chapter 16.

1

The Best of California

by Erika Lenkert, Mary Anne Moore,
Matthew R. Poole & Stephanie Avnet Yates

In my early 20s, I took the requisite college student's pilgrimage to Europe, exploring its finer train stations and sleeping on the premier park benches from London to Istanbul. I was relatively anonymous—just another tanned and skinny, blond and blue-eyed American lugging around 60 pounds of backpack. That is, until I crossed over into the former Eastern Bloc.

The reaction was dramatic, almost palpable. Like Moses parting the sea, I would wander through the crowded streets of Prague and citizens would stop, stare, and sidestep as if a scarlet *A* was emblazoned across my chest. It wasn't until a man who spoke faltering English finally approached me that I discovered the reason for my newfound celebrity status.

"Eh, you. Where you from? No, no. Let me guess." He steps back, gives a cursory examination followed by pregnant pause. "Ah. I've got it! California! You're from California, no?" A gleam in his eyes as I tell him that, yes, he's quite correct. "Wonderful! Wonderful!" A dozen or so pilsners later with my loquacious new friend and it all becomes clear to me: To him, I truly am a celebrity—a rich, convertible-driving surfer who spends most his days lazing on the beach, fending off hordes of buxom blondes while I argue with my agent via my portable phone. The myth is complete. I *am* the Beach Boys. I *am* *Baywatch*. Status by association. The tentacles of Hollywood have done what no NATO pact could achieve—they've leapfrogged the staid issues of capitalism versus communism by offering a far more potent narcotic: the alluring mystique of sun-drenched California, of movie stars strolling down Sunset Boulevard, of beautiful women in tight shorts and bikini tops roller-skating along Venice Beach. In short, they've bought what we're selling.

Of course, the allure is understandable. It really is warm and sunny most days of the year, movie stars actually do abound in Los Angeles, and you can't swing a cat by its tail without hitting a roller-blading babe in Venice Beach. This part of the California mystique—however exaggerated it may be—truly does exist, and it's not hard to find.

But there's more—a lot more—to California that isn't scripted, sanitized, and squeezed through a cathode-ray tube to the world's millions of mesmerized masses. Beyond the glitter and glamour of Hollywood is an incredibly diverse state that, if it ever seceded from the Union, would be one of the most productive and powerful nations in the world. We've got it all: misty redwood forests, an incredibly verdant Central Valley teeming with agriculture, the mighty Sierra Nevada Mountain Range, eerily fascinating deserts, a host of world-renowned cities, and, of course, hundreds of miles of stunning coastline.

And despite the endemic crime, pollution, traffic, and bowel-shaking earthquakes that California is famous for, we're still the golden child of the United States, America's spoiled rich kid whom everyone else either loves or loathes.

(Neighboring Oregon, for example, sells lots of license-plate rims that proudly state, "I hate California.") But, truth be told, we really don't care what anyone thinks of us. Californians *know* they live in one of the most diverse and interesting places in the world, and we're proud of the state we call home.

Granted, there's no guarantee that you'll bump into Arnold Schwarzenegger or learn how to surf, but if you have a little time, a little money, and—most importantly—an adventurous spirit, then Erika, Stephanie, Mary Anne, and I will help guide you through one of the most fulfilling vacations of your life. The four of us travel the world for a living, but we *choose* to live in California, simply because there's no other place on earth that has so much to offer.

—*Matthew R. Poole*

1 The Best of Natural California

- **Año Nuevo State Reserve:** Nature enthusiasts come from all over the world to this spot 22 miles north of Santa Cruz to view the elephant seal colony. Pups are born from December through March, and molting follows between April and August. You can also spot sea lions in spring and summer, whales in winter and spring, plus more than 250 bird species. See chapter 5.

- **Point Reyes National Seashore:** This extraordinarily scenic stretch of coast and wetlands is one of the best bird-watching spots in California for shorebirds, songbirds, and waterfowl, as well as osprey and red-shouldered hawks. There's a rainbow-hued wildflower garden, too, and you might catch a glimpse of a whale from the Point Reyes Lighthouse. See chapter 7.

- **Redwood National & State Parks:** A wildlife enthusiast's dream. More than 300 bird species and 100 mammals can be seen, many of them year-round. Also watch (or watch out!) for black bears in summer. See chapter 7.

- **Mt. Shasta:** One of the most spectacular sights in all of Northern California is the mighty volcano Mt. Shasta, a solitary tower of rock and snow rising thousands of feet above the valley floor. And if you're in good shape, it makes for an exhilarating climb as well. See chapter 8.

- **Lake Tahoe:** One of the world's most magnificent bodies of fresh water, sparkling Lake Tahoe is famous for its pure, azure water and incredible volume. In fact, it's so deep that the water it contains—close to 40 trillion gallons—could cover the entire state of California to a depth of $14\frac{1}{2}$ inches. See chapter 8.

- **Yosemite National Park:** You're in for the ultimate treat at Yosemite. Nothing in the state—maybe even the world—compares to this vast wilderness playground and its miles of rivers, lakes, peaks, and valleys. With 3 out of 10 of the world's tallest waterfalls, the largest single granite monolith in the world, and some of the world's largest trees, Yosemite is one of the most fantastic natural places on the planet. You'll have a sweeping 180° view of it all from high atop Glacier Point, where a majestic High Sierra panorama unfolds at 3,200 feet. See chapter 9.

- **Elkhorn Slough** (Moss Landing): It's as close as you'll ever get to feeling like you're on a *National Geographic* adventure. Captain Gideon's 2-hour cruise takes you into the heart of the northern California shore's wildlife reserve, where you'll encounter dozens of otters and harbor seals and hundreds of bird species. See chapter 11.

- **The Big Sur Coast:** Rock-strewn beaches, towering cliffs, and redwood forests combine to form what may be the world's most dramatic coastal panorama. Our favorite vantage point for taking it all in is Garrapata State Park, a 2,879-acre preserve that lords over 4 spectacular miles of coastline. See chapter 11.

- **Point Lobos State Reserve:** Take Calif. 1 about 4 miles south of Carmel to view harbor seals, sea lions, and sea otters at play. From December to May, gray whales pass by on their migration south. The area is filled with nature walks. See chapter 11.

- **Cachuma Lake:** Situated on mountainous and scenic Calif. 154, halfway between Solvang and Santa Barbara, is this stunning winter home to dozens of American bald eagles. Loons, white pelicans, and Canadian geese are some of the other migratory birds that call this glassy lake home part of the year. See chapter 12.

- **Channel Islands National Park:** This is California in its most natural state. Paddle a kayak into sea caves; camp among indigenous island fox and seabirds; and swim, snorkel, or scuba dive tide pools and kelp forests teeming with wildlife. The channel waters are prime for whale-watching, and winter brings elephant seal mating season, when you'll see them and their sea lion cousins sunbathing on cove beaches. See chapter 12.

- **Joshua Tree National Park:** You'll find awesome rock formations, groves of flowering cacti and stately Joshua trees, ancient Native American petroglyphs, and shifting sand dunes in this desert wonderland—and a brilliant night sky, if you choose to camp here. See chapter 15.

- **Death Valley National Park:** Its inhospitable climate makes it the state's most unlikely tourist attraction—but the same conditions that thwarted settlers create some of the most dramatic landscapes you'll ever see. Mesmerizing rock formations, ever-changing dry lake beds, and often stifling heat provide the setting for relics of hardy 19th-century borax miners and (fool-) hardy dwellers from the 1930s. See chapter 15.

- **Torrey Pines State Reserve:** Poised on a majestic cliff overlooking the Pacific Ocean, this reserve is home to the rare Torrey pine. Exhibits on the local ecology are housed in the visitor center, and numerous hiking trails fan out throughout the park. See chapter 16.

- **Anza-Borrego Desert State Park:** The largest state park in the lower 48 states attracts the most visitors during the spring wildflower season, when a kaleidoscopic carpet blankets the desert floor. Others come year-round to hike the more than 100 miles of designated trails. See chapter 16.

2 The Best Beaches

- **Sonoma Coast State Beaches:** Stretching about 10 miles from Bodega Bay to Jenner, these beaches attract more than 300 species of birds. From December through September, look for osprey. Seal pups can be spotted from March through June, and the gray whale from December through April. See chapter 7.

- **Drake's Beach:** A massive stretch of white sand at Point Reyes National Seashore, west of Inverness. Winds and choppy seas make it rough for swimmers, but sun worshippers can have their Marin County tan for the day. If the rangers say it's all right, beach driftwood can make a romantic campfire in the early evening. See chapter 7.

- **Santa Cruz Beaches:** Northern California's answer to the south state's fun-in-the-sun beach scene, Santa Cruz has 29 miles of beaches varied enough to please all comers—surfers, swimmers, fishers, sailboarders, the sand pail and shovel set, and the bikini and biceps crowd. For starters, just walk down the steps from the famous Boardwalk to the mile-long, white sand Main Beach, complete with summer lifeguards and golden oldie tunes drifting over the sand from the Boardwalk's live concerts. See chapter 11.

- **Sand Dollar Beach:** The best Big Sur beach lies beyond Pacific Valley—ideal for swimming and surfing, with a panoramic view of Cone Peak, one of the coast's highest mountains. See chapter 11.

- **Pfeiffer Beach:** This is one of Big Sur's best-kept secrets. It can be accessed via an unmarked paved road on the right-hand side of Calif. 1, 1 mile south of Pfeiffer State Park. There are no signs, so you'll have to do some sleuthing, but once you've parked behind the trail of cars on the side of the road and made it to the beach, you'll know why locals want to keep this spot all to themselves. See chapter 11.

- **Santa Barbara's East Beach:** This wide swath of clean white sand hosts beach umbrellas, sandcastle builders, and spirited volleyball games. A grassy, parklike median keeps the happy beachgoers insulated from busy Cabrillo Boulevard. On Sundays, local artists display their wares beneath the elegant palm trees. See chapter 12.

- **Malibu's Legendary Beaches:** Zuma and Surfrider Beaches served as inspiration for the 1960s surf music that embodies the Southern California beach experience. Surfrider, just up from Malibu Pier, is home to L.A.'s best waves. Zuma is loaded with amenities, including snack bars, restrooms, and jungle gyms. In addition to some of the state's best sunbathing, you can walk in front of the Malibu Colony, a star-studded enclave of multimillion-dollar homes set on this seductively curvaceous stretch of coast. See chapter 13.

- **Hermosa City Beach:** This is one of L.A.'s top beaches for family outings. It's also popular with the volleyball set. It offers wide sands, a paved boardwalk ("The Strand") that's great for strolling and biking, and has loads of amenities—including plenty of parking. See chapter 13.

- **La Jolla's Beaches:** Roughly translated, *La Jolla* means "the jewel," and the beaches of La Jolla's cliff-lined coast truly are gems. Each has a distinct personality: Surfers love Windansea's waves; Torrey Pines and La Jolla Shores are popular for swimming and sunbathing; and Black's Beach is San Diego's unofficial (and illegal) nude beach. See chapter 16.

- **Coronado Beach:** On the west side of Coronado extending to the Hotel del Coronado, this beautiful beach is uncrowded and great for watching the sunset. Marilyn Monroe romped in the surf here during the filming of *Some Like It Hot.* See chapter 16.

3 The Best Golf Courses

- **Pebble Beach Golf Links:** The famous 17-Mile Drive is the site of 10 national championships and the winter telecast of the celebrity-laden AT&T Pebble Beach National Pro-Am. The raging nearby Pacific and a scenic backdrop of the Del Monte Forest justify astronomical greens fees. See chapter 11.
- **Spyglass Hill** (Pebble Beach): Five holes border the ocean, and the rest extend deep within Del Monte Forest. The holes here have been called "long and unforgiving" by golf magazines. Its slope rating of 143 makes it one of the toughest courses in California. See chapter 11.
- **Poppy Hills** (Pebble Beach): *Golf Digest* has called this Robert Trent Jones, Jr.–designed course "one of the world's top 20 courses." Also used for AT&T festivities, it cuts right through the pines of Del Monte Forest. One golf pro said the course is "long and tough on short hitters." It's maintained in state-of-the-art condition and, unlike some of its competitors, is rarely overcrowded. See chapter 11.
- **The Links at Spanish Bay:** Perched along the 17-Mile Drive, the Links were also designed by Robert Trent Jones, Jr., with a little help from Tom Watson and former USGA president Frank Tatum. Their aim was to simulate the experience of playing golf on true Scottish links. Its fescue grasses and natural fairways lead to rolls and unexpected bounces for your ball. Holes 14 through 18—taking you to the sea and back again through high dunes— call for some trick shot making, but make the whole experience worthwhile. See chapter 11.
- **Westin Mission Hills Resort, Pete Dye Course** (Rancho Mirage): Since 1987, when course-architect Pete Dye sculpted this links-style, par-70 challenger, players have wrangled with the pot bunkers, hidden pin placements, and carries over water that are his classic trademarks. Rolling fairways and railroad ties also characterize Dye's 6,706-yard classic. The course takes full scenic advantage of the lavender hills all around. See chapter 15.
- **PGA West TPC Stadium Course** (La Quinta): The par-3 17th hole has a picturesque island green where Lee Trevino made Skins Game history with a spectacular hole-in-one. The rest of Pete Dye's 7,261-yard design is flat with huge bunkers, lots of water, and severe mounding throughout. The PGA West is part of the La Quinta Resort & Club, which received *Golf* magazine's 1994 Gold Medal Award for the total golf-resort experience. See chapter 15.
- **Torrey Pines Golf Course** (La Jolla): Two gorgeous 18-hole championship courses overlook the ocean and provide players with plenty of challenge. In February, the Buick Invitational Tournament is held here; the rest of the year, these popular municipal courses are open to everybody. See chapter 16.
- **Coronado Municipal Golf Course (San Diego):** This 18-hole, par-72 municipal course overlooking Glorietta Bay is located to the left of the Coronado Bay Bridge. It's the first thing you see when you arrive in Coronado—a fabulous welcome for duffers. See chapter 16.

4 The Best Offbeat Travel Experiences

- **Hot-Air Ballooning over Napa Valley:** It's all the rage, and for good reason: Northern California's temperate weather allows for ballooning year-round, and the valley is simply beautiful from up high. Flights are best right after sunrise, when the air is calm and cool. Hotels throughout the valley can arrange a trip aloft for you, or you can book one directly with **Bonaventura Balloon Company** (*©* **800/FLY-NAPA**). Sometimes there's a catered champagne brunch at the end of the adventure. See chapter 6.

- **Taking a Mud Bath in Calistoga:** In this town's famous volcanic-ash mud—mixed with mineral water—you can get buck naked and covered in gooey mud. At a dozen or so places you can immerse yourself in the mud, followed by a mineral-water shower and a whirlpool bath, and then a steam bath. It's perhaps the most relaxing experience in California. See chapter 6.

- **Rafting Scenic Northern California Rivers:** You can white-water raft through thrilling cascades of racing water or float peacefully through tranquil vistas of blue skies, deep forests, and abundant wildlife. California rivers are rated—from easy to unrunnable—to make sure you know what you are getting into. The fastest flows are in the spring, naturally. Depending on the river and the time of year, some trips are okay for children over 6. Guided tours are safest. **Ahwahnee Whitewater** (*©* **800/ 359-9790**) offers a variety of river trips around the Yosemite area, from a half day to overnighters, from April through September. See chapter 9.

- **Panning for Gold in the Gold Country:** In the southern Gold Country, you can dig into living history and pan for gold. Several companies, including **Gold Prospecting Adventures** (*©* **800/ 596-0009** or 209/984-4653) in Jamestown, offer dredging lessons and gold-panning tours. You'll quickly learn that this adventure is back-breaking labor. But who knows? You might get lucky and launch a new gold rush. See chapter 10.

- **Discovering Downtown L.A.'s Public Art:** The wealth of public art on display in downtown Los Angeles is one of the city's best-kept secrets. Some works make political or social commentary (the black experience as represented by the life of former slave Biddy Mason in a multimedia exhibit between Broadway and Spring Streets, just south of Third Street). Others are abstract and open to a variety of interpretations. Pershing Square, a formerly untended eyesore bounded by Fifth, Sixth, Olive, and Hill Streets, has been reincarnated as a modern sculpture garden. See chapter 13.

- **Riding the Amtrak Rails Along the Southern California Coast:** Relive the golden age of train travel and see the natural beauty of California, avoiding the crowded highways at the same time. Spanish-style Union Station, a marble-floored Streamline Moderne masterpiece, is the Los Angeles hub. Trains run between L.A. and the romantic mission towns of San Juan Capistrano, San Diego, Santa Barbara, and San Luis Obispo. The scenery includes lush valleys, a windswept coastline, and the occasional urban stretch. Call Amtrak (© **800/ USA-RAIL**) for information.

• **Skydiving over Southern California:** Enjoy a bird's-eye view of the Southland. Local schools offer instruction at all levels (including tandem jumps for first-timers). At the **California City Skydive Center** (© 800/2-JUMP-HI) in the Mojave Desert, you can soar through the same skies as the space shuttle, which lands at nearby Edwards Air Force Base. Hemet and Perris are home to world-renowned schools—**Skydiving Adventures** at Hemet-Ryan Airport (© 800/526-9682) and the **Perris Valley Skydiving School** (©800/832-8818)—as is Skylark Airport at Lake Elsinore, where you'll find **Jim Wallace Skydiving** (© 800/795-DIVE).

• **Getting Up Close to the Desert's Gigantic Windmills:** Anyone who's driven through the desert near Palm Springs has marveled at these looming structures. Curiosity proved to be the mother of invention, and now visitors have a chance to see, touch, and learn about the surprisingly efficient power generators, why they're clustered here, and just what is the difference between wind *turbines* and wind *mills*. See chapter 15.

• **Climb Into Sunny Jim Cave (La Jolla):** Get in touch with your inner pirate when you descend a precarious staircase through solid rock, emerging inside an enormous sea cave—rumored to have once been a landing for Prohibition-era bootleggers—on the La Jolla coast. Hand-carved nearly 100 years ago, the tunnel is safer than it feels (honest!), and offers a cool treat . . . though not for the faint-of-heart. See chapter 16.

5 The Best of Small-Town California

• **St. Helena:** A small town in the heart of the Napa Valley, St. Helena is known for its Main Street, which is lined with Victorian storefronts featuring intriguing wares. In a horse and buggy, Robert Louis Stevenson and his new bride, the cantankerous Fanny, made their way down this street. Come for the old-timey, tranquil mood and the wonderful food. See chapter 6.

• **Mendocino:** An artists' colony with a New England flavor, Mendocino served as the backdrop for *Murder, She Wrote.* Perched on the cliff tops above the Pacific Ocean, it's filled with small art galleries, general stores, weathered wooden houses, and elbow-to-elbow tourists. See chapter 7.

• **Arcata:** If you're losing your faith in America, a few days spent at this northern California coastal town will surely restore it. Arcata has it all: its own redwood forest and bird marsh, a charming town square, great family-owned restaurants, and even its own minor-league baseball team, which draws the whole town together for an afternoon of pure camaraderie. See chapter 7.

• **Nevada City:** The whole town is a national historic landmark and the best place to understand gold-rush fever. Settled in 1849, it offers fine dining and shopping and a stock of multi-gabled Victorian frame houses of the Old West. Relics of the cannibalistic Donner Party are on display at the 1861 Firehouse No. 1. See chapter 10.

• **Pacific Grove:** You can escape the Monterey crowds by heading just 2 miles west to Pacific Grove, which is known for its tranquil waterfront location and quiet, unspoiled air. Thousands of monarch butterflies flock here between October and March to make their winter home in Washington Park. See chapter 11.

- **Cambria:** Near Hearst Castle, Cambria benefits from a constant stream of visitors, who bring the right amount of sophistication to this picturesque coastal town. Moonstone Beach holds a string of seaside lodges; farther north are dozens of sunbathing elephant seals, while the village itself is filled with charming B&Bs, artists' studios and galleries, and friendly shops. See chapter 12.

- **Ojai:** When Hollywood needed a Shangri-La for the movie *Lost Horizon,* filmmakers drove north to idyllic Ojai Valley, an unspoiled hideaway of eucalyptus groves and small ranches warmly nestled among soft, green hills. Ojai is the amiable village at the valley's heart. It's a mecca for artists, free spirits, and weary city folk in need of a restful weekend in the country. See chapter 12.

- **Ventura:** This charming mission town is filled with colorful Victorians. It's also home to a pleasantly eclectic old Main Street lined with thrift and antiques shops, used-record stores, friendly diners, and even old-time saloons operating beneath broken-down, second-story hotels. Don't miss the historic mission on its landscaped

plaza, and the deco-era Greek Revival San Buenaventura City Hall looming over the town, bedecked with smiling stone faces of the founding Franciscan friars. See chapter 12.

- **Avalon:** This crescent-shaped hamlet on idyllic Santa Catalina Island may welcome the summer influx of city-savvy tourists, but off-season visitors get to see a close-knit community that cherishes its isolation. Phone numbers are given in four digits here (the entire island shares a single exchange), and many residents rarely bother traveling to the mainland. There are very few cars, lots of cozy cafes and friendly pubs, a charming art-deco history, and the sparkling blue Pacific everywhere you look—you might not want to leave, either! See chapter 14.

- **Julian:** This old mining town in the Cuyamaca Mountains near San Diego is well known today for its wildflower fields, the fall apple harvest, and tasty flavored breads from Dudley's Bakery. There's plenty of pioneer history here, too, including a local-history museum, a schoolhouse built around 1888, and mining demonstrations. A smattering of antiques shops, plenty of barbecue, and an old-fashioned soda fountain operating since 1886 round out the experience. See chapter 16.

6 The Best Family Vacation Experiences

- **San Francisco:** The City by the Bay is filled with unexpected pleasures for every member of the family. Ride the cable cars that "climb halfway to the stars" and visit the Exploratorium, the California Academy of Sciences (which includes the Steinhart Aquarium), the zoo, the ships at the National Maritime Museum,

Golden Gate Park, Sony's Metreon Entertainment Center, and much more. See chapter 4.

- **Lake Tahoe:** California's Disneyland of outdoor adventure, Lake Tahoe has loads of family-fun things to do. Skiing, snowboarding, hiking, tobogganing, swimming, fishing, boating, water-skiing, mountain biking—the list is nearly endless. Even the casinos cater to kids while mom and pop play the slots. See chapter 8.

- **Yosemite National Park:** Camping or staying in a cabin in Yosemite is a premier family attraction in California. Sites are scattered over 17 different campgrounds, and the rugged beauty of the Sierra Nevada Mountains surrounds you. During the day, the family calendar is packed with hiking, bicycling, white-water rafting, and even mountaineering to rugged, snowy peaks. See chapter 9.
- **Santa Cruz:** Surfing, sea kayaking, hiking, fishing, and great shopping, not to mention those fantastic beaches and the legendary amusement park on the boardwalk—this wonderfully funky bayside town has everything you need for the perfect family vacation. See chapter 11.
- **Monterey:** It's been called "Disneyland-by-the-Sea" due to its wealth of family-friendly activities, including those on Cannery Row and Fisherman's Wharf. Be sure to check out the state-of-the-art aquarium. See chapter 11.
- **Big Bear Lake:** Families flock year-round to this lake in the San Bernardino Mountains, and not just for the skiing. Horseback riding, miniature golf, water sports,

and the Alpine Slide (kind of a snowless bobsled) are fun alternatives, and you can see and learn about native wildlife at the Moonridge Animal Park. The recently expanded village has a movie theater, arcade, and dozens of cutesy bear-themed businesses. The area's woodsy cabins are perfect for families. See chapter 14.

- **Disneyland:** The "Happiest Place on Earth" is family entertainment at its best, joined in 2001 by a brand-new sister theme park, California Adventure. Whether you're wowed by Disney animation, thrilled by the roller-coaster rides, or interested in the history and hidden secrets of this pop-culture icon, you won't walk away disappointed. Stay at one of the resort's on-site hotels (connected directly to the park by monorail), and take advantage of early entrance to Disneyland. See chapter 14.
- **San Diego Zoo, Wild Animal Park, & SeaWorld:** San Diego boasts three of the world's best animal attractions. At the zoo, animals live in creatively designed habitats such as Tiger River and Hippo Beach. At the Wild Animal Park, 3,000 animals roam freely over 2,200 acres. And SeaWorld, with its ever-changing animal shows and exhibits, is an aquatic wonderland. See chapter 16.

7 The Best Architectural Landmarks

- **The Civic Center** (San Francisco): The creation of designers John Bakewell, Jr., and Arthur Brown, Jr., this is perhaps the most beautiful beaux-arts complex in America. See chapter 4.
- **The Painted Ladies** (San Francisco): The so-called Painted Ladies are the city's famous, ornately decorated Victorian homes. Check out the brilliant beauties around

Alamo Square. Most of the extant 14,000 structures date from the second half of the 19th century. See chapter 4.

- **Winchester Mystery House** (San Jose): The heiress to the Winchester rifle fortune, Sarah Winchester, created one of the major "Believe It or Not?" curiosities of California, a 160-room Victorian mansion. It's been called the "world's strangest monument to a woman's fear." When a fortune-teller told her she wouldn't die if she continued to build onto her house, her mansion underwent construction day and night from 1884 to 1922. She did die eventually, and the hammers were silenced. See chapter 5.

- **The Carson House** (Eureka): A splendidly flamboyant Victorian— and one of the state's most photographed Queen Anne–style structures. It was built in 1885 by the Newsom brothers for William Carson, the local timber baron. Today, it's the headquarters of a men's club. See chapter 7.

- **California State Capitol** (Sacramento): Built in 1869 and completely renovated in 1976, the dazzling white capitol building has the original statuary (which was lost for a while) restored along its eaves; historical rooms furnished with antiques from the original offices; a strangely interesting collection of portraits of California governors (don't miss Jerry Brown); and a dome that from the inside looks like a Fabergé egg. It also has a few oddities such as gargoyles hidden in the ornate moldings. See chapter 10.

- **Mission San Carlos Borromeo del Rio Carmelo** (Carmel): The second mission founded in California in 1770 by Father Junípero Serra (who is buried here) is perhaps the most beautiful. Its stone church and tower dome have been authentically restored, and a peaceful garden of California poppies adjoins the church. Sights include an early kitchen and the founding father's spartan sleeping quarters. See chapter 11.

- **The Theme Building at Los Angeles International Airport:** The spacey *Jetsons*-style "Theme Building," which once loomed over underdeveloped LAX, still holds court in the center of the airport and unmistakably signals your arrival. Enjoy the view of arriving and departing jets from the building's observation deck or its groovy *Star Trek*–ish Encounter restaurant and bar, whose eerie purple neon floods the surrounding area after dark. See chapter 13.

- **Tail o' the Pup** (Los Angeles): At first glance, you might not think twice about this hot dog-shaped bit of kitsch on West Hollywood's San Vicente Boulevard, just across from the Beverly Center. But locals adored this closet-sized wiener dispensary so much that when it was threatened by the developer's bulldozer, they spoke out en masse to save it. One of the few remaining examples of 1950s representational architecture, the "little dog that could" also serves up a great Baseball Special. See chapter 13.

- **The Gamble House** (Pasadena): The Smithsonian Institution calls this Pasadena landmark, built in 1908, "one of the most important houses in the United States." Architects Charles and Henry Greene created a masterpiece of the Japanese-influenced Arts and Crafts movement. Tours are conducted of the spectacular interior, designed by the Greenes, down to the last piece of teak furniture and coordinating Tiffany lamp, and executed with impeccable craftsmanship. After you're done, stroll the immediate neighborhood to view several more Greene-and-Greene creations. See chapter 13.

- **Balboa Park** (San Diego): These Spanish-Mayan–style buildings were originally built as temporary structures for the Panama–California Exposition between 1915 and 1916. Set amidst the vast hilly terrain of one of the country's finest city parks, the ornately decorated and imposing facades have a special magic. Although some have been rebuilt over the years, many of the original buildings still remain, housing San Diego's finest museums. See chapter 16.

- **Hotel del Coronado** (Coronado): The "Hotel Del" stands in all its ornate Victorian red-tiled glory on some of the loveliest beach in Southern California. Built in 1888, it's one of the largest remaining wooden structures in the world. Even if you're not staying, stop by to take a detailed tour of the splendidly restored interiors, elegant grounds, and fascinating mini-museum of the hotel's spirited history. On your way to Coronado, you can't miss the soaring Coronado Bay Bridge, an architectural landmark in its own right. See chapter 16.

8 The Best Museums

- **The Exploratorium** (San Francisco): The hands-on, interactive Exploratorium boasts 650 exhibits that help show how things work. You use all your senses and stretch them to a new dimension. Every exhibit is designed to be useful. See chapter 4.
- **The Oakland Museum:** This one might be dubbed the "Museum of California." The colorful people and history of the Golden State, and its sometimes overpowering art and culture, are all here. Everything from the region's first inhabitants to today's urban violence is depicted. See chapter 5.
- **California State Railroad Museum** (Sacramento): Old Sacramento's biggest attraction, the 100,000-square-foot museum was once the terminus of the Transcontinental and Sacramento Valley railways. The largest museum of its type in the United States, it displays 21 locomotives and railroad cars, among other attractions. One sleeping car simulates travel, with all the swaying and flashing lights of lonely towns passed in the night. See chapter 10.
- **J. Paul Getty Museum at the Getty Center** (Los Angeles): Since opening in 1997, the Getty has been deluged by visitors eager to see whether this ambitiously conceived (14 years and $1 billion in the making) complex fulfills its promise as new cultural cornerstone of L.A. Besides boasting a permanent art collection and notable visiting exhibits, the center is a striking—and starkly futuristic—architectural landmark. From its picturesque vantage point, the Getty offers panoramic city and ocean views. See chapter 13.
- **Autry Museum of Western Heritage** (Los Angeles): This one's a treat for both young and old. Relive California's historic cowboy past and see how the period has been depicted by Hollywood through the years, from Disney cartoon re-creations to founder Gene Autry's "singing cowboy" films to popular 1960s TV series. Highlights include a life-size woolly mammoth and a glimmering vault of ornate frontier firearms. See chapter 13.
- **Petersen Automotive Museum** (Los Angeles): This museum is a natural for Los Angeles, a city whose personality is so entwined with the popularity of the car. Impeccably restored vintage autos are displayed in life-size dioramas accurate to the last period detail (including an authentic 1930s–era service station). Upstairs galleries house movie-star and motion-picture vehicles, car-related

artwork, and visiting exhibits. See chapter 13.

- **Museum of Contemporary Art (MCA)** (San Diego): MCA is actually one museum with two locations: one in La Jolla, the other downtown. Perched on a seaside cliff, the La Jolla branch wins praise for outstanding views, site-specific outdoor sculpture, and the recent restoration of the museum's facade, a 1916 Irving Gill–designed home originally built for benefactor Ellen Browning Scripps. The permanent collection is known internationally, and focuses primarily on work produced since 1950. See chapter 16.

- **The Museums of Balboa Park** (San Diego): Located in a relaxed, verdant setting, these museums offer a unique variety of cultural experiences. Highlights include the Aerospace Historical Center, Museum of Man, Museum of Photographic Arts, Model Railroad Museum, Natural History Museum, and the lily pond and Botanical Building. Check in at the House of Hospitality for a map and "Passport to Balboa Park," a low-cost pass to a combination of the museums. See chapter 16.

9 The Best Luxury Hotels & Resorts

- **Ritz-Carlton San Francisco** (San Francisco; ✆ 800/241-3333): Two short blocks from the top of Nob Hill, San Francisco's Ritz is world-renowned among discerning travelers for its superfluously accommodating staff, luxurious amenities, and top-rated restaurant. Another bonus is the most lavish brunch in town, served on Sundays in the Terrace Room or on the patio amidst blooming rose bushes. See chapter 4.

- **Auberge du Soleil** (Rutherford; ✆ 707/963-1211): The "Inn of the Sun," a Relais & Châteaux member in a 33-acre olive grove, stands above the vineyards of Napa Valley. This French country–style inn is the Wine Country's best resort. Each of the spacious villas is named after a region of France and exudes an ambiance of romantic exclusivity. See chapter 6.

- **Meadowood Napa Valley Resort** (St. Helena; ✆ 800/458-8080): A retreat of charm and style, this 256-acre Wine Country estate was inspired by New England's grand turn-of-the-century cottages.

With its plethora of sports facilities and stress-relieving treatments, it attracts such clients as megabuck novelist Danielle Steele. See chapter 6.

- **The Estate by the Elderberries** (Oakhurst; ✆ 559/683-6860): Close to Yosemite, the Château du Sureau and Erna's Elderberry House, established in 1984, evoke the best of Europe. Exquisite furnishings, individually decorated rooms, and a cuisine worthy of the stars make for a memorable lodging and dining experience at this gateway to the wilderness. See chapter 9.

- **Casa Palmero Resort** (Pebble Beach; ✆ 800/654-9300): A small, ultra-luxury resort on the first tee of the Pebble Beach Golf Course, Casa Palmero has just 24 cottages and suites, all very intimate and private. In addition, you have the splendors of Pebble Beach, its fabulous golf links, fine restaurants, and gorgeous scenery to amuse you. See chapter 11.

- **Post Ranch Inn** (Big Sur; ✆ 800/527-2200): The freestanding, architecturally sophisticated cabins—which virtually hang over the cliffs of Big Sur—combined with first-rate amenities, hiking trails, spectacular views, a top-notch restaurant, and a celestial outdoor heated pool make this one of the most exclusive—and romantic—resorts we've ever visited. See chapter 11.

- **Ventana Inn and Spa** (Big Sur; ✆ **800/628-6500**): A luxurious wilderness resort on 243 mountainous, oceanfront acres, this place is chic, tranquil, and hip— the pioneer sylvan retreat at Big Sur is a magnet for celebrities. Accommodations in one- and two-story buildings—each "worthy of the wild"—blend in with the dramatic Big Sur coastline. The cuisine is first-rate. See chapter 11.

- **Four Seasons Biltmore** (Santa Barbara; ✆ **800/332-3442**): Open since 1927, the Biltmore has palm-studded formal gardens and a prime beachfront location along "America's Riviera." Meander through the elegant Spanish-Moorish arcades and walkways, all accented by exquisite Mexican tile, and then play croquet on manicured lawns or relax at the Coral Casino Beach and Cabana Club. The rooms are the epitome of refined luxury, and the service couldn't be more friendly and accommodating. See chapter 12.

- **Hotel Bel-Air** (Los Angeles; ✆ **800/648-4097**): Nestled in the foothills above UCLA, this is the choice of visiting European royalty, world leaders, and top celebrities. The graceful hotel was built in the 1920s, its grounds landscaped like a fairy-tale kingdom: Stone footbridges pass over koi-filled streams, flowering trees surround a swan-filled pond, and flagstone paths lead to richly traditional rooms. See chapter 13.

- **The Inn on Mount Ada** (Santa Catalina Island; ✆ **800/608-7669**): This former mansion of the wealthy Wrigley family is one of the most exclusive B&B experiences you'll ever have. With only six guest rooms, the hilltop inn's hefty rates include all your meals (and thoughtful snacks laid out each afternoon), plus the use of a golf cart to putter around this auto-eschewing island paradise. You'll feel like an honored guest at a friend's Mediterranean villa. See chapter 14.

- **Ritz-Carlton Laguna Niguel** (Dana Point; ✆ **800/241-3333**): This jewel in the Ritz-Carlton chain is well known for its warmth, charm, picture-perfect setting, and impeccable service. On dramatic cliffs overlooking 2 miles of prime beach, the Ritz is done in an easy yet elegant nautical-seashore decor, accented by well-chosen antiques and fine art. See chapter 14.

- **La Quinta Resort & Club** (La Quinta; ✆ **800/854-1271**): This luxury resort, set in a grove of palms at the base of the rocky Santa Rosa Mountains, is surrounded by some of the desert's best golf courses. Single-story, Spanish-style cottages are surrounded by a gardenlike setting and 24 "private" swimming pools. The tranquil lounge and library in the unaltered original hacienda hearkens back to the early days of the resort, when Clark Gable, Greta Garbo, and other luminaries regularly escaped to the seclusion of La Quinta's casitas. See chapter 15.

- **La Valencia Hotel** (La Jolla; ✆ **800/451-0772**): Meticulously preserved to look just as it has since opening in 1926, this elegant Spanish-Moorish grande dame is still the choice of celebrities and the centerpiece of La Jolla's charming clifftop "village." The hotel's rich history and lavish good taste are reflected everywhere, and the ocean views are stupendous. See chapter 16.

10 The Best Affordable Small Hotels & Inns

- **The Laurel Inn** (San Francisco; ✆ **800/552-8735** or 415/567-8467): Fashionable digs with Zenlike accouterments and ample amenities don't get any cheaper than they do at this posh Pacific Heights neighborhood motel. Runner-up is favorite standby **Hotel Bohème** (San Francisco; ✆ **415/433-9111**). The rooms may be small and lack extra amenities and parking, but there's no prettier rooms the heart of North Beach. Plus, you need only step outside your door to find some of the city's best cafes, restaurants, and nightlife. See chapter 4.

- **St. Orres** (Gualala; ✆ **707/884-3303**): Designed in a Russian style—complete with two Kremlin-esque onion-domed towers—St. Orres offers secluded accommodations constructed from century-old timbers salvaged from a nearby mill. One of the most eye-catching inns on California's North Coast. See chapter 7.

- **Albion River Inn** (Albion; ✆ **800/479-7944**): Easily one of the best rooms-with-a-view on the California coast, the Albion River Inn is dripping with romance. Perched on a cliff overlooking the rugged shoreline, most of the luxuriously appointed rooms have Jacuzzi tubs for two, elevated to window level. Add champagne and you're guaranteed to have a night you won't soon forget. See chapter 7.

- **Olallieberry Inn** (Cambria; ✆ **888/927-3222**): Nestled in the charming town of Cambria, this 1873 Greek Revival house, furnished in a romantic floral-and-lace Victorian style, is a perfect base for exploring Hearst Castle. The gracious innkeepers have your comfort and convenience at heart, providing everything from directions to Moonstone Beach to restaurant recommendations—and a scrumptious breakfast in the morning, of course. See chapter 12.

- **Cottage Inn by the Sea** (Pismo Beach; ✆ **888/440-8400;** www.cottage-inn.com): Feeling more intimate than its 80 rooms would suggest, this affordable seaside hotel is perched above the crashing waves of Pismo Beach with rolling green ranchland as a backdrop. It's the antithesis of the chain motel conformity usually found at this price range, filled with thoughtful touches and better-than-average decor. A retro farmhouse-themed breakfast room is fully stocked each morning; the morning meal is complimentary. See chapter 12.

- L.A. is home to two upstart hangouts, catering to an MTV generation with more style than bucks: **The Standard** (✆ **323/650-9090**) is a Warhol-hued party place combining 1970s chic, 1960s architecture, and jet-age modernity with touches like a barbershop/tattoo parlor in the lobby. Across town, **Avalon Hotel** (✆ **800/535-4715**) exudes a postwar Hollywood glamour accented with mid-century modern furnishings and a sophisticated 1950s aura inspired by the hotel's classic lines. Both offer top-of-the-line luxury amenities—at ultra-reasonable rates. See chapter 13.

- **Casa Malibu** (Malibu; ⓒ **800/ 831-0858**): This beachfront motel will fool you from the front. Its cheesy 1970s entrance, right on noisy Pacific Coast Highway, belies the quiet, restful charm found within. Situated around the courtyard garden are 21 rooms, many with private decks above the Malibu sands. Rooftops and balconies are festooned with bougainvillea vines, creating an effect reminiscent of a Mexican seaside village. There's easy beach access, and one elegant suite that was Lana Turner's favorite. See chapter 13.

- **Casa Cody** (Palm Springs; ⓒ **760/320-9346**): You'll feel more like a house guest at this 1920s Spanish-style *casa* that's blessed with peaceful, blossoming grounds and two swimming pools. The Southwestern-style rooms are large and equipped for extended stays, and the hotel is just a couple of easy blocks from the heart of the action. See chapter 15.

- **Gaslamp Plaza Suites** (San Diego; ⓒ **800/874-8770**): This impeccably restored Victorian at the center of the vibrant Gaslamp Quarter still boasts the exquisite interiors (the finest wood, marble, etched glass) that must've cost a fortune in 1913. The hotel carries itself with an elegance and drama that belie its bargain rates; room appointments say "indulgence" rather than "economy," too. See chapter 16.

11 The Best Places to Stay with the Kids

- **The Lost Whale Bed & Breakfast Inn** (Trinidad; ⓒ **800/677- 7859**): Parents will love the beautiful inn and the outdoor spa, and kids will love the enclosed play area and the menagerie of horses, goats, and other animals down the road. It has a private beach, and it's near interesting redwood parks. Best of all, no one has to cook because a fabulous breakfast is included. See chapter 7.

- **KOA Kamping Kabins** (Point Arena; ⓒ **800/562-4188**): Once you see the adorable little log cabins at this KOA campground, you can't help but admit that, rich or poor, this is one cool way to spend the weekend on the coast. Rustic is the key word here: mattresses, a heater, and a light bulb are the standard amenities. All you need is some bedding (or sleeping bags), cooking and eating utensils, and a bag of charcoal for the barbecue out on the front porch. See chapter 7.

- **Camping at Yosemite's Tuolumne Meadows** (ⓒ **800/ 436-7275**): It's especially memorable in late spring, when the meadow is carpeted with wildflowers. At an elevation of 8,600 feet, this is the largest alpine meadow in the High Sierra and a gateway to the "high country." A large campground with a full-scale naturalist program is operated here by park authorities. True adventurers should backpack into the wilderness. See chapter 9.

- **Columbia City Hotel and Fallon Hotel** (Columbia; ⓒ **800/ 532-1479**): Some parents may roll their eyes a bit at this preserved gold rush town that looks like a television setting, but it's really rather remarkable with rides on a 100-year-old stagecoach, a working blacksmith shop, lots of relics from mining days to peruse, and Victorian hotels that are reasonably priced and dish up a great buffet breakfast. Cars are barred from the dusty main street so everybody wanders up and down gawking just like they used to. See chapter 10.

- **Oceanfront Camping at Big Sur:** Kirk Creek Campground, about 3 miles north of Pacific Valley, offers camping with dramatic ocean views and access to the beach. But there are dozens more—take your pick. See chapter 11.
- **Grey Squirrel Resort** (Big Bear Lake; ⓒ **800/381-5569;** www. greysquirrel.com): Like a camp for kids and adults alike, this cluster of kitchen-equipped cottages near the lake and Big Bear's charming village offers economical lodgings for a single night or the entire season (winter or summer). Enjoy a heated, enclosed pool, fire pit, barbecues, volleyball and basketball courts—plus nearby skiing, boat rental, and plenty of other family recreation. See chapter 14.
- **Disneyland Resort Hotels** (Anaheim; ⓒ **714/956-MICKEY;** www.disneyland.com): The Holy

Grail of Disneygoers has always been the "Official Hotel of the Magic Kingdom," including the original Disneyland Hotel and newcomers Paradise Pier Hotel and the Grand Californian. An easy monorail or tram ride to the parks' main gate (the Grand Californian even opens directly into California Adventure) means you'll be able to return to your room anytime, whether to take a much-needed nap or to change your soaked shorts after a water ride. Because they're attractions unto themselves, these hotels are the very best choice for Disney-bound families with small children. See chapter 14.

- **Crystal Pier Hotel** (San Diego; ⓒ **800/748-5894**): Occupying a historic private pier that extends into the Pacific Ocean, this property affords guests the unusual experience of actually sleeping *over* the ocean in a darling cottage. Ideal for beach-loving families, who can enjoy the soothing sound of waves or head out for boardwalk action; beach gear is even available for rental. See chapter 16.

12 The Best Restaurants

- **San Francisco's Finest:** We can't choose! It's practically sacrilege to even attempt to name the "top" San Francisco restaurant. But for a perfect combo of great food and atmosphere, we always count on **Boulevard** (ⓒ 415/543-6084), **Restaurant Gary Danko** (ⓒ 415/749-2060), **Zuni Cafe** (ⓒ 415/552-2522) and **Kokkari** (ⓒ 415/981-0983). See chapter 4.
- **Chez Panisse** (Berkeley; ⓒ **510/548-5525**): This is the culinary domain of Alice Waters, often called "the queen of California cuisine." Her food captivates the

senses and the imagination. Although originally inspired by the Mediterranean, her kitchen has found its own style. Even Bill Clinton deserted the Big Mac for some Chez Panisse delights, such as grilled fish wrapped in fig leaves with red-wine sauce, and Seckel pears poached in red wine with burnt caramel. See chapter 5.

- **Bistro Don Giovanni** (Napa ⓒ 707/224-3300): Shhh.... Don't tell anyone, but in this Napa Valley dining room you can get an incredible meal without a reservation. Just drop into the cheery, large restaurant, wait for a seat at the bar, and order off the fantastic Italian menu. It does the trick every time. See chapter 6.

- **The French Laundry** (Yountville; © 707/944-2380): The best restaurant in the Wine Country also happens to be one of the top-ranked restaurants in the nation. Renowned chef and owner Thomas Keller, dubbed "Chef of the Nation" in 1997 by judges of the James Beard Award, offers a multicourse masterpiece that almost justifies the 6-month waiting list (though we offer some tips on how to skip the wait). See chapter 6.
- **Terra** (St. Helena; © 707/963-8931): One of the Napa Valley's premier dining rooms is the creation of Lissa Doumani and her Japanese husband, Hiro Sone. It's on every gastronome's tour of the Wine Country, a celebration of the region's bounty—sublime, flavorful, well crafted. The wine list is a tribute to the Golden State, emphasizing nearly unknown selections from the small estates. See chapter 6.
- **Pangaea** (Point Arena; © 707/882-3001): North Coast locals have been going nuts about chef/owner Shannon Hughes' wondrously fresh, inventive, and organically grown cuisine. Pork confit, served on a potato tart with homemade apricot chutney; Thai-style crab cakes served with a Thai green-curry coconut sauce; Niman-Schell burgers topped with organic cheese and greens, caramelized onions, and Thai chili sauce—it's all fantastic. Even the decor is a work of art. See chapter 7.
- **Erna's Elderberry House** (Oakhurst; © 559/683-6800): It's like a beacon shining across the culinary wasteland of the region around Yosemite. The six-course menu—which changes nightly—is an almost perfect blend of continental and Californian. The food is bountiful, and as fully satisfying as the elegant European ambiance. Fresh, fresh, fresh—and no natural flavor is cooked beyond recognition. Ingredients are deftly and skillfully handled to bring out their natural flavors. See chapter 9.
- **bouchon** (Santa Barbara; © 805/730-1160): With an always-intriguing seasonal menu derived from Santa Barbara County's Wine Country and abundant fresh ingredients, this intimate restaurant (whose name means *wine cork*) lies hidden behind a grandiose shrubbery portal in the heart of downtown. The food and service are always impeccable, and an experienced staff stands ready to help coordinate by-the-glass (or even half-glass) wines for each course, should you desire. See chapter 12.
- **The Ranch House** (Ojai; © 805/646-2360): This charming restaurant has been placing its emphasis on using the freshest vegetables, fruits, and herbs since it opened its doors in 1965, long before it became a national craze. If you stroll through the lush herb garden before your meal, you might later recognize the freshly snipped sprigs that will aromatically transform your simple meat, fish, or game dish into a work of art. See chapter 12.
- **Patina** (Los Angeles; © 323/467-1108): The flagship restaurant of superchef Joachim Splichal, who also conceived the (slightly) more affordable Pinot eateries, Patina's menu consistently wows otherwise jaded Angelenos, who

keep coming back to this beautifully comfortable Cal-French dining room. Meticulously chosen seasonal menus are always fine-tuned to perfection, featuring partridge, pheasant, or other game in winter, and spotlighting exotic vegetables and tropical fish in summer. See chapter 13.

- **Röckenwagner** (Santa Monica; © 310/399-6504): L.A.'s gossipy tongues regularly wag about handsome chef Hans Röckenwagner, but he seems more concerned with maintaining the culinary perfection that propelled him from obscurity in funky Venice to this gallery-like space on Santa Monica's trendy Main Street. Although he trained in Europe, Röckenwagner co-opts ethnic dishes from around the world and elevates them to culinary works of multicultural art. Don't be surprised to find Scandinavian treats like spätzle, Knödel, and smoked salmon sharing space with Pacific Rim elements like mangoes, wasabi, and hoisin. See chapter 13.

- **Azzura Point** (Coronado; © 935/424-4477): With its plushly upholstered, gilded, and view-endowed setting, this stylishly contemporary hotel dining room wins continual raves from deep-pocketed San Diego foodies willing to cross the bay for inventive and artistic creations from Azzura Point's pedigreed chefs. For chic fine cuisine, it's definitely the best in town. See chapter 16.

- **George's at the Cove/George's Ocean Terrace** (La Jolla; © 858/454-4244; www.georgesatthecove.com): Tasty smoked chicken-broccoli-black bean soup is an enduring dish; it's on the menu at the fancy downstairs dining room *and* the breezy upstairs cafe. The two also share an *aah*-inspiring ocean view and attentive service. The downstairs kitchen turns up the finesse factor for inventive and formal California cuisine, while the cafe offers crowd-pleasing versions. See chapter 16.

13 The Best Culinary Experiences

- **A Dim Sum Lunch, San Francisco Style:** Eating a dim sum lunch is like Christmas morning, only the continual stream of presents is edible, including the wrappers. Throughout the meal, waiters stop at your table and offer an exotic selection of appetizer-size Chinese dishes—from dumplings and pot stickers to salt-fried shrimp, shark fin soup, and stuffed eggplant. No one this side of China does dim sum as well as San Francisco. Our favorite place to indulge is **Ton Kiang** (© 415/387-8273). See chapter 4.

- **Dungeness Crab at San Francisco's Fisherman's Wharf:** Crabs, which are best consumed as soon as possible after being cooked, emerge right from boiling pots onto your plate. You crack the shells and pick the delectable meat out. Gastronomes treasure even the edible organs (crab butter) inside the carapace. See chapter 4.

- **Grazing at San Francisco's Farmers Market:** Head to San Francisco's Embarcadero on Tuesday or Saturday morning and join the locals as they feast on the freshest vegetables, fruits, and prepared foods from some of the city's beloved restaurants (© 415/353-5650). See chapter 4.

- **A San Francisco Burrito:** No matter where we go in California, we just can't find a burrito as luscious as those served throughout

San Francisco. The tortilla-wrapped meal takes on a gourmet dimension here: flavored tortillas; fresh-grilled meats, fish, and vegetables; three types of beans; a symphony of salsas; guacamole; and sour cream all tidily tucked in the perfect to-go feast. See chapter 4.

- **A Decadent Meal in the Wine Country:** The Wine Country atmosphere sets a better stage for indulgent dining than anywhere else in the state. Add the best wines and some of the most talented chefs in the nation and you've got what we consider the ultimate dining experience. Deep-pocketed diners simply must reserve an evening at **The French Laundry** (St. Helena; ℂ 707/944-2380)—if, that is, they can get through to a reservationist. More moderately priced memories can be made at **Mustards Grill** (ℂ 707/944-2424), **Bistro Jeanty** (ℂ 707/944-0103), and Tra Vigne's **The Cantinetta** (ℂ 707/963-8888). See chapter 6.
- **Gourmet Food Shopping in St. Helena:** This is gourmet grocery shopping at its finest. New York's **Dean & DeLuca** (ℂ 707/967-9980) opened its gastronomic warehouse in 1997 as a world's fair of foods, where everything is beautifully displayed and often painfully pricey. If you're into food, you've got to check this place out. Across the street is the **Oakville Grocery Co.** (ℂ 707/944-8802), which has a small-town vibe and crowds liable to send any claustrophobe into a rage. You'll find shelves crammed with perfect picnic provisions. See chapter 6.
- **Tomales Bay Oysters: Johnson's Oyster Farm** (ℂ 415/669-1149) sells its farm-fresh oysters—by the dozen or the hundreds—for a fraction of the price you'd pay at a restaurant. Our modus operandi is to 1) buy a couple dozen, 2) head for an empty campsite along the bay, 3) fire up the barbecue pit (don't forget the charcoal), 4) split and 'cue the little guys, 5) slather them in Johnson's special sauce, and then 6) slurp 'em down—yum. See chapter 7.

- **A Sunset Horseback Ride Through Griffith Park to a Mexican Feast:** This culinary/equine excursion departs Friday evenings from Beachwood Stables in the Hollywood Hills just before dusk, winding up in Burbank at the modest but tasty—especially coming off the trail!—Viva Restaurant. Tie up your steed outside and saunter in for a steaming plate of enchiladas accompanied by an ice-cold cerveza, just like the real *vaqueros* (cowboys). For information, call the Sunset Ranch at ℂ **323/464-9612.** For more information about horseback riding in Griffith Park, see chapter 13.
- **Grand Central Market** (Los Angeles; ℂ **213/624-2378**): Fresh-produce stands, exotic spice and condiment vendors, butchers and fishmongers, and prepared-food counters create a noisy, fragrant, vaguely comforting atmosphere in this L.A. mainstay. The gem of the airy, cavernous complex is the fresh juice bar at the southwest corner. A market fixture for many years, it dispenses dozens of varieties from an elaborate system of wall spigots (just like an old-fashioned soda fountain), deftly blending unlikely but heavenly combinations. See chapter 13.
- **Sunday Champagne Brunch Aboard the *Queen Mary*** (Long Beach; ℂ **562/435-3511** or 562/432-6964): This elegant ocean liner was the largest, finest vessel when she was built in 1934, and

the grandeur of those Atlantic-crossing days remains. A sumptuous buffet-style feast, accompanied by harp soloist and ice sculpture, is presented in the richly wood-furnished, first-class dining room. Walk off your overindulgence on the spectacular teak decks and through the Art Deco interiors. See chapter 14.

• **A Date with the Coachella Valley:** Some 95% of the world's dates are farmed here in the desert. While the groves of date palms make evocative scenery, it's their savory fruit that draws visitors to the National Date Festival in Indio each February. Amid the Arabian Nights Parade and dusty camel races, you can feast on an exotic array of plump Medjool, amber Deglet Noor, caramel-like Halawy, and buttery Empress dates. The rest of the year, date farms and markets throughout the valley sell dates from the season's harvest, as well as date milkshakes, sticky-date coconut rolls, and more. See chapter 15.

• **San Diego County Farmers Markets:** The bountiful harvest of San Diego County is sold on various days at moveable markets throughout the area. Finds are fresh local fruits, vegetables, and flowers, as well as specialty items such as raw apple cider (in the fall), macadamia nuts, and rhubarb pies. See chapter 16.

14 The Best of the Performing Arts & Special Events

• **The San Francisco Opera:** This world-class company performs at the War Memorial Opera House, which is modeled after the Opéra Garnier in Paris. The opera season opens with a gala in September and runs through December. This was the first municipal opera in the United States, and its brilliant productions have members have been acclaimed by critics throughout the world. See chapter 4.

• **The American Conservatory Theater** (San Francisco): The ACT is one of the nation's leading regional theaters, dating from 1967. It's been called the American equivalent of the British National Theatre, the Berliner Ensemble, and the Comédie Française in Paris. Both classical and experimental works are brilliantly performed. See chapter 4.

• **The Monterey Jazz Festival:** When the third weekend of September rolls around, the Monterey Fairgrounds hosts this fabled classic, drawing jazz fans from around the world. The 3-day festival (which is usually sold out about a month in advance) is known for presenting the sweetest jazz west of the Mississippi. It even draws fans from that city of jazz, New Orleans. See chapter 2.

• **The Carmel Bach Festival:** For more than 50 years, Carmel has hosted an annual 3-week celebration honoring Johann Sebastian Bach and his contemporaries. It culminates in a candlelit concert in the chapel of the Carmel Mission. It starts in mid-July, and you must order tickets way in advance. For details about Carmel and the mission, see chapter 11.

• **The Hollywood Bowl:** This iconic outdoor amphitheater is the summer home of the Los Angeles Philharmonic, a stage for visiting virtuosos—including the occasional pop star—and the setting for several splendid fireworks shows throughout the summer. It's customary to feast on a gourmet picnic before the performance, either at your seat or on the grounds; at evening's end, the aisles are littered with empty wine bottles. Those lucky enough to obtain a box seat can set their own private table. See chapter 13.

- **The Viper Room:** Head to this West Hollywood closet for a glimpse of L.A.'s hippest scene. Owner Johnny Depp took this small but historic club space on the famous Sunset Strip and gave it an atmospheric Art Deco vibe. Visiting celebrities and musicians can be found mingling and listening to live bands every night of the week. After midnight or so, don't be surprised if big-name recording artists take the stage for an impromptu jam. See chapter 13.

- **The Groundling Theater** (Hollywood): Many Groundling alumni have hit the big time, graduating to *Saturday Night Live,* TV sitcoms, and motion pictures. The ensemble is best known for split-second improvisation and offbeat, irreverent original skits, all performed in its small, intimate theater on Melrose Avenue. You're bound to bust a gut here. See chapter 13.

- **Festival of Arts & Pageant of the Masters** (Laguna Beach): These events draw enormous crowds to the Orange County coast every July and August. Begun in 1932 by a handful of area painters, the festival has grown to showcase hundreds of artists. In the evening, crowds marvel at the Pageant of the Masters' *tableaux vivants,* in which costumed townsfolk pose convincingly inside a giant frame and depict famous works of art, accompanied by music and narration. See chapter 14.

- **Old Globe Theatre** (San Diego): This Tony Award–winning theater, fashioned after Shakespeare's original stage, produced the revival of *Damn Yankees,* and has billed such notable performers as John Goodman, Marsha Mason, Cliff Robertson, Jon Voight, and Christopher Walken. See chapter 16.

- **La Jolla Playhouse:** Winner of the 1993 Tony Award for Outstanding American Regional Theater, the LJ Playhouse stages six productions each year in its 400-seat Mandell Weiss Theater and 400-seat Mandell Weiss Forum on the campus of UCSD. Expect a fair share of nationally acclaimed directors and highly touted revivals, such as when Matthew Broderick starred in *How to Succeed in Business Without Really Trying* before it went on to Broadway accolades. See chapter 16.

15 The Best Websites

- **@LA** (**www.at-la.com**): This exceptional search engine (much used by savvy locals) provides links to almost 60,000 sites in thousands of categories relation to all of southern California.

- **California National Parks** (**www.nps.gov/parklists/ca.html**): California has preserved much of its glorious heritage in its parks. The state is home to about two dozen national parks, monuments, seashores, and recreation areas. The National Park Service's index includes detailed information on visiting, camping, getting around, and recommended activities.

- **CitySearch San Francisco** (**bayarea.citysearch.com**): The substantial articles and listings cover all of the city's entertainment highlights. The events calendar links to goings-on throughout the Bay Area; the Visitor section includes tips on getting around.

- **The Disneyland Resort (www. disneyland.com)**: Check out the resorts, dining facilities, travel package options, and activities and rides in the Magic Kingdom. Get specific hours and ride closures in advance by selecting the day of your visit; this site is guaranteed to rev up your enthusiasm level.

- **Los Angeles Times (www.latimes. com)**: California's leading newspaper keeps you up to date on local and statewide happenings. The Calendar section combines features from the *Times* with up-to-date entertainment listings and ticket information from Ticketmaster and CitySearch.

- **Oakland.com   (www.oakland. com)**: This site offers numerous links to attractions, shopping, and the arts around Oakland; in addition, its Dining section offers detailed descriptions and recommendations.

- **San Diego Zoo (www.sandiego zoo.com)**: The zoo site is organized by exhibit, with descriptions and photos previewing all the resident critters. Details are provided on tours, plus direction and other logistical information.

2

Planning Your Trip to California

by Stephanie Avnet Yates

In the pages that follow, we've compiled everything you need to know to handle the practical details of planning your trip in advance—from making campsite reservations to finding great deals on the Internet, plus a calendar of events and much more.

1 Visitor Information & Money

VISITOR INFORMATION

For information on the state as a whole, contact the **California Office of Tourism,** 801 K St., Suite 1600, Sacramento, CA 95812 (② **800/862-2543;** www.gocalif.ca.gov), and ask for a free information packet. In addition, almost every city and town in the state has a dedicated tourist bureau or chamber of commerce that will be happy to send you information on its particular parcel. These are listed under the appropriate headings in the geographically organized chapters that follow.

International travelers should also see chapter 3, "For International Visitors," for entry requirements and other pertinent information.

INFORMATION ON CALIFORNIA'S PARKS To find out more about California's national parks, contact the **Western Region Information Center,** National Park Service, Fort Mason, Building 201, San Francisco, CA 94123 (② **415/556-0560;** www.nps.gov). Reservations can be made at national park campsites by calling ② **800/365-2267** (800/436-7275 for Yosemite) or logging on to **http://reservations.nps.gov.**

For information on state parks, contact the **Department of Parks and Recreation,** P.O. Box 942896, Sacramento, CA 94296-0001 (② **916/653-6995;** http://cal-parks.ca.gov). Ten thousand campsites are on the department's reservation system, and can be booked up to 8 weeks in advance by calling **Park-Net** at ② **800/444-7275.** You can also get reservations information online at **www.park-net.com/usa/xca.**

For information on fishing and hunting licenses, contact the **California Department of Fish and Game,** License and Revenue Branch, 3211 S St., Sacramento, CA 95816 (② **916/227-2244**).

MONEY

Wells Fargo Bank is linked with the Star, Cirrus/MasterCard, and Instant Cash systems; it has hundreds of ATMs at branches and in-store locations. To find the one nearest you, call ② **800/869-3557** or visit the website at **www.wellsfargo.com/findus.** Other statewide banks include Bank of America (which accepts PLUS, Star, and Interlink cards). To locate other ATMs in the **Cirrus** system, call ② **800/424-7787** or search online at **www.mastercard.com;** to find a **PLUS** ATM, call ② **800/843-7587** or visit **www.visa.com.** Be sure to check your bank's daily

> **_Tips_ Plan Ahead for the Unexpected**
>
> Before you leave home, make photocopies—two sets—of your IDs (including passports for international travelers), credit cards (front and back), and plane tickets or itinerary confirmations. Leave one set at home where a trusted friend can fax it to you if necessary, and carry one set with you separately from wallets and purses. In case of emergency, you'll have proof of your identity, everything necessary to cancel and replace your credit cards, and a receipt for your plane trip home!

withdrawal limit before you depart. Also, be warned that a Santa Monica city ordinance prohibiting banks from charging ATM fees has led some banks to limit access to their machines to bank customers only.

2 When to Go

WEATHER California's climate is so varied that it's impossible to generalize about the state as a whole.

San Francisco's temperate marine climate means relatively mild weather year-round. In summer, temperatures rarely top 70°F (pack sweaters, even in August), and the city's famous fog rolls in most mornings and evenings. In winter, the mercury seldom falls below freezing, and snow is almost unheard of. Because of San Francisco's fog, summer rarely sees more than a few hot days in a row. Head a few miles inland, though, and it's likely to be clear and hot.

The Central Coast shares San Francisco's climate, although it gets warmer as you get farther south. Seasonal changes are less pronounced south of San Luis Obispo, where temperatures remain relatively stable year-round. The North Coast is rainier and foggier; winters tend to be mild but wet.

Summers are refreshingly cool around Lake Tahoe and in the Shasta Cascades—a perfect climate for hiking, camping, and other outdoor activities and a popular escape for residents of California's sweltering deserts and valleys who are looking to beat the heat. Skiers flock to this area for terrific snowfall from late November to early April.

Southern California—including Los Angeles and San Diego—is usually much warmer than the Bay Area, and it gets significantly more sun. This is the place to hit the beach. Even in winter, daytime thermometer readings regularly reach into the 60s and warmer. Summers can be stifling inland, but southern California's coastal communities are always comfortable. The area's limited rainfall is generally seen between January and mid-April, and is rarely intense enough to be more than a slight inconvenience. It's possible to sunbathe throughout the year, but only die-hard enthusiasts and wet-suited surfers venture into the ocean in winter. The water is warmest in summer and fall, but even then, the Pacific is too chilly for many.

The deserts, including Palm Springs and the desert national parks, are sizzling hot in summer; temperatures regularly top 100°F. Winter is the time to visit the desert resorts (and remember, it gets surprisingly cold at night in the desert).

San Francisco's Average Temperatures (°F)

	Jan	Feb	Mar	Apr	May	June	July	Aug	Sept	Oct	Nov	Dec
Avg. High	56	59	60	61	63	64	64	65	69	68	63	57
Avg. Low	46	48	49	49	51	53	53	54	56	55	52	47

Los Angeles's Average Temperatures (°F)

	Jan	Feb	Mar	Apr	May	June	July	Aug	Sept	Oct	Nov	Dec
Avg. High	65	66	67	69	72	75	81	81	81	77	73	69
Avg. Low	46	48	49	52	54	57	60	60	59	55	51	49

AVOIDING THE CROWDS If you're planning a summertime visit, you're not alone. The period between Memorial Day and Labor Day is the height of the tourism season virtually everywhere in the state—except for desert areas like Palm Springs and Death Valley, where sizzling temperatures keep all but the hardiest bargain-hunters away. California's pleasant summer weather (with relatively low humidity) has a lot to do with these numbers, but the season is also popular simply because that's when most people, especially families with kids, get to take that precious vacation time. So, naturally, prices are highest between May and September in much of the state, and can fall dramatically outside of that period—exceptions to this rule include the aforementioned deserts and winter ski resorts. *Insider tip:* What Californians know, however, is the best time to travel the state is autumn—roughly late September through early December—when crowds drop off, "shoulder season" rates kick in, and winter rains are still months away. In fact, you might be lucky enough to enjoy the renewed warm days of "Indian summer" that often occur during the autumn season.

CALIFORNIA CALENDAR OF EVENTS

January

Tournament of Roses, Pasadena. A spectacular parade down Colorado Boulevard, with lavish floats, music, and extraordinary equestrian entries, followed by the Rose Bowl Game. Call ✆ **626/449-4100** or visit www.tournamentofroses.com for details, or just stay home and watch it on TV (you'll have a better view). January 1.

Bob Hope Chrysler Classic, Palm Springs Desert Resorts. 2002 marks the 43rd year of this weeklong PGA golf tournament, which raises money for charity and includes a celebrity-studded Pro-Am. For spectator information and tickets, call ✆ **888/MR-BHOPE** or 760/346-8184. Mid- to late January.

AT&T Pebble Beach National Pro-Am, Pebble Beach. A PGA-sponsored tour where pros are teamed with celebrities to compete on three world-famous golf courses. Call ✆ **800/541-9091** or 831/649-1533, or visit www.attpbgolf.com. January 28 to February 3, 2002.

February

Chinese New Year Festival & Parade. The largest Chinese New Year festival in the United States is in San Francisco. The celebration includes a Golden Dragon parade with lion dancing, marching bands, street fair, flower sale, and festive food. Call ✆ **415/982-3000** or 415/391-9680. In 2002, the New Year begins February 12; the parade will be February 16.

L.A.'s celebration is colorful as well, with dragon dancers parading

Whale-Watching

Each winter, pods of California gray whales making their annual migration from their Alaskan feeding grounds to breeding lagoons at the southern tip of Baja pass close by California shores; if you've ever been lucky enough to spot one of these graceful behemoths, you'll understand why whale-watching is such an eagerly anticipated activity. From December through March, you can view this spectacular parade from land or sea. Recommended spots include **Point Reyes National Seashore** (© 415/669-1534), where an historic lighthouse offers whale- and elephant seal–viewing; **Monterey Peninsula,** where January's WhaleFest (© 831/644-7588) celebrates these special mammals from the Monterey Aquarium down through Big Sur; **Point Vicente Lighthouse and Interpretive Center** (© 562/377-5370), on the windswept Palos Verdes Peninsula south of Los Angeles; and San Diego's **Cabrillo National Monument** (© 619/557-5450; www.nps.gov/cabr), which offers a glassed-in observatory and educational whale exhibits.

Boat excursions depart from a number of locations, including **Morro Bay** (Virg's Landing, © 800/762-5263 or 805/772-1222), **Santa Barbara** (The Condor, © 888/77-WHALE or 805/963-3564), **Ventura Harbor** (Island Packers, © 805/642-1393; www.islandpackers.com), and **San Diego** (San Diego Harbor Excursions, © 800/442-7847 or 619/234-4111). Also in San Diego, the **Natural History Museum** (© 619/232-3821, ext. 203; www.sdnhm.org) offers fascinating, naturalist-led, half-day whale-watching trips for passengers 12 and older.

through the streets of downtown's Chinatown. Chinese opera and other events are scheduled. For this year's schedule, contact the Chinese Chamber of Commerce at © **213/ 617-0396.**

National Date Festival, Indio. Crowds gather to celebrate the Coachella Valley desert's most beloved cash crop with appropriately themed events like camel and ostrich races, the Blessing of the Date Garden, and festive Arabian Nights pageants. Plenty of date-sampling booths are set up, along with rides, food vendors, and other county-fair trappings. Call © **800/811-3247** or 760/863-8247, or visit www.datefest. org. Two weeks in February.

Mustard Festival, Napa Valley. Celebrating the blossom of yellow-petalled mustard flowers, which coat the valley during February and March, the event was originally conceived to drum up interest in visiting during this once-slow season. The festival has evolved into 6 weeks of events ranging from a kick-off gourmet gala at the CIA Greystone to a wine auction, golf benefit, recipe and photography competitions, and plenty of food and wine celebrations. For information and a schedule of events, call © **707/ 259-9020** or 707/938-1133, or visit online at www.mustardfestival. com. February and March.

March

Return of the Swallows, San Juan Capistrano. Each St. Joseph's Day (March 19), visitors flock to this charming village for the arrival of the mission's loyal flock of swallows that will nest and remain until October. The celebration includes a parade, dances, and special programs. Call ℂ **949/248-2048** for details.

Santa Barbara International Film Festival. For 10 days each March, pretty Santa Barbara does its best impression of Cannes. There's a flurry of foreign and independent film premieres, personal appearances by noted actors and directors, and symposia on hot cinematic topics. For a rundown of events, call ℂ **805/963-0023;** www.sbfilm festival.org. Mid-March.

Nabisco Championship, Rancho Mirage. This 32-year-old LPGA golf tournament (formerly known as the Nabisco Dinah Shore) takes place near Palm Springs. After the celebrity Pro-Am early in the week, the best female pros get down to business. For further information, call ℂ **760/324-4546;** www. nabiscochampionship.com. Other special-interest events for women usually take place around the Dinah Shore, including the country's largest annual lesbian gathering. Last week of March.

Redwood Coast Dixieland Jazz Festival, Eureka. Three days of jazz featuring 12 of the best Dixieland groups, including a variety of jam sessions. Call ℂ **707/445-3378.** Late March.

April

San Francisco International Film Festival. One of the oldest film festivals in the United States, featuring more than 100 films and videos from more than 30 countries. Tickets are relatively inexpensive, and screenings are very accessible to the general public during 2 weeks early in the month. Call ℂ **415/931-FILM;** www.sfiff.org.

Toyota Grand Prix, Long Beach. An exciting weekend of Indy-class auto racing and entertainment in and around downtown Long Beach, drawing world-class drivers from the United States and Europe. Contact the **Grand Prix Association** at ℂ **888/52-SPEED** or 562/981-2600; www.longbeachgp. com. Mid-April.

Renaissance Pleasure Faire, San Bernardino. One of America's largest Renaissance festivals, this annual happening is set in Glen Helen Regional Park in L.A.'s relatively remote countryside. Performers (and many attendees) dress in 16th-century costume and revel in this festive re-creation of a medieval English village. For ticket information, call ℂ **800/52-FAIRE;** http:// renaissance-faire.com. Weekends from late April to Memorial Day.

Ramona Pageant, Hemet. A unique outdoor play that portrays the lives of the Southern California Mission Indians. The play was adapted from Helen Hunt Jackson's 1884 novel *Ramona.* Call ℂ **909/658-3111** or visit www. ramonapageant.com for details. Late April to early May.

Del Mar National Horse Show. Horse-and-rider teams compete in national championships at the Del Mar Fairgrounds. Call ℂ **858/ 792-4288** or 858/755-1161 for more information. Late April to early May.

May

Cinco de Mayo. A weeklong celebration of one of Mexico's most jubilant holidays takes place throughout the city of Los Angeles near May 5. The fiesta's carnival-like atmosphere is created by large crowds, live music, dances, and food. The main festivities are held in El Pueblo de Los Angeles State Historic Park, downtown, with other events around the city. Call ℰ 213/485-6855 for information. There's also a Cinco de Mayo celebration in San Diego, featuring folkloric music, dance, food, and historical reenactments. It's held in Old Town. Call ℰ 619/296-3161 for more information.

Calaveras County Fair and Jumping Frog Jubilee, Angels Camp. The event inspired by Mark Twain's story "The Celebrated Jumping Frog of Calaveras County." Entrants from all over the world arrive with their frog participants. There's also a children's parade, livestock competition, rodeo, carnival, and fireworks. Call ℰ 209/736-2561; www.frogtown. org. Third weekend in May.

Bay to Breakers Foot Race, San Francisco. One of the city's most popular annual events, it's really more fun than run. Thousands of entrants show up dressed—or undressed—in their best costumes for the approximately 7½-mile run. Call ℰ 415/777-7770; www. baytobreakers.com. Third Sunday of May.

Paso Robles Wine Festival. What began as a small, neighborly gathering has grown into the largest outdoor wine tasting in California. The 3-day event features winery open houses and tastings, a golf tournament, 5K run and 10K bike ride, concerts, plus a carnival-like festival in downtown's City Park. For a schedule of events and fees, call ℰ 800/549-WINE; www.pasowine. com. Third weekend in May.

Carnival, San Francisco. The Mission District's largest annual event is a 2-day series of festivities that culminates with a parade on Mission Street over Memorial Day weekend. More than half a million spectators line the route, and the samba musicians and dancers continue to play on 14th Street, near Harrison, at the end of the march. Call the **Mission Economic and Cultural Association** at ℰ 415/826-1401. Memorial Day weekend.

June

Playboy Jazz Festival, Los Angeles. Bill Cosby is the traditional Master of Ceremonies, presiding over top artists at the Hollywood Bowl. Call ℰ 310/246-4000. Mid-June.

Lesbian & Gay Freedom Day Parade. It's celebrated all over the state, but San Francisco's party draws up to half a million participants. The parade's start and finish have been moved around in recent years to accommodate road construction, but traditionally it begins and ends at Civic Center Plaza, where hundreds of food, art, and information booths are set up around several sound stages. Call ℰ 415/864-3733 for information. Usually the third or last Sunday of June.

Ojai Music Festival. This 5-day event has been drawing world-class classical and jazz personalities to the open-air Libbey Bowl since 1947. Past events have featured Igor Stravinsky, Aaron Copland, and the Juilliard String Quartet. Seats (and local lodgings) fill up quickly; call ℰ 805/646-2094 for more information, or log onto www. ojaifestival.org. First half of June.

Mariachi USA Festival, Los Angeles. A 2-day family-oriented celebration of Mexican culture and tradition at the Hollywood Bowl, where festival-goers pack their picnic baskets and enjoy music, ballet folklorico, and related performances by special guests. Call ℰ 323/848-7717. Late June.

July

Mammoth Lakes Jazz Jubilee. A 4-day festival featuring 20 bands on 10 different stages, plus food, drink, and dancing—all under the pine trees and stars. Call ℂ **800/367-6572** or 760/934-2478. Second weekend in July.

Festival of Arts & Pageant of the Masters, Laguna Beach. A fantastic performance-art production in which live actors re-create famous Old Masters paintings. Other festivities include live music, crafts sales, art demonstrations and workshops, and the grass-roots Sawdust Festival across the street. Grounds admission is $3; pageant tickets range from $15 to $40. Call ℂ **800/487-FEST** or 949/494-1145, or check out www.foapom.com. July through August.

Gilroy Garlic Festival. A gourmet food fair with more than 85 booths serving garlicky food from almost every ethnic background, plus close to 100 arts, crafts, and entertainment booths. Call ℂ **831/842-1625;** www.gilroygarlicfestival.com. Last full weekend in July.

Shakespeare at the Beach, Lake Tahoe. A bewitching experience of the Bard at Sand Harbor on the shore beneath the stars. Call ℂ **702/832-1606.** Three weeks in late July and August.

Beach Festival, Huntington Beach. Two straight weeks of fun in the sun, featuring two surfing competitions—the U.S. Open of Surfing *and* the world-class Pro of Surfing—plus several extreme sport events such as in-line skating, BMX biking, skateboarding, and more. Includes entertainment, food, tons of product booths and giveaways—and plenty of tanned, swimsuit-clad bodies of both sexes. For more information, cal ℂ **949/885-8200,** or log onto www.hbvisit.com. End of July.

August

Old Spanish Days Fiesta, Santa Barbara. The city's biggest annual event, this 5-day festival features a grand parade with horse-drawn carriages, music and dance performances, *mercados* (marketplaces), and a rodeo. Call ℂ **805/962-8101;** www.oldspanishdays-fiesta.org. Early August.

Nisei Week Japanese Festival, Los Angeles. This week-long celebration of Japanese culture and heritage is held in Little Tokyo at the Japanese American Cultural and Community Center Plaza. Festivities include parades, food, music, arts, and crafts. Call ℂ **213/687-7193.** Mid-August.

California State Fair, Sacramento. At the California Exposition Grounds, a gala celebration with livestock, carnival food, exhibits, entertainment on 10 different stages, plus thoroughbred racing and a 1-mile monorail for panoramic views over the scope of it all. Call ℂ **916/263-FAIR;** www.bigfun.org. Late August to early September.

September

Sausalito Art Festival. A juried exhibit of more than 180 artists. It's accompanied by music provided by Bay Area jazz, rock, and blues performers and international cuisine enhanced by wines from some 50 different Napa and Sonoma producers. Call ℂ **415/332-3555** for information. Labor Day weekend.

San Diego Street Scene. The historic Gaslamp Quarter is transformed by this 3-day extravaganza featuring food, dance, international character, and live music on 12 separate stages. Saturday is set aside as an all-ages day; attendees must be

21 and over the other 2 days. Call ☏ 619/557-0505 for more information. First weekend after Labor Day.

Monterey Jazz Festival. Features top names in traditional and modern jazz. One of the oldest annual jazz festivals in the world. Call ☏ 800/307-3378 or 831/373-0244. Mid-September.

Los Angeles County Fair. Horse racing, arts, agricultural displays, celebrity entertainment, and carnival rides are among the attractions of the largest county fair in the world, held at the Los Angeles County Fair and Exposition Center, in Pomona. Call ☏ 909/623-3111 or visit www.fairplex.com for information. Throughout September.

Danish Days, Solvang. Since 1936 this 3-day event has been celebrating old-world customs and pageantry with a parade, gymnastics exhibitions by local schoolchildren, demonstrations of traditional Danish arts and crafts, and plenty of *aebleskivers* (Danish fritters) and *medisterpolse* (Danish sausage). Call ☏ 800/GO-SOLVANG for further information.

Watts Towers Day of the Drum Festival, Los Angeles. Celebrating the historic role of drums and drummers, this event features a variety of unique performances, from Afro-Cuban folkloricos to East Indian tabla players. Call ☏ 213/847-4646. Late September.

October

Catalina Island Jazz Trax Festival. Great contemporary jazz artists travel to the island to play in the legendary Avalon Casino Ballroom. The festival is held over two consecutive 3-day weekends. Call ☏ 888/330-5252 or visit www.jazztrax.com for advance ticket sales and a schedule of performers. Early October.

Sonoma County Harvest Fair, Sonoma County Fairgrounds. A 3-day celebration of the harvest with exhibitions, art shows, and annual judging of the local wines. Call ☏ 707/545-4203. Dates vary.

The Half Moon Bay Art & Pumpkin Festival, Half Moon Bay. The festival features a Great Pumpkin Parade, pie-eating contests, a pumpkin-carving competition, arts and crafts, and all manner of squash cuisine. The highlight of the event is the Giant Pumpkin weigh-in contest, won recently by an 875-pound monster. Colorful to the extreme. For exact date and details, call the **Pumpkin Hotline** at ☏ 650/726-9652.

Western Regional Final Championship Rodeo, Lakeside. Top cowboys from 11 western states compete in seven rodeo events, including calf roping, barrel racing, bull riding, team roping, and steer wrestling. Held at the Lakeside Rodeo Grounds, Calif. 67 and Mapleview Avenue, Lakeside. Call ☏ 619/561-4331. Mid-October.

Halloween, San Francisco. The City by the Bay celebrates with a fantastical parade organized at Market and Castro, and a mixed gay-straight crowd revels in costumes of extraordinary imagination. October 31.

November

Doo Dah Parade, Pasadena. An outrageous spoof of the Rose Parade, featuring participants such as the Precision Briefcase Drill Team and a kazoo band. Call ☏ 626/449-3689. Sunday before Thanksgiving.

Hollywood Christmas Parade. This spectacular star-studded parade marches through the heart of Hollywood. For information call ☏ 323/469-2337. Sunday after Thanksgiving.

December

How the Grinch Stole Christmas,
San Diego. In honor of the late
Theodor Geisel ("Dr. Seuss," a former San Diego resident), the lobby
of Loews Coronado Bay Resort is
transformed into Whoville, where
the Cat in the Hat assembles eager
young audiences for regular readings of the beloved Christmas story.
Punch and cookies are served at
this free event, and carolers also
perform following each reading.
For more information, call ✆ **619/
424-4000.** December 1 to 24.

Christmas Boat Parade of Lights.
Following longstanding tradition,
sailors love to decorate their craft
with colorful lights for the holidays.
Several southern California harbors
hold nighttime parades to showcase
these creations, which range from
tiny dinghies draped with a single
strand of lights to showy yachts
with entire Nativity scenes twinkling on deck. Call the following
for schedules and information: **Ventura Harbor** (✆ 805/642-6746),
Marina Del Rey (Los Angeles;
✆ 310/821-0555), **Long Beach**
(✆ 562/435-4093), **Huntington
Harbour** (✆ 714/840-7542),
Mission Bay (San Diego; ✆ 619/
276-8200).

New Year's Eve Torchlight Parade,
Big Bear Lake. Watch dozens of
nighttime skiers follow a serpentine
path down Snow Summit's ski slopes
bearing glowing torches—it's one of
the state's loveliest traditions. Afterward, the party continues indoors
with live bands and plenty to eat and
drink. For more information on this
21-and-over event, call ✆ **909/
866-5766;** www.snowsummit.com.

3 Tips for Travelers with Special Needs

**FOR TRAVELERS WITH DIS-
ABILITIES** California's spirit of
tolerance and diversity has made it a
welcoming place for travelers with
disabilities. Strict construction
codes make most public facilities and
attractions extremely accessible
(though some historic sites and older
buildings simply can't accommodate
drastic remodeling), and the city
provides many services for those with
disabilities.

A little advance planning is always
useful. There are more resources out
there than ever before. *A World of
Options,* a 658-page book for travelers
with disabilities, covers everything
from biking trips to scuba outfitters. It
costs $45 (less for members) and is
available from **Mobility International
USA,** P.O. Box 10767, Eugene, OR
97440 (✆ **541/343-1284,** voice and
TDD; www.miusa.org). Annual membership for Mobility International is
$35, which includes their quarterly
newsletter, *Over the Rainbow.*

You can join **The Society for
Accessible Travel & Hospitality**
(SATH), 347 Fifth Ave., Suite 610,
New York, NY 10016 (✆ **212/
447-7284;** www.sath.org), for $45
annually, $30 for seniors and students,
to gain access to a vast network of
connections in the travel industry. The
society provides information sheets on
travel destinations and referrals to tour
operators that specialize in travelers
with disabilities. Its quarterly magazine, *Open World,* is full of good
information and resources. A year's
subscription is included with
membership, or costs $18 ($35 outside the U.S.).

Access-Able Travel Source is a
homegrown online tip sheet that
offers a comprehensive online index of
accessible hotels, restaurants, attractions, and disabled-service providers
around the country; log onto
www.access-able.com or call ✆ **303/
232-2979.**

CAR RENTALS   Many of the major car-rental companies now offer hand-controlled cars for drivers with disabilities. **Avis** can provide such a vehicle at any of its locations in the United States with 48-hour advance notice; **Hertz** requires between 24 and 72 hours of advance reservation at most of its locations. **Wheelchair Getaways** (© 800/642-2042; www.wheelchair-getaways.com) rents specialized vans with wheelchair lifts and other features for those with disabilities in more than 100 cities across the United States.

FOR GAY & LESBIAN TRAVELERS   The **International Gay & Lesbian Travel Association** (IGLTA) (© 800/448-8550 or 954/776-2626; fax 954/776-3303; www.iglta.org) links travelers with the appropriate gay-friendly service organization or tour specialist. With around 1,200 members, it offers quarterly newsletters, marketing mailings, and a membership directory that's updated quarterly.

There are also two good, biannual English-language gay guidebooks, both focused on gay men but including information for lesbians as well. You can get the *Spartacus International Gay Guide* or *Odysseus* from most gay and lesbian bookstores, or order them online from **amazon.com**.

There are many gay-oriented publications with information and up-to-date listings, including *The Advocate,* a biweekly national magazine. *Out and About* (© 800/929-2268; www.outandabout.com), hailed for its "straight" and savvy reporting on gay travel, offers guidebooks and a monthly newsletter packed with good information on the gay and lesbian scene. The newsletter's been praised by everybody from *Travel & Leisure* to *The New York Times;* a year's subscription costs $49.

FOR SENIORS   Nearly every attraction in California offers a senior discount; age requirements vary, and specific prices are discussed throughout this book. Public transportation and movie theaters also have reduced rates. Don't be shy about asking for discounts, but always carry some kind of identification, such as a driver's license, that shows your date of birth. Also, mention the fact that you're a senior citizen when you first make your travel reservations. For example, both **Amtrak** (© 800/USA-RAIL; www.amtrak.com) and **Greyhound** (© 800/752-4841; www. greyhound.com) offer discounts to persons over 62.

Members of the **American Association of Retired Persons** (AARP), 601 E St. NW, Washington, DC 20049 (© 800/424-3410 or 202/434-2277; www.aarp.org), get discounts not only on hotels but on airfares and car rentals too. AARP also offers members a wide range of other special benefits, including *Modern Maturity* magazine and a monthly newsletter; membership is only $10 per year.

The Mature Traveler, a monthly 12-page newsletter on senior citizen travel, is a valuable resource. It is available by subscription ($30 a year) from GEM Publishing Group, Box 50400, Reno, NV 89513-0400. GEM also publishes *The Book of Deals,* a collection of more than 1,000 senior discounts on airlines, lodging, tours, and attractions around the country; it's available for $7.95 by calling © 800/460-6676. Another helpful publication is *101 Tips for the Mature Traveler,* available free from Grand Circle Travel, 347 Congress St., Suite 3A, Boston, MA 02210 (© 800/221-2610 or 617/350-7500; www.gct.com). Also check your newsstand for the quarterly magazine *Travel 50 & Beyond.*

FOR FAMILIES   Several books offer tips on traveling with kids. *Family Travel* (Lanier Publishing

International) and *How to Take Great Trips with Your Kids* (The Harvard Common Press) are full of good general advice. *The Unofficial Guide to California with Kids* (Hungry Minds, Inc.) is an excellent resource that covers the entire state. It rates and ranks attractions for each age group, lists dozens of family-friendly accommodations and restaurants, and suggests lots of beaches and activities that are fun for the whole clan.

Family Travel Times is published six times a year (© **888/822-4388** or 212/477-5524; www.familytraveltimes. com), and includes a weekly call-in service for subscribers. Subscriptions are $39 a year.

4 Getting There

BY PLANE

All major U.S. carriers serve the San Francisco, Sacramento, San Jose, Los Angeles, John Wayne (Orange County), and San Diego airports. They include **American** (© 800/ 433-7300), **Continental** (© 800/ 525-0280), **Delta** (© 800/221-1212), **Northwest** (© 800/225-2525), **Southwest** (© 800/435-9792), **United** (© 800/241-6522), and **US Airways** (© 800/428-4322). The lowest round-trip fares to the West Coast from New York fluctuate between about $350 and $500; from Chicago, they range from $300 to $400. International travelers should also see "Getting to the United States," in chapter 3, for information on overseas flights into California. For details on air travel within California, see "Getting Around," later in this chapter.

FINDING THE BEST AIRFARE

Passengers who can book their tickets in advance, stay over Saturday night, or travel at off-peak hours will pay a fraction of the full fare. Airlines periodically lower prices on their most popular routes. Check your newspaper for advertised discounts or call the airlines directly and ask if any **promotional rates** or special fares are available. If your schedule is flexible, ask if you can secure a cheaper fare by staying an extra day or by flying midweek. (Many airlines won't volunteer this information.)

Consolidators—wholesalers who buy tickets in bulk at a discount—offer some of the best deals around. Their ads usually run in the Sunday travel section of your newspaper, and many have set up online reservations systems. There are lots of fly-by-night consolidators, though, and problems can range from disputing never-received tickets to finding you have no seat booked when you get to the airport. Play it safe by going with a reputable business; our favorite has always been **Cheap Tickets** (© 800/ 377-1000; www.cheaptickets.com).

It's possible to get some great deals on airfares, hotels, and car rentals via **Internet travel agencies.** Two of the better-respected virtual travel agents are **Travelocity** (www.travelocity.com) and **Microsoft Expedia** (www.expedia. com). See "Planning Your Trip Online," below, for more information on resources on the Web.

BY CAR

Here are some handy driving times if you're on one of those see-the-USA car trips. From Phoenix, it's about 6 hours to Los Angeles on I-10. Las Vegas is 265 miles northeast of Los Angeles (about a 4-hour drive).

San Francisco is 227 miles southwest of Reno, Nevada, and 577 miles northwest of Las Vegas. It's a long day's drive 640 miles south from Portland, Oregon, on I-5. The drive between San Francisco and L.A. takes about 6 hours on I-5, closer to 8 hours on the more scenic U.S. 101.

> **Tips A Road-Trip Tip**
>
> If you're planning a road trip, it's a good idea to be a member of the **Automobile Association of America (AAA)**. Members (only those who carry their cards with them) not only receive free roadside assistance, but also have access to a wealth of free travel information, including detailed maps. Also, many hotels and attractions throughout California offer discounts to AAA members—always inquire. Call © **800/922-8228** or your local branch for membership information.

BY TRAIN

Amtrak (© **800/USA-RAIL;** www. amtrak.com) connects California with about 500 American cities. The *Sunset Limited* is Amtrak's regularly scheduled transcontinental service, originating in Florida and making 52 stops along the way as it passes through Alabama, Mississippi, Louisiana, Texas, New Mexico, and Arizona before arriving in Los Angeles 2 days later. The train, which runs three times weekly, features reclining seats, a sightseeing car with large windows, and a full-service dining car. Round-trip coach fares begin at around $300; several varieties of sleeping compartments are also available for an extra charge.

Amtrak's *Coast Starlight* travels along the Pacific Coast between Seattle and Los Angeles. This stylish train (and wonderfully scenic route) has been steadily growing in popularity; for more information, see "Getting Around," later in this chapter.

PACKAGE TOURS

Independent fly and drive packages (no escorted tour groups, just a bulk rate on your airfare, hotel, and possibly rental car) are offered by **American Airlines Vacations** (© **800/321-2121**; www.aavacations.com), **Continental Airlines Vacations** (© 800/634-5555; www.coolvacations.com), **Delta Vacations** (© 800/872-7786; www.deltavacations.com), **Southwest Airlines Vacations** (© 800/423-5683; www.swavacations.com), or **United Vacations** (© 800/328-6877; www. unitedvacations.com).

In addition to these airline agencies, travel package services are offered to Amex customers at **American Express Travel** (© 800/AXP-6898; www. americanexpress.com/travel), which books packages through various vendors, including Continental Vacations and Delta Vacations. Or contact **Liberty Travel** (© 888/271-1584; www.libertytravel.com), one of the oldest and biggest packagers; they offer great deals—with or without air—to the many popular California destinations, including San Diego and Disneyland. At press time, the buzz was about **Travelution** (© 800/903-1616; www.travelution.com), the latest travel-planning tool from ultra-experienced Rosenbluth Travel. With 24/7 service by phone or online, Travelution.com even features Fare-Guard, which notifies you if a better priced airfare becomes available and allows you to rebook your flight.

Availability varies widely based upon season and demand, but it always pays to investigate what these major air carriers are offering to encourage you to fly with them. The packages are best suited to travelers who can be flexible in the following ways:

- Try not to be too picky about your hotel. That's not to say packages force you to stay in dumps—quite the contrary, they often include some premier hostelries—but you'll have a limited selection. Pinpoint roughly where you'd like to stay (within a region or city), and ask if there's a participating hotel there. The biggest hotel chains and resorts also offer package deals. If you already know where you want to stay, call the hotel itself and ask if it can offer land-air packages.

- If you can schedule your departure and arrival so you're not flying on the weekend, airfares will usually be at least $25 to $50 lower per person. And it goes without saying that the popular season, summer, is the most restrictive season, though package deals can still save you some money over booking separately.

- Engage the reservationist in conversation, mentioning all the activities you're considering for your visit. All of the companies have access to various goodies they can hitch to your package for far less than you'd pay separately. Examples include tickets to Universal Studios or Disneyland; passes for city tours, studio tours, and other excursions; tickets for theater events; car-rental upgrades; and more.

5 Planning Your Trip Online

With a mouse, a modem, and a certain do-it-yourself determination, Internet users can tap into the same travel-planning databases that were once accessible only to travel agents. Sites such as **Travelocity, Expedia,** and **Orbitz** allow consumers to comparison shop for airfares, book flights, learn of last-minute bargains, and reserve hotel rooms and rental cars.

But don't fire your travel agent just yet. Although online booking sites offer tips and hard data to help you bargain shop, they cannot endow you with the hard-earned experience that makes a seasoned, reliable travel agent an invaluable resource, even in the Internet age. And for consumers with a complex itinerary, a trusty travel agent is still the best way to arrange the most direct flights to and from the best airports.

Still, there's no denying the Internet's emergence as a powerful tool in researching and plotting travel time. The benefits of researching your trip online can be well worth the effort:

- **Last-minute specials,** known as "E-savers," such as weekend deals or Internet-only fares, are offered by airlines to fill empty seats. Most of these are announced on Tuesday or Wednesday and must be purchased online. They are only valid for travel that weekend, but some can be booked weeks or months in advance. Sign up for weekly e-mail alerts at airline websites or check megasites that compile comprehensive lists of E-savers, such as Smarter Living (http://smarterliving.com) or WebFlyer (www.webflyer.com).

- Some sites will send you **e-mail notification** when a cheap fare becomes available to your favorite destination. Some will also tell you when fares to a particular destination are lowest.

- The best of the travel planning sites are now **highly personalized;** they track your frequent-flier miles, and store your seating and meal preferences, tentative itineraries, and credit-card information, letting you plan trips or check agendas quickly.

- All major airlines offer **incentives**—bonus frequent-flier miles, Internet-only discounts, sometimes even free cell phone rentals—when you purchase online or buy an e-ticket.

- Advances in mobile technology provide business travelers and

Frommers.com: The Complete Travel Resource

For an excellent travel planning resource, we highly recommend **Arthur Frommer's Budget Travel Online** (www.frommers.com). We're a little biased, of course, but we guarantee you'll find the travel tips, reviews, monthly vacation giveaways, and online-booking capabilities thoroughly indispensable. Among the special features are: **"Ask the Expert"** bulletin boards, where Frommer's authors answer your questions via online postings; **Arthur Frommer's Daily Newsletter,** for the latest travel bargains and inside travel secrets; and Frommer's **"Destinations" archive,** where you'll get expert travel tips, hotel and dining recommendations, and advice on the sights to see for more than 200 destinations around the globe. Once your research is done, the **Online Reservation System** (www.frommers.com/booktravelnow) takes you to Frommer's favorite sites for booking your vacation at affordable prices.

other frequent travelers with **the ability to check flight status, change plans, or get specific directions** from handheld computing devices, mobile phones, and pagers. Some sites will e-mail or page a passenger if a flight is delayed.

TRAVEL PLANNING & BOOKING SITES

The best travel planning and booking sites cast a wide net, offering domestic and international flights, hotel and rental-car bookings, plus news, destination information, and deals on cruises and vacation packages. Keep in mind that free (one-time) registration is often required for booking. Because several airlines are no longer willing to pay commissions on tickets sold by online travel agencies, be aware that these online agencies will either charge a $10 surcharge if you book a ticket on that carrier—or neglect to offer those air carriers' offerings.

The sites in this section are not intended to be a comprehensive list, but rather a discriminating selection to get you started. Recognition is

given to sites based on their content value and ease of use and is not paid for—unlike some website rankings, which are based on payment. Remember: This is a press-time snapshot of leading websites—some undoubtedly will have evolved or moved by the time you read this.

- **Travelocity** (www.travelocity.com or http://frommers.travelocity.com) and **Expedia** (www.expedia.com) are the most longstanding and reputable sites, each offering excellent selections and searches for complete vacation packages. Travelers search by destination and dates coupled with how much they are willing to spend.
- The latest buzz in the online travel world is about **Orbitz** (www.orbitz.com), a site launched by United, Delta, Northwest, American, and Continental airlines. It shows all possible fares for your desired trip, offering fares lower than those available through travel agents. (Stay tuned: At press time, travel agency associations were waging an antitrust battle against this site.)

- **Qixo** (www.qixo.com) is another powerful search engine that allows you to search for flights and hotel rooms on 20 other travel-planning sites (such as Travelocity) at once. Qixo sorts results by price, after which you can book your travel directly through the site.

SMART E-SHOPPING

The savvy traveler is one armed with good information. Here are a few tips to help you navigate the Internet successfully and safely:

- **Know when sales start.** Last-minute deals may vanish in minutes. If you have a favorite booking site or airline, find out when last-minute deals are released to the public. (For example, Southwest's specials are posted every Tuesday at 12:01am central time.)
- **Shop around.** Compare results from different sites and airlines—and against a travel agent's best fare, if you can. If possible, try a range of times and alternate airports before you make a purchase.
- **Follow the rules of the trade.** Book in advance, and choose an off-peak time and date if possible. Some sites will tell you when fares to a particular destination tend to be cheapest.
- **Stay secure.** Book only through secure sites (some airline sites are not secure). Look for a key icon (Netscape) or a padlock (Internet Explorer) at the bottom of your web browser before you enter credit card information or other personal data.
- **Avoid online auctions.** Sites that auction airline tickets and frequent-flier miles are the number-one perpetrators of Internet fraud, according to the National Consumers League.
- **Maintain a paper trail.** If you book an e-ticket, print out a confirmation, or write down your confirmation number, and keep it safe and accessible—or your trip could be a virtual one!

ONLINE TRAVELER'S TOOLBOX

Veteran travelers usually carry some essential items to make their trips easier. Following is a selection of online tools to bookmark and use:

- **Intellicast** (www.intellicast.com). Weather forecasts for all 50 states and cities around the world.
- **Mapquest** (www.mapquest.com). This best of the mapping sites lets you choose a specific address or destination, and in seconds, returns a map along with detailed directions.
- **Cybercafes.com** (www.cybercafes. com) or Net Café Guide (www. netcafeguide.com/mapindex.htm). Locate Internet cafes at hundreds of locations around the globe. Catch up on your e-mail and log onto the Web for a few dollars per hour.

6 Getting Around

BY CAR

California's freeway signs frequently indicate direction by naming a town rather than a point on the compass. If you've never heard of Canoga Park, you might be in trouble—unless you have a map. The best state road guide is the comprehensive **Thomas Bros. California Road Atlas,** a 300-plus-page book of maps with schematics of towns and cities statewide. It costs about $23, a good investment if you plan to do a lot of exploring. Smaller, accordion-style maps are handy for the

Sample Distances Between Key California Cities:

San Francisco

87 miles SW of Sacramento	321 miles NW of Santa Barbara
115 miles NW of Monterey	379 miles NW of Los Angeles
278 miles SE of Eureka	548 miles NW of San Diego

Sacramento

87 miles NE of San Francisco	383 miles N of Los Angeles
185 miles NE of Monterey	391 miles NE of Santa Barbara
304 miles SE of Eureka	484 miles NW of Palm Springs

Los Angeles

96 miles SE of Santa Barbara	379 miles SE of San Francisco
103 miles W of Palm Springs	383 miles S of Sacramento
120 miles NW of San Diego	659 miles SE of Eureka
332 miles SE of Monterey	

state as a whole or for individual cities and regions; you'll find a very useful one inserted in the back of this book.

If you're heading into the Sierra or Shasta-Cascades for a winter ski trip, top up on antifreeze and carry snow chains for your tires. (Chains are mandatory in certain areas.)

DRIVING RULES California law requires both drivers and passengers to wear seat belts. Children under 4 years or 40 pounds must be secured in an approved child safety seat. Motorcyclists must wear a helmet. Auto insurance is mandatory; the car's registration and proof of insurance must be carried in the car.

You can turn right at a red light, unless otherwise indicated—but be sure to come to a complete stop first. Pedestrians always have the right-of-way.

Many California freeways have designated carpool lanes, also known as High Occupancy Vehicle (HOV) lanes or "diamond" lanes. Some require two passengers, others three. Most on-ramps are metered during even light congestion to regulate the flow of traffic onto the freeway; cars in HOV lanes can pass the signal without stopping. All other drivers are required to observe the stoplights—fines begin at around $271.

CAR-RENTAL AGENCIES California is one of the cheapest places in the United States to rent a car. The best-known firms, with locations throughout the state and at most major airports, include **Alamo** (© 800/327-9633), **Avis** (© 800/331-1212), **Budget** (© 800/527-0700), **Dollar** (© 800/800-3665), **Hertz** (© 800/654-3131), **National** (© 800/227-7368), and **Thrifty** (© 800/367-2277).

Many rental agencies have begun offering a variety of essential or just helpful extras, such as cellular phones, child seats, and specially equipped vehicles for travelers with disabilities. Ask about additional fees when you make your reservation.

DEMYSTIFYING RENTER'S INSURANCE Before you drive off in a rental car, be sure you're insured. Hasty assumptions about your personal auto insurance or a rental agency's additional coverage could end up costing you tens of thousands of dollars—even if you're involved in an accident that was clearly the fault of another driver.

If you already hold a **private auto insurance** policy, you are most likely covered in the United States for loss of or damage to a rental car, and liability in case of injury to any other party involved in an accident. Be sure to find out whether you're covered in the area you're visiting, whether your policy extends to all persons who will be driving the rental car, how much liability is covered in case an outside party is injured in an accident, and whether the type of vehicle you are renting is included under your contract. (Rental trucks, sport-utility vehicles, and luxury vehicles or sports cars may not be covered.)

Most **major credit cards** provide some degree of coverage as well—provided they were used to pay for the rental. Terms vary widely, however, so be sure to call your credit card company directly before you rent.

If you're **uninsured,** your credit card may provide primary coverage as long as you decline the rental agency's insurance. This means that the credit card may cover damage or theft of a rental car for the full cost of the vehicle. (In a few states, however, theft is not covered; ask specifically about state law where you will be renting and driving.) If you already have insurance, your credit card may provide secondary coverage—which basically covers your deductible.

Credit cards **will not cover liability,** or the cost of injury to an outside party and/or damage to an outside party's vehicle. If you do not hold an insurance policy, you may seriously want to consider purchasing additional liability insurance from your rental company. Be sure to check the terms, however: Some rental agencies only cover liability if the renter is not at fault.

The basic insurance coverage offered by most car-rental companies, known as the **Loss/Damage Waiver (LDW)** or **Collision Damage Waiver (CDW),** can cost as much as $20 per day. It usually covers the full value of the vehicle with no deductible if an outside party causes an accident or other damage to the rental car. Liability coverage varies according to the company policy and state law, but the minimum is usually at least $15,000. If you are at fault in an accident, however, you will be covered for the full replacement value of the car but not for liability. In California, you can buy additional liability coverage for such cases. Most rental companies will require a police report in order to process any claims you file, but your private insurer will not be notified of the accident.

BY PLANE

In addition to the major carriers listed earlier in "Getting There," several smaller airlines provide service within

---

✓ Tips **Bicycling Tours**

Combine an interest in biking with California's spectacular scenery by signing up for a weeklong or weekend tour with **Backroads,** 801 Cedar St., Berkeley, CA 94710 (© **800/GO-ACTIVE** or 510/527-1555; www.backroads. com). Focusing on coastal routes, Wine-Country rides, and even a microbrew program, the tours vary in difficulty and comfort; some are camping trips, while others accommodate you in luxury B&Bs. Professional leaders accompany each group, while a support van trails with gear, baggage, and provisions. Tours include all meals and overnight accommodations, and range in price from $150 to $275 per day (per person).

The *Coast Starlight:* All Aboard for Nostalgia

If you're traveling by rail along the California coast, or even as far north as Seattle, treat yourself to a ride aboard Amtrak's luxurious *Coast Starlight.* In an effort to recapture the glory days of 1940s Streamline luxury liners, Amtrak is pulling out all the stops on these double-decker Superliners, complete with a gourmet dining car, first-class and coach lounge cars, standard and deluxe sleeping compartments, and enough diversions (including feature-length films, live entertainment, games for kids and adults, and a full bar) to make the overnight, 2-day trip a pleasure. All sleeping-car fares include three meals daily, prepared fresh onboard with an emphasis on regional flavor, and wines from vintners in Washington, Oregon, and California as well as seasonal specials from along the *Coast Starlight*'s route.

The highlight of the journey is the exceptional scenery you'll enjoy from the upper-level, panoramic windows of the coach and observation cars. Sweeping views of lushly green Washington State, California's rugged coastline, rural farmland, bucolic rolling hills, sparkling beaches, and charming railroad stations all provide a memorable travelogue. For travelers who believe the journey itself is as important as the destination, this excursion fits the bill perfectly.

While coach tickets are comparable to airplane fares, the surcharge for sleeping compartments adds considerably to the cost of the trip. All fares quoted are for one-way adult tickets. Children ages 2 to 15 travel for half price, and seniors 62 and older receive a 15% discount. Coach fare buys assigned seating in surprisingly comfortable upper-level reclining chairs. Blankets and pillows are offered in the evening, and fold-up leg rests help make sleeping more comfortable than you might imagine. Between San Francisco and Los Angeles, one-way adult coach fare ranges from $54 to $77; between Seattle and L.A., it's $102 to $170. Based on travel between Seattle and L.A., a standard sleeping compartment for two adds $255, a deluxe with private bathroom is $525, and a family sleeper for two adults and two kids (no bathroom) is $485.

It's advisable to book several months ahead for peak periods (summer, weekends, and holidays). Since the splendid views depend on daylight, also consider carefully before traveling during the very short days of winter. For information and tickets, call **Amtrak (*©* 800/USA-RAIL)** or visit its special *Coast Starlight* website at **www.coaststarlight.com**.

the state, including **American Eagle** (*©* 800/433-7300), **Skywest** (*©* 800/453-9417), **Shuttle by United** (*©* 800/241-6522), and **US Airways Express** (*©* 800/428-4322). The round-trip fare between Los Angeles and San Francisco ranges from $79 to $200. See the section titled "Orientation" in each city's chapter for further information.

BY TRAIN

Amtrak (*©* 800/USA-RAIL; www.amtrak.com) runs trains up and down the California coast, connecting San Diego, Los Angeles, and San Francisco, and all points in between. There are multiple trains each day, and rates fluctuate according to season and special promotions. One-way fares for popular segments can range from $20 (Los Angeles–Santa Barbara) to $23 (Los Angeles–San Diego) to $85 (San Francisco–Los Angeles). Also see "The *Coast Starlight:* All Aboard for Nostalgia" above.

7 Recommended Reading

by Matthew R. Poole

There's no shortage of reading material about the history and culture of California, one of the most romanticized places on earth. Almost from the beginning, novelists and poets were an essential part of California's cultural mosaic, and the works they've created offer a fascinating window into the lives and legends that have greatly influenced California's inception and fervid growth.

HISTORICAL   PERSPECTIVES Readers are spoiled for choices when it comes to fictionalized accounts of California's pioneers. Salinas native John Steinbeck, one of the state's best-known authors, paints a vivid portrayal of proletarian life in the early to mid-1900s. His *Grapes of Wrath* remains the classic account of itinerant farm laborers coming to California in the midst of the Great Depression. *Cannery Row* has forever made the Monterey waterfront famous, and *East of Eden* offers insight into the way of life in the Salinas Valley.

Famed humorist and storyteller Mark Twain penned vivid tales during California's gold rush era, including one of his most popular works, "The Celebrated Jumping Frog of Calaveras County" (an annual Gold Country competition that still has legs). Other good gold rush reads include Bret Harte's *The Luck of Roaring Camp,* a sentimental tale of hard-luck miners and their false toughness, and J. S. Holliday's *The World Rushed In,* one of the finest nonfiction accounts of the gold rush still in print.

San Francisco was also a popular setting for many early works, including Twain's *San Francisco,* a collection of articles that glorified "the liveliest, heartiest community on our continent." It was also the birthplace of Jack London, who wrote several short stories of his younger days as an oyster pirate on the San Francisco Bay, as well as *Martin Eden,* his semi-autobiographical account of life along the Oakland shores.

A much-heralded anthology containing selections from writers representing all the varied cultures in California's diverse history, *The Literature of California: Writings from the Golden State,* was recently published by the University of California Press.

Finally, for what some critics consider the best novel ever written about Hollywood, turn to Nathanael West's *The Day of the Locust,* a savage and satirical look at 1930s life on the fringes of the film industry.

MYSTERY & MAYHEM For all you mystery buffs headed to California, two must-reads include Frank Norris's *McTeague: A Story of San Francisco,* a violent tale of love and greed set at the turn of the century, and Dashiell Hammett's *The Maltese Falcon,* a steamy detective novel that captures the seedier side of San Francisco in the 1920s (you can even take a walking tour of Hammett's famous haunts). Another favorite is Raymond Chandler's *The Big Sleep,* in which private dick Philip Marlowe plies the seedier side of Los Angeles in the 1930s.

California has always been a hotbed for alternative—and, more often than not, controversial—literary styles.

Joan Didion, in her novel *Slouching Toward Bethlehem,* and Hunter S. Thompson, in his columns for the *San Francisco Examiner* (brought together in the collection *Generation of Swine*), both used a "new journalistic" approach in their studies of San Francisco in the 1960s. Tom Wolfe's early work *The Electric Kool-Aid Acid Test* follows the Hell's Angels, the Grateful Dead, and Ken Kesey's Merry Pranksters as they ride through the hallucinogenic 1960s. Meanwhile, Beat writers Allen Ginsberg and Jack Kerouac were penning protests against political conservatism—and promoting their bohemian lifestyle—in the former's controversial poem "Howl" (daringly published by Lawrence Ferlinghetti, poet and owner of City Lights in San Francisco's North Beach district) and the latter's famous tale of American adventure, *On the Road.*

CONTEMPORARY FICTION If you're interested in a contemporary look back at four generations in the life of an American family, you can do no better than Wallace Stegner's *Angle of Repose.* The winner of the Pulitzer Prize in 1971, this work chronicles the lives of pioneers on the western frontier. Among Stegner's many other works of fiction and nonfiction about the West is his novel *All the Little Live Things,* which explores the conflicts faced by retired literary agent Joe Allston; the book is set in the San Francisco Bay Area of the 1960s. *The Spectator Bird* (winner of the 1976 National Book Award) revisits Allston's character as he reflects on his life and his memories of a search for his roots.

SPECIAL-INTEREST   READS
Geology buffs will want to pack a copy of *Assembling California,* John McPhee's fascinating observation of California's complex geological history. Most of this volume was previously published in *The New Yorker.* Mike Davis's *City of Quartz* and *Ecology of Fear* offer a critical perspective on the social and natural history of Los Angeles.

Outdoor enthusiasts have literally dozens of sporting books to choose from, but most comprehensive is Foghorn Press's excellent outdoor series—*California Camping, California Fishing, California Golf, California Beaches,* and *California Hiking*—available at every major bookstore in the state. Another recommended choice is *Frommer's Great Outdoor Guide to Northern California.*

 FAST FACTS: California

Earthquakes In the rare event of an earthquake, you should know a few simple precautions that every California schoolchild is taught: If you're in a tall building, don't run outside; instead, move away from windows and toward the building's center. Crouch under a desk or table, or stand against a wall or under a doorway. If you're in bed, get under the bed or stand in a doorway, or crouch under a sturdy piece of furniture. When exiting the building, use stairwells, *not* elevators.

If you're in your car, pull over to the side of the road and stop, but wait until you're away from bridges or overpasses, as well as telephone or power poles and lines. Stay in your car.

If you're out walking, stay outside and away from trees, power lines, and the sides of buildings.

Emergencies To reach the police, ambulance service, or fire department, dial © **911.** No coins are needed at pay phones for 911 calls.

Liquor Laws Liquor and grocery stores, as well as some drugstores, can legally sell packaged alcoholic beverages between 6am and 2am. Most restaurants, nightclubs, and bars are licensed to serve alcoholic beverages during the same hours. The legal age for the purchase and consumption of alcoholic beverages is 21; proof of age is strictly enforced.

Taxes California's state sales tax is 7%. Some cities include an additional percentage, so tax varies throughout the state. Hotel taxes are almost always higher than tariffs levied on goods and services.

Time California and the entire West Coast are in the Pacific time zone, 3 hours earlier than the East Coast.

3

For International Visitors

by Matthew R. Poole & Mary Anne Moore

The pervasiveness of American culture around the world may make you feel that you know the United States pretty well, but leaving your own country still requires an additional degree of planning. This chapter will help prepare you for the more common problems that visitors to California may encounter.

1 Preparing for Your Trip

ENTRY REQUIREMENTS

Immigration laws are always a political issue in the United States, and the following requirements may have changed somewhat by the time you plan your trip. Check at any U.S. embassy or consulate for current information and requirements. You can also plug into the **U.S. State Department's** website at **www.state.gov**.

VISAS The U.S. State Department has a **Visa Waiver Program** allowing citizens of certain countries to enter the United States without a visa for stays of up to 90 days. At press time these included Andorra, Argentina, Australia, Austria, Belgium, Brunei, Denmark, Finland, France, Germany, Iceland, Ireland, Italy, Japan, Liechtenstein, Luxembourg, Monaco, the Netherlands, New Zealand, Norway, San Marino, Singapore, Slovenia, Spain, Sweden, Switzerland, the United Kingdom, and Uruguay. Citizens of these countries need a valid passport, proof of financial solvency, and a round-trip air or cruise ticket in their possession upon arrival. If they first enter the United States, they may also visit Mexico, Canada, Bermuda, and/or the Caribbean islands and return to the United States without a visa. Further information is available from any U.S. embassy or consulate. Canadian citizens may enter the United States without visas; they need only proof of residence.

Citizens of all other countries must have (1) a valid passport that expires at least 6 months later than the scheduled end of their visit to the United States, and (2) a visitor visa, which may be obtained with a nonrefundable US$45 application fee from any U.S. consulate.

To obtain a visa, the traveler must submit a completed application form (either in person or by mail) with a 1½-inch-square photo, and must demonstrate binding ties to a residence abroad. Usually you can get a visa at once or within 24 hours, but it may take longer during the summer rush from June through August. If you cannot go in person, contact the nearest U.S. embassy or consulate for directions on applying by mail. Your travel agent or airline office may also be able to provide you with visa applications and instructions. The U.S. consulate or embassy that issues your visa will determine whether you will be issued a multiple- or single-entry visa and any restrictions regarding the length of your stay.

British subjects can obtain up-to-date passport and visa information by calling the **U.S. Embassy Visa Information Line** (© 0891/200-290) or the **London Passport Office** (© 0990/210-410 for recorded information).

IMMIGRATION QUESTIONS

Telephone operators will answer your inquiries regarding U.S. immigration policies or laws at the **Immigration and Naturalization Service's Customer Information Center** (© 800/375-5283). Representatives are available from 9am to 3pm, Monday through Friday. The INS also runs a 24-hour automated information service, for commonly asked questions at the same number.

MEDICAL REQUIREMENTS

Unless you're arriving from an area known to be suffering from an epidemic (particularly cholera or yellow fever), inoculations or vaccinations are not required for entry into the United States. If you have a disease that requires treatment with narcotics or syringe-administered medications, carry a valid signed prescription from your physician to allay any suspicions that you may be smuggling narcotics (a serious offense that carries severe penalties in the United States). See "Insurance" below for information on health insurance for your trip.

For HIV-positive visitors, requirements for entering the United States are somewhat vague and change frequently. According to the publication *HIV and Immigrants: A Manual for AIDS Service Providers,* although the Immigration & Naturalization Service (INS) doesn't require a medical exam for everyone trying to come into the United States, INS officials may keep out people who they suspect are HIV positive. INS may stop people because they look sick or because they are carrying AIDS/HIV medicine.

If an HIV-positive non-citizen applying for a non-immigrant visa knows that HIV is a communicable disease of public health significance but checks "No" on the question about communicable diseases, INS may deny the visa because it thinks the applicant committed fraud. If a non-immigrant visa applicant checks "Yes," or if INS suspects the person is HIV positive, it will deny the visa unless the applicant asks for a special waiver for visitors. This waiver is for people visiting the United States for a short time, to attend a conference, for instance, to visit close relatives, or to receive medical treatment. It can be a confusing situation, so for up-to-the-minute information concerning HIV-positive travelers, contact the Center for Disease Control's **National AIDS Hotline** (© **800/342-AIDS,** in Spanish 800/344-7432, or a TGY line for the hearing impaired 800/243-7889) or the **Gay Men's Health Crisis** (© **212/367-1000;** www.gmhc.org).

DRIVER'S LICENSES

Foreign driver's licenses are recognized in California, although you may want to get an international driver's license if your home license is not written in English.

PASSPORTS

Safeguard your passport in an inconspicuous, inaccessible place like a money belt. If you lose it, visit the nearest consulate of your native country as soon as possible for a replacement. Passport applications are downloadable from the Internet sites listed below.

For Residents of Canada You can pick up a passport application at one of 29 regional passport offices or most travel agencies. The passport is valid for 5 years and costs C$60. Children under 16 may be included on a parent's passport but need their own to travel unaccompanied by the parent. Applications, which must be accompanied by two identical passport-sized photographs and proof of Canadian citizenship, are available at travel agencies throughout Canada or from the central

Passport Office, Department of Foreign Affairs and International Trade, Ottawa K1A 0G3 (℃ **800/567-6868;** www.dfait-maeci.gc.ca). Processing takes 5 to 10 days if you apply in person, or about 3 weeks by mail.

For Residents of the United Kingdom To pick up an application for a regular 10-year passport (the Visitor's Passport has been abolished), visit your nearest passport office, major post office, or travel agency. You can also contact the **UK Passport Agency** at (℃ **0870/521-0410**) or search its website at www.open.gov.uk/ukpass/ukpass. htm).Passports are £28 for adults and £14.80 for children under 6.

For Residents of Ireland You can apply for a 10-year passport, costing IR£45, at the **Passport Office,** Setanta Centre, Molesworth Street, Dublin 2 (℃ **01/671-1633;** www.irlgov.ie). Those under age 18 and over 65 must apply for a IR£10 3-year passport. You can also apply at 1A South Mall, Cork (℃ **021/272-525**), or over the counter at most main post offices.

For Residents of Australia Apply at your local post office or passport office or search the government website at www.passports.gov.au. Passports for adults are A$132 and for those under 18, A$66.

For Residents of New Zealand You can pick up a passport application at any travel agency or Link Centre. For more info, contact the **Passport Office,** P.O. Box 805, Wellington (℃ **0800/ 225-050;** www.passports.govt.nz). Passports for adults are NZ$80 and for those under 16, NZ$40.

CUSTOMS
WHAT YOU CAN BRING IN
Every visitor over 21 years of age may bring in, free of duty, the following: (1) 1 liter of wine or hard liquor; (2) 200 cigarettes, 100 cigars (but not from Cuba), or 3 pounds of smoking tobacco; and (3) $100 worth of gifts.

These exemptions are offered to travelers who spend at least 72 hours in the United States and who have not claimed them within the preceding 6 months. It is altogether forbidden to bring into the country foodstuffs (particularly fruit, cooked meats, and canned goods) and plants (vegetables, seeds, tropical plants, and the like). Foreign tourists may bring in or take out up to $10,000 in U.S. or foreign currency with no formalities; larger sums must be declared to U.S. Customs on entering or leaving, which includes filing form CM 4790. For more specific information regarding U.S. Customs, call your nearest U.S. embassy or consulate, call **U.S. Customs** (℃ **202/927-1770**), or visit the website at www.customs.gov.

WHAT YOU CAN TAKE HOME
U.K. citizens returning from the United States have a customs allowance of 200 cigarettes, 50 cigars, or 250 grams of smoking tobacco; 2 liters of still table wine; and 1 liter of spirits or strong liqueurs (over 22% volume), or 2 liters of fortified wine, sparkling wine or other liqueurs; 60cc (ml) perfume; 250cc (ml) toilet water; and £145 worth of all other goods, including gifts and souvenirs. People under 17 cannot have the tobacco or alcohol allowance. For more information, contact HM Customs & Excise at (℃ **0845/010-9000** (from outside the U.K., 44/20-8910-3744), or consult the website at www.hmce.gov.uk.

For a clear summary of **Canadian** rules, write for the booklet *I Declare,* issued by **Canada Customs & Revenue Agency** (℃ **800/467-9999;** www.ccra-adrc.gc.ca). Canada allows its citizens a $500 exemption, and you're allowed to bring back duty-free 200 cigarettes, 2.2 pounds of tobacco, 50 cigars, and 40 imperial ounces of liquor. In addition, you're allowed to mail gifts to Canada from abroad at the rate of C$60 a day, provided they're unsolicited and don't contain alcohol or tobacco (write on the package "Unsolicited gift, under $60 value"). All valuables should be declared on the Y-38 form before departure from Canada, including serial numbers of valuables you already own, such as expensive foreign cameras. *Note:* The $500 exemption can only be used once a year and only after an absence of 7 days.

The duty-free allowance in **Australia** is A$400 or, for those under 18, A$200. Personal property mailed home should be marked "Australian goods returned" to avoid payment of duty. Upon returning to Australia, citizens can bring in 250 cigarettes or 250 grams of loose tobacco, and 1,125 milliliters of alcohol. If you're returning with valuable goods you already own, such as foreign-made cameras, you should file form B263. A helpful brochure, available from Australian consulates or Customs offices, is *Know Before You Go.* For more information, contact **Australian Customs Services** at ✆ **1300/363-263,** or visit the website at www.customs.gov.au.

The duty-free allowance for **New Zealand** is NZ$700. Citizens over 17 can bring in 200 cigarettes, or 50 cigars, or 250 grams of tobacco (or a mixture of all three if their combined weight doesn't exceed 250 grams); plus 4.5 liters of wine and beer, or 1.125 liters of liquor. New Zealand currency does not carry import or export restrictions. Fill out a certificate of export, listing the valuables you are taking out of the country; that way, you can bring them back without paying duty. Most questions are answered in a free pamphlet available at New Zealand consulates and Customs offices: *New Zealand Customs Guide for Travellers, Notice no. 4.* For more information, contact **New Zealand Customs,** The Customhouse, 17-21 Whitmore St., Box 2218, Wellington (✆ **04/473-6099** or 0800/428-786; www.customs.govt.nz).

INSURANCE

Although it's not required of travelers, health insurance is highly recommended. Unlike many European countries, the United States does not usually offer free or low-cost medical care to its citizens or visitors. Doctors and hospitals are expensive, and in most cases will require advance payment or proof of coverage before they render their services. Other policies can cover everything from the loss or theft of your baggage and trip cancellation to the guarantee of bail in case you're arrested. Good policies will also cover the costs of an accident, repatriation, or death. Packages such as **Europ Assistance** in Europe are sold by automobile clubs and travel agencies at attractive rates. **Worldwide Assistance Services, Inc. (**✆ **800/ 821-2828**) is the agent for Europ Assistance in the United States.

Though lack of health insurance may prevent you from being admitted to a hospital in non-emergencies, don't worry about being left on a street corner to die: The American way is to fix you now and bill the living daylights out of you later.

British travelers will notice that most big travel agents offer their own insurance, which they'll probably try to sell you when you book a holiday. Think before you sign. Britain's Consumers' Association recommends that you insist on seeing the policy and reading the fine print before buying travel insurance. The **Association of British Insurers (**✆ **020/7600-3333**) gives advice by phone and publishes the free *Holiday Insurance,* a guide to policy provisions and prices. You might also shop around for better deals: Try **Columbus Travel Insurance Ltd. (**✆ **020/7375-0011**) or, for students, **Campus Travel (**✆ **020/ 7730-2101**).

Canadians should check with their provincial health plan offices or call **HealthCanada (**✆ **613/957-2991**) to find out the extent of their coverage and what documentation and receipts they must take home in case they are treated in the United States.

MONEY

CURRENCY The U.S. monetary system is painfully simple: The most common bills (all ugly, all green) are the $1 (colloquially, a "buck"), $5, $10, and $20 denominations. There are also $2 bills (seldom encountered), $50 bills, and $100 bills (the last two are usually not welcome as payment for small purchases). Note that newly designed bills are now in circulation. Despite rumors to the contrary, the old-style bills are still legal tender.

There are six denominations of coins: 1¢ (1 cent, or a penny), 5¢ (5 cents, or a nickel), 10¢ (10 cents, or a dime), 25¢ (25 cents, or a quarter), 50¢ (50 cents, or a half dollar), and the $1 coins, of which there are three types in circulation (the older, large silver dollar, the small Susan B. Anthony coin, and the golden Sacajawea coin).

Note: The "foreign-exchange bureaus" so common in Europe are rare even at airports in the United States, and nonexistent outside major cities. It's best not to change foreign money (or traveler's checks denominated in a currency other than U.S. dollars) at a small-town bank, or even a branch in a big city; in fact, leave any currency other than U.S. dollars at home—it may prove a greater nuisance to you than it's worth.

TRAVELER'S CHECKS Though traveler's checks are widely accepted, make sure that they're denominated in U.S. dollars, as foreign-currency checks are often difficult to exchange. The three traveler's checks that are most widely recognized—and least likely to be denied—are **Visa, American Express,** and **Thomas Cook.** Be sure to record the numbers of the checks, and keep that information

separately in case they get lost or stolen. Most California businesses are pretty good about taking traveler's checks, but you're better off cashing them in at a bank (in small amounts, of course) and paying in cash. *Remember:* You'll need identification, such as a driver's license or passport, to change a traveler's check.

CREDIT CARDS & ATMS Credit cards are the most widely used form of payment in the United States: **Visa** (BarclayCard in Britain), **MasterCard** (EuroCard in Europe, Access in Britain, and Chargex in Canada), **American Express, Diners Club, Discover,** and **Carte Blanche.** You must have a credit or charge card to rent a car. There are a handful of stores and restaurants in California that do not take credit cards, however, so be sure to ask in advance. Most businesses display a sticker near their entrances to let you know which cards they accept. (*Note:* Often businesses require a minimum purchase price, usually around $10, for use of a credit card.)

It is strongly recommended that you bring at least one major credit card. Hotels, car-rental companies, and airlines usually require a credit card imprint as a deposit against expenses, and in an emergency a credit card can be priceless.

You'll find automated teller machines (ATMs) on just about every block—at least in almost every town—in California and across the country. Some ATMs will allow you to draw U.S. currency against your bank and credit cards. Check with your bank before leaving home, and remember that you will need your personal identification number (PIN) to do so. Most accept Visa, MasterCard, and American Express, as well as ATM cards from other U.S. banks. Expect to be charged up to $3 per transaction, however, if you're not using your own bank's ATM. *Tip:* One way around these fees is to ask for cash back at grocery stores that accept ATM cards and don't charge usage fees. Of course, you'll have to purchase something first.

MONEYGRAMS If you have a financial emergency, you can also have someone wire money to you very quickly via Western Union. There are numerous offices throughout California; call ℭ **800/325-6000** for the one nearest you.

SAFETY

While tourist areas in California are generally safe, U.S. urban areas tend to be less safe than those in Europe or Japan. You should always stay alert. This is particularly true of large U.S. cities. It's wise to ask your hotel front desk staff or the city's or area's tourist office if you're in doubt about which neighborhoods are safe.

Avoid deserted areas, especially at night, and don't go into public parks at night unless there's a concert or similar occasion that will attract a crowd.

Avoid carrying valuables with you on the street, and don't display expensive cameras or electronic equipment. If you're using a map, consult it inconspicuously—or better yet, try to study it before you leave your room. Hold on to your pocketbook, and place your billfold in an inside pocket. In theaters, restaurants, and other public places, keep your possessions in sight.

Remember also that hotels are open to the public, and in a large hotel, security may not be able to screen everyone entering. Always lock your room door—don't assume that once inside your hotel you are automatically safe and no longer need to be aware of your surroundings.

Driving safety is important, too; question your rental agency about personal safety and ask for a traveler-safety brochure when you pick up your car. Obtain written directions—or a map with the route clearly marked—from the agency showing how to get to your destination. (Many agencies now offer the option of renting a cellular phone for the duration of your car rental; check with the rental agent when you pick up the car.) And, if possible, arrive and depart during daylight hours.

Recently, more and more crime has involved cars and drivers. If you drive off a highway into a doubtful neighborhood, leave the area as quickly as possible. If you have an accident, even on the highway, stay in your car with the doors locked until you assess the situation or until the police arrive. If you're bumped from behind on the street or are involved in a minor accident with no injuries and the situation appears to be suspicious, motion to the other driver to follow you. Never get out of your car in such situations. Go directly to the nearest police precinct, well-lit service station, or 24-hour store.

Always try to park in well-lit and well-traveled areas if possible. If you leave your rental car unlocked and empty of your valuables, you're probably safer than locking your car with valuables in plain view. Never leave any packages or valuables in sight. If someone attempts to rob you or steal your car, don't try to resist the thief—report the incident to the police department immediately by calling ℭ **911.**

2 Getting to the United States

Visitors arriving by air, no matter what the port of entry, should cultivate patience and resignation before setting foot on U.S. soil. Getting through immigration control may take as long as 2 hours on some days, especially on summer weekends, so be sure to have this guidebook or something else to read handy. Add the time it takes to clear Customs, and you'll see that you should make a 2- to 3-hour allowance for delays when you plan your connections between international and domestic flights.

In contrast, for the traveler arriving by car or rail from Canada, the border-crossing formalities have been streamlined to the vanishing point. People traveling by air from Canada, Bermuda, and some places in the Caribbean can sometimes clear Customs and Immigration at the point of departure, which is much quicker.

AIRLINES

See "Getting There," in chapter 2, "Planning Your Trip to California," for tips on finding the best airfare. Overseas visitors can also take advantage of the APEX (Advance Purchase Excursion) reductions offered by all major U.S. and European carriers.

FROM THE UNITED KINGDOM & IRELAND Many airlines offer service from the United Kingdom or Ireland to the United States. If possible, try to book a direct flight. Airlines that offer direct flights from London include British Airways, United, and Virgin Atlantic. Airlines that do not have direct flights from London to Los Angeles or San Francisco can book you on a connecting flight. You can make reservations by calling the following numbers in London: **American Airlines** (© 020/8572-5555 in London or 0845/778-9789), **British Airways** (© 0345/222-111), **Continental Airlines** (© 0800/776-464), **Delta Air Lines** (© 0800/414-767), **United Airlines** (© 0845/844-4777), and **Virgin Atlantic** (© 01293/747-747.

Residents of Ireland can call **Aer Lingus** (© 01-886-8888 in Dublin).

FROM AUSTRALIA & NEW ZEALAND **Qantas** (© 13-13-13 in Australia) has direct flights from Sydney to Los Angeles and San Francisco. You can also take **United** (© 131-777) from Australia to Los Angeles and San Francisco.

Air New Zealand (© 0800/737-000) offers service to Los Angeles International Airport.

FROM CANADA Canadian readers might also consider Air Canada (© 888/247-2262), which offers direct service from Toronto, Montreal, Calgary, and Vancouver to San Francisco, Sacramento, Los Angeles, and San Diego. Many American carriers also offer similar routes.

3 Getting Around the United States

BY PLANE Some large airlines (for example, Northwest and Delta) offer travelers on their transatlantic or transpacific flights special discount tickets under the name **Visit USA,** allowing mostly one-way travel from one U.S. destination to another at very low prices. These discount tickets are not sold in the United States and must be purchased abroad in conjunction with your international ticket. This system is the best, easiest, and fastest way to see the United States at a low cost. You should get information well in advance from your travel agent or the office of the airline concerned, because the conditions attached to these discount tickets can be changed without advance notice.

BY TRAIN International visitors can also buy a **USA Railpass,** good for 15 or 30 days of unlimited travel on **Amtrak** (© 800/USA-RAIL; www.amtrak.com). The pass is available through many foreign travel agents. Prices at press time for a 15-day pass are $295 off-peak, $440 peak; a 30-day pass costs $385 off-peak, $550 peak. (With a foreign passport, you can also buy passes at some Amtrak offices in the United States, including locations in San Francisco, Los Angeles, Chicago, New York, Miami, Boston, and Washington, D.C.) Reservations are generally required and should be made for each part of your trip as early as possible.

BY BUS Although bus travel is often the most economical form of public transit for short hops between U.S. cities, it can also be slow and uncomfortable—certainly not an option for everyone (particularly when Amtrak, which is far more luxurious, offers reasonable rates). **Greyhound/Trailways** (© **800/231-2222;** www.greyhound.com), the sole nationwide bus line, offers an **Ameripass** (© **888/454-7277**) for unlimited travel for 7 days at $185, 15 days at $285, 30 days at $385, and 60 days at $509. Passes must be purchased at a Greyhound terminal. Special rates are available for seniors and students.

BY CAR The most cost-effective, convenient, and comfortable way to travel around the United States—especially California—is by car. The Interstate highway system connects cities and towns all over the country; in addition to these high-speed, limited-access roadways, there's an extensive network of federal, state, and local highways and roads. California has no toll roads, but it does charge a toll fee at many major bridges. Some of the national car rental companies that have offices in California include **Alamo** (© 800/327-9633), **Avis** (© 800/831-2847), **Budget** (© 800/527-0700), **Dollar** (© 800/800-4000), **Hertz** (© 800/654-3131), **National** (© 800/227-7368), and **Thrifty** (© 800/847-4389).

If you plan on renting a car in the United States, you probably won't need the services of an additional automobile organization. If you plan to buy or borrow a car, automobile association membership is recommended. **AAA,** the **American Automobile Association** (© **800/922-8228** for Northern California and © **800/924-6141** for Southern California), is the country's largest auto club and supplies its members with maps, insurance, and, most important, emergency road service. The cost of joining runs from $66 for singles to $93 for two members, but if you're a member of a foreign auto club with reciprocal arrangements, you can enjoy free AAA service in America. See "Getting There" in chapter 2 for more information.

 FAST FACTS: For the International Traveler

Automobile Organizations Auto clubs will supply maps, suggested routes, guidebooks, accident and bail-bond insurance, and emergency road service. The **American Automobile Association (AAA)** is the major auto club in the United States. If you belong to an auto club in your home country, inquire about AAA reciprocity before you leave. You may be able to join AAA even if you're not a member of a reciprocal club; to inquire, call AAA at the previous numbers listed earlier in this chapter. AAA is actually an organization of regional auto clubs, so look under "AAA Automobile Club" in the White Pages of the phone directory. The San Francisco AAA headquarters is at 150 Van Ness Ave., San Francisco, CA 94102 (© **800/922-8228**). AAA's nationwide emergency road service telephone number is © **800/AAA-HELP.**

Business Hours Offices are usually open Monday through Friday from 9am to 5pm. Banks are open Monday through Friday from 9am to 3pm or later and sometimes Saturday mornings. Stores, especially those in shopping complexes, tend to stay open late—until about 9pm on weekdays and 6pm on weekends.

Currency & Currency Exchange See "Entry Requirements" and "Money" under "Preparing for Your Trip," earlier in this chapter.

Drinking Laws The legal age for purchase and consumption of alcoholic beverages is 21; proof of age is required and often requested at bars, nightclubs, and restaurants, so it's always a good idea to bring ID when you go out. In California, liquor is sold in supermarkets and grocery and liquor stores daily from 6am to 2am. Licensed restaurants are permitted to sell alcohol during the same hours. Note that many eateries are licensed only for beer and wine.

Do not carry open containers of alcohol in your car or any public area that isn't zoned for alcohol consumption (and very few exist in California). The police can, and probably will, fine you on the spot. And nothing will ruin your trip faster than getting a citation for DUI ("driving under the influence"), so don't even think about driving while intoxicated.

Electricity Like Canada, the United States uses 110 to 120 volts AC (60 cycles), compared to 220 to 240 volts AC (50 cycles) in most of Europe, Australia, and New Zealand. If your small appliances use 220 to 240 volts, you'll need a 110-volt transformer and a plug adapter with two flat parallel pins to operate them here. Downward converters that change 220 to 240 volts to 110 to 120 volts are difficult to find in the United States, so bring one with you.

Embassies & Consulates All embassies are located in the nation's capital, Washington, D.C. Some consulates are located in major U.S. cities, and most nations have a mission to the United Nations in New York City. If your country isn't listed below, call for directory information in Washington, D.C. (© **202/555-1212**) for the number of your national embassy.

The embassy of **Australia** is at 1601 Massachusetts Ave. NW, Washington, DC 20036 (© **202/797-3000**; www.austemb.org). There are consulates in New York, Atlanta, Honolulu, Los Angeles, and San Francisco.

The embassy of **Canada** is at 501 Pennsylvania Ave. NW, Washington, D.C. 20001 (© **202/682-1740**; www.canadianembassy.org). Other Canadian consulates are in Atlanta, Boston, Buffalo, Chicago, Dallas, Detroit, Los Angeles, Miami, Minneapolis, New York, and Seattle.

The embassy of **Ireland** is at 2234 Massachusetts Ave. NW, Washington, DC 20008 (© **202/462-3939**; www.irelandemb.org). Irish consulates are in Boston, Chicago, New York, and San Francisco.

The embassy of **Japan** is at 2520 Massachusetts Ave. NW, Washington, DC 20008 (© **202/238-6700**; www.embjapan.org). Japanese consulates are located in Anchorage, Atlanta, Boston, Chicago, Denver, Detroit, Guam, Honolulu, Houston, Kansas City, Los Angeles, Miami, New Orleans, New York, Portland, San Francisco, and Seattle.

The embassy of **New Zealand** is at 37 Observatory Circle NW, Washington, DC 20008 (© **202/328-4800**; www.nzemb.org). New Zealand consulates are in Atlanta, Boston, Chicago, Guam, Houston, Los Angeles, New York, Sacramento, Salt Lake City, San Diego, San Francisco, and Seattle.

The embassy of the **United Kingdom** is at 3100 Massachusetts Ave. NW, Washington, DC 20008 (© **202/588-6500**; www.britainusa.com). Other British consulates are in Atlanta, Boston, Chicago, Cleveland, Houston, Los Angeles, New York, San Francisco, and Seattle.

Emergencies Call © **911** to report a fire, call the police, or get an ambulance anywhere in the United States. This is a toll-free call (no coins are required at public telephones).

If you encounter traveler's problems, check the local telephone directory to find an office of the **Traveler's Aid Society,** a nationwide, nonprofit, social-service organization geared to helping travelers in difficult straits. Its services might include reuniting families separated while traveling, providing food and/or shelter to people stranded without cash, or even emotional counseling. If you're in trouble, seek them out.

Gasoline (Petrol) Petrol is known as gasoline (or simply "gas") in the United States, and petrol stations are known as both gas stations and service stations. Gasoline costs less than it does in Europe (about $1.90 per gallon in California at press time, but fluctuating), and taxes are already included in the printed price. One U.S. gallon equals 3.8 liters or 0.85 Imperial gallons.

Holidays Banks, government offices, post offices, and many stores, restaurants, and museums are closed on the following legal national holidays: January 1 (New Year's Day), the third Monday in January (Martin Luther King, Jr., Day), the third Monday in February (Presidents' Day, Washington's Birthday), the last Monday in May (Memorial Day), July 4 (Independence Day), the first Monday in September (Labor Day), the second Monday in October (Columbus Day), November 11 (Veterans' Day/Armistice Day), the fourth Thursday in November (Thanksgiving Day), and December 25 (Christmas). Also, the Tuesday following the first Monday in November is Election Day and is a federal government holiday in presidential-election years (held every 4 years, and next in 2004).

Legal Aid The foreign tourist will probably never become involved with the American legal system. If you are "pulled over" for a minor infraction (for example, of the highway code, such as speeding), never attempt to pay the fine directly to a police officer; this could be construed as attempted bribery, a much more serious crime. Pay fines by mail, or directly into the hands of the clerk of the court. If accused of a more serious offense, say and do nothing before consulting a lawyer. Here the burden is on the state to prove a person's guilt beyond a reasonable doubt, and everyone has the right to remain silent, whether he or she is suspected of a crime or actually arrested. Once arrested, a person can make one telephone call to a party of his or her choice. Call your embassy or consulate.

Mail If you aren't sure what your address will be in the United States, mail can be sent to you, in your name, c/o General Delivery at the main post office of the city or region where you expect to be. (Call ✆ **800/ 275-8777** or visit www.usps.gov for information on the nearest post office.) The addressee must pick mail up in person and must produce proof of identity (driver's license, passport, for example). Most post offices will hold your mail for up to 1 month, and are typically open Monday through Friday from 8am to 6pm, and Saturday from 9am to 3pm.

Generally found at intersections, mailboxes are blue with a red-and-white stripe and carry the inscription U.S. MAIL. If your mail is addressed to a U.S. destination, don't forget to add the five-digit postal code (or zip code) after the two-letter abbreviation of the state to which the mail is addressed (CA for California).

At press time, domestic postage rates are 20¢ for a postcard and 34¢ for a letter. For international mail, a first-class letter of up to one-half ounce costs 60¢ to Canada and Mexico); a first-class postcard costs 50¢ to

Canada and Mexico); and a preprinted postal aerogramme costs 70¢ to Canada and Mexico.

Smoking Heavy smokers are in for a tough time in California. There is no smoking allowed in public buildings, sports arenas, elevators, theaters, banks, lobbies, restaurants, offices, stores, bed-and-breakfasts, most small hotels, and bars. Yes, that's right, you can't even smoke in a bar in California—the only exception being a bar where drinks are served solely by the owner of the establishment.

Taxes In the United States, there is no value-added tax (VAT) or other indirect tax at the national level. Every state, county, and city has the right to levy its own local tax on all purchases (which can vary from 4% to 10%), including hotel and restaurant checks, airport tax, and so on.

Telephone, Telegraph, Telex & Fax The telephone system in the United States is run by private corporations, so rates, especially for long-distance service and operator-assisted calls, can vary widely. Generally, hotel surcharges on long-distance and local calls are astronomical, so you're usually better off using a **public pay telephone,** which you'll find clearly marked in most public buildings and private establishments as well as on the street. Convenience grocery stores and gas stations always have them. Many convenience groceries and packaging services sell **prepaid calling cards** in denominations up to $50; these can be the least expensive way to call home. Many public phones at airports now accept American Express, MasterCard, and Visa. **Local calls** made from public pay phones in most locales cost 35¢. Pay phones do not accept pennies, and few will take anything larger than a quarter

Most long-distance and international calls can be dialed directly from any phone. **For calls within the United States and to Canada,** dial 1 followed by the area code and the seven-digit number. **For other international calls,** dial 011 followed by the country code, city code, and the telephone number of the person you are calling.

Calls to area codes **800, 888,** and **877** are toll-free. However, calls to numbers in area codes **700** and **900** (chat lines, bulletin boards, "dating" services, and so on) can be very expensive—usually a charge of 95¢ to $3 or more per minute, and they sometimes have minimum charges that can run as high as $15 or more.

For reversed-charge or collect calls, and for person-to-person calls, dial 📞 **0** (zero, not the letter *O*) followed by the area code and number you want; an operator will then come on the line, and you should specify that you are calling collect, or person-to-person, or both. If your operator-assisted call is international, ask for the overseas operator.

For local directory assistance ("information"), dial 📞 **411;** for long-distance information, dial 1, then the appropriate area code and 555-1212.

Telegraph & telex services are provided primarily by Western Union. You can bring your telegram into the nearest Western Union office (there are hundreds across the country) or dictate it over the phone (📞 **800/325-6000**). You can also telegraph money or have it telegraphed to you very quickly over the Western Union system, but this service can cost as much as 15% to 20% of the amount sent.

Most hotels have **fax machines** available for guest use (be sure to ask about the charge to use it), and many hotel rooms are even wired for guests' fax machines. A less-expensive way to send and receive faxes may be at stores such as Mail Boxes, Etc., a national chain of packing service shops (look in the Yellow Pages directory under "Packing Services").

There are two kinds of telephone directories in the United States. The so-called **White Pages** lists private households and business subscribers in alphabetic order. The inside front cover lists emergency numbers for police, fire, ambulance, the Coast Guard, poison-control center, crime-victims hotline, and so on. The first few pages will tell you how to make long-distance and international calls, complete with country codes and area codes. Government numbers are usually printed on blue paper within the White Pages. Printed on yellow paper, the so-called **Yellow Pages** lists all local services, businesses, industries, and houses of worship according to activity with an index at the front or back. (Drugstores/pharmacies and restaurants are also listed by geographic location.) The Yellow Pages also includes city plans or detailed area maps, postal zip codes, and public transportation routes.

Time The continental United States is divided into **four time zones:** eastern standard time (EST), central standard time (CST), mountain standard time (MST), and Pacific standard time (PST). Alaska and Hawaii have their own zones. For example, noon in New York City (EST) is 11am in Chicago (CST), 10am in Denver (MST), 9am in Los Angeles (PST), 8am in Anchorage (AST), and 7am in Honolulu (HST). All of California is on Pacific standard time, which is 8 hours behind Greenwich mean time.

Daylight saving time is in effect from 1am on the first Sunday in April through 1am the last Sunday in October, except in Arizona, Hawaii, part of Indiana, and Puerto Rico. Daylight saving time moves the clock 1 hour ahead of standard time.

Tipping Tipping is so ingrained in the American way of life that the annual income tax of tip-earning service personnel is based on how much they should have received in light of their employers' gross revenues. Accordingly, they may have to pay tax on a tip you didn't actually give them.

Here are some tipping guidelines:$1 to $2 per bag to hotel bellhops and chamber staff; $1 to the valet parking attendant every time you get your car; 15% to 20% of the check to service staff in restaurants, bars, and nightclubs; 10% to 15% of the tab to bartenders; $1 per item to checkroom attendants; and 15% of the fare to cab drivers.

Tipping theater ushers, gas-station attendants, and cafeteria and fast-food restaurant employees isn't expected.

Toilets You won't find public toilets or "restrooms" on the streets in most U.S. cities (though San Francisco is experimenting with French-style public toilets), but they can be found in hotel lobbies, bars, restaurants, museums, department stores, railway and bus stations, and service stations. Note, however, that restaurants and bars in resorts or heavily visited areas may reserve their restrooms for the use of their patrons. Some establishments display a notice that toilets are for the use of patrons only. You can ignore this sign or, better yet, avoid arguments by paying for a cup of coffee or a soft drink, which will qualify you as a patron. Large hotels and fast-food restaurants are probably the best bet for good, clean facilities. If possible, avoid the toilets at parks and beaches, which tend to be dirty.

4

San Francisco

by Erika Lenkert

Consistently rated one of the top tourist destinations in the world, San Francisco abounds in multiple dimensions. Its famous, thrilling streets go up, and they go down; its multifarious citizens—and their adopted cultures, architectures, and cuisines—hail from San Antonio to Singapore; and its politics range from hyper-liberalism to an ever-encroaching wave of conservatism. Even something as mundane as fog takes on a new dimension as it creeps from the ocean and slowly envelops San Francisco in a resplendent blanket of mist.

From an outsider's perspective, San Francisco is still very much the city it's reputed to be. The restaurant scene is booming, boutiques abound, the Castro is the Castro, liberalism is hip, and all the goings-on in the unique neighborhoods take place against picture-perfect backdrops of famous bridges, bay vistas, cable cars, and colorful only-in-San-Francisco city life. But from an insider's view, the historic City by the Bay is striving to maintain its identity while embracing an evolution spawned by a burgeoning new economy, dot-commercialization (and

its recent downfall), and the slew of new residents who just don't want to live anywhere else. The result? Out-of-this-universe housing prices, a growing community of 20-something millionaires, and commercial and residential expansion to make room for the deep-pocketed masses. Even the sting of mass layoffs in the high-tech industry and stock market correction hasn't put a damper on the growing pains that resulted from a 7.3% population growth over 10 years of the already crowded city.

But that's nothing for you to worry about—so long as you're prepared to pay the high hotel and restaurant prices that come along with the San Francisco's status as the nation's favorite city destination. In fact, it makes a visit here even more exciting (minus the traffic, of course).

You'll still encounter classic San Francisco: Feel the cool blast of salt air as you stroll across the Golden Gate, stuff yourself on dim sum, and walk along the beach, pierce your nose, see a play, rent a Harley—the list is endless. It's all happening in San Francisco, and everyone's invited.

1 Orientation

ARRIVING
BY PLANE

Two major airports serve the Bay Area: San Francisco International and Oakland International. All the major car rental companies have desks at the airports; see "Getting Around" later in this chapter for details on car rentals.

SAN FRANCISCO INTERNATIONAL AIRPORT San Francisco International Airport, located 14 miles south of downtown directly on U.S. 101, is served by almost four dozen major scheduled carriers. Travel time to downtown during commuter rush hours is about 50 minutes; at other times it's about 20 to 25 minutes.

The airport offers a toll-free hot line available Monday through Friday from 7am to 5pm (PST) for information on ground transportation (© **800/736-2008**). The line is answered by a real person who will provide you with a rundown of all your options for getting into the city from the airport. Each of the three main terminals also has a desk where you can get the same information.

A cab from the airport to downtown will cost $28 to $32, plus tip. **SFO Airporter** buses (© **650/624-0500**) depart from outside the lower-level baggage claim area to downtown San Francisco every 15 to 30 minutes from 6:15am to midnight. They stop at several Union Square–area hotels, including the Grand Hyatt, San Francisco Hilton, San Francisco Marriott, Westin St. Francis, Parc Fifty-Five, Hyatt Regency, and Sheraton Palace. No reservations are needed. The cost is $12 each way; children under age 2 ride free.

Other private shuttle companies offer door-to-door airport service, in which you share a van with a few other passengers. **SuperShuttle** (© **415/558-8500**) will take you anywhere in the city, charging $14.50 to a residence or business, plus $8 for each additional person; and $40 to charter an entire van for up to seven passengers. Keep in mind that this shuttle demands they pick you up 2 hours before your flight, 3 hours during holidays.

The San Mateo County Transit system, **SamTrans** (© **800/660-4287** in northern California, or 650/508-6200; www.samtrans.com), runs two buses between the airport and the Transbay Terminal at First and Mission Streets. The 292 bus costs $2.20 and makes the trip in about 55 minutes. The KX bus costs $3 and takes only 35 minutes but permits only one carry-on bag. Both buses run daily. The 292 starts at 5:27am, and the KX starts at 6:03am. Both run frequently until 8pm, then hourly until about midnight.

OAKLAND INTERNATIONAL AIRPORT   Located about 5 miles south of downtown Oakland, at the Hagenberger Road exit off Calif. 17 (I-880), Oakland International Airport (© **510/577-4000**) is used primarily by passengers with East Bay destinations. Many San Franciscans, however, prefer this less-crowded, accessible airport when flying during busy periods. Without traffic, a car or taxi ride to the airport is a quick 20 to 30 minutes; with traffic, give yourself at least an hour.

Again, taxis from the airport to downtown San Francisco are expensive, costing approximately $45, plus tip.

Bayporter Express (© **415/467-1800**) is a shuttle service that charges $23 for the first person, $10 for each additional person to downtown San Francisco (it costs more to outer areas of town). Shuttles, usually located to the right of the airport exit, will take you to the city for around $20 per person. These are independently owned and prices vary, so ask and make any negotiations (sometimes possible) before you ride.

The cheapest way to downtown San Francisco (and easiest during traffic snarls) involves taking the shuttle bus from the airport to **BART** (Bay Area Rapid Transit; © **510/464-6000**). The **AirBART** shuttle bus runs about every 15 minutes Monday through Saturday from 6am to 11:30pm and Sunday from 8:30am to 11:30pm, stopping in front of Terminals 1 and 2 near the ground transportation signs. The cost is $2 for the 10-minute ride to BART's Coliseum terminal. BART fares vary, depending on your destination; the trip to downtown San Francisco costs $2.75 and takes 20 minutes once on board. The entire excursion should take around 45 minutes.

San Francisco at a Glance

San Francisco Bay

Fisherman's Wharf

Pier 41 (Ferries to Alcatraz)

Pier 39

Fort Mason

Aquatic Park

Jefferson St.

Beach St.

Ghirardelli Square

NORTH BEACH

Marina Blvd.

MARINA DISTRICT

Bay St.

RUSSIAN HILL

Columbus Ave.

Coit Tower

The Embarcadero

Chestnut St.

Lombard St.

101

"Crookedest Street"

TELEGRAPH HILL

COW HOLLOW

Van Ness Ave.

Polk St.

Hyde St.

Taylor St.

Grant Ave.

Kearny St.

Battery St.

Union St.

Gough St.

PACIFIC HEIGHTS

Broadway

CHINATOWN

FINANCIAL DISTRICT

Washington St.

Transbay Transit Terminal

NOB HILL

California St.

Sacramento St.

Franklin St.

101

Sutter St.

UNION SQUARE

Powell St.

Yerba Buena Gardens

Fillmore St.

Divisadero St.

Post St.

Geary St.

Moscone Convention Center

1st St.

Geary Blvd.

JAPANTOWN

WESTERN ADDITION

Turk St.

CIVIC CENTER

Mission St.

Howard St.

Folsom St.

Harrison St.

3rd St.

Masonic St.

Golden Gate Ave.

Fulton St.

SOMA

4th St.

5th St.

Alamo Square

Fell St.

8th St.

9th St.

Bryant St.

6th St.

Oak St.

10th St.

7th St.

Haight St.

Market St.

HAIGHT-ASHBURY

Stanyan St.

Cole St.

Ashbury St.

14th St.

101

280

17th St.

THE CASTRO

17th St.

Church St.

Dolores St.

Mission St.

South Van Ness Ave.

MISSION DISTRICT

Potrero Ave.

POTRERO HILL

Claredon Ave.

Castro St.

Deharo St.

Connecticut St.

Twin Peaks

Portola Dr.

24th St.

Clipper St.

101

BY CAR

San Francisco is accessible via several major highways: **U.S. 101** and **Calif. 1** from the north and south; and **I-80** and **I-580** from the northeast and east, respectively. If you drive from Los Angeles, you can either take the longer coastal route along Calif. 1/U.S. 101 (437 miles, or 11 hours), or the inland route along I-5 to I-580 (389 miles, or 7 hours). From Mendocino, it's a little over 3 hours along Calif. 1, and about 3¼ hours along U.S. 101; and from Sacramento, it's 88 miles, or 1½ hours, along I-80.

BY TRAIN

San Francisco–bound **Amtrak** (✆ **800/USA-RAIL;** www.amtrak.com) trains leave from New York and cross the country via Chicago. The journey takes about 3½ days, and seats sell quickly. At this writing, the lowest round-trip fare costs anywhere from $381 to $600 from New York and from $335 to $570 from Chicago. These heavily restricted tickets are good for 45 to 180 days and allow up to three stops along the way, depending on your ticket.

Round-trip tickets from Los Angeles can be purchased for as little as $88 or as much as $148. Trains actually arrive in Emeryville, just north of Oakland, and connect with regularly scheduled buses to San Francisco's Ferry Building and Cal Train station in downtown San Francisco.

Cal Train (✆ **800/660-4287** or 415/546-4461) operates train services between San Francisco and the towns of the peninsula. The city depot is at 700 Fourth St., at Townsend Street.

VISITOR INFORMATION

The **San Francisco Visitor Information Center,** Hallidie Plaza, 900 Market St. (at Powell St.), Lower Level, San Francisco, CA 94102 (✆ **415/283-0177;** www.sfvisitor.org), is the best source for any kind of specialized information about the city. Even if you don't have a specific question, you may want to send them $3 for their 100-page magazine, *The San Francisco Book.*

CITY LAYOUT

San Francisco occupies the tip of a 32-mile-long peninsula between San Francisco Bay and the Pacific Ocean. Its land area measures about 46 square miles. Twin Peaks, in the geographic center of the city, is more than 900 feet high.

San Francisco may seem confusing at first, but it quickly becomes easy to negotiate. The city's downtown streets are arranged in a simple grid pattern, with the exception of Market Street and Columbus Avenue, which cut across the grid at right angles to each other. Hills appear to distort this pattern, however, and can be disorienting. But as you learn your way around, these same hills will become your landmarks and reference points.

MAIN ARTERIES & STREETS   **Market Street** is San Francisco's main thoroughfare. Most of the city's buses travel this route on their way to the Financial District from the outer neighborhoods to the west and south. The tall office buildings clustered downtown are at the northeast end of Market; 1 block beyond lie the Embarcadero and the Bay.

The **Embarcadero** curves along San Francisco Bay from south of the Bay Bridge to the northeast perimeter of the city and terminates at Fisherman's Wharf, the famous tourist-oriented pier. Aquatic Park, Fort Mason, and the Golden Gate National Recreation Area are located farther on around the bay, occupying the northernmost point of the peninsula.

From the eastern perimeter of Fort Mason, **Van Ness Avenue** runs due south, back to Market Street.

NEIGHBORHOODS & DISTRICTS IN BRIEF

Union Square Union Square is the commercial hub of the city. Most major hotels and department stores are crammed into the area surrounding the actual square (named for a series of violent pro-union mass demonstrations staged here on the eve of the Civil War), with a plethora of upscale boutiques, restaurants, and galleries tucked between the larger buildings.

Nob Hill/Russian Hill Bounded by Bush, Larkin, Pacific, and Stockton Streets, Nob Hill is the genteel, well-heeled district of the city, still occupied by the major power brokers and the neighborhood businesses they frequent. Russian Hill extends from Pacific to Bay and from Polk to Mason. It's marked by steep streets, lush gardens, and high-rises occupied by both the moneyed and the more bohemian.

SoMa No part of San Francisco has been more affected by recent development than South of Market (dubbed "SoMa"). The once desolate area is the hub of dot-commercialization and $750,000 lofts, as well as urban entertainment à la the Museum of Modern Art and Yerba Buena Gardens. It is officially demarcated by the Embarcadero, Highway 101, and Market Street, with the greatest concentrations of interest around Yerba Buena Center, along Folsom and Harrison Streets between Steuart and Sixth, and Brannan and Market. Along the waterfront are an array of restaurants and the new and absolutely fab Pacific Bell Park. Farther west, around Folsom between Seventh and 11th Streets, is where much of the city's night-clubbing occurs.

Financial District East of Union Square, this area bordered by the Embarcadero, Market, Third, Kearny, and Washington Streets is the city's business district and stomping grounds for many major corporations. The pointy TransAmerica Pyramid, at Montgomery and Clay Streets, is one of the area's most conspicuous features. To its east stands the sprawling Embarcadero Center, an $8\frac{1}{2}$-acre complex housing offices, shops, and restaurants. Farther east still is the World Trade Center, standing adjacent to the old Ferry Building, the city's pre-bridge transportation hub. Ferries to Sausalito and Larkspur still leave from this point.

Chinatown The official entrance to Chinatown is marked by a large red-and-green gate on Grant Avenue at Bush Street. Beyond lies a 24-block labyrinth, bordered by Broadway, Bush, Kearny, and Stockton Streets, filled with restaurants, markets, temples, and shops—and, of course, a substantial percentage of San Francisco's Chinese residents. Chinatown is a great place for urban exploration all along Stockton, Grant, and Portsmouth Square, and the alleys that lead off them like Ross and Waverly. This area is jam-packed, so don't even think about driving around here.

North Beach The Italian quarter, which stretches from Montgomery and Jackson to Bay Street, is one of the best places in the city to grab a coffee, pull up a cafe chair, and do some serious people watching. Nightlife is equally happening:

Restaurants, bars, and clubs along Columbus and Grant Avenues attract folks from all over the Bay Area to fight for a parking place and romp through the festive neighborhood. Down Columbus toward the Financial District are the remains of the city's Beat generation landmarks, including Lawrence Ferlinghetti's City Lights Bookstore and Vesuvio's Bar. Broadway—a short strip of sex joints—cuts through the heart of the district. Telegraph Hill looms over the east side of North Beach, topped by Coit Tower, one of San Francisco's best vantage points.

Fisherman's Wharf North Beach runs into Fisherman's Wharf, which was once the busy heart of the city's great harbor and waterfront industries. Today, it is a tacky-but-attractive tourist area with little if any authentic waterfront life, except for recreational boating and some friendly sea lions.

Marina District Created on land-fill for the Pan Pacific Exposition of 1915, the Marina boasts some of the best views of the Golden Gate, as well as plenty of grassy fields alongside San Francisco Bay. Streets are lined with elegant, Mediter-ranean-style homes and apart-ments, which are inhabited by the city's well-to-do singles and wealthy families. Here, too, are the Palace of Fine Arts, the Exploratorium, and Fort Mason Center. The main street is Chestnut between Franklin and Lyon, which is lined with shops, cafes, and boutiques. Because of its landfill foundation, the Marina was one of the city's hardest-hit districts in the 1989 quake.

Cow Hollow Located west of Van Ness Avenue, between Russian Hill and the Presidio, this flat area sup-ported 30 dairy farms in 1861. Today, Cow Hollow is largely residential and occupied by the city's young and yuppie. Its two primary commercial thoroughfares are Lombard Street, known for its many relatively inexpensive motels; and Union Street, a flourishing shopping sector filled with restau-rants, pubs, cafes, and shops.

Pacific Heights The ultra-elite, such as the Gettys and Danielle Steel—and those lucky enough to buy before the real-estate boom—reside in the mansions and homes that make up Pacific Heights. When the rich meander out of their fortresses, they wander down to Union Street, a long stretch of bou-tiques, restaurants, cafes, and bars.

Japantown Bounded by Octavia, Fillmore, California, and Geary, Japantown shelters only a small percentage of the city's Japanese population, but it's still a cultural experience (albeit rather anticlimac-tic) to explore these few square blocks and the shops and restau-rants within them.

Civic Center Although millions of dollars have been expended on brick sidewalks, ornate lampposts, and elaborate street plantings, the southwestern section of Market Street remains downright dilapi-dated. The Civic Center, at the "bottom" of Market Street, is an exception. This large complex of buildings includes the domed City Hall, the Opera House, Davies Symphony Hall, and the city's main library. The landscaped plaza connecting the buildings is the staging area for San Francisco's demonstrations for or against just about everything.

Haight-Ashbury Part trendy, part nostalgic, part funky, the Haight, as it's most commonly known, was the soul of the psychedelic and free-loving 1960s and the center of the counterculture movement. Today, the neighborhood straddling upper Haight Street on the eastern border of Golden Gate Park is more gentrified, but the commercial area still harbors all walks of life. Leftover aging hippies mingle outside Ben & Jerry's ice-cream shop (where they may still be talking about Jerry Garcia) with grungy, begging street kids, nondescript marijuana dealers, and people with Day-Glo hair. But you don't need to be a freak or wear tie-dye to enjoy the Haight: The food, shops, and bars cover all tastes. From Haight, walk south on Cole Street for a more peaceful and quaint neighborhood experience.

Richmond & Sunset Districts San Francisco's suburbs of sorts, these are the city's largest and most populous districts, consisting mainly of homes, small shops, and neighborhood restaurants. Though both districts border Golden Gate Park and Ocean Beach, only a small percentage of tourists venture into "The Avenues," as this area is referred to by locals.

The Castro One of the liveliest streets in town, Castro is practically synonymous with San Francisco's gay community. Located at the very end of Market Street, between 17th and 18th Streets, the Castro supports dozens of shops, restaurants, and bars catering to the gay community. Open-minded straight people are welcome, too.

Mission District This is another area greatly affected by the city's new wealth. The Mexican and Latin American populations, along with their cuisine, traditions, and art, still make the Mission District a vibrant area to visit. Some parts of the neighborhood are still poor and sprinkled with the homeless, gangs, and drug addicts, but more and more young urbanites are infiltrating, moving into the "reasonably" priced rentals (reasonable is a relative term) and forging the endless oh-so-hot restaurants and bars that stretch from 16th Street and Valencia to 25th and Mission Streets. Less adventurous tourists still duck into Mission Dolores, cruise by a few of the 200+ amazing murals, and head back downtown. Don't be afraid to visit this area, but do use caution at night.

2 Getting Around

BY PUBLIC TRANSPORTATION

The San Francisco Municipal Railway, better known as **Muni** (© 415/ 673-6864), operates the city's cable cars, buses, and Metro streetcars. Together, these three public transportation services crisscross the entire city, making San Francisco fully accessible to everyone. Buses and Metro streetcars cost $1 for adults, 35¢ for children ages 5 to 17, and 35¢ for seniors over 65. Cable cars cost $3 ($1 for seniors from 9pm to midnight and from 6 to 7am). Needless to say, they're packed primarily with tourists. Exact change is required on all vehicles except cable cars.

For detailed route information, phone Muni or consult the bus map at the front of the Yellow Pages. If you plan on making extensive use of public transportation, you may want to invest in a comprehensive route map ($2), sold at the San Francisco Visitor Information Center (see "Visitor Information" in the "Orientation" section, earlier in this chapter) and in many downtown retail outlets.

Muni **discount passes,** called "Passports," entitle holders to unlimited rides on buses, Metro streetcars, and cable cars. A Passport costs $6 for 1 day, and $10 or $15 for 3 or 7 consecutive days. As a bonus, your Passport also entitles you

San Francisco Mass Transit

Cable Car
Bus Line
BART/Muni stop

San Francisco Bay

BART

Ferry Terminal — 7 9 21 71

Transbay Terminal

5 38L
42

The Embarcadero

BART/Muni Embarcadero — 1

Second St.

Third St.

9 71

9X 15
45 30
45 30

Fourth St.

Broadway

30X

Montgomery St.

30X
41 30X
9X
15

Grant Ave.

Stockton St.
30 9X

Powell St.

Mason St.

UNION SQUARE

BART/Muni Powell

9
7
5
71

Francisco St.

TELEGRAPH HILL

NORTH BEACH

CHINATOWN

15
45

Columbus Ave.

32

15

30

Jones St.

12 83

27

NOB HILL

27

38

FISHERMAN'S WHARF

42

RUSSIAN HILL

41 45

Hyde St.

Larkin St.

Sutte St.

Post St.

Geary St.

38

30

Polk St.

Van Ness Ave.

42

1

Franklin St.

42

30X

Gough St.

12

Octavia St.

1

Francisco St.

Lombard St.

30

30X

PACIFIC HEIGHTS

42

Laguna St.

Buchanan St.

Sacramento St.

California St.

Pine St.

Bush St.

JAPANTOWN

38

45

41

12

Beach St.

Bay St.

Webster St.

Fillmore St.

Steiner St.

Pierce St.

Scot St.

Geary Expwy

IMPORTANT BUS LINES FOR TRAVELERS

5 Civic Center, Alamo Square Historic District, Golden Gate Park

21 Via Haight & Market to Golden Gate Park, Haight-Ashbury
71

38 Via Geary Blvd. to Japan Center, Richmond District, Lincoln Park

30 North Beach, Union Square, Fisherman's Wharf

15 Via Kearney to North Beach, Chinatown

41 Via Union St. to the Presidio, Pacific Heights
45

32 Via Embarcadero to Fisherman's Wharf, Financial District
42

to admission discounts at 24 of the city's major attractions, including the Asian Art Museum, the California Academy of Sciences, and the Japanese Tea Garden (all in Golden Gate Park); the Museum of Modern Art; Coit Tower; the Exploratorium; the zoo; and the National Maritime Museum and Historic Ships. Among the places where you can purchase a Passport are the San Francisco Visitor Information Center, the Holiday Inn Civic Center, and the Tix Bay Area booth at Union Square.

BY CABLE CAR   San Francisco's cable cars may not be the most practical means of transport, but these rolling historic landmarks sure are a fun ride. There are only three lines in the city, and they're all concentrated in the downtown area. The most scenic, and exciting, is the **Powell-Hyde line,** which follows a zigzag route from the corner of Powell and Market Streets, over both Nob Hill and Russian Hill, to a turntable at gaslit Victorian Square in front of Aquatic Park. The **Powell-Mason line** starts at the same intersection and climbs over Nob Hill before descending to Bay Street, just 3 blocks from Fisherman's Wharf. The least scenic is the **California Street line,** which begins at the foot of Market Street and runs a straight course through Chinatown and over Nob Hill to Van Ness Avenue. All riders must exit at the last stop and wait in line for the return trip. The cable car system operates daily from approximately 6:30am to 12:30am.

BY BUS   Buses reach almost every corner of San Francisco and travel over the bridges to Marin County and Oakland. All are numbered and display their destinations on the front. Stops are designated by signs, curb markings, and yellow bands on adjacent utility poles, and most bus shelters exhibit Muni's transportation map and schedule. Many buses travel along Market Street or pass near Union Square and run daily from about 6am to midnight, after which there is infrequent all-night "Owl" service. If you can help it, for safety purposes avoid taking buses late at night.

Popular tourist routes are nos. 5, 7, and 71, all of which run to Golden Gate Park; 41 and 45, which travel along Union Street; and 30, which runs between Union Square and Ghirardelli Square.

BY METRO STREETCAR   Five of Muni's six Metro streetcar lines, designated J, K, L, M, and N, run underground downtown and on the street in the outer neighborhoods. The sleek railcars make the same stops as BART (see below) along Market Street, including Embarcadero Station (in the Financial District), Montgomery and Powell Streets (both near Union Square), and the Civic Center (near City Hall). Past the Civic Center, the routes branch off in different directions: The J line will take you to Mission Dolores; the K, L, and M lines to Castro Street; and the N line parallels Golden Gate Park and now extends all the way to the Embarcadero. Metros run about every 15 minutes, more frequently during rush hours. Service is offered Monday to Friday from 5am to 12:30am, on Saturday from 6am to 12:20am, and on Sunday from 8am to 12:20am. The L and N lines operate all day and all night.

The most recent streetcar additions are not newcomers at all, but San Francisco's beloved 1930s streetcars. The beautiful, rejuvenated multicolored cars on the F Market line now run along the Embarcadero from Fisherman's Wharf to Market Street, and then to the Castro and back. It's a quick and charming way to get up and downtown without any hassle.

BY BART   BART, an acronym for **Bay Area Rapid Transit (© 650/ 992-2278**), is a futuristic-looking, high-speed rail network that connects San

Francisco with the East Bay—Oakland, Richmond, Concord, and Fremont. Four stations are located along Market Street (see "By Metro Streetcar," above). Fares range from $1.10 to $4.30, depending on how far you go. Tickets are dispensed from machines in the stations and are magnetically encoded with a dollar amount. Computerized exits automatically deduct the correct fare. Children 4 and under ride free. Trains run every 15 to 20 minutes, Monday through Friday from 4am to midnight, Saturday from 6am to midnight, and Sunday from 8am to midnight.

A $2.5 billion, 33-mile BART extension, currently under construction, includes a southern line that is planned to extend all the way to San Francisco International Airport. It will open, presumably, around the year 2005.

BY TAXI

If you're downtown during rush hours or leaving from a major hotel, it won't be hard to hail a cab—just look for the lighted sign on the roof that indicates if one is available. Otherwise, it's a good idea to call one of the following companies to arrange a ride: **Veteran's Cab** (© 415/552-1300), **Luxor Cabs** (© 415/282-4141), or **Yellow Cab** (© 415/626-2345). Rates are approximately $2.50 for the first mile and $1.80 for each mile thereafter.

BY CAR

With the city becoming more crowded by the minute, a car can be your worst nightmare—you're likely to end up stuck in traffic with lots of aggressive and frustrated drivers, pay upward of $25 a day in parking, and spend a good portion of your vacation looking for a parking space. But if you want to venture outside of the city, driving is the best way to go.

RENTALS The major car-rental companies operating in the city include **Alamo** (© 800/327-9633), **Avis** (© 800/331-1212), **Budget** (© 800/527-0700), **Dollar** (© 800/800-3665), **Hertz** (© 800/654-3131), **National** (© 800/CAR-RENT), and **Thrifty** (© 800/535-1391).

PARKING If you want to have a relaxing vacation here, don't even attempt to find street parking downtown or in Nob Hill, North Beach, or Chinatown; by Fisherman's Wharf; or on Telegraph Hill. Park in a garage or take a cab or a bus. If you do find street parking, pay attention to street signs that will explain when you can park and for how long. Be especially careful not to park in zones that are tow areas during rush hours.

When parking on a hill, apply the hand brake, put the car in gear, and *curb your wheels*—toward the curb when facing downhill, away from the curb when facing uphill. Curbing your wheels will not only prevent a possible "runaway," but also keep you from getting a ticket—an expensive fine that is aggressively enforced.

 FAST FACTS: San Francisco

American Express For travel arrangements, traveler's checks, currency exchange, and other member services, American Express has an office 455 Market St. at First Street (tel] **415/536-2600**), open Monday through Friday from 8:30am to 5:30pm and Saturday from 9am to 2pm. To report lost or stolen traveler's checks, call © **800/221-7282**. For American Express Global Assist, call © **800/554-2639**.

Dentist In the event of a dental emergency, see your hotel concierge or contact the **San Francisco Dental Society** (© **415/421-1435**) for a referral to a specialist. The **San Francisco Dental Office**, 131 Steuart St. (© **415/777-5115**), between Mission and Howard Streets, offers emergency service and comprehensive dental care Monday, Tuesday, and Friday from 8am to 4:30pm, Wednesday and Thursday from 10:30am to 6:30pm.

Doctor **Saint Francis Memorial Hospital,** 900 Hyde St., between Bush and Pine Streets on Nob Hill (© **415/353-6000**), provides 24-hour emergency-care service. The hospital also operates a physician-referral service (© **800/333-1355**).

Drugstores See "Pharmacies," below.

Emergencies Dial © **911** for the police, an ambulance, or the fire department.

Pharmacies There are **Walgreens** drugstores all over town, including one at 135 Powell St. (© **415/391-4433**). The store is open Monday through Saturday from 8am to midnight and Sunday from 9am to 10pm, but the pharmacy has more limited hours: Monday through Friday from 8am to 8:30pm, Saturday from 9am to 5pm, and Sunday from 10am to 6pm. The branch on Divisadero Street at Lombard (© **415/931-6415**) has a 24-hour pharmacy. The pharmacy at **Merrill's,** 805 Market St. (© **415/431-5466**), is open Monday through Friday from 8:30am to 6:30pm and Saturday from 9:30am to 5:30pm, while the rest of the drugstore is open Monday to Friday 7am to 9pm, Saturday 8am to 7pm, and Sunday 9:30am to 6pm.

Police For emergencies, dial © **911** from any phone; no coins are needed. For other matters, call © **415/553-0123.**

Post Office There are dozens of post offices located all around the city. The closest office to Union Square is inside Macy's department store, 170 O'Farrell St. (© **800/275-8777**).

Safety Few locals would recommend walking alone late at night in certain areas, particularly the Tenderloin, between Union Square and the Civic Center. Compared with similar areas in other cities, however, even this section of San Francisco is relatively tranquil. Other areas where you should be particularly alert are the Mission District, around 16th and Mission Streets; the lower Fillmore area, around lower Haight Street; and the SoMa area south of Market Street.

Taxes An 8.5% sales tax is added at the register for all goods and services purchased in San Francisco. The city hotel tax is a whopping 14%. There is no airport tax.

Transit Information Call **Muni** at © **415/673-6864** Monday through Friday between 7am and 5pm and Saturday and Sunday between 9am and 5pm. At other times, recorded information is available.

Useful Telephone Numbers **Tourist information** (© 415/283-0176); **highway conditions** (© 800/427-7623); **MovieFone** (© 415/777-FILM).

Weather Call © **831/656-1725** to find out when the next fog bank is rolling in.

3 Accommodations

San Francisco is an extensive—albeit expensive—hotel town, especially considering its relatively small size. We can't cover them all in this guide, so if you'd like a larger selection, check out *Frommer's San Francisco,* which has dozens of other options.

Most of the hotels listed below are within easy walking distance of Union Square, and accessible via cable car. Union Square is near the city's major shops, the Financial District, and all transportation. Prices listed below do not include state and city taxes, which total 14%.

The price categories below reflect the prices of double rooms during the high season, which runs approximately from April through September. (In reality, rates don't vary much because the city is so popular year-round.) But remember: These are rack (or published) rates; you can almost always get a better deal if you inquire about packages, weekend discounts, corporate rates, and family plans.

Bed-and-Breakfast California, 12711 McCartysville Place, Saratoga, CA 95070 (© **800/872-4500** or 408/867-9662; fax 408/867-0907; www. bbintl.com), offers a selection of accommodations priced from $70 to $140 per night (2-night minimum). Choices range from simple rooms in private homes to luxurious, full-service carriage houses, houseboats, and Victorian homes. **San Francisco Reservations,** 360 22nd Street, Suite 300, Oakland, CA 94612 (© **800/677-1500** or 510/628-4450; www.hotelres.com), arranges reservations at more than 300 of San Francisco's hotels and often offers discounted rates.

In addition to the hotels listed below, we also recommend those represented by the reasonably priced and fashionable **Joie de Vivre** hotel chain (© 800/ SF-TRIPS; www.sftrips.com) and **Personality Hotels** (© 800/553-1900; www.personalityhotels.com), which spiffs up older buildings in central locales. Pricier options include those from the **Kimpton Group,** such as the **Juliana Hotel** (© 800/328-3880) and the new **Hotel Serrano** (© 415/885-2500), the latter of which opened in mid-1999; and the stately **Donatello** (© 800/ 227-3184). The **San Francisco Hilton & Towers** (© 800/445-8667) and **San Francisco Marriott** (© 800/ 228-9290) both have impersonal convention-hotel ambiance, but are conveniently located downtown and have enough rooms to sleep thousands.

UNION SQUARE
VERY EXPENSIVE

Campton Place Hotel ★★★   With a $10 million room renovation completed by the end of 2000, this already fabulous luxury boutique hotel offers some of the best accommodations in town—not to mention the most expensive. Along with gutting the rooms and replacing the furnishings with limestone, pear wood, and more Italian-modern and Asian-influenced decor, management changed the rooms' layout for the better. By eliminating 17 of the once-cramped rooms they made the new 110 units more spacious. Two executive suites and one luxury suite push the haute envelope to even more luxurious heights. Discriminating returning guests will still fine superlative service, extra-large beds, exquisite bathrooms, bathrobes, top-notch toiletries, slippers, and every necessity and whim that's made Campton Place a favored temporary address.

340 Stockton St. (between Post and Sutter Sts.), San Francisco, CA 94108. © **800/235-4300** or 415/ 781-5555. Fax 415/955-5536. www.camptonplace.com. 110 units. $335–$460 double; from $550–$2,000 suite. American breakfast $19. AE, DC, MC, V. Valet parking $32. Cable car: Powell-Hyde and Powell-Mason

San Francisco Accommodations

Abigail Hotel **35**
Andrews Hotel **21**
Campton Place Hotel **31**
Clarion Bedford Inn **22**
Commodore International **20**
Edward II Inn & Pub **5**
Fairmont Hotel & Tower **17**
Golden Gate Hotel **19**
Harbor Court **33**
Hotel Bohème **13**
Hotel del Sol **7**
Hotel Diva **26**
Hotel Griffon **33**
Hotel Majestic **3**
Hotel Monaco **24**
Hotel Triton **16**
Huntington Hotel **18**
Inn on Castro **1**
Kensington Park Hotel **29**
King George Hotel **27**
The Laurel **4**
Mandarin Oriental **14**
Marina Inn **8**
Mark Hopkins Intercontinental **17**
Maxwell **26**
Palace Hotel **32**
Parker House **2**
Phoenix Hotel **36**
Prescott Hotel **28**
Queen Anne Hotel **3**
Ritz-Carlton **15**
San Remo Hotel **12**
Savoy Hotel **23**
Sheraton at Fisherman's Wharf **10**
Sir Francis Drake **29**
Tuscan Inn **11**
Union Street Inn **6**
W San Francisco Hotel **34**
Warwick Regis **25**
Westin St. Francis **30**
Wharf Inn **9**

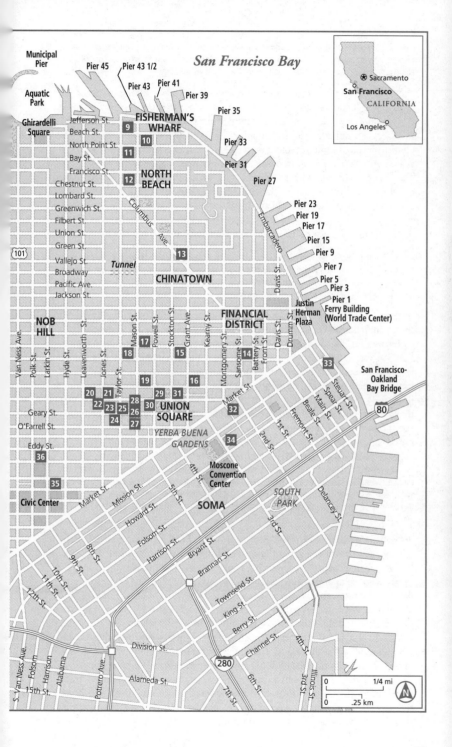

lines (1 block west). Bus: 2, 3, 4, 30, or 45. **Amenities:** The excellent restaurant/bar is French to accentuate revered chef Laurent Manrique's style; access to nearby health club; concierge; courtesy car; secretarial services; 24-hour room service; in-room massage; babysitting; laundry service; same-day dry cleaning. *In room:* A/C, TV w/ movie rentals, fax, dataport, minibar, hair dryer, iron, safe.

Hotel Monaco ★★ This remodeled 1910 beaux arts building is one of the divas among Union Square's luxury hotels. In 1995, the Kimpton Group poured $24 million into the cozy main lobby with a two-story French inglenook fireplace, and rather small but vibrant and sexy guest rooms with canopy beds, Chinese-inspired armoires, bamboo writing desks, and bold stripes. As playful as it is serious, the hotel offers nifty extras like Web TV and two-line phones. The decor, combined with its breathtaking restaurant The Grand Cafe, make this a favorite luxury hotel in the city. The only downside is that many rooms are way too small (especially for the price).

501 Geary Blvd. (at Taylor St.), San Francisco, CA 94102. © **800/214-4220** or 415/292-0100. Fax 415 /292-0111. www.monaco-sf.com. 201 units. $259–$319 double; from $369–$479 suite. Rates include evening wine hour. Call for discounted rates. AE, DC, DISC, MC, V. Valet parking $28. Bus: 2, 3, 4, 27, or 38. Pets accepted. **Amenities:** The adjoining Grand Cafe restaurant is a grand space with sky-high ceilings, elaborate 1920s and 1930s style, an amazing collection of local art, and okay French-inspired cuisine; exercise room; Jacuzzi; sauna; concierge; courtesy car; business center; room service (6:30am–11pm); in-room massage; laundry service; dry cleaning. *In room:* A/C, TV, fax, dataport, minibar, hair dryer, iron, safe.

Prescott Hotel ★★ It may be small, but boutique Prescott has some big things going for it. The staff treats you like royalty, rooms are attractively unfrilly and masculine, location (just a block from Union Square) is perfect, and limited room service is provided by one of the most popular restaurants in the city, Postrio (see complete review in "Dining" section, later in this chapter). Dark tones of green, plum, and burgundy blend well with the cherrywood furnishings in each of the soundproofed rooms; the view, alas, isn't so pleasant. The very small bathrooms contain terry robes and hair dryers, but only the suites have Jacuzzi bathtubs. Concierge-level guests are pampered with free continental breakfast, evening cocktails, and even head and shoulder massages.

545 Post St. (between Mason and Taylor Sts.), San Francisco, CA 94102. © **800/283-7322** or 415/563-0303. Fax 415/563-6831. 164 units. $270–$325 double; $300 concierge-level double (including breakfast and evening cocktail reception); from $365 suite. AE, DC, DISC, MC, V. Valet parking $30. Cable car: Powell-Hyde and Powell-Mason lines (1 block east). Bus: 2, 3, 4, 30, 38, or 45. **Amenities:** 1 restaurant/bar; small exercise room; concierge; limited courtesy car; limited room service. *In room:* TV w/ pay movies, minibar, hair dryer, iron, safe.

Westin St. Francis ★★ *Kids* Although the St. Francis is too massive to offer the personal service you get at the smaller deluxe hotels on Nob Hill, few other hotels in San Francisco can match its majestic aura. It sounds corny, but the St. Francis is so intertwined with the city's past that it truly is San Francisco: Stroll through the vast, ornate lobby and you can feel 100 years of history oozing from its hand-carved redwood paneling. The hotel did a massive $50 million renovation in 1996 and threw in another $60 million in 1999, replacing the carpeting, furniture, and bedding in every main building guest room, gussying up the lobby, and restoring the facade. Today, the rooms in the Tower, which was built in the 1970s and renovated in 2001, evoke a contemporary design in the vein of W Hotel style. The historic main building accentuates its history with traditional, more elegant ambiance, high ceilings, and crown molding. Even if you stay elsewhere, it's worth a visit if only to partake of high tea at the Compass Rose, one of San Francisco's most enduring and enjoyable traditions.

The Westin Kids Club program means that when families check in the kids receive age-specific gifts.

335 Powell St. (between Geary and Post Sts.), San Francisco, CA 94102. © **800/WESTIN-1** or 415/397-7000. Fax 415/774-0124. 1,194 units. Main building: $249–$499 double; from $650 suite. Tower: $389–$549 double; from $850 suite. Extra person $30. Continental breakfast $15–$18. AE, DC, DISC, MC, V. Valet parking $40. Cable car: Powell-Hyde and Powell-Mason lines (direct stop). Bus: 2, 3, 4, 30, 38, 45, or 76. Pets accepted; $30 fee. **Amenities:** 3 American/California restaurants (Compass Rose, Dewey's pub, and St. Francis Café); new $2.1 million health club; spa; concierge; car-rental desk; business center; 24-hour room service. *In room:* A/C, TV, dataport, minibar, fridge, hair dryer.

EXPENSIVE

Hotel Diva ⭑   The Diva is the prima donna of San Francisco's affordable modern hotels. A profusion of curvaceous glass, marble, and steel marks the Euro-tech lobby; the minimalist rooms, spotless and neat, are softened with utterly fashionable "Italian modern" furnishings of monochromatic colors, silver, and wood. Personally, I find the hotel a little on the cold side (figuratively speaking). But toys and services abound, including VCRs (with a discreet video vending machine), Nintendo, and breakfast delivered to your room. *Insider tip:* Reserve one of the rooms ending in "09," which have extra-large bathrooms with vanity mirrors and makeup tables. The downside: views that make you want to keep the chic curtains closed.

440 Geary St. (between Mason and Taylor Sts.), San Francisco, CA 94102. © **800/553-1900** or 415/885-0200. Fax 415/346-6613. www.hoteldiva.com. 111 units. $189 double; $229 junior suite; $550 suite. Rates include continental breakfast. AE, DC, DISC, MC, V. Parking $27. Cable car: Powell-Mason line. Bus: 38 or 38L. **Amenities:** Exercise room; concierge; secretarial services; limited room service from nearby California Pizza Kitchen; laundry service; dry cleaning. *In room:* A/C, TV/VCR, fax, dataport, CD player, minibar, hair dryer, iron, safe.

Hotel Triton ⭑⭑   Described as chic, retro-futuristic, and even neo-Baroque, the Triton begs attention, from the Daliesque lobby and designer suites à la Jerry Garcia, Joe Boxer, and Wyland (the ocean artist) to the New York hip clientele lounging in the funky lobby. Two dozen environmentally sensitive "Eco-Rooms"—with biodegradable soaps, filtered water and air, and all-natural linens—were also installed to please the tree-hugger in all of us. *A mild caveat:* Don't expect perfection; many of the rooms could use a little touching up here and there, and service isn't as snappy as it could be. If you can live with this, and want to inject a little fun and style into your stay, then come join Dorothy and Toto for a trip far from Kansas.

342 Grant Ave. (at Bush St.), San Francisco, CA 94108. © **800/433-6611** or 415/394-0500. Fax 415/394-0555. www.hotel-tritonsf.com. 140 units. $219–$269 double; $329 suite. AE, DC, DISC, MC, V. Parking $28. Cable car: Powell-Hyde and Powell-Mason lines (2 blocks west). Pets accepted; $50 fee. **Amenities:** Café de la Presse, a European-style newsstand and outdoor cafe, serves breakfast, lunch, and dinner; exercise room; business center; room service 7am–11pm; same-day laundry service/dry cleaning. *In room:* A/C, TV, dataport, minibar, coffeemaker, hair dryer, iron.

The Kensington Park Hotel ⭑⭑   The Kensington's age shows, but its cheery, eager-to-please staff, tasteful accommodations, central location, and easy access to downstairs hot-shot restaurant Farallon has made this place so popular that in the past 4 years, the rates have practically doubled. Still, the value is decent. The recently upgraded rooms are indeed handsome with traditional mahogany furniture, enormous armoires, and dark sophisticated colors—far more attractive than most hotel furnishings. Bathrooms may be small, but they're sweetly appointed in brass and marble. For the best view, ask for an upper corner room. One big complaint: Every time we visit, the front desk is understaffed. The adjoining seafood restaurant, Farallon, is one of downtown's hottest restaurants (see "Dining" section, later in chapter for details).

450 Post St. (between Powell and Mason Sts.), San Francisco, CA 94102. ℂ **800/553-1900** or 415/788-6400. Fax 415/399-9484. www.personalityhotels.com. 89 units. $175–$205 double; $550 suite. Extra person $10. Rates include continental breakfast; afternoon tea, sherry, and cookies. AE, DC, DISC, MC, V. Valet parking $28. Cable car: Powell-Hyde and Powell-Mason lines (½ block east). **Amenities:** 1 adjoining restaurant, Farallon (see "Dining" for details); access to nearby health club; concierge; business center; babysitting; room service (limited); laundry service; same-day dry cleaning. *In room:* TV, fax, dataport, fridge, hair dryer, iron.

Sir Francis Drake ★★
It took a change of ownership and a multimillion-dollar restoration to save the Sir Francis Drake from becoming a Starbucks, but the stately old queen is again housing guests. Granted, the venerable septuagenarian is still showing signs of age—the owners admitted there was more work to be done and threw another $5 million into room renovations in early 1999. But the price of imperfection certainly shows in the room rate: a good $100 less per night than its Nob Hill cousins. The new Sir Francis Drake is a hotel for people who are willing to trade a chipped bathroom tile or oddly matched furniture for the opportunity to vacation in pseudo-grand fashion. Allow Tom Sweeny, the ebullient (and legendary) Beefeater doorman, to handle your bags as you enter the elegant, captivating lobby. Sip cocktails at the superchic Starlight Lounge overlooking the city. Dine at Scala's Bistro, one of the hottest restaurants downtown. In short, live like the king or queen of Union Square without all the pomp, circumstance, and credit card bills.

450 Powell St. (at Sutter St.), San Francisco, CA 94102. ℂ **800/227-5480** or 415/392-7755. Fax 415/391-8719. www.sirfrancisdrake.com. 417 units. $235–$269 double; $500–$700 suite. AE, DC, DISC, MC, V. Valet parking $24. Cable car: Powell-Hyde and Powell-Mason lines (direct stop). Bus: 2, 3, 4, 45, or 76. **Amenities:** Scala's Bistro serves good Italian cuisine in a stylish setting; the Parisian-style Café Expresso does an equally commendable job serving coffees, pastries, and sandwiches daily; the Starlight Room on the 21st floor offers cocktails, entertainment, and dancing nightly with a panoramic view of the city; exercise room; concierge; limited room service; same-day laundry and dry cleaning. *In room:* A/C, TV w/ pay movies, dataport, minibar, hair dryer, iron on request.

MODERATE

The Andrews Hotel ★
As is fitting with Euro-style hotels, the accommodations are small but well maintained and comfortable; lace curtains and fresh flowers in each room add a light touch. Some units have shower only, and bathrooms in general tend to be tiny—but for the location and price, the Andrews is a good, safe bet for an enjoyable stay in the city. An added bonus is the adjoining Fino Bar and Ristorante, which offer complimentary wine to hotel guests in the evening.

624 Post St. (between Jones and Taylor Sts.), San Francisco, CA 94109. ℂ **800/926-3739** or 415/563-6877. Fax 415/928-6919. www.andrewshotel.com. 48 units (some with shower only). $99–$145 double; $139–$175 superior rooms. Rates include continental breakfast and evening wine. AE, DC, MC, V. Self-parking $20. Cable car: Powell-Hyde and Powell-Mason lines (3 blocks east). Bus: 2, 3, 4, 30, 38, or 45. **Amenities:** Access to nearby health club; concierge; room service from 5:30–9:30pm; babysitting; self-service laundromat; laundry service; dry cleaning. *In room:* TV, hair dryer on request, iron.

The Clarion Bedford Hotel ★★ *Value*
For the price and location (3 blocks from Union Square), the 17-story Bedford offers a darn good deal. Your hard-earned dollars will get you a large, spotless, recently renovated room (a third were updated as recently as 2001) with flowery decor that's not exactly en vogue but definitely in fine taste, as well as service from an enthusiastic, attentive, and professional staff. Each unit is well furnished with a king, a queen, or two double beds; a writing desk; an armchair; in-room coffee; and a well-stocked honor bar

> ### (Kids Family-Friendly Hotels
>
> **Westin St. Francis** (*see p. 76*)   All children under 12 are given a Kids Club hat on arrival, and special sports bottles and complimentary refills in the restaurants. Those ages 3 to 7 also get fun stuff like dinosaur soaps and sponges, and coloring books.
>
> **The Wharf Inn** (*see p. 85*)   No whining about when you'll get there 'cause you're already there—right smack dab in the middle of the wharf. Plus, parking is free, and there's no charge for packing along an extra monster.

with plenty of munchies. Big closets are a trade for the small bathrooms. Most rooms are sunny and bright and have priceless views of the city (the higher the floor, the better the view).

761 Post St. (between Leavenworth and Jones Sts.), San Francisco, CA 94109. ℂ **800/252-7466** or 415/673-6040. Fax 415/563-6739. www.hotelbedford.com. 144 units. $159–$199 double; from $209 suite. Continental breakfast $8.50. AE, DC, DISC, MC, V. Valet parking $25. Cable car: Powell-Hyde and Powell-Mason lines (4 blocks east). Bus: 2, 3, 4, or 27. Pets under 25 pounds welcome for a $50 deposit. **Amenities:** 1 lobby cafe/deli; secretarial services; room service (breakfast only); laundry service; dry cleaning. *In room:* TV w/ pay movies, dataport, minibar, coffeemaker, hair dryer, iron.

The Commodore International ★★   If you're looking to pump a little fun and fantasy into your vacation, this low-budget trendy spot is the place. Stealing the show is the Red Room, a swank and dim bar and lounge that's ruby red through and through. Adjoining is the stylish Titanic Café, a cute little diner serving buckwheat griddlecakes, Vietnamese tofu sandwiches, and salads. The "Neo-Deco" rooms, all of which have been undergoing continued upgrades through 2001, feature bright colors, whimsical furnishings, pretty artwork, and recently refurbished bathrooms.

825 Sutter St. (at Jones St.), San Francisco, CA 94109. ℂ **800/338-6848** or 415/923-6800. Fax 415/923-6804. www.thecommodorehotel.com. 113 units. $125–$169 double. AE, DC, MC, V. Parking $22. Bus: 2, 3, 4, 27, or 76. **Amenities:** 1 diner serving breakfast and lunch; access to nearby health club ($15 per day); concierge; laundry service and same-day dry cleaning. *In room:* TV, dataport, fridge on request, coffeemaker, hair dryer.

King George Hotel ★★ (*Value*   Built in 1914 for the Panama-Pacific Exhibition when rooms went for $1 per night, this utterly delightful hotel has fared well over the years, continuing to draw a mostly European clientele. The location—surrounded by cable-car lines, the Theater District, Union Square, and dozens of restaurants—is superb, and the rooms are surprisingly quiet for such a busy area. Though rooms can be small, a complete room renovation in 1999 made the most of the space with new mattresses, desks, Nintendo, and a handsome studylike ambiance. All units are also meticulously clean, and bathrooms have hair dryers and lovely amenities. A big hit since it started a few years back is the hotel's English afternoon tea, served in the Windsor Tea Room from 3 to 6:30pm.

334 Mason St. (between Geary and O'Farrell Sts.), San Francisco, CA 94102. ℂ **800/288-6005** or 415/781-5050. Fax 415/835-5991. www.kinggeorge.com. 141 units. $160 double; $240 suite. Breakfast $6.50–$8. Special-value packages available seasonally. AE, DC, DISC, MC, V. Self-parking $18. Cable car:

Powell-Hyde and Powell-Mason lines (1 block west). Bus: 2, 3, 4, 30, 38, or 45. **Amenities:** Complimentary access to health club ½ block away; concierge; secretarial services; 24-hour room service; same-day laundry service and dry cleaning. *In room:* TV w/ pay movies, dataport, hair dryer, iron, safe.

The Maxwell 𝒜   When new management renovated this hotel a few years ago in a style they call "theater-deco-fused-with-Victoriana," the results were a chic-boutique blend of velvets, brocades, and rich color and patterns. Rooms come with upholstered chairs, hand-painted lamps, luxurious pillows, boldly tiled sinks, and respectable prints hanging on the walls. Other pluses are writing desks, hair dryers, and two phones. The adjoining Max's On The Square Restaurant looks great, but its American fare and service are nothing to write home about.

386 Geary St. (at Mason St.), San Francisco, CA 94102. ✆ **888/734-6299** or 415/986-2000. Fax 415/397-2447. 153 units. $185–$235 double; $295–$595 suite. Extra person $15. Corporate discounts available. AE, DC, DISC, MC, V. Parking $22. Cable car: Powell-Hyde and Powell-Mason lines (1 block east). Bus: 2, 3, 4, 30, 38, or 45. **Amenities:** Swank Max's on the Square serves American cuisine; concierge; meeting facilities; limited room service; laundry service and dry cleaning. *In room:* A/C, TV w/ pay movies, dataport, hair dryer, iron.

The Savoy Hotel 𝒜   A European-style hotel through and through, the Savoy is a lovely and affordable option downtown. A few years ago it was clear the hotel hasn't kept up with the wear associated with brisk business. However, rooms have been renovated and while they are still cozy French provincial, with some 18th-century period furnishings, featherbeds, and goose-down pillows, they now incorporate contemporary designs and upgraded textiles. Rooms can be small, but each has beautiful patterned draperies, triple sheets, full-length mirrors, and two-line telephones. Rates include late-afternoon cookies, sherry, and tea, served in the Brasserie Savoy, a dependable seafood restaurant.

580 Geary St. (between Taylor and Jones Sts.), San Francisco, CA 94102. ✆ **800/227-4223** or 415/441-2700. Fax 415/441-0124. www.thesavoyhotel.com. 83 units. $149–$189 double; from $205 suite. Ask about package, government, senior, and corporate rates. AE, DC, DISC, MC, V. Parking $18. Bus: 2, 3, 4, 27, or 38. **Amenities:** 1 seafood restaurant; concierge; laundry service; dry cleaning. *In room:* TV, dataport, hair dryer, iron.

The Warwick Regis 𝒜 *(Value)*   Louis XVI may have been a rotten monarch, but he certainly had taste. Fashioned in the style of pre-Revolutionary France, the Warwick is awash with pristine French and English antiques, Italian marble, chandeliers, four-poster beds, hand-carved headboards, and the like. The result is an expensive-looking hotel that, for all its pleasantries and perks, is surprisingly affordable when compared to its Union Square neighbors. Honeymooners should splurge on a fireplace room, which has a canopy bed.

490 Geary St. (between Mason and Taylor Sts.), San Francisco, CA 94102. ✆ **800/827-3447** or 415/928-7900. Fax 415/441-8788. www.warwicksf.com. 80 units. $159–$215 double; $199–$289 suite. Rates include continental breakfast. AE, DC, DISC, MC, V. Parking $23. Cable car: Powell-Hyde and Powell-Mason lines. Bus: 2, 3, 4, 27, or 38. **Amenities:** 1 restaurant; access to nearby health club ($10 per day); concierge; business center; secretarial services; 24-hour room service; babysitting; laundry service; dry cleaning. *In room:* TV, dataport, minibar, hair dryer, iron, safe.

INEXPENSIVE

Golden Gate Hotel 𝒜𝒜   Among San Francisco's small hotels occupying historic turn-of-the-century buildings are some real gems, and the Golden Gate Hotel is one of them. It's 2 blocks north of Union Square and 2 blocks down (literally) from the crest of Nob Hill, with cable car stops at the corner for easy access to Fisherman's Wharf and Chinatown. (The city's theaters and best restaurants are also within walking distance.) But the best thing about the Golden Gate Hotel is that it's a family-run establishment: John and Renate Kenaston are hospitable innkeepers who take obvious pleasure in making their guests comfortable. Each individually decorated room has handsome antique furnishings (plenty of wicker) from the early 1900s, quilted bedspreads, and fresh flowers. (Request a room with a clawfoot tub if you enjoy a good, hot soak.) All rooms have phones, and complimentary afternoon tea is served daily from 4 to 7pm, and guests are welcome to use the house fax and computer free of charge.

775 Bush St. (between Powell and Mason Sts.), San Francisco, CA 94108. ℂ **800/835-1118** or 415/392-3702. Fax 415/392-6202. www.goldengatehotel.com. 23 units, 14 with bathroom. $85 double without bathroom; $130 double with bathroom. Rates include continental breakfast and afternoon tea. AE, DC, MC, V. Self-parking $15. Cable car: Powell-Hyde and Powell-Mason lines (1 block east). Bus: 2, 3, 4, 30, 38, or 45. Powell & Market BART. **Amenities:** Access to health club 1 block away; laundry service and dry cleaning next door. *In room:* TV, dataport, hair dryer upon request.

NOB HILL
VERY EXPENSIVE

Fairmont Hotel & Tower 🏰🏰   The granddaddy of Nob Hill's ritzy hotels, the Fairmont wins top honors for the most awe-inspiring lobby in San Francisco. Even if you're not staying here, it's worth a trip to gape at its massive marble columns, vaulted ceilings, velvet chairs, gilded mirrors, and spectacular wraparound staircase. In previous years the rooms fell short, but thanks to an $85 million renovation completed in 2001, the glamour carries to guest rooms where everything is brand spanking new and in good taste. In addition to the expected luxuries, expect such extras as goose-down pillows, electric shoe buffers, large walk-in closets, and multi-line phones with voice mail. Whatever you do, make a point of getting to the Tonga Room, a fantastically kitsch, Disneyland-like tropical bar and restaurant where happy hour hops and rain falls every 20 minutes.

950 Mason St. (at California St.), San Francisco, CA 94108. ℂ **800/527-4727** or 415/772-5000. Fax 415/772-5013. www.fairmont.com. 600 units. Main building $289–$409 double, from $500 suite; Tower $269–$359 double, from $800 suite. Extra person $30. Continental breakfast $14. AE, DC, DISC, MC, V. Parking $30. Cable car: California St. line (direct stop). **Amenities:** Laurel Court restaurant serves French contemporary cuisine; Tonga Room bar/restaurant; health club ($15 daily); 24-hour concierge; tour desk; car-rental desk; business center; shopping arcade; salon; 24-hour room service; massage; babysitting; same-day laundry service and dry cleaning. *In room:* A/C, TV w/ pay movies, fax, dataport, some with kitchenette, minibar, coffeemaker, hair dryer, iron, safe.

Huntington Hotel 🏰🏰🏰   The stately Huntington has long been a favorite retreat for Hollywood stars and political VIPs who desire privacy and security. Family-owned since 1924—a real rarity among large hotels—this place eschews pomp and circumstance; absolute privacy and unobtrusive service are its mainstays. Though the elaborate 19th-century–style lobby is rather petite, the apartment-like guest rooms are quite large and feature Brunschwig and Fils fabrics, French antiques, and city views. Prices are steep, but special offers such as the Romance Package, which includes champagne, sherry, and limousine service, make the Huntington worth considering for a special occasion.

1075 California St. (between Mason and Taylor Sts.), San Francisco, CA 94108. ℂ **800/227-4683** or 415/474-5400. Fax 415/474-6227. www.huntingtonhotel.com. 140 units. $285–$430 double; $485–$1000 suite. Continental breakfast $15. Special packages available. AE, DC, DISC, MC, V. Valet parking $19.50. Cable car: California St. line (direct stop). Bus: 1. **Amenities:** The Big Four restaurant offers expensive contemporary American cuisine; live piano music plays nightly in the lounge; indoor heated pool (for ages 16 and up); health club; new spa; sauna; concierge; massage; babysitting; same-day laundry service/dry cleaning. *In room:* A/C, TV w/ pay movies, fax, dataport, some kitchenette, minibar, some fridge, hair dryer, iron, safe.

Mark Hopkins Intercontinental 🏰🏰   Built in 1926 on the spot where railroad millionaire Mark Hopkins's turreted mansion once stood, the 19-story Mark Hopkins is one of the city's most classy historic luxury hotels. A complete room renovation in 2000 resulted in exceedingly comfortable neoclassical rooms with all the fancy amenities you'd expect from a world-class hotel, including custom furniture, plush fabrics, sumptuous bathrooms, and extraordinary city views. Luxury suites, added in early 2001, are twice the size of most San Francisco apartments and cost close to a month's rent per night. The Top of the Mark, a fantastic bar and lounge, where Pacific-bound servicemen went to toast their good-bye to the States during World War II, underwent a $1.5 million renovation. Now, dancing to live jazz or swing, enjoying afternoon tea or brunch, and dining on the newly added three-course price-fixed dinner Thursday through Saturday is done in spruced, old-fashioned style. (Romantics, this place is for you.)

1 Nob Hill (at California and Mason Sts.), San Francisco, CA 94108. © 800/327-0200 or 415/392-3434. Fax 415/421-3302. www.markhopkins.net. 382 units. $380–$500 double; from $610 suite; from $2500 luxury suite. Breakfast buffet $24. AE, DC, DISC, MC, V. Valet parking $27. Cable car: California St. line (direct stop). Bus: 1. **Amenities:** The outstanding Top of the Mark lounge serves afternoon tea, cocktails, and dinner Thurs–Sat; formal Nob Hill Restaurant offers California-French cuisine nightly and a full buffet breakfast each morning; the Nob Hill Terrace serves lunch, cocktails, and dinner daily; exercise room; concierge; car-rental desk; business center; secretarial services; 24-hour room service; massage; babysitting; laundry service and dry cleaning. In room: A/C, TV, dataport, minibar, coffeemaker, hair dryer, iron, safe.

Ritz-Carlton 𝄄𝄄𝄄   Ranked among the top hotels in the world (as well as the top hotel in the city) by readers of *Condé Nast Traveler*, the Ritz-Carlton has been the benchmark of San Francisco luxury hotels since it opened in 1991. A Nob Hill landmark, it's outfitted with the finest furnishings, fabrics, and artwork, and the rooms offer every possible amenity and service, from Italian-marble bathrooms with double sinks to plush terry robes. The more expensive rooms offer good views of the city. Club rooms have a dedicated concierge, separate elevator-key access, and complimentary buffet meals throughout the day.

600 Stockton St. (between Pine and California Sts.), San Francisco, CA 94108. © 800/241-3333 or 415/296-7465. Fax 415/986-1268. www.ritzcarlton.com. 336 units. $475–$575 double; $595–$695 club-level double; from $700 suite. Buffet breakfast $18; Sun brunch $55. Weekend discounts and packages available. AE, DC, DISC, MC, V. Parking $45. Cable car: Powell-Hyde and Powell-Mason lines (direct stop). **Amenities:** 2 restaurants, 1 bar; indoor heated pool; outstanding health club; Jacuzzi; sauna; concierge; courtesy car; business center; secretarial services; 24-hour room service; in-room massage & manicure; babysitting; same-day laundry service and dry cleaning. In room: A/C, TV w/ pay movies, dataport, minibar, hair dryer, iron, safe.

SOMA
VERY EXPENSIVE
The Harbor Court 𝄄𝄄   When the Embarcadero Freeway was torn down after the Big One in 1989, one of the major benefactors was this hotel, whose backyard view went from a wall of cement to a dazzling view of the Bay Bridge (a bay-view room costs extra). Located just off the Embarcadero at the edge of the Financial District, this former YMCA books a lot of corporate travelers, but anyone who prefers stylish, high-quality accommodations—half-canopy beds, large armoires, writing desks, soundproof windows—and a lively scene—will be very content here.

165 Steuart St. (between Mission and Howard Sts.), San Francisco, CA 94105. © 800/346-0555 in the U.S., or 415/882-1300. Fax 415/882-1313. www.harborcourthotel.com. 131 units. $165–$399 double. Continental breakfast $12. AE, DC, MC, V. Parking $28. Muni Metro: Embarcadero. Bus: 14, 32, or 80X. Pets accepted. **Amenities:** Large, heated indoor pool; access to health club next door; courtesy car; room service (breakfast only); same-day laundry service and dry cleaning. In room: A/C, TV, fax, dataport, minibar, hair dryer, iron, safe.

W San Francisco Hotel 𝄄𝄄𝄄   Starwood Hotels & Resorts' 31-story, 423-room property adjacent to the San Francisco Museum of Modern Art is the most hip hotel in town (at least until Ian Schrager unveils his newly renovated Clift

Hotel). Sophisticated, sleek, and stylish, its octagonal, three-story glass entrance and lobby give way to a great lounge and two bars. The interior has a residential feel in the guest rooms, and a hip, urban style throughout. All guest rooms offer a "luxury" bed with goose-down comforters and pillows, an oversized dark wood desk, upholstered chaise lounge, plus louvered blinds opening to usually great city views. Rooms also feature a compact media wall complete with Sony CD and video cassette players with an extensive CD library, 27-inch color TV, plus Internet service via an infrared keyboard and portable two-line phones. Bathrooms are supersleek and stocked with Aveda products.

181 Third St. (between Mission and Howard Sts.), San Francisco, CA 94103. © 800/877-WHOTEL or 415/777-5300. Fax 415/817-7800. www.whotels.com. 423 units. From $399 double; from $900 suite. AE, DC, DISC, MC, V. Valet parking $33. Muni Metro: J, K, L, or M to Montgomery. Bus: 15, 30, or 45. **Amenities:** 1 hip but unimpressive restaurant, 2 bars; heated atrium pool and whirlpool; fitness center; 24-hour concierge; business center; secretarial services; 24-hour room service; same-day laundry/dry cleaning. *In room:* A/C, TV/VCR w/ pay movies and Internet access, fax, dataport, minibar, coffeemaker, hair dryer, iron, safe, portable two-line phone with conference calling and voice mail.

FINANCIAL DISTRICT
VERY EXPENSIVE
The Mandarin Oriental 𝄞𝄞𝄞 *Finds*   The common areas here are a bit cold and impersonal, but the rooms are superfluously appointed and the views divine, making this a top choice for luxury travelers. The large rooms are located between the 38th and 48th floors of a high-rise, which affords them extraordinary views. Not all units have tub-side views (get one that does and you'll never forget it!), but all have well-stocked marble bathrooms that include such luxuries as terry- and cotton-cloth robes, makeup mirrors, and silk slippers. The less opulent rooms are done in a kind of reserved-contemporary decor with Asian accents. Don't miss out on the Asian teatime, complete with a bento box of uncommonly delicious goodies.

222 Sansome St. (between Pine and California Sts.), San Francisco, CA 94104. © 800/622-0404 or 415/276-9888. Fax 415/433-0289. www.mandarinoriental.com. 158 units. $475–$495 double; $675–$700 signature rooms; from $1,400 suite. Continental breakfast $18. AE, DC, DISC, MC, V. Valet parking $34. Muni Metro: J, K, L, or M to Montgomery. Bus: All Market St. buses. **Amenities:** 1 restaurant, 1 bar; fitness center; concierge; car-rental; business center; 24-hour room service; in-room massage; laundry service; same-day dry cleaning. *In room:* A/C, TV w/ pay movies, CD player, fax, dataport, minibar, hair dryer, iron, safe.

The Palace Hotel 𝄞   Every time you walk through these doors, you'll be reminded how incredibly majestic old luxury really is. The original 1875 Palace was rebuilt after the 1906 quake; the most spectacular attribute is still the old regal lobby and the Garden Court, a San Francisco landmark that has been restored to its original heart-stopping grandeur. Regrettably, the rooms have that standardized, chain-hotel appearance.

2 New Montgomery St. (at Market St.), San Francisco, CA 94105. © 800/325-3535 or 415/512-1111. Fax 415/543-0671. www.sfpalace.com. 551 units. $300–$560 double; from $550 suite. Extra person $40. Continental breakfast $16; deluxe continental $18. Children under 18 sharing existing bedding free in parents' room. Weekend rates and packages available. AE, DC, DISC, MC, V. Parking $30. Muni Metro: All Market St. trams. Bus: All Market St. buses. **Amenities:** 4 restaurants; health club with a skylight-covered heated lap pool; whirlpool; sauna; concierge; business center; lobby-level shops; 24-hour room service; laundry and dry cleaning. *In room:* A/C, TV w/ pay movies, dataport, minibar, hair dryer, iron, safe.

NORTH BEACH
MODERATE
The Hotel Bohème 𝄞𝄞 *Finds*   North Beach romance awaits you at the Bohème. Although located in the center of North Beach, this recently renovated

hotel's style and demeanor are more reminiscent of a prestigious home in upscale Nob Hill. The decor evokes the Beat generation, which flourished here in the 1950s; rooms are small but hopelessly romantic, with gauze-draped canopies and walls artistically accented with lavender, sage green, black, and pumpkin. The staff is ultra-hospitable, and bonuses include free sherry in the lobby each afternoon. Take note: While bathrooms are sweet, they're also absolutely tiny (no tubs). *Tip:* Request a room off the street side; they're quieter.

444 Columbus Ave. (between Vallejo and Green Sts.), San Francisco, CA 94133. ✆ 415/433-9111. Fax 415/ 362-6292. www.hotelboheme.com. 15 units. $164–$174 double. Rates include afternoon sherry. AE, DISC, DC, MC, V. Parking $27.50 at nearby public garage. Cable car: Powell-Mason line. Bus: 12, 15, 30, 41, 45, or 83. **Amenities:** Concierge. *In room:* TV, dataport, hair dryer.

INEXPENSIVE

The San Remo Hotel 🌟🌟 *Value* Located in a quiet North Beach neighborhood and within walking distance of Fisherman's Wharf, this small European-style pensione is one of the best budget hotels in San Francisco. The rooms are small and bathrooms shared, but all is forgiven when it comes time to pay the bill. Rooms are decorated in a cozy country style with brass and iron beds, armoires, and wicker furnishings; most have ceiling fans. The shared bathrooms, each immaculately clean, feature clawfoot tubs and brass pull-chain toilets with oak tanks and brass fixtures. If the penthouse is available, book it: You won't find a more romantic place to stay in San Francisco for so little money. (It's got its own bathroom, TV, fridge, and patio.)

2237 Mason St. (at Chestnut St.), San Francisco, CA 94133. ✆ 800/352-REMO or 415/776-8688. Fax 415/ 776-2811. www.sanremohotel.com. 62 units, 61 with shared bathroom. $60–$90 double; $150 suite. AE, DC, MC, V. Parking $10–$12. Cable car: Powell-Mason line. Bus: 15, 22, 30, or 42. **Amenities:** Access to nearby health club; tour desk; self-service laundromat. *In room:* Ceiling fan.

FISHERMAN'S WHARF
EXPENSIVE

Sheraton Fisherman's Wharf Hotel 🌟 Built in the mid-1970s, this modern, four-story hotel offers the reliable comforts of a Sheraton in San Francisco's most popular tourist area. In other words, the clean, modern rooms, which were completely renovated in 1995, are comfortable and well equipped but nothing unique to the city. The Corporate Floor caters exclusively to business travelers.

2500 Mason St. (between Beach and North Point Sts.), San Francisco, CA 94133. ✆ 800/325-3535 or 415/362-5500. Fax 415/956-5275. www.sheratonatthewharf.com. 525 units. $165–$380 double; from $550–$1,000 suite. Extra person $20. Continental breakfast $17. AE, DC, DISC, MC, V. Valet parking $26. Cable car: Powell-Mason line (1 block east, 2 blocks south). Bus: 15, 32, or 42. **Amenities:** 1 restaurant, 1 bar; outdoor heated pool; exercise room; concierge; business center; salon; car-rental desk; room service (6am–midnight); dry cleaning and laundry. *In room:* A/C, TV, fax (in club-level rooms), dataport, coffeemaker, hair dryer.

The Tuscan Inn 🌟🌟 The Tuscan is the best hotel at Fisherman's Wharf. Like an island of respectability in a sea of touristy schlock, it offers a level of style and comfort far beyond its neighbors. Splurge on parking—cheaper than the wharf's outrageously priced garages—and then make your way toward the plush lobby warmed by a grand fireplace. Even the rooms, each equipped with writing desks and armchairs, are a cut above competing neighborhood hotels. The only caveat is the lack of views—a small price to pay for a good hotel in a great location. The adjoining Cafe Pescatore, which is open for breakfast, lunch, and dinner, serves standard Italian fare in an airy setting.

425 North Point St. (at Mason St.), San Francisco, CA 94133. ✆ 800/648-4626 or 415/561-1100. Fax 415/ 561-1199. www.tuscaninn.com. 221 units. $189–$269 double; $279–$339 suite. Rates include coffee, tea,

and evening fireside wine reception. AE, DC, DISC, MC, V. Parking $22. Cable car: Powell-Mason line. Bus: 15, 32, or 42. Pets welcome for $50 fee. **Amenities:** Access to nearby gym; concierge; courtesy car; secretarial services; room service (7am–9:30pm); same-day laundry and dry cleaning. *In room:* A/C, TV w/ pay movies, dataport, minibar, hair dryer, iron.

MODERATE

The Wharf Inn ✿✿ *(Kids)* My top choice for good-value lodging at Fisherman's Wharf, the Wharf Inn boasts newly refurbished rooms, done in handsome tones of forest green, burgundy, and pale yellow, come with all the standard amenities, including complimentary coffee and tea. Its main attribute, however, is its location—right smack dab in the middle of the wharf, 2 blocks away from Pier 39 and the cable-car turnaround, and within walking distance of the Embarcadero and North Beach. The inn is ideal for car-bound families, as parking is free (that saves $25 a day right off the bat) and there's no charge for packing along an extra person.

2601 Mason St. (at Beach St.), San Francisco, CA 94133. ✆ **800/548-9918** or 415/673-7411. Fax 415/776-2181. www.wharfinn.com. 51 units. $99–$199 double; penthouse $270–$399. AE, DC, DISC, MC, V. Free parking. Cable car: Powell-Mason line. Bus: 15, 32, or 42, Metro: F. **Amenities:** Access to nearby health club ($10 per day); concierge; tour desk. *In room:* TV, hair dryer on request.

COW HOLLOW/PACIFIC HEIGHTS
EXPENSIVE

Union Street Inn ✿✿ This two-story Edwardian may front the perpetually busy (and chichi) Union Street, but it's quiet as a church on the inside. All individually decorated rooms are comfortably furnished, and most come with canopied or brass beds with down comforters, fresh flowers, bay windows (beg for one with a view of the garden), and private bathrooms (a few even have Jacuzzi tubs). An extended continental breakfast is served in the parlor, in your room, or on an outdoor terrace overlooking a lovely English garden. The ultimate honeymoon retreat is the private carriage house behind the inn, but any room at this warm, friendly place is guaranteed to please.

2229 Union St. (between Fillmore and Steiner Sts.), San Francisco, CA 94123. ✆ **415/346-0424.** Fax 415/922-8046. www.unionstreetinn.com. 5 units, 1 cottage. $159–$239 standard double; $255 cottage. Rates include breakfast, hors d'oeuvres, and evening beverages. AE, MC, V. Parking $15. Bus: 22, 28, 41, 45, or 47. *In room:* TV.

MODERATE

Hotel Del Sol ✿✿ *(Value)* Two-level Hotel del Sol's sunshine theme attracts a youngish clientele to its hip motel. With a centerpiece courtyard and pool and the Miami-Beach-style use of vibrant color, as in the yellow, red, orange, and blue exterior, the atmosphere two blocks off busy (and bland) Lombard is unexpectedly festive. Fair weather fun doesn't stop at the front door of the 54 spacious rooms, which boast equally colorful interior decor (read: loud) to the unexpected extras like a CD player and tips to the town's happenings and shopping meccas.

3100 Webster St., at Greenwich St., San Francisco, CA 94123.✆877/433-5765 or 415/921-5520. Fax 415/931-4137. www.thehoteldelsol.com. 57 units, including 10 one-bedroom suites. $119–$165 double; $160–$235 suite. AE, DC, DIS, MC, V. Bus: 22, 28, 41, 43, 45, or 76. **Amenities:** Heated outdoor pool; sauna. *In room:* TV, dataport, kitchenettes in some rooms, coffeemaker, iron.

The Laurel ✿✿ *(Value)* If you don't mind being out of the downtown area, this motel is one of the most tranquil, lovely, new, and affordable places to rest your head. Tucked just beyond the southernmost tip of the Presidio and its winding roads shaded by eucalyptus, the outside isn't impressive. But inside it's tres chic and modern, with Zen-like influences. Some rooms have excellent city views and all have CD players, VCRs, and spiffy bathrooms. But wait! There's more: concierge services, complimentary continental breakfast, 24-hour coffee and tea service, access to nearby fitness facilities, pet-friendly rooms, and topping it off, free parking and a hip bar/lounge called G!

444 Presidio Ave. (at Masonic Ave.), San Francisco, CA 94115. © **800/552-8735** or 415/567-8467. Fax 415/928-1866. www.thelaurelinn.com. 49 units. $135–$165 double. Rates include continental breakfast, afternoon lemonade and cookies. AE, DC, DISC, MC, V. Free parking. Muni Metro: 1, 3, 4, 43. Pets accepted. **Amenities:** 1 bar; access to health club across the street; concierge; self-service laundromat; iron. *In room:* TV/VCR, dataport, kitchenette in some rooms, hair dryer.

INEXPENSIVE

Edward II Inn & Suites 🌟🌟   This three-story, self-styled "English Country" inn has a room for almost anyone's budget, ranging from pensione rooms with shared bathrooms to luxuriously appointed suites and cottages with living rooms, kitchens, and whirlpool tubs. Originally built to house guests who attended the 1915 Pan-Pacific Exposition, it's now run by innkeepers Denise and Bob Holland, who have done a fantastic job maintaining its worldly charm. Regardless of their rate, all rooms are spotlessly clean and comfortably appointed with cozy antique furnishings and plenty of fresh flowers. The only caveat is that its Lombard Street location is usually congested with traffic, but nearby Chestnut and Union Streets offer some of the best shopping and dining in the city. The price includes continental breakfast, and there's an adjoining pub.

3155 Scott St. (at Lombard St.), San Francisco, CA 94123. © **800/473-2846** or 415/922-3000. Fax 415/931-5784. www.edwardii.com. 32 units, 21 with bathroom. $77–$85 double with shared bathroom, $110 double with private bathroom; $185–$235 suite or cottage. Rates include continental breakfast and evening sherry. AE, MC, V. Self-parking $10 across the street. Bus: 28, 43, or 76. **Amenities:** 1 bar (open Thurs–Sat). *In room:* TV, hair dryer/iron available on request.

The Marina Inn 🌟🌟 *Value*   How this 1924 four-story Victorian offers so much for so little is mystifying. Each guest room looks as though it's been culled from a country-furnishings catalog, complete with rustic pinewood furniture, a four-poster bed with silk-soft comforter, and pretty wallpaper. There are even high-class touches that many expensive hotels don't include: new remote-control TVs discreetly hidden in pine cabinetry, full bathtubs with showers, and nightly turndown service with chocolates on your pillow. Add to that complimentary continental breakfast, afternoon sherry, friendly service, and an armada of nearby shops and restaurants, and there you have it: our number-one choice for Best Overall Value. *Note:* Be sure to request one of the quieter rooms away from busy Lombard Street.

3110 Octavia St. (at Lombard St.), San Francisco, CA 94123. © **800/274-1420** or 415/928-1000. Fax 415/928-5909. www.marinainn.com. 40 units. Nov–Feb $65–$105 double; Mar–May $75–$125 double; June–Oct $85–$135 double. Rates include continental breakfast and afternoon sherry. AE, MC, V. Bus: 28, 30, 43, or 76. *In room:* TV, hair dryer/iron on request.

JAPANTOWN & ENVIRONS
EXPENSIVE

The Hotel Majestic 🌟🌟   The Majestic, built in 1902, meets every professional need while retaining a seriously opulent ambiance of a luxurious old-world hotel. The lobby alone will sweep you into another era with its tapestries, brocades, Corinthian columns, and intricate, lavish detail. Rooms are furnished with French and English antiques, the centerpiece of each being a large four-poster canopy bed; you'll also find mirrored armoires and antique reproductions. All drapes, fabrics, carpet, and bedspreads were replaced in 1997, and half the bathrooms and guest rooms underwent a $2 million renovation in 1999. But they're still sprucing up in early 2002. Extras include a well-lit full-size desk and bathrobes; some rooms also have fireplaces and easy access to a fantastic and intimate bar and elegant California-Asian restaurant, Perlot.

1500 Sutter St. (between Octavia and Gough Sts.), San Francisco, CA 94109. © **800/869-8966** or 415/441-1100. Fax 415/673-7331. www.thehotelmajestic.com. 58 units. $175–$285 double; from $350 suite. Continental breakfast $8.50. Rates include complimentary coffee in lobby 6:30–9am and wine and appetizers 4–6pm. Group, government, corporate, and relocation rates available. AE, DC, DISC, MC, V. Valet parking $23. Bus: 2, 4, 42, 47, or 49. **Amenities:** 1 restaurant, 1 bar; access to nearby health club ($10 per day); concierge; 24-hour room service; in-room massage; babysitting; same-day dry cleaning and laundry service. *In room:* A/C, TV, dataport, honor basket; fridges in some rooms; hair dryer, iron.

MODERATE

The Queen Anne Hotel ✶✶   This majestic 1890 Victorian is a charming boutique hotel that remains true to its heritage and emulates San Francisco's golden days. The lavish "grand salon" greets you with English oak paneling and antiques; rooms follow suit with antique armoires, marble-top dressers, and other period pieces. Some have corner turret bay windows that look out onto tree-lined streets, plus separate parlor areas and wet bars; others have cozy reading nooks and fireplaces. All rooms have phones in the bathroom, computer hookups, and fridges. You can relax in the parlor, with its impressive floor-to-ceiling fireplace, or in the hotel library. Amenities include room service, concierge, and complimentary afternoon tea and sherry. There's also access to an off-premises health club with a lap pool.

1590 Sutter St. (between Gough and Octavia Sts.), San Francisco, CA 94109. © **800/227-3970** or 415/441-2828. Fax 415/775-5212. www.queenanne.com. 48 units. $139–$199 double; $199–$315 suite. Extra person $10. Rates include continental breakfast and afternoon tea and sherry. AE, DC, DISC, MC, V. Parking $14. Bus: 2, 3, or 4. **Amenities:** Access to nearby health club; 24-hour concierge; business center; same-day dry cleaning. *In room:* TV, dataport, hair dryer, iron, safe.

CIVIC CENTER
MODERATE

The Phoenix Hotel ✶✶   Situated on the fringes of the less-than-pleasant Tenderloin District, this retro-1950s-style choice—which has been described by *People* as the hippest hotel in town—is a gathering place for visiting rockers, writers, and filmmakers who crave a dose of southern California on their trips to San Francisco. The focal point of the pastel-painted Palm Springs–style hotel is a heated, paisley-muraled pool set in a modern-sculpture garden. The rooms, while far from plush, are comfortably outfitted with bamboo furnishings and original local art. In addition to the usual amenities, the inn's own closed-circuit channel shows films exclusively made in or about San Francisco. Services include on-site massage, concierge, laundry/valet, and—woo hoo!—free parking. Backflip, a superswank cocktail lounge, serves "cocktail cuisine."

601 Eddy St. (at Larkin St.), San Francisco, CA 94109. © **800/248-9466** or 415/776-1380. Fax 415/885-3109. www.sftrips.com. 44 units. $125–$145 double; $175–$195 suite. Rates include continental breakfast. AE, DC, MC, V. Free parking. Bus: 19, 31, 38, 42, or 47. **Amenities:** 1 restaurant, 1 bar; heated outdoor pool; concierge; tour desk; limited room service; in-room massage; same-day laundry and dry cleaning. *In room:* TV, dataport, hair dryer and iron available on request.

INEXPENSIVE

The Abigail Hotel ✶✶ *Value*   Although it doesn't get much press, the Abigail is one of the better medium-priced hotels in the city; what it lacks in luxury it more than makes up for in charm. The rooms, while on the small side, are clean, cute, and comfortably furnished with cozy antiques and down comforters.

Morning coffee, and pastries greet you in the beautiful faux-marble lobby, while lunch and dinner are served in the chichi organic restaurant, Millennium.

246 McAllister St. (between Hyde and Larkin Sts.), San Francisco, CA 94102. ☎ 800/243-6510 or 415/626-6500. Fax 415/626-6580. www.abigailhotel.com. 61 units. $115–$159 standard double; $125–$189 deluxe double; $350 suite. Extra person $10. Rates include continental breakfast. AE, DC, DISC, MC, V. Valet parking $20. Muni Metro: All Market St. trams. Bus: All Market St. buses. **Amenities:** 1 restaurant, 1 bar; access to nearby health club; concierge. *In room:* TV, dataport, hair dryer, iron; fridge upon request.

THE CASTRO
MODERATE

The Parker House ☆☆☆   This is the best B&B option in the Castro, and one of the best in the entire city. The gay-friendly 5,000-square-foot, 1909 beautifully restored Edwardian home is a few blocks from the heart of Castro's action. The bright, cheery urban compound boasts period antiques, and spacious guest rooms wonderfully appointed with smart, patterned furnishings, voice mail, robes, and a spotless private bath (plus amenities) en suite or across the hall. A fire burns nightly in the cozy living room, and guests are welcome to make themselves at home in the wood-paneled common library (with fireplace and piano), sunny breakfast room overlooking the garden, formal dining room, and spacious garden with fountains and a steam room.

520 Church St. (between 17th and 18th Sts.), San Francisco, CA 94114. ☎ 888/520-PARK or 415/621-3222. Fax 415/621-4139. www.parkerguesthouse.com. 10 units. $120–$180 double; $200 junior suite. Rates include extended continental breakfast. AE, DISC, MC, V. Muni Metro: J Church. Bus: 22, 33. Self-parking $15. **Amenities:** Access to nearby health club; steam room; concierge. *In room:* TV, dataport, hair dryer.

4 Dining

San Francisco's dining scene is one of the best in the world. Since our space is limited, we had to make tough choices, but the end result is a cross section of San Francisco's best restaurants in every price range. For a greater selection of reviews, see *Frommer's San Francisco.*

Note: If you want a table at a top restaurant, make your reservation weeks in advance—perhaps through www.OpenTable.com, which gives real-time reservations to many Bay Area establishments.

UNION SQUARE
EXPENSIVE

Farallon ☆ *Overrated* COASTAL CUISINE/SEAFOOD   While this seafood restaurant is hands-down the most whimsical in its stunning oceanic decor, the high price tag and the fine but not mind-blowing food make it a better cocktail and appetizer or lunch stop than dinner choice. Handblown jellyfish lamps, kelp bed–like back-lit columns, glass clam shells, sea-urchin light fixtures, a sea-life mosaic floor, and a tentacle-encircled bar set the scene for chef Mark Franz's seafood. Starters range from the expected (oysters) to the more ambitious, like the iced Atlantic and Pacific shellfish indulgence, a cornucopia of oysters, clams, crayfish, prawns, mussels, and scallops with a horseradish mignonette ($21.50 per person). While most main courses—such as sautéed black bass with wild mushroom ragout, leek risotto, and pesto or grilled monkfish loin with truffled cauliflower puree, saffron jus, and lobster aioli—stick with the seaside theme, meat and game eaters have at least one option. The wine list (more than 300 by the bottle, 24 by the glass) is impressive. Reserve well in advance.

450 Post St. (between Mason and Powell Sts., adjoining the Kensington Park Hotel). ☎ 415/956-6969. www.farallonrestaurant.com. Reservations recommended. Main courses $10.50–$16.25 lunch; $22–$32

dinner. AE, DC, DISC, MC, V. Tues–Sat 11:30am–2:30pm; Tues–Sat 2:30–5pm (bistro menu); Mon–Wed 5:30–10:30pm; Thurs–Sat 5:30–11pm; Sun 5–10pm. Valet parking $12. Bus: 2, 3, 4, or 38.

Masa's ★★★ FRENCH   One of the city's veteran contenders for best French restaurant underwent major changes in early 2001, including a new chef and updated interior. Executive Chef Ron Siegel deftly designs three-, six-, and nine-course tasting menus within an almost startlingly trendy (think hip hotelier Ian Schrager) room. Fortunately, beyond the small, minimalist bar and illuminated white curtains one thing has remained the same: a dedication to culinary excellence. Anticipate delicate seared scallops elevated both literally and figuratively by microgreens and a dab of decadent uni (sea urchin) and savory skate balanced atop a short rib ravioli bathed in a mushroom jus. Desserts are too precious and are better to look at than they are to eat. But the candy cart, which is wheeled by so you may select lollipops, chocolates, and mini cookies, almost makes up for it.

In the Hotel Vintage Court, 648 Bush St. (at Stockton St.). ℰ **800/258-7694** or 415/989-7154. Reservations required and accepted up to 3 weeks in advance. Fixed-price dinner $60–$105. AE, DC, DISC, MC, V. Tues–Sat 5:30–9:30pm. Closed first 2 weeks in Jan, first week in July. Cable car: Powell-Mason and Powell-Hyde lines. Valet parking: $9. Bus: 2, 3, 4, 30, or 45.

Postrio ★★ AMERICAN   Over 10 years after Wolfgang Puck launched the trend for large, glamorous downtown dining rooms, it's still a rare night when brother chefs Mitchell and Steven Rosenthal don't perform to a full house. But eating is only half the reason you come to Postrio. After squeezing through the perpetually swinging bar—which, in its own right, dishes out excellent pizzas from a wood-burning oven—you're forced to make a grand entrance down the antebellum staircase to the cavernous dining room below. (It's everyone's 15 seconds of fame, so make sure your fly is zipped.) Pure Hollywood, for sure, but fun. The menu combines Italian, Asian, French, and California styles with mixed results. The desserts, each artistically sculpted, are the highlight of the evening.

In the Prescott Hotel, 545 Post St. (between Mason and Taylor Sts.). ℰ **415/776-7825.** Reservations recommended. Main courses $6–$16 breakfast; $12–$16 lunch; $24–$36 dinner. AE, DC, DISC, MC, V. Mon–Fri 7–10am; Mon–Sat 11:30am–2pm; Sun brunch 11am–2pm; Sun–Wed 5:30–10pm; Thurs–Sat 5:30–10:30pm. Bar menu daily 11:30am–11:30pm, open til 2am. Cable car: Powell-Mason and Powell-Hyde lines. Bus: 2, 3, 4, or 38.

MODERATE

Kuleto's ★★ ITALIAN   It's not a destination restaurant, but if you're downtown and hungry, Kuleto's is a great place to feast. Skip the wait for a table, muscle a seat at the antipasto bar, and fill up on appetizers, which are often better than the entrees. For a main course, try penne pasta drenched in tangy lamb-sausage marinara sauce, clam linguini (generously overloaded with fresh clams), or any of the fresh-fish specials grilled over hardwoods. If you don't arrive by 6pm, expect to wait—this place fills up fast.

In the Villa Florence Hotel, 221 Powell St. (between Geary and O'Farrell Sts.). ℰ **415/397-7720.** Reservations recommended. Breakfast $5–$10; main courses $10–$20. AE, DC, MC, V. Mon–Fri 7–10:30am; Sat–Sun 8–10:30am; daily 11:30am–11pm. Cable car: Powell-Mason and Powell-Hyde lines. Muni Metro: Powell. Bus: 2, 3, 4, or 38.

Le Colonial ★★ *Finds* VIETNAMESE   Sexy, French-Vietnamese plantation environs and delicious—albeit pricey—Vietnamese food make this an excellent choice for an all-around fun experience. One of my favorite reasons to enter the long dining room and beautiful front patio is the sea bass. Wrapped in banana leaf with glass noodles, ginger, scallions, and cilantro, the buttery fish is genuine bliss.

Then again, the vibrant flavors of tender wok-seared beef tenderloin with watercress onion salad are outstanding as well. I can't say enough about the upstairs lounge, where romance reigns, with cozy couches, seductive surroundings (and, often, live jazz), and a kicked-back cocktail crowd of swank professionals.

20 Cosmo Place (off Taylor St., between Post and Sutter Sts.). ℂ **415/931-3600.** Reservations recommended. Main courses $14–$33. AE, DC, DISC, MC, V. Sun–Wed 5:30–10pm; Thurs–Sat 5:30–11pm. Valet parking $5 first hour, $2 each additional half hour. Bus: 2, 3, 4, or 27.

Scala's Bistro ⋆⋆ FRENCH/ITALIAN   This latest venture by husband-and-wife team Giovanni (the host) and Donna (the chef) Scala is one of the better restaurants in Union Square. The Parisian-bistro/old-world atmosphere has just the right balance of elegance and informality, which means it's perfectly okay to have some fun here (and apparently most people do). Donna puts together a fantastic array of Italian and French dishes that are priced surprisingly low. Start with the Earth and Surf calamari appetizer or grilled portobello mushrooms. Generous portions of the moist, rich duck-leg confit will satisfy hungry appetites, but if you can only order one thing, make it Scala's signature dish: the seared salmon resting on a bed of creamy buttermilk mashed potatoes and ensconced with a tomato, chive, and white-wine sauce. Finish with the creamy Bostini cream pie, a dreamy combo of vanilla custard and orange chiffon cake with a warm chocolate glaze.

In the Sir Francis Drake hotel, 432 Powell St. (at Sutter St.). ℂ **415/395-8555.** Reservations recommended. Breakfast $7–$10; lunch and dinner main courses $12–$24. AE, DC, DISC, MC, V. Daily 8am–midnight. Cable car: Powell-Hyde line. Bus: 2, 3, 4, 30, 45, or 76.

INEXPENSIVE

Café Claude ⋆⋆ FRENCH   For a little bit of Paris off Powell Street, try Café Claude, a crowded and lively restaurant tucked into a narrow lane near Union Square. With prices topping out at about $12 for main courses such as *poussin rôti* (roast Cornish hen with potatoes and aïoli), French shepherd's pie, or *poisson du jour* (fish of the day), Café Claude is a good value. There is live jazz Thursday and Friday from 8 to 11pm and Saturday from 7 to 10pm. Outdoor seating is available when the weather permits.

7 Claude Lane (off Sutter St.). ℂ **415/392-3515.** www.cafeclaude.com. Reservations recommended. Main courses $7–$13. AE, DC, DISC, MC, V. Mon 11:30am–2:30pm; Tues–Wed 11:30am–10pm; Thurs–Fri 11:30am–10:30pm; Sat 11:30am–11:30pm. Cable car: Powell-Mason and Powell-Hyde lines.

RUSSIAN HILL
INEXPENSIVE

Swan Oyster Depot ⋆⋆ *Finds* SEAFOOD   Swan Oyster Depot is a unique San Francisco dining experience you shouldn't miss. Opened in 1912, this tiny hole-in-the-wall boasts only 20 or so seats, jammed cheek-by-jowl along a long marble bar. Most patrons come for a quick cup of chowder or a plate of oysters on the half shell that arrive chilling on crushed ice. The menu is limited to fresh crab, shrimp, oyster, clam cocktails, Maine lobster, and Boston-style clam chowder, all of which are exceedingly fresh. *Note:* Don't let the lunchtime line dissuade you—it moves fast.

1517 Polk St. (between California and Sacramento Sts.). ℂ **415/673-1101.** Reservations not accepted. Seafood cocktails $5–$8; clams and oysters on the half shell $6–$7.50 per half dozen. No credit cards. Mon–Sat 8am–5:30pm. Bus: 27.

SOMA
EXPENSIVE

Boulevard ★★★ *Finds* AMERICAN   Master restaurant designer Pat Kuleto and one of the nation's top chefs Nancy Oaks teamed up in 1993 to create one of San Francisco's most exciting restaurants, and Boulevard is still one of my— and the city's—all-time favorites. What's the winning combination? The dramatic Belle Époque interior combined with Oaks's well-sculpted, mouthwatering dishes. Starters alone could make a perfect meal, especially if you indulge in the sweetbreads wrapped in prosciutto on watercress and Lola Rose lettuce with garlic croutons and a whole-grain mustard vinaigrette; Sonoma foie gras with elderberry syrup, toast, and Bosc pear salad; or Maine sea scallops on garlic mashed potato croustade with truffle and portobello mushroom relish. The nine or so main courses are equally creative and might include pan-roasted miso-glazed sea bass with asparagus salad, Japanese rice, and shiitake-mushroom broth, or spit-roasted cider-cured pork loin with sweet potato–swirled mashed potatoes and sautéed baby red chard. Vegetarian items, such as wild mushroom risotto with fresh chanterelles and Parmesan, are also offered. Three levels of formality—bar, open kitchen, and main dining room—keep things from getting too snobby.

1 Mission St. (between Embarcadero and Steuart Sts.). ℂ **415/543-6084.** Reservations recommended. Main courses $19–$30. AE, DC, DISC, MC, V. Mon–Fri 11:30am–2pm; Sun–Wed 5:30–10pm; Thurs–Sat 5:30–10:30pm. Valet parking $10. Bus: 15, 30, 32, 42, or 45.

Fifth Floor Restaurant ★★★ MODERN FRENCH   Executive Chef George Morrone (who opened Aqua and has reigned at L.A.'s Hotel Bel-Air) has enjoyed a stellar reputation since this fancy spot hit the ground running in 1999. Like the decor—swathed in rich color and fabric, red leather and velvet banquettes, Frette linens, zebra-striped carpeting, and an intended Parisian 1930s club-like atmosphere ensconcing the 75 seats—his menu features all things luxurious: Kobe beef; foie gras; sea urchin (accompanied by salmon Paillard, East Coast Belon oyster, and Diver scallop); caviar; his signature "tuna foie gras;" suckling pig à l'orange; milk-fed veal steak with Madeira glazed sweet-breads, curry oil, and jasmine rice—the list goes on. The food, while giving a nod to the classics, takes it one step further into a world of pure and modern indulgence. In other words, if you want a memorable meal and can afford to pay through the nose for it, this is your place. The outstanding wine list, overseen by sommelier Rajat Parr who is big on little wineries and specialties from Burgundy, offers 250-plus selections that are equally lavish.

In the Hotel Palomar, 12 Fourth St. (at Market St.). ℂ **415/348-1555.** Reservations required. Main courses $24–$39. AE, DC, DISC, MC, V. Mon–Thurs 5:30–10pm; Fri–Sat 5:30–11pm. Valet parking: $10. Bus: All Market St. buses.

MODERATE

bacar ★★ AMERICAN BRASSERIE   No other dining room makes wine as integral to the meal as popular new bacar. Up to 250 eclectic, fashionable diners pack into the warehouse-restaurant's three distinct areas—the casual (loud) downstairs salon, the bustling bar and loud mezzanine, or the more quiet upstairs, which looks down on the mezzanine's action—for chef Arnold Eric Wong's "American Brasserie" (i.e., French Bistro with a California twist) cuisine. During a recent visit, cod cakes and roasted mussels were lovely, while fried smelt was bland. Skate atop picholine olives and roasted peppers and *osso buco* were outstanding. Just as much fun is the wine selection, which gives you 1,000 choices. Around 100 come by the glass, 2-ounce pour, or 250- or 500-milileter decanter, and Wine Director Debbie Zachareas is almost always available to introduce you to new and exciting options. Vibrant in both energy and design, bacar is definitely the hot spot right now, so don't be surprised if even with a reservation you have to wait for a table.

448 Brannan St., at Third St. ☎ **415/904-4100.** Reservations recommended. Main courses $12–$29. AE, MC, V. Daily 5:30pm–1am. Valet (at dinner only) $9. Bus: 15, 30, 45, 76, 81.

Fringale Restaurant ★★ *Value* FRENCH   Still one of San Francisco's better restaurants for the money a decade after opening, Fringale—colloquial French for "sudden urge to eat"—has enjoyed a waiting list since the day chef and co-owner Gerald Hirigoyen opened this small bistro. Within the small and airy dining environment, guests begin their meal with steamed mussels with fried garlic vinaigrette, or roasted quail with apple risotto and foie gras. Among the 10 courses on the seasonally changing menu, you might find rack of lamb with potato gratin or pork tenderloin confit with cabbage and onion and apple marmalade. Desserts are worth savoring, too, particularly the Gateau Basque (which has won me many culinary friends since I began preparing it myself, with the help of Hirigoyen's cookbook). The mostly French waiters provide charming service, and prices are surprisingly reasonable for such high-quality cuisine.

570 Fourth St. (between Brannan and Bryant Sts.). ☎ **415/543-0573.** Reservations recommended. Main courses $4–$12 lunch; $11–$21 dinner. AE, MC, V. Mon–Fri 11:30am–3pm; Mon–Sat 5:30–10:30pm. Bus: 30 or 45.

Yank Sing ★★ CHINESE/DIM SUM   Loosely translated as "a delight of the heart," Yank Sing does great dim sum. Like most good dim sum meals, at Yank Sing you get to choose the small dishes from a cart that's continually wheeled around the dining room. Confident, experienced servers take the nervousness out of novices—they're good at guessing your gastric threshold. Most dim sum dishes are dumplings, filled with tasty concoctions of pork, beef, fish, or vegetables. Spareribs, stuffed crab claws, scallion pancakes, pork buns, and other palate-pleasers complete the menu.

101 Spear St. (at Mission St. at Rincon Center). ☎ **415/957-9300.** Dim sum $2.65–$3.40 for 3–4 pieces. AE, DC, MC, V. Mon–Fri 11am–3pm; Sun 11am–2:30pm. Cable car: California St. line. Bus: 1 or 42.

INEXPENSIVE

AsiaSF ★ CALIFORNIA/ASIAN   At AsiaSF you'll be entertained by Asian men—dressed as women—who lip-sync show tunes as they dish out an excellent grilled shrimp and herb salad, Asian-influenced hamburgers, pot stickers, duck quesadillas, and chicken sate. Fortunately, the food and the atmosphere are as colorful as the staff, which means a night here is more than a meal—it's a very happening event.

201 9th St. (at Howard St.). ☎ **415/255-8889.** Reservations recommended. Main courses $7–$18. AE, DC, MC, V ($20 minimum). Daily 5–10pm. Bus: 9, 12, 42, or 47.

Manora's ★ THAI   Ever-bustling Manora's cranks out dependable Thai to an eclectic mix of local diners. It's perpetually packed (unless you come early), so you'll be seated sardine-like at one of the cramped but well-appointed tables. During the dinner rush, the noise level can make conversation among larger parties almost impossible, but the food is so good, you'll probably prefer to turn toward your plate and stuff your face. Start with tangy soup or chicken satay. Follow with any of the wonderful dinner dishes—which should be shared—and a side of rice. There are endless options, including a vast array of vegetarian plates. *Tip:* Come before 7pm or after 9pm if you don't want a loud, rushed meal.

1600 Folsom St. (at 12th St.). © **415/861-6224.** Reservations recommended for 4 or more. Main courses $7–$12. MC, V. Mon–Fri 11:30am–2:30pm; Mon–Sat 5:30–10:30pm; Sun 5–10pm. Bus: 9, 12, or 47.

FINANCIAL DISTRICT
EXPENSIVE

Aqua ★★★ SEAFOOD   Without question, Aqua remains San Francisco's finest seafood restaurant. Heralded chef Michael Mina dazzles his customers with a bewildering juxtaposition of earth and sea in his seasonally changing menus. The ahi tartare, for example, is mixed tableside with pears, pine nuts, quail egg, and mint—it's truly divine and one of the best I've ever had. The roasted spot prawn with crab stuffing, citrus hollandaise, and hot and sour vinaigrette is deliciously creative, the miso-marinated Chilean sea bass and grilled medaillons of ahi tuna and foie gras in Pinot sauce are other show stoppers. Desserts are equally impressive, particularly the Aqua soufflé-of-the-day. Our only complaint: The dining room is rather stark and noisy.

252 California St. (between Battery and Front Sts.). © **415/956-9662.** Reservations required. Main courses $26–$45; 5-course tasting menu $75; 8-course tasting menu $95; vegetarian tasting menu $55. AE, DC, MC, V. Mon–Fri 11:30am–2pm; Mon–Sat 5:30–10:30pm. Bus: All Market St. buses.

MODERATE

Kokkari ★★★ *Value* GREEK   It figures that it would take a French chef to make Greek food fabulous, and executive chef Jean Alberti, the mastermind behind the moussaka, does exactly that. In truth, there are few restaurants I continually like as much as Kokkari ("Ko-car-ee"). The love affair begins with the setting: a beautifully rustic living room–like dining area with a commanding fireplace and oversized furnishings and ends with Alberti's traditional Aegean dishes. Hearty eaters should opt for the to-die-for moussaka (eggplant, lamb, potato, and béchamel). Another boon: quail stuffed with winter greens served on oven-roasted leeks, orzo, and wild rice *pilafi.* Don't leave without sinking your fork into an order of *Kalithopita,* the most velvety chocolate cake you'll ever eat.

200 Jackson St. (at Front St.). © **415/981-0983.** Reservations recommended. Main courses $16.50–$32.50. www.kokkari.com. AE, DC, MC, V. Mon–Fri lunch 11:30am–2:30pm, bar menu 2:30–5:30pm; dinner Mon–Thurs 5:30–10pm; Fri 5:30–11pm and Sat 5–11pm. Valet parking (dinner only) $8. Bus: 12, 15, 41, 42, or 83.

CHINATOWN
INEXPENSIVE

House of Nanking ★ CHINESE   To its legion of fans, the wait at this dive— sometimes up to an hour—is worth what's on the plate. When the line is reasonable, I drop by for a plate of pot stickers and chef-owner Peter Fang's signature shrimp-and-green-onion pancake, served with peanut sauce. You can select from a good number of pork, rice, beef, seafood, chicken, or vegetable dishes, but I suggest you trust the waiter when he recommends a special, or simply point to what looks good on someone else's table. Even with an expansion that doubled the space, seating is tight, so prepare to be bumped around a bit and don't expect good service—it's all part of the Nanking experience.

919 Kearny St. (at Columbus Ave.). © **415/421-1429.** Main courses $6–$12. MC, V. Mon–Fri 11am–10pm; Sat noon–10pm; Sun 4–10pm. Bus: 9, 12, 15, or 30.

Dining with the Sun on Your Face at Belden Place

San Francisco has always been woefully lacking in the alfresco dining department. One exception, however, is Belden Place, an adorable little brick alley in the heart of the Financial District that is closed to everything but foot traffic. When the weather is agreeable, the restaurants that line the alley break out the big umbrellas, tables, and chairs à la Boulevard St-Michel and voilà—a bit of Paris just off Pine Street.

A handful of adorable cafes line Belden Place and offer a wide variety of cuisine. There's **Cafe Bastille,** 22 Belden Place (✆ **415/986-5673**), your classic French bistro and fun speakeasy basement serving excellent crepes, mussels, and French onion soup along with live jazz on weekends; **Cafe Tiramisu,** 28 Belden Place (✆ **415/421-7044**), a stylish Italian hot spot serving addictive risottos and gnocchi; and **Plouf,** 40 Belden Place (✆ **415/986-6491**), which specializes in big bowls of mussels slathered in a choice of seven sauces as well as fresh seafood.

R&G Lounge ★★ CHINESE   If you want a sure thing in Chinatown, go directly to two-story R&G Lounge. During lunch, both plainly decorated floors are packed with hungry neighborhood workers who go straight to the $5 rice plate specials. But even then you can order from the dinner menu, which features legendary (and very greasy and rich) deep-fried salt and pepper crab. Personal favorites include R&G Special Beef, which melts in your mouth and explodes with the tangy flavor of the accompanying sauce or savory seafood in a clay pot, delicious classic roast duck, and the adzuki bean pudding finale.

631B Kearny St. (at Clay St.). ✆ 415/982-7877. Reservations recommended. Main courses $7–$25. AE, MC, V. Mon–Fri 11am–10pm; Sat 11:30am–10:30pm; Sun 11:30am–9:30pm. Bus: 1, 9AX, 9BX, 12, or 15.

NORTH BEACH
MODERATE

Enrico's ★ MEDITERRANEAN   Enrico's is the most fun sidewalk restaurant and supper club destination on this North Beach strip. Families might want to skip this one, but anyone with an appreciation for live jazz (played nightly), late-night noshing, and people-watching from the outdoor patio would be quite content spending an alfresco evening under the heat lamps. (However, the best view of the band is from inside.) Chewy brick-oven pizza, a handful of pastas, zesty tapas, and thick steaks are hot items on the menu, which changes monthly.

504 Broadway (at Kearny St.). ✆ 415/982-6223. Reservations recommended. Main courses $8–$13 lunch; $13–$19 dinner. AE, DC, DISC, MC, V. Sun–Thurs 11:30am–11:30pm; Fri–Sat 11:30am–12:30am; bar daily 11:30am–1:30am or earlier depending on patronage. Valet parking $7 at lunch, $10 at dinner. Bus: 12, 15, 30, or 83.

Moose's ★★ Value MEDITERRANEAN/CALIFORNIA   A big blue neon moose marks your arrival to North Beach's most schmoozy restaurant, where Nob Hill socialites and local politicians come to dine and be seen. But convivial Moose's is not just an image. The food on recent visits has been very, very good. Appetizers include a truly good Caesar salad and a perfect Dungeness crab cake with apple salad and meyer lemon aioli). Main courses (especially meats) tend to be lovingly prepared. Try the commendable center-cut pork loin chop with creamy yellow grits and apple and onion compote, or the grilled Arctic char with baby artichokes, black trumpet mushrooms, and lobster sauce. Other reasons to love Moose's: They make a darned good hamburger, have a casual bar and live jazz nightly, and serve Sunday brunch.

1652 Stockton St. (between Filbert and Union Sts.). (✆ **800/28-MOOSE** or 415/989-7800. www.mooses.com. Reservations recommended. Main courses $13–$26. AE, DC, MC, V. Mon–Wed 5:30–10pm; Thurs 11:30am–10pm; Fri 11:30am–11:30pm; Sat 11:30am–11:30pm (bar menu 2:30–5:30pm); Sun 10am–10pm (bar menu 2:30–5pm). Valet parking $6 lunch, $9 dinner for 3 hr. Bus: 15, 30, 41, or 45.

INEXPENSIVE

L'Osteria del Forno ★★ ITALIAN   L'Osteria del Forno might be only slightly larger than a walk-in closet, but it's one of the top three authentic Italian restaurants in North Beach. Peer in the window facing Columbus Avenue, and you'll probably see two Italian women with their hair up, sweating from the heat of the brick-lined oven, which cranks out the best focaccia (and focaccia sandwiches) in the city. There's no pomp or circumstance: Locals come here strictly to eat. The menu features a variety of superb pizzas, salads, soups, and fresh pastas, plus a good selection of daily specials (pray for the roast pork braised in milk), which includes a roast of the day, pasta, and ravioli. Small baskets of warm focaccia keep you going until the arrival of the entrees, which should always be accompanied by a glass of Italian red. Good news for folks on the go: You can get pizza by the slice.

519 Columbus Ave. (between Green and Union Sts.). (✆ **415/982-1124.** Reservations not accepted. Sandwiches $5.50–$6.50; pizzas $10–$17; main courses $6–$11. No credit cards. Sun–Mon and Wed–Thurs 11:30am–10pm; Fri–Sat 11:30am–10:30pm. Bus: 15 or 41.

Mario's Bohemian Cigar Store ★ Finds ITALIAN   Across the street from Washington Square is one of North Beach's most popular neighborhood hangouts. The century-old bar—small, well worn, and perpetually busy—is best known for its focaccia sandwiches, including meatball and eggplant. Wash it all down with an excellent cappuccino or a house Campari as you watch the tourists stroll by. And yes, they do sell cigars (although you can't smoke 'em inside).

566 Columbus Ave. (at Union St.). (✆ **415/362-0536.** Sandwiches $6.75–$7.25. No credit cards. Daily 10am–11pm. Closed Dec 24–Jan 1. Bus: 15, 30, 41, or 45.

Pasta Pomodoro ★★ Value Kids ITALIAN   If you're looking for a good, cheap meal in North Beach—or anywhere else in town, for that matter—this San Francisco chain can't be beat. There's usually a 20-minute wait for a table, but after you're seated you'll be surprised at how promptly you're served. Every dish is fresh and sizable, and best of all, they cost a third of what you'll pay elsewhere. Winners include the spaghetti *frutti di mare* made with calamari, mussels, scallops, tomato, garlic and wine, or *cavatappi pollo* with roast chicken, sun-dried tomatoes, cream, mushrooms, and Parmesan—both are under $7.

There are 12 other locations, including 2027 Chestnut St., at Fillmore Street (✆ **415/474-3400**); 2304 Market St., at 16th Street (✆ **415/558-8123**); 3611 California St. (✆ **415/831-0900**); and 816 Irving St., between 9th and 10th Streets (✆ **415/566-0900**).

655 Union St. (at Columbus Ave.). (✆ **415/399-0300.** Reservations not accepted. Main courses $4.60–$10.50. MC, V. Mon–Thurs 11am–11pm; Fri 11am–midnight; Sat noon–midnight; Sun noon–11pm. Cable car: Powell-Mason line. Bus: 15, 30, 41, or 45.

FISHERMAN'S WHARF
EXPENSIVE

Restaurant Gary Danko ★★★ Finds MODERN CLASSIC   Gary Danko, who received the James Beard Foundation award for Best Chef in California and made San Francisco's Ritz-Carlton Dining Room the top dining destination during his reign from 1991 to 1996, still tops the charts after his 1999 opening. Within the romantic yet unfussy wood, split-dining room thoughtfulness is woven into the experience with the intricacy of a master embroiderer. The three- to six-course price-fixed menu is freestyle, so whether you want a sampling of appetizers or a flight of meat courses, you need only ask. Top picks? Glazed oysters, which were as creamy as the light accompanying sauce graced with leeks and intricately carved "zucchini pearls"; seared foie gras with peaches, caramelized onions, and verjus sauce; and adventurous Moroccan spiced squab with chermoula and orange-cumin carrots. Diners at the small bar have the option of ordering a la carte and everyone has access to the stellar, but expensive, wine list. If after dinner you have the will to pass on the glorious cheese cart or caramel almond peaches with buttermilk ice cream prepared tableside, a plate of petit fours reminds you that Gary Danko is one sweet and memorable meal.

800 North Point St. (at Hyde St.). ✆ 415/749-2060. www.garydanko.com. Reservations required. 3- to 6-course fixed-price menu $55–$74. AE, DC, MC, V. Sun–Wed 5:30–9:30pm; Thurs–Sat 5:30–10pm. Bus: 42.

MODERATE

Ana Mandara ✶✶ *(Kids* VIETNAMESE   Don Johnson is part owner but the real star is the Vietnamese food in an outstandingly beautiful setting. Amid a shuttered room with mood lighting, palm trees, and Vietnamese-inspired decor, diners (mostly tourists) splurge on crisp spring rolls; Dungeness crab with zesty lemon sauce; buttery Chilean sea bass, lovingly wrapped and steamed in banana leaf with shiitake mushrooms and miso sauce; a sculptural "lobster tower" with rice, avocado, and daikon sprouts; and wok-charred tournedos of beef tenderloin with sweet onions and peppercress.

891 Beach St. (at Polk St.). ✆ 415/771-6800. Reservations recommended. Main courses $18–$28. AE, DISC, MC, V. Mon–Fri 11:30am–2pm; Sun–Thurs 5:30–9:30pm; Fri–Sat 5:30–10:30pm. Valet parking $8. Bus: 19, 30, 32, or 42.

MARINA DISTRICT, COW HOLLOW, & PACIFIC HEIGHTS
EXPENSIVE

La Folie ✶✶ *(Finds* FRENCH   My mother and I call this unintimidating, cozy, relaxed French restaurant "the house of foie gras" because on our first visit virtually every dish overflowed with the ultrarich delicacy. But in truth, while foie gras is still celebrated, there's more to chef Roland Passot's fantastic menu: melt-in-your-mouth starters such as the roast quail and—drum roll please—foie gras with salad, wild mushrooms, and roasted garlic, and very generous main courses such as rôti of quail and squab stuffed with wild mushrooms and wrapped in crispy potato strings, or roast venison with vegetables, quince, and huckleberry sauce. The country-French decor is tasteful but not too serious, with whimsical chandeliers and a cloudy sky painted overhead. Finish off with any of the delectable desserts and when you're done you're sure to loosen your belt a few notches.

2316 Polk St. (between Green and Union Sts.). ✆ 415/776-5577. Reservations recommended. Main courses $32–$48; 4-course tasting menu $75; 10-course chef's tasting menu (order in advance for whole table) $120 per person; vegetarian tasting menu $55. AE, DC, DISC, MC, V. Mon–Sat 5:30–10pm. Bus: 19, 41, 45, 47, 49, or 76.

MODERATE

Ella's ✶✶ *(Kids* AMERICAN/BREAKFAST   Although this homey American restaurant serves (quiet) dinners on weeknights, it's well known throughout town as the undisputed king of breakfasts. Unfortunately, its acclaim means you're likely to wait up to an hour on weekends. But midweek and in the wee hours of morning, it's possible to slide into a counter or table seat in the colorful split dining room and lose yourself in outstanding and obscenely generous servings of chicken hash, crisped to perfection and served with eggs any way you like them, with fluffy buttermilk biscuits. Pancakes, omelets, and the short list of other breakfast essentials are equally revered. Service can be slow, but at least the busboys are quick to fill coffee cups. Come lunchtime and the far more mellow dinner, solid entrees like salads or grilled salmon with mashed potatoes remind you what's great about good old American cooking.

500 Presidio Ave. (at California St.). ℭ **415/441-5669.** For parties of 8 or more reservations are accepted for breakfast and are always accepted for lunch and dinner. Main courses $2.75–$8.25 breakfast; $9–$17 dinner. AE, MC, V. Mon–Fri 7am–9pm; Sat–Sun 8:30am–2pm. Bus: 1, 5, or 43.

Florio ★★ FRENCH/ITALIAN BISTRO   When I'm in the mood for a good meal without hoopla, I head directly to bistro-like Florio. It's not only because the staff is friendly, or because if it's booked I can always eat at the bar, or even because the place is small enough that I don't feel like I'm being rushed in and out as quickly as possible. The real reason is because I'm addicted to the shrimp and white bean salad, steak frites, and virtually every other little comfort dish that makes its way to the table. The wines by the glass (and by the bottle) always disappoint, but I don't care. I pull up a chair, make myself at home, and enjoy casual and cozy surroundings and consistently satisfying food. I suggest you do the same.

1915 Fillmore St. (between Pine and Bush Sts.). ℭ **415/775-4300.** Reservations recommended. Most main courses $17–$20. AE, MC, V. Sun–Thurs 5:30–10pm; Fri–Sat 5:30–11pm. Bus: 22, 41, or 45.

Greens Restaurant, Fort Mason ★★ *Finds* VEGETARIAN   Knowledgeable locals swear by Greens, where executive chef Annie Somerville (author of *Fields of Greens*) cooks with the seasons, using produce from Green Gulch Farm and other local organic farms. Located in an old warehouse, with enormous windows overlooking the bridge and the bay, the restaurant is both a pioneer and a legend. A weeknight dinner might start with such appetizers as tomato lentil soup with spinach and parmesan cheese or ricotta and white corn griddle cakes with asiago, smoked mozzarella, and scallions. Entrees include such choices as spring-vegetable risotto with asparagus, peas, shiitake and crimini mushrooms, and Parmesan cheese; or Sri Lankan curry made of new potatoes, cauliflower, carrots, peppers, and snap peas stewed with tomatoes, coconut milk, ginger, and Sri Lankan spices.

A special four-course dinner is served on Saturday. Adjacent to the restaurant, Greens To Go bakery sells homemade breads, sandwiches, soups, salads, and pastries.

Building A, Fort Mason Center (enter Fort Mason opposite the Safeway at Buchanan and Marina Sts.). ℭ **415/771-6222.** Reservations recommended 2 weeks in advance. Main courses $8–$13 lunch, $13–$18 dinner; fixed-priced dinner $45; brunch $8–$12. DISC, MC, V. Tues–Fri 11:30am–2pm; Sat 11:30am–2:30pm and 5:30–9pm; Sun 10am–2pm; Mon–Fri 5:30–9:30pm. Greens To Go Mon–Fri 8am–9:30pm; Sat 8am–4:30pm; Sun 9am–3:30pm. Bus: 28 or 30.

Pane e Vino ★★ *Kids* ITALIAN   The authentic Italian food is consistently excellent (try not to fill up on the outstanding breads), the prices reasonable, and the mostly Italian-accented staff always smooth and efficient under pressure. The two small dining rooms—separated by an open kitchen from which heavenly aromas emanate—offer only limited seating, so expect a wait even if you have reservations. The wide selection of appetizers includes a fine carpaccio and the hugely popular chilled artichoke stuffed with bread and tomatoes and served with vinaigrette. A favorite, the antipasti of mixed grilled vegetables, always spurs a fork fight. A similarly broad selection of pastas is available, including a flavorful *pennette alla boscaiola* with porcini mushrooms and pancetta in a tomato cream sauce. Other specialties include a chicken breast marinated in lime juice and herbs. Top dessert picks are any of the Italian ice creams, the crème caramel, and the creamy tiramisu.

3011 Steiner St. (at Union St.). ⓒ **415/346-2111**. Reservations recommended. Main courses $8.50–$20. AE, MC, V. Mon–Thurs 11:30am–3pm and 5–10pm; Fri–Sat 11:30am–10pm; Sun 5–10pm. Valet parking (Mon–Sat evenings only) $8. Bus: 41 or 45.

INEXPENSIVE

Andalé Taqueria ⭐⭐ *Value Kids* MEXICAN Andalé (Spanish for "hurry up") offers incredible high-end fast food for the health-conscious and the just plain hungry in an attractive and casual setting. Lard, preservatives, or canned items are eschewed for salad dressings made with double virgin olive oil; whole vegetarian beans (not refried); skinless chicken; salsas and aguas frescas made from fresh fruits and veggies; and mesquite-grilled meats. Add the location (on a sunny shopping stretch), sophisticated decor, full bar, and check-me-out patio seating (complete with corner fireplace), and it's no wonder the good-looking, fitness-fanatic Marina District considers this place home. Cafeteria-style service keeps prices low.

2150 Chestnut St. (between Steiner and Pierce Sts.). ⓒ **415/749-0506**. Reservations not accepted. Most dishes $5.25–$9.50. AE, MC, V. Mon–Thurs and Sun 11am–10pm; Fri–Sat 11am–11pm. Bus: 22, 28, 30, 30X, 43, 76, or 82X.

Eliza's ⭐⭐ *Value Kids* CHINESE Despite the humorous train-wreck-like design of modern architecture, glass art, and color, this perennially packed neighborhood haunt serves some of the freshest, best-tasting Chinese in town. Unlike most comparable options, here the atmosphere (albeit unintentionally funky) and presentation parallel the food. The fantastically fresh soups, salads, seafood, pork, chicken, duck, and such specials as spicy eggplant are outstanding and served on beautiful Italian plates. (Get the sea bass with black bean sauce and go straight to heaven!) I often come at midday and order the wonderful kung pao chicken lunch special: a mixture of tender chicken, peanuts, chili peppers, subtly hot sauce, and perfectly crunchy vegetables. It's one of 21 main-course choices that come with rice and soup for around $5. The place is also jumping at night, so prepare to stand in line.

2877 California St. (at Broderick St.). ⓒ **415/621-4819**. Reservations not accepted. Main courses $4.50–$5.15 lunch; $5.25–$9 dinner. MC, V ($10 minimum). Mon–Fri 11am–3pm and 5–9:45pm; Sat 11am–9:45pm. Bus: 6, 7, 21, 66, or 71.

Mel's Diner ⭐⭐ *Kids* AMERICAN Sure, it's contrived, touristy, and nowhere near healthy, but when you get that urge for a chocolate shake and banana cream pie at the stroke of midnight—or when you want to entertain the kids—no other place in the city comes through like Mel's Diner. Modeled after a classic 1950s diner, right down to the nickel jukebox at each table, Mel's harks back to the halcyon days when cholesterol and fried foods didn't jab your guilty conscience with every greasy, wonderful bite. Too bad the prices don't reflect the '50s; a burger with fries and a Coke runs about $8.

There's another Mel's at 3355 Geary St., at Stanyan Street (ⓒ **415/ 387-2244**); it's open 6am to 3am Thursday through Saturday.

2165 Lombard St. (at Fillmore St.). ⓒ **415/921-3039**. Reservations accepted. Main courses $4–$5.50 breakfast; $6–$8 lunch; $8–$12 dinner. No credit cards. Sun–Wed 6am–2am; Thurs 6am–3am; Fri–Sat 24-hr. Bus: 22, 30, or 43.

Pluto's ★ *Value* CALIFORNIA Pluto's combines assembly-line efficiency with three-star quality. The result is cheap, fresh, high-quality fare ranging from humongous salads with a dozen choices of toppings to oven-roasted poultry and grilled meats (the flank steak is great), sandwiches, and a wide array of sides like crispy garlic potato rings, seasonal veggies, and barbecued chicken wings. Drinks include cappuccino, tea, sodas, bottled brews, and Napa wines, and desserts are homemade. The ordering system can be bewildering to newcomers: Grab a checklist and hand it to the food servers, who will check off your order and relay it to the cashier. Seating is limited during the rush, but the turnover is fairly fast. A second location is at 627 Irving St., at 7th Avenue (𝒞 **415/753-8867**).

3258 Scott St. (at Chestnut St.). 𝒞 **415/7-PLUTOS**. Reservations not accepted. Main courses $3.50–$5.75. MC, V. Mon–Thurs 11:30am–10pm; Fri 11:30am–11pm; Sat 9:30am–11pm; Sun 9:30am–10pm. Bus: 28, 30, 42, or 76.

CIVIC CENTER
EXPENSIVE

Jardinière ★★ FRENCH/CALIFORNIA Jardinière is not only the pre-ferred pre- and post-symphony dining spot; it also happens to be the perfect setting for a cocktail. The sexy dining room is run by a culinary dream team con-sisting of owner-chef Traci Des Jardins and owner-designer Pat Kuleto. On most evenings the two-story brick structure is abuzz with an older crowd (including regular Mayor Brown) who sip bubbly at the centerpiece mahogany bar or watch the scene discreetly from the upstairs circular balcony. The restaurant's cham-pagne theme is integrated via twinkling lights and fun ice buckets built into the balcony railing, making the atmosphere conducive to throwing back a few in the best of style—especially when there's live jazz.

Actually, cocktailing is my preferred reason to visit here. While the daily changing menu is lovely and might include seared scallops with truffled potatoes and truffle reduction, its famed truffled chicken potpie, venison with celery root red wine, braised cabbage, and juniper sauce, the atmosphere just doesn't have enough warmth for me. But anyone in search of a quality meal will not be dis-appointed. Kudos also to the great wine selection—many by the glass and over 300 bottles.

300 Grove St. (at Franklin St.). 𝒞 **415/861-5555**. Reservations recommended. Main courses $21–$29; 6-course tasting menu $75. AE, DC, DISC, MC, V. Daily 5–10:30pm. Valet parking $10. Bus: 19 or 21.

MODERATE

Absinthe ★★ *Value* SOUTHERN FRENCH This Hayes Valley hot spot is a sexy, fun, *and* reasonably priced restaurant preferred by everyone from the the-atergoing crowd to the young and chic. Decor is scrumptious brasserie and the fare is tasty—from the specialty cocktails, and good wine list to the slew of seafood starters, including oysters and cold seafood platters. Appetizers range from classic (Caesar salad, French onion soup) to modern luxe (perhaps grilled asparagus with black-truffled mayonnaise, or lamb's lettuce with pickled beets and walnuts). Main courses are equally satisfying, with the likes of coq au vin to an excellent burger.

398 Hayes St. (at Gough St.). 𝒞 **415/551-1590**. Reservations recommended. Breakfast $6–$12; most main courses $8.50–$18 at lunch, $9–$20 at dinner. AE, DC, DISC, MC, V. Tues–Fri 7:30am–1am (bar menu 3pm–1am); Sat 11am–1am (brunch until 3pm, bar menu 3pm–1am); Sun 11am–10:30pm (brunch until 3pm, bar menu 3pm–10:30pm). Valet parking (Tues–Sat) $6 with dinner, $18 without. Bus: 21.

Hayes Street Grill ★★ SEAFOOD For well over a decade this small, no-nonsense seafood restaurant (owned and operated by revered food writer and chef Patricia Unterman) has maintained a solid reputation among San Francisco's picky epicureans for its impeccably fresh and straightforwardly prepared fish. Choices ranging from Hawaiian swordfish to Puget Sound salmon—cooked to perfection, naturally—are matched with your sauce of choice (Szechuan peanut, tomatillo salsa, or shallot butter) and a side of their signature french fries. Fancier seafood specials are available too, such as paella with clams, mussels, scallops, calamari, chorizo, and saffron rice, as well as an impressive selection of garden-fresh salads and local grilled meats. Finish with the outstanding crème brûlée.

320 Hayes St. (near Franklin St.). ℂ **415/863-5545.** Reservations recommended. Main courses $14.50–$25. AE, DC, DISC, MC, V. Mon–Fri 11:30am–2pm; Mon–Thurs 5–9:30pm; Fri 5–10:30pm; Sat 5:30–10:30pm; Sun 5–8:30pm. Bus: 19, 31, or 38.

Zuni Café ★★ *Finds* MEDITERRANEAN Delicious, trend-setting Zuni Café is, and probably always will be, a local favorite. Its expanse of windows and prime lower Castro location guarantee good people-watching, but even better is the action within: attractive 30- and 40-somethings crowding in for the flavors of chef Judy Rodgers's incredibly satisfying Mediterranean-influenced menu. For the full effect, stand at the bustling, copper-topped bar, order a glass of wine and a few oysters from the oyster menu. (A dozen or so varieties are on hand at all times.) Then take a seat amidst the exposed-brick, two-level maze of little dining rooms. Although the changing menu always includes meat (such as New York steak with Belgian endive gratin) and fish (grilled or braised in the kitchen's brick oven), the proven winners are Rodgers's brick-oven-roasted chicken for two with Tuscan-style bread salad, the polenta with mascarpone, and the hamburger on grilled rosemary focaccia bread (a strong contender for the city's best burger).

1658 Market St. (at Franklin St.). ℂ **415/552-2522.** Reservations recommended. Main courses $15–$24. AE, MC, V. Tues–Sat 11:30am–midnight; Sun 11am–11pm. Valet parking $7. Muni Metro: All Market St. trams. Bus: 6, 7, 71, or 75.

HAIGHT-ASHBURY
INEXPENSIVE

Cha Cha Cha ★★ *Value* CARIBBEAN Put your name on the mile-long list, crowd into the minuscule bar, and drink sangria while you wait. When you finally get seated (generally at least an hour later), you'll dine in a loud—and I mean *loud*—dining room with Santería altars, banana trees, and plastic tropical tablecloths. Do as we do and order from the tapas menu, sharing such dishes as one of the city's best fried calamari, fried new potatoes, Cajun shrimp, and mussels in saffron broth, all of which are accompanied by rich, luscious sauces. This is the kind of place where you can take friends in a partying mood, let your hair down, and make an evening of it. If you want all the flavor without the festivities, come during lunch.

A second, larger location is open in the Mission at 2327 Mission St., between 19th and 20th Streets (ℂ **415/648-0504**).

1801 Haight St. (at Shrader St.). ℂ **415/386-5758.** Reservations not accepted. Tapas $4.50–$8.75; main courses $9–$15. MC, V. Daily 11:30am–4pm; Sun–Thurs 5–11pm; Fri–Sat 5–11:30pm. Muni Metro: N. Bus: 6, 7, 66, 71, or 73.

Thep Phanom ★★ THAI By successfully incorporating flavors from India, China, Burma, Malaysia, and more recently the West, Thep Phanom has risen through the ranks to become one of the best Thai restaurants in San Francisco. (The line out the front door proves it's no secret.) Start with the signature dish, *ped swan*—boneless duck in a light honey sauce served on a bed of spinach. *Larb ped* (minced duck salad), velvety basil-spiked seafood curry served on banana leaves, and spicy *yum plamuk* (calamari salad) are also recommended. The Haight location attracts an eclectic crowd; the atmosphere is informal, and the decor quite tasteful.

400 Waller St. (at Fillmore St.). ℭ **415/431-2526.** Reservations recommended. Main courses $8–$12. AE, DC, DISC, MC, V. Daily 5:30–10:30pm. Bus: 6, 7, 22, 66, or 71.

RICHMOND & SUNSET DISTRICTS
INEXPENSIVE

Ton Kiang ★★ *Finds* **Kids** CHINESE/DIM SUM   Ton Kiang is the number-one place in the city to do dim sum. Wait in line (which is out the door anytime between 11am and 1:30pm), get a table on the first or second floor, and say yes to dozens of delicacies, which are brought to the table for your approval. From stuffed crab claws, roast Peking duck, and a gazillion dumpling selections (including scallop and vegetable, shrimp, and beef) to the delicious and hard-to-find *doa miu* (snow pea sprouts flash-sautéed with garlic and peanut oil), shark-fin soup, and a mesmerizing mango pudding, every tray of morsels coming from the kitchen is an absolute delight. Though it's hard to get past the dim sum, which is served all day everyday, the full menu of Hakka cuisine is worth investigation as well. This is definitely one of my favorite places to do lunch, and it happens to have an unusually friendly staff.

5821 Geary Blvd. (between 22nd and 23rd Aves.). ℭ **415/387-8273.** Reservations accepted for parties of 8 or more. Dim sum $2–$5.50. AE, MC, V. Mon–Sat 10:30am–10pm, Sun 9am–10pm. Bus: 38.

THE CASTRO
MODERATE

Mecca ★★ *Finds* AMERICAN   In 1996, Mecca entered the scene in a decadent swirl of chocolate-brown velvet, stainless steel, cement, and brown Naugahyde, unveiling the kind of industrial-chic supper club that makes you want to order a martini just so you'll match the ambiance. A night here promises a live DJ spinning hot grooves (or live entertainment on Mondays), and a fine American meal served at tables tucked into several dining nooks. Menu options include such classic starters as Osetra caviar, oysters on the half shell, and Caesar salad, as well as more creative dishes like stir-fried clams with garlic and minced pork in a black-bean sauce. Main courses include shrimp and lemongrass-crusted Chilean sea bass, rosemary-grilled rack of lamb, and soft-shell crabs with white corn salsa and Creole mustard vinaigrette. The food is very good, but it's that only-in–San Francisco vibe that makes this place the smokin' hot spot in the Castro.

2029 Market St. (between 14th and Church Sts.). ℭ **415/621-7000.** www.sfmecca.com. Reservations recommended. Main courses $16–$32. AE, DC, MC, V. Mon–Thurs 5–11pm; Fri–Sat 5pm–midnight; Sun 4–10pm. Valet parking $8. Muni Metro: F, K, L, or M. Bus: 8, 22, 24, or 37.

INEXPENSIVE

Firewood Café ★★ *Value* ITALIAN/AMERICAN   One of the sharpest rooms in the neighborhood, the colorful Firewood put its money in the essentials and eliminated extra overhead. There are no waiters or waitresses; everyone orders at the counter and then relaxes at the single family-style table, one of the small tables facing the huge street-side windows, or in the cheery back dining room. Fresh salads ($6.75) come with a choice of three "fixins" ranging from caramelized onions to spiced walnuts, and three gourmet dressing options. Pastas might include three tortellini selections, such as roasted chicken and mortadella. There are gourmet pizzas, calamari with lemon-garlic aïoli, and an herb-roasted half or whole chicken with roasted new potatoes. Wines are reasonably priced and yummy desserts top off at $2.95.

4248 18th St. (at Diamond St.). © 415/252-0999. Reservations not accepted. Main courses $6.25–$9. MC, V. Daily 11am–11pm. Muni Metro: F, K, L, or M. Bus: 8, 33, 35, or 37.

MISSION DISTRICT
MODERATE

Foreign Cinema ✶✶ FRENCH BISTRO   This place is so chic that it's hard to believe it's a San Francisco restaurant. An indoor seat is a lovely place to watch San Francisco's most fashionable; outdoors (heated, partially covered, but still chilly), the enormous foreign film showing on the side of an adjoining building steals the show. Food can be uneven, but usually good enough to merit a visit and might include asparagus salad with truffle vinaigrette, frogs' legs, herb-crusted chicken breast with garlic mashed potatoes, roasted duck breast with black mission figs, rosemary marinated lamb loin with potato gratin, and lobster and monkfish bouillabaisse with coral aïoli. Truth be told, even if the food sucked, I'd come here. It's just that cool. By the way, if you have to wait for your table, consider stepping next door to the new adjoining bar, Lazslo's.

2534 Mission St. (between 21st and 22nd Sts.). © 415/648-7600. www.foreigncinema.com. Reservations recommended. Main courses $14–$21. MC, V. Tues–Sun 5:30–11pm. Valet parking $6. Bus: 14, 14L, or 49.

The Slanted Door ✶✶✶ *Finds* VIETNAMESE   This place is so popular that Mick Jagger and President Clinton made stopovers last time they hit town. Why? Despite the sometimes can't-be-bothered staff, the colorful industrial-chic warehouse serves incredibly fresh and flavorful Vietnamese food. Pull up a modern, color-washed chair and order anything from clay-pot catfish or amazing green papaya salad to one of the inexpensive lunch rice dishes topped with grilled shrimp or stir-fried eggplant or go full boar with steamed chicken with black-bean sauce, long beans with shrimp, or vegetarian noodles sautéed with mushrooms, lily buds, tofu, bamboo, and shiitake mushrooms.

584 Valencia St. (at 17th St.). © 415/861-8032. Reservations recommended. Main courses $6.50–$15.50 lunch; $7–$20 dinner. MC, V. Tues–Sun 11:30am–3pm; Sun–Thurs 5:30–10pm; Fri–Sat 5:30–10:30pm. Valet parking (dinner only) $7. Bus: 22, 26, 33, 49, or 53. BART: 16th St. Station.

Universal Café ✶✶ *Finds* AMERICAN/FRENCH   Not only does the intimate, rather cramped place look good—suave and stylish, with thick floor-to-ceiling windows and a row of tables running the length of the restaurant and paralleling the bar and open kitchen—it also attracts a nightly gaggle of locals. They come for phenomenal focaccia sandwiches (such as moist and memorable salmon), huge leafy salads, and inventive thin-crust pizzas at lunch. Superb dinner dishes include braised duck leg on a bed of creamy polenta; sea bass served with risotto, spinach, and caramelized onions; and hearty pot roast with lumpy mashed potatoes and fresh veggies. Granted, it's on the way to nowhere, but if you want an authentic small-restaurant charming San Francisco experience, this is as good as it gets.

2814 19th St. (at Bryant St.). © 415/821-4608. Reservations recommended for dinner. Main courses $2–$8 breakfast (full on weekends, continental on weekdays); $7–$15 lunch; $11–$24 dinner. AE, MC, V. Tues–Fri 11:30am–2:30pm; Sat–Sun 9am–2:30pm; Tues–Thurs 6–10pm; Fri–Sat 6–11pm; Sun 5:30–10pm. Bus: 27.

INEXPENSIVE
Delfina ✶✶ *Finds* SEASONAL ITALIAN   Delfina eschews bells, whistles, big-time design, and fancy preparations for something that used to be utterly San

Francisco: straightforward simplicity and a small-business feel. Unpretentious atmosphere, unreasonably reasonable prices, and chef and co-owner Craig Stoll's ultrafresh seasonal Italian cuisine mean you're in for a price-painless and delicious experience from the minute you're seated by Craig's wife Ann Spencer to the time you receive your surprisingly low (by local standards) bill. The menu may feature Niman Ranch flat-iron steak with french fries; roasted chicken with Yukon gold mashed potatoes and shiitake mushrooms; and Alaskan halibut roasted on a fig leaf with yellow wax beans and tarragon butter. The only downside: It's impossible to find parking—literally—and there's no valet.

3621 18th St. (between Dolores and Guererro Sts.). © 415/552-4055. Reservations required. Main courses $9–$18.25. MC, V. Mon–Thurs 5:30–10pm; Fri–Sat 5:30–11pm. Bus: 26, 33; Metro: J.

Taquerias La Cumbre ★★ MEXICAN While most restaurants gussy up their gastronomic goods with million-dollar decor and glamorous gimmicks, La Cumbre's celebrity is the burrito. Craftily constructed with fresh pork, steak, chicken, or vegetables, plus cheese, beans, rice, salsa, and maybe a dash of guacamole or sour cream, there is hardly a better ultracheap meal. That it's served in a cafeteria-like brick-lined room with overly shellacked tables and chairs is all the better: There's no mistaking the attraction here.

515 Valencia St. (between 16th and 17th Sts.). © 415/863-8205. Reservations not accepted. Tacos and burritos $2.50–$5.50; dinner plates $5–$7. DISC, MC, V. Mon–Sat 11am–10pm; Sun noon–9pm. BART: Mission. Bus: 14, 22, 33, 49, or 53.

5 The Top Attractions

MAJOR SAN FRANCISCO SIGHTS

Alcatraz Island ★★★ Visible from Fisherman's Wharf, Alcatraz Island (a.k.a. "The Rock") has seen a checkered history. It was discovered in 1775 by Juan Manuel Ayala, who named it after the many pelicans that nested on the island. From the 1850s to 1933, when the army vacated the island, it served as a military post protecting the bay shoreline. In 1934, the buildings of the military outpost were converted into a maximum-security prison. Given the sheer cliffs, treacherous tides and currents, and frigid temperatures of the waters, it was believed to be a totally escape-proof prison. Among the famous gangsters who were penned in cell blocks A through D were Al Capone; Robert Stroud, the so-called Birdman of Alcatraz (because he was an expert in ornithological diseases); Machine Gun Kelly; and Alvin Karpis. It cost a fortune to keep them imprisoned here because all supplies, including water, had to be shipped in. In 1963, after an apparent escape in which no bodies were recovered, the government closed the prison, and in 1972 it became part of the Golden Gate National Recreation Area. The wildlife that was driven away during the military and prison years has begun to return—the black-crested night heron and other seabirds are nesting here again—and a new trail has been built that passes through the island's nature areas. Tours, including an audio tour of the prison block and a slide show, are given by the park's rangers, who entertain their guests with interesting anecdotes.

It's a popular excursion and space is limited, so purchase tickets as far in advance as possible. The tour is operated by **Blue & Gold Fleet** (© **415/705-5555;** www.blueandgoldfleet.com) and can be charged to American Express, Master-Card, or Visa ($2.25 per ticket service charge on phone orders). You can also buy tickets in advance from the Blue & Gold ticket office on Pier 41.

Major San Francisco Sights

San Francisco Bay

Pier 41
(Ferries to Alcatraz)

FISHERMAN'S WHARF

Jefferson St.

Ghirardelli
Square

Beach St.

NORTH BEACH

Marina Blvd.

**MARINA
DISTRICT**

Bay St.

RUSSIAN HILL

Columbus Ave.

Chestnut St.

Lombard St.

"Crookedest
Street"

**TELEGRAPH
HILL**

COW HOLLOW

Union St.

PACIFIC HEIGHTS

Broadway

Washington St.

CHINATOWN

**FINANCIAL
DISTRICT**

The Embarcadero

Battery St.

Sacramento St.
California St.

NOB HILL

Sutter St.
Post St.
Geary St.

Union
Square

1st St.

Lincoln Blvd.

Presidio Ave.

Lyon St.

Divisadero St.

Fillmore St.

Gough St.

Franklin St.

Van Ness Ave.

Polk St.

Hyde St.

Taylor St.

Powell St.

Grant Ave.

Kearny St.

Geary Blvd.

**WESTERN
ADDITION**

JAPANTOWN

Mission St.

Howard St.

Folsom St.

Harrison St.

Moscone
Convention
Center

Masonic St.

Turk St.

Golden Gate Ave.

**CIVIC
CENTER**

SOMA

Fulton St.

Alamo
Square

Fell St.

Market St.

8th St.

9th St.

10th St.

Bryant St.

4th St.

5th St.

6th St.

7th St.

3rd St.

Oak St.

Haight St.

**HAIGHT-
ASHBURY**

14th St.

17th St.

Stanyan St.

Cole St.

Ashbury St.

Castro St.

Church St.

Dolores St.

Mission St.

South Van Ness Ave.

17th St.

**MISSION
DISTRICT**

Potrero Ave.

**POTRERO
HILL**

THE CASTRO

Clarendon Ave.

Twin
Peaks

Portola Dr.

24th St.

Clipper St.

Deharo St.

Connecticut St.

105

Wear comfortable shoes and take a heavy sweater or windbreaker—even when the sun's out, it's cold. The National Park Service also notes that there are a lot of steps to climb on the tour.

Pier 41, near Fisherman's Wharf. © **415/773-1188** (info only). Admission (includes ferry trip and audio tour) $13.25 adults with headset, $9.25 without; $11.50 seniors 62 and older with headset, $7.50 without; $8 children 5–11 with headset, $6 without. Winter daily 9:30am–2:15pm; summer daily 9:15am–4:15pm. Advance purchase advised; evening tours are available; call for information. Ferries depart at 15 and 45 min. after the hour. Arrive at least 20 min. before sailing time.

Cable Cars ✦✦✦ Designated official historic landmarks by the National Park Service in 1964, the city's beloved cable cars clank across the hills like mobile museum pieces. Each weighs about 6 tons and is hauled along by a steel cable, enclosed under the street in a center rail. They move at a constant 9½ miles per hour—never more, never less. This may strike you as slow, but it doesn't feel that way when you're cresting an almost perpendicular hill and looking down at what seems like a bobsled dive straight into the ocean. But in spite of the thrills, they're perfectly safe.

© **415/673-6864.** www.sfcablecar.com. The Powell-Hyde and Powell-Mason lines begin at Powell and Market Sts.; the California St. line begins at the foot of Market St. Fare $3.

Coit Tower ✦✦ In a city known for its panoramic views and vantage points, Coit Tower is "The Peak." If it's a clear day, it's wonderful to get here by walking up the Filbert Steps (thereby avoiding a traffic nightmare), and then taking in the panoramic views of the city and bay at the base of the tower. (In fact, we'd recommend not paying the admission and going to the top; the view is just as good from the parking area and you can see the murals for free.) Completed in 1933, the tower is the legacy of Lillie Hitchcock Coit, a wealthy eccentric who left San Francisco a $125,000 bequest. Inside the base of the tower are the impressive WPA murals titled *Life in California, 1934,* which were completed during the New Deal by more than 25 artists, many of whom had studied under master muralist Diego Rivera.

Atop Telegraph Hill. © **415/362-0808.** Admission (to the top of the tower) $3.75 adults, $2.50 seniors, $1.50 children 6–12. Daily 10am–6pm. Bus: 39.

The Exploratorium ✦ *Kids* This fun, hands-on science fair contains more than 650 permanent exhibits that explore everything from color theory to Einstein's theory of relativity. Optics is demonstrated in booths where you can see a bust of a statue in three dimensions—but when you try to touch it, you discover it isn't there! The same surreal experience occurs with an image of yourself: When you stretch your hand forward, a hand comes out to touch you, and the hands pass in midair. Every exhibit is designed to be used. You can whisper into a concave reflector and have a friend hear you 60 feet away, or you can design your own animated abstract art—using sound.

3601 Lyon St., in the Palace of Fine Arts (at Marina Blvd.). © **415/563-7337** or 415/561-0360 (recorded information). www.exploratorium.edu. Admission $9 adults, $7 seniors and college students with ID, $5 children 6–17, $2.50 children 3–5, children under 3 free. Free to all first Wed of each month. AE, MC, V. Summer (Memorial Day–Labor Day) and holidays, Mon–Tues and Thurs–Sun 10am–6pm; Wed 10am–9pm. Rest of the year Tues and Thurs–Sun 10am–5pm; Wed 10am–9pm. Closed Thanksgiving and Dec 25. Free parking. Bus: 30 from Stockton St. to the Marina stop.

Golden Gate Bridge ✦✦✦ With its gracefully swung single span, spidery bracing cables, and sky-high twin towers, the bridge looks more like a work of abstract art than one of the greatest practical engineering feats of the 20th century. Construction began in May 1937 and was completed at the then-colossal cost of $35 million. Contrary to pessimistic predictions, the bridge neither collapsed in a gale or earthquake nor proved to be a white elephant. A symbol of hope when the country was afflicted with widespread unemployment, the Golden Gate single-handedly changed the Bay Area's economic life, encouraging the development of areas north of San Francisco.

The mile-long steel link (longer if you factor in the approach), which reaches a height of 746 feet above the water, is an awesome bridge to cross. You can park in the lot at the foot of the bridge on the city side, and then make the crossing by foot. Back in your car, continue to Marin's Vista Point, at the bridge's northern end. Look back and you'll be rewarded with one of the most famous cityscape views in the world. Millions of pedestrians walk across the bridge each year. You can walk out onto the span from either end. Note that it's usually windy and cold, and the bridge vibrates. Still, walking even a short way is one of the best ways to experience the immense scale of the structure.

Bridge-bound Golden Gate Transit buses (© 415/923-2000) depart daily every 30–60 min. during the day for Marin County, starting from the Transbay Terminal (Mission and First Sts.) and stopping at Market and Seventh Sts., at the Civic Center, and along Van Ness Ave. and Lombard St. $1.50–$6.

San Francisco Museum of Modern Art (MOMA) ⊛ MOMA's collection consists of more than 15,000 works, including close to 5,000 paintings and sculptures by artists such as Henri Matisse, Jackson Pollock, and Willem de Kooning. Other artists represented include Diego Rivera, Georgia O'Keeffe, Paul Klee, the Fauvists, and exceptional holdings of Richard Diebenkorn. MOMA was also one of the first to recognize photography as a major art form; its extensive collection includes more than 9,000 photographs by such notables as Ansel Adams, Alfred Stieglitz, Edward Weston, and Henri Cartier-Bresson. Phone for current details of upcoming special events and whatever you do, check out the fabulous MuseumStore.

151 Third St. (2 blocks south of Market St., across from Yerba Buena Gardens). © 415/357-4000. Admission $10 adults, $7 seniors, $6 students over 12 with ID, free for children under 12. Half price for all Thurs 6–9pm; free to all first Tues of each month. Thurs 10am–9pm; Fri–Tues 10am–6pm. Closed major holidays. Muni Metro: J, K, L, or M to Montgomery Station. Bus: 15, 30, or 45.

Yerba Buena Center for the Arts & Yerba Buena Gardens ⊛⊛ (Kids) An urban interactive wonderland, Yerba Buena could keep you busy all day with its 5-acre garden and cafes, and consists of the **Center for the Arts** (www.yerbabuenaarts.org), which presents music, theater, dance, and visual arts; **Galleries and Arts Forum,** which features three galleries and a space designed specially for dance; **Zeum** (© 415/777-2800; www.zeum.org), a part of the children's addition that includes a cafe, interactive cultural center, ice-skating rink, fabulous 1906 historic carousel, and interactive play and learning garden; Sony's futuristic retail and entertainment mecca **Metreon Entertainment Center** (© 415/537-3400), a 350,000-square-foot complex housing movie theaters, an **IMAX** theater, small restaurants, interactive attractions (including a restaurant and attraction that features Maurice Sendak's *Where the Wild Things Are*), and shops; a virtual bowling alley; and a child-care center.

701 Mission St. © 415/978-2700 or 415/978-ARTS (box office). www.yerbabuenaarts.org. Admission $6 adults, $3 seniors and students. Free to all first Thurs of each month 5–8pm. Tues–Wed and Sat–Sun 11am–6pm; Thurs–Fri 11am–8pm. Muni Metro: Powell or Montgomery. Bus: 30, 45, or 9X.

GOLDEN GATE PARK ⊛⊛⊛

Everybody loves Golden Gate Park: people, dogs, birds, frogs, turtles, bison, trees, bushes, and flowers. Literally everything feels unified here in San

Francisco's enormous arboreal front yard, conveniently located between Fulton Street and Lincoln Way with the main entrance at Fell and Stanyan Streets.

Totaling 1,017 acres, Golden Gate Park is a truly magical place. Spend one sunny day stretched out on the grass along JFK Drive, have a good read in Shakespeare Garden, or stroll around Stow Lake and you, too, will understand the allure. It's an interactive botanical symphony—and everyone is invited to play in the orchestra.

The park is made up of hundreds of gardens and attractions linked by wooded paths and paved roads. While many sites worth seeing are clearly visible, the park has infinite hidden treasures, so make your first stop the **McLaren Lodge and Park Headquarters** (© 415/831-2700) if you want detailed information on the park.

Of the dozens of special gardens in the park, most recognized are the Rhododendron Dell, the Rose Garden, the Strybing Arboretum (see below), and, at the western edge of the park, a springtime array of thousands of tulips and daffodils around the Dutch windmill. An incredible, lower-key attraction is AIDS Memorial Grove, a peaceful place for reflection near the northeastern side of the park.

In addition to the highlights discussed below, the park contains several recreational facilities: tennis courts; baseball, soccer, and polo fields; a golf course; riding stables; and fly-casting pools.

If you plan to visit all the park's attractions, consider buying the Culture Pass, which enables you to visit lots of San Francisco museums plus all of the park's museums. The cost is $33.75 for adults, $26.75 for seniors, and $24.75 for youths. For further information, call © 415/391-2000. Enter the park at Kezar Drive, an extension of Fell Street. Bus: 16AX, BX, 5, 6, 7, 66, or 71.

MUSEUMS INSIDE THE PARK

California Academy of Sciences *Kids*   Clustered around the Music Concourse in Golden Gate Park are three outstanding world-class museums and exhibitions that are guaranteed to entertain every member of the family.

The **Steinhart Aquarium** is the most diverse aquarium in the world, housing some 14,000 specimens, including amphibians, reptiles, marine mammals, penguins, and much more. Youngsters will love the California tide pool and a hands-on area where they can touch starfish and sea urchins. The living coral reef is the largest display of its kind in the country. In the Fish Roundabout, visitors are surrounded by fast-swimming schools of fish kept in a 100,000-gallon tank.

The **Morrison Planetarium** projects sky shows on its 65-foot domed ceiling as well as laser light shows. Approximately four major exhibits, with titles such as *Star Death: The Birth of Black Holes* and *The Universe Unveiled,* are presented each year. Related cosmos exhibits are located in the adjacent Earth and Space Hall. Sky shows are featured at 2pm Monday through Friday and hourly on Saturday, Sunday, and holidays (call © 415/750-7141 for more information).

The **Natural History Museum** includes several halls displaying classic dioramas of fauna in their habitats. The Wattis Hall of Human Cultures traces the evolution of different human cultures and how they adapted to their natural environment; the "Wild California" exhibition in Meyer Hall includes a 14,000-gallon aquarium and seabird rookery, life-size battling elephant seals, and two larger-than-life views of microscopic life forms; in McBean-Peterson Hall, visitors can walk through an exhibit tracing the course of 3½ billion years of evolution, from the earliest life forms to the present day; and in the Hohfeld

Golden Gate Park

Stanyan St.

McLaren Lodge (Park HQ)

Arguello Blvd.

4th Ave.

6th Ave.

8th Ave.

10th Ave.

12th Ave.

Park Presidio Blvd.

15th Ave.

J.F. Kennedy Dr.

Conservatory Dr.

Lily Pond

Middle Dr. E.

Tennis Courts

Children's Playground

Bowling Green Dr.

Lawn Bowling

Kezar Stadium and Pavilion

M.L. King Dr.

AIDS Memorial Grove

9th Ave.

Way

Funston Ave.

Lincoln

1/4 mi

0.25 km

Stow Lake Dr.

Strawberry Hill

Stow Lake

Park Presidio By-Pass Dr.

Fulton St.

Cross-Over Dr.

Transverse Dr.

19th Ave.

St.

St.

Overlook Dr.

Elk Glen Lake

Mallard Lake

25th St.

Balboa

Cabrillo

St.

St.

Marx Meadow

Lloyd Lake

Speedway Meadow

Middle Dr.

Lindley Meadow

Metson Lake

M.L. King Dr.

26th Ave.

Irving

Judah

Golden Gate Park Stadium
Polo Field

Medson Rd.

Way

33rd Ave.

Speckels Lake Dr.

Spreckels Lake

J.F. Kennedy Dr.

Buffalo Paddock

Middle Lake

Fly Casting Pool

South Lake

Sunset Blvd.

Lincoln

Way

39th Ave.

Fulton St.

Chain of Lakes Dr.

41st Ave

43rd Ave.

North Lake

Golf Course

45th Ave.

47th Ave.

La Playa Ave.

Esplanade

Great Highway

Ocean Beach

PACIFIC OCEAN

Asian Art Museum **3**
Beach Chalet **14**
Boat House **9**
Buffalo Paddock **11**
California Academy of Sciences,
Steinhart Aquarium, and
Morrison Planetarium **5**
Conservatory of Flowers **1**

Dutch Windmill **13**
Golden Gate Golf Course **12**
Japanese Tea Garden **7**
McLaren Memorial Rhododendron Dell **2**
Music Concourse **4**
Riding Stables **10**
Stow Lake **8**
Strybing Arboreturum & Botanical Gardens **6**

Union Square

SAN FRANCISCO

Golden Gate Park

Candlestick Park

Earth and Space Hall, visitors can experience a simulation of two of San Francisco's biggest earthquakes, determine what their weight would be on other planets, see a real moon rock, and learn about the rotation of the planet at a replica of Foucault's Pendulum (the original one is in Paris).

On the Music Concourse of Golden Gate Park. ℂ 415/750-7145 for recorded information. Admission (aquarium, Natural History Museum, and Planetarium) $8.50 adults, $5.50 seniors 65+ and students 12–17, $2 children 4–11, free for children under 4. Free to all first Wed of each month. Planetarium shows $2.50 adults, $1.25 seniors 65+ and children under 18. Labor Day–Memorial Day daily 10am–5pm; Memorial Day–Labor Day daily 9am–6pm; first Wed of each month 10am–9pm. Muni Metro: N to Golden Gate Park. Bus: 5, 44, or 71.

OTHER PARK HIGHLIGHTS

BEACH CHALET   First listed on the National Register of Historic places in 1981, the Spanish-Colonial Beach Chalet, 1000 Great Hwy., at the west end of Golden Gate Park near Fulton Street (ℂ **415/386-8439**), was designed by the architect Willis Polk in 1925. Built with a 200-seat restaurant upstairs and a public lounge and changing rooms on the first floor, it was a popular stopover for generations of beachgoers. In the late 1930s, the federal government's Works Progress Administration (WPA) commissioned Lucien Labaudt (who also painted Coit Tower's frescoes) to create incredible frescoes, mosaics, and wood carvings of San Francisco life. After decades of use, the chalet grew old and worn, forcing its closure in 1981; but in December 1996, the historic Beach Chalet reopened its doors, and through the original mosaics and new literature and displays, it continues to celebrate the city's heritage. The upstairs restaurant is far too modern to wax historical, but it's a great place to stop for a house-made brew and a glimpse of the expansive Pacific.

CONSERVATORY OF FLOWERS (1878)   This striking assemblage of glass and iron, modeled on the famous glass house at Kew Gardens in London, usually exhibits a rotating display of plants and shrubs. Unfortunately, it's closed to visitors until further notice, but the exterior architecture and surrounding gardens alone are worth a look.

JAPANESE TEA GARDEN (1894)   Developed for the 1894 Midwinter Exposition, this garden would be a quiet place with cherry trees, shrubs, and bonsai crisscrossed by winding paths and high-arched bridges crossing over pools of water—were it not for the hordes of tourists and screaming children who can all but destroy any semblance of peace. Come early to enjoy the focal points and places for contemplation, including the massive bronze Buddha that was cast in Japan in 1790 and donated by the Gump family, the Shinto wooden pagoda, and the Wishing Bridge, which reflected in the water looks as though it completes a circle. The garden is open daily November through February 8:30am to 5pm (teahouse 10am to 4:30pm), March through October 8:30am to 6pm (teahouse 10am to 5:30pm). For information on admissions, call ℂ **415/752-4227**. For the teahouse, call ℂ **415/752-1171.**

STRYBING ARBORETUM & BOTANICAL GARDENS   Some 6,000 plant species grow here, among them rare species, very ancient plants in a special "primitive garden," and a grove of California redwoods. Open Monday to Friday 8am to 4:30pm, and Saturday and Sunday 10am to 5pm. For more information, call ℂ **415/753-7090.**

STOW LAKE & STRAWBERRY HILL ⚲ *Kids*   Rent a paddleboat, rowboat, or motorboat here and cruise around the circular lake as painters create still lifes and joggers pass along the grassy shoreline. Ducks waddle around waiting to be fed, and turtles bathe on rocks and logs. Strawberry Hill, the 430-foot-high artificial island that lies at the center of Stow Lake, is a perfect picnic spot and boasts a bird's-eye view of San Francisco and the bay. It also has a waterfall and peace pagoda. To reach the boathouse, call ☎ **415/752-0347.** Boat rentals are available daily from 9am to 4pm.

6 Exploring the City
SPECIAL POINTS OF INTEREST

Mission Dolores ★ This is the oldest structure in the city, built on order of Franciscan Father Junípero Serra by Father Francisco Palou. It was constructed of 36,000 sunbaked bricks and dedicated in June 1776 at the northern terminus of El Camino Real, the Spanish road from Mexico to California. It's a moving place to visit, with its cool, serene buildings with thick adobe walls and especially the cemetery and gardens where the early settlers are buried.

16th St. (at Dolores St.). ☎ 415/621-8203. Donations appreciated. May–Oct daily 9am–4:30pm; Nov–Apr daily 9am–4pm; Good Friday 9am–noon. Closed Thanksgiving, Dec 25. Muni Metro: J. Bus: 14, 22, 26, or 53 to the corner of Church and 16th Sts.

Lombard Street Known (erroneously) as the "crookedest street in the world," the whimsically winding block of Lombard Street puts smiles on the faces of thousands of visitors each year. The elevation is so steep that the road has to snake back and forth to make a descent possible.

Between Hyde and Leavenworth Sts.

ARCHITECTURAL HIGHLIGHTS

The **Alamo Square Historic District** contains many of the city's 14,000 Victorian **"Painted Ladies,"** homes that have been restored and ornately painted by residents. The small area—bordered by Divisadero Street on the west, Golden Gate Avenue on the north, Webster Street on the east, and Fell Street on the south, about 10 blocks west of the Civic Center—has one of the city's largest concentrations of these. One of the most famous views of San Francisco, which you'll see on postcards and posters all around the city, depicts sharp-edged Financial District skyscrapers behind a row of Victorians. This view can be seen from Alamo Square at Fulton and Steiner Streets.

Built in 1881 to a design by Brown and Bakewell, **City Hall** and the **Civic Center** are part of a "City Beautiful" complex done in the beaux arts style. The dome rises to a height of 308 feet on the exterior and is ornamented with occuli and topped by a lantern. The interior rotunda soars 112 feet and is finished in oak, marble, and limestone with a monumental marble staircase leading to the second floor; City Hall is worth seeking as it just underwent a total renovation and retrofitting.

The **Flood Mansion,** 1000 California St., at Mason Street, was built between 1885 and 1886 for James Clair Flood, who, thanks to the Comstock Lode, rose from being a bartender to being one of the city's wealthiest men. The house cost $1.5 million (the fence alone carried a price tag of $30,000!). It was designed by Augustus Laver and modified by Willis Polk after the earthquake to accommodate the Pacific Union Club.

The **Octagon House,** 2645 Gough St., at Union Street (☎ **415/441-7512**), is an eight-sided, cupola-topped house dating from 1861. Its features are extraordinary, especially the circular staircase and ceiling medallion. Inside, you'll find furniture, silverware, and American pewter from the colonial and Federal periods. There are also some historic documents, including signatures of

54 of the 56 signers of the Declaration of Independence. Even if you're not able to visit during open hours, this strange structure is worth a look. It's open on the second Sunday and second and fourth Thursdays of each month (except January) from noon to 3pm; closed January and holidays.

The **Palace of Fine Arts,** on Baker between Jefferson and Bay Streets, is the only building to survive from the Pan-Pacific Exhibition of 1915. Constructed by Bernard Maybeck, it was rebuilt in concrete using molds taken from the original in the 1950s. It now houses the Exploratorium (see "The Top Attractions," earlier in this chapter).

The **TransAmerica Pyramid,** 600 Montgomery St., between Clay and Washington Streets, is the tallest structure in San Francisco's skyline—48 stories tall and capped by a 212-foot spire.

Although the **San Francisco–Oakland Bay Bridge** is visually less appealing than the Golden Gate Bridge (see "The Top Attractions," earlier in this chapter), it is in many ways more spectacular. Opened in 1936, before the Golden Gate, it's 8¼ miles long, one of the world's longest steel bridges. It's not a single bridge at all, but actually a dovetailed series of spans joined in midbay—at Yerba Buena Island—by one of the world's largest (in diameter) tunnels. To the west of Yerba Buena, the bridge is really two separate suspension bridges, joined at a central anchorage. East of the island is a 1,400-foot cantilever span, followed by a succession of truss bridges.

A CHURCH

Glide Memorial United Methodist Church ★ *Moments*   There would be nothing special about this plain, Tenderloin-area church if it weren't for its exhilarating pastor, Cecil Williams. Williams's enthusiastic and uplifting preaching and singing with the homeless and poor people of the neighborhood crosses all socioeconomic boundaries and has attracted nationwide fame. Go for an uplifting experience.

330 Ellis St. (west of Union Square.). ⓒ **415/771-6300.** Services Sun at 9 and 11am. Muni Metro: Powell. Bus: 37.

MUSEUMS

Also see "The Top Attractions," earlier in this chapter.

California Palace of the Legion of Honor ★★   Designed as a memorial to California's World War I casualties, the neoclassical structure is an exact replica of the Legion of Honor Palace in Paris, right down to the inscription *honneur et patrie* above the portal. Reopened after a 2-year, $29-million renovation and seismic upgrading project that was stalled by the discovery of almost 300 turn-of-the-century coffins, the museum's collection contains paintings, sculpture, and decorative arts from Europe, as well as international tapestries, prints, and drawings. The chronological display of more than 800 years of European art includes a fine collection of Rodin sculpture.

In Lincoln Park (34th Ave. and Clement St.). ⓒ **415/750-3600** or 415/863-3330 (recorded information). Admission $8 adults, $6 seniors 65 and over, $5 youths 12–17, free for children under 12. Fees may be higher for special exhibitions. Free to all second Wed of each month (9:30am–8:45pm). Tues–Sun 9:30am–5pm. Bus: 18 or 38.

San Francisco Maritime National Historical Park *Kids*   Shaped like an Art Deco ship and located near Fisherman's Wharf, the National Maritime Museum is filled with sailing, whaling, and fishing lore. Exhibits include intricate model craft, scrimshaw, and a collection of shipwreck photographs and historic marine scenes, including an 1851 snapshot of hundreds of abandoned ships, deserted en masse by crews dashing off to participate in the gold rush. The museum's walls are lined with finely carved, painted wooden figureheads from old wind-jammers.

Two blocks east, at Aquatic Park's Hyde Street Pier, are several historic ships that are open to the public. The *Balclutha*, one of the last surviving square-riggers, was built in Glasgow, Scotland, in 1886 and was used to carry grain from California around Cape Horn at a near-record speed of 300 miles a day; it rounded the treacherous Cape 17 times in its career. Visitors are invited to spin the wheel, squint at the compass, and imagine they're weathering a mighty storm. Kids can climb into the bunking quarters, visit the "slop chest" (galley to you, matey), and read the sea chanties (clean ones only) that decorate the walls.

The 1890 *Eureka* still carries a cargo of nostalgia for San Franciscans. It was the last of 50 paddle-wheeled ferries that regularly plied the bay; it made its final trip in 1957. Restored to its original splendor, the side-wheeler is loaded with deck cargo, including antique cars and trucks.

At the pier's small-boat shop, visitors can follow the restoration progress of historic boats from the museum's collection. It's behind the maritime bookstore on your right as you approach the ships.

At the foot of Polk St. (near Fisherman's Wharf). ☏ 415/556-3002. Museum free; ships $5 adults, $2 seniors over 62 and children 12–17, free for children under 12. Museum daily 10am–5pm. Ships on Hyde St. Pier May 15–Sept 15 daily 9:30am–5:30pm; Sept 16–May 14 daily 9:30am–5pm. Closed Jan 1, Thanksgiving, Dec 25. Cable car: Powell-Hyde St. line to the last stop. Bus: 19, 30, 32, 42, or 47.

NEIGHBORHOODS WORTH SEEKING OUT

THE CASTRO   Castro Street around Market and 18th Streets is the center of the city's gay community, which is catered to by the many stores, restaurants, bars, and other institutions here. Among the landmarks are Harvey Milk Plaza, the Quilt Project, and the Castro Theatre, a 1920s movie palace. (See "Organized Tours," later in this chapter for details on a walking tour of the area.)

CHINATOWN   California Street to Broadway and Kearny to Stockton Street are the boundaries of today's Chinatown. San Francisco is home to the second-largest community of Chinese in the United States, but the majority of them do not live and work in these 24 blocks, although they do return to shop and dine here on weekends.

The gateway at Grant and Bush marks the entry to Chinatown. Walk up Grant, which has become the tourist face of Chinatown, to California Street and Old St. Mary's.

The heart of Chinatown is at **Portsmouth Square,** where you'll find Chinese locals playing board games (often gambling) or just sitting quietly. This square was the center of early San Francisco and the spot where the American flag was first raised on July 9, 1846. From the square, Washington Street leads up to Waverly Place, where you can see three temples.

Explore the area at your leisure, or see "Organized Tours," later in this chapter, if you'd like to join a walking tour.

FISHERMAN'S WHARF & THE NORTHERN WATERFRONT   Few cities in America are as adept at wholesaling their historical sites as San Francisco, which has converted Fisherman's Wharf into one of the most popular tourist destinations in the world. Unless you come really early in the morning, you won't find any traces of the traditional waterfront life that once existed here; the only serious fishing going on is for tourist dollars. A small fleet of fewer than

Finds   **Amazing Graze at the Farmers Market**

There's no better way to enjoy a bright San Francisco morning than strolling and snacking through this gourmet street market ★★. Every Saturday from 8:30am to 1:30pm, northern California fruit, vegetable, bread, and dairy vendors join local restaurateurs in selling fresh, delicious edibles along the Embarcadero at Green Street (about a 15-minute walk from Fisherman's Wharf). You can also pick up locally made vinegars and oils, which make wonderful gifts. There's another market on Tuesday at Justin Herman Plaza (Market Street and Embarcadero) from 10:30am to 2:30pm. For more information, call ℂ **415/353-5650;** to get there, take bus 2, 7, 8, 9, 14, 21, 31, 32, 66, or 71.

---

30 boats still operates from here, but basically Fisherman's Wharf has been converted into one long shopping mall stretching from Ghirardelli Square at the west end to Pier 39 at the east. Some people love it, others can't get far enough away from it, but most agree that Fisherman's Wharf, for better or for worse, has to be seen at least once in a lifetime.

Ghirardelli Square, at 900 North Point, between Polk and Larkin Streets (ℂ **415/ 775-5500**), is best known as the former chocolate-and-spice factory of Domingo Ghirardelli. The factory has been converted into a 10-level mall containing more than 50 stores and 11 dining establishments. Scheduled street performers play regularly in the West Plaza. The stores generally stay open until 8 or 9pm in the summer and 6 or 7pm in the winter.

The Cannery, at 2801 Leavenworth St. (ℂ **415/771-3112;** www.thecannery.com), was built in 1894 as a fruit-canning plant and converted in the 1960s into a mall containing more than 50 shops and several restaurants and galleries. Vendors' stalls and sidewalk cafes are set up in the courtyard amid a grove of century-old olive trees, and on summer weekends, street performers are out in force entertaining tourists.

Pier 39, on the waterfront at Embarcadero and Beach Street (ℂ **415/ 981-8030**), is a 4½-acre waterfront complex, a few blocks east of Fisherman's Wharf. Ostensibly a re-creation of a turn-of-the-century street scene, it features walkways of aged and weathered wood salvaged from demolished piers. But don't expect a slice of old-time maritime life. This is the busiest mall of the group, with more than 100 touristy stores. In addition, there are 20 or so restaurants and snack outlets, some with good views of the bay.

In recent years some 600 California **sea lions** have taken up residence on the adjacent floating docks. They sun themselves and honk and bellow playfully. The latest major addition to Fisherman's Wharf is **Aquarium of the Bay,** a $38-million, 707,000-gallon marine attraction filled with sharks, stingrays, and more, all witnessed via a moving footpath that transports visitors through clear acrylic tunnels.

The shops are open daily from 10:30am to 8:30pm. Cable car: Powell-Mason line to Bay Street.

THE MISSION DISTRICT   Once inhabited almost entirely by Irish immigrants, the Mission is now the center of the city's Latino community and the city's dot-commercialization, an oblong area stretching roughly from 14th to 30th Streets between Potrero Avenue in the east and Dolores on the west. Some of the city's finest Victorians still stand in the outer areas, though many seem strangely out of place in the mostly lower-income neighborhoods. The heart of the community lies along 24th Street between Van Ness and Potrero, where dozens of excellent ethnic restaurants, bakeries, bars, and specialty stores attract a hip crowd from all over the city. Strolling through the Mission District at night should be done cautiously on the outskirts, but it's quite safe during the day and highly recommended.

For even better insight into the community, go to the **Precita Eyes Mural Arts Center,** 2981 24th, between Harrison Street and Alabama Street (© **415/ 285-2287**), and take one of the hour-long tours conducted on Saturday at 11am and 1:30pm and Sunday at 1:30pm, which cost $10 for adults, $8 for students with ID, $5 for seniors, and $2 for under-18s. You'll see 85 murals in an 8-block walk. Every year it also holds a Mural Awareness Month (usually in May) when tours are given daily. Most tours leave from its second and newer location at 2981 24th St; call to confirm. (at Harrison Street; © **415/285-2287**).

At 16th and Dolores is the **Mission San Francisco de Assisi** (better known as **Mission Dolores**), which is the city's oldest surviving building (see the separate listing, earlier in this chapter under "Exploring the City") and the district's namesake.

NOB HILL   When the cable car was invented in 1873, this hill became the most exclusive residential area in the city. The Big Four and the Comstock Bonanza kings built their mansions here, but the structures were all destroyed by the 1906 earthquake and fire. Only the Flood Mansion, which serves today as the Pacific Union Club, and the Fairmont (which was under construction when the earthquake struck) were spared. The area is now home to some of the city's most upscale hotels as well as Grace Cathedral, which stands on the Crocker Mansion site. Stroll around and enjoy the views, and perhaps pay a visit to Huntington Park.

NORTH BEACH   In the late 1800s, an enormous influx of Italian immigrants into North Beach firmly established this aromatic area as San Francisco's "Little Italy." Today, dozens of Italian restaurants and coffeehouses continue to flourish in what is still the center of the city's Italian community. Walk down Columbus Avenue any given morning and you're bound to be bombarded with the wonderful aromas of roasting coffee and savory pasta sauces. Though there are some interesting shops and bookstores in the area, it's the eclectic little cafes, delis, bakeries, and coffee shops that give North Beach its Italian-bohemian character.

For a proper perspective of North Beach, sign up for a guided Javawalk with coffee-nut Elaine Sosa (see "Organized Tours," later in this chapter).

PARKS, GARDENS & ZOOS
In addition to **Golden Gate Park** (see "The Top Attractions," earlier in this chapter) and **Golden Gate National Recreation Area** and the **Presidio** (see section 8, later in this chapter), San Francisco boasts more than 2,000 additional acres of parkland, most of which are perfect for picnicking.

Lincoln Park, at Clement Street and 34th Avenue, a personal favorite, occupies 270 acres on the northwestern side of the city and contains the California Palace of the Legion of Honor (see "Museums," earlier in this chapter) and a scenic 18-hole municipal golf course. But the most dramatic features of the park are the 200-foot cliffs that overlook the Golden Gate Bridge and San Francisco Bay. Take bus no. 38 from Union Square to 33rd and Geary Streets, and then transfer to bus no. 18 into the park.

San Francisco Zoo & Children's Zoo   Located between the Pacific Ocean and Lake Merced, in the southwest corner of the city, the San Francisco Zoo houses more than 1,000 inhabitants, which are contained in landscaped enclosures guarded by concealed moats. The Primate Discovery Center is particularly noteworthy for its many rare and endangered species. Expansive outdoor atriums, sprawling meadows, and a midnight world for exotic nocturnal primates house such species as the ruffed-tailed lemur, black-and-white colobus monkeys, patas monkeys, and emperor tamarins, pint-size primates distinguished by their long, majestic mustaches.

Other highlights include Koala Crossing, housing kangaroos, emus, and walleroos; Gorilla World, one of the world's largest exhibits of these gentle giants; and Penguin Island, home to a large breeding colony of Magellanic penguins. The Feline Conservation Center is a wooded sanctuary and breeding facility for the zoo's endangered snow leopards, Persian leopards, and other jungle cats. And the Lion House is home to rare Sumatran and Siberian tigers, a rare white Bengal tiger, and the African lions (you can watch them being fed at 2pm Tuesday through Sunday).

At the Children's Zoo, adjacent to the main park, the barnyard is alive with domestic animals such as sheep, goats, ponies, and a llama. Also of interest is the Insect Zoo, which showcases a multitude of insect species, including the hissing cockroach and walking sticks.

Sloat Blvd. and 45th Ave. ☎ 415/753-7080. www.sfzoo.org. Admission to main zoo and children's zoo $9 adults, $6 seniors and youths 12–17, $3 children 3–11, free for children under 3 accompanied by an adult. Free to all first Wed of each month, except $2 fee for children's zoo. Carousel $2. Main zoo daily 10am–5pm. Children's Zoo Mon–Fri 11am–4pm; Sat–Sun 10:30am–4:30pm. Muni Metro: L from downtown Market St. to the end of the line.

7 Organized Tours

ORIENTATION TOURS
THE 49-MILE SCENIC DRIVE

The self-guided, 49-mile drive is one easy way to orient yourself and to grasp the beauty of San Francisco and its extraordinary location. Beginning in the city, it follows a rough circle around the bay and passes virtually all the best-known sights, from Chinatown and the Golden Gate Bridge to Ocean Beach, Seal Rocks, Golden Gate Park, and Twin Peaks. Originally designed for the benefit of visitors to San Francisco's 1939 and 1940 Golden Gate International Exposition, the route is marked with blue-and-white seagull signs. Although it makes an excellent half-day tour, this mini-excursion can easily take longer if you decide, for example, to stop to walk across the Golden Gate Bridge or to have tea in Golden Gate Park's Japanese Tea Garden.

The San Francisco Visitor Information Center, at Powell and Market Streets, distributes free route maps. Since a few of the Scenic Drive marker signs are missing, the map will come in handy. Try to avoid the downtown area during the weekday rush hours from 7 to 9am and 4 to 6pm.

BOAT TOURS

One of the best ways to look at San Francisco is from a boat bobbing on the bay. The **Blue & Gold Fleet** tours the bay year-round in a sleek, 400-passenger sightseeing boat, complete with food and beverage facilities. The fully narrated, 1¼-hour cruise passes beneath the Golden Gate and Bay bridges, and comes within yards of Alcatraz Island. Frequent daily departures from Pier 41 begin at 10am in summer and 11am in winter. Tickets cost $18 for adults, $14 for kids

12 to 17 and seniors over 62, $10 for kids 5 to 11; children under 5 sail free. For recorded information, call © 415/773-1188; for tickets, which cost an additional $2.25 each when ordered via phone, call © 415/705-5555 or visit www.blueandgoldfleet.com.

The **Red & White Fleet** also offers daily bay cruises, which depart from Pier 43½ and travel under the Golden Gate Bridge and past the Marin Headlands, Sausalito, Tiburon, Angel Island, and Alcatraz. Prices are $18 for adults, $14 for seniors over 60 and kids 12 to 18, and $10 for children 5 to 11. Call © 415/ 447-0597 for information, or check out the website at www.redandwhite.com.

SPECIAL-INTEREST WALKING TOURS

AN INSIDER'S TOUR OF CHINATOWN   Founded by author, TV personality, cooking instructor, and restaurant critic Shirley Fong-Torres, **Wok Wiz Chinatown Walking Tours** (© 415/981-8989; www.wokwiz.com) takes you into nooks and crannies not usually seen by tourists. Each guide is intimately acquainted with all of Chinatown's back ways, alleys, and small businesses as well as the area's history, folklore, culture, and food. The 2½-hour tours are conducted daily from 10am to 1:30pm and include a dim sum (Chinese) lunch. Groups are generally held to a maximum of 12, and reservations are essential. Prices (including lunch) are $39 for adults, $35 for seniors 60 and older, and $37 for children under 12. Additional tours are offered.

NORTH BEACH CAFE SOIREE   Self-described "coffeehouse lizard" Elaine Sosa leads **Javawalk,** a 2-hour walking tour. Aside from visiting cafes, Javawalk also serves up a good share of historical and architectural trivia. Sosa keeps the tour interactive and fun, and it's obvious that she knows a wealth of tales and trivia about the history of coffee and its North Beach roots. Tours are given Tuesday through Saturday at 10am. The price is $20 for adults and $10 for kids 12 and under. For information and reservations, call © 415/673-9255.

THE VICTORIAN LEGACY   Jay Gifford, founder of **Victorian Homes Historical Walking Tour** (© 415/252-9485) and San Francisco resident for 2 decades, portrays his enthusiasm and love of San Francisco throughout this highly entertaining 2½-hour tour. Set at a very leisurely place, it incorporates a wealth of interesting knowledge about San Francisco's Victorian architecture, as well as the city's storied history—particularly the periods just before and after the great earthquake and fire of 1906. You'll stroll through the neighborhoods of Japantown, the Western Addition (where you can take a break to cruise the trendy shops on Fillmore Street), and onward to Pacific Heights and Cow Hollow. In the process you'll see more than 200 meticulously restored Victorians, including the one where *Mrs. Doubtfire* was filmed. Jay's guests often find they are the only ones on the quiet neighborhood streets, where tour buses are forbidden. The tour ends with a trolley ride back to Union Square, passing though North Beach and Chinatown. Tours, which start at Union Square at 11am, are offered daily year-round and cost $20 per person. Reservations are required. You can preview the tour at **www.victorianwalk.com.**

8 Golden Gate National Recreation Area & the Presidio

GOLDEN GATE NATIONAL RECREATION AREA
No urban shoreline is as stunning as San Francisco's. Golden Gate National Recreation Area, which wraps around the northern and western edges of the city and is run by the National Park Service, lets visitors fully enjoy it. Along this shoreline are several landmarks, and from its edge visitors have views of the bay

Golden Gate National Recreation Area & the Presidio

and the ocean. Muni provides transportation to most sites, including Aquatic Park, the Cliff House, and Ocean Beach. For more information, see "Outdoor Pursuits," below, or contact the **National Park Service** (© **415/556-0560**).

Here's a brief rundown of the major features of the recreation area, starting at the northern section and moving westward around the coastline:

Aquatic Park, adjacent to the Hyde Street Pier, is a small swimming beach, although it's not that appealing and the water's ridiculously cold.

Fort Mason Center occupies an area from Bay Street to the shoreline and consists of several buildings and piers, which were used during World War II. Today, they're occupied by a variety of museums, theaters, and organizations, as well as by **Greens** vegetarian restaurant (see "Dining," earlier in this chapter), which affords views of the Golden Gate Bridge. For information on Fort Mason Center events, call © **415/441-5706.**

Farther west along the bay at the northern end of Fillmore, **Marina Green** is a favorite spot for flying kites or watching the sailboats on the bay. Next stop along the bay is the St. Francis Yacht Club. From here begins the 3½-mile paved **Golden Gate Promenade,** a favorite biking and hiking path, which sweeps along Crissy Field, leading ultimately to Fort Point under the Golden Gate Bridge. This Promenade defines the outer limits of the Presidio (see below).

Fort Point (© **415/556-1693**), a National Historic Site sitting directly under the Golden Gate Bridge, was built in 1853 to protect the narrow entrance to the

Jugglers, dancers and an assortment of acrobats fill the street.

She shoots you a wide-eyed look as a seven-foot cartoon character approaches.

What brought you here was wanting the kids

to see something magical while they still believed in magic.

America Online Keyword: Travel

With 700 airlines, 50,000 hotels and over 5,000 cruise and vaca-

tion getaways, you can now go places you've always dreamed of.

Travelocity.com
A Sabre Company
Go Virtually Anywhere.

"WORLD'S LEADING TRAVEL WEB SITE, 5 YEARS IN A ROW." WORLD TRAVEL AWARDS

harbor. You might recognize it from Alfred Hitchcock's *Vertigo;* the master of suspense filmed some of the most important scenes here. During the Civil War, the brick Fort Point was manned by 140 men and 90 pieces of artillery to prevent a Confederate takeover of California. Rangers in Civil War regalia lead regular tours and sometimes fire the old cannons.

Lincoln Boulevard sweeps around the western edge of the bay to two of the most popular beaches in San Francisco. **Baker Beach,** a small and beautiful strand just outside the Golden Gate where the waves roll ashore, is a fine spot for sunbathing, walking, or fishing—it's packed on sunny days. Because of the cold water and the roaring currents that pour out of the bay twice a day, swimming is not advised here for any but the most confident. (You'll also see some nude sunbathers here.) Here you can pick up the **Coastal Trail,** which leads through the Presidio (see below). A short distance from Baker, **China Beach** is a small cove where swimming is permitted. Changing rooms, showers, a sundeck, and restrooms are available.

A little farther around the coast appears **Land's End,** looking out to Pyramid Rock. Both a lower and an upper trail provide hiking opportunities amid windswept cypress and pines on the cliffs above the Pacific.

Still farther along the coast lie **Point Lobos,** the **Sutro Baths,** and the **Cliff House.** The latter has been serving refreshments to visitors since 1863. Here you can view the **Seal Rocks,** home to a colony of sea lions and many marine birds.

The **visitor center** here (© 415/556-8642) is open daily from 10am to 5pm. The kids will enjoy the **Musée Mecanique** (© 415/386-1170), an authentic old-fashioned arcade with 150 coin-operated amusements. Only traces of the Sutro Baths remain today northeast of the Cliff House. This swimming facility was a major summer attraction that could accommodate 24,000 people, but it burned down in 1966. A little farther inland at the western end of California Street is **Lincoln Park,** which contains a golf course and the Palace of the Legion of Honor.

From the Cliff House, the Esplanade continues south along the 4-mile-long **Ocean Beach,** which is not suitable for swimming. At the southern end of Ocean Beach is another area of the park around **Fort Funston** where there's an easy loop trail across the cliffs (for information, call the ranger station at © 415/239-2366). Here, too, you can watch the hang gliders taking advantage of the high cliffs and strong winds.

Farther south along I-280, **Sweeney Ridge,** which can only be reached by car, affords sweeping views of the coastline from the many trails that crisscross these 1,000 acres of land. It was from here that the expedition led by Don Gaspar de Portolá first saw San Francisco Bay in 1769. It's located in Pacifica and can be reached via Sneath Lane off Calif. 35 (Skyline Blvd.) in San Bruno.

THE PRESIDIO

In October 1994, the Presidio was transferred from the U.S. Army to the National Park Service and became one of a handful of urban national parks that combines historical, architectural, and natural elements into one giant arboreal expanse—not to mention a previously private golf course and a home for George Lucas's production company.

The 1,480-acre area incorporates a variety of terrain—coastal scrub, dunes, and prairie grasslands that shelter many rare plants and more than 150 species of birds, some of which nest here. There are also more than 350 historic buildings, a national cemetery, and a variety of terrain and natural habitats. The National Park Service offers a number of walking and biking tours around the Presidio; reservations are required.

Walkers and joggers will enjoy the forests of the Presidio. It was once a bleak field of wind-blasted rock, sand, and grass, but in a strangely humanitarian gesture, 60,000 trees were planted in the 1880s to make the place more livable for the troops. Today, on the 2-mile **Ecology Loop Trail,** walkers can see more than 30 different species of those trees, including redwood, spruce, cypress, and acacias. Hikers can follow the 2½-mile **Coastal Trail** from Fort Point along this part of the coastline all the way to Land's End. It follows the bluff top from Baker Beach to the southern base of the Golden Gate Bridge.

Crissy Field is a former airfield that in recent years has become known as one of the see-and-be-seen proving grounds of California's windsurfing culture. Between March and October, hundreds come to try their hand. The beach here provides easy water access and plenty of room to rig up, but is not recommended for the inexperienced. This is also a popular place for joggers en route from the Marina District to Fort Point and back. At the west end of Crissy Field is a pier that can be used for fishing and crabbing.

The Presidio is currently undergoing major changes so that it may pay for its upkeep. For schedules, maps, and general information about ongoing developments at the Presidio, the best source is the **Golden Gate National Recreation Area Headquarters** at Fort Mason, Building 102, San Francisco, CA 94123

(© **415/556-0560**). For additional information, call the **Visitor Information Center** at © **415/561-4323.** Take the 28, 76, or 82X bus.

9 Outdoor Pursuits

The prime places to enjoy all kinds of recreational activities in San Francisco have already been described earlier in this chapter. See "The Top Attractions," earlier in this chapter for a complete description of Golden Gate Park, and section 8 for complete details on Golden Gate National Recreation Area and the Presidio.

BEACHES   There are only two beaches in San Francisco that are safe for swimming: **Aquatic Park,** which is a ridiculously small patch of sand adjacent to the Hyde Park Pier, and **China Beach,** a small cove on the western edge of the South Bay. But dip in at your own risk—there are no lifeguards on duty, and the water is painfully cold.

Baker Beach, a small, beautiful strand just outside the Golden Gate, isn't the best place for swimming due to strong currents, but it's great for sunning, walking, picnicking, or fishing. It's wonderful to sit here on a sunny day and take in the view of the bridge. You'll climb down a very long flight of stairs from the street to reach the beach.

Ocean Beach, at the end of Golden Gate Park, on the westernmost side of the city, is San Francisco's largest beach (4 miles long). Just offshore, at the northern end of the beach in front of the Cliff House, are the jagged Seal Rocks, which are inhabited by various shore birds and a large colony of barking sea lions. Bring binoculars for a close-up view. Ocean Beach is for strolling or sunning, but don't swim here—tides are tricky, and each year bathers and surfers drown in the rough waters.

BICYCLING   Two city-designated bike routes are maintained by the Recreation and Parks Department. One winds for 7½ miles through Golden Gate Park to Lake Merced; the other traverses the city, starting in the south, and follows a route over the Golden Gate Bridge. A bike map is available from the San Francisco Visitor Information Center and from bicycle shops all around town.

A massive new seawall, constructed to buffer Ocean Beach from storm-driven waves, doubles as a public walk and bikeway along 5 waterfront blocks of the Great Highway between Noriega and Santiago Streets. It's an easy ride from the Cliff House or Golden Gate Park.

There's also great biking in the Presidio. From here, you can venture across the Golden Gate Bridge and into the Marin hills.

Avenue Cyclery at 756 Stanyan Street, at Page Street (© **415/668-8016**) rents bikes for $5 per hour or $25 per day and is open daily April through September from 10am to 7pm and October through March from 10am to 6pm.

CITY STAIR-CLIMBING   You don't need a StairMaster in San Francisco. The **Filbert Street Steps,** 377 of them running between Sansome Street and Telegraph Hill, scale the eastern face of Telegraph Hill, from Sansome and Filbert past charming 19th-century cottages and lush gardens. Napier Lane, a narrow wooden plank walkway, leads to Montgomery Street. Turn right and follow the path to the end of the cul-de-sac, where another stairway continues to Telegraph's panoramic summit.

The **Lyon Street Steps,** between Green Street and Broadway, comprise another historic stairway street, containing four steep sets of stairs totaling 288 steps. Begin at Green Street and climb all the way up, past manicured hedges and flower gardens, to an iron gate that opens into the Presidio. A block east, on Baker Street, another set of 369 steps descends to Green Street.

GOLF **Golden Gate Park Course,** 47th Avenue and Fulton Street (℃ **415/ 751-8987**), is a nine-hole, par-27 course over 1,357 yards. All holes are par 3, tightly set, and well trapped with small greens. Greens fees are very reasonable: $10 per person Monday through Friday and $13 Saturday and Sunday. The course is open daily from 6am to dusk.

Lincoln Park Golf Course, 34th Avenue and Clement Street (℃ **415/ 221-9911**), San Francisco's prettiest municipal course, has terrific views and fairways lined with Monterey cypress trees. Its 18 holes encompass 5,081 yards, for a par 68. Greens fees are $23 per person Monday through Friday and $27 Saturday and Sunday. The course is open daily from 6:30am to dusk.

SKATING Although people skate in Golden Gate Park all week long, Sunday is best, when John F. Kennedy Drive, between Kezar Drive and Transverse Road, is closed to cars. A smooth "skate pad" is located on your right, just past the Conservatory. **Skates on Haight,** 1818 Haight St. (℃ **415/752-8376**), is the best place to rent either in-line or conventional skates and is located only a block from the park. Protective wrist guards and kneepads are included free. The cost is $6 per hour for in-line or "conventionals," $24 for all-day use. A major credit card and ID deposit are required.

10 Shopping

Store hours vary, but are generally Monday through Saturday from 10am to 6pm and Sunday from noon to 5pm. Most department stores stay open later, as do shops around Fisherman's Wharf.

Sales tax in San Francisco is 8½%. If you live out of state and buy an expensive item, consider having the store ship it home for you. You'll have to pay for its transport, but will escape paying the sales tax.

UNION SQUARE & ENVIRONS San Francisco's most congested and popular shopping mecca is centered around Union Square. Most of the big department stores and many high-end specialty shops are in this area. Be sure to venture to Grant Avenue, Post and Sutter Streets, and Maiden Lane.

If you're into art, pick up *The San Francisco Gallery Guide,* a comprehensive, bimonthly publication listing the city's current shows (most of which are downtown). It's available free by mail; send a self-addressed stamped envelope to San Francisco Bay Area Gallery Guide, 1369 Fulton St., San Francisco, CA 94117 (℃ **415/921-1600**). You can also pick one up at the San Francisco Visitor Information Center at 900 Market St. (at Powell Street).

One of our favorite galleries is the **Catharine Clark Gallery,** on the second floor at 49 Geary St., between Kearny and Grant Streets (℃ **415/399-1439**). It exhibits up-and-coming contemporary artists, mainly from California, and nurtures beginning collectors by offering an unusual interest-free purchasing plan.

Of the area's specialty stores, century-old **Gump's,** 135 Post St., between Kearny Street and Grant Avenue (℃ **415/982-1616**), is a must-visit. A virtual treasure trove of household items and gifts, it offers a collection of Asian antiquities, contemporary art glass, exquisite jade and pearl jewelry, and more.

Music aficionados will choose to get lost in **Virgin Megastore,** Market Street at Stockton (℃ **415/397-4525**), with thousands of CDs (including an impressive collection of imports), videos, laser discs, and a multimedia department. Its literary equivalent is nearby **Borders Books & Music,** 400 Post St., at Powell (© **415/399-1633**), which has thousands of titles and a cafe.

While the department stores have plenty of clothes, real fashion fiends will want to check out the boutiques. For men, **Cable Car Clothiers,** 246 Sutter St., between Grant Avenue and Kearny Street (© **415/397-4740**), is a popular stop for traditional attire, such as three-button suits with natural shoulders, Aquascutum coats, McGeorge sweaters, and Atkinson ties. The most fashionable-modern-rather-than-corporate man heads to **MAC,** 5 Claude Lane, off Sutter Street between Grant Avenue and Kearny Street (© **415/837-0615**), where imported tailored suits come in designs by London's Paul Smith, Belgium's SO, Italy's Alberto Biani, and New York's John Bartlett. (Their women's store is located at 1543 Grant Ave., between Filbert and Union Streets; © **415/837-1604.**)

Wilkes Bashford, 375 Sutter St., at Stockton Street (© **415/986-4380**), is one of the most expensive and well-known clothing stores in the city, offering fashions for both sexes. It stocks only the finest clothes (which can often be seen on Mayor Willie Brown), including men's Kiton and Brioni suits (at $2,500 and up, they're considered some of the most expensive suits in the world).

For what we consider the best in women's fashions, check out **Métier,** 355 Sutter St., between Grant and Stockton Streets (© **415/989-5395**). Its inventory of European ready-to-wear lines is expensive, but in the best taste; featured designers include Italian designer Anna Molinari, Alberto Biani, and Los Angeles designer Katayone Adeli, as well as a distinguished collection of antique-style, high-end jewelry from L.A.'s Kathie Waterman and ultrapopular custom-designed poetry jewelry by Jeanine Payer.

CHINATOWN When you pass under the gate to Chinatown on Grant Avenue, say good-bye to the world of fashion and hello to a swarm of cheap tourist shops selling everything from linen and jade to plastic toys and $2 slippers. The real gems are tucked on side streets or in small, one-person shops selling Chinese herbs, original art, and jewelry. Grant Avenue is the area's main thoroughfare, and side streets between Bush Street and Columbus Avenue are full of restaurants, markets, and eclectic shops. Walking is best, since traffic through this area is slow at best and parking is next to impossible. Most of the stores in Chinatown are open daily from 10am to 10pm. The area is serviced by bus lines 9X, 15, 30, 41, and 45.

Of the endless array of trinket shops scattered through the compact neighborhood, two worth noting are **Eastwind Books & Arts,** 1435 Stockton St., at Columbus Avenue (© **415/772-5877** Chinese department, 415/772-5899 English department; e-mail: info@eastwindsf.com), which carries an incredible selection of Chinese books, stationery, and stamps, as well as Asian-American and English books covering everything from health and cooking to martial arts and medicine. At the mystical **Ten Ren Tea Company,** 949 Grant Ave., between Washington and Jackson Streets (© **415/362-0656**), you can enjoy a steaming cup of roselle tea, made of black tea and hibiscus, while you browse the selection of almost 50 traditional and herbal teas and related paraphernalia.

SOMA Though this area isn't suitable for strolling, you'll find almost all the discount shopping in warehouse spaces south of Market. You can pick up a discount-shopping guide at most major hotels. Many buses pass through this area, including routes 9, 12, 14, 15, 19, 26, 27, 30, 42, 45, and 76.

An all-time favorite is the **SFMOMA MuseumStore,** 151 Third St., 2 blocks south of Market Street, across from Yerba Buena Gardens (© **415/357-4035**). Its array of artistic cards, books, jewelry, housewares, knickknacks, and creative tokens of San Francisco makes this one of the locals' favorite shops. It also offers far more tasteful mementos than most Fisherman's Wharf options.

Fashionable bargain hunters head to **Jeremys,** 2 South Park, at Second Street between Bryant and Brannan Streets (✆ **415/882-4929**), where top designer fashions from shoes to suits come at rock-bottom prices. For the more adventurous thrift-shopper, there's the **North Face** discount outlet, 1325 Howard St., between Ninth and Tenth Streets (✆ **415/626-6444**). The sporting, camping, and hiking equipment is still expensive, but the skiwear, boots, sweaters, and goods such as tents, packs, and sleeping bags are far less expensive than if you buy them at a retail shop.

Another worthy stop is the **Wine Club San Francisco,** 953 Harrison St., between Fifth and Sixth Streets (✆ **415/512-9086**), which offers bargain prices on more than 1,200 domestic and foreign wines. Bottles cost from $4 to $1,100.

HAYES VALLEY It may not be the prettiest area in town, but while most neighborhoods cater to more conservative or trendy shoppers, lower Hayes Street, between Octavia and Gough, celebrates anything vintage, artistic, or downright funky. Though still in its developmental stage, it's definitely the most interesting new shopping area in town, with furniture and glass stores, thrift shops, trendy shoe stores, and men's and women's clothiers. There are also lots of great antiques shops south on Octavia and on nearby Market Street. Bus lines include nos. 16AX, 16BX, and 21.

If you have a fetish for foot fashions, you must check out **Bulo,** 437A Hayes St., at Gough Street (✆ **415/864-3244**), which carries nothing but imported Italian men's and women's shoes that run the gamut from casual to dressy, reserved to wildly funky. Shop for the sale items unless you're ready to drop around $200 per pair.

THE CASTRO You could easily spend all day wandering through the home and men's-clothing shops of the Castro. Buses serving this area include nos. 8, 24, 33, 35, and 37.

Citizen Clothing, 536 Castro St., between 18th and 19th Streets (✆ **415/ 558-9429**), is a popular shop for stylish casual clothing.

Our favorite chocolate shop, **Joseph Schmidt Confections,** 3489 16th St., at Sanchez Street (✆ **415/861-8682**), adds a whole new dimension to designer chocolate. Here the sinful sweets take the shape of exquisite sculptural masterpieces that are so beautiful, you'll be hesitant to bite the head off your adorable chocolate panda bear. Prices are also remarkably reasonable.

UNION STREET Union Street, from Fillmore to Van Ness, caters to the upper middle–class crowd. It's a great place to stroll; to window-shop the plethora of boutiques, cafes, and restaurants; and to watch the beautiful people parade by. Bus lines include nos. 22, 41, 42, and 45.

Among the dozens of fashion and home boutiques is **Three Bags Full,** 2181 Union St., at Fillmore (✆ **415/567-5753**), where expensive, handmade, and one-of-a-kind knitwear is both playful and extravagant.

CHESTNUT STREET Parallel to and a few blocks north of Union Street, Chestnut is a younger Union Street, with endless shopping and dining choices, and the ever-tanned, superfit population of postgraduate singles who hang around cafes and scope each other out. The area is serviced by bus lines 22, 28, 30, 41, 42, 43, and 76.

FISHERMAN'S WHARF & ENVIRONS   The tourist-oriented malls—Ghirardelli Square, Pier 39, the Cannery, and the Anchorage—run along Jefferson Street and include hundreds of shops, restaurants, and attractions.

Locals tend to avoid this part of town, but do venture to **Cost Plus Imports,** 2552 Taylor St., between North Point and Bay Streets (℅ **415/928-6200**), a vast warehouse crammed to the rafters with Chinese baskets, Indian camel bells, Malaysian batik scarves, and innumerable other items from Algeria to Zanzibar. There's also a decent wine section. Adjoining is a **Barnes & Noble** "superstore," at 2550 Taylor, between Bay and North Point (℅ **415/292-6762**).

FILLMORE STREET   Some of the best shopping in town is packed into 5 blocks of Fillmore Street in Pacific Heights. From Jackson to Sutter Streets, Fillmore is the perfect place to grab a bite and peruse the high-priced boutiques, crafts shops, and incredible houseware stores. It's serviced by bus lines 1, 2, 3, 4, 12, 22, and 24.

One of our absolute favorite housewares shops is **Fillamento,** 2185 Fillmore St., at Sacramento Street (℅ **415/931-2224**), which is always packed with shoppers searching for the most classic, artistic, and refined home items. Whether you're looking to set a good table or revamp your bedroom, you'll find it all here. Head south a few blocks on Fillmore to incredible **Zinc Details,** 1905 Fillmore St., between Bush and Pine Streets (℅ **415/776-2100**), which has an amazing collection of locally handcrafted glass vases, pendant lights, ceramics, and furniture. Each piece is a true work of art created specifically for the store (except vintage items).

HAIGHT STREET   Green hair, spiked hair, no hair, or mohair—even the hippies look conservative next to Haight Street's dramatic fashion freaks. The shopping in the 6 blocks of upper Haight Street, between Central Avenue and Stanyan Street, reflects its clientele and offers everything from incense and European and American street styles to furniture and vintage and ubertrendy clothing. Bus lines 7, 66, 71, and 73 run down Haight Street. The Muni Metro N line stops at Waller Street and at Cole Street.

Less wearable, but equally collectable are the oldies-but-goodies at **Recycled Records,** 1377 Haight St., between Central and Masonic Streets (℅ **415/ 626-4075**). Easily one of the best used-record stores in the city, this loud shop has a good selection of promotional CDs and cases of used classic rock LPs. Sheet music, tour programs, and old *TV Guides* are also sold.

NORTH BEACH   Along with a great cup of coffee, Grant and Columbus Avenues cater to their hip clientele with a small but worthy selection of boutiques and specialty shops.

You can pick up a great gift for yourself or anyone else at **Biordi Art Imports,** 412 Columbus Ave., at Vallejo Street (℅ **415/392-8096**). Its Italian Majolica pottery is both exquisite and unique.

For a dose of local color, join the brooding literary types who browse **City Lights Booksellers & Publishers,** 261 Columbus Ave., at Broadway (℅ **415/ 362-8193**), the famous bookstore owned by renowned Beat-generation poet Lawrence Ferlinghetti. The shelves here are stocked with a comprehensive collection of art, poetry, and political paperbacks, as well as more mainstream books.

Fun mementos are for sale at **Quantity Postcards,** 1441 Grant St., at Green Street (℅ **415/986-8866**), where you'll find the perfect postcard for literally everyone you know, as well as some depictions of old San Francisco and movie stars, plus Day-Glo posters featuring concert-poster artist Frank Kozik.

CHINA BASIN   The only reason to come to the southeastern tip of the city is to dine at one of the shipyard-front restaurants or to shop at the **Esprit Outlet Store,** 499 Illinois St., at 16th Street (© **415/957-2550**). Fashionable bargain hunters will revel in the Esprit collections and Susie Tompkins merchandise, which are available here at 30% or more off regular prices. In addition to clothes, there are accessories, shoes, and assorted other items.

11 San Francisco After Dark

For up-to-date nightlife information, turn to the *San Francisco Weekly* and the *San Francisco Bay Guardian,* both of which contain comprehensive current listings. They're available free at bars and restaurants, and from street-corner boxes all around the city. *Where,* a free tourist monthly, also has information on programs and performance times; it's available in most of the city's finer hotels. The Sunday edition of the *San Francisco Examiner and Chronicle* also features a "Datebook" section, printed on pink paper, with information and listings on the week's upcoming events.

GETTING TICKETS   Half-price tickets to theater, dance, and music performances are available from **Tix Bay Area** (© **415/433-7827**) on the day of the show only; tickets for Sunday and Monday events, if available, are sold on Saturday. Tix also sells advance, full-price tickets for most performance halls, sporting events, concerts, and clubs. A service charge, ranging from $1 to $3, is levied on each ticket. Only cash or traveler's checks are accepted for half-price tickets; Visa and MasterCard are accepted for full-price tickets. Tix is located inside the Union Square Garage (on Geary Street at Powell Street). It's open Tuesday through Thursday from 11am to 6pm, Friday and Saturday from 11am to 7pm.

Tickets to most theater and dance events can also be obtained through **City Box Office,** 153 Kearny St., Suite 402 (© **415/392-4400**). American Express, MasterCard, and Visa are accepted.

BASS Ticketmaster (© **415/478-2277**) sells tickets to concerts, sporting events, plays, and special events. Downtown BASS Ticketmaster outlets can be found at Tix Bay Area (see above) and at **Warehouse** stores throughout the city. The most convenient location is at 30 Powell St.

THE PERFORMING ARTS

American Conservatory Theater (A.C.T.)   A.C.T. made its debut in 1967
and quickly established itself as the city's premier resident theater group. The troupe is so venerated that A.C.T. has been compared to the superb British National Theatre, the Berliner Ensemble, and the Comédie Française. The A.C.T. season runs from September through July and features both classical and experimental works. Performing at the Geary Theater, 415 Geary St. (at Mason St.). © 415/749-2ACT. www.act-sfbay.com.Tickets $11–$65.

The Magic Theatre   The highly acclaimed Magic Theatre continues to be a
major West Coast company dedicated to presenting the works of new playwrights; over the years it has nurtured the talents of such luminaries as Sam Shepard and Jon Robin Baitz. Shepard's Pulitzer Prize–winning play *Buried Child* premiered here. A more recent production included Shepard's *The Late Henry Moss* starring Nick Nolte, Sean Penn, and Woody Harrelson. The season usually runs from September through July; performances are offered Wednesday

through Sunday. Performing at Building D, Fort Mason Center, Marina Blvd. (at Buchanan St.). © 415/441-8822. www.magictheater.org. Tickets $8–$30. Discounts for students and seniors.

Philharmonia Baroque Orchestra   Acclaimed by the *New York Times* as "the country's leading early music orchestra," Philharmonia Baroque performs in San Francisco and all around the Bay Area. The season lasts from September through April. Performing in Herbst Theater, 401 Van Ness Ave. © 415/392-4400 (box office) or 415/252-1288 (administrative offices). www.philharmonia.org. Tickets $30–$42.

San Francisco Ballet   Founded in 1933, the San Francisco Ballet is the oldest professional ballet company in the United States and regarded as one of the country's finest, performing an eclectic repertoire of full-length, neoclassical, and contemporary ballets. Even the *New York Times* proclaimed, "The San Francisco Ballet under Helgi Tomasson's leadership is one of the spectacular success stories of the arts in America." The season runs from February through June. All performances are accompanied by the San Francisco Ballet Orchestra. War Memorial Opera House, 301 Van Ness Ave. (at Grove St.). © 415/865-2000 for tickets and information. Tickets $10–$110.

San Francisco Opera   The San Francisco Opera was the first municipal opera in the United States, and is one of the city's cultural icons. All productions have English supertitles. The season starts in September and lasts just 14 weeks. Performances are held most evenings, except Monday, with matinees on Sundays. Tickets go on sale as early as June, and the best seats quickly sell out. Unless Pavarotti or Domingo is in town, some less-coveted seats are usually available until curtain time. War Memorial Opera House, 301 Van Ness Ave. (at Grove St.). © 415/864-3330 (box office). www.sfopera.com. Tickets $23–$165.

San Francisco Symphony   Founded in 1911, the internationally respected San Francisco Symphony has long been an important part of this city's cultural life under such legendary conductors as Pierre Monteux and Seiji Ozawa. In 1995, Michael Tilson Thomas took over from Herbert Blomstedt and has already led the orchestra to new heights, crafting an exciting repertoire of classical and modern music. The season runs from September through June; tickets are very hard to come by, but there's usually someone outside the hall trying to sell their tickets the night of the show. Summer symphony activities include a Composer Festival and a Summer Pops series. Performing at Davies Symphony Hall, 201 Van Ness Ave. (at Grove St.). © 415/864-6000 (box office). Tickets $12–$73.

COMEDY & CABARET

Beach Blanket Babylon *Finds*   Now a San Francisco tradition, Beach Blanket Babylon is best known for its outrageous costumes and oversize headdresses. It's been playing almost 22 years now, and still almost every performance sells out. It's wise to write for tickets at least 3 weeks in advance, or obtain them through Tix (see above). At Club Fugazi, Beach Blanket Babylon Blvd., 678 Green St. (between Powell St. and Columbus Ave.). © 415/421-4222. Tickets $20–$55.

Cobb's Comedy Club   Located in the Cannery at Fisherman's Wharf, Cobb's features such national headliners as George Wallace, Emo Philips, and Jake Johannsen. There's comedy every night, including a 15-comedian All-Pro Monday showcase (a 3-hour marathon). Cobb's is open to those 18 and over, and occasionally to kids ages 16 and 17 if they're accompanied by a parent or legal guardian (call ahead first). The Cannery, 2801 Leavenworth St. (at Beach St.). © 415/928-4320. Cover Mon–Wed $10, Thurs and Sun $10–$13, Fri–Sat $13–$15. 2-beverage minimum nightly. Validated parking at Anchorage Shopping Center Garage.

THE CLUB & MUSIC SCENE
ROCK & BLUES CLUBS

Biscuits & Blues With a crisp, blow-your-eardrums-out sound system, a New Orleans–speakeasy (albeit commercial) appeal, and a nightly line-up of live entertainment, there's no better place to muse the blues than at this basement-cum-nightclub. 401 Mason (at Geary St.). ℂ **415/292-2583.** Cover (during performances) $5–$15.

Blue Bar Whether you're passing by North Beach or finishing a night at Reed Hearon's Black Cat Cafe (see "Dining," earlier in this chapter, for a review), you should drop into this cozy-chic, live jazz and blues venue with cushy couches and laid-back atmosphere. The restaurant's full menu is available here—a plus for late-night eaters and a bummer for those who come exclusively for the music. Below the Black Cat Cafe, 501 Broadway (at Kearny St.). ℂ **415/981-2233.** Cover $5 Wed–Sun.

The Fillmore *(Finds)* Reopened after years of neglect, The Fillmore, made famous by promoter Bill Graham in the 1960s, is once again attracting big names. Check the local listings in magazines, or call the theater for information on upcoming events. 1805 Geary Blvd. (at Fillmore St.). ℂ **415/346-6000.** www.thefillmore.com. Tickets $9–$25.

Lou's Pier 47 Club There are few locals in the place, but Lou's happens to be a good old-fashioned casual spot where you can let your hair down with Cajun seafood (downstairs), other tourists, and live jazz, blues, rock, and country bands (upstairs). Major happy-hour specials (Monday through Friday from 4 to 7pm) and a vacation attitude make the place one of the more sloppy happy spots near the Wharf. There's no cover for the first band, which plays nightly from 4 to 8pm, but it will cost you for the second, which comes on at 9pm. 300 Jefferson St. (at Jones St.). ℂ **415/771-5687.** Cover $5–$10.

Slim's Co-owned by musician Boz Scaggs, who sometimes takes the stage under the name "Presidio Slim," this glitzy restaurant and bar seats 300, serves California cuisine, and specializes in excellent American music—homegrown rock, jazz, blues, and alternative—almost nightly. 333 11th St. (at Folsom St.). ℂ **415/522-0333.** www.slims-sf.com. Cover free–$20. 2-drink minimum when seated at a table.

JAZZ & LATIN CLUBS

Cafe du Nord *(Finds)* Although it's been around since 1907, this basement-cum-supper-club has finally been recognized as a respectable jazz venue. With a younger generation now appreciating the music, the place is often packed, from the 40-foot mahogany bar to the back room with a pool table. Du Nord is even putting out its own compilation CDs now, which are definitely worth purchasing. 2170 Market St. (at Sanchez St.). ℂ **415/861-5016.** Nominal cover varies.

Jazz at Pearl's This is one of the best venues for jazz in the city. Ribs and chicken are served with the sounds, too, with prices ranging from $4 to $12. The live jams last until 2am nightly. 256 Columbus Ave. (at Broadway). ℂ **415/ 291-8255.** No cover. 2-drink minimum.

DANCE CLUBS

Club Ten 15 Get decked out and plan for a late-nighter if you're headed to this enormous party warehouse. Three levels and dance floors offer a variety of venues, complete with a 20- and 30-something gyrating mass who live for the DJs' pounding house, disco, and acid-jazz music. Each night is a different club that attracts its own crowd, ranging from yuppie to hip-hop. 1015 Folsom St. (at Sixth St.). ℂ **415/431-1200.** Cover $5–$15.

Nickie's Bar-be-cue   Don't show up here for dinner; the only hot thing you'll find is the small, crowded dance floor. But don't let that stop you from checking it out. Nickie's is a sure thing. Every time we come here, the old-school disco hits are in full force, casually dressed happy dancers lose all inhibitions, and the crowd is mixed with all types of friendly San Franciscans. This place is perpetually hot, so dress accordingly and don't expect a full bar—it's beer and wine only. 460 Haight St. (between Fillmore and Webster Sts.). ✆ 415/621-6508. www.nickies.com. Cover $3–$5.

Paradise Lounge   Labyrinthine Paradise features three dance floors simultaneously vibrating to different beats. Smaller, auxiliary spaces include a pool room with half a dozen tables. Poetry readings are also given. 1501 Folsom St. (at 11th St.). ✆ 415/861-6906. Cover $3–$15.

SUPPER CLUBS

If you can eat dinner, listen to live music, and dance (or at least wiggle in your chair) in the same room, it's a supper club—that's our criteria.

Harry Denton's Starlight Room   Come dressed to the nines or in casual attire to this old-fashioned cocktail-lounge-turned-nightclub, where tourists and locals sip drinks at sunset and boogie down to live swing and big-band tunes after dark. The room is classic 1930s San Francisco, with red-velvet banquettes, chandeliers, and fabulous views. But what really attracts flocks of all ages is a night of Harry Denton–style fun, which usually includes plenty of drinking and unrestrained dancing. At the Sir Francis Drake Hotel, 450 Powell St., 21st floor. ✆ 415/395-8595. Cover $5 Wed–Thurs after 7pm, $10 Fri–Sat after 8pm.

Julie's Supper Club   Julie's is a longtime standby for cocktails and late dining. Divided into two rooms, the vibe is very 1950s cartoon, with a space-aged *Jetsons* appeal. Good-looking singles prowl, cocktails in hand, as live music plays by the front door. The food is hit-or-miss, but the atmosphere is definitely a casual and playful winner with a little interesting history—this building is one location where the Symbionese Liberation Army held Patty Hearst hostage back in the 1970s. Menu items range from $9 to $20. 1123 Folsom St. (at Seventh St.). ✆ 415/861-0707. $5 cover on weekends.

RETRO CLUBS

Club Deluxe   Before the recent 1940s trend hit the city, Deluxe and its fedora-wearing clientele had been celebrating the bygone era for years. And fortunately, even with all the retro-hype, the vibe here hasn't changed. Expect an eclectic mix of throw-backs and generic San Franciscans in the intimate, smoky bar and adjoining lounge, and live jazz or blues most nights. Although many regulars dress the part, there's no attitude here—so come as you like. 1511 Haight St. (at Ashbury St.). ✆ 415/552-6949. Cover $2–$10.

THE BAR SCENE

Finding your idea of a comfortable bar has a lot to do with picking a neighborhood filled with your kind of people and investigating that area. There are hundreds of bars throughout San Francisco, and although many are obscurely located and can't be classified by their neighborhood, the following is a general description of what you'll find and where:

- **Chestnut and Union Street** bars attract a post-collegiate crowd.
- Young alternatives frequent **Mission District** haunts.
- **Upper Haight** caters to eclectic neighborhood cocktailers.
- **Lower Haight** is skate- and snowboarder grungy.

- Tourists mix with theatergoers and thirsty businesspeople in **downtown** pubs.
- **North Beach** serves all types.
- **Castro** caters to gay locals and tourists.
- **South of Market (SoMa)** offers an eclectic mix.

Backflip   Adjoining the rock-'n'-roll Phoenix Hotel, this shimmering aqua-blue cocktail lounge—designed to induce the illusion that you're carousing in the deep end—serves "cocktail fare" to mostly young, fashionable types, so please don't order a Cosmopolitan. 601 Eddy St. (at Larkin St.). © 415/771-FLIP.

The Bubble Lounge   Toasting the town is a nightly event at this relatively new champagne bar. With 300 champagnes (and around 30 by the glass), brick walls, couches, velvet curtains, and a pool table within its two levels, there's plenty of pop in this fizzy lounge. 714 Montgomery St. (at Columbus Ave.). © 415/434-4204.

The Red Room   At one time the hottest cocktail lounge in town (though it's cooled off a bit), this ultra-modern, Big Apple–style bar and lounge reflects no other spectrum but ruby red. Really, you gotta see this one. 825 Sutter St. (at Jones St.). © 415/346-7666.

Spec's   Its incognito locale on Saroyan Place, a tiny alley at 250 Columbus Ave., makes Spec's less of a walk-in bar and more of a lively locals' hangout. Its funky decor—maritime flags that hang from the ceiling, exposed brick walls lined with posters, photos, and various oddities—gives it character that intrigues every visitor. A "museum," displayed under glass, contains memorabilia and items brought back by seamen who drop in between sails, and the clientele is funky enough to keep you preoccupied while you drink a beer. 12 Saroyan Place (off Columbus Ave.). © 415/421-4112.

Tosca *(Finds*   Open daily from 5pm to 2am, Tosca is a low-key and large popular watering hole for local politicos, writers, media types, incognito visiting celebrities such as Johnny Depp or Nicholas Cage, and similar cognoscenti of unassuming classics. Equipped with dim lights, red leather booths, high ceilings, and the requisite vintage jukebox spilling out Italian arias, it's everything you'd expect an old North Beach legend to be. 242 Columbus Ave. (between Broadway and Pacific Ave.). © 415/986-9651.

Vesuvio   Situated along Jack Kerouac Alley across from the famed City Lights Bookstore, this renowned literary beatnik hangout isn't just riding its historic coattails. Popular with neighborhood writers, artists, songsters, and wanna-bes, Vesuvio is crowded with self-proclaimed philosophers, along with everyone else ranging from longshoremen and cab drivers to businesspeople. 255 Columbus Ave. (at Broadway). © 415/362-3370.

BREWPUBS

Gordon-Biersch Brewery   Popular with the young Republican crowd (loose ties and tight skirts predominate), this modern, two-tiered brewery and restaurant attracts a more upscale clientele than your typical beer garden. The food—beer-braised lamb shank, baby-back ribs, lemon roasted half chicken—is pretty good, but it's the gourmet lagers and ales that account for the line out the door. *One caveat:* When the lower-level bar fills up, you practically have to shout to be heard. 2 Harrison St. (on the Embarcadero). © 415/243-8246.

San Francisco Brewing Company   The bar is one of the city's few remaining old saloons, aglow with stained-glass windows, tile floors, skylights, a mahogany bar, and a massive overhead fan running the full length of the bar—a bizarre contraption crafted from brass and palm fronds. Menu items range from $3.70 (curiously, for edamame) to $20 for a full rack of baby back ribs with all the fixings. The happy-hour special, a dollar per 10-ounce microbrew beer (or $1.75 a pint), runs daily from 4 to 6pm and midnight to 1am. 155 Columbus Ave. (at Pacific St.). 🕐 415/434-3344. www.sfbrewing.com.

Thirsty Bear Brewing Company   Seven superb, handcrafted varieties of brew, ranging from a fruit-flavored Strawberry Ale to a steak-in-a-cup stout, are always on tap at this stylish high-ceilinged brick edifice. Excellent Spanish food, too. Pool tables and dartboards are upstairs, and live music (jazz, flamenco, blues, alternative, and classical) can be heard most nights. 661 Howard St. (1 block east of the Moscone Center). 🕐 415/974-0905.

COCKTAILS WITH A VIEW

The Carnelian Room   On the 52nd floor of the Bank of America building, the Carnelian Room offers uninterrupted views of the city. From a window-front table you feel as if you can reach out, pluck up the TransAmerica Pyramid, and stir your martini with it. *Note:* The restaurant has the most extensive wine list in the city—1,275 selections to be exact. 555 California St., in the Bank of America Building (between Kearny and Montgomery Sts.). 🕐 415/433-7500. Jacket and tie required for men.

Cityscape   When you sit under the glass roof and sip a drink here, it feels as though you're out under the stars and enjoying views of the bay. There's nightly dancing to a DJ's picks from 10pm. The mirrored columns and floor-to-ceiling draperies help create an elegant and romantic ambiance. Atop Hilton Tower I, 333 O'Farrell St. (at Mason St.), 46th floor. 🕐 415/923-5002.

Equinox   The sales "hook" of the Hyatt's rooftop Equinox is a revolving floor that gives each table a 360° panoramic view of the city every 45 minutes. In addition to cocktails, dinner is served daily. In the Hyatt Regency Hotel, 5 Embarcadero Center. 🕐 415/788-1234.

Harry Denton's Starlight Room. See "Supper Clubs," above, for a full review. Atop the Sir Francis Drake Hotel, 450 Powell St., 21st floor. 🕐 415/395-8595.

Top of the Mark *(Finds)*   This is one of the most famous cocktail lounges in the world. During World War II, it was considered de rigueur for Pacific-bound servicemen to toast their good-byes to the States here. The spectacular glass-walled room features an unparalleled view. Appetizers and live entertainment is offered at 8:30pm nightly, when there's a $6 to $10 cover. Drink prices range from $6 to $8. In the Mark Hopkins Intercontinental, 1 Nob Hill (between California and Mason Sts.). 🕐 415/616-6916.

GAY AND LESBIAN BARS & CLUBS

The Café   When this place first got jumping, it was the only predominantly lesbian dance club on Saturday nights in the city. But once the guys found out how much fun the girls were having, they joined the party. Today, it's still a very happening mixed gay and lesbian scene with two bars; a steamy, free-spirited dance floor; and a small patio. 2367 Market St. (at Castro St.). 🕐 415/861-3846.

The EndUp   It's a different nightclub every night of the week, but regardless of who's throwing the party, the place is always jumping with the DJs blasting tunes. There are two pool tables, a flaming fireplace, an outdoor patio, and a mob of gyrating souls on the dance floor. Some nights are straight, so call for gay nights. 401 Sixth St. (at Harrison St.). 🕐 415/357-0827. Cover varies.

The Stud The Stud has been around for over 30 years, is one of the most successful gay establishments in town, and is mellow enough for straights as well as gays. The interior has an antiques-shop look and a miniature train circling over the bar and dance floor. Music here is a balanced mix of old and new, and nights vary from cabaret and oldies to disco. Call in advance for the evening's venue. Drink prices range from $1.25 to $5.75. 399 Ninth St. (at Harrison St.). ⓒ 415/863-6623. Cover $2–$6 Fri–Sat.

Twin Peaks Tavern Right at the intersection of Castro, 17th, and Market Streets is one of the Castro's most famous gay hangouts, which caters to an older crowd and is considered the first gay bar in America. Because of its relatively small size and desirable location, the place becomes fairly crowded and convivial by 8pm, earlier than many neighboring bars. 401 Castro St. (at 17th and Market Sts.). ⓒ 415/864-9470. No cover.

The San Francisco Bay Area

by Erika Lenkert

Without question, the Bay City is captivating. But don't let it ensnare you to the point of ignoring its environs, which contain a multitude of natural spectacles like Mount Tamalpais and Muir Woods; scenic communities like Tiburon, Sausalito, and Half Moon Bay; and cities like gritty Oakland and its youth-oriented next-door neighbor, Berkeley. A little farther north stretch the valleys of Napa and Sonoma, the finest wine region in the nation (see chapter 6, "The Wine Country"). And to the south lie high-tech Silicon Valley and San Jose, northern California's largest city.

1 Berkeley

10 miles NE of San Francisco

Until recently, the University of California at Berkeley and its first-rate academic standards, 17 Nobel Prize winners (7 of which are currently on staff), and protests that led to the most well-known student riots in U.S. history were the primary reasons that Berkeley is something more than a quaint, sleepy town east of the big city. But the race to find affordable Bay Area housing has made the East Bay portal even more of a hub. Today, there's still hippie idealism in the air, but the radicals have aged; the 1960s are only present in tie-dye and paraphernalia shops (which are rapidly being taken over by national chains along Telegraph Avenue), and the students suffer from less angst. Meanwhile, upscale restaurants, shops, and communities continue to flourish. All in all, it's an entertaining town with all types of people, a beautiful campus, vast parks, and some incredible restaurants.

ESSENTIALS

GETTING THERE The Berkeley **BART (Bay Area Rapid Transit)** station is 2 blocks from the university. The fare from San Francisco is less than $3. For information, call BART at © **510/793-2278.**

If you're coming **by car** from San Francisco, take I-80 east to the University Avenue exit. Count on walking some distance, as you won't find a parking spot near the university.

VISITOR INFORMATION The **Berkeley Convention and Visitors Bureau,** 2015 Center St., Berkeley, CA 94703 (© **800/847-4823** or 510/549-7040), can answer your questions and even find accommodations for you. Call the **Visitor Hotline** (© **510/549-8710**) for information on events and happenings in Berkeley.

EXPLORING THE UNIVERSITY & ENVIRONS

Hanging out is the preferred Berkeley pastime, and the best place to do it is on **Telegraph Avenue,** the street that leads to the campus' southern entrance. Most of the action lies between Bancroft Way and Ashby Avenue, where coffeehouses, restaurants, shops, great book and record stores, and crafts booths swarm with life.

Pretend you're local: Plant yourself at a cafe, sip a latte, and ponder something intellectual while you survey the town's unique population bustling by. Bibliophiles must stop at **Cody's Books,** 2454 Telegraph Ave. (*C* **510/845-7852**), to peruse its gargantuan selection of titles, independent-press books, and magazines.

UC Berkeley itself is worth a stroll as well. It's a beautiful old campus with plenty of woodsy paths, architecturally noteworthy buildings, and 32,000 students scurrying to and from classes. Among the architectural highlights of the campus are a number of buildings by Bernard Maybeck, Bakewell and Brown, and John Galen Howard. Contact the **Visitor Information Center,** 101 University Hall, 2200 University Ave., at Oxford Street (*C* **510/642-5215**), to join a free, regularly scheduled campus tour (Monday through Saturday at 10am and 1pm, Sunday at 1pm; no tours offered from mid-December to mid-January), or stop by the office and pick up a self-guided walking-tour brochure. If you're interested in notable off-campus buildings, contact the **Berkeley Convention and Visitors Bureau** (*C* **510/549-7040**) for an architectural walking-tour brochure.

You'll find the university's southern entrance at the northern end of Telegraph Avenue, at Bancroft Way. Walk through the main entrance into **Sproul Plaza.** Here, when school is in session, you'll encounter the gamut of Berkeley's inhabitants as well as the **Student Union,** complete with a bookstore, cafes, and information desk on the second floor, where you can pick up a free map of Berkeley along with the local student newspaper (also found in dispensers throughout campus). You might be lucky enough to stumble upon some impromptu musicians or a heated—and sometimes absurd—debate. There's always something going on, so stretch out on the grass for a few minutes and take in the Berkeley vibe.

For viewing more traditional art forms, there are some noteworthy museums here, too. The **Lawrence Hall of Science,** Centennial Drive near Grizzly Peak (*C* **510/ 642-5132**), offering hands-on science exploration, is open from 10am to 5pm daily and is a wonderful place to watch the sunset. Admission is $7 for adults; $5 for seniors, students, and children 7 to 18; $3 for children 3 to 6; free for kids under 3. The **University Art Museum,** 2626 Bancroft Way (*C* **510/ 642-0808**), is open from 11am to 5pm on Wednesday and Friday through Sunday, and Thursday from 11am to 9pm. Admission is $6 for adults; $4 for seniors, students, and children 12 to 17; and free for kids under 12 and U.C. students. This museum includes a substantial collection of Hans Hofmann paintings, a sculpture garden, and the **Pacific Film Archive,** main entrance at 2625 Durant Ave. (*C* **510/642-1124**).

OFF-CAMPUS ATTRACTIONS

PARKS Unbeknownst to many travelers, Berkeley has some of the most extensive and beautiful parks around. If you enjoy hiking, getting a breath of California air, and sniffing a few roses, or just want to wear out the kids, jump in your car and make your way to **Tilden Park** (*C* **510/843-2137**), where you'll find plenty of flora and fauna, hiking trails, an old steam train and merry-go-round, a farm and nature area for kids, and a chilly tree-encircled lake. On the way, stop at the colorful terraced **Rose Garden,** located in north Berkeley on Euclid Avenue between Bay View and Eunice Street.

The San Francisco Bay Area

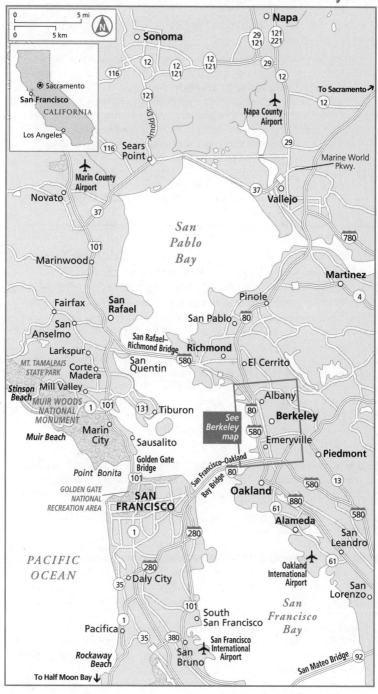

0   5 mi
0   5 km

N

Sonoma

Napa

29
121

121
221

12

12
121

12
121

29

12

To Sacramento

116

121

Arnold Dr.

Napa County
Airport

29

Sears
Point

116

Marine World
Pkwy.

Marin County
Airport

37

Vallejo

Novato

37

San
Pablo
Bay

780

101

Marinwood

Martinez

Pinole

4

Fairfax

San
Rafael

San Pablo

80

San
Anselmo

San Rafael–
Richmond Bridge

Richmond

Larkspur

580

El Cerrito

MT. TAMALPAIS
STATE PARK

Corte
Madera

San
Quentin

Stinson
Beach

Mill Valley

Albany

MUIR WOODS
NATIONAL
MONUMENT

1

101

131

Tiburon

80

See
Berkeley
map

Berkeley

580

Muir Beach

Marin
City

Emeryville

Piedmont

Sausalito

Golden Gate
Bridge

San Francisco–Oakland

Point Bonita

101

Bay Bridge

80

Oakland

580

13

GOLDEN GATE
NATIONAL
RECREATION AREA

SAN
FRANCISCO

880

580

61

PACIFIC
OCEAN

1

280

Alameda

San
Leandro

280

35

Daly City

Oakland
International
Airport

61

San
Lorenzo

San
Francisco
Bay

101

South
San Francisco

Pacifica

1

35

380

San Francisco
International
Airport

Rockaway
Beach

San
Bruno

San Mateo Bridge

92

To Half Moon Bay

135

(Finds **Sweet Sensations at Berkeley's New Chocolate Factory**

If you haven't had chocolate nibs you haven't lived—at least that's what chocoholics are likely to discover upon visiting Scharffen Berger Chocolate Maker (© **510/981-4050;** www.scharffenberger.com), California's runaway-success chocolatier that opened its factory and retail shop doors in Berkeley in mid-2001. Within the brick building visitors can not only taste the "nibs" or crunchy roasted and shelled cocoa beans, but also see how the famous chocolate company uses vintage European equipment during regularly scheduled tours (call for details). And let's not forget there are plenty of tasty products, from candy bars to cocoa powder and chocolate sauce, available in the retail shop. The factory is located at 914 Heinz Avenue; from I-80 East take the Ashby Ave exit, turn left on 7th Street, and right on Heinz.

Another worthy nature excursion is the **University of California Botanical Garden,** in Strawberry Canyon on Centennial Drive (© **510/642-3343**), which features a vast collection of plant life ranging from cacti to redwoods.

SHOPPING If you're itching to exercise your credit cards, head to one of two places. **College Avenue** from Dwight all the way down to the Oakland border is crammed with eclectic boutiques, antiques shops, and restaurants. The other option is **Fourth Street** in west Berkeley, just 2 blocks north of the University Avenue exit off I-80, where you can grab a cup of java, read the paper at a patio table, and then hit the **Crate & Barrel Outlet,** 1785 Fourth St., between Hearst and Virginia (© **510/528-5500**), where prices are 30% to 70% off retail, or any of the small, wonderful stores crammed with imported and locally made housewares. Nearby is **REI,** the Bay Area's favorite outdoor outfitter, at 1338 San Pablo Ave., near Gilman Street (© **510/527-4140**).

WHERE TO STAY
Bed-and-Breakfast California (© **800/872-4500** or 408/867-9662; fax 408/867-0907; www.bbintl.com), books visitors into private homes and apartments in the Berkeley area. The cost ranges from $95 to $300 per night, and there's a 2-night minimum.

WHERE TO DINE
EXPENSIVE
Chez Panisse ✦✦✦ CALIFORNIA California cuisine is greatly a product of Alice Waters's genius. Read the menus posted outside and you'll understand why. Most of the produce and meat comes from local farms and is organically produced, and after all these years, Alice still attends to her restaurant with great integrity and innovation.

Alice's creations are served in a delightful redwood and stucco cottage with a brick terrace filled with flowering potted plants. There are two separate dining areas—the upstairs cafe and the downstairs restaurant, both offering Mediterranean-inspired cuisine.

In the upstairs cafe you'll pass a tempting display of pastries and fruit, and large bouquets of fresh flowers, which adorn an oak bar. At lunch or dinner, a

Berkeley

RICHMOND

EL CERRITO

KENSINGTON

TILDEN REGIONAL PARK

To Sacramento & Napa Valley

Moeser Ln.

Point Isabel Regional Shoreline

El Cerrito Plaza BART

Solano Ave Shopping District

CONTRA COSTA CO.
ALAMEDA CO.

ALBANY

Solano Ave.

Marin Ave.

BERKELEY

Golden Gate Fields

CESAR E. CHAVEZ PARK

Gilman Ave.
Gilman Shopping Pocket

Hopkins St.

North Berkeley Shopping District

North Berkeley BART

Cedar Ave.

Berkeley Marina

Virginia Ave.

University Ave.

Hearst Ave.

UNIVERSITY OF CALIFORNIA AT BERKELEY

Berkeley BART

AQUATIC PARK

Bancroft Way
Channing Way
Dwight Way

Clark Kerr Campus

CLAREMONT CANYON REGIONAL PRESERVE

San Francisco Bay

SAN PABLO PARK

Derby St.

Ashby Ave.
Ashby BART

Alcatraz Avenue

Rockridge BART

EMERYVILLE

OAKLAND

To Bay Bridge/ San Francisco

Mac Arthur BART

MOSSWOOD PARK

0   3/4 mi
0   0.75 km

To Downtown Oakland

To East Oakland & Stockton

Berkeley Convention & Visitors Bureau **6**

College Avenue **1**

Fourth Street Shopping District **7**

Lawrence Hall of Science **4**

Rose Garden **8**

Telegraph Avenue **2**

Tilden Regional Park **9**

University Art Museum **3**

University of California Botanical Garden **3**

University Visitor Center **5**

delicately smoked gravlax or a roasted eggplant soup with pesto, followed by lamb ragout garnished with apricots, onions, and spices served with couscous, might be featured.

The cozy downstairs restaurant, strewn with blossoming floral bouquets, is an appropriately warm environment to indulge in the fixed-price, four-course gourmet dinner, which is served Tuesday to Thursday. Friday and Saturday, it's four courses plus an aperitif, and Monday is bargain night with a three-course dinner for $39.

The menu, which changes daily, is posted outside the restaurant each Saturday for the following week. Meals are complemented by an excellent wine list.

1517 Shattuck Ave. (between Cedar and Vine). ✆ 510/548-5525; cafe reservations 415/548-5049. Fax 510/548-0140. www.chezpanisse.com. Reservations essential. Restaurant fixed-price menu $45–$75; cafe main courses $15–$25. AE, DC, DISC, MC, V. Restaurant seatings Mon–Sat 6–6:30pm and 8:30–9:30pm. Cafe Mon–Thurs 11:30am–3pm and 5–10:30pm; Fri–Sat 11:30am–3:30pm and 5–11:30pm. From I-80 north, take the University Ave. exit and turn left onto Shattuck Ave. BART: Berkeley.

MODERATE

Cafe Rouge ✿✿ BISTRO   After cooking at San Francisco's renowned Zuni Cafe for 10 years, chef and owner Marsha McBride launched her own restaurant, a sort of Zuni East. She brought former staff members and some of the restaurant's flavor with her, and now her sparse, loft-like dining room serves salads, rotisserie chicken with oil and thyme, grilled lamb chops, steaks, and homemade sausages. East Bay carnivores are especially happy with the burger; like Zuni's, it's top-notch.

1782 Fourth St. (between Delaware and Hearst). ✆ **510/525-1440.** Reservations recommended. Main courses $9.50–$24. AE, MC, V. Mon–Sat 11:30am–3pm; Tues–Sat 3–5pm (interim menu); Tues–Thurs 5:30–9:30pm; Fri–Sat 5:30–10:30pm; Sun 5–9pm.

O Chamé ✿✿ JAPANESE   Spare and plain in its decor, with ochre-colored walls marked with etched patterns, this spot has a meditative air to complement the traditional and experimental Japanese-inspired cuisine coveted by lovers of "clean," light food. The menu, which changes daily, offers meal-in-a-bowl dishes (from $10 to $17.50) that allow a choice of soba or udon noodles in a clear soup with a variety of toppings—from shrimp and wakame seaweed to beef with burdock root and carrot; appetizers and salads, which include a flavorful melding of grilled shiitake mushrooms and sweet peppers and portobello mushrooms, watercress, and green-onion pancakes; a sashimi of the day; and specials that range from $10 to $17.50 and always include a delicious roasted salmon.

1830 Fourth St. (near Hearst). ✆ **510/841-8783.** Reservations recommended Fri–Sat. Main courses $9–$18.50. AE, DC, MC, V. Mon–Sat 11:30am–3pm; Mon–Thurs 5:30–9pm; Fri–Sat 5:30–9:30pm.

Rivoli ✿✿ (Finds CALIFORNIA   One of the favored dinner destinations in the East Bay, Rivoli offers top-notch food at amazingly reasonable prices. The owners have done the most with an otherwise uninteresting space by creating a warm, intimate dining room, which overlooks a sweet little garden with visiting raccoons and possums, and is preceded by a wine bar near the entrance. Aside from a few house favorites, the menu changes entirely every 3 weeks to serve whatever's freshest and in season; the wine list follows suit with around a dozen by-the-glass options hand-picked to match the food. While many love it, I wasn't thrilled with the portobello-mushroom fritter, which in my mind was a glorified variation of the fried zucchini stick. However, there are plenty of dishes that shine, including artichoke lasagne with ricotta, mint salsa, and tomato sauce; and braised lamb shank with green garlic risotto, sautéed spinach, and oven-dried tomatoes. Finish the evening with an assortment of cheeses or a warm chocolate truffle torte with hazelnut ice cream, orange crème anglaise, and chocolate sauce.

1539 Solano Ave. ℭ **510/526-2542.** www.rivolirestaurant.com. Reservations recommended. Main courses $14–$17. AE, DISC, MC, V. Mon–Thurs 5:30–9:30pm; Fri 5:30–10pm; Sat 5–10pm; Sun 5–9pm.

INEXPENSIVE

Cambodiana's ⊛ CAMBODIAN For those who relish the spicy cuisine of Cambodia, this is quite a find. The decor is as colorful as the fare—brilliant blue, yellow, and green walls with Breuer-style chairs. Especially tasty choices include curry (chicken, beef, and so on), and Naga dishes with a sauce of tamarind, turmeric, lemongrass, shrimp paste, coconut-milk galinga, shallot, lemon leaf, sugar, and green chili. This sauce may smother salmon, prawns, chicken, or steak. Another tempting dish is chicken *chaktomuk,* prepared with pineapple, red peppers, and zucchini in soy and oyster sauce. There are plenty of vegetarian and low-cal options.

2156 University Ave. (between Shattuck and Oxford). ℭ **510/843-4630.** Reservations recommended. Main courses $6.50–$15. AE, DC, MC, V. Tues–Fri 11:30am–9pm; Sat–Sun 5–9:30pm.

2 Oakland

10 miles E of San Francisco

Although it's less than a dozen miles from San Francisco, the city of Oakland is worlds apart from its sister city across the bay. Originally little more than a cluster of ranches and farms, Oakland's size and stature exploded practically overnight as the last mile of transcontinental railroad track was laid down. Major shipping ports soon followed, and to this day Oakland has retained its hold as one of the busiest industrial ports on the West Coast.

The price for all this economic success, however, has been Oakland's lowbrow reputation as a predominantly working-class city, forever in the shadow of San Francisco's chic spotlight. However, with progressive Mayor Jerry Brown at the helm and housing prices and weather far more inviting than they are in San Francisco, "Oaktown" is in a renaissance, and its future continues to look brighter and brighter with plenty of pleasant surprises for those who venture this way. Rent a sailboat on Lake Merritt, stroll along the waterfront, explore the fantastic Oakland Museum—they're all great reasons to hop the bay and spend a fog-free day exploring one of California's largest and most ethnically diverse cities.

ESSENTIALS

GETTING THERE **Bay Area Rapid Transit (BART)** makes the trip from San Francisco to Oakland through one of the longest underwater transit tunnels in the world. Fares range from $1 to $4, depending on your station of origin; children 4 and under ride free. BART trains operate Monday through Friday from 4am to midnight, Saturday from 6am to midnight, and Sunday from 8am to midnight. Exit at the 12th Street station for downtown Oakland.

By car from San Francisco, take I-80 across the San Francisco–Oakland Bay Bridge and follow the signs to downtown Oakland. Exit at Grand Avenue South for the Lake Merritt area.

CITY LAYOUT Downtown Oakland is bordered by Grand Avenue on the north, I-980 on the west, Inner Harbor on the south, and Lake Merritt on the east. Between these landmarks are three BART stations (12th Street, 19th Street, and Lake Merritt), City Hall, the Oakland Museum, Jack London Square, and several other sights.

WHAT TO SEE & DO

Lake Merritt is Oakland's primary tourist attraction along with Jack London Square (see below). Three and a half miles in circumference, the tidal lagoon was bridged and dammed in the 1860s and is now a wildlife refuge that's home to flocks of migrating ducks, herons, and geese. It's surrounded on three sides by the 122-acre **Lakeside Park,** a popular place to picnic, feed the ducks, and escape the fog. At the **Sailboat House** (© **510/444-3807**), in Lakeside Park along the north shore, you can rent sailboats, rowboats, pedal boats, and canoes for $6 to $12 per hour. Another option is to take an hour-long gondola ride with **Gondola Servizio** (**510/663-6603;** www.gondolaservizio.com). Experienced gondoliers will serenade you as you glide across the lake; the cost is $55 for two or $65 including an antipasto picnic.

Another site worth visiting is Oakland's **Paramount Theatre,** 2025 Broadway (© **510/893-2300**), an outstanding example of art-deco architecture and decor. Built in 1931 and authentically restored in 1973, it now functions as the city's main performing arts center featuring incredible talent like Nina Simone and Buena Vista Social Club. Guided tours of the 3,000-seat theater are given the first and third Saturdays of each month, excluding holidays. No reservations are necessary; just show up at 10am at the box-office entrance on 21st Street at Broadway. Cameras are allowed, and admission is $1.

If you take pleasure from strolling sailboat-filled wharves or are a die-hard fan of Jack London, you might actually enjoy a visit to **Jack London Square.** Oakland's only patent tourist area, this low-key version of San Francisco's Fisherman's Wharf shamelessly plays up the fact that Jack London spent most of his youth along this waterfront. The square fronts the harbor, housing a tourist-tacky complex of boutiques and eateries that are about as far away from the "call of the wild" as you can get. Most are open Monday through Saturday from 10am to 7pm (some restaurants stay open later). In the center of the square is a small reconstructed version of the Yukon cabin in which Jack London lived while prospecting in the Klondike during the gold rush of 1897.

In the middle of Jack London Square you'll find a more authentic memorial, **Heinold's First and Last Chance Saloon**—a funky, friendly little bar and historic landmark that's actually worth a visit. This is where London did some of his writing and most of his drinking; the corner table he used has remained exactly as it was nearly a century ago. Also in the square are the mast and nameplate from the USS *Oakland,* a ship that saw extensive action in the Pacific during World War II, and a wonderful museum filled with interesting London memorabilia.

The square is located at Broadway and Embarcadero. Take I-880 to Broadway, turn south, and go to the end. Via BART, get off at the 12th Street station, then walk south along Broadway (about half a mile) or take bus no. 51a to the foot of Broadway.

Oakland Museum of California ⊛   Located 2 blocks south of the lake, this museum includes just about everything you'd want to know about the state and its people, history, culture, geology, art, environment, and ecology. Inside a low-swept, modern building set among sweeping gardens and terraces, it's actually three museums in one: exhibitions of works by California artists from Bierstadt to Diebenkorn; collections of artifacts from California's history, from Pomo Indian basketry to Country Joe McDonald's guitar; and re-creations of California habitats from the coast to the mountains. The museum holds major shows of California artists, like the recent exhibit of photography: "Capturing Light," masterpieces of California photography from 1860 to 2000, Bob Walker's "The Art of Environmental Photography," and "Every Worker is An Organizer," which took a look at California's farm labor and the resurgence of the United Farm Workers. There are 45-minute guided tours leaving the gallery information desks on request or by appointment. There is also a fine cafe, a **gallery** (© **510/834-2296**) selling works by California artists, and a book and gift shop. The cafe is open Wednesday to Saturday from 10am to 4pm and Sunday from noon to 4pm.

WHERE TO STAY

Lake Merritt Hotel ☆☆   Six-floor Lake Merritt Hotel is so delightfully charming in its Art Deco glory, it's impossible not to love the place. The completely renovated (new beds!) rooms and suites are cheery; many rooms overlook Lake Merritt, which is across the street. The decor is fresh with bright colors, fun lampshades, Deco-style armoires, new bathrooms (but old tile) and lots of homey touches and amenities. The suites are full-blown apartments. Completing the cozy picture are the comfy and swank sitting area—all dark with high ceiling and grand piano—and the beautiful restaurant, Madison's, which offers astounding lakefront views from huge picture windows.

1800 Madison St. (at 17th Street), Oakland, CA 94612. © **800/933-4683** or 510/832-2300. Fax 510/832-7150. www.lakemerritthotel.com. 52 units. $179–$289 double. AE, DC, MC, V. Valet parking $14. **Amenities:** 1 restaurant; complimentary passes to nearby health club; concierge; shuttle service; room service; same-day dry cleaning. *In room:* TV, dataport, fridge, coffeemaker, hair dryer, iron, safe; suites have kitchenettes.

WHERE TO DINE

Bay Wolf ☆☆☆ CALIFORNIA   Bay Wolf, one of Oakland's most venerable and revered restaurants, has been going strong for more than 2 decades. This converted brown Victorian is a comfortably familiar sight for most East Bay diners, who have been coming here for years to let chef/owner Michael Wilds do the cooking. Bay Wolf's reputation for simple yet sagacious preparations using only fresh ingredients remains. Main courses vary from a much-revered Liberty Ranch duck with blood oranges, braised endive, and lentils; flavorful seafood stew seasoned with saffron and brimful of cracked Dungeness crab, prawns, rockfish, and mussels; and tender braised *osso bucco* with creamy polenta and gremolata. Informal service means you can leave the tie at home. Heat lamps on the front deck allow for open-air evening dining—a treat San Franciscans rarely experience.

3853 Piedmont Ave. (off Broadway between 40th St. and MacArthur Blvd.). © **510/655-6004.** www.baywolf.com. Reservations recommended. Main courses $16.75–$22. AE, MC, V. Mon–Fri 11:30am–2pm and 6–9pm; Sat–Sun 5:30–9:30pm.

Citron ☆☆ FRENCH/MEDITERRANEAN   This petite, adorable French bistro was an instant smash when it first opened in 1992, and it continues to draw raves for its small yet enticingly eclectic menu. Chef Chris Rossi draws the flavors of France, Italy, and Spain together with fresh California produce for Chez Panisse–like results. Although the menu changes every few weeks, dishes range from Sonoma rack of lamb, which is grilled then baked with an aïoli-breadcrumb crust and served atop grilled ratatouille Provencal with waffle-cut potato chips or Spicy Bayou seafood stew brimming with fried oysters, shrimp, snapper, and bell pepper and tomato sauce. The fresh salads and Citron "40 clove" chicken are also superb.

5484 College Ave. (off the northeast end of Broadway between Taft and Lawton Sts.). ℂ 510/653-5484. Reservations recommended. Main courses $18–$28; 3-course fixed-price menu (Sun–Wed only) $26–$32. AE, DC, DISC, MC, V. Mon–Thurs 5:30–9:30pm; Fri 5:30–10pm; Sat 5–10pm; Sun 5–9pm.

Oliveto Cafe & Restaurant ✦✦ ITALIAN   It's been years since Paul Bertolli, former chef at the world-renowned Chez Panisse restaurant, jumped ship to open one of the top Italian restaurants in the Bay Area (certainly the best in Oakland). But time hasn't changed this restaurant's popularity. During the week it's a mad-house at lunchtime, when BART commuters pile in for the wood-fired pizzas and tapas served at the restaurant's lower-level cafe. The upstairs restaurant—suavely bedecked with neo-Florentine decor and a partial open kitchen—is slightly more civil, packed nightly with fans of Bertolli's house-made pastas, sausages, and pro-sciutto. A noteworthy addition include a wood-burning oven, flame-broiled rotisserie from which an assortment of pricey grills, braises, and roasts anchor the daily changing menu. But it's the reasonably priced pastas, pizzetas, and awesome salads that offer the most bang for your buck. *Tip*: There's free parking in the lot at the rear of the Market Hall building.

Rockridge Market Hall, 5655 College Ave. (off the northeast end of Broadway at Shafter/Keith St., across from the Rockridge BART station). ℂ 510/547-5356. Reservations recommended for restaurant. Main courses $16–$30. AE, DC, MC, V. Mon–Fri 11:30am–2pm; Mon–Wed 5:30–9pm; Thurs–Sat 5:30–10pm; Sun 5–9pm.

3 Sausalito

5 miles N of San Francisco

Just off the northern end of the Golden Gate Bridge is the eclectic little town of Sausalito, a slightly bohemian, nonchalant, and studiedly quaint adjunct to San Francisco. With approximately 7,500 residents, Sausalito feels rather like St. Tropez on the French Riviera—minus the starlets and the European aristocracy. It has its quota of paper millionaires, but they rub their permanently suntanned shoulders with a good number of hard-up artists, struggling authors, shipyard workers, and fishers. Next to the swank restaurants, plush bars, and antiques shops and galleries, you'll see hamburger joints, beer parlors, and secondhand bookstores.

Above all, Sausalito has scenery and sunshine, for once you cross the Golden Gate Bridge you're out of the San Francisco fog patch and under blue California sky (we hope). Almost all the tourist action, which is basically limited to window-shopping and eating, takes place at sea level on Bridgeway.

ESSENTIALS

GETTING THERE   The **Golden Gate Ferry Service** fleet, Ferry Building (ℂ 415/923-2000), operates between the San Francisco Ferry Building, at the foot of Market Street, and downtown Sausalito. Service is frequent, departing at reasonable intervals every day of the year except New Year's Day, Thanksgiving Day, and Christmas Day. Phone for an exact schedule. The ride takes a half hour, and one-way fares are $5 for adults; $3.75 for kids 6 to 12; $2.50 for sen-iors and passengers with disabilities; and free for children under 6. Family rates are available on weekends.

Ferries of the **Blue & Gold Fleet** (ℂ 415/705-5555) leave from Pier 41 (Fisherman's Wharf) and cost $12 round-trip; half price for kids 5 to 11. Boats run on a seasonal schedule; phone for departure information.

By car from San Francisco, take U.S. 101 north, then the first right after the Golden Gate Bridge (Alexander exit). Alexander becomes Bridgeway in Sausalito.

EXPLORING THE TOWN

Sausalito is a mecca for shoppers seeking handmade, original, and offbeat clothes and footwear, as well as arts and crafts. The town's best shops are found in the alleys, malls, and second-floor boutiques reached by steep, narrow staircases on and off **Bridgeway,** Sausalito's main touring strip, which runs along the water. Those in the know make a quick detour to **Caledonia Street,** which runs parallel to and 1 block inland from Bridgeway. Not only is it less congested, but there's also a far better selection of cafes and shops.

Bay Model Visitors Center *(Kids)* The U.S. Army Corps of Engineers uses this high-tech, 1¹/₂-acre model of San Francisco's bay and delta to resolve problems and observe the impact changes in water flow will have. The model reproduces (in scale) the rise and fall of tides, the flows and currents of water, and the mixing of fresh water and saltwater, and indicates trends in sediment movement. There's a 10-minute film and a tour, but the most interesting time to visit is when it's in use, so call ahead.

2100 Bridgeway. © **415/332-3871.** Free admission. Labor Day–Memorial Day Tues–Sat 9am–4pm; Memorial Day–Labor Day Tues–Fri 9am–4pm, Sat–Sun and holidays 10am–5pm.

WHERE TO STAY

Casa Madrona *(★★)* Sooner or later most visitors to Sausalito look up and wonder at the ornate mansion on the hill. It's part of Casa Madrona, a hideaway by the bay built in 1885 by a wealthy lumber baron. Successive renovations and extensions have added a rambling, New England–style building to the hillside below the main house. Now a certified historic landmark, the hotel offers rooms, suites, and cottages, which are accessed by steep, gorgeously landscaped pathways. The 16 newest units are each uniquely decorated by different local designers. The "1,000 Cranes" is Asian in theme, with lots of ash wood and lacquer. "Artist's Loft" is reminiscent of a rustic Parisian artist's studio complete with easel and paints. "Summer House" is decked out in white wicker. Other rooms in the mansion are decorated in a variety of styles; some have Jacuzzis, and others have fireplaces. The newest rooms overlook the water with panoramic views of the San Francisco skyline and bay.

801 Bridgeway, Sausalito, CA 94965. © **800/567-9524** or 415/332-0502. Fax 415/332-2537. www. casamadrona.com. 34 units. $188–$275 double; $340 Madrona Villa suite. Rates include breakfast (served 7:30–9:30am). 2-night minimum stay on weekends Oct–Mar, 3-night minimum anytime from Apr–Sept. AE, MC, V. Valet parking $12. Ferry: Walk across the street from the landing. From U.S. 101 north, take the first right after the Golden Gate Bridge (Alexander exit); Alexander becomes Bridgeway. **Amenities:** 1 romantic restaurant, Mikayla, serving great West Coast cuisine with equally impressive bay views; Jacuzzi; concierge; room service (breakfast and dinner); babysitting; laundry service; dry cleaning. *In room:* TV, dataport, minibar, coffeemaker, hair dryer.

The Inn Above Tide *(★★)* Perched directly over the bay atop well-grounded pilings, this former luxury apartment complex underwent a $4-million transformation into one of Sausalito's—if not the Bay Area's—finest accommodations. It's the view that clinches it: Every room comes with an unparalleled panorama of the San Francisco Bay, including a postcard-quality vista of the city glimmering in the distance. Should you manage to tear yourself away from your private deck (I was tempted to drag my mattress outside), you'll find that 22 of the sumptuously appointed rooms sport a romantic little fireplace; some have a vast sunken tub with Jacuzzi jets, remote-control air-conditioning, and wondrously comfortable queen- or king-size beds. Soothing shades of pale green and blue highlight the decor, which blends in well with the bayscape outside. Be sure to request that your breakfast and newspaper be delivered to your deck, and then cancel your early appointments: On sunny mornings, nobody checks out early.

30 El Portal (next to the Sausalito Ferry Landing), Sausalito, CA 94965. ℭ **800/893-8433** or 415/332-9535. Fax 415/332-6714. www.innabovetide.com. 30 units. $235–$600 double. Rates include continental breakfast and evening wine and cheese. 2-night minimum stay on weekends. AE, DC, MC, V. Valet parking $12. **Amenities:** Limited concierge; in-room massage; same-day laundry service and dry cleaning. *In room:* A/C, TV, dataport, minibar, fridge, hair dryer, iron.

WHERE TO DINE

Guernica ✦ FRENCH/BASQUE   Established in 1976, Guernica is one of those funky old kinds of restaurants that you'd probably pass up for something more chic and modern down the street if you didn't know better. What? You don't know about Guernica's legendary Paella Valenciana? Well, now you do, so be sure to call ahead and order it in advance, and bring a partner 'cause it's served for two but will feed three. Begin with an appetizer of artichoke hearts or escargots. Other main courses range from pork loin "New Orleans style" to a hearty Rack of Lamb Guernica. Rich desserts include such in-season specialties as strawberry tart, peach Melba, and Basque-style rice pudding.

2009 Bridgeway. ℭ **415/332-1512.** Reservations recommended. Main courses $11.75–$22. AE, MC, V. Tues–Sun 5–10pm. From U.S. 101 north, take the first right after the Golden Gate Bridge (Alexander exit); Alexander becomes Bridgeway in Sausalito.

Ondine ✦ ASIAN/FRENCH   Sausalito's fanciest restaurant entered the scene in 1999, delighting Marin diners with its stunning bay views and creative fusion cuisine. The East-meets-West delights of Japanese-trained chef Seiji Wakabayashi, who hails from Wolfgang Puck's Spago, can't dissuade your gaze toward the panoramic vista of the Alcatraz, Angel Island, Bay Bridge, and Tiburon. But the view on the plate is worth attention as well. Chef "Waka" takes kung-pao cooking to new heights: His luxurious version includes lobster, shrimp, and squid sausage with peanuts, Thai basil, and chiles. Grilled tuna and rock shrimp risotto goes exotic, with coconut-banana curry sauce. Salmon? Perhaps sesame-crusted and served with ginger-sake beurre blanc. Desserts, also whipped up by Waka, are almost as sweet and decadent as the view.

558 Bridgeway. ℭ **415/331-1133.** www.ondinerestaurant.com. Reservations recommended. Main courses $24–$35. AE, DC, MC, V. Mon–Fri 5:30–10pm; Sat–Sun 5–10pm. Valet parking $4 for the first two hours.

4 Angel Island & Tiburon

8 miles N of San Francisco

A federal and state wildlife refuge, **Angel Island** is the largest of the San Francisco Bay's three islets (the others being Alcatraz and Yerba Buena). The island has been, at various times, a prison, a quarantine station for immigrants, a missile base, and even a favorite site for duels. Nowadays, though, most of the people who visit here are content with picnicking on the large green lawn that fronts the docking area. Loaded with the appropriate recreational supplies, they claim a barbecue, plop their fannies down on the lush green grass, and while away an afternoon free of phones, televisions, and traffic. Hiking, mountain biking, and guided tram tours are also popular activities.

   Tiburon, situated on a peninsula of the same name, looks like a cross between a fishing village and a Hollywood Western set—imagine San Francisco reduced to toy dimensions. This seacoast town rambles over a series of green hills and ends up at a spindly, multicolored pier on the waterfront, like a Fisherman's Wharf in miniature. But in reality, it's an extremely plush patch of yacht-club suburbia, as you'll see by both the marine craft and the homes of their owners. **Main Street** is lined with ramshackle, color-splashed old frame houses that shelter chic boutiques, souvenir stores, antiques shops, and art galleries. Other roads are narrow, winding, and hilly, leading up to dramatically situated homes. The view of San Francisco's skyline and the islands in the bay is a good enough reason to pay the precious price to live here.

ESSENTIALS

GETTING THERE   Ferries of the **Blue & Gold Fleet** (© 415/705-5555) leave from Pier 41 (Fisherman's Wharf) and travel to both Angel Island and Tiburon. Boats run on a seasonal schedule; phone for departure information. The round-trip fare is $10.50 to Angel Island or Tiburon, half price for kids 5 to 11, and free for kids under 5. Catch the **Tiburon–Angel Island Ferry** (© 415/435-2131) to Angel Island from the dock located at Tiburon Boulevard and Main Street. The 15-minute round-trip, which only runs on weekends, costs $5.50 for adults, $4.50 for children 5 to 11, $1 for bikes. One child under 5 is free with each paying adult.

   By car from San Francisco, take U.S. 101 to the Tiburon/Highway 131 exit, then follow Tiburon Boulevard all the way into downtown, a 40-minute drive from San Francisco.

ANGEL ISLAND

Passengers disembark from the ferry at **Ayala Cove,** a small marina abutting a huge lawn area equipped with tables, benches, barbecue pits, and restrooms. Also at Ayala Cove are a small store, gift shop, cafe (with surprisingly good grub), and an overpriced mountain-bike rental shop (helmets included).

   Among the 12 miles of Angel Island's hiking and mountain-bike trails is the **Perimeter Road,** a partly paved path that circles the island and winds its way past disused troop barracks, former gun emplacements, and other military buildings; several turnoffs lead up to the top of Mount Livermore, 776 feet above the bay.

   Sometimes referred to as the "Ellis Island of the West," from 1910 to 1940 Angel Island was used as a holding area for Chinese immigrants awaiting their citizenship papers. You can still see some faded Chinese characters on the walls of the barracks where the immigrants were held. During the warmer months, you can camp at a limited number of sites; reservations are required and can be obtained by calling © **800/444-7275.**

   Also offered at Angel Island are guided **sea-kayak tours.** The all-day trips, which include a catered lunch, combine the thrill of paddling stable one-, two-, or three-person kayaks with an informative, naturalist-led tour that encircles the island (conditions permitting). All equipment is provided, kids are welcome, and no experience is necessary. Rates run about $100 per person; a shorter trip takes 2½ hours and costs $75 per person. For more information, call **Sea Trek** (© **415/332-8494**).

   The most recent tour addition is the 1-hour **Angel Island Tram Tour** (© **925/ 426-3058,** www.angelisland.com), which costs $11.50 for adults, $10.50 for seniors, and $7.50 for children 6 to 12; children under 6 are free. For recorded information on **Angel Island State Park,** call © **415/435-1915.**

TIBURON

The main thing to do in Tiburon is stroll along the waterfront, pop into the stores, and spend an easy $50 on drinks and appetizers before heading back to the city. For a taste of the Wine Country, stop in at **Windsor Vineyards,** 72 Main St. (© **800/214-9463** or 415/435-3113), which has a Victorian tasting room dating back to 1888. Thirty-five choices are available for a free tasting. Wine accessories and gifts—glasses, cork pullers, gourmet sauces, posters, and maps—are also for sale. Carry-packs (which hold six bottles) are available; ask about personalized labels for your own selections. The shop is open Sunday to Thursday from 10am to 6pm and Friday to Saturday until 7pm.

WHERE TO DINE

Guaymas MEXICAN   Guaymas offers authentic Mexican regional cuisine and a spectacular panoramic view of San Francisco and the bay. In good weather, the two outdoor patios are almost always packed with diners soaking in the sun and scene. Inside, colorful Mexican artwork aids the festive scene. Should you feel chilled, to the rear of the dining room is a beehive-shaped adobe fireplace.

Guaymas is named after a fishing village on Mexico's Sea of Cortez, and both the town and the restaurant are famous for their *camarones* (giant shrimp). In addition, the restaurant features ceviche, handmade tamales, and charcoal-grilled beef, seafood, and fowl. Save room for dessert, especially the outrageously scrumptious fritter with "drunken" bananas and ice cream. In addition to a good selection of California wines, the restaurant offers an exceptional variety of tequilas, Mexican beers, and mineral waters flavored with flowers, grains, and fruits.

5 Main St. © 415/435-6300. Reservations recommended. Main courses $12–$20. AE, DC, DISC, MC, V. Mon–Thurs 11:30am–10pm; Fri–Sat 11:30am–11pm; Sun 10:30am–10pm. Ferry: Walk about 10 paces from the landing. From U.S. 101, exit at Tiburon/Hwy. 131; follow Tiburon Blvd. 5 miles and turn right onto Main St. Restaurant is behind the bakery.

Sam's Anchor Café ⊹ *(Finds* SEAFOOD   Summer Sundays are liveliest in Tiburon, when weekend boaters tie up at the docks of waterside restaurants like this one. Sam's is the kind of place where you and your cronies can take off your shoes and have a fun, relaxed time eating burgers and drinking margaritas outside on the pier. The fare is typical—sandwiches, salads, and seafood such as deep-fried oysters—but the quality and selection is inconsequential: beers, burgers, and a designated driver are all you really need.

27 Main St. © 415/435-4527. Main courses $8–$24. AE, DC, DISC, MC, V. Mon–Thurs 11am–10pm; Fri 11am–10:30pm; Sat 10am–10:30pm; Sun 9:30am–10pm. Ferry: Walk from the landing. From U.S. 101, exit at Tiburon/Hwy. 131, follow Tiburon Blvd. 4 miles, and turn right onto Main St.

5 Muir Woods & Mount Tamalpais

12 miles N of the Golden Gate Bridge

While the rest of Marin County's redwood forests were being devoured to feed the building spree in San Francisco around the turn of the century, the trees of Muir Woods, in a remote ravine on the flanks of Mount Tamalpais, escaped destruction in favor of easier pickings.

MUIR WOODS

Although the magnificent California redwoods have been successfully transplanted to five continents, their homeland is a 500-mile strip along the mountainous coast of southwestern Oregon and northern California. The coast redwood, or *Sequoia sempervirens,* is the tallest tree in the immediate region, and the largest-known specimen (located in the Redwood National Forest) towers 367.8 feet. It has an even larger relative, the *Sequoiadendron giganteum* of the California Sierra Nevada, but the coastal variety is stunning enough. Soaring toward the sky like a wooden cathedral, seeing it is an experience you won't soon forget.

Granted, Muir Woods is tiny compared to the Redwood National Forest farther north, but you can still get a pretty good idea of what it must have been like when these redwood giants dominated the entire coastal region. What is truly amazing is that they exist a mere 6 miles (as the crow flies) from San Francisco; close enough, unfortunately, that tour buses arrive in droves on the weekends. You can, however, avoid the masses by hiking up the **Ocean View Trail** and returning via the **Fern Creek Trail**—a moderate hike that shows off the woods' best sides and leaves the tour-bus crowd behind.

To reach Muir Woods from San Francisco, cross the Golden Gate Bridge heading north on U.S. 101, take the Stinson Beach/Calif. 1 exit heading west, and follow the signs (and the traffic). The park is open daily from 8am to sunset; the entrance fee is $2 per person 17 years or older. There's a small gift shop, educational displays, and docent-led tours that you're welcome to stand in on. For more information, call the **Muir Woods information line** (© **415/388-2595**).

If you don't have a car, you can book a bus trip with the **Red & White Fleet,** which takes you straight to Muir Woods via the Golden Gate Bridge, and on the way back makes a short stop in Sausalito. The 3½-hour tours run several times daily and cost $33 for adults, $16 for children 5 though 11, and kids under 5 are free. Call for more information and specific departure times (© **877/855-5506** or 415/447-0597).

MOUNT TAMALPAIS

The birthplace of mountain biking, Mount Tam—as the locals call it—is the Bay Area's favorite outdoor playground and the most dominant mountain in the region. Most every local has his or her secret trail and scenic overlook, as well as an opinion on the dilemma between mountain bikers and hikers (a touchy subject around here). The main trails—mostly fire roads—see a lot of foot and bicycle traffic on the weekends, particularly on clear, sunny days when you can see a hundred miles in all directions, from the foothills of the Sierra to the western horizon. It's a great place to escape from the city for a leisurely hike and to soak in the breathtaking views of the bay.

To get to Mount Tamalpais **by car,** cross the Golden Gate Bridge heading north on U.S. 101 and take the Stinson Beach/Calif. 1 exit. Follow the shoreline highway about 2½ miles and turn onto the Panoramic Highway heading west. After about 5½ miles, turn onto Pantoll Road and continue for about a mile to Ridgecrest Boulevard. Ridgecrest winds to a parking lot below East Peak. From here, it's a 15-minute hike up to the top.

6 Half Moon Bay

28 miles SW of San Francisco

A mere 45-minute drive from the teeming streets of San Francisco is a heavenly little seaside hamlet called Half Moon Bay, one of the finest—and friendliest—small towns on the California coast. While other coastal communities like Bolinas take strides to make tourists unwelcome, Half Moon Bay residents are disarmingly amicable, bestowing greetings on anyone and everyone who stops for a visit.

Only in the last decade has Half Moon Bay begun to capitalize on its golden beaches, mild climate, and close proximity to San Francisco, so you won't find the ultra-touristy machinations that result in gaudy theme parks and time-share condos. What you will find, however, is a peaceful, unfettered slice of textbook California: pristine beaches, redwood forests, nature preserves, rustic fishing harbors, horse ranches, organic farms, and a host of superb inns and restaurants—everything you need for the perfect weekend getaway.

Note: Temperatures rarely venture into the 70s in Half Moon Bay, so be sure to pack for cool (and often wet) weather.

ESSENTIALS

GETTING THERE   There's no public transportation from San Francisco to Half Moon Bay. There are two ways to get here by car: the fast way and the scenic way. To save time, take Calif. 92 west from either I-280 or U.S. 101 out of San Francisco, which will take you over a small mountain range and drop you directly into Half Moon Bay. A better—and far prettier—route is via Calif. 1, which technically starts at the south end of the Golden Gate Bridge and veers southwest to the shoreline a few miles south of Daly City. Both routes to Half Moon Bay are clearly marked with numerous signs, so don't worry about getting lost.

Downtown Half Moon Bay, however, is easy to miss since it's not on Calif. 1, but a few hundred yards inland. Head 2 blocks up Calif. 92 from the Calif. 1 intersection, then turn south at the Shell gas station onto Main Street until you cross a small bridge. For more information, call the **Half Moon Bay Coastside Chamber of Commerce** (© 650/726-8380; www.halfmoonbaychamber.org).

EXPLORING HALF MOON BAY & ENVIRONS

The best things to do in Half Moon Bay are the same things the locals do. For example, there's a wonderful **paved beach trail** that winds 3 miles from Half Moon Bay to picturesque Pillar Point Harbor, where you can watch the trawlers unload their daily catch. Walking, biking, jogging, and skating are all kosher, and be sure to keep a lookout for dolphins and whales. Bicycles can be rented from the **Bicyclery,** 101A & B Main St. (© 650/726-6000), in downtown Half Moon Bay. Prices range from $8 to $12 an hour to $25 to $30 per day.

Half Moon Bay is also known for its organically grown produce, and the best place to stock up on fruits and vegetables is the **Andreotti Family Farm,** 329 Kelly Ave., off Calif. 1 (© 650/726-9461), a charming old-fashioned outfit that's been in business since 1926. Every Friday, Saturday, and Sunday, a member of the Andreotti family slides open the door to their weathered old barn at 10am sharp to reveal a cornucopia of strawberries, artichokes, cucumbers, and more. Head toward the beach and you'll see the barn on your right-hand side. It's open until 6pm year-round.

BEACHES & PRESERVES   The 4-mile arc of golden-colored sand that rings Half Moon Bay is broken up into three state-run beaches—Dunes, Venice, and Francis—all part of **Half Moon Bay State Beach.** There's a $5-per-vehicle entrance fee for all three beaches. Though surfing is allowed, swimming isn't a good idea unless you happen to be cold-blooded.

A few miles farther north on Calif. 1 is the **Fitzgerald Marine Reserve,** one of the most diverse tidal basins on the West Coast, as well as one of the safest, thanks to a wave-buffering rock terrace 50 yards from the beach. Call © 650/728-3584 before coming to find out when it's low tide (all the sea creatures are hidden at high tide) and to get information on the docent-led tour schedules (usually offered on Saturdays). Rubber-soled shoes are recommended. It's located at the west end of California Avenue off Calif. 1 in Moss Beach.

Sixteen miles south of Half Moon Bay on Calif. 1 (at the turnoff to Pescadero) is the **Pescadero Marsh Natural Preserve,** one of the few remaining natural marshes left on the central California coast. Part of the Pacific flyway, it's a resting stop for nearly 200 bird species, including great blue herons that nest in the northern row of eucalyptus trees. Passing through the marsh is the mile-long **Sequoia Audubon Trail,** accessible from the parking lot at Pescadero State Beach on Calif. 1 (the trail starts below the Pescadero Creek Bridge). Docent-led tours take place every Saturday at 10:30am and every Sunday at 1pm, weather permitting.

Starting in December and continuing through March, the **Año Nuevo State Reserve** is home to one of California's most amazing animal attractions: the hallowed breeding grounds of the northern elephant seal. Every winter, people reserve tickets months in advance for a chance to witness a fearsome clash between the 2½-ton bulls over mating privileges among the harems of females. Reservations are required for the 2½-hour naturalist-led tours (held rain or shine December 15 to March 31). For tickets and tour information, call ℂ **800/ 444-4445.** Even if it's not mating season, you can still see the elephant seals lolling around the shore almost year-round, particularly between April and August when they come ashore to molt.

OUTDOOR PURSUITS   One of the most popular activities in town is horseback riding along the beach. **Sea Horse Ranch** (a.k.a. Friendly Acres Horse Ranch), on Calif. 1 a mile north of Half Moon Bay (ℂ **650/726-2362** or 650/726-8550), offers guided and unguided rides along the beach or on well-worn trails for about $40. Hours are daily from 8am to 6pm.

For golfers, there's **Half Moon Bay Golf Links,** 2000 Fairway Dr., at the south end of Half Moon Bay next to the Half Moon Bay Lodge (ℂ **650/ 726-6384**). Designed by Arnold Palmer, the oceanside 18-hole course has been rated among the top 100 courses in the country, as well as the best in the Bay Area. Greens fees range from $132.50 to $153.70. Reserve your tee time as far in advance as possible.

SHOPPING   Main Street is a shopper's paradise. Dozens of small stores and boutiques line the quarter-mile strip, selling everything from feed and tack to custom furniture and camping gear. From north to south, must-see stops include the **Buffalo Shirt Company,** 315 Main St. (ℂ **650/726-3194**), which carries a fine selection of casual wear, Indian rugs, and outdoor gear; **Cartwheels,** 330 Main St. (ℂ **650/726-6060**), a nifty store specializing in rustic wood furniture, rugs, and toys; and **Half Moon Bay Feed & Fuel,** 331 Main St. (ℂ **650/726-4814**), a great place to pick up a treat for your pet.

Cunha's Country Store, 448 Main St. (ℂ **650/726-4071**), the town's beloved grocery and general store, is a mandatory stop for regular visitors from the Bay Area. And, of course, what would Half Moon Bay be without a good bookstore like **Coastside Books,** 432 Main St. (ℂ **650/726-5889**), which also carries a fair selection of children's books and postcards. End your shopping spree with a stop at **Cottage Industries,** 621 Main St. (ℂ **650/712-8078**), to marvel at the high-quality handcrafted furniture.

WHERE TO STAY

Beach House Inn ✿   While the facade has a rather unimaginative Cape Cod look, the rooms at this three-story hotel are surprisingly well designed and decorated with modern prints, stylish furnishings, soothing yellow tones, and spectacular views of the bay and harbor. Every room comes fully loaded with a wood-burning fireplace, king-size bed and sleeper sofa, large bathroom, stereo with CD player, private patio or deck access, two color TVs and a VCR, *four* telephones with dataports and voice mail, and a kitchenette with microwave and fridge. Facilities include a heated pool, oceanview whirlpool, fitness room, and sauna. *Tip:* Opt for one of the corner rooms, which offer a more expansive view for the same price.

4100 N. Cabrillo Hwy. (Hwy. 1), Half Moon Bay, CA 94019. © 800/315-9366 or 650/712-0220. Fax 650/712-0693. www.beach-house.com. 54 units. $199–$350 double. Rates include continental breakfast. AE, DC, DISC, MC, V. From Half Moon Bay, go 3 miles north on Hwy. 1. **Amenities:** Heated outdoor pool; exercise room; oceanview whirlpool; concierge; room service (lunch and dinner); in-room massage; same-day laundry and dry cleaning. *In room:* TV, dataport, kitchenette, minibar, fridge, coffeemaker, hair dryer.

Cypress Inn on Miramar Beach ★★   A favorite place to stay in Half Moon Bay, the Cypress Inn is blissfully free of Victorian charm (nary a lace curtain in *this* joint). Instead you have a modern, artistically designed and decorated building infused with colorful native folk art and rustic furniture made of pine and heavy wicker. Each room has a billowy feather bed, private balcony, gas fireplace, private bathroom, and unobstructed ocean view. Adjacent to the inn are four Beach House rooms equipped with built-in stereo systems and hidden TVs, though they lack the Santa-Fe-meets-California effect that we adore in the main house. The ace in the hole is, however, that it's the only B&B perched right on the beach.

407 Mirada Rd., Half Moon Bay, CA 94019. © 800/83-BEACH or 650/726-6002. Fax 650/712-0380. 12 units. TV. $215–$365 double. Rates include breakfast; tea, wine, and hors d'oeuvres; after-dinner treats. AE, DISC, MC, V. From the junction of Hwys. 92 and 1, go 3 miles north, then turn west and follow Medio to the end; hotel is at Medio and Mirada. **Amenities:** Room service (breakfast only); in-room massage. *In room:* TV, hair dryer; some rooms have coffeemakers, and iron and ironing boards are available on request.

Seal Cove Inn ★★   Before Karen Herbert and her husband, Rick, opened this top-notch B&B, she was the writer and publisher of Karen Brown's Country Inns Series, so you can bet she knows what it takes to create and run a superior bed-and-breakfast. The result is a stately, sophisticated B&B that harmoniously blends California, New England, and European influences in a spectacular setting. All rooms have wood-burning fireplaces, country antiques, original watercolors, grandfather clocks, hidden televisions with VCRs, and refrigerators stocked with free beverages. They overlook distant cypress trees and a colorful half-acre wildflower garden dotted with birdhouses. You'll find coffee and a newspaper outside your door in the morning, brandy and sherry by the living-room fireplace in the evening, and chocolates beside your turned-down bed at night. The ocean is just a short walk away.

221 Cypress Ave., Half Moon Bay, CA 94038. © 650/728-4114. Fax 650/728-4116. www.sealcoveinn.com. 10 units. $200–$300 double. Rates include breakfast, wine, and sherry. AE, DISC, MC, V. The inn is 6 miles north of Half Moon Bay off Hwy. 1; follow signs to Moss Beach Distillery. **Amenities:** Concierge. *In room:* TV, fax, minibar, hair dryer.

WHERE TO DINE

Pasta Moon ★★ ITALIAN   When visitors ask, "Where is the best place to eat around here?" the inevitable answer is Pasta Moon, a handsome nouveau Italian restaurant in downtown Half Moon Bay. It specializes in making everything from scratch and using only the freshest ingredients. Pasta dishes, which are always freshly made and perfectly cooked, earn the highest recommendations. They include house-made linguine with diver sea scallops, anchovies, garlic, chili flakes, and olive oil and penne with spicy lamb sausage with Swiss chard tomato sauce and fresh ricotta cheese. For dessert, try the wonderful tiramisu, with its layers of Marsala-and-espresso–soaked ladyfingers and creamy mascarpone.

315 Main St., Half Moon Bay. ℂ 650/726-5125. Reservations recommended. Main courses $15–$25. AE, DISC, MC, V. Mon–Fri 11:30am–2:30pm; Sat noon–3pm; Sun brunch 11am–2:30pm; Sun–Thurs 5:30–9:30pm; Fri–Sat 5:30–10pm.

7 San Jose

45 miles SE of San Francisco

Some may mourn the San Jose of yesterday, a sleepy small town of orchards, crops, and cattle, but those days are long gone. Founded in 1717 and previously dwelling in the shadows of San Francisco, San Jose is now northern California's largest city. With surveys that declare it one of the safest and sunniest cities in the country and rank it the fifth most popular place to live in America, San Jose is a force to be reckoned with. Today, the prosperity of Silicon Valley has transformed what was once an agricultural backwater into a thriving city of restaurants, shops, a state-of-the-art light-rail system, a sports arena (go Sharks!), and a reputable art scene.

ESSENTIALS

GETTING THERE   BART (ℂ 510/465-2278) travels from San Francisco to Fremont in 1¼ hours; you can take a bus from there. **Cal Train** (ℂ 800/ 660-4287 or 408/271-4980) operates frequently from San Francisco and takes about 1 hour and 25 minutes.

VISITOR INFORMATION   For information, contact the **San Jose Visitors Information & Business Center,** located in the San Jose McEvery Convention Center, 150 W. San Carlos St., San Jose, CA 95113 (ℂ **408/977-0900;** www. sanjose.org).

GETTING AROUND   Light Rail (ℂ **408/321-2300**) is your best option for getting around. A ticket is good for 2 hours and stops include Paramount's Great America, the Convention Center, and downtown museums. Fares are $1.25 for adults, 70¢ for children ages 5 to 17, 40¢ for seniors and disabled, and children age 4 and under ride for free. Or you can use the historic trolleys, which operate in a loop around downtown (in summer only). Tickets can be purchased at Light Rail stations.

MUSEUMS WORTH SEEKING OUT

Children's Discovery Museum *Kids*   Here the kids will find more than 150 interactive exhibits, as well as shows and workshops, which explore science, humanities, arts, and technology. ZoomZone consists of science and art activities designed by kids for kids; Bubbalogna, an exhibit that explores the whimsical and scientifically intriguing world of bubbles, draws rave reviews. Smaller kids enjoy dressing up in costumes and playing on the fire truck.

180 Woz Way. ℂ 408/298-5437. www.cdm.org. Admission $6 adults, $5 for seniors, $6 children 1–17. Tues–Sat 10am–5pm; Sun noon–5pm.

San Jose Historical Museum   Twenty-six original and replica buildings on 25 acres in Kelley Park have been restored to represent life in 1880s San Jose. The usual cast of characters is here—the doctor, the printer, the postmaster— with an occasional local surprise, such as the 1888 Chinese temple and the original Stevens fruit barn.

1650 Senter Rd. ℰ **408/287-2290.** Admission $6 adults, $5 seniors, $4 children 6–17, free for children under 6. Tues–Sun noon–5pm.

San Jose Museum of Art ✸　This contemporary art museum features post-1980 works as well as older contemporary art from its permanent collection. Exhibitions include *Parallels and Intersections: A Remarkable History of Women Artists in California* (from 1950 to 2000), which debuts in July 2002 as well as new media shows and solo exhibitions. The renovated Historic Wing now includes a cafe, bookstore, and education center. Public tours of exhibitions are offered every day at 12:30 and 2:30pm. On the second Saturday of each month at 12:30pm, the public gallery tour is signed for deaf and hearing-impaired visitors. Groups are asked to call and make reservations at least 1 week in advance.

110 S. Market St. ℰ **408/294-2787** or 408/271-6840. www.sjmusart.org. Free admission. Tues–Thurs and Sat–Sun 11am–5pm; Fri 11am–10pm.

Rosicrucian Egyptian Museum & Planetarium　The Rosicrucian is associated with an educational organization that traces its origins back to the ancient Egyptians, who strongly believed in the afterlife and reincarnation. On display are human and animal mummies, funerary boats, and canopic jars, as well as jewelry, pottery, and bronze tools. There's also a replica of a noble Egyptian's tomb. *Note:* At press time, the Planetarium was closed for earthquake renovation; call for more information.

1342 Naglee Ave. ℰ **408/947-3636.** Museum admission $9 adults, $7 seniors, $5 children 5–10, free for children under 5. Tues–Fri 10am–5pm; Sat–Sun 11am–6pm; closed major holidays. Planetarium admission $4 adults, $3 children; call for show times.

Tech Museum of Innovation ✸ *Kids*　Now housed in a 132,000-square-foot facility, the Tech Museum allows visitors to grapple with the latest in modern technology. You can create your own virtual roller-coaster ride, survive an earthquake on a giant shake table, operate an underwater ROV (remotely operated vehicle) à la *Titanic,* and play with tons of other cool high-tech stuff. There's also an IMAX Dome Theater, Jet Pack simulator, and Virtual Bobsled ride, the same used to train Olympic competitors.

201 S. Market St., downtown at the corner of Park and Market Sts. ℰ **408/294-TECH.** www.thetech.org. Admission $8 adults, $7 seniors 65 and over, $6 children 3–12, free for children under 3; additional fee for IMAX shows. Daily 10am–5pm.

THEME PARK THRILLS

Paramount's Great America, Great America Parkway (off U.S. 101), Santa Clara (ℰ **408/988-1776**), provides 100 acres of family entertainment. A pretty cool place to lose your lunch, the park includes such favorites as the *Top Gun* suspended jet coaster, the *Seventh Portal,* a 3-D motion-simulator adventure, a 3-acre Nickelodeon Center for children, "Drop Zone" (the world's tallest free-fall ride), the Xtreme Skyflyer, which combines skydiving with hang gliding, and the new Pyscho Mouse roller coaster and go-carts. Be sure to check for concerts and special events. Admission is $42.99 for adults and children ages 7–17; $36.99 for seniors age 60 and over; and $32.99 for children 3 to 6. Parking is $9 per vehicle. Open Saturday and Sunday from 10am to 8pm from March 15 to May 29; daily from 10am to 10pm from June through August; and Saturday and Sunday from 10am to 9pm from August 30 to October 18. (The park closes earlier than 8pm on weekdays, and the schedule is subject to change due to weather, so be sure to call ahead.) From San Francisco, take U.S. 101 south for about 45 miles to the Great America Parkway exit.

The Winchester Mystery House: A Monument to One Woman's Paranoia

Begun in 1884, the **Winchester Mystery House,** 525 S. Winchester Blvd., at the intersection of I-280 and Hwy. 17, San Jose (© **408/ 247-2101**), is the legacy of Sarah L. Winchester, widow of the son of the famous rifle magnate. After the deaths of her husband and baby daughter, Mrs. Winchester consulted with a seer, who proclaimed that the family had been targeted by the evil spirits of those killed with Winchester repeaters, who would only be appeased by perpetual construction on the Winchester mansion. Convinced that she'd live as long as the building continued, the widow used much of her $20-million inheritance to finance the construction, which went on 24 hours a day, 7 days a week, 365 days a year, for 38 years. (Ricki Lake would love to have her as a guest.)

As you can probably guess, this is no ordinary home. With 160 rooms, it sprawls across a half-dozen acres. And it's full of disturbing features: a staircase leading nowhere, a Tiffany window with a spider's web design, and doors that open onto blank walls. There are 13 bathrooms, 13 windows and doors in the old sewing room, 13 palms lining the main driveway, 13 hooks in the séance room, and chandeliers with 13 lights. Such schemes were designed to confound the spirits that seemed to plague the heiress.

Tours of the house and grounds are $15.95 for adults, $12.95 for seniors age 65 and over, $9.95 for children 6 to 12, and free for kids under 6; a behind-the-scenes tour is also offered for guests over 12. Tours leave about every 20 to 30 minutes and last around 65 minutes. The house is open daily from 9am to 8pm in the summer (winter hours vary; call ahead).

WHERE TO STAY

Fairmont   Ideally situated near the Convention Center and the Center of Performing Arts, this hotel is in a landmark building. A popular spot to have afternoon tea or cocktails, the lobby attracts many who are just passing through. The hotel places an emphasis on comfort: The guest rooms offer many modern features such as fax and high-speed modem lines, while other amenities include 24-hour room service, a concierge, laundry and valet service, and a rooftop pool surrounded by tropical foliage. There are three restaurants. Their most high-end restaurant, The Grill, serves steakhouse cuisine; there's also a Chinese restaurant and a coffee shop that's nicely accented with a massive marble soda fountain.

170 S. Market St., San Jose, CA 95113. © **800/527-4727** or 408/998-1900. Fax 408/287-1648. 541 units. $229–$459 double; $359–$1,800 suite. AE, DC, DISC, MC, V. **Amenities:** 3 restaurants: grill, Chinese, and seasonal cuisine, 1 bar; heated outdoor pool; health club; spa; sauna; concierge; car-rental desk; business center; secretarial services; 24-hour room service; in-room massage; same-day laundry service and dry cleaning. *In room:* A/C, TV w/pay movies (suites have VCR and fax), dataport, minibar, hair dryer, iron.

WHERE TO DINE

Emile's ✦✦ CONTEMPORARY EUROPEAN   The kitchen uses the Bay Area's bounty of local produce to create exceptional contemporary cuisine at

Emile's, a San Jose institution for fine dining for the last 28 years. Mirrors, recessed lighting, and large, bold floral arrangements create an elegant atmosphere. To start, try the seared and peppered Sonoma foie gras with seared apples and arugula salad, or an interesting variation on French onion soup, made with Parmesan and Gruyère cheese. Follow with a roasted pork tenderloin served with toasted pearl couscous, or perhaps the seared salmon with baby artichokes, trumpet mushrooms, and a veal stock reduction. For dessert, go with the warm chocolate truffle cake with raspberry sorbet.

545 S. Second St. ℂ **408/289-1960.** www.emiles.com. Reservations recommended. Main courses $25–$34. AE, DC, DISC, MC, V. Tues–Sat 6:30–10pm.

Paolo's ✮ NORTHERN ITALIAN   Paolo's attracts a business crowd at lunchtime and a rather cultured crowd in the evening. The cuisine is refined northern Italian, with innovative flourishes. Among the appetizers, for instance, the tuna carpaccio with capers, olives, anchovy, sage, basil, and basil oil. The main dishes might include sea scallops baked in foil with romaine lettuce, black truffle, herbs, and pancetta or veal saltimbocca (veal stuffed with sage, fontina, Vald'osta cheese and covered with marsala wine sauce and forest mushrooms). Desserts also stretch beyond the typical Italian favorites to include a chocolate torte with orange-caramel sauce, or semifreddo of cookies and cream with vanilla bean gelato and shaved Italian chocolate. An extensive wine list features more than 600 selections.

333 W. San Carlos St. ℂ **408/294-2558.** Reservations recommended. Main courses $13–$28. AE, DC, DISC, MC, V. Mon–Fri 11am–2:30pm; Mon–Sat 5:30–10pm.

The Wine Country

by Erika Lenkert

California's Napa and Sonoma Valleys are two of the most famous wine-growing regions in the world, and two of our favorite places to visit in the state. The workaday valleys that are a way of life for thousands of vintners are also the ultimate retreat for wine lovers and romantics. Hundreds of wineries are nestled among the vines, and most are open to visitors. But even if you don't want to wine-taste, the fresh country air, beautiful rolling countryside, and world-class restaurants and spas are reasons enough to come. If you can, plan on spending more than a day here; you'll need a couple of days just to get to know one of the valleys. No matter how long you stay, you'll probably never get enough of the Wine Country's romantic, indulgent atmosphere.

While Napa and Sonoma are close to each other (about a half-hour drive apart), each is attraction-packed enough that your best bet is to focus on just one of the valleys, especially if your time is limited. We recommend that you read about each below, then decide which one is right for you—unless, of course, you're lucky enough to have time to explore both.

1 Napa Valley

The most obvious distinction between the two valleys is size—Napa Valley dwarfs Sonoma Valley both in population, number of wineries, and sheer volume of tourism (and in summertime, serious traffic). Napa is definitely the more commercial of the two, with dozens more wineries, spas (some at far cheaper rates), and a far superior selection of fine restaurants, hotels, and quintessential Wine Country activities like hot-air ballooning, all of which are set amidst rolling, mustard flower-covered hills and vast stretches of vineyards. And if your goal is to really learn about the wonderful world of winemaking, world-class wineries such as Sterling and Robert Mondavi offer the most interesting and edifying wine tours in North America, if not the world. The combined attractions make Napa the place to come for the ultimate Wine Country experience.

Napa Valley is relatively condensed. It's just 25 miles long, which means you can venture from one end to the other in less than a half hour (traffic permitting). Conveniently, most of the large wineries—as well as most of the hotels, shops, and restaurants—are located along a single road, Calif. 29, which starts at the mouth of the Napa River, near the north end of San Francisco Bay, and continues north to Calistoga and the top of the growing region. Every Napa Valley town and winery can be reached from this main thoroughfare.

The Ins & Outs of Shipping Wine Home

Perhaps the only thing more complex than that $600 case of cabernet you just purchased are the rules and regulations regarding shipping it home. Due to absurd and forever fluctuating "reciprocity laws"—which were supposedly created to protect the business of the country's wine distributors—wine shipping is limited by state regulations that vary in each of the 50 states. Shipping rules also vary from winery to winery. Hence, depending on which state you live in, sending even a single bottle of wine can be a truly Kafkaesque experience.

To avoid major hassles, do your homework before you buy. Talk to wineries, shipping companies, and the companies below about whether they can ship. Be skeptical of any winery that tells you it can ship to nonreciprocal states—if they run into problems, you'll never get your wine. Find out if you can order the wine on the Internet through a wine e-commerce site. If you have to find a shipping company yourself, keep in mind that it's technically illegal to box your own wine and send it to a nonreciprocal state; the shippers could lose their license, and you could lose your wine. However, if you do get stuck shipping illegally (not that we're recommending you do that), you might want to disguise your box and head to a post office, UPS, or other shipping company outside of the Wine Country area; it's far less obvious that you're shipping wine from, say, Vallejo or San Francisco than from Napa Valley.

Aero Packing, 122 Dodd Court, American Canyon (south of the city of Napa (© **707/554-2088**), will pack and ship wine and insures the first $50 (it's 50¢ extra per $100 beyond the first $50). Ground shipping of one case to Los Angeles is $22.50; to Florida, $54. Currently does not ship to a handful of states, including Kentucky and Utah.

The **St. Helena Mailing Center,** 1241 Adams St., at Highway 29, St. Helena (© **707/963-2686**), tells us that they will pack and ship anywhere in the United States. Rates are around $21 per case for ground delivery to Los Angeles, $66 to New York. While those who live in reciprocal states insure their package for up to $100, the Mailing Center does not insure packages shipped to nonreciprocal states. However, it's no big deal; each bottle is packed in Styrofoam and should make it home without a problem.

Mail Boxes, Etc., 19229 Sonoma Hwy., at Verano Street, Sonoma (© **707/935-3438**), claims it will ship your wine to any state.

The **Wine Exchange of Sonoma,** 452 First St. E., between East Napa and East Spain Streets, Sonoma (© **707/938-1794**), will ship your wine, but you must buy an equal amount of the same wine at the store (which they assured us would be in stock, and probably at a better rate).

ESSENTIALS
GETTING THERE From San Francisco, cross the Golden Gate Bridge and continue north on U.S. 101. Turn east on Calif. 37 (toward Vallejo), then north on Calif. 29, the main road through Napa Valley.

The Wine Country

Arrowood **25**	Gloria Ferrer Champagne Caves **29**	Raymond Vineyard & Cellar **8**
Beaulieu Vineyard **12**	Grgich Hills Cellar **11**	Robert Mondavi Winery **14**
Benziger Family Winery **24**	The Hess Collection **22**	St. Supéry Winery **15**
Beringer Vineyard **5**	Joseph Phelps Vineyards **10**	Schramsberg **3**
Buena Vista Winery **28**	Kenwood Vineyards **23**	Sebastiani Vineyards **27**
Cakebread Cellars **15**	Kunde Estate Winery **23**	Silver Oak **18**
Charles Krug Winery **6**	Niebaum-Coppola **13**	Stag's Leap Wine Cellars **20**
Château St. Jean **23**	Opus One **16**	Sterling Vineyards **2**
Clos Pegase **1**	PlumpJack Winery **17**	Trefethen Vineyards **21**
Domaine Chandon **19**	Prager Wines & Port Works **9**	V. Sattui Winery **7**
Frank Family Vineyards **4**	Ravenswood Winery **26**	Viansa Winery **30**

VISITOR INFORMATION   You can get Wine Country maps and brochures from the **Wine Institute** at 425 Market St., Suite 1000, San Francisco, CA 94105 (℡ **415/512-0151**). Once in Napa Valley, stop first at the **Napa Conference & Visitors Bureau,** 1310 Town Center Mall, Napa, CA 94559 (℡ **707/226-7459**), and pick up the slick *Napa Valley Guide,* or call in advance to order its $10 package, which includes the guide plus a bunch of brochures, a map, *Four Perfect Days in the Wine Country Itinerary,* and hot-air balloon discount coupons. If you want less to recycle, call **Vintage Publications,** 2929 Conifer Court, Napa, CA 94558 (℡ **800/651-8953**), to order just the guide, which costs $6, plus $3 for shipping within the United States. If you don't want to pay the bucks for the official publications, point your browser to **www. napavalley.com/nvcvb.html**, the NVCVB's official site, which has much of the same information for free.

WHEN TO GO   The beauty of the valley is striking any time of the year, but it's most memorable in September and October when the grapes are being pressed and the wineries are in full production. Another great time to come is the spring, when the mustard flowers are in full bloom and the tourist season hasn't yet begun; you'll find less traffic and fewer crowds at the wineries and restaurants, and better deals on hotel rooms. While winter is beautiful and promises the best budget rates, the vines are dormant and rain is likely, so bring appropriate shoes and an umbrella. Summer? Say hello to hot weather and lots of traffic.

TOURING THE VALLEY & WINERIES

The Napa Valley has more than 250 wineries, each offering distinct wines, atmosphere, and experience—so touring the valley takes a little planning. Decide what you're most interested in and chart your path from there. Ask locals which vintners have the type of experience you're looking for. Whatever you do, plan to visit no more than four or five wineries in one day. Above all, take it slowly. The Wine Country should never be rushed; like a great glass of wine, it should be savored.

Most wineries offer tours daily from 10am to 4:30pm. Tours usually chart the process of winemaking from the grafting and harvesting of the vines to the pressing of the grapes and the blending and aging of the wines in oak casks. They vary in length, detail, and formality, depending on the winery. Most tours are free.

The towns and wineries below are organized geographically, from south to north along Calif. 29, from Napa village to Calistoga. We've included a handful of our favorites below; for a complete list of wineries, be sure to pick up one of the free guides to the valley (see "Essentials," above).

THE CITY OF NAPA

The city of Napa serves as the commercial center of the Wine Country and the gateway to Napa Valley. Most visitors whiz right past it on their way the to the heart of the valley, but if you do veer off the highway, you'll be surprised to discover a small but burgeoning community of 63,000 residents and some of the most affordable accommodations in the area. Unfortunately, any small-town charm Napa may exude is all but squelched by the used car lots and warehouse superstores surrounding the turn-of-the-century neighborhoods. Just a few minutes north of town, the quintessential Wine Country atmosphere envelops you instantly.

Tips The World According to Wine

Despite downtown's renovations and restorations, the hottest reason to make a detour into downtown Napa is **COPIA: The American Center for Wine, Food, & the Arts,** 500 First Street (© **707/259-1600;** www.copia. org). Scheduled to open in November 2001, the 12-acre, $70 million project promises to "explore our culture, highlighting American innovations and investigating our distinctive approach to food and drink" through classes, exhibitions, and demonstrations in everything from enology to cuisine and history.

Anyone with an appreciation for art absolutely must visit the **di Rosa Preserve,** which through a private tour explores the collection and 53-acre grounds of Rene and Veronica di Rosa, who have been collecting contemporary American art for more than 40 years. Their world-renowned collection features over 1,500 works in all media by more than 600 Greater Bay Area artists. Their treasures are displayed practically everywhere, from along the shores of their 30-acre lake to each nook and cranny of their century-old winery-turned-residence, adjoining building, two additional galleries, and gardens. It's located at 5200 Sonoma Hwy. (Calif. 121/12). Visits are by appointment only, when a maximum of 25 guests are guided through the preserve. Each tour lasts 2 to 2½ hours and costs $10 per person. Call © **707/226-5991** for reservations.

Antiques hounds should plan to spend at least an hour at **Red Hen's** co-op collection of antiques. You'll find everything from baseball cards to living room sets, and prices are remarkably affordable. You can't miss this enormous red barn–style building at 5091 St. Helena Hwy., on Calif. 29 at Oak Knoll Avenue West (© **707/257-0822**). It's open daily from 10am to 5:30pm.

South of downtown Napa, 1.3 miles east of Calif. 29 on Calif. 12, is the **Chardonnay Golf Club** (© **707/257-8950**), a challenging 36-hole land-links golf complex with first-class service. There are three nines of similar challenge, all starting at the clubhouse so that you can play the 18 of your choice. You pay just one fee, which makes you a member for the day. Privileges include the use of a golf cart, the practice range (including a bucket of balls), and services usually found only at a private club. Starting times can be reserved up to 2 weeks in advance. Greens fees (including mandatory cart and practice balls) are $70 Monday through Friday, $95 weekends and holidays; at 2pm, fees go down to $45 and $60 respectively, and at 4pm they go to $35. Limited space is available to play the private course, which goes for $125 per person.

The Hess Collection ★★ *Finds* No place in the valley brings together art and wine better than this combination winery and art gallery on the side of Mount Veeder. Swiss art collector Donald Hess acquired the old Christian Brothers Winery in 1978; along with producing wine, he also funded a huge restoration and expansion project to honor wine and the fine arts. The result is a working winery interspersed with gloriously lit rooms that exhibit his truly stunning art collection; the free self-guided tour takes you through these galleries as it introduces you to the winemaking process.

For a $3 tasting fee you can sample the winery's current cabernet and chardonnay as well as one other featured wine. If you want to take some with you, by-the-bottle prices start at $9.95 for the second-label Hess select brand, while most other selections range from $15 to $35.

Riding the Napa Valley Wine Train

You don't have to worry about drinking and driving if you tour the Wine Country aboard the **Napa Valley Wine Train,** a rolling restaurant that makes a leisurely 3-hour, 36-mile journey through the vineyards of Napa, Yountville, Oakville, Rutherford, and St. Helena. You'll love riding in the vintage-style cars, each finished with polished mahogany paneling and etched-glass partitions.

During the trip, optional gourmet meals are served complete with all the finery—damask linen, bone china, silver flatware, and etched crystal. The fixed menus consist of three to five courses. In addition to the dining rooms, the train pulls a Wine Tasting Car, a Deli Car, and four 50-passenger lounges. One trip offers an optional stop in Yountville and at the Grgich Winery in Rutherford for a tour of the barreling, bottling, and wine-making process, followed by a tasting.

The train departs from the **McKinstry Street Depot,** 1275 McKinstry St. (near First Street and Soscol Avenue), Napa (© **800/427-4124** or 707/253-2111; www.winetrain.com). Train fare and travel packages range from $29.50 for a daytime ride without a meal to $110 for a multi-course gourmet wine dinner. Departures are Monday through Friday at 11:30am; Saturday, Sunday, and holidays at 9am (brunch) and 12:30pm; Wednesday through Friday and Sunday and holidays at 6:30pm; and Saturday and Sunday at 6pm. (The schedule is reduced in January and February.) *Tip:* Sit on the west side for the best views. Fair warning: Photos are taken before you board (to be sold to you later), so if you want this moment captured on film, be prepared.

4411 Redwood Rd., Napa. © **707/255-1144.** www.hesscollection.com. Daily 10am–4pm. Closed first week of January. From Hwy. 29 north, exit at Redwood Rd. west and follow Redwood Rd. for 6½ miles.

Trefethen Vineyards   Listed on the National Register of Historic Places, the vineyard's main building was constructed in 1886 and remains Napa's only wooden, gravity-powered winery. The bucolic brick courtyard is surrounded by oak and cork trees, and free wine samples are distributed in the brick-floored, wood-beamed tasting room. Although Trefethen is one of the valley's oldest wineries, it did not produce its first chardonnay until 1973—but thank goodness it did. Its whites and reds are both award winners and a pleasure to the palate.

1160 Oak Knoll Ave. (east of Hwy. 29), Napa. © **707/255-7700.** www.trefethen.com. Daily 10am–4:30pm. Tours by appointment only.

Stag's Leap Wine Cellars   Founded in 1972, Stag's Leap shocked the oeno-logical world in 1976 when its 1973 cabernet won first place over French wines in a Parisian blind tasting. For $5 per person, you can be the judge of the winery's current releases, or you can fork over another fiver for one of Stag's Leap's best-known wines, Cabernet Sauvignon Cask 23 (when available). The 1-hour tour runs through everything from the vineyard to production facilities and ends with a tasting; by the time you visit, it could also include their new caves, which premiered in mid-2001, and ends with a tasting.

YOUNTVILLE

The town of Yountville was founded by the first white American to settle in the valley, George Calvert Yount. While it lacks the small-town charm of neighboring St. Helena and Calistoga—primarily because it has no rambunctious main street—it does serve as a good base for exploring the valley, and it's home to a handful of excellent wineries, inns, boutiques, and a small stretch of fab restaurants, including world-renowned The French Laundry.

Domaine Chandon ★★ *Finds*   The valley's most renowned sparkling winery was founded in 1973 by French champagne house Moët et Chandon. The grounds suit Domaine Chandon's reputation perfectly—this is the kind of place where the world's wealthy might stroll the beautifully manicured gardens under the shade of a delicate parasol, stop at the outdoor patio for sips of the famous sparkling wine, then glide into the dining room for a world-class luncheon.

Bubbly is sold by the glass ($8 to $12) and served with complimentary bread and spread. The comprehensive tour of the facilities is worth the time. In addition to a shop, there's a small gallery housing artifacts from Moët et Chandon that depict the history of champagnes and revolving art exhibits (available for purchase), which in 2001 included watercolor works of French artist Guy Buffet, and an impressive and formal French-inspired restaurant, which tends to require reservations.

1 California Dr. (at Hwy. 29), Yountville. ℂ **707/944-2280.** www.chandonusa.com. Jan–Mar Wed–Sun 10am–6pm; Apr–Dec daily 10am–6pm. Free tours every hour on the hour from 11am to 5pm; no reservations necessary.

OAKVILLE

Driving farther north on the St. Helena Highway (Calif. 29) brings you to the Oakville Cross Road and the famous picnic-fare favorite **Oakville Grocery Co.** (see " Gourmet Picnics, Napa Style," later in this chapter).

Robert Mondavi Winery ★ *Finds*   At Mondavi's magnificent mission-style facility, almost every variable in the wine-making process is controlled by computer (fascinating to watch!). After the tour, you can taste the results in selected current wines, free of charge, but anyone really interested in learning more about wine should explore their extensive array of more in-depth tours and tastings offered for a fee and by appointment. You can also taste without taking the tour, but it will cost you: The Rose Garden (an outdoor tasting area open in summer) offers an etched Reidel glass and three wines for $10; tastings in the ToKalon Room go from $3 for a 3-ounce taste to $25 for a rare library wine.

Fridays feature an "Art of Wine and Food" program, which includes a slide presentation on wine history, a tour, and a three-course luncheon with wine pairing; the cost is around $65, and you must reserve in advance. The Vineyard Room usually features an art show; in summer, the winery also hosts some great outdoor jazz concerts. Call to learn about upcoming events.

7801 St. Helena Hwy. (Hwy. 29), Oakville. ℂ **800/MONDAVI** or 707/226-1395. www.robertmondaviwinery. com. May–Oct daily 9:30am–5:30pm; Nov–Apr daily 9:30am–4:30pm. Reservations recommended for guided tour; book 1 week ahead, especially for weekend tours.

Opus One   A visit to Opus One is a very serious and stately affair. Robert Mondavi and Baroness Phillipe de Rothschild are to thank for this winery, which caters to one ultra-premium wine offered here for a whopping $25 per 4-ounce taste (and a painful $140 per bottle). Architecture buffs in particular will appreciate the tour, which takes in both the impressive

Hot-Air Ballooning over the Valley

Admit it—floating across lush green pastures in a hot-air balloon is something you've always dreamed of doing. Well, here's your chance, because believe it or not, Napa Valley is the busiest hot-air balloon "flight corridor" in the *world*. Northern California's temperate weather allows for ballooning year-round, and on summer weekends in the valley, it's a rare day when you don't see at least one of the colorful airships floating above the vineyards.

Trips usually depart early in the morning, when the air is cooler and the balloons have better lift. (*Note:* When weather conditions aren't optimal, balloon companies often launch flights from locations up to an hour's drive outside of the valley. You won't know until the morning of the flight, but you should be able to cancel on the spot if you desire.) Flight paths vary with the direction and speed of the changing breezes, so "chase" crews on the ground must follow the balloons to their undetermined destinations. Most flights last about an hour and end with a traditional champagne celebration and breakfast. Reservations are required and should be made far in advance. Prices range from $165 to $195 per person for the basic package, which includes shuttle service from your hotel. Wedding, wine tasting, picnic, and lodging packages are also available. For more information or reservations, call Napa's **Bonaventura Balloon Company** (© **800/FLY-NAPA**), a highly reputable organization owned and operated by master pilot Joyce Bowen.

Greco-Roman-meets-20th-century building and the no-holds-barred ultra-high-tech production and aging facilities.

Wine lovers happily fork over the cash for a taste: It's likely to be one of the most memorable reds you'll ever sample. Grab your glass and head to the redwood rooftop deck to enjoy the view—definitely the most kicked-back spot in the whole place!

7900 St. Helena Hwy. (Hwy. 29), Oakville. © 707/944-9442. www.opusonewinery.com. Daily 10:30am–3:30pm. Tours by appointment only; in high season, book a month in advance.

RUTHERFORD

If you so much as blink after Oakville, you're likely to overlook Rutherford, the next small town that borders on St. Helena. Rutherford has its share of spectacular wineries, but you won't see most of them while driving along Calif. 29.

Silver Oak Cellars   Twenty-five years ago, an oil man from Colorado, Ray Duncan, and a former Christian Brothers monk, Justin Meyer, formed a partnership and a mission to create the finest cabernet sauvignon in the world. "We still haven't produced the best bottle of cabernet sauvignon of which Silver Oak is capable," admits Meyer, but this small winery is still the Wine Country's undisputed king of cabernet.

A narrow tree-lined road leads to the handsome Mediterranean-style winery, where roughly 40,000 cases of 100% varietal cab are produced annually. (An additional 10,000 cases are produced annually from their Alexander Valley winery in Geyserville.) The elegant tasting room is refreshingly quiet and soothing, adorned with redwood panels stripped from old wine tanks and warmed by a wood fire. Tastings and tours are $10, which includes a beautiful German-made burgundy glass. At press time, only two wines were released: a 1996 Alexander Valley and a 1995 Napa Valley. If the $50- and $80-per-bottle price tags are a bit much, for half the price you can take home one of the winery's non-cab releases—a velvety Meyer Family Port.

915 Oakville Cross Rd. (at Money Rd.), Oakville. *C* **707/944-8808**. www.silveroak.com. Tasting room Mon–Sat 9am–4pm. Tours Mon–Fri at 1:30pm, by appointment only.

PlumpJack Winery If most wineries are like a traditional and refined Brooks Brothers suit, PlumpJack stands out as the Todd Oldham of wine tasting: chic, colorful, a little wild, and popular with a young and old crowd. Like the franchise's PlumpJack restaurant and wine shop in San Francisco and its resort in Tahoe, this playfully medieval winery is a welcome diversion from the same old, same old. But with Getty bucks behind what was once Villa Mt. Eden winery, the budget covers far more than just atmosphere: There's some serious wine-making going on here, too. For $5 you can sample the cabernet, sangiovese, and chardonnay—each an impressive product from a winery that's only been open to the public since mid-1997. The few vintages for sale currently range from $28 to $50. There are no tours or picnic spots, but this refreshingly stylized and friendly facility will make you want to hang out for a while nonetheless.

620 Oakville Cross Rd. (just west of the Silverado Trail), Oakville. *C* **707/945-1220**. www.plumpjack.com. Daily 10am–4pm.

Cakebread Cellars This winery's moniker is actually the owners' surname, but it suits the wines produced here, where the focus is on making wine that pairs well with food. They've done such a good job that a majority of their 85,000 annual cases go directly to restaurants, which means only a select few wine drinkers get to take home a bottle. Even if you've found their label in your local wine store, your choice has been limited: Just three varieties are distributed nationally. Here you can sample the sauvignon blanc, chardonnay, cabernet, and merlot, most of which are made from Napa Valley grapes. Prices range from an affordable $15.25 for a bottle of the 1999 sauvignon blanc to a pricey $85 for the 1995 reserve cab, but the average bottle sells for just a little more than $20. In the tasting room, a large barnlike space, the hospitable hosts pour either a $5 or $10 sampling; both include a keepsake wineglass.

8300 St. Helena Hwy. (Hwy. 29), Rutherford. *C* **800/588-0298** or 707/963-5221. www.cakebread.com. Daily 10am–4:30pm. Tours by appointment only.

St. Supéry Winery The outside may look like a modern corporate office building, but inside you'll find a functional and welcoming winery that encourages first-time wine tasters to learn more about oenology. On the self-guided tour, you can wander through the demonstration vineyard and learn about growing techniques. Inside, kids gravitate toward "SmellaVision," an interactive display that teaches you how to identify different wine ingredients. Adjoining is the Atkinson House, which chronicles more than 100 years of winemaking history. For $5 you'll get lifetime tasting privileges, and though they probably won't be pouring their ever-popular Moscato dessert wine, the sauvignon blanc, chardonnay, and cab flow freely. Even the prices make visitors feel at home: Many bottles go for around $15, although the 1997 Dollarhide Ranch cabernet will set you back $70.

8440 St. Helena Hwy. (Hwy. 29), Rutherford. © **800/942-0809** or 707/963-4507. www.stsupery.com. Daily 9:30am–5pm (until 6pm during summer). Tours three times daily.

Niebaum-Coppola ★ *Finds* Hollywood meets Napa Valley at Francis Ford Coppola's historic winery (pronounced *nee*-bomb *coh*-pa-la), previously Inglenook Vineyards. Coppola bought and restored the beautiful 1880s ivy-draped stone winery and surrounding property to its historic dimensions, gilding it with the glitz and glamour you'd expect from Tinseltown in the process. On display are Academy Awards and memorabilia from his movies.

In spite of all the Hollywood hullabaloo, wine is not forgotten. Available for tasting are a Rubicon (a blend of three grapes, aged for more than 5 years), cabernet franc, merlot, chardonnay, zinfandel, and others, all made from organically grown grapes and ranging from around $12 to more than $80. There's also a wide variety of expensive and affordable gift items. The steep $7.50-per-person tasting fee might make you wonder whether a movie is included in the price—it's not, but you'll at least get to keep the souvenir glass. And at $20 a pop for the château and garden tour, you've gotta wonder whether you're *funding* his next film. But the grounds are indeed spectacular, and the 1½-hour journey includes a private tasting and glass.

Regardless, do visit the grounds—they're absolutely stunning, it costs nothing to stroll, and you're welcome to picnic at any of the designated garden sites.

1991 St. Helena Hwy. (Hwy. 29), Rutherford. © **707/968-1100.** www.niebaum-coppola.com. Daily 10am–5pm (until 6pm Memorial Day–Labor Day). Tours daily at 10:30am and 2:30pm.

Beaulieu Vineyard Bordeaux native Georges de Latour founded the third-oldest continuously operating winery in Napa Valley in 1900—and, with the help of legendary oenologist André Tchelistcheff, produced world-class, award-winning wines that have been served by every president of the United States since Franklin D. Roosevelt. The brick-and-redwood tasting room isn't much to look at, but with Beaulieu's (pronounced *bowl*-you) stellar reputation, they have no need to impress visually. They do, however, offer tastings for $5 as well as a variety of bottles under $20. The Private Reserve Tasting Room offers a "flight" of reserve wines to taste for $25—but if you want to take a bottle to go, it may cost as much as $130. A free tour explains the winemaking process and the vineyard's history. No reservations are necessary.

1960 St. Helena Hwy. (Hwy. 29), Rutherford. © **707/967-5230.** www.bvwine.com. Daily 10am–5pm. Tours daily 11am–4pm.

Grgich Hills Cellar Yugoslavian émigré Miljenko (Mike) Grgich made his presence known to the world when his Château Montelena chardonnay bested the top French white burgundies at the famous 1976 Paris tasting. Since then, this master vintner has teamed up with Austin Hills (of the Hills Brothers coffee fortune) and started this extremely successful and respected winery in Rutherford.

The ivy-covered stucco building isn't much to behold, and the tasting room is even less appealing, but people don't come here for the scenery: As you might expect, Grgich's (pronounced *grr*-gitch) chardonnays are legendary—and priced accordingly. The smart buys, however, are Grgich's outstanding zinfandel and cabernet sauvignon, which are priced at around $23 and $50, respectively. The winery also produces a fantastic fumé blanc for as little as $18 a bottle. Before you leave, be sure to poke your head into the barrel-aging room and inhale the divine aroma. Tastings cost $5 on weekends, which includes the glass, and are free on weekdays.

1829 St. Helena Hwy. (Hwy. 29), north of Rutherford Cross Rd., Rutherford. ℭ **707/963-2784.** www.grgich. com. Daily 9:30am–4:30pm. Free tours by appointment only, Mon–Fri 11am and 2pm, Sat–Sun 11am and 1:30pm.

ST. HELENA

This quiet, attractive little town, located 17 miles north of Napa on Calif. 29, is home to a slew of beautiful old homes as well as first-rate restaurants and accommodations. The former Seventh Day Adventist village manages to maintain a pseudo–Old West feel while simultaneously catering to upscale shoppers with deep pockets—hence **Vanderbilt and Company,** 1429 Main St., between Adams and Pine Streets (ℭ **707/963-1010**), purveyor of gorgeous cookware and fine housewares; open daily from 9:30am to 5:30pm.

Shopaholics won't be able to avoid at least one sharp turn off Calif. 29 for a stop at the **St. Helena Premium Outlets,** located 2 miles north of downtown St. Helena (ℭ **707/963-7282**), whose stores include Donna Karan, Coach, Movado, London Fog, and more; open daily from 10am to 6pm.

One last favorite stop: **Napa Valley Olive Oil Manufacturing Company,** 835 Charter Oak Rd., at the end of the road behind Tra Vigne restaurant (ℭ **707/963-4173**). This tiny market presses and bottles its own oils and sells them at a fraction of the price you'll pay elsewhere. They also have an extensive selection of Italian cooking ingredients, imported snacks, and excellent deals on exotic mushrooms.

If you'd like to go **bicycling,** the quieter northern end of the valley is an ideal place to rent a bike and ride the Silverado Trail. **St. Helena Cyclery,** 1156 Main St. (ℭ **707/963-7736**), rents bikes for $7 per hour or $25 a day, including rear rack and picnic bag.

Raymond Vineyard & Cellar As fourth-generation vintners from Napa Valley and relations of the Beringers, brothers Walter and Roy Raymond have had plenty of time to develop terrific wines and an excellent wine-tasting experience. The short drive through vineyards to reach Raymond's friendly, unintimidating cellar is case in point: Passing the heavy-hanging grapes makes you feel you're really in the thick of things. Then comes the spacious, warm room, complete with dining table and chairs—a perfect setting for sampling the four tiers of wines, most of which are free for the tasting and well priced to appeal to all levels of wine drinkers: The Amber Hill label starts at $8 a bottle for the chardonnay and $11 for the cab; the reserves are priced in the low $30s, while the "Generations" cab costs $60. The winery has a great gift selection, which includes barbecue sauces, mustard, a chocolate wine syrup, and a gooey hazelnut merlot fudge sauce. Private reserve tastings cost $2.50.

849 Zinfandel Lane (off Hwy. 29 or the Silverado Trail), St. Helena. ℭ **800/525-2659** or 707/963-3141. www. raymondwine.com. Daily 10am–4pm. Tours by appointment only.

V. Sattui Winery *(Kids)* At this combination winery and enormous gourmet deli (pronounced vee sa-*too*-ee), you can fill up on wine, pâté, and cheese samples without ever reaching for your pocketbook. The gourmet store stocks more than 200 cheeses, sandwich meats, breads, exotic salads, and delicious desserts, such as a white chocolate cheesecake.

Meanwhile, the long wine bar in the back offers everything from chardonnay, sauvignon blanc, Riesling, cabernet, and zinfandel to a tasty Madeira and a muscat dessert wine. Their wines aren't distributed, so if you taste something you simply must have, buy it. (If you buy a case, ask to talk with a manager, who'll give you access to the less crowded, more exclusive private tasting room.)

Wine prices start around $9, with many in the $13 range; reserves top out at around $75. V. Sattui's expansive, lively, and grassy picnic facilities make this a favorite for families. *Note:* To use the facilities, food and wine must be purchased here.

1111 White Lane (at Hwy. 29), St. Helena. ℂ 707/963-7774. www.vsattui.com. Winter daily 9am–5pm; summer daily 9am–6pm.

Joseph Phelps Vineyards ★ Visitors interested in intimate, comprehensive tours and a knockout tasting should schedule a tour at this stellar winery. The winery was founded in 1973 and has since become a major player in both the region and the worldwide wine market. Phelps himself is attributed with a long list of valley firsts, including launching the syrah varietal in the valley and extending the 1970s Berkeley food revolution (led by Alice Waters) up to the Wine Country via his store, the Oakville Grocery Co. (see "Gourmet Picnics, Napa Style," later in this chapter). The tour and tasting are only available via reservation, and the location—a quick and unmarked turn off the Silverado Trail in Spring Valley—is impossible to find unless you're looking for it.

Those in the know come to this modern, state-of-the-art winery and find an air of seriousness that hangs heavier than harvest grapes. Fortunately, the mood lightens as the well-educated tour guide explains the details of what you're tasting while pouring samples of five to six wines, which may include Riesling, sauvignon blanc, gewürztraminer, syrah, merlot, zin, and cab. Unfortunately, some wines are so popular that they sell out quickly; come late in the season and you may not be able to taste or buy them. The three excellently located picnic tables, on the terrace overlooking the valley, are available by reservation.

Taplin Rd. (off the Silverado Trail), P.O. Box 1031, St. Helena. ℂ 800/707-5789. www.jpvwines.com. Mon–Sat 9am–5pm; Sun 9am–4pm. Tours and tastings by appointment only; tasting $5 per person, $10 per person for reserve tastings.

Prager Winery & Port Works If you want a real down-home, off-the-beaten-track experience, Prager's can't be beat. Turn the corner from Sutter Home and roll into the small gravel parking lot. Pull open the creaky old wooden door, pass the oak barrels, and you'll quickly come upon the clapboard tasting room. Most days, your host will be Jim Prager himself, who's a sort of modern-day Santa Claus in both looks and demeanor, but you won't have to sit on his lap for your wish to come true. Just fork over $5 (refundable with purchase) and he'll pour you samples of his delicious $25 Sweet Claire dessert wine, a late-harvest Johannisberg Riesling, the recently released 10-year-old port (which costs $45 per bottle and has won various awards), and a few other yummy selections. Also available is "Prager Chocolate Drizzle," a chocolate liqueur that tops ice creams and other desserts.

1281 Lewelling Lane (just west of Hwy. 29, behind Sutter Home), St. Helena. ℂ 800/969-PORT or 707/963-7678. www.pragerport.com. Daily 10:30am–4:30pm.

Beringer Vineyards Follow the line of cars just north of St. Helena's business district to Beringer Vineyards, where everyone stops at the remarkable Rhine House to taste wine and view the hand-dug tunnels carved out of the mountainside. Founded in 1876 by brothers Jacob and Frederick, this is the oldest continuously operating winery in the Napa Valley—it was open even during Prohibition, when Beringer kept afloat by making "sacramental" wines. While their white zinfandel is still the winery's most popular nationwide seller, their reserve chardonnay is regularly high-ranked among top California wines. Three-dollar tastings of current vintages are soon to be conducted in new facilities, but for now are held in the gift shop, where there's also a large selection of bottles for less than $20. Reserve wines are available on the second floor of the Rhine House for a fee of $2 to $10 per taste.

2000 Main St. (Hwy. 29), St. Helena. ℭ 707/963-7115. www.beringervineyards.com. Off-season daily 9:30am–5pm (last tour 4pm, last tasting 4:30pm); summer 9:30am–6pm (last tour 5pm, last tasting 5:30pm). $5 45-min. tours every 30 min. (free for anyone under 21 and accompanied by an adult); no reservations necessary.

Charles Krug Winery   Founded in 1861, Krug was the first winery built in the valley and is today owned by the family of Peter Mondavi (yes, Robert is his brother). It's worth paying your respects here with a $3 tour, which takes just under an hour and encompasses a walk through the historical redwood Italianate wine cellar, built in 1874, as well as the vineyards, where you'll learn more about grapes and varietals. The tour ends with a tasting in the retail center. But you don't have to tour to taste: Just stop by and fork over $3 to sip current releases, $5 to sample reserves; you'll also get a souvenir glass. On the grounds are picnic facilities with umbrella-shaded tables overlooking vineyards or the historic wine cellar. At press time tours were not being given due to renovations, so call to confirm before arriving for a tour.

2800 St. Helena Hwy. (just north of the tunnel of trees at the northern end of St. Helena), St. Helena. ℭ 707/963-5057. www.charleskrugwinery.com. Daily 10:30am–5pm. Tours daily at 11:30am, 1:30, and 3:30pm.

CALISTOGA

The last tourist town in Napa Valley was named by Sam Brannan, entrepreneur extraordinaire and California's first millionaire. After making a bundle supplying miners during the gold rush, he went on to take advantage of the natural geothermal springs at the north end of the Napa Valley by building a hotel and spa here in 1859. Flubbing up a speech in which he compared this natural California wonder to New York State's Saratoga Springs resort, he serendipitously coined the name "Calistoga," and it stuck. Today, this small, simple resort town with 4,700-plus residents and an old-time main street (no building along the 6-block stretch is more than two stories high) is popular with city folk who come here to unwind. Calistoga is a great place to relax and indulge in mineral waters, mud baths, Jacuzzis, massages, and, of course, wine. The vibe is more casual—and a little groovier—than you'll find in neighboring towns to the south.

Old Faithful Geyser of California, 1299 Tubbs Lane (ℭ 707/942-6463), is one of only three "old faithful" geysers in the world. It's been blowing off steam at regular intervals for as long as anyone can remember. The 350°F water spews out to a height of about 60 feet every 40 minutes, day and night (varying with natural influences such as barometric pressure, the moon, tides, and tectonic stresses). The performance lasts about a minute, and you can watch the show as many times as you wish. Bring along a picnic lunch to munch on between spews. An exhibit hall, gift shop, and snack bar are open every day. Admission is $6 for adults, $5 for seniors, $2 for children ages 6 to 12, and free for children under 6. Open daily from 9am to 6pm (to 5pm in winter). To get here, follow the signs from downtown Calistoga; it's between Calif. 29 and Calif. 128.

You won't see thousands of trees turned into stone, but you'll still find many interesting petrified specimens at the **Petrified Forest,** 4100 Petrified Forest Rd. (ℭ 707/942-6667). Volcanic ash blanketed this area after the eruption of Mount St. Helena three million years ago. As a result, you'll find redwoods that have turned to rock through the slow infiltration of silicas and other minerals, as well as petrified seashells, clams, and marine life indicating that water covered this area even before the redwood forest. Admission is $5 for adults, $4 for seniors and children 11 to 17, $2 for children ages 4 to 11, and free for children under 4. Open daily from 10am to 5:30pm (to 4:30pm in winter). Heading north from Calistoga on Calif. 128, turn left onto Petrified Forest Road, just past Lincoln Street.

Cycling enthusiasts can rent bikes from **Getaway Adventures BHK** (Biking, Hiking, and Kayaking), 1117 Lincoln Ave. (✆ **800/499-BIKE** or 707/763-3040; www.getawayadventures.com). Full-day tours cost $105 and include lunch and a visit to four or five wineries; downhill cruises (about half the price) are available for people who hate to pedal. Bike rental without a tour costs $9 an hour, $20 per half day, or $28 per day.

If you like horses and venturing through cool, misty forests, then $40 will seem like a bargain for a 1½-hour ride with a friendly tour guide from **Napa Valley Trail Rides** (✆ **707/996-8566;** www.napasonomatrailrides.com). After you've been saddled and schooled in the basics of horse handling at the stable, you'll be led on a leisurely stroll (with the occasional trot thrown in for excitement) through beautiful Bothe–Napa Valley State Park, located off Calif. 29 near Calistoga. Also offered are a Western Barbecue Ride, Sunset Ride, Full Moon Ride, and Gourmet Boxed Lunch Ride & Winery Tour.

Frank Family Vineyards (aka Kornell) "Wine dudes" Bob, Danny, Dennis, and Rich will do practically anything to maintain their self-proclaimed reputation as the "friendliest winery in the valley." They'll serve you all the bubbly you want (four to six varieties: brut, blanc de blanc, blanc de noir, and extra-dry reserve, all ranging from $20 to $70 a bottle). They guarantee that you'll never wait more than 10 minutes to take the free 20-minute tour of the oldest champagne cellar in the region, and even offer up a great story about Marie Antoinette's champagne-glass design.

The tasting room is casual-modern, but the stone cellar (listed on the National Register of Historic Places) captures the essence of the Wine Country's history. Meander into the Back Room, where chardonnay, zinfandel, and cabernet are poured. Behind the tasting room is a choice picnic area, situated under the oaks and overlooking the vineyards.

1091 Larkmead Lane (just off the Silverado Trail), Calistoga. ✆ **707/942-0859.** Daily 10am–5pm; tours by appointment.

Schramsberg *Finds* This 200-acre champagne estate, a landmark once frequented by Robert Louis Stevenson, has a wonderful old-world feel and is one of our all-time favorite places to explore. Schramsberg is the label that presidents serve when toasting dignitaries from around the globe, and there's plenty of historic memorabilia in the front room to prove it. But the real mystique begins when you enter the champagne caves, which wind 2½ miles (the longest in North America, they say) and were partly hand-carved by Chinese laborers in the 1800s. The caves have an authentic Tom Sawyer ambiance, complete with dangling cobwebs and seemingly endless passageways; you can't help but feel you're on an adventure. The comprehensive, unintimidating tour ends in a charming tasting room, where you'll sit around a big table and sample several surprisingly varied selections of bubbly. Tasting prices are a bit dear at $10 per person, but it's money well spent. Note, however, that tastings are only offered to those who take the free tour, and you must reserve a spot in advance.

1400 Schramsberg Rd. (off Hwy. 29), Calistoga. ✆ **707/942-2414.** www.schramsberg.com. Daily 10am–4pm. Tours and tastings by appointment only.

Find the New You—in a Calistoga Mud Bath

The one thing you should do while you're in Calistoga is what people have been doing here for the last 150 years: Take a mud bath. The natural baths are composed of local volcanic ash, imported peat, and naturally boiling mineral hot-springs water, all mulled together to produce a thick mud that simmers at a temperature of about 104°F. Follow your soak in the mud with a warm mineral-water shower, a whirlpool bath, a visit to the steam room, and a relaxing blanket-wrap. The outcome: a rejuvenated, revitalized, squeaky-clean new you.

Indulge yourself at any of these Calistoga spas: **Dr. Wilkinson's Hot Springs,** 1507 Lincoln Ave. (© 707/942-4102); **Golden Haven Hot Springs Spa,** 1713 Lake St. (© 707/942-6793); **Calistoga Spa Hot Springs,** 1006 Washington St. (© 707/942-6269); **Calistoga Village Inn & Spa,** 1880 Lincoln Ave. (© 707/942-0991); **Indian Springs Resort,** 1712 Lincoln Ave. (© 707/942-4913); **Nance's Hot Springs,** 1614 Lincoln Ave. (© 707/ 942-6211); or **Roman Spa Motel,** 1300 Washington St. (© 707/942-4441).

Clos Pegase *(Finds)* Renowned architect Michael Graves designed this incredible oasis, which integrates art, 20,000 square feet of aging caves, and a luxurious hilltop private home on its 450 acres. Viewing the art here is as much the point as tasting the wines, which cost $2.50 to $5 per three premium wines. Bottles cost from $13 for the 2000 Vin Gris Merlot to as much as $75 for the 1997 Hommage Artist Series Reserve, an extremely limited blend of the winery's finest lots of cabernet sauvignon and merlot. The grounds at Clos Pegase (pronounced *clo* pay-*goss*) feature an impressive sculpture garden as well as scenic picnic spots.

1060 Dunaweal Lane (off Hwy. 29 or the Silverado Trail), Calistoga. © **707/942-4981.** www.clospegase. com. Daily 10:30am–5pm. Tours daily at 11am and 2pm with no reservation necessary.

Sterling Vineyards *(Kids)* No, you don't need climbing shoes to reach this dazzling white Mediterranean-style winery, perched 300 feet up on a rocky knoll. Just hand over $6 and you'll arrive via aerial tram, which offers dazzling bucolic views along the way. If you've been here before, even before embarking you'll notice major changes due to a complete renovation in 2001. Once you're back on land, follow the self-guided tour (the most comprehensive in the entire Wine Country) of the winemaking process. The winery produces more than 200,000 cases per year. If you're not into taking the tram or you have kids in tow, visit anyway; there's an elevator that can take you to the tasting room and kids get a goodie bag and a hearty welcome (a rarity at wineries). Samples at the panoramic tasting room are included in the tram fare. Expect to pay anywhere from $10 to $60 for a souvenir bottle ($20 is the average)

1111 Dunaweal Lane (off Hwy. 29, just south of Calistoga), Calistoga. © **707/942-3344.** www. sterlingvineyards.com. Daily 10:30am–4:30pm.

WHERE TO STAY

Accommodations here run the gamut—from motels and B&Bs to world-class luxury retreats—and all are easily accessible from the main highway. While we recommend shacking up in the more romantically pastoral areas such as

St. Helena, there's no question you're going to find better deals in the towns of Napa or laid-back Calistoga.

Keep in mind that during the high season—between June and November—most hotels charge peak rates and sell out completely on weekends; many have a 2-night minimum. If you need help organizing your Wine Country vacation, contact one of the following companies: **Accommodation Referral Bed & Breakfast Exchange** (✆ **800/240-8466,** 800/499-8466 in California, or 707/965-3400), which also represents hotels and inns; **Bed & Breakfast Inns of Napa Valley** (✆ **707/944-4444**), an association of B&Bs that provides inn descriptions and makes reservations; or **Napa Valley Reservations Unlimited** (✆ **800/251-NAPA** or 707/252-1985), which is also a source for everything from hot-air balloon and glider rides to wine-tasting tours by limousine.

VERY EXPENSIVE

Auberge du Soleil ★★★   This spectacular Relais & Châteaux property, set high above the Napa Valley in a 33-acre olive grove, is quiet, indulgent, and luxuriously romantic. The Mediterranean-style rooms are large enough to get lost in—and you might want to once you discover all the amenities. The bathtub alone—an enormous hot tub with a skylight overhead—will entice you to grab a glass of complimentary California red and settle in for awhile. A wood-burning fireplace is surrounded by oversized, cushy furniture—the ideal place to relax and listen to CDs (the stereo comes with a few selections, and there's also a VCR). Fresh flowers, original art, terra-cotta floors, and natural-wood and leather furnishings whisk you out of the Wine Country and into the Southwest. Each sun-washed private deck has views of the valley that are nothing less than spectacular. Those with money to burn should opt for the $2,000-per-night cottage suite; the 1,800-square-foot hideaway's got two fireplaces, two full baths, a den, and a patio Jacuzzi. Now *that's* living. All guests have access to a celestial swimming pool, new exercise room, and the most fabulous (and new) spa in the Wine Country, which opened in 2001. Only guests can use the spa, but if you want to get all the romantic grandeur of Auberge, have lunch on the patio at the wonderful restaurant overlooking the valley

180 Rutherford Hill Rd., Rutherford, CA 94573. ✆ **800/348-5406** or 707/963-1211. Fax 707/963-8764. www.aubergedusoleil.com. 50 units. $350–$600 double. AE, DC, DISC, MC, V. From Hwy 29 in Rutherford, turn right on California 128 and go 3 miles to the Silverado Trail; turn left and head north about 200 yd. To Rutherford Hill Rd.; turn right. **Amenities:** 1 restaurant; 3 outdoor pools ranging from hot to cold; 3 tennis courts; health club and full-service spa; salon; sauna; bikes; concierge; secretarial services; 24-hour room service; massage; same-day laundry service and dry cleaning. *In room:* A/C, TV/VCR w/ pay movies, dataport, kitchenette, minibar, fridge, coffeemaker, hair dryer, iron.

The Inn at Southbridge ★★   Eschewing the lace-and-latticework theme that plagues most Wine Country inns, the Inn at Southbridge takes an unswervingly modern, pragmatic approach to accommodating its guests. Instead of stuffed teddy bears, you'll find terry-cloth robes, fireplaces, bathroom skylights, down comforters, private balconies, and a host of other little luxuries. The decor is upscale Pottery Barn—trendy, and for some a welcome departure from quaintly traditional hotel-style stuff. Functional touches include voice mail and fax modems. One notable bummer: The hotel is located along the highway, so it lacks that reclusive feel many other upscale hotels offer.

1020 Main St., St. Helena, CA 94574. ✆ **800/520-6800** or 707/967-9400. Fax 707/967-9486. $290–$445 double. AE, DC. MC, V. **Amenities:** 1 restaurant; large heated outdoor pool; excellent health club and full-service spa; Jacuzzi; concierge; limited room service; massage; same-day laundry service and dry cleaning. *In room:* A/C, TV, dataport, minibar, coffeemaker, hair dryer, iron.

Tips **Accommodations Tip**

Wherever tourist dollars are to be had, you're sure to find big hotels with familiar names, catering to independent vacationers, business travelers, and groups. **Embassy Suites**, 1075 California Blvd., Napa, CA 94559 (© **800/362-2779** or 707/253-9540; www.embassysuites.com), offers 205 of its usual two-room suites. Each has a kitchenette, coffeemaker, modem capability, and two TVs; there are indoor and outdoor pools and a restaurant. Rates range from $190 to $280 and include cooked-to-order breakfast. The 191-room **Napa Valley Marriott**, 3425 Solano Ave., Napa, CA 94558 (© **800/228-9290** or 707/253-7433; www.marriott.com), has lighted tennis courts, an exercise room, a heated outdoor pool and spa, and two restaurants; rates range from $154 to $320.

Meadowood Napa Valley ★★★ *Finds*   Less reclusive than Auberge du Soleil, Meadowood is the summer camp for wealthy grown-ups. The resort, tucked away on 250 acres of pristine mountainside amidst a forest of madrone and oak trees, is quiet and exclusive enough to make you forget that busy wineries are just 10 minutes away. Rooms, furnished with American country classics, have beamed ceilings, private patios, stone fireplaces, and wilderness views; many are individual suite-lodges that are so far removed from the common areas that you must drive to get to them (lazier folks can opt for more centrally located accommodations). You can spend your days playing golf, tennis, or croquet; lounging around the pools or spa; or hiking the surrounding areas. Those who actually want to leave the property to do some wine tasting can check in with John Thoreen, the hotel's wine tutor, whose sole purpose is to help guests better understand and enjoy Napa Valley wines.

900 Meadowood Lane, St. Helena, CA 94574. © **800/458-8080** or 707/963-3646. Fax 707/963-3532. www. meadowood.com. 85 units. $360–$590 double; 1-bedroom suite from $580; 2-bedroom from $910; 3-bedroom from $1,265; 4-bedroom from $1,620. Ask about promotional offers and off-season rates. 2-night minimum stay on weekends. AE, DISC, DC, MC, V. **Amenities:** 2 restaurants; 2 large, heated outdoor pools; golf course; 7 tennis courts; 2 croquet lawns; health club and full-service spa; Jacuzzi; sauna; concierge; secretarial services; room service; same-day laundry service and dry cleaning. *In room:* A/C, TV, dataport, kitchenettes in some rooms, minibar, coffeemaker, hair dryer, iron.

Napa River Inn ★★   Downtown Napa's newest and most luxury hotel manages an old-world boutique feel through most of its three-buildings housing 66 rooms. The main building, part of the newly renovated Napa Mill and Hatt Market, is an 1884 historic landmark. Each of the fantastically appointed rooms is exceedingly romantic with burgundy-colored walls, original brick, wood furnishings, plush fabrics, and seats in front of the gas fireplace. A gilded clawfoot tub beckons in the luxury bathroom. The newest addition is a brand-new building with bright and airy accommodations overlooking the Napa River. Less luxurious, but equally well-appointed are the mustard-and-brown colored rooms that also overlook the riverfront, but have a nautical theme and less daylight. Extra perks abound and include complimentary vouchers to a full breakfast and evening cocktails at one of the adjoining restaurants. A small, but excellent spa is located in the hotel's parking lot.

500 Main St., Napa, CA 94599. © **707/251-8500** or 877/251-8500. www.napariverinn.com. 66 units. $149–$300 double. AE, DC, DIS, MC, V. **Amenities:** 1 American restaurant; concierge; business services; same-day laundry service/dry cleaning. *In room:* A/C, TV, CD, clock radio, dataport, coffeemaker, hair dryer, iron, safe.

Napa Valley Lodge ★★ *Finds*   Many frequent visitors compare this contemporary hotel to the town's popular Vintage Inn, noting that it's even more personable and accommodating. The lodge is just off Calif. 29, though they do a good job of disguising it. Facilities include a pool, redwood sauna, and small exercise room; the newly upgraded guest rooms are large, ultra-clean, and better appointed than many in the area. Many have vaulted ceilings and 33 have fireplaces. All come with a king- or queen-size bed, wicker furnishings, coffeemaker, robes, and either a private balcony or a patio, and all the bathrooms include a vanity area and nice tile work. The cheapest rooms are at ground level; these are smaller and get less sunlight than those on the second floor. Extras include concierge, on-demand video, afternoon tea and cookies in the lobby, Friday-evening wine tasting in the library, and a full champagne breakfast—with all this, it's no wonder ACCOMMODATIONS gave the Napa Valley Lodge the four-diamond award for excellence. Ask about winter discounts—they can be as much as 30%.

2230 Madison St., Yountville, CA 94599. ✆ 800/368-2468 or 707/944-2468. Fax 707/944-9362. www. woodsidehotels.com. 55 units. $282–$585 double. Rates include champagne breakfast buffet. AE, DC, DISC, MC, V. **Amenities:** Heated outdoor pool; Jacuzzi; redwood sauna; small exercise room. *In room:* A/C, TV w/ pay movies, dataport, minibar, coffeemaker, hair dryer, iron.

MODERATE

Cedar Gables Inn ★★ *Finds*   Innkeepers Margaret and Craig Snasdell have developed quite a following with their cozy, romantic B&B in Old Town Napa. The Victorian was built in 1892, and rooms reflect the era with rich tapestries and stunning gilded antiques. Five rooms have fireplaces; five have whirlpool tubs; and all feature queen-size brass, wooden, or iron beds. Guests meet each evening in front of the roaring fireplace in the family room for complimentary wine and cheese. At other times, it's a perfect place to cuddle up and watch the large-screen TV.

486 Coombs St., Napa, CA 94559. ✆ 800/309-7969 or 707/224-7969. Fax 707/224-4838. www. cedargablesinn.com. 9 units. $169–$279 double; winter $129–$249 double. Rates include full breakfast and port. AE, DISC, MC, V. From Hwy. 29 north, exit onto First St. and follow signs to downtown; turn right onto Coombs St.; the house is at the corner of Oak St. *In room:* A/C, TV, dataport, hair dryer, iron.

Cottage Grove Inn ★★   Standing in two parallel rows at the end of the main strip in Calistoga are the perfect couples' retreats—cottages that, although located on a residential street, seem well removed from the action once you've stepped across the threshold. Each compact guest house comes complete with a wood-burning fireplace, homey furnishings (perfect for curling up in front of the fire), cozy quilts, and an enormous bathroom with a skylight and a deep, two-person Jacuzzi tub, plus such niceties as gourmet coffee, stereo with CD player, VCR (a video library is on-site), wet bar, and fridge. Smokers beware— it's not allowed inside, but you can puff all you want on the small front porch. Several major spas are within walking distance. This is our top pick if you want to do the Calistoga spa scene in comfort and style. One cabin is accessible for travelers with disabilities.

1711 Lincoln Ave., Calistoga, CA 94515. ✆ 800/799-2284 or 707/942-8400. Fax 707/942-2653. www. cottagegrove.com. 16 cottages. $235–$295 double. Rates include continental breakfast and evening wine and cheese. AE, DC, DISC, MC, V. *In room:* A/C, TV/VCR, stereo, dataport, fridge, coffeemaker, hair dryer.

Maison Fleurie ★★   Maison Fleurie is one of the prettiest hotels in the Wine Country, a trio of beautiful 1873 brick-and-fieldstone buildings overlaid with ivy. Seven rooms are located in the main house—a charming Provençal replica complete with thick brick walls, terra-cotta tile, and paned windows—while the remaining rooms are split between the old bakery building and the carriage house. All have private bathrooms, and some feature private balconies, patios, sitting areas, Jacuzzis, and fireplaces. Breakfast is served in the quaint little dining room; afterward, you're welcome to wander the landscaped grounds, use the pool or outdoor spa, or borrow a mountain bike (free of charge) to ride around town, returning in time for afternoon hors d'oeuvres. It's truly impossible not to enjoy your stay at Maison Fleurie.

6529 Yount St. (between Washington St. and Yountville Cross Rd.), Yountville, CA 94599. ℂ 800/788-0369 or 707/944-2056. Fax 707/944-9342. www.foursisters.com. 13 units. $110–$260 double. Rates include full breakfast and afternoon hors d'oeuvres. AE, DC, MC, V. **Amenities:** Heated outdoor pool; Jacuzzi; free bikes. *In room:* A/C, TV, dataport, hair dryer, iron.

Rancho Caymus Inn ⬮ This Spanish-style hacienda, with two floors opening onto wisteria-covered balconies, was the creation of sculptor Mary Tilden Morton (of Morton Salt). Morton wanted each room in the hacienda to be a work of art, so she hired the most skilled craftspeople of her day. She designed the adobe fireplaces herself, and wandered through Mexico and South America purchasing artifacts for the property.

Guest rooms are situated around a whimsical garden courtyard with an enormous outdoor fireplace. The mix-and-match interior decor is on the funky side, with overly varnished dark-wood furnishings and braided rugs. The inn is cozy, however, and rooms are decent-size, split-level suites with queen beds. Other amenities include wet bars, sofa beds in the sitting areas, and small private patios. Most of the suites have fireplaces, and five have kitchenettes and whirlpool tubs. A complimentary continental breakfast, which includes fresh fruit, granola, orange juice, and breads, is served in the inn's dining room.

Since chef Ken Frank's La Toque opened here, this funky inn has also become a dining destination (see "Where to Dine," below, for complete details).

1140 Rutherford Rd. (P.O. Box 78), Rutherford, CA 94573. ℂ 800/845-1777 or 707/963-1777. Fax 707/963-5387. www.ranchocaymus.com. 26 suites. $155–$255 double; from $285 master suite; $385 2-bedroom suite. Rates include continental breakfast. AE, DC, MC, V. From Hwy. 29 north, turn right onto Rutherford Rd./Calif. 128 E.; the hotel is on your left. **Amenities:** 1 restaurant. *In room:* A/C, TV, dataport, kitchenettes in some rooms, minibar, fridges in some rooms, hair dryer, iron.

Wine Country Inn ⬮⬮ Just off the highway behind Freemark Abbey Vineyard, this attractive wood-and-stone inn, complete with a French-style mansard roof and turret, overlooks a pastoral landscape of Napa Valley vineyards. The individually decorated rooms are outfitted with iron or brass beds, antique furnishings, and handmade quilts; most have fireplaces and private terraces overlooking the valley, while others have private hot tubs. One of the inn's best features, besides the absence of TVs, is the outdoor pool (heated year-round), which is attractively landscaped into the hillside.

Another favorite is the selection of suites, which come with stereos, plenty of space, and lots of privacy. Wine and appetizers are served nightly, along with a big dash of hotel-staff hospitality in the inviting living room. A full buffet breakfast is served there, too. *Note:* Half the bathrooms have showers only. Ongoing renovations ensure updated rooms, and new luxury cottages are slated to open in 2002.

1152 Lodi Lane, St. Helena, CA 94574. ℂ 707/963-7077. Fax 707/963-9018. www.wine-country-inn.com. 24 units (12 with shower only). $130–$345 double. Rates include breakfast and appetizers. MC, V. **Amenities:** Heated outdoor pool; Jacuzzi; concierge. *In room:* A/C, stereo, hair dryer.

INEXPENSIVE

Along with the listings below, we also recommend **Napa Valley Railway Inn,** 6503 Washington St., adjacent to the Vintage 1870 shopping complex, Yountville (© **707/944-2000**), which rents private railway cars converted into adorable hotel rooms; and **Dr. Wilkinson's Hot Springs,** 1507 Lincoln Ave. (© **707/942-4102**), which recently underwent a major renovation.

Calistoga Spa Hot Springs. ⚡ *Kids*   Very few hotels in the Wine Country welcome children, which is why we strongly recommend the Calistoga Spa Hot Springs for families. Even if you don't have kids in tow, it's still a great bargain, offering unpretentious yet clean and comfortable rooms with kitchenettes, as well as a plethora of spa facilities ranging from exercise rooms to four naturally heated outdoor mineral pools, aerobic facilities, volcanic-ash mud baths, mineral baths, steam baths, blanket wraps, massage sessions, and more. All of Calistoga's best shops and restaurants are within easy walking distance, and you can even whip up your own grub at the barbecues set up near the large pool and patio area.

1006 Washington St. (at Gerrard St.), Calistoga, CA 94515. © **707/942-6269**. www.calistogaspa.com. 57 units, 1 family unit. Winter $90 double, $110 family unit; summer $110 double, $130 family unit. MC, V. **Amenities:** 3 heated outdoor pools; kids' wading pool; exercise room; spa. *In room:* A/C, TV, kitchenette, fridge, coffeemaker, hair dryer on request; iron.

Chablis Inn ⚡   There's no way around it. If you want to sleep cheaply in a town where the average room goes for upwards of $200 per night in high season, you're going to have to motel it. But look on the bright side: Since your room is likely to be little more than a crashing pad after a day of eating and drinking, a clean bed and a remote control are all you'll really need. But Chablis offers much more than that. Each of the superclean motel-style rooms has a new mattress, fridge, and coffeemaker; some even boast kitchenettes and/ or whirlpool tubs. Guests have access to an outdoor heated pool and Jacuzzi, plus a basic continental breakfast. Friendly owner Ken Patel is on hand most of the time and is constantly upgrading his tidy highway-side hostelry.

3360 Solano Ave., Napa, CA 94558. © **707/257-1944**. Fax 707/226-6862. www.chablisinn.com. 34 units. Apr to mid-Nov $80–$150 double; mid-Nov to Mar $70–$120 double. Rates include continental breakfast. AE, DC, DISC, MC, V. **Amenities:** Heated outdoor pool; Jacuzzi. *In room:* A/C, TV, dataports in some rooms, kitchenettes in some rooms, fridge, coffeemaker, hair dryer.

El Bonita Motel ⚡ *Kids*   This 1930s Art Deco motel was built a bit too close to Calif. 29 for comfort, but the 2½ acres of beautifully landscaped gardens behind the place (away from the road) help even the score. The rooms, while small, are spotlessly clean and decorated with new furnishings; all have microwaves and coffeemakers, and some have kitchens or whirlpool bathtubs. Families, attracted to the larger bungalows with kitchenettes, often regard El Bonita as one of the best values in Napa Valley—especially considering the heated outdoor pool, Jacuzzi, sauna, and massage facility.

195 Main St. (at El Bonita Ave.), St. Helena, CA 94574. © **800/541-3284** or 707/963-3216. Fax 707/963-8838. www.elbonita.com. 41 units. $89–$259 double. Rates include continental breakfast. AE, DC, DISC, MC, V. **Amenities:** Heated outdoor pool; spa; Jacuzzi. *In room:* A/C, TV, fridge, coffeemaker, hair dryer, iron.

White Sulphur Springs Retreat & Spa ⚡⚡ *Value*   If your idea of the ultimate vacation is a cozy cabin set among 330 acres of creeks, waterfalls, hot springs, hiking trails, and redwood, madrone, and fir trees, paradise is a short winding drive away from downtown St. Helena. Established in 1852, Sulphur Springs claims to be the oldest resort in California. Guests stay at the inn or in small and large creek-side cabins, which were recently renovated. Each is decorated with simple but homey furnishings; some have fireplaces or wood-burning stoves, and/or kitchenettes. From here you can venture off on a hike; take a dip in the natural hot sulphur spring; lounge by the pool; sit under a tree and watch for deer, foxes, raccoons, spotted owls, or woodpeckers; or schedule a day of massage, aromatherapy, and other spa treatments in the spa, which underwent upgrading and expansion in 2001. *Note:* No RVs are allowed without advance notice.

3100 White Sulphur Springs Rd., St. Helena, CA 94574. © **800/593-8873** in CA or 707/963-8588. Fax 707/ 963-2890. www.whitesulphursprings.com. 28 units, 14 with bathroom; 9 cottages. Carriage House (shared bathroom) $90–$110 double; Inn $115–$155 double; Creekside Cottages $155–$245. Extra person $15. Off-season and midweek discounts available. 2-night minimum stay on weekends Apr–Oct and all holidays. MC, V. **Amenities:** Heated outdoor pool; spa. *In room:* A/C, TV, hair dryer.

Wine Valley Lodge ★ *Value*   Dollar for dollar, the Wine Valley Lodge offers the most for the least in all of Wine Country. Located at the south end of town in a quiet residential neighborhood, the mission-style motel is extremely well kept and accessible, just a short drive from Calif. 29 and the wineries to the north. Soft pastels dominate the color scheme, featured prominently in the matching quilted bedspreads, furniture, and objets d'art. The clincher on the whole deal is a fetching little oasis in the center courtyard, consisting of a sun deck, barbe-cue, and pool flanked by a cadre of odd teacup-shaped hedges. A $500,000 room renovation, completed in 2000, resulted in new furnishings in most rooms.

200 S. Coombs St. (between First and Imola Sts.), Napa, CA 94559. © **800/696-7911** or 707/224-7911. www.winevalleylodge.com. 54 units. $69–$119 double; $120–$165 deluxe. AE, DC, DISC, MC, V. **Amenities:** Heated outdoor pool. *In room:* A/C, TV.

WHERE TO DINE

To best enjoy Napa's restaurant scene, keep one thing in mind: *reserve—* especially for seats in a more renowned room.

EXPENSIVE

Auberge du Soleil ★★ *Finds* CONTINENTAL/CALIFORNIA   There is no better restaurant view than that at Auberge du Soleil. Perched on a hillside over-looking the valley, alfresco dining rises to an entirely new level here, particularly on warm summer afternoons at sunset. In fact, we recommend coming during the day (request terrace seating) to join the wealthy patrons, many of whom have emerged from their uberluxury guest rooms and are slinking to a table to dine above the vines. The kitchen, which welcomed a new chef in late 2000, is turning out seasonal dishes such as well-prepared sautéed sweetbreads, venison loin with butternut squash, stuffed squab, and roasted saddle of lamb—nothing mind-blowing, but certainly good. While the interior is warm, bustling, and formal enough that some folks wear ties, personally, come dinnertime I'd rather drop big bucks at La Toque, where the food is more creative and even.

180 Rutherford Hill Rd., Rutherford. © **707/963-1211.** Reservations recommended. Main courses $17–$20 lunch; $25–$30 dinner. AE, DISC, MC, V. Daily 7–11am, 11:30am–2:30pm, and 6–9:30pm.

The French Laundry ★★★ CLASSIC AMERICAN/FRENCH   It's almost futile to include this restaurant, since the likelihood of securing a reservation— or getting through on the reservation line for that matter—is about as likely as driving Highway 29 without passing a winery. But, several years after renowned chef and owner Thomas Keller bought the place and caught the attention of epicureans worldwide (including the judges of the James Beard Awards, who dubbed him 1997's "Chef of the Nation"), the discreet restaurant is still the hottest dinner ticket *in the world*. So, at least you can read about it. *Tip:* If you can't get a reservation, try walking in—on occasion folks don't make their reservation and tables open up—especially during lunch on rainy days.

Here the atmosphere is as serious as the diners who quietly swoon over the ongoing parade of precious bite-size delights delivered to the table. Technically, the prix-fixe menu offers a choice of five or nine courses (including a vegetarian menu), but after a slew of cameo appearances from the kitchen, everyone starts to lose count. Signature dishes include Keller's "tongue in cheek" (a marinated and braised round of sliced lamb tongue and tender beef cheeks) and "macaroni and cheese" (sweet butter-poached Maine lobster with creamy lobster broth and orzo with mascarpone cheese). Portions are small, but only because Keller wants his guests to taste as many different things as possible—nobody leaves hungry. The excellent staff is well acquainted with the wide selection of regional wines; the house charges a $50 corkage fee if you choose to bring your own bottle. On warm summer nights, request a table in the flower-filled garden. But keep in mind, The French Laundry experience focuses on food in such a way that it is most appreciated by serious foodies who revel in four-hour meals and unparalleled culinary artistry.

6640 Washington St. (at Creek St.), Yountville. ℭ **707/944-2380.** Reservations required. Vegetarian menu $80; 5-course menu $90; chef's 9-course tasting menu $105. AE, MC, V. Fri–Sun 11am–1pm; daily 5:30–9:30pm.

La Toque ✸✸✸ FRENCH-INSPIRED   Don't come here without an appetite or a nice outfit. Renowned Ken Frank left Los Angeles's Fenix at the Argyle Hotel to open one of the Wine Country's most formal dining rooms—and once you sit down to the five-course extravaganza you can't refrain from gobbling up all the delicious—and generous—creations that come your way. Each table at the elegant restaurant adjoining Rancho Caymus Inn is well spaced, making plenty of room to showcase Frank's memorable and innovative French-inspired cuisine. The menu might feature an incredible Indian spice–rubbed foie gras with Madras carrot puree (one of the best I've had);melt-in-your-mouth yellowfin tuna with braised daikon, red wine, and sautéed pea sprouts; knock-out Maine lobster with creamy orzo and lobster cabernet sauce; and, should you find room and the extra few bucks for the cheese course, delicious selections served with walnut bread. For an additional $32 per person, my party drank splendid and well-paired wines with each course. Alas, we did not have room for desserts of chocolate panna cotta with vanilla Anglaise and toasted pineapple fritter with vanilla bean ice cream, but we couldn't help but eat it anyway.

1140 Rutherford Cross Rd., Rutherford. ℭ **707/963-9770.** www.latoque.com. Reservations recommended. Fixed-price menu $72. Wed–Sun 5:30–10pm.

Terra ✸✸✸ CONTEMPORARY AMERICAN   St. Helena's restaurant of choice is the creation of Lissa Doumani and her husband, Hiro Sone, a master chef who hails from Japan and once worked with Wolfgang Puck at L.A.'s original Spago. Sone makes full use of the region's bounty; he seems to know how to coax every nuance of flavor from his fine local ingredients. The simple stone-walled dining room is a perfect foil for the extraordinary food. Among the appetizers, the terrine of foie gras with fig and endive salad and the home-smoked salmon with potato latkes, sour cream, and caviar are the stars of the show. The main dishes successfully fuse different cooking styles: Try the grilled salmon with Thai red-curry sauce or the sake-marinated sea bass with shrimp dumplings in shiso broth. Recommended finales? Tiramisu and an out-of-this-world-heavenly orange risotto in brandy snap with passion fruit sauce, which are some of the best I've tasted.

1345 Railroad Ave. (between Adams and Hunt Sts.), St. Helena. ℂ 707/963-8931. www.terrarestaurant. com. Reservations recommended. Main courses $18.50–$26. DC, MC, V. Sun–Mon and Wed–Thurs 6–9:30pm; Fri–Sat 6–10pm. Closed for 2 weeks in early January.

MODERATE

All Seasons Café ✶✶ CALIFORNIA Wine Country devotees often wend their way to the All Seasons Café in downtown Calistoga because of its extensive wine list and knowledgeable staff. The trick here is to buy a bottle of wine from the cafe's wine shop, then bring it to your table; the cafe adds a corkage fee of around $10 instead of doubling the price of the bottle (as they do at most restaurants). The diverse menu ranges from pizzas and pastas to such main courses as braised lamb shank *osso buco* in an orange, Madeira, and tomato sauce. Anything with the house-smoked salmon or spiced sausages is also a safe bet. Chef John Coss saves his guests from any major faux pas by matching wines to his dishes on the menu, so you know what's just right for smoked salmon and Crescenza cheese pizza.

1400 Lincoln Ave. (at Washington St.), Calistoga. ℂ 707/942-9111. Reservations recommended on weekends. Main courses $7.50–$13 lunch; $10.25–$19 dinner. MC, V. Mon–Tues and Thurs–Fri 11am–3pm; daily 5:30–9pm. Wine shop Thurs–Tues 11am–7pm.

Bistro Don Giovanni ✶✶ *Value* REGIONAL ITALIAN Donna and Giovanni Scala—who also run Scala's Bistro in San Francisco—own this bright, bustling, and cheery Italian restaurant, which also happens to be one of our favorite restaurants in Napa Valley. The menu features pastas, risottos, pizzas (baked in a wood-burning oven), and a half dozen other main courses. Every time I grab a menu, I can't get past the beet and haricots verte salad and pasta with duck Bolognese. On the rare occasion that I do, I am equally smitten with outstanding thin-crust pizzas fresh from the wood-burning oven, seared salmon filet perched atop a tower of buttermilk mashed potatoes, and steak frites. Alfresco dining on the patio is available—and highly recommended on a warm, sunny day.

4110 St. Helena Hwy. (Hwy. 29, just north of Salvador Ave.), Napa. ℂ 707/224-3300. Reservations recommended. Main courses $12–$23.50. AE, DC, DIS, MC, V. Sun–Thurs 11:30am–10pm; Fri–Sat 11:30am–11pm.

Bistro Jeanty ✶✶ FRENCH BISTRO This casual, warm bistro with muted buttercup walls and two dining rooms divided by the bar is the brainchild of chef Phillipe Jeanty, who a few years back left his highly reputed 18-year post at Domaine Chandon to open one of the hottest (and most moderately priced) new restaurants in town. Jeanty was previously known for formal French cooking, but his charming and cheery bistro offers far more laid-back but equally worship-worthy fare. Outstanding classic French bistro fare comes in the form of an all-day menu, which includes everything from his legendary tomato soup in a puff pastry, foie gras paté, steak tartare, and house smoked trout with potato slices basking in an olive and lite vinegar and oil bath to daube de boeuf simmered in red wine and served with mashed potatoes, fresh peas, and baby carrots; and cassoulet with white beans, fennel sausage, pork, and duck leg. I'll return frequently for the decadent fall-off-the-bone coq au vin with an earthy, smoky red wine sauce and delicate deep-fried smelt special, which came in a wax-paper cone accompanied by a seasoned mayo dipping sauce. I, like most San Franciscans, consider this place a must-stop on the Wine Country itinerary.

6510 Washington St., Yountville. ℂ 707/944-0103. Reservations recommended. Appetizers $4.50–$7.50, most main courses $13.75–$18.50. MC, V. Daily 11:30am–10:30pm. Closed Thanksgiving, Dec 25.

Bouchon ⚹ FRENCH BISTRO   Perhaps to appease the crowds who never get a reservation at The French Laundry, Thomas Keller teamed up with his brother Joseph to open a far more casual French brasserie called Bouchon. You'll have to call in advance for an opportunity to sample the French fare, which is served in a dining room designed by Adam Tihany (who also conceptualized New York's Le Cirque 2000). Along with a raw bar, expect steak frite, mussels marinieres, grilled cheese sandwiches, and other heavenly French classics at far more down-to-earth prices and atmosphere. We do like this place, but far prefer Bistro Jeanty. An added bonus (especially for restless residents) is the late hours.

6534 Washington St. (at Humbolt), Yountville. ℂ 707/944-8037. Reservations recommended. Main courses $12–$17. AE, DC, MC, V. Daily 11:30am–2pm and 5:30–10:45pm.

Catahoula ⚹ AMERICAN/SOUTHERN   The domain of chef Jan Birnbaum, formerly of New York's Quilted Giraffe and San Francisco's Campton Place, this restaurant is the current favorite in town. And for good reason: It's the only place in Napa where you can get a decent rooster gumbo. You'd have to travel all over Louisiana to find another pan-fried jalapeño-pecan catfish like this one. Catahoula is funky and fun, and the food that comes out of the wood-burning oven—like the roast duck with chili-cilantro potatoes or the whole roasted fish with lemon broth, orzo, and escarole—is exciting (and usually spicy). Start with the spicy gumbo ya ya with andouille sausage, and finish with what may be a first for many non-Southerners—buttermilk ice cream.

1457 Lincoln Ave. (between Washington and Fairway Sts.), Calistoga. ℂ 707/942-2275. Reservations recommended. Main courses $11–$22. DISC, MC, V. Sat–Sun 10am–3:30pm; daily 5:30–10:30pm.

Mustards Grill ⚹⚹ CALIFORNIA   Mustards, the quintessential Wine Country restaurant, is a safe bet for anyone in search of a casual atmosphere and quality food that's not overly adventurous. Housed in a convivial, barn-style space, it offers an 11-page wine list and an ambitious chalkboard list of specials. Our party started out with a wonderfully light seared ahi tuna. Although the tea-smoked Peking duck with almond onion sauce and grilled rabbit with potatoes, fennel, and saffron broth were tempting, we opted for a moist, perfectly flavored grilled chicken breast with mashed potatoes and fresh herbs. The menu includes something for everyone, from gourmands and vegetarians to good old burger lovers.

7399 St. Helena Hwy. (Hwy. 29), Yountville. ℂ 707/944-2424. Reservations recommended. Main courses $11–$27. DC, DISC, MC, V. Mon–Thurs 11:30am–9:30pm; Fri 11:30am–10pm; Sat 11am–10pm; Sun 11am–9:30pm.

Piatti ⚹ ⟨Kids⟩ ITALIAN   This local favorite—the first (and best) of a swiftly growing northern California chain—is known for serving excellent, reasonably priced food in a rustic Italian-style setting. For the perfect meal, start with a salad of morning-cut field greens mixed with white corn and Napa Valley strawberry crostini, accompanied by a bowl of the spaghetti squash and sweet-potato soup. Though the restaurant offers a wide array of superb pastas and pizzas, it's the wood-oven-roasted duck, basted with a sweet cherry sauce and served over a bed of citrus risotto, that brings back the regulars. There are far fancier and more intimate restaurants in the valley, but none where you can fill up on such outstanding fare at these prices. *Note:* Piatti also offers patio dining year-round, weather permitting.

6480 Washington St. (between Washington and Oak Sts.), Yountville. ℂ 707/944-2070. Reservations recommended. Main courses $10–$19. AE, DC, MC, V. Sun–Thurs 11:30am–10pm; Fri–Sat 11:30am–11pm.

Tra Vigne Restaurant ✿✿✿ ITALIAN   Tra Vigne's combination of good ultra-fresh food, high-energy atmosphere, gorgeous patio seating, all-day service, and "reasonable" prices makes this restaurant a long-standing favorite among visitors and locals. Whether guests are in the Tuscany-evoking courtyard (heated on cold nights) or in the center of the bustling scene, they're usually thrilled just to have a seat. Though the wonderful bread served with house-made flavored olive oils is tempting, save room for partner and executive chef Carmen Quagliata's robust California dishes, such as standbys like short ribs; frito misto; irresistible oven-roasted polenta with cheese, mushrooms, and balsamic reduction; and outstanding whole roasted fish. If you're lucky, our favorite will be on the menu: Angry Sand Dab, a spicy celebration of chili oil, crisp and crunchy fried basil, lemon zest, baby jalapeños, garlic slivers, and white beans. Equally tempting are the fresh pastas—such as spaghettini with cuttlefish Bolognese and spring onions—and delicious desserts.

The adjoining Cantinetta offers a small selection of sandwiches, pizzas, and lighter meals, and an exciting new wine program, which features 100 by-the-glass selections.

1050 Charter Oak Ave., St. Helena. ℂ 707/963-4444. Reservations recommended. Main courses $12.50–$22. DC, DISC, MC, V. Daily 11:30am–10pm.

Wappo Bar & Bistro ✿✿ GLOBAL   One of the best alfresco dining experiences in the Wine Country is under Wappo's honeysuckle-and-vine-covered arbor, but you'll also be comfortable inside this small bistro at one of the well-spaced, well-polished tables. The menu offers a wide range of choices, from Chilean sea bass with mint chutney to roast rabbit with oven tomato tagliarini. Desserts of choice are the black-bottom coconut cream pie and the strawberry rhubarb pie.

1226B Washington St. (off Lincoln Ave.), Calistoga. ℂ 707/942-4712. Main courses $13.50–$19.75. AE, MC, V. Wed–Mon 11:30am–2:30pm and 6–9:30pm.

Wine Spectator Greystone Restaurant ✿ WINE COUNTRY CUISINE This place offers a combination visual and culinary feast that's unparalleled in the area, if not the state. The room itself is an enormous stone-walled former winery, but the festive decor and heavenly aromas warm the space up. Cooking islands—complete with scurrying chefs, steaming pots, and rotating chicken—provide edible entertainment. New head chef Todd Humphries (formerly of Campton Place in San Francisco) has put his own mark on the California Wine Country cuisine. The "tastings" (appetizer) menu features these fresh ingredients–inspired dishes, including a perfect calamari sautéed with smoked paprika, garlic, and rosemary; a fine seafood and white bean salad; and an unimpressive mushroom piroshki with caramelized onions. Portions are small but affordable; pastas and salads are a bit heftier. Main courses, such as a crispy fried lamb shank with cranberry beans, cherry tomatoes, and spinach, are well portioned, but we recommend you opt for a barrage of appetizers for your table to share. You should also order the "Flights of Fancy," where for $14 to $20 you can sample three 3-ounce pours of local wines such as white rhones, pinot, or zinfandel. (Wines by the glass are from the same selection, which, annoyingly, does not list by-the-glass prices.) While the food is serious, the atmosphere is playful—casual enough that you'll feel comfortable in jeans or shorts.

Gourmet Picnics, Napa Style

You could easily plan your whole trip around restaurant reservations. But put together one of the world's best gourmet picnics, and the valley's your oyster.

One of the finest gourmet food stores in the Wine Country, if not all of California, is the **Oakville Grocery Co.,** 7856 St. Helena Hwy., at Oakville Cross Road (📞 707/944-8802). Here you can put together the provisions for a memorable picnic—or, if you give them at least 24 hours' notice, the staff can prepare a picnic basket for you. The store, with its small-town vibe and claustrophobia-inducing crowds, is crammed with the best breads and the choicest selection of cheeses in the northern Bay Area, as well as patés, cold cuts, crackers, top-quality olive oils, fresh foie gras, smoked Norwegian salmon, fresh caviar (Beluga, Sevruga, Osetra), and, of course, an exceptional selection of California wines. The Grocery Co. is open daily from 9am to 6pm; it also has an espresso bar tucked in the corner (open daily from 7am to 3pm), offering breakfast and lunch items, house-baked pastries, and 15 wines available by the glass or for tasting.

Another of our favorite places to fill a picnic basket is New York City's version of a swank European marketplace, **Dean & Deluca,** 607 South Main St. (Calif. 29), north of Zinfandel Lane and south of Sulphur Springs Road in St. Helena (📞 707/967-9980). The ultimate gourmet grocery store is more like a world's fair of foods, where everything is beautifully displayed and often painfully pricey. But even if you choose not to buy, this place is definitely worth a browse. Check out the 200 domestic and imported cheeses; shelves of tapenades, pastas, oils, hand-packed dried herbs and spices, chocolates, sauces, and cookware; an espresso bar; one hell of a bakery section; and more. The wine shop boasts a 1,200-label collection. Hours are Monday through Saturday from 10am to 7pm (the espresso bar is open from 8am to 7pm), and Sunday from 10am to 6pm.

At the Culinary Institute of America at Greystone, 2555 Main St., St. Helena. 📞 707/967-1010. Reservations recommended. Tastings $5–$8; main courses $14–$24. AE, DC, MC, V. Daily 11:30am–10pm.

INEXPENSIVE

The Cantinetta 👪 WINE BAR/ITALIAN DELI   Regardless of where we dine while in the valley, we always make a point of stopping at The Cantinetta for an espresso and a snack. Part cafe, part shop, and part wine bar, it's a casual place with a few tables and a counter. The focaccias (we've never had better in our lives!), pasta salads, and pastries are outstanding, and there's also a selection of cookies and other wonderful treats, flavored oils (free tastings), wines, and an array of gourmet items, many of which were created here. You can also get great picnic grub to go, but it'd be sinful not to sample at least a few wines from their 100-plus bottle list.

At Tra Vigne Restaurant, 1050 Charter Oak Ave., St. Helena. 📞 707/963-8888. Main courses $4–$7. DC, DISC, MC, V. Daily 11:30am–6pm.

Smokehouse Café ★★ *(Kids)*   There are some darned good spareribs and house-smoked meats coming from this little kitchen in Calistoga. But that doesn't mean you shouldn't start with the Sacramento delta crawfish cakes and husk-roasted Cheyenne corn, then move on to the slow pig sandwich, a half slab of ribs, or homemade sausages—all of which take up to a week to prepare (not while you wait, luckily). The clincher is the fluffy all-you-can-eat cornbread dipped in pure cane syrup, which comes with every full-plate dinner. Kids are especially catered to—a rarity in these parts—and patio dining is available in summer.

1458 Lincoln Ave., Calistoga. ✆ **707/942-6060.** Main courses $8–$21. MC, V. Daily 8:30am–9pm (closed for dinner Tues–Wed Jan–Feb).

2 Sonoma Valley

Sonoma is often thought of as the "other" Wine Country, forever in the shadow of Napa Valley. Truth is, it's a very different experience. Sonoma still manages to maintain a backcountry ambiance thanks to its much lower density of wineries, restaurants, and hotels; because it's far less traveled than its neighbor to the east, it offers a more genuine "escape from it all" experience. Small, family-owned wineries are its mainstay, just like in the old days of winemaking, when everyone started with the intention of going broke and loved every minute of it. Unlike the rigidly structured tours at many of Napa Valley's corporate-owned wineries, tastings and tours on the Sonoma side of the Mayacamas Mountains are usually free and low-key, and come with plenty of friendly banter between the winemakers and their guests.

ESSENTIALS
GETTING THERE   From San Francisco, cross the Golden Gate Bridge and stay on U.S. 101 north. Exit at Calif. 37; after 10 miles, turn north onto Calif. 121. After another 10 miles, turn north onto Calif. 12 (Broadway), which will take you directly into the town of Sonoma.

VISITOR INFORMATION   While you're in Sonoma, stop by the **Sonoma Valley Visitors Bureau,** 453 First St. E. (✆ **707/996-1090;** www.sonomavalley. com). It's open daily from 9am to 7pm in summer and from 9am to 5pm in winter. An additional **Visitors Bureau** is located a few miles south of the square at 25200 Arnold Dr. (Calif. 121), at the entrance to Viansa Winery (✆ **707/996-5793;** www.sonomavalley.com); it's open daily from 9am to 7pm in summer and 9am to 5pm in winter.

If you prefer some advance information, you can contact the Sonoma Valley Visitors Bureau to order the $2 *Sonoma Valley Visitors Guide,* which lists most every lodging, winery, and restaurant in the valley.

WHEN TO GO   See "When to Go" in the Napa section, earlier in this chapter.

TOURING THE VALLEY & WINERIES
Sonoma Valley is currently home to about 35 wineries (including California's first winery, Buena Vista, founded in 1857) and 13,000 acres of vineyards, which produce roughly 25 types of wines totaling more than 5 million cases a year.

The towns and wineries covered below are organized geographically from south to north, starting at the intersection of Calif. 37 and Calif. 121 in the Carneros District and ending in Kenwood. The wineries here tend to be a little more spread out than they are in Napa, but they're easy to find. Still, it's best to decide which wineries you're most interested in and devise a touring strategy before you set out so you don't find yourself doing a lot of backtracking.

We've reviewed our favorite Sonoma Valley wineries here—more than enough to keep you busy tasting wine for a long weekend. For a complete list of local wineries, pick up one of the free guides to the valley available at the Sonoma Valley Visitors Bureau (see "Visitor Information," above).

THE CARNEROS DISTRICT

As you approach the Wine Country from the south, you must first pass through the Carneros District, a cool, windswept region that borders the San Pablo Bay and marks the entrance to both Napa and Sonoma Valleys. Until the latter part of the 20th century, this mixture of marsh, sloughs, and rolling hills was mainly used as sheep pasture (*carneros* means sheep in Spanish). After experimental plantings yielded slow-growing yet high-quality grapes—particularly chardonnay and pinot noir—several Napa and Sonoma wineries expanded their plantings here, eventually establishing the Carneros District as an American Viticultural Appellation.

Viansa Winery and Italian Marketplace ✦   This sprawling Tuscany-style villa is perched atop a knoll overlooking the entire lower valley. Viansa is the brainchild of Sam and Vicki Sebastiani, who left the family dynasty to create their own temple to food and wine (*Viansa* being a contraction of Vicki and Sam). While Sam, a third-generation winemaker, runs the winery, Vicky manages the marketplace, a large room crammed with a cornucopia of high-quality preserves, mustards, olive oils, pastas, salads, breads, desserts, Italian tableware, cookbooks, and wine-related gifts.

The winery, which does an extensive mail-order business through its Tuscany Club (worth joining if you love getting mail and good wine), has quickly established a favorable reputation for its cabernet, sauvignon blanc, and chardonnay, blended from premium Napa and Sonoma grapes. Sam is also experimenting with Italian grape varieties such as muscat canelli, sangiovese, and nebbiolo, most of which are sold exclusively at the winery. Free tastings are poured at the east end of the marketplace, and the self-guided tour includes a trip through the underground barrel-aging cellar adorned with colorful hand-painted murals.

25200 Arnold Dr. (Calif. 121), Sonoma. ✆ **800/995-4740** or 707/935-4700. www.viansa.com. Daily 10am–5pm; summer 9am–5:30pm. Daily self-guided tours.

Gloria Ferrer Champagne Caves *(Finds*   When you have it up to here with chardonnays and pinots, it's time to pay a visit to Gloria Ferrer, the grande dame of the Wine Country's sparkling-wine producers. Who's Gloria, you ask? She's the wife of José Ferrer, whose family has been making sparkling wine for the past 5 centuries and whose company, Freixenet, is the largest producer of sparkling wine in the world.

Glimmering like Oz high atop a gently sloping hill, the estate overlooks the verdant Carneros District; on a sunny day, enjoying a glass of dry Brut while soaking in the magnificent views is a must.

If you're unfamiliar with the term *méthode champenoise,* be sure to take the free 30-minute tour of the fermenting tanks, bottling line, and caves brimming with racks of yeast-laden bottles. Afterwards, retire to the elegant tasting room for a flute of Brut or Cuvée ($3 to $6 a glass, $16 and up per bottle), find an empty chair on the veranda, and say, "Ahhh. *This* is the life." There are picnic tables, but it's usually too windy up here for comfort, and you have to purchase a bottle of their sparkling wine to reserve a table.

23555 Carneros Hwy. (Calif. 121), Sonoma. (C) **707/996-7256.** www.gloriaferrer.com. Daily 10am–5:30pm. Tours daily 11am–4pm.

SONOMA

At the northern boundary of the Carneros District along Calif. 12 is the center-piece of Sonoma Valley, the midsized town of Sonoma, which owes much of its appeal to Mexican general Mariano Guadalupe Vallejo. It was Vallejo who fash-ioned this pleasant, slow-paced community after a typical Mexican village—right down to its central plaza, Sonoma's geographical and commercial center. The plaza sits at the top of a T formed by Broadway (Calif. 12) and Napa Street. Most of the surrounding streets form a grid pattern around this axis, making Sonoma easy to negotiate. The plaza's Bear Flag Monument marks the spot where the crude Bear Flag was raised in 1846, signaling the end of Mexican rule; the symbol was later adopted by the state of California and placed on its flag. The 8-acre park at the center of the plaza, complete with two ponds populated with ducks and geese, is perfect for an afternoon siesta in the cool shade.

The best way to see the town of Sonoma is to follow the **Sonoma Walking Tour** map, provided by the Sonoma League for Historic Preservation. Tour highlights include General Vallejo's 1852 Victorian-style home; the Sonoma Barracks, erected in 1836 to house Mexican army troops; and the Blue Wing Inn, an 1840 hostelry built to accommodate travelers—including John Fremont, Kit Carson, and Ulysses S. Grant—and new settlers while they erected homes in Sonoma. You can purchase the $2.75 map at the Vasquez House, located at 414 First St. E., between East Napa and East Spain Streets ((C) **707/938-0510**), open Wednesday through Sunday from 1:30 to 4:30pm.

The **Mission San Francisco Solano de Sonoma,** on Sonoma Plaza at the corner of First Street East and Spain Street ((C) **707/938-9560**), was founded in 1823. It was the northernmost, and last, mission built in California. It was also the only one established on the northern coast by the Mexican rulers, who wished to protect their territory from expansionist Russian fur traders. It's now part of Sonoma State Historic Park. Admission is $3 for adults, $2 for children ages 6 to 12, and free for children under 6. It's open daily from 10am to 5pm except Thanksgiving, Christmas, and New Year's Day.

Sebastiani Vineyards Winery   What started in 1904, when Samuele Sebastiani began producing his first wines, has, in three successive generations, now grown into a small empire and Sonoma County's largest winery, producing some *six million* cases a year. At press time the interesting, informative 25-minute tour was not offered due to renovations, which are scheduled to be complete by fall 2001. Call to confirm that you can see the winery's original turn-of-the-century crusher and press as well as the world's largest collection of oak-barrel carvings, crafted by local artist Earle Brown. If you don't want to take the tour, head straight for the charmingly rustic tasting room, where you can sample an extensive selection of wines sans tasting fee. Bottle prices are very reasonable, ranging from $8 to $60. A picnic area is adjacent to the cellars, though a far more scenic spot is located across the parking lot in Sebastiani's Cherryblock Vineyards.

389 Fourth St. E., Sonoma. (C) **800/888-5532** or 707/938-5532. www.sebastiani.com. Daily 10am–5pm. Tours 10:30am–4pm, every 30 min. in summer, every 45–60 min. in winter; no reservations necessary.

Buena Vista Winery The patriarch of California wineries was founded in 1857 by Count Agoston Haraszthy, the Hungarian émigré who is universally regarded as the father of California's wine industry. A close friend of General Vallejo, Haraszthy returned from Europe in 1861 with 100,000 of the finest vine cuttings, which he made available to all winegrowers. Although Buena Vista's winemaking now takes place at an ultra-modern facility in the Carneros District, the winery still maintains a complimentary tasting room inside the restored 1862 Press House—a beautiful stone-crafted room brimming with wines, wine-related gifts, and accessories (as well as a small art gallery along the inner balcony).

Tastings are free for most wines, $3 for the really good stuff. There's also a self-guided tour that you can follow any time during operating hours; a "Historical Presentation," offered daily at 2pm, details the life and times of the count.

18000 Old Winery Rd. (off E. Napa St., slightly northeast of downtown), Sonoma. © **800/926-1266** or 707/938-1266. www.buenavistawinery.com. Daily 10am–5pm. Self-guided tours only.

Ravenswood Winery Compared to old heavies like Sebastiani and Buena Vista, Ravenswood is a relative newcomer to the Sonoma wine scene, but it has quickly established itself as the sine qua non of zinfandel. In fact, Ravenswood is the first winery in the United States to focus primarily on zins, which make up about three quarters of its 150,000-case production; it also produces merlot, cabernet sauvignon, and a small amount of chardonnay.

The winery is smartly designed—recessed into the Sonoma hillside to protect its treasures from the simmering summers. Tours follow the winemaking process from grape to glass, and include a visit into the aromatic oak-barrel-aging rooms. A gourmet "Barbecue Overlooking the Vineyards" is held each weekend (from 11am to 4:30pm, from Memorial Day to the end of September; call for details and reservations), though you're welcome to enjoy your own picnic at any of their tables. Tastings are free and generous.

18701 Gehricke Rd. (off Lovall Valley Rd.), Sonoma. © **800/NO-WIMPY** or 707/938-1960. www.ravenswood-wine.com. Daily 10am–4:30pm. Tours by reservation only.

GLEN ELLEN

About 7 miles north of Sonoma on Calif. 12 is the town of Glen Ellen, which, though just a fraction of the size of Sonoma, is home to several of the valley's finest wineries, restaurants, and inns. Aside from the addition of a few new restaurants, this charming Wine Country town hasn't changed much since the days when Jack London settled on his Beauty Ranch, about a mile west. If you haven't yet decided where you want to set up camp during your visit to the Wine Country, we highly recommend this lovable little town.

Hikers, horseback riders, and picnickers will enjoy **Jack London State Historic Park,** 2400 London Ranch Rd., off Arnold Drive (© **707/938-5216**). Within its 800 acres, which were once home to the renowned writer, you'll find 9 miles of trails, the remains of London's burned-down dream house, preserved structures, a museum, and plenty of ideal picnic spots. The park is open daily from 10am to 7pm in summer, from 10am to 5pm in winter; the museum is open year-round from 10am to 5pm. Admission $3 per car or $2 per seniors' car.

Arrowood Vineyards & Winery Richard Arrowood had already established a reputation as a master winemaker at Château St. Jean before he and his wife, Alis Demers Arrowood, set out on their own in 1986. Their utterly picturesque winery is perched on a gently rising hillside lined with perfectly manicured vineyards. Tastings take place in the Hospitality House, the newer of Arrowood's two stately gray-and-white buildings fashioned after New England farmhouses, complete with wraparound porches. Richard's focus is on making world-class wine with minimal intervention, and his results are impressive: More than one of his current releases has scored over 90 points. Mind you, such excellence doesn't come cheaply: Prices start at $26 for a 1997 chardonnay and quickly climb to the mid- to high 30s. Tastings are $3.

14347 Sonoma Hwy. (Calif. 12), Glen Ellen. ℂ 707/938-5170. www.arrowoodvineyards.com. Daily 10am–4:30pm. Tours by appointment only, daily at 10:30am and 2:30pm.

Benziger Family Winery *(Finds)* A visit here confirms that you are indeed visiting a "family" winery; at any given time three generations of Benzigers (pronounced *ben*-zigger) may be running around tending to chores, and you're instantly made to feel as if you're part of the clan. The pastoral, user-friendly property features an exceptional self-guided tour ("The most comprehensive tour in the wine industry," exclaims *Wine Spectator*), gardens, an art gallery, and a spacious tasting room manned by an amiable staff. The free 40-minute tram tour, pulled by a beefy tractor, is both informative and fun as it winds through the estate vineyards before making a champagne-tasting pit stop on a scenic bluff. *Tip:* Tram tickets—a hot item in the summer—are available on a first-come, first-served basis, so either arrive early or stop by in the morning to pick up afternoon tickets.

Tastings of the standard-release wines are free. The winery offers several scenic picnic spots.

1883 London Ranch Rd. (off Arnold Dr., on the way to Jack London State Historic Park), Glen Ellen. ℂ 800/989-8890 or 707/935-3000. www.benziger.com. Tasting room daily 10am–5pm. $5 tram tours daily (weather permitting) at 11:30am, 12:30, 2, and 3:30pm.

KENWOOD

A few miles north of Glen Ellen along Calif. 12 is the tiny town of Kenwood, the northernmost outpost of the Sonoma Valley. The town itself consists of little more than a few restaurants, wineries, and modest homes recessed into the wooded hillsides.

Kunde Estate Winery Expect a friendly, unintimidating welcome at this scenic winery, run by four generations of the Kundes since 1904. One of the largest grape suppliers in the area, the Kunde family (pronounced *kun*-dee) converted 800 acres of their 2,000-acre ranch to growing ultra-premium-quality grapes, which they provide to about 30 Sonoma and Napa wineries. Hence, all their wines are "estate" (made from grapes grown on their own property). The free new-release tastings are offered in a spiffy new 17,000-square-foot winemaking facility. Private tours are available by appointment, but the picnic tables and man-made pond can be spontaneously enjoyed.

10155 Sonoma Hwy., Kenwood. ℂ 707/833-5501. www.kunde.com. Tastings daily 10:30am–4pm. Cave tours Fri–Sun approximately every half hour from 11am–4pm.

Kenwood Vineyards Kenwood's history dates back to 1906, when the Pagani brothers made their living selling wine straight from the barrel and into the jug. In 1970, the Lee family bought the place and converted the aging winery into a modern, high-production facility concealed in the original barn-like buildings. Since then, Kenwood's wines have earned a solid reputation for consistent quality with each of their varietals: cabernet sauvignon, chardonnay, zinfandel, pinot noir, merlot, and their most popular wine, sauvignon blanc—a crisp, light wine with hints of melon.

Though the winery looks rather modest in size, its output is staggering: 400,000 cases of ultra-premium wines fermented in 60 steel tanks and 7,000 French and American oak barrels. Popular with wine collectors is winemaker Michael Lee's Artist Series cabernet sauvignon, a limited production from the winery's best vineyards featuring labels with original artwork by renowned artists. The tasting room, housed in one of the old barns, offers free tastings of most varieties, as well as gift items for sale.

9592 Sonoma Hwy. (Calif. 12), Kenwood. © 707/833-5891. www.kenwoodvineyards.com. Daily 10am–4:30pm. Tours at 11:30am and 2:30pm daily.

Château St. Jean *(Finds)*   Château St. Jean is notable for its exceptionally beautiful buildings, landscaped grounds, and elegant tasting room. Among California wineries, it's a pioneer in vineyard designation—the procedure of making wine from, and naming it for, a single vineyard. A private drive takes you to what was once a 250-acre country retreat built in 1920; a well-manicured lawn overlooking the meticulously maintained vineyards is now a picnic area, complete with a fountain and picnic tables. There's a self-guided tour with detailed and photographic descriptions of the winemaking process. When you're done, be sure to walk to the top of the faux medieval tower for a magnificent view of the valley.

Back in the elegant tasting room—split into three areas to better handle the traffic—you can sample Château St. Jean's wide array of wines. They range from chardonnays and cabernet sauvignon to fumé blanc, merlot, Johannesburg Riesling, and Gewürztraminer. (Don't miss a rare tasting of late-harvest wines—you'll be amazed what a little more time on the vine can do.) Tastings are $5 per person.

8555 Sonoma Hwy. (Calif. 12), Kenwood. © 800/543-7572 or 707/833-4134. www.chateaustjean.com. Tasting daily 10am–6pm. At the foot of Sugarloaf Ridge, just north of Kenwood and east of Hwy. 12.

WHERE TO STAY

If you're having trouble finding a vacancy, try calling the **Sonoma Valley Visitors Bureau** at © **707/996-1090.** They'll try to refer you to a lodging that has a room to spare, but they won't make reservations for you. Another option is calling the **Bed and Breakfast Association of Sonoma Valley** (© **800/969-4667**), which will refer you to a member B&B and make reservations for you as well.

VERY EXPENSIVE

Gaige House Inn ✦✦✦ *(Finds)*   The Gaige House is the best B&B I've ever stayed in. The inn's owners, Ken Burnet, Jr., and Greg Nemrow, turned what was already a fine bed-and-breakfast into the finest in the Wine Country, and they've done it by offering a level of service, amenities, and decor normally associated with outrageously expensive resorts (and without the snobbery). Breakfast and afternoon appetizers are made with herbs from the inn's garden and prepared by a chef who was featured at the James Beard House in 2001. Firm mattresses are graced with wondrously silk-soft linens and premium down comforters, and even the furniture and artwork are of museum quality. Behind the inn is a 1½-acre oasis with perfectly manicured lawns, a 40-foot-long swimming pool, and a creek-side hammock shaded by a majestic Heritage oak. All 11 rooms, each artistically designed in a plantation theme with Asian and Indonesian influences, have private bathrooms, direct-dial phones, and king- or queen-size beds; two rooms have Jacuzzi tubs, and several have fireplaces. On sunny days, breakfast is served at individual tables on the large terrace. Evenings are best spent in the reading parlor sipping premium wines. They recently added an outdoor hot tub and two additional suites in the creek-side house.

13540 Arnold Dr., Glen Ellen, CA 95442. © **800/935-0237** or 707/935-0237. Fax 707/935-6411. www.gaige. com. 15 units. Summer $170–$525 double. Rates include full breakfast and evening wines. AE, DC, DISC, MC, V. **Amenities:** Large heated pool; in-room massage. *In room:* A/C, TV, fax, dataport, hair dryer, iron, safe.

Kenwood Inn & Spa ★★
Inspired by the villas of Tuscany, the honey-colored Italian-style buildings, flower-filled flagstone courtyard, and pastoral views of vineyard-covered hills are enough to make any northern Italian homesick. Every spacious room here is lavishly and exquisitely decorated with imported tapestries, velvets, and antiques; each has a fireplace, balcony (unless you're on the ground floor), feather bed, CD player, and down comforter—but no phone or TV, so you can relax. A minor caveat is road noise, which you're unlikely to hear from your room, but can be slightly heard over the tranquil piped-in music around the courtyard and pool.

An impressive two-course gourmet breakfast is served poolside or in the Mediterranean-style dining room; ours consisted of a poached egg accompanied by light, flavorful potatoes, red bell peppers, and other roasted vegetables, all artfully arranged, followed by a delicious homemade scone with fresh berries and a small lemon tart.

10400 Sonoma Hwy., Kenwood, CA 95452. © **800/353-6966** or 707/833-1293. Fax 707/833-1247. www. kenwoodinn.com. 12 units. Apr–Oct $295–$475 double; Nov–Mar $265–$425 double. Rates include gourmet breakfast and bottle of wine. 2-night minimum on weekends Apr–Oct. AE, MC, V. **Amenities:** Heated outdoor pool; full-service spa; concierge. *In room:* CD plyaer, hair dryer, iron. No phone.

Sonoma Mission Inn, Spa & Country Club ★★★
Set on 12 meticulously groomed acres, Wine Country's most extensive superspa, the Sonoma Mission Inn, consists of a massive three-story replica of a Spanish mission (well, aside from the pink paint job) built in 1927, an array of satellite wings housing numerous superluxury suites, and, of course, the world-class spa facilities, which include pools filled with naturally heated artesian mineral water. It's a popular retreat for the wealthy and the well known, so don't be surprised if you see Barbra Streisand or Harrison Ford strolling around in skivvies. Big changes have occurred since the resort changed ownership a few years ago, including 70 new guest rooms and suites, a new $20 million spa facility (you won't even recognize the old one), and the acquisition of the Sonoma Golf Club.

The modern rooms are furnished with plantation-style shutters, ceiling fans, down comforters, and such extra amenities as bathroom scales, hair dryers, and oversize bath towels. The Wine Country rooms feature king-size beds, desks, refrigerators, and huge limestone and marble bathrooms; some offer wood-burning fireplaces, and many have balconies. The older, slightly smaller Historic Inn rooms are sweetly appointed with homey furnishings, and most have queen-size beds. For the ultimate in luxury, however, the opulently appointed (and brand new) Mission Suites are the way to go.

18140 Sonoma Hwy. (Calif. 12), P.O. Box 1447, Sonoma, CA 94576. © **800/862-4945** or 707/938-9000. Fax 707/935-1205. www.sonomamissioninn.com. 230 units. $299–$1,200 double. AE, DC, MC, V. From central Sonoma, drive 3 miles north on Highway 12 and turn left on Boyes Blvd. **Amenities:** 2 restaurants (American, California/Spa Cuisine); 2 large, heated outdoor pools; golf course; tennis courts; health club and spa; Jacuzzi; sauna; bike rental; business center; concierge; salon; room service (6am–11pm); babysitting; same-day laundry service/dry cleaning. *In room:* A/C, TV, dataport, minibar, hair dryer, iron, safe.

MODERATE

Beltane Ranch ★ *Finds*
The word "Ranch" conjures up an image of a big ol' two-story house in the middle of hundreds of rolling acres; the kind of place

where you laze away the day in a hammock watching the grass grow or pitching horseshoes in the garden. Well, friend, you can have all that and more at the Beltane Ranch, a century-old, buttercup-yellow manor that's been everything from a bunkhouse to a brothel to a turkey farm. You simply can't help but feel your tensions ease away as you kick your feet up on the shady wraparound porch overlooking the vineyards, sipping a cool, fruity chardonnay. Each room is uniquely decorated with American and European antiques; all have private bathrooms, sitting areas, and separate entrances. A big country breakfast is served in the garden on the porch overlooking the vineyards. For exercise, you can play tennis on the private court or hike the trails meandering through the 1,600-acre estate. *Tip:* Request one of the upstairs rooms, which has the best views.

11775 Sonoma Hwy. (Hwy. 12), Glen Ellen, CA 95442. © 707/996-6501. www.beltaneranch.com. 5 units, 1 cottage. $130–$180 double; cottage $220. Rates include full breakfast. No credit cards; personal checks accepted. **Amenities:** Tennis court. *In room:* No phone.

El Dorado Hotel This place may look like a 19th-century Wild West relic from the outside, but inside it's all 20th-century deluxe. Each modern, handsomely appointed guest room—designed by the same folks who put together the ultra-exclusive Auberge du Soleil resort in Rutherford (see "Where to Stay" in section 1)—has French windows and tiny terraces; some offer lovely views of the plaza, while others overlook the hotel's private courtyard and heated lap pool. All rooms (except those for guests with disabilities) are on the second floor, and have private baths with plush towels and hair dryers. The two rooms on the ground floor are off the private courtyard, and each has a partially enclosed patio. Breakfast, served either inside or out in the courtyard, includes coffee, fruits, and freshly baked breads and pastries. Within the hotel is Piatti, a popular restaurant serving regional Italian cuisine.

405 First St. W., Sonoma, CA 95476. © 800/289-3031 or 707/996-3030. Fax 707/996-3148. www.hoteleldorado.com. 27 units. Summer $220–$265 double; winter $195–$235 double. Rates include continental breakfast and bottle of wine. AE, MC, V. **Amenities:** 1 restaurant; heated outdoor pool; access to nearby health club; bike rental; concierge; room service (11:30am–10pm); laundry service; dry cleaning. *In room:* A/C, TV, dataport, hair dryer.

Glenelly Inn This former 1916 railroad inn is positively drenched in serenity. Located well off the main highway on an oak-studded hillside, the inn comes with everything you would expect from a country retreat—long verandas with comfy wicker chairs and views of the verdant Sonoma hillsides; a hearty country breakfast served beside a large cobblestone fireplace; and bright, immaculate rooms with private entrances, authentic antiques, old-fashioned clawfoot tubs, Scandinavian down comforters, firm mattresses, and ceiling fans. The simmering hot tub is ensconced within a grapevine- and rose-covered arbor.

5131 Warm Springs Rd. (off Arnold Dr.), Glen Ellen, CA 95442. © 707/996-6720. Fax 707/996-5227. www.glenelly.com. 8 units. $135–$190 double. Rates include full breakfast. MC, V. *In room:* No phone.

INEXPENSIVE

Sonoma Hotel This cute little historic hotel on Sonoma's tree-lined town plaza places an emphasis on 19th-century elegance and comfort. Built in 1880 by German immigrant Henry Weyl, each of the attractive guest rooms is decorated in early California style with French country furnishings, antique beds, and period decorations. In a bow to modern luxuries, recent additions include private bathrooms in each of the rooms, as well as cable TVs, phones with dataports, and (this is crucial) air conditioning. Perks include fresh coffee and pastries in the morning and complimentary wine and cheese in the evening.

Also within the hotel is the girl & the fig (see "Where to Dine," below), a popular restaurant serving California-French cuisine.

110 W. Spain St., Sonoma, CA 95476. © **800/468-6016** or 707/996-2996. Fax 707/996-7014. www. sonomahotel.com. 16 units. Summer $110–$245 double; winter Sun–Thurs $95–$170 double, Fri–Sat $115–$195 double. Rates include continental breakfast and evening wine and cheese. AE, DC, MC, V. *In room:* A/C, TV, dataport.

Victorian Garden Inn ⍟ Proprietor Donna Lewis runs what is easily the cutest B&B in Sonoma Valley. A small picket fence and wall of trees enclose an adorable Victorian garden brimming with bowers of violets, roses, camellias, and peonies, all shaded under flowering fruit trees. Four guest rooms—three in the century-old water tower and one in the main house, an 1870s Greek Revival farmhouse—are in keeping with the Victorian theme: white wicker furniture, floral prints, padded armchairs, and clawfoot tubs. The most popular rooms are in the Top o' the Tower, which has its own entrance and view overlooking the garden, and the Woodcutter's Cottage, which has its own entrance and garden view, plus a sofa and armchairs set in front of the fireplace. A breakfast of croissants, muffins, gourmet coffee, and fruit picked from the garden is served at the dining table, in the garden, or in your room; evening wine and sherry are served in the parlor. Leisure time can be spent in the pool or along the shaded wraparound porch.

316 E. Napa St., Sonoma, CA 95476. © **800/543-5339** or 707/996-5339. Fax 707/996-1689. www. victoriangardeninn.com. 4 units. $125–$240 double. Rates include continental breakfast. AE, DC, MC, V. **Amenities:** Outdoor pool; business center; concierge; room service (8am–5pm); laundry service; dry cleaning. *In room:* A/C.

WHERE TO DINE

Though Sonoma Valley has far fewer visitors than Napa Valley, its restaurants are often equally as crowded, so be sure to make reservations in advance.

EXPENSIVE

Depot Hotel–Cucina Rustica Restaurant ⍟ NORTHERN ITALIAN Michael Ghilarducci has been the chef and owner here for the past 14 years, which means he's either independently wealthy or a darn good cook. Fortunately, it's the latter. Located a block north of the plaza in a handsome, historic 1870 stone building, the Depot Hotel offers pleasant outdoor dining in an Italian garden complete with a reflection pool and cascading Roman fountain. The menu is unwaveringly Italian, filled with a plethora of classic dishes such as spaghetti Bolognese and veal alla parmigiana. Start with the bounteous antipasto misto and end the feast with a dish of Michael's handmade Italian ice cream and fresh-fruit sorbets.

241 First St. W. (off Spain St.), Sonoma. © **707/938-2980.** www.depothotel.com. Reservations recommended. Main courses $17–$20. AE, DISC, MC, V. Wed–Fri 11:30am–5pm; Wed–Sun 5–9pm.

the girl & the fig ⍟⍟ COUNTRY FRENCH Already well established in its new downtown Sonoma digs (it used to be in Glen Ellen), this is the new home for Sondra Bernstein's (the girl) beloved and cozy restaurant. Here the cuisine is nouveau country with French nuances, and yes, figs are sure to be on the menu in one form or another. The wonderful winter fig salad contains arugula, pecans, dried figs, Laura Chenel goat cheese, and fig-and-port vinaigrette. Chef John Toulze uses garden-fresh produce and local meats, poultry, and fish whenever possible, in dishes such as pork tenderloin with a potato-leek pancake and roasted beets, and sea scallops with lobster-scented risotto. For dessert, try

Gourmet Picnics, Sonoma Style

Sure, Sonoma has plenty of restaurants, but when the weather's warm, there's no better way to have lunch in the Wine Country than by toting a picnic basket to your favorite winery and basking under the sweet Sonoma sunshine. Even Sonoma's central plaza, with its many picnic tables, is a good spot to set up a gourmet spread.

But first you need grub, so head to the venerable **Sonoma Cheese Factory,** on the plaza at 2 Spain St. (© **707/996-1000**), to stock up for an alfresco fete. The factory offers award-winning house-made cheeses and an extraordinary variety of imported meats and cheeses; a few are set out for tasting every day. Also available are caviar, gourmet salads, paté, and homemade Sonoma Jack cheese. Pick up some good, inexpensive sandwiches, such as fire-roasted pork loin or New York steak. While you're there, you can watch a narrated slide show about the cheese-making process. The factory is open Monday through Friday from 11am to 5:30pm, Saturday and Sunday from 11am to 6pm.

the warm pear galette topped with gingered crème fraîche, a glass of Quady Essensia Orange Muscat, and a sliver of raclette from the cheese cart. Sondra knows her wines, and will be happy to choose the best accompaniment to your meal.

110 West Spain St. © 707/938-3634. www.thegirlandthefig.com. Reservations recommended. Main courses $12–$19. AE, MC, V. Daily 11:30am–11pm.

Glen Ellen Inn Restaurant ✯ CALIFORNIA Christian and Karen Bertrand run this popular Glen Ellen restaurant. The dining room is so quaint and cozy that you feel as if you're dining in their home, but that's exactly the place's charm. Garden seating is the favored choice on sunny days, but the covered, heated patio is always welcoming. First courses from Christian's open kitchen might include a wild-mushroom-and-sausage "purse" served in a brandy cream sauce and warm goat-cheese croquettes. Main courses change with the seasons, but might range from linguine with artichoke hearts and feta to stellar late-harvest ravioli stuffed with pumpkin, walnuts, and sun-dried cranberries on a bed of butternut squash. Other favorites include the marinated pork tenderloin on smoked mozzarella polenta, topped with roasted pepper onion compote, and the utterly tender Nebraska corn-fed filet mignon in a foie gras-brandy reduction sauce. The wine list offers numerous Sonoma selections, as well as more than a dozen wines by the glass. *Tip:* There's a small parking lot behind the restaurant.

13670 Arnold Dr., Glen Ellen. © 707/996-6409. www.glenelleninn.com. Reservations recommended. Main courses $12–$22. AE, MC, V. Daily 5:30–9:30pm. Closed Mon–Thurs last week in Jan.

Kenwood Restaurant & Bar ✯✯ CALIFORNIA/CONTINENTAL This is what California Wine Country dining should be (but what it often, disappointingly, is not). From the terrace of the Kenwood Restaurant, diners enjoy a view of the vineyards set against Sugarloaf Ridge as they imbibe Sonoma's finest at umbrella-covered tables. On nippy days, you can retreat inside to the

Sonoma-style roadhouse, with its shiny wood floors, pine ceiling, vibrant art-work, and cushioned rattan chairs set at white-cloth-covered tables. Chef Max Schacher serves first-rate cuisine, perfectly balanced between tradition and inno-vation, and complemented by a reasonably priced wine list. Great starters are the Dungeness crab cake with herb mayonnaise; the superfresh sashimi with ginger, soy, and wasabi; and the wonderful Caesar salad. Main-dish choices might include poached salmon in a creamy caper sauce, prawns with saffron Pernod sauce, or braised Sonoma rabbit with grilled polenta. But the Kenwood doesn't take itself too seriously: Sandwiches and burgers also are available.

9900 Sonoma Hwy., Kenwood. © 707/833-6326. Reservations recommended. Main courses $13–$26. MC, V. Tues–Sun 11:30am–9pm.

Mission Grill CALIFORNIA/SPA   The Grille, one of the most well-known restaurants in the Wine Country, has long suffered from a solid reputation for serving high-caliber spa cuisine. The problem, of course, is the word "spa," which conjures up visions of blue-haired ladies eating boiled vegetables and soybean salads. Fortunately, the Grille has found a solution: Toni Robertson, the former award-winning Executive Chef at the five-star Pan Pacific Hotel in Singapore (as well as stints in South Africa, Maui, Beverly Hills, and Chicago). Her emphasis is on healthy, uncomplicated cuisine that relies on fresh ingredi-ents and natural flavors. Typical selections from the seasonally changing menu range from lean medallions of ostrich served with a ragout of fingerling pota-toes, artichokes, and dried tomatoes to roasted sea bass with saffron fettuccine and grilled Liberty duck breast in a roasted plum sauce. Service is professional yet friendly, and the wine list is extensive and expensive.

At Sonoma Mission Inn, 18140 Sonoma Hwy., Sonoma. © 707/938-9000. Reservations recommended. Main courses $22.50–$27. AE, DC, MC, V. Sun brunch 10am–2pm. Daily 6–9:30pm.

MODERATE

Della Santina's ★★ ITALIAN   Those of you who just can't take another expensive, chichi California meal should follow the locals to this friendly, tradi-tional Italian restaurant. Every classic Tuscan dish we tried was refreshingly authentic and well flavored—without overbearing sauces or one *hint* of California pretentiousness. Start with traditional antipasti, especially the sliced mozzarella and tomatoes or the delicious white beans. The nine pasta dishes are, again, wonderfully authentic (gnocchi lovers, rejoice!). The spit-roasted meat dishes are a local favorite (though we found them a bit overcooked), and for those who can't choose among chicken, pork, turkey, rabbit, or duck, there's a selection that offers a choice of three. Don't worry about breaking your bank on a bottle of wine, as most of the savory choices here go for under $25.

133 E. Napa St. (just east of the square), Sonoma. © 707/935-0576. Reservations recommended. Main courses $9–$15. AE, DISC, MC, V. Daily 11:30am–3pm and 5–9:30pm.

Cafe La Haye ★★★ ECLECTIC   Well-prepared, wholesome food, an expe-rienced wait staff, friendly owners, soothing atmosphere, and reasonable prices—including a modestly priced wine list—make La Haye a favorite. Within the small split-level dining room pleasantly decorated with hardwood floors, an exposed-beam ceiling, and revolving contemporary artwork, the vibe is small-business. The straightforward, seasonally inspired cuisine, which chefs bring forth from the tiny open kitchen, is delicious and wonderfully well priced. Although the menu is small, it offers just enough options. Expect a risotto special, pasta such as fresh tagliarini with butternut squash, proscuitto, sage, and garlic cream, and pan-roasted chicken breast, perhaps with goat cheese-herb stuffing, caramelized shallot jus, and fennel mashed potatoes. Meat eaters are sure to be pleased with filet of beef seared with black pepper-lavender sauce served with gorgonzola-potato gratin, and no one can resist the creative salads. Sunday brunch includes a handful of creative breakfast and lunch dishes.

140 E. Napa St., Sonoma. (☎ **707/935-5994**. Reservations recommended. Main courses $12–$20. MC, V. Tues–Sat 5:30–9pm; Sun brunch 9:30am–2pm.

Mucca ✸✸ AMERICAN   Rustic-romantic Mucca brings comfort dining to ultra-charming Wine Country heights with soul-satisfying food served in a spiffed-up barn setting. Make a point of saddling up at the cow-patterned bar before pulling up a chair at a linen-draped table in front of a blazing fire (winter) and indulge in simply delicious dishes such as homemade mozzarella with olive oil and thyme, steamed mussels, and grilled T-bone steaks of lamb, pork, and double-cut beef.

14301 Arnold Dr, Glen Ellen (☎ **707/938-3451**. Reservations recommended. Main courses $15–$24. MC, V. Thurs–Sun 5:30–10pm.

Piatti ITALIAN   Piatti has built a steadfast and true clientele by consistently serving large portions of good Italian food at fair prices in a festive setting. The restaurant occupies the ground floor of the El Dorado Hotel at the northwest corner of Sonoma Plaza (just follow your nose). Good pizzas and braised meats—such as the superb lamb shank flavored with a rich port-wine sauce and fresh mint—emerge from a wood-burning oven. Also offered is an array of satisfying pastas, a favorite being the cannelloni stuffed with roasted veal, spinach, porcini mushrooms, and ricotta. Granted, there are fancier and more intimate restaurants in the valley, but none that can fill you up with such good food at these prices. And if the sun is out, be sure to dine alfresco on Piatti's courtyard.

405 First St. W., Sonoma. (☎ **707/996-2351**. Reservations recommended. Main courses $10–$19. AE, DC, MC, V. Sun–Thurs 11:30am–10pm; Fri–Sat 11:30am–11pm.

INEXPENSIVE

Cucina Viansa ✸✸ ITALIAN DELI   Cucina Viansa is the sexiest thing going in Sonoma, a suave deli and wine bar owned by Sam and Vicki Sebastiani, who also run Viansa Winery (see "Touring the Valley & Wineries" in section 2, earlier in this chapter). It's a visual masterpiece, with shiny black-and-white-checkered flooring, long counters of Italian marble, track lighting, and a center deli and wine bar where a crew of young men slice meats, pour wines, and scoop gelato. Start by sampling the preserves and jams near the entrance, then wander the aisle and choose among the armada of cured meats, cheese, fruit, pastas, salads, and breads lining the deli. Popular choices are the hefty sandwiches on herbed focaccia bread or the herb-marinated rotisserie chickens served by the half with your choice of pasta or salad. Roasted turkey, duck, pork, lamb, and rabbit also are available. Opposite the deli is the wine bar, featuring all of Viansa's current wine releases for both tasting and purchase, as well as a small selection of microbrewed beers on tap. On your way out, stop at the gelateria and treat yourself to some intense Italian ice cream. *Note:* Cucina Viansa also hosts live jazz bands every Friday and Saturday night from 6 to 11pm.

400 First St. E., Sonoma. (☎ **707/935-5656**. Deli items $5–$9. AE, DISC, MC, V. Sun–Thurs 10am–6pm; Fri–Sat 10am–11pm.

The Northern Coast

by Matthew R. Poole & Mary Anne Moore

Heading north from San Francisco, you'll come upon a California that hardly resembles the southern part of the state. It's an entirely different landscape, in climate as well as flora and fauna. You can forget about California's fabled surfing-and-bikini scene this far north; instead, you'll find miles and miles of rugged coastline with broad beaches and tiny bays harboring dramatic rock formations—from chimney stacks to bridges and blowholes—carved by the ocean waves.

You may think you've arrived in Alaska when you hit the beaches of northern California. Take a dip in the sea and you'll soon agree with the locals: When it comes to swimming, the Arctic waters along the north coast are best left to the sea lions. But that doesn't mean you can't enjoy the beaches, whether by strolling along the water or taking in the panoramic views of towering cliffs and seascapes. And unlike their southern counterparts, the beaches along the north coast are not likely to be crowded, even in summer.

The best time to visit is in the spring or fall. In spring, the headlands are carpeted with wildflowers—golden poppy, iris, and sea foam—and in fall, the sun shines clear and bright. Summers are typically cool and windy, with the ubiquitous fog burning off by the afternoon.

The most scenic way to reach Stinson Beach, Gualala, Mendocino, and points north is to drive along the coast via Calif. 1. The larger freeway, U.S. 101, runs inland through Healdsburg and Cloverdale and is much faster, but doesn't provide the spectacular views of coastal cliffs and windswept beaches you will see on Calif. 1. A good compromise if you're headed to, say, Mendocino, is to take U.S. 101 to Cloverdale, then cut over on Calif. 128 to the coast.

Oh, and one last thing: Dress warmly.

1 Point Reyes National Seashore ★★★

35 miles NW of San Francisco

The National Seashore system was created to protect rural and undeveloped stretches of the coast from the pressures brought on by soaring real-estate values and increasing population. Nowhere is the success of the system more evident than at Point Reyes. Residents of the surrounding towns—**Inverness, Point Reyes Station,** and **Olema**—have steadfastly resisted runaway development. You won't find any strip malls or fast-food joints here—just laid-back coastal towns with cafes and country inns where gentle living prevails.

The park, a 71,000-acre hammer-shaped peninsula jutting 10 miles into the Pacific and backed by Tomales Bay, is loaded with wildlife, ranging from tule elk, birds, and bobcats to gray whales, sea lions, and great white sharks. Aside from its beautiful scenery, it also boasts historical treasures that offer a window into California's coastal past, including lighthouses, turn-of-the-century dairies and ranches, the site of Sir Francis Drake's 1579 landing, plus a complete replica of a coastal Miwok Indian village.

Though the peninsula's people and wildlife live in harmony above the ground, the situation beneath the soil is much more volatile. The infamous San Andreas Fault separates Point Reyes—the northernmost landmass on the Pacific Plate—from the rest of California, which rests on the North American Plate. Point Reyes is making its way toward Alaska at a rate of about 2 inches per year, but there have been times when it has moved much faster. In 1906, Point Reyes jumped north almost 20 feet in an instant, leveling San Francisco and jolting the rest of the state. The half-mile **Earthquake Trail,** near the Bear Valley Visitor Center, illustrates this geological drama with a loop through an area torn by the slipping fault. Shattered fences, rifts in the ground, and a barn knocked off its foundation by the quake illustrate how alive the earth is here. If that doesn't convince you, a seismograph in the visitor center will.

ESSENTIALS

GETTING THERE   Point Reyes is only 35 miles northwest of San Francisco, but it takes at least 90 minutes to reach by car (it's all the small towns, not the topography, that slow you down). The easiest route is via Sir Francis Drake Boulevard from U.S. 101 south of San Rafael; it takes its sweet time getting to Point Reyes, but does so without any detours. For a much longer but more scenic route, take the Stinson Beach/Calif. 1 exit off U.S. 101 just south of Sausalito and follow Calif. 1 north.

VISITOR INFORMATION   As soon as you arrive at Point Reyes, stop at the **Bear Valley Visitor Center** (© **415/464-5100;** www.nps.gov/pore) on Bear Valley Road (look for the small sign posted just north of Olema on Calif. 1) and pick up a free Point Reyes trail map. The rangers here are extremely friendly and helpful, and can answer any questions you have about the National Seashore. Be sure to check out the great natural history and cultural displays as well. It's open Monday through Friday from 9am to 5pm, Saturday and Sunday from 8am to 5pm.

CAMPING PERMITS   Entrance to the park is free. Camping is $10 per site per night, and permits are required; reservations can be made up to 3 months in advance by calling © **415/663-8054,** Monday through Friday from 9am to 2pm.

WHAT TO SEE & DO

When heading out to any part of the Point Reyes coast, expect to spend the day surrounded by nature at its finest. The park encompasses several surf-pounded beaches, bird estuaries, open swaths of land with roaming elk, and the Point Reyes lighthouse—a favorite among visitors who are awestruck by the spectacular views of the coast. But bear in mind that, as beautiful as the wilderness can be, it's also untameable. Waters in these areas are not only bone chilling and home to a vast array of sea life, including sharks, but are also unpredictable and dangerous. There are no lifeguards on duty, and waves and riptides strongly discourage swimming. Pets are not permitted on any of the area's trails.

By far the most popular—and crowded—attraction at Point Reyes National Seashore is the venerable **Point Reyes Lighthouse** ⨁, located at the westernmost tip of Point Reyes. Even if you plan to forego the 308 steps down to the lighthouse, it's still worth the visit to marvel at the dramatic scenery, which includes thousands of common murres and prides of sea lions that bask on the

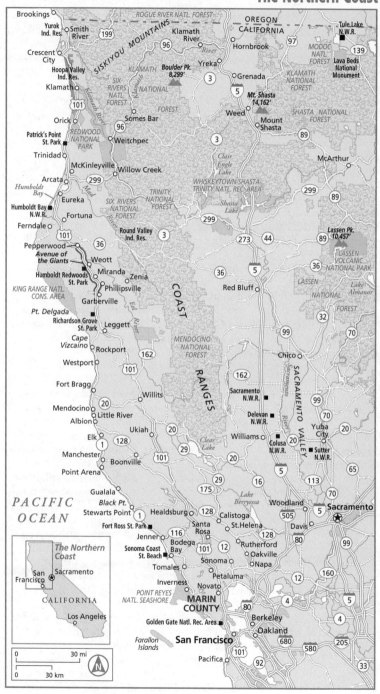

Brookings

Yurok
Ind. Res.
Smith
River
199

ROGUE RIVER NATL. FOREST

OREGON
CALIFORNIA

Tule Lake
N.W.R.

Klamath
River
96

SISKIYOU MOUNTAINS

Hornbrook

97

MODOC
NATL.
FOREST

139

Crescent
City

River

Boulder Pk.
8,299'

Yreka

Grenada

KLAMATH
NATIONAL
FOREST

Lava Beds
National
Monument

Hoopa Valley
Ind. Res.

KLAMATH

3

Klamath

SIX
RIVERS
NATL.
FOREST

NATIONAL

Mt. Shasta
14,162'

Klamath River

FOREST

Weed

Mount
Shasta

SHASTA NATIONAL
FOREST

101

Somes Bar

89

Orick

96

Weitchpec

3

McArthur

Patrick's Point
St. Park

REDWOOD
NATIONAL
PARK

Clair
Engle
Lake

Trinidad

McKinleyville
Willow Creek

WHISKEYTOWN-SHASTA-
TRINITY NATL. REC. AREA

299

89

Arcata
299

TRINITY
NATIONAL
FOREST

Humboldt
Bay

Eureka

SIX RIVERS
NATIONAL
FOREST

Shasta
Lake

Humboldt Bay
N.W.R.

Fortuna

Ferndale

Round Valley
Ind. Res.

3

299

273

44

Lassen Pk.
10,457'

89

101

Pepperwood
36

LASSEN
VOLCANIC
NATIONAL PARK

Avenue of
the Giants
Weott
Miranda
Zenia

36

5

LASSEN

Humboldt Redwoods
St. Park
Phillipsville

Red Bluff

NATIONAL

32

Lake
Almanor

KING RANGE NATL.
CONS. AREA
Garberville

FOREST

70

Pt. Delgada
Richardson Grove
St. Park
Leggett

MENDOCINO
NATIONAL
FOREST

99

Cape
Vizcaino
Rockport

162

COAST

Chico

Westport

SACRAMENTO

89

101

162

Fort Bragg

RANGES

Sacramento
N.W.R.

99

Willits

Mendocino

20

Delevan
N.W.R.

70

Little River

Sacramento River

Yuba
City

20

Albion

Ukiah

20

Williams

Colusa
N.W.R.

20

Elk

1

128

Clear
Lake

20

Sutter
N.W.R.

65

Manchester

Boonville

29

16

5

113

70

Point Arena

101

29

175

Gualala

Lake
Berryessa

Woodland

5

Sacramento

Black Pt.

128

Healdsburg

Stewarts Point

1

Calistoga

505

Fort Ross St. Park

Santa
Rosa

St.Helena

Davis

80

Jenner

116

Bodega
Bay
101

Rutherford

128

99

Sonoma Coast
St. Beach

12

Oakville

Napa

160

Tomales

Sonoma

Inverness

Petaluma

12

POINT REYES
NATL. SEASHORE

Novato

MARIN
COUNTY

4

5

80

Berkeley

4

Golden Gate Natl. Rec. Area

680

205

Farallon
Islands

San Francisco

Oakland

580

Pacifica

101

92

33

*PACIFIC
OCEAN*

The Northern
Coast

San
Francisco

Sacramento

CALIFORNIA

Los Angeles

0   30 mi
0   30 km

N

rocks far below (binoculars come in handy). The lighthouse visitor center (© **415/669-1534**) is open Thursday through Monday from 10am to 4:30pm, weather permitting.

The lighthouse is also the top spot on the California coast to observe **gray whales** as they make their southward and northward migration along the coast from January through April. The annual round-trip is 10,000 miles—one of the longest mammal migrations known. The whales head south in December and January, and return north in March. *Tip:* If you plan to drive out to the lighthouse to whale-watch, arrive early as parking is limited. If possible, come on a weekday. On a weekend or holiday from December through April (weather permitting), it's wise to park at the Drake's Beach Visitor Center and take the shuttle bus to the lighthouse, which is $3.50 for adults, free for kids 12 and under. Dress warmly—it's often quite cold and windy—and bring binoculars.

Whale-watching is far from the only activity offered at the Point Reyes National Seashore. Rangers conduct many different tours on weekends: You can walk along the **Bear Valley Trail,** spotting the wildlife at the ocean's edge; see the waterfowl at **Fivebrooks Pond;** explore tide pools; view some of North America's most beautiful ducks in the wetlands of **Limantour;** hike to the promontory overlooking **Chimney Rock** to see the sea lions, elephant seals, harbor seals, and seabirds; or take a self-guided walk along the **San Andreas Fault** to observe the site of the epicenter of the 1906 earthquake and learn about the regional geology. And this is just a sampling. Since tours vary seasonally, you can either call the **Bear Valley Visitor Center** (© **415/464-5100**) or request a copy of *Park Paper,* which includes a schedule of activities and other useful information. Many of the tours are suitable for travelers with disabilities.

North and South **Point Reyes Beach** face the Pacific and withstand the full brunt of ocean tides and winds—so much so that the water is far too rough for even wading. Until a few years ago, entering the water was actually illegal, but persistent surfers went to court for their right to shred the mighty waves. Today, the park service strongly advises against taking on the tides, so play it safe and stroll the coastline. Along the southern coast, the waters of **Drake's Beach** ★ can be as tranquil and serene as Point Reyes's are turbulent. Locals come here to sun and picnic; occasionally a hearty soul ventures into the cold waters of Drake's Bay. But keep in mind that storms generally come inland from the south and almost always hit Drake's before moving north or south. A powerful weather front can turn wispy waves into torrential tides.

Some of the park's best—and least crowded—highlights can only be approached on foot, such as **Alamere Falls** ★, a freshwater stream that cascades down a 40-foot bluff onto Wildcat Beach, or **Tomales Point Trail** ★, which passes through the Tule Elk Reserve, a protected haven for roaming herds of tule elk that once numbered in the thousands. Hiking most of the trails usually ends up being an all-day outing, however, so it's best to split a 2-day trip within Point Reyes National Seashore into a "by car" day and a "by foot" day.

If you're into bird-watching, you definitely want to visit the **Point Reyes Bird Observatory** ★ (© **415/868-1221**), one of the few full-time ornithological research stations in the United States, located at the southeast end of the park on Mesa Road. This is where ornithologists keep an eye on more than 400 feathered species. Admission to the visitor center and nature trail is free, and visitors are welcome to observe the tricky process of catching and banding the birds. It's open daily from 15 minutes after sunrise until sunset. Banding hours vary seasonally; call © **415/868-0655** for exact times.

Point Reyes National Seashore & Bodega Bay

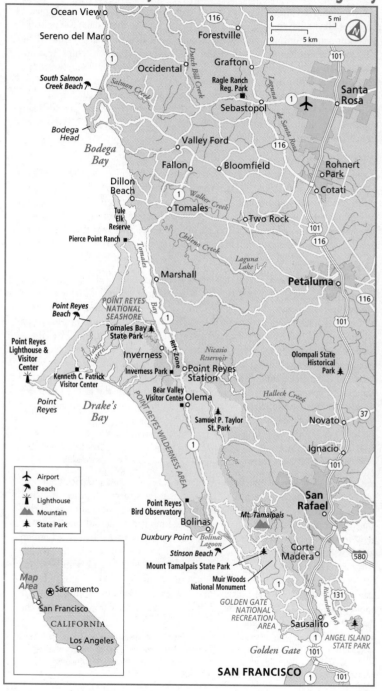

Ocean View
Sereno del Mar
116
Forestville
1
Occidental
Grafton
101
South Salmon Creek Beach
Salmon Creek
Dutch Bill Creek
Ragle Ranch Reg. Park
Santa Rosa
Sebastopol
Bodega Head
Valley Ford
Laguna de Santa Rosa
116
Bodega Bay
Fallon
Bloomfield
Rohnert Park
Dillon Beach
1
Walker Creek
Cotati
Tule Elk Reserve
Tomales
Two Rock
101
Pierce Point Ranch
Chileno Creek
116
Laguna Lake
Tomales Bay
Marshall
Petaluma
116
Point Reyes Beach
POINT REYES NATIONAL SEASHORE
1
101
Tomales Bay State Park
Rift Zone
Nicasio Reservoir
Olompali State Historical Park
Point Reyes Lighthouse & Visitor Center
Inverness
Drakes Estero
Inverness Park
Point Reyes Station
Kenneth C. Patrick Visitor Center
Halleck Creek
Point Reyes
Drake's Bay
Bear Valley Visitor Center
Olema
Novato
37
Samuel P. Taylor St. Park
POINT REYES WILDERNESS AREA
Ignacio
101
1
Point Reyes Bird Observatory
San Rafael
580
✈ Airport
🏖 Beach
Lighthouse
▲ Mountain
🌲 State Park
Bolinas
Mt. Tamalpais
Duxbury Point
Bolinas Lagoon
Corte Madera
131
Stinson Beach
Mount Tamalpais State Park
Richardson Bay
Muir Woods National Monument
1
Map Area
Sacramento
GOLDEN GATE NATIONAL RECREATION AREA
Sausalito
San Francisco
CALIFORNIA
ANGEL ISLAND STATE PARK
Los Angeles
Golden Gate
101
SAN FRANCISCO
1
101

0   5 mi
0   5 km

One of our favorite things to do in Point Reyes is paddle through placid **Tomales Bay,** a haven for migrating birds and marine mammals. Kayak trips, including sunset outings, full-moon paddles, and day trips, are organized by **Tomales Bay Sea Kayaking** (© 415/663-1743; www.tamalsaka.com). Instruction, clinics, and boat delivery are available, and all ages and levels are welcome. Prices start at $50 per person for tours. Half-day rentals begin at $35 for one, $50 for two. Don't worry, the kayaks are very stable, and there are no waves to contend with. The launching point is located on Calif. 1 at the Marshall Boatworks in Marshall, 8 miles north of Point Reyes Station. It's open 7 days a week from 9am to 6pm.

WHERE TO STAY

If you're having trouble finding a vacancy, **Inns of Marin** (© 800/887-2880 or 415/663-2000) and **West Marin Network** (© 415/663-9543) are two reputable services that will help you find accommodations, ranging from one-room cottages to inns and complete vacation homes. Keep in mind that many places here have a 2-night minimum, although in slow season they may make an exception. They'll also refer you to restaurants, hiking, and attractions in the area.

EXPENSIVE

Blackthorne Inn ★★ This elaborate redwood home with its octagonal widow's walk, spiral staircase, turrets, and multiple decks looks more like a superdeluxe tree house than a B&B. Our favorite—and the most expensive— unit is the Eagle's Nest, an octagonal room enclosed by glass and topped with a private sundeck with a catwalk leading to the private bathroom. The largest room is the Forest View, a two-room suite complete with deck, which has a private entrance and a sitting area facing the woods; it's furnished with white wicker and natural rattan, and decorated with floral fabrics and modern lithographs. All have private baths. The main sitting room in the house features a large stone fireplace, skylight, wet bar, and stained-glass windows, and is surrounded by a huge deck.

266 Vallejo Ave. (off Sir Francis Drake Blvd., south of Inverness), Inverness Park, P.O. Box 712, Inverness, CA 94937. © 415/663-8621. Fax 415/663-8635. www.blackthorneinn.com. 4 units. $175–$325 double. Rates include buffet breakfast. MC, V. **Amenities:** Nearby golf course; hot tub. *In room:* Coffeemaker.

Manka's Inverness Lodge ★★ If there were ever a reason to pack your bags and leave San Francisco for a day or two, this is it. A former hunting and fishing lodge, Manka's Inverness Lodge looks like something out of a Hans Christian Andersen fairy tale, right down to the tree-limb bedsteads and cooks roasting venison sausage in front of the hearth. It's all terribly romantic in a Jack London sort of way, and tastefully done as well. The lodge consists of an excellent restaurant on the first floor, four rooms upstairs (Rooms 1 and 2 come with large private decks), four rooms in the Redwood Annex, and two spacious one-bedroom cabins located behind the lodge. For the ultimate romantic splurge, inquire about these secluded cabins: Fishing and Manka's, or at the water's edge, the Boathouse and Chicken Ranch.

30 Callendar Way (On Argyle St. off Sir Francis Drake Blvd., 1½ blocks north of downtown Inverness), P.O. Box 1110, Inverness, CA 94937. © 800/58-LODGE or 415/669-1034. Fax 415/669-1598. www.mankas.com. 12 units. $185–$465. MC, V. **Amenities:** Restaurant; bike rental; limited room service; in-room massage. *In room:* TV in some units, kitchenette, fridge, coffeemaker, hair dryer; no phone.

MODERATE

An English Oak Bed and Breakfast ★ This venerable two-story turn-of-the-century farmhouse has survived everything from a major earthquake to a recent forest fire, which is lucky for you because you'll be hard-pressed to find a better B&B for the price in Point Reyes. Loaded with charm, right down to the profusion of flowers and vines outside and comfy chairs fronting a toasty-warm wood-burning stove inside, it's in a great location, too, with two good restaurants within walking distance and the entire national seashore at your doorstep. One of the units is a private cottage with two futon couches in the living area, suitable for children.

88 Bear Valley Rd., Olema, CA 94950. © 415/663-1777. www.anenglishoak.com. 4 units. $95–$160 double. Rates include breakfast. AE, DISC, MC, V. *In room:* Coffeemaker in some units, hair dryer, iron. Cottage has A/C, TV, fully equipped kitchen.

Point Reyes Country Inn & Stables ⊙   Are you and your horse dreaming of a country getaway? Then book a room at Point Reyes Country Inn & Stables, a ranch-style home on 4 acres that offers pastoral accommodations for two- and four-legged guests (horses only), plus access to plenty of hiking and riding trails. Each of the six B&B rooms has a private bathroom and either a balcony or a garden. The innkeepers have also added two studios (with kitchens) above the stables, plus they rent out two cottages on Tomales Bay equipped with decks, stocked kitchens, fireplaces, and a shared dock.

12050 Calif. 1 (P.O. Box 501), Point Reyes Station, CA 94956. © 415/663-9696. Fax 415/663-8888. www.ptreyescountryinn.com. 10 units. $95–$115 studio; $110–$170 double; $190–$200 cottage. $10–$15 per horse. Rates include breakfast with the 6 B&B rooms, breakfast provisions in the cottages. MC, V. **Amenities:** Nearby golf course. *In room:* No phone. Studios and cottages with kitchens.

INEXPENSIVE

Point Reyes Hostel *Value*   Located deep within Point Reyes National Seashore, this beautiful old ranch-style complex has 44 dormitory-style accommodations, including one room that's reserved for families (though at least one child must be 5 years old or younger). There are also two common rooms, each warmed by wood-burning stoves on chilly nights, as well as a fully equipped kitchen, barbecue (BYO charcoal), and patio. If you don't mind sharing your sleeping quarters with strangers, this is a deal that can't be beat. Reservations (and earplugs) are strongly recommended.

Off Limantour Rd., P.O. Box 247, Point Reyes Station, CA 94956. © 415/663-8811. www.norcalhostels.org. 44 bunks; 1 private room for parent(s) with child age 5 and under. $14 per adult, $7 per child under 17 with parents. 5 nights out of 30 maximum stay. MC, V. Reception hours 7:30–10am and 4:30–9:30pm daily.

WHERE TO DINE

The Gray Whale *Value* ITALIAN   For more than a decade, the Gray Whale has been a popular pit stop for Bay Areans heading to the lighthouse at Point Reyes. Why so popular? First off, it's cheap: Sandwiches—such as the roasted eggplant with pesto and mozzarella—are under $7, as are most of the salads and pastas. Second, it's pretty good: Personal favorites are the specialty pizzas, such as the Californian (artichoke hearts, fresh basil, and tomatoes) and the Vegetarian (baked eggplant, roasted onions and romas, broccoli, and piles of freshly grated Parmesan cheese). Veteran hikers and mountain bikers stop by for an espresso booster, sipped on the small patio overlooking the block-long town of Inverness.

12781 Sir Francis Drake Blvd., Inverness. © 415/669-1244. Main courses $5–$10. MC, V. Daily 11am–8pm.

Manka's Inverness Lodge ⊙⊙ CALIFORNIA/WILD GAME   Manka's reputation is built in large part on its restaurant, which dominates the bottom floor of the lodge. The restaurant dinners are prix fixe, and the specialty of the house is fire-grilled wild game, although if you call ahead you may be able to arrange something tamer. The seasonal menu features such things as pheasant with a Madeira jus, mashed potatoes, and a wild huckleberry jam; black buck antelope chops with sweet corn salsa; or everybody's favorite, pan-seared elk tenderloin. The restaurant's boast is that the majority of the fish, fruits, and vegetables it serves are grown and raised or caught within 15 minutes of its kitchen. The wine cellar features more than 150 selections.

On Argyle Street (off Sir Francis Drake Blvd., 1½ blocks north of downtown Inverness), Inverness. © 800/58-LODGE or 415/669-1034. Reservations recommended. Prix fixe menu Thurs, Fri, Sun $48 per person; Sat $68 per person; Mon $32 per person. MC, V. Thurs–Mon 6–9pm.

Station House Café 🟊 AMERICAN   This friendly, low-key establishment has been a local favorite for more than 2 decades, thanks to its open kitchen, outdoor garden dining area (key on sunny days), and live music on weekends. Breakfast dishes range from a hangtown fry with local Johnson's oysters and bacon to eggs served with creamed spinach to mashed-potato pancakes. Lunch and dinner specials might include fettuccine with fresh local mussels steamed in a white-wine-and-butter sauce, or two-cheese polenta served with fresh spinach sauté and grilled garlic-buttered tomato—all made from local produce, seafood, and organically raised Niman-Schell Farms beef. Fresh salmon is also always on the menu. The cafe has an extensive list of California wines, plus local and imported beers.

Main St., Point Reyes Station. © 415/663-1515. Reservations recommended. Breakfast $4.50–$8; main courses $9–$22. DISC, MC, V. Sun–Thurs 8am–9pm; Fri–Sat 8am–10pm. Closed Wed in winter.

Taqueria La Quinta *Value* MEXICAN   Fresh, fast, good, and cheap: What more could you ask for in a restaurant? Taqueria La Quinta has been one of our favorite lunch stops in downtown Point Reyes for years and years. A huge selection of Mexican-American standards are posted above the counter. Our favorite is chili verde in a spicy tomatillo sauce with a side of handmade corn tortillas. Those in the know inquire about the seafood specials. Since it's all self-serve, you can skip the tip, but watch out for the salsa—that sucker's hot.

11285 Calif. 1 (at Third and Main Sts.), Point Reyes Station. © 415/663-8868. Main courses $5–$9. No credit cards. Wed–Mon 11:30am–7:30pm.

2 Along the Sonoma Coast

BODEGA BAY

Beyond the tip of the Point Reyes peninsula, the road curves around toward the coastal village of Bodega Bay, which supports a fishing fleet of around 300 boats. It's a good place to stop for lunch or a stroll around town. Despite the droves of tourists who arrive on summer weekends, Bodega Bay is still a mostly working-class fishing town—the sort of place where most people start their day before dawn mending nets, rigging fishing poles, and talking shop. There are several interesting shops and galleries, though the best show in town—especially for kids—is at **Tides Wharf,** where the fishing boats come in to unload their daily catch, which is promptly gutted and packed in ice.

   Bodega Head State Park 🟊 is a great vantage point for whale-watching during the annual migration season from January through April. At **Doran Beach,** there's a large bird sanctuary (willets, curlews, godwits, and more), and the University of California Marine Biology Lab (© 707/875-2211) next door conducts guided tours of its lab projects on Friday afternoons between 2 and 4pm. (Suggested donation is $2.)

   The **Bodega Harbour Golf Links,** at 21301 Heron Dr. (© 707/875-3538), enjoys a panoramic ocean-side setting. It's an 18-hole Scottish-style course

designed by Robert Trent Jones, Jr. A warm-up center and practice facility is free
of charge to registered golfers. Rates range from $60 with cart Monday through
Thursday, $70 on Friday, and $90 on weekends. If golfing isn't your thing, you
can go horseback riding through some spectacular coastal scenery by contacting
Chanslor Horse Stables (© **707/875-3333**), which also has pony rides for the
kids. It's open daily from 9am to 5pm.

One of the bay's major events is the **Fisherman's Festival** in April. Local fishing boats, decorated with ribbons and banners, sail out for a Blessing of the
Fleet, while up to 25,000 landlubbers enjoy music, a lamb-and-oyster barbecue,
and an arts-and-crafts fair.

A few miles inland on Calif. 1 (toward Petaluma) is the tiny town of **Bodega**
(pop. 100), famous as the setting of Alfred Hitchcock's *The Birds,* which was
filmed here in 1961. Fans will want to visit the Potter School House and St.
Teresa's Church.

For more information about these festivals and other goings-on in Bodega
Bay, call or stop in at the **Bodega Bay Area Visitors Center,** 850 Calif. 1,
Bodega Bay, CA 94923 (© **707/875-3866;** www.bodegabay.org). It has lots of
brochures about the town and the surrounding area, including maps of the
Sonoma Coast State Beaches and the best local fishing spots.

WHERE TO STAY

Bodega Bay Lodge and Spa 🏵🏵   Located near Doran Beach State Park,
this is the best hotel in Bodega Bay. Every room has a private balcony with
sweeping views of the bay and bird-filled marshes; fireplaces; and plush furnishings and fabrics. If you can afford the elbow room, opt for one of the luxury
suites. Guests have complimentary access to a fitness center and sauna, as well
as to a beautiful fieldstone spa and heated pool perched above the bay and
surrounded by flower gardens. The lodge's Duck Club Restaurant also enjoys a
reputation as Bodega Bay's finest. Large picture windows take advantage of the
bay view, a sublimely romantic setting for Sonoma County cuisine such as
roasted Petaluma duck and fresh fish caught by the Bodega fleet.

103 Calif. 1, Bodega Bay, CA 94923. © **800/368-2468** or 707/ 875-3525. Fax 650/875-2428. www.
woodsidehotels.com. 84 units. Sun–Thurs $210–$240 double, $400 suite; Fri–Sat $235–$285 double, $450
suite. 2-night minimum on weekends. AE, DC, DISC, MC, V. **Amenities:** Restaurant; heated outdoor pool with
ocean view; nearby golf course; complimentary access to full service spa and fitness center; bike rental;
concierge; room service; in-room massage; babysitting; laundry facilities. *In room:* A/C, TV w/ pay movies, fax,
dataport, minibar, fridge, coffeemaker, hair dryer, iron, safe.

Inn at the Tides 🏵   The larger of Bodega Bay's two upscale lodgings, the
other being Bodega Bay Lodge, the Inn at the Tides consists of a cluster of
condo-like wood complexes perched on the side of a gently sloping hill. The selling point here is the view; each unit is staggered just enough to guarantee a view
of the bay across the highway. The rooms are tastefully modern and the inn's
amenities are first-rate, such as the strikingly attractive indoor-outdoor pool.
The Bay View Restaurant is open Wednesday through Sunday for dinner only,
offering ocean views, a well prepared albeit traditional choice of entrees, and a
romantic, somewhat formal ambiance.

800 Coast Hwy. 1 (P.O. Box 640), Bodega Bay, CA 94923. © **800/541-7788** or 707/875-2751. Fax 707/
875-3285. www.innatthetides.com. 86 units. Summer Sun–Thurs $169–$249; Fri–Sat $199–$284. Winter
rates drop about 20%. Rates include continental breakfast. Golf packages available. AE, DC, DISC, MC, V.
Amenities: Restaurant; indoor heated pool; outdoor pool; nearby golf course; exercise room; whirlpool spa;
Finnish sauna; room service; in-room massage; babysitting (with advance notice); self-service laundry room.
In room: TV w/ pay movies, minibar, coffeemaker, hair dryer, iron.

WHERE TO DINE

In addition to the following choices, see "Where to Stay," above, for hotel restaurants.

Breakers Café CALIFORNIA   If you're a big breakfast eater, the Breakers Café is your best bet in Bodega Bay. Omelets, Belgian waffles, baked polenta, house-baked muffins, and even good ol' biscuits and gravy are served in a pleasant greenhouse-style dining room filled with a profusion of healthy plants and diffused sunlight. The cafe also offers a modest lunch-and-dinner menu, ranging from above-average sandwiches and burgers to fresh pastas, locally caught seafood, and a small selection of vegetarian dishes. Prices run a bit steep for the seafood choices, but most items are under $10. If the weather's warm, ask for a table on the patio.

1400 Calif. 1, Bodega Bay. ℂ 707/875-2513. Main courses $7–$20. MC, V. Daily 9am–9pm, but hours vary seasonally.

Lucas Wharf Deli ⋆ *Value* DELI   We always stop here whenever we pass through Bodega Bay. Most visitors don't even give it a glance as they head into the adjacent restaurant, but that's because they don't know about the big bowls of fresh, tangy crab cioppino doled out, in season, for only $5.25 a pint—a third of the restaurant price. It's a fabulously messy affair, best devoured at the nearby picnic tables. Fish and chips are available year-round. The deli is also open for breakfast.

595 Calif. 1, Bodega Bay. ℂ 707/875-3562. Deli items $4–$10. MC, V. Mon–Thurs 9am–6pm; Fri–Sun 9am–7pm.

Tides Wharf Restaurant SEAFOOD/PASTA   In summer, as many as 1,000 diners a day pass through the Tides Wharf. Back in the early 1960s, it served as one of the settings for Hitchcock's *The Birds,* but don't expect the weather-beaten, board-and-batten luncheonette you saw in the movie—a $6 million renovation gentrified, enlarged, and redecorated the place beyond recognition. The best tables offer views overlooking the ocean, and the bill of fare is what you might expect at a seaside eatery: oysters on the half shell, clam chowder, and all the fish that the owners (who send their own fishing boat out into the Pacific every day) can dredge up from the cold blue waters offshore. Prime rib, pasta, and poultry dishes are available as well. Adjacent to the restaurant are a fish-processing plant, snack bar, and gift shop.

835 Calif. 1. ℂ 707/875-3652. Main courses $13.50–$37. AE, DISC, MC, V. Mon–Fri 7:30am–9pm; Sat–Sun 7am–9:30.

THE SONOMA COAST STATE BEACHES, JENNER & FORT ROSS STATE HISTORIC PARK ⋆⋆

Along 13 winding miles of Calif. 1—from Bodega Bay to Goat Rock Beach in Jenner—stretch the Sonoma Coast State Beaches. These beaches are ideal for walking, tide pooling, abalone picking, fishing, and bird-watching for such species as great blue heron, cormorant, osprey, and pelican. Each beach is clearly marked from the road, and numerous pullouts are provided for parking. Even if you don't stop at any of the beaches, the drive alone is spectacular.

At **Jenner,** the Russian River empties into the ocean. **Penny Island,** in the river's estuary, is home to otters and many species of birds; a colony of harbor seals lives out on the ocean rocks. **Goat Rock Beach** is a popular breeding ground for the seals; pupping season begins in March and lasts until June.

From Jenner, a 12-mile drive along some very dramatic coastline will bring you to **Fort Ross State Historic Park** (© **707/847-3286**), a reconstruction of the fort that was established here in 1812 by the Russians as a base for seal and otter hunting (it was abandoned in 1842). At the visitor center, you can view the silver samovars and elaborate table services that the Russians used. The fenced compound contains several buildings, including the first Russian Orthodox church ever built on the North American continent outside Alaska. A short history lesson about the fort is offered at 11:30am, 1:30pm, and 3:30pm between Memorial Day and Labor Day, and at noon and 2pm the rest of the year. Call ahead to be sure. The park also offers beach trails and picnic grounds on more than 1,000 acres. Admission is free, parking is $2.

North from Fort Ross, the road continues to **Salt Point State Park** (© **707/ 847-3221**). This 3,500-acre expanse contains 30 campsites, 14 miles of hiking trails, dozens of tide pools, a pygmy forest, and old Pomo village sites. Your best bet is to pull off the highway any place that catches your eye and start exploring on foot. At the north end of the park, head inland on Kruse Ranch Road to the 317-acre **Kruse Rhododendron Reserve** (© **707/847-3221**), a forested grove of wild pink and purple flowers where the *Rhododendron californicum* grow up to a height of 18 feet under the redwood-and-fir canopy.

WHERE TO STAY

Jenner Inn ✦   The worst-kept secret on the north coast is Jenner Inn, a hodgepodge of individually designed and decorated houses and cottages scattered along the coast and inland along the Russian River. Couples from the Bay Area who want to stay along the coast for a night, but dread the long drive to Mendocino, usually wend their way here for an easy weekend getaway. Most of the houses are subdivided into suites, while second honeymooners vie for the ultra private oceanfront cottages. Wicker furniture, wood paneling, and private bathrooms and entrances are standard, though each lodging has its own distinct personality: Some have kitchens, while others have fireplaces, porches, or private decks. Naturally, the private cottages overlooking the Pacific are the priciest, but for about $130 most people are content with one of the small suites. A complimentary breakfast is served in the main lodge. In addition to the bed-and-breakfast accommodations, the inn rents out vacation homes located along the river, within Jenner Canyon, or overlooking the ocean.

10400 Calif. 1 (P.O. Box 69), Jenner, CA 95450. © **800/732-2377** or 707/865-2377. Fax 707/865-0829. www. jennerinn.com. 22 units (including 2 vacation homes). $95–$375 double. Rates include extended continental breakfast. AE, MC, V. *In room:* Fridge, coffeemaker, hair dryer, iron, some units with kitchen; no phone.

WHERE TO DINE

River's End INTERNATIONAL   Outwardly unpretentious yet deceptively urbane, this small seaside restaurant offers an artfully rustic setting, with big windows overlooking the coast (seals and sea lions might happen to be cavorting offshore). The menu, which changes monthly, is wonderfully eclectic, offering everything from coconut shrimp, pheasant breast, racklets of elk, seafood, and steaks. Local Sonoma products—game, lamb, poultry, vegetables—are used whenever possible, including Sonoma microbrews and wines. After dinner, take the remainder of your wine to the outside deck and enjoy the sunset.

Calif. 1, Jenner. © **707/865-2484.** Reservations recommended. Main courses $13–$28. MC, V. Summer Thurs–Mon 11:30am–9:30pm. Winter (Nov–Apr) Fri–Sun noon–9:30pm.

Sizzling Tandoor *Value* INDIAN   Something of a non-sequitur along a rather desolate stretch of Calif. 1 between Bodega Bay and Jenner, the Sizzling Tandoor serves huge, inexpensive plates of classic Indian cuisine. The lonely location, though peculiar, is superb: Perched high atop a windswept hill, the restaurant boasts an exquisite view of the Russian River far below. The large array of curries and kabobs are accompanied by soup, vegetables, pulao rice, and the best naan (Indian bread) we've ever had. Even if you're not hungry, order some naan to go—it makes the perfect road snack.

9960 Calif. 1, at the south end of the Russian River Bridge, Jenner. © **707/865-0625.** Main courses $9–$13.50. AE, DISC, MC, V. Mon–Thurs 11:30am–9:00pm; Fri–Sun 11:30am–9:30pm.

GUALALA & POINT ARENA

Back on Calif. 1 heading north, you'll pass through Sea Ranch, a series of condominium beach developments, before you reach the small coastal community of Gualala (pronounced wah-*la*-la). Back in the old days, Gualala was an industrious, vivacious logging town. A few real-life suspender-wearing lumberjacks still end their day at the Gualala Hotel's saloon, but for the most part this coastal town's main role is providing gas, groceries, and hardware for area residents. Just outside of town are several excellent parks, hiking trails, and about 10 or so public beaches that are ideal for sunbathing.

The **Gualala River,** adjacent to the town of the same name, is suitable for canoeing, rafting, and kayaking, because all powerboats and jet skis are forbidden. Along its banks you're likely to see osprey, herons, egrets, and ducks; steelhead, salmon, and river otters make their home in the waters. Canoes and kayaks can be rented in Gualala for 2 hours, a half day, or a full day from **Adventure Rents** (© **888/881-4386** or 707/884-4386, www.adventurerents. com), in downtown Gualala on Calif. 1 north of the Chevron. A double kayak or canoe (which seats two to five persons) costs $50 for 2 hours, $60 for a half day, and $70 for a whole day (single kayaks cost half as much).

Point Arena lies a few miles north of Gualala. Most folks stop here for the view at the **Point Arena Lighthouse** ★ (© **707/882-2777**), which was built in 1870 after 10 ships ran aground here on a single night during a storm. A $3-per-person fee ($1 for children under 12) covers parking, entrance to the lighthouse museum, and a surprisingly interesting tour of the six-story, 145-step lighthouse. It's open daily from 10am to 3:30pm, May through October, but closed on weekdays in December and January; call for times during the other months.

WHERE TO STAY

St. Orres ★★ An extraordinary Russian-style building—complete with two onion-domed towers—St. Orres lies 1½ miles north of Gualala. The complex was built in 1972 with century-old timbers salvaged from a nearby mill. It offers secluded cottage-style accommodations on 42 acres, as well as eight rooms in the main building (these rooms are handcrafted and share three bathrooms decorated in brilliant colors). Other units are very private. Some have wet bars, sitting areas with Franklin stoves, and French doors leading to decks with a distant ocean view. Seven cottages border St. Orres Creek and have exclusive use of a spa facility that includes a hot tub, sauna, and sundeck. The most luxurious is Pine Haven, with two bedrooms, two redwood decks, two bathrooms, a tiled breakfast area, a beach-stone fireplace, and a wet bar. A new cottage, the Black Chanterelle, is as exotic as it sounds with domes, a sauna and Jacuzzi, a fireplace, and an ocean view. Full breakfast is delivered to the cottages. The hotel's restaurant, open for dinner only, is located in a dramatic setting below one of the main building's onion domes. Light filters through stained-glass windows onto strands of ivy that cascade down from the upper balcony. The menu is inspired by Pacific Northwest cuisine and includes wild boar, pheasant, venison, quail, and rack of lamb.

36601 Calif. 1, P.O. Box 523, Gualala, CA 95445. © 707/884-3303. Fax 707/884-1840. www.saintorres.com. 8 units (sharing 3 bathrooms), plus 13 cottages. $80–$95 double; $110–$235 cottage double. Rates include full breakfast. MC, V. **Amenities:** Restaurant, bar; nearby golf course; Jacuzzi; sauna; bike rental; in-room massage; babysitting. *In room:* Fridge, coffeemaker, hair dryer, iron; some units with kitchenettes.

WHERE TO DINE

The Food Company *Value* DELI   If the St. Orres restaurant (see above) is out of your price range, you'll be happy to know that you can have an equally romantic lunch or dinner just down the road for a fraction of the price. Place your order at the deli counter, grab a bottle of wine from the rack, then head to the adjacent garden and plop your collective fannies at one of the picnic tables. The menu offers a dizzying array of specials from around the globe—corn tamales, Greek moussaka, lamb curry, quiche Lorraine, pasta puttanesca—as well as fresh-baked breads, pastries, and sandwiches. Better yet, order it all to go and head for the beach.

38411 Calif. 1 at Robinsons Reef Rd., Gualala. © 707/884-1800. $7–$12. MC, V. Daily 8–10:30am; Sun–Thurs 11am–7pm; Fri–Sat 11am–8pm (closing hours flexible).

Pangaea *Finds* ECLECTIC   North-coast locals have been raving about this place since the day it opened. Chef and owner Shannon Hughes, an expatriate of both the St. Orres and Old Milano Hotel restaurants, decided it was time to do her own thing, and boy is she doing it well. Everything that comes out of her kitchen is wondrously fresh, inventive, and organically grown and/or raised. Try the succulent pork confit, served on a potato tart with homemade apricot chutney. And how's this for a $5 salad: organic greens in a vinaigrette of toasted shallots, sherry vinegar, and Italian mountain Gorgonzola. Hughes has become famous for her Thai-style crab cakes made with ginger scallions and served with a Thai green-curry coconut sauce. Even her burgers are beyond reproach, made with Niman-Schell beef, organic cheese and greens, caramelized onions and Thai chili sauce, garlic-roasted red potatoes, and homemade ketchup. Desserts—strawberry-rhubarb crisp à la mode, lemon-curd tart with a blood-orange sauce—are equally impressive, as is the hip decor.

250 Main St., Point Arena. © 707/882-3001. Reservations recommended. Main courses $17–$26. No credit cards. Wed–Sun 6–9pm.

NORTH FROM POINT ARENA

Driving north from Point Arena, you'll pass Elk (a good place to stop for lunch), Manchester, Albion, and Little River on your way to Mendocino.

WHERE TO STAY

Greenwood Pier Inn ✦   Perched on the edge of a dramatic bluff, the Greenwood Pier Inn is an eclectic, New Age kind of place. It's the unique domain of Kendrick Petty, who owns and operates this quartet of cafe, country store, garden shop, and accommodations. Kendrick is an artist and passionate gardener whose collages, tiles, and marble work can be seen in the interiors of several of the buildings in the complex and also outside in the gardens. Of the accommodations, which are in various buildings in addition to the main inn, the Cliffhouse is our top choice: a seaside redwood cabin complete with a fireplace, a large deck, and an upper-level bathtub with ocean views. All the rooms have private decks, fireplaces or wood burners, and lie within 100 feet of the cliff edge. A beautiful new building, called The Tower, has 3 levels: a two-person Jacuzzi at the bottom, an incredible deck overlooking the ocean on the second level, and, up a library ladder, there's a full-size bed facing an ocean view. A continental breakfast is delivered to your room; breakfast, lunch and dinner— roast pork loin, grilled rack of lamb, grilled Chilean sea bass—are served daily in the cafe.

5928 Calif. 1 (P.O. Box 336), Elk, CA 95432. ℭ **707/877-9997.** Fax 707/877-3439. www.greenwoodpierinn. com. 12 units. $130–$300 double. Rates include continental breakfast. AE, MC, V. Pets accepted in some rooms for $15 per night. **Amenities:** Restaurant; nearby golf course; Jacuzzi with ocean view; in-room massage. *In room:* Fridge, coffeemaker; some units with hair dryers; no phone.

Harbor House ⭐⭐   While the Greenwood Pier Inn is New Age, the darkly beautiful, redwood-sided two-story Harbor House is very traditional. It was built in 1916 by the president of the Goodyear Redwood Lumber Co. as a hide-away for corporate executives. This is not a hotel, but an upscale inn offering 3 acres of gardens, access to a private beach, and views overlooking the Pacific. None of the units has a TV or phone, and that's how guests here like it. Five of the rooms in the main building have their own fireplaces, many are furnished with antiques originally purchased by the lumber executives, and all have private bathrooms. The four cottages tend to be small, but have fireplaces and private decks. Set dinners, included in the rates, change nightly and feature California and Pacific Northwest cuisines, making use of local herbs, freshly baked breads, and vegetables from the inn's own gardens.

5600 S. Calif. 1 (P.O. Box 369), Elk, CA 95432. ℭ **800/720-7474** or 707/877-3203. Fax 707/877-3452. www.theharborhouseinn.com. 10 units. $225–$415 double (winter rates are considerably less). Extra person $100. Rates include full breakfast and 4-course dinner. AE, MC, V. **Amenities:** Restaurant; nearby golf course; in-room massage. *In room:* A/C; cottages have coffeemakers, hair dryer, iron; no phone.

KOA Kamping Kabins *(Kids*   What? You expect me to stay at a Kampgrounds of America?! You bet. Once you see these neat little log "kabins," you can't help but admit that, rich or poor, this is one great way to spend a weekend on the coast. The cabins have one or two bedrooms with log-frame double beds or bunk beds for the kids and sleep four to six people respectively. Rustic is the key word here: Mattresses, a heater, and a light bulb are your standard amenities. Beyond that, you're on your own, but basically all you need is some bedding or a sleeping bag, cooking and eating utensils, and a bag of charcoal for the barbe-cue in front of the cabin. Enjoy your meal at the picnic table or on the front porch in the log porch swing. If this is all a little too spartan for you, opt for one of the fully furnished "kottages," both decked out with private bathrooms, fire-places, comfy beds and other creature comforts. Hot showers, bathrooms, laundry facilities, a small store, and a swimming pool are a short walk away, as is Manchester Beach. It's kid heaven.

On Kinney Rd. (off Calif. 1, 5 miles north of Point Arena). ℭ **800/562-4188** or 707/882-2375. Fax 707/ 882-3104. www.manchesterbeachkoa.com. 24 cabins plus 2 cottages. $46–$54 cabin; $120 cottage (up to 4 people). AE, DISC, MC, V. **Amenities:** Heated outdoor pool (seasonal); spa; children's center and playground; laundry facilities. *In room:* Cottages have TV, kitchenette; no phone.

WHERE TO DINE

Ledford House ⭐ CALIFORNIA/FRENCH   If James Beard were alive today, he'd feel right at home at this innovative but simply decorated restaurant overlooking the pounding surf of the Pacific from a bluff above. The kitchen offers self-styled "New American cuisine," experimenting with the bounty of the Golden State to fashion rich combinations and harmonious flavors. One part of the menu is reserved primarily for the pastas and hearty stews suitable to this far northern setting, such as Antoine's cassoulet, a jumble of pork, lamb, garlic sausage, and duck confit slowly cooked with white beans. Although the menu changes seasonally, for a taste of California try the salmon primavera with lemon-caper butter, or the crisp-roasted duckling with wild huckleberry sauce. Evenings bring live jazz in the cocktail lounge.

3000 N. Calif. 1, Albion. © 707/937-0282. www.ledfordhouse.com. Reservations recommended. Main courses $22–$26. AE, MC, V. Wed–Sun 5–9pm.

3 Mendocino ✶✶✶

166 miles N of San Francisco

Mendocino is, to our minds, *the* premier destination on California's north coast. Despite (or because of) its relative isolation, it emerged as one of northern California's major centers for the arts in the 1950s. It's easy to see why artists were—and still are—attracted to this idyllic community, a cluster of New England–style sea captain's homes and small stores set on headlands overlooking the ocean.

At the height of the logging boom, Mendocino became an important and active port. Its population was about 3,500, and eight hotels were built, along with 17 saloons and more than a dozen bordellos. Today, it has only about 1,000 residents, most of whom reside on the north end of town. On summer weekends, the population seems more like 10,000, as hordes of tourists drive up from the Bay Area—but despite the crowds, Mendocino still manages to retain its small-town charm.

ESSENTIALS
GETTING THERE   The fastest route from San Francisco is via U.S. 101 north to Cloverdale. Then take Calif. 128 west to Calif. 1, then go north along the coast. It's about a 4-hour drive. (You could also take U.S. 101 all the way to Ukiah or Willits, and cut over to the west from there.) The most scenic route from the Bay Area, if you have the time and your stomach doesn't mind the twists and turns, is to take Calif. 1 north along the coast the entire way; it's at least a 5- to 6-hour drive.

VISITOR INFORMATION   You can stock up on lots of free brochures and maps at the **Fort Bragg/Mendocino Coast Chamber of Commerce,** 332 N. Main St. (P.O. Box 1141), Fort Bragg, CA 95437 (© **800/726-2780** or 707/961-6300; www.mendocinocoast.com). Pick up a copy of the center's monthly magazine, *Arts and Entertainment,* which lists upcoming events throughout Mendocino. It's available at numerous stores and cafes, including the Mendocino Bakery, Gallery Bookshop, and Mendocino Art Center.

EXPLORING THE TOWN
Stroll through town, enjoy the architecture, and browse through the dozens of galleries and shops. Our favorites include the **Highlight Gallery,** 45052 Main St. (© **707/937-3132**), for its handmade furniture, pottery, and other craft work; and the **Gallery Bookshop & Bookwinkle's Children's Books,** at Main and Kasten Streets (© **707/937-2665**), one of the best independent bookstores in northern California, with a wonderful selection of books for children and adults. Another popular stop is **Mendocino Jams & Preserves,** 440 Main St. (© **800/708-1196** or 707/937-1037), which offers free tastings of its natural, locally made gourmet wares on little bread chips.

After exploring the town, walk out on the headlands that wrap around the town and constitute **Mendocino Headlands State Park** ✯. (The visitor center for the park is in the Ford House on Main Street; ✆ 707/937-5397.) Three miles of trails wind through the park, giving visitors panoramic views of sea arches and hidden grottoes. If you're here at the right time of year, the area will be blanketed with wildflowers; when we last stopped by, we could pick fresh blackberries beside the trails. The headlands are home to many unique species of birds, including black oystercatchers. Behind the Mendocino Presbyterian Church on Main Street is a trail leading to stairs that take you down to the beach, a small but picturesque stretch of sand where driftwood formations have washed ashore.

On the south side of town, **Big River Beach** is accessible from Calif. 1; it's good for picnicking, walking, and sunbathing.

In town, stop by the **Mendocino Art Center,** 45200 Little Lake St. (✆ 707/ 937-5818), the town's unofficial cultural headquarters. It's also known for its gardens, three galleries, and shops that display and sell local fine arts and crafts. Admission is free; open daily from 10am to 5pm.

For a special treat, go to **Sweetwater Spa & Inn,** 955 Ukiah St. (✆ 800/ 300-4140 or 707/937-4140; www.sweetwaterspa.com), which offers group and private saunas and hot-tub soaks by the hour. Additional services include Swedish or deep-tissue massages. Reservations are recommended. Private tub prices are $10 per person per half hour, $13 per person per hour. Group tub prices are $8.50 per person with no time limit. Special discounts are available on Wednesdays. Open Monday through Thursday from 1 to 10pm, Friday and Sunday from noon to 10pm, Saturdays and holidays from noon to 11pm.

OUTDOOR PURSUITS

Explore the Big River by renting a canoe, kayak, or outrigger from **Catch a Canoe & Bicycles Too** (✆ 707/937-0273), located on the grounds of the Stanford Inn by the Sea (see "Where to Stay," below). If you're lucky, you'll see some osprey, blue herons, harbor seals, deer, and wood ducks. These same folks will also rent you a mountain bike (of much better quality than your usual bike rental), so you can head up Calif. 1 and explore the nearby state parks on two wheels.

Horseback riding (both English and western) on the beach and into the redwoods is offered by **Ricochet Ridge Ranch,** 24201 N. Calif. 1, Fort Bragg (✆ 888/873-5777 or 707/964-PONY; www.horse-vacation.com). Prices range from $40 for a 2-hour beach ride to $195 for an all-day beach and redwoods trail ride.

In addition to Mendocino Headlands State Park (see "Exploring the Town," above), there are several other state parks near Mendocino; all are within an easy drive or bike ride and make for a good day's outing. Information on all the parks' features, including maps of each one, is found in a brochure called *Mendocino Coast State Parks,* available from the visitor center in Fort Bragg. These areas include **Manchester State Park,** located where the San Andreas Fault sweeps to the sea; **Jughandle State Reserve;** and **Van Damme State Park** ✯, with a sheltered, easily accessible beach.

Our favorite of these parks, located directly on Calif. 1 just north of Mendocino, is **Russian Gulch State Park** ✯✯. It's one of the region's most spectacular parks, where roaring waves crash against the cliffs that protect the park's California coastal redwoods. The most popular attraction is the **Punch Bowl,** a collapsed sea cave that forms a tunnel through which waves crash, creating throaty echoes. Inland, there's a scenic paved bike path, and visitors can also hike along miles of trails, including a gentle, well-marked 3-mile **Waterfall Loop** that winds past tall redwoods and damp green foliage to a 36-foot-high waterfall. Admission is $2 and camping is $12 per night. Call ℂ **800/444-7275** for reservations; for general state park information, call ℂ **707/937-5804** or visit www.cal-parks.ca.gov.

Fort Bragg is just a short distance up the coast; deep-sea fishing charters are available from its harbor.

WHERE TO STAY
EXPENSIVE
Stanford Inn by the Sea 🌟🌟   Just south of Mendocino, this rustic but ever-so-sumptuous lodge occupies 11 acres of land abutting the Big River. The grounds are captivating, with tiers of elaborate gardens, a pond for ducks and geese, and fenced pastures containing horses, curious llamas, and old gnarled apple trees. The solarium-style indoor hot tub and pool surrounded by tropical plants is gorgeous. The luxuriously furnished rooms come with special touches such as thick robes, down comforters, fresh flowers, and works by local artists. All have fireplaces or stoves and private decks from which you can gaze on the Pacific. Second honeymooners should inquire about the romantic River Cottage; families will want the big ol' renovated barn. Pets are welcome here and receive the royal treatment. The inn recently added a small massage studio, individual and group yoga lessons, and the only totally vegetarian restaurant on the Mendocino coast, which has become a big hit with both guests and locals.

N. Calif. 1 and Comptche Ukiah Rd. (P.O. Box 487), Mendocino, CA 95460. ℂ **800/331-8884** or 707/937-5615. Fax 707/937-0305. www.stanfordinn.com. 33 units. $235–$295 double; $310–$720 suite. Rates include breakfast. AE, DC, DISC, MC, V. Pets accepted with $25 fee. **Amenities:** Vegetarian restaurant; nearby golf course; solarium-style pool, spa, and sauna; exercise room; kayak and canoe rental; complimentary mountain bikes; concierge; courtesy car; business center; secretarial services; evening room service; in-room massage. *In room:* TV/VCR w/ pay movies, dataport, fridge, coffeemaker, hair dryer, iron; some units with kitchenette, minibar.

MODERATE
Agate Cove Inn 🌟🌟   Good luck trying to find an accommodation with a more beautiful coastal setting than Agate Cove Inn's. Words can barely convey the almost surreal splendor of the view from the inn's front lawn, a sweeping, unfettered vista of the sea and its surging waves crashing onto the dramatic bluffs. Situate yourself on one of the Adirondack chairs with a good book, and you'll never want to leave. The inn consists of a main house trimmed in blue and white, surrounded by a bevy of single and duplex cottages. All but one of the 10 spacious units have views of the ocean, king- or queen-size beds, down comforters, CD players, fireplaces, and private decks. In the morning, a fantastic country breakfast is served in the main house's enclosed porch (yes, with the same ocean view).

11201 N. Lansing St. (P.O. Box 1150), Mendocino, CA 95460. ℂ **800/527-3111** or 707/937-0551. Fax 707/937-0550. www.agatecove.com. 10 units. $119–$269 double. Rates include full breakfast. AE, MC, V. **Amenities:** Nearby golf course; concierge; activities desk; in-room massage. *In room:* TV/VCR w/ complimentary videos, hair dryer; no phone.

Joshua Grindle Inn 🌟🌟   When it was built in 1879, this stately Victorian was one of the most substantial and impressive houses in Mendocino, owned by the town's wealthiest banker. Now the oldest B&B in Mendocino, it features redwood siding, a wraparound porch, and large emerald lawns. From its prettily planted gardens, there's a view across the village to the distant bay. There are five rooms in the main house, two in the cottage, and three in the water tower. All have well-lit, comfortably arranged sitting areas; some offer fireplaces, three have deep-soak tubs, and three have a whirlpool tubs. Each is individually decorated: The library, for example, has a New England feel with its four-poster pine bed, floor-to-ceiling bookcase, and 19th-century tiles around the fireplace depicting Aesop's fables. Sherry, sweets, and tea are served in the parlor in front of the fireplace; breakfast is offered in the dining room. In addition to the inn, the proprietors also have a beautiful two-bedroom, two-bathroom oceanview rental home with floor-to-ceiling windows, a large kitchen, and a wood-burning fireplace. It's located a few minutes north of Mendocino, and rates range from $245 to $375 depending on occupancy.

44800 Little Lake Rd. (P.O. Box 647), Mendocino, CA 95460. ℂ 800/GRINDLE or 707/937-4143. www. joshgrin.com. 10 units. June–Oct and Fri–Sun year-round $130–$245 double; Nov–May Mon–Thurs $115–$195. Rates include full breakfast. MC, V. **Amenities:** Nearby golf course; concierge. *In room:* Hair dryer, some units with TV/DVD; no phone.

MacCallum House ☆☆

An historic 1882 gingerbread Victorian mansion, MacCallum House is one of Mendocino's top accommodations. Originally owned by local matriarch Daisy MacCallum, the house still bears the imprint of this daughter of the town's richest lumber baron. It remained in the family until 1974, when it was turned into a B&B. Now owned by resident proprietors Melanie and Joe Redding, the home has been preserved with all of its original furnishings and contents—right down to Daisy's Christmas cards and books of pressed flowers. Boasting the occasional Tiffany lamp or authentic Persian carpet, each uniquely decorated guest room is exquisitely furnished with many original pieces—a Franklin stove, a handmade quilt, a cushioned rocking chair, or a child's cradle. All have private bathrooms, many equipped with clawfoot or spa tubs for two. The luxurious barn suite, complete with a stone fireplace, can accommodate up to six adults. The popular dinner restaurant on the premises serves California cuisine.

45020 Albion St. (P.O. Box 206), Mendocino, CA 95460. ℂ 800/609-0492 or 707/937-0289. Fax 707/ 964-2243. www.maccallumhouse.com. 19 units. $100–$195 double. Extra person $15. AE, MC, V. **Amenities:** Restaurant, cafe, bar; concierge. *In room:* Some units with fridge, coffeemaker.

Mendocino Hotel & Garden Suites ☆

Right in the heart of town, this 1878 hotel evokes California's gold-rush days. Beveled-glass doors open into a Victorian-style lobby and parlor where you might expect to see Mae West. The hotel's decor combines antiques and reproductions, like the oak reception desk from a demolished Kansas bank. Remington paintings, stained-glass lamps, and Persian carpets contribute to the Wild West aura. Guest rooms feature hand-painted French porcelain sinks with floral designs, quaint wallpaper, old-fashioned beds and armoires, and photographs and memorabilia of historic Mendocino. About half the rooms are located in four handsome small buildings behind the main house. Many of the deluxe rooms have fireplaces, as well as modern bathrooms and good views. Suites have an additional parlor, as well as a fireplace or balcony.

45080 Main St. (P.O. Box 587), Mendocino, CA 95460. ℂ 800/ 548-0513 or 707/937-0511. Fax 707/ 937-0513. www.mendocinohotel.com. 51 units, 37 with private bathroom. $85 double with shared bathroom, $120–$205 double with private bathroom; $275 suite. Extra person $20. AE, MC, V. **Amenities:** 2 restaurants, 2 bars; room service; in-room massage. *In room:* TV, hair dryer.

INEXPENSIVE

Mendocino Village Inn & Spa ⋆   This historic Victorian Inn is just across the street from the headlands, overlooking the ocean and the Big River beach. A garden of flowers, plants, and frog ponds fronts the large blue-and-white guest house, which was built in 1882 by a local doctor and later occupied by famed local artist Emmy Lou Packard. Each pretty room is individually decorated. The Queen Anne Room features a four-poster canopy bed and other Victorian furnishings, and the sentimental Madge's Room is named for a child who etched her name in the window glass almost a century ago (you can still see it). Except for two attic units, all have private bathrooms, and four rooms have private outside entrances. Complimentary beverages are served in the evening, and all guests have spa privileges at the nearby Sweetwater Spa.

44860 Main St. (P.O. Box 626), Mendocino, CA 95460. ℭ 800/882-7029 or 707/937-0246. www.mendocinoinn. com. 12 units. $75–$85 double with shared bathroom, $110–$185 double with private bathroom; $165 Water Tower suite. Winter midweek discounts. Rates include full breakfast and evening refreshments. MC, V. **Amenities:** Spa privileges at adjacent Sweetwater Spa; room service; massage discount at spa.

IN NEARBY ALBION & LITTLE RIVER

Albion River Inn and Restaurant ⋆⋆   A quarter mile north of Albion (or 6 miles south of Mendocino), this modern, beautiful inn overlooks the mouth of the Albion River from a bluff some 90 feet above the Pacific. The view is, of course, spectacular. A plaintive harbor horn in the area adds to the seaside atmosphere. (If you are a light sleeper, earplugs are provided). The rooms are attractively decorated in a contemporary style with comfortable furnishings; all have ocean views, and most have decks. You'll find wingbacks placed in front of the fireplaces, down comforters on the queen and king-size beds, well-lit desks, binoculars for wildlife viewing, CD players, and bathrobes. *Insider tip:* If you really want to impress your sweetie, reserve one of the rooms with a spa tub for two, which has a large picture window offering dazzling views of the coast. The cuisine at the inn's respected restaurant changes daily, featuring fresh local produce whenever possible, but the view from the tables remains the same: stellar. The award-winning wine list is also impressive. Evenings, soft piano music adds to the romantic atmosphere.

3790 N. Calif. 1 (P.O. Box 100), Albion, CA 95410. ℭ 800/479-7944 or 707/937-1919. Fax: 707/937-2604. www.albionriverinn.com. 20 units. $180–$220 double; $260–$280 spa suite. Rates include full breakfast. AE, DC, DISC, MC, V. **Amenities:** Restaurant. *In room:* Fridge, coffeemaker, hair dryer, iron.

Glendeven ⋆⋆   Named one of the 12 best inns in America by *Country Inns* magazine, this 1867 farmhouse has been converted into a place of exceptional style and comfort. Accommodations are spread across 2½ acres that encompass the main house, the Carriage House Suite, and an addition known as Stevenscroft. Each room is individually decorated with a well-balanced mixture of antiques and contemporary pieces, and original art. Most have ocean views, fireplaces and porches. Etta's Suite in the Farmhouse includes an antique walnut bed, while the Eastlin and Carriage House suites are furnished with king-size feather beds. The four rooms in the Stevenscroft annex are also spacious and beautifully furnished. A vacation rental house, La Bella Vista, has two bedrooms, two baths, a kitchen, Jacuzzi, and its namesake beautiful view of the ocean and surrounding gardens. Adjacent to the inn are the numerous fern-lined canyon trails to the ocean and beaches of Van Damme State Park.

8205 N. Hwy. 1, Little River, CA 95456. ℭ 800/822-4536 or 707/937-0083. Fax 707/937-6108. www.glendeven. com. 10 units. Weekend and summer rates $135–$225. Ask about off season midweek specials. Rates include full breakfast. AE, DISC, MC, V. **Amenities:** In-room massage (with notice). *In room:* Hair dryer; no phone.

Heritage House ★★   Famous as the site of the romantic movie *Same Time, Next Year*, most of the rooms at this traditional country club–style property have great views of the ocean and rugged coastline. Thirty-seven seafront acres of lush gardens house a variety of accommodations ranging from the merely attractive to frankly lush. Only three guest rooms are located in the ivy-covered New England–style main building; the other accommodations are in cottages grouped two to four under one common roof. Rooms are individually decorated with original antiques and locally made furnishings, with every kind of amenity including bathrobes, umbrellas, wine splits, and newspaper delivery. Most have wood-burning fireplaces or stoves, private decks, sitting areas, and ocean views; several suites have wet bars and Jacuzzis. Wooded trails wind along the dramatic coastline, offering spectacular scenery. The reliable Heritage House dining room is in a magnificent setting overlooking the ocean, features a seasonal menu, and has a highly touted wine cellar.

5200 N. Calif. 1, Little River, CA 95456. ℭ **800/235-5885** or 707/937-5885. Fax 707/937-0318.www. heritagehouseinn.com. 66 units. Summer $145–$425 double; winter $130–$375 double. Extra person $20. AE, MC, V. **Amenities:** Restaurant; concierge; tour and activities desk; in-room massage. *In room:* Fax, dataport, fridge, coffeemaker, hair dryer, iron; no phone.

WHERE TO DINE
EXPENSIVE
Café Beaujolais ★★★ AMERICAN/FRENCH   This is one of Mendocino's— if not northern California's—top dining choices. The venerable French country–style tavern is set in a turn-of-the-century house; rose-colored carnivalglass chandeliers add a burnish to the oak floors and the heavy oak tables adorned with flowers. On warm summer nights, request a table at the enclosed deck overlooking the "designer" gardens.

Though Café Beaujolais started out as a breakfast and lunch place, it's strictly a dinner house now. (Yes, their famed weekend brunch has been discontinued.) The menu changes weekly and usually lists about five main courses, such as wild sturgeon filet pan-roasted with truffle emulsion sauce, roast free-range duck with wild-huckleberry sauce, or broiled Wildwood Ranch pork loin chop with yam purée. The restaurant usually closes for a winter vacation in December and/or January.

961 Ukiah St. ℭ **707/937-5614.** Fax 707/937-3656. www.cafebeaujolais.com. Reservations recommended. Main courses $18–$27. AE, DISC, MC, V. Daily 5:45–9pm.

The 955 Ukiah Street Restaurant ★★ CALIFORNIA/FRENCH   Shortly after this building's construction in the 1960s, the region's most famous painter, Emmy Lou Packard, commandeered its premises as an art studio for the creation of a series of giant murals. Today, it's a large but surprisingly cozy restaurant, accented with massive railway ties and vaulted ceilings. Ask for a window table overlooking the gardens. The cuisine is creative and reasonably priced, a worthy alternative to the perpetually booked Café Beaujolais next door. It's hard to pick a favorite dish from the menu, although the phyllo-wrapped red snapper with pesto and lime has a zesty tang, while the crispy duck with ginger, apples, and a Calvados sauce would earn enthusiastic friends in Normandy.

955 Ukiah St. ℭ **707/937-1955.** www.955restaurant.com. Reservations recommended. Main courses $12–$26. MC, V. Wed–Sun 6–10pm.

MODERATE
Bay View Café ★ AMERICAN   This reasonably priced cafe is one of the most popular in town. From the second-floor dining area of the cafe, there's a

sweeping view of the Pacific and faraway headlands; to reach it, climb a flight of stairs running up the outside of the town's antique water tower, then detour sideways. Surrounded by dozens of ferns suspended from the ceiling, you'll find a menu with Southwestern selections (the marinated chicken breast is very popular), a good array of sandwiches (our favorite is the hot crabmeat with avocado slices), fish and chips, and the fresh catch of the day. Breakfast ranges from the basic bacon 'n' eggs to eggs Florentine and honey-wheat pancakes.

45040 Main St. ℭ **707/937-4197.** Reservations not accepted. Main courses $6–$15. No credit cards. Summer daily 8am–9pm; winter Mon–Thurs 8am–3pm, Fri–Sun 8am–9pm.

The Moosse Café ✚ CALIFORNIA BISTRO   This petite cafe set in a New England–style home is another one of the most popular restaurants in Mendocino. In 1995, the place was gutted and redone, resulting in an attractive, modern interior. The menu, which changes seasonally, boasts many local items such as organic herbs and vegetables, as in the outstanding Caesar salad. We also enjoyed the roast chicken with garlic mashed potatoes and the swordfish special, which came with a pile of fresh vegetables. Other popular entrees are the mixed seafood cakes served over basmati rice with a roasted red pepper remoulade, and the lavender-smoked double-thick pork chop served with roasted yam and apple puree. Service is friendly; our only complaint is that the tables are a bit too close together, especially if it's crowded.

390 Kasten St. (at Albion St.). ℭ **707/937-4323.** Reservations recommended for dinner. Main courses $13–$19. MC, V. Daily 11:30am–3:30pm and 5:30–9pm except Fri–Sat and holidays when closing time is 10pm.

INEXPENSIVE

You'd be surprised what $5 will get you for lunch if you know where to go. **Tote Fete Bakery** (ℭ **707/937-3140**) has a wonderful little carryout booth at the corner of Albion and Lansing Streets. We like the foil-wrapped barbecue chicken sandwiches, but the pizza, focaccia bread, and twice-baked potatoes are also good choices. Dine at the stand-up counter, or opt for a picnic at the headlands down the street.

Regardless of preference—beef, chicken, turkey, or veggie—burger lovers won't be let down at **Mendo Burgers** (ℭ **707/937-1111**), arguably the best burger joint on the north coast. A side of thick, fresh-cut fries is mandatory, as is a pile of napkins. Hidden behind the Mendocino Bakery and Café at 10483 Lansing St., it's a little hard to find, but well worth searching out.

In the back of the **Little River Market** (ℭ **707/937-5133**), located directly across from the Little River Inn on Calif. 1, is a trio of small tables overlooking the beautiful Mendocino coastline. Order a tamale, sandwich, or whatever else is on the menu at the tiny deli inside the market, or buy a loaf of legendary Café Beaujolais bread sold at the front counter and your favorite spread.

4 Fort Bragg

10 miles N of Mendocino, 176 miles N of San Francisco

As Mendocino coast's commercial center—hence the site of most of the area's fast-food restaurants and supermarkets—Fort Bragg is far more down to earth than Mendocino. Inexpensive motels and cheap eats used to be its only attractions, but over the past few years, gentrification has quickly spread throughout the town as the logging and fishing industries have continued to decline. With no room left to open new shops in Mendocino, many gallery, boutique, and restaurant owners have moved up the road. The result is a huge increase in Fort

Bragg's tourist trade, particularly during the annual Whale Festival in March and Paul Bunyan Days over Labor Day weekend.

To explore the town properly, make your first stop the **Fort Bragg/Mendocino Coast Chamber of Commerce,** 332 N. Main St. (P.O. Box 1141), Fort Bragg, CA 95437 (© **800/726-2780** or 707/961-6300; www.mendocinocoast.com), and pick up a free walking map. The friendly staff can answer any questions about Mendocino, Fort Bragg, and the surrounding region.

SHOPPING & EXPLORING THE AREA

The town doesn't boast as many well-coiffed stores and galleries as its dainty cousin to the south, but it does have some worthwhile shopping spots. **Antiques shops** line Franklin Street between Laurel and Redwood (a.k.a. "Antiques Row"), and several boutiques are housed within the newly refurbished **Union Lumber Company Store,** an impressive edifice built almost entirely with hand-crafted redwoods (on the corner of Main and Redwood Streets.).

For the Shell of It, 344 N. Main St. (© 707/961-0461), stocks handmade jewelry, chimes, and collectibles made of shells or designed around a nautical theme, as well as rocks, gems, minerals, and fossils. The **Hot Pepper Jelly Company,** 330 N. Main St. (© 707/961-1422), is famous for its assortment of Mendocino food products—dozens of varieties of pepper jelly, plus local mustards, syrups, and biscotti along with hand-painted porcelain bowls, unusual baskets, and more. The **Mendocino Chocolate Company,** 542 N. Main St. (© 707/964-8800), makes and sells homemade chocolates and truffles, which it ships all over the world. Painters, jewelers, sculptors, weavers, potters, woodworkers, and other local artists display their works at **Northcoast Artists,** 362 N. Main St. (© 707/964-8266). At **Windsong,** 324 N. Main St. (© 707/ 964-2050), predominantly a nice used bookstore, you'll also find a clutter of colorful kites, cards, candles, and other gifts.

Fort Bragg is also the home of the **Mendocino Coast Botanical Gardens,** 18220 N. Calif. 1 (© 707/964-4352), about 7 miles north of Mendocino. This cliff-top public garden, set among the pines along the rugged coast, nurtures rhododendrons, fuchsias, azaleas, and a multitude of flowering shrubs. The area contains bridges, streams, canyons, dells, picnic areas, and trails for easy walking. Admission is $6 for adults, $5 for seniors ages 60 and over, $3 for children 13 to 17, $1 for children 6 to 12, and free for children 5 and under. (Children under 18 must be accompanied by an adult.) Open March through October daily from 9am to 5pm, November through February daily from 9am to 4pm.

From Fort Bragg, the **Skunk Train** ☆ (© **800/77-SKUNK** or 707/964-6371) gives riders a fine tour of the area's redwoods. Locals have always said of the logging trains, "You can smell 'em before you can see 'em," which explains the nickname. The trains, which can be boarded at the Fort Bragg Depot at the foot of Laurel Avenue in Fort Bragg (2 blocks from the Grey Whale Inn), travel 40 miles inland along the Redwood Highway (U.S. 101) to Willits. It's a scenic route through the redwood forest, crossing 31 bridges and trestles and cutting through two deep tunnels. The round-trip takes about 8 hours, allowing plenty of time for lunch in Willits before you return on the afternoon train. The trains run full-day trips daily from Memorial Day weekend through the last weekend in October, but call for exact times, as schedules vary. Half-day trips are offered daily from March 1 through the end of November. During the summer months, it's a good idea to make advance reservations. Tickets cost $39 for a full-day trip, from $29 to $39 for a half-day trip, depending whether you ride the steam engine, diesel, or motor car; children ages 3 to 16 board for $22 full day, $16–18 half day. Serious train buffs can ride in the locomotive cab with the engineer for $99.95. Family packages are also available.

Also worth checking out is the **North Coast Brewing Company,** 455 N. Main St. (© **707/964-2739**), which offers free tours of the brewery Monday through Friday at 1 pm. Across the street is the Brewing Company's pub, open for lunch and dinner (see "Where to Dine," below).

OUTDOOR PURSUITS

Fort Bragg is the county's sportfishing center. Just south of town, **Noyo Fishing Center,** 32440 N. Harbor, Noyo (© **707/964-3000**), is a good place to buy tackle and the best source of information on local fishing boats. Lots of party boats leave from the town's harbor, as do whale-watching tours.

Lost Coast Kayaking, located in Van Damme State Park (© **707/ 937-2434**), offers kayak tours of the coastline's numerous sea caves. All the necessary equipment is provided; all you need to bring is a bathing suit and about $45 for the 2-hour tour (closed during the winter).

Three miles north of Fort Bragg, off Calif. 1, lies **MacKerricher State Park** (© **707/937-5804**), a popular place for biking, hiking, and horseback riding. This enormous 1,700-acre park has 142 campsites and 8 miles of shoreline. For a true biking or hiking venture, travel the 8-mile-long "Haul Road," an old logging road (partly washed out, but safe) that provides fine ocean vistas all the way to Ten Mile River. Harbor seals make their home at the park's Laguna Point Seal Watching Station.

WHERE TO STAY

Beachcomber Motel *(Value)*   If the room rates in Mendocino have you reconsidering a visit to the coast, the Beachcomber Motel may be just what you're looking for. Granted, the rather plain guest rooms lack the fancy antique and lace accouterments you'll find at most B&Bs in the area, but they are definitely spacious, comfortable, and equipped with the basic necessities. None of this really matters, though, since you'll be spending most of your time on the huge back deck that overlooks the cool blue Pacific and gorgeous sunsets. Better yet, directly across from the motel are MacKerricher State Park's miles of beaches and dunes. If you really want to save a bundle, get a room with a kitchenette, stock up on groceries, and make use of the large barbecue area. Low-end rates are for a standard room with no ocean view and the top rate is for the deluxe suite with king bed, Jacuzzi, fireplace, and ocean view. Three units here are wheelchair accessible.

1111 N. Main St., Fort Bragg, CA 95437. © **800/400-7873** or 707/964-2402. Fax 707/964-8925. www. thebeachcombermotel.com. 75 units. $49–$250 double. Rates include continental breakfast. AE, DC, DISC, MC, V. Pets welcome with $10 fee. **Amenities:** Exercise room. *In room:* TV/VCR, dataport, fridge, coffeemaker; suites have kitchenettes.

Colombi Motel *(Value)*   Considering a room here costs about a quarter of the average room rate in Mendocino, the Colombi Motel is what we travel writers call a real score. For only 50 bones, you get a lot for your money at this humble little motel just off Fort Bragg's main strip: It's clean and neat, has all the essentials (including some with kitchens), and you even get your own covered carport. Families will want to reserve one of the two-bedroom units that sleep up to six. Across the street is a Laundromat, a small cafe serving good Mexican food, and the Colombi Market, which is where the motel's guests check in.

600 East Oak St., Fort Bragg, CA 95437. © **707/964-5773**. Fax 707/964-5627. 22 units. $35–$85 double. MC, V. *In room:* A/C, TV, fridge; some units with kitchens.

Grey Whale Inn ✪ Located in downtown Fort Bragg and a short walk from the beach, this charming B&B was originally built as a hospital in 1915, hence the wide hallways and large guest rooms. The handsome redwood building is now a well-run, relaxed inn, furnished with antiques, handmade quilts, and plenty of local art. Each room is unique: Two have ocean views, four have fireplaces, one has a whirlpool tub, three have private decks, and one offers a shower with wheelchair access. The buffet breakfast includes a hot entree, homemade bread or coffee cake, and fresh fruit.

615 N. Main St., Fort Bragg, CA 95437. ℂ **800/382-7244** or 707/964-0640. Fax 707/964-4408. www.greywhaleinn.com. 14 units. $120–$220 double. Discounted winter rates available midweek Nov–Mar. Rates include buffet breakfast. AE, DISC, MC, V. *In room:* TV, coffeemaker, hair dryer; some units with VCR, kitchenette, fridge.

WHERE TO DINE

North Coast Brewing Company ✪ AMERICAN This homey brewpub is the most happening place in town, especially during happy hour, when the bar and dark-wood tables are occupied by boisterous locals. The building that houses the pub is a dignified, century-old redwood structure, which in previous lives has functioned as a mortuary, an annex to the local Presbyterian church, an art studio, and administration offices for the College of the Redwoods. Nine different types of beer are available year-round, in addition to seasonal brews. Standard fare such as burgers and barbecued chicken sandwiches are supplemented by more substantial dishes, ranging from linguine with smoked mushrooms to grilled sirloin pepper steak. After lunch, browse the retail shop or take a free tour of the brewery (see "Shopping & Exploring the Area," above).

444 N. Main St. ℂ **707/964-3400.** Reservations accepted for large parties only. Main courses $7–$22. AE, DISC, MC, V. Daily noon–11pm.

The Restaurant *(Kids* PACIFIC NORTHWEST/CALIFORNIA One of the oldest family-run restaurants on the coast, this small, unpretentious Fort Bragg landmark is known for its good dinners and Sunday brunches. The eclectic menu offers dishes from just about every corner of the planet: New York strip steak, a Provençal-style fish stew, and Margarita chicken marinated in tequila and lime juice. There are also a few vegetarian specialties, including grilled polenta with melted mozzarella and sautéed mushrooms, topped with tomato-herb sauce and Parmesan cheese. A nicely priced kids' menu is available. The comfortable booth section is the best place to sit if you want to keep an eye on the entertainment—courtesy of ebullient chef Jim Larsen—in the kitchen.

418 N. Main St. ℂ **707/964-9800.** Reservations recommended. Dinner $12.50–$21.50; Sun brunch $5–$10. MC, V. Thurs–Tues 5–9pm; Sun brunch 10am–1pm.

Viraporn's Thai Café THAI Born in northern Thailand, Viraporn Lobell attended cooking school and apprenticed in restaurants in her homeland before coming to the United States. After working at Mendocino's premier restaurant, Café Beaujolais, she opened her own restaurant in Fort Bragg, giving local Thai-food fans good reason to cheer. Viraporn works wonders with Thai mainstays such as pad thai, lemongrass soup, spring rolls, and satays, all of which have a pleasant balance of the five traditional Thai flavors of tart, bitter, hot, sweet, and salty. Viraporn also whips up some wonderful curry dishes, best washed down with a cool, super-sweet Thai iced tea.

500 S. Main St. (across from PayLess off Calif. 1). ℂ **707/964-7931.** Main courses $3.95–$9.95. No credit cards. Wed–Mon 11:30am–2:30pm and 5–9pm.

5 The Avenue of the Giants ⋆⋆

From Fort Bragg, Calif. 1 continues north along the shoreline for about 30 miles before turning inland to Leggett and the Redwood Highway (U.S. 101), which runs north to Garberville. Six miles beyond Garberville, the Avenue of the Giants (Calif. 254) begins around Phillipsville. The Avenue of the Giants is one of the most spectacular scenic routes in the West, cutting along the Eel River through the 51,000-acre Humboldt Redwoods State Park. It roughly parallels U.S. 101, and there are about a half dozen interchanges between the two roads if you don't want to drive the whole thing. The Avenue ends just south of Scotia; from here, it's only about 10 miles to the turnoff to Ferndale, about 5 miles west of U.S. 101.

For more information or a detailed map of the area, go to the **Humboldt Redwood State Park Visitor Center,** P.O. Box 276, Weott, CA 95571 (© **707/ 946-2263**), just north of Hidden Springs State Campground, 2 miles south of Weott, in the center of the Avenue of the Giants.

Thirty-three miles long, the Avenue of the Giants was left intact for sightseers when the freeway was built. The giants, of course, are the majestic coast redwoods (*Sequoia sempervirens*); more than 50,000 acres of them makes up the most outstanding display in the redwood belt. Their rough-bark columns climb 100 feet or more without a branch and soar to a total height of more than 340 feet. With their immunity to insects and fire-resistant bark, they have survived for thousands of years. The oldest dated coast redwood is more than 2,200 years old.

The state park has three **campgrounds** with 248 campsites: Hidden Springs, half a mile south of Myers Flat; Burlington, 2 miles south of Weott, near park headquarters; and Albee Creek State Campground, 5 miles west of U.S. 101 on the Mattole Road north of Weott. Reservations are advised in the summer months; call **ReserveAmerica** at © **800/444-7272.** Remaining sites are on a first-come, first-served basis. You'll also come across picnic and swimming facilities, motels, resorts, restaurants, and numerous rest and parking areas.

Sadly, the route has several tacky attractions that attempt to turn the trees into some kind of freak show. Our suggestion is to skip these and appreciate the trees by taking advantage of the trails and the campgrounds off the beaten path. As you drive along, you'll see numerous parking areas with short loop trails leading into the forest. From south to north, the first of these "attractions" is the **Chimney Tree,** where J. R. R. Tolkien's Hobbit is rumored to reside. This living, hollow redwood is more than 1,500 years old. Nearby are a gift shop and a burger place. Then there's the **One-Log House,** a small apartment-like house built inside a log. At Myers Flat midway along the Avenue, you can also drive your car through a living redwood at the **Shrine Drive-Thru Tree.**

A few miles north of Weott is **Founders Grove,** named in honor of those who established the Save the Redwoods League in 1918. Farther north, close to the end of the Avenue, stands the 950-year-old **Immortal Tree,** just north of Redcrest. Near Pepperwood at the end of the Avenue, the **Drury Trail** and the **Percy French Trail** are two good short hikes. The park itself is also good for mountain biking. Ask the rangers for details. For more information, contact Humboldt Redwoods State Park (© **707/946-2409**).

WHERE TO STAY & DINE NEAR THE SOUTHERN ENTRANCE TO THE AVENUE OF THE GIANTS

Benbow Inn ⋆⋆   This elegant National Historic Landmark, overlooking the Eel River and surrounded by marvelous gardens, has housed such notable persons as Eleanor Roosevelt, Herbert Hoover, and Charles Laughton. Constructed in 1926 in a mock Tudor style, it's named after the well-to-do family who built it. Guests enter through a grand hall and into the sumptuous lobby with its huge fireplace surrounded by cushy sofas, grandfather clocks, Oriental carpets, and cherry-wood wainscoting. Rooms vary in size and amenities, though all are tastefully decorated with period antiques; the deluxe units have fireplaces, Jacuzzis, private entrances and patios. The Honeymoon Cottage is the most popular accommodation, with its vaulted ceilings, canopy bed, wood-burning fireplace, and private patio overlooking the river. A comfortable annex with elegant woodwork was added in the 1980s. Beautiful Benbow Lake State Park is right out the front door. Complimentary afternoon tea and scones are served in the lobby at 3pm, hors d'oeuvres in the lounge at 5pm, and port wine at 9pm—all very proper, of course. The dramatic high-ceilinged dining room opens onto a spacious terrace and offers internationally inspired main courses.

445 Lake Benbow Dr., Garberville, CA 95542. © **800/355-3301** or 707/923-2124. Fax 707/923-2122. www.benbowinn.com. 55 units. $130–$245 double; $325 cottage. AE, DISC, MC, V. **Amenities:** Restaurant, bar; nearby golf course; complimentary bikes; guided day hikes; courtesy car; babysitting (with advance notice). *In room:* A/C, coffeemaker, hair dryer, iron; some units with TV/VCR, minibar, fridge.

FERNDALE 🏕

The village of Ferndale, beyond the Avenue of the Giants and west of U.S. 101, has been declared a historic landmark because of its many Victorian homes and storefronts (which include a smithy and a saddlery). About 5 miles inland from the coast and close to the redwood belt, Ferndale is one of the best-preserved Victorian hamlets in northern California. Despite its unbearably cute shops, it is nonetheless a vital part of the northern coastal tourist circuit.

What's less readily known about this small town is that it has a number of artists in residence and is home to one of California's oddest happenings, the **World Championship Great Arcata to Ferndale Cross-Country Kinetic Sculpture Race,** a bizarre 3-day event held every Memorial Day weekend. The race, which draws more than 10,000 spectators, is run 38 miles over land, sand, mud, and water in whimsically designed, handmade, people-powered vehicles that have to be seen to be believed—dragons, Christmas trees, flying saucers, pyramids to mention but a few. Awards range from Best Art to Best Engineering to Best Bribe and as the Grand Prizes are worth about $14.98, inspired madness is the only incentive. Stop in at the museum at 780 Main St. if you want to see a few past race entries, although they're poor, pale facsimiles of the contrivances in glorious action.

WHERE TO STAY

Gingerbread Mansion 🏕🏕   This peach-and-yellow structure with stained glass and other fine architectural details is one of Ferndale's most frequently photographed Victorians, built in 1899 as the home of a local doctor and his family. Run by Ken Torbert, it's beautifully furnished with antiques. Some of the large guest rooms have two old-fashioned clawfoot tubs for bubble baths for two, and others offer fireplaces. Our favorite room is the attic-level Empire Suite, a lavish spare-no-expense blowout with Ionic columns, massage-jet shower, two fireplaces, and a king-size bed draped with Royal Sateen fabric. The new ultra-luxurious Veneto Room is also very impressive. Bathrobes and thick, extra-large towels are provided. Beds are turned down for the night, and you'll find hand-dipped chocolates on the nightstand. When you rise, there's morning coffee or tea outside your door, enough to sustain you until your breakfast of fruit, cheese, muffins, breads, cakes, and a baked egg dish. Afternoon tea with sandwiches, pastries, and fresh fruit are also served.

400 Berding St. (P.O. Box 40), Ferndale, CA 95536. ℂ **800/952-4136** or 707/786-4000. Fax 707/786-4381. www.gingerbread-mansion.com. 11 units. $150–$210 double; $170–$385 suite. Extra person $40. Rates include full breakfast and afternoon tea. AE, MC, V. **Amenities:** In-room massage with advance notice. *In room:* Hair dryer; no phone.

WHERE TO DINE

Curley's Grill ✪ CALIFORNIA GRILL   This bright and lively restaurant specializes in California-inspired grilled foods, but don't think for a moment that the menu is limited to steaks, prime rib, and barbecued baby-back ribs. Owner Curley Tait also grills up such items as polenta with a sausage-tomato sauce, a medley of Pacific seafish, crab cakes, and some of the freshest vegetables on the California coast. Curley has added homemade breads and desserts to the menu as well. Curley's also offers an interesting selection of California wines, and has a Victorian-style full bar area.

400 Ocean St., inside the Victorian Inn. ℂ **707/786-9696.** Main courses $9–$18. DISC, MC, V. Daily 11:30am–9pm; breakfast Sat–Sun 8–11am.

6 Eureka & Environs ✪

Eureka is 296 miles N of San Francisco.

EUREKA

On first glance, Eureka (pop. 27,000) doesn't look very appealing: Fast-food restaurants, cheap motels, and shopping malls predominate on the main thoroughfare. But if you turn west off U.S. 101 anywhere between A and M Streets, you'll discover **Old Town Eureka** along the waterfront, which is worth exploring. It has a large number of Victorian buildings, a museum, and some good-quality stores and restaurants. A new waterfront boardwalk is under construction.

For more visitor information, contact or visit the **Eureka/Humboldt County Convention and Visitors Bureau,** 1034 Second St., Eureka, CA 95501 (ℂ **800/ 346-3482** or 707/443-5097; www.redwoodvisitor.org), or the **Eureka Chamber of Commerce,** 2112 Broadway, Eureka, CA 95501 (ℂ **800/356-6381** or 707/442-3738).

The **Clarke Memorial Museum,** 240 E St. (ℂ **707/443-1947**), has a fine collection of Native American baskets and other historic artifacts. The other popular attraction is the extraordinary architectural gem, the **Carson House** ✪, built from 1884 to 1886 for lumber baron William Carson. A three-story conglomeration of ornamentation, its design is a mélange of styles—Queen Anne, Italianate, Stick, and Eastlake. It took 100 men more than 2 years to build. Today it's a private club, so you can only marvel at the exterior of this 18-room mansion—said to be the most photographed Victorian home in the United States—from the sidewalk. Across the street stands the **"Pink Lady,"** designed for William Carson as a wedding present for his son. Both testify to the wealth that was once made in Eureka's lumber trade. As early as 1856, there were already seven sawmills producing 2 million board feet of lumber every month. A lovingly restored building in Old Town now houses the **Morris Graves Museum of Art,** 636 F St., Eureka (ℂ **707/442-0278**), with four galleries showcasing local artists as well as traveling exhibitions.

Humboldt Bay, where the town stands, was discovered by white settlers in 1850. In 1853, Fort Humboldt was established to protect settlers from local

Native American communities. Ulysses S. Grant was stationed here for 5 months until he resigned after serious disputes with his commanding officer about his drinking. The fort was abandoned in 1870. Today, the fort offers a self-guided trail past a series of logging exhibits, plus a reconstructed surgeon's quarters and a restored fort hospital, used today as a museum housing Native American artifacts and military and pioneer paraphernalia. **Fort Humboldt State Historic Park** is located at 3431 Fort Ave. (℗ **707/445-6567**). Admission is free; it's open daily from 9am to 4pm.

OUTDOOR PURSUITS

Humboldt Bay supplies a large portion of California's fish, and Eureka has a fishing fleet of about 200 boats. To get a better view (and perspective) of the bay and surrounding waters, you can board skipper Leroy Zerlang's *Madaket*—said to be the oldest passenger-carrying vessel in operation in the United States—for a 75-minute **Humboldt Bay Harbor Cruise** (℗ **707/445-1910**), departing from the foot of L Street in downtown Eureka. Tickets are $10.50 per person, free for children ages 4 and under. (For its returning fans, the *Madaket* was recently relocated from its long-time C Street location because of the construction of the new waterfront boardwalk.)

For more active water recreation, kayaks, canoes, and sailboats can be rented from **Hum Boats,** on F Street (℗ **707/443-5157**), which also provides tours and lessons.

Humboldt County is also suitable for biking because it's relatively uncongested. Bikes can be rented from **Pro Sport Center,** 508 Myrtle Ave. (℗ **707/443-6328**). Fishing, diving, biking, and hiking information are also available here.

Humboldt Bay is an important stopover point along the Pacific Flyway and is the winter home for thousands of migratory birds. South of town, the **Humboldt Bay National Wildlife Refuge** ⍟, 1020 Ranch Rd., Loleta (℗ **707/ 733-5406**), provides an opportunity to see many of the 200 or so species that live in the marshes and willow groves—including Pacific black brant, western sandpiper, northern harrier, great blue heron, and green-winged teal. The egret rookery on the bay, best viewed from Woodley Island Marina across the bay en route to Samoa, is spectacular. Peak viewing for most species of waterbirds and raptors is between September and March. The refuge's entrance is off U.S. 101 north at the Hookton Road exit. Cross the overpass and turn right onto Ranch Road.

WHERE TO STAY

Abigail's Elegant Victorian Mansion Bed & Breakfast ⍟ For anyone interested in Victorian history and design, this is a special experience; those who just want comfort, service, a true gourmet breakfast, and a lovely garden will also find this lodging ideal. The 1888 house, a National Historic Landmark, is the labor of love of owners Doug and Lily Vieyra, who have combed the country for the fabrics and designs that now provide the most authentic Victorian atmosphere we have ever encountered in the United States. The wallpapers are extraordinary—brilliant blues, golds, jades, and reds in intricate patterns that feature peacocks and mythological figures. Doug pays attention to every detail, from the butler who greets you in morning dress to the silent movies and period music on the phonograph. Each unit is individually furnished: The Van Gogh room contains the Belgian bedroom suite of Lily's mother. The Lily Langtry room, named after the actress and king's mistress who stayed here when she performed locally, features a four-poster bed and Langtry memorabilia. Guests can play croquet on the manicured lawn, where ice-cream sodas and lemonade are served in the afternoon.

1406 C St. (at 14th St.), Eureka, CA 95501. ℂ **707/444-3144.** Fax 707/442-3295. www.eureka-california. com. 4 units. $95–$215 double. Additional person $40–$50. Rates include breakfast. MC, V. **Amenities:** Sauna; complimentary bikes; Swedish massage; laundry services. *In room:* A/C.

Hotel Carter, Carter House, Bell Cottage & Carter Cottage ★★★   At

the north end of Eureka's Old Town is the original building that launched Carter's renowned hostelry empire: the Carter House. Copied from a famous 1884 San Francisco Victorian, it was constructed by Mark Carter as a family home in 1982. Soon afterwards, Mark and his wife, Christi Carter, began taking guests, and before long they built a lovely hotel across the street, the Hotel Carter. Later, the pretty Victorian Bell Cottage was acquired, and most recently the ultra-luxurious Carter Cottage.

The 23 rooms in the large, full-service Hotel Carter have modern furnishings and pine four-posters. The suites have such luxury appointments as fireplaces and Jacuzzis, and distant views of the waterfront can be seen from the tubs. There are seven rooms in the original Carter House, which is furnished with antiques, Oriental rugs, and modern artwork. The Bell Cottage's rooms are also individually decorated in grand Victorian fashion. If you really want to splurge, however, reserve the Carter Cottage, a small home that's been converted into one of the most luxurious lodgings in northern California, a mini-mansion replete with a chef's kitchen, two fireplaces, a grand bathroom with a whirlpool tub for two, a private deck, and even a wine cellar. On the ground level of the Hotel Carter is one of Eureka's finest restaurants, Restaurant 301 (see "Where to Dine," below).

301 L St., Eureka, CA 95501. ℂ **800/404-1390** or 707/444-8062. Fax 707/444-8067. www.carterhouse.com. 32 units. $125–$187 double; $297–$326 suite; $497 Carter Cottage. Packages available. AE, DC, DISC, MC, V. From U.S. 101 north, turn left onto L St. and go to Third St. **Amenities:** Restaurant, wine shop; nearby golf course; activities desk; in-room massage; babysitting; laundry service. *In room:* A/C, TV/VCR w/ pay movies, hair dryer, iron; some units with kitchens.

WHERE TO DINE
Ramone's Bakery & Café *Value* BAKERY   Ramone's combines a bakery on
one side with a small cafe on the other. The baked items are extraordinary—try any one of the croissants, Danish, or muffins, and you won't be disappointed. Alas, the once-popular cafe has closed down, but you can still find a few lunch specials to choose from among the breads and pastries, such as soups, salads, sandwiches, and more. At any time of the day, it's a great place to stop in for a light, inexpensive meal and cup of coffee. There's a second bakery location at 2223 Harrison St., in Eureka, as well as one in Arcata at 747 13th St., at Wildberries Marketplace.

209 E St. (in Old Town). ℂ **707/445-2923.** Main courses $4–$6. No credit cards. Cafe Mon–Sat 7am–6pm; Sun 7am–4pm.

Restaurant 301 ★★★ CALIFORNIA   The large, light, and airy dining
room adjacent to the hotel's lobby has tall windows looking out on the waterfront. It's the best restaurant in the area, with most of the herbs and many of the vegetables picked fresh from the hotel's organic gardens across the street. At dinner, diners may order either a la carte or off the Discovery Menu, a highly recommended prix-fixe five-course dinner menu that pairs each course with suggested wines by the glass. A typical dinner may begin with an artichoke, green lentil, and fennel salad, followed by a warm chèvre cake appetizer, then on to a grilled duck breast served with a seasonal fruit and zinfandel sauce. The cuisine

also displays Asian accents, as in the chicken with spicy peanut sauce and the tiger prawns with sesame, ginger, and soy. If you're an oyster lover, start with a few Humboldt Bay oysters roasted with barbecue sauce. There's an excellent and extensive wine list, courtesy of the 301 Wine Shop within the hotel.

In the Hotel Carter, 301 L St. ✆ **800/404-1390** or 707/444-8062. Reservations required. Main courses $18–$26. AE, DC, DISC, MC, V. Breakfast daily 7:30–10am; dinner daily 6–9pm.

Samoa Cookhouse ✿ *(Finds* AMERICAN   During the lumber industry's heyday, cookhouses (like this one dating from 1885) were common, serving as community centers. Here the mill men and longshoremen at the Hammond Lumber Company came to chow down on three hot meals before, during, and after their 12-hour workday. The food is still hearty—though not necessarily healthy by today's waist-conscious standards—and served family style at long tables covered with red-checkered cloths. Nobody leaves hungry. The price includes soup, salad, fresh-baked bread, the main course, and dessert (usually pie). The lunch-and-dinner menu still features a different dish each day—roast beef, fried or barbecued chicken, ham, or pork chops. Breakfast typically includes eggs, potatoes, sausage, bacon, pancakes, and all the orange juice and coffee you can drink. Adjacent to the dining room is a small museum featuring memorabilia from the lumbering era. This is the last cookhouse in the West. Bring the kids before it vanishes into history.

Cookhouse Rd., Samoa. ✆ **707/442-1659.** www.humboldtdining.com/cookhouse/. Reservations accepted for large groups only. Main courses $7.45–$11.95. AE, DISC, MC, V. Mon–Sat 7am–3:30pm and 5–10pm; Sun 7am–10pm (closes an hour earlier in winter). From U.S. 101, take Samoa Bridge to the end and turn left on Samoa Rd., then take the first left.

ARCATA ✿
From Eureka it's only 7 miles to Arcata, one of our favorite towns on the northern coast. Sort of a cross between Mayberry and Berkeley, it has an undeniable small-town flavor—right down to the bucolic town square—yet it possesses that intellectual and environmentally conscious esprit de corps so characteristic of university towns (Arcata is the home of Humboldt State University).

There are loads of family-type things to do here. On Wednesday, Friday, and Saturday evenings between June and July, Arcata's semipro baseball team, the **Humboldt Crabs,** partake in America's favorite pastime at Arcata Ballpark, at Ninth and F Streets. Also worth a stop: the kid-friendly **Humboldt State University Natural History Museum,** 1315 G St. (✆ 707/826-4479), which is open Tuesday through Saturday from 10am to 5pm; **Tin Can Mailman,** at 10th and H Streets (✆ 707/822-1307), a wonderful used-book store with more than 130,000 titles; **Redwood Park** (east end of 11th Street), which has an outstanding playground for kids and miles of forested hiking trails; and the **Humboldt Brewing Company,** 10th and I Streets (✆ 707/826-BREW), creators of the heavenly Red Nectar Ale (call for tour information).

A few miles north of Willow Creek lies the Hoopa Indian Reservation. In the Hoopa Shopping Center, the **Hoopa Tribal Museum** (✆ 530/625-4110) archives the culture and history of the native people of northern California, including their ceremonial regalia, basketry, canoes, and tools. Hours are Monday through Friday from 8am to noon and 1 to 5pm year-round, and in summer on Saturdays from 10am to 4pm.

OUTDOOR PURSUITS
The **Arcata Marsh and Wildlife Sanctuary** ✿, at the foot of South I Street (✆ 707/826-2359), is a thought-provoking excursion. The 154-acre sanctuary—which

doubles as Arcata's integrated wetland wastewater treatment plant—is a stopover for marsh wrens, egrets, and other waterfowl, including the rare Arctic loon. Each Saturday at 8:30am and 2pm there are free 1-hour guided tours starting at the cul-de-sac at the foot of South I Street. The town populace is very proud of its environmentally-pleasing wastewater solution, boasting that "Arcata Residents Flush With Pride."

Heading east from Arcata, Calif. 299 leads to the Trinity River in the heart of **Six Rivers National Forest.** Willow Creek and Somes Bar are the prime recreational centers for the area. Here visitors can sign up for canoeing, rafting, and kayaking trips with such outfitters as **Aurora River Adventures,** in Willow Creek (𝄡 **800/562-8475;** www.rafting4fun.com), which offers some offbeat, educationally oriented excursions that are great for kids, as well as gnarly Class V trips for the more daring. They also rent equipment for self-guided adventures.

WHERE TO STAY

Hotel Arcata *Value* This is the town's most prominent hotel, and many guests are parents visiting their ungrateful offspring at Humboldt State University. Located at the northeast corner of the town plaza, the Hotel Arcata consists of a handsome turn-of-the-century brick facade and an equally charming lobby (the staff is quite friendly as well). The individually decorated rooms range from small singles starting at a modest $66, and twice that amount for a large Executive Suite that overlooks the plaza. The mini-suites are the quietest, and a bargain at $88. On the premises, under different management, is a Japanese restaurant, Tomo. If you can't afford the more sumptuous Lady Anne B&B (see below), this is definitely the next best choice.

708 Ninth St., Arcata, CA 95521. 𝄡 800/344-1221 or 707/826-0217. Fax 707/826-1737. www.hotelarcata. com. 32 units. $66–$110 double; $116–$138 executive suite. Rates include continental breakfast. AE, DC, DISC, MC, V. Pets accepted with $5-a-day fee and $50 deposit. **Amenities:** Restaurant; free passes to nearby indoor pool and health club; salon; executive suites. *In room:* TV, dataport, coffeemaker.

The Lady Anne 𝄢 Easily Arcata's finest lodging, this Queen Anne–style bed-and-breakfast is kept in top-notch condition by innkeepers Sharon Ferrett and Sam Pennisi, who also served a term as Arcata's mayor. The large, cozy guest rooms are individually decorated with period antiques, lace curtains, Oriental rugs, and English stained glass. For second honeymooners, there's the Lady Sarah Angela Room with its four-poster bed and pleasant bay view. Breakfast is served in the grand dining room, warmed on winter mornings by a toasty fire. On summer afternoons, you can lounge on the veranda with a book or play a game of croquet on the front lawn. Several good dining options are only a few blocks away at Arcata Plaza.

902 14th St., Arcata, CA 95521. 𝄡 707/822-2797. www.humboldt1.com/~ladyanne. 5 units. $90–$110 double. Rates include breakfast. MC, V. *In room:* Hair dryer, iron; no phone.

WHERE TO DINE

Abruzzi ITALIAN The best way to review your dining options in Arcata is to stroll downtown to Jacoby's Storehouse, a converted mid-19th-century brick warehouse located at the southwest corner of the town plaza, and ponder the menus posted outside the Abruzzi and Plaza Grill (see below). Abruzzi is generally acknowledged as the best Italian restaurant in town. Replete with dark woods and dim lighting, it has all the makings for a romantic dinner. Specialties include range-fed veal picatta and sea scallops with langostinos tossed with cheese tortellini. Well-seasoned filet steaks are available as well. The standout dessert is the chocolate paradiso, a dense chocolate cake set in a pool of champagne mousseline. All meals begin with a basket of warm bread sticks, focaccia, and a baguette that you can smell all the way down the street.

Jacoby's Storehouse (at the corner of Eighth and H Sts.). ✆ **707/826-2345.** Reservations recommended. Main courses $9–$22. AE, DISC, MC, V. Daily 5:30–9pm.

Folie Douce ✦ BISTRO Humboldt Hip meets Cuisine Chic at Folie Douce, the most energized and inventive restaurant in town. Designer wood-oven-fired pizza is its mainstay, such as the grilled duck sausage fennel, chèvre, and sundried tomato pizza, or the spicy shrimp with fontina, mozzarella, and scallions combo. But the appetizers and entrees are equally intriguing. The highlight of your vacation may well be the artichoke-heart cheesecake appetizer, followed by a plate of grilled wild rice polenta in a light cream sauce. Other heartier menu items range from a fat filet mignon to roast duck. The restaurant has a serious wine list. This small, festive off-street eatery is extremely popular, so be sure to make reservations.

1551 G St (between 15th and 16th Sts.). ✆ **707/822-1042.** Reservations recommended. Main courses $9–$27. AE, DISC, MC, V. Tues–Thurs 5:30–9pm; Fri–Sat 5:30–10pm.

Plaza Grill *Kids* AMERICAN If the prices at Abruzzi are a bit more than you care to spend, consider the Plaza Grill, located directly above Abruzzi. Despite efforts to make it more upscale, it can't seem to shake its image as a college-student burger joint, but a nice one. The menu is more substantial than you'd think, with a choice of salads, sandwiches, burgers, fish platters, chicken specialties, steaks, and all kinds of coffee drinks. There's a very reasonably priced children's menu.

Jacoby's Storehouse (at the corner of Eighth and H Sts.). ✆ **707/826-0860.** Main courses $7–$17. AE, DISC, MC, V. Sun–Thurs 5–8:30pm; Fri 5–11; Sat 5–10:30pm.

TRINIDAD & PATRICK'S POINT STATE PARK ✦

Back on U.S. 101 north of Arcata, you'll come to **Trinidad,** a tiny coastal fishing village of some 400 people. One of the smallest incorporated cities in California, it occupies a peninsula 25 miles north of Eureka. If you're not into fishing, there's little to do in town except poke around at the handful of shops, walk along the busy pier, and wish you owned a house here.

Five miles north of Trinidad takes you to the 640-acre **Patrick's Point State Park** ✦, 4150 Patrick's Point Dr. (✆ **707/677-3570**), which has one of the finest ocean access points in the north at sandy **Agate Beach.** It's suitable for driftwood picking, rockhounding, and camping on a sheltered bluff. The park contains a re-creation of a Sumeg Village, which is actively used by the Yurok people and neighboring tribes. A self-guided tour takes you to replicas of family homes and sweat houses.

WHERE TO STAY

The Lost Whale Bed and Breakfast Inn ✦✦ *Kids* This modern version of a blue-and-gray Cape Cod–style house is set on 4 acres of seafront land studded with firs, alders, spruces, and redwoods. Its owners welcome children (there's a playground and pygmy goat farm on the premises) and adults (there's also a Jacuzzi with a view of the sea), and claim that it's the only hotel in the state of California with its own private beach. Afternoon tea and an artfully prepared and presented breakfast are included in the rates. The decor is eclectic, with lots of paintings, plus an outdoor deck facing the surf. Part of the grounds is devoted to a kitchen garden with fresh herbs and vegetables. Families should inquire about the furnished homes—including a wonderful farmhouse—that the innkeepers also rent out. A recent addition is a rebuilt beach trail with stairs and handrails.

3452 Patrick's Point Dr., Trinidad, CA 95570. *C* **800/677-7859** or 707/677-3425. Fax 707/677-0284. www.lostwhaleinn.com. 8 units. Summer $162–$192 double; winter $132–$162 double. Rates include country breakfast and afternoon tea. AE, DISC, MC, V. **Amenities:** Jacuzzi with ocean view; children's playground and playhouse; game room; business center. *In room:* No phone.

Trinidad Bay Bed & Breakfast *★* Set 175 feet above the ocean, all rooms at this picturesque Cape Cod–style home have sweeping views of Trinidad Bay. On a clear day, you can see up to 65 miles of the rugged coastline. Your hosts are Corlene and Don Blue (Cordon Blue to their friends), two innkeepers who have created what many visitors think is the most charming inn around. Rare for an older B&B, all the rooms have private bathrooms. Decor throughout is an eclectic mix of New England–style antiques and a collection of antique clocks. If it's available, opt for the Mauve Fireplace Suite, with its wraparound window, large wood-burning fireplace, king-size bed, and private entrance.

560 Edwards St. (P.O. Box 849), Trinidad, CA 95570-0849. *C* **707/677-0840.** Fax 707/677-9245. www. trinidadbaybnb.com. 4 units. Summer $150–$180 double; winter $135–$165. Rates include breakfast. MC, V. Closed Dec–Jan. *In room:* Fridge; coffeemaker; hair dryer; iron; no phone.

Trinidad Inn *Value* There's a bevy of inexpensive motels in these parts, but the Trinidad Inn is the best of the lot. It's located 2 miles north of Trinidad on a serene stretch of road ensconced by a towering cadre of aromatic redwoods. Both the motel's exterior—trimmed in pretty shades of white and blue—and guest rooms are impeccably maintained. Each room is unique: Some are family units that hold up to four persons, while others offer a comfortable queen bed, and private bath for as little as $70 per night (access to the adjoining kitchen is an extra $10). Our favorite room for couples is number 10, an adorable little cottage complete with a full kitchen, living room, private bath, bedroom, and small patio. Each morning, Anna, the manager, serves fresh coffee, tea, and homemade raspberry scones and muffins under the gazebo in the flower-filled garden. Guests are free to use the picnic table and barbecue, or wander through the adjacent forest to the beaches a short stroll away.

1170 Patrick's Point Dr., Trinidad, CA 95570. *C* **707/677-3349.** www.trinidadinn.com. 10 units. $70–$130 double. Rates include continental breakfast. AE, DC, DISC, MC, V. Pets may be accepted with $10 fee and $20 deposit. From U.S. 101, take the Trinidad exit and head 2 miles north on Patrick's Point Dr. *In room:* TV; no phone.

WHERE TO DINE

Larrupin Café *★★* AMERICAN Located on a quiet country road 2 miles north of Trinidad, this highly popular and wondrously decorated restaurant sports an eclectic blend of Indonesian and African artifacts mingled with colorful urns full of exotic flowers and romantic candlelit tables. The recently added new patio with a reflecting pool and bamboo fencing is a charmer. Dinner starts with an appetizer board stocked with gravlax, paté, dark pumpernickel, apple slices, and sauce, followed by a red- and green-leaf salad tossed with a Gorgonzola vinaigrette. Many menu items are barbecued over mesquite fires, such as a hefty cut of halibut that's been basted with lemon butter and served with mustard-flavored dill sauce, and the fantastic pork ribs served with a side of sweet and spicy barbecue sauce. Another recommended dish is the barbecued Cornish game hen served with an orange-and-brandy glaze. For appetizers, the barbecued oysters are divine, especially in winter, when the fireplace casts a much welcomed warmth. Heaven is a slice of pecan-chocolate pie topped with hot buttered rum sauce, or the sinfully good triple-layer chocolate cake layered with caramel and whipped cream.

1658 Patrick's Point Dr. ⓒ 707/677-0230. Reservations recommended. Main courses $15–$22. No credit cards. Wed–Mon 5–9pm.

The Seascape Restaurant *Finds* CALIFORNIA   Established in the 1940s, this is an endearingly unpretentious cross between a cafe and a diner, with three dining rooms, great ocean views, overworked but cheerful waitresses, and a nostalgic aura. Folks pop in for coffee or snacks from early morning until after sundown, but by far the biggest seller here is the Trinidad Bay Platter ($17.95). Heaped with halibut, scallops, and shrimp, and accompanied by salad and rice pilaf, it's even more popular than the prawn brochette, which draws a close second.

Beside the Pier at the foot of Bay St. ⓒ 707/677-3762. Full dinners $8–$22. DISC, MC, V. Daily 7am–9pm.

ORICK

From Trinidad, it's about another 15 miles to Orick. You can't miss it: Just look for the dozens of burl stands alongside the road. Carved with chisels and chain saws, these former redwood logs have been transformed into just about every creature you can imagine—perhaps a gift for your mother-in-law?

At the south end of Orick is the town's saving grace, the sleek **Redwood National Park Information Center** ✵ (ⓒ **707/464-6101,** ext. 5265). If you plan to spend any amount of time exploring the park, stop here first and pick up a free map; the displays of fauna and wildlife aren't too bad, either. It's open daily from 9am to 5pm.

The first of the parks that make up Redwood National Park, Prairie Creek, is 6 miles north of Orick. About 14 miles farther on is the mouth of the **Klamath River,** famous for its salmon, trout, and steelhead. Tours aboard a jet boat take visitors upriver from the estuary to view bear, deer, elk, osprey, hawks, otters, and more along the riverbanks. Rates for the 30-mile scenic trip (offered May 1 to October 30) are $20 for adults, $10 for children ages 4 to 11, and free for kids under 4. For more information and reservations, contact **Klamath River Jet Boat Tours,** Klamath (ⓒ **800/887-JETS** or 707/482-7775).

A more serene alternative to exploring the Klamath is taking a ranger-led **kayak tour.** Offered only during the summer months (and only if they have enough money in their budget), the trip costs about $50 and includes all the requisite kayak gear. For more information, call the Redwood National Park Information Center at the phone number listed above.

From Klamath, it's another 20 miles to Crescent City, gateway to the other parks that make up Redwood National Park.

7 Crescent City

79 miles N of Eureka, 375 miles N of San Francisco

Crescent City itself has little to offer, but it makes a good base for exploring Redwood National Park and the Smith River, one of the great recreational rivers of the West. The **Battery Point Lighthouse,** at the foot of A Street (ⓒ **707/464-3089**), which is accessible on foot only at low tide, houses a museum with exhibits on the coast's history. Tours of the lighthouse ($2 for adults, 50¢ for children) are offered Wednesday through Sunday from 10am to 4pm, tides permitting, from April through September.

Another draw is the **Smith River National Recreation Area** ✵, east of Jedediah Smith State Park and part of Six Rivers National Forest. The Area

Headquarters is at 10600 U.S. 199, Gasquet (© **707/457-3131**), which is reached via U.S. 199 from Crescent City (19 miles; about a 30-minute drive). Maps of the forest can be obtained here, at the Supervisor's Office in Eureka, or at either of the Redwood National Park centers in Orick and Crescent City.

The 300,000-plus acres of wilderness offer camping at five modest-sized campgrounds (all with fewer than 50 sites) along the Smith River. Sixteen trails attract hikers from across the country. The easiest short trail is the **McClendon Ford,** which is 2 miles long and drops from 1,000 to 800 feet in elevation to the south fork of the river. Other activities include mountain biking, white-water rafting, kayaking, and fishing for salmon and trout.

For information, contact the **Crescent City–Del Norte County Chamber of Commerce,** 1001 Front St., Crescent City, CA 95531 (© **800/343-8300** or 707/464-3174).

WHERE TO STAY

Crescent Beach Motel _(Value_   Crescent City doesn't have any fancy hotels or bed-and-breakfasts, but it does have lots of modestly priced motels, the best of which is the Crescent Beach Motel. Near the highway, about 1 mile south of town, this single-story structure is the only local motel set directly on the beach. The freshly remodeled and refurbished rooms are clean and simple. Four of the units face the highway; try to get one of the others, all of which have sliding-glass doors to decks and a small lawn area overlooking the bay. One of the city's most popular restaurants, the Beachcomber (see "Where to Dine," below), is located next door.

1455 Redwood Hwy. S. (U.S. 101), Crescent City, CA 95531. © 707/464-5436. www.visitor-mags.com/crescent. 27 units. Summer $73–$83 double; winter $49–$57 double. AE, DISC, MC, V. _In room:_ TV; no phone.

Curly Redwood Lodge _(Value_   This is a blast from the past, the kind of place where you might have stayed as a kid during one of those cross-country vacations in the family station wagon. It was built in 1957 on grasslands across from the town's harbor, and is completely trimmed with lumber from a single ancient redwood. Although they're not full of the latest high-tech gadgets, the bedrooms are among the largest and best-soundproofed in town, and certainly the most evocative of a bygone, more innocent age. In winter, about a third of the rooms (the ones upstairs) are locked and sealed. Overall, the aura is more akin to Oregon than anything you might imagine in California.

701 Redwood Hwy. S. (U.S. 101), Crescent City, CA 95531. © 707/464-2137. Fax 707/464-1655. www.curlyredwoodlodge.com. 36 units. Summer $60–$86 double; winter $39–$68 double. Winter rates include breakfast. AE, DC, MC, V. _In room:_ TV.

WHERE TO DINE

Beachcomber SEAFOOD   The decor is as predictably nautical as the name implies: rough-cut planking and a scattering of driftwood, fishnets, and buoys dangling above a dimly lit space. The restaurant lies beside the beach, 2 miles south of Crescent City's center. The cuisine is a joy to fish lovers who prefer not to mask the flavor of their seafood with complicated sauces. Most of the dishes are grilled over madrone-wood barbecue pits, a technique perfected since this place was established in 1975. Pacific salmon, halibut, lingcod, shark, sturgeon, Pacific snapper, oysters, and steamer clams are house specialties that have visitors lining up, especially on Friday and Saturday nights.

1400 U.S. 101. © 707/464-2205. Reservations recommended. Main courses $6–$15. MC, V. Thurs–Tues 5–9pm. Closed Dec–Jan, part of Feb.

Harbor View Grotto Restaurant & Lounge SEAFOOD/STEAKS This restaurant has been specializing in fresh seafood at market prices since 1961. It has distant views of the ocean and harbor from the dining room and lounge. The "light eaters" menu includes a choice of a cup of white chowder (made fresh daily) or salad, a main course, and vegetables; heartier appetites can choose from among three different cuts of prime rib. Menu items include fresh, locally caught fish like Pacific snapper and salmon. Crab or shrimp Louis, as well as crabmeat or shrimp sandwiches, are popular in season.

150 Starfish Way. ℂ 707/464-3815. Reservations recommended. Main courses $4–$9 lunch; $6–$20 dinner. DISC, MC, V. Daily 11:30am–9pm, later in the summer months.

8 Redwood National & State Parks ★★

40 miles N of Eureka, 336 miles N of San Francisco.

It's impossible to explain the feeling you get in the old-growth forests of Redwood National and State Parks without resorting to Alice-in-Wonderland comparisons. Like a tropical rain forest, the redwood forest is a multistoried affair, the tall trees being only the top layer. Everything seems big, misty, and primeval—flowering bushes cover the ground, 10-foot-tall ferns line the creeks, and the smells are rich and musty. It's so *Jurassic Park* that you can't help but half expect to turn the corner and see a dinosaur.

When Archibald Menzies first noted the botanical existence of the coast redwood in 1794, more than two million acres of redwood forest carpeted California and Oregon. By 1965, heavy logging had reduced that to 300,000 acres, and it was obvious something had to be done if any redwoods were to survive. The state created several parks around individual groves in the 1920s, and in 1968, the federal government created Redwood National Park. In May 1994, the National Park Service and the California Department of Parks and Recreation signed an agreement to manage these four redwood parks cooperatively, hence the Redwood National *and* State Parks.

Although logging of old-growth redwoods in the region is still a major bone of contention among the government, private landowners, and environmentalists, it's an auspicious sign that contention even exists, a sign that perhaps we have all learned to see the forest *and* the trees for what they are—the undisputed monarchs of all living things, a thriving link to the age of dinosaurs, and a humble reminder that the age of mankind is but a hiccup in time to the venerable *Sequoia sempervirens*.

ESSENTIALS

GETTING THERE & GATEWAYS The southern gateway to the Redwood National and State Parks is the town of Orick, which you can identify by the dozens of burl stands alongside the road. U.S. 101 runs right through the middle of town. The northern gateway to the park is Crescent City, your best bet for a cheap motel, gas, fast food, and outdoor supplies.

INFORMATION In Orick you'll find the **Redwood Information Center,** P.O. Box 7, Orick, CA 95555 (ℂ **707/464-6101,** ext. 5265), one of California's rare examples of well-placed tax dollars (though some may dispute this because it's located near a floodplain and within a tsunami zone). Stop here and pick up a free map; it's open daily from 9am to 5pm. If you missed the Orick center, don't worry: About 10 miles farther north on U.S. 101 is the **Prairie Creek Visitor Center** (ℂ **707/464-6101,** ext. 5300), which carries all the same

Redwood National & State Parks

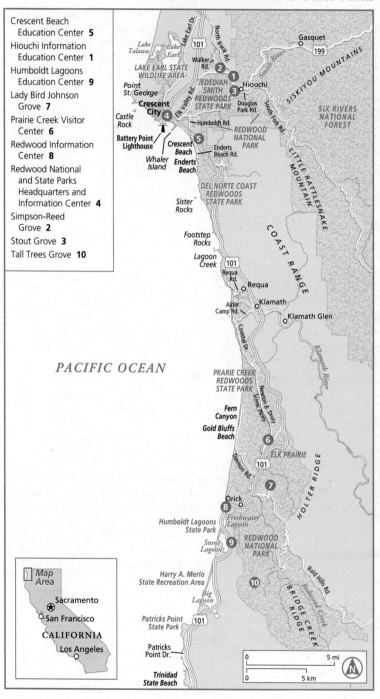

Crescent Beach
  Education Center **5**
Hiouchi Information
  Education Center **1**
Humboldt Lagoons
  Education Center **9**
Lady Bird Johnson
  Grove **7**
Prairie Creek Visitor
  Center **6**
Redwood Information
  Center **8**
Redwood National
  and State Parks
  Headquarters and
  Information Center **4**
Simpson-Reed
  Grove **2**
Stout Grove **3**
Tall Trees Grove **10**

PACIFIC OCEAN

Lake Earl Dr.
North Bank Rd.
Smith River
Gasquet
199
Lake
Talawa
Lake
Earl
101
Walker
Rd.
LAKE EARL STATE
WILDLIFE AREA
Point
St. George
Castle
Rock
Crescent
City
Battery Point
Lighthouse
Whaler
Island
Elk Valley Rd.
JEDEDIAH
SMITH
REDWOODS
STATE PARK
Hiouchi
Douglas
Park Rd.
South Fork Rd.
Humboldt Rd.
Crescent
Beach
Enderts
Beach
Enderts
Beach Rd.
REDWOOD
NATIONAL
PARK
SISKIYOU MOUNTAINS
SIX RIVERS
NATIONAL
FOREST
LITTLE RATTLESNAKE MOUNTAIN
COAST RANGE
DEL NORTE COAST
REDWOODS
STATE PARK
Sister
Rocks
Footstep
Rocks
Lagoon
Creek
101
Requa
Rd.
Requa
Alder
Camp Rd.
Klamath
Klamath Glen
Coastal Dr.
Klamath River
PRARIE CREEK
REDWOODS
STATE PARK
Newton B. Drury Scenic Pkwy.
Fern
Canyon
Gold Bluffs
Beach
ELK PRAIRIE
Davison Rd.
101
HOLTER RIDGE
Orick
Freshwater
Lagoon
Humboldt Lagoons
State Park
Stone
Lagoon
REDWOOD
NATIONAL
PARK
Bald Hills Rd.
BRIDGE CREEK RIDGE
Redwood Creek
Harry A. Merlo
State Recreation Area
Big
Lagoon
Patricks Point
State Park
101
Patricks
Point Dr.
Trinidad
State Beach

Map
Area
Sacramento
San Francisco
CALIFORNIA
Los Angeles

0   5 mi
0   5 km

maps and information. It's open daily from 9am to 5pm in summer, daily from 10am to 4pm (sometimes later) in winter.

Before touring the park, pick up a free guide at the **Redwood National and State Parks Headquarters and Information Center,** 1111 Second St. (at K Street), Crescent City, CA 95531 (℃ **707/464-6101,** ext. 5064). It's open daily from 9am to 5pm.

If you happen to be arriving via U.S. 199 from Oregon, the rangers manning the **Hiouchi Information Station** (℃ **707/464-6101,** ext. 5067) and **Jedediah Smith Visitor Center** (℃ **707/464-6101,** ext. 5113) can also supply you with the necessary maps and advice. Both are open daily in summer from 9am to 5pm, and in winter when staffing is available.

For more information about the Redwood National and State Parks, visit their website at **www.nps.gov/redw.**

FEES & PERMITS   Admission to the national park is free, but to enter any of the three state parks (which contain the best redwood groves), you'll have to pay a $2 day-use fee, which is good at all three. The camping fee is $12 for drive-in sites. (Reservations are highly recommended in summer.) Walk-in sites are free, though a permit is required.

RANGER PROGRAMS   The park service runs interpretive programs—from trees to tide pools, legends to landforms—at the Hiouchi, Crescent Beach, and Redwood information centers during summer months, as well as year-round at the park headquarters in Crescent City. State rangers lead campfire programs and numerous other activities throughout the year as well. Call the **Parks Information** service for both the national and state parks (℃ **707/464-6101,** ext. 5265) to get current schedules and events.

EXPLORING THE PARKS BY CAR

If you're approaching the park from the south, be sure to take the detour along U.S. 101 called the **Newton B. Drury Scenic Parkway** ⭐, which passes through dazzling groves of redwoods and elk-filled meadows before leading back onto the highway 8 miles later. Another spectacular route is the **Coastal Drive** ⭐, which winds through stands of redwoods and offers grand views of the Pacific.

The most amazing car-friendly trail in all the Redwood National and State Parks is the hidden, well-maintained gravel **Howland Hill Road** ⭐⭐ that winds for about 12 miles through Jedediah Smith Redwoods State Park. It's an unforgettable journey through an unbelievably spectacular old-growth redwood forest—considered by many to be one of the most beautiful areas in the world. To get here from U.S. 101, keep an eye out for the 76 gas station at the south end of Crescent City; just before the station, turn right on Elk Valley Road, and follow it to Howland Hill Road, which will be on your right. After driving through the park, you'll end up at U.S. 199 near the town of Hiouchi, and from here it's a short jaunt west to get back to U.S. 101. Plan at least 2 to 3 hours for the 45-mile round-trip, or all day if you want to do some hiking or mountain biking in the park. This drive is not recommended for trailers and motor homes.

SPORTS & OUTDOOR PURSUITS

BEACHES, WHALE-WATCHING & BIRD-WATCHING   The park's beaches vary from long white-sand strands to cobblestone pocket coves. The water temperature is in the high 40s to low 50s year-round; it's often rough out there, so swimmers and surfers should be prepared for adverse conditions.

Crescent Beach is a long sandy beach just 2 miles south of Crescent City that's popular with beachcombers, surf fishermen, and surfers. Just south of Crescent Beach is **Endert's Beach,** a protected spot with a hike-in campground and tide pools at the southern end of the beach.

High coastal overlooks (like Klamath overlook and Crescent Beach overlook) make great whale-watching outposts during the southern migration in December and January and the return migration in March and April. The northern sea cliffs also provide valuable nesting sites for marine birds like auklets, puffins, murres, and cormorants. Birders will thrill at the park's freshwater lagoons as well. These coastal lagoons are some of the most pristine shorebird and waterfowl habitats left, and are chock-full of hundreds of different species.

HIKING   The park's official map and guide, available at any of the information centers, provides a fairly good layout of hiking trails within the park. Regardless of how short or long your hike may be, dress warmly and bring plenty of water and sunscreen. Pets are prohibited on all of the park's trails.

The most popular walk is the short, heavily traveled **Fern Canyon Trail** ✪, which leads to an unbelievably lush grotto of lady, deer, chain, sword, five-finger, and maidenhair ferns clinging to 50-foot-high vertical walls divided by a babbling brook. It's only about a 1½-mile walk from Gold Bluffs Beach, but be prepared to scramble across the creek several times on your way via small footbridges.

The **Lady Bird Johnson Grove Loop** ✪ is an easy, 1-hour self-guided tour that loops 1 mile around a glorious lush grove of mature redwoods. It's the site at which the national park was dedicated by Lady Bird Johnson in 1968. Also an easy trek is the **Yurok Loop Nature Trail** at Lagoon Creek. The 1-mile self-guided trail gradually climbs to the top of rugged sea bluff (with wonderful panoramic views of the Pacific) before looping back to the parking lot. If someone's willing to act as shuttle driver, have him or her meet you at the Requa Trailhead and take the 4-mile coastal trail to the mouth of the Klamath. And for the whiner in your group, there's **Big Tree Trail,** a quarter-mile paved trail leading to a really big tree.

Tall Trees Trail leads to the one of the world's tallest trees—perhaps 365 feet tall, 14 feet in diameter, and more than 600 years old. This was once touted as the tallest tree in the world, but new candidates keep popping up and this proud giant has also lost a couple of feet. Now, who knows? It's still worth it to see the contender. You'll have to go to the Redwood Information Center near Orick (see "Essentials" above) to obtain a free map and permit to drive to the trailhead of Tall Trees Grove. Only 50 permits are issued per day on a first-come, first-served basis because of a small parking area. After driving to the trailhead, you have to walk a steep 1⅓ miles down into the grove. The trail round-trip is 3.2 miles.

WILDLIFE VIEWING   One of the most striking aspects of Prairie Creek Redwoods State Park is its 200- to 300-strong herd of **Roosevelt elk** ✪, usually found in the appropriately named Elk Prairie in the southern end of the park. These gigantic beasts can weigh 1,000 pounds, and the bulls carry huge antlers from spring to fall. Elk are also sometimes found at Gold Bluffs Beach—it's an incredible rush to suddenly come upon them out of the fog or after a turn in the trail. Nearly a hundred **black bears** also call the park home, but are seldom seen. Unlike those at Yosemite and Yellowstone, these bears are still afraid of people. Keep them that way by giving them a wide berth, observing food-storage etiquette while camping, and disposing of garbage properly.

CAMPING & ACCOMMODATIONS

Five small campgrounds are located in the national park proper. Four of the walk-in (more like backpack-in) camps—Little Bald Hills, Nickel Creek, Flint Ridge, and Butler Creek—are free, and only one (the Redwood Creek Gravel Bar) requires a permit from the visitor center in advance.

Most car campsites are in the **Prairie Creek** and **Jedediah Smith State Parks,** which lie entirely inside the national park. Prairie Creek contains two campgrounds, at Elk Prairie and Gold Bluffs Beach. Sites are $12 per night and can be reserved by calling the ReserveAmerica reservations system (✆ **800/ 444-7275;** www.reserveamerica.com). It helps if you know what campground and if possible which site you would like.

If the camping areas above are all filled, try the **Mill Creek Campground,** in Del Norte Coast Redwoods State Park (part of RNSP), located 7 miles south of Crescent City on U.S. 101, which has 145 tent or RV sites. The walk-in tent sites are actually quite nice, situated amidst the forest. Fees are $12 per night. The ReserveAmerica system (see above) handles reservations for this campground as well.

A number of bed-and-breakfasts and funky roadside motels are available in the surrounding communities of Crescent City, Orick, and Klamath. The **Crescent City/Del Norte Chamber of Commerce** (✆ **800/343-8300**) can probably steer you toward the proper match.

Redwood National Park AYH Hostel *Value* The only lodging actually within the park, this turn-of-the-century settler's homestead was remodeled in 1987 to accommodate 30 guests dormitory style (that is, bunks and shared bathrooms). The location of this hostel is perfect, a mere 100 yards from the beach, and surrounded by hiking trails leading along the Redwood Coast (the staff leads nature walks and is well versed in local history). A couple's room is available, for an additional $10, with advance notice, and the hostel even takes reservations by credit card (strongly recommended in the summer). The nightly rate includes use of the showers, common room with VCR and videos, redwood deck, self-help common kitchen, laundry room, dining room, pellet stove, and bicycle storage.

14480 U.S. 101 (at U.S. 101 and Wilson Creek Rd., across from False Klamath Cove), Klamath, CA 95548. ✆ **800/909-4776 ext. 74** or 707/482-8265. Fax 707/482-4665. www.norcalhostels.org. 28 bunks, 1 couple's room. $14–$16. DISC, MC, V.

The Far North: Lake Tahoe, the Shasta Cascades & Lassen Volcanic National Park

by Matthew R. Poole & Mary Anne Moore

Dominated by the eternally snow-capped Mount Shasta—visible for 100 miles around on a clear day—California's upper northern territory is among the least-toured sections of the state. Often referred to as "the Far North," this vast region stretches from the rice fields north of Sacramento all the way to the Oregon border. In fact, the area is so immense that the state of Ohio would fit comfortably within its borders.

The Far North is a virtual outdoor playground for the adventurous traveler, offering myriad inexpensive recreational activities such as hiking, climbing, skiing, white-water rafting, and mountain biking. Other attractions, both artificial and natural, range from the amazing Shasta Dam to Lava

Beds National Monument, which has dozens of caves to explore, and Lassen Volcanic National Park, a towering laboratory of volcanic phenomena.

Directly south of the Cascade Range is one of the most popular recreational regions in the Golden State: Lake Tahoe. Situated at 6,225 feet above sea level in the Sierra Nevada Mountains, it straddles the border between Nevada and California. Although the lake has been marred by overdevelopment—particularly along the casino-riddled southern shore—the western and eastern coastlines still provide quiet havens for hiking and cycling. The surrounding mountains offer some of the best skiing in the United States at more than a dozen resorts.

1 Lake Tahoe ★★★

107 miles E of Sacramento, 192 miles E of San Francisco, 45 miles SW of Reno, NV

Lake Tahoe is one of our great national treasures. It's not only stunningly beautiful, but the air is crisp and clear, and the sun shines 80% of the time. In summer, you can enjoy boating and watersports, sandy beaches, bicycling, golf, tennis, hiking, camping, ballooning, horseback riding, rock climbing, bungee jumping, parasailing, skating—the array of possibilities is endless. In winter, with an average snowfall of 409 inches, Lake Tahoe is one of the nation's premier ski destinations, offering 15 downhill resorts and 10 cross-country ski centers. There's also snowboarding, ice-skating, snowshoeing, snowmobiling, sleigh riding, sledding, and snow play. Year-round activities include fishing, Vegas-style gambling, and big name entertainment in the casinos.

Then there is the lake. It's disputable whether Lake Tahoe is the most beautiful lake in the world, but it's hard to imagine any spot as lovely. When Mark

A Tale of Two Shores

Before you visit Tahoe for the first time, it's important to know that there's a huge difference between the North and the South Shores. Don't let the "City" in North Shore's "Tahoe City" fool you: The entire town can be driven through in a couple of minutes, whereas South Lake Tahoe is brimming with high-rise casinos, motels, and mini-malls. Where you choose to stay is important because driving from one end of the lake to the other takes an hour or more in the summer and can be downright treacherous in the winter.

So which side is for you? If you're here for gambling or entertainment, stay south: The selection of casinos is better and there's more action. If it's the great outdoors you're after, or simply a relaxing retreat, head north. The scenic North Shore offers a better selection of quality resorts and vacation rentals, while the bustling South Shore shoots for quantity, offering more lodging options, often at better rates. The woodsy West Shore has the most camping spots, while the East Shore has been protected from development and has no commercial activity.

Wherever you stay, you'll find no shortage of water and mountain sporting activities. The lake is crowded during the summer and ski seasons, so plan far ahead. It's much easier to get reservations for the spring and fall, and the rates are significantly lower. There are numerous vacation homes and condominiums available to rent. Call the visitor centers bureaus or visit the websites listed below under "Visitor Information" for a list of rental agents.

Twain first saw it, he declared it "the fairest picture the whole earth affords." Famed for its crystal clear water (a white dinner plate at the depth of 75 ft. would be clearly visible from the surface) and its size, 22 miles long and 12 miles wide, it is the largest alpine lake in North America. Its average depth is 989 feet with the deepest point being 1,645 feet, containing enough water to cover the entire state of California to a depth of 14½ inches. Surrounded by the majestic peaks of the Sierra Nevadas, its waters seem to soak up the colors of the sky and the mountains, creating a kaleidoscope of sparkling blues, greens, and purples. It's a sight that will lure you back year after year.

ESSENTIALS

GETTING THERE   It's a 4-hour drive from San Francisco; take I-80 east to Sacramento, then U.S. 50 to the South Shore, or I-80 east to Calif. 89 or Calif. 267 to the North Shore. Be prepared for snow in the winter. During heavy storms, you won't be permitted to pass the checkpoints without 4-wheel drive or chains. From Los Angeles, it's a grueling 9-hour drive; take I-5 through the Central Valley to Sacramento, and then follow the directions above.

Reno-Tahoe International Airport (45 min. to North Shore, 90 min. to South Shore) offers regularly scheduled service by 10 major airlines, including **American** (© 800/433-7300), **Delta** (© 800/221-1212), and **United** (© 800/241-6522). Rent a car or take a shuttle up to the lake: **No Stress Express**

Lake Tahoe & Environs

To the Gold Country and Sacramento
Donner Lake
To Reno
80
Sugar Bowl
Donner Peak
Donner Memorial State Park
Truckee
Martis Creek Lake
TOIYABE NATIONAL FOREST
431
Washoe Lake
Lookout Mtn.
267
Northstar-at-Tahoe
Mt. Pluto
Carnelian Bay
Crystal Bay
Incline
Diamond Peak
395
TAHOE
89
Squaw Valley USA
Lake Forest
28
Marlette Lake
Lake Tahoe State Park
NATIONAL
Alpine Meadows
Tahoe City
Homewood
Homewood
Lake Tahoe
Carson City
FOREST
Pacific Crest Trail
Truckee River
Centerville
89
Tahoma
Glenbrook
28
50
Rubicon River
Sugar Pine Point State Park
TOIYABE
Carson River
ELDORADO NATIONAL FOREST
D.L. Bliss State Park
Zephyr Cove
50
NATIONAL
FOREST
395
Desolation Wilderness Area
Emerald Bay State Park
Stateline
NEVADA
CALIFORNIA
E. Fk. Carson R.
89
Heavenly Resort
Fallen Leaf Lake
South Lake Tahoe
W. Fk. Carson R.
50
ELDORADO NATIONAL FOREST
89
50
89
Twin Bridges
89
ELDORADO NATIONAL FOREST
Woodfords
Washoe Indian Reservation
88
Skiing
State Park
Kirkwood
Kirkwood
TOIYABE NATIONAL FOREST
88
Kit Carson
Caples Lake
Markleeville
Emigrant Lake
Pacific Crest Trail
Grover Hot Springs State Park
Sacramento
Map Area
San Francisco
CALIFORNIA
Los Angeles
Moklumne Wilderness Area
4
TOIYABE NATIONAL FOREST

0   5 mi
0   5 km

Tips **Tahoe Traffic**

Like Yosemite, Tahoe is an extremely sensitive environmental area. All who love it work toward preserving its ethereal beauty. "Keep Tahoe Blue" bumper stickers are everywhere, and land-use issues are a source of constant debate. What has evolved is a philosophy of urban renewal rather than urban expansion, and the hugely popular vacation town of South Lake Tahoe is benefiting from an ambitious makeover now in progress. The area's spruce-up is not just visual: Environmental remedies have been factored in the new design. Aging buildings are being replaced with attractive lodgings, a retail and restaurant plaza, a multiplex movie theater, an open-air skating rink, and a central transit facility. A recently completed $20 million Heavenly Valley Ski Resort gondola is a focal point for the project, featuring state-of-the-art cars holding up to eight people that can take you from the South Shore downtown area up to an observation deck at 9,200 feet on Heavenly Mountain. During this period of major reconstruction in the already bustling area, visitors should be prepared for a few more traffic snarls and other minor inconveniences.

(© **888/48885;**www.nostressexpress.com) serves the North and West Shores; **Tahoe Casino Express** (© **800/446-6128**) serves the South Shore (1-day advance reservations recommended). To get to the lake, take U.S. 395 South to either Rte. 431 for the North Shore or U.S. 50 for the South Shore. While all of the roads leading to the lake are scenic, the panoramic views as you descend into the Lake Tahoe Basin from Rte. 431 are spectacular. Pull into the overlook and enjoy the moment.

Amtrak (© **800/USA-RAIL**) stops in Truckee, 10 miles north of the lake. Public transportation (TART or Truce Trolley) is available from the train depot, or you can take a taxi to the North Shore. **Greyhound Bus Lines** (© **800/ 231-2222**) serves both Truckee and South Lake Tahoe with daily arrivals from San Francisco and Sacramento.

VISITOR INFORMATION   If you are in Tahoe City, stop by the **Visitor Service Center,** 245 North Lake Blvd. (© **800/824-6348** or 530/583-3494; www.tahoefun.org). In Incline Village, go to the **Incline Village/Crystal Bay Visitors Center,** 969 Tahoe Blvd. (© **800/468-2463** or 775/832-1606; www. gotahoe.com). In South Lake Tahoe, go to the **Lake Tahoe Visitors Authority,** 1156 Ski Run Blvd. (© **800/288-2463** or 530/544-5050; www.virtualtahoe. com), or to the **South Lake Tahoe Chamber of Commerce,** 3066 Lake Tahoe Blvd. (© **530/541-5255;** www.tahoeinfo.com). Countless other websites are chock full of information about Lake Tahoe, including www.skilaketahoe.com, www. laketahoeconcierge.com, or www.tahoevacationguide.com.

SKIING & SNOWBOARDING

With the largest concentration of ski resorts in North America, Lake Tahoe offers California's best skiing. The ski season typically lasts from November to May and frequently extends into the summer. Lift tickets last winter ranged from $38 to $57 per day for adults and from free to $29 for children, with special rates for teens and seniors. Tickets go up every year, but bargains are available. Many resorts, hotels, and motels, offer special ski packages. Contact the visitor centers or visit the websites listed in "Visitor Information," above, to look for these great values. The ski resorts all offer instruction for adults and children, equipment rental, special terrain courses for snowboarding, and restaurants. Most have free shuttles.

Alpine Meadows ★★★ *Kids*   In addition to its 12 lifts, this world-class resort has recently installed a beginner surface lift designed especially for children, novice skiers, and snowboarders. With more than 100 runs over 2,000 acres, Alpine has something for everyone: unique kid's programs and a family ski zone, as well as its "wild side," for the double black diamond crowd. You can get a great bargain through its Bed and Board package, which provides lift tickets and lodging (© **800/949-3296**). Alpine also offers ski and snowboard instruction for all ages, excellent snowboarding terrain parks, snowshoe rentals, snow play areas, and special events like the funky Wayne Wong World Hot Dog Skiing Championship.

2600 Alpine Meadows Rd., Tahoe City, CA 96145. © **800/441-4423** or 530/583-4232. www.skialpine.com.

Diamond Peak ★ *Value*   This smaller and less expensive ($41 lift ticket!) resort has spectacular lake views and prides itself on being a premier destination for families. Whether your child chooses to ski or snowboard, there will be some something available, including a snow play program for the younger ones who aren't quite ready to learn to ski yet. Kids love the snowboard park and sledding area. Located in the heart of the quiet, upscale community of Incline Village, this is a great choice for a low-key, less crowded, and beautiful skiing adventure. The Diamond Peak Cross Country and Snowshoe Center (same telephone number), just east of Incline Village on NV Rte. 431, is absolutely gorgeous and even allows dogs to share in the fun in the afternoon.

1210 Ski Way, Incline Village, NV 89451. © **775/832-1177** or 775/831-3249. www.diamondpeak.com.

Heavenly Resort ★★ *Kids*   This hugely popular resort has 4,800 skiable acres, 27 lifts (including a 50-passenger aerial tram), 82 runs, and the highest elevation (10,000 feet) of any resort at the lake. Skiers of all levels will find something here to challenge them. One hundred percent of the mountain is available to snowboarders, along with a snowboard park and specially constructed terrain features. Heavenly offers day care for infants through 6 years, child care and ski combinations for ages 3 to 5, and full-day programs for older kids. It's the only ski resort on the South Shore. With the nearby arcades, recreation centers, bowling alleys, and movie theaters, this is a good choice if you have teenagers or if you want to visit the big casinos.

P.O. Box 2180 (on Ski Run Blvd.), Stateline, NV 89449. © **775/586-7000**. www.skiheavenly.com.

Homewood Mountain Resort ★ *Value*   Homewood is one of our favorite small ski areas, a homey little resort with 1,260 acres, 56 trails, 8 lifts, and great lake views. It's a good family resort with child care for ages 2 to 6 and ski schools for ages 4 to 12. Lift tickets were only $38 last winter, and children under 10 skied free when accompanied by an adult.

5145 W. Lake Blvd., Homewood, CA 96141 (6 miles south of Tahoe City and 19 miles north of South Lake Tahoe on Calif. 89). © **530/525-2992**. www.skihomewood.com.

Kirkwood ★★★ *Kids*   Kirkwood's only drawback is that it's 30 miles from South Lake Tahoe; otherwise, it's one of the top ski areas in Tahoe, with lots of snow and excellent spring skiing. It has 2,300 skiable acres, 12 lifts, and 65 trails. Many programs are offered for the children, including child care for the younger ones (ages 2 to 6). The Cross Country Ski Center (© **209/258-7248**) is one of the best around, offering lessons for all ages, and spectacular scenery. Kirkwood is also ideal for summertime hiking, horseback riding, mountain biking, and rock climbing. With ample lodging (© **800/967-7500**) and dining options, this is a wonderful year-round vacation destination. There's a free shuttle service to South Lake Tahoe.

Off Hwy. 88 at Carson Pass, P.O Box 1, Kirkwood, CA 95646. © **209/258-6000**. www.kirkwood.com.

Northstar-at-Tahoe ★★ *Kids*   With 63 runs covering 2,400 acres on two mountains, Northstar is consistently rated among the top Far West resorts. Its sophisticated series of lifts, including an express gondola, insure speedy access to the slopes and short lift lines. Whatever age or experience level, you will find something here. Guided snowcat tours test the skills of expert skiers and snowboarders on 200 acres of ungroomed, out-of-boundary terrain. The Learning Center offers coaching in skiing, snowboarding, cross-country, and the new snow toys. Child care (ages 2 to 6) is provided as well as instruction for the younger set, including the new "magic carpet" lift and special "Paw" courses. It's hard to imagine more ways to have fun in the snow than you will find at Northstar—skiing, snowboarding, cross country, telemarking, dog sled tours, sleigh rides, tubing, snowmobile tours, and an amazing evening adventure park called Polaris Park. Check out the snow toys such as the snowscoot, the skifox, the snowbike, and the amazing Zorb, a 9½-foot plastic ball that carries a harnessed-in thrill seeker on an exciting 30- to 40-second ride down a special course.

P.O. Box 129, Truckee, CA 96160 (6 miles north of Kings Beach). © **800/466-6784** or 530/562-1010. www.skinorthstar.com.

Squaw Valley USA ★★★ *Kids*   Site of the 1960 Olympic Winter Games, Squaw is one of the world's finest year-round resorts. Skiing is spread across six peaks with one of the most advanced lift systems in the world providing access to over 4,000 acres of skiable terrain—70% geared toward beginners and intermediates and 30% for the advanced, expert, and/or insane. Children's World offers child care (reservations required, © **530/581-7280**, between 1 and 4pm.) and snow school. For nonskiers and skiers alike, High Camp, at the top of the cable car, has the Olympic Ice Pavilion (year-round ice-skating), a swimming lagoon and spa (spring and summer), snow tubing, snowboarding school, bungee jumping, restaurants, and bars. Squaw also has an arcade, cinema, climbing wall, and Central Park (a snowboarder's dream). The Cross-Country Ski Center (© **530/583-6300**) has 400 beautiful acres of groomed trails. For those who can't get enough of a good thing, Squaw offers free night skiing with the purchase of a full-day lift ticket. Children ages 12 and under ski for only $5.

Olympic Valley, CA 96146 (6 miles north of Tahoe City). © **800/545-4350** or 530/583-6985. www. squaw.com.

Sugar Bowl ★★ *Kids*   If you are driving from the Bay Area or Sacramento on I-80 and don't want to drive all the way to Tahoe, Sugarbowl is an excellent place to ski. This medium-size resort (13 lifts, 1,500 skiable acres) offers child care, ski school, snowboard parks, and lodging at the foot of the mountains. It was a popular hideaway for the Hollywood jet set of the 1940s and '50s.

P.O. Box 5, Norden, CA 95724 (3 miles east of the Soda Springs/Norden exit of I-80). © **530/426-9000**. www.sugarbowl.com.

OTHER WINTER FUN

CROSS-COUNTRY SKIING   In addition to the major resorts, here are some excellent choices. **Royal Gorge Cross Country Ski Resort** ★★★, Soda Springs, near Sugar Bowl (© **800/500-3871** or 800/666-3871; www.royalgorge.com), has 90 trails (203 miles), including 28 novice trails and four ski lifts, and is one of the largest and best cross country resorts anywhere. **Tahoe Cross Country Ski Center** ⚓, 925 Country Club Dr., Tahoe City (© **530/583-5475;** www.tahoexc.org) is a small (14 trails), full-service ski center run by a nonprofit community group and is easy and convenient to North Shore visitors. **Spooner Lake Cross Country Ski Area** ⚓, near the intersection of Highway 28 and U.S. 50 on the East Shore (© **888/858-8844;** www.spoonerlake.com), is a quiet, full-service ski center off the beaten path, but it offers some of the most scenic skiing at the lake.

ICE-SKATING   Accessible only by a scenic tram ride (included in the admission fee of $19 for adults, $10 for children), **Squaw Valley's High Camp** ⚓⚓ (© **530/583-6985**) has one of the world's most beautiful and unusual ice rinks. It's open daily, year-round, from 11am to 9pm.

SNOWMOBILING   Snowmobile rental and tours are available at several locations in the Lake Tahoe Area. Call ahead for reservations and directions. The **Zephyr Cove Snowmobile Center** (© **775/588-3833**), 760 U.S. 50, about 4 miles northeast of the casinos, offers several tours daily for all experience levels. The cost for a standard 2-hour tour is $89 for a single rider, $124 for two. **Snowmobiling Unlimited** (© **530/583-7192**) offers backcountry tours from Brockway Summit, about 3 miles north of Kings Beach on Calif. 267, $85 for one, $115 for two. **TC Snomos,** 205 River Rd., Tahoe City (© **530/581-3906**), starts its tours right in Tahoe City, and charges $75 for one and $100 for two.

SNOWPLAY   For snow play other than at the big resorts try the **North Tahoe Regional Park,** at the top of National Avenue off Highway 28, Tahoe Vista (© **530/546-6115**). This ultimate snow play hill has a $5 fee that includes choice of sled, tube, or saucer. **Taylor Creek Snow Park,** off Calif. 89 in South Lake Tahoe (© **530/573-2674**), is run by the U.S. Forest Service. Bring your own equipment for sledding and tubing.

SUMMER ACTIVITIES

BALLOONING   See the lake and mountains from 8,000 to 10,000 feet above with **Lake Tahoe Balloons** (© **800/872-9294**) in South Lake Tahoe ($175 per person for a 1-hour tour and brunch).

BEACHES   Here are a few popular spots around the lake. All have sandy beaches, picnic areas, and restrooms; many have playgrounds. Remember that this is an alpine lake so the water is very cold.

> **Commons Beach Park:** Downtown Tahoe City, free movie (Fridays at dusk)
> **Kings Beach State Recreation Center:** Highway 28 in Kings Beach
> **Sand Harbor:** 4 miles south of Incline Village on Highway 28; lifeguards
> **D. L. Bliss State Park:** South of Meeks Bay on Calif. 89; camping, trails
> **Sugar Pine Point:** Calif. 89, just south of Tahoma; camping, trails, pier
> **Baldwin Beach:** Calif. 89, 4 miles north of South Lake Tahoe
> **Connolly Beach:** U.S. 50 at Timber Cove Lodge; boat launches
> **El Dorado Beach:** Between Rufus Allen and Lakeview in South Lake Tahoe
> **Pope Beach:** Calif. 89, 2 miles north of South Lake Tahoe
> **Zephyr Cove Beach:** U.S. 50 at Zephyr Cove

BICYCLING   There are many miles of paved bicycle paths around the lake. Incline Village has a lovely, easy 2½-mile path along Lakeshore Boulevard. This is a safe choice for younger children. In Tahoe City, you can follow the path in three directions. The one that follows Truckee River is a relaxing, beautiful ride. On the South Shore, the Pope-Baldwin bike path runs parallel to Calif. 89 through Camp Richardson and the Tallac Historic Site. Nearby in South Lake Tahoe, a paved pathway runs from El Dorado Beach along the lake, paralleling U.S. 50. You can rent a bicycle from any of the shops listed below.

MOUNTAIN BIKING   Biking is big at Lake Tahoe. For serious mountain bikers, there is a dizzying choice of trails. At both **Northstar** (② **530/562-1010**) and **Squaw Valley** (② **530/583-6985**) you can take the cable car (Squaw) or chairlift (Northstar) up with your bike and ride the trails all the way down. For other trails, check with one of the bicycle rental shops for maps and information. Here are a few good ones: **North: The Back Country,** 255 N. Lake Blvd., Tahoe City (② 530/581-5861); **Olympic Bike Shop,** 620 N. Lake Blvd., Tahoe City (② 530/581-2500); **Tahoe Bike & Ski,** 8499 N. Lake Blvd., Kings Beach (② 530/546-7437); **Porter's Sports Shop,** 885 Tahoe Blvd., Incline Village (② 775/831-3500); **South: Anderson's Bike Rental,** 645 Emerald Bay Rd. (② 530/541-0500); **Lakeview Sports,** 3131 Hwy. 50 at El Dorado Beach (② 530/544-0183). Another great choice is **Cyclepaths Mountain Bike Adventures,** 1785 West Lake Blvd. in Tahoe Park, a few miles south of Tahoe City (② **800/780-BIKE;** www.cyclepaths.com), where you can arrange a guided off-road tour. Whether you're into hardcore downhill single track or easy-going scenic outings, the expert guides will provide you with all the necessary equipment, food, and transportation. They offer day tours ($29 and up), weekenders ($199), and 3- and 5-day adventure camps (rates vary).

BOAT RENTALS, WATERSPORTS & PARASAILING   Nothing beats actually getting out on the water. Take a guided tour, go off on your own, or just paddle around. Here are a few reliable choices: **Zephyr Cove Marina** (② **775/588-3833**) is the lake's largest marina. It's the home of the paddle wheeler M.S. *Dixie II* and the catamaran *Woodwind II.* Here you can parasail (② 775/588-3530), charter sportfishing trips (② 775/586-9338), or take guided tours. You can also rent motorized boats, pontoon boats, pedal boats, kayaks, canoes, water ski equipment, and jet skis. **Tahoe City Marina** (② **530/583-1039**), 700 N. Lake Blvd., Tahoe City, rents motorized boats, sailboats, and fishing boats. Sailboat cruises are available. This is also the location for **Lake Tahoe Parasailing** (② **530/583-7245**). **Lighthouse Water Sports,** 950 N. Lake Blvd., Tahoe (② **530/583-7245**), rents jet skis, paddleboats, and canoes. **Tahoe Paddle and Oar,** North Lake Beach Center, 7860 N. Lake Blvd., Kings Beach (② **530/531-3029**), is a good place to rent kayaks, canoes, pedal boats, and windsurfing equipment. Paddling around on a calm day in the clear waters of Crystal Bay is great fun. **Action Water Sports** has two locations: 3411 Lake Tahoe Blvd. at Timber Cove Marina, South Lake Tahoe (② **530/544-2942**); and across from the Hyatt in Incline Village (② **775/831-4386**). Rent boats, kayaks, jet skis, paddleboats, and other water toys here. Parasailing and guided tours are also available. **Camp Richardson Marina,** 1900 Jameson Beach Rd., off Calif. 89 on the South Shore (② **530/542-6570**), located on a long sandy beach, rents power and ski boats, jet skis, kayaks, and paddleboats. It also offers fishing charters, ski school, cruises on the *Woodwind I* sailboat, and guided raft and kayak tours to Emerald Bay. **SunSports,** 3564 Lake Tahoe Blvd., South Lake Tahoe (② **530/541-6000**), provides rentals, tours, and lessons for kayaking, rafting, sailing, and scuba diving.

CAMPING   If you have an appetite for the great outdoors, here are a few of the many good campgrounds at Tahoe:

D. L. Bliss State Park (© 530/525-7277), on the western shore, has 168 campsites, fine beaches, and hiking trails.

Sugar Pine Point State Park (© 530/525-7982), also on the western shore, offers 175 campsites, a picnic area, a beach, a nature center, and cross-country skiing, and is open year-round.

Campground by the Lake (© 530/542-6059), 1150 Rufus Allen Blvd., South Lake Tahoe, features 170 campsites, a boat ramp, a gym, and a history museum.

Zephyr Cove RV Park and Campground (© 775/588-6644), located at Zephyr Cove Resort on U.S. 50, has a beach, a marina, and complete facilities.

FISHING   The cold, clear waters of Lake Tahoe are home to kokanee salmon and rainbow, brown, and Mackinaw trout. With lots of hiding places in the deep water, fishing here is a challenge, and many anglers opt to use a guide or charter boat. There are dozens of charter companies offering daily excursions. Rates run about $65 for a half day to $95 for a whole day (bait, tackle, fish cleaning and food included). On the North Shore try: **Mickey's Big Mack Charters** (Sierra Boat Company, Carnelian Bay) (© 530/546-4444); or **Reel Deal Sportfishing,** Tahoe City (© 530/581-0924). On the South Shore try: **Avid Fisherman,** Zephyr Cove, (© 775/588-7675); **Blue Ribbon Fishing Charters,** Tahoe Keys Marina (© 530/541-8801); or **Tahoe Sportfishing,** 900 Ski Run Blvd. (© 800/696-7797 or 530/541-5448).

FITNESS CENTERS & SPAS   Soak your tired body at the end of the day at the **North Tahoe Beach Center,** 7860 North Lake Blvd., Kings Beach (© **530/ 546-2566**). Besides a full line of exercise equipment, the center boasts a huge 26-foot spa, saunas, weight gym, TV, Ping-Pong, fireplace, lockers, and showers, all for $7 for adults and $3 for children. The **Incline Recreation Center,** 980 Incline Way, Incline Village (© **775/832-1310**) is a gorgeous new facility with a heated indoor Olympic-size swimming pool, aerobics, basketball gym, cardiovascular fitness room, lounge, fireplace, and on-site child care. The fee is $11 for adults and $6 for children.

GOLF   With its world-class golf courses, mild summer weather, and magnificent scenery, Lake Tahoe is a golfer's paradise. All of these courses are very busy in the summer so call far in advance for tee times. Starting at the north end of the lake, there are four highly rated courses: **Incline Village Championship Course,** 955 Fairway Blvd.; the smaller **Incline Village Mountain (Executive) Course,** 690 Wilson Way (© 775/832-1144 for both); **Northstar,** 6 miles north of Kings Beach (© 530/562-2490); and **Squaw Creek,** 6 miles north of Tahoe City (© 800/327-3353). In the south, there's **Edgewood,** U.S. 50 at Lake Parkway, Stateline, NV (© 775/588-3566), home of the Celebrity Golf Championship; and **Lake Tahoe Golf Course,** 2500 Emerald Bay Rd., South Lake Tahoe, CA (© 530/577-0788). In addition, there are some good nine-hole municipal courses: **Old Brockway Golf Course,** 7900 N. Lake Blvd., Kings Beach (© 530/546-9909); **Tahoe City Golf Course,** 251 N. Lake Blvd., Tahoe City (© 530/583-1516); and **Bijou Municipal Golf Course,** 3436 Fairway Ave., South Lake Tahoe (© 530/542-6097).

HIKING   The mountains surrounding Lake Tahoe are crisscrossed with hiking trails graded for all levels of experience. Before setting out, you may wish to contact the local visitor centers or sporting goods shops for a map and more in-depth information on particular trails, or hire a guide. Try **Tahoe Trips & Trails** (✆ 530/583-4506) for short and long guided hikes. Everything is provided: food, drinks, transportation, and great information about the lake. Going on your own? Some of the most popular short hikes in the area are:

> **Eagle Falls/Eagle Lake:** This easy trail is well marked and begins at Eagle Picnic Area, directly across Calif. 89 from Emerald Bay.
>
> **Emerald Bay/Vikingsholm:** The trail begins in the parking lot (on the east side of Calif. 89 at Emerald Bay) and goes down to Vikingsholm, a replica of a medieval Scandinavian castle.
>
> **Nevada Shoreline:** Begin at the paved parking lot on the left side of Highway 28, 2.9 miles south of Sand Harbor. The trail drops to the beach and follows the shoreline, passing Chimney Beach, Secret Harbor, and Whale Beach. The trail eventually connects to a service road that can be followed back up to the parking area.
>
> **Shirley Lake:** Take the tram at Squaw Valley up to High Camp and hike down or vice-versa. The trail begins at the end of Squaw Creek Road, next to the cable car building.

HORSEBACK RIDING   Most stables offer a variety of guided trail rides and lessons for individuals, families, and groups. Choose the one that appeals to your sense of adventure: 1- to 2-hour trail rides; breakfast, lunch, or dinner rides; half-day, day, overnight, and extended pack trips. Expect to pay $20 to $25 for a 1-hour ride; $6 for a half-hour pony ride. Saddle up and savor the scenery. Try **Alpine Meadows Stables,** Alpine Meadows Rd., Tahoe City (✆ 530/583-3905); **Northstar Stables,** Highway 267, 6 miles north of Kings Beach (✆ 530/562-2480); **Squaw Valley Stables,** 1525 Squaw Valley Rd., north of Tahoe City (✆ 530/583-7433); **Camp Richardson Corral,** Calif. 89, South Lake Tahoe (✆ 530/541-3113); or **Zephyr Cove Stables,** Zephyr Cove Resort, U.S. 50 at Zephyr Cove (✆ 775/588-5664).

IN-LINE SKATING   Although there are many trails around the lake, the best one for blading is the well-paved bicycle- and pedestrian-only path that hugs the Truckee River between Tahoe City and Squaw Valley. Skates and protective gear can be rented for $12 per half day, $18 full day, from the nearby **Squaw Valley Sport Shop,** 170 N. Lake Blvd., Tahoe City (✆ **530/583-6278**).

RIVER RAFTING   For a swift but gentle ride down the Truckee River (the lake's only outlet), try **Truckee River Raft Rental,** 185 River Rd., Tahoe City (✆ **530/583-0123**). Only available in the summer, the rates are $25 for adults and $20 for children (5 years and up).

TENNIS   The mild summer weather at Lake Tahoe is perfect for great tennis. If you want to sharpen your skills, **Northstar** (✆ **530/562-0321**) offers several excellent tennis packages for its guests only. **Squaw Creek** (✆ **530/581-6694**) tennis courts are open to the public for $12 an hour. **Kirkwood, Caesar's,** and **Harvey's** all feature tennis courts for a fee. Budget-minded players looking for good local courts should visit Tahoe Lake School, Grove Street, Tahoe City, or Tahoe Regional Park, at the end of National Avenue in Tahoe Vista. South Tahoe Intermediate School on Lyons Avenue has eight lighted courts and charges a manageable $3 per hour. South Tahoe High School, 1735 Lake Tahoe Blvd., has free courts.

LAKE CRUISES

If you can possibly fit a cruise into your vacation plans, you won't regret it. It's one of the best ways to see the lake. **M.S. *Dixie II,*** Zephyr Cove Marina, 4 miles north of the casinos on U.S. 50 (© 775/882-0786), is a 570-passenger vessel with bars, a dance floor, and a full dining room. Scenic cruises cost $23 for adults, $7 for children. They also have champagne brunch and breakfast cruises ($25), dinner cruises ($39), and sunset dinner-dance cruises ($49). **Hornblower's *Tahoe Queen*** (© 800/238-2463 or 530/541-3364), departing from the Marina Village at Ski Run Boulevard in South Lake Tahoe, is an authentic paddle wheeler with a capacity of 500. It offers Emerald Bay sightseeing tours ($18 for adult, $8 for children) and dinner cruises ($32), as well as full-service charters. Live music, buffet breakfast, dinner, and appetizers are all available on board. The **Hornblower Ski Shuttle** ($85, including lift ticket, food, and ground transportation) is the world's only known water-borne ski shuttle. On the way to Squaw Valley enjoy a breakfast buffet, and on the way home experience a fun-filled après-ski party. This ski shuttle allows skiers staying on the South Shore an opportunity to ski one of the finest resorts on the North Shore without the hassle. Buses pick up passengers from their hotels in the morning and drop them off at night. The ***Tahoe Gal*** (© 800/218-2464 or 530/583-0141), departing from the Lighthouse Marina (behind Safeway) in Tahoe City, is the only cruise boat on the North Shore. Cruises include Scenic Shoreline ($15 for adults, $5 for children) and Emerald Bay ($20 for adults, $8 for children). Dinner is available for an additional $15 for adults and $5 for children. **Woodwind Sailing Cruises** (© 888/867-6394) specializes in daily sightseeing cruises ($22 for adults, $20 for seniors, $10 for children), sunset champagne cruises ($28), weddings, and charters. The Woodwind fleet includes the original ***Woodwind I,*** a 30-passenger Searunner trimaran sailing to Emerald Bay from Camp Richardson Marina in South Lake Tahoe, and the new ***Woodwind II,*** a 50-passenger Searunner catamaran sailing from Zephyr Cove Marina.

A DRIVE AROUND THE LAKE

Overwhelmed by all of the choices? Get in your car and take a leisurely drive around the lake. It's only a 72-mile trip, but you should plan on taking several hours, even in the best of weather. In the worst of weather, don't try it! Parts of the road, if not closed, can be icy and dangerous. On a mild day though, it will be a memorable experience. If your car sports a tape deck, consider buying *Drive Around the Lake,* a drive-along audio cassette that contains facts, legends, places of interest, and just about everything else you could possible want to know about the lake. It's available at numerous gift shops or at the **South Lake Tahoe Chamber of Commerce,** 3066 Lake Tahoe Blvd. (© 530/541-5255; www. tahoeinfo.com), which is closed on Sundays.

We'll start at the California-Nevada border in South Lake Tahoe and loop around the western shore on Calif. 89 to Tahoe City and beyond. U.S. 50, which runs along the south shore, is an ugly, overdeveloped strip that obliterates any view of the lake. Keep heading west, and you will soon be free of this ugly stretch.

First stop is the **Tallac Historic Site,** site of the former Tallac Resort and a cluster of rustic 100-year-old mansions that provide a fascinating glimpse into Tahoe's past. In its heyday, the resort included two large hotels, a casino, and numerous outbuildings. Throughout the summer here, the Valhalla Festival of

Arts and Music (℃ **530/541-4975**) showcases jazz, bluegrass, rock, mariachi, and classical music. Summer highlights include June's Valhalla Renaissance Festival, July's Native American Fine Arts Festival, and August's Great Gatsby Festival.

From here the highway winds northward along the shore until you reach **Cascade Lake** on the left and **Emerald Bay** ✸✸ on the right. The Emerald Bay Lookout is a spectacular picture-taking spot. Emerald Bay's deep green water is the site of the only island in Lake Tahoe, Fannette Island. The small structure atop the island is the teahouse, built by Ms. Lora Knight, who also constructed **Vikingsholm** ✸, a 38-room Scandinavian Castle built in 1929, located at the head of Emerald Bay. Tours ($3) of this unique structure are available in summer. Even if you don't want to take the tour, it's a lovely walk from the parking area down to the beach and the mansion's grounds. Just remember that you have to walk back up. Across the highway, there's another parking area. From here, it's a short, steep ¼-mile hike to a footbridge above **Eagle Falls**. Then it's about a mile farther up to **Eagle Lake.**

Continuing on, it's only about 2 miles to **D. L. Bliss State Park** (℃ **530/ 525-7982**), where you'll find one of the lake's best beaches. It gets crowded in the summer, so arrive early to get a parking place. The park also contains 168 campsites and several trails, including one along the shoreline.

In about 7 miles you will reach **Sugar Pine State Park** (℃ **530/525-7232**), the largest (2,000 acres) of the lake's parks and also the only one that has year-round camping. In summer, you can visit the beaches in the park plus a nature center and miles of trails; in winter, there's cross-country skiing on well-maintained trails.

Continuing on through the small town of **Homewood** (site of the ski resort), **Sunnyside,** on the right, is a pleasant place to stop for a lakeside lunch. Or, if you feel like taking a stroll, drive on to Tahoe City where there is a lovely paved path along the Truckee River. Check out the big trout at **Fanny Bridge** ✸ first. If you would like to see **Squaw Valley** and **Alpine Meadows,** take a left at Calif. 89. A ride on the Squaw Valley cable car (℃ **530/583-6985**) will reward you with incredible vistas from 2,000 feet above the valley floor. It operates year-round and costs $16 for adults, $13 for seniors, and $5 for children under 13. Back on Calif. 28, as you leave **Tahoe City,** you will pass a string of interesting, small malls, 700 through 850 North Lake Blvd. If you enjoy just wandering around, this is a good area to stop and eat, watch the activity at the **Tahoe City Marina** (parasailing, cruises on the *Tahoe Gal,* and boat rental), or visit the interesting shops.

Continuing around the lake on Calif. 28, you'll reach Carnelian Bay, Tahoe Vista, and Kings Beach before crossing the state line into Nevada. **Kings Beach State Recreation Area** ✸ (℃ **530/546-7248**) is a long, wide beach and picnic area. It is jammed in the summer with sunbathers and swimmers. As you approach **Crystal Bay,** you will immediately know you have crossed the state line by the string of small casinos that suddenly appear. The **Cal-Neva Lodge** on the right was once owned by Frank Sinatra and has a very colorful, celebrity-filled history. The state line goes right through the lodge, and gambling is allowed only on the Nevada side. This is worth stopping to see.

Your journey next takes you to woodsy Incline Village, probably the most beautiful community on the lake. Take a right on Lakeshore Boulevard to view the elegant estates. Lunch or dinner time? The magnificent **Lone Eagle Grille** (see "Where to Dine," below), at Lakeshore and Country Club Drive, offers panoramic lake views as well as good food.

Remember Hoss and Little Joe? The **Ponderosa Ranch** (© 775/831-0691) off Highway 28 at the east end of Incline Village, home to television's *Bonanza,* features the Cartwright Ranch House, an entire Old West town complete with working blacksmiths, a saloon, a haywagon breakfast, a shootin' gallery, and even live gunfights. It's open daily from April to October; admission is $9.50 for adults, free for children under 12.

The East Shore of the lake is largely undeveloped and very scenic. Drive about 4 miles south of Incline Village to **Sand Harbor** ✵ (© 775/831-0494), one of the lake's best-loved beaches, home to the very popular **Lake Tahoe Shakespeare Festival** (© 800/74-SHOWS) every August. In addition to turquoise blue water dotted with big boulders and a wide sandy beach, you'll find nature trails, picnic areas, and boating.

Going south you will come to an outcropping called **Cave Rock** where the highway passes through 25 yards of solid stone. Farther along is **Zephyr Cove Resort and Marina,** home to the M.S. *Dixie II* and a beehive of watersports activity. You'll then return to Stateline and South Lake Tahoe, your original starting point.

WHERE TO STAY
SOUTH SHORE & SOUTH LAKE TAHOE
Expensive
Black Bear Inn ✵✵   Nestled on a wooded acre near Heavenly Ski Resort, this charming new lodge offers luxury accommodations, a tranquil setting, and a convenient location. The Great Room, with its beamed ceilings, grand piano, country antiques, and large rock fireplace, is relaxing after a long day of activities. Sit by the fire and enjoy the tempting array of goodies served during wine hour or soak your tired body in the sheltered Jacuzzi. Breakfast is an event in itself, offering such treats as fresh-baked muffins, eggs Benedict, and delicious omelets. The spacious guest rooms all have a king-size bed, private bathroom, and gas fireplace.

1202 Ski Run Blvd., South Lake Tahoe, CA 96150. © 877/232-7466 or 530/544-4451. www.tahoeblackbear. com. 5 lodge rooms, 3 cabins. $225–$275 lodge rooms; $25–$495 cabins. Rates include full breakfast. MC, V. **Amenities:** Nearby golf course; Jacuzzi. *In room:* A/C, TV/VCR, dataport, hair dryer. Cabins also include kitchenette, fridge, coffeemaker.

Caesar's Tahoe ✵   This 16-story hotel, built in the early 1980s, has the glitter, the glitz, and the campy references to Roman mythology that Caesar's Palace in Las Vegas has perfected for decades. It has a full casino with sports booking, the Circus Maximus showroom featuring top-name entertainment, a lagoon-style indoor pool, plus indoor and outdoor wedding chapels. If you feel like kicking up your heels, go to Nero 2000 to dance the night away. It has live music and the biggest dance floor around. Planet Hollywood, chock full of Hollywood memorabilia, is another favorite hangout. Finally, you can even indulge yourself with a cruise around the lake on the *Odyssey,* Caesar's own luxury yacht, or get married on it, if that's your heart's desire.

55 U.S. 50, P.O. Box 5800, Lake Tahoe, NV 89449. © 800/648-3353 or 775/588-3515. www.caesars.com. 440 units. $75–$250 double; $375–$650 suite. Packages available. AE, DC, MC, V. **Amenities:** 6 restaurants; 4 lounges; indoor pool; 3 outdoor tennis courts; health club; spa; Jacuzzi; sauna; ski rental; bike rental; video arcade; concierge; activities desk; car-rental desk; business center; secretarial services; shopping arcade; salon; 24 hour room service; in-room massage; babysitting; dry cleaning; executive level rooms. *In room:* A/C, TV, dataport, fridge (upon request), coffeemaker, hair dryer, iron, safe. Suites also have kitchenettes and minibars.

Embassy Suites Resort ★★ (Kids) A Bavarian-style hotel of character, Embassy Suites rises nine floors, the roofline pierced with a double layer of dormers. Family skiers fill up the place in winter. Kids 18 and under stay free. The one- and two-bedroom suites all have microwaves, dining room tables, and wet bars. Complimentary cooked-to-order breakfasts are served in a garden atrium. For wining and dining, try Zachary's, Pasquale's wood-fired pizzas, or Turtles sports bar, which opens onto an outdoor deck and turns into a disco later in the evening.

4130 Lake Tahoe Blvd., South Lake Tahoe, CA 96150. ☎ **800/988-9820** or 530/544-540. Fax 530/544-4900. www.embassy-suites.com. 400 suites. $149–$359 double. Rates include full breakfast and evening cocktail reception. Special packages available. AE, DC, DISC, MC, V. **Amenities:** Restaurant, pizzeria, sports bar; indoor pool; health club; spa; Jacuzzi; dry sauna; watersports equipment rental; concierge; car-rental desk; limited room service; in-room massage; babysitting; same-day dry cleaning; executive level rooms. *In room:* A/C, TV/VCR, dataport, minibar, fridge, coffeemaker, hair dryer, iron.

Harrah's Casino Hotel ★★ (Kids) Understatement is not a word that comes to mind when you visit Harrah's, Tahoe's most highly rated hotel and casino, and its complete remodeling has made what was already luxurious and glitzy even more so. Harrah's takes great pride in its special blend of luxury, beauty, unparalleled guest service, and casino entertainment. The large rooms have two bathrooms, each with its own TV and telephone so you won't miss anything while bathing, and those thick, fluffy, white towels Sinatra always demanded. Most have bay windows overlooking the lake or the mountains. With families in mind, the casino has an enormous fun center with the latest in video and arcade games, virtual reality, and an indoor "playscape" for young children. Weddings and parties can be arranged aboard the private yacht, the *Tahoe Star*. The legendary South Shore Room features showbiz stars, and, in case you've forgotten what you're there for, the casino is a gambler's dream.

P.O. Box 8, Stateline, NV 89449. ☎ **800/427-7247** or 775/588-6611. Fax 775/586-6607. www.harrahstahoe. com. 540 units. $109–$209 double; $229–$329 suite. Packages available. AE, DC, DISC, MC, V. **Amenities:** 4 restaurants, a cafe, a deli, a coffeehouse; indoor pool; full service health club and spa; family fun center; game room; video arcade; concierge; shopping arcade; salon; 24 hour room service; in-room massage; same-day dry cleaning; executive level rooms. *In room:* A/C, TV/VCR, minibar, fridge, coffeemaker, hair dryer, iron, safe.

Harveys Casino Resort, Lake Tahoe ★ (Kids) With its two towers and 740 rooms, Harveys is the largest hotel in Tahoe. It features an 88,000-square-foot casino (Tahoe's largest), eight restaurants, and a cabaret with some of the most glittering, bespangled entertainment in town. More than a hotel, Harveys is like a city unto itself. There's a children's day camp, beauty and barber shops, and even a wedding chapel should you get the urge. Heck, you never have to see the real world again. Try to get a room between the 15th and 19th floors in the newer Lake tower, where every unit has a view of both Lake Tahoe and the surrounding Sierra.

U.S. 50 at Stateline Ave. (P.O. Box 128), Stateline, NV 89449. ☎ **800/HARVEYS** or 775/588-2411. Fax 775/ 588-6643. www.harveystahoe.com. 740 units. $89–$299 double; $299–$699 suite. AE, DC, DISC, MC, V. **Amenities:** 8 restaurants, 10 bars; outdoor heated pool; nearby golf course; health club; spa; Jacuzzi; sauna; watersports equipment rental; children's day camp; video arcade; concierge; car-rental desk; business center; shopping arcade; salon; 24 hour room service; in-room massage; laundry service; same-day dry cleaning. *In room:* A/C, TV w/ pay movies, dataport, minibar, coffeemaker, hair dryer, iron, safe.

Tahoe Seasons Resort ★★ Big, modern, and loaded with luxuries, the Tahoe Seasons lies in a relatively uncongested residential neighborhood at the base of the Heavenly Valley Ski Resort, 2 miles from Tahoe's casinos. Every unit here is a spacious, attractive suite, sleeping up to four in the smaller one and six in the larger one. Most have gas fireplaces, and all have huge whirlpool spas complete with shoji screens. Skiing isn't the only activity around here: Play a round of tennis on the roof or hop aboard the free casino shuttles.

3901 Saddle Rd., off Ski Run Blvd. (P.O. Box 5656), South Lake Tahoe, CA 96157. ℂ 800/540-4874 or 530/541-6700. Fax 530/541-7342. www.tahoeseasons.com. 160 suites. Summer $170–$240; winter $180–$250; spring and fall $122–$200. Seasonal packages available. AE, DC, DISC, MC, V. **Amenities:** Restaurant, pub; outdoor heated pool; nearby golf course; 2 rooftop tennis courts; complimentary use of health club at Harveys Resort; game room; concierge; tour and activities desk; courtesy car; room service; in-room massage; same-day dry cleaning. *In room:* A/C, TV/VCR, dataport, fridge, coffeemaker, hair dryer (on request), iron.

Moderate

Best Western Station House Inn *(Value)*   Nestled amid pines, this is one of the few hotels in town that has its own private "gated" beach on the lake. The rooms are neat and pleasant, the grounds and the large, pretty swimming pool are inviting, and it even has its own award-winning restaurant, LewMarNel's. The complimentary cooked-to-order breakfast and free shuttle service make this a particularly good value.

901 Park Ave., South Lake Tahoe, CA 96150. ℂ 800/822-5953 or 530/542-1101. Fax 530/542-1714. www.stationhouseinn.com. 100 units. $98–$138 double; $135–$165 suite; $200–$275 cabin. Rates include full breakfast. Packages available. AE, DC, DISC, MC, V. **Amenities:** Restaurant; heated outdoor pool; Jacuzzi; babysitting. *In room:* A/C, TV, coffeemaker, hair dryer.

Camp Richardson Resort ✦ *(Kids)*   If you are planning a family vacation, a reunion, or just a weekend getaway, Camp Richardson has it all. Located on a long sandy beach on the southwest shore, this rustic, woodsy resort offers a wide array of activities as well as several lodging and dining choices. Its two restaurants offer lakeside dining, but there are also more informal dining options, plus a general store, a candy store, and an ice cream parlor. The sports center rents all the seasonal equipment you need. You can ski right along the shore here, or try scaling the rock-climbing wall. The full service marina rents power and ski boats, jet skis, kayaks, and paddleboats, and also offers guided tours, cruises, and chartered fishing trips. There's even a stable for horseback riding. Lodging options include a hotel, cabins, a beachside inn, a marina duplex, tent campgrounds, and an RV park. The children will fall into bed exhausted at night with all of the available organized activities. Cabins are only rented by the week in the summer and fill up quickly, so plan early.

Jameson Beach Rd. (P.O. Box 9028), South Lake Tahoe, CA, 96158. ℂ 800/544-1801 or 530/541-1801. Fax 530/541-1802. www.camprichardson.com. $65–$175 hotel; $90–170 cabins per day, $565–$1,625 per week in summer. Camping or RV hookup, $17–$26 per day. **Amenities:** 2 restaurants, deli, cafe; marina; Jacuzzi; sports center with bike, snowshoe, and ski rental; children's program; tour and activities desk. *In room:* Coffeemaker. Inn has TV; duplex has TV, kitchen; cabin has kitchen. Hotel and cabins have no phone.

Horizon Casino Resort *(Value)*   Horizon is not as well known as the other casinos, but it charges less for basically the same facilities. The lobby is a sea of white marble and mirrors, and the rooms are tastefully decorated. The upper floors of the two towers naturally open onto the best views of mountains and the lake. Besides the casino, it has a multiplex movie theater, a cabaret, lounge, and nightclub, and restaurants ranging from buffet to gourmet.

U.S. 50 (P.O. Box C), Lake Tahoe, NV 89449. ℂ 800/648-3322 or 775/588-6211. Fax 775/588-0349. www.horizoncasino.com. 539 units. Summer $119–$169 double; winter $99–$169 double; $250–$500 suite. Children under 12 stay free. Packages available. AE, DISC, DC, MC, V. **Amenities:** 3 restaurants; large heated outdoor pool; nearby golf course; health club; 3 Jacuzzis; bike and ski rental; video arcade; concierge; car-rental desk; business center; shopping arcade; salon; 24 hour room service; in-room massage; babysitting; laundry service; same-day dry cleaning; executive level rooms. *In room:* A/C, TV w/ pay movies, dataport. Suites have minibar, fridge, coffeemaker, hair dryer, iron.

Lakeland Village Beach & Mountain Resort ★ *Kids*   This resort is a good choice for families. Clustered on 19 lightly forested acres of prime shoreline property, the half-residential apartment/half-holiday resort complex was built in the 1970s. The layout is a complicated labyrinth of redwood buildings that blend into the surrounding landscape. The only drawback is the proximity to traffic headed into Lake Tahoe, although some units are quieter than those in the main lodge, which lies adjacent to the road. The units, ranging from studios to four-bedroom lakeside apartments, are streamlined California architecture, and many have upstairs sleeping lofts. All rooms come with fully equipped kitchens and fireplaces. Perks include a large private beach opening directly onto the lake, access to a boat dock, and free shuttle service.

3535 Lake Tahoe Blvd., South Lake Tahoe, CA 96150. © **800/822-5969** or 530/544-1685. Fax 530/541-6278. 212 condo units. $88–$290 double; $135–$975 for a 1–4 bedroom townhouse. Children stay free. AE, MC, V. **Amenities:** 2 heated outdoor pools; nearby golf course; 2 outdoor tennis courts; 2 Jacuzzis; sauna; children's play area and wading pool; seasonal concierge; room service; laundry service; same-day dry cleaning. *In room:* TV/VCR, dataport, kitchen, fridge, coffeemaker, hair dryer, iron. Lodge has A/C.

Inexpensive

Viking Motor Lodge ★ *Value*   You get a lot for your money here: agreeable accommodations, access to a private beach, and an easy walk to the casinos and the Heavenly gondola. Nothing fancy, but the rooms are clean and pleasant, and have all the standard conveniences. If you're traveling with kids, you may want one of the units with a kitchen.

4083 Cedar Ave., South Lake Tahoe, CA 96150. © **800/288-4083** or 530/541-5155. Fax 530/541-5643. www.tahoeviking.com. 76 units, including 14 with kitchen. $49–89 double. Children under 12 free. Continental breakfast included. Packages available. AE, DC, DISC, MC, V. **Amenities:** Outdoor heated pool; nearby golf course; Jacuzzi. *In room:* TV/VCR, dataport, fridge (on request), coffeemaker, hair dryer, iron. Some units with kitchen.

Holiday Lodge *Kids*   Budget-minded travelers will appreciate all of the amenities offered here. Spread out on 4 acres, it's only 1 block to the casinos, 4 blocks to the lake, and seconds away from the new Heavenly Valley gondola. This well-maintained lodge has indoor and outdoor pools, a children's play area, kitchen units, and laundry facilities. It even has a family barbecue area. On the other hand, if you want to cook and wash clothes, why'd you leave home?

4095 Laurel Ave., South Lake Tahoe, CA 96150. © **800/544-4095** (in CA only) or 530/544-4101. Fax 530/ 542-4932. www.holidaylodge.com. 165 units. $45–$225 double. Continental breakfast included. Packages available. AE, MC, V. **Amenities:** Heated indoor and outdoor pools; nearby golf course; indoor Jacuzzi and sauna; children's play area; game room; concierge; activities desk; laundry facilities. *In room:* A/C, TV. Some units with VCR, kitchen, minibar, fridge.

NORTH SHORE/TAHOE CITY
Expensive

Hyatt Regency Lake Tahoe ★★ *Kids*   If you like to gamble but hate gauche, glitzy casinos, you'll like the Hyatt in Incline Village. Located amid towering pines and mountains on the lake's pristine northeast shore, it's far, far classier and quieter than the casino-hotels you'll find along Stateline. All of the rooms have wonderful views accompanied by all of the special little touches that are the very definition of elegance. The resort's private beach, loaded with water toys— catamaran cruises, boat rentals, jet skis, parasailing—is available only to guests. The adjoining Lakeside Cottages are a wee bit o' heaven for families—or honeymooners—who want beachfront access and large, comfortable rooms with unobstructed panoramas of the lake. A bonus for families is the popular Camp Hyatt, which lets kids ages 3 to 12 get a break from their parents for the day. In addition to its other restaurants, the Lone Eagle Grille is one of the most beautiful restaurants on the lake (see "Where to Dine," later in this chapter). Be sure to take a walk (or a run) down Lakeshore Boulevard to see the magnificent estates fronting the lake.

Country Club at Lakeshore (P.O. Box 3239), Incline Village, NV 89450. © **888/899-5019** or 775/832-1234. Fax 775/831-7508. www.laketahoehyatt.com. 458 units, including 24 cottages. $115–$285 double; $395–$850 cottages. Packages available. AE, DC, DISC, MC, V. **Amenities:** 4 restaurants; outdoor heated pool; nearby golf course; complete health and fitness club; Jacuzzi; steam room; watersports equipment rental; bike rental; children's program; video arcade; concierge; tour and activities desk; car-rental desk; business center; room service; in-room massage; laundry service; same day dry cleaning; executive level rooms. *In room:* A/C, TV w/ pay movies, dataport, minibar, fridge, coffeemaker, hair dryer, iron, safe.

PlumpJack Squaw Valley Inn ★★★   Part ski chalet, part boutique hotel, PlumpJack Squaw Valley Inn is easily Tahoe's most refined and elegant hotel and restaurant. Granted, it lacks the fancy toys offered by its competitor across the valley, the Resort at Squaw Creek (see below), but the PlumpJack is unquestionably more genteel, a tribute to the melding of artistry and hostelry. The entire hotel is draped in muted, earthy tones; swirling sconces and sculpted metal accents are brain-candy for the eyes, while the rest of your body parts are soothingly enveloped in thick hooded robes, terry-cloth slippers, and down comforters atop expensive mattresses. Each room has mountain views for your pampered body to contemplate. The inn's equally fine restaurant, PlumpJacks Cafe, is reviewed under "Where to Dine," later in this chapter.

1920 Squaw Valley Rd. (P.O. Box 2407), Olympic Valley, CA 96146. © **800/323-7666** or 530/583-1576. Fax 530/583-1734. www.plumpjack.com. 61 units. Summer $150–$370; winter $150–$545. Rates include continental breakfast. AE, DC, DISC, MC, V. **Amenities:** Restaurant, bar; heated outdoor pool (seasonal); nearby golf course; tennis court; 2 Jacuzzis; bike rental; concierge; room service; in-room massage; laundry service; same-day dry cleaning; executive level rooms. *In room:* TV w/ pay movies, dataport, minibar, fridge, hair dryer. Suites with coffeemaker; 1 unit available with kitchenette.

The Resort at Squaw Creek ★★★ *(Kids)*   The most deluxe resort on the lake is the $130-million Resort at Squaw Creek. You can't beat the resort's ski-in/ski-out access to Squaw Valley skiing—in fact, a chairlift lands just outside the door. Don't ski? Don't worry. There are lots of other sports facilities to keep active travelers happy including 20 miles of groomed cross-country skiing trails (marked for hiking and biking in the summer), an ice-skating rink, and, in summer, a world-class golf course and an equestrian center with riding stables. Particularly good for families, trained counselors lead a "Mountain Buddies" program for kids ages 4 to 13, offering different activities every day. While the standard guest rooms are not particularly spacious, they're well equipped with attractive furnishings, original artwork, and even windows with beautiful views that open to let in the mountain air. Suites come in all different sizes and configurations.

400 Squaw Creek Rd., Olympic Valley, CA 96146. © **800/403-4434** or 530/583-6300. Fax 530/581-6632. www.squawcreek.com. 403 units. $250–$395 double; $450–$1,900 suite. Packages available. AE, DC, DISC, MC, V. Valet parking $15; free self-parking. **Amenities:** 4 restaurants, 1 deli, 4 bars; 3 pools (1 heated); world class golf course; 2 outdoor tennis courts; health club; region's largest spa; indoor and outdoor Jacuzzis; dry saunas; bike rental; children's program; video arcade; concierge; activities desk; courtesy car; business center; secretarial services; shopping arcade; salon; room service; in-room massage; babysitting; laundry service; same-day dry cleaning. *In room:* A/C, TV w/ pay movies, dataport, minibar, coffeemaker, hair dryer, iron. Some units with kitchen.

The Shore House ★★   This romantic little bed-and-breakfast inn, right on the lake, is a real charmer. Each individually decorated room has its own entrance, handmade log furniture, knotty pine walls, a gas-log fireplace, and a blissfully comfortable feather bed. Guests have access to a private beach and landscaped lawn that overlook the lake. Boat owners can even make use of its six buoys and private dock. Planning on tying the knot? No problem: The charming hosts can help. Marty's a minister of the Universal Life Church; Barb can provide the marriage license; they have a pretty area for small, romantic weddings, and even a Honeymoon cottage with a two-person spa tub.

7170 N. Lake Blvd. (P.O. Box 499), Tahoe Vista, CA 96148. ℂ 800/207-5160 or 530/546-7270. Fax 530/546-7130. www.tahoeinn.com. 8 units, 1 cottage. $160–$240 double; $225–$285 cottage. Rates include full breakfast. DISC, MC, V. **Amenities:** Jacuzzi; in-room massage. *In room:* A/C, fridge, hair dryer; no phone.

Moderate

Cal-Neva Resort, Spa & Casino ⍟

You might guess from its name that the state line runs right through this hotel, but you could never imagine its colorful, sometimes scandalous history. Ownership has been passed around by names like "Pretty Boy," "Babyface," and Sinatra, who built the famed Celebrity Room where many big names sang for their supper. It's here that Marilyn Monroe is alleged to have had her rendezvous with John F. Kennedy (you can even see the secret tunnel). There's more. Somebody really should make a movie about this place. Respectability, however, has laid claim to the Cal-Neva, and it is now a popular (and reputable) lakeside resort. Almost all of the rooms in the lodge have lake views and are quite elegantly decorated. Besides the casino (on the Nevada side of the hotel, of course), the Cal-Neva offers the full array of sport and spa options, a complete wedding planning service, and two wedding chapels. Even if you don't stay here, stop by and take a look.

2 Stateline Rd. (Box 368), Crystal Bay, NV 89402-0368. ℂ 800/225-6382 or 775/832-4000. Fax 775/831-9007. www.calnevaresort.com. 168 units, 20 suites 9 chalets, 3 bungalows. $95–$185 double; $219–$399 suite, chalet or bungalow. Packages available. AE, DC, DISC, MC, V. **Amenities:** Restaurant; heated outdoor pool; nearby golf course; 2 outdoor tennis courts; full service European health spa; Jacuzzi; large video arcade; concierge; business center; salon; room service. *In room:* A/C, TV, fax, dataport, coffeemaker, hair dryer, iron.

Meeks Bay Resort ⍟

Rustic Meeks Bay Resort is one of the oldest hostelries on the lake and something of a historical landmark. Opened as a public campground in 1920, its sweeping lakefront location boasts one of the finest beaches on the lake. During the next 50 years, the resort grew to include cabins and other improvements, and attracted many celebrities from southern California. Acquired by the U.S. Forest Service in 1974, the property is open during summers only. Most rentals are on a weekly basis and consist of modest cabins perched near the lake. Facilities include a full marina with boat rentals, a campground with RV access ($20 a night, 4-night minimum), a beachfront snack bar, a playground, and a visitor center with a cultural display, coffee bar, and retail store. The Kehlet House set on a rock that juts out into the lake is the resort's prime accommodation. Owned at one time by William Hewlett, co-founder of the Hewlett-Packard Corporation, and later the summer residence of billionaire Gordon Getty, it has seven bedrooms, three bathrooms, a large kitchen, a living room, and water on three sides. The entire house is rented by the week, sleeps a dozen, and costs $3,850. Make all reservations here early.

P.O. Box 787, Tahoma, CA 96142 ℂ 877/326-3357 or 530/525-6946. Fax 530/525-4028. www.meeksbayresort.com. 21 units and 28 campsites. $85–$195 double per night; $770–$1,650 per week. AE, MC, V. Open May–Oct only. **Amenities:** Watersports equipment rental. *In room:* Log cabins have kitchens.

Northstar-at-Tahoe Resort ⍟⍟⍟ (Kids)

The folks at Northstar continue to come up with even more ways to have fun year-round—the list of activities is mind-boggling. Priding itself on being the ultimate, self-contained, family destination, there is something here for everyone. The Northstar Village and

Lodge are surrounded by a honeycomb of fully equipped redwood condos and vacation homes, all nestled among the pines. Lodging options range from a hotel room in the lodge to a five-bedroom house, with every size in between. Summer activities include golf, swimming, tennis, mountain biking, hiking, fly-fishing, rock climbing, rope courses, and horseback riding. See "Skiing and Snowboarding," earlier in this chapter for winter activities.

Off Hwy. 267, Box 129, Northstar-at-Tahoe, CA 96160. ✆ **800/466-6784** or 530/562-1010. Fax 530/562-2215. www.skinorthstar.com. 262 units. $195–$325 double in lodge; $178–$989 condos, homes. Packages available. AE, DISC, MC, V. **Amenities:** Restaurant, cafe, deli, bar; outdoor heated pool; heated lap pool year-round; kiddie pool; golf course on site; 10 tennis courts; health club; 3 outdoor Jacuzzis; sauna; bike rental; children and teen center; game room/video arcade; tour and activities desk; business center; babysitting; laundry facilities. *In room:* TV/VCR, coffeemaker, hair dryer, iron. Condos have kitchens.

River Ranch Lodge & Restaurant ★★   The River Ranch Lodge has long been one of our favorite places to stay in Lake Tahoe. Situated alongside the Truckee River, the lodge is mere minutes away from Alpine Meadows and Squaw Valley ski resorts, and a short drive (or ride along the bike path) into Tahoe City. The best rooms in this rustic lodge have balconies that overlook the river. All have a handsome mountain home decor, lodgepole pine furniture, and down comforters. Rooms 9 and 10, the farthest from the road, are our top choices. In summer, guests relax under umbrellas on the huge patio overlooking the river, working down burgers and beer while watching the rafters float by. During the ski season, the River Ranch's spectacular circular cocktail lounge and dining area, which cantilevers over the river, is an immensely popular après-ski hangout. Also a big hit is the handsome River Ranch Lodge Restaurant, which serves fresh seafood, steaks, rack of lamb, and more exotic meats such as wood-oven-roasted Montana elk loin with a dried-cherry/port sauce.

On Calif. 89, at Alpine Meadows Rd. (P.O. Box 197), Tahoe City, CA 94145. ✆ **800/535-9900** or 530/583-4264. Fax 530/583-7237. www.riverranchlodge.com. 19 units. $65–$150 double. Rates include continental breakfast. Packages available. AE, MC, V. **Amenities:** Restaurant, bar; golf course nearby; concierge. *In room:* TV, dataport, iron.

Sunnyside Lodge ★★   Built as a private home in 1908, this hotel and restaurant, one of the grand old lodges still left on the lake, stands 2 miles south of Tahoe City. It looks very much like a giant wooden cabin, complete with dormers, steep pitched roofs, and natural-wood siding. Stretching across the building, a large deck fronts a tiny marina and gravel beach. The place is rustic but fairly sophisticated. The newly remodeled Lakefront rooms, the most desirable, go for about $15 more than the others, and are well worth the added expense. Five units have rock fireplaces. Most of the lodge's ground floor is dominated by the popular Sunnyside Restaurant (see "Where to Dine," later in this chapter).

1850 W. Lake Blvd. (P.O. Box 5969), Tahoe City, CA 96145. ✆ **800/822-2754** or 530/583-7200. Fax 530/583-2551. www.sunnysideresort.com. 23 units. $90–$225 double. Continental breakfast included. Packages available. AE, MC, V. **Amenities:** Restaurant and bar; nearby golf course; watersports equipment rental; room service. *In room:* TV/VCR, hair dryer, iron. Some units with fridge.

Tahoma Meadows Bed & Breakfast *Kids*   Nothing glitzy about this historic bed & breakfast, just some cute little red cabins nestled on a gentle forest slope. Many have clawfoot tubs, and all have gas fireplaces and lots of rustic charm. The largest cabin, Treehouse, sleeps six and is ideal for families.

6821 W. Lake Blvd. (P.O. Box 810), 8½ miles from Tahoe City, Homewood, CA 96141. ✆ **800/355-1596** or 530/525-1553. www.tahomameadows.com. 13 units. $95–$225 double. Rates include full breakfast. AE, DISC, MC, V. Pets accepted in some units with $25 fee. **Amenities:** Cafe; nearby golf course. *In room:* TV/VCR, some units with kitchen. No phone.

Inexpensive

Ferrari's Crown Resort *(Value)* If you are looking for convenient, lakefront accommodations at a reasonable price, this family-operated motel is a great choice. The Ferrari family has proudly offered a warm family atmosphere to its guests since 1957. Family suites are completely equipped with kitchenettes and gas fireplaces, and can sleep up to seven. Nothing fancy here, but this place is well run, the rooms are very inviting, and you can't beat the location. Plan a trip during the off-season to take advantage of their great bargain rates.

8200 N. Lake Blvd. (P.O. Box 845), Kings Beach, CA 96143. © **800/645-2260** or 530/546-3388. Fax 530/546-3851. www.tahoecrown.com. 45 units. $45–$95 double; $70–$210 2-bedroom suites or lakefront rooms. Packages available. AE, DISC, MC, V. **Amenities:** Heated outdoor pool (seasonal); nearby golf course; free passes to nearby health club; Jacuzzi. *In room:* A/C, TV. Some units with stocked kitchenettes, fridge, coffeemaker, hair dryer, iron.

Lake of the Sky Motor Inn *(Value)* This remodeled 1960s-style A-frame motel in the heart of Tahoe City offers decent accommodations in a central location, only steps away from shops and restaurants. Just the basics here, but the housekeeping is good and the comfort level in tiptop motor-inn tradition. Some rooms have lake views, and there's an attractively landscaped picnic and barbecue area.

955 N. Lake Blvd. (P.O. Box 227), Tahoe City, CA 96145. © **530/583-3305.** Fax 530/583-7621. 23 units. $59–$129 double. Children under 12 stay free. Rates include continental breakfast. AE, DC, DISC, MC, V. **Amenities:** Heated outdoor pool (seasonal); nearby golf course. *In room:* TV, dataport. Some units with fridge.

WHERE TO DINE
SOUTH SHORE/SOUTH LAKE TAHOE
Expensive

Evan's American Gourmet Café ✹✹✹ AMERICAN/CONTINENTAL After a dinner at Evan's, you'll feel you've had not just a good meal but a great dining experience. The restaurant's impeccable service, award-winning wine list, and unyielding attention to detail serve as a perfect backdrop for the creative culinary artistry of Chef Aaron Maffit. The philosophy here is to use only the finest, freshest ingredients and not overwhelm them with heavy sauces or over-stylized culinary technique. The cuisine is an original blend of styles from around the world, with each dish being an artistic creation. For appetizers, typical choices are sautéed Dungeness crab cakes on roasted red pepper puree with crème fraîche or foie gras on crispy spice bread with port and apple cider fumet. Entrees might include breast and confit leg of duck with roast onion and savory bread pudding and hazelnut sauce, or roast Cevena venison with balsamic roast cherries, fresh tarragon, and lacquered root vegetables. If you have room, the desserts are luscious as well as beautiful. Seats are limited in this cozy little restaurant so be sure to call ahead for reservations.

536 Emerald Bay Rd., South Lake Tahoe. © **530/542-1990.** Reservations required (must confirm by 4pm). Main courses $18–$25. Open daily for dinner at 5:30pm. DC, DISC, MC, V.

Fresh Ketch ✹✹ SEAFOOD Ensconced in a small marina at the foot of Tahoe Keys Boulevard, Fresh Ketch has long been regarded as South Lake's premier seafood restaurant. Try to get a window table so you can watch the marina activities. For starters, we always order half a dozen oysters and the seared ahi tuna with ponzu and wasabi dipping sauces. Then it's on to the sautéed sea bass encrusted with pistachio, herbs, and garlic, or the big ol' Alaskan king crab, steamed in the shell and served with the requisite drawn butter. There's also a modest selection of meat and poultry dishes, including a great surf-and-turf of petite mignon and lobster. For dessert, the calorie fest continues with a big slice of Kimo's Hula Pie. Prices are a bit steep, but you can always join the locals at the bar and order off the extensive bar menu, which offers everything from blackened mahimahi to fresh-fish tacos and fish-and-chips, all for under $10. There's also live music Friday and Saturday evenings.

2433 Venice Dr. ☎ 530/541-5683. Reservations recommended. Main courses $17–$24, market price for crab and lobster. AE, DC, DISC, MC, V. Daily 11:30am–10pm (bar open until midnight).

Moderate

Cantina Bar & Grill ✸ MEXICAN   The Cantina Bar & Grill is a favorite local hangout and serves the best Mexican food in South Lake. With friendly service, three sports televisions, and 30 kinds of beer, joviality reigns. The menu is well priced and extensive, offering Cal-Mex specialties such as tacos, burritos, and enchiladas along with a half-dozen Southwestern dishes such as smoked chicken polenta and grilled pork chops with jalapeño mashed potatoes. The steak fajitas get a thumbs-up, as do the barbecued baby back ribs. To demonstrate their sense of whimsy and eclectic ethnic appeal, they offer an Oriental chicken salad, a Southwestern Reuben sandwich, a French dip, and a stir-fry wrap as well as a few vegetarian selections.

765 Emerald Bay Rd. ☎ 530/544-1233. Main courses $8–$15. MC, V. Daily 11:30am–10:30pm (bar open until midnight).

Scusa! ✸ ITALIAN   This is one of the best-loved Italian restaurants at Tahoe. The decor is nothing to write home about, but the fresh pasta and other Italian dishes are excellent. The menu might include offerings such as chicken picatta; smoked chicken and ravioli; stuffed eggplant; and baked penne pasta with smoked mozzarella, prosciutto, baked garlic cloves, and a focaccia crust.

1142 Ski Run Blvd. ☎ 530/542-0100. Main courses $9–$18. AE, DISC, MC, V. Daily 5–10pm.

Inexpensive

Sprouts Natural Foods Café ✸✸ *Value* HEALTH FOOD/JUICES   Sprouts owner Tyler Cannon has filled a much-needed niche in South Lake, serving wholesome food that looks good, tastes good, and *is* good. Most everything is made in-house, including the soups, smoothies, and fresh-squeezed juices. Menu items range from rice bowls to sandwiches (try the Real Tahoe Turkey), huge burritos, coffee drinks, muffins, fresh-fruit smoothies, and a marvelous mayo-free tuna sandwich made with yogurt and packed with fresh veggies. Order from the counter, then scramble for a vacant seat (outdoor tables are coveted). This is also an excellent place to pack a picnic lunch.

3123 Harrison Ave. (at U.S. 50 and Alameda St., next to Lakeview Sports). ☎ 530/541-6969. Meals $4.50–$6.75. No credit cards. Daily 8am–10pm.

Yellow Sub *Value* SANDWICHES   When it comes to picnic supplies, there's stiff competition in South Lake Tahoe: three sandwich shops on this single block alone. Still, our favorite is Yellow Sub, voted Best Deli Sandwich Shop by readers of the *Tahoe Daily Tribune*. It offers a whopping 21 versions of overstuffed subs—made in 6-inch and 12-inch varieties—as well as several kinds of wraps. The shop is hidden in a small shopping center across from the El Dorado Campground.

983 Tallac Ave. (at U.S. 50). ☎ 530/541-8808. Sandwiches and wraps $3.20–$7.05. No credit cards. Daily 10:30am–10pm.

NORTH SHORE/TAHOE CITY
Expensive

Lone Eagle Grille ★★★ AMERICAN   If you want to see the most beautiful restaurant in all of Tahoe, don't miss the Lone Eagle Grille, right on the lake in Incline Village. Superlatives are inadequate to describe this architectural delight. It captures the charm of a grand "Old Tahoe" lodge with its massive stone fire-places and towering open beamed ceilings while offering stunning lake views through its expansive windows. For lunch you can choose from an extensive selection of soups, salads, pastas, pizzas, specialty sandwiches, and a few main dishes. The French onion soup and the spit-roasted chicken are particularly good. In addition to the highly recommended items from the specialty grille, the dinner menu might include chili-lime sea bass, ginger-roasted duck, or stuffed Sonoma chicken breast. Great pride is taken in the wine list, and the service is attentive and friendly. Candlelit tables, a roaring fire, magnificent scenery, good food and wine—it just doesn't get better than this.

111 Country Club Dr. (across from the Hyatt), Incline Village, NV. © 775/832-3250. Reservations recommended. Lunch $9–$14; dinner $19–$35 brunch $25, includes champagne. Daily 11:30am–2:30pm, 6–10pm; Sunday brunch 10:30am–2:30pm.

PlumpJack Café ★★★ MODERN AMERICAN   Squaw Valley's investors have spent oodles of money trying to turn the ski resort into a world-class destination, and one major step in the right direction is the sleek and sexy PlumpJack Café. Although dinner prices have dropped slightly (guests balked at the original outrageous rates), none of PlumpJack's high standards have diminished. Expect impeccable service regardless of your attire (this is, after all, a ski resort), and heady menu choices ranging from risotto with shiitake mushrooms and fava beans to roasted rabbit atop a golden potato puree, plus a fabulous dish of braised oxtail paired with horseradish mashed potatoes and carrots. Those already familiar with PlumpJack in San Francisco know that the reasonably priced wine list is among the nation's best.

In the PlumpJack Squaw Valley Inn, 1920 Squaw Valley Rd., Squaw Valley. © 530/583-1576. Reservations recommended. Main courses $17–$20. AE, MC, V. Daily 7am–10pm, 11:30am–2:30pm, and 5:30–10pm.

Sunsets on the Lake ★★ NORTHERN ITALIAN/CALIFORNIA   Here's something appealing: a lakeside restaurant in Tahoe where the food is as spectacular as the view. A rustic, romantic ambiance is created by a large fireplace, white-clothed tables, and—of course—a panoramic lake view. Recommended dishes include Chef Orlady's fantastic braised lamb shank, a hefty hunk of tender lamb perfectly complemented by shiitake mushrooms, caramelized vegetables, and garlic mashed potatoes. If the duck is among the specials, order it: Each tender slice explodes with flavor. When the snow melts, the heated outdoor deck and "Island Bar" are open for dining and drinks. Heck, they even provide blankets for an especially cozy sunset cocktail hour.

7360 N. Lake Blvd. (at North Tahoe Marina), Tahoe Vista. © 530/546-3640. Reservations recommended. Main courses $18–$24. AE, DC, DISC, MC, V. Winter daily 5–10pm; June 25–Sept 7 daily 11:30am–midnight.

Wolfdale's ★★ CALIFORNIA/JAPANESE   Wolfdale's has long been one of Tahoe's finest restaurants. The innovative chefs know how to put a personal spin on regional ingredients, fusing flavors and textures of the East and the West. Although the menu changes frequently, a "cuisine unique" experience—as they're fond of calling it— might begin with tea-smoked duck with peanut noodles and mango chutney or sashimi with ginger and wasabi. The spinach salad tossed with smoked local trout, olives, and grated eggs is particularly memorable.

Main courses are equally inventive, such as grilled game hen with Thai dipping sauce, or Alaskan halibut and sea scallops wrapped in Swiss chard with leek sauce.

640 N. Lake Blvd., Tahoe City. ℂ 530/583-5700. Reservations recommended. Main courses $18–$24. DISC, MC, V. Wed–Mon 6pm–10pm (open daily July–Aug).

Moderate

Café 333 ✿✿ ECLECTIC AMERICAN   The cuisine at this chic little cafe has been described as contemporary French country style with a San Francisco flair. Whatever you call it, the food is outstanding. If you're tired of the same old breakfasts, you'll love your choices here. Try the Breakfast Strata ("Bread Pudding" baked with prosciutto, spinach, tomato, basil, mascarpone, Parmesan and cream), the chicken hash, or the caramelized apple French toast. Gourmet coffees, baked goods, and creative omelets also grace the menu. For lunch you can't go wrong with any of their tasty salads, sandwiches, or pastas. The dinner menu might include grilled vegetable risotto or salmon with fresh herbed gnocchi and Gorgonzola sauce. The desserts are made in-house and include such goodies as crème brûlée, caramel chocolate pecan pie, and berry shortcake. They need more room to accommodate their enthusiastic guests, but the ambiance is so cheerful that somehow you don't mind sometimes rubbing elbows.

333 Village Blvd., Incline Village. ℂ 775/832-7333. Breakfast $7–$9; lunch $8–$12; dinner $15–$24. Daily 7:30am–3pm and 5:30pm–9pm.

Gar Woods Grill & Pier ✿ AMERICAN   Named after the builder of those beautiful mahogany race boats that used to grace the lake in the 1930s and '40s, Gar Woods attempts to capture the nostalgia and atmosphere of that old wooden boat era. Whether folks are watching Monday night football or drinking a famous "Wet Woody," it seems like there is always something festive going on in the bar. And on a sunny day, it's great fun to sit out on the lakeside deck to enjoy the good food and good cheer. The menu is wide-ranging, covering everything from a shrimp and lobster bisque to a pepper and garlic turkey burger with curly fries. Appetizers go from beer-battered coconut prawns to sashimi. Dinner entrees include nothing out of the ordinary, but the preparation is good and the service is friendly. Try the sumptuous Sunday brunch—it's more food than you could ever imagine for $25.

5000 N. Lake Blvd., Carnelian Bay. ℂ 530/546-3366. Lunch $9–$14; dinner $14–$27; brunch $25. AE, DISC, MC, V. Mon–Sat 11:30am–10pm, Sun 10:30am–10pm.

Sunnyside Restaurant ✿ SEAFOOD/AMERICAN   In summer, when the sun is shining, there's no more highly coveted table in Tahoe than one on Sunnyside's lakeside veranda. Guests can also dine in the lodge's more traditional dining room with its 1930s aura. Nothing out of the ordinary here: The lunch menu has fresh pastas, burgers, chicken, and fish sandwiches, together with a variety of soups and salads. Dinners are fancier, with such main courses as Australian lobster tail, lamb chops with roasted-garlic chutney butter, and fresh salmon oven-baked on a cedar plank.

At the Sunnyside Lodge, 1850 W. Lake Blvd., Tahoe City. ℂ 530/583-7200. Main courses $14–$24. AE, DISC, MC, V. Oct–June daily 4–9:30pm; July–Sept daily 11am–9:30pm, Fri–Sat 'til 10pm; Sun brunch 9:30am–2pm.

Inexpensive

Bridgetender Tavern and Grill *Value* PUB FARE   Although it's located in one of the most popular tourist areas in North Lake, the Bridgetender is a locals' hangout through and through. Still, they're surprisingly tolerant of out-of-towners, who come for the cheap grub and huge selection of draft beers. The tavern is built around a trio of Ponderosa pines that blend with the decor so well you hardly notice them. Big burly burgers, salads, pork ribs, and such round out the menu, and the daily beer specials—posted on the wall in Day-Glo colors—are definitely worth going over. In summer, dine outside among the pines.

30 W. Lake Blvd. (at Fanny Bridge), Tahoe City. ℭ 530/583-3342. Burgers, salads, and ribs $5–$8. MC, V. Daily 11am–2am.

Fire Sign Café ⋆ *Value* AMERICAN   Choosing a place to have breakfast in North Tahoe is a no-brainer. Since the late 1970s, the Fire Sign Café has been the locals' choice—which explains the lines out the door on weekends. Just about everything is made from scratch, such as the delicious coffee cake that accompanies the big plates of bacon and eggs or blackberry-buckwheat pancakes. Even the salmon for chef and owner Bob Young's legendary salmon omelet is smoked in-house. Lunch—burgers, salads, sandwiches, burritos, and more—is also quite popular, particularly when the outdoor patio is open.

1785 W. Lake Blvd., Tahoe City. ℭ 530/583-0871. Breakfast and lunch $4–$9. MC, V. Daily 7am–3pm.

Izzy's Burger Spa *Value* BURGERS   It's just a simple, wooden A-frame building containing a small short-order grill, but Izzy's Burger Spa flips an unusually hefty and tasty burger and an equally enticing grilled chicken-breast sandwich. On a sunny day, the best seats are at the picnic tables set out front.

100 W. Lake Blvd. (at Fanny Bridge), Tahoe City. ℭ 530/583-4111. Burgers $4–$7. No credit cards. Daily 11am–7pm.

TAHOE AFTER DARK

Tahoe is not particularly known for its nightlife, although there's always something going on in the showrooms of the major casino hotels on the South Shore. Call **Harrah's** (ℭ 775/588-6611), **Harvey's** (ℭ 775/588-2411), **Caesar's** (ℭ 775/588-3515), and the **Horizon** (ℭ 775/588-6211) for current show schedules and prices. Most cocktail shows cost $15 to $40. On the North Shore, there's usually live music nightly in **Bullwhackers Pub,** at the Resort at Squaw Creek (ℭ 530/583-6300), 5 miles west of Tahoe City. The **Pierce Street Annex,** 850 North Lake Blvd. (ℭ 530/583-5800), behind the Safeway in Tahoe City, has pool tables, shuffleboard, and DJ dancing every night. It's one of the livelier places around. The college crowd will feel at home at **Elevations,** 877 North Lake Blvd., across from Safeway (ℭ 530/583-4867), which has the cheapest drinks in town and live rock music most nights.

2 Mount Shasta & the Cascades ⋆⋆

274 miles N of San Francisco

Chances are, your first glimpse of Mount Shasta's majestic, snowcapped peak will result in a twang of awe. A dormant volcano with a 17-mile-diameter base, it stands in virtual isolation 14,162 feet above the sea. When John Muir first saw Shasta from 50 miles away in 1874, he wrote: "[I] was alone and weary. Yet my blood turned to wine, and I have not been weary since." He went on to describe it as "the pole star of the landscape," which indeed it is.

Keep in mind, however, that dining and lodging in these parts lean more toward sustenance than indulgence: It's the fresh air, not fresh fish, that lures visitors this far north. You can leave the dinner jacket at home—all that's really required when visiting the Far North are a pair of broken-in hiking boots, binoculars (the bald eagle is a common sight in these parts), some warm clothing, and an adventurous spirit.

Redding/Mt. Shasta Area

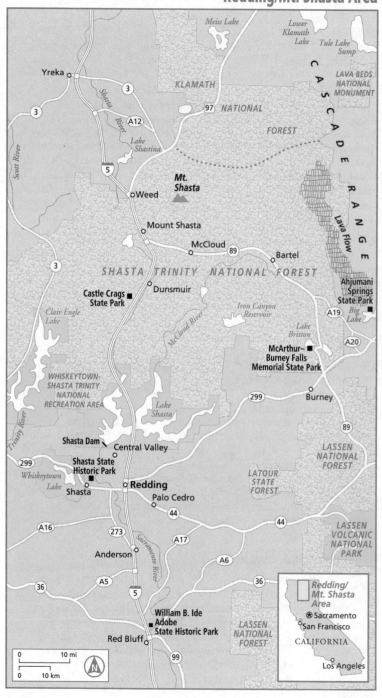

Meiss Lake

Lower Klamath Lake

Tule Lake Sump

C A S C A D E

LAVA BEDS NATIONAL MONUMENT

Yreka

3

KLAMATH

97

NATIONAL

FOREST

A12

Shasta River

Scott River

Lake Shastina

5

Mt. Shasta

Weed

Lava Flow

R A N G E

Mount Shasta

McCloud

89

Bartel

3

SHASTA TRINITY NATIONAL FOREST

Dunsmuir

Castle Crags State Park

Clair Engle Lake

McCloud River

Iron Canyon Reservoir

Ahjumani Springs State Park

A19

Big Lake

Lake Britton

A20

WHISKEYTOWN-SHASTA TRINITY NATIONAL RECREATION AREA

Trinity River

Lake Shasta

McArthur–Burney Falls Memorial State Park

299

Burney

89

Shasta Dam

Central Valley

Shasta State Historic Park

299

Whiskeytown Lake

Shasta

Redding

Palo Cedro

44

LASSEN NATIONAL FOREST

LATOUR STATE FOREST

44

LASSEN VOLCANIC NATIONAL PARK

A16

273

A17

Sacramento River

Anderson

A6

36

A5

5

36

William B. Ide Adobe State Historic Park

LASSEN NATIONAL FOREST

Red Bluff

99

0   10 mi

0   10 km

N

Redding/ Mt. Shasta Area

⊗ Sacramento

San Francisco

CALIFORNIA

Los Angeles

257

ESSENTIALS

GETTING THERE   From San Francisco, take I-80 to I-505 to I-5 to Redding. From the coast, pick up Calif. 299 east a few miles north of Arcata to Redding.

Redding Municipal Airport, 6751 Woodrum Circle (© 530/224-4399), is serviced by **United Express** (© 800/241-6522) and **Horizon Air** (© 800/547-9308). **Amtrak** (© 800/USA-RAIL) stops in Dunsmuir and Redding.

VISITOR INFORMATION   Regional information can be obtained from the following organizations: **Shasta Cascade Wonderland Association,** 1699 Calif. 273, Anderson, CA 96007 (© 800/474-2782 or 530/365-7500; www.shastacascade.org); **Mount Shasta Visitors Bureau,** 300 Pine St., Mount Shasta, CA 96067 (© 800/926-4865 or 530/926-4865; www.mtshasta.com); **Redding Convention and Visitors Bureau,** 777 Auditorium Dr., Redding, CA 96001 (© 800/874-7562 or 530/225-4100; www.ci.redding.ca.us); **Trinity County Chamber of Commerce,** 210 N. Main St., P.O. Box 517, Weaverville, CA 96093 (© 800/487-4648 or 530/623-6101; www.trinitycounty.com).

REDDING

The major town and gateway to the region is Redding, the hub of the panoramic Shasta-Cascade region, lying at the top of the Sacramento Valley. From here, you can either turn westward into the wilderness forest of Trinity and the Klamath Mountains, or north and east into the Cascades and Shasta Trinity National Forest.

In Redding, with its fast-food joints, gas stations, and cheap motels, summer heat generally hovers around 100°F. A city of some 80,000, Redding is the transportation hub of the upper reaches of northern California. It has little of interest; it's mainly useful as a base for exploring the natural wonders nearby. Information is available from the **Redding Convention and Visitors Bureau,** 777 Auditorium Dr., Redding, CA 96001 (© **800/874-7562** or 530/225-4100; www.ci.redding.ca.us), west of I-5 on Calif. 299. It's open Monday through Friday from 8am to 5pm. Ahead and northeast, Mount Shasta rises to a height of more than 14,000 feet. From Redding, I-5 cuts north over the Pit River Bridge, crossing Lake Shasta and leading eventually to the mount itself. Before striking north, however, you may want to explore **Lake Shasta** and see **Shasta Dam.** Another option is to take a detour west of Redding to Weaverville, Whiskeytown–Shasta Trinity National Recreation Area, and Trinity Lake (see "Whiskeytown National Recreation Area," below).

About 3 miles west, stop at the old mining town of **Shasta,** which has been converted into a state historic park (© **530/243-8194**). Shasta was founded on

 The Republic of California

En route to Mount Shasta from the south, you may want to stop near Red Bluff at **William B. Ide Adobe State Historic Park,** 21659 Adobe Rd. (© 530/529-8599), for a picnic along the Sacramento River and a visit to an adobe home dating back to 1852. The 4-acre park commemorates William B. Ide, the Republic of California's first and only president. The Republic of California was proclaimed on June 14, 1846 following the Bear Flag Rebellion and lasted only 3 weeks. In summer, the park is open from 8am to sunset, the house from noon to 4pm; call ahead in winter. Parking is $3 per vehicle.

Shasta vs. Shasta

Don't confuse the old mining town, Shasta, located a few miles west of Redding, with the much larger community, Mount Shasta, a major tourist destination located on Interstate 5 near the base of Mount Shasta.

gold and was the "Queen City" of the northern mines in the Klamath Range. Its life was short, and it expired in 1872 when the Central Pacific Railroad bypassed it in favor of Redding. Today, the business district is a ghost town, complete with a restored general store and a Masonic hall. The 1861 courthouse has been converted into a museum where you can view the jail and a gallows out back, as well as a remarkable collection of California art assembled by Mae Helen Bacon Boggs. The collection includes works by Maynard Dixon, Grace Hudson, and many others. It's open Wednesday through Sunday from 10am to 5pm. Admission is $2 for adults, $1 for children ages 6 to 12.

Continue along Calif. 299 west to Calif. 3 north, which will take you to Weaverville and then to the west side of the lake and Trinity Center.

WHERE TO STAY
In addition to Tiffany House (see below), Redding has a **Doubletree Motor Inn** (✆ **800/222-8733** or 530/221-8700) and a **La Quinta Inn** (✆ **800/ NU-ROOMS** or 530/221-8200). Both are fine choices.

Tiffany House Bed and Breakfast Inn   Despite the fact that this two-story gray-and-white house wasn't built until 1939, everyone in town refers to it as a Victorian. A sweeping view of the Lassen Mountain Range is visible from every guest room and cottage, as well as from the oversize deck, which seems to float above the garden in back. There's also a Music Room with piano; Victorian Parlor with fireplace, games, and puzzles; and even a swimming pool. Each guest room is appointed with a queen-size bed and antique furnishings, and all have private bathrooms and soft robes. Top choice is the secluded Lavinia's Cottage, which has a 7-foot spa tub, sitting area, and magnificent laurel-wreath iron bed.

1510 Barbara Rd., Redding, CA 96003. ✆ **530/244-3225.** www.sylvia.com/tiffany.htm. 4 units. $85–$105 double; $135 cottage. Rates include full breakfast. AE, DISC, MC, V. **Amenities:** Outdoor pool; nearby golf course; Jacuzzi; game room. *In room:* A/C, hair dryer; no phone.

WHERE TO DINE
Jack's Grill ✎ STEAK HOUSE   This building was originally constructed in 1835 as a secondhand-clothing store. The second floor served as a brothel in the late 1930s, and an entrepreneur named Jack Young set up the main floor as a steak house (his establishment serviced all of a body's needs, you might say). Today, it's a local favorite. Waiting for a table over drinks in the bar is part of the fun. Good old-fashioned red meat is supplemented by a couple of seafood dishes, such as deep-fried jumbo prawns and ocean scallops. It's a very fetching spot, with good, honest tavern food and a jovial crowd. Be prepared to wait on weekends.

1743 California St. ✆ **530/241-5826.** Reservations not accepted. Main courses $9.15–$22.25. AE, DISC, MC, V. Mon–Sat 4–11pm.

WEAVERVILLE
Weaverville was a gold-mining town in the 1850s, and part of the history of the place is captured at the **Jake Jackson Memorial Museum–Trinity County**

Historical Park, 508 Main St. (① **530/623-5211**). The collection of memorabilia, from firearms to household items, is interesting for what it reveals about the residents of the town—Native Americans, miners, pioneers, and especially the Chinese. In the gold-rush era, the town was half Chinese, with a Chinatown of about 2,500 residents. Admission is free, but a donation of $1 is suggested.

Across the parking lot, you can view the oldest continuously used Taoist temple in California at the **Joss House State Historic Park** (① **530/623-5284**). This well-preserved temple was built by immigrant Chinese miners in 1874. Admission is $2 for adults, Admission is $1 for adults, free for children ages 16 and under.

WHERE TO DINE

LaGrangeCafé 🌟🌟 *(Finds)* CREATIVE TRADITIONAL CUISINE Weaverville isn't exactly a star in the culinary firmament, but there is one bright spot. This is far and away the best food in town. Heck, it would be considered really good in Redding, Sacramento, or Tahoe. Recently relocated from its original home down the street, the restaurant now has digs worthy of its cuisine. It's in Weaverville's historic district; two adjoining buildings were combined and stripped down to the original old brick walls to make a spacious, attractive dining area with a sit-down bar. Chef and owner Sharon Heryford's menu includes the local favorite—chicken enchiladas with marinated tri-tip—plus seasonal items such as the local rabbit, braised with mushrooms, fresh herbs, and white wine. The tender Duane's Chicken served with wheat pilaf is also popular. The interesting menu includes other things like buffalo steaks, venison bratwurst, and wild boar sausages. Heryford's buffalo ragout won third place in a national contest. The 135-plus selections on the wine list make it one of the strongest in Northern California. Desserts, like a sinfully rich banana cream pie and that quintessential comfort food, bread pudding, are all made on the premises.

226 Main St. ① **530/623-5325.** Main courses $10–$25. AE, DISC, MC, V. Mon–Thurs 11am–9pm; Fri–Sun 11am–10pm.

THE TRINITY ALPS

West of Weaverville stretch the Trinity Alps, with Thompson Peak rising to more than 9,000 feet. The second-largest wilderness area in the state lies between the Trinity and Salmon Rivers and contains more than 55 lakes and streams. Its alpine scenery makes it popular with hikers and backpackers. You can access the **Pacific Crest Trail** west of Mount Shasta at Parks Creek, South Fork Road, or Whalen Road, and also from Castle Crags State Park. For trail and other information, contact the forest service at Weaverville (① **530/623-2121**).

The Fifth Season, 300 N. Mount Shasta Blvd. (① **530/926-3606**), offers mountaineering and backpack rentals and will provide trail maps and other information concerning Shasta's outdoor activities.

Living Waters Recreation (① **530/926-5446**) offers half-day to 2-day rafting trips on the Upper Sacramento, Klamath, Trinity, and Salmon Rivers. **Trinity River Rafting Company,** on Calif. 299W in Big Flat (① **800/ 30-RIVER** or 530/623-3033), also operates local white-water trips.

For additional outfitters and information, contact the **Trinity County Chamber of Commerce,** 210 N. Main St. (P.O. Box 517), Weaverville, CA 96093 (① **800/487-4648** or 530/623-6101; www.trinitycounty.com).

WHISKEYTOWN NATIONAL RECREATION AREA

In adjacent Shasta County, Whiskeytown National Recreation Area is on the eastern shore of Trinity Lake, a quiet and relatively uncrowded lake with 157 miles of shoreline. When this reservoir was created, it was officially named Clair Engle, after the politician who created it. But locals insist on calling it Trinity after the name of the river that used to rush through the region past the towns of Minersville, Stringtown, and an earlier Whiskeytown. All of these were destroyed when the river was dammed. They now lie submerged under the lake's glassy surface.

Both Trinity Lake and the Whiskeytown National Recreation Area are in the Shasta Trinity National Forest, 1.3 million acres of wilderness with 1,269 miles of hiking trails. For information on trails, contact **Shasta Trinity National Forest** (© **530/246-5222**).

LAKE SHASTA

Heading north on I-5 from Redding, travel about 12 miles and take the Shasta Dam Boulevard exit to the **Shasta Dam and Power Plant** ✸ (© **530/ 275-4463**), which has an overflow spillway that is three times higher than Niagara Falls. The huge dam—3,460 feet long, 602 feet high, and 883 feet thick at its base—holds back the waters of the Sacramento, Pit, and McCloud Rivers. A dramatic sight indeed, it is a vital component of the Central Valley water project. At the visitor center is a series of photographs and displays covering the dam's construction period. You can either walk or drive over the dam, but far more interesting are the free 1-hour tours given daily from 9am to 5pm on the hour in the summer, and at 10am, noon, and 2pm from Labor Day to Memorial Day. The guided tour takes you deep within the dam's many chilly corridors (not a good place for claustrophobes) and below the spillway. It's an entertaining way to beat the summer heat.

Lake Shasta has 370 miles of shoreline and attracts anglers (bass, trout, and king salmon), water-skiers, and other boating enthusiasts—2 million, in fact, in summer. The best way to enjoy the lake is aboard a houseboat; they can be rented from several companies, including **Antlers Resort & Marina,** P.O. Box 140, Antlers Rd., Lakehead, CA 96051 (© **800/238-3924**); and **Packers Bay Marina,** 16814 Packers Bay Rd., Lakehead, CA 96051 (© **800/331-3137** or 530/275-5570). There is a 1-week minimum during the summer, and 3- to 4-day minimum during the off-season.

While you're here, you can visit **Lake Shasta Caverns** (© **530/238-2341**). These caves contain 20-foot-high stalactite and stalagmite formations—60-foot-wide curtains of them in the great Cathedral Room. To see the caves, drive about 15 miles north of Redding on I-5 to the O'Brien/Shasta Caverns exit. A ferry will take you across the lake and a short bus ride will follow to the cave entrance for a 2-hour-long tour. Admission is $17 for adults, $9 for children ages 4–12, and free for kids under 4. The caverns are open daily year-round.

For information about the Lake Shasta region, contact the **Redding Convention and Visitors Bureau,** 777 Auditorium Dr., Redding, CA 96001 (© **800/874-7562** or 530/225-4100), west of I-5 on Calif. 299. It's open Monday through Friday from 8am to 5pm.

MOUNT SHASTA

A volcanic mountain with eight glaciers, **Mount Shasta** ✸✸✸ is a towering peak of legend and lore. It stands alone, always snowcapped, unshadowed by other mountains—visible from 125 miles away. Although it's been dormant since 1786, eruptions cannot be ruled out, and indeed, hot sulfur springs bubble at the summit. The springs saved John Muir on his third ascent of the mountain in 1875. Caught in a severe snowstorm, he and his partner took turns submersing themselves in the hot mud to survive.

Many New Agers are convinced that Mount Shasta is the center of an incredible energy vortex. These devotees flock to the foot of the mountain. In 1987, the foothills were host to the worldwide Harmonic Convergence, calling for a planetary union and a new phase of universal harmony. Yoga, massage, meditation, and metaphysics are all the rage here. These New Agers seem to coexist harmoniously with those whose metaphysical leanings begin and end with Dolly Parton song lyrics.

Those who don't want to climb can drive up to about 7,900 feet. From the town of Mount Shasta, drive 14 miles up the Everitt Memorial Highway to the end of the road near Panther Meadow. At the **Everitt Vista Turnout,** you'll be able to stop and see the Sacramento River Canyon, the Eddy Mountains to the west, and glimpses of Mount Lassen to the south. You can also take the short hike through the forests to a lava outcrop overlooking the McCloud area.

Continue on to **Bunny Flat,** a major access point for climbing in summer and also for cross-country skiing and sledding in winter. The highway ends at the Old Ski Bowl Vista, providing panoramic views of Mount Lassen, Castle Crags, and the Trinity Mountains.

While in Mount Shasta, visit the **Fish Hatchery** at 3 N. Old State Rd. (© 530/ 926-2215), which was built in 1888. Here you can observe rainbow and brown trout being hatched to stock rivers and streams statewide—millions are born here annually. You can feed them via coin-operated food dispensers, and observe the spawning process on certain Tuesdays during the fall and winter. Admission is free; hours are daily from 8am to sunset. Adjacent to the hatchery is the **Sisson Museum** (© 530/926-5508), which displays a smattering of local-history exhibits. It's open daily year-round, from 10am to 4pm in summer, from 1 to 4pm in winter; admission is free.

OUTDOOR PURSUITS

GOLF & TENNIS   Golfers should head for the 27-hole Robert Trent Jones, Jr., golf course at **Lake Shastina Golf Resort,** 5925 Country Club Dr., Weed (© 800/358-4653 or 530/938-3201), or the 18-hole course at **Mount Shasta Resort,** 1000 Siskiyou Lake Blvd., Mount Shasta (© 800/958-3363 or 530/ 926-3030); the resort also has tennis courts.

MOUNTAIN CLIMBING   Mount Shasta attracts thousands of hikers from around the world each year, from timid first-timers to serious mountaineers who search for the most difficult paths up. The hike isn't technically difficult, but it's a demanding ascent that takes about 8 hours of continuous exertion, particularly when the snow softens up. (*Tip:* Start early, while the snow is still firm.) Before setting out, hikers must secure a permit by signing in at the trailhead or at the **Mount Shasta Ranger District** office, which also gives out plenty of good advice for amateur climbers. The office is at 204 W. Alma St., off North Mount Shasta Boulevard in Mount Shasta (© 530/926-4511; www.r5.fs.fed.us/shasta-trinity). Be sure to wear good hiking shoes and carry crampons and an ice ax, a first-aid kit, a quart of water per person, and a flashlight in case it takes longer than anticipated. Sunblock is an absolute necessity. All the requisite equipment can be rented at **The Fifth Season,** 300 N. Mount Shasta Blvd. (© 530/ 926-3606). (By the way, for those mere mortals who just want to hike and don't feel compelled to summit, there are lots of low elevation trails.)

Weather can be extremely unpredictable, and every year hikers die on this dormant volcano, usually from making stupid mistakes. For **weather and climbing conditions,** call ✆ **530/926-5555** for recorded information. Traditionally, climbers make the ascent from the Sierra Lodge at Horse Camp, which can be reached from the town of Mount Shasta via Alma Street and the Everitt Memorial Highway or from Bunny Flat.

For more information as well as supervised trips, contact **Shasta Mountain Guides,** 1938 Hill Rd. (✆ **530/926-3117**). This outfitter offers a 2-day climb that follows the traditional John Muir route and costs $268. It also offers a glacier climb and rock climbing in Castle Crags State Park, backpacking trips, plus cross-country and telemark skiing. You can take its basic rock-climbing course for $78, mountaineering course for $78, or one of its 3-day ski and snowboard descents for $368.

Also nearby is **Castle Crags State Park** (✆ **530/235-2684**), a 4,300-acre park with 64 campsites and 28 miles of hiking trails. Here, granite crags that were formed 225 million years ago tower more than 6,500 feet above the Sacramento River. The park is filled with dogwood, oak, cedar, and pine as well as tiger lilies, azaleas, and orchids in summer. You can walk the 1-mile Indian Creek nature trail or take the easy 1-mile Root Creek Trail. The entrance fee is $5 per vehicle per day. Castle Craggs is off I-5, about 50 miles north of Redding.

OTHER WARM-WEATHER ACTIVITIES Mount Shasta offers some excellent **mountain biking.** In the summer, ride the chairlifts to the top of Mount Shasta Ski Park and bike down the trails. An all-day chairlift pass is only $12 (✆ **530/926-8610**). Another good source for renting mountain bikes and getting trail information is **Shasta Cycling** (✆ **530/938-3002**).

For fishing information or guided trips, call **Jack Trout Flyfishing Guide** (✆ **530/926-4540**). Two other recommended sources are **Mount Shasta Fly Fishing** (✆ **530/926-6648**) and **Hart's Guide Service** (✆ **530/926-2431**).

SKIING In winter, visitors can ski at **Mount Shasta Board & Ski Park,** 104 Siskiyou Ave., Mount Shasta (✆ **530/926-8610;** www.skipark.com), which has 31 runs with 80% snowmaking, three triple chairlifts, and a surface lift. Lift tickets are $31 on weekends, $26 during the week. There's also a Nordic ski center with 15½ miles of groomed trails, as well as a Terrain Park that's geared toward snowboarders. The Learning Center offers instruction for adults and children. In summer, you can ride the chairlifts to scenic views, mountain bike down the trails (an all-day pass is $15), or practice on the two-story climbing wall. Access to the park is 10 miles east of Mount Shasta (the town) on Calif. 89. For information, call ✆ **530/926-8610**.

WATERSPORTS The source of the headwaters of the Sacramento River accumulates in **Lake Siskiyou,** a popular spot for boating, swimming, and fishing—and a great vantage point for photographs of Mount Shasta and its reflection. Water-skiing and jet-skiing are not allowed, but windsurfing is, and boat rentals are offered at **Lake Siskiyou Camp Resort,** 4239 W. A. Barr Rd., Mount Shasta (✆ **888/926-2618** or 530/926-2618).

WHERE TO STAY

Best Western Tree House Just off the main highway, this motor inn is one of the best places to stay in the town of Mount Shasta, and it keeps its prices low. The lobby and refurbished rooms, some with decks and fridges, are pleasant enough, plus there's a huge indoor pool, usually deserted, making this a family favorite. Downhill and cross-country ski areas are 10 miles away.

111 Morgan Way (at I-5 and Lake St.), Mount Shasta, CA 96067. © **800/545-7164** or 530/926-3101. Fax 530/926-3542. www.bestwestern.com. 95 units. $82–$125 double. AE, DC, MC, V. **Amenities:** Restaurant, bar; indoor pool; nearby golf course; exercise room; Jacuzzi; video arcade; business center; secretarial services. *In room:* A/C, TV, fridge, coffeemaker, hair dryer, iron.

McCloud Guest House ✦

Off Calif. 89, west of McCloud, and set among the oak and pine trees of Mount Shasta's lower slopes, this graceful old home has a wraparound veranda and dormer windows, and overlooks beautifully groomed grounds. Built in 1907 as a residence for the president of the McCloud River Lumber Company, the handsome house was nicely restored in 1984 and changed ownership in 1999. Upstairs, there's a large comfortable parlor with an antique pool table from the Hearst Collection. Off the parlor are five individually decorated rooms with white iron beds. Three of the rooms have clawfoot tubs; the other two have showers only. The new innkeepers take great pride in the creative gourmet breakfasts served in the leaded- and stained-glassed dining room. In addition to a whipped fruit drink, fresh fruit, and homemade pastries, the menu might include a California soufflé or Belgian waffles.

606 W. Colombero Dr. (P.O. Box 1510), McCloud, CA 96057. © **877/964-3160** or 530/964-3160. Fax 530/964-3202. www.mccloudguesthouse.com. 5 units, $95–$130 double. Rates include a full breakfast. MC, V. **Amenities:** Nearby golf course; sauna; massage upon request. *In room:* Iron; no phone.

Mount Shasta Ranch B&B ✦

Mount Shasta Ranch was conceived and built in 1923 by one of the country's most famous horse trainers and racing tycoons, H. D. ("Curley") Brown, as the centerpiece of a private retreat and thoroughbred-horse ranch. Despite the encroachment of nearby buildings, the main house and its annex are still available as a cozy B&B with touches of nostalgia, the occasional antique, and spectacular views of Mount Shasta. Four bedrooms (the ones with private bathrooms) lie in the main house; the remaining five share two bathrooms in the carriage house. It's a 3-minute trek to the shores of nearby Lake Siskiyou (15 minutes to the ski slopes), or you could stay here to enjoy the Jacuzzi, Ping-Pong tables, pool table, darts, and horseshoes.

1008 W. A. Barr Rd., Mount Shasta, CA 96067. © **530/926-3870.** Fax 530/926-6882. www.stayinshasta.com. 10 units, 5 with private bathroom; 1 cottage. $55–$80 double with shared bathroom, $110 double with bathroom; $115 cottage for 2. Country breakfast included (except cottage). Pets allowed with $10 fee. AE, DISC, MC, V. Take Central Mount Shasta exit off I-5 to W. A. Barr Rd. **Amenities:** Nearby golf course; Jacuzzi; game room. *In room:* A/C, TV; 2 units with kitchen. No phone.

Railroad Park Resort *(Kids)*

Lying a quarter of a mile from the Sacramento River, this is an offbeat place that kids will enjoy. It's located at the foot of Castle Crags and contains a campground and RV park, four rustic cabins, and the Caboose Motel. Railroad cabooses have been converted into rooms, leaving their pipes, ladders, and lofts in place. Located around the fenced-in kidney-shaped pool, they're furnished with modern brass beds, table and chairs, dressers. The restaurant and lounge are also in vintage railroad cars.

100 Railroad Park Rd., Dunsmuir, CA 96025. © **800/974-RAIL** or 530/235-4440. Fax 530/235-4470. www.rrpark.com. 27 units. $85–$100 double. $10 less off season. Extra person $10. AE, DISC, MC, V. Take Railroad Park exit off I-5, 1 mile south of Dunsmuir. Pets allowed with $10 fee. **Amenities:** Restaurant and lounge; outdoor pool; Jacuzzi; game room; laundry facilities. *In room:* A/C, TV, fridge, coffeemaker; some units with minibar. Some cabins with kitchen.

Stewart Mineral Springs Resort *(Finds)*

Stewart Mineral Springs is one of the most unusual health spas in California, loaded with lore and legends. It lies above cold-water springs that Native Americans valued for their healing powers. Don't expect anything approaching a European spa or big-city luxury here.

Everything is deliberately rustic, with as few intrusions from the urban world as possible (no phones or TVs). Designed in a somewhat haphazard compound of about a dozen buildings, 4 miles west of the town of Weed, it occupies a 37-acre site of sloping, forested land accented with ponds, gazebos, and decorative bridges and is riddled with hiking and nature trails, freshwater streams, and a swimming hole.

Activities revolve around hiking, nature watching, and taking the healing waters of the legendary springs. The bathhouse is the curative headquarters of the resort and contains 13 private rooms where water from the springs is heated and run into tubs for soaking. A staff member will describe the rituals for you: A 20-minute soak is followed by a visit to a nearby sauna and an immersion in the chilly waters of Parks Creek, just outside the bathhouse. Other feel-good options include massages ($30 per half-hour session). On Saturdays, medicine man Walking Eagle guides guests on a spiritual journey within the Native American Purification Sweat Lodge. If you opt for treatment and R&R here, you won't be alone. Despite its rusticity, the place has been discovered by young Hollywood, including many soap actors, San Francisco 49ers football players, and local newscasters.

4617 Stewart Springs Rd., Weed, CA 96094. © 530/938-2222. Fax 530/938-4283. www.starhawk.com/ stewart. 6 teepees (for up to 4 persons), 4 motel rooms, 6 apt units, 5 cabins with kitchens, and a large A-frame house (suitable for 10 persons). $24 double teepee; $44–$74 double in motel, apts., and cabins; $325 for house. $5 for each extra person. DISC, MC, V. Pets accepted with $25 fee. **Amenities:** Restaurant (not open in winter); spa; sauna; massage. *In room:* No phone. Cabins and some units with kitchens, coffeemakers.

WHERE TO DINE

The Bagel Cafe and Bakery *Value* AMERICAN   This is the hands-down winner for a low-cost meal in Mount Shasta. Packed daily with locals, the lively little cafe serves the best coffee in the region, as well as wonderful pizza by-the-slice, soups, salads, sandwiches, and desserts; and you can "build a bagel" sandwich. If you're planning on spending the day out in the great outdoors, stop here first for a large coffee and sandwich to go.

315 N. Mount Shasta Blvd., Mount Shasta © 530/926-1414. Sandwiches/salads $5–$7. No credit cards. Daily from 7am–5pm. *AQ: No closing time?*

Café Maddalena ★★★ *Finds* SARDINIAN/MEDITERRANEAN COUNTRY COOKING   Owner and chef Maddalena Serra, who hails from Sardinia, has created a wonderful restaurant in the refurbished old railroad quarter of Dunsmuir. The smells wafting from this small place will literally draw you in. Maddalena cooks in full sight of the happy, satisfied (and stuffed) customers, preparing dishes like pasta Marco—fresh fettuccine with shrimp, tomatoes, cream, and herbs all wrapped in flaky dough and baked in a pizza oven. Everything is made fresh daily, including the breads and desserts. Try the deceptively simple yet utterly scrumptious *panna cotta,* a cream flan with lemon, vanilla, and caramelized sugar. A memorable and special place.

5801 Sacramento Ave., Dunsmuir. © 530/235-2725. Reservations strongly recommended. Main courses $10–$19. MC, V. Thurs–Sun 5pm–10pm. Closed mid-Dec–April.

Lily's ★ AMERICAN   Set in a white-clapboard, turn-of-the-century house in a residential neighborhood south of the town center, this friendly little restaurant has a front porch, a picket fence, a back garden, and dining in two rooms inside and two patios out. It's popular for breakfast, when chunky breads, omelets, and polenta fritters start the morning off right. Lunch and dinner dishes—tamale pie, chicken curry, scampi al roma, and kung-pao shrimp salad—span the globe. Popular dishes are the enchiladas *suizas* stuffed with shrimp, crab, and fresh spinach, and Chicken Rosie, a tender breast of chicken simmered with raspberries, hazelnut liqueur, and cream.

1013 S. Mount Shasta Blvd., Mount Shasta. ② **530/926-3372.** Reservations recommended. Breakfast $6–$10; lunch $6–$10; dinner $11–$21. AE, DISC, MC, V. Mon–Fri 7am–9pm, Sat–Sun 7am–9:30pm.

MCARTHUR–BURNEY FALLS MEMORIAL STATE PARK ⭑

On its way to Lassen Volcanic National Park (see below) from Mount Shasta, Calif. 89 east loops back south to **McArthur–Burney Falls Memorial State Park** (② **530/335-2777**). One of the most spectacular features of this 910-acre park is **Burney Falls** ⭑⭑, an absolutely gorgeous waterfall that cascades over a 129-foot cliff. Theodore Roosevelt once called the falls "the eighth wonder of the world." Giant springs lying a few hundred yards upstream feed the falls and keep them flowing—100 million gallons every day—even during California's legendary dry spells.

The half-mile **Headwater Trail** will take you to a good vantage point above the falls. If you're lucky, you can observe the black swifts that nest in the mossy crevices behind the cascade. Other birds to look for include barn and great horned owls, the belted kingfisher, the common flicker, and even the Oregon junco. The year-round park also has 5 miles of nature trails, 128 campsites, picnicking grounds, and good fishing for bass, crappie, brown trout, rainbow trout, and brook trout. For **camping reservations,** call ② **800/444-PARK (7275).**

From here, Lassen Volcanic National Park lies about 40 miles south.

3 Lassen Volcanic National Park ⭑

45 miles E of Redding, 255 miles NE of San Francisco

Stashed away in the far northeastern corner of California, Lassen Volcanic National Park is a remarkable reminder that North America is still forming, and that the ground below is alive with the forces of creation and, sometimes, destruction. Lassen Peak is the southernmost peak in a chain of volcanoes (including Mount Saint Helens) that stretches all the way from British Columbia.

Although it's dormant, 10,457-foot **Lassen Peak** is still very much alive. It last awakened in May 1914, beginning a cycle of eruptions that spit lava, steam, and ash until 1921. The eruption climaxed in 1915 when Lassen blew its top, sending a mushroom cloud of ash 7 miles high that was seen from hundreds of miles away. The peak itself has been dormant for nearly three quarters of a century now, but the area still boils with a ferocious intensity: Hot springs, fumaroles, geysers, and mud pots are all indicators that Lassen hasn't had its last word. Monitoring of geothermal features in the park shows that they are getting hotter, not cooler, and some scientists take this as a sign that the next big eruption in the Cascades is likely to happen here.

Until then, the park gives visitors an interesting chance to watch a landscape recover from the massive destruction brought on by an eruption. To the north of Lassen Peak is the aptly named **Devastated Area,** a huge swath of volcanic destruction steadily repopulating with conifer forests. Forest botanists have revised their earlier theories that forests must be preceded by herbaceous growth after watching the Devastated Area immediately revegetate with a diverse mix of eight different conifer species, four more than were present before the blast.

The 108,000-acre park is a place of great beauty. The flora and fauna here are an interesting mix of species from the Cascade Range, which stretches north from Lassen, and species from the Sierra Nevada Range, which stretches south.

Lassen Volcanic National Park

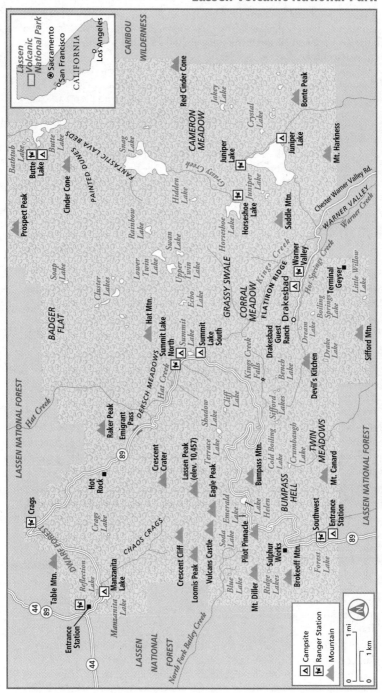

The resulting blend accounts for an enormous diversity of plants: 715 distinct species have been identified in the park. Although it is snowbound in winter, Lassen is an important summer feeding ground for transient herds of mule deer and numerous black bears.

In addition to the volcano and all its geothermal features, Lassen Volcanic National Park includes miles of hiking trails, 50 beautiful alpine lakes, large meadows, cinder cones, lush forests, cross-country skiing, and great backcountry camping. In fact, three quarters of the park is designated wilderness.

And crowds? Forget it. Lassen is one of the least-visited national parks in the lower 48 states, so crowd control isn't as big a consideration here as in other places. Unless you're here on the Fourth of July or Labor Day weekend, you won't encounter anything that could rightly be called a crowd. Even then, you can escape the hordes simply by skipping the popular sites like Bumpass Hell or the Sulphur Works and heading a few miles down any of the backcountry trails.

ESSENTIALS

GETTING THERE   One of the reasons Lassen Volcanic National Park is one of the least visited national parks is its remote location. The most foolproof route here is to take Calif. 44 east from Redding, which leads directly to the northern gateway to the park. A shortcut if you're coming from the south along I-5 is Calif. 36 in Red Bluff, which leads to the park's southern gateway. If you're arriving from the east via I-80, take the U.S. 395 turnoff at Reno and head to Susanville. Depending on which end of the park you're shooting for, take either Calif. 44 (to the northwest entrance) or Calif. 36 (to the southwest entrance) from Susanville. The $5-per-car entrance fee, valid for a week, comes with a copy of the *Lassen Park Guide,* a handy little newsletter listing activities, hikes, and points of interest. Camping fees range from $8 to $14.

Only one major road, Calif. 89 (a.k.a. the Park Road), crosses the park in a 39-mile half circle with entrances and visitor centers at either end.

Most visitors enter the park at the southwest entrance station, drive through the park, and leave through the northwest entrance, or vice versa. Two other entrances lead to remote portions of the park. Warner Valley is reached from the south on the road from Chester. The Butte Lake entrance is reached by a cut-off road from Calif. 44 between Calif. 89 and Susanville.

VISITOR INFORMATION   **Ranger stations** are clustered near each entrance and provide the full spectrum of interpretive displays, ranger-led walks, informational leaflets, and emergency help. The largest **visitor center** is located just inside the northwest entrance station at the Loomis Museum. The park information number for all requests is ✆ **530/595-4444,** or you can visit www.nps.gov/lavo or write Lassen Volcanic National Park, P.O. Box 100, Mineral, CA 96063-0100.

Because of the dangers posed by the park's thermal features, rangers ask that you remain on trails at all times. Fires are allowed in campgrounds only; please make sure they're dead before leaving them. Mountain bikes are prohibited on all trails.

WEATHER   Lassen Volcanic National Park is in one of the coldest places in California. Winter begins in late October and doesn't release its grip until June. Even in the summer, you should plan for possible rain and snow. Temperatures at night can drop below freezing at any time. Winter, however, shows a different and beautiful side of Lassen that more people are starting to appreciate. Since most of the park is over a mile high and the highest point is 10,457 feet, snow accumulates in incredible quantities. Don't be surprised to find snowbanks lining the Park Road into July.

EXPLORING THE PARK

The highlight of Lassen is, of course, the volcano and all of its offshoots: boiling springs, fumaroles, mud pots, and more. You can see many of the most interesting sites in a day, making it possible to visit Lassen as a short detour from I-5 or US 395 on the way to or from Oregon. Available at park visitor centers, the *Road Guide to Lassen Park* is a great traveling companion that will explain a lot of the features you'll see as you traverse the park.

Bumpass Hell ✿, a 1½-mile walk off the Park Road in the southern part of the park, is the largest single geothermal site in the park—16 acres of bubbling mud pots cloaked in a stench of rotten-egg-smelling sulfur. The hike leads you through a quiet and peaceful meadow of wildflowers and chirping birds before arriving at the geothermal site. The name comes from an early Lassen traveler, Bumpass, who lost a leg after he took a shortcut through the area while hunting and plunged into a boiling pool. Stay on the wooden catwalks that safely guide visitors past the pyrite pools, steam vents, and noisy fumaroles, and you won't suffer Bumpass's fate.

Sulphur Works ✿ is another stinky, steamy example of Lassen's residual heat. Two miles from the southwest park exit, the ground roars with seething gases escaping from the ground.

Boiling Springs Lake and **Devil's Kitchen** are two of the more remote geothermal sites; they're located in the Warner Valley section of the park, which can be reached by hiking from the main road or entering the park through Warner Valley Road from the small town of Chester.

OUTDOOR PURSUITS

In addition to the activities below, free naturalist programs are offered daily in the summer, highlighting everything from flora and fauna to geologic history and volcanic processes. For more information, call the **park headquarters** at ✆ **530/595-4444.**

CANOEING & KAYAKING Paddlers can take canoes, rowboats, and kayaks on any of the park lakes except Reflection, Emerald, Helen, and Boiling Springs. Motors, including electric motors, are strictly prohibited on all park waters. Park lakes are full of trout, and fishing is popular. You must have a current California fishing license, which you can obtain in Red Bluff at **Lassen Ranch and Home Store,** 22660 Antelope Rd. (✆ **530/527-6960**).

CROSS-COUNTRY SKIING The park road usually closes due to snow in November, and most years it doesn't open until June, so cross-country skiers have their run of the park. Snowmobiles were once allowed but are now forbidden. Marked trails of all skill levels leave from Manzanita Lake at the north end of the park and Lassen Chalet at the south. Most visitors come to the southwest entrance, where the ski chalet offers lessons, rental gear, and a warm place to stay. Popular trips are the beginners' trails to Lake Helen or Summit Lake. More advanced skiers can make the trek into Bumpass Hell, a steaming valley of sulfuric mud pots and fumaroles.

You can also ski the popular 30-mile course of the Park Road in an overnight trek, but doing this involves a long car shuttle. For safety reasons, the park requires all skiers to register at the ranger stations before heading into the backcountry, whether for an overnight or just the day. For more information or to hire a guide, call **Lassen Ski Touring** (✆ **530/595-3376**).

HIKING   Most Lassen visitors drive through in a day or two, see the geothermal hot spots, and move on. That leaves 150 miles of trails and expanses of backcountry to the few who take the time to get off-road. The *Lassen Trails* booklet available at the visitor centers gives good descriptions of some of the most popular hikes and backpacking destinations. Anyone spending the night in the backcountry must have a wilderness permit issued at the ranger stations. And don't forget to bring plenty of water, sunscreen, and warm clothing.

The most popular hike in the park is the **Lassen Peak Trail** ✿, a 2½-mile climb from the Park Road to the top of the peak. The trail may sound short, but it's steep and generally covered with snow until late summer. At an elevation of 10,457 feet, though, you'll get a view of the surrounding wilderness that's worth every step of the way. On clear days, you can see south all the way to Sutter Buttes near Yuba City and north into the Cascades. The round-trip takes about 4 to 5 hours.

Running a close second in popularity is **Bumpass Hell Trail.** This 1½-mile walk off the Park Road in the southern part of the park deposits you right in the middle of the largest single geothermal site in the park. (See "Exploring the Park," above.)

The **Cinder Cone Trail,** located in the northeast corner of the park, is another worthy hike, best reached from Butte Lake Campground at the far northeast corner of the park. If 4 miles seems too short, you can extend the hike (and shorten the drive) by walking in about 8 miles from Summit Lake on the Park Road. Now dormant, Cinder Cone is generally accepted as the source of mysterious flashing lights that were seen by early settlers to the area in the 1850s. Black and charred-looking, Cinder Cone is bare of any sort of life and surrounded by dunes of multihued volcanic ash.

SNOWSHOEING   From January through March, park naturalists give free 2-hour eco-adventure snowshoe hikes across Lassen's snowpacked hills. The tours take place on Saturdays at 1:30pm at the Lassen Chalet, located at the park's southwestern entrance. You must be at least 8 years old, be warmly dressed, and be wearing boots. Snowshoes are provided free of charge on a first-come, first-served basis, although a $1 donation is requested for upkeep. For more details, call park headquarters (✆ **530/ 595-4444,** ext. 5133).

CAMPING

Car campers have their choice of seven park campgrounds with a total of 375 sites, more than enough to handle the trickle of visitors who come to Lassen every summer. In fact, so few people camp in Lassen that there is no reservations system except for at the **Lost Creek Group Campground,** and stays are granted a generous 14-day limit. Sites do fill up on weekends, so your best bet is to get to the park early on Friday to secure a place to stay. If the park is packed, there are 43 campgrounds in surrounding Lassen National Forest, so you're bound to find a site somewhere.

By far the most "civilized" campground in the park is at **Manzanita Lake,** where you can find hot showers, electrical hookups, flush toilets, and a camper store. When Manzanita fills up, rangers open the **Crags Campground** overflow camp, about 5 miles away and much more basic. Further within the park along Calif. 89 is **Summit Lake Campgrounds,** located on the north and south ends of Summit Lake. It's a pretty spot, often frequented by deer, and it's a launching point for some excellent day hikes.

On the southern end of the park you'll find **Southwest Campground,** a walk-in camp directly adjacent to the Lassen Chalet parking lot.

The two remote entrances to Lassen and Warner Valley have their own primitive campgrounds with pit toilets and no water, but the price is right—free.

Backcountry camping is allowed almost everywhere, and traffic is light. Ask about closed areas when you get your wilderness permit, which are issued at the ranger stations and required for anyone spending the night in the backcountry.

WHERE TO STAY
INSIDE THE PARK

Drakesbad Guest Ranch ★★★ *Finds*   The only lodge operating within Lassen Park is Drakesbad Guest Ranch, hidden in a high mountain valley inside the park and surrounded by meadows, lakes, and streams. It's famous for its rustic cabins, lodge, and steaming thermal swimming pool, fed by a natural hot spring and open 24 hours a day. Drakesbad is as deluxe as a place with some electricity and no phones can be, with handmade quilts on every bed and kerosene lamps to read by. Full meal service is available—and it's very good. Since the lodge is extremely popular and only open from June through mid-October, reservations are booked as far as 2 years in advance (although May or June are good times to call to take advantage of cancellations).

c/o California Guest Services, 2150 N. Main St. no. 5, Red Bluff, CA 96080. ✆ 530/529-1512. Fax 530/ 529-4511. www.drakesbad.com. 19 units. $112–$135 per person, double occupancy. Rates include meals. DISC, MC, V. Open early June to early Oct. **Amenities:** Restaurant; hot spring–fed swimming pool; children's center. *In room:* No phone.

NEAR THE PARK

The Bidwell House ★★   In 1901, General John Bidwell, a California senator who made three unsuccessful bids for the U.S. presidency, built a country retreat and summer home for his beloved young wife, Annie. After her death, when Chester had developed into a prosperous logging hamlet, the building, with its farmhouse-style design and spacious veranda, was converted into the headquarters for a local ranch. Today, the house sits at the extreme eastern end of Chester, adjacent to a rolling meadow. The lake is visible across the road, and inside, Ian and Kim James maintain one of the most charming B&Bs in the region. Seven of the rooms have Jacuzzi tubs, and three offer wood-burning stoves. Breakfast is presented with fanfare and many gourmet touches, including home-baked breads and scrumptious omelets.

1 Main St. (P.O. Box 1790), Chester, CA 96020. ✆ 530/258-3338. www.bidwellhouse.com. 14 units, 12 with private bathroom. $75–$150 double; $165 for cabin (sleeps 6). Rates include full breakfast. MC, V. **Amenities:** Nearby golf course. *In room:* TV.

Lassen Mineral Lodge *Kids*   A mere 9 miles south of Lassen Volcanic National Park's southern entrance, the Lassen Mineral Lodge offers 20 motel-style accommodations in a forested setting. In summer, the lodge is almost always bustling with guests and customers who venture into the gift shop, ski shop, general store, and full-service restaurant and bar. This is probably the best lodging option for families in the Lassen area.

On Hwy. 36E (P.O. Box 160), Mineral, CA 96063. ✆ 530/595-4422. Fax 530/595-4452. www.minerallodge. com. 20 units. $65–$85 double. AE, DISC, MC, V. **Amenities:** Restaurant and saloon; laundry facilities. *In room:* Some units with kitchens. No phone.

Mill Creek Resort *Kids*   Set deep within the forest, the Mill Creek Resort is that rustic mountain retreat you've always dreamed of while slaving away in the office. A homey country general store and coffee shop serve as the resort's center, a good place to stock up on food while exploring Lassen Volcanic National Park. Nine housekeeping cabins, available on a daily or weekly basis, are clean, cute, and outfitted with vintage 1930s and '40s furniture, including kitchens (a good thing, since restaurants are scarce in this region). Pets are welcome, too.

1 Calif. 172 (3 miles south of Calif. 36), Mill Creek, CA 96061. © 888/595-4449 or 530/595-4449. www. millcreekresort.net. 9 units. $75–$100 per cabin. No credit cards. Pets accepted. **Amenities:** Bike rental; laundry facility (open May–Oct.). *In room:* Kitchen, coffeemaker; no phone.

WHERE TO DINE
INSIDE THE PARK
The only restaurant within Lassen Volcanic National Park (besides the Drakesbad Guest Ranch; see above) is the **Summer Chalet Café** (© **530/595-3376**), which serves inexpensive, basic breakfasts, as well as sandwiches and burgers for lunch. Located at the park's south entrance, it's open daily from 8am to 6pm (grill closes at 4pm, however), May to mid-October, weather permitting.

NEAR THE PARK
When you're this far into the wilderness, the question isn't *which* restaurant to choose, but *if* there is a restaurant to choose. If bacon and eggs, sandwiches, steaks, chicken, burgers, pizza, and salads aren't part of your diet, you're in big trouble unless you packed your own grub.

Deciding where you're going to eat near Lassen Volcanic National Park depends mostly on which side you're on, north or south. Near the north entrance to the park in the town of Old Station is **Uncle Runt's Place** (© **530/ 335-7177**), which serves your standard steaks, chicken, burgers, and sandwiches for lunch and dinner. At the south entrance to the park, the closest restaurant is the **Lassen Mineral Lodge** (see "Where to Stay," above) in the town of Mineral, which serves the usual uninspired American fare.

The best approach, however, is to stay at a B&B or lodge that offers meals to its guests—such as the **Bidwell House** or **Drakesbad Guest Ranch**—or at least provides a kitchen to cook your own meals, such as the **Mill Creek Resort** (see above). Food and camping supplies are available at the **Manzanita Lake Camper Store** (© **530/335-7557;** closed in winter) located at the north entrance to the park, or **Lassen Mineral Lodge,** on Calif. 36 in Mineral, at the southern end of the park (© **530/595-4422**). They also sell or rent just about every outdoor toy you'd ever want to play with in Lassen Park, including cross-country and alpine ski equipment.

4 Lava Beds National Monument

324 miles NE of San Francisco, 50 miles NE of Mount Shasta

Lava Beds takes a while to grow on you. It's a seemingly desolate place with high plateaus, cinder cones, and rolling hills covered with lava cinders, sagebrush, and twisted junipers. Miles of land just like it cover most of this corner of California. So why, asks the first-time visitor, is this a national monument? The answer lies underground.

The earth here is like Swiss cheese, so porous in places that it actually makes a hollow sound. When lava pours from a shield volcano, it doesn't cool all at once; the outer edges cool first and the core keeps flowing, forming underground tunnels like a giant pipeline system.

More than 330 lava-tube caves lace the earth at Lava Beds—caves that are open to the public to explore on their own or with park rangers. Whereas most caves lend themselves to a fear of getting lost with their huge chambers, multiple entrances, and bizarre topography, these are simple, relatively easy-to-follow tunnels with little room to go wrong. Once inside, you'll feel that this would be a great place for a game of hide-and-seek.

ESSENTIALS

GETTING THERE   The best access to the park it from Highway 139, 4 miles south of Tulelake.

VISITOR INFORMATION   Call the **Lava Beds National Monument** headquarters (© **530/667-2282;** www.nps.gov) for information on ranger-led hikes, cave trips, and campfire programs. The visitor center is located at the southern end of the park.

ENTRY FEES   The entry fee is $4 per vehicle for 7 days, and camping is $10 a day.

WHEN TO GO   Park elevations range from 4,000 to 5,700 feet, and this part of California can get cold any time of year. Summer is the best time to visit, with average temperatures in the 70s; winter temperatures plunge down to about 40°F in the day and as low as 20°F by night. Summer is also the best time to participate in ranger-led hikes, cave trips, and campfire programs.

EXPLORING THE PARK

A hike to **Schonchin Butte** (three quarters of a mile each way) will give you a good perspective on the wildly stark beauty of the monument and nearby Tule Lake Valley. Wildlife lovers should keep their eyes peeled for terrestrial animals like mule deer, coyote, marmots, and squirrels, while watching overhead for bald eagles, 24 species of hawks, and enormous flocks of ducks and geese headed to the Klamath Basin, one of the largest waterfowl wintering grounds in the Lower 48. Sometimes the sky goes dark with ducks and geese during the peak migrations.

The caves at **Lava Beds** are open to the public with very little restriction or hassle. All you need to see most of them are a good flashlight or headlamp, sturdy walking shoes, and a sense of adventure. Many of the caves are entered by ladders or stairs; others still by holes in the side of a hill. Once inside, walk far enough to round a corner, and then shut off your light—a chilling experience, to say the least.

One-way **Cave Loop Road,** just southwest of the visitor center, is where you'll find many of the best cave hikes. About 15 lava tubes have been marked and made accessible. Two are ice caves, where the air temperature remains below freezing year-round and ice crystals form on the walls. If exploring on your own gives you the creeps, check out **Mushpot Cave.** Almost adjacent to the visitor center, this cave has been outfitted with lights and a smooth walkway; you'll have plenty of company.

Hardened spelunkers will find enough remote and relatively unexplored caves in the monument to keep themselves busy. Many caves require specialized climbing gear.

Above ground, several trails crisscross the monument. The longest of these, the 8.2-mile (one-way) **Lyons Trail,** spans the wildest part of the monument, where you are likely to see plenty of animals. The 3.4-mile (one-way) **Whitney Butte Trail** leads from Merill Cave along the shoulder of 5,000-foot Whitney Butte to the edge of the Callahan Lava Flow and monument boundary.

PICNICKING, CAMPING & ACCOMMODATIONS

The 43-unit **Indian Well Campground** near the visitor center has spaces for tents and small RVs year-round, with water available only during the summer. The rest of the year, you'll have to carry water from the nearby visitor center.

Two **picnic grounds,** Fleener Chimneys and Captain Jacks Stronghold, have tables but no water; open fires are prohibited.

There are no hotels or lodges in the monument, but numerous services are available in nearby Tulelake and Klamath Falls. For more information, call or write Lava Beds National Monument, P.O. Box 867, Tulelake, CA 96134 (© **530/ 667-2282**).

9

The High Sierra: Yosemite, Mammoth Lakes & Sequoia/Kings Canyon

by Matthew R. Poole & Mary Anne Moore

The national parks of California's Sierra are a mecca for travelers from around the globe. The big attraction is Yosemite, of course, but the entire region is packed with natural wonders and adventures.

It was in Yosemite that naturalist John Muir found "the most songful streams in the world . . . the noblest forests, the loftiest granite domes, the deepest ice-sculpted canyons." Even today, few visitors would disagree with Muir's early impressions as they explore this land of towering cliffs, alpine lakes, river beaches, and dazzling fields of snow in winter. Yosemite Valley, lush with waterfalls and dramatic peaks reaching toward the sky, is the most central and accessible part of the park, stretching for some 7 miles from Wawona Tunnel in the west to Curry Village in the east. If you visit during spring or early fall, you'll encounter fewer problems with crowds and have more opportunities to see the park's splendor the way it was meant to be seen.

Across the heart of the Sierra Nevada, in east-central California, Sequoia and Kings Canyon National Parks comprise a vast, mountainous region that stretches some 1,300 square miles, taking in the giant sequoias for which they're fabled. This is a land of alpine lakes, granite peaks, and deep canyons. At 14,495 feet, Mount Whitney is the highest point in the lower 48 states.

Another big attraction in the area is Mammoth Lakes, one of the major playgrounds of California, where you can enjoy dozens of recreational activities in a setting of lakes, streams, waterfalls, and rugged meadows. Glaciers in unrecorded times carved out much of this panoramic region.

Because of the vast popularity of the parks, facilities can be strained at peak visiting times. Always make your reservations in advance if possible (and that definitely includes camping).

1 Yosemite's Gateways

The good news: Towns on each gateway's periphery are virtually built around the tourism industry. They offer plenty of places to stay and eat and have natural wonders of their own. The bad news: If you stay here, reaching any point within the park requires at least a half-hour drive (usually closer to an hour), which is especially frustrating during high season, when motor homes and overall congestion cause traffic to move at a snail's pace. A new, controversial park plan is being debated that would cut the number of day-use parking places in the park from 1,600 to 550, encourage bus and shuttle usage, reduce lodging rooms from 1,260 to 981, restore 180 acres to their natural state, and eliminate a 3.2-mile section of road to be replaced with a foot and bike trail.

In the meantime, there's no shortage of options to encourage you to help the park by leaving your car at your lodging or a parking area and entering on convenient, inexpensive buses (and then moving around the valley floor on free, readily available shuttles). The Yosemite Area Regional Transit System (YARTS) (© 877/989-2787; www.yarts.com) provides round-trip transit service from communities within Mariposa, Merced, and Mono Counties to Yosemite. The Merced route along Highway 140 operates year-round, although the winter schedule is limited. Fares for riding YARTS vary, but generally range from $7 to $15 round-trip for adults, including entrance to the park, with discounts for children and seniors. Summer routes originate at Coulterville, Mammoth Lake and Lee Vining, and Wawona. For information on the Highway 120 east service (Mammoth Lakes to Yosemite Valley call © 800/626-6684, from May until it snows (typically September or October).

Should you need to reserve accommodations outside the park, choose based on which gate offers you easiest access. Our selections below are grouped by the three most popular entrances: The west entrances are Big Oak Flat (via Calif. 120), which is 88 miles east of Manteca and accommodates traffic from San Francisco, and Arch Rock (via Calif. 140), which is 75 miles northeast of Merced and is the easiest route from central California. The South Entrance is Wawona (via Calif. 41), which is 64 miles north of Fresno and the passage leading from southern California.

BIG OAK FLAT ENTRANCE

The Big Oak Flat entrance is 150 miles east of San Francisco and 130 miles southeast of Sacramento. Among the string of small communities along the way is charming **Groveland** (23 miles from the park's entrance), a throwback to gold-mining days, complete with rednecks, the oldest saloon in the state, and at least some semblance of a real town. It'll take around an hour to reach the park entrance from Groveland, but at least there's some extracurricular activity if you're planning to stay in the area awhile. Big Oak Flat has a few hotels as well, but no town. Call the visitor information number below for details.

GETTING THERE   If you're driving from San Francisco, take I-580 (which turns into I-205) to Manteca, then Calif. 120 east.

VISITOR INFORMATION   Contact the **Hwy. 120 Chamber of Commerce** (© 800/449-9120) for an exhaustive list of hotels, motels, cabins, RV parks, and campsites in the area.

WHERE TO STAY & DINE

Besides the places mentioned below, there are not a lot of great dining options. Ask anyone in town, and they'll point you to more offerings.

Evergreen Lodge ✿ *Kids*   This has been a favorite rustic retreat for everyone from families to bikers for over 75 years. The 22 cabins offer the basic necessities and are well dispersed along a wooded grove. But what's great about this place is its surroundings: It's only 8 miles from Yosemite's entrance and has a fun log-cabin lodge and bar where dinner is served and where dudes in 10-gallon hats shoot pool. (On warm nights, it's best to enjoy a pitcher of beer and some barbecue on the outdoor patio.) There are endless hiking trails and, in summer, access to tennis courts, a pool (major family fun), and horseback riding. Though officially in Groveland, the lodge is 40 minutes east of downtown.

33160 Evergreen Rd. (at Calif. 120), Groveland, CA 95321. ℂ 800/ **935-6343** or 209/379-2606. Fax 209/ 379-2607. www.evergreenlodge.com. 22 units. Apr–Oct $69–$79 double; $79–$95 cabin (with 1 queen and 2 single beds); $89–$105 2-bedroom cottage. Rates include continental breakfast. AE, DISC, MC, V. Closed in winter. From San Francisco, take I-580 E. (which turns into I-205) to Manteca; take Calif. 120 E. through Groveland; turn left at Hetch Hetchy/Evergreen Rd. **Amenities:** Restaurant, bar, deli; heated outdoor pool and tennis courts at neighboring Camp Mather for day-use fee (summer only). *In room:* TV.

The Groveland Hotel ★   Constructed around 1850, this adorable historic hotel complements the surroundings of the Wild West–like town. Rooms are sweetly appointed with antiques as well as modern amenities, and the suite has a spa tub and fireplace. The staff is both friendly and accommodating. The most expensive, fanciest, and best restaurant in town is on the premises, and the supercool Iron Door Saloon (the other place to eat well) is across the street. Smoking is not permitted in this hotel.

18767 Main St. (P.O. Box 289), Groveland, CA 95321. ℂ 800/**273-3314** or 209/962-4000. Fax 209/ 962-6674. www.groveland.com. 17 units. $135–$155 double; $210 suite. Rates include extended continental breakfast. AE, DC, DISC, MC, V. Pets permitted. **Amenities:** Restaurant; nearby golf course; small game room; concierge; business center; secretarial service; limited room service; babysitting; laundry service. *In room:* A/C, dataport, minibar, coffeemaker, hair dryer, iron; some units with TV/VCR.

ARCH ROCK ENTRANCE

This is the most heavily used entrance to the park, offering easy access to the valley.

GETTING THERE   Arch Rock is 75 miles northeast of Merced. If you're driving from central California, take I-5 to Calif. 99 to Merced, then Calif. 140 east through El Portal.

Greyhound (ℂ **800/231-222**) and Amtrak (ℂ **800/872-7245**) have routes to Fresno from many cities. VIA, the Yosemite–Amtrak Connection/Gray Line, offers service from Merced Amtrak Passenger Station to Yosemite Valley Visitor Center and Yosemite Lodge. Coaches, which can be wheelchair-lift equipped with advance notice, provide several round trips daily between Merced and Yosemite (ℂ **800/369-PARK** or ℂ 209/384-1315 from outside CA; www. via-adventures.com).

WHERE TO STAY

Yosemite View Lodge   Once you've come this far, you're practically at the gate, so it's literally shocking to drive onto this gargantuan compound amidst the otherwise awesome natural surroundings. But the crowds need to stay some-where, and this mega-motel under perpetual construction is scheduled to eventually offer around 500 rooms. The motel-style units include fridges, microwaves, and HBO; some offer kitchenettes, river views, balconies, and fireplaces. The indoor pool is very popular with kids. There's also a general store. The restaurant provides okay food, but it would be pricey for a family. If this place is booked, they also represent other good properties in the vicinity, although they're not nearly as close to the entrance. Call ahead for information or check out the helpful website which also provides weather and road conditions.

11136 Hwy. 140 (P.O. Box D), El Portal, CA 95318. ℂ 800/**321-5261** or 209/379-2681. Fax 209/379-2704. www.yosemite-motels.com. 279 units. Apr–Oct $109–$169 double; Nov–Mar $82–$129 double. 2-night minimum during holidays. MC, V. Pets permitted for $5 per night. **Amenities:** Restaurant, pizza parlor, lounge; indoor and outdoor heated pools; 4 Jacuzzis; tour and activities desk. *In room:* A/C, TV, fridge, microwave.

SOUTH ENTRANCE

The South Entrance is 332 miles north of Los Angeles, 190 miles east of San Francisco, 59 miles north of Fresno, and 33 miles south of Yosemite Valley. Fish

Camp and Oakhurst are the closest towns to the South Entrance at Wawona. This entrance to the valley leads through the Wawona Tunnel to the **Tunnel View** where you must stop to admire the panorama. If you've never been to Yosemite before, we promise this is the view you will never, ever forget.

GETTING THERE   If you're driving from Los Angeles, take I-5 to Calif. 99 north, then Calif. 41 north. Fresno-Yosemite International Airport, in nearby Fresno, is 90 miles south of Yosemite. The airport is served by Alaska Airlines, America West, American, Continental, Delta, Horizon, and United; all major car companies are represented at the airport.

VISITOR INFORMATION   Ask the **Yosemite Sierra Visitors Bureau,** 40637 Calif. 41, Oakhurst, CA 93644 (✆ **559/683-4636;** www.yosemite-sierra. org), for a helpful brochure on the area, and be sure to check out its excellent online guide.

WHERE TO STAY & DINE

If you can't afford to eat at the opulent Erna's Elderberry House in Oakhurst (see below), try the charming **Three Sisters Café,** 39993 Hwy. 41 (✆ **559/ 642-2253**), for breakfast, lunch, or dinner. For more dining and lodging options, contact the Visitors Bureau, above.

The Estate by the Elderberries ✸✸✸   Its kudos say it all: five diamonds, five stars, and hailed by *Zagat* as one of the top three small hotels in the United States. This is the ultimate in luxurious lodging, decadent dining, and exclusivity, and it's only a 20-minute drive from the South Entrance to Yosemite along Calif. 41. The house—"built to look old"—dates only from 1991 and is set back off the road on the crest of a hill. From the renowned restaurant, a pathway leads through fragrant gardens to the house, which resembles a French château, complete with turret and terra-cotta tile roof.

The interior is exquisitely furnished with fine antiques, rugs, and fabrics. Each individually decorated room has a wood-burning fireplace, wrought-iron balcony, and CD player with a selection of CDs. Beds are covered in the finest Italian linens and down comforters; some rooms have whirlpool tubs. This is where Hollywood's elite often head for their escapes. Celebrities escaping Los Angeles will be especially fond of the $2,800-per-night Villa Sureau ($2,500 without the butler), a two-bedroom, two-bathroom luxury villa with a library, full kitchen, and 24-hour butler service. The restaurant on the premises, **Erna's Elderberry House**, is famous in its own right, offering impeccable food, ambiance, and service. The six-course prix-fixe menu ($75) changes daily.

48688 Victoria Lane (P.O. Box 577), Oakhurst, CA 93644. ✆ 559/683-6860 (Château du Sureau), or 559/683-6800 (Erna's Elderberry House restaurant). Fax 559/683-0800. www.chateaudusureau.com. 10 units. $325–$510 double. Rates include full European breakfast. Extra person $75. AE, DISC, MC, V. **Amenities:** Restaurant, bar; outdoor pool; nearby golf course; spa services; concierge; activities desk; 24-hour room service; in-room massage; laundry service; same-day dry cleaning. *In room:* A/C, TV/VCR (on request), hair dryer.

Hound's Tooth Inn ✸   This recently built bed-and-breakfast is in a great location for visitors to Yosemite as it's only 12 miles from the southern entrance. It's very nice and has comfortable, pretty rooms, some with spas or fireplaces. It's decorated in a Victorian style with a mix of reproductions and antiques, wallpaper, lace valances, and original art. The favorite rooms are the Hound's Tooth, with a king bed, fireplace, and view of the Sierra; and the Tower, with a romantic decor complete with white sheer netting, rattan chairs, and a spa. Kids are welcome by prior arrangement.

42071 Hwy. 41, Oakhurst, CA 93644. ℂ **559/642-6600** or 888/642-6610. Fax 559/658-2946. www. houndstoothinn.com. 12 units, plus cottage. $95–$165 double; $225 cottage. Extra person $20. Rates include full breakfast. AE, DC, DISC, MC, V. *In room:* A/C, TV/VCR, hair dryer, iron. Some units with kitchenette, mini-bar, fridge, coffeemaker.

The Narrow Gauge Inn   If you want to stay in a place that celebrates the mountain atmosphere, book a room at this very friendly inn, just 4 miles south of the park entrance. All of the superclean motel-style units have a rustic cabin feel, complete with A-frame ceilings, little balconies or decks, antiques, quilts, and lace curtains; some have wood-paneled walls. The higher the price of the room, the cuter it gets. (Room nos. 16 through 26 are the best and most secluded; they look directly into forest.) There are hiking trails on the property, as well as a wonderfully old-fashioned, lodge-style restaurant and buffalo bar, serving "Old California Rancho Cuisine," open daily from 5:30 to 9pm.

48571 Calif. 41, Fish Camp, CA 93623. ℂ **888/644-9050** or 559/683-7720. Fax 559/683-2139. www. narrowgaugeinn.com. 25 units. Apr–Oct $100–130 double. Extra person $10. Children under 6 stay free in parents' room. Continental breakfast included. AE, DISC, MC, V. Pets permitted for a $25 fee. **Amenities:** Restaurant, bar; outdoor heated pool (seasonal); Jacuzzi (seasonal). *In room:* Satellite TV, dataport, coffeemaker.

Tenaya Lodge ⋆⋆ *Kids*   Tenaya Lodge is the best resort outside the southern entrance to Yosemite; it's particularly idyllic for families. Camp Tenaya For Kids has nature hikes, arts and crafts, games, and music seven days a week from Memorial Day to Labor Day and on Friday and Saturday evenings. The three- and four-story complex, which is run by the Marriott chain, is set on a 35-acre tract of forested land a few miles outside the national park. Inside, the decor is a cross between an Adirondack hunting lodge and a Southwestern pueblo, with a lobby dominated by a massive river-rock fireplace rising three stories. The ultramodern rooms definitely do the trick with nice furnishings and roomy, well-appointed bathrooms.

1122 Calif. 41, Fish Camp, CA 93623. ℂ **800/635-5807** or 559/683-6555. Fax 559/683-8684. www. tenayalodge.com. 244 units. Winter from $139 double; summer from $239 double add $60–$250 for suite. Buffet breakfast $12.95 per person. Children 17 and under stay free in parents' room. AE, DC, DISC, MC, V. Pets permitted for $50 per night. **Amenities:** Two restaurants, deli; indoor and outdoor pools; two nearby golf courses; exercise room; full service spa; indoor and outdoor Jacuzzis; bike rental; children's program; game room; video arcade; activities desk; business center; secretarial services; room service; massage; babysitting; laundry facilities; dry cleaning; executive level rooms. *In room:* A/C, TV w/ pay movies, dataport, minibar, fridge, coffeemaker, hair dryer, iron, safe.

2 Yosemite National Park ⋆⋆⋆

Yosemite is a place of record-setting statistics: the highest waterfall in North America and three of the world's 10 tallest waterfalls (Upper Yosemite Fall, Ribbon Fall, and Sentinel Falls); the tallest and largest single granite monolith in the world (El Capitan); the most recognizable mountain (Half Dome); one of the world's largest trees (the Grizzly Giant in the Mariposa Grove); and literally thousands of rare plant and animal species. But trying to explain its majesty is impossible: This is a place you simply must experience firsthand.

What sets the valley apart is its incredible geology. The Sierra Nevada was formed between 10 and 80 million years ago, when a tremendous geological uplift pushed layers of granite lying under the ocean up into an impressive mountain range. Cracks and rifts in the rock gave erosion a start at carving canyons and valleys. Then, during the last ice age, at least three glaciers flowed

> ## ⌒ *Moments* White-Water Rafting on the Tuolumne
>
> One of the most depressing facts about Yosemite tourism is that few folks do more than get out of their car, take a brief walk around the valley floor, "ooh" and "ah," snap some photos, and go back to their hotel. But if you really want to experience the wonders of the outdoors, contact **Ahwahnee Whitewater**, P.O. Box 1161, Columbia, CA 95310 (© **800/ 359-9790** or 209/533-1401; www.ahwahnee.com). Its rafting trips offer one of the best ways to truly interact with nature—especially if you're not the type to throw on a backpack and hoof it. The 1- to 3-day trips are ideal for white-water rebels in the spring (when the melting snow makes the ride most exciting) and for families later in the season. Although the trip doesn't go through the park, it's still an all-wilderness adventure— except they make the arrangements, provide and cook the food (gourmet by camping standards), steer the rafts, and practically hand you an experience you'll never forget. All you need to do is reserve well in advance, and if you're going on an overnight trip (highly recommended!), bring a tent, sleeping bag, and a few other camping accouterments—and get ready for the time of your life.

through the valley, shearing vertical faces of stone and hauling away the rubble. The last glacier retreated 10,000 to 15,000 years ago, but left its legacy in the incredible number and size of the waterfalls pouring into the valley from hanging side canyons. From the 4,000-foot-high valley floor, the 8,000-foot tops of El Capitan, Half Dome, and Glacier Point look like the top of the world, but they're small in comparison to the highest mountains in the park, some of which reach over 13,000 feet. The 7-square-mile valley is really a huge bathtub drain for the combined runoff of hundreds of square miles of snow-covered peaks (which explains why the valley flooded during the great storm of 1997).

High-country creeks flush with snowmelt catapult over the abyss left by the glaciers and form an outrageous variety of falls, from tiny ribbons that never reach the ground to the torrents of Nevada and Vernal falls. Combined with the shadows and lighting of the deep valley, the effect of all this falling water is mesmerizing. All that vertical stone gets put to use by hundreds who flock to the park for some of the finest climbing anywhere.

The valley is also home to beautiful meadows and the Merced River. When the last glacier retreated, its debris dammed the Merced and formed a lake. Eventually, sediment from the river filled the lake and created the rich and level valley floor we see today. Tiny Mirror Lake was created later by rockfall that dammed up Tenaya Creek; the addition of a man-made dam in 1890 made it more of a lake than a pond. Rafters and inner-tubers enjoy the slow-moving Merced during the heat of summer.

Deer and **coyote** frequent the valley, often causing vehicular mayhem as one heavy-footed tourist slams on brakes to whip out the Handi-cam while another rubbernecker, also mesmerized, drives right into him. Metal crunches, tempers flare, and the deer daintily hops away.

Bears, too, are at home in the valley. Grizzlies are gone from the park now, but black bears are plentiful—and hungry for your food. Bears will rip into cars that have even the smallest treats inside, including things you think are safe

STANISLAUS NATIONAL FOREST

108

KENNEDY MEADOW

TOIYABE NATIONAL FOREST

395

Bridgeport Reservoir

EMIGRANT WILDERNESS

Buckeye Creek

Bridgeport

Cherry Creek

STUBBLEFIELD CANYON

Pacific Crest Trail

JACK MAIN CANYON

KERRICK CANYON

MATTERHORN CANYON

Twin Lakes Rd.

Twin Lakes

HOOVER WILDERNESS

Lake Eleanor

Lake Eleanor

Hetch Hetchy Reservoir

POOPENAUT VALLEY

Tuolumne R.

YOSEMITE

RODGERS CANYON

VIRGINIA CANYON

Virginia Lakes

Virginia Lakes Rd.

Lundy Lake Rd.

Lundy Lake

INYO NATIONAL FOREST

GRAND CANYON OF THE TUOLUMNE RIVER

COLD CANYON

Glen Aulin High Sierra Camp

Tioga Pass

Mather

Camp Mather

To Manteca

ASPEN VALLEY

Big Oak Flat Entrance

120

Crane Flat

Tamarack Flat

White Wolf

NATIONAL

Tuolumne River

Lembert Dome

Tuolumne Meadows Visitor Center

120

Tioga Pass Entrance

May Lake

Porcupine Creek

120

Tenaya Lake

LYELL CANYON

Yosemite Creek

South Fork Tuolumne River

El Capitan

Yosemite Falls

PARK

TENAYA CANYON

John Muir Trail

Sunrise

CATHEDRAL RANGE

Vogelsang

Yosemite Village

Half Dome

Yosemite Falls

YOSEMITE VALLEY

STANISLAUS NATIONAL FOREST

Arch Rock Entrance

140

El Portal

Chinquapin

To Merced

Glacier Point

Little Yosemite Valley

Merced R.

Merced Lake

ANSEL ADAMS WILDERNESS

RITTER RANGE

Glacier Point Rd.

Bridalveil Falls

Bridalveil Creek

Bridalveil Creek

Badger Pass Ski Area

41

SIERRA NATIONAL FOREST

S. Fork Merced R.

Pioneer Yosemite History Center

Buck Camp

Wawona

Wawona Information Center

Mariposa Grove

South Entrance

△ Campground

▲ High Sierra camp (By reservation only)

🚩 Ranger Station

49

0   5 mi

0   5 km

N

Fish Camp

41

To Oakhurst & Fresno

SIERRA NATIONAL FOREST

Sacramento

San Francisco

Map Area

CALIFORNIA

Los Angeles

inside your car's trunk! Last year, by September there were 490 incidents, and four bears had to be killed when they became too aggressive and destructive. If that doesn't deter you, you should know there is a fine of up to $5,000 for feeding park animals and your car can be impounded. There are food storage lockers throughout the park.

Right in the middle of the valley's thickest urban cluster is the **Valley Visitor Center** (© 209/372-0200; www.nps.gov/yose), with exhibits that will teach you about glacial geology, history, and the park's flora and fauna. Check out the **Indian Cultural Museum** next door for insight into what life in the park was once like. Excellent exhibits highlight the Miwok and Paiute cultures that thrived here. The Ansel Adams Gallery displays the famous photographer's prints as well as other artists' works. You'll also find much history and memorabilia from the career of nature writer John Muir, one of the founders of the conservation movement.

While it's easy to let the tremendous beauty of the valley monopolize your attention, remember that 95% of Yosemite is wilderness. Of the 4 million visitors who come to the park each year, very few ever venture more than a mile from their cars. That leaves most of Yosemite's 750,000 acres open for anyone adventurous enough to hike a few miles. Even though the valley is a hands-down winner for dramatic freak-of-nature displays, the high country offers a more subtle kind of beauty: glacial lakes, roaring rivers, and miles of granite spires and domes. In the park's southwest corner, the Mariposa Grove is a striking forest of rare sequoias, the world's largest trees, as well as several meadows and the rushing south fork of the Merced River.

Tenaya Lake and Tuolumne Meadows are two of the most popular highcountry destinations, as well as starting points for many great trails to the backcountry. Since this area of the park is under snow from November through June, summer is really more like spring. From snowmelt to the first snowfall, the high country explodes with wildflowers and long-dormant wildlife trying to make the most of the short season.

ESSENTIALS

ENTRY POINTS   There are four main entrances to the park. Most valley visitors enter through the **Arch Rock Entrance** on Calif. 140. The best entrance for Wawona is the **South Entrance** on Calif. 41 from Oakhurst. If you're going to the high country, you'll save a lot of time by coming in through the **Big Oak Flat Entrance,** which puts you straight onto Tioga Road without forcing you to deal with the congested valley. The **Tioga Pass Entrance** is open only in summer and is only really relevant if you're coming from the east side of the Sierra (in which case it's your only choice). A fifth, little-used entrance is the **Hetch Hetchy Entrance** in the euphonious Poopenaut Valley, on a dead-end road.

FEES   It costs $20 per car per week to enter the park or $10 per person per week. Annual Yosemite Passes are a steal at only $40. Wilderness permits are free, but reserving them requires a $3 fee per person. If you are 62 or older and you haven't purchased a lifetime Golden Age Passport for $10, what are you waiting for? You can apply for this passport here (or at any other national park or national forest), and you must show reasonable proof of age.

GAS   There are no gas stations in Yosemite Valley, so be sure and fill up at a gas station before entering the park.

VISITOR CENTERS & INFORMATION   There's a central, 24-hour recorded information line for the park (© 209/372-0200; www.nps.gov/yose).

All visitor-related service lines, including hotels and information, can be accessed by touch-tone phone at ℂ **209/372-1000,** or www.yosemitepark.com.

By far, the biggest visitor center is the **Valley Visitor Center** (ℂ **209/ 372-0200**). The **Wawona Information Station** (ℂ **209/375-9501**) gives general park information (closed in winter). For interesting biological and geological displays about the High Sierra, as well as trail advice, the **Tuolumne Meadows Visitor Center** (ℂ **209/372-0263**) is great (closed in winter). All can provide you with maps, plus more newspapers, books, and photocopied leaflets than you'll ever read.

REGULATIONS   Rangers in the Yosemite Valley spend more time being cops than being rangers. They even have their own jail, so don't do anything here you wouldn't do in your hometown. Despite the pressure, park regulations are pretty simple: Wilderness permits are required for all overnight backpacking trips; fishing licenses are required; utilize proper food-storage methods in bear country; don't collect firewood in the valley; no off-road bicycle riding; dogs are allowed in the park but must be leashed and are forbidden from trails; and, don't feed the animals.

SEASONS   Winter is one of the nicest times to visit the valley. It isn't crowded, as it is in summer, and a dusting of snow provides a stark contrast to all that granite. To see the waterfalls at their best, come in spring when snowmelt is at its peak. Fall can be cool, but it's beautiful and much less crowded than summer. Sunshine seekers will love summer—if they can tolerate the crowds.

The high country is under about 20 feet of snow from November through May, so unless you're snow camping, summer is pretty much the only season to pitch a tent. Even in summer, thundershowers are a frequent occurrence, sometimes with a magnificent lightning show. Mosquitoes can be a plague during the peak of summer, but the situation improves after the first freeze.

RANGER PROGRAMS   Even though they're overworked just trying to keep the peace, Yosemite's wonderful rangers also take time to lead a number of educational and interpretive programs ranging from backcountry hikes to fireside talks to snow-country survival clinics. Call the main park information number with specific requests for the season and park area you'll be visiting. Also a great service are the free painting, drawing, and photography classes offered spring to fall at the Art Activity Center next to the Museum Gallery in the valley.

AVOIDING THE CROWDS   Unfortunately, popularity isn't always the greatest thing for wild places. Over the last 20 years, Yosemite Valley has set records for the worst crowding, noise, crime, and traffic in any California national park.

The park covers more than 1,000 square miles, but most visitors flock to the floor of Yosemite Valley, the 1-mile-wide, 7-mile-long freak of glacial scouring that tore a deep and steep valley from the solid granite of the Sierra Nevada. It becomes a total zoo between Memorial Day and Labor Day. Cars line up bumper to bumper on almost any busy weekend. In 1995, Yosemite's superintendent closed the entrances to the park 11 times between Memorial Day and mid-August when the number of visitors reached the park's quota; she turned away 10,000 vehicles.

Our best advice is to try to come before Memorial Day or after Labor Day. If you must go in summer, do your part to help out. It's not so much the numbers of people that are ruining the valley, but their insistence on driving from attraction to attraction within the valley. Once you're here, park your car, then bike, hike, or ride the shuttle buses. You can rent bicycles at **Curry Village** (✆ 209/372-8319) and **Yosemite Lodge** (✆ 209/372-1208) in summer. It may take longer to get from point A to point B, but you're in one of the most gorgeous places on earth—so why hurry?

EXPLORING THE PARK
THE VALLEY

First-time visitors are often completely dumbstruck as they enter the valley from the west. The first two things you'll see are the delicate and beautiful **Bridalveil Fall** ✸✸ and the immense face of **El Capitan** ✸✸, a stunning and anything-but-delicate 3,593-foot-tall solid-granite rock. A short trail leads to the base of Bridalveil, which at 620 feet tall is only a medium-size fall by park standards, but one of the prettiest.

This is a perfect chance to get those knee-jerk tourist impulses under control early: Resist the temptation to rush around bagging sights like they're feathers for your cap. Instead, take your time and look around. One of the best things about the valley is that many of its most famous features are visible from all over. Instead of rushing to the base of every waterfall or famous rock face and getting a crick in your neck from staring straight up, go to the visitor center and spend a half hour learning something about the features of the valley. Buy the excellent *Map and Guide to Yosemite Valley* for $2.50; it describes many hikes and short nature walks. Then go take a look. Walking and biking are the best ways to get around. To cover longer distances, the park shuttles run frequently around the east end of the valley.

If you absolutely must see it all and want to have someone tell you what you're seeing, the **Valley Floor Tour** is a 2-hour narrated bus or open-air tram tour (depending on the season) that provides an introduction to the valley's natural history, geology, and human culture. Fees are $20 for adults, $15 for kids ages 5 to 12, and kids under 5 are free, although they may have to sit on a parent's lap. Purchase tickets at valley hotels or call ✆ 209/372-1240 for advance reservations.

Three quarters of a mile from the visitor center is the **Ahwahnee.** Unlike the rest of the hotel accommodations in the park (see "Accommodations in the Park," later in this chapter), the Ahwahnee actually lives up to its surroundings. The native granite-and-timber lodge was built in 1927 and reflects an era when grand hotels were, well, grand. Fireplaces bigger than most Manhattan studio apartments warm the immense common rooms. Parlors and halls are filled with antique Native American rugs. Don't worry about what you're wearing unless you're going to dinner—this is Yosemite, after all.

The best single view in the valley is from **Sentinel Bridge** ✸ over the Merced River. At sunset, Half Dome's face functions as a projection screen for all the sinking sun's hues from yellow to pink to dark purple, and the river reflects it all. Ansel Adams took one of his most famous photographs from this very spot.

The **Nature Center at Happy Isles** ✸ has great hands-on nature exhibits for kids, plus a wheelchair-accessible path along the banks of the Merced River.

VALLEY WALKS & HIKES   Yosemite Falls is within a short stroll of the visitor center. You can actually see it better elsewhere in the valley, but it's really impressive to stand at the base of all that falling water. The wind, noise, and blowing spray generated when millions of gallons catapult 2,425 feet through space onto the rocks below are sometimes so overwhelming you can barely stand on the bridge.

If you want more, the **Upper Yosemite Fall Trail** ✿ zigzags 3½ miles from Sunnyside Campground to the top of Upper Yosemite Fall. This trail gives you an inkling of the weird, vertically oriented world climbers enter when they head up Yosemite's sheer walls. As you climb this narrow switchback trail, the valley floor drops away until people below look like ants, but the top doesn't appear any closer. It's a little unnerving at first, but braving it promises indescribable rewards. Plan on spending all day on this 7-mile round-trip trail because of the incredibly steep climb.

A mile-long trail leads from the Valley Stables (take the shuttle; no car parking) to **Mirror Lake** ✿. The already tiny lake is gradually becoming a meadow as it fills with silt, but the reflections of the valley walls and sky on its surface remain one of the park's most unforgettable sights.

Also accessible from the Valley Stables or nearby Happy Isles is the best valley hike of all—the **John Muir Trail** ✿✿ to Vernal and Nevada falls. It follows the Sierra crest 200 miles south to Mount Whitney, but you only need go 1½ miles round-trip to get a great view of 317-foot Vernal Fall. Add another 1½ miles and 1,000 vertical feet for the climb to the top of Vernal Fall on the **Mist Trail** ✿, where you'll get wet as you climb directly alongside the falls. On top of Vernal and before the base of Nevada Fall is a beautiful little valley and deep pool. For a truly outrageous view of the valley and one heck of a workout, continue on up the Mist Trail to the top of Nevada Fall. From 2,000 feet above Happy Isles where you began, it's a dizzying view straight down the face of the fall. To the east is an interesting profile perspective of Half Dome. Return either by the Mist Trail or the slightly easier John Muir Trail for a 7-mile round-trip hike.

Half Dome ✿✿✿ may look insurmountable to anyone but an expert rock climber, yet thousands every year take the strenuous-but-popular cable route up the backside. It's almost 17 miles round-trip and a 4,900-foot elevation gain from Happy Isle on the John Muir Trail. Many do it in a day, starting at first light and rushing home to beat nightfall. A more relaxed strategy is to camp in the backpacking campground in Little Yosemite Valley just past Nevada Fall. From here, the summit is within easy striking distance of the base of Half Dome. If you plan to spend the night, you need a Wilderness Pass (see "Camping," below). You must climb up a very steep granite face using steel cables installed by the park service. In summer, boards are installed as crossbeams, but they're still far apart. Wear shoes with lots of traction and bring your own leather gloves for the cables (your hands will thank you). The view from the top is an unbeatable vista of the high country, Tenaya Canyon, Glacier Point, and the awe-inspiring abyss of the valley below. When you shuffle up to the overhanging lip for a look down the face, be extremely careful not to kick rocks or anything else onto the climbers below, who are earning this view the hard way.

THE SOUTHWEST CORNER

This corner of the park is densely forested and gently sculpted in comparison to the stark granite that makes up so much of Yosemite. Coming from the valley, Calif. 41 takes you to **Tunnel View** ✿✿✿, site of a famous Ansel Adams photograph, and the best scenic outlook of the valley accessible by car. Virtually the whole valley is laid out below: Half Dome and Yosemite Falls straight ahead in the distance, Bridalveil to the right, and El Capitan to the left.

A few miles past the tunnel, Glacier Point Road turns off to the east. Closed in winter, this winding road leads to a picnic area at **Glacier Point** ✿✿, site of another fabulous view of the valley, this time 3,000 feet below. Schedule at least an hour to drive here from the valley and an hour or two to absorb the view.

This is a good place to study the glacial scouring of the valley below; the Glacier Point perspective makes it easy to picture the valley filled with sheets of ice.

Some 30 miles south of the valley on Calif. 41 are the **Wawona Hotel** and the **Pioneer Yosemite History Center.** The Wawona was built in 1879 and is the oldest hotel in the park. Its Victorian architecture evokes a time when travelers spent several days in horse-drawn wagons to get here. The Pioneer Center is a collection of early homesteading log buildings across the river from the Wawona.

One of the primary reasons Yosemite was first set aside as a park was the **Mariposa Grove** ✪ of giant sequoias. (Many good trails lead through the grove.) These huge trees have personalities that match their gargantuan size. Single limbs on the biggest tree in the grove, the Grizzly Giant, are 10 feet thick. The tree itself is 209 feet tall, 32 feet in diameter, and more than 2,700 years old. Totally out of proportion with the size of the trees are the tiny cones of the sequoia. Smaller than a baseball and tightly closed, the cones won't release their cargo of seeds until opened by fire.

THE HIGH COUNTRY ✪✪✪

The high country of Yosemite is stunning. Dome after dome of beautifully crystalline granite reflects the sunlight above deep-green meadows and icy-cold rivers.

Tioga Pass is the gateway to the high country. At times, it clings to the side of steep rock faces; in other places, it weaves through canyon bottoms. Several good campgrounds make it a pleasing overnight alternative to fighting summertime crowds in the valley, although use is increasing here, too. **Tenaya Lake** ✪ is a popular windsurfing, fishing, canoeing, sailing, and swimming spot. The water is very chilly. Many good hikes lead into the high country from here, and the granite domes surrounding the lake are popular with climbers. Fishing here varies greatly from year to year.

Near the top of Tioga Pass is beautiful **Tuolumne Meadows** ✪✪. This enormous meadow covering several square miles is bordered by the Tuolumne River on one side and spectacular granite peaks on the other. The meadow is cut by many stream channels full of trout, and herds of mule deer are almost always present. The **Tuolumne Meadows Lodge** and store are a welcome counterpoint to the overdeveloped valley. In winter, the canvas roofs are removed and the buildings fill with snow. You can buy last-minute backpacking supplies here, and there's a basic burgers-and-fries cafe.

TUOLUMNE MEADOWS HIKES & WALKS   So many hikes lead from here into the backcountry that it's impossible to do them justice. A good trail passes an icy-cold spring and traverses several meadows.

On the far bank of the Tuolumne from the meadow, a trail leads downriver, eventually passing through the grand canyon of the Tuolumne and exiting at Hetch Hetchy. Shorter hikes will take you downriver past rapids and cascades.

An interesting geological quirk is the **Soda Springs** on the far side of Tuolumne Meadow from the road. This bubbling spring gushes carbonated water from a hole in the ground; a small log cabin marks its site.

For a great selection of Yosemite high-country hikes and backpacking trips, consult some of the specialized guidebooks to the area. Two of the best are published by Wilderness Press: *Tuolumne Meadows,* a hiking guide by Jeffrey B. Shaffer and Thomas Winnett; and *Yosemite National Park,* by Thomas Winnett and Jason Winnett.

SPORTS & OUTDOOR PURSUITS

BICYCLING   With 10 miles of bike paths in addition to the valley roads, biking is the perfect way to go. You can rent them at the **Yosemite Lodge** (© **209/372-1208** or **Curry Village** (© **209/372-8319**) for $5.25 per hour or $20 per day. You can also rent bike trailers for little kids, $10.50 an hour or $33 a day. All trails in the park are closed to mountain bikes.

FISHING   The Merced River from Happy Isles downstream to the Pohono Bridge is catch-and-release only for native rainbow trout, and barbless hooks are required. Brown trout limits are five fish per day and ten in possession. Trout season begins on the last Saturday in April and continues through November 15. A California license is required and must be displayed by everyone 16 years old and above. Licenses are obtainable in the park at the Yosemite Village Sport Shop © **209/372-1286.**

HORSEBACK RIDING   Three stables offer scenic day rides and multiday pack excursions in the park. **Yosemite Valley Stables** (© **209/372-8348**) is open spring through fall. The other two—**Wawona** (© **209/375-6502**) and **Tuolumne Stables** (© **209/372-8427**)—operate only in summer. Day rides run from $35 to $70, depending on length. Multi-day backcountry trips cost roughly $100 per day and must be booked almost a year in advance. The park wranglers can also be hired to make resupply drops at any of the backcountry High Sierra Camps if you want to arrange for a food drop while on an extended trip.

ICE-SKATING   In winter, the **Curry Village Ice Rink** (© **209/372-8341**) is a lot of fun. It's outdoors and melts quickly when the weather warms up. Rates are $5 for adults and $4.50 for children. Skate rentals are available for $2.

ROCK CLIMBING   Much of the most important technical advancement in rock climbing came out of the highly competitive Yosemite Valley climbing scene of the 1970s and 1980s. Though other places have taken some of the limelight, Yosemite is still one of the most desirable climbing destinations in the world.

The **Yosemite Mountaineering School** (© **209/372-8444;** www.yosemite mountaineering.com) runs classes for beginners through advanced climbers. Considered one of the best climbing schools in the world, it offers private lessons for $170 per person per day, $90 for two people per day, $70 for three or more people per day, that will teach you basic body moves and rappelling, and will take you on a single-pitch climb. Classes run from early spring to early October in the valley, during summer in Tuolumne Meadows.

SKIING & SNOWSHOEING   Opened in 1935, **Badger Pass** (© **209/ 372-8430;** www.yosemitepark.com) is the oldest operating ski area in California. It's nice for families. Four chairs and one rope tow cover a compact mountain of beginner and intermediate runs. At $28 per weekend day for adults and $16 for children ($25 and $14.50 midweek), it's a great place to learn how to ski or snowboard. There are naturalist-led winter children's programs and even babysitting.

Yosemite is also a popular destination for cross-country skiers and snowshoers. Both the Badger Pass ski school and the mountaineering school run trips and lessons for all abilities, ranging from basic technique to trans-Sierra crossings. There are two ski-huts available on guided cross-country tours, including the spiffy **Glacier Point Hut** with its massive stone fireplace, beamed ceilings, and bunk beds; for information, call © **209/372-8444.** Then there's the **Ostrander Hut** with 25 bunks, and you have to pack in your own supplies,

(C) **209/372-0740.** If you're on your own, Crane Flat is a good place to go, as is the groomed track up to Glacier Point, a 20-mile round-trip self-guided tour.

CAMPING

Campgrounds in Yosemite can be reserved up to 5 months in advance through the **National Park Reservation Service** (*(C)* **800/436-7275;** http://reservations.nps.gov/). During the busy season, all valley campsites sell out within hours of becoming available on the service.

Backpacking into the wilderness and camping is always the least crowded option and takes less planning than reserving a campground. If you plan to backpack and camp in the wilderness, you must get a free **Wilderness Pass** (and still pay the park entrance fee). At least 40% of each trailhead quota is allocated up to 24 hours in advance; the rest is available by mail. Write to the Wilderness Center, P.O. Box 545, Yosemite, CA 95389, and specify the dates and trailheads of entry and exit, principal destination, number of people, and any accompanying animals; include a $5 per person advance-registration fee. You may also secure a pass by calling *(C)* **209/372-0740.**

VALLEY CAMPGROUNDS

Until January 1997, the park had five car campgrounds that were always full except in the dead of winter. Now the park has half the number of campsites available, and getting a reservation on short notice takes a minor miracle. (Yosemite Valley lost almost half of its 900 camping spaces in a freak winter storm that washed several campsites downstream and buried hundreds more beneath a foot of silt.)

The 2½ campgrounds that remain—**North Pines, Upper Pines,** and half of **Lower Pines**—charge $18 per night. All have drinking water, flush toilets, pay phones, fire pits, and a heavy ranger presence. Showers are available for a small fee at Curry Village. Upper Pines, North Pines, and Lower Pines allow small RVs (less than 40 feet long). If you're expecting a real nature experience, skip camping in the valley unless you like doing so with 4,000 strangers.

Camp 4 (previously named Sunnyside camp ground) is a year-round, walk-in campground in the valley and fills up with climbers since it's only $5 per night. Hard-core climbers used to live here for months at a time, but the park service has cracked down on that. It still has a much more bohemian atmosphere than any of the other campgrounds.

CAMPGROUNDS ELSEWHERE IN THE PARK

Outside the valley, things start looking up for campers. Two car campgrounds near the south entrance of the park, **Wawona** and **Bridalveil Creek,** offer a total of 210 sites with all the amenities. Wawona is open year-round, and reservations are required May through September; otherwise, it's first-come, first-served (call the National Park Reservation Service at *(C)* **800/436-7275**). Family sites at Wawona are $18 per night, and group sites, which hold up to 30 people, are $40 per night. Because it sits well above snow line at more than 7,000 feet, Bridalveil is open in summer only. Its rates are $12 per night for first-come, first-served sites, and $40 for group sites.

Crane Flat, Hodgdon Meadow, and Tamarack Flat are all in the western corner of the park near the Big Oak Flat Entrance. **Crane Flat** is the nearest to the valley, about a half-hour drive, with 166 sites, water, flush toilets, and fire pits. Its rates are $18 per night, and it's open from June through September. **Hodgdon Meadow** is directly adjacent to the Big Oak Flat Entrance at 4,800

Tips   **Securing Accommodations**

All hotel reservations can be made exactly 366 days in advance. Call Yosemite Concessions Services at (*C*) **559/252-4848** in the morning 366 days before your intended arrival for the best chance of securing your reservation. If you don't plan far in advance, it's good to call anyway—cancellations may leave new openings. Online reservations may be booked through **www.yosemitepark.com**. Keep in mind that reservations held without deposit must be confirmed on the scheduled day of arrival by 4pm. Otherwise, you'll lose your reservation.

feet elevation. It's open year-round, charges $18 per night, and requires reservations May through September through NPRS (*C* **800/436-7275**). Facilities include flush toilets, running water, a ranger station, and pay phones. It's one of the least crowded low-elevation car campgrounds, but there's not a lot to do here. **Tamarack Flat** is a waterless, 52-site campground with pit toilets; open June through October. It's a bargain at $8 per night.

Tuolumne Meadows, White Wolf, Yosemite Creek, and Porcupine Flat are all above 8,000 feet and open in summer only. **Tuolumne Meadows** *⚔* is the largest campground in the park, with more than 300 spaces, but it absorbs the crowd well and has all the amenities, including campfire programs and slide shows in the outdoor amphitheater. You will, however, feel sardine-packed between hundreds of other visitors. Half of the sites are reserved in advance; the rest are set aside on a first-come, first-served basis. Rates are $15 per night.

White Wolf, west of Tuolumne Meadows, is the other full-service campground in the high country, with 87 sites available for $18 per night for family sites, $40 for group sites. It offers a drier climate than the meadow and doesn't fill up as quickly. Sites are available on a first-come, first-served basis.

Two primitive camps, **Porcupine Flat** and **Yosemite Creek,** are the last to fill up in the park. Both have pit toilets but no running water, and charge $8 per night on a first-come, first-served basis.

ACCOMMODATIONS IN THE PARK

Yosemite Concessions Services, 5410 E. Home Ave., Fresno, CA 93727 (*C* **559/252-4848**), operates all accommodations within the park and accepts all major credit cards. The reservations office is open Monday through Friday from 7am to 6pm, Saturday and Sunday 8am to 5pm (PST). For more lodging options and information or to make an online reservation request, visit its website at **www.yosemitepark.com**.

An intriguing option bridging the gap between backpacking and staying in a hotel is Yosemite's five backcountry **High Sierra Camps** (*C* **559/253-5674**). The five camps—Glen Aulin, May Lake, Sunrise, Merced Lake, and Vogelsang—make for good individual destinations. Or you can link several together, because they're arranged in a loose loop about a 10-mile hike from one another. Guests bunk dormitory style in canvas tents; each camp has bathrooms and showers. Unguided stays cost $94 per night, per person; guided trips start at $375 for 4 nights (rates include breakfast and dinner). Due to the enormous popularity of these camps, reservations are booked by lottery. Applications are accepted from October 15 to November 30. The lottery is then held in December and the winning applicants are notified by the end of March.

The Ahwahnee Hotel ★★★ A National Historic Landmark noted for its striking architecture, the grand Ahwahnee is one of the most romantic and beautiful hotels in California. With its great lounge, grand gourmet dining room, outstanding views, and high-digit prices, it's a special-occasion sort of affair. Try to reserve one of the more spacious cottages, which cost the same as rooms in the main hotel. For the price you're paying, the hotel's guest rooms, although pleasant in warm woods and Indian motif fabrics, may seem simple to the point of austerity. On the other hand, when you can look out your window and see Half Dome, Yosemite Falls, or Glacier Point, why bother with fripperies?

℘ 559/252-4848. Fax 559/456-0542. www.yosemitepark.com. 123 units, including 24 cottages. $342–$665 double. Children 12 and under free. Extra person $20. AE, DC, DISC, MC, V. No pets but there is a small kennel at the park stables. **Amenities:** Restaurant and lounge; heated outdoor pool; nearby golf course; tennis courts; Jacuzzi; concierge; tour desk; room service; babysitting (need 2 weeks advance notice; child must be potty-trained and at least 2 yrs. old). *In room:* A/C, TV, coffeemaker, hair dryer, iron. Cottages also have fridge and ceiling fans instead of A/C.

Curry Village *Kids* Accommodations at Curry Village, which celebrated its 100th birthday in 1999, range from a few motel-type rooms or heated wood cabins with private bathrooms to canvas tent cabins with central baths. Ironically, the older wood cabins are the nicest. The tent cabins have wood floors and canvas walls. Without a real wall to stop noise, they lack any sort of privacy, but they're fun in that summer-camp sort of way. You'll have to sustain yourself with fast food from the village concessions, as no cooking is allowed in the rooms.

℘ 559/252-4848. Fax 559/456-0542. 628 units. $53–$158 double. Children 12 and under free. Extra person $7–$10, tent cabins $4. AE, DC, DISC, MC, V. **Amenities:** Buffet-style dining from spring to fall, fast food court; heated outdoor pool; nearby golf course; bike rental; tour/activities desk. *In room:* No phone.

Wawona Hotel ★ If the Ahwahnee doesn't fit your plans or your pocketbook, the Wawona is the next best thing. Also a National Historic Landmark, the Wawona is a romantic throwback to another century. However, old-world charm has its ups and downs. Private bathrooms were not a big hit in the 19th century, rooms were small to hold in heat, there were no TVs or telephones, and walls were thin—and all of the above still applies today. Still, the Wawona is charming and less commercial than other accommodations on the valley floor.

℘ 559/252-4848. 104 units. $105 double without private bathroom; $158 double with private bathroom. Children 12 and under free. Extra person $16. AE, DC, DISC, MC, V. **Amenities:** Restaurant; outdoor pool; golf course on site; tennis court. *In room:* Iron; no phone.

Yosemite Lodge The next step down in valley accommodations, Yosemite Lodge is not actually a lodge but a large, more modern complex with two types of accommodations. The larger "Lodge" rooms with outdoor balconies have striking views of Yosemite Falls. Indeed the largest bonus—and curse—is that every room's front yard is the valley floor, which means you're near glorious larger-than-life natural attractions and equally gargantuan crowds.

℘ 559/252-4848. 245 units. $134–$158 double. Children 12 and under free. Extra person $10–$12. AE, DC, DISC, MC, V. **Amenities:** 2 restaurants, bar, food court; heated outdoor pool; nearby golf course; bike rental; tour/activities desk; babysitting.

3 Mammoth Lakes ★★

40 miles E of Yosemite, 319 miles E of San Francisco, 325 miles NE of Los Angeles

High in the Sierra, just southeast of Yosemite, Mammoth Lakes is surrounded by glacier-carved, pine-covered peaks that soar up from flower-filled meadows. It's an alpine region of sweeping beauty and one of California's favorite playgrounds for hiking, biking, horseback riding, skiing, and more. It's also home to one of the top-rated ski resorts in the world. Mammoth Mountain is higher at 11,053 feet than either Squaw or Heavenly so the snow stays firm longer in the year for spring skiing. You won't find the long lift lines that you find at Tahoe, either. There's more mountain and fewer people.

ESSENTIALS

GETTING THERE   It's a 6-hour drive from San Francisco via Calif. 120 over the Tioga Pass in Yosemite (closed in winter); 5 hours north of Los Angeles via Calif. 14 and U.S. 395; and 3 hours south of Reno, Nevada, via U.S. 395. In winter, Mammoth is accessible via U.S. 395 from the north or the south.

Mammoth Air Charter (© 760/934-4279) offers charter flights to the area. It services Mammoth Lakes Airport on U.S. 395. The closest international airport is Reno-Tahoe Airport (© 775/328-6400). See "Lake Tahoe" in chapter 8 for airlines that service the Reno-Tahoe Airport.

VISITOR INFORMATION   Contact the **Mammoth Lakes Visitors Bureau,** Calif. 203 (P.O. Box 48), Mammoth Lakes, CA 93546 (© 800/ 367-6572, 888/466-2666, or 760/ 934-2712; www.visitmammoth.com).

OUTDOOR PURSUITS

Mammoth Lakes is at the heart of several wilderness areas and is cut through by the San Joaquin and Owens Rivers. Mammoth Mountain overlooks the Ansel Adams Wilderness Area to the west and the John Muir Wilderness Area to the southeast, and beyond to the Inyo National Forest and the Sierra National Forest.

The **Mammoth Mountain Ski Area** ⭑⭑ (© 888/462-6668 or 760/ 934-2571; www.mammothmountain.com) is the central focus for both summer and winter activities. Visitors can ride the lifts to see panoramic vistas; those who want an active adventure have a world of options. If you do hit the slopes in winter, you may want to contact **Mammoth Area Shuttle** (MAS); call © 760/934-0678 for transportation to and from town and the ski area. The shuttle makes convenient stops throughout town and eliminates the long wait you may encounter if you take your own car.

The park's recently renovated, state-of-the-art **Panorama Gondola** provides great viewing every day, winter or summer, weather permitting. Tickets are $16 for adults, $12 for seniors, $8 for children ages 7 to 12; kids under 7 ride free. The gondola carries eight passengers and stops midway up the mountain and at the summit with dazzling 360° views. In summer, you can use the gondola to gain access to the myriad hiking and biking trails on the mountain.

DOWNHILL SKIING, CROSS-COUNTRY SKIING & SNOWBOARDING In winter, Mammoth Mountain has more than 3,500 skiable acres, a 3,100-foot vertical drop, 150 trails (32 with snowmaking), and 30 lifts, including seven high-speed quads. The terrain is 30% beginner, 40% intermediate, and 30% advanced. It's known for power sun, ideal spring skiing conditions, and anywhere from 8 to 12 feet of snow.

There's a cross-country ski center at **Tamarack Lodge** (© 760/934-2442; www.tamaracklodge.com), and for the non-skiers there's snowmobiling, dogsledding, snowshoeing, and sleigh rides.

If you're renting equipment, you'll save money if you do it in town instead of at the resort. Try **Sandy's Ski & Sports** (© 760/934-7518), on Calif. 203 next to Schat's Bakery, for all types of winter equipment; and **Wave Rave Snowboard**

Shop, on Main Street (Calif. 203; ℂ **760/934-2471**), for snowboards and accessories.

The **June Mountain Ski Area** ⚜ (ℂ **760/648-7733;** www.junemountain. com), 20 minutes north of Mammoth, is smaller and offers many summer activities. It has 500 skiable acres, a 2,590-foot vertical drop, 35 trails, and eight lifts, including high-speed quads. The terrain is 35% beginner, 45% intermediate, and 20% advanced. It's at the center of a chain of lakes—Grant, Silver, Gull, and June—which can be viewed on a scenic driving loop around Calif. 158. It's especially beautiful in the fall when the aspens are ablaze with gold.

HIKING   Trails abound in the Mammoth Lakes Basin area. They include the half-mile-long **Panorama Dome Trail,** which is just past the turnoff to Twin Lakes on Lake Mary Road, leading to the top of a plateau that provides a view of the Owens Valley and Lakes Basin. Another trail of interest is the 5-mile-long **Duck Lake Trail,** starting at the end of the Coldwater Creek parking lot with switchbacks across Duck Pass past several lakes to Duck Lake. The head of the **Inyo Craters Trail** is reached via a gravel road, off the Mammoth Scenic Loop Road. This trail takes you to the edge of these craters and a sign that explains how they were created.

For additional trail information and maps, contact the **Mammoth Ranger Station** (ℂ **760/924-5500**). For equipment and maps, go to **Footloose Sports Center,** at the corner of Canyon and Minaret (ℂ **760/934-2400**), which also rents in-line skates and mountain bikes.

KAYAKING   Kayaks are available at Crowley Lake from **Caldera Kayaks** (ℂ **760/935-4942;** www.calderakayak.com), starting at $30 a day. This outfitter also offers tours on Crowley and Mono Lakes and provides instruction as well.

MOUNTAIN BIKING   In summer, the mountain becomes one huge bike park and climbing playground. The bike park is famous for its **Kamikaze Downhill Trail,** an obstacle arena and slalom course where riders can test their balance and skill. Of course, there are also lots of trails for gentler folk who just want to commune with nature and get a little exercise. Bike shuttles will haul you and your bike to the lower mountain trails, if you want to skip the uphill part, or the gondola will take you to the summit and you get down any way you can. There's also an area designed for kids. The park operates daily from 9am to 6pm, during summer months. A 1-day pass with unlimited access to the gondola, bike shuttle, and trail system is $27 for adults, $14 for kids ages 12 and under. For the trail system only, it's $10 for adults, $5 for children 12 and under. There's a variety of rent-and-ride packages available; for more information, call ℂ **800/MAMMOTH** or visit www.mammothmountain.com.

In town, mountain bikes can also be rented from the **Footloose Sports Center,** at the corner of Canyon and Minaret (ℂ **760/934-2400**). The **NORBA National Mountain Bike Championships** are held here in summer.

PACK TRIPS   The region is also an equestrian's paradise, and numerous outfitters offer pack trips. Among them are **Red's Meadows Pack Station,** Red's Meadows, past Minaret Vista (ℂ **800/292-7758** or 760/934-2345); **Mammoth Lakes Pack Outfit,** Lake Mary Road, past Twin Lakes (ℂ **760/934-2434**), which offers 1- to 6-day riding trips and semiannual horse drives, plus other wilderness workshops; and **McGee Creek Pack Station,** McGee Creek Road, Crowley Lake (ℂ **760/935-4324**).

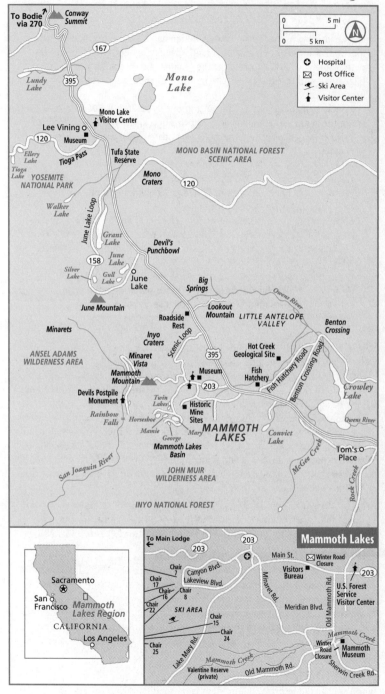

Mammoth Lakes Region

Hospital
Post Office
Ski Area
Visitor Center

To Bodie via 270

Conway Summit

167

Mono Lake

Lundy Lake

395

Mono Lake Visitor Center

Lee Vining
Museum

120

Ellery Lake

Tioga Pass

Tioga Lake

YOSEMITE NATIONAL PARK

Tufa State Reserve

MONO BASIN NATIONAL FOREST SCENIC AREA

Mono Craters

120

Walker Lake

June Lake Loop

Grant Lake

Devil's Punchbowl

158

June Lake

Silver Lake

Gull Lake

June Lake

June Mountain

Big Springs

Owens River

Lookout Mountain

LITTLE ANTELOPE VALLEY

Benton Crossing

Roadside Rest

Minarets

Inyo Craters

Scenic Loop

395

Hot Creek Geological Site

Fish Hatchery Road

Benton Crossing Road

ANSEL ADAMS WILDERNESS AREA

Minaret Vista

Mammoth Mountain

Museum

Fish Hatchery

Crowley Lake

Devils Postpile Monument

203

Owens River

Rainbow Falls

Twin Lakes

Horseshoe

Historic Mine Sites

MAMMOTH LAKES

Convict Lake

Tom's Place

Mamie

Mary

McGee Creek

Rock Creek

San Joaquin River

George

Mammoth Lakes Basin

JOHN MUIR WILDERNESS AREA

INYO NATIONAL FOREST

Sacramento

San Francisco

Mammoth Lakes Region

CALIFORNIA

Los Angeles

Mammoth Lakes

To Main Lodge

203

203

Main St.

Winter Road Closure

Visitors Bureau

203

Chair 7

Canyon Blvd.

Lakeview Blvd.

Chair 17

Chair 16

Chair 8

Minaret Rd.

U.S. Forest Service Visitor Center

Old Mammoth Rd.

Meridian Blvd.

Chair 22

SKI AREA

Chair 15

Chair 24

Chair 25

Lake Mary Rd.

Mammoth Creek

Winter Road Closure

Mammoth Museum

Valentine Reserve (private)

Old Mammoth Rd.

Sherwin Creek Rd.

Tips Winter Driving in the Sierra

Winter driving in the Sierra Nevada Range can be dangerous. While the most hazardous roads are often closed, others are negotiable by vehicles with four-wheel drive or with tire chains. Be prepared for sudden blizzards, and protect yourself by taking these important pre-trip precautions:

- Check road conditions before setting out by calling © **800/427-7623.**
- Let the rental car company you rent through know you're planning to drive in snow, and ask whether the antifreeze is prepared for cold climates.
- Make sure your heater and defroster work.
- Always carry chains. If there's a blizzard, the police will not allow vehicles without chains on certain highways. You'll have to pay about $40 to "chain up" at the side of the road.
- Recommended items include an ice scraper, a small shovel, sand or burlap for traction if you get stuck, warm blankets, and an extra car key (it's surprisingly common for motorists to lock their keys in the car while chaining up).
- Don't think winter ends in March. At the end of last April, snow was up to 7 feet high on the sides of the roads leading to the valley, and cold temperatures made more snowfall a very real possibility.

TROUT FISHING   Mammoth Lakes Basin sits in a canyon a couple of miles west of town. Here are the lakes—Mary, Mamie, Horseshoe, George, and Twin—that have made the region known for trout fishing. Southeast of town, Crowley Lake is also famous for trout fishing, as are the San Joaquin and Owens Rivers. In addition, there are plenty of other lakes in which to spin your reel.

For fishing information and guides, contact **Rick's Sport Center,** at Calif. 203 and Center Street (© **760/934-3416**); **The Trout Fitter,** in the Shell Mart Center at Main Street and Old Mammoth Road (© **760/924-3676**); or **Kittredge Sports,** Main Street and Forest Trail (© **760/934-7566**), which rents equipment, supplies guides, teaches fly-fishing, and offers backcountry trips and packages.

OTHER SUMMERTIME FUN   Golf can be enjoyed at **Snowcreek Golf Course,** Old Mammoth Road (© **760/934-6633**). Adventurers can also go hot-air ballooning with the **Mammoth Ballooning Co.** (© **760/934-7188**).

EXPLORING THE SURROUNDING AREA

Bodie ✦, one of the most authentic ghost towns in the West, lies about an hour's drive north of Mammoth, past the Tioga Pass entrance to Yosemite. In 1870, more than 10,000 people lived in Bodie; today, it's an eerie shell. En route to Bodie, you'll pass **Mono Lake** ✦, near Lee Vining, which has startling tufa towers arising from its surface—limestone deposits formed by underground springs. It's a major bird-watching area—about 300 species nest or stop here during their migrations.

WHERE TO STAY

If you stay at the resort, you'll be steps from the lifts each morning. If you opt for the town, you're closer to the restaurants and nightlife. Regardless, they're within a 5-minute drive from each other, so whatever you choose, you're never too far from the action.

There are more than 700 campsites available in the area. These sites open on varying dates in June, depending on the weather. The largest campgrounds are at Twin Lakes and Cold Water (both in the Mammoth Lakes Basin), Convict Lake, and Red's Meadow. For additional information, call the **Mammoth Ranger Station** (② 760/924-5500).

Holiday Inn ✦   This faux alpine lodge is Mammoth's newest hotel. A woodsy exterior with a river-rock base gives the three-story hotel a rustic appeal, while the interior boasts a more contemporary atmosphere. The generically decorated guest rooms contain all the comfort and amenities you could want, and come in variety of configurations, including a King/Kid suite with bunk beds. The suites offer a little extra room and Jacuzzi tubs. A spacious honeymoon suite caters to those who want romance in the great outdoors.

3236 Main St. (behind the Chevron station), Mammoth Lakes, CA 93546. ② 800/HOLIDAY or 866/924-1234 or 760/924-1234. Fax 760/934-3626. www.mammothholidayinn.com. 72 units. $129–$349 double and suite. Packages available. AE, DC, DISC, MC, V. **Amenities:** Cafe, bar; indoor heated pool; nearby golf course; exercise room; Jacuzzi; room service; laundry facility. *In room:* A/C, TV, dataport, fridge, coffeemaker, hair dryer, iron. Some units with VCR, kitchenette.

Mammoth Mountain Inn ✦ *Kids*   Located opposite the ski lodge at the base of the ski resort, the inn started out in 1954 as only one building, but was expanded a decade later into a larger, glossier complex. Though it was remodeled in the early 1990s, it still retains the rustic charm you'd expect from a mountain resort. Rooms, which were recently upgraded with new carpets and furnishings, are well equipped and pleasantly furnished, but not exactly inspired. Families love this place for its day-care activities, cribs ($10 one-time charge), playground, box lunches for picnics, games room, and even picnic tables. There's also an array of sports facilities, including bicycles, fishing or hiking guides, downhill or cross-country skiing, sleighing, horseback riding, and hay-wagon rides. Extras include free airport transportation and occasional entertainment.

Minaret Rd. (P.O. Box 353), Mammoth Lakes, CA 93546. ② 800/228-4947 or 760/934-2581. Fax 760/934-0701. www.mammothmountain.com. 173 units, 40 condos (some suitable for up to 13 people). Winter $115–$220 double; from $220–$500 condo. Summer $99–$130 double; from $145 condo. Ski and mountain-biking packages available. AE, MC, V. **Amenities:** Restaurant, bar; heated outdoor pool; nearby golf course; two indoor and one outdoor whirlpool spas; mountain bike rental; day-care center; game room; video arcade; concierge; 24-hour room service; babysitting; laundry facility; executive level rooms. *In room:* TV (VCR in 1 and 2 bedroom units), dataport, coffeemaker, hair dryer, iron. Some units with kitchen.

Motel 6 *Value*   The rooms may be small, but accommodations here are the nicest around in this price range. Although quarters are a bit more cramped than some other options, factor in the pool, vending machines, and free coffee in the lobby, and you've got all you really need to set up camp.

3372 Main St. (P.O. Box 1260), Mammoth Lakes, CA 93546. ② 800/4-MOTEL-6 or 760/934-6660. Fax 760/934-6989. www.motel6.com. 151 units. Winter $50–$60 double; summer from $55 double. Extra person $6. AARP discounts. AE, DC, DISC, MC, V. Pets accepted (1 pet per room). **Amenities:** Heated outdoor pool (summer only); laundry facilities. *In room:* A/C, TV, dataport.

Sherwin Villas *Value*   Just outside the center of town on Old Mammoth Road is this cluster of woodsy condos, perfect for larger families or groups of friends traveling together. Here you'll find one-, two-, three-, and four-bedroom units, each with a fully stocked kitchen, fireplace, linens, and access to the sauna, Jacuzzi, pool, tennis courts, and free ski shuttle that will take you to the slopes (a 5-minute drive away). Considering how many people you can pack into these apartments—and that if you stay 4 weekday nights, the fifth night is free—it's a good deal. When making reservations, make sure you specify exactly what you're looking for; each condo is independently owned and varies dramatically in both decor and quality.

P.O. Box 2249, Mammoth Lakes, CA 93546. ℭ **800/228-5291** or 760/934-4773. www.mammothsherwinvillas. com. 70 condos. 1-bedroom unit for up to 4 people $100–$120 winter, from $95 summer; 2-bedroom loft for up to 6 people $140–$190 winter, from $115 summer; 3-bedroom unit for up to 8 people $155–$220 winter, from $135 summer; 4-bedroom unit for up to 10 people $195–$260 winter, from $155 summer. Extra person $10. MC, V. **Amenities:** Outdoor pool; tennis courts; 2 Jacuzzis; Finnish sauna; game room. *In room:* TV, fully stocked kitchen. Phone on request.

Sierra Lodge (Value) In the heart of the resort town near the ski shuttle, this two-story inn offers clean, modern surroundings; rock-built fireplaces in the public areas; and a sincere effort to please its guests. Rooms are large and equipped with a kitchenette and utensils, but are unfortunately decorated in upscale-motel style. Still, everything is spotless and rooms have small patios or balconies. Facilities include a fireside room for relaxing. Continental breakfast is the only meal served, but many restaurants are nearby. Smoking is not permitted.

3540 Main St. (Calif. 203)(P.O. Box 9228), Mammoth Lakes, CA 93546. ℭ **800/356-5711** or 760/934-8881. Fax 760/934-7231. www.sierralodge.com. 35 units. $85–$159 double. Rates include continental breakfast. MC, V. Pets accepted $10 per night with $100 deposit. **Amenities:** Nearby golf course; outdoor Jacuzzi. *In room:* TV, kitchenette, fridge, hair dryer.

Tamarack Lodge & Resort The lodge and cabin accommodations at this rustic lakeside retreat are nothing fancy, but that's exactly what's kept guests coming here since the 1920s. Folks relax in front of the fire in the sitting room or hang out in their rooms, which are intentionally rustic with knotty-pine walls and modern furnishings. The cabins, which can accommodate two to nine people, are dotted around the property and offer a variety of configurations, from studios with wood-burning stove and shower to two-bedroom/two-bathroom accommodations with fireplace. Each cabin has a fully equipped kitchen. In the main lodge, there are rooms both with private bathrooms and with shared bathrooms. The lodge has a very popular cross-country ski center with more than 25 miles of trails and skating lanes, ski rentals, and a ski school. Boat and canoe rentals are also available. The dining room, overlooking Twin Lakes, offers California and continental fare.

Twin Lakes Rd., off Lake Mary Rd. (P.O. Box 69), Mammoth Lakes, CA 93546. ℭ **800/237-6879** or 760/ 934-2442. Fax 760/934-2281. www.tamaracklodge.com. 11 units, 6 with bathroom; 27 cabins. $85–$150 double; $115–$340 cabin. AE, MC, V. **Amenities:** French restaurant; nearby golf course. *In room:* Fax, fridge, coffeemaker, iron; cabins have kitchens.

WHERE TO DINE

Nevados ₰₰ EUROPEAN/CALIFORNIA What makes this restaurant a favorite with the locals? Well, owner/host Tim Dawson is on hand nightly to ensure that their every need is met; the innovative cuisine is fresh and homemade; and the tasty bread is house-baked. The clincher, though, is the fixed-price meal, which consists of a first course such as scallop-crab cakes, duck confit salad, or tuna sashimi; a main course featuring the likes of rosemary rack of lamb or grilled New York steak; and dessert (love that warm-pear-and-almond tart). Throw in the casual-but-sweet ambiance (white tablecloths, candles, and French country murals) and the extensive selection of wines, single-malt scotches, and single-batch bourbons, and it's no wonder this is the hangout for ski instructors and race coaches.

Main St. (at Minaret Rd.). © **760/934-4466.** Reservations recommended. Main courses $15–$25; fixed-price meal $33. AE, DC, DISC, MC, V. Daily 5:30–9:30pm.

The Restaurant at Convict Lake 🌟🌟 CONTINENTAL/FRENCH   After years of remaining a local secret, this place was awarded 4-star status by ACCOMMODATIONS. With only 20 others in the state enjoying similar recognition, you can bet you'd better make reservations. The rustic-but-elegant dining room's ambiance—surrounded by mountains amidst tiny wood cabins and a lake—makes for one heck of a special backdrop for this romantic dining diversion 5 miles south of the town of Mammoth Lakes. Within the woodsy, plank-sided cabin with a copper-hooded, freestanding fireplace and windows overlooking a forest of aspen, you can try such classic dishes as duck breast with Grand Marnier and sun-dried-cherry sauce, garnished with candied-orange zest. In season, the venison, pan-seared with kalamata olives, toasted cumin, and oven-dried tomatoes and served with a fine herb glaze, is worth the trip here.

Convict Lake Rd. © **760/934-3803.** Reservations recommended. Main courses $14–$28. AE, MC, V. Summer daily 11am–2pm; year-round daily 5:30–9:30pm.

Shogun 🌟 JAPANESE   Sushi and tempura in an alpine setting may seem out of context, but this authentic Japanese restaurant, located on the second floor of a strip mall, consistently packs in both tourists and locals. Diners at the eight-seat sushi bar sup on sashimi, handrolls, and a variety of sushi creations. Delicate tempura, sweet and tangy teriyaki dishes, and grilled yakitori skewers are offered individually or as combination dinners. Those with a hearty appetite can order the Boat Dinner, which includes beef and chicken teriyaki, tempura, tonkatsu, sashimi or salmon, and dessert for $17.50 per person (minimum two people). Sake, beer, and cocktails are also available.

Old Mammoth Rd. (in the Sierra Center Mall). © **760/934-3970.** Reservations recommended. Main courses $8.95–$17.50. AE, DC, DISC, MC, V. Mon–Sun 5–9:30pm.

Skadi 🌟🌟 ECLECTIC   The mini-mall where this restaurant is located (half a mile south of Mammoth Lake's center) may not be the home of the Viking goddess of skiing and hunting whose name this restaurant bears, but she wouldn't have cared once she saw the view—it encompasses most of the mountains for miles around. This universal favorite is perfect for an après-ski cocktail at the 14-seat bar, a snack from the substantial selection of appetizers and desserts, or a full-blown dinner on the town.

The decor has a big-city postmodern aura that's a welcome change after all that local alpine rusticity. Main courses are self-proclaimed "Alpine cuisine" and include such dishes as smoked trout Napoleon or grilled venison with lingonberries and a game sauce. Finish the evening with crème brûlée or the frozen macadamia-nut parfait.

587 Old Mammoth Rd. (in the Sherwin Plaza III shopping mall). © **760/934-3902.** Reservations recommended. Main courses $14–$22. AE, MC, V. Thurs–Sun 5:30–10pm.

Whiskey Creek AMERICAN   If you favor surf-and-turf fare combined with alpine atmosphere, you've found your dining spot. The building's wraparound windows encompass a view of the snow-clad mountains, and the menu is known for its beef, baby-back ribs, tequila shrimp, and lemon-garlic chicken.

Although the dining room may offer a peaceful experience, the upstairs brew-pub is a whole different world. The upstairs Mammoth Brewing Company and its live music (every night from 9pm until at least 1am) make this place the number one spot to mingle, slam suds, and get happy. (Think very crowded, post-collegiate frat party.) The cover ranges from free to $5.

24 Lake Mary Rd. (at Minaret Rd.). ℂ 760/934-2555. Reservations recommended. Main courses $12–$22. AE, DC, DISC, MC, V. Daily 5–10pm (summer 5:30); bar stays open until 2am.

4 Devils Postpile National Monument ⦿

10 miles W of Mammoth, 50 miles E of Yosemite's eastern boundary

Just a few miles outside the town of Mammoth Lakes, Devils Postpile National Monument is home to one of nature's most curious geological spectacles. Formed when molten lava cracked as it cooled, the 60-foot-high, blue-gray basalt columns that form the postpile look more like some sort of enormous eerie pipe organ or a jumble of giant pencil leads than anything you'd expect to see made from stone. The mostly six-sided columns formed underground and were exposed when glaciers scoured this valley in the last Ice Age, some 10,000 years ago. Similar examples of columnar basalt are found in Ireland and Scotland.

Because of its high elevation (7,900 feet) and heavy snowfall, the monument is open only from summer until early fall. The weather in summer is usually clear and warm, but afternoon thundershowers can soak the unprepared. Nights are still cold, so bring good tents and sleeping bags if you'll be camping. The Mammoth Lakes region is famous for its beautiful lakes—but unfortunately all that water also means lots of mosquitoes. Plan for them.

GETTING THERE   From late June to early September, cars are prohibited in the monument between 7:30am and 5:30pm because of the small roads' inability to handle the traffic. Visitors must take a shuttle bus from the Mammoth Mountain Inn to and from locations in the monument. While it takes some planning, the resulting peace and quiet are well worth the trouble and make you wonder why the park service hasn't implemented similar programs at Yosemite Valley and other traffic hot spots.

HIKING   There's more to Devils Postpile than a bunch of rocks, no matter how impressive they might be. Located on the banks of the San Joaquin River in the heart of a landscape of granite peaks and crystalline mountain lakes, the 800-acre park is a gateway to a hiker's paradise. Short paths lead from here to the top of the postpile and to **Soda Springs,** a spring of cold carbonated water.

A longer hike (about 1¼ miles) from the separate Rainbow Falls Trailhead will take you to spectacular **Rainbow Falls** ⦿, where the entire middle fork of the San Joaquin plunges 101 feet from a lava cliff. From the trail, a stairway and short trail lead to the base of the falls and swimming holes below.

The **John Muir Trail,** which connects Yosemite National Park with Kings Canyon and Sequoia National Parks, and the **Pacific Crest Trail** both run through here. Named after the famous conservationist and author who is largely credited with saving Yosemite and popularizing the Sierra Nevada as a place worth preserving, the 211-mile John Muir Trail traverses some of the most rugged and remote parts of the Sierra. There are two accesses to it in Devils Postpile, one via the ranger station, the other from the Rainbow Falls Trailhead. From here, you can hike as far as your feet will take you north or south. *Note:* Mountain bikes are not permitted on trails.

CAMPING   While most visitors stay in or around Mammoth Lakes, the monument does maintain a 21-site campground with piped water, flush toilets, fire pits, and picnic tables on a first-come, first-served basis. Rates are $8 per night. Bears are common in the park, so take proper food-storage measures.

Leashed pets are permitted on trails and in camp. Call the **National Park Service** (📞 **760/934-2289;** www.nps.gov/depo/depomain.htm) for details, but don't expect an answer during winter—the park is closed. There are several other U.S. Forest Service campgrounds nearby, including **Red's Meadow** and **Upper Soda Springs.**

5 En Route to Sequoia & Kings Canyon

Though **Visalia** is the official "gateway" and the city closest to Sequoia and Kings Canyon National Parks, it's still 40 minutes to the park entrance. Much closer to the entrance is the small town of **Three Rivers,** which though charming, until recently had little more than a few mediocre restaurants, coffee shops, and motels to offer visitors. That's about to change with the opening of the **Shoshone Inn,** which will eventually have 60 lodging units in addition to its two restaurants. (See "Where to Dine," below).

ESSENTIALS
GETTING THERE   If you're driving from San Francisco, take I-580 east to I-5 south to Calif. 198 east. The trip takes about 5 hours.

The Visalia Municipal Airport, 9500 Airport Dr. No. 1, is served by **Shuttle by United** (📞 **800/241-6522).**

Amtrak (📞 **800/USA-RAIL)** stops at nearby Hanford, and there's a shuttle from there to Visalia.

VISITOR INFORMATION   Contact the **Visalia Chamber of Commerce** (📞 **559/734-5486;** www.cvbvisalia.com).

WHERE TO STAY
In Three Rivers try the **Holiday Inn Express,** 40820 Sierra Dr. (Calif. 198), Three Rivers, CA 93271 (📞 **800/HOLIDAY** or 559/561-9000), which has an outpost here. For other options, contact **The Reservation Centre** (📞 **559/ 561-0410;** www.sequoiapark.com).

Ben Maddox House ✫   Set on a residential street of Victorian homes, 4 blocks from the town's main street, the Ben Maddox House is an impressive sight. Its triangular gable is punctuated with a round window and two extremely tall palm trees looming over the front yard. The house, built in 1876, is constructed of redwood, and its rooms retain their original dark-oak trim and white-oak floors. The guest rooms contain 18th- and 19th-century furnishings, and the two front rooms have French doors leading to two small porch sitting areas. A full made-to-order breakfast is part of the treat.

601 N. Encina St., Visalia, CA 93291. 📞 800/401-9800 or 559/739-0721. Fax 559/625-0420. www. benmaddoxhouse.com. 4 units. $70–$85 single; $85–$105 double. Rates include breakfast. AE, DISC, MC, V. **Amenities:** Outdoor pool; nearby golf course. *In room:* A/C, TV w/ pay movies, dataport, fridge, hair dryer, iron.

Radisson Hotel   Seven blocks from the town center, the eight-story Radisson is the finest hotel in Visalia and a family favorite for those en route to Sequoia and Kings Canyon National Parks. Some of the attractively furnished rooms open onto balconies. This is not the most glamorous Radisson in California, but it's serviceable in every way. The restaurant serves breakfast, lunch, and dinner, with last seating at 10pm. The local bar provides entertainment on Friday and Saturday nights.

300 S. Court St., Visalia, CA 93291. 📞 800/333-3333 or 559/636-1111. Fax 559/636-8224. www.radisson. com/visaliaca. 201 units. $125–$150 double; $239–$469 suite. Extra person $15. Cribs provided free. AE, DC, MC, V. **Amenities:** Restaurant; bar; large pool; complete fitness center; Jacuzzi; bike use; room service (until 2am); executive level rooms. *In room:* A/C, TV/VCR w/ pay movies, dataport, coffeemaker, iron.

WHERE TO DINE

Shoshone Inn *★★* *(Finds)* CALIFORNIA/MEDITERRANEAN   News flash: A hot, new destination resort is nearing completion. This new inn on the banks of the Kaweah River and at the gateway to Sequoia National Park is still under construction, but it's largely finished and it's gorgeous. With 3 feet thick white mission-style walls, Saltillo tile floors, Shoshone Indian–theme wall hangings and statuary, and a huge central fireplace constructed of rock from the Kaweah river bed, the inn is almost as lovely as its 14-acre site. The inn has two restaurants. The Monachi Café, open now and serving breakfast, lunch, and dinner, is aimed at bistro-style family dining, offering a variety of dishes ranging from chicken, fish, ribs, and pasta to gourmet hamburgers. Le Provencal, a smaller, newly-opened dining room, serves dinner only and aims at a slightly more formal ambiance. The menu focuses on sautéed specialties, fresh fish, and Italian dishes. There's also a full bar and a wine cellar.

40387 Sierra Drive, Three Rivers. ✆ **559/561-8000.** Monachi Café reservations ✆ **559/561-CAFE;** Le Provencal reservations ✆ **559/561-1234.** www.shoshoneinn.com. Reservations recommended. Main courses cafe $10–$23; dining room $15–$30. Cafe open daily 6:30am–10pm; dining room Wed–Sat 5:30–10pm.

The Vintage Press *★★* AMERICAN/CONTINENTAL   This has long been the best restaurant within a surrounding 100-mile radius, a culinary stopover of widely acknowledged merit in the gastronomic wasteland between Los Angeles and San Francisco. The design is reminiscent of a fin de siècle gin mill in gold-rush San Francisco, with a bar imported from that city manufactured by the Brunswick Company (of bowling-alley fame), lots of antiques bought at local auctions, and glittering panels of leaded glass and mirrors. The place is big enough (250 seats) to feed a boatload of gold-rush hopefuls and has a bustling bar and lounge where a pianist presents live music Thursday through Saturday from 5:30 to 9pm.

The menu is supplemented by daily specials—a zesty rack of lamb roasted in a cabernet sauce with rosemary and pistachios, for example. The regular menu offers about a dozen meat and fish dishes, with steaks as well as such choices as red snapper with lemon, almonds, and capers, or pork tenderloin with Dijon mustard, red chili, and honey. To start, we recommend farm-raised fresh oysters on the half shell or the wild mushrooms with cognac in puff pastry.

216 N. Willis St. ✆ **559/733-3033.** Reservations recommended. Main courses $13–$30. AE, DC, MC, V. Mon–Thurs 11:30am–2pm and 6–10:30pm; Fri–Sat 11:30am–2pm and 6–11pm; Sun 10am–2pm and 5–9pm.

6 Sequoia & Kings Canyon National Parks *★★*

30 miles E of Visalia

Only 200 road miles separate Yosemite from Sequoia and Kings Canyon National Parks, but they're worlds apart. While the National Park Service has taken every opportunity to modernize, accessorize, and urbanize Yosemite, resulting in a frenetic tourist scene much like the cities so many of us strive to escape, at Sequoia and Kings Canyon, they've treated the wilderness beauty of the parks with respect and care. Only one road, the Generals Highway, loops through the area, and no road traverses the Sierra here. The park service recommends that vehicles over 22 feet long avoid the steep and windy stretch between Potwisha Campground and the Giant Forest in Sequoia National Park. Generally speaking, the park is much less accessible by car than most, but spectacular for those willing to head out on foot.

Sequoia & Kings Canyon National Parks

Tips   **National Parks vs. National Forests: What You Don't Know Can Cost You**

Sierra, Inyo, and Sequoia National Forests surround Kings Canyon and Sequoia National Parks. What's the difference between a national park and a national forest? National parks are intended to strictly preserve natural and historic features, in addition to providing areas of easy-on-the-land recreation. National forests, on the other hand, operate under a multiple use concept, sometimes including the harvesting of commodities such as lumber and minerals. National parks and national forests have different rules, and if you plan to travel in the area for a while you should know them. Legal activity in a forest can earn you a fine in a park.

Parks forbid hunting; forests usually allow it. Dogs can be taken on forest trails, but not in parks. You can only camp in numbered sites in designated areas in parks; in the forest it's either campgrounds or, unless posted otherwise, near roadsides. You can ride your bike on a forest trail; in parks you must stay on the roads and helmets are required for persons 18 and younger. To protect the ecosystem in parks, you can't disturb anything—plants, pine cones, or rocks. In the forest, collecting a few things for personal use is permitted.

For more information, contact the **National Park Service** at © 559/565-3341, or the **Forest Service** at © 559/784-1500.

The Sierra Nevada tilts upward as it runs south. **Mount Whitney,** at 14,494 feet (the highest point in the lower 48 states), is just one of many high peaks in Sequoia and Kings Canyon. The **Pacific Crest Trail** also reaches its highest point here, crossing north to south through both parks. In addition to rocky, snow-covered peaks, Sequoia and Kings Canyon are home to the largest groves of giant sequoias in the Sierra Nevada, as well as the headwaters of the Kern, Kaweah, and Kings Rivers. A few small, high-country lakes are home to some of the only remaining pure-strain golden trout. Bears, deer, and numerous smaller animals and birds depend on the parks' miles of wild habitat for year-round breeding and feeding grounds.

Technically two separate parks, Sequoia and Kings Canyon are contiguous and managed jointly from the park headquarters at Ash Mountain, just past the entrance on Calif. 198 east of Visalia.

ESSENTIALS
Most visitors make a loop through the parks by entering at Grant Grove and leaving through Ash Mountain, or vice versa.

ENTRANCE FEES   A $10-per-car fee is good for 7 days' entry at any park entrance. An annual pass costs $20; the Golden Age pass offers lifetime access for seniors 62 and over for $10; and blind or permanently disabled visitors get free entry with the Golden Access pass.

VISITOR CENTERS & INFORMATION   The **Lodgepole** and **Grant Grove** visitor centers are the largest, with a full selection of park information and displays about the history, biology, and geology of this incredible place. Some time spent here will pay off by letting you decide which parts of the parks you most want to concentrate on. For visitor information before you go, call © 559/565-3341, or visit www.nps.gov/seki.

AVOIDING THE CROWDS   To escape the crowds and see less-used areas of the parks, enter on one of the dead-end roads to Mineral King or Cedar Grove (both open only in summer), or South Fork. The lack of through traffic makes these parts of the parks incredibly peaceful even at full capacity, and they're gateways to some of the best hiking.

RANGER PROGRAMS   Park rangers offer hikes, campfire talks, and slide shows at several campgrounds and visitor centers during the summer.

REGULATIONS   Mountain bikes and dogs are forbidden on all park trails (dogs are only permitted in developed areas, but must be leashed). The park service allows firewood gathering at campgrounds, although supplies can be scarce. Removing wood from living or standing trees is forbidden.

WILDERNESS PERMITS   Wilderness permits are required for overnight backpacking trips in the parks. You can reserve the $10 permits in advance by writing the Wilderness Office, Superintendent, Sequoia and Kings Canyon National Parks, HCR 89 Box 60, Three Rivers, CA 93271 (© **559/565-3708**). You must reserve permits for climbing Mount Whitney via the Inyo National Forest. Reservations can be made by filling out an application form, preferably downloaded and printed from the park website (www.r5.fs.fed.us/inyo), and sending it to the Wilderness Reservations Office, Inyo National Forest, 873 North Main, Bishop, CA 93514. At this writing, there is an experimental phone reservation system in progress. Reservations by phone will be accepted from 1pm to 5pm Monday through Friday at © **760/873-2483.** Applications for the Mt. Whitney trail are $15 a person.

THE SEASONS   In the high altitudes, where most Sequoia and Kings Canyon visitors are headed, the summers are short and the winters cold. Snow in July and August, although rare, is not unheard of. At mid-elevations, where the sequoias grow, spring can come as early as April and as late as June. Afternoon showers are occasional. In winter, only the main roads into the parks are usually open; the climate can range from bitter cold to pleasant and can change minute by minute. The Generals Highway between Sequoia and Kings Canyon closes for plowing during and after snowstorms. Be ready for anything if you head into the backcountry on skis. In summer, poison oak and rattlesnakes are common in lower elevations, and mosquitoes are plentiful in all wet areas.

EXPLORING THE PARKS

There are some 75 groves of giant sequoias in the parks, but the easiest places to see the trees are **Grant Grove** ⊛, in Kings Canyon near the park entrance on Calif. 180 from Fresno, or **Giant Forest** ⊛, a huge grove of trees containing 40 miles of footpaths, located 16 miles from the entrance to Sequoia National Park on Calif. 198. Saving the sequoias was one of the reasons Sequoia National Park was created in 1890 at the request of San Joaquin Valley residents, making it the second-oldest national park in the United States.

The 2-mile **Congress Trail** loop in Giant Forest starts at the base of the **General Sherman Tree** ⊛, the largest living thing in the world. Single branches

---

(*Tips* **Fill 'er Up**

Note that there are no gas stations in the parks, so be sure to fill up your gas tank before you enter.

---

of this monster are more than 7 feet thick. Each year, it grows enough wood to make a 60-foot-tall tree of normal dimensions. Other trees in the grove are nearly as large, and many of the peaceful-looking trees have also been saddled with strangely militaristic and political monikers like General Lee and Lincoln. Longer trails lead to remote reaches of the grove and nearby meadows.

Unlike the coast redwoods, which reproduce by sprouting or by seeds, giant sequoias only reproduce by seed. Adult sequoias rarely die of diseases and are protected from most fire by thick bark. The huge trees have surprisingly shallow roots, and most die from toppling when their roots are damaged for some reason and can no longer support them. These groves, like the ones in Yosemite, were explored by conservationist and nature writer John Muir, who named the Giant Forest.

Besides the sequoia groves, Sequoia and Kings Canyon are home to the most pristine wilderness in the Sierra Nevada. At **Road's End** on the Kings Canyon Highway (open from late May to early November), you can stand by the banks of the Kings River and stare up at granite walls rising thousands of feet above the river, the deepest canyon in the United States.

Near Giant Forest Village, **Moro Rock** is a 6,725-foot-tall granite dome formed by exfoliation of layers of the rock. A quarter-mile trail scales the dome for a spectacular view of the adjacent Canyon of the Middle Fork of the Kaweah. The trail gains 300 feet in 400 yards, so be ready for a climb.

Crystal Cave ✿ is located 15 miles from the Calif. 198 park entrance and an additional 7 miles to cave parking. Here you can take a 50-minute tour of Crystal's beautiful marble interior. The tour is $8 for adults, $6 for seniors, $3 for children ages 6 to 12, and free for kids 6 and under. Tickets are not sold at the cave and must be purchased at the Lodgepole or Foothills visitor centers at least 1½ hours in advance. Be sure to wear sturdy shoes and bring a jacket. For information, call ✆ **559/565-3759.** The cave is open summers mid-May through late September from 11 am to 4pm.

Boyden Cavern, on Calif. 180 in neighboring Sequoia National Forest, is a large cave where you can take a 45-minute tour to see stalactites and stalagmites. A fee is charged; call ✆ **209/736-2708** for details or check the website at www.caverntours.com. The cave is open April through October from 10 am to 5pm.

HIKING THE PARKS

Hiking and backpacking are what these parks are really all about. Some 700 miles of trails connect canyons, lakes, and high alpine meadows and snowfields.

When traveling overnight inside the parks' boundaries, overnight and/or day-use permits are required. If you want to do serious overnight backpacking, see "Essentials: Wilderness Permits," above.

Some of the park's most impressive hikes start in the **Mineral King** section in the southern end of Sequoia. Beginning at 7,800 feet, trails lead onward and upward to destinations like Sawtooth Pass, Crystal Lake, and the old White Chief Trail to the now-defunct White Chief Mine. Once an unsuccessful silver-mining town in the 1870s, Mineral King was the center of a pitched battle in the late 1970s when developers sought to build a huge ski resort here. They were defeated when Congress added Mineral King to Sequoia National Park, and the wilderness remains unspoiled.

The **John Muir Trail,** which begins in Yosemite Valley, ends at Mount Whitney. For many miles it coincides with the **Pacific Crest Trail** as it skirts the highest peaks in the park. This is the most difficult part of the Pacific Crest, remaining above 10,000 feet most of the time and crossing 12,000-foot-tall passes.

Other hikers like to explore the northern part of Kings Canyon from **Cedar Grove** and **Road's End.** The **Paradise Valley Trail,** leading to beautiful Mist Falls, is a fairly easy day trip by park standards. The **Copper Creek Trail** immediately rises into the high wilderness around Granite Pass at 10,673 feet, one of the most strenuous day hikes in the parks.

If the altitude and steepness are too much for you at these trailheads, try some of the longer hikes in **Giant Forest** or **Grant Grove.** These forests are woven with interlocking loops that allow you to take as short or as long a hike as you want. The 6-mile **Trail of the Sequoias** in Giant Forest will take you to the grove's far-eastern end, where you'll find some of the finest trees. In Grant Grove, a 100-foot walk through the hollow trunk of the **Fallen Monarch** makes a fascinating side trip. The tree has been used for shelter for more than 100 years and is tall enough inside that you can walk through without bending over.

Perhaps the most traversed trail to the park is the **Whitney Portal Trail.** It runs from east of Sequoia near Lone Pine, through Inyo National Forest, to Sequoia's boundary, the summit of Mount Whitney. Though it's a straightforward walk to the summit and it's possible to bag it in a very long day hike, you'd better be in really good shape before attempting it. Almost half the people who attempt Whitney, including those who camp partway up, don't reach the summit. Weather, altitude, and fatigue can conspire to stop even the most prepared party. For more information, you can contact the **Mt. Whitney Ranger Station** at ✆ **760/876-6200.** For wilderness permits, see "Essentials" at the beginning of this section.

The official park map and guide has good road maps for the parks, but for serious hiking you'll want to check out *Sierra South: 100 Back-Country Trips,* by Thomas Winnett and Jason Winnett (Wilderness Press). Another good guide is *Kings Canyon Country,* a hiking handbook by Ginny and Lew Clark. The Grant Grove, Lodgepole, Cedar Grove, Foothills, and Mineral King visitor centers all sell a complete selection of maps and guidebooks to the parks. Books and maps are also available by mail through the **Sequoia Natural History Association** (✆ **559/565-3759**).

OTHER OUTDOOR PURSUITS

FISHING   Trout fishing in the lower altitudes is fairly limited; most fishing takes place along the banks of the Kings and Kaweah Rivers. A few high-country lakes are refuges for trout and are not stocked with hatchery fish. Before venturing into the high country, inquire at a ranger station about the area you'll be visiting to find out about closures or specific regulations. A California fishing license is required for everyone over 16 years old. Tackle and licenses are available at several park stores.

RAFTING & KAYAKING   Only fairly recently have professional outfitters begun taking experienced rafters and kayakers down the Class IV and V Kaweah and Upper Kings Rivers outside the parks. Check The Reservation Center website (www.sequoiapark.com) for a good list of companies running trips. Rafting and kayaking here are only for the very adventurous.

SKIING & SNOWSHOEING   **Wolverton,** 2 miles north of the General Sherman tree, has a snow-play and cross-country ski area. You can rent skis and snowshoes at the Lodgepole Market. In the **Giant Forest** and **Grant Grove** areas, there are about 50 miles of marked cross-country trails. Rangers offer naturalist talks and snowshoe walks some weekends. Rental equipment (including snowshoes) and lessons are available at the Grant Grove Market. For more information on cross-country skiing, sledding, or snowshoeing at Grant Grove, call © **559/335-5500;** for Wolverton, call © **559/565-3435.** Kids can sled and play in the snow-play areas near Wolverton and at Big Stump, Columbine, and Azalea in Grant Grove.

The Sequoia Natural History Association operates the **Pear Lake Ski Hut** for snowshoers and cross-country skiers, which can accommodate up to 10 people. Use of the facility is by lottery. For further information, call © **559/565-3759.**

CAMPING

There are 13 campgrounds in the parks, offering the most convenient and economical accommodations here, although none have hookups. Only two accept reservations: **Lodgepole Campground** and **Dorst Campground** in Sequoia (© **800/365-2267**). Others are first-come, first-served, and often fill up on weekends. Three campgrounds—Azalea, Lodgepole, and Potwisha—are open year-round. The rest are open from snowmelt through September. Call © **559/565-3341** for camping information. Even in summer, campers should prepare for rain and cold temperatures. Bring a good tent and warm sleeping bags. Also note that due to bears, proper food storage is required.

Two large campgrounds in Sequoia are **Dorst** and **Lodgepole.** Both are close to Giant Forest. Lodgepole is within a short stroll of a restaurant, market, showers, laundry, and visitor center. With more than 200 sites each, they tend to be the noisiest campgrounds in Sequoia. Lodgepole charges $14 per night and Dorst charges $16 per night.

Smaller and more peaceful are **South Fork, Potwisha, Buckeye Flat, Atwell Mill,** and **Cold Springs.** Atwell Mill and Cold Springs have pit toilets and cost $8 per night. Potwisha and Buckeye Flat, with flush toilets and sinks, charge $14. South Fork, with pit toilets and no drinking water, charges $8.

Campers in the remote Cedar Grove area of Kings Canyon National Park in the Kings River gorge can choose from **Moraine, Sentinel, Sheep Creek,** and **Canyon View,** which also has a group camp. All four have flush toilets and are convenient to some of the parks' best hiking. Sites are $14. The small **Cedar Grove Village** offers a restaurant, motel, showers, and store. Sites are $14.

Three campgrounds in the Grant Grove area will put you near the sequoias without the noise and crowds of Giant Forest Village. All three—**Sunset, Azalea,** and **Crystal Springs**—have flush toilets and phones. The area has an RV disposal site, a visitor center, and showers nearby. The charge is $14 per site.

LODGING

Lodging in the parks ranges from rustic cabins (with no bathrooms or heat) to brand new rooms with all the modern comforts—well, maybe not all—hot tubs aren't mentioned anywhere. New structures are increasing both the numbers of rooms available and the general comfort level. There are a dizzying array of types of rooms and cabins with prices that change seasonally. Your best bet is to check the Web for the location and accommodation that best suits your needs, and then call for the current price. Lodging in Kings Canyon is operated by the park concessionaire, Kings Canyon Park Services Co., P.O. Box 909, Kings Canyon National Park, CA 93633 (© **559/335-5500** for information and reservations; www.sequoia-kingscanyon.com).

Cedar Grove Lodge on the Kings River in the eastern section of Kings Canyon in Cedar Grove Village has 18 motel-style rooms and is open from early

May to early October. Each room has two queen-size beds and a private bath-room. Grant Grove Village, on Calif. 180 30 miles northwest of Giant Forest, offers a variety of cabins with private or shared bathrooms and tent cabins. A recently added lodge offers 24 rooms and 6 suites in a 2-story building in the forest; no pets are allowed. The newest lodge in Kings Canyon is named after John Muir, and has 30 rooms with two queen beds and a private bathroom. The lodge features an extensive collection of Muir's writings, and paintings and photographs of his journeys decorate the walls.

Sequoia National Park is in the process of eliminating the old lodgings at Giant Forest and replacing them with new facilities. The attractive **Wuksachi Village & Lodge** ⊀, 64740 Wuksachi Way in Lodgepole, Sequoia National Park (© **888/252-5757** or 559/565-0340; www.visitsequoia.com) is Sequoia's most recent addition. It's open year-round, offering 102 rooms within the park from $82 to $159 off-season, and from $132 to $225 during peak season (April 1 to November 30). Rooms in the cedar and stone, mountain-themed lodge have two queens or a king and a sofa bed. Children under 12 can stay free in their parents' room. The Wuksachi Lodge dining room serves surprisingly good lunches and dinners, including a thoughtful kids' menu. The lodge offers winter ski promotions such as cross-country skis or snowshoes for two adults as part of the room rates. Unfortunately, you have to leave your (four-legged) furry friends at home.

10

Sacramento, the Gold Country & the Central Valley

by Matthew R. Poole & Mary Anne Moore

On the morning of January 24, 1848, a carpenter named James Marshall was working on John Sutter's mill in Coloma when he made an exciting discovery: He stumbled upon a gold nugget on the south fork of the American River. Despite Sutter's wishes to keep the find a secret, word leaked out—a word that would change the fate of California almost overnight: *Gold!*

The news spread like wildfire, and a frenzy seized the nation: The gold rush was on. Within 3 years, the population of the state grew from a meager 15,000 to more than 265,000. Most of these newcomers were single men under the age of 40, and not far behind were the thousands of merchants, bankers, and women who made their fortunes catering to the miners, most of whom went bust in their search for instant wealth.

Sacramento grew quickly as a supply town at the base of the surrounding goldfields. The Gold Country boom lasted less than a decade; the gold supply was quickly exhausted, and many towns shrank or disappeared. Sacramento, however, continued to grow as the fertile Central Valley south of it exploited another source of wealth, becoming the vegetable and fruit garden of the nation.

A trip along Calif. 49 from the northern mines to the southern mines will give visitors a sense of what life might have been like on the rough mining frontier. The towns along this route seem frozen in time, with the main streets boasting raised wooden sidewalks, double-porched buildings, ornate saloons, and Victorian storefronts. Each town tells a similar story of sudden wealth and explosive growth, yet each has also left behind its own unique imprint. Any fan of movie Westerns will recognize the setting—hundreds, perhaps even thousands, of films have been shot in these parts.

At the base of the Gold Country's rolling hills is the sprawling and decidedly flat Central Valley. Some 240 miles long and 50 miles wide, it's California's agricultural breadbasket, the source of much of the bounty that is shipped across the nation and overseas. Much of the history of California has revolved around the struggle for control of the water used to irrigate the valley (it receives less than 10 inches of rainfall per year) and make this inland desert bloom. Despite the scarcity of water, a breathtaking panorama of orange and pistachio groves, grapevines, and strawberry fields stretches uninterrupted for miles.

1 Sacramento ✦

90 miles E of San Francisco

Sacramento, with a metropolitan population of 1,782,000, is one of the state's fastest growing areas. In addition to being the state capital, it is a thriving shipping and processing center for the fruit, vegetables, rice, wheat, and dairy goods that are produced in the fertile Central Valley. In the past decade, it's also become an area of high-tech spillover from Silicon Valley, and more recently, a suburb for Bay Area workers seeking affordable homes. This prosperous and politically charged city has broad, tree-shaded streets lined with some impressive Victorians and well-crafted bungalows. At its heart sits the capitol building—Sacramento's main attraction—in a well-maintained park replete with flower gardens and curious squirrels. It's far from a tourist town, but it does have its share of touristy activities. Visitors and locals alike enjoy spending the day walking through Old Sacramento or floating down the American River.

ESSENTIALS

GETTING THERE   If you're driving from San Francisco, Sacramento is located about 90 miles east on I-80. From Los Angeles, take I-5 through the Central Valley directly into Sacramento. From North Lake Tahoe, get on I-80 west, and from South Lake Tahoe take U.S. 50.

Sacramento International Airport (© 916/929-5411), 12 miles northwest of downtown Sacramento, is served by about a dozen airlines, including **American** (© 800/433-7300), **Alaska** (© 800/426-0333), **America West** (© 800/235-9292), **Continental** © 800/523-3273, **Delta** (© 800/221-1212), **Northwest** (© 800/225-2525), **Southwest** (© 800/435-9792), **TWA** (© 800/ 221-2000), and **United** (© 800/241-6522).

Taxi and Shuttle Service (© **916/362-5525**) will get you from the airport to downtown; it charges a flat rate of $15 to the capital, a bargain compared to the $25 a conventional taxi would cost.

Amtrak (© **800/USA-RAIL**) trains serve Sacramento daily.

VISITOR INFORMATION   The **Sacramento Convention and Visitors Bureau,** 1303 J St., Sacramento, CA 95814 (© **916/264-7777;** fax 916/ 264-7788), provides plenty of helpful information for tourists. Once in the city, visitors can also stop by the **Old Sacramento Visitor Center,** 1101 Second St. (© **916/442-7644**), in Old Sacramento; it's usually open daily from 10am to 5pm.

ORIENTATION   Suburbia sprawls around Sacramento, but its downtown area is relatively compact. Getting around the city is made easy by a grid-like pattern of streets that are designated by numbers or letters. The capitol building, on 10th Street between N and L Streets, is the key landmark. From the front of the capitol, M Street—which is at this point called Capitol Mall—runs 10 straight blocks to Old Sacramento, the oldest section of the city.

EXPLORING THE CAPITAL & ENVIRONS

In town, you'll want to stroll around **Old Sacramento** ⊕, 4 square blocks at the foot of the downtown area that have become a major tourist attraction. These blocks contain more than 100 restored buildings (California's largest restoration project), including restaurants and shops. Although the area has cobblestone streets, wooden sidewalks, and authentic gold rush–era architecture, the high concentration of T-shirt shops and other gimmicky stores has turned it into a sort of historical amusement park. Nonetheless, there are interesting things to see here, such as where the Pony Express ended and the transcontinental railroad—and the Republican Party—began. The **Railroad Museum** (see below) is the dream of railroad buffs, and the **Sacramento Jazz Festival,** mostly Dixieland, is famous for attracting over 100 bands that congregate here from

> ### Kids Where the Wild Things Are
>
> The best place to take your kids on a sunny afternoon in Sacramento is **Fairytale Town,** at William Land Park, Land Park Drive and Sutterville Road (*©* **916/264-5233**). Although the slides and other climbing toys are pretty basic and showing their age, little guys seem to think it's the best place in the world. After you've explored every nook and cranny, cross the street to the **Sacramento Zoo** (*©* **916/264-5885**), buy a big spool of cotton candy, and see the animals. Adjacent to Fairytale Town, there's also a small, but pleasant **Funderland** amusement park (*©* **916/456-0115**) with inexpensive, kid-sized rides, open all week in summer months and on spring and fall weekends when the weather is nice.

around the world for 4 days of madness over the Memorial Day weekend. While you're meandering, stop at the **Discovery Museum** ✸ at 101 I St. (*©* **916/264-7057;** www.thediscovery.org), which houses hands-on exhibits of California's history, highlighting the valley's agricultural gold rush as well as the real one in 1849. It's open Tuesday through Sunday from 10am to 5pm. Admission is $5 for adults, $4 for seniors over 60, $4 for kids ages 13 to 17, $3 for kids 6 to 12, and free for kids under 6.

California State Capitol ✸✸✸   Closely resembling a scale model of the U.S. Capitol in Washington, D.C., the beautiful, domed California state capitol was built in 1869 and massively renovated in 1976. (Some of the restored sections are temporarily closed to repair extensive damage inflicted by a truck driver who purposefully decided to drive his semi into one of the entrances.) Sacramento's most distinctive landmark, the capitol has been the stage of many important political dramas in California history. Guided tours provide insight into both the building's architecture and the workings of the government it houses.

10th St. (between N and L Sts.). *©* **916/324-0333.** Free admission. Daily 9am–5pm. Tours offered every hour on the hour until 4pm. Closed Thanksgiving, Christmas, and New Year's Day.

California State Railroad Museum ✸✸✸   Well worth visiting, this museum is one of the highlights of Old Sacramento. You won't miss much if you bypass the memorabilia displays and head straight for the museum's 105 shiny locomotives and rail cars, beautiful antiques that are true works of art. Afterward, you can watch a film on the history of the western railroads that's quite good, then peruse related exhibits that tell the amazing story of the building of the transcontinental railroad. This museum is not just for train buffs: Over half a million people visit each year, and even the hordes of schoolchildren that typically mob this place shouldn't dissuade you from visiting one of the largest and best railroad museums in the country.

From April through September, on weekends and holidays from 11am to 5pm, **steam locomotive rides** carry passengers 6 miles along the Sacramento River. Trains depart on the hour from the Central Pacific Freight Depot in Old Sacramento, at K and Front Streets. Fares are $6 for adults and children ages 13 and older and $3 for children 6 to 12.

125 I St. (at Second St.). *©* **916/445-6645.** Fax 916/327-5655. www.californiastaterailroadmuseum.org. Admission $3 adults 17 and older, free for children 16 and under. Daily 10am–5pm. Closed Thanksgiving, Christmas, and New Year's Day.

Downtown Sacramento

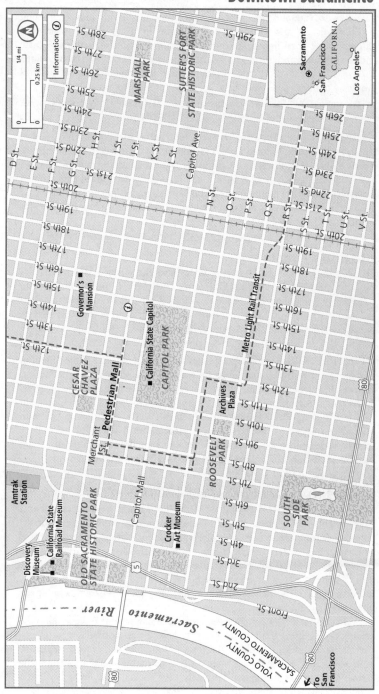

Crocker Art Museum ✸ This museum houses a truly outstanding collection of California art, as well as temporary exhibits from around the world. The museum itself is an imposing century-old Italianate building, with an ornate interior of carved and inlaid woods. The Crocker Mansion Wing, the museum's most recent addition, is modeled after the Crocker family home and contains works by northern California artists from 1945 to the present.

216 O St. (at Third St.). ℂ **916/264-5423.** Admission $6 adults, $3 children 7–17, free for children under 7. Tues–Wed and Fri–Sun 10am–5pm; Thurs 10am–9pm. Closed Mondays and major holidays.

Sutter's Fort State Historic Park ✸ John Sutter established this outpost in 1839, and the park, restored to its 1846 appearance, aims to recapture the pioneering spirit of 19th-century California. The usual exhibits are on hand—a blacksmith's forge, cooperage, bakery, and jail—and a self-guided audio tour is available. Historic demonstrations and live reenactments in costume are staged daily from Memorial Day to Labor Day, when admissions are bumped to $3 for adults and $1 for children ages 6 to 16.

2701 L St. ℂ **916/445-4422.** Admission $1 adults, free for children 16 and under. Daily 10am–5pm.

OUTDOOR PURSUITS

BICYCLING One good thing about a town that's as flat as a tortilla: It's perfect for exploring on a bike. One of the best places to ride is through Old Sacramento and along the 22-mile American River Parkway, which runs right through it. If you didn't bring your own wheels, the friendly guys at **City Bicycle Works,** 2419 K St., at 24th Street (ℂ **916/447-2453**), will rent you one for about $15 a day and point you in the right direction.

RIVER RAFTING Sacramento lies nestled at the confluence of the American and Sacramento Rivers, and rafting on the clear blue water of the American is immensely popular, especially on warm weekends. Several Sacramento-area outfitters rent rafts for 4 to 15 persons, along with life jackets and paddles for about $12 to $15 per person. Their shuttles drop you and your entourage upstream and meet you 3 to 4 hours later at a predetermined point downstream. A recommended outfitter is **American River Raft Rentals,** 11257 S. Bridge St. (at Sunrise Ave.), Rancho Cordova (ℂ **916/635-6400;** www.raftrentals.com).

WHERE TO STAY
EXPENSIVE

Amber House Bed-and-Breakfast ✸✸ Just 8 blocks from the capitol on a quiet neighborhood street, Amber House offers lovely, individually decorated rooms possessing all the amenities you could wish for. Named for famous artists, musicians, and writers, accommodations are located in two adjacent historic houses: the Poet's Refuge, a well-crafted 1905 home with five rooms, and the Artist's Retreat, a Mediterranean-style house built in 1913. A third addition—an old colonial-revival home called the Musician's Manor—is across the street, and its Mozart Room is the B&B's best, containing a four-poster queen bed, a heart-shaped Jacuzzi, a private patio, and three bay windows overlooking the tree-shaded street. A beautiful living room and library are available for guests' use. A full breakfast is served at the time and location you request—either in your room, in the large dining room, or outside on the veranda. Coffee and a newspaper are brought to your door early every morning, as are freshly baked cookies and wine or champagne every evening.

1315 22nd St., Sacramento, CA 95816. ℂ **800/755-6526** or 916/444-8085. Fax 916/552-6529. www. amberhouse.com. 14 units. $159–$289 double. Rates include breakfast. AE, DC, DISC, MC, V. **Amenities:**

Complimentary bike use; concierge; in-room massage; laundry service; same-day dry cleaning. *In room:* A/C, TV/VCR, dataport, hair dryer, iron.

Grand Sacramento Hotel ★ Sacramento's newest convention hotel opened in May 2001 with words of high praise for its high-tech amenities, a million dollar public art collection, and the preservation of a beloved landmark. The hotel's 504 rooms are in a shiny new, 26 story building adjoining a three-story building which was originally Sacramento's public market from 1920 to the 1960s. This historic structure, designed by Julia Morgan, architect for Hearst Castle, was a favorite gathering place for three generation of Sacramentans. Now housing the lobby, bar, and two restaurants, the site is once again a downtown focal point for residents and travelers alike. The rooms are new convention-type hotel rooms, a mite anonymous, but not unpleasant.

1230 J St., Sacramento, CA 95814. ℂ **800/325-3535** or 916/447-1700. Fax 916/477-1701. www.sheraton. com. 504 units. $119–$275 double; from $350 suite. AE, DC, DISC, MC, V. Self-parking $10; valet parking $15. **Amenities:** 2 restaurants, bar; heated outdoor pool; health club; concierge; car-rental desk; business center; full service salon; room service; in-room massage; babysitting; laundry service; same-day dry cleaning; club level rooms. *In room:* A/C, TV w/ pay movies, dataport, minibar, coffeemaker, hair dryer, iron.

Hyatt Regency Sacramento ★★ Sacramento's top hotel stands right in the heart of downtown, directly across from the California state capitol and adjacent to the convention center. It's the high-status address for visiting politicos and is popular with conventioneers as well, as its facilities and services are unmatched in the city. While the rooms themselves are not terribly distinctive, they conform to a very high standard and come with all the amenities you expect from Hyatt. The best are the corner units with views facing the state capitol.

1209 L St., Sacramento, CA 95814. ℂ **800/233-1234** or 916/443-1234. Fax 916/321-3799. www. sacramento.hyatt.com. 503 units. $220–$260 double; from $375 suite. AE, DC, DISC, MC, V. Self-parking $10; valet parking $15. **Amenities:** 2 restaurants, bar; heated outdoor pool; nearby golf course; health club; Jacuzzi; concierge; car-rental desk; business center; full service salon; room service; in-room massage; babysitting; laundry service; same-day dry cleaning; executive level rooms. *In room:* A/C, TV w/ pay movies, dataport, minibar, fridge (upon request), coffeemaker, hair dryer, iron.

MODERATE

Best Western Sutter House *Value* You would never know from the plain, motel-like exterior that this is one of the best values in Sacramento. Rooms here are as up-to-date as any offered by upscale hotels such as the Hilton or the Hyatt, including well-coordinated furnishings and lots of amenities. There's a pool in the courtyard, and complimentary coffee and pastries are served each morning in the lobby.

1100 H St., Sacramento, CA 95814. ℂ **800/830-1314** or 916/441-1314. Fax 916/441-5961. 98 units. $85–$160 double. Rates include continental breakfast. AE, DC, DISC, MC, V. **Amenities:** Solar heated outdoor pool; access to fitness center; room service; same-day dry cleaning; executive level rooms. *In room:* A/C, TV, fax, dataport, fridge, coffeemaker, hair dryer, iron.

Delta King Riverboat ★ The *Delta King* carried passengers between San Francisco and Sacramento in the 1930s. Permanently moored in Sacramento since 1984, the riverboat is now a somewhat gimmicky but nonetheless charming hotel. Staying here can be quite a novelty, but the staterooms in a boat are ultra-cozy and may bother landlubbers, especially if you're planning to spend a lot of time in your room. All units are nearly identical and have private bathrooms and low ceilings. The captain's quarters, a particularly pricey suite, is a unique, mahogany-paneled stateroom, complete with an observation platform and private deck.

The Pilothouse Restaurant is popular for local office parties. When the weather is nice, there's dining on outside decks with views of colorful Old Sacramento. Live entertainment is presented below decks in two shipboard venues on Friday and Saturday nights. In the *Mark Twain Lounge*, "Suspect's Murder Mystery," an interactive whodunit, challenges the audience to reveal the true murderer, played by period actors. It's $35 per person to attend, but that includes dinner, tax, and gratuity. Drinks, of course, are extra. Or for $14 a person you can see a local production of a Broadway play in the 75-seat *Delta King Theater.*

1000 Front St., Old Sacramento, CA 95814. ✆ **800/825-5464** or 916/444-5464. www.deltaking.com. 44 units. Sun–Thurs $119–$139 double, $400 captain's quarters; Fri–Sat $169 double, $400 captain's quarters. Rates include continental breakfast. AE, DC, DISC, MC, V. **Amenities:** Restaurant, lounge, dinner theatre; laundry service; same-day dry cleaning. *In room:* A/C, TV, dataport, hair dryer, iron.

Sterling Hotel 🌟🌟   Set in the heart of Sacramento, 3 blocks from the capitol, this inn occupies a white-fronted Victorian mansion originally built in the 1890s and heavily renovated in 1995. The Sterling has all the charm of a small, well-managed, sophisticated inn, with a carefully tended flowering yard, tasteful decor, designer furnishings, Italian marble, and a Jacuzzi in every room. The Chanterelle, which serves well-prepared California regional cuisine in a dignified setting, is known as one of Sacramento's better restaurants.

1300 H St., Sacramento, CA 95814. ✆ **800/365-7660** or 916/448-1300. Fax 916/448-8066. www.sterling-hotel.com. 17 units. Sun–Thurs $179–$199 double; $325 suite. Fri–Sat $199–$249 double; $325 suite. Rates include continental breakfast. AE, DC, MC, V. **Amenities:** Restaurant; Jacuzzi; room service. *In room:* A/C, TV w/ pay movies, dataport, hair dryer, iron; most units with fridge.

INEXPENSIVE

The Sacramento Vagabond Inn *Value*   A reliable choice within walking distance of the state capitol, the Vagabond Inn has a host of free features, including local phone calls, weekday newspapers, and continental breakfast. Bedrooms are clean and comfortable, but not exceptional—it's the economical rates and the convenient location that make it worth your while. There's an adjoining 24-hour Denny's restaurant as well.

909 Third St., Sacramento, CA 95814. ✆ **800/522-1555** or 916/446-1481. Fax 916/448-0364. 108 units. $85 double. Extra person $10. Children under 19 stay free in parents' room. Rates include continental breakfast. AE, DC, DISC, MC, V. **Amenities:** Restaurant; heated pool; nearby golf course; laundry service; same-day dry cleaning. *In room:* A/C, TV, coffeemaker, hair dryer, iron; some units with fridge.

WHERE TO DINE
EXPENSIVE

Biba 🌟🌟🌟 ITALIAN   Locals flock to this sleek neo–Art Deco restaurant to sample the classical Italian cuisine of Bologna-born owner Biba Caggiano, who recently published her eighth cookbook. Although the menu changes seasonally, you can expect to find about 10 pastas and an equal number of main courses. There might be a delicate pappardelle with a fresh-seafood sauce, or a more pungent spaghetti alla Siciliana, which combines eggplant, tomatoes, capers, garlic, and anchovies. For a main course, the classic *osso buco* Milanese served with a soft, creamy polenta is excellent, but save room for the double-chocolate trifle made with dark and white chocolate, Grand Marnier–soaked pound cake, and raspberry puree.

2801 Capitol Ave. ✆ **916/455-2422.** www.biba-restaurant.com. Main courses $17–$23. AE, DC, MC, V. Mon–Fri 11:30am–2:30pm; Mon–Thurs 5:30–9:30pm; Fri–Sat 5:30–10:30pm.

Twenty Eight ★★ CALIFORNIA   Named after the restaurant's cross street, Twenty Eight is a contender for the city's best restaurant. This place is serious about food, going so far as to bake its own bread and grow many of the veggies served. The menu, which changes seasonally, serves such tempting fare as pork loin carefully grilled to that magic spot between rare and overdone, served on a bed of polenta with sage and blue cheese. Other notable entrees include sweet-pea ravioli with hedgehog mushrooms; pan-seared fresh daily scallops with mashed potatoes, caramelized shallots, and vanilla oil; and grilled quail with an artichoke and a salad of mustard greens and blood oranges. It's a popular hangout for lobbyists and legislators, and because it only seats 55, reservations are a must.

2730 N St. ✆ **916/456-2800.** Reservations recommended. Main courses $15–$28. AE, DISC, MC, V. Mon–Sat 5–10pm.

MODERATE

Harlow's ★ MEDITERRANEAN/CALIFORNIA   This comfortable, casual, and very popular supper club has a 1930s air that might have pleased Jean Harlow herself. If you've got a hot date for the night, suggest meeting at the bar: It's one of Sacramento's most fashionable places to see and be seen. The Italian dishes are very good here—ranging from the simple house-made smoked-chicken ravioli to the elaborate veal Portofino stuffed with chicken, hot salami, and Parmesan and baked in a sherry-mushroom-cream sauce. Top it all off with the chocolate paté, and lean back and enjoy the live music (swing, salsa, reggae, and R&B) that starts nightly at 10pm. After dinner, join the party upstairs at the MoMo Lounge, where you can often find some of Sacramento's best jazz groups.

2708 J St. ✆ **916/441-4693.** Main courses $12–$24. AE, MC, V. Wed–Sun 5:30–9pm.

Paragary's Bar and Oven ★★ MEDITERRANEAN   Occupying two distinct dining rooms just across the street from Twenty Eight, Paragary's is widely considered the best moderately priced restaurant in Sacramento's downtown area. During good weather, the best seats are outside amid the gorgeous fountains and plantings of the courtyard; other seating options include the formal fireplace room and the brightly lit cafe. The same menu is served no matter where you sit, with some of the best dishes coming from the kitchen's wood-burning pizza oven. But this is more than a gourmet pizza parlor, as evidenced by the grilled rib-eye steak with mashed potatoes, portobello mushrooms, and grilled leeks, or the hand-cut rosemary noodles with seared chicken, pancetta, artichokes, leeks, and garlic.

1401 28th St. ✆ **916/457-5737.** Main courses $12–$20. AE, DC, DISC, MC, V. Mon–Thurs 11:30am–11pm; Fri 11:30am–midnight; Sat 4:30pm–midnight; Sun 4:30–10pm.

33rd Street Bistro ★ BISTRO   Seattle transplants Fred Haynes (chef) and his brother Matt (manager) have taken an old brick building and transformed it into a bistro that's been a raging success from the day it opened. And it's popular for all the right reasons—the food is good (and priced right), the staff is friendly and helpful, and the ambiance is warm and cheerful. Selections include a variety of Italian grilled sandwiches and house favorites such as wood-roasted vegetables with sun-dried tomatoes and goat-cheese crostini; Uncle Bum's jerk ribs with Jamaican barbecue sauce and key-lime crème fraîche; and wood-roasted pork loin with ancho-chili butter and linguisa risotto.

3301 Folsom Blvd. (at 33rd St.). ✆ **916/455-2282.** Main courses $8–$17. AE, MC, V. Sun–Thurs 8am–10pm; Fri and Sat 8am–11pm.

INEXPENSIVE

Fox & Goose Public House ★★ *(Value* ENGLISH PUB   The Fox is your classic British pub, right down to the dartboard, giant picture of the queen, and numerous varieties of beers from across the pond. The soups at lunch are excellent, and the specials often include bangers and mash, Welsh rarebit, and Cornish pasties. The burnt cream dessert is famous. Either arrive early for lunch or be prepared for a wait, as locals love this place (no reservations taken and they won't even seat you until all the members of your party have arrived). Equally popular breakfasts include kippers, grilled tomatoes, and crumpets, as well as the ubiquitous waffles, omelets, and French toast. There's live entertainment by local bands 6 nights a week, as well as pub grub like fish and chips and hamburgers Monday through Friday from 5:30 to 9:30pm.

1001 R St. (at 10th St.). © **916/443-8825.** Reservations not accepted. Main courses $4–$7. AE, MC, V. Mon–Fri 7am–2pm; Sat–Sun 8am–1pm. Bar stays open until midnight Mon–Thurs, until 2am Fri–Sat.

Tower Café INTERNATIONAL   The Tower Café gets its name from the building in which it's located: a grand old 1939 movie house with a tall Art Deco spire. The restaurant occupies the same space in which a small mom-and-pop music store once stood. This former resident, Tower Records, has since grown into America's second-largest record retailer. While it's unlikely that Tower Café will share the phenomenal success of its predecessor, it's popular with locals. The multi-cultural decor—kind of Art Deco meets *National Geographic*— is a feast for the eyes. Dishes reflect a variety of international flavors, from the Jamaican jerk chicken to Shanghai chow mein. Sometimes the food is good, but sometimes you wonder what's going on in the kitchen. On warm days, it seems as if everyone in the city is lunching here on the large outdoor deck (in fact, recent patrons included the president and his staff), so people watching can be a real treat.

1518 Broadway. © **916/441-0222.** Main courses $8–$14. AE, MC, V. Sun–Thurs 8am–10pm; Fri and Sat 8am–10:30pm, with dessert and drinks only until 11:30pm.

2 The Gold Country ★★

Cutting a serpentine swath for nearly 350 miles along aptly numbered Calif. 49, the Gold Country stretches from Sierra City to the foothills of Yosemite. Much of this rugged region still retains its '49er ambiance: Mining sites, horse ranches, and Wild West saloons are common sights in these parts. Along with its numerous ghost towns and gold rush–era architecture, it's enough to make Gene Autry or Roy Rogers feel right at home.

The town of Placerville, 44 miles east of Sacramento at the intersection of U.S. 50 and Calif. 49, is in the approximate center of the Gold Country. To the north are the classic old mining towns of Grass Valley and Nevada City, while in the central and southern Gold Country are such well-preserved towns as Amador City, Sutter Creek, Columbia, and Jamestown, to name just a few.

In fact, the Gold Country is so immense that it would take weeks to thoroughly explore. But rather than provide an exhaustive list of each and every town, we have instead narrowed our coverage to include three of our favorite regions, each of which can be thoroughly explored in just 2 or 3 days: the utterly charming side-by-side towns of Nevada City and Grass Valley to the north; the well-preserved gold-rush communities of Amador City, Sutter Creek, and Jackson, in the central Gold Country; and at the southern end of Gold Country, the

To Nevada City & Grass Valley
Bowman
Applegate
80
Newcastle
193
Foresthill
Loomis
49
Auburn
Rocklin
80
Rubicon River
TAHOE NATIONAL FOREST
5
99
Rio Linda
Roseville
Carmichael
193
Georgetown
FOLSOM STATE REC. AREA
Granite Bay
49
193
Coloma
ELDORADO NATIONAL FOREST
American River
Folsom Reservoir
Marshall Gold Discovery State Hist. Park
E9
Sacramento
Rancho Cordova
Folsom
Placerville
Florin
99
El Dorado Hills
Cameron Park
50
Diamond Springs
Camino
Union Valley Res.
Pollock Pines
Echo Lake
Elk Grove
16
El Dorado
South Fork American River
5
E13
Cosumnes River
49
E16
American River
50
Galt
104
Plymouth
E16
88
Amador City
Lodi
99
Ione
124
49
Indian Grinding Rocks State Hist. Park
88
Mokelumne River
Sutter Creek
88
Comanche Res.
Jackson
Volcano
88
Lockeford
12
Pardee Res.
West Point
88
Mokelumne River
TOIYABE NATIONAL FOREST
Salt Springs Res.
Valley Springs
Mokelumne Hill
26
Linden
26
26
New Hogan Res.
San Andreas
Calaveras Big Trees State Park
4
J6
J14
49
Arnold
STANISLAUS NATIONAL FOREST
4
Woodward Res.
Mercer Caverns
4
J7
Murphys
Stanislaus River
Beardsleys Res.
J6
4
New Melones Lake U.S. Bureau of Reclamation
Angels Camp
Columbia State Historic Park
108
Escalon
New Melones Lake
49
Columbia
J14
Tulloch Res.
Tuttletown
Sugar Pine
Mi-Wuk Village
Pinecrest
Oakdale
Sonora
108
108
TOIYABE NATIONAL FOREST
Riverbank
Jamestown
Twain Harte
132
Waterford
49
Tuolumne
Modesto Lake
132
Cherry Lake
YOSEMITE NATIONAL PARK
Turlock Lake St. Rec. Area
Lake Don Pedro
120
Tuolumne River
Lake Eleanor
J17
Turlock Lake
132
Hetch Hetchy Res.
McConnell St. Rec. Area
J16
Grand Canyon of the Tuolumne
Livingston
Couterville
Lake McLure
SIERRA NATIONAL FOREST
59
Merced River
99
Winton
49
Atwater
J16
Bagby Rec. Area
140
Sacramento
The Gold Country
140
J7
Merced National Wildlife Refuge
Merced
San Francisco
CALIFORNIA
59
99
Planada
140
Mariposa
Los Angeles
Le Grand
49

✈ Airport
🌲 State Park

0   10 mi
0   10 km

wonderfully authentic neighboring mining towns of Angels Camp, Murphys, Columbia, Sonora, and Jamestown.

Any of these three regions will provide an excellent base for exploring and experiencing the Gold Country, whether you're intent on panning for gold, exploring old mines and caverns, or rafting the area's many white-water rivers. In fact, the Gold Country is one of the most underrated and least congested tourist destinations in California, a winning combination of Old West ambiance, adorable (and affordable) bed-and-breakfasts, and outdoor adventures galore.

THE NORTHERN GOLD COUNTRY: NEVADA CITY & GRASS VALLEY

Lying about 60 miles northeast of Sacramento, Nevada City and Grass Valley are far and away the top tourist destinations of the northern Gold Country.

These two historic towns were at the center of the hard-rock mining fields of northern California. Grass Valley, in fact, was California's richest mining town, producing more than a billion dollars worth of gold. Both are attractive, although we usually spend most of our time traipsing through Nevada City. Its wealth of Victorian homes and storefronts makes it one of the most appealing small towns in California, particularly in the fall when the maple trees are ablaze with color. (In fact, its entire downtown has been designated a National Historic Landmark.)

It's easy to get here. If you're driving from San Francisco, take I-80 to the Calif. 49 turnoff in Auburn and follow the signs. For information about the area, go to—or call in advance—the **Grass Valley/Nevada County Chamber of Commerce,** 248 Mill St., Grass Valley, CA 95945 (© **800/655-4667** (CA only) or 530/273-4667), or the **Nevada City Chamber of Commerce,** 132 Main St., Nevada City, CA 95959 (© **800/655-NJOY** or 530/265-2692; www. nevadacitychamber.com).

NEVADA CITY ★★

Rumors of miners pulling a pound of gold a day out of Deer Creek brought thousands of fortune seekers to the area in 1849. Within a year, Nevada City was a boisterous town of 10,000, the third largest city in California. In its heyday, everyone who was anyone visited this rollicking Western outpost with its busy red-light district. Mark Twain lectured here in 1866, telling the audience about his trips to the Sandwich Islands (Hawaii). Former President Herbert Hoover also lived and worked here as a gold miner.

Pick up a walking-tour map at the **Chamber of Commerce,** 132 Main St., and stroll the streets lined with impressive Victorian buildings, including the **Firehouse Number 1 Museum,** 214 Main St. (© **530/265-5468**), complete with bell tower, gingerbread decoration, a small museum that displays mementos from the Donner Party, a Maidu Indian basket collection, and an altar from a temple originally located in the Chinese section of Grass Valley. Admission is free. It's open in summer daily from 11am to 4pm; winter hours (from November 1 to April 1) are Thursday through Sunday from 11am to 4pm. The **National Hotel** (built between 1854 and 1856) is here (we always stop in at the handsome gold rush–era bar for a refresher), as is the **Nevada Theatre** (1865), one of the oldest theaters in the nation still operating as such. Today, it's home to the Foothill Theatre Company.

If you want to see the source of much of the city's wealth, visit **Malakoff Diggins State Historic Park** ★, 23579 N. Bloomfield Rd. (© **530/265-2740**), 28 miles northeast of Nevada City. Once the world's largest hydraulic gold mine, it's an awesome (some might say disturbing) spectacle of hydraulic mining—nearly half a mountain has been washed away by powerful jets of water, leaving behind a 600-foot-deep canyon of exposed rock. In the 1870s, North Bloomfield, then located in the middle of this park, had a population of 1,500. Some of the buildings have been reconstructed and refurnished to show what life was like then. The 3,000-acre park also offers several hiking trails, swimming at Blair Lake, and 30 campsites that can be reserved through **Reserve America** (© **800/ 444-7275;** www.reserveamerica.com). The museum is open daily in summer from 10am to 5pm, in winter on weekends only from 10am to 4pm. To reach the park, take Calif. 49 toward Downieville for 11 miles. Turn right onto Tyler-Foote Crossing Road for 17 miles. The name will change to Curzon Grade and then to Backbone. Turn right onto Derbec Road and into the park. The fee is $2 per car.

Another 6 miles up Calif. 49 from the Malakoff Diggins turnoff will bring you to Pleasant Valley Road, the exit that will take you (in about 7 miles) to one of the most impressive **covered bridges** in the country. Built in 1862, it's 225 feet long and was crossed by many a stagecoach (in autumn, it makes for a spectacular photo opportunity).

Where to Stay

Deer Creek Inn Bed & Breakfast ⊛★ An 1860 three-floor Victorian overlooking Deer Creek and within walking distance of downtown Nevada City, this inn feels like a warm home-away-from-home. The individually decorated rooms, most with private verandas facing the creek or town, are furnished with assorted antiques and four-poster or canopy beds with down comforters. Most bathrooms have clawfoot tubs. A full breakfast is served either out on the deck or in the formal dining room. Guests are invited to try a little panning of their own, fish, play croquet, or simply relax and enjoy the lawn and landscaped rose gardens along the creek.

116 Nevada St., Nevada City, CA 95959. © **800/655-0363** or 530/265-0363. Fax 530/265-0980. www. deercreekinn.com. 5 units. $100–$165 double. Rates include breakfast. AE, MC, V. **Amenities:** Nearby golf course; bike rental. *In room:* A/C; phone on request.

Emma Nevada House ⊛★★ One of the finest—and prettiest—B&Bs in the Gold Country, Emma Nevada House is a picture-perfect Victorian that was the childhood home of 19th-century opera star Emma Nevada. You'll like everything about Emma Nevada: the quiet location, sun-drenched decks, wraparound porch, understated decor, and particularly breakfast, which is served in the beautiful hexagonal Sun Room. The guest rooms range from small and intimate to large and luxurious; all have private bathrooms and queen-size beds. Top choice for honeymooners is the Empress's Chamber, with its large wall of windows, soothing ivory and burgundy tones, and—of course—the Jacuzzi tub for two. You'll also like the fact that the shops and restaurants of Nevada City's Historic District are only a short walk away.

528 E. Broad St., Nevada City, CA 95959. © **800/916-EMMA** or 530/265-4415. Fax 530/265-4416. www. emmanevadahouse.com. 6 units. $110–$170 double. Rates include breakfast. AE, MC, V. **Amenities:** Concierge. *In room:* A/C, hair dryer, iron; phone on request.

National Hotel You can't miss this classic three-story Victorian, the oldest hotel in continuous operation west of the Rocky Mountains, and it shows its age. Some folks feel this makes it more historic and authentic, others may opt for more upscale and restored lodgings. It's located near what was once the center of the town's red-light district. The lobby is full of mementos from that era, hence the grandfather clock and early square piano. The suites are replete with gold rush–era antiques and large, cozy beds. Most rooms have private bathrooms, and some come with canopy beds and romantic love seats. A definite bonus during typically sweltering summers is the secluded swimming pool filled with cool mountain water.

The hotel's Victorian dining room, which serves traditional items such as prime rib, steaks, lobster tail, and homemade desserts, also has a gold-rush atmosphere; tables, for example, are lit with coal oil lamps. The hotel provides live entertainment on Friday and Saturday nights. There's also a popular Sunday brunch, one of the best in the county.

211 Broad St., Nevada City, CA 95959. ② 530/265-4551. Fax 530/265-2445. 42 units, 30 with private bathroom. $75 double with bathroom; from $119 suite with bathroom. AE, MC, V. **Amenities:** Restaurant, bar; outdoor pool; business center; room service. *In room:* A/C, TV, dataport.

Red Castle Historic Lodgings ✪   This elegant, comfortable hillside inn occupies a four-story Gothic Revival brick house built in 1860, situated in a secluded spot with a panoramic view of the town. The highlight of the week is the Sunday "Conversations with Mark Twain," in which guests can engage the great author (or at least a reasonable facsimile) in conversation while enjoying breakfast or afternoon tea. The house retains its original woodwork, plaster moldings, ceiling medallions, and much of the handmade glass. It lacks any modern intrusions, such as TVs and phones. Guests enjoy bountiful five-course buffet breakfasts and relax on the verandas that encircle the first two floors of the house and overlook the rose gardens. Our favorite rooms are the Garden Room, with a canopy bed and French doors leading into the gardens, and the three-room garret suite tucked under the eaves, furnished with sleigh beds and featuring Gothic arched windows.

109 Prospect St., Nevada City, CA 95959. ② 800/761-4766 or 530/265-5135. www.historic-lodgings.com. 7 units. $110–$165 double. Rates include breakfast. MC, V. *In room:* A/C; no phone.

Where to Dine

Citronée ✪✪ REGIONAL AMERICAN/INTERNATIONAL   After being underserved with serious restaurants for some years, Nevada City has taken a leap forward with two new, notable temples to fine cuisine—Citronée and New Moon (see below). It took a review by *The New York Times* to get California food mavens to turn their appetites from Napa and San Francisco to Citronée and the Gold Country. And Owner and Chef Robert Perez's new restaurant is indeed worth exploring. For example, at lunch the barbecued brisket sandwich topped with white cheddar cheese on chipotle focaccia served with cayenne-dusted waffle potato chips is a must try; or, at dinner, the highly acclaimed appetizer of rare seared ahi tuna with a crust of black and white sesame seeds served with a soy chili vinaigrette and wasabi crème fraîche or the oven-roasted Maui onion stuffed with sautéed wild mushrooms on a bed of creamy polenta with a thyme lavender honey sauce. Mmm. And if that isn't enough, ask for the special menu gastronomique, a five-course surprise menu specially chosen each night to drive you out of your mind. *Wine Spectator* magazine recently awarded Citronée its award of excellence for their selection of over 140 wines.

320 Broad St. ② 530/265-5697. Reservations recommended. Main courses $13–$25. AE, MC, V. Mon–Thurs 5:30–9:30 or 10:30pm; Sat 5–9:30 or 10:30pm.

Country Rose Café ✪ COUNTRY FRENCH   The flowery country-French atmosphere of this popular Nevada City restaurant belies a serious (and seriously priced) menu put together by owner and chef Michael Johns. Dinner selections, written on a huge board that's lugged over to your table soon after you've been seated, are mostly French with a dash of Italian, Mexican, and American dishes. Skip the typical pastas and head straight for John's specialty—fresh fish prepared in a myriad of classic styles such as filet of sole dore, swordfish oskar, and sea bass with garlic-basil sauce. Other regular menu items include filet mignon, lobster, rack of lamb, and roast game hen, all served with soup or salad. Both lunch (handled by Michael's son Dave) and dinner are served on the pretty walled-in patio in the summer, so be sure to request alfresco seating when making a reservation.

300 Commercial St. (**) 530/265-6252. Reservations recommended. Main courses $14–$31. AE, DC, MC, V. Daily 11am–2:30pm; Sun–Thurs 5–9pm; Fri–Sat 5–10pm; Sun brunch 11am–2:30pm.

Friar Tucks ✪ INTERNATIONAL   A local favorite for nearly a quarter of a century, this restaurant consists of a series of rustic, dimly lit rooms furnished with high-backed oak booths. The eclectic menu changes weekly, offering everything from French fondues and Swiss meatballs to teriyaki steak, rack of lamb, fresh seafood, filet mignon, and roast duck. Request a table in the dining room that overlooks Nevada City's Historic District. The accompanying wine list recently won its third *Wine Spectator* Award of Excellence. With the flavor and ambiance of a British pub, the bar is a popular local hangout; a guitar player entertains nightly from 7pm.

111 N. Pine St. (**) 530/265-9093. Main courses $16–$24. AE, MC, V. Sun–Thurs 5–9:30pm; Fri–Sat 5–10pm.

Kirby's Creekside Restaurant & Bar ✪ INTERNATIONAL   After being royally thumped by the floods of 1997, Kirby's Creekside is better than ever serving a wide variety of steak, seafood, pasta, and chicken accompanied by the sights and sounds of Deer Creek, which literally flows underneath the restaurant's large wood deck. If possible, forego the low-ceilinged dining room for a far more romantic table outdoors. For starters, try the fresh-pumpkin ravioli in sage cream sauce or steamed mussels with chive sauce and sherry aïoli. Recommended dinner choices include the oven-roasted leg of lamb with honey-thyme sauce, and the stuffed pork loin with orange port sauce; or take a chance with the "Chef's Grand Creation: unique and exotic creations supremely chosen by the chef." Lunch is more modest—sandwiches, burgers, salads, and half a dozen hot entrees, all surprisingly inexpensive.

101 Broad St. (**) 530/265-3445. Reservations suggested. Main courses $14–$25. AE, DISC, MC, V. Mon–Thurs 11:30am–2:30pm and 5–9:30pm; Fri–Sat 11:30am–2:30pm and 5–10pm; Sun 10am–2:30pm and 5–8:30pm.

New Moon ✪✪ AMERICAN/INTERNATIONAL   After a five-year hiatus Nevada City's favorite chef, Peter Selaya, is back in the kitchen with a new restaurant and a menu of imaginatively prepared items that feature free-range and antibiotic-free meats and poultry, house-baked breads, and house-made fresh pastas using organic flours and grains, and local organic vegetables when available—which is regularly in this hotbed of natural foodstuffs. So not only is the food healthy, it actually tastes great! Dinner entrees include the likes of a lean Niman Ranch top sirloin cap grilled with a roast garlic zinfandel and rosemary sauce, or fresh line-caught, wild salmon pan-seared with julienne vegetables and a beurre blanc verjus. The raviolis with different stuffings are made fresh daily, as are the house-made desserts. Fresh strawberry Napoleons recently tasted were beyond delicious. Nevada City's balmy climate makes the front deck a great place to dine and people watch.

203 York St. (**) 530/265-6399. Reservations recommended. Main courses $15–$21. AE, DC, MC, V. Tues–Fri 11:30am–2pm; Tues–Sun 5–8pm (or later).

GRASS VALLEY ✷

In contrast to Nevada City's "tourist town" image, Grass Valley is the commercial and retail center of the region. The **Empire Mine State Historic Park** ✷, 10791 E. Empire St., Grass Valley (✆ **530/273-8522**), the largest and richest gold mine in California, is just outside of town. This mine, which once had 367 miles of underground shafts, produced an estimated 5.8 million ounces of gold between 1850 and 1956, when it closed. Here you can look down the shaft of the mine, walk around the mine yard, and stroll through the gardens of the mine owner. From March through November, tours are given daily, and a mining movie is shown. You can also enjoy picnicking, cycling, mountain biking, or hiking in the 784-acre park. It's open year-round except for Thanksgiving, Christmas, and New Year's Day. Admission to the park, tour, and museum is $1 for adults and children, and dogs are free.

In town, visitors can pick up a walking-tour map at the **Chamber of Commerce,** 248 Mill St., and explore the historic downtown area along Mill and Main Streets. There are also a few museums that California-history and gold-mining buffs will want to visit: the **Grass Valley Museum,** 410 S. Church St., adjacent to St. Joseph's Cultural Center (✆ **530/273-5509**); the **North Star Mining Museum,** at the south end of Mill Street at Allison Ranch Road (✆ **530/273-4255**); and the **Video History Museum,** in the center of Memorial Park off Calif. 174 (✆ **530/274-1126**), which houses a collection of old films of the region from the 1920s.

Grass Valley was, for a time, the home of **Lola Montez,** singer, dancer, and paramour of the rich and famous. A fully restored home that she bought and occupied in 1853 can be viewed at 248 Mill St., now the site of Grass Valley's Chamber of Commerce. **Lotta Crabtree,** Montez's famous protégé, lived down the street at 238 Mill St., now an apartment house. Also pop into the **Holbrooke Hotel,** 212 Main St., to see the signature of Mark Twain, who stayed here, as did five U.S. presidents. The saloon has been in continuous use since 1852, and it's the place to meet the locals and have a tall cold one.

The surrounding region offers many recreational opportunities on its rivers and lakes and in the Tahoe National Forest. You can enjoy fishing, swimming, and boating at **Scotts Flat Lake** near Nevada City (east on Calif. 20) and at **Rollins Lake** on Calif. 174, between Grass Valley and Colfax. White-water rafting is available on several rivers. **Tributary Whitewater Tours,** 20480 Woodbury Dr., Grass Valley, CA 95949 (✆ **800/672-3846** or 530/346-6812; www.whitewatertours.com), offers half- to 3-day trips from March through October. The region is also ideal for mountain biking. The chambers of commerce publish a trail guide, but there's nowhere to rent a bike in either Nevada City or Grass Valley, so bring your own wheels. For regional hiking information, contact **Tahoe National Forest Headquarters,** at Coyote Street and Calif. 49 in Nevada City (✆ **530/265-4531**).

Where to Stay

Holbrooke Hotel ✷   This Victorian-era white-clapboard building was a rollicking saloon during the gold-rush days, and then evolved into a place for exhausted miners to "rack out." The oldest and most historic hotel in town, it has hosted a number of legendary figures since opening its doors: Ulysses Grant, Mark Twain, Benjamin Harrison, and Grover Cleveland, among others. Seventeen of the rooms lie within the main building. The remainder are in an adjacent annex, a house occupied long ago by the hotel's owner. Each guest room is decorated with an eclectic collection of gold rush–era furniture and antiques. All have cable TVs tucked away in armoires, and most bathrooms have clawfoot tubs. If you can, reserve one of the larger Veranda rooms that face Main Street and have access to the balconies, it's well worth the few extra dollars.

212 W. Main St., Grass Valley, CA 95945. ☎ **800/933-7077** or 530/273-1353. Fax 530/273-0434. www. holbrooke.com. 28 units. $58–$115 double; $100–$155 suite. Rates include breakfast. AE, DC, DISC, MC, V. **Amenities:** Restaurant, saloon; business center; salon. *In room:* A/C, TV.

Where to Dine

Arletta's at the Holbrooke AMERICAN   This elegant hotel dining room is the most formal place in town—an ironic twist, given its past life as a gold-rush saloon and a flophouse for drunken miners. In its way, it's the most authentic and nostalgic restaurant in a town filled with worthy hardworking competitors. Items on the ever-changing menu range from braised pork loin with red chile applesauce to grilled breast of chicken stuffed with boursin cheese, pine nuts, and roasted red peppers. Lunch prices are lower, ranging from $6.95 for a BLT with applewood smoked bacon to $8.95 for a tasty spinach pasta with portobello mushrooms, roasted garlic, red peppers, julienne vegetables, herbs, Parmesan cheese, and rock shrimp.

212 W. Main St. (in the Holbrooke Hotel). ☎ **530/273-1353.** Reservations recommended on Fri–Sat nights. Main courses $12.50–$23. AE, DC, DISC, MC, V. Daily 11:30am–2pm and 5:30–9pm; Sun 10am–2pm and 5–8:30pm.

Tofanelli's (Value) INTERNATIONAL   If a diet of meat and potatoes isn't your cup of tea, head to Tofanelli's, which specializes in good—and good for you—entrees for brunch, lunch, and dinner. You'll like the setting, a bright, cheery trio of dining areas (atrium, outdoor patio, and dining room) separated by exposed brick walls and decorated with beautiful prints and paintings. Specials on the menu, such as Gorgonzola ravioli topped with garlic cream sauce or pad Thai noodles with fresh ginger and marinated beef, change weekly, but you can always rely on Tofanelli classics like Linda's famous vegetarian lasagna and the popular veggie burger. And yes, they serve good ol' New York steak, too. Don't you dare depart without a slice of Katherine's chocolate cake.

302 W. Main St. ☎ **530/272-1468.** Main courses $7–$15. AE, MC, V. Mon–Fri 7am–8:30pm; Sat brunch 8:30am–3pm, dinner 5–9pm; Sun brunch 8:30am–3pm, dinner 5–8:30pm.

THE CENTRAL GOLD COUNTRY: AMADOR CITY, SUTTER CREEK & JACKSON

Though Placerville is technically the center of the Gold Country, it's the small trio of towns a few miles to the south—Amador City, Sutter Creek, and Jackson—that are far and away the most appealing destination in this beautiful region of rolling hills, dotted with solitary oaks and granite outcroppings. When the mining boom went bust, most of the towns were abandoned; nowadays, most of these restored gold-rush towns rely solely on tourism (hence the rapid conversion of many Victorian homes into B&Bs), though a few mines have reopened recently and are reportedly making a profit.

One of the advantages of staying in this area, 55 miles southeast of Sacramento, is that both the northern and southern regions of the Gold Country are only a few hours' drive away (via very winding roads, however). If you're intent on seeing as much of the Gold Country as possible in a few days' time, any one of these three towns will suffice as a good home base.

To reach Amador City, Sutter Creek, or Jackson from Placerville, head south along Calif. 49 past Plymouth and Drytown. If you're coming straight here from Sacramento, take U.S. 50 to Placerville and head south on Calif. 49; Calif. 16

from Sacramento is another option, but only slightly faster. For more information about any of these towns, contact the **Amador County Chamber of Commerce,** 125 Peek St., Jackson (© **209/223-0350;** www.amadorcounty chamber.com).

AMADOR CITY ✮

Once a bustling mining town, Amador City is now devoted mostly to dredging up tourist dollars. Although Amador City sounds large and impressive, it is in fact so tiny that it holds the title as the smallest incorporated city in California. Local merchants have made the most of a refurbished block-long boardwalk, converting the historic false-fronted buildings into a gallery of sorts; the stores sell everything from turn-of-the-century antiques and folk art to handcrafted furniture, gold-rush memorabilia, rare books, and Native American crafts. Parking can be difficult, however, especially in summer.

Where to Stay & Dine

Imperial Hotel ✮   Proprietors Bruce Sherrill and Dale Martin did a brilliant job restoring this stately century-old brick hotel and restaurant, located at the foot of Main Street overlooking Amador City. The individually decorated rooms—all with private bathrooms—are furnished with brass, iron, or pine beds and numerous antiques; two come with private balconies. Our favorite room features hand-painted, whimsical furnishings by local artist John Johannsen. The Imperial Hotel restaurant, serving Mediterranean/California cuisine, has a sterling reputation, and hotel guests can take advantage of room service when it's open from 5 to 9pm. The restaurant is worth a detour, even if you aren't staying here.

Main St. (Calif. 49), P.O. Box 195, Amador City, CA 95601-0195. © **800/242-5594** or 209/267-9172. Fax 209/ 267-9249. www.imperialamador.com. 6 units. $85–$115 double. Rates include breakfast. AE, DISC, MC, V. Located right on Calif. 49, in an 1879 brick Victorian building. **Amenities:** Restaurant, bar; room service; in-room massage. *In room:* A/C, hair dryer; no phone.

SUTTER CREEK ✮

The self-proclaimed "nicest little town in the Mother Lode," Sutter Creek was named after sawmill owner John Sutter, employer of James Marshall (the first white man to discover gold in California). Railroad baron Leland Stanford made his fortune at Sutter Creek's Lincoln Mine, and then invested his millions to both build the transcontinental railroad and fund his successful campaign to become governor of California.

The town is a real charmer, lined with beautiful 19th-century buildings in pristine condition, including **Downs Mansion,** the former home of the foreman at Stanford's mine (now a private residence on Spanish St., across from the Immaculate Conception Church), and the landmark **Knight's Foundry,** 81 Eureka St., off Main Street (no phone), the last water-powered foundry and machine shop in the nation. There are also numerous shops and galleries along Main Street, though finding a free parking space can be a real challenge on summer weekends.

Where to Stay & Dine

The Foxes ✮✮   This 1857 clapboard house is Sutter Creek's most elegant hostelry. The seven rooms are all uniquely decorated, each with a queen-size bed and down comforters. Four rooms, including the Garden Room and the Fox Den, have wood-burning fireplaces. The Fox Den also has a little library of its own, while the Victorian suite features a 9-foot-tall Renaissance Revival bed and a separate sitting room. All have private bathrooms. Breakfast, cooked to order and delivered on silver service along with the morning paper, can be served in your room or in the gazebo in the garden.

77 Main St. (P.O. Box 159), Sutter Creek, CA 95685. © 800/987-3344 or 209/267-5882. Fax 209/267-0712. www.foxesinn.com. 7 units. $135–$195 double. Rates include breakfast. DISC, MC, V. *In room:* A/C, hair dryer; most units with TV/VCR and fridge. No phone.

Grey Gables Inn *★* The Grey Gables Inn is a postcard-perfect replica of a Victorian manor made all the more English by Roger and Sue Garlick, two amicable British expatriates who relish being innkeepers. The two-story B&B is surrounded by terraces of colorful gardens and embellished with fountains and vine-covered arbors. "A touch of the English countryside," says Sue. Each of the plushly carpeted guest rooms is named after a British poet; the Byron Room, for example, features hues of deep green and burgundy, dark-wood furnishings, and a Renaissance Revival bed. Aside from the king-size bed in the Brontë Room and Victorian Suite, all rooms have queen beds, gas-log fireplaces, large armoires, and private bathrooms (a few with clawfoot tubs). Breakfast, delivered on fine English bone china, is served either in the formal dining room adjacent to the Victorian parlor or in your room. The only flaw in an otherwise perfect B&B is the bit-too-close proximity to heavily traveled Calif. 49, but once inside you'll hardly notice. The shops and restaurants of Sutter Creek are within walking distance.

161 Hanford St., Sutter Creek, CA 95685. © 800/473-9422 or 209/267-1039. Fax 209/267-0998. www.greygables.com. 8 units. $105–$180 double. AE, DC, DISC, MC, V. *In room:* A/C, hair dryer; no phone.

Zinfandels *★★* CALIFORNIA   Greg and Kelley West's Zinfandels has received nothing but kudos since it first opened in July 1996. Greg, a 6-year veteran of Greens Restaurant (a highly respected vegetarian restaurant in San Francisco; see chapter 4, "San Francisco"), is responsible for the entrees, while his wife, Kelley, bakes the breads and pastries. Though the emphasis is on low-fat vegetarian fare such as butternut-squash risotto with pancetta, leeks, crimini mushrooms, and spinach, West also offers a trio of fresh fish, chicken, and beef dishes ranging from cannelloni filled with lamb sausage, chard, and smoked mozzarella to Petrale sole with a citrus-ginger beurre blanc. The menu changes monthly to take advantage of seasonal produce from local farms, and even the wines—paired with each dish—are provided by local wineries such as Sobon and Karly. An appealing alternative to a full sit-down dinner is the wine-tasting-appetizer-dessert room downstairs.

51 Hanford St. © 209/267-5008. www.zinfood.com. Reservations recommended. Main courses $16.95–$24.95. AE, DISC, MC, V. Thurs–Sun 5:30–9:30pm.

JACKSON *★*

Jackson, the county seat of Amador County, is far livelier than its neighboring towns to the north. (It was the last place in California to outlaw prostitution.) Be sure to take time to stroll through the center of town, browsing in the stores and admiring the Victorian architecture. Although the Kennedy and Argonaut mines ultimately produced more than $140 million in gold, Jackson initially earned its place in the gold rush as a supply center. That history is apparent in the town's wide Main Street, lined by tall buildings adorned with intricate iron railings.

Make no mistake: This is not a ghost town, but rather a modern mini-city that has worked to preserve its pre-Victorian influence. At the southern end of the street is the famous **National Hotel**, 2 Water St., at Main Street (© 209/223-0500), rumored to be California's oldest continuously operating hotel since it opened its doors in 1862. Will Rogers, John Wayne, Leland Stanford, and

Coloma: Where the Gold Rush Began

Located on Calif. 49 between Auburn and Placerville, the town of Coloma ✦ is so small, placid, and unpretentious that it's hard to imagine the significant role it played in the rapid development of California and the West. For it was here that James Marshall, working on John Sutter's mill, first discovered that there was gold aplenty in the foothills of California. Over the next 50 years, 125 *million* ounces of gold were taken from the Sierra foothills, an amount worth a staggering $50 billion today.

Although Marshall and Sutter tried to keep the discovery secret, word soon leaked out. Sam Brannan, who ran a general store at Fort Sutter, secured some gold samples himself—as well as significant amounts of choice Coloma real estate—and then headed for San Francisco, where he ran through the streets shouting, "Gold! Gold! Gold! From the American River!" San Francisco rapidly emptied as men rushed off to seek their fortunes at the mines (and make Sam Brannan's as well).

Coloma was quickly mined out, but its boom brought 10,000 people to the settlement and lasted long enough for residents to build a schoolhouse, a gunsmith, a general store, and a tiny, tin-roofed post office. The miners also planted oak and mimosa trees that shade the street during hot summers. About 70% of this quiet, pretty town lies in the **Marshall Gold Discovery State Historic Park** (© 530/622-3470), which preserves the spot where James Wilson Marshall discovered gold along the banks of the south fork of the American River.

Farther up Main Street is a huge replica of the mill Marshall was building when he made his discovery. The largest building in town, the mill is powered by electricity during the summer. Other attractions in the park include the **Gold Discovery Museum,** which relates the story of the gold rush, and a number of Chinese stores, all that remain of the once sizable local Chinese community. The park also has three picnic areas, four trails, recreational gold panning, and a number of buildings and exhibits relating the way of life that prevailed here in the 19th century. Admission is $5 per vehicle; hours are daily from 10am to 5pm, except on major holidays.

Folks also come here for white-water thrills on the American River. (Coloma is a popular launching point.) **White Water Connection,** in Coloma (© 530/622-6446), offers half- to 2-day trips down the frothy forks of the American River. It's great fun and one of the Gold Country's best outdoor attractions.

many other celebrities and big-time politicos of the 19th century stayed here. Today, the hotel's **Louisiana House Bar**—a cool, dark establishment where weary travelers can rest while a honky-tonk pianist beats out ragtime tunes and classic oldies—does a brisk business (alas, the guest rooms aren't nearly as enjoyable).

The **Amador County Museum,** a huge brick building at 225 Church St. (© **209/223-6386**), is where Will Rogers filmed *Boys Will Be Boys* in 1920.

Today, the former home of Armistead Calvin Brown and his 11 children is filled with mining memorabilia and information on two local mines, the Kennedy and the Argonaut, that were among the deepest and richest in the nation. Within the museum is a working large-scale model of the Kennedy. The museum is open Wednesday through Sunday from 10am to 4pm; admission is by a contribution of any amount. Tours of the museum cost $2 and are offered Saturday and Sunday on the hour from 11am to 3pm.

If you would rather see the real thing, head to the **Kennedy Tailing Wheels Park,** site of the famous Kennedy and Argonaut mines, the deepest in the Mother Lode. The mines have been closed for decades, but the huge tailing wheels and head frames, used to convey mine debris over the hills to a settling pond, remain. To reach the park, take Main Street to Jackson Gate Road, just north of Jackson (no phone).

A few miles south of Jackson on Calif. 49 is one of the most evocative mining towns of the region: **Mokelumne Hill** ★. The town basically consists of one street overlooking a valley with a few old buildings, and somehow its sad, abandoned air has the mark of authenticity. At one time, the hill was dotted with tents and wood-and-tar-paper shacks, and the town boasted a population of 15,000, including an old French quarter and a Chinatown. But now many of its former residents are merely memorialized in the town's Protestant, Jewish, and Catholic cemeteries.

Where to Stay & Dine

Court Street Inn ★   Two blocks from Main Street, this Victorian beauty— listed on the National Register of Historic Places—was built in 1870 and is brimming with elegant details such as eyelash shutters, embossed ceilings, and a marble fireplace. Our favorite room is Burgundy Court, with its oak-mantled fireplace and handsome four-poster king-size bed. Romantics will like the Bordeaux Court's private sitting room and four-poster wicker bed, or the separate and secluded Chablis Court with its own private terrace, skylight, and corner fireplace. The guest rooms are very nicely decorated; all have down bedding, and some have fireplaces and whirlpool or clawfoot tubs. The separate two-story/two-bedroom Indian House cottage can accommodate up to four guests. There's a porch where guests can relax outside, and an outdoor Jacuzzi that's ideal for stargazing. A full homemade breakfast (served outside on the terrace on sunny days) and complimentary evening refreshments are included in the room rate.

215 Court St., Jackson, CA 95642. © 800/200-0416 or 209/223-0416. Fax 209/223-5429. www.courtstreetinn. com. 6 units, 1 cottage. $110–$150 double, $170–$220 cottage. Rates include breakfast. AE, DISC, MC, V. **Amenities:** Jacuzzi. *In room:* A/C, TV on request, iron; no phone.

Mel and Faye's Diner (Value AMERICAN   How can anybody not love a classic old diner? In business since 1956, Mel and Faye have been cranking out the best diner food in the Gold Country for so long that it's okay to not feel guilty for salivating over the thought of a sloppy double cheeseburger smothered with onions and special sauce and washed down with a large chocolate shake, and could you please add a large side of fries with that, and how much is a slice of pie? It's a time-honored Jackson tradition.

205 Calif. 49 (at Main St.). © 209/223-0853. Menu items $4–$8. DISC, MC, V. Daily 4:45am–10pm.

Upstairs Restaurant & Streetside Bistro ★ INTERNATIONAL   This adorable little restaurant offers a limited menu that changes weekly, but you might stumble on some true culinary gems, such as pasta puttanesca with tomato-basil fettuccine and fresh Roma tomatoes, or julienned duck served with

A Visit to Volcano

About a dozen miles east of Jackson on Calif. 88 is the enchantingly decrepit town of Volcano ⭑, one of the most authentic ghost towns in the central Sierra. The town got its name in 1848, after miners mistook the origins of the enormous craggy boulders that lie in the center of town. The dark rock and blind window frames of a few backless, ivy-covered buildings give the town's main thoroughfare a haunted look. Sprinkled between boarded-up buildings, about 100 residents do business in the same sagging storefronts that a population of 8,000 frequented nearly 150 years ago.

One thing you'll notice about Volcano is the overwhelming silence of its streets. But the tiny, now-quiet burg has a rich history: Not only was this boomtown once home to 17 hotels, courts of quick justice, and the state's first lending library and astronomical observatory, but Volcano gold also supported the Union during the Civil War. Residents even smuggled a huge cannon to the front line in a hearse (it was never used). The story goes that had the enthusiastic blues fired it, it was so overcharged that "Old Abe" would have exploded. The cannon sits in the town center today, under a rusting weather vane.

Looming over the small buildings is the stately **St. George Hotel** ⭑ (© 209/296-4458; www.stgeorgehotel.com), a three-story, balconied building that testifies to the $90 million in gold mined in and around the town. Its ivy-covered brick and shuttered windows will remind you of colonial New England. In 1998 new owners took over the run-down 20-room hotel and have totally turned it around. The restaurant serves brunch on Sunday, and dinner Thursday through Sunday. Even if you're not hungry, stop in for a libation at the classic old bar, the Whiskey Flat Saloon.

In summer, the **Volcano Theatre Company** performs at the town's outdoor amphitheater, hidden behind stone facades on Main Street, a block north of the St. George Hotel. It's a wonderful Gold Country experience. For information on upcoming performances, call © 209/296-2525. And in early spring, hundreds of people come from all around to picnic amid the nearly half million daffodils in bloom on **Daffodil Hill**, a 4-acre ranch 3 miles north of Volcano (follow the sign on Ram's Horn Grade; no phone).

a blackberry-ginger sauce. Layne McCollum, a graduate of California's Culinary Academy, is known as the town's finest and most sophisticated chef, with a reputation for imaginative and innovative cuisine. Crisp white linens, bowls of fresh flowers, and background music provide a romantic backdrop to the restaurant's 12 candlelit tables. Lunch—quiche, soups, salads, and gourmet sandwiches such as smoked pork loin with red chili pesto on chipotle—is served until about 2:30pm in the bright, cheery Streetside Bistro, which is tastefully outfitted with wrought-iron furniture, tile flooring, and colorful oil paintings.

164 Main St. © 209/223-3342. Reservations recommended. Main courses $16–$30. AE, DISC, MC, V. Wed–Sun 11:30am–2:30pm, and 5:30–9pm.

THE SOUTHERN GOLD COUNTRY: ANGELS CAMP, MURPHYS, COLUMBIA, SONORA & JAMESTOWN

No other region in the Gold Country offers more to see and do than these towns in the south, 86 miles southeast of Sacramento. From exploring enormous caverns to riding in the stagecoach and panning for real gold, the neighboring towns of Angels Camp, Murphys, Columbia, Sonora, and Jamestown offer a cornucopia of gold rush–related sites, museums, and activities. It's a great place to bring the family (kids love roaming around the dusty car-free streets of Columbia), and the region offers some of the best lodgings and restaurants in the Gold Country. In short, if you're the Type-A sort who needs to stay active, the southern Gold Country is for you.

To reach any of these towns from Sacramento, head south on Calif. 99 to Stockton, then take Calif. 4 east directly into Angels Camp. (From here, it's a short, scenic drive to all the other towns.) For a much longer but more scenic route, take U.S. 50 east to Placerville and head south on Calif. 49, which also takes you directly to Angels Camp.

ANGELS CAMP ✪

You've probably heard of Angels Camp, the town that inspired Mark Twain to pen "The Celebrated Jumping Frog of Calaveras County." This pretty, peaceful Gold Country community is built on hills that are honeycombed with mine tunnels. In the 1880s and 1890s, five mines were located along Main Street—Sultana, Angel's, Lightner, Utica, and Stickle—and the town echoed with noise as more than 200 stamps crushed the ore. Between 1886 and 1910, the five mines generated close to $20 million.

But a far-more lasting legacy than the town's gold production is the **Jumping Frog Jubilee,** started in 1928 to mark the paving of the town's streets. To this day, the ribbiting competition takes place every third weekend in May. The record, 21 feet, 5¾ inches, was jumped in 1986 by "Rosie the Ribbiter," beating the old world record by 4½ inches. Livestock exhibitions, pageants, cook-offs, arm-wrestling tournaments, live music, carnival rides, a rodeo, and plenty of beer and wine keep the thousands of spectators entertained between jump-offs. (Heck, you can even rent a frog if you forget to pack one.) For more information and entry forms ($5 per frog), call the Jumping Frog Jubilee headquarters at ✆ **209/736-2561.**

Where to Stay & Dine

B of A Cafe AMERICAN   Katherine Reese, who also runs the Cooper House Bed & Breakfast Inn (see below), has done a marvelous job restoring and converting this 1936 Bank of America building into a bright, cheerful cafe. Using leftover banking curios, she decorated the walls with polished teller windows and converted the vault into a wine-tasting room. Lunch items range from country-style quiche du jour and gourmet baby-green salad to roasted eggplant sandwiches on multigrain bread. Dinners include lemon rosemary chicken, prime rib, and mesquite-marinated baby-back ribs. Daily specials include fresh fish, pasta, and vegetables, and all entrees come with fresh bread, soup or salad, and Kathy's Famous Herbed Roasted Red Potatoes.

1262 S. Main St. ✆ 209/736-0765. Main courses $9–$15. MC, V. Daily 8am–4pm, Sat and Sun 5:30–9pm.

Camps ✪ FUSION   Located on the edge of a sprawling golf resort on the western fringes of Angels Camp is Camps, the culinary feather in the cap of Greenhorn Creek, one of northern California's newest destination retreats. The restaurant's architects have successfully integrated the building into its natural surroundings by constructing the outer walls with locally mined rhyolite and painting it in natural earth tones. The interior is furnished with leather armchairs, wicker, and antique woods. The best seats in the house are on the spacious veranda overlooking the golf course, the perfect setting for executive chef Robert Smith's fusion cuisine, a culinary composition that pairs local produce with European, Asian, and Caribbean influences. Though the menu changes seasonally, a typical dish may be macadamia-crusted halibut with a mandarin orange beurre blanc. The house salas with American field greens, toasted pistachios, julienned red onions and a raspberry vinaigrette is marvelous, as is the duck à la orange served with a traditional brigade sauce and wild rice.

676 McCauley Ranch Rd. (½ mile west of Calif. 4/Calif. 49 junction off Angel Oaks Dr.). © **209/736-8181.** Reservations recommended. Main courses $14.50–$24. AE, MC, V. Tues–Sat 11:30am–3pm; Wed–Sun 5:30–9pm; Sun brunch 11am–3pm.

Cooper House Bed & Breakfast Inn ⍟   Once the home and office of a prominent community physician, Dr. George P. Cooper, the Cooper House is now Angels Camp's only B&B. This small Arts and Crafts home is mercifully positioned well away from the hustle and bustle of the town's Main Street. Owner and innkeeper Kathy Reese maintains three units, all with private bathrooms. The Zinfandel Suite has its own private entrance and deck, and the Chardonnay Suite has a king-size bed, antique clawfoot bathtub, and a private deck. The third bedroom, the Cabernet Suite, is mid-size, with a queen bed, adjoining sunroom, and splendid garden view.

1184 Church St. (P.O. Box 1388), Angels Camp, CA 95222. © **800/225-3764,** ext. 326, or 209/736-2145. 3 units. $105 double. Rates include breakfast. DISC, MC, V. *In room:* A/C.

MURPHYS ⍟

From Angels Camp, a 20-minute drive east along Calif. 4 takes you to Murphys, one of our favorite Gold Country towns. Legend has it Murphys started as a former trading post set up by brothers Dan and John Murphy in cooperation with local Indians (John married the chief's daughter). These days, its peaceful community is made up of gingerbread Victorians shaded by tall locust trees bordering narrow streets. Be sure to take a stroll down Main Street, stopping in **Grounds** for a bite to eat (see "Where to Dine," below) and perhaps a cool draft of Murphys Red—direct from **Murphys Brewing Company**—at the rustic saloon within Murphys Historic Hotel and Lodge.

While you're here, you might also want to check out **Ironstone Vineyards,** 1894 Six Mile Rd., 1 mile south of downtown Murphys (© **209/728-1251**), a veritable wine theme park built by the Kautz family. It boasts an enormous tasting room, jewelry shop, museum housing the largest crystalline gold piece in existence, gallery, amphitheater, music room, caverns, park and gardens, and even a culinary center. It's open daily from 10am to 5pm.

Also in the vicinity—just off Calif. 4, 1 mile north of Murphys off Sheep Ranch Road—are the **Mercer Caverns** (© **209/728-2101**). These caverns, discovered in 1885 by Walter Mercer, contain a variety of geological formations—crystalline stalactites and stalagmites—in a series of descending chambers. Tours of the well-lit caverns take about 55 minutes. From Memorial Day through September, hours are Sunday through Thursday from 9am to 6pm, Friday and Saturday from 9am to 8pm; October through May, Sunday through Thursday from 10am to 4:30pm, Friday and Saturday from 10am to 6pm. Admission is $8 for adults, $4 for children ages 5 to 11, and free for children under 5.

Fifteen miles east of Murphys up Calif. 4 is **Calaveras Big Trees State Park** ✹ (© **209/795-2334**), where you can witness giant sequoias that are among the biggest and oldest living things on earth. It's a popular summer retreat that offers camping, swimming, hiking, and fishing along the Stanislaus River. It's open daily; admission is $2 per car for day use.

Where to Stay & Dine

Dunbar House, 1880 ✹✹   This pretty Italianate home, built in 1880 for the bride of a local businessman, is one of the finest B&Bs in the Gold Country. The inviting front porch, which overlooks the exquisite gardens, is decorated with wicker furniture and hanging baskets of ivy. Inside, the emphasis is on comfort and elegance. The recently redecorated rooms are furnished with quality antiques and equipped with every possible amenity. Beds have lace-trimmed linens and down comforters, and each room has a wood-burning stove and fridge stocked with mineral water and a complimentary bottle of wine. Our favorite room, the Cedar, is a fabulous two-room suite with a private sun porch, whirlpool tub, and complimentary champagne. We also like the Sugar Pine suite, with its private balcony in the trees. Lemonade and cookies are offered in the afternoon, appetizers and wine in the early evening. Breakfast is served in your room, the dining room, or the garden.

271 Jones St., Murphys, CA 95247. © **800/692-6006** or 209/728-2897. Fax 209/728-1451. www.dunbarhouse. com. 5 units. $155–$215 double. Rates include breakfast and afternoon appetizers. AE, MC, V. *In room:* A/C, TV/VCR, hair dryer, iron.

Grounds ✹ ECLECTIC   When River Klass moved here from the East Coast to open his own place, Murphys' restaurant-challenged residents heaved a collective sigh of relief. Its nickname is the "Rude Boy Cafe," after Klass's acerbic wit, but you'll find only happy smiles and friendly service from the energetic staff. The majority of Grounds's business is with the locals, who have become addicted to the potato pancakes that come with every made-to-order omelet. For lunch, try the sausage sandwich on house-baked bread or the grilled eggplant sandwich stuffed with smoked mozzarella and fresh basil. Although the menus change twice a week, typical dinner choices include fettuccine topped with sautéed shrimp, halibut, and mussels in a garlic cream sauce; grilled halibut served with rock shrimp and spinach dumplings; and a big, fat Angus rib eye served with fresh grilled vegetables and garlic mashed potatoes. The wine list is equally impressive (and reasonably priced). The long, narrow dining rooms are bright and airy with pinewood furnishings, wood floors, and an open kitchen. On sunny days, request a table on the back patio.

402 Main St. © **209/728-8663.** Reservations recommended. Main courses $7.50–$15.50. AE, DISC, MC, V. Mon–Tues 7am–4pm; Wed–Sat 7am–9pm; Sun 8am–9pm.

COLUMBIA

Though a little hokey and contrived, **Columbia State Historic Park** ✹✹ (© **209/532-4301** for the museum) is the best-maintained gold-rush town in the Mother Lode (as well as one of the most popular, so expect crowds in the summer). At one point, this boisterous mining town was the state's second largest city (and only two votes shy of becoming the state capital over Sacramento). When gold mining no longer panned out in the late 1850s, most of the town's 15,000 residents departed, leaving much of the mining equipment and buildings in place. In 1945, the entire town was turned into a Historic Park.

As a result, Columbia has been preserved and functions much as it did in the 1850s, with stagecoach rides, Western-style Victorian hotels and saloons, a

---

Fun Fact **How to Pan for Gold**

Find a gold pan, ideally a 12- to 15-inch steel pan. Place the pan over an oven burner, or better yet, in a campfire. This will darken the pan, making it easier to see any flakes of placer gold (many gold pans come already blackened). Find some gravel, sand, or dirt in a stream that looks promising or feels lucky. Scoop dirt into the pan until it's nearly full, then place it under water and keep it there while you break up the clumps of mud and clay and toss out any stones. Then grasp the pan with both hands. Holding it level, rotate it in swirling motions. This will cause the heavier gold to loosen and settle to the bottom of the pan. Drain off the dirty water and loose stuff. Keep doing this until gold and heavier minerals called "black sand" are left in the pan. Carefully inspect the black sand for nuggets or speck traces of gold. Who knows? You just might get lucky.

If this all seems too much to try on your own, you can sign up for a gold-panning lesson with Jamestown's **Gold Prospecting Adventures** (*©* **209/984-4653**). The hour-long instruction costs about $15, and yes, you get to keep any gold you might find.

---

newspaper office, a working blacksmith's forge, a Wells Fargo express office, and numerous other relics of California's early mining days. Cars are banned from its dusty streets, giving the shady town an authentic and noncommercial feel. Merchants still do business behind some storefronts, as horse, stagecoach, and pedestrian traffic wanders by.

If Columbia's heat and dust get to you, pull up a stool at the **Jack Douglass Saloon** (no phone) on Main Street, open daily from 10am to 5pm. Inside the swinging doors of the classic Western bar, you can sample homemade sarsaparilla and wild cherry, drinks the saloon has been serving since 1857. The storefront's large shuttered windows open onto a dusty main street, so put up your boots, relax awhile, and watch the stagecoach go by.

Where to Stay & Dine

City Hotel *℞ (Kids)*   Established in 1856, the historic City Hotel was fully restored in 1975 by the State of California, the nonprofit City Hotel Corporation, and Columbia College, and is now run as a sort of on-the-job training center for hospitality-management students (hence the eager-to-please staff). It's a big, beautiful building, complete with a stately parlor furnished with Victorian sofas, antiques, and Oriental rugs. The largest guest rooms have two balconies overlooking Main Street; the units off the parlor are also spacious. The hallway rooms are smaller, but still nicely furnished with Renaissance Revival beds and antiques. Each room has a sink and toilet, but the shower rooms are separate. A large buffet breakfast is served in the dining room. The hotel also runs a fine-dining restaurant serving classic continental cuisine (roast rack of lamb, grilled salmon, and smoked duck breast) Tuesday through Sunday, as well as the What Cheer saloon. Noise from the saloon, though perhaps not as loud as when the customers packed pistolas, does travel upstairs, so if you're a light sleeper, bring earplugs.

Main St. (P.O. Box 1870), Columbia State Park, CA 95310. *©* **800/532-1479** or 209/532-1479. Fax 209/532-7027. www.cityhotel.com. 10 units, all with shared shower rooms. $105–$125 double. Rates include breakfast. AE, DISC, MC, V. **Amenities:** Restaurant (open Tues–Sun), saloon; nearby golf course. *In room:* A/C; no phone.

Fallon Hotel ⚜ *Kids*   Opened in 1857, this hotel has been restored and decorated to evoke the 1890s. The classic two-story building retains many of its original antiques and furniture. The largest rooms are those along the front upper balcony. Only one unit has a full bathroom; the rest have a private sink and toilet, and showers are down the hall. Rooms are furnished with high-backed Victorian beds, marble-topped dressers, rockers, and similar oak pieces. A full breakfast is served in the downstairs parlor.

Washington St. (P.O. Box 1870), Columbia State Park, CA 95310. ℂ 800/532-1479 or 209/532-1470. Fax 209/532-7027. www.cityhotel.com. 14 units, 13 with shared bathroom. $60–$125 double. Rates include breakfast. AE, DISC, MC, V. **Amenities:** Ice cream parlor; nearby golf course. *In room:* A/C; no phone.

SONORA

Located a few miles south of Columbia, Sonora is the largest town in the southern Gold Country. (You'll know you've arrived when traffic starts to crawl.) Back in the gold-rush days, Sonora and Columbia were the two richest towns in the Mother Lode. Dozens of stores and small cafes line the main thoroughfare. If you can find a parking space, it's worth your while to spend an hour or two checking out the sites, including the 19th-century **St. James Episcopal Church,** at the top of Washington Street, and the **Tuolumne County Museum and History Center,** 158 W. Bradford Ave. (ℂ **209/532-1317**), located in the 1857 County Jail. Admission is free, and it's open daily year-round: Sunday to Friday 10am to 4pm; Saturday 10am to 3:30pm.

Where to Dine

Good Heavens ⚜ *Value* AMERICAN   This small, homey cafe, beloved by locals, recently changed owners. Lets hope the quality stays high. The lunch menu features a variety of hearty sandwiches and the price includes both soup and salad. At dinnertime there are six salads to choose from as well as pastas, grilled steaks, and the famous Mama's meatloaf topped with Acapulco sauce and served with mashed potatoes and veggies.

49 N. Washington St. ℂ **209/532-3663.** Main courses $4–$12 lunch; $10–$18 dinner. MC, V. Wed–Sat 11:30am–3pm and 5–8:30pm; Sun 11am–3pm.

La Torre's North Beach Café ITALIAN   Chef and owner Terry La Torre has turned this former auto-parts store into one of the most popular restaurants in Sonora. A longtime local and progeny of San Francisco restaurateurs, the well-rounded, mustachioed La Torre can usually be found draped in chef's whites, barking orders to his amiable staff. The place is almost always abuzz with customers who come to eat La Torre's cooking and to bask in his infectious banter. The menu is predominantly Italian, including a dozen or so pastas, fresh fish, veal, chicken, and steaks. The combination of fair prices, good food, and classic La Torre histrionics makes North Beach Café worth searching out.

14317 Mono Way/Calif. 108 (from central Sonora, go 3 miles east on Calif. 108). ℂ **209/536-1852.** Main courses $7.50–$13.50. Daily 11am–9pm. AE, MC, V.

JAMESTOWN ⚜

About 4 miles southwest of Sonora on Calif. 49 is Jamestown, a 4-block-long town of old-fashioned storefronts and two charming turn-of-the-century hotels. Yes, there's gold in these parts, too, as the marker commemorating the discovery of a 75-pound nugget will attest (panning nearby Woods Creek is a popular pastime among both locals and tourists). If Jamestown looks eerily familiar to you, that's probably because you've seen it in the movies or on television. It's one of Hollywood's favorite Western movie sets; scenes from such films as *Butch Cassidy and the Sundance Kid* were shot here.

Jamestown's most popular attraction is the **Railtown 1897 State Historic Park** ✸, a train buff's paradise featuring three original Sierra steam locomotives. These great machines were used in many a movie and television show, including *High Noon, Little House on the Prairie, Bonanza,* and *My Little Chickadee.* The trains at the roundhouse are on display daily year-round. Call for information on weekend rides and guided tours. The Depot Store and Museum are open daily from 9:30am to 4:30pm. The park is located near the center of town, on Fifth Avenue at Reservoir Road (© **209/984-3953**).

Where to Stay & Dine

Jamestown Hotel ✸   The most worked-over building in town, the Jamestown was originally built in 1858; it burned down and was rebuilt twice before 1915. To achieve the old-fashioned, brick-fronted Victorian look it sports today, its owners ripped out a lot of stucco and Spanish-revival paraphernalia. Much of the lower floor is devoted to the front office, bar, and restaurant, the Jenny Lind Room. The second floor contains a cadre of cozy bedrooms outfitted with antiques acquired along both coasts of North America. All of the spacious rooms are loaded with nostalgic charm; a few have sitting rooms, and all have a private bathroom (some with clawfoot tubs). The most popular has its own balcony. The street-level rooms are the most luxurious, outfitted with whirlpool tubs, private patios, and individual heat and A/C controls.

18153 Main St. (P.O. Box 539), Jamestown, CA 95327. © **800/205-4901** or 209/984-3902. Fax 209/984-4149. www.jamestownhotel.com. 10 units. $110–$135 double. Rates include continental breakfast. AE, DC, DISC, MC, V. **Amenities:** Restaurant, bar; activities desk; business center. *In room:* A/C, hair dryer, iron.

1859 Historic National Hotel ✸   Located in the center of town, this two-story classic Western hotel has been operating since 1859, making it one of the 10 oldest continuously operating hotels in the state. The saloon has its original 19th-century redwood bar, and you can imagine what it must have been like when miners traded gold dust for drinks. The rooms above are outfitted with numerous period antiques, as well as oak furnishings and brass beds. A recent addition is an authentic "Soaking Room," a private room equipped with a sort of 1800s clawfoot Jacuzzi for two (when cowboys longed for a good, hot soak). All units have private bathrooms. The restaurant on the main floor serves continental cuisine with a California influence, such as brandy-apple pork, ruby trout amandine, and blackened prime rib with sautéed prawns.

77 Main St. (P.O. Box 502), Jamestown, CA 95327. © **800/894-3446** or 209/984-3446. Fax 209/984-5620. www.national-hotel.com. 9 units. $90–$130 double. Rates include buffet breakfast. AE, DC, DISC, MC, V. Pets accepted $10 per night. **Amenities:** Restaurant, saloon; nearby golf course; concierge; tour/activities desk; business center; secretarial services; room service; in-room massage. *In room:* A/C, TV, dataport, coffeemaker, hair dryer.

3 The Central Valley & Sierra National Forest

The Central Valley (also known as the San Joaquin Valley) is about as far as you can get from California's glamorous movie-stars-in-stretch-limos image. This hot, flat strip of farms, dairies, fast-food joints, cheap motels, and truck stops stretches for some 225 miles from Bakersfield to Redding. The 18,000-square-mile valley is central to the economy of the Golden State, in part because of its cultivated and irrigated fields, orchards, pastures, and vineyards.

The major traffic arteries through the valley are Calif. 99 and I-5. Calif. 99 links the agricultural communities, while I-5 provides access routes to the roadside attractions in the valley. Rivers cutting through the valley offer fishing, boating, house-boating on the delta, and white-water rafting on the rapids. And once you get off the freeways, the valley's spectacular landscapes provide unrivaled natural beauty. Many visitors drive through in spring just to view the orchards in bloom.

The Central Valley also stands on the doorstep of some of America's greatest attractions, the most well known being Yosemite National Park. See chapter 9 for coverage of two Central Valley towns, Merced and Visalia, which are good gateways to Yosemite, Sequoia, and Kings Canyon, respectively.

Fresno, although not much in itself, is on the doorstep of the Sierra National Forest and nearby natural attractions like the Millerton Lake State Recreation Area.

FRESNO

The running joke in California is that Fresno is the "gateway to Bakersfield." For most visitors, Fresno, located 185 miles southeast of San Francisco, is just a place to pass through en route to the state parks; it can, however, be a good place to stop for food and lodging, and it makes a good base for exploring the Sierra National Forest (see below).

Founded in 1874 in the geographic center of the state, Fresno lies in the heart of the Central Valley and has experienced incredible growth in recent years. Like most growing cities, it has been plagued by an increase in crime, drugs, and urban sprawl.

As the seat of Fresno County, the city handles more than $3 billion annually in agricultural production. It also contains Sun Maid, the world's largest dried-fruit packing plant, and Guild, one of the country's largest wineries.

If you have any reason at all to be in Fresno, try to visit between late February and late March so you can drive the **Fresno County Blossom Trail** ✦. This 62-mile, self-guided tour takes in the beauty of California's agrarian bounty at its peak. The trail courses through fruit orchards in full bloom and citrus groves with lovely orange blossoms and a heady natural perfume. The **Fresno Convention and Visitors Bureau,** 847 M St., 3rd floor, in Fresno (✆ **800/ 788-0836** or 559/233-0836), supplies full details, including a map.

WHERE TO STAY & DINE

San Joaquin ✦   Set on the northern edge of Fresno, this full-service hotel was conceived as an apartment complex in the 1970s. Around 1985, a lobby was added, the floor plans were adjusted, and the place was reconfigured as an all-suite hotel. Suites range from junior 1-bedroom suites to 3-bedroom suites with kitchens, and each is outfitted in a slightly different style, with light, contemporary colors and furniture. Room service is available from an independently managed restaurant down the street.

1309 W. Shaw Ave., Fresno, CA 93711. ✆ **800/775-1309** or 559/225-1309. Fax 559/225-6021. www. sanjoaquinhotel.com. 68 suites. $89–$195 suite. Rates include breakfast and evening hospitality. AE, DC, DISC, MC, V. **Amenities:** Outdoor pool; Jacuzzi; business center; room service; laundry service. *In room:* A/C, TV/VCR, dataport, kitchen, fridge, coffeemaker, hair dryer, iron.

Veni, Vidi, Vici ✦ CALIFORNIA CUISINE   The most innovative and creative restaurant in Fresno occupies a prominent position about 6 miles south of the commercial center, in a funky neighborhood known as the Tower District. The place's rustic exterior strikes an interesting contrast to the polished and artful interior on the other side of the 15-foot doors, where the decor is accented with exposed brick walls, hanging mirrors, and chandeliers fashioned from twisted wire and metal leaves.

The menu changes often, but might include roasted loin of pork with Chinese black beans and citrus-flavored glaze, served with grilled portobello mushrooms, sun-dried tomatoes, risotto, and red-pepper coulis; or a wild-mushroom lasagna with preserved tomato sauce. There are also fresh fish specials nightly. This is the only restaurant in Fresno that makes its own ice cream (the flavor of the day when we arrived was Technicolor lime sorbet). Have a scoop or two with the restaurant's perennial dessert favorite: bittersweet chocolate cake.

1116 N. Fulton. (© 559/266-5510. Reservations recommended. Main courses $19–$26. AE, DC, DISC, MC, V. Tues–Sun 5:30–10pm (late-night menu Fri–Sat 10pm–midnight).

SIERRA NATIONAL FOREST 🕸🕸

Leaving Fresno's taco joints, used-car lots, and tract houses behind, an hour's drive and 45 miles northeast gets you to the Sierra National Forest, a land of lakes and coniferous forests lying between Yosemite, Sequoia, and Kings Canyon National Parks. The entire eastern portion of the park is still unspoiled wilderness protected by the government. Development—some of it, unfortunately, beside the bigger lakes and reservoirs—is confined to the western side.

The 1.3-million-acre forest contains 528,000 acres of wilderness. The Sierra's five wilderness areas include Ansel Adams, Dinkey Lakes, John Muir, Kaiser, and Monarch (see below). The forest offers plenty of opportunities for fishing, swimming, sailing, boating, camping, water-skiing, white-water rafting, kayaking, and horseback riding, all regulated by certain guidelines. Downhill and cross-country skiing, as well as hunting, are also available, depending on the season. Backpackers looking to retreat to the wilderness will find solace here, as the park is traversed by some 1,100 miles of forest hiking trails.

ESSENTIALS

GETTING THERE   After visiting the ranger station at Oakhurst, take Calif. 41 to Calif. 49, the major road into the northern part of the national forest. This is more convenient for visitors approaching the park from northern California. Calif. 168 via Clovis is the primary route from Fresno if you're headed for Shaver Lake. There is no approach road from the eastern Sierra, only from the west.

INFORMATION & PERMITS   To learn about hiking, camping, or other activities, or to obtain the fire and wilderness permits needed for backcountry jaunts, visit one of the ranger stations in the park's western section. These include **Mariposa and Minarets Ranger Station,** 57003 North Fork (© **559/877-2218**); and the **Pineridge Ranger Station,** 29688 Auberry Rd., Prather (© **559/855-5360**).

SUPPLIES   Shaver Lake is one place where you can stock up on goods and supplies if you're going into the wilderness, but stores in Fresno carry much of the same stuff at lower prices. Cheaper supplies are also available in the town of Clovis outside Fresno (which you must pass through en route to the forest), especially at the **Peacock Market,** at Tollhouse Road (Third St.) and Sunnyside Avenue (© **559/299-6627**).

WEATHER   In the lower elevations, summer temperatures can frequently reach 100°F, but in the higher elevations, more comfortable temperatures in the 70s and 80s are the norm.

THE MAJOR WILDERNESS & RECREATION AREAS

ANSEL ADAMS WILDERNESS   Divided between the Sierra and Inyo national forests, this wilderness area covers 228,500 acres. Elevations range from

3,500 to 13,157 feet. The frost-free period extends from mid-July through August, the best time for a visit to the park's upper altitudes.

Ansel Adams is dotted with scenic alpine vistas, including steep-walled gorges and barren granite peaks. There are several small glaciers in the north and some fairly large lakes on the eastern slope of the precipitous Ritter Range. This vast wilderness has excellent stream and lake fishing, especially for rainbow, golden, and brook trout, and offers challenging mountain climbing on the Minarets Range. The wilderness is accessed by the Tioga Pass Road in the north, U.S. 395 and Reds Meadow Road in the east, the Minarets Highway in the west, and Calif. 168 to High Sierra in the south.

DINKEY LAKES WILDERNESS The 30,000-acre Dinkey Lakes area was created in 1984 and occupies the western slope of the Sierra Nevada, southeast of Huntington Lake and just northwest of Courtright Reservoir. Most of the timbered, rolling terrain here is 8,000 feet above sea level, reaching its highest point (10,619 feet) at Three Sisters Peak. Sixteen lakes are clustered in the west-central region. You can reach the area on Kaiser Pass Road (north), Red/Coyote Jeep Road (west), Rock Creek Road (southwest), or Courtright Reservoir (southeast), generally from mid-June to late October.

JOHN MUIR WILDERNESS Occupying 584,000 acres in the Sierra and Inyo National Forests, John Muir Wilderness—named after the turn-of-the-century naturalist—extends southeast from Mammoth Lakes along the crest of the Sierra Nevada for 30 miles before forking around the boundary of Kings Canyon National Park to Crown Valley and Mount Whitney. Elevations range from 4,000 to 14,496 feet at Mount Whitney, with many of the area's peaks surpassing 12,000 feet. The wilderness can be accessed from numerous points west of US 395 between Mammoth Lake and Independence.

Split by deep canyons, the wilderness is also a land of meadows (especially beautiful when wildflowers bloom), lakes, and streams. The south and middle forks of the San Joaquin River, the north fork of Kings River, and many creeks draining into Owens Valley originate in the John Muir Wilderness. Mountain hemlock, red and white fir, and whitebark and western pine dot the park's landscape. Temperatures vary wildly throughout any 24-hour period: Summer temperatures range from 25°F to 85°F, and the only really frost-free period is between mid-July and August. The higher elevations are marked by barren expanses of granite splashed with many glacially carved lakes.

KAISER WILDERNESS Immediately north of Huntington Lake and some 70 miles northeast of Fresno, Kaiser is a 22,700-acre forest tract commanding a view of the central Sierra Nevada. It was named after Kaiser Ridge, which divides the area into two different regions. Four trailheads provide easy access to the wilderness, but the northern half is much more open than the forested southern half; the primary point of entry is the Sample Meadow Campground. All other lakes are approached cross-country. Winter storms begin to blow in late October, and the grounds are generally snow-covered until early June.

MONARCH WILDERNESS Monarch is located at the southern end of the John Muir Wilderness, on the western border of Sequoia/Kings Canyon national Park, approximately 65 miles east of Fresno via Calif. 180. The area extends across 45,000 acres in the Sierra and Sequoia National Forests. The Sierra National Forest portion of the region—about 21,000 acres—is very rugged and hard to traverse. Steep slopes climb from the middle and main forks of Kings River, with elevations increasing from 2,400 to more than 10,000 feet.

Rock outcroppings are found throughout Monarch, and most of the lower elevations are mainly chaparral covered with pine stands near the tops of the higher peaks. Monarch is located at the southern end of the John Muir Wilderness, on the western border of Sequoia-Kinds Canyon National Park, approximately 65 miles east of Fresno via Calif. 180.

HUNTINGTON LAKE RECREATION AREA   At 7,000 feet, this area is a 2-hour drive east of Fresno via Calif. 168. The lake is one of the reservoirs in the Big Creek Hydroelectric System and has 14 miles of shoreline. It's a popular recreational area, offering camping, hiking, picnicking, sailing, swimming, windsurfing, fishing, and horseback riding—or you can just appreciate the beauty. The main summer season stretches from Memorial Day to Labor Day. There are seven campgrounds and four picnic areas in the Huntington Lake Basin, plus numerous hiking and riding trails.

NEIDER GROVE OF GIANT SEQUOIAS ⭐   This 1,540-acre tract in the Sierra National Forest contains 101 mature giant sequoias in the center of the Sequoia Range, south of Yosemite National Park. A visitor center stands near the Neider Grove Campground, with historical relics and displays, including two restored log cabins. The Bull Buck Tree—at one time thought to be the largest in the world—is 246 feet high and has a circumference at ground level of 99 feet. There's a mile-long, self-guided walk along the "Shadow of the Giants" National Recreational Trail in the southwest corner of the grove.

OUTDOOR PURSUITS

CAMPING   The Sierra National Forest seems like one vast campsite. Options range from unembellished, primitive wilderness camps to developed and often crowded campgrounds with snack bars, flush toilets, bathhouses, and hookups for RVs. For information and reservations, call the **National Recreation Reservation Service** toll-free at ☎ **877/444-6777,** or visit its website at www.reserveusa.com.

The major campgrounds are the Shaver Lake area; the Huntington Lake area (which has seven family campgrounds open from the end of June to Labor Day that must be reserved in advance); the Florence and Edison Lake area (first-come, first-served); the Dinkey Creek area (family and group camping); the Wishon and Courtright area (four campgrounds; first-come, first-served); the Pine Flat Reservoir (in the Sierra foothills, with two first-come, first-served campgrounds); and Upper Kings River, east of Pine Flat Reservoir (family campgrounds; first-come, first-served).

FISHING   The many streams of the Sierra are home to rainbow, golden, brown, and brook trout. The best freshwater angling is in the Pineridge and Kings River Rangers District. At the lower elevations, Shaver Lake, Bass Lake, and Pine Flat Reservoirs are known for their black-bass fishing. Questions about fishing in the national forest can be directed to the **California Department of Fish and Game,** 1234 E. Shaw Ave., Fresno, CA 93710 (☎ **559/243-4005**).

SKIING   Lying 65 miles northeast of Fresno on Calif. 168 in the Sierra National Forest, the **Sierra Summit Ski Area** offers mildly challenging alpine skiing, as well as marked trails for cross-country skiing and snowmobiling. The resort area has two triple and three double chairlifts, plus four surface lifts and 30 runs, the longest of which extends for 2¼ miles. There's a vertical drop-off at 1,600 feet. Other facilities include a lodge, snack bar, cafeteria, restaurant, and bar, all open daily from mid-November until mid-April. For resort information or a ski report, call ☎ **559/893-3311.**

The **Pineridge Ranger Station** (© 559/855-5360) also maintains several marked cross-country trails along Calif. 168, ranging from a 1-mile tour for beginners to a 6-mile trail for more advanced skiers.

WHITE-WATER RAFTING   The Upper Kings River, east of Pine Flat Reservoir, offers a 10-mile rafting run through Garnet Dike to Kirch Flat Campground. Rafting season is from late April to mid-July, with the highest waters in late May and early June. To get there, take Belmont Avenue in Fresno east (toward Pine Flat Reservoir) for about 63 miles. For more information about guided rafting trips on the Kings River, call **Kings River Expeditions** (© 559/233-4881).

11

The Monterey Peninsula & the Big Sur Coast

by Matthew R. Poole & Mary Anne Moore

The Monterey Peninsula and the Big Sur coast comprise one of the world's most spectacular shorelines, skirted with cypress trees, rugged shores, and crescent-shaped bays. Monterey reels in visitors with its world-class aquarium and array of outdoor activities. Pacific Grove is so peaceful and quaint that the butterflies choose it as their yearly mating ground. Pebble Beach attracts the world's golfing elite, and although packed with tourists who come for the beaches, shops, and restaurants, tiny Carmel-by-the-Sea somehow remains romantic and sweet. Big Sur's dramatic and majestic coast, backed by pristine redwood forests and rolling hills, is one of the most breathtaking and tranquil environments on earth. And if you're traveling on Calif. 1 (which you should be), the magnificent coastline will guide you all the way through the region.

This chapter begins with Santa Cruz, located at the northwestern end of Monterey Bay. It's one of our favorite coastal destinations and home of the famous Santa Cruz Beach Boardwalk. Across Monterey Bay at the northern tip of the Monterey Peninsula are the seaside communities of Monterey and Pacific Grove, while Pebble Beach and Carmel-by-the-Sea hug the peninsula's south coast along Carmel Bay. Between the north and south coasts, which are only about 5 miles apart, are numerous golf courses, some of the state's most stunning homes and hotels, and 17-Mile Drive, one of the most scenic coastal roads in the world.

Inland lies Carmel Valley, with its elegant inns and resorts, golf courses, and guaranteed sunshine, even when the coast is socked in with fog. Farther down the coast along Calif. 1 is Big Sur, a stunning 90-mile stretch of coast south of the Monterey Peninsula and west of the Santa Lucia Mountains.

1 Santa Cruz ★★

77 miles SE of San Francisco

For a small bayside city, Santa Cruz has a lot to offer. The main show, of course, is the Beach Boardwalk, the West Coast's only seaside amusement park, which attracts millions of visitors each year. But past the arcades and cotton candy is a surprisingly diverse and energetic city that has a little something for everyone. Shopping, hiking, mountain biking, sailing, fishing, kayaking, surfing, wine tasting, golfing, whale-watching—the list of things to do here is almost endless, making Santa Cruz one of the premier family destinations on the California coast.

ESSENTIALS

GETTING THERE   Santa Cruz is 77 miles southeast of San Francisco. The most scenic route to Santa Cruz is along Calif. 1 from San Francisco, which, aside from the "you fall, you die" stretch called Devil's Slide, allows you to cruise at a steady 50 m.p.h. along the coast. Faster but far less romantic is Calif. 17, which is accessed near San Jose from I-280, I-880, or U.S. 101, and literally ends at the foot of the boardwalk. The exception to this rule is on weekend mornings, when Calif. 17 tends to logjam with Bay Area beachgoers while Calif. 1 remains relatively uncrowded.

VISITOR INFORMATION   For information, contact the **Santa Cruz County Conference and Visitors Council,** 1201 Ocean St., Santa Cruz, CA 95060 (© **800/833-3494** or 831/425-1234; www.santacruzca.org), open Monday through Saturday from 9am to 5pm, Sunday from 10am to 4pm.

SPECIAL EVENTS   Special events include the Santa Cruz Hot and Cool Jazz Festival in July (© **831/474-7407**), Shakespeare Santa Cruz in July and August (© **831/459-2121**), and Cabrillo Music Festival in August (© **831/426-6966**).

EXPLORING SANTA CRUZ: BEACHES, HIKING, FISHING & MORE

A charming, old-fashioned amusement park, the **Santa Cruz Beach Boardwalk** 🐾🐾 (© **831/426-7433**) draws more than 3 million visitors a year to its 30 rides and multitudes of arcades, shops, and restaurants. The park has two national landmarks—a 1924 wooden Giant Dipper roller coaster and a 1911 carousel complete with hand-carved wooden horses and a 342-pipe organ band. It's open daily in the summer (from Memorial Day weekend through Labor Day) and on weekends and holidays throughout the spring and fall, from 11am (noon sometimes in winter). Admission to the boardwalk is free, but an all-day "unlimited rides" pass will set you back $22.95. Check the Boardwalk calendar © **831/ 423-5590;** www.beachboardwalk.com) for special discounts, concerts and events, and up-to-date info on hours, which can often vary.

Here, too, is **Neptune's Kingdom,** 400 Beach St. (© **831/426-7433**), an enormous indoor family recreation center whose main feature is a two-story miniature golf course. Also on Beach Street is the **Municipal Wharf** (© **831/ 420-6025**), lined with shops and restaurants—a beachfront strip that is serenaded by the sea lions below. You can also crab and fish from here. Most shops are open daily from 7am to 9pm, the wharf daily from 5am to 2am. **Stagnaro's** (© **831/427-2334**) operates fishing and whale-watching trips from the wharf year-round, as well as hour-long narrated bay cruises for a mere $7 for adults, $5 for kids.

Farther down on West Cliff Drive, you'll come to a favorite surfing spot, **Steamer Lane,** where you can watch pro surfers shredding the waves. If you want to find out more about this local sport that's been practiced here for 100 years, go to the **Santa Cruz Surfing Museum,** at the memorial lighthouse (© **831/420-6289**), open Wednesday through Monday from noon to 4pm. Antique surfboards, videos, photographs, and other memorabilia depict the history and evolution of surfing around the world.

Continue along West Cliff and you'll eventually reach **Natural Bridges State Beach,** 2531 W. Cliff Dr. (© **831/423-4609**), a large sandy beach with nearby tide pools and hiking trails. It's also home to a large colony of monarch butterflies that cluster and mate in the nearby eucalyptus grove.

Other Santa Cruz beaches worth noting are **Bonny Doon,** at Bonny Doon Road and Calif. 1, an uncrowded sandy beach and a major surfing spot accessible by a steep walkway; **Pleasure Point Beach,** East Cliff Drive at Pleasure Point Drive; and **Twin Lakes State Beach,** which is ideal for sunning and also provides access to Schwann Lagoon, a bird sanctuary.

In addition to hosting many cultural and sporting events, the University of California at Santa Cruz also features the **Long Marine Laboratory and Aquarium,** 100 Shaffer Rd., at the northwest end of Delaware Avenue (✆ 831/459-3800), where you can observe the activities of marine scientists and the species kept in tide-pool touch tanks and aquariums. Visitors get to learn firsthand how real marine scientists study the seas at the **Marine Discovery Center.** Hours are Tuesday through Sunday from 1 to 4pm; admission is $2 for adults, free for kids under 17.

The **Santa Cruz Harbor,** 135 Fifth Ave. (✆ 831/475-6161), is the place to head for boat rentals, open boat fishing (cod, shark, and salmon), and whale-watching trips. Operators include **Santa Cruz Sportfishing Inc.** (✆ 831/426-4690) and **Shamrock Charters,** 2210 E. Cliff Dr. (✆ 831/476-2648). Even if you're not into fishing, it's worth a walk down the harbor to browse through the numerous shops and restaurants.

Bikes—mountain, kids', tandem, hybrid—are available by the hour, day, or week from various bike rental shops in convenient locations around the city. For a list of shops, call the **Santa Cruz Visitors Council** at ✆ 800/833-3494, or check the website at www.santacruzca.org. Figure on paying $25 a day, which includes helmets, locks, and packs.

There are several public golf courses, the best being the **Pasatiempo Golf Club,** at 18 Clubhouse Rd. (✆ 831/459-9155; www.pasatiempo.com), which is rated among the top 100 courses in the United States. Greens fees are $115 Monday through Friday, $125 Saturday and Sunday.

Sea kayaking is also available. Outfitters include **Kayak Connection,** 413 Lake Ave. No. 4 (✆ 831/479-1121), and **Venture Quest Kayaking** (✆ 831/427-2267), which rent single, double, and triple kayaks at Building No. 2 on the wharf and at 125 Beach St. across from the wharf. Classes, wildlife tours, and moonlight paddles are also available.

Surfing equipment can be rented at the **Cowell's Beach 'n' Bikini Surf Shop,** 109 Beach St. (✆ 831/427-2355), and also from the **Club Ed Surf School** (✆ 831/459-9283), on Cowell Beach in front of the West Coast Santa Cruz Hotel (formerly the Dream Inn). Both companies offer surf lessons: Club Ed's rates are $80 for a 2-hour group session, $80 for private lessons (equipment included), and $950 for a 7-day surf camp, and Cowell's costs $70 for a 2-hour group lesson and includes the use of a board and wet suit.

IN NEARBY CAPITOLA ✩

South along the coast lies the small, attractive community of **Capitola** at the mouth of the Soquel Creek, which is a spawning ground for steelhead and salmon. You can fish without a license from the **Capitola Wharf,** 1400 Wharf Rd. (✆ 831/462-2208), or you can rent a fishing boat from **Capitola Boat and Bait** (✆ 831/462-2208).

Capitola Beach fronts the Esplanade ✆ 831/475-7300. Surf-fishing and clamming are popular pastimes at Capitola's **New Brighton State Beach,** 1500 State Park Dr. (✆ 831/464-6330), where camping is also allowed.

Other Capitola pastimes? **Antiquing!** Explore the many stores along Soquel Drive between 41st and Capitola Avenues.

Still farther south around the bay is **Aptos** ⊛, home to the 10,000-acre **Forest of Nisene Marks State Park** (ⓒ **831/763-7063**), which has hiking trails that wind through redwoods and past abandoned mining camps. Mountain bikers and leashed dogs are also welcome. This was the infamous epicenter of the 1989 earthquake. It's located at the end of Aptos Creek Road off Soquel Drive and is open year-round from sunrise to sunset.

In the redwood-forested mountains behind Santa Cruz, there are quite a few wineries, although visitors may not be familiar with the labels because the output is small and consumed locally. Most wineries are clustered around Boulder Creek and Felton or around Capitola. All offer tours by appointment; some feature regular tastings, including the **Bargetto Winery,** 3535 N. Main, Soquel (ⓒ **831/475-2258**), which has a courtyard wine-tasting area overlooking the creek. For additional information, contact the **Santa Cruz Mountains Winegrowers Association** (ⓒ **831/479-WINE**).

WHERE TO STAY

Two **Travelodges** (ⓒ 800/578-7878; www.travelodge.com), two **Best Westerns** (ⓒ 800/528-1234; www.bestwestern.com), two **Super 8s** (ⓒ 800/800-8000; www.super8.com), and an **Econo Lodge** (ⓒ 800/553-2666; www.hotelchoice. com) provide moderate- and budget-priced accommodations in addition to the more inspiring choices below.

Casa Blanca Inn   Across from the wharf in a heavily trafficked area, this motel along the waterfront was once the Mediterranean-style Cerf Mansion, dating from 1918. Other motel-style accommodations have grown up around the main building. Originally the home of a federal judge, it offers individually decorated bedrooms, some with brass beds and velvet draperies. Some units contain fireplaces and terraces, and all are equipped with microwaves. Most of the rooms have views of the water. A restaurant on the premises (see "Where to Dine," below) serves California-continental cuisine in a romantic oceanview setting.

101 Main St. (at the corner of Beach St.), Santa Cruz, CA 95060. ⓒ **800/644-1570** or 831/423-1570. Fax 831/423-0235. www.casablanca-santacruz.com. 33 units. High season (summer) $96–$300 double; low season $78–$295 double. AE, DC, DISC, MC, V. **Amenities:** Restaurant, bar; nearby golf course; room service; laundry service. *In room:* TV, dataport, minibar, fridge, coffeemaker, hair dryer, iron, safe; some units with full kitchen.

Darling House ⊛   This lovely Spanish-style house, designed in 1910 by William Weeks (architect of Santa Cruz's Coconut Grove), has a panoramic view of the Pacific Ocean and is situated in a quiet residential area within walking distance of the Boardwalk and lighthouse. The gardens are fragrant with citrus and orchids, and contain some stately palms as well. From the tiled front veranda, guests enter an elegant interior, the focal point of which is the dining room hand-crafted from tiger oak. The house boasts fine architectural features throughout, such as beveled glass, antiques, and handsome fireplaces. Each of the eight rooms is individually decorated; although all have sinks, only two come with private bathrooms. The Pacific Ocean room, decorated like a sea captain's quarters, features a fireplace, telescope, and one of the finest ocean views in Santa Cruz. Breakfast includes oven-fresh breads and pastries, fruit, and homemade granola made with walnuts from the Darling's own farm.

314 W. Cliff Dr., Santa Cruz, CA 95060. ⓒ **831/458-1958.** www.darlinghouse.com. 8 units (2 with private bathroom). $95 double without bathroom; $260 double with bathroom. Rates include breakfast. AE, DISC, MC, V. **Amenities:** Concierge.

Edgewater Beach Motel   If the other two inns listed here are booked, consider the Edgewater Beach Motel. It looks like a time capsule from the 1960s, which, oddly enough, makes it all the more appealing (how they kept the furnishings in such prime condition is a mystery). The motel offers a range of accommodations, from family suites with kitchens to rooms with fireplaces; most have microwaves and all have fridges. The Edgewater also sports a nice pool, sundeck, and barbecue area, but the real bonus is the location—the Santa Cruz Beach Boardwalk is only a block away. *Tip:* Inquire about the Edgewater's off-season mini-vacation packages, which can save you a bundle on room rates. Smoking is not permitted in any of the rooms.

525 Second St., Santa Cruz, CA 95060. ℂ **831/423-0440.** www.edgewaterbeachmotel.com. 17 units. Winter $85–$219 double; summer $139–$299 double. AE, DC, DISC, MC, V. **Amenities:** Outdoor heated pool. *In room:* TV/VCR, fridge, coffeemaker; suites with fully equipped kitchen.

IN NEARBY CAPITOLA

The Inn at Depot Hill 🏵🏵🏵   Located a few blocks from the bay front, this converted railroad station has been beautifully designed and decorated with great attention to detail, thanks to innkeeper extraordinaire Suzanne Lankes. Sporting fine fabrics and linens, all rooms and suites have wood-burning fireplaces, VCRs and stereos, phones with fax and modem capabilities, bathrobes, hair dryers, two-person showers, and full bathrooms. Most have private patios with private Jacuzzis (guests in the other rooms share a common Jacuzzi, and sign up for times). Perhaps you'll check into the Portofino Room, patterned after an Italian villa right down to the frescoes and stone cherub, or the Stratford-on-Avon, a replica of an English cottage.

The evening wine and hors d'oeuvres and the breakfast are of similar prime quality, and can be enjoyed either in your room or out back in the garden courtyard on wrought-iron tables shaded by market umbrellas.

250 Monterey Ave. (near Park Ave.), Capitola, CA 95010. ℂ **800/57-B-AND-B** (572-2632) or 831/462-3376. Fax 831/462-3697. www.innatdepothill.com. 12 units. $235–$325 double. Rates include breakfast, afternoon tea or wine, hors d'oeuvres, and after-dinner dessert. AE, DC, DISC, MC, V. **Amenities:** Jacuzzi; room service. *In room:* A/C, TV/VCR, dataport, hair dryer.

WHERE TO DINE

Bittersweet Bistro 🏵🏵 CALIFORNIA   What started out as a tiny operation within a small strip development has grown into one of the most popular restaurants in the Santa Cruz region. The relocation to bigger digs in Rio Del Mar hasn't tarnished chef and owner Thomas Vinolus's reputation for serving exceptional cuisine. The menu offers a wide array of carefully crafted dishes, ranging from pizzas from the wood-fired oven to grilled lamb porterhouse in a sun-dried cranberry demi glace. Fresh fish is Vinolus's forte, however, such as the Monterey Bay halibut, baked in parchment over fresh vegetables, or the roasted Chelis River wild sturgeon finished with an exotic mushroom sauce. Co-proprietor and wine director Elizabeth Vinolus has put together an exceptional wine list and often hosts winemaker dinners. "Bistro Hour" is from 3 to 6pm every afternoon, featuring half-price specials on gourmet pizzettas and special pricing on all wines by the glass, beer, and spirits.

787 Rio Del Mar Blvd., Aptos (about 10 miles SE of Santa Cruz on Calif. 1). ℂ **831/662-9799.** www. bittersweetbistro.com. Reservations recommended. Main courses $18–$24. AE, MC, V. Daily "bistro" lunch 3–6pm; dinner 5:30–10pm; Sun brunch 10am–2pm.

Café El Palomar MEXICAN   If both O'Mei and Bittersweet Bistro are out of your price range, then head to the Santa Cruz Harbor and seat yourself at one of the seven tables at Café El Palomar. An offshoot of the far fancier El Palomar restaurant in the Pacific Garden Mall, the Café serves the standard Mexican fare—chimichangas, burritos, tacos, chorizo, and more—for breakfast, lunch, and dinner. For the money, it's mucho bueno grub.

2222 E. Cliff Dr. (at the Santa Cruz Harbor). ⓒ **831/462-4248.** Main courses $4–$6. MC, V. Daily 7am–7pm (7am–5pm winter).

Casa Blanca Restaurant ⓕ CALIFORNIA/CONTINENTAL   The candle-lit dining room at the Casa Blanca Inn was obviously built for romance, right down to the stellar views of the shimmering bay. The menu offers your classic fancy fare such as rack of lamb, grilled salmon, and sautéed chicken breast, but most folks come here primarily for the ambiance. For a fiery start, try the fire-roasted Anaheim chili stuffed with herbed chèvre and served with tomatillo salsa. Among the 10 or so main courses, we'd recommend any of the fresh seafood dishes, perhaps the red snapper sautéed with capers, scallions, and lime sauce. The award-winning book-length wine list is excellent.

101 Main St. (at Beach St.). ⓒ **831/426-9063.** Reservations recommended. Main courses $15–$23. AE, DC, DISC, MC, V. Daily 5–9:30pm.

O'Mei ⓕⓕ PROVINCIAL SICHUAN   O'Mei's (pronounced *oh-may*) mini-mall location may not be very inviting, but the fantastic food served here more than makes up for it. The menu features some unusual specialties such as Chengdu-bean-curd sea bass in a spicy *dou-ban* sauce (a rich, velvety wine-chili sauce), apricot-almond chicken, and lichee pi-pa bean-curd balls, along with more familiar dishes like chicken with cashews or beef with asparagus. Dinner starts with a dim sum–style tray of exotic vegetarian offerings such as sesame-cilantro-eggplant salad or pan-roasted peppers with feta cheese. A recommended dish is the sliced rock cod in black-bean and sweet-pepper sauce, followed by a scoop of black-sesame ice cream.

2316 Mission St. (where Calif. 1 turns into Mission St.). ⓒ **831/425-8458.** Reservations recommended. Main courses $9.25–$18.95. AE, MC, V. Mon–Fri 11:30am–2pm; Sun–Thurs 5–9pm; Fri–Sat 5–10pm.

IN NEARBY CAPITOLA
Shadowbrook ⓕ AMERICAN/CONTINENTAL   Shadowbrook, one of Capitola's most venerable and romantic restaurants, occupies a serene setting above Soquel Creek. To reach the restaurant, diners either have to take the cable-driven "hillavator" down or walk the long, steep bank of steps beside a running waterfall. At the bottom is a log cabin built in the 1920s, which has been enlarged and now contains a series of dining rooms on different levels: the wood-paneled Wine Cellar, the airy Garden Room, the Fireplace Room, and the creek-side Greenhouse.

The menu doesn't hold many surprises, featuring thick-cut prime rib and steaks along with seafood such as scampi and grilled trout, plus pasta dishes including shellfish linguine and porcini ravioli. Prawn cocktail, deep-fried arti-choke hearts, and baked brie are among the appetizers. Standout desserts are the mud pie and chocolate torte with raspberry sauce. If you don't have the time, appetite, or budget for a big sit-down dinner, grab a seat in the lounge and nosh on appetizers and light entrees prepared in the restaurant's wood-fired oven.

1750 Wharf Rd., Capitola. ⓒ **831/475-1511.** Fax 831/475-7664. www.shadowbrook-capitola.com. Reser-vations recommended. Main courses $13–$24. AE, DC, DISC, MC, V. Mon–Fri 11:30am–9:30pm; Sat 4:30–10:30pm; Sun 10am–2:30pm and 4:30–9pm.

A SIDE TRIP TO MISSION SAN JUAN BAUTISTA

On U.S. 101, **San Juan Bautista** ✮ is a charming mission town that works hard to honor its pioneer heritage by retaining the flavor of a 19th-century village. The mission complex is perched in a picturesque farming valley, surrounded by the restored buildings of the original city plaza.

From U.S. 101, take Calif. 156 east (south) to the center of town to the mission itself, which was founded in 1797. Here you'll see the largest church in the mission chain and the only one in continuous service since its founding. The padres here inspired many Native Americans to convert, creating one of the largest congregations in all of California. The small museum contains many musical instruments and transcriptions, evidence of the mission's musical focus—it once boasted a formidable Native American boys' choir. Mission San Juan Bautista is open daily year-round from 9:30am to 4:45pm. Suggested donation is $1 per person. For further information, call ℂ **831/623-4528.**

East of the church, perched at the edge of an abrupt drop created by the movement of the San Andreas Fault, is a marker pointing out the path of the old **El Camino Real.** Accompanying the marker are seismographic measuring equipment and an earthquake science exhibit.

In addition to the mission, there's much to see on the restored city plaza. Be sure to visit the **San Juan Bautista State Historic Park.** The park is comprised of not only the old Plaza Hotel with its classic frontier barroom and furnished rooms, but also the Plaza Hall, its adjoining stables and blacksmith shop, and the Castro House, where the Breen family lived after traveling here with the ill-fated Donner Party in 1846. Allow 1½ to 2 hours to see the entire plaza. Admission to the park buildings is $2 for adults, $1 for children ages 6 to 12 (separate from your charge to the mission). Hours are daily 10am to 4:30pm. For further information (including event schedules), call ℂ **831/623-4881.**

2 Monterey ✮✮

45 miles S of Santa Cruz, 116 miles S of San Francisco, 335 miles N of Los Angeles

Originally settled in 1770, Monterey was one of the West Coast's first European settlements, and the capital of California under the Spanish, Mexican, and American flags. California's state constitution was drafted here in 1849, paving the way for admission to the Union a year later. In fact, many buildings from the early colonial era still stand. A major whaling center in the 1800s, Monterey eventually became the sardine capital of the Western Hemisphere when the first packing plant was built in 1900. By 1913, the boats were bringing in 25 tons of sardines a night to the 18 canneries. The gritty lives of the mostly working-class residents were forever captured by local hero John Steinbeck in his 1945 novel *Cannery Row.*

After the sardines disappeared, Monterey was forced to fish for tourist dollars instead; hence, an array of boutiques, knickknack stores, and theme restaurants now reside in converted sardine factories along the bay. Granted, plenty of history and heritage remains along Cannery Row, but you'll have to weed though the tourist schlock to find them. Its saving grace is the world-class aquarium and beautiful Monterey Bay, where sea lions and otters still frolic in abundance.

As you distance yourself from the Row, however, you'll soon discover that Monterey is a pleasant seaside community, replete with magnificent vistas, historic architecture, stately Victorians, and a number of quality lodgings and restaurants. More important, Monterey is only a short drive from Pacific Grove,

Carmel, Pebble Beach, and Big Sur, and the lodgings here are far less expensive, which makes it a great place to set up base while exploring the Monterey coast.

ESSENTIALS

GETTING THERE   The region's most convenient runway, at the **Monterey Peninsula Airport** (© 831/648-7000), is 3 miles east of Monterey on Calif. 68. **American Eagle** (© 800/433-7300), **Northwest** (© 800/225-2525), **United** (© 800/241-6522), and **US Airways** (© 800/428-4322) have daily flights in and out of Monterey.

Many area hotels offer free airport shuttle service. If you take a taxi, it will cost about $10 to $15 to get to a peninsula hotel. Several national car rental companies have airport locations, including **Dollar** (© 800/800-4000) and **Hertz** (© 800/654-3131).

VISITOR INFORMATION   The **Monterey Peninsula Visitors and Convention Bureau** (© 831/649-1770; www.monterey.com) has two visitor centers: one located in the lobby of the Maritime Museum at Custom House Plaza near Fisherman's Wharf, and the other at Lake El Estero on Camino El Estero. Both locations, open daily, offer an array of good maps, as well as free pamphlets and publications, including an excellent visitors' guide and the magazine *Coast Weekly.*

GETTING AROUND   The **Waterfront Area Visitor Express (WAVE)** operates each year from Memorial Day weekend through Labor Day and takes passengers to and from the aquarium and other waterfront attractions. Stops are located at many hotels and motels in Monterey and Pacific Grove. The cost of $1.50 for adults and 75¢ for kids and seniors gets you unlimited rides all day between 9am and 6pm and eliminates the stress of parking in crowded downtown. For further information, call **Monterey Salinas Transit** (© 831/899-2555).

EXPLORING MONTEREY

The **National Steinbeck Center** ❀ is not in town, but if you're a fan, you'll want to make the 20-mile drive northeast from Monterey on Calif. 68 to One Main St. in Salinas (© **831/775-4721;** www.steinbeck.org). A new $11-million, 37,000-square-foot museum opened in mid-1998, offering walk-through interactive exhibits, a changing exhibition gallery, an orientation theater presenting a 10-minute video on Steinbeck's life, educational programs, a gift shop, and a cafe. Admission is $7.95 for adults, $6.95 for seniors over 62, $5.95 for children ages 13 to 17, $3 for children 6 to 12, and free for children under 6. Hours are daily from 10am to 5pm.

If you're traipsing through Monterey on a Tuesday afternoon, be sure to check out the **Old Monterey Marketplace** on Alvarado Street, from Pearl to Del Monte Streets, open from 4 to 8pm (until 7pm in winter). More than 100 vendors participate in this farmers' market, bringing food, music, crafts, and entertainment together for an afternoon of flavorful festivities.

Monterey Bay Aquarium ❀❀❀ *(Kids)*   The site of one of the world's most spectacular aquariums was not chosen at random. It sits on the border of one of the largest underwater canyons on earth (wider and deeper than even the Grand Canyon) and is surrounded by incredibly diverse local marine life. The Monterey Bay Aquarium is one of the best exhibit aquariums in the world, and one of the largest, too—home to more than 350,000 marine animals and plants. One of the living museum's main exhibits is a three-story, 335,000-gallon tank, with clear acrylic walls that give visitors an unmatched look at local sea life. A

The Monterey Peninsula

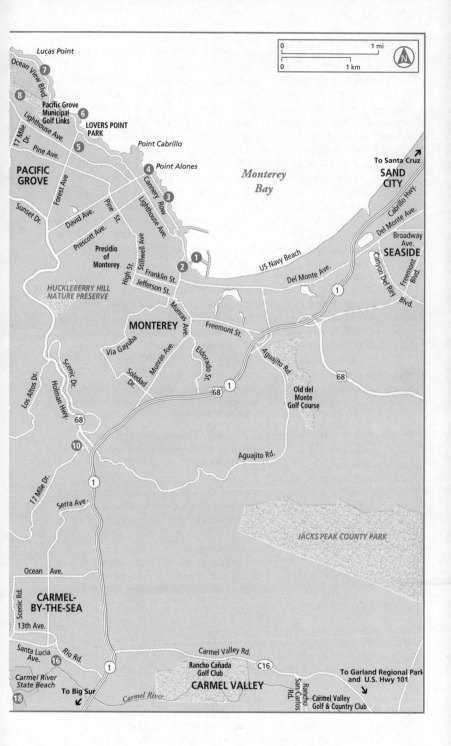

Lucas Point

Ocean View Blvd. **7**

8

Pacific Grove
Municipal
Golf Links **6**

Lighthouse Ave.

17 Mile Dr.

Pine Ave. **5**

**PACIFIC
GROVE**

Forest Ave.

Sunset Dr.

David Ave.

Prescott Ave.

Pine St.

Stillwell Ave.

Cannery Row

Lighthouse Ave.

**LOVERS POINT
PARK**

Point Cabrillo

Point Alones **4**

3

Presidio
of
Monterey

High St.

Franklin St.

Jefferson St.

2

1

*Monterey
Bay*

US Navy Beach

Del Monte Ave.

To Santa Cruz

**SAND
CITY**

Cabrillo Hwy.

Del Monte Ave.

Broadway
Ave.

SEASIDE

Canyon Del Rey

Fremont
Blvd.

1

*HUCKLEBERRY HILL
NATURE PRESERVE*

MONTEREY

Munras Ave.

Via Gayuba

Freemont St.

Munras Ave.

Eldorado St.

Aguajito Rd.

68

Los Altos Dr.

Scenic Dr.

Holman Hwy.

Soledad
Dr.

68

1

68

Old del
Monte
Golf Course

68

10

17 Mile Dr.

1

Serra Ave.

Aguajito Rd.

JACKS PEAK COUNTY PARK

Ocean Ave.

**CARMEL-
BY-THE-SEA**

Scenic Rd.

13th Ave.

Santa Lucia
Ave. **16**

Rio Rd.

1

*Carmel River
State Beach*

18

To Big Sur

Carmel River

Carmel Valley Rd.

Rancho Cañada
Golf Club

C16

CARMEL VALLEY

Rancho
San Carlos
Rd.

To Garland Regional Park
and U.S. Hwy 101

Carmel Valley
Golf & Country Club

0   1 mi
0   1 km

towering kelp forest, which rises from the floor of this oceanic zoo, gently waves with the water as hundreds of leopard sharks, sardines, anchovies, and other fish swim back and forth in an endless game of hide-and-seek.

The outstanding Outer Bay exhibit features creatures that inhabit the open ocean. This tank—holding a million gallons of water—houses yellowfin tuna, large green sea turtles, barracuda, sharks, the very cool giant ocean sunfish, and schools of bonito. The Outer Bay's jellyfish exhibit is guaranteed to amaze, and kids will love Flippers, Flukes, and Fun, a learning area for families.

The Mysteries of the Deep exhibit is the largest collection of live deep-sea species in the world—many of which have never been on display anywhere. The 7,000-square-foot exhibit highlights the underwater life collected from waters as deep as 3,300 feet, including such creatures as spider crabs, ratfish, filetail catsharks, predatory tunicates, mushroom corals, and California king crabs.

New this year is the Splash Zone exhibit (designed for families with kids up to 9 years old), which features black footed penguins, invertebrates, and fish whose habitats are coral reefs and the cooler waters and rocky shores of northern California.

Additional exhibits re-create other undersea habitats found in Monterey Bay. Everyone falls in love with the sea otters playing in their two-story exhibit. There are also coastal streams, tidal pools, a sand beach, and a petting pool, where you can touch living bat rays and handle sea stars. Visitors can also watch a live video link that regularly transmits from a deep-sea research submarine maneuvering thousands of feet below the surface of Monterey Bay.

Tip: You can avoid lines at the gate by calling © **800/756-3737** or **831/648-4888** outside California and ordering tickets in advance.

886 Cannery Row. © **800/756-3737** or 831/648-4888. Fax 831/648-4810. www.montereybayaquarium.org. Admission $15.95 adults, $13.95 students and seniors 65 and over, $7.95 visitors with disabilities and children 3–12, free for children under 3. AE, MC, V. Daily 10am–6pm.

Fisherman's Wharf   Just like San Francisco's Fisherman's Wharf, this wooden pier is jam-packed with craft and gift shops, boating and fishing operations, fish markets, and seafood restaurants—all trawling for tourist dollars. But Monterey's wharf does have redeeming qualities: The natural surroundings are so beautiful that if you cast your view toward the bobbing boats and surfacing sea lions, you might not even notice the hordes of tourists around you. Grab some clam chowder in a sourdough bread bowl and find a seaside perch along the pier. Or, when the wind picks up, find a bayfront seat at one of the seafood restaurants (see "Where to Dine," later in this section).

If the seaside sights have got you itching to set sail, boats depart regularly from Fisherman's Wharf and will lead you on a number of ocean adventures. See "Outdoor Pursuits," below, for details on some of the offerings.

99 Pacific St. © **831/649-6544**.

Cannery Row   Once the center for an industrial sardine-packing operation immortalized by John Steinbeck as "a poem, a stink, a grating noise, a quality of light, a tone, a habit, a nostalgia, a dream," this area today is better described as a strip congested with wandering tourists, tacky gift shops, overpriced seafood restaurants, and an overall parking nightmare. What changed it so dramatically? The silver sardines suddenly disappeared from Monterey's waters in 1948 as a result of overfishing, changing currents, and pollution. Fishermen left, canneries closed, and the Row fell into disrepair. But curious tourists continued to visit Steinbeck's fabled area, and where there are tourists, there are capitalists.

After visiting Cannery Row in the 1960s, Steinbeck wrote, "The beaches are clean where they once festered with fish guts and flies. The canneries that once put up a sickening stench are gone, their places filled with restaurants, antique shops, and the like. They fish for tourists now, not pilchards, and that species they are not likely to wipe out." And we couldn't put it any better.

Between David and Drake Aves. (℅ 831/373-1902.

FOLLOWING THE PATH OF HISTORY

The dozen or so historic buildings clustered around Fisherman's Wharf and the adjacent town collectively comprise the "Path of History," a tour that examines 1800s architecture and lifestyle. Many of the buildings are a part of the **Monterey State Historic Park** ✦, 20 Custom House Plaza (℅ **831/649-7118**). Highlights include the **Custom House,** which was constructed around 1827 and is the oldest government building in California, and the **Maritime Museum of Monterey,** 5 Custom House Plaza (℅ **831/373-2469**), which showcases ship models and other collections that relate the area's seafaring history, including a two-story-high, 10,000-pound Fresnel lens, used for nearly 80 years at the Point Sur lighthouse. Admission is $3 for adults, $2 for seniors and youths ages 13 to 18, free for children under 13; open daily from 10am to 5pm.

You can go the self-guided route by picking up a free tour booklet at the Monterey Peninsula Visitors and Convention Bureau (see above), the Cooper-Molera Adobe (at the corner of Polk and Munras Sts.), and various other locations. You may also opt to take the guided tour, which departs several times daily. The price is $5 for adults, $3 for youths ages 13 to 18, $2 for children 6 to 12, free for children under 6. Call ℅ **831/649-7118** for exact schedule information, or visit the **State Park Visitor Center** at Stanton Center, 5 Custom House Plaza. A free film on the history of Monterey is shown here every 20 minutes.

MONTEREY WINE COUNTRY

The congestion and price of Napa and Sonoma vineyards and the increasingly lucrative and romantic occupation of winemaking have forced industry newcomers to plant their grapes elsewhere. Fortunately, much of the California coast offers perfect growing conditions. Nowadays, if you visit any area between Monterey and Santa Barbara, there's easy access to new appellations and a variety of boutique vintners making respectable wines. Stop by **A Taste of Monterey,** 700 Cannery Row (℅ **831/646-5446**), daily between 11am and 6pm to learn about and taste locally produced wines in front of huge bayfront windows. This is also the place to get a map and winery touring information.

OUTDOOR PURSUITS

Cast your hook on a deep sea–fishing expedition. Among the operators are **Chris' Fishing Trips,** 48 Fisherman's Wharf (℅ **831/375-5951**), which offers large party boats. Cod and salmon are the main catches, with separate boats leaving daily. Full-day excursions cost $38 weekdays and $40 weekends per person for cod, $48 weekdays and $50 weekends for salmon. Call for a complete price list and departure schedule.

Sam's Fishing Fleet, 84 Fisherman's Wharf (℅ **831/372-0577**), offers fishing excursions for cod, salmon, and whatever else is running, as well as whale-watching tours. Make reservations and bring a lunch. Departures are Monday through Friday at 5am and 7:30am (salmon-fishing boats leave earlier), Saturday and Sunday at 7am. Check-in is 45 minutes prior to departure. Prices for cod are $35, $20 for children 12 and under; weekend and holiday rates are

$38 for adults, $23 for children. Prices for salmon are $45 weekdays, $50 on weekends. Equipment rental costs a bit extra.

Several outfitters rent kayaks for a spin around the bay. Contact **Monterey Bay Kayaks,** 693 Del Monte Ave. (© **800/649-5357** or 831/373-5357; www.montereykayaks.com), on Del Monte Beach north of Fisherman's Wharf, which offers instruction as well as natural-history tours that introduce visitors to the Monterey Bay National Marine Sanctuary. Prices start at $50 for the tours, rentals from $25. A second store is at nearby Moss Landing, offering guided tours of Elkhorn Slough, one of the last remaining estuaries in California (see below). Call © **800/655-6367** for more information.

For bikes and in-line skates as well as kayak tours and rentals, contact **Adventures by the Sea,** 299 Cannery Row (© **831/372-1807**). Bikes cost $6 per hour or $24 per day; kayaks are $25 per person, or $45 for a 2½-hour tour; and skates are $12 for 2 hours, $24 for a day. Adventures by the Sea also has other locations at 201 Alvarado Mall (© **831/648-7235**) at the Doubletree Hotel, and on the beach at Lovers Point in Pacific Grove.

Experienced scuba divers wishing to go out on an excursion can contact **Monterey Bay Dive Center,** 225 Cannery Row (© **831/656-0454**), which arranges personal dives with a divemaster and has scheduled weekend dives. **Aquarius Dive Shop,** 2040 Del Monte Ave. (© **831/375-1933**), also has regularly scheduled trips and divemasters. Certification cards are essential.

North of Monterey at Marina State Beach, you can learn to hang glide during a 3-hour course that includes a minimum of five flights with **Western Hang Gliders,** Calif. 1 at Reservation Road, Marina (© **831/384-2622**). The cost is $98. Tandem flights, paragliding, and ultralights are available, too.

Need to keep the kids busy, or feeling playful yourself? The **Dennis the Menace Playground** ⚓ at Camino El Estero and Del Monte Avenue, near Lake Estero, © **831/646-3860,** is an old-fashioned playground created by Pacific Grove resident and famous cartoonist Hank Ketcham. It has bridges to cross, tunnels to climb through, and an authentic Southern Pacific Railroad engine teeming with wanna-be conductors. There's also a hot dog and burger stand, and a big lake where you can rent paddleboats or feed the ducks. The park is open daily from 10am to sunset.

WHERE TO STAY

It seems there are only three types of choices for accommodations in Monterey: lace-and-flowers B&Bs, large corporate hotels with only a slight beachy feel (if even that), or run-of-the-mill motel digs. Consider which area you'd like to be in—beach, Cannery Row, wharf, secluded, central, and so forth—as well as how much you want to spend; then check out the options below or contact the reservations service **Time to Coast** (© **800/555-WAVE;** www.timetocoast.com), which represents about 30 lodging facilities in Monterey.

EXPENSIVE

In addition to the choices below, there are two chain hotels conveniently located near Fisherman's Wharf: The **Monterey Marriott,** 350 Calle Principal, at Del Monte Blvd. (© **800/228-9290** or 831/649-4234; www.marriott.com), offers some rooms with bay views, an outdoor pool, health club, Jacuzzi, and saunas. There's also the **Doubletree Hotel at Fisherman's Wharf,** 2 Portola Plaza (© **800/222-8733** or 831/649-4511; www.doubletree.com). Less centrally located, but great for families and golfers, is the enormous **Hyatt Regency Monterey** resort, 1 Old Golf Course Rd. (© **800/233-1234** or 831/372-1234;

Kids The Otters, Seals & Birds of the Elkhorn Slough

One of our favorite stops along the coast is Moss Landing, which is 25 minutes north of Monterey on Calif. 1. Along the virtually one-street town are a few adorable down-home restaurants and antiques shops. But what really attracts us is Captain Yohn Gideon's **Elkhorn Slough Safari.** For $26 for adults or $19 for children under 15, friendly Cap'n Gideon loads guests onto a 27-foot pontoon boat (safe for old and young) and embarks on a 2-hour tour of the wondrous Elkhorn Slough Wildlife Reserve, which, by the way, is like jumping into a *National Geographic* special. It's not uncommon to see a "raft" of up to 50 otters feet-up and sunning themselves, an abundance of lounging harbor seals, and hundreds of species of waterfowl and migratory shorebirds. An onboard naturalist answers questions, Cap'n educates on the surroundings, and binoculars are available. For reservations, schedules, and information, call ✆ **831/633-5555** or check out **www.elkhornslough.com**.

---

www.hyatt.com). It adjoins the Del Monte Golf Course and has three pools, two Jacuzzis, a gym, tennis courts, and two restaurants. All three hotels are popular with business travelers and conventioneers.

Hotel Pacific ★★ Although it's not even remotely waterfront (it's close to the wharf and across the street from the Monterey Conference Center), this is our favorite upscale choice in Monterey. Beyond the elegant Spanish-Mediterranean architecture of the common areas, each unit is situated in one of 16 buildings clustered around courtyards and compact gardens complete with spas and fountains. The cozy Southwestern-style junior suites have fluffy down comforters atop four-poster feather beds (for the full effect, request a canopied bed), rustically stylish decor, terra cotta–tiled floors, and a fireplace surrounded by a cushy couch and seats. Add to that two TVs, three phones, and gourmet coffee and tea—all of which make this a place where you'll want to hibernate awhile. Tiny closets are one of the few downsides.

300 Pacific St., Monterey, CA 93940. ✆ **800/554-5542** or 831/373-5700. Fax 831/373-6921. www.hotel pacific.com. 105 suites. $229–$409 suite for 2. Rates include continental breakfast and afternoon tea. AE, DC, DISC, MC, V. Free parking. **Amenities:** Nearby golf course; 2 Jacuzzis; room service; in-room massage; laundry service; same-day dry cleaning. *In room:* TV/VCR, minibar, coffeemaker, hair dryer, iron.

Monterey Plaza Hotel and Spa ★★ One of the most formal hotels in town, the Monterey Plaza is comprised of three buildings—two on the water and one across the street—that are connected by a second-story enclosed "skywalk." The public areas are elegantly decorated with imported marble, Brazilian teak, and attractive artwork. The stately bedrooms are more upscale-corporate than most around town and have double or king beds, decor reminiscent of 19th-century Biedermeier, and Italian marble bathrooms. Many units have balconies overlooking the water (sea otters included in the view). The least desirable rooms are across the street from the ocean. Extras include terry robes and an attentive and professional staff.

400 Cannery Row, Monterey, CA 93940. ✆ **800/334-3999** in CA, 800/631-1339 outside of CA, or 831/646-1700. Fax 831/656-0439. www.woodsidehotels.com. 290 units. $185–$505 double; $510–$2,500 suite. Children 17 and under stay free in parents' room. Packages available. AE, DC, DISC, MC, V. Parking $14 per day. From Calif. 1, take the Soledad Dr. exit and follow the signs to Cannery Row. **Amenities:** 2 restaurants; nearby golf course; fully equipped fitness center; full service European-style spa; Jacuzzi; dry sauna; concierge;

tour desk; business center; secretarial services; shopping arcade; 24-hour room service; in-room massage; laundry service; same-day dry cleaning; executive-level rooms. *In room:* TV w/ pay movies, dataport, fully stocked minibar, fridge, coffeemaker, hair dryer, iron.

Old Monterey Inn ✦✦ Proprietors Ann and Gene Swett did a masterful job of converting their comfortable three-story family home into a vine-covered Tudor-style country inn. Although it's away from the surf, it's a perfect choice for romantics, with rose gardens, a bubbling brook, and brick-and-flagstone walkways shaded by a panoply of oaks. All but one guest room enjoy peaceful garden views and cozy beds with goose-down comforters and pillows. Most units also have feather beds and wood-burning fireplaces, and two open onto private patios. The guest rooms are all charmingly furnished and unique in character; two of our favorites are the Library and the Serengeti Room. Special touches are evident throughout, including fresh fruit, flowers, and candies, sachets by the pillow, and books and magazines. The private cottage out back has an English country look and comes with a double Jacuzzi, linen-and-lace-draped king-size bed, wood-burning fireplace, sitting area, and private patio.

Breakfast, prepared by Gene, is also stellar, consisting of perhaps orange French toast, soufflé, or Belgian waffles. It's served in your room, the dining room, or the rose garden. The Swetts will also provide picnic blankets and towels for the beach. At 5pm, guests retire to the living room for wine and hors d'oeuvres in front of a blazing fire.

500 Martin St. (off Pacific Ave.), Monterey, CA 93940. ✆ **800/350-2344** or 831/375-8284. Fax 831/375-6730. www.oldmontereyinn.com. 9 units, 1 cottage. $200–$300 double; from $300 cottage. Rates include full breakfast and evening wine and hors d'oeuvres. MC, V. Free parking. From Calif. 1, take the Soledad Dr. exit and turn right onto Pacific Ave., then left onto Martin St. **Amenities:** Nearby golf course; passes to nearby health club; Jacuzzi; concierge; tour desk; in-room massage. *In room:* Dataport, hair dryer, iron; some units with TV/VCR.

Spindrift Inn ✦ Down in the middle of honky-tonk Cannery Row, but right along a narrow stretch of beach, this four-story hotel is an island of continental style in a sea of commercialism. It's elegant and well maintained, and the rooms are sweetly decorated with feather beds (a few with canopies), hardwood floors, wood-burning fireplaces, and either cushioned window seats or private balconies. The luxurious bathrooms are adorned with marble and brass fixtures. Extras include terry robes and *two* phones. The ocean views are definitely worth the additional cost, although the place is still painfully expensive for what it offers—unless, of course, you get a deal (same goes for the Monterey Bay Inn).

652 Cannery Row, Monterey, CA 93940. ✆ **800/841-1879** or 831/646-8900. Fax 831/646-5342. www.spindriftinn.com. 42 units. $199–$329 double with Cannery Row view; $329–$459 double with ocean view. Rates include continental breakfast delivered to your room and afternoon tea. Parking $7. AE, DC, DISC, MC, V. **Amenities:** 2 restaurants, bar; nearby golf course; room service; in-room massage; same-day dry cleaning. *In room:* TV/VCR, fully stocked minibar, coffeemaker, hair dryer.

MODERATE

Munras Avenue and northern Fremont Avenue are lined with moderate and inexpensive family-style motels, some independently owned and some chains. They're not as central as the downtown options, and atmosphere is seriously lacking on Fremont Avenue, but if transportation's not an issue, you can save a bundle by staying in one of these areas. If the selections below are full, try calling **Best Western** (✆ **800/528-1234**) for several other options. There's also the **Cypress Gardens Inn,** 1150 Munras Ave. (✆ **831/373-2761**), with a pool, Jacuzzi, free movie channels, and continental breakfast; dogs are welcome.

Fireside Lodge   Location is the primary advantage of this hotel near Fisherman's Wharf and downtown. The room furnishings are relatively standard, but make an attempt at coziness with wicker chairs set around the gas-heated brick fireplace. Families on a budget will appreciate the kitchen facilities, plus the continental breakfast served daily in the hotel's lobby will ease the food bill, too.

1131 10th St., Monterey, CA 93940. ℂ 800/722-2624 (in CA) or 831/373-4172. Fax 831/655-5640. www. montereyfireside.com. 24 units. $69–$225 double. Rates include continental breakfast. AE, DC, DISC, MC, V. Pets accepted $10 (under 20 lbs.), $20 (over 20 lbs.). **Amenities:** Nearby golf course; Jacuzzi. *In room:* TV, dataport, kitchenette, fridge.

The Jabberwock Bed & Breakfast ✮   One of the better B&Bs in the area, the Jabberwock (named after a poem in Lewis Carroll's *Through the Looking Glass*) is 4 short blocks from Cannery Row. Although centrally located, the property is tranquil, and its half-acre garden with waterfalls offers a welcome respite from the downtown crowds. The seven rooms are individually furnished, some more elegantly than others, but all with goose-down comforters and pillows. The Toves Room has a huge walnut Victorian bed; the Borogrove has a fireplace and a view of Monterey Bay; the Mimsey has a fine ocean view from its window seat; and the Wabe has an Austrian carved bed. A full breakfast is served in the dining room or in your own room. Evening hors d'oeuvres are offered on the veranda, and a Vorpal rabbit tucks each guest in with cookies and milk.

598 Laine St., Monterey, CA 93940. ℂ 888/428-7253 or 831/372-4777. Fax 831/655-2946. www. jabberwockinn.com. 7 units (5 with bathroom). $115 double without private bathroom; $210–$235 double with private bathroom. Rates include full breakfast, afternoon aperitifs, and bedtime cookies. MC, V. **Amenities:** Nearby golf course; Jacuzzi; concierge; activities desk; in-room massage. *In room:* Hair dryer; no phone.

INEXPENSIVE

Opt for a motel to get the best rates in this town. Some reliable options are **Motel 6** (ℂ 800/4-MOTEL6), **Super 8** (ℂ 800/800-8000), or **Best Western** (ℂ 800/528-1234).

Cypress Tree Inn *Value*   Although it's not centrally located (2 miles from downtown), if you're on a budget and have transportation, you won't be sorry if you stay here. The large rooms are spotless, and all but one has a combination tub and shower. Nine also have Jacuzzis. There's no shampoo, or in-room treats other than the taffy left by the maid, but the hostelry does have a handy coin-op laundry. RV spaces are also available.

2227 N. Fremont St., Monterey, CA 93940. ℂ 831/372-7586. Fax 831/372-2940. www.cypresstreeinn.com. 55 units. $52–$129 double. AE, DC, DISC, MC, V. **Amenities:** Nearby golf course; Jacuzzi; sauna; laundry facilities. *In room:* TV, dataport, fridge; some units with kitchen or kitchenette.

WHERE TO DINE

Bubba Gump Shrimp Co. Restaurant & Market AMERICAN   Culinary cognoscenti will flee in disgust at the sight of this tourist haven, but the fact is, lots of folks love this place. It could be the location—near the aquarium and offering a million-dollar unobstructed bayfront view—or the old boatyard decor that attracts visitors in droves. But it's more likely the entertainment value: Gump's (as in Forrest Gump) is packed with movie gimmicks and memorabilia. The food, unfortunately, is far less exciting. As the roll of paper towels at each table suggests, you're guaranteed a go with grease, which is likely to arrive in the form of fried and buttered-up seafood. The "Bucket of Boat Trash," for example, is shrimp and lobster tails cooked and served in a bucket with a side of fries and coleslaw. There are also pork chops, a veggie dish, salads, and burgers. The "market" referred to in the moniker is a gift shop packed with T-shirts, caps, and, of course, boxes of chocolate.

720 Cannery Row (at Prescott). (C) 831/373-1884. Fax 831/373-1139. www.bubbagump.com. Main courses $7.95–$24.99. AE, DC, DISC, MC, V. Daily 11am–11pm.

Cafe Fina ✿ ITALIAN/SEAFOOD   While other pier-side restaurants lure tourists with little more than an outstanding view, Cafe Fina's mesquite-grilled meats, well-prepared fresh fish, brick-oven pizzas, and an array of delicious salads and pastas give even locals a reason to head to the wharf. Combine the food with a million-dollar vista and a casual atmosphere, and Cafe Fina ranks hands down as the best choice on the pier.

47 Fisherman's Wharf. (C) 831/372-5200. Fax 831/3725209. www.cafefina.com. Reservations recommended. Main courses $14–$19. AE, DC, DISC, MC, V. Mon–Fri 11:30am–2:30pm and 5–9:30pm; Sat–Sun 11:30am–4pm and 4 –9:30pm.

John Pisto's Whaling Station Prime Steaks & Seafood AMERICAN/ STEAK HOUSE   If you insist on eating on Cannery Row, come to this touristy restaurant known for its New York, porterhouse, and other steaks grilled over oak and mesquite. A 28-year tradition guarantees you an artichoke vinaigrette appetizer before your main course, which ranges from pasta and chicken to jumbo live Maine lobsters and live local abalone.

763 Wave St. (between Prescott and Irving Aves.). (C) 831/373-3778. Fax 831/373-2460. Reservations recommended on weekends. Main courses start at $21.95. AE, DC, DISC, MC, V. Daily from 5–10pm. From Calif. 1, take the Soledad Dr. exit and follow the signs toward Cannery Row; turn left on Wave St. 1 block before Cannery Row. Free valet parking on weekends.

Montrio ✿✿ AMERICAN BISTRO   Big-city sophistication meets old Monterey here. The enormous dining room is definitely the sharpest in town, mixing chic style with a playful canopied vineyard of modern light fixtures, clouds hanging from the ceiling, and the buzz of well-dressed diners. You can watch chefs scurry around in the open kitchen, but you're more likely to keep your eyes on the tasty dishes, such as the crispy Dungeness crab cakes with spicy rémoulade; succulent grilled pork chops with apple, pear, and currant compote; or an oven-roasted portobello mushroom with polenta and ragout of vegetables. Finish the evening with passion-fruit gratin with wild-berry coulis.

414 Calle Principal (at Franklin). (C) 831/648-8880. www.montrio.com. Reservations recommended. Main courses $12–$25. AE, DISC, MC, V. Mon–Thurs 11:30am–10pm; Fri–Sat 11:30am–11pm; Sun 5–10pm.

Stokes Restaurant and Bar ✿✿ CALIFORNIA/MEDITERRANEAN This historic adobe and board-and-batten house, built in 1833 for the town doctor, has been converted into one of Monterey's finest restaurants. It's quite the handsome establishment, consisting of a bar and several large dining rooms, all outfitted with terra-cotta floors, bleached-wood plank ceilings, and Southwestern-style wood chairs and tables. It's the perfect rustic-yet-contemporary showcase for chef Brandon Miller's carefully crafted California-Mediterranean fare—butternut-squash soup with apple cider and maple crème fraîche; cassoulet of duck confit and homemade currant sausage with chestnut beans; and grilled lavender-infused pork chops with savory bread pudding and pear chutney. Desserts are equally dreamy, such as the warm apricot clafouti and the warm banana-rum bread pudding with vanilla crème Anglaise. Highly recommended is the prix-fixe dinner, offered nightly for around $35. The wine list is excellent as well.

500 Hartnell St. (at Madison St). © **831/373-1110.** Fax 831/373-1202. www.stokesadobe.com. Reservations recommended. Main courses $12–$19. AE, DC, DISC, MC, V. Mon–Thurs 11:30am–10pm; Fri–Sat 11:30am–10:30pm; Sun 4–10pm.

Tarpy's Roadhouse ★★ CALIFORNIA/AMERICAN   Always a mandatory stop when we're passing through Monterey is this lively Southwestern-style restaurant located a few miles east of downtown (and definitely worth the detour). The very handsome dining room has stylish yet soothingly rustic decor. On sunny afternoons, patrons relax under market umbrellas on the huge outdoor patio, sipping margaritas and munching on Tarpy's legendary Caesar salad. Come nightfall, the place fills quickly with tourists and locals who pile in for the hefty plate of bourbon-molasses pork chops or Dijon-crusted lamb loin. There's also a modest selection of fresh fish, shellfish, and vegetable dishes, but it's the good ol' meat 'n' potato mainstays that sell the best. (The thick, juicy meatloaf with garlic mashers and fresh veggies is a bargain at $14.)

2999 Monterey-Salinas Hwy. (at Calif. 68 and Canyon del Rey near the Monterey Airport). © **831/647-1444.** Fax 831/647-1103. www.tarpys.com. Reservations recommended for dinner. Most main courses $14–$30. AE, DISC, MC, V. Daily 11:30am–10pm.

Wharfside Restaurant & Lounge SEAFOOD   While the fresh seafood is okay, the real attraction is the Wharfside's casual upstairs dining room, which offers a nautical decor and a great view from the end of Fisherman's Wharf (there's also downstairs and upper-deck outdoor seating). Choose from six different varieties of ravioli (made on the premises), such specialties as a combination bouillabaisse, and any of the house-made desserts. Daily specials usually include fresh seasonal fish, beef, and pasta. Clam chowder, sandwiches (including hot crab), and pizzas are on the regular menu.

60 Fisherman's Wharf, Monterey. © **831/375-3956.** Fax 831/375-2967. Reservations recommended. Main courses $11–$20. AE, DC, DISC, MC, V. Daily 11am–10pm. Closed the first 10 days of Dec.

3 Pacific Grove ★★

42 miles S of Santa Cruz, 113 miles S of San Francisco, 338 miles N of Los Angeles

Some compare 2.6-square-mile Pacific Grove—the locals call it "P.G."—to Carmel as it was 20 years ago. Although tourists wind their way through here on oceanfront trails and dining excursions, the town remains quaint and peaceful—amazing considering that Monterey is a stone's throw away (a quarter of the Monterey Bay Aquarium is actually in Pacific Grove). While neighboring Monterey is comparatively congested and cosmopolitan, Pacific Grove is a community sprinkled with historic homes, blooming flowers, and the kind of tranquility that inspires butterflies to flutter about and deer to meander fearlessly across the road in search of another garden to graze.

ESSENTIALS

VISITOR INFORMATION   Although the town is small, there is the **Pacific Grove Chamber of Commerce,** at the corner of Forest and Central Avenues (© **800/656-6650** or 831/373-3304; www.pacificgrove.org).

ORIENTATION   Lighthouse Avenue is the Grove's principal thoroughfare, running from Monterey to the lighthouse at the very point of the peninsula. Lighthouse Avenue is bisected by Forest Avenue, which runs from Calif. 1 (where it's called Holman Highway, or Calif. 68) to Lover's Point, an extension of land that sticks out into the bay in the middle of Pacific Grove.

EXPLORING THE TOWN

Pacific Grove is a town to be strolled, so park the car, put on your walking shoes, and make an afternoon of it. Meander around George Washington Park and along the waterfront around the point.

The **Point Pinos Lighthouse** ⋆, at the tip of the peninsula on Ocean View Boulevard (© 831/625-4419), is the oldest working lighthouse on the West Coast. Its 50,000-candlepower beacon has illuminated the rocky shores since February 1, 1855, when Pacific Grove was little more than a pine forest. The museum and grounds are open, free to visitors, Thursday through Sunday from 1 to 4pm.

Marine Gardens Park ⋆, a stretch of shoreline along Ocean View Boulevard on Monterey Bay and the Pacific, is renowned not only for its ocean views and colorful flowers, but also for its fascinating tide-pool seaweed beds. Walk out to **Lover's Point** (named after Lovers of Jesus, not groping teenagers) and watch the sea otters playing in the kelp beds and cracking open an occasional abalone for lunch.

An excellent shorter alternative, or complement, to the 17-Mile Drive (see section 4 later in this chapter) is the scenic drive or bike ride along Pacific Grove's **Ocean View Boulevard** ⋆. This coastal stretch starts near Monterey's Cannery Row and follows the Pacific around to the lighthouse point. Here it turns into Sunset Drive, which runs along secluded **Asilomar State Beach** ⋆ (© 831/648-3130). Park on Sunset and explore the trails, dunes, and tide pools of this sandy stretch of shore. You might find purple shore crabs, green anemone, sea bats, starfish, and limpets, as well as all kinds of kelp and algae. The 11 buildings of the conference center established here by the YWCA in 1913 are historic landmarks that were designed by noted architect Julia Morgan. If you follow this route during winter, a furious sea rages and crashes against the rocks.

To learn more about the marine and other natural life of the region, stop in at the **Pacific Grove Museum of Natural History,** 165 Forest Ave. (© 831/648-3116). It has displays on monarch butterflies and their migration, stuffed examples of the local birds and mammals, and temporary exhibits and special events. Admission is free; hours are Tuesday through Sunday from 10am to 4:30pm.

Pacific Grove is widely known as "Butterfly Town, USA," a reference to the thousands of **monarch butterflies** that migrate here from November to February, traveling from as far away as Alaska. Many settle in the Monarch Grove sanctuary, a eucalyptus stand on Grove Acre Avenue off Lighthouse Avenue. George Washington Park, at Pine Avenue and Alder Street, is also famous for its "butterfly trees." To reach these sites, the butterflies may travel as far as 2,000 miles, covering 100 miles a day at an altitude of 10,000 feet. Collectors beware: The town imposes strict fines for molesting butterflies.

Just as Ocean View Boulevard serves as an alternative to the 17-Mile Drive, the **Pacific Grove Municipal Golf Course,** 77 Asilomar Ave. (© 831/648-3177), serves as a reasonably priced alternative to the high-priced courses at Pebble Beach. The back nine holes of this 5,500-yard, par-70 course overlook the sea and offer the added challenge of coping with the winds. Views are panoramic, and the fairways and greens are better maintained than most semi-private courses. There's a restaurant, pro shop, and driving range. Eighteen holes start at $25 Monday through Thursday and $35 Friday through Sunday and holidays; twilight rates are available. Optional carts cost $25.

The **American Tin Cannery Factory Premium Outlets,** 125 Ocean View Blvd., around the corner from the Monterey Bay Aquarium (© 831/372-1442), is a huge converted warehouse housing 40 factory-outlet shops. Labels represented here include Anne Klein, Joan & David, Bass Shoes, Reebok, Carter's Childrenswear, Royal Doulton, Jones New York, Maidenform, London Fog, Woolrich, and Carole Little. It's open Sunday through Thursday from 10am to 6pm, Friday and Saturday from 10am to 8pm.

WHERE TO STAY

If you're having trouble finding a vacancy, try calling **Resort II Me** (© 800/757-5646), a local reservations service that offers free recommendations of Monterey Bay–area hotels in all price ranges.

EXPENSIVE

Martine Inn ✯✯ One glance at the lavish Victorian interior and the incredible bay views and you'll know why this Mediterranean-style inn is one of the best B&Bs in the area. Enjoy the vista via binoculars that the management leaves out for guests, or stroll the bayfront promenade. You'll have to pay more if you want a fireplace and ocean view, though every room is a winner. Request a room with a bathtub if it matters to you; some have only a shower. The inn also maintains an adjacent Victorian cottage, which has been converted into a luxury suite. A full breakfast is served at lace-covered tables in the large front room; hors d'oeuvres are served in the evening. Guests also have access to two additional sitting quarters: a small room downstairs overlooking the ocean and a larger room with shelves of books.

255 Ocean View Blvd., Pacific Grove, CA 93950. © 800/852-5588 or 831/373-3388. Fax 831/373-3896. www.martineinn.com. 23 units. $170–$300 double. Rates include full breakfast and evening hors d'oeuvres. AE, DISC, MC, V. **Amenities:** Nearby golf course; Jacuzzi; game room; concierge; tour desk; room service; in-room massage and babysitting upon request. *In room:* Fridge, hair dryer.

Seven Gables Inn ✯✯ This is one of the most opulent B&Bs we've ever seen. Named after the seven gables that cap the hotel, the compound of Victorian buildings was constructed in 1886 by the Chase family (as in Chase Manhattan Bank). Outside is the coast road overlooking the sea; inside is a valuable collection of mostly European antiques. Everything here is luxurious and gilded, including the oceanview rooms, which are scattered among the main house, cottages (including a two-bedroom option), and the guesthouse. The accommodations are linked by verdant gardens filled with roses and marble sculpture. Afternoon tea is accompanied by an array of pastries and homemade chocolates. If the hotel's booked, ask about the Grand View Inn, a slightly less ornate but comparable B&B next door that's run by the same owners.

555 Ocean View Blvd., Pacific Grove, CA 93950. © 831/372-4341. www.pginns.com. 14 units. $175–$385 double. Rates include breakfast and afternoon tea. 2-night minimum on weekends. MC, V. **Amenities:** Nearby golf course. *In room:* Hair dryer; some units with fridge, 1 unit with kitchenette. No phone.

MODERATE

Centrella Inn ✯ A couple of blocks from the waterfront and from Lover's Point Beach, the two-story Centrella is an old turreted Victorian that was built as a boardinghouse in 1889. Today, the rooms are decorated in Victorian style, but they're somewhat plain—iron beds, side table, floor lamp, and armoire—although the bathrooms do have clawfoot tubs. In the back, connected to the house by brick walkways, are several private cottages and suites with fireplaces, and separate bedrooms and bathrooms. Two have private decks; the others offer decks facing the rose garden and patio, which is set with umbrella tables and chairs.

612 Central Ave., Pacific Grove, CA 93950. ℂ **800/233-3372** or 831/372-3372. Fax 831/372-2036. www. centrellainn.com. 26 units. $129–$239 double; $189–$259 suites and cottages. Rates include buffet breakfast and evening hors d'oeuvres. AE, DISC, MC, V. **Amenities:** Nearby golf course. *In room:* TVs in cottages; no phone.

Gosby House ℛ

Originally a boardinghouse for Methodist ministers, this Victorian was built in 1888, 3 blocks from the bay. It's still one of the most charming Victorians in town, with individually decorated rooms, floral-print wallpapers, lacy pillows, and antique furnishings. Twelve guest rooms have fireplaces, and all come with the inn's trademark teddy bears. Especially noteworthy are the two Carriage House rooms, which come with fireplace, balcony, and extra-large bathroom with spa tub. The house has a separate dining room and parlor, where guests gather for breakfast and complimentary wine and hors d'oeuvres in the afternoon. Other amenities include complimentary newspaper, twice-daily maid service, and bicycles.

643 Lighthouse Ave., Pacific Grove, CA 93950. ℂ **800/527-8828** or 831/375-1287. Fax 831/655-9621. www. foursisters.com. 22 units (20 with bathroom). $115 double without bathroom; $90–$170 double with bathroom. Rates include full breakfast and afternoon wine and hors d'oeuvres. AE, DC, MC, V. From Calif. 1, take Calif. 68 to Pacific Grove, where it turns into Forest Ave.; continue on Forest to Lighthouse Ave., turn left, and go 3 blocks. **Amenities:** Nearby golf course; complimentary bike use. *In room:* Hair dryer; Carriage House has TV/VCR, fridge, coffeemaker.

Green Gables Inn ℛℛ

This beautiful 1888 Queen Anne–style mansion, which is decorated like an English country inn, forgoes opulence (and in some cases private bathrooms) to allow for reasonable rates and less formal accommodations. The rooms are divided between the main building and the carriage houses behind it. The Carriage House rooms, which are better for families, have large private bathrooms with Jacuzzi tubs. All accommodations are individually decorated with dainty furnishings, including some antiques and an occasional poster bed. Most rooms in the original home have ocean views and share two immaculate bathrooms. There's an antique carousel horse in the comfortable parlor, where complimentary wine, tea, and hors d'oeuvres are served each afternoon.

104 Fifth St., Pacific Grove, CA 93950. ℂ **800/722-1774** or 831/375-2095. Fax 831/375-5437. www.four sisters.com. 11 units (7 with bathroom). $120–$150 double without bathroom, $160–$180 double with bathroom; $200–$260 suite. Rates include full breakfast and afternoon wine and hors d'oeuvres. AE, DC, MC, V. From Calif. 1, take the Pacific Grove exit (Calif. 68) and continue to the Pacific Ocean; turn right on Ocean View Blvd. and drive half a mile to Fifth St. **Amenities:** Complimentary bike use. *In room:* Iron.

Pacific Grove Inn

Five blocks from the beach, this renovated 1904 Queen Anne–style mansion is one of the town's bevy of painted ladies. Despite heavy Victorian embellishments, the accommodations feel light and airy. Rooms come with queen- or king-size beds, and fireplaces. Afternoon tea is served in the parlor.

581 Pine Ave., Pacific Grove, CA 93950. ℂ **800/732-2825** or 831/375-2825. Fax 831/375-0752. 16 units. $98–$138 double; $135–$200 suite. Rates include buffet breakfast and afternoon tea. AE, DC, DISC, MC, V. From Calif. 1, take the Pacific Grove exit (Calif. 68) to the corner of Pine and Forest Aves. **Amenities:** Nearby golf course. *In room:* TV/VCR, fridge, safe.

INEXPENSIVE

The Wilkies Inn ℛ *Value* This motel consistently charges less than the other hotels in town, gets an A+ for service, and is located on a quiet tree-lined street with a resident deer who often drops by for breakfast (but please don't feed him). The motel boasts well-kept furnishings and carpets, and stylish bedspreads. All the squeaky-clean rooms come with microwaves and free HBO and local calls. Some have partial ocean views.

1038 Lighthouse Ave., Pacific Grove, CA 93950. © **866/372-5960** or 831/372-5960. Fax 831/655-1681. 24 units. $49–$210 double. Extra person $10. 2-night minimum on weekends. Rates include continental breakfast. Packages available. AE, DISC, MC, V. **Amenities:** Nearby golf course. *In room:* TV/VCR, fridge, coffeemaker, hair dryer, iron.

WHERE TO DINE
EXPENSIVE
Fandango ★★ MEDITERRANEAN   Provincial Mediterranean specialties from Spain to Greece to North Africa spice up the menu with such offerings as seafood paella with North African couscous (the recipe has been in the owner's family for almost 200 years), cassoulet maison, cannelloni Niçoise, and a Greek-style lamb shank. You'll feel transported straight to Europe in one of the five upstairs and downstairs dining rooms, cozied by roaring fires, wood tables, and antiqued walls. There's an award-winning international wine list with 450 options and a dessert menu that includes a Grand Marnier soufflé with fresh raspberry puree sauce and profiteroles. In winter, ask to be seated in the fireplace dining room, and in summer, request the terrace room—but whenever you come, expect everything here to be lively and colorful, from the regional decor to the owner himself.

223 17th St. © **831/372-3456.** Fax 831/372-2673. www.fandangorestaurant.com. Reservations recommended. Main courses $11–$24. AE, DC, DISC, MC, V. Mon–Sat 11am–3pm; Sun 10am–2:30pm; daily 5–9:30pm. From Calif. 1, take the Pacific Grove exit (Calif. 68), turn left on Lighthouse Ave., and continue a block to 17th St.

Joe Rombi's ★ ITALIAN   In an area where most restaurants pack 'em in, Joe Rombi's offers a refreshingly intimate dining room with dimmed lights and enormous French antique posters. The food here is very fresh. (Lasagnas and pastas are made that day.) Once seated at one of the 11 tables, you'll immediately be served a basket of fresh house-made focaccia to munch on while you peruse the limited menu of appetizers, soups, salads, pizzas, pastas, and four main courses (some of which come with soup and salad). Go with the fish of the day—we had a halibut dish that any upscale San Francisco restaurant would be proud to serve.

208 17th St. (at Lighthouse Ave.). © **831/373-2416.** Fax 831/373-2106. www.joerombis.com. Reservations recommended. Main courses $12–$21. AE, MC, V. Wed–Sun 5–10pm.

The Old Bath House ★ CONTINENTAL   Romance is in the air at this restored Victorian restaurant, perched on the edge of the earth overlooking Lover's Point. It may be pricey and frequented by tourists, but dinner here is a stately affair with knockout bay views, superb service, and competently prepared cuisine. Popular starters are the grilled prawns and wild-boar sausage. Main courses range from soy-ginger-glazed filet mignon to braised petrale sole and veal medaillons crusted with pistachios. The signature dish is the duck merlot, served with apples and a raspberry-merlot sauce. End your decadent dinner with a plate of hot pecan ice-cream fritters.

620 Ocean View Blvd. © **831/375-5195.** Fax 831/375-5379. www.oldbathhouse.com. Reservations required. Main courses $19.50–$29.50. AE, DC, DISC, MC, V. Mon–Fri 5–10:30pm; Sat 4–11pm; Sun 4–10:30pm.

MODERATE

The Fishwife at Asilomar Beach ⊛ _Kids_ SEAFOOD   The Fishwife is the ideal dining spot for anyone looking for a casual, affordable, and quality meal. The restaurant dates from the 1830s, when a sailor's wife started a small food market that became famous for its Boston clam chowder. Today, locals still return for the savory soup as well as some of the finest seafood in Pacific Grove. Two best-sellers at dinner are calamari steak sautéed with shallots, garlic, tomatoes, and white wine; and prawns Belize, served sizzling with red onions, tomatoes, fresh Serrano chilies, jicama, lime juice, and cashews. Steak and pasta dishes are also available, and all main courses come with vegetables, bread, black beans, and rice or potatoes. Kids get their own color-in menu, which has smaller portions for less than $6.

1996½ Sunset Dr. (at Asilomar Beach). ✆ 831/375-7107. Fax 831/375-7107. www.fishwife.com. Main courses $8.95–$14.95. AE, DISC, MC, V. Mon–Sat 11am–10pm; Sun 10am–10pm. From Calif. 1, take the Pacific Grove exit (Calif. 68) and stay left until it becomes Sunset Dr.; the restaurant will be on your left about 1 mile ahead, as you approach Asilomar Beach.

Peppers Mexicali Café ⊛ MEXICAN/LATIN AMERICAN   Peppers is a casual, festive place serving good food at reasonable prices. The inviting dining room has wooden floors and tables, pepper art visible from every vantage point, and a perpetual crowd of diners who come to suck up beers and savor spicy specialties such as well-balanced seafood tacos and fajitas or house-made tamales and chiles rellenos. Other fire-starters include the snapper Yucatán, which is cooked with chilies, citrus cilantro, and tomatoes; and grilled prawns with lime-cilantro dressing. More than a dozen daily specials are offered as well, such as Mexican seafood paella and grilled mahimahi tacos. Add a substantial selection of cervezas, an addicting compilation of chips and salsa, and a friendly staff, and your taste buds are bound to bellow "Ole!"

170 Forest Ave. ✆ 831/373-6892. Fax 831/373-5467. Reservations recommended. Main courses $7–$15. AE, DC, DISC, MC, V. Mon and Wed–Thurs 11:30am–10pm; Fri–Sat 11:30am–10:30pm; Sun 4–10pm.

INEXPENSIVE

First Awakenings ⊛ _Value_ AMERICAN   What was once a dank canning factory is now a bright, huge, open restaurant offering one of the cheapest and healthiest breakfasts in the area. Eye-openers include eight varieties of omelets; granola with nuts, fruit, and yogurt; walnut and wheat pancakes; "gourmet" pancakes; and raisin French toast. At lunch, there's a fine choice of salads and a slew of sandwiches ranging from albacore to zucchini. On sunny days, take advantage of the outdoor patio tables.

In the American Tin Cannery, 125 Ocean View Blvd. ✆ 831/372-1125. Reservations not accepted. Breakfast $3–$7; lunch $5–$7. AE, DISC, MC, V. Daily 7am–2:30pm. From Calif. 1, take the Pacific Grove exit (Calif. 68) and turn right onto Lighthouse Ave.; after a mile turn left onto Eardley Ave., and take it to the corner of Ocean View.

4 Pebble Beach & the 17-Mile Drive ⊛⊛⊛

Pebble Beach is a world unto itself. Polo shirts, golf shoes, and big bankrolls are standard here, and if you have to ask how costly accommodations and greens fees are, you definitely can't afford them. In this elite golfers' paradise, endless grassy fairways are interrupted only by a few luxury resorts and cliffs where the ocean meets the land. In winter, it's also the site of the AT&T Pebble Beach National Pro-Am, a celebrity tournament originally launched in 1937 by crooner Bing Crosby.

THE 17-MILE DRIVE 𝒢𝒢

The beautiful 17-Mile Drive demands a leisurely afternoon. Pack a picnic or make lunch reservations at pricey Roy's in the Inn at Spanish Bay (see "Where to Stay & Dine," below), fork over $7.50 to enter the drive, and prepare to see some of the most exclusive coastal real estate in California.

The drive can be entered from any of five gates: two from Pacific Grove to the north, one from Carmel to the south, or two from Monterey to the east. The most convenient entrance from Calif. 1 is just off the main road at the Holman Highway exit. You may beat traffic by entering at the Carmel Gate and doing the tour backward.

Admission to the drive includes an informative map that lists 26 points of interest along the way. Aside from homes of the ultra-rich, highlights include **Seal and Bird Rocks,** where you can see countless gulls, cormorants, and other offshore birds as well as seals and sea lions; and **Cypress Point Lookout,** which affords a 20-mile view all the way to the Big Sur Lighthouse on a clear day. Also visible is the famous **Lone Cypress** tree, inspiration to so many artists and photographers, which you can admire from afar but to which you can no longer walk. The drive also traverses the **Del Monte Forest,** thick with tame black-tailed deer and often described as some "billionaire's private game preserve."

One of the best ways to see 17-Mile Drive is by bike, but the ride toward Carmel is all downhill, so unless you're in great shape, arrange for a ride back. For further information, call the Pebble Beach Resort at ✆ **831/624-3811.**

GREAT GOLF COURSES

Locals tell us it's almost impossible to get a tee time unless you're staying at the golf resort. If you're one of the lucky few, you can choose from several famous courses along the 17-Mile Drive.

PEBBLE BEACH GOLF LINKS 𝒢𝒢𝒢   The most famous course is Pebble Beach Golf Links (✆ **800/654-9300**) at the Lodge at Pebble Beach (see "Where to Stay & Dine," below). It's home in winter to the AT&T Pebble Beach National Pro-Am, a celebrity-laden tournament televised around the world. Jack Nicklaus has claimed, "If I could play only one course for the rest of my life, this would be it." He should know; he won both the 1961 U.S. Amateur and the 1972 U.S. Open here. Indeed, 10 national championships have been decided here. Herbert Warren Wind, dean of 20th-century golf writers, said, "There is no finer seaside golf course in creation"—and that includes the legendary Old Course at St. Andrews in Scotland. Built in 1919, this 18-hole course is 6,799 yards and par 72. It's precariously perched over a rugged ocean. Greens fees are a staggering $320 plus cart fee.

SPYGLASS HILL GOLF COURSE 𝒢𝒢   Also frequented by celebrities is this course at Stevenson Drive and Spyglass Hill Road (✆ **800/654-9300**). Its slope rating of 143 means that it's one of the toughest courses in California. It's a justifiably famous links: 6,859 yards and par 72 with five oceanfront holes. The rest reach deep into the Del Monte Forest. Greens fees are $250 plus cart, $195 for guests of the Lodge or the Inn (see "Where to Stay & Dine," below). Reservations for non-guests should be made a month in advance. There's an excellent Grill Room on the grounds.

POPPY HILLS 𝒢𝒢   This 18-hole, 6,219-yard course on 17-Mile Drive (✆ **831/625-2035**) was named one of the world's top 20 by *Golf Digest*. It was designed by Robert Trent Jones, Jr., in 1986. Greens fees are $115 Monday through Thursday and $130 Friday, Saturday and Sunday, plus $30 for the cart rental. You can make reservations 30 days in advance.

THE LINKS AT SPANISH BAY ✪✪ Lying on the north end of 17-Mile Drive at the Pebble Beach Resort and Inn at Spanish Bay (✆ **800/654-9300**), this is the most easily booked course. Serious golfers say it's the most challenging of the Pebble Beach links. Robert Trent Jones, Jr., Tom Watson, and Frank Tatum (former USGA president) designed it to duplicate a Scottish links course. Greens fees are $210. Cart rental is an additional $25. Reservations can be made 60 days in advance.

DEL MONTE GOLF COURSE ✪ At 1300 Sylvan Rd. (✆ **831/373-2700**) lies the oldest course west of the Mississippi, charging some of the most "reasonable" greens fees: $80 per player ($70 for resort guests), plus a cart rental of $18. The course, often cited in magazines for its "grace and charm," is relatively short—only 6,339 yards. This seldom-advertised course, which is located at the Hyatt east of Monterey, is part of the Pebble Beach complex, but is not along 17-Mile Drive.

WHERE TO STAY & DINE

Casa Palmero Resort ✪✪✪ The Casa Palmero is a small, ultra-luxury resort on the first tee of the Pebble Beach Golf Links. The two-story villa is the newest firmament in the dazzling sister properties, which include the Inn at Spanish Bay and the Lodge at Pebble Beach. The more intimate and private of the three, Casa Palmero is fashioned as an Old World European villa with cool stucco walls, window boxes dripping bougainvillea, every modern creature comfort, and a staff to anticipate your every wish. It has 24 cottages and suites with varying amenities including French doors opening onto private garden spas, oversized window box sofas, wood-burning fireplaces, and oversized soaking tubs that open to the main room. "Convivial" areas, places you can hang out your with your friends, include a trellised patio, library, billiards parlor, living room, private dining room, executive boardroom and small conference room, intimate courtyards with fountains, and lavish outdoor pool pavilion.

1518 Cypress Dr. (on 17-Mile Dr.), Pebble Beach, CA 93953. ✆ 800/654-9300 or 831/622-6650. Fax 831/622-6655. www.pebblebeach.com. 24 units. $595–$1,900. $18.50 gratuity added. Rates include continental breakfast and evening hors d'oeuvres and cocktails. AE, DC, DISC, MC, V. From Calif. 1 south, turn west onto Calif.68 and south onto 17-Mile Dr., and follow the coastal road to the hotel. **Amenities:** 3 restaurants; outdoor heated pool; golf course on site; 12 tennis courts; health club; full service spa; Jacuzzi; sauna; bike rental; concierge; 24-hour room service; in-room massage; babysitting; laundry service; same-day dry cleaning; executive-level rooms. In room: TV/VCR w/ pay movies, dataport, minibar, fridge, coffeemaker, hair dryer, iron, safe.

The Inn at Spanish Bay ✪✪✪ Surrounded by the renowned Links at Spanish Bay golf course, the Inn at Spanish Bay is a plush three- and four-story lowrise, set on 236 manicured acres 10 miles north of the Lodge at Pebble Beach. Approximately half the rooms face the ocean and are more expensive than their counterparts, which overlook the forest. Each unit contains about 600 square feet of floor space and has a private fireplace and either an outdoor deck or a patio. The bathrooms are finished in Italian marble; the custom-made furnishings include four-poster beds with down comforters. Our favorite time here is dusk, when a bagpiper strolls the terrace with a skirling tribute to Scotland.

2700 17-Mile Dr., Pebble Beach, CA 93953. ✆ 800/654-9300 or 831/647-7500. Fax 831/644-7960. www.pebblebeach.com. 276 units. $350–$500 double; from $1,750–$2,165 2-bedroom suite. $18.50 gratuity added. AE, DC, MC, V. From Calif. 1 south, turn west onto Calif. 68 and south onto 17-Mile Dr.; the hotel is on your right, just past the toll plaza. **Amenities:** 3 restaurants; bar/lounge; heated outdoor pool; golf course on site; 8 outdoor tennis courts (2 lit at night); health club; full service spa; Jacuzzi; sauna; bike rental; concierge; tour desk; business center; shopping arcade; 24-hour room service; in-room massage; babysitting; laundry service; same-day dry cleaning; executive-level rooms. *In room:* TV/VCR w/ pay movies, dataport, minibar, fridge, coffeemaker, hair dryer, iron; most units with safe.

The Lodge at Pebble Beach ★★   For the combined cost of greens fees and a room here, you could easily create a professional putting green in your own backyard—and still have some money left over. But if you're a dedicated hacker, you've got to play here at least once. Look on the bright side—at least you can expect ultra-plush, recently revamped rooms, which are equipped with every conceivable amenity, including wood-burning fireplaces. Most are in two-story cottage clusters, with anywhere from 8 to 12 units in each. Those opening onto the ocean carry the highest price tags.

1700 17-Mile Dr., Pebble Beach, CA 93953. © **800/654-9300** or 831/624-3811. Fax 831/644-7960. www. pebblebeach.com. 173 units. $395–$500 double; from $1,250 suite. $15 gratuity added. AE, DC, DISC, MC, V. From Calif. 1 south, turn west on Calif. 68, turn south onto 17-Mile Dr., and follow the coastal road to the hotel. **Amenities:** 4 restaurants, bar/lounge; heated outdoor pool; golf course on site; 12 tennis courts; health club; full service spa; Jacuzzis; sauna; bike rental; children's center; concierge; tour desk; courtesy car; business center; shopping arcade; 24-hour room service; in-room massage; babysitting; laundry service; same-day dry cleaning; executive-level rooms. *In room:* TV/VCR w/ pay movies, dataport, minibar, fridge, coffeemaker, hair dryer, iron; most units with safe.

5 Carmel-by-the-Sea ★★

5 miles S of Monterey, 121 miles S of San Francisco, 33 miles N of Big Sur

If you visited the town officially known as Carmel-by-the-Sea dozens of years ago, you're likely to be of the school that criticizes its present-day overcommercialization. Carmel began as an artists' colony that attracted such luminaries as Robinson Jeffers, Sinclair Lewis, Robert Louis Stevenson, Ansel Adams, William Rose Benet, and Mary Austin. It was a nonconformist enclave where residents resisted assigned street numbers and lighting (they carried lanterns, which they considered more romantic).

Today, Carmel may not be the bohemian artists' village of seasoned travelers' memories, but it's still an adorable (albeit touristy) town that knows how to celebrate its surroundings. Vibrant wildflower gardens flourish along each residential street, gnarled cypress trees reach up from white sandy beaches, and at the end of each day tourists magically disappear and the town—for a split second—feels undiscovered.

It's still intimate enough that there's no need for street numbers. Carmel's inns, restaurants, boutiques, and art galleries all identify their locations only by cross streets. A few hints such as Saks Fifth Avenue, convertible roadsters cruising through town, intolerable traffic, and lofty B&B rates indicate we're not in Kansas anymore, but rather a well-preserved upscale tourist haven.

If you're interested in saving a few dollars, we recommend staying in quaint Pacific Grove. It's only a few miles away, has better rates, and you can easily daytrip into crowded Carmel.

ESSENTIALS

The **Carmel Business Association,** P.O. Box 4444, Carmel, CA 93921 (© **831/ 624-2522;** www.carmelcalifornia.org), is located on San Carlos between Fifth and Sixth Streets. It distributes local maps, brochures, and publications. Pick up a copy of the *Guide to Carmel* and a schedule of local events. Hours are Monday through Friday from 9am to 5pm. On weekends, an information booth is set up from 11am to 3pm at Carmel Plaza, on Ocean Avenue between Junipero and San Carlos Streets.

EXPLORING THE TOWN

A wonderful stretch of white sand backed by cypress trees, **Carmel Beach City Park** ★★ is a wee bit o' heaven on earth (though the jammed parking lot can feel more like a visit to a car rally). There's plenty of room for families, surfers, and dogs with their owners (yes, pooches are allowed to run off-leash here). If the parking lot is full, there are some spaces on Ocean Avenue, but take heed: They're generally good for 90-minute parking only, and you will get a ticket if you park for the day.

Farther south around the promontory, **Carmel River State Beach** ★ is a less crowded option, with white sand and dunes, plus a bird sanctuary where brown pelicans, black oystercatchers, cormorants, gulls, curlews, godwits, and sanderlings make their home.

The **Mission San Carlos Borromeo del Rio Carmelo** ★★, on Basilica Rio Road at Lasuen Drive, off Calif. 1 (© **831/624-3600;** www.carmelmission.org), is the burial ground of Father Junípero Serra and the second-oldest of the 21 Spanish missions he established. Founded in 1771 on a scenic site overlooking the Carmel River, it remains one of the largest and most interesting of California's missions. The stone church, with its gracefully curving walls and Moorish bell tower, was begun in 1793. Its walls are covered with a lime plaster made of burnt seashells. The old mission kitchen, the first library in California, the high altar, and the flower gardens are all worth visiting. More than 3,000 Native Americans are buried in the adjacent cemetery; their graves are decorated with seashells. The mission is open June through August, Monday through Saturday from 9:30am to 7:30pm, Sunday from 10:30am to 7:30pm; in other months, Monday through Saturday from 9:30am to 4:30pm, Sunday from 10:30am to 4:30pm. A $2 donation is requested.

One of Carmel's prettiest homes and gardens is **Tor House** ★, 26304 Ocean View Ave. (© **831/624-1813;** www.torhouse.org), built by California poet Robinson Jeffers. Situated on Carmel Point, the house dates from 1918 and includes a 40-foot tower containing stones from around the world, which are embedded in the walls (there's even one from the Great Wall of China). Inside, an old porthole is reputed to have come from the ship on which Napoleon escaped from Elba in 1815. No photography is allowed. Admission is by guided tour only, and reservations are requested. It's $7 for adults, $4 for college students, and $2 for high-school students (no children under 12). Open on Friday and Saturday from 10am to 3pm.

If the tourists aren't lying on the beach in Carmel, then they're probably **shopping**—the sine qua non of Carmel activities. You'll be surprised at the number of shops packed into this small town—more than 500 boutiques offering unique fashions, baskets, housewares, imported goods, and a veritable cornucopia of art galleries. Most of the commercial action is packed along the small stretch of Ocean Avenue between Junipero and San Antonio Avenues.

If you want to tour the galleries, pick up a copy of the *Carmel Gallery Guide* from the Carmel Business Association (see "Essentials," above).

Serious shoppers should also head south a few miles to the **Crossroads Shopping Center** (from Calif. 1 south, take the Rio Rd. exit west for 1 block and turn right onto Crossroads Blvd.). As far as malls go, this is a great one, with oodles of shopping and a few good restaurants.

WHERE TO STAY

If you're traveling with pets, your best bet is **The Cypress Inn,** Lincoln and Seventh (P.O. Box Y), Carmel-by-the-Sea, CA 93921 (© **800/443-7443** or 831/624-3871; www.cypress-inn.com), which is a moderately priced option run by owner and actress Doris Day.

EXPENSIVE

Carriage House Inn ★★   The luxurious atmosphere and superfluous pampering make this one of our top picks in the "downtown" area. Each room comes with a wood-burning fireplace and king-size bed with down comforter. Most of the second-floor rooms have sunken tubs and vaulted beam ceilings; first-floor rooms have single whirlpool tubs. Not only is breakfast delivered to guest rooms, but there's also wine and hors d'oeuvres served in the afternoon and cappuccino, wine, and cheese in the evening. Plus, while almost all choices in the area are frill-and-lace, the Carriage House is a more mature, formal, yet cozy environment.

Junipero St., between Seventh and Eighth Aves. (P.O. Box 1900), Carmel, CA 93921. © 800/433-4732 or 831/625-2585. Fax 831/624-0974. www.ibts-carriagehouse.com. 13 units. $209–$375 double; $259–$399 suite. Rates include continental breakfast and afternoon wine and hors d'oeuvres. Free parking for every room. AE, DISC, MC, V. From Calif. 1, exit onto Ocean Ave. and turn left onto Junipero St. Amenities: Nearby golf course; concierge. *In room:* TV/VCR, minibar, coffeemaker, hair dryer, iron, safe.

Highlands Inn, Park Hyatt Carmel ★   Four miles south of Carmel on a 12-acre cliff overlooking Point Lobos, this one- and two-story inn has attracted everyone from celebrities—Madonna, Sammy Hagar, Walt Disney, Marlon Brando—to honeymooners and business executives. It's rustic yet luxurious, with wildflowers gracing its pathways, plenty of character, and a charming, exclusive atmosphere. The old-style main lounge dates from 1916 and has panoramic coastal vistas. The guest rooms are distributed throughout a cluster of buildings terraced into the hillside. Expect modern decor with natural-wood furnishings. Most units have decks or balconies and wood-burning fireplaces. The suites come with Jacuzzi tubs and fully equipped kitchens; four rooms have showers only.

120 Highlands Dr., Carmel, CA 93923. © 800/682-4811 or 831/620-1234. Fax 831/626-8105. www.highlands-inn.com. 142 units. $195 double; $250–$585 spa suite; $675–$915 2-bedroom, full oceanview spa suite. AE, DC, DISC, MC, V. Dogs under 15 lbs. with $75 fee. **Amenities:** 2 restaurants, lounge; outdoor heated pool; nearby golf course; exercise room; 3 outdoor Jacuzzis; complimentary bike use; concierge; tour/activities desk; car rental desk; business center; secretarial services; room service; in-room massage; babysitting; laundry service; same-day dry cleaning; executive level rooms. *In room:* TV w/ pay movies (VCR on request), minibar, fridge, coffeemaker, hair dryer, iron, safe; suites with kitchens.

La Playa ★   Only 2 blocks from the beach and yet within walking distance of town, the four-story La Playa is a romantic, Mediterranean-style villa built in 1904. Norwegian artist Christopher Jorgensen ordered its construction for his bride, an heiress of the Ghirardelli chocolate dynasty. The stylish lobby sets the elegant tone with its terra-cotta floors, Oriental rugs, and white marble fireplace. In the courtyard, walkways lead through beautifully landscaped grounds that surround a heated pool. Compared to the splendor of the lobby and grounds, the standard guest rooms are a bit of a disappointment. The walls are thin and the furnishings perfunctory. The luxury cottages are an improvement—all have kitchens, wet bars, and garden patios, and most have wood-burning fireplaces—but yes, they're expensive.

Camino Real and Eighth Ave. (P.O. Box 900), Carmel, CA 93921. © 800/582-8900 or 831/624-6476. Fax 831/624-7966. www.laplayahotel.com. 80 units. $155–$295 double; $295–$595 suite or cottage. Complimentary valet parking. AE, DC, MC, V. **Amenities:** Restaurant, bar; outdoor heated pool; nearby golf course; bike rental; concierge; business center; room service; babysitting; same-day dry cleaning. *In room:* TV, fridge, hair dryer, iron; cottages have full kitchen, limited room service.

Mission Ranch 🐾🐾   If you want to stay a bit off the beaten track, consider this converted 1850s dairy farm, which was purchased and restored by Clint Eastwood to preserve the vista of the nearby wetlands stretching out to the bay. The ranch's accommodations are spaciously scattered amid different structures, both old and new, and surrounded by wetlands and grazing sheep. Guest rooms range from "regulars" in the main barn (which are less desirable) to meadow-view units, each with a vista across the fields to the bay. As befits a ranch, rooms are decorated in a provincial style, with carved wooden beds bedecked with handmade quilts. Most are equipped with whirlpool baths, fireplaces, and decks or patios. The Martin Family farmhouse contains six units, all arranged around a central parlor, while the Bunkhouse (the oldest structure on the property) contains separate living and dining areas, bedrooms, and a fridge. Even if you're not staying here, call for a table at the Restaurant at Mission Ranch; see "Where to Dine," below.

26270 Dolores St., Carmel, CA 93923. ☎ **800/538-8221** or 831/624-6436. Fax 831/626-4163. 31 units. $95–$275 double. Rates include continental breakfast. AE, MC, V. **Amenities:** Restaurant; 6 tennis courts; exercise room; babysitting; laundry service; dry cleaning. *In room:* TV, dataport, coffeemaker, hair dryer, iron; some units with fridge.

MODERATE

Carmel Sands Lodge 🐾   The Sands is a motor lodge, but it's decorated better than most and is located on a quiet street in Carmel. The modern rooms have pretty bedspreads and updated furnishings; some have fireplaces and wet bars. There's a small pool, but it's practically in the center courtyard parking lot. Several restaurants are nearby. We like the quaint location here better than that of the comparable Carmel Village Inn.

San Carlos and Fifth (P.O. Box 951), Carmel, CA 93921. ☎ **800/252-1255** or 831/624-1255. Fax 831/624-2576. www.carmelsandslodge.com. 38 units. July–Oct $98–$189 double; Nov–June $68–$169 double. AE, DC, DISC, MC, V. From Ocean Ave., take a right onto San Carlos and go 2 blocks. **Amenities:** Restaurant; heated pool (seasonal); nearby golf course. *In room:* TV; some units with minibar, fridge, coffeemaker, hair dryer.

Carmel Village Inn 🐾   Well run and centrally located, the Village Inn is basically a motor lodge. The rooms, arranged around a courtyard and parking lot lined with potted geraniums, are outfitted with bland but functional decor. The guest rooms come equipped with fridges. Breakfast, accompanied by the morning newspaper, is served in the downstairs lounge.

Ocean Ave. and Junipero St. (P.O. Box 5275), Carmel, CA 93921. ☎ **800/346-3864** or 831/624-3864. Fax 831/626-6763. www.carmelvillageinn.com. 53 units. $69–$190 double; $89–$380 triple or quad; from $108 suite. Rates include continental breakfast. AE, MC, V. From Calif. 1, exit onto Ocean Ave. and continue straight to Junipero St. **Amenities:** Babysitting. *In room:* Fax, kitchenette.

Cobblestone Inn 🐾   The Cobblestone may not be Victorian like other properties owned by the Four Sisters Inns, but it's just as flowery, well kept, and cute, with hand-stenciled wall decorations, fireplaces, and a trademark abundance of teddy bears. The first floor is completely constructed of stones taken from the Carmel River (hence the inn's name), and the rooms encircle a slate courtyard; some look out onto the brick patio where breakfast is occasionally served. The guest rooms vary in size; some can be small, and only the Honeymoon suite comes with a bathtub, but the largest units include a wet bar, sofa, and separate bedroom. Guests have the use of a comfortable living room with large stone fireplace and enjoy complimentary wine, hors d'oeuvres, coffee, and cookies. Extras include daily maid and turndown service and morning newspaper.

Junipero St., between Seventh and Eighth Aves., 1½ blocks from Ocean Ave. (P.O. Box 3185), Carmel, CA 93921. ℂ 800/833-8836 or 831/625-5222. Fax 831/625-0478. www.foursisters.com. 24 units. $125–$200 double; from $250 suite. Rates include full breakfast and afternoon hors d'oeuvres. AE, DC, MC, V. **Amenities:** Complimentary bike use. *In room:* TV, fridge, hair dryer; some units with coffeemaker. Honeymoon suite with VCR.

Normandy Inn ✮   Three blocks from the beach, this French Provincial-style hotel is like something out of a storybook, especially with the array of colorful flowers that brighten up the property. Some of the guest rooms show their age a little, but are well appointed with French country decor and down comforters. Some have fireplaces and/or kitchenettes. The tiny heated pool is banked by a sweet flower garden.

The three large family-style units are an especially good deal and accommodate up to eight; each one has three bedrooms, two bathrooms, a fully equipped kitchen, a dining room, a living room with a fireplace, and a back porch. Be sure to reserve far in advance, especially in summer.

Ocean Ave., between Monte Verde and Casanova Sts. (P.O. Box 1706), Carmel, CA 93921. ℂ 800/343-3825 or 831/624-3825. Fax 831/624-4614. www.normandyinncarmel.com. 48 units. $99–$279 double; $169–$500 suites and cottages. Rates include continental breakfast. Extra person $10. AE, DC, MC, V. From Calif. 1, exit onto Ocean Ave. and continue straight for 5 blocks past Junipero St. **Amenities:** Outdoor pool (seasonal); nearby golf course. *In room:* TV, coffeemaker, hair dryer, iron; some units with kitchenette. 3 family-style units with fully equipped kitchens.

Sandpiper Inn by the Sea ✮   A garden of flowers welcomes visitors to this quiet, relaxing, mid-scale Carmel standby that's been in business for more than 60 years. The inn's rooms, from which you can hear the surf, offer a range of well-kept accommodations. The highest priced are corner rooms with four-poster beds and plenty of windows framing the ocean view. All are decorated with handsome country antiques and fresh flowers that are changed daily; three have fireplaces. Carmel's fabled white-sand beaches are a mere 100 yards away.

2408 Bay View Ave., Carmel, CA 93923. ℂ 800/633-6433 or 831/624-6433. Fax 831/624-5964. www. sandpiper-inn.com. 17 units. $95–$285 double. Rates include extended continental breakfast and afternoon sherry/tea. AE, DISC, MC, V. **Amenities:** Nearby golf course; concierge; tour desk. *In room:* No phone.

WHERE TO DINE
EXPENSIVE

Anton & Michel ✮ EUROPEAN/CONTINENTAL   This elegant restaurant, just across from Carmel Plaza, serves traditional French cuisine in one of the most formal rooms in town. During the day, it's best to dine fountain-side on the patio or encased in the glass-wrapped terrace. The view is equally charming in the evening, when the courtyard is lit and the fountain's water sparkles with reflections. Decorated with French chandelier lamps and original oil paintings, the main dining room is a formal affair—but, as in most restaurants in town, patrons' attire need not match it. Appetizers include crab cakes with cilantro-pesto aïoli or delicate ravioli filled with ricotta cheese and spinach. Specialties include rack of lamb with an herb-Dijon mustard au jus, medaillons of ahi tuna with a black pepper and sesame seed crust, and more eclectic items such as a chicken breast Jerusalem, sautéed with olive oil, white wine, cream, and artichoke hearts. The award-winning wine list is impressive.

At Court of the Fountain, Mission St. (between Ocean and Seventh Aves.). ℂ 831/624-2406. www.carmels best.com. Reservations recommended. Main courses $22–$35. AE, DC, DISC, MC, V. Daily 11:30am–3pm and 5:30–9:30pm.

Casanova ✿ NORTHERN ITALIAN/SOUTHERN FRENCH   It's the European ambiance that makes this place special. The building, which once belonged to Charlie Chaplin's cook, is divided into three Belgian chalet–style dining rooms that serve as the perfect setting for leaning over a bottle of red wine and creating vacation memories. More festive folk step back to the Old World–style covered patio where it's bustling and crowded. Because all dinner entrees include antipasto and a choice of appetizers (such as baked stuffed eggplant with rice, herbs, cheese, and tomatoes), prices here are not a bad deal (at least in overpriced Carmel). The menu features typical Mediterranean cuisine: paella, homemade pastas, meats, and fish. Casanova also boasts an award-winning wine cellar featuring more than 1,600 French, California, German, and Italian wines.

Fifth Ave. (between San Carlos and Mission Sts.). © **831/625-0501.** Fax 831/625-9799 Reservations recommended. 3-course dinner $21.75–$40. MC, V. Mon–Sat 11:30am–3pm; Sun 10am–3pm; Sun–Thurs 5–10pm; Fri–Sat 5–10:30pm. From Calif. 1, take the Ocean Ave. exit and turn right on Mission, then left onto Fifth Ave.

The Restaurant at Mission Ranch ✿✿ AMERICAN   Clint Eastwood bought this rustic out-of-the-way property in 1986 and restored the ranch-style building to its original integrity, and although the chance of seeing him brings in some folks, it's the views, quality food, and merry atmosphere that really make the place special. The wooden building is encased with large windows that accentuate the wonderful view of the marshlands, grazing sheep, and bay beyond. Warm days make patio dining the prime choice, but the key time to come is at sunset, when the sky is transforming and happy hour is in full swing (you'll find some of the cheapest drinks around, and Clint often stops by when he's in town). As you'd expect from the ranch motif, meat is king here: Burgers are freshly ground on-site, and prime rib with twice-baked potato and vegetables is the favored dish. There are, of course, wonderful seafood, chicken, and vegetarian options as well; and all dinners include soup or salad. Entertainment is provided at the piano bar, where locals and tourists have been known to croon their favorites. The Sunday buffet brunch with live jazz piano is also hugely popular; be sure to reserve.

At Mission Ranch, 26270 Dolores St. © **831/625-9040.** Fax 831/625-5502. Reservations recommended. Most main courses $16.95–$26.95. MC, V. Mon–Fri 4:30–9:45pm; Sat 11am–2:30pm and 4:30–9:30pm; Sun 9:30am–1:30pm and 4:30–9:30pm; bar stays open until midnight.

Robert's Boulevard Bistro ✿ FRENCH   Chef/owner Robert Kincaid was at renowned Fresh Cream before he went solo and wowed locals with hard-to-beat ambiance and quality food. The decor—sophisticated country French with antiqued walls, dried flowers, and divided dining rooms—is cozy and romantic (especially if you grab a booth), and the three-course lunch deal has got to be one of the best in town ($20 gets you a starter such as country sausage in a puff pastry, one of five main courses such as spicy blackened swordfish, and a dessert). There are no deals at dinner, just delightful offerings such as crab dumplings, award-winning crisp roast duck, roast rack of lamb with a mustard crust, and serious desserts that may be worth the price tag.

Crossroads Shopping Village, 217 Crossroads Blvd. © **831/624-9626.** Reservations recommended for dinner. Fixed-price early bistro lunch $19.95; dinner main courses $19–$35. AE, DC, DISC, MC, V. Sun–Fri 4–10pm; Sat 5–10pm. From Calif. 1, turn east on Rio Rd.; go 1 block and turn right into Crossroads Center, then left on Crossroads Blvd.

MODERATE

Flying Fish Grill ✿ PACIFIC RIM/SEAFOOD   We always feel more confident when a restaurant's kitchen is actually run by its owner—and a dinner experience here will confirm that chef/proprietor Kenny Fukumoto is in the house. Dark, romantic, and Asian-influenced, the dining room has an intimate atmosphere with redwood booths (built by Kenny) and fish hanging (flying?) from the ceiling. The cuisine features fresh seafood with exquisite Japanese accents. Start with sushi, tempura, or any of the other exotic and tantalizing taste teasers. Then prepare your tongue for seriously sensational main courses. House favorites include a savory rare peppered ahi, blackened and served with mustard-and sesame-soy vinaigrette and angel hair pasta; and a pan-fried almond sea bass with whipped potatoes, Chinese cabbage, and rock shrimp stir-fry.

In Carmel Plaza, Mission St. (between Ocean and Seventh Aves.). ✆ **831/625-1962.** Reservations recommended. Main courses $15–$24. AE, DISC, MC, V. Wed–Mon 5–10pm.

Grasing's Coastal Cuisine ✿ CALIFORNIA   When chef Kurt Grasing and renowned Bay Area restaurateur Narsai David teamed together to open Grasing's Coastal Cuisine, the result was one of Carmel's best new restaurants. The bright, split-room dining area is simple yet stylish, with buttercup yellow walls, beaded lamps, and colorful artwork. Grasing's menu also reflects a stylish simplicity; ultra-fresh ingredients gleaned from California's coast and central valley regions are displayed in a modest fashion that belie an intense combination of textures and flavors. The warm Napa Salad, for example, appears ordinary enough, but "when I took it off the menu," says Grasing, "I still made 30 a night." Two other dishes that have generated such interest are the lobster risotto made with pearl pasta (rather than arborio rice, for a smoother texture) and the Bronzed Salmon served in a garlic cream sauce. Even the bread, which comes fresh from Gail's Bakery in Aptos, is fantastic. When the sun's out, request a table at the dog-friendly patio, and be sure to inquire about the very reasonable prix-fixe meal.

Sixth St. (at Mission St.). ✆ **831/624-6562.** Reservations recommended. Main courses $16.50–$25.50. AE, MC, V. Daily 11am–4pm and 5–10pm.

Il Fornaio ✿ ITALIAN   We don't care if it is a chain—Il Fornaio is still one of our favorite restaurants because we know we're guaranteed a well-prepared mocha and thick chocolate-dipped biscotti at every outpost. There's also a great selection of salads (go with the simple house salad with shaved Parmesan, croutons, and a tangy light dressing), pastas, pizzas, and rotisserie chicken, duck, and rabbit fresh from the brick oven. The house-made breads and seeded breadsticks alone are reasons enough to come. We must admit that we were disappointed with the tasty-but-measly $11 lasagna, so skip it and start with the seared swordfish antipasto with roast pepper and Dijon mustard, or decadent grilled polenta with sautéed wild mushrooms, provolone, and Italian truffle oil. Move on to a gourmet pizza or pasta. The large airy dining room and sunny terrace offer charming and diverse atmosphere. The Panetteria, a retail bakery, is the perfect place to pick up a gourmet picnic or have a breakfast snack.

Ocean Ave. (at Monte Verde). ✆ **831/622-5100,** or 831/622-5115 for the bakery. Main courses $9.95–$24.95. AE, DC, MC, V. Restaurant open 11:30am–10pm; Sat and Sun brunch 8am–2pm.

La Bohème ✿ FRENCH COUNTRY   Like a set from Disney's "It's a Small World," La Bohème mimics a French street with cartoony asymmetrical shingled house facades and a painted blue sky overhead. Thankfully, the similarity stops with the decor, and there are no dolls singing anywhere—in French or English. Dinner here is utterly romantic French cuisine, served at cramped tables set with floral-print cloths in bright colors, hand-painted dinnerware, and vibrant bouquets. Dinner is a three-course, fixed-price feast consisting of a large salad, a tureen of soup, and a main dish (perhaps roast breast of duckling with green peppercorn sauce or filet mignon with cognac-cream sauce). Vegetarian specials are also available nightly. Homemade desserts and fresh coffee are sold separately, and are usually worth the extra expense.

Dolores St. and Seventh Ave. ⓒ **831/624-7500.** www.laboheme.com. Reservations not accepted. prix-fixe, 3-course dinner $23.75. MC, V. Daily 5:30–10pm. From Calif. 1, exit onto Ocean Ave. and turn left onto Dolores St.

Rio Grill ⓐⓐ AMERICAN   The food or the festive atmosphere (a cartoon mural of famous locals such as Clint Eastwood and the late Bing Crosby, plus playful sculpture, cactus, and other vibrant art) has kept this place popular with even the locals for the past several years. The whimsical nature of the modern Santa Fe–style dining room belies the kitchen's serious preparations, which include homemade soups; a rich quesadilla with almonds, cheeses, and smoked-tomato salsa; barbecued baby-back ribs from a wood-burning oven; and fresh fish from an open oak grill. The restaurant's good selection of wines includes some rare California vintages and covers a broad price range.

Crossroads Shopping Center, 101 Crossroads Blvd. ⓒ **831/625-5436.** www.riogrill.com. Reservations recommended. Main courses $8–$25. AE, DISC, MC, V. Sun–Thurs 11:30am–10:30pm; Fri–Sat 11:30am–11pm. From Calif. 1, take the Rio Rd. exit west for 1 block and turn right onto Crossroads Blvd.

INEXPENSIVE

Caffè Napoli ⓐ *Value* ITALIAN   The decor here is so quintessentially Italiana, with flags, gingham tablecloths, garlic, and baskets overhead, that we expected a flour-coated pot-bellied Padrino Napoli to emerge from the kitchen, embrace us wholeheartedly, and exclaim "Mangia! Mangia!" as he slapped down a bowl overflowing with sauce-drenched pasta. Of course there is no Padrino here, and we received no welcoming hug, but we did indulge in the fine Italian fare that keeps locals coming back for more.

Ocean Ave. (between Dolores and Lincoln). ⓒ **831/625-4033.** Reservations recommended. Main courses $10–$20. MC, V. Daily 11:30am–9pm.

6 Carmel Valley

3 miles SE of Carmel-by-the-Sea

Inland from Carmel stretches Carmel Valley, where wealthy folks retreat beyond the reach of the coastal fog and mist. It's a scenic and perpetually sunny valley of rolling hills dotted with manicured golf courses and many a horse ranch.

Hike the trails in **Garland Regional Park,** 8 miles east of Carmel on Carmel Valley Road (dogs are welcome off-leash). The sun really bakes you out here, so bring lots of water. You could also sign up for a trail ride or riding lesson at the **Holman Ranch,** 60 Holman Rd. (ⓒ **831/659-6054**), 12 miles east of Calif. 1.

Golf is offered at several resorts and courses in the valley, notably at **Quail Lodge,** 8205 Valley Green Dr. (ⓒ **800/538-9516** or 831/620-8858), and **Rancho Cañada Golf Club,** Carmel Valley Rd. (ⓒ **831/624-0111**).

While you're in the valley, taste the wines at the **Château Julien Winery,** 8940 Carmel Valley Rd. (ⓒ **831/624-2600**), which is open daily.

WHERE TO STAY

Quail Lodge Resort and Golf Club ⓐⓐ   Lying in the foothills of the Santa Lucia Range, Quail Lodge has already received five-star ratings for 20 years running. Its pastoral setting encompasses more than 850 acres of sparkling lakes, secluded woodlands, and rolling meadows. The guest rooms are in two-story balconied wings, with terraces overlooking the pool or one of the 10 man-made lakes, or in cottages holding five units each. Executive villas are the most expensive and luxurious accommodations.

The guest rooms are decorated in warm earth tones jazzed up with floral and striped patterns. Higher-priced accommodations, on the upper floors, have cathedral ceilings. Every room has a separate dressing area and an ample balcony; some have fireplaces and wet bars. All units have coffeemakers, supplied with freshly ground beans; a fresh-fruit plate is delivered to each room per day as well. Afternoon tea is served in the lobby from 3 to 5pm.

8205 Valley Greens Dr., Carmel, CA 93923. (© **888/828-8787** or 831/624-2888. Fax 831/624-3726. www. quail-lodge-resort.com. 100 units. Apr–Nov $295 double; $975 deluxe room/suite. Extra person $35. Call for winter specials. Packages available. AE, DC, DISC, MC, V. Pets accepted for $100 fee per stay. $25 fee per extra pet. Pet amenities and doggie treats included. From Calif. 1 north, past the Carmel exits (after which the highway narrows to 2 lanes), turn left on Carmel Valley Rd. and continue 3 miles to Valley Greens Dr. **Amenities:** 3 restaurants, 2 bars; 2 outdoor pools (1 heated); golf course on site; 4 tennis courts; exercise room; spa services; Jacuzzi; bike rental; concierge; business center; room service; in-room massage; babysitting; laundry service; same-day dry cleaning; executive-level rooms. *In room:* TV w/ pay movies, dataport, minibar, coffeemaker, hair dryer.

7 The Big Sur Coast ✶✶✶

3 miles S of Carmel-by-the-Sea, 123 miles S of San Francisco, 87 miles N of Hearst Castle

Big Sur is more than a drive along one of the most dramatic coastlines on earth or a peaceful repose amid a forest of towering California redwoods. It's a stretch of vast wilderness so overwhelmingly beautiful—especially when the fog glows in the moonlight—that it enchants all who walk its majestic paths. It's also home to a particular breed of nature lover who prefers a rustic lifestyle to the rest of California's offerings. When the 1997 and 1998 El Niño storms caused landslides and major road damage, cutting the area off from civilization for months, reports from Big Sur were unusual: Some residents fled, vowing never to return; others loved it even though their incomes were temporarily all but eliminated. The remaining residents rejoiced in the temporary solitude; Post Ranch, the area's ultimate luxury resort, shared the impromptu intimacy with deep-pocketed guests by flying them in via helicopter (for an extra fee, of course). (Highway 1 was damaged and closed again by storms in 2000, primarily south of Big Sur, but most of it has been reopened at this writing.) Such is the price paid for living among the untamable California wilderness. The reopened roads are packed again, and driving through the region is painfully slow; rubberneckers admiring the view and nervous Nellies fearing the cliffs can't help but drive with their foot on the brakes.

Although there is an actual Big Sur Village approximately 25 miles south of Carmel, "Big Sur" refers to the entire 90-mile stretch of coastline between Carmel and San Simeon, blessed on one side by the majestic Santa Lucia Range and on the other by the rocky Pacific coastline. It's one of the most romantic and relaxing places on earth, and if you need respite from the rat race, we can recommend no better place to find it (although Yosemite, if you hike past the crowds, is equally rejuvenating). There's little more to do than explore the mountains and beaches, or just perch yourself atop the cliffs and take in the California sea air— but spend a few days here and you'll find that you need nothing else.

ESSENTIALS

VISITOR INFORMATION   Contact the **Monterey Peninsula Visitors and Convention Bureau** (© 831/649-1770; www.monterey.com) for specialized information on places and events in Big Sur.

ORIENTATION   Most of this stretch is state park, and Calif. 1 runs its entire length, hugging the ocean the whole way. Restaurants, hotels, and sights are easy to spot—most are situated directly on the highway—but without major towns as reference points, their addresses can be obscure. For the purposes of orientation, we'll use the River Inn as our mileage guide. Located 29 miles south of Monterey on Calif. 1, the inn is generally considered to mark the northern end of Big Sur.

EXPLORING THE BIG SUR COAST

Big Sur offers visitors a profusion of tranquility and natural beauty—ideal for hiking, picnicking, camping, fishing, and beachcombing.

The first settlers arrived here only a century ago, and the present highway was built in 1937, making the area accessible by car. (Electricity arrived only in the 1950s, and it's still not available in the remote inland mountains.) Big Sur's mysterious, misty beauty has inspired several modern spiritual movements (the Esalen Institute was the birthplace of the human potential movement). Even the tourist bureau bills the area as a place in which "to slow down . . . to meditate . . . to catch up with your soul." Take the board's advice and take your time—nothing better lies ahead.

The region affords a bounty of wilderness adventure opportunities. The inland **Ventana Wilderness,** which is maintained by the U.S. Forest Service, contains 167,323 acres straddling the Santa Lucia Mountains and is characterized by steep-sided ridges separated by V-shaped valleys. The streams that cascade through the area are marked by waterfalls, deep pools, and thermal springs. The wilderness offers 237 miles of hiking trails that lead to 55 designated trail camps—a backpacker's paradise. One of the easiest trails to access is the **Pine Ridge Trail** at Big Sur station (© **831/667-2315**).

From Carmel, the first stop along Calif. 1 is **Point Lobos State Reserve** ★★ (© **831/624-4909**), 3 miles south of Carmel. Sea lions, harbor seals, sea otters, and thousands of seabirds reside in this 1,276-acre reserve. Between December and May, you can also spot migrating California gray whales just offshore. Trails follow the shoreline and lead to hidden coves. Note that parking is limited; on weekends especially, you need to arrive early to secure a place.

From here, cross the Soberanes Creek, passing **Garrapata State Park** © **831/ 624-4909,** a 2,879-acre preserve with 4 miles of coastline. It's unmarked and undeveloped, though the trails are maintained. To explore them, you'll need to park at one of the turnouts on Calif. 1 near Soberanes Point and hike in.

Ten miles south of Carmel, you'll arrive at North Abalone Cove. From here, Palo Colorado Road leads back into the wilderness to the first of the Forest Service camping areas at **Bottchers Gap** ($10 to camp, $5 to park overnight).

Continuing south, about 13 miles from of Carmel, you'll cross the **Bixby Bridge** and see the **Point Sur Lighthouse** off in the distance. The Bixby Bridge, one of the world's highest single-span concrete bridges, towers nearly 270 feet above Bixby Creek Canyon, and offers gorgeous canyon and ocean views from several observation alcoves at regular intervals along the bridge. The lighthouse, which sits 361 feet above the surf on a volcanic rock promontory, was built in 1889, when only a horse trail provided access to this part of the world. Tours,

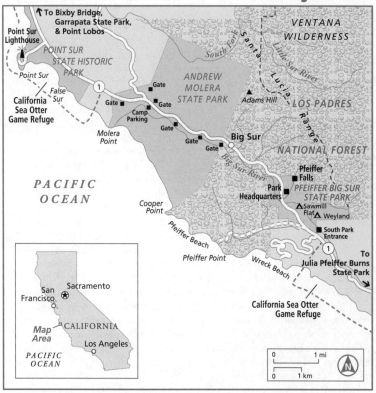

which take 2 to 3 hours and involve a steep half-mile hike each way, are scheduled on most weekends. For information, call © **831/625-4419.** Admission is $5 for adults, $3 for youths ages 13 to 17, $2 for children 5 to 12, and free for kids under 5.

About 3 miles south of the lighthouse is **Andrew Molera State Park (© 831/ 667-2315),** the largest state park on the Big Sur Coast at 4,800 acres. It's much less crowded than Pfeiffer–Big Sur (see below). Miles of trails meander through meadows and along beaches and bluffs. Hikers and cyclists use the primitive trail camp about a third of a mile from the parking area. **Molera Big Sur Trail Rides (© 800/942-5486** or 831/625-5486) offers coastal trail rides daily from April to December, or until the rains come. There are trails through the park for horseback riders of all levels of experience. Cost of rides vary but are usually $36 per hour. The 2½-mile-long beach, which is sheltered from the wind by a bluff, is accessible via a mile-long path flanked in spring by wildflowers and offers excellent tide pooling. You can walk the entire length of the beach at low tide; otherwise take the bluff trail above the beach. The park also has campgrounds.

Back on Calif. 1, you'll soon reach the village of Big Sur, where commercial services are available.

About 26 miles south of Carmel you'll come to **Big Sur Station (© 831/ 667-2315),** where you can pick up maps and other information about the region. It's located a quarter mile past the entrance to **Pfeiffer–Big Sur State Park** ⚅ **(© 800/444-7275** or 831/667-2315), an 810-acre park that offers 218 camping sites along the Big Sur River, picnicking, fishing, and hiking. It's a scenic park of redwoods, conifers, oaks, and open meadows. For this reason, it gets very crowded. The Big Sur Lodge in the park has cabins with fireplaces and other facilities (see "Where to Stay" and the "Camping in Big Sur" box, below). Admission to the park is $5, and it's open daily from dawn to dusk.

Exactly 1¹⁄₁₀-mile south of the entrance to Pfeiffer–Big Sur State Park is the turnoff to Sycamore Canyon Road (unmarked), which will take you 2 winding miles down to beautiful **Pfeiffer Beach** ⊛, a great place to soak in the sun on the wide expanse of golden sand. It's open for day-use only, there's no fee, and it's the only beach accessible by car (but not motorhomes).

Back on Calif. 1, the road travels 11 miles past Sea Lion Cove to Julia Pfeiffer Burns State Park. High above the ocean is the famous **Nepenthe** restaurant (see "Where to Dine," later in this chapter), the retreat bought by Orson Welles for Rita Hayworth in 1944. A few miles farther south is the **Coast Gallery** (© 831/667-2301), the premier local art gallery, which shows lithographs of works by Henry Miller. The gallery's casual Coast Cafe offers simple serve-your-self lunches of soup, sandwiches, baked goods, and coffee drinks. Miller fans will also want to stop at the **Henry Miller Memorial Library** (© 831/667-2574) on Calif. 1, 30 miles south of Carmel and a quarter mile south of Nepenthe restaurant. The library displays and sells books and artwork by Miller and houses a permanent collection of first editions. It also serves as a community art center, hosting concerts, poetry readings, and art exhibitions (check its upcoming events at www.henrymiller.org). The rear gallery room is a video-viewing space where films about Henry Miller can be seen. There's a sculpture garden, plus tables on the adjacent lawn where visitors can rest and enjoy the surroundings. Admission is free; hours are Tuesday and Wednesday 2 to 6pm, Thursday through Sunday from 11am to 5pm.

Julia Pfeiffer Burns State Park ⊛⊛ (© 831/667-2315) encompasses some of Big Sur's most spectacular coastline. To get a closer look, take the trail from the parking area at McWay Canyon, which leads under the highway to a bluff overlooking an 80-foot-high McWay Waterfall dropping directly into the ocean. It's less crowded here than at Pfeiffer–Big Sur, and there are miles of trails to explore in the 3,580-acre park. Scuba divers can apply for permits to explore the 1,680-acre underwater reserve.

From here, the road skirts the Ventana Wilderness, passing Anderson and Marble Peaks and the Esalen Institute, before crossing the Big Creek Bridge to Lucia and several campgrounds farther south. **Kirk Creek Campground** ⊛, about 3 miles north of Pacific Valley, offers camping with ocean views and beach access. Beyond Pacific Valley, the **Sand Dollar Beach** ⊛ picnic area is a good place to stop and enjoy the coastal view and take a stroll. A half-mile trail leads down to the sheltered beach, from which there's a fine view of Cone Peak, one of the coast's highest mountains. Two miles south of Sand Dollar is **Jade Cove,** a popular spot for rock hounds. From here, it's about another 27 miles past the Piedras Blancas Light Station to San Simeon.

WHERE TO STAY

Only a handful of Big Sur's accommodations offer the kind of pampering and luxury you'd expect in a fine urban hotel; even direct-dial phones and TVs (often considered gauche in these parts) are rare. Big Sur hotels are especially busy in summer, when advance reservations are required. There are more accommodations than those listed here, so if you're having trouble securing a room or a site, contact the visitors bureau (listed in the "Essentials" section earlier in this chapter) for other options.

Big Sur Lodge *(Kids)*   A family-friendly place, the Big Sur Lodge—sheltered by towering redwoods, sycamores, and broad-leafed maples—is situated in the enormous state park. The rustic motel-style cabins are huge, with high peaked cedar- and redwood-beamed ceilings. They're clean and heated, and have private bathrooms and reserved parking spaces. Some have fireplaces. All offer porches or decks with views of the redwoods or the Santa Lucia Range.

An advantage to staying here is that you're entitled to free use of all the facilities of the park, including hiking, barbecue pits, and picnic areas. In addition, the lodge has its own grocery store and laundry facilities.

In Pfeiffer–Big Sur State Park, Calif. 1 (P.O. Box 190), Big Sur, CA 93920. ℂ 800/424-4787 or 831/667-3100. Fax 831/667-3110. www.bigsurlodge.com. 61 cottages. $89–$139 cottage for 2; $119–$199 cottage with kitchen or fireplace; $139–$219 cabin with kitchen and fireplace. Rates include park entrance fees. AE, MC, V. From Carmel, take Calif. 1 south 26 miles. **Amenities:** Restaurant; heated outdoor pool (seasonal); laundry facilities. *In room:* Coffeemaker; no phone. Some units with fully equipped kitchens.

Deetjen's Big Sur Inn ✿   Man, is this place cute. In the 1930s, before Calif. 1 was built, this homestead was an overnight stopping place on the coastal wagon road. It was begun by Norwegian homesteader Helmuth Deetjen, who over the years built several units constructed from hand-hewn logs and lumber. Folks either love or hate the accommodations, which are set in a redwood canyon. They're rustic, cozy, and adorable with their old-fashioned furnishings and down-home feel. But those who want extensive creature comforts should go elsewhere. Single-wall construction means that the rooms are far from soundproof, so children under 12 are allowed only if families reserve both rooms of a two-room building. There's no insulation, so prepare to crank up the fire or wood-burning stove. *Tip:* The cabins near the river offer the most privacy.

The restaurant is a local favorite and consists of four intimate, English country inn–style rooms lit by candlelight (See "Where to Dine," below).

Calif. 1, Big Sur, CA 93920. ℂ 831/667-2377. 20 units (15 with bathroom). $90 double with shared bathroom; $90–$195 double with private bathroom. MC, V. **Amenities:** Restaurant. *In room:* No phone.

Post Ranch Inn ✿✿✿   This is one of our very favorite places to stay on the planet. Perched on 98 acres of pristine seaside ridges 1,200 feet above the Pacific, this romantic resort opened in 1992 and was instantly declared one of the world's finest retreats. What's the big deal? The Post Ranch doesn't attempt to beat its stunning natural surroundings, but rather to join them. The wood-and-glass guest cottages are built around existing trees—some are elevated on stilts to avoid damaging native redwood root structures—and the ultra-private Ocean and Coast cottages are so close to the edge of the earth, you get the impression that you've joined the clouds (imagine that from your private spa tub). Other cottages face the woodlands and are equally impressive in design. Each room contains a fireplace, terrace, massage table, cassette and CD player, and wet bar filled with complimentary goodies. The bathrooms, fashioned out of slate and granite, feature spa tubs. There's also a small workout room, the best "hot tub" we've ever encountered (it's on a cliff and seems to join the sky), a mediocre pool, and sundecks on the premises. The only drawback is that the vibe can be stuffy, which is due more to the clientele than the staff. The Sierra Mar restaurant is open only to guests for continental breakfasts, and to the public nightly for dinner. It, too, has floor-to-ceiling views of the ocean.

Camping in Big Sur

Big Sur is one of the most spectacular places in the state for camping. One of the most glorious settings can be found at **Pfeiffer–Big Sur State Park,** on Calif. 1, 26 miles south of Carmel (✆ 800/444-7275 or 831/667-2315; fax 831/667-2886). The 810-acre state park offers hundreds of secluded, woodsy sites on hundreds of acres of redwood forest. Hiking trails, streams, and the river are steps away from your sleeping bag, and the most modern amenities are the 25¢ showers (for 3 minutes). Water faucets are located between sites, and each spot has its own picnic table and fire pit. There are, however, no RV hookups or electricity. Riverfront sites are most coveted, but others promise more seclusion among the shaded hillsides of the park. Campfire programs and nature walks are also offered. At the entrance are a store, gift shop, restaurant, and cafe. There's a total of 218 sites (fees are $20 for regular sites, $23 for riverside sites). Rates include park entrance fees. Senior discounts are available, and dogs are permitted ($1 per night extra).

The entrance to the **Ventana Campground,** on Calif. 1, 28 miles south of Carmel and 4¼ miles south of the River Inn (✆ **831/667-2712;** www.ventanabigsur.com), is adjacent to the entrance to the resort of the same name, but the comparison stops there. This is pure rusticity. The 75 campsites, on 40 acres of a redwood canyon, are set along a hillside and spaced well apart for privacy. Each is shaded by towering trees and has a picnic table and fire ring, but offers no electricity, RV hookups, or river access. There are, however, three bathhouses with hot showers (25¢ fee), which are conveniently located. To reserve a space, call and charge on a credit card (MasterCard or Visa) one night's deposit. Or you

Calif. 1 (P.O. Box 219), Big Sur, CA 93920. ✆ **800/527-2200** or 831/667-2200. Fax 831/667-2824. www.postranchinn.com. 30 units. $455–$835 double. Rates include continental breakfast. AE, MC, V. **Amenities:** Restaurant, bar/lounge; outdoor heated pool; exercise room; spa services; cliffside Jacuzzi; game room; concierge; activities desk; room service; in-room massage. *In room:* A/C, minibar, coffeemaker, hair dryer, iron, safe.

Ventana Inn and Spa 🏵🏵🏵   Luxuriously rustic and utterly romantic, Ventana has been a wildly popular wilderness outpost for more than 20 years, and with good reason. Located on 243 mountainous oceanfront acres, Ventana has an elegance that's atypical of the region, and has continually attracted famous guests such as Barbra Streisand, Goldie Hawn, and Francis Ford Coppola since its opening in 1975.

The accommodations, in one- and two-story, natural-wood buildings along winding, wildflower-flanked paths, blend in with the magical Big Sur countryside. The extensive grounds are dotted with hammocks and hand-carved benches, which are strategically located under shady trees and at vista points. The guest rooms are divinely decorated in warm, cozy luxury, with private terraces or balconies overlooking the ocean or forest. Most rooms offer wood-burning fireplaces, and some have Jacuzzis and high cathedral ceilings. A small fitness center offers the basics—but you'll be more inspired to hike the grounds, where you'll not only find plenty of pastoral respite, but also a pool, a rustic can mail a check for the deposit along with the dates you'd like to stay and a stamped, self-addressed envelope at least 2 weeks in advance (earlier during peak months). Rates are $25 for a site for two with one vehicle; $35 per night weekends. An additional person is $5 extra, and it'll cost you $5 to bring Fido. Rates include entrance fee for your car. Open April through October.

Big Sur Campground and Cabins is on Calif. 1, 26 miles south of Carmel (a half-mile south of the River Inn; ℂ **831/667-2322**). The sites are cramped, so the feel is more like a camping village than an intimate retreat. However, it's very well maintained and perfect for families, who love the playground, river swimming, and inner-tube rentals. Each campsite has its own wood-burning fire pit, picnic table, and fresh-water faucet within 25 feet of the pitching area. There are also RV water and electric hookups available. Facilities include bathhouses with hot showers, laundry facilities, an aged volleyball/basketball court, and a grocery store. There are 81 tent sites (30 RV-ready with electricity and water hookup), plus 13 cabins (all with shower). The all-wood cabins are absolutely adorable, with stylish country furnishings, wood-burning ovens, patios, and full kitchens. Rates are $26 for a tent site for two, $30 for an RV hookup (plus $3 extra for electricity and water), $50 for a tent cabin (bed, but no heat or plumbing), or $93 to $187 for a cabin for two. Rates include entrance for your car. MasterCard and Visa are accepted. Pets cost $4 for campsites and $12 for tent-cabins; pets are not allowed in the other cabins. Open year-round.

library, and clothing-optional tanning decks and spa tubs. This, along with Post Ranch, is one of the best retreats in the region, if not the state. But we can't say which is better. We prefer the rooms at Post Ranch, but the laid-back energy and the extensive grounds at Ventana. Families take heed: Children are permitted, but not exactly embraced.

Ventana's restaurant, Cielo, is an incredibly romantic and first-rate dining experience (see "Where to Dine," below, for complete details).

Calif. 1, Big Sur, CA 93920. ℂ **800/628-6500** or 831/667-2331. Fax 831/667-0573. www.ventanainn.com. 59 units. $340–$850 double; from $575 suite. Rates include continental breakfast and afternoon wine and cheese. AE, DC, DISC, MC, V. **Amenities:** Restaurant; 2 heated outdoor pools; exercise room; full spa with 2 Japanese hot baths; sauna; concierge; room service; in-room massage; laundry service; executive-level rooms. In room: A/C, TV/VCR, minibar, fridge, coffeemaker, hair dryer, iron, safe.

WHERE TO DINE

In addition to the following choices, you should try the **Big Sur Bakery and Restaurant** on Calif. 1, just past the post office and a mile south of Pfeiffer–Big Sur State Park (ℂ **831/667-0520**). It offers friendly service and healthy fare, ranging from wood-fired pizzas and portobello mushroom burgers at lunch to salmon, tuna, and chicken selections at dinner. All the pastries are freshly baked on the premises, along with hearth-baked breads. It's open daily from 8am to 10pm, but they close early on Mondays

Big Sur River Inn CALIFORNIA/AMERICAN   Popular with everyone from families to bikers, the River Inn is an unpretentious, rustic, down-home restaurant that's got something for all tastes. Trying to seat a small army? No problem. Want to watch sports on TV at a local bar? Pull up a stool. Looking to snag a few rays from a deck right beside the Big Sur River? Break out the suntan lotion. In winter, the wooden dining room is the prime spot; on summer days, some folks grab their patio chair and a cocktail and hang out literally midstream. Along with the local color, attractions include a full bar and good ol' American breakfasts (steak and eggs, omelets, pancakes, and so on, plus espresso, with most dishes for around $6), lunches (an array of salads, sandwiches, and baby-back ribs, or fish and chips), and dinners (fresh catch, pastas, burgers, or ribs).

On Calif. 1, 2 miles north of Pfeiffer–Big Sur State Park. © 831/667-2700. Fax 831/667-2743. www.bigsur riverinn.com. Main courses $8.75–$14.50 lunch; $8.95–$28 dinner. AE, DC, MC, V. Daily 8am–10pm; 8am–9pm in winter.

Café Kevah SOUTHWEST/CALIFORNIA   Located one level below Nepenthe, Café Kevah offers the same celestial view (at a fraction of the price), a more casual environment, and—depending on your taste—better food. Seating is entirely outdoors—a downside when the biting fog rolls in, but perfect on a clear day. You can order breakfast or lunch from the small shack of a kitchen, then grab an umbrella-shaded table, and enjoy the feast for your eyes and taste buds. Fare here is more eclectic than Nepenthe's, with such choices as homemade granola, pastries, baby greens with broiled salmon and papaya, chicken brochettes, omelets, and new potato hash. It ain't cheap, but innovative cuisine, the view, and a surprisingly decent mocha make it a worthwhile stopover. Don't forget to bring a coat.

On Calif. 1, 28 miles south of Carmel (5 miles south of the River Inn). © 831/667-2344. Appetizers $6.25–$11.50; main courses $10.75–$17.50. Daily 9am–3pm, 3:30pm weekends. Grill closes at 4pm for coffee and dessert. Closes when it rains. AE, MC, V.

Cielo Restaurant ★★ CALIFORNIA   Like the resort, Ventana's restaurant is woodsy but extravagant, and is an excellent place to dine alfresco at lunch or for a romantic dinner. The airy cedar interior is divided into two spaces: the lounge, where a wooden bar and cocktail tables look onto a roaring fire and through picturesque windows; and the dining room, which overlooks the mountains and/or the ocean. But in summer it's the outdoor patio, with its views of the ocean expanse and 50 miles of Big Sur coast, that's the coveted lunch spot. Unlike some costly restaurants in the area, a meal here is as gratifying as the surroundings. Lunch offers sandwiches, burgers, and an array of gourmet salads, as well as main courses such as grilled Atlantic salmon; dinner includes stellar starters like a perfectly dressed Caesar salad and a well-balanced chanterelle mushroom risotto, and main courses such as seared ahi tuna or roasted duck breast with hazelnut risotto and sun-dried cherry sauce.

At Ventana Inn and Spa, Calif. 1, Big Sur. © 831/667-4242. Fax 831/667-2287. www.ventanainn.com. Reservations recommended for dinner. Main courses $11–$17 lunch; $23–$32 dinner. AE, DC, DISC, MC, V. Mon–Fri noon–3pm; Sat–Sun 11am–3:30pm; daily 6–9pm.

Deetjen's Big Sur Inn Restaurant ★ AMERICAN   With the feel of an English farmhouse, this cozy, country setting is the perfect venue for the delicious comfort food and friendly service that you'll find here. Mornings start off with a jump after a cup of the delicious and strong coffee, and breakfast offers all the basics: omelets, eggs Benedict, pancakes, and granola, most of which come piled high with breakfast potatoes. Dinner is highly regarded by locals, and might include lamb au jus and twice-baked potatoes; grilled chicken with mushrooms and a garlic Marsala sauce; and roast duckling with brandy, peppercorn, and molasses sauce.

On Calif. 1. © **831/667-2378.** Reservations recommended. Main courses $4.25–$11.75 breakfast; $15–$33 dinner. MC, V. Daily 8am–noon and 6–9pm.

Nepenthe AMERICAN Stop by Nepenthe for two reasons: The views are outrageous, and the atmosphere rocks. Sitting 808 feet above sea level along the cliffs overlooking the ocean, Nepenthe is naturally celestial—especially when fog lingers above the water below. On a warm day, join the crowds on the terrace. On colder days, go the indoor route: The redwood-and-adobe structure offers a warmer and equally magical view, and with its big wood-burning fireplace, redwood ceilings, and large bayfront windows, the atmosphere is something you can't find anywhere else.

Unfortunately, that's not been our experience with the fare. We would scoff at an $11 burger (without fries!), $16 swordfish sandwich, and a $4 draft Budweiser anywhere else—but we'd cough up the cash all over again for an afternoon here. (Think of it as nominal admission to dine at heights only angels usually enjoy.) Lunch is adequate and basic: burgers, sandwiches, and salads. Dinner main courses include steak, broiled chicken, and fresh fish prepared any number of ways, though we suggest you come only for lunch and spend big dinner bucks elsewhere.

Calif. 1, 28 miles south of Carmel (5 miles south of the River Inn). © **831/667-2345.** Fax 831/667-2394. www.nepenthebigsur.com. Reservations accepted only for parties of 5 or more. Main courses $9–$25. AE, MC, V. Daily 11:30am–10pm.

8 Pinnacles National Monument ⓧ

58 miles SE of Monterey

Once a little-known outpost of the national park system, Pinnacles National Monument has become one of the most popular weekend climbing destinations in central California over the past decade. The mild winter climate and plentiful routes make this a perfect off-season training ground for climbers. It's also a popular haven for campers, hikers, and nature lovers. One of the most unique chaparral ecosystems in the world supports a large community of plant and animal life here, including one of California's largest breeding populations of raptors.

The Pinnacles themselves—hundreds of towering crags, spires, and hoodoos—are seemingly out of place in the voluptuously rolling hills of the coast range. And they are, in fact, out of place, part of the eroded remains of a volcano formed 23 million years ago 195 miles south in the middle of the Mojave Desert. It was carried here by the movement of the San Andreas Fault, which runs just east of the park. (The other half of the volcano remains in the Mojave.)

You could spend days here without getting bored, but it's possible to cover the most interesting features in a weekend. With a single hike, you can go from the lush oak woodland around the Bear Gulch Visitor Center to the dry and desolate crags of the high peaks, then back down through a half-mile-long cave complete with underground waterfalls.

ESSENTIALS

GETTING THERE   Two entrances lead to the park. The **West Entrance** from Soledad and U.S. 101 is a dry, dusty, winding single-lane road (not suitable for trailers) with the best drive-up view of the park. It doesn't connect with the east side.

The alternative route is via the **East Entrance.** Unless you're coming from nearby, take the longer drive on Calif. 25 to enter through the east. Because most of the peaks of the Pinnacles face east and the watershed drains east, most of the interesting hikes and geologic features are on this side. No road crosses the park.

FEES   Park entrance fees, which are good for 7 days, are $2 per person or $5 per car.

VISITOR CENTER   The first place you should go upon entering the park from the east is the **Bear Gulch Visitor Center** (© **831/389-4485**)), open daily from 8am to 4:30pm. This small center is rich with exhibits on the park's history, wildlife, and geology, and also has a great selection of nature handbooks and climbing guides for the Pinnacles. Climbers should check with rangers about closures and other information before heading out: Many routes are closed during hawk- and falcon-nesting season, and rangers like to know how many climbers are in the park.

Adjacent to the visitor center, the Bear Gulch picnic ground is a great place to fuel up before setting out on a hike or, if you're not planning to leave your car, one of the best places to gaze up at dramatic spires of the high peaks (the ultimate spot is from the west side).

REGULATIONS & WARNINGS   Beware of poison oak, particularly in Bear Gulch. Rattlesnakes are common throughout the park but rarely seen. Bikes and dogs are prohibited on all trails, and no backcountry camping is allowed anywhere in the park.

Hiking through this variety of landscapes demands versatility. Come prepared with a good pair of hiking shoes, snacks, lots of water, and a flashlight.

Daytime temperatures often exceed 100°F in summer, so the best time of year to visit is spring, when the wildflowers are blooming, or in the fall. Crowds are common during spring weekends.

HIKING & EXPLORING THE PARK

To see most of the park in a single, moderately strenuous morning, take the **Condor Gulch Trail** from the visitor center. As you climb quickly out of the parking area, the Pinnacles's wind-sculpted spires seem to grow taller. In less than 2 miles, you're among them, and Condor Gulch intersects with the **High Peaks Trail.** The view from the top spans miles: the Salinas Valley to your west, the Pinnacles below, and miles of coast to the east. After traversing the high peaks (including stretches of footholds carved in steep rock faces) for about a mile, the trail drops back toward the visitor center via a valley filled with eerie-looking hoodoos.

In another 1½ miles, you'll reach the reservoir marking the top of **Bear Gulch Cave,** which closes occasionally; in 1998, it closed due both to storm damage and to accommodate migrating Townsend bats, who in the past two years have come here to have their babies. It's usually open, but if you want to explore, you'll need your flashlight and you might get wet; still, this 0.6-mile-long talus cave is a thrill. From the end of the cave you're just a short walk (through the most popular climbing area of the park) away from the visitor center. It's also possible to hike just Bear Gulch and the cave, then return via the **Moses Spring Trail.** It's about 2 miles round-trip, but you'll miss the view from the top.

If you're coming from the West Entrance, the **Juniper Canyon Trail** is a short (1.2 miles), but very steep, blast to the top of the high peaks. You'll definitely earn the view. Otherwise, try the short **Balconies Trail** to the monument's other talus cave, **Balconies Cave.** Flashlights are required here, too.

CAMPING

The park's campground on the west side was demolished by El Niño storms in 1997 and 1998 and is not scheduled for repair. Now the only campground is the privately run **Pinnacles Campground, Inc.,** on the east side (© 831/389-4462; www.pinncamp.com), which charges $5 per person, $7 for two people, with a $14 minimum on Friday and Saturday nights. It's just outside the park (off Calif. 25, 32 miles south of Hollister), with lots of privacy and space between sites, plus showers, a store, and a pool. It's close enough so you can hike into the park from the campground, though it will add a few miles to your outing. Though private campgrounds are often overdeveloped, the management here saw the benefits of leaving the surroundings natural. Dogs are not recommended, but you can bring them if you're willing to pay a $10 leash deposit. *Note:* No animals are allowed at Pinnacles.

12

The Central Coast

by Stephanie Avnet Yates

California's Central Coast—a spectacular amalgam of beaches, lakes, and mountains—is the state's most diverse region. The narrow strip of coast that runs for more than 100 miles from San Simeon to Ventura spans several climate zones and is home to an eclectic mix of students, middle-class workers, retirees, farmers, computer techies, and fishermen. The ride along Calif. 1, which follows the ocean cliffs, is almost always packed with rental cars, RVs, and bicycles. Traffic may give your brakes a workout, but it also allows you to take longer looks at one of the most spectacular vistas in the world.

Whether you're driving up from Los Angeles or down from San Francisco, Calif. 1 is the most scenic and leisurely route. (U.S. 101 gets you there faster, but is less picturesque.) Most bicyclists pedal from north to south, the direction of the prevailing winds. Those in cars may prefer to drive south to north, so they can get a better look at the coastline as it unfolds toward the west. No matter which direction you drive, break out the camera—you're about to experience unparalleled beauty, California style.

1 San Simeon: Hearst Castle

205 miles S of San Francisco (via Calif. 1), 254 miles NW of Los Angeles

Few places on earth compare to **Hearst Castle.** The 165-room estate of publishing magnate William Randolph Hearst, situated high above the coastal village of San Simeon atop a hill he called La Cuesta Encantada ("the Enchanted Hill"), is an ego trip par excellence. One of the last great estates of America's Gilded Age, it's an astounding, completely over-the-top monument to wealth—and to the power that money brings.

Hearst Castle is a sprawling compound of structures, constructed over 28 years in a Mediterranean Revival architectural style, set in undeniably magical surroundings. The focal point of the estate is the you-have-to-see-it-to-believe-it **Casa Grande,** a 100-plus-room mansion brimming with priceless art and antiques. Hearst acquired most of his vast European collection via New York auction houses, where he bought entire rooms (including walls, ceilings, and floors) and shipped them here. The result is an old-world castle done in a priceless mix-and-match style. You'll see fantastic 400-year-old Spanish and Italian ceilings, enormous 500-year-old fireplace mantels, 16th-century Florentine bedsteads, Renaissance paintings, Flemish tapestries, and innumerable other treasures.

Three opulent "guest houses" also contain magnificent works of art. A lavish private movie theater was used to screen first-run films twice nightly—once for employees, and again for the guests and host.

The Central Coast

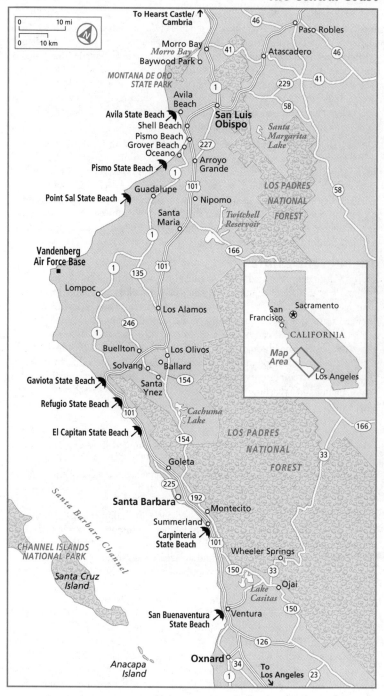

0   10 mi
0   10 km

To Hearst Castle/
Cambria

Paso Robles
Morro Bay
Morro Bay
Baywood Park
Atascadero

MONTANA DE ORO
STATE PARK

Avila
Beach
San Luis
Obispo
Avila State Beach
Shell Beach
Pismo Beach
Grover Beach
Oceano
Pismo State Beach
Arroyo
Grande

*Santa
Margarita
Lake*

LOS PADRES

NATIONAL

FOREST

Guadalupe
Nipomo
Point Sal State Beach
Santa
Maria
*Twitchell
Reservoir*

Vandenberg
Air Force Base

Lompoc

Los Alamos

Buellton
Los Olivos
Solvang
Ballard
Gaviota State Beach
Santa
Ynez
Refugio State Beach
El Capitan State Beach

*Cachuma
Lake*

LOS PADRES

NATIONAL

FOREST

Goleta

Santa Barbara
Montecito
Summerland
Carpinteria
State Beach
Wheeler Springs

CHANNEL ISLANDS
NATIONAL PARK

Santa Barbara Channel

*Santa Cruz
Island*

Ojai
*Lake
Casitas*

San Buenaventura
State Beach
Ventura

*Anacapa
Island*

Oxnard

To
Los Angeles

San
Francisco
Sacramento

CALIFORNIA

Map
Area

Los Angeles

And then there are the swimming pools. The Roman-inspired indoor pool has intricate mosaic work, Carrara-marble replicas of Greek gods and goddesses, and alabaster globe lamps that create the illusion of moonlight. The breathtaking outdoor Greco-Roman Neptune pool, flanked by marble colonnades that frame the distant sea, is one of the mansion's most memorable features.

In 1957, in exchange for a massive tax write-off, the Hearst Corporation donated the estate to the state of California (while retaining ownership of approximately 80,000 acres); the California Department of Parks and Recreation now administers it as a State Historic Monument.

GETTING THERE Hearst Castle is located directly on Calif. 1, about 42 miles north of San Luis Obispo and 94 miles south of Monterey. From San Francisco or Monterey, take U.S. 101 south to Paso Robles, then Calif. 46 west to Calif. 1, and Calif. 1 north to the castle. From Los Angeles, take U.S. 101 north to San Luis Obispo, then Calif. 1 north to the castle. Park in the visitor center parking lot; a bus will take you the 5 miles up the hill to the estate. The movie theater and visitor center adjoin the parking lot and are easily accessible without heading up to the actual estate.

TOURING THE ESTATE

Hearst Castle can be visited only by guided tours, which are conducted daily beginning at 8:20am, except on New Year's Day, Thanksgiving, and Christmas. Two to six tours leave every hour, depending on the season. Allow 2 hours between starting times if you plan on taking more than one tour. Reservations are recommended and can be made up to 8 weeks in advance. Tickets can be purchased by phone through **California Reservations** (© **800/444-4445**). Daytime tours are $10 for adults, $5 for children ages 6 to 12, and free for children under 6. Evening tours are $20 for adults, $10 for children 6 to 12, and free for children under 6. To get information online, go to **www.hearstcastle. org**. Four distinct daytime tours are offered on a daily basis, each lasting almost 2 hours.

Tour 1 is usually recommended for first-time visitors and is the first to get booked up. In addition to the swimming pools, this tour visits several rooms on the ground floor of the main house (known as Casa Grande), including Hearst's private theater, where you'll see some home movies taken during the castle's heyday. You'll get to see the sculptures and flowers in the gardens and the formal esplanade, as well as the largest guesthouse, Casa del Sol.

Tour 2 focuses on Casa Grande's upper floors, including Hearst's opulent library, private suite of rooms, and lots of fabulous bathrooms. Ongoing efforts are made to lend a lived-in look to the house; examples are the lifelike food displayed in the kitchen and pantry, and vintage sewing equipment in Marion Davies' suite. Although Tour 1 is commonly recommended for first-timers, Tour 2 is a perfectly fine choice if you're only planning to take one tour, particularly if your interest lies more in the home's private areas.

Tour 3 delves into the complex construction and subsequent alterations of Hearst Castle. You'll visit Casa del Monte, a guesthouse unaltered from its original design, then head to the North Wing of Casa Grande, the last portion of the property to be completed, to see the contrast in styles. A video called *The Building of a Dream,* which uses film and photographs from the 1920s and 1930s to go behind the scenes of the construction process, is shown. Tour 3 is especially fascinating for architecture buffs and detail hounds, but shouldn't be the first and only tour you take if you've never visited the castle before.

Tour 4 is dedicated to the estate's gardens, terraces, and walkways, and is only offered from April through October. You'll also tour the Casa del Mar guesthouse, the wine cellar of Casa Grande, and the colorful dressing rooms at the Neptune Pool. Like Tour 3, this one is best taken after you've seen some of the more essential areas of the estate.

Evening tours are held most Friday and Saturday nights during spring and fall. These last about 30 minutes longer than the daytime tours, and visit highlights of the main house, the largest and most elaborate guesthouse, and the estate's pools and gardens, which are illuminated by hundreds of restored light fixtures. The pools in particular are most breathtaking when seen this way. The entire living-history experience is enhanced by docents dressed in period costume assuming a variety of roles.

Tip: Because these are walking tours, be sure to wear comfortable shoes— you'll be walking about a half mile per tour, which includes between 150 and 400 steps to climb or descend. (Wheelchair tours are available by calling ℂ **805/ 927-2020** at least 10 days in advance.)

The latest addition to the estate is the giant-screen **Hearst Castle National Geographic Theatre,** which you can visit regardless of whether you take a tour. Films include *Hearst Castle: Building the Dream,* among others. For current information, call ℂ **805/927-6811** or visit the website at www.ngtheater.com. The Hearst film shows hourly at half past the hour, and tickets cost $7.50 for adults and $5.50 for children 12 and under.

WHAT TO SEE & DO IN NEARBY CAMBRIA

After driving for close to an hour without passing anything but lush green hills and nature at its most glorious (especially from Calif. 46 off U.S. 101), it's a remarkably quaint surprise to roll into the adorable coastal minitown of Cambria, just south of San Simeon. Cambria, known as an artists' colony, is so charming that the town itself is reason enough to make the drive. With little more than 3 blocks worth of shops, restaurants, and a handful of B&Bs, Cambria is the perfect place to escape the everyday, enjoy the endless expanses of pristine coastal terrain, and meander through little shops selling local artwork and antiques.

Gray whales pass through the area from late December to early February, and for the past few years hundreds of elephant seals have made the shore just north of the Hearst Castle entrance their year-round playground—much to the delight of locals and nature enthusiasts. Keep your distance from these mammoth mammals: They're a protected species and can be dangerous if molested. There is a parking lot, and docents are usually on hand to answer questions. The beaches and coves are also wonderful places for humans to frolic as well. For more information on Cambria, check out **www.cambria-online.com,** or call the chamber of commerce at ℂ **805/927-3624.**

SHOPPING

Shopping is a major pastime in the village; boutique owners are hyper-savvy about keeping their merchandise current—and priced just a hair lower than L.A. or San Francisco. This close-knit community has always attracted artists and artisans of the highest quality; for the finest handcrafted glass artworks, from affordable jewelry to investment-scale sculpture, head to **Seekers Collection & Gallery,** 4090 Burton Dr. (ℂ **805/927-4352;** www.seekersglass.com). Nearby, at **Moonstones Gallery,** 4070 Burton Dr. (ℂ **805/927-3447**), you'll find a selection of works ranging from woven crafts to jewelry and an exceptional

Fun Fact   **Weekends at the Ranch: William Randolph Hearst & the Legacy of Hearst Castle**

The lavish palace that William Randolph Hearst always referred to simply as "the ranch" took root in 1919. William Randolph ("W. R." to his friends) had inherited 275,000 acres from his father, mining baron George Hearst, and was well on his way to building a formidable media empire. He often escaped to a spot known as "Camp Hill" on his newly acquired lands in the Santa Lucia Mountains above the village of San Simeon, the site of boyhood family outings. Complaining that "I get tired of going up there and camping in tents," Hearst hired architect Julia Morgan to design the retreat that would become one of the most famous private homes in the world.

An art collector with indiscriminate taste and inexhaustible funds, Hearst overwhelmed Morgan with interiors and furnishings from the ancestral collections of Europe. Each week, railroad cars carrying fragments of Roman temples, lavish doors and carved ceilings from Italian monasteries, Flemish tapestries, hastily rolled paintings by the old masters, ancient Persian rugs, and antique French furniture arrived—5 tons at a time—in San Simeon. *Citizen Kane,* which depicts a Hearst-like mogul with a similarly excessive estate called Xanadu, has a memorable scene of hoarded priceless treasures warehoused in dusty piles, stretching as far as the eye can see. Like Kane, Hearst, once described as a man with an "edifice complex," purchased so much that only a fraction of what he bought was ever installed in the estate.

In 1925, Hearst separated from his wife and began to spend time in Los Angeles overseeing his movie company, Cosmopolitan Pictures. His principal starlet, Marion Davies, became W. R.'s constant companion and hostess at Hearst Castle; this would be her main role for the rest of his life. The ranch soon became a playground for the Hollywood crowd as well as dignitaries like Winston Churchill and playwright George Bernard Shaw, who is said to have wryly remarked of the estate, "This is the way God would have done it if He had the money."

collection of woodcarvings and other crafts. If a visit to the nearby Paso Robles Wine Country has inspired you, **Fermentations,** 4056 Burton Dr. (© 805/927-7141) has wines, wine accessories and gifts, plus Wine Country gourmet goodies open for tasting. Women who appreciate casual style and ease of care mustn't miss **Leslie Mark,** 4070 Burton Dr. (© 805/927-1434; www.lesliemark.com) and her deceptively simple line of versatile cotton and rayon separates. Across the street, **Heart's Ease,** 4101 Burton Dr. (© 800/266-4372 or 805/927-5224), is located inside a quaint historic cottage and is packed with an abundance of garden delights, apothecary herbs, and custom-blended potpourris.

WHERE TO STAY

Cambria's popularity in summertime and on holiday weekends makes advance planning a necessity. If our favorites below are full, try one of these recommended

Despite its opulence, Hearst promoted "the ranch" as a casual weekend home. He regularly laid the massive refectory table in the dining room with paper napkins and bottled ketchup and pickles to evoke a rustic camplike atmosphere. In Hearst's beautiful library, his priceless collection of ancient Greek pottery—one of the greatest collections of its kind in the world—is arranged casually among the rare volumes, like knickknacks.

The Hollywood crowd would take Hearst's private railway car from Los Angeles to San Luis Obispo, where a fleet of limousines waited to transport them to San Simeon. Those who didn't come by train were treated to a flight on Hearst's private plane from the Burbank airport (MGM head Irving Thalberg and his wife, Norma Shearer, preferred this mode of transportation). Hearst, an avid aviator, had a sizable landing strip built; Charles Lindbergh used it when he flew up for a visit in the summer of 1928.

Oh, if the walls could talk. Atop one of the castle's looming towers are the hexagonal Celestial Suites. One was a favorite of Clark Gable and Carole Lombard, who would be startled out of their romantic slumber by the clamor of 18 carillon bells directly overhead. David Niven, a frequent guest, was one of the unknown number who defied teetotally Hearst's edict against liquor in private rooms; Niven was called upon more than once to explain the several "empties" under the bed (which Cardinal Richelieu once owned and slept in) in his customary suite.

W. R. Hearst and Marion Davies hosted frequent costume parties at the ranch, which were as intricately planned as a movie production. The most legendary, the Circus Party, was held to celebrate W. R.'s 75th birthday on April 29, 1938. Much of Hollywood attended to honor the tycoon, including grande dame Bette Davis—dressed as a bearded lady.

alternatives: **Captain's Cove Inn,** 6454 Moonstone Beach Dr. (© **800/781-COVE** or 805/927-8581; www.thegrid.net/captainscove) is a small beachfront B&B whose motel-style exterior belies the array of creature comforts cheerily provided by the family owners; or **Cambria Pines Lodge,** 2905 Burton Dr. (© **800/445-6868** or 805/927-4200; www.cambriapineslodge.com), a summer camp, lodge-style compound with terrific family facilities nestled in the pines just a few blocks from the center of town. The **Ragged Point Inn,** 19019 Highway 1 (© **805/927-4502;** fax 805/927-8862) is located 15 miles north of Hearst Castle, and offers sweeping ocean views from each room.

Best Western Cavalier Oceanfront Resort ☆ *Kids*   Of the dozen or so budget and midrange motels clustered along Highway 1 near Hearst Castle, this surprisingly nice chain is the only one that's actually oceanfront. Sprawled across a gentle slope, the hotel invites guests to huddle around cliffside bonfires each evening. Every room—whether you choose a basic double or opt for extras such as a fireplace, ocean view, wet bar, or oceanfront terrace—features an array of amenities (tape rentals for the VCR are conveniently next door). The Cavalier is top-notch in its class, and a terrific choice for Castle-bound families.

9415 Hearst Dr. (Calif. 1), San Simeon, CA 93452. ℰ **800/826-8168** or 805/927-4688. Fax 805/927-6472. www.cavalierresort.com. 90 units. $99–$189 double. AE, DC, DISC, MC, V. Pets welcome. **Amenities:** Restaurant; 2 outdoor heated (and windshielded) pools; Jacuzzi; exercise room; concierge; room service (7am to 9pm); self-service Laundromat. *In room:* TV/VCR, dataport, minibar, coffeemaker, hair dryer, iron.

FogCatcher Inn ✹ *(Value* You'll spot the FogCatcher by its faux English architecture (though a contemporary hotel), that fits right in with the mish-mash of styles on funky Moonstone Beach. The U-shaped building is situated so many rooms have unencumbered views of the crashing waves across the street; some gaze oceanward over a sea of parked cars, and others are hopelessly landlocked—be sure to inquire when reserving.

Though rates vary wildly according to view, each room interior sports identical amenities and comforts. Immaculately maintained and furnished in a comfy cottage style with oversize pine furniture, each room is made cozier by a gas fireplace and also boasts a microwave oven. Unlike many comparably priced Moonstone Beach lodgings, the FogCatcher has a heated swimming pool and Jacuzzi; stop by the breakfast room in the morning for basic coffee, juice, and muffins to start the day.

6400 Moonstone Beach Dr., Cambria, CA 93428. ℰ **800/425-4121** or 805/927-1400. Fax 805/927-0204. 60 units. $115–$275 double. Substantial midweek and off-season discounts available. Rates include continental breakfast. AE, DISC, MC, V. **Amenities:** Outdoor heated pool; Jacuzzi. *In room:* TV, minibar, fridge, coffeemaker.

J. Patrick House ✹ Hidden in a pine-filled residential neighborhood overlooking Cambria's village, this picture-perfect B&B is cozy, elegant, and welcoming. The main house is an authentic two-story log cabin, where each afternoon innkeepers Ann and John host wine and hors d'oeuvres next to the living room fireplace, and each morning serve breakfast by windows overlooking a hummingbird-filled garden. Most guest rooms are in the adjacent carriage house, and feature wood-burning fireplaces, feather duvets, bedtime milk and cookies, and country elements like knotty pine, bent-twig furniture, calico prints, and hand-stitched quilts. Amenities like phone, fax, and guest fridge are available in the common area; hair dryers and irons will be provided upon request.

2990 Burton Dr., Cambria, CA 93428. ℰ **800/341-5258** or 805/927-3812. Fax 805/927-6759. www.jpatrick house.com. 8 units. $135–$200 double. Seasonal discounts and packages available. Rates include full breakfast, afternoon hors d'oeuvres, and evening milk and cookies. DISC, MC, V. *In room:* No phone.

Olallieberry Inn ✹✹ This 1873 Greek Revival house is our favorite B&B in the area. The grounds are perfectly manicured but bloom whimsically; in the afternoon the aromas of baked Brie and homemade bread (served during the wine hour) waft through the main house, and the staff does everything imaginable to make your stay special. They also have a passion for cooking and gardening, but the decor doesn't fall by the wayside: Victorian floral-and-lace reigns, and the guest rooms are lovingly and individually appointed. Each has its own private bathroom, although some are across or down the hall. Rooms in a newer adjoining building overlook a creek; they're remarkably charming and have a fireplace and private deck. The delicious full breakfast—accompanied by olallieberry jam, of course—is gourmet all the way. *Note:* Amenities like phone, fax, and guest fridge are available in the common area; hair dryers, irons, and bathrobes are cheerfully provided if you ask.

2476 Main St., Cambria, CA 93428. ℂ **888/927-3222** or 805/927-3222. Fax 805/927-0202. www.olallieberry. com. 9 units. $95–$165 double; $180–$190 cottage suite. Rates include full breakfast and evening wine and hors d'oeuvres. AE, MC, V. *In room:* No phone.

WHERE TO DINE

Tiny Cambria boasts an unusual concentration of superb restaurants. (The town's eateries repeatedly dominate Zagat's mere two pages of Central Coast listings.) In addition to the restaurants listed below, consider **Bistro Sole,** 1980 Main St. (tel] **805/927-0887**), a quaint and cozy bungalow with a sophisticated decor and eclectic California cuisine; **Moonstone Beach Bar & Grill,** 6550 Moonstone Beach Dr. (ℂ **805/927-3859**), whose incredible view must be what accounts for prices on the expensive side for this tasty but casual restaurant—stick to breakfast or lunch; or local institution **Linn's Main Binn,** 2277 Main St. (ℂ **805/927-0371**), a casual all-day diner featuring hearty homemade pot pies, fresh-from-the-farm salads, breakfast treats, and Linn's famous fruit pies.

Robin's ⊕ ECLECTIC   Robin's is a restaurant with something for everyone, from exotic dishes from Mexico, Thailand, India, and beyond to more straightforward preparations like a tasty salad or juicy steak and an array of vegetarian dishes. Offerings include a salmon-bisque appetizer; porcini ravioli with roasted-pepper-cream sauce, fresh spinach, basil, and Parmesan; and other flavorful combinations such as Tandoori prawns with basmati brown rice, fruit chutney, and chapati. Don't miss dessert—try the espresso-soaked cake with mascarpone mousse and shaved chocolate or vanilla-custard bread pudding.

4095 Burton Dr., Cambria. ℂ **805/927-5007.** www.robinsrestaurant.com. Reservations recommended. Main courses $9–$19. MC, V. Daily 11am–9pm (open late in summer).

Sea Chest Oyster Bar ⊕ SEAFOOD   Feeling like a dozen other seaside old-salt hangouts, the strangely familiar Sea Chest is a must for seafood lovers. Sporting a crusty nautical kitsch and warm, welcoming atmosphere, this gray clapboard cottage even has a game-filled lounge complete with cribbage, checkers, and chess to keep you amused during the inevitable wait for a table. Oysters are the main attraction: on the half shell, oyster stew, oysters Casino, oysters Rockefeller, or "devils on horseback" (with wine, garlic, and bacon). The menu is also filled with very fresh seafood from local and worldwide waters: steamed New Zealand green-lipped mussels, clams in several preparations, halibut, salmon, lobster, scampi, plus whatever looked good off the boats that morning. There's a respectable list of microbrewed and imported beers, along with a selection of Central Coast wines. *Note:* If you don't enjoy seafood, stay away—there's not even a token steak on this menu!

6216 Moonstone Beach Dr. ℂ **805/927-4514.** Reservations not accepted. Main courses $9–$17. No credit cards. Wed–Mon 5:30–9pm (open Tues May–Sept only).

Sow's Ear Café ⊕⊕ AMERICAN   This tiny old cottage at the center of the village has been transformed into a warm, romantic hideaway. The best tables are in the fireside front room, lit just enough to highlight its rustic wood-and-brick decor; pigs appear everywhere, in oil paintings, small ceramic or cast-iron models, and the woodcut sow logo. Though the menu features plenty of contemporary California cuisine, the most popular dishes are American country favorites given a contemporary lift; these include a warmly satisfying chicken-fried steak with gravy, chicken and dumplings, and zesty baby pork ribs. Other standouts are parchment-wrapped salmon, and pork loin glazed with chunky olallieberry chutney. Every meal begins with the restaurant's signature marbled bread baked in terra-cotta flowerpots, and the wine list is among the area's best.

Early birds (5–6pm nightly) choose from six dinners from $11 to $13.

2248 Main St. ℃ **805/927-4865.** Reservations recommended. Main courses $14–$22. AE, DISC, MC, V. Daily 5–9:30pm.

2 Morro Bay

124 miles S of Monterey, 235 miles S of San Francisco (via Calif. 1), 220 miles N of Los Angeles

Morro Bay is separated from the ocean by a long peninsula of towering sand dunes. It's best known for dramatic **Morro Rock,** an enormous egg-shaped monolith that juts out of the water just offshore. Across from the rock, a monstrous oceanfront electrical plant mars the visual appeal of the otherwise pristine bay, which is filled with birds, sea mammals, and calm water offering plenty of recreational activities.

Other than gawking at the amazing "Gibraltar of the Pacific," there's not all that much to see in the town itself. Motels, shops, and restaurants line the waterfront Embarcadero and adjacent blocks, but the town's best feature is its natural surroundings; the beaches and wildlife sanctuaries can be quite peaceful and wondrous.

EXPLORING THE AREA

The **Morro Bay Chamber of Commerce,** 880 Main St., Morro Bay, CA 93442 (℃ **800/231-0592** or 805/772-4467; www.morrobay.com), offers armfuls of area information. It's open Monday through Friday from 8:30am to 5pm and Saturday from 10am to 3pm.

Most visitors come to Morro Bay to ogle **Morro Rock,** the much-photographed Central Coast icon that anchors the mouth of the waterway. This ancient towering landmark, whose name comes from the Spanish word for a Moorish turban, is a volcanic remnant inhabited by the endangered peregrine falcon and other migratory birds.

BEACHES   Popular **Atascadero State Beach,** just north of Morro Rock, has gentle waves and lovely views. Restrooms, showers, and dressing rooms are available. Just north of Atascadero is **Morro Strand State Beach,** a long, sandy stretch with normally gentle surf. Restrooms and picnic tables are available here. Morro Strand has its own campgrounds; for information, call ℃ **805/772-2560,** or reserve a spot through Park-Net (℃ **800/444-7275;** www.park-net.com).

STATE PARKS   Cabrillo Peak, located in the lovely **Morro Bay State Park** (℃ **805/772-7434**), makes for a terrific day hike and offers fantastic 360° views from its summit. There's a faint zigzagging trail, but the best way to reach the top is by bushwhacking straight up the gentle slope—a hike that takes about 2 hours round-trip. To reach the trailhead, take Calif. 1 south and turn left at the Morro Bay State Park/Montana de Oro State Park exit. Follow South Bay Boulevard for three quarters of a mile, then take the left fork another half a mile to the Cabrillo Peak dirt parking lot, located on your left. The park also offers camping and a decent public golf course called Morro Bay, which charges $28 to $35 for greens fees (℃ **805/782-8060**).

South of Morro Bay in Los Osos is **Montana de Oro State Park** ("Mountain of Gold"), fondly known as "petite Big Sur" because of its stony cliffs and rugged terrain. There's great swimming at Spooner's Cove and lots of easy hiking trails here, including some that lead to spectacular coastal vistas or hidden forest streams. The Hazard Reef Trail will take you up on the Morro Bay Sandspit dunes. The park's campground is in the trees, across from the beach. For information, call the park rangers (© **805/528-0513**), or reserve a spot through Park-Net (© **800/444-7275;** www.park-net.com).

ON THE WATER   You can venture out on a kayak tour with **Kayaks of Morro Bay** (© **805/772-1119**), which is located on the Embarcadero at Pacific St. If you've always yearned for sailing lessons, call ahead to the **Sailing Center of Morro Bay** (© **805/772-6446**). It's next to Morro Bay Yacht Club and offers everything from 1-day intro classes to weeklong series and scheduled sunset sails.

IN TOWN   The Embarcadero is also home to the **Giant Chessboard,** whose 3-foot-tall redwood pieces were inspired by open-air boards in Germany. Nearby is the **Morro Bay Aquarium,** 595 Embarcadero (© **805/772-7647**), a modest operation notable for the injured or abandoned sea otters, seals, and sea lions it rescues and rehabilitates. During their stay, all the animals learn to perform tricks for a morsel of fishy food (50¢ per bag).

WHERE TO STAY

Baywood Bed & Breakfast Inn *(Finds*   Located south of Morro Bay in Baywood Park, facing out onto Morro's "back bay," this two-story gray inn is a converted 1970s garden-style office building with spacious B&B suites, each furnished in a distinctive (over-the-top) theme and Grandma-style flair. Every room has a private entrance, gas fireplace, and microwave (plus a fridge stocked with complimentary sodas and snacks); all but a few have bay views. Included in your stay is a full breakfast each morning and a late-afternoon wine and cheese reception highlighted by a room tour. If you're looking for solitude, Baywood Park suits the bill; there are a couple of decent restaurants on the block, and pretty Montana de Oro is close by.

1370 Second St. (2½ blocks so. of Santa Ysabel Ave.), Baywood Park, CA 93402. © **805/528-8888.** Fax 805/ 528-8887. www.baywoodinn.com. 15 units. $80–$110 double; $110–$160 suite. Rates include full breakfast and afternoon wine and cheese. Extra person $15. MC, V. *In room:* TV/VCR, kitchenette, minibar, coffeemaker, hair dryer.

The Inn at Morro Bay   Despite a sleek brochure that hints at snooty glamour, this comfortable and affordable resort is smart enough to let its splendid natural surroundings be the focus of attention. Situated directly on the water, the inn's two-story Cape Cod–style buildings have contemporary interiors amid a quiet garden setting. The inn has quietly been enhancing itself with a spa ambiance; new features include an on-site massage center and private balcony Jacuzzis for some guest quarters. Rates vary wildly according to view, with the best rooms enjoying unobstructed views of Morro Rock plus convenient access to a bayfront sundeck; those in back face the swimming pool, gardens, and eucalyptus-forested golf course at Morro Bay State Park (see above). The hotel has a romantic bayside lounge and California/Mediterranean restaurant.

60 State Park Rd., Morro Bay, CA 93442. © **800/321-9566** or 805/772-5651. Fax 805/772-4779. www.innat morrobay.com. 98 units. $99–$299 double. Midweek and seasonal discounts available. AE, DISC, MC, V. Take Main St. south, past park entrance. **Amenities:** 2 restaurants; lounge; outdoor heated pool; full-service spa; nearby golf and water recreation; complimentary bicycles; concierge; room service (7am to 10pm); in-room massage; babysitting; dry cleaning/laundry service. *In room:* TV, dataport, fridge, coffeemaker, hair dryer, iron.

WHERE TO DINE

Hofbrau *(Value* GERMAN/AMERICAN   When you're hungry in Morro Bay and want something other than fish and chips, Hofbrau is the place. Although they do serve the standard wharfside fare, the star here is the roast beef French Dip (their strategically placed carving station ensures its popularity). Those in the know order the mini sandwich, which is a dollar less and just an inch shorter. As the name would suggest, they have a nice selection of beers as well as a kids' menu with six choices at $3.49, making this a great value for families.

571 Embarcadero, Morro Bay. ✆ 805/772-2411. Reservations not accepted. Most items $4.25–$8.75. AE, DISC, MC, V. Sun–Thurs 11am–8:30pm; Fri–Sat 11am–9pm.

Windows on the Water 𝒢 CALIFORNIA   If you're looking for a special meal in town, you'll find Morro Bay's best at this respected restaurant that takes full advantage of prime waterfront views with its airy, high-ceilinged, multilevel space. But chef Gerard Robert's cuisine—a California/French/Mediterranean hybrid incorporating local fresh seafood and produce—is the main attraction. On a given evening, the menu might include seared halibut in a Dijon crust off-set by sweet-tangy orange marmalade and tequila sauce, shellfish braised in champagne and tossed with house-made fettuccine, or pheasant breast enveloped in prosciutto and Brie atop a Riesling reduction sauce. The wine list is composed of the choicest Central Coast vintages and select French bottles. The Saturday-Sunday brunch is a rich prix fixe indulgence if you're celebrating.

699 Embarcadero (in Marina Square). ✆ 805/772-0677. Reservations recommended. Main courses $14–$26; brunch $19.95 ($12.95 for kids). AE, DC, DISC, MC, V. Daily 5–10pm; Sat–Sun 11am–2pm.

3 San Luis Obispo

38 miles S of Cambria, 226 miles S of San Francisco, 198 miles N of Los Angeles

Because the actual town of San Luis Obispo is not visible from U.S. 101, even many Californians don't know that it's more than another fast food-and-gasoline stopover on the highway. But its "secret" location is part of what helps this relaxed yet vital college town keep its charm and character intact.

San Luis Obispo (SLO to locals) is neatly tucked into the mountains about halfway between San Francisco and Los Angeles. It's surrounded by green, pristine mountain ranges and filled with a mix of college kids, big-city transplants, dot.com entrepreneurs, and friendly agricultural folk.

The town grew up around an 18th-century mission, and its dozens of historic landmarks, Victorian homes, shops, and restaurants are its primary attractions for visitors. Today, it's still quaint, almost undiscovered, and best ventured on foot. It also makes a good base for an extensive exploration of the region as a whole. To the west of town, a short drive away, are some of the state's prettiest swimming beaches; to the north and south you'll find the Central Coast's Wine Country, home to dozens of respectable wineries and bucolic scenery.

ESSENTIALS

GETTING THERE   U.S. 101, one of the state's primary north-south road-ways, runs right through San Luis Obispo; it's the fastest land route here from anywhere. If you're driving down along the coast, Calif. 1 is the way to go for its natural beauty and oceanfront cliffs. If you're entering the city from the east, take Calif. 46 or 41 to U.S. 101, then go south.

VISITOR INFORMATION   The **San Luis Obispo Visitors Center,** 1039 Chorro St. (✆ **805/781-2777;** www.VisitSLO.com), is located downtown, between Monterey and Higuera Streets. It offers a colorful, comprehensive *Visitors Guide* and the self-guided *Mission Plaza Walking Tour.* The center is open

Sunday and Monday from 10am to 5pm, Tuesday and Wednesday from 8am to 5pm, Thursday and Friday from 8am to 8pm, and Saturday from 10am to 8pm.

ORIENTATION   San Luis Obispo is about 10 miles inland, at the junction of Calif. 1 and U.S. 101. The downtown is laid out in a grid, roughly centered around the historic mission and its Mission Plaza (see below). Most of the main tourist sights are around the mission, within the small triangle created by U.S. 101 and Santa Rosa and Marsh Streets.

EXPLORING THE TOWN

Before heading downtown, definitely make a pit stop at the perpetually pink **Madonna Inn,** 100 Madonna Rd., off U.S. 101 (**℡ 805/543-3000**), if for no other reason than to use its unique public restrooms (the men's has a waterfall urinal; the women's is a barrage of crimson and pink). Every over-the-top inch of this place is an exercise in excess, from the dining room, complete with pink leather booths, pink table linens, and colored sugar that's—you guessed it— piquantly pink, to the rock-walled, cavelike guest rooms (see "Where to Stay," below, for a complete review).

Once downtown, you can ride the free trolley that does a repeat loop through the downtown area daily from noon to 5pm. (Stops are well marked.)

Ah Louis Store   Mr. Ah Louis was a Cantonese immigrant who was lured to California by gold fever in 1856. Emerging from the mines empty handed, he soon began a lucrative career as a labor contractor, hiring and organizing Chinese crews that built the railroad. In 1874, he opened this store. Today, the store is rarely open, but if it is you can browse the clutter of Asian merchandise.

800 Palm St. (at Chorro St.). ℡ 805/543-4332. Open hours vary; serious shoppers phone in advance.

Farmers Market ⊛   If you're lucky enough to be in town on a Thursday, take an evening stroll down Higuera Street, when the county's largest weekly street fair fills four downtown city blocks. You'll find much more here than fresh-picked produce—there's an ever-changing array of street entertainment, open-pit barbecues, food stands, and market stalls selling fresh flowers, cider, and other seasonal goodies. Surrounding stores stay open until 9pm.

Higuera St. (between Osos and Nipomo Sts.). Thurs 6:30–9pm (rain or shine).

Mission San Luis Obispo de Tolosa   Founded by Father Junípero Serra in 1772, California's fifth mission was built with adobe bricks by Native American Chumash people. It remains one of the prettiest and most interesting structures in the Franciscan chain. Serra chose this valley for the site of his fifth mission based on tales told to him of friendly natives and bountiful food (including grizzly bears). Here the traditional red-tile roof was first used atop a California mission, after the original thatched tule roofs repeatedly fell to hostile Native Americans' burning arrows. The former padres' quarters are now an excellent museum chronicling both Native American and missionary life through all eras of the mission's use. Allow about 30 to 45 minutes to tour the mission and its grounds.

Mission Plaza, a pretty garden with brick paths and park benches fronting a meandering creek in which children love to wade, still functions as San Luis Obispo's town square. It's the focal point for local festivities and activities, from live concerts to poetry readings and dance and theater productions. Check at the visitor center (see "Essentials," above) to find out what's on when you're in town.

At the south end of Mission Plaza you'll find the **San Luis Obispo Art Center** (© 805/543-8562), whose three galleries display and sell an array of California-made art. Admission is free; hours are Tuesday through Sunday from 11am to 5pm.

751 Palm St. © 805/781-8220. www.oldmissionslo.org. Free admission ($2 donation requested). Summer daily 9am–5pm (sometimes later); winter daily 9am–4pm.

San Luis Obispo Children's Museum *Kids* This terrific children's museum features a playhouse for toddlers, an authentic reproduction of a Native American Chumash cave dwelling, a music room, a computer corner, a pint-sized bank and post office, and over 20 interactive exhibits rotated on a regular basis. Special events like mask making, sing-alongs, and stage-makeup classes are scheduled regularly; call for a list of events.

1010 Nipomo St. (at Monterey St.). © 805/544-KIDS. www.slonet.org/~slokids. Admission $4.75 adults and children 2 and older, free for children under 2. Thurs[nd[Sat 11am–5pm; Sun noon–4pm.

SHOPPING

You'll find SLO resembles a smaller version of Santa Barbara, where unique boutiques and specialty shops are interspersed with recognized names and finer chains. With an influx of new residents, big-name businesses have been popping up all over the place: Look for the Gap, Barnes & Noble, Victoria's Secret, and Starbucks on SLO's charming tree-lined streets. The best place to exercise your credit cards is on the downtown streets surrounding the mission, specifically the 5 blocks of **Higuera Street** from Nipomo to Osos Streets, as well as a short stretch of **Monterey Street** between Chorro and Osos Streets.

On Higuera Street, check out **Hands Gallery,** 777 Higuera St. (© 805/543-1921), which has a playful, bright collection of local and international art. Trinkets range from glass candies to vases, jewelry, and ceramics and can be viewed or purchased Monday through Wednesday from 10am to 6pm, Thursday through Saturday from 10am to 9pm, and Sunday from 11am to 5pm.

ATTRACTIONS OUTSIDE OF TOWN

There are dozens of **wineries** in the area that offer tastings and tours daily and make for a fun country diversion. See "The Central Coast Wine Country: Paso Robles & the Santa Ynez Valley," later in this chapter, for further details. If you don't have time to tour the wineries or would like more information before heading out to taste, you can visit **The Wine Guy,** 1817 Osos St. by the train station (© 805/546-VINO). Local wine guru Ron Rawlinson, who teaches enology at Cal Poly and even hosts a local radio show devoted to all things wine, is a one-stop source of information, supplies, and anecdotes on the Central Coast wine industry; he also stocks a comprehensive array of bottles, including unknown limited-production gems.

WHERE TO STAY

In addition to what's listed below, there's a pristine branch of **Holiday Inn Express** (© 800/465-4329 or 805/544-8600), a reliable **Motel 6** (© 800/4-MOTEL-6 or 805/541-6992), and 34 sweet motel-style units at the **Apple Farm Trellis Court** (© 800/255-2040 or 805/544-2040).

Adobe Inn Okay, it's not *actually* adobe—or even remotely close for that matter—but new owners have taken this old motor inn and given it a creatively homey atmosphere at unbeatable prices. Each spotless room is individually decorated in Southwestern style with quirky additions such as playfully painted cupboards or a window-side reading nook. Breakfast is served in a clean dining area that unfortunately faces the street, but coffee snobs will delight in the strong, locally roasted blend. Plants adorn the inn's exterior. The owners go out of their way to make guests happy and offer a slew of packages that explore the surrounding areas and attractions.

1473 Monterey St., San Luis Obispo, CA 93401. © 800/676-1588 or 805/549-0321. Fax 805/549-0383. www.adobeinns.com. 15 units (8 with kitchenette, but no stove). $59–$125 double. Rates include breakfast. Extra person $6 in winter, $10 in summer. AE, DISC, MC, V. **Amenities:** Complimentary bicycles. *In room:* TV, dataport, coffeemaker, hair dryer, iron; some with kitchenette (no stove).

Apple Farm Inn ✿✿   Ultra-popular, the Apple Farm Inn is a peaceful getaway in a Disney-plantation kind of way. Every square inch of the immaculate Victorian-style farmhouse is cheek-pinchingly cute with floral wallpaper, fresh flowers, and sugar-sweet colorful touches. No two rooms are alike, although each has a gas fireplace, large well-equipped bathroom, pine antiques, lavish country decor, and either a canopy four-poster or brass bed. Some bedrooms open onto cozy turreted sitting areas with romantic window seats; others have bay windows and a view of San Luis Creek, where a working mill spins its huge wheel to power an apple press. The outstanding service here includes nightly turndown and a morning wake-up knock, delivered with complimentary coffee or tea and a newspaper. Other features include complimentary cribs and train and airport shuttle service. Cider is always on hand in the lobby. The hotel shares a name with their on-site restaurant, one of Highway 101's best-loved pit stops.

Those who want the bang without the requisite bucks can opt for the adjoining motel-style **Apple Farm Trellis Court**, which shares the inn's wonderful grounds. Rooms are smaller, but are well decorated and have gas fireplaces; rates include a continental breakfast and are just half as much as the inn.

2015 Monterey St., San Luis Obispo, CA 93401. © 800/255-2040 or 805/544-2040. Fax 805/546-9495. www.applefarm.com. 69 units. $160–$289 double. AE, DISC, MC, V. **Amenities** Restaurant; outdoor heated pool; Jacuzzi; dry cleaning/laundry service. *In room:* AC, TV w/ pay movies, dataport.

Garden Street Inn ✿   SLO's prettiest (and most-polished) bed-and-breakfast is this gracious Italianate/Queen Anne downtown. Built in 1887 and completely restored in 1990, the house is a monument to gentility and to the good taste of owners Dan and Kathy Smith. Each bedroom and suite is decorated with well-chosen antique armoires, opulent fabric or paper wall coverings, and vintage memorabilia. Choose one with a clawfoot tub, fireplace, whirlpool bath, or private deck—whatever suits your fancy. Breakfast is served in the stained-glass morning room, and each evening wine and cheese are laid out for guests. A well-stocked library is always available.

1212 Garden St. (between Marsh and Pacific), San Luis Obispo, CA 93401. © 800/488-2045 or 805/ 545-9802. Fax 805/545-9403. www.gardenstreetinn.com. 13 units. $110–$180 double. Rates include full breakfast and evening wine and cheese. AE, MC, V. *In room:* A/C, dataport.

Madonna Inn ✿   This one you've got to see for yourself. The creative imaginations of owners Alex and Phyllis Madonna gave birth to the wildest—and most superfluously garish—fantasy world this side of Graceland. The only decor consistency throughout the hotel is its color scheme, which is perpetual pink. Beyond that, it's a free-for-all. Although tongue-in-cheek, this place can seem tired and tacky, and some of the rooms could use updating. However, the lobby men's room with its rock-waterfall urinal and clamshell sinks is a must-see. One guest room features a trapezoidal bed—it's 5 feet long on one side and 6 feet long on the other. "Rock" rooms with zebra- or tiger-patterned bedspreads and stonelike showers and fireplaces conjure up thoughts of a Flintstones's Playboy palace. There are also blue rooms, red rooms, and over-the-top Spanish, Italian, Irish, Alps, Currier and Ives, Native American, Swiss, and hunting rooms. The cocktail lounges are also outlandishly ornate. Even if you don't stay here, stop by and check it out. One caveat: The Madonna Inn, surprisingly, lacks a swimming pool.

100 Madonna Rd. (off U.S. 101), San Luis Obispo, CA 93405. © 800/543-9666 or 805/543-3000. Fax 805/543-1800. www.madonnainn.com. 134 units. $147–$248 double; from $210 suite. AE, MC, V. **Amenities:** Restaurant, coffee shop, 2 lounges. *In room:* TV, coffeemaker.

WHERE TO DINE

Big Sky Cafe ✿ AMERICAN   The folk-artsy fervor of San Luis really shines at this Southwestern mirage, where local art and a blue, star-studded ceiling surround diners who come for fresh, healthy food. The menu is self-classified "modern food," a category that here means a dizzying international selection including Caribbean shrimp tacos with chipotle-lime yogurt, Thai curry pasta tossed with sautéed tiger shrimp, chilled sesame ginger noodles, and breakfast's red-flannel turkey hash—a beet-fortified ragout topped with basil-Parmesan glazed eggs. Big Sky's owner also runs L.A.'s funky Gumbo Pot, whose Cajun-Creole influences spice up the menu at every turn; in fact, this might be the only Central Coast outlet for decent jambalaya, gumbo, or authentically airy beignets.

1121 Broad St. © 805/545-5401. www.bigskycafe.com. Reservations not necessary. Main courses $9–$17; salads and sandwiches $6–$10; breakfast $5–$9. AE, MC, V. Mon–Sat 7am–10pm; Sun 8am–9pm.

Buona Tavola ✿✿ NORTHERN ITALIAN   While most choices in town are burger-and-sandwich casual, Buona Tavola offers well-prepared Italian food in a more upscale setting. You can stroll in wearing jeans, but the dining room, with checkerboard floors and original artwork, is warmer and more intimate than other spots in town. There's also backyard-terrace seating where you can enjoy your meal surrounded by magnolias, ficus, and grapevines. The menu boasts a number of salads on the antipasti list. Favorite pastas include *agnolotti de scampi allo zafferano,* which is house-made pockets filled with scampi, then served in a cream-saffron sauce; *linguini fradiavolo* served with Manila clams, mussels, and river shrimp in a spicy tomato sauce; or the classic *timballo di parma,* a vegetarian delight baked with two cheeses. Don't worry—once you've gotten past trying to pronounce your desired dish, the rest of the evening should be both relaxing and satisfying.

1037 Monterey St. © 805/545-8000. Reservations recommended. Main courses $12–$23. AE, DISC, MC, V. Mon–Fri 11:30am–2:30pm; Sun–Thurs 5:30–9:30pm; Fri–Sat 5:30–10pm.

Mondéo Pronto (Value INTERNATIONAL   Mondéo Pronto provides patrons an affordable bite of international fillings in a burrito-type wrap. But unlike most "wrap" restaurants in California, this place goes a step beyond by paying attention to detail with presentation and freshness. Choices range from Americana versions like the Mardi Gras (a tomato tortilla packed with Cajun sausage, rock shrimp, Creole veggies, and jambalaya sauce) to Mediterranean selections like the Sicilian, with grilled portobello mushrooms, herb polenta, veggies, goat cheese, olives, capers, and sun-dried tomato pesto. "Fusion bowls" satisfy non-wrappers with such combinations as basil scampi, a lovely shrimp dish over bow-tie pasta with pesto, marinara, pine nuts, and herbs. Big bonuses: Everything on the kids' menu is under $3, and as the menu states, "Substitutions and sides are no problem."

893 Higuera St. (in the plaza). © 805/544-2956. Most items $5–$7. MC, V. Sun–Wed 11am–9pm; Thurs–Sat 11am–10pm.

Mo's Smokehouse BBQ ★★ BARBECUE   Just about everyone in SLO is a devotee of this place, whose reputation and great barbecue belie its humble ambiance. It's not fancy, but you name it, it's here—pork or baby-back ribs, BBQ beef, and chicken in either a mild or hot sauce, all accompanied by baked beans, bread, potato salad, or coleslaw. To top off this delectable deal, practically everything on the menu is under $10.

970 Higuera St. (at Osos St.). (© **805/544-6193**. Reservations not necessary. Most items $4.95–$13. AE, MC, V. Sun–Wed 11am–9pm; Thurs–Sat 11am–10pm.

Thai-rrific THAI   Although on Higuera Street, Thai-rrific is a bit removed from the downtown action—but once you step inside this cute, ivy-covered building, the aroma will convince you you've made a worthy diversion. Fine examples of authentic Bangkok-style cuisine are the ginger beef, garlic noodles, and our favorite, lemongrass chicken (grilled chicken breasts topped with lemongrass cream sauce, roasted chilies, and peanuts). Don't overlook the great array of tasty appetizers and salads, including the grilled shrimp or beef with cucumber, lime, and chili. An impressive wine list rounds out the offerings. Prices here are a little higher than at most Thai restaurants, but well worth it.

208 Higuera St. (© **805/541-THAI**. Reservations not accepted. Most dishes $7–$13. MC, V. Mon–Fri 11:30am–2pm; Mon–Sat 5–9pm.

4 Pismo Beach

13 miles S of San Luis Obispo

Just outside San Luis Obispo, on Pismo's 23-mile stretch of prime beachfront, flip-flops are the shoes of choice and surf wear is the dominant fashion. It's all about beach life here, so bring your bathing suit, your board, and a good book.

If building sandcastles or tanning isn't your idea of a tantalizing time, you can explore isolated dunes, cliff-sheltered tide pools, and old pirate coves. Bring your dog (Fido's welcome here) and play an endless game of fetch. Or go fishing—it's permitted from Pismo Beach Pier, which also offers arcade entertainment, bowling, and billiards. Pismo is also the only beach in the area that allows all-terrain vehicles on the dunes.

Because the town itself consists of little more than tourist shops and surf-and-turf restaurants, nearby San Luis Obispo is a far more charming place to stay. But if all you want are a few lazy days on a beautiful beach at half the price of an oceanfront room in Santa Barbara, Pismo is the perfect choice.

ESSENTIALS

The **Pismo Beach Chamber of Commerce and Visitors Bureau,** 581 Dolliver St., Pismo Beach, CA 93449 (© **800/443-7778** or 805/773-4382), offers free brochures and information on local attractions, lodging, and dining. The office is open Monday through Saturday from 9am to 5pm and Sunday from 10am to 4pm. You can peruse their information on the Web at **www.classic california.com**.

WHAT TO SEE & DO

Beaches in Pismo are exceptionally wide, making them some of the best in the state for sunning and playing. The beach north of Grand Avenue is popular with families and joggers. North of Wadsworth Street, the coast becomes dramatically rugged as it rambles northward to Shell Beach and Pirates Cove.

Pismo Beach was once one of the most famous places in America for **clamming,** but the famed "Pismo clam" reached near-extinction in the mid-1980s due to overzealous harvesting. If you'd like to get your feet wet digging for bivalves, you'll need to obtain a license and follow strict guidelines. Or come for the annual **Clam Festival;** held at the pier each October since 1946, the celebration features a chowder cook-off, sand-sculpture contest, and Miss Pismo Beach pageant.

If **fishing** is more your style, you'll be pleased to know that no license is required to fish from Pismo Beach Pier. Catches here are largely bottom fish like red snapper and lingcod. There's a bait-and-tackle shop on the pier.

Livery Stables, 1207 Silver Spur Place (© **805/489-8100**), in Oceano (about 5 minutes south of Pismo Beach), is one of the very few places in the state that rents horses for riding on the beach. Horses go for $20 per hour and can be ridden at your own pace, or you can opt for a guided ride.

You can hike along the **Guadalupe-Nipomo Dunes** year-round. This 18-mile strip of coastline 20 minutes south of Pismo has the highest beach dunes in the West. It's a great place for observing native plants and birds, including the California brown pelican, one of 200 species that migrate here each year.

From late November to February, tens of thousands of migrating **monarch butterflies** take up residence in the area's eucalyptus and Monterey pine-tree groves. The colorful butterflies form dense clusters on the trees, each hanging with its wings over the one below it, providing warmth and shelter for the entire group. During the monarchs' stay, naturalists at Pismo State Beach conduct 45-minute narrative walks every Saturday and Sunday at 11am and 2pm (call © **805/772-2694** for tour information). Most of the "butterfly trees" are located on Calif. 1, between Pismo Beach and Grover Beach, to the south.

WHERE TO STAY

Cottage Inn by the Sea ☞ One of Pismo Beach's newest cliffside lodgings, the Cottage Inn is a good, moderately priced choice for couples and families alike. With its rounded thatched roofs and Laura Ashley–style decor, the country charm is evident both inside and out. Rooms, which are refreshingly clean and spacious, range both in price and style from traditional to ocean view. All come with the amenities of a romantic inn (including fireplaces), yet have the modern conveniences as well (like in-room microwaves and other amenities). This seaside retreat is one of the best in town.

2351 Price St., Pismo Beach, CA 93449. © **888/440-8400** or 805/773-4617. Fax 805/773-8336. www.cottage-inn.com. 80 units. $139–$219 double Memorial Day through Labor Day; $89–$179 off-season. Rates include deluxe continental breakfast. Extra person $10. AF, DC, DISC, MC, V. Pets accepted for $10 fee per night. **Amenities:** Oceanfront heated pool and Jacuzzi. *In room:* TV w/ pay movies and Nintendo, fridge, coffeemaker, hair dryer, iron, safe.

Kon Tiki Inn *Value* The over-the-top Polynesian architecture of this three-story gem is easy to spot from the freeway, and upon closer examination evokes memories of 1960s Waikiki hotels. Rooms are modest, small, and simply furnished with unremarkable faux bamboo furniture, yet each has an oceanfront balcony or patio. Outside, vast lawns slope gently toward the cliffs, broken only by the wind-shielded, kidney-shaped swimming pool flanked by twin Jacuzzis. This humble hotel—which is privately owned and does no advertising—has a sandy beach with stairway access, and lacks the highway noise that plagues many neighbors. Room service is provided by Steamers of Pismo next door (see "Where to Dine," below).

1621 Price St., Pismo Beach, CA 93449. ℂ **888/KON-TIKI** or 805/773-4833. Fax 805/773-6541. www.
kontikiinn.com. 86 units. $74–$89 double. Extra person $14. AE, DISC, MC, V. **Amenities:** Outdoor heated
pool; 2 Jacuzzis; beach access; access to nearby health club; room service; laundry service. *In room:* TV w/ pay
movies, dataport, fridge, coffeemaker.

SeaVenture Resort ⊛ If luxury accommodations overlooking the beach
and an outdoor spa on your private deck sound like heaven to you, head for
SeaVenture, a 7-year-old resort providing the most luxurious accommodations
in Pismo. Once in your room, you need only drag your tired traveling feet
through the thick forest-green carpeting and past the white country furnishings
and feather bed, and turn on your gas fireplace to begin what promises to be a
relaxing stay. Then rent a movie from the video library, schedule a massage, or
simply bathe your weary bones in your own outdoor hydrotherapy spa tub.
With the beach right outside your door, there's not much more you could ask
for—although there is, in fact, more provided: plush robes, a wet bar, continental breakfast delivered to your room, and a restaurant on the premises with a
lovely brunch. Most rooms have ocean views and many have a private balcony
overlooking the beach.

100 Ocean View Ave., Pismo Beach, CA 93449. ℂ **800/662-5545** or 805/773-4994. Fax 805/773-0924.
www.seaventure.com. 50 units. $129–$349 double. Rates include continental breakfast. AE, DC, DISC, MC, V.
Take U.S. 101 to the Price St. exit and turn west onto Ocean View (at the beach). **Amenities:** Restaurant;
outdoor heated pool; massage center; complimentary bicycles; room service (5 to 9pm); dry cleaning/laundry
service. *In room:* TV/VCR, dataport, minibar, coffeemaker, hair dryer, iron.

WHERE TO DINE

Local icon **F. McLintocks** has a lock on Pismo with two crowd-pleasing oceanview eateries: **F. McLintocks Saloon & Dining House,** 750 Mattie Rd. (across
Hwy. 101; ℂ **805/773-1892**), for stick-to-your-ribs, ranch-style meals in a
corny Old West setting; and **Steamers of Pismo,** 1601 Price St. (ℂ **805/
773-4711**), a recently opened warehouse-style space with "Miles of Clams" and
plenty for landlubbers too.

Guiseppe's ⊛ SOUTHERN ITALIAN This is the region's best southern
Italian restaurant—would you believe owner Guiseppe DiFronza started it as his
senior project at Cal Poly University? It's true, and DiFronza's love of (and
expertise at) cuisine from the Pugliese region (an Adriatic seaport) continues to
bring diners a taste of the Italian countryside. Along with the fresh homemade
bread baked in a wood-burning oven imported from Italy, Guiseppe's classic fare
uses authentic recipes, imported ingredients, and organically grown produce;
the extensive menu of antipasti, salads, pizzas, pastas, fish, and steak makes it
virtually impossible to not find something you like. Highlights of our meal
included linguine with shrimp, scallops, pancetta, and garlic in a vodka cream
sauce, and seared ahi with a peppercorn crust and garlic-caper aïoli.

891 Price St. ℂ **805/773-2870.** Reservations not accepted. Main courses $6–$10 lunch; $9–$22 dinner. AE,
DISC, MC, V. Daily 11:30am–3pm; Sun–Thurs 4:30–10pm; Fri–Sat 4:30–11pm.

Splash Cafe AMERICAN This beachy burger stand, with a short menu and
just a few tables, gets high marks for its award-winning clam chowder, served in
a sourdough bread bowl. Fish and chips, burgers, hot dogs, and grilled ahi sandwiches are also available. Far-flung aficionados know that Splash will ship its
chowder frozen, overnight anywhere in the country (sourdough loaves, too).

197 Pomeroy St. (near Pismo Beach Pier). ℂ **805/773-4653.** www.splashcafe.com. Most items
$2.50–$5.95. MC, V. Daily 10am–8pm.

5 The Central Coast Wine Country: Paso Robles & the Santa Ynez Valley

Paso Robles: 29 miles N of San Luis Obispo; Solvang: 60 miles S of San Luis Obispo

When people talk about California wines, you can normally assume they mean those from the Napa and Sonoma regions north of San Francisco. But here in California, and increasingly across the country, wine lovers are becoming more aware of vintages coming from California's Central Coast wineries, located in the dewy green hills and sun-kissed valleys of San Luis Obispo and Santa Barbara counties. The Central Coast is coming into its own as a respected wine region, and offers another excuse to visit some of the state's most beautifully scenic countryside. Wine snobs might tell you that Central Coast wines cannot compare to those from the northern appellations, where precious vintages can age to sublime flavor and astronomical price, but if you're in the market for bottles in the $15-to-$25 range that are ready to drink within a couple of years, then trust me—you'll love what this up-and-comer has to offer.

PASO ROBLES

Welcome to Paso Robles—"pass through the oaks"—so named for the clusters of oak trees liberally scattered throughout the rolling hills of this inland region. The town has a faintly checkered past: It was established in 1870 by Drury James, uncle of outlaw Jesse James (who reportedly hid out in tunnels under the original Paso Robles Inn). In 1913, pianist Ignace Paderewski came to live in Paso Robles, where he brought zinfandel vines for his ranch (zinfandel is now the most successful varietal among area wineries) and played often in the Paso Robles Inn, which today maintains a small exhibit in his honor in the lobby. Paderewski really wasn't here for long, returning to Poland after World War I, but the town today treats him like a native son, and fans gather each year at the Paderewski Festival in March.

ESSENTIALS

GETTING THERE/ORIENTATION   Paso Robles lies along U.S. 101; there's an exit for the town's main business thoroughfare, Spring Street. Calif. 46 intersects, and briefly joins, U.S. 101. Many wineries are located on the winding roads off Calif. 46 on either side—try to cluster your visit according to this destination, visiting one side and then the other. You'll be able to feel how the weather on the western side, which is cooler due to higher elevations and frequent coastal fog, differs from the hotter east side, on a flat plain leading inland; winemakers bicker constantly over which conditions are "better" for wine grapes.

VISITOR INFORMATION   For a complete list of area wineries, tasting rooms, and seasonal events, contact the **Paso Robles Vintners and Growers Association,** 1940 Spring St. (P.O. Box 324), Paso Robles, CA 93447 (© **800/ 549-WINE** or 805/239-8463; fax 805/237-6439; www.pasowine.com). Additional information on the area is offered by the **Paso Robles Chamber of Commerce,** 1225 Park St., Paso Robles, CA 93446 (© **800/406-4040** or 805/ 238-0506; fax 805/238-0527; www.pasorobleschamber.com).

TOURING THE LOCAL WINERIES

They've been tending vines in Paso Robles's fertile foothills since the turn of the century—the 19th century, that is. For decades, the area was overlooked by wine aficionados, even though in 1983 it was granted its own "Paso Robles" appellation (the official government designation of a recognized wine-producing region; "Napa Valley" and "Sonoma County" are probably more familiar appellations). But somewhere around 1992, wine grapes surpassed lettuce as San Luis Obispo County's primary cash crop, and there are now almost 40 wineries and more than 100 vineyards (which grow grapes but do not produce their own wine from them).

Wine touring in Paso Robles is reminiscent of another, unhurried time. Because not all wine enthusiasts are wine experts, an advantage of the area is its friendly attitude and small crowds, which make it easy to learn more about the winemaking process as you go along. Enjoy the relaxed rural atmosphere along two-lane country roads, driving leisurely from winery to winery and, more often than not, chatting with the winemaker while tasting his product.

Eberle Winery   Owner Gary Eberle, who's been making Paso Robles wine since 1973, is sometimes called the "grandfather of Paso Robles's Wine Country" because many of the recent new vintners in the area honed their craft working under his tutelage. A visit to Eberle Winery includes a tour through its underground caves, where hundreds of aging barrels share space with the Wild Boar Room, site of Eberle's monthly winemaker dinners featuring guest chefs from around the country (always held on Saturday nights; the prix-fixe meal is around $80, including wine). Call for a current events schedule.

Hwy. 46 E. (3½ miles east of U.S. 101). ✆ **805/238-9607.** www.eberlewinery.com. Complimentary tastings daily 10am–5pm (until 6pm in summer).

EOS Estate Winery at Arciero Vineyards   Follow the checkered flag to the 800 acres of wine grapes owned by former race car driver Frank Arciero, Sr. Arciero was drawn to the area by its resemblance to his native Italy; he passed through on his way to Laguna Seca, a racetrack near Salinas. (Trivia buffs will know it as James Dean's intended destination in 1955, when he was killed in nearby Cholame while driving his silver Porsche.) The label specializes in Italian varietals (nebbiolo, sangiovese) and blends; the facility includes a self-guided tour, a race car exhibit, spectacular rose gardens, and a picnic area.

Hwy. 46 E. (6 miles east of U.S. 101). ✆ **805/239-2562.** www.eosvintage.com. Complimentary tastings daily 10am–5pm (until 6pm summer weekends).

Justin Vineyards & Winery ★★★   At the end of a scenic country road lies Justin and Deborah Baldwin's boutique winery, and even a casual glance shows how much love and dedication the ex–Los Angelenos have put into their operation. The tasting room, dining room, offices, and even winemaking barns have a stylish Tuscan flair. Justin's flagship wine is Isosceles, a Bordeaux-style blend that's pricier than most area wines but exudes sophistication—and earns *Wine Spectator* raves. Also worth a try is their port-style dessert wine, called Obtuse.

For an extra-special treat, the winery has a three-suite B&B called the **JUST Inn.** Impeccably outfitted, the inn has an undeniable serenity, and you can even have a romantic gourmet dinner prepared for you with advance notice. Room rates are $225 to $275—and worth every precious penny. *Insider tip:* When space permits, Justin's intimate private dining room is also open to the public; if you're celebrating—or just want to have the best meal of your trip—call for advance reservations.

11680 Chimney Rock Rd. (15 miles west of U.S. 101). ✆ **805/237-4150;** www.justinwine.com. Tastings Mon–Fri 11am–4pm; Sat–Sun 10am–5pm. Tasting fee $3, includes souvenir glass.

Meridian Vineyards ★   The local vintner with the largest profile is also the Central Coast's best-known label, producing more cases each year than all the other Paso wineries *combined.* Veteran winemaker Chuck Ortman brought a respected Napa Valley pedigree to Meridian; as a result, here's where you'll get the most Napa-like tasting experience. In addition to a grand tasting room, there's a man-made lake surrounded by rolling lawns, where picnicking is encouraged.

Hwy. 46 E. (7 miles east of U.S. 101). 𝒞 805/237-6000. www.meridianvineyards.com. Complimentary tastings daily 10am–5pm.

Tobin James Cellars 𝒞𝒞 Winemaker Tobin James is a walking contradiction. A lifelong wine expert who claims to wear the same pair of khaki shorts every day, Toby has patterned his winery in the spirit of local bad boys, the James Gang. The tasting room has a Wild West theme, a 100-year-old saloon bar, and blaring country music, all serving to dispel the wine-snob atmosphere that prevails at so many other wineries. Tobin James's particular expertise lies in the production of a "user-friendly" zinfandel; the late-harvest dessert wine from zinfandel grapes is smooth and spicy.

8950 Union Rd. (at Hwy. 46 E., 8 miles east of U.S. 101). 𝒞 **805/239-2204.** www.tobinjames.com. Complimentary tastings daily 10am–6pm.

Treana Winery 𝒞𝒞 There's a spit and polish about this sleek player in the Paso wine game. The Hope family's elegant tasting room now features a gourmet deli for picnickers, an adjacent cigar gazebo (a relaxed room of tropical palms and wicker invoking 1950s Cuba), and the luxurious Arbor Inn bed-and-breakfast set among the vines (see "Where to Stay," below). With the help of a Napa-alumnus winemaker, Treana is turning out some of the best reds around, including cabernets rich in character, plus a portlike late-harvest merlot that's sweet, smooth, and complex.

2175 Arbor Rd. (at Hwy. 46 W., 1 mile west of U.S. 101). 𝒞 805/238-6979. Complimentary tastings daily 10am–5pm.

York Mountain Winery *(Finds)* If you're impressed by "firsts" and "onlys," don't miss York Mountain. It was the first winery established in the area (in 1882 by Andrew York, on land originally deeded by President Ulysses S. Grant) and is the oldest continuously operating vintner, as well as the only producer in the "York Mountain" viticulture appellation. In the 100-year-old stone tasting room, look for a dry chardonnay with a complex, spicy aroma, and award-winning cabernet sauvignons, the best of which are the reserve bottlings from hand-chosen grapes.

7505 York Mountain Rd. (off Hwy. 46 W., 7 miles west of U.S. 101). 𝒞 **805/238-3925.** Tasting fee $1. Tastings daily 10am–5pm.

OTHER DIVERSIONS IN THE PASO ROBLES AREA

The fragrance emanating from **Sycamore Farms,** Hwy. 46 W., 3 miles west of U.S. 101 (𝒞 **800/576-5288** or 805/238-5288), is that of hundreds of herbs, grown for culinary, medicinal, and decorative purposes. Learn about them at the farm's walk-through garden; it also sells fresh-cut and dried herbs, nursery seedlings to transplant at home, and a bevy of herbal vinegars, olive oils, mustards, herbal soaps, and potpourri. Hours are daily from 10:30am to 5:30pm, except Christmas Day and from January 4 to 14.

It requires some advance planning, but nothing beats the exhilaration of seeing the Wine Country at sunrise from the serenity of a hot-air balloon. **Seventh Heaven Balloons** (𝒞 **805/687-8459**) operates on select weekends throughout the year, offering two flights daily followed by champagne brunch. The package price is $139 per person; reservations are suggested at least 4 weeks in advance.

WHERE TO STAY

Adelaide Inn *Value* Tended with loving care that's rare among lower-priced accommodations, the Adelaide Inn stands out from other motels. Although it's situated adjacent to freeway-close gas stations and coffee shops, special attention has been given to isolate this quiet, lushly landscaped property from its bustling surroundings. The rooms are clean and comfortable with extra warmth, and the motel has a safe, welcoming ambiance. Unexpected comforts include complimentary newspaper, fruit and muffins, and in-room amenities for the business traveler. Facilities include summertime water diversions and even a putting green.

1215 Ysabel Ave., Paso Robles, CA 93446. © **800/549-PASO** or 805/238-2770. Fax 805/238-3497. www. adelaideinn.com. 67 units. $45–$80 double. Extra person $6. Rates include morning coffee and muffins. AE, DC, DISC, MC, V. From U.S. 101, exit Hwy. 46 E. Turn west at 24th St.; the hotel is just west of the freeway. **Amenities:** Heated outdoor pool; Jacuzzi; sauna; self-service laundromat; dry cleaning/laundry service. *In room:* A/C, TV w/ pay movies, dataport, fridge, coffeemaker, hair dryer, iron.

The Arbor Inn *★* The guest book at this elegant B&B sports more than its share of honeymooners drawn by the splendid setting and luxurious treatment. Located at Treana Winery (see "Touring the Local Wineries," above), this three-story clapboard house looks like a cross between Queen Anne and Southern-plantation styles, but is furnished in formal English country. It's a brand-new building, so rooms are spacious and bathrooms ultra-modern; the main floor (including two guest rooms) is fully wheelchair accessible. Every room has a private balcony overlooking Treana's vineyards, plus a gas fireplace, fresh flowers, and terry robes; morning coffee is left discreetly outside your door in insulated carafes.

2130 Arbor Rd. (P.O. Box 3260), Paso Robles, CA 93447. © **805/227-4673.** 9 units. $140–$205 double; $245 suite. Extra person $65. Rates include full breakfast, afternoon wine and hors d'oeuvres, and evening cookies. MC, V. From U.S. 101, exit Hwy. 46 W. Continue 1 mile to Arbor Rd. *In room:* A/C, TV, hair dryer.

Paso Robles Inn This Mission Revival–style inn was built to replace the 1891 Stanford White masterpiece, El Paso De Robles Hotel, that burned to the ground in 1940. Photos of the grand landmark in its heyday line the Spanish-tiled lobby and adjacent dining room and cocktail lounge. A creek meanders through the oak-shaded property, and two-story motel units are scattered across the tranquil and lovely grounds. Well shielded from street noise, these rooms are simple but boast creature comforts (shiny new bathrooms, gas fireplaces, and microwaves in many rooms) added in a massive 2000 update that, unfortunately, removed much of their nostalgic charm. The best rooms here are worth the extra bucks: newly built "Spa Rooms" with fireplaces and privacy-shielded outdoor Jacuzzis supplied by the property's mineral springs. Convenient carports are located behind each building. Skip the overpriced Hot Springs Grill in favor of the retro-flavored Coffee Shop, both served by the same kitchen. *Insider tip:* Avoid room numbers beginning with 1 or 2—they're too close to the street.

1103 Spring St., Paso Robles, CA 93446. © **805/238-2660.** www.pasoroblesinn.com. 100 units. $125–$165 double (May–Sept); $95–$115 rest of year. Spa room $175–$235. Midweek discounts available. Extra person $10. AE, DC, DISC, MC, V. **Amenities:** 2 restaurants; lounge; outdoor heated pool; Jacuzzi; business center; room service (7am to 8pm); dry cleaning/laundry service. *In room:* A/C, TV w/ pay movies, dataport, fridge, coffeemaker, hair dryer, iron; bathrobes in spa rooms.

WHERE TO DINE

Bistro Laurent *★* FRENCH/CALIFORNIA Executive chef Laurent Grangien's sophisticated bistro initially caused quite a stir in this town unaccustomed to such innovations as a chef's tasting menu. But once the dust settled, everyone kept returning for the unpretentious neighborhood atmosphere, delicious recipes, and reasonable (by L.A. or San Francisco standards) prices. Whet your appetite with a complimentary teaser hors d'oeuvre (goat-cheese toasts, for example) before plunging into dishes like rosemary-garlic chicken, pork loin bathed in peppercorn sauce, or ahi tuna in red-wine reduction. "Twilight dinners" are served nightly until 6:30pm.

1202 Pine St., Paso Robles. © 805/226-8191. Reservations recommended. Main courses $5–$12 lunch; $15–$23 dinner. MC, V. Mon–Sat 11:30am–2:30pm and 5:30–10pm.

Busi's on the Park CALIFORNIA/ECLECTIC   The name may sound snooty and scenic, but Busi's is neither. It's just a comfortable, tavernlike joint across the street from downtown's City Park, but the capable kitchen draws a big local crowd. A short seasonal menu highlights fresh local ingredients; eclectic offerings include Southwestern chicken salad with refreshing cilantro-lime crema; Chinese stir-fried beef tinged with orange and sesame; pan-roasted salmon with oriental salsa; and a superior cannelloni that utilizes freshly made basil-egg pasta, roasted tomato sauce, and sautéed spinach. Weekend brunch runs the gamut from French toast or Spanish frittata to Thai noodle salad or saffron mussels.

1122 Pine St., Paso Robles. © 805/238-1390. Reservations recommended on weekends. Main courses $10–$25. AE, MC, V. Tues–Fri 5–9pm; Sat–Sun 10am–2pm and 5–9pm.

McPhee's Grill ✶✶ CALIFORNIA GRILL   When Ian McPhee left Ian's restaurant in Cambria and launched this one, it didn't take long for word to get out. McPhee's is worth the short drive to the historic town of Templeton. The converted old saloon features contemporary country decor, an open kitchen, and indoor and outdoor dining. The menu offers a half-dozen appetizers such as a duck quesadilla, artichoke fritters, and a zingy greens-and-grapefruit salad with Maytag bleu cheese and spiced nuts. Gourmet pizza, pasta, an amazing macadamia-crusted salmon, and four varieties of tender, juicy steaks cooked to perfection round out the Americana-with-a-twist style menu. Especially impressive are the prices; it's rare that a restaurant "dedicated to great food and great service" offers the majority of its dishes for under $16. A champagne buffet brunch is offered on Sundays. McPhee's is one of the very best in the region, and families will appreciate the economical kids' menu.

416 Main St., Templeton. © 805/434-3204. Reservations recommended. Main courses $6–$12 lunch; $12–$24 dinner; brunch $12.95 adults, $6.95 for kids under 10. MC, V. Daily 11:30–2pm and 5–9pm.

THE SANTA YNEZ VALLEY

Welcome to the Santa Ynez Valley, an idyllic domain of oak-covered hills and uncrowded roads set against a mountain backdrop. This is beautiful country, where the clear blue sky achieves a brilliance unheard of in California's smog-clogged cities. In the Santa Ynez Valley, the pace is a little slower, and the locals a little friendlier. Don't expect to find yokels gnawing on hay, though—this is gentleman-farmer country, where some of the nicest ranches are gated and have video surveillance, and even Disney's Davy Crockett is a respected winemaker. This balance of old-fashioned living and modern sophistication is what makes the area enjoyable; you can wallow in simple pleasures one day and go wine tasting the next.

Los Olivos is a good ol'-fashioned country town right in the middle of Wine Country. There's a big flagpole in the center of the town's intersection, and stretches of boardwalk stand in for sidewalk here and there, giving the town a Wild West air. If you saw TV's *Return to Mayberry,* that was Los Olivos standing in for Andy Griffith's sentimental Southern hamlet. But these days, the town's storefronts feature art galleries, stylish cafes, and wine-tasting rooms; you'll see more Land Rovers than John Deeres in this upscale retreat.

Finds **Gourmet Picnics, Paso Robles–Style**

You'll find everything you need for a casual snack or sophisticated picnic at Paso Robles's new **Odyssey Culinary Provisions,** 1214 Pine St. (© 805/ 237-7516). A sandwich board features gourmet deli selections on focaccia and other fresh-baked breads, and refrigerated cases yield up inventive salads, cheeses, salami, olives, and other delicacies. Mustards, crackers, chocolates, and pastries line the shelves, along with baskets and knapsacks to hold your feast. Odyssey is also the place to come for freshbrewed coffee and espresso drinks. It's open Sunday through Thursday from 7am to 7pm, Friday and Saturday from 7am to 11pm.

Just minutes away from one another, Los Olivos, Santa Ynez, Ballard, Solvang, and Buellton each make an excellent base for touring the wineries of this fertile area.

ESSENTIALS

GETTING THERE From U.S. 101, take Calif. 246 east 4 miles to reach Solvang, Santa Ynez, and Ballard. Los Olivos is located on Calif. 154 about 2 miles from U.S. 101. Lake Cachuma is also on Calif. 154, traveling southeast toward Santa Barbara.

VISITOR INFORMATION Contact the **Santa Barbara County Vintners Association,** 3669 Sagunto St., Unit 101 (P.O. Box 1558), Santa Ynez, CA 93460 (© **800/218-0881** or 805/688-0881; www.sbcountywines.com), for its *Winery Touring Map.* Hours are Monday through Friday from 9am to 5pm. The **Solvang Visitor Bureau,** 1511 Mission Dr., at Fifth Street (P.O. Box 70), Solvang, CA 93464 (© **800/GO-SOLVANG** or 805/688-6144; www.solvang usa.com), has additional information on the Santa Ynez Valley. It's open daily from 10am to 4pm.

ORIENTATION U.S. 101, Calif. 246, and Calif. 154 form a triangle enclosing the towns of the Santa Ynez Valley. Calif. 246 becomes Mission Drive within Solvang city limits, then continues east past the mission toward Santa Ynez. Alamo Pintado Road connects Solvang with Los Olivos, whose commercial stretch is located along 3 blocks of Grand Avenue. Foxen Canyon Road continues north from downtown Los Olivos.

TOURING THE LOCAL WINERIES

Santa Barbara County has a 200-year tradition of growing grapes and making wine—an art originally practiced by Franciscan friars at the area's missions—but only in the past 20 to 30 years have wine-grape fields begun to approach the size of other crops that do so well in these fertile inland valleys.

Geography makes the area well suited for successful vineyards: The Santa Ynez and San Rafael mountain ranges are transverse (east-west) ranges, which allows ocean breezes to flow through, keeping the climate temperate. Variations in temperature and humidity within the valley create many microclimates, and vintners have learned how to cultivate nearly all the classic grape varietals. Today, you'll find about 25 vintners in the Santa Ynez Valley area, most of which have tasting rooms—a few offer tours of their operations as well. If you'd like to start with a winery tour to acquaint yourself with viticulture, Gainey Vineyard or Firestone Vineyard are good bets (see below). And if you'd like to sample wines without driving around, head to **Los Olivos Tasting Room & Wine Shop,**

2905 Grand Ave. ((C) **805/688-7406**), located in the heart of town, or **Los Olivos Wine & Spirits Emporium,** 2531 Grand Ave. ((C) **805/688-4409;** www.sbwines.com), a friendly barn in a field half a mile away. Both offer a wide selection of vintners, including those—such as Au Bon Climat and Qupé—who don't have their own tasting rooms.

The Brander Vineyard Winemaker Fred Brander has been making a name for himself since 1976; although the winery's production is small, his is a name you'll see frequently on local wine lists. Brander is among the valley's most pleasant wineries, with a friendly family of staff. The best bets are Cuvee Nicolas, which is a 100% sauvignon blanc from low-yielding vines; or choose a high-density cabernet from the cellar for full-bodied perfection.

2401 Refugio Rd., Los Olivos. (C) 805/688-2455. www.brander.com. Tastings daily 10am–4pm (till 5pm in summer). Tasting fee of $3 includes souvenir glass and is applied toward any purchase.

Fess Parker Winery & Vineyard (★) You loved him as a child, now see what Hollywood's Davy Crockett/Daniel Boone is up to. Fess Parker has made a big name for himself in Santa Barbara County, with resort hotels, cattle ranches, and now an eponymous winery that's turning out some critically acclaimed syrahs, among other varietals. Look for the syrah and chardonnay American Tradition Reserve vintages in the tasting room. Parker's grandiose complex, shaded by the largest oak tree we've ever seen, also features picnic tables on a breezy terrace and an extensive gift shop where you can even buy—you guessed it—coonskin caps!

6200 Foxen Canyon Rd., Los Olivos. (C) 800/841-1104 or 805/688-1545. www.fessparker.com. Tastings daily 10am–5pm; tours daily at 11am, 1, and 3pm. Tasting fee $3.

Firestone Vineyard Probably the largest producers in Santa Barbara County, this operation started by Brooks Firestone (of tire-manufacturing fame) now includes two "second" labels. Its wines are affordable and reasonably good, and it's started experimenting with Chilean-grown grapes, some of which can be excellent. Firestone's tasting room and gift shop are a three-ring circus of merchandise, but it offers a quick, worthwhile tour and free tastings.

5000 Zaca Station Rd., Los Olivos. (C) 805/688-3940. www.firestonewine.com. Tastings daily 10am–5pm; tours hourly Sat–Sun.

The Gainey Vineyard (★) This slick operation is one of the most-visited wineries in the valley, thanks to its prime location on Calif. 246 and its in-depth tours, offered daily. It has every hallmark of a visitor-oriented winery: a terra cotta–tiled tasting room, plenty of logo merchandise, and a deli case for impromptu lunches at the picnic tables in a secluded vineyard garden. It bottles the most popular varietals—chardonnay, cabernet sauvignon, pinot noir, sauvignon blanc—and offers them at moderate prices.

3950 E. Calif. 246, Santa Ynez. (C) 805/688-0558. Tastings daily 10am–5pm; tours daily 11am, 1, 2, and 3pm. No reservations required. Tasting fee $5, includes souvenir glass.

Sunstone Vineyards and Winery (★★★) Take a rambling drive down to this locally well-known winery, whose gracious wisteria-wrapped stone tasting room belies the dirt road you take to reach it. Sunstone is nestled in an oak grove overlooking the river, boasting a splendid view from the lavender-fringed picnic courtyard. Inside, try its flagship merlot or treasured reserve vintages; there's also a fine selection of gourmet foods, logo ware, and cigars.

125 Refugio Rd., Santa Ynez. (C) 800/313-WINE or 805/688-WINE. www.sunstonewinery.com. Tastings daily 10am–4pm. Tasting fee $3–$5, includes souvenir glass.

Zaca Mesa Winery ★★   One of the region's old-timers, Zaca Mesa has been in business since 1972, so we can forgive the hippie/New Age mumbo-jumbo pleasantly interwoven with the well-honed vintages. Situated on a unique plateau that the Spanish named *la zaca mesa* (the restful place), this winery's 750 acres are uniquely beautiful—a fact it celebrates with two easy nature trails for visitors. You'll also find picnic tables and a giant lawn chessboard. Inside, look for the usual syrah and chardonnay offerings jazzed up with experimental Rhône varietals like grenache, roussanne, and voignier.

6905 Foxen Canyon Rd., Los Olivos. ✆ **800/350-7972** or 805/688-9339. www.zacamesa.com. Complimentary tastings daily 10am–4pm; call for tour schedule.

A TASTE OF DENMARK: SOLVANG

The valley's largest town is also one of the state's most popular tourist stops, and Solvang takes a lot of flack for being a Disney-fied version of its founders' vision. Everything here that *can* be Danish *is* Danish: You've never seen so many windmills, cobblestone streets, wooden shoes, and so much gingerbread trim—even the sidewalk trash cans look like little Danish farmhouses with pitched-roof lids.

To reach Solvang from U.S. 101 south, turn east (left) onto Calif. 246 at Buellton; it's a well-marked 20-minute drive along an extremely scenic two-lane road. From Santa Barbara, take U.S. 101 north to Calif. 154, a truly breathtaking 45-minute drive over San Marcos Pass. For a destination guide or hotel information, contact the **Solvang Conference and Visitors Bureau** (see "Essentials," above).

One way to weed through the unabashed tourism here for a little authentic history is to visit the **Elverhøj Museum,** 1624 Elverhoy Way (✆ **805/686-1211**), a warm and welcoming place devoted to Danish culture and Solvang history. Set in a traditional handcrafted Scandinavian-style home, and featuring many original old-world furnishings, this little museum can be fully appreciated in 30 minutes or less. Hours are Wednesday through Sunday from 1 to 4pm; a $2 donation is suggested.

Solvang has always been renowned for its traditional and delectable pastries, and the best bakery in town is **Birkholm's Bakery,** 1555 Mission Dr. (✆ **805/688-3872**). It's the oldest, opened in 1951 and still family-run. In addition to sticky pastries, sweet rolls, fresh bread, and fresh-brewed coffee, Birkholm's sells its trademark blue-and-white waxed tub of Danish butter cookies ($7.95 each). Hours are daily from 8am to 5:30pm.

Old Mission Santa Ines   Just on the edge of town, and one of the few buildings without a windmill or other Scandinavian fanfare, this Spanish mission was founded by Franciscan friars in 1804 and is still in use for daily services. Most of the original structure, painstakingly constructed of adobe by Native Americans, has been destroyed; the reconstruction features the ornately tiled and painted chapel typical of the Spanish missions and an extensive museum display of mission artifacts and Franciscan vestment robes.

1760 Mission Dr., Solvang. ✆ **805/688-4815**. $3 donation requested, free for children under 16. Summer Mon–Fri 9am–7pm, Sat 9am–4pm, Sun 1:30–5:30pm; winter Sun–Fri 9am–5:30pm. Sat 9am–4pm. From downtown Solvang, take Calif. 246 1 mile east to Mission Dr.

CACHUMA LAKE: A BALD EAGLE HABITAT

Created in 1953 by damming the Santa Ynez River, this picturesque reservoir running along Calif. 154 is the primary water source for Santa Barbara County. It's also the centerpiece of a 6,600-acre county park with a flourishing wildlife population and well-developed recreational facilities. Cachuma has, through both agreeable climate and diligent ranger efforts, become a notable habitat for resident and migratory birds, including rarely sighted bald eagles, which migrate south from as far as Alaska in search of food.

One of the best ways to appreciate this fine-feathered bounty is to take one of the naturalist-led **Eagle Cruises** of the lake, offered between November and February. The 48-foot *Osprey* was specially designed for wildlife observation, with unobstructed views from nearly every seat. During the rest of the year, rangers lead **Wildlife Cruises** around the lake, helping you spot resident waterfowl, grazing deer, and the elusive bobcats and mountain lions that live here. Eagle Cruises depart Wednesday through Sunday at 10am, with additional cruises Friday and Saturday at 2pm. Wildlife Cruises run Friday and Saturday at 3pm, and Saturday and Sunday at 10am. All cruises are 2 hours long. In addition to the park day-use fee of $5 per car, the fare is $10 for adults and $5 for children 12 and under. Reservations are recommended for all cruises; call the **Santa Barbara County Parks Department** (☎ **805/686-5050;** www.sbparks.com).

The recreational opportunities at Cachuma don't stop there; campers, boaters, and fishermen will find abundant facilities. Contact the **Lake Cachuma Recreation Area** (☎ **805/686-5054**) for more information.

WHERE TO STAY

Ballard Inn 🐾🐾   This two-story inn may look 100 years old, but it's actually of modern construction, offering both contemporary comforts and charming country details like wicker rockers on a wraparound porch. The entry and parlors are tastefully furnished with a comfortable mix of antiques and reproductions; sumptuous wallpaper and fabrics lend a cozy touch, and hand-hooked rugs, bent-twig furniture, and vintage accessories lend character to the house. The guest rooms upstairs are similarly unique—some have fireplaces and/or private balconies, and all have well-stocked bathrooms, many featuring a separate antique washbasin in the bedroom. The best (and most expensive) unit is the Mountain Room, a minisuite decorated in rich forest green and outfitted with a fireplace and private balcony. In addition to cooked-to-order breakfast and a wine-and-hors d'oeuvres reception, you'll be treated to evening coffee and tea, plus addictive chocolate cookies on your nightstand at bedtime.

The inn's restaurant, Cafe Chardonnay, is tucked into a cozy room downstairs by a crackling fire; the California-style seasonal menu can include grilled meats, seafood pastas, and catch-of-the-day specials. *Note:* The inn staff doesn't accept gratuities; instead, a 10% service charge is added at checkout.

2436 Baseline Ave., Ballard, CA 93463. ☎ **800/638-2466** or 805/688-7770. Fax 805/688-9560. www.ballardinn.com. 15 units. $195–$275 double. Rates include full breakfast, afternoon wine and hors d'oeuvres, and evening coffee and tea. Packages and midweek discounts available. AE, MC, V. Take Alamo Pintado Rd. to Baseline; the inn is half a block east of the intersection. **Amenities:** Restaurant; bicycle rental; activities desk; in-room massage. *In room:* A/C, hair dryer, iron.

Inn at Petersen Village 🐾   If you think every hotel in Solvang has a kitschy, Danish theme, then step off the street right into this quiet, tasteful, and affordable hotel. Rooms are decorated in a European country motif, with print wallpaper, canopy beds, and mahogany-hued furniture. But it's the little touches that impress the most, like lighted magnifying mirrors, bathroom lights controlled by dimmers, free coffee and tea service to your room, and the complimentary food that's nearly always laid out in the hotel's friendly piano lounge. Some rooms overlook a bustling courtyard of shops, while others face Solvang's scenic hills. All are designed so everyone's happy: Smaller units have private balconies, those with noisier views are more spacious, and so on.

Picnicking in the Santa Ynez Valley

You can assemble a picnic lunch at the **Santa Ynez Valley Market,** on Calif. 154 about a mile east of Los Olivos (📞 **805/688-5115**), where a fresh deli counter prepares simple sandwiches and side salads, plus buckets of fried chicken. With a little advance notice, it'll prepare box lunches that include a sandwich, chips, a piece of fruit, and a cookie, for $7.50 each. The market is open daily from 7am to 8pm.

Los Olivos offers easy-to-carry, eat-at-room-temperature goodies packed up with all the necessary utensils. At **Panino,** 2900 Grand Ave. (📞 **805/688-9304**), choose from 31 gourmet sandwiches priced from $6 to $8, all served on Panino's fresh-baked, Italian-style bread; varieties include grilled chicken with sun-dried tomatoes, fresh basil, and provolone, or English Stilton with Asian pear on fresh walnut bread. Open Monday through Friday from 10am to 4pm, Saturday and Sunday from 9am to 5pm.

1576 Mission Dr., Solvang, CA 93463. 📞 **800/321-8985** or 805/688-3121. Fax 805/688-5732. www. peterseninn.com. 42 units. $145–$265 double. Extra person $15. Rates include breakfast buffet, evening wine and hors d'oeuvres, and dessert buffet. Midweek and AAA discounts available. AE, MC, V. **Amenities:** Courtyard lounge. *In room:* A/C, TV, dataport, hair dryer, iron.

Royal Scandinavian Inn   If you're looking for a traditional, full-service hotel, this attractive and comfortable mainstay in Solvang is nicely located away from the congested main drag. Popular with business conventions and leisure groups, the Royal Scandinavian Inn has an all-day restaurant and cocktail lounge and is within walking distance of downtown Solvang; the championship Alisal River Golf Course is next door. Rooms are furnished in a vaguely Danish country decor, but are otherwise unremarkable; bathrooms are up-to-date. Ask for a room overlooking the courtyard—the view extends to the foothills beyond.

400 Alisal Rd. (P.O. Box 30), Solvang, CA 93464. 📞 **800/624-5572** or 805/688-8000. Fax 805/688-0761. www.solvangrsi.com. 133 units. Feb–Nov $104–$154 double, from $159 suite; Dec to mid-Feb $99–$134 double, from $149 suite. Extra person $10. Golf packages available. AE, DC, DISC, MC, V. **Amenities:** Restaurant, lounge; outdoor pool; Jacuzzi; fitness room; nearby golf; business center; room service (7am–10pm); dry cleaning/laundry service. *In room:* A/C, TV w/ pay movies, fax, fridge, coffeemaker, hair dryer, iron.

WHERE TO DINE

If you're looking for traditional Danish fare in Solvang, head for **Bit o' Denmark,** 473 Alisal Rd. (📞 **805/688-5426**). Its smorgasbord may not be the largest in town, but it's the freshest and highest quality; you can also order from the regular menu. It's open daily from 9am to 9pm; the smorgasbord costs $8.95 at lunch, $12.95 at dinner. **The Hitching Post,** 406 East Hwy. 246, Buellton (📞 **805/688-0676**) is the Valley's mecca for meat lovers; within these western-themed surroundings steaks are grilled to perfection over an oakwood pit, and—fittingly—the house label wine is better than you'd expect.

Mattei's Tavern   AMERICAN/CONTINENTAL   Mattei's is proud of its stagecoach past, and this rambling white Victorian submerged in climbing wisteria has successfully retained its historic charm. It's well known throughout the county for fun and good food; rumors abound of high-stakes poker games in Mattei's back room, where many an early rancher literally "lost the farm." You'll find fine steaks on the menu, along with Australian lobster tail, rainbow trout, burgers, prime-rib chili, a dill-tinged tomato bisque, and chicken picatta, marsala, or teriyaki.

Calif. 154, Los Olivos. ℂ **805/688-4820.** Reservations suggested on weekends. Dinner $15–$35. MC, V. Daily 5:30–9pm; Sat–Sun noon–2:30pm.

Paula's Pancake House *(Kids* AMERICAN/DANISH   Morning means one thing in Solvang, and that's Paula's three-page menu of *just breakfast!* There are wafer-thin Danish pancakes, served plain and simple, sweet and fruity, or with sausage and eggs; plus buttermilk pancakes, whole-wheat/honey pancakes, fresh-baked waffles, sourdough French toast, and every omelet and egg dish imaginable, including some south-of-the-border salsa-fied specials. Paula's is friendly and casual, plunked in the heart of town so that patio diners can watch the whole wacky world go by.

1531 Mission Dr., Solvang. ℂ **805/688-2867.** Most menu items under $7. AE, DISC, MC, V. Daily 6am–3pm.

6 Santa Barbara

45 miles S of Solvang, 105 miles S of San Luis Obispo, 92 miles NW of Los Angeles

Santa Barbara is nestled between palm-lined Pacific beaches and the sloping foothills of the Santa Ynez Mountains. This prosperous resort community presents a mosaic of whitewashed stucco and red tile roofs and a gracious, relaxed attitude that has earned it the sobriquet "American Riviera." It's ideal for kicking back on white-sand beaches, prowling the shops and galleries that line the village's pristine, historic streets, and relaxing over a good meal in one of many top-notch cafes and restaurants.

Downtown Santa Barbara is distinctive for its Spanish-Mediterranean architecture. But it wasn't always this way. Santa Barbara had a thriving Native American Chumash population for hundreds, if not thousands, of years. The European era began in the late 18th century, around a Spanish *presidio* (fort) that's been reconstructed in its original spot. The earliest architectural hodge-podge was destroyed in 1925 by a powerful earthquake that leveled the business district. Out of the rubble rose the Spanish-Mediterranean town of today, a stylish planned community that continues to enforce strict building codes.

Visit Santa Barbara's waterfront on a Sunday, and you're sure to see the weekly **Waterfront Arts and Crafts Show,** one of the city's best-loved traditions. Since 1965, artists, craftspeople, and street performers have been lining grassy Chase Palm Park, along Cabrillo Boulevard.

ESSENTIALS
GETTING THERE   By car, U.S. 101 runs right through Santa Barbara; it's the fastest and most direct route from north or south (1½ hours from Los Angeles, 6 hours from San Francisco).

The **Santa Barbara Municipal Airport** (ℂ 805/967-7111) is located in Goleta, about 10 minutes north of downtown Santa Barbara. Airlines serving Santa Barbara include **American Eagle** (ℂ 800/433-7300), **AmericaWest Airlines** (ℂ 800/235-9292), **United** (ℂ 800/241-6522), and **US Airways Express** (ℂ 800/428-4322). **Yellow Cab** (ℂ 805/965-5111) and other metered taxis line up outside the terminal; the fare is about $22 (without tip) to downtown.

By train, **Amtrak** (ℂ **800/USA-RAIL;** www.amtrak.com) offers daily service to Santa Barbara. Trains arrive and depart from the **Santa Barbara Rail Station,** 209 State St. (ℂ **805/963-1015**). Fares can be as low as $40 (round-trip) from Los Angeles's Union Station.

Santa Barbara

ORIENTATION   State Street, the city's primary commercial thoroughfare, is the geographic center of town. It ends at Stearns Wharf and Cabrillo Street; the latter runs along the ocean and separates the city's beaches from touristy hotels and restaurants. Electric shuttles (25¢ fare) provide frequent service along these two routes if you'd rather leave the car behind.

VISITOR INFORMATION   The **Santa Barbara Visitor Information Center,** 1 Santa Barbara St., Santa Barbara, CA 93101 (C **800/927-4688** to order a free destination guide, or 805/965-3021; www.santabarbaraca.com), is on the ocean, at the corner of Cabrillo Street. The center distributes maps, brochures, an events calendar, and information. It's open Monday to Saturday from 9am to 4pm and Sunday from 10am to 4pm.

Be sure you pick up a copy of *The Independent,* Santa Barbara's free weekly, with hip articles and events listings; and *Explore Santa Barbara,* a compact visitor's guide published by the local paper, *New-Press.* Both are also available at shops and sidewalk racks throughout town.

EXPLORING THE TOWN
HISTORIC DOWNTOWN

Following a devastating 1925 earthquake, city planners decreed that all new construction would follow codes of Spanish and mission-style architecture. In time, the adobe-textured walls, rounded archways, artfully glazed tilework and terra-cotta rooftops would come to symbolize the Mediterranean ambience that still characterizes Santa Barbara. The architecture also gave a name to the **Red Tile Tour,** a self-guided walking tour of historic downtown. The visitor center (see "Visitor Information," above) has a map and guide of the tour, which can take anywhere from 1 to 3 hours, including time to visit some of the buildings, and covers about 12 blocks in total. Some of the highlights are destinations in their own right.

Santa Barbara County Courthouse ⊛   Built in 1929, this grand "palace" is considered the local flagship of Spanish colonial revival architecture. It's certainly the most flamboyant example, with impressive facades, beamed ceilings, striking murals, an 85-foot-high observation clock tower, and formal sunken gardens. Free guided tours are offered on Monday, Tuesday, and Friday at 10:30am and Monday through Saturday at 2pm.

1100 Anacapa St. C **805/962-6464.** Free admission. Mon–Fri 8am–5pm; Sat, Sun, and holidays 10am–4:45pm.

Santa Barbara Museum of Art ⊛   This little jewel of a museum feels more like the private gallery of a wealthy collector. Its leaning is toward early–20th-century Western American paintings and 19th- and 20th-century Asian art, but the best displays might be the antiquities and Chinese ceramics collections. In addition, there are often visiting exhibits featuring small but excellent collections from other establishments. Free docent-led gallery tours are given Tuesday to Saturday at 1pm, and exhibition tours are given Wednesday, Thursday, and Saturday at noon.

1130 State St. C **805/963-4364.** www.sbmuseart.org. Admission $5 adults, $3 seniors (over age 65), $2 students and children 6–17, free for children under 6. Free for everyone Thurs and the 1st Sun of each month. Tues–Wed and Fri–Sat 11am–5pm; Thurs 11am–9pm; Sun noon–5pm.

ELSEWHERE IN THE CITY

Santa Barbara Botanic Garden *(Finds*   The Botanic Garden is devoted entirely to indigenous California plants. More than 5½ miles of meandering trails on 65 acres offer glimpses of cacti, redwoods, wildflowers, and much more, many arranged in representational habitats or landscapes. The gardens were established in 1926. You'll catch the very best color and aroma just after spring showers. Docent tours are offered daily at 2pm, with additional tours on Thursday, Saturday, and Sunday at 10:30am.

1212 Mission Canyon Rd. (a short drive uphill from the mission). *C* **805/682-4726.** www.sbbg.org. Admission $5 adults, $3 children 13–18 and seniors (over 60), $1 children 5–12, free for children under 5. Mon–Fri 9am–5pm; Sat–Sun 9am–6pm.

Santa Barbara Mission *✯✯* Established in 1786 by Father Junípero Serra and built by the Chumash Indians, this is a very rare example in physical form of the blending of Indian and Hispanic spirituality. This hilltop structure is called the "Queen of the Missions" for its twin bell towers and graceful beauty. It overlooks the town and the Channel Islands beyond. Brochures are available in six languages, and docent-guided tours can be arranged in advance ($1 extra per person).

Laguna and Los Olivos Sts. *C* **805/682-4149.** www.sbmission.org. Admission $3 adults, free for children under 16. Daily 9am–5pm.

Santa Barbara Zoological Gardens *(Kids* When you're driving around the bend on Cabrillo Boulevard, look up—you might spot the head of a giraffe poking up through the palms. This zoo is a thoroughly charming, pint-sized place, where all 700 animals can be seen in about 30 minutes. Most of the animals live in natural, open settings. There are also a children's Discovery Area, a miniature train ride, and a small carousel. The picnic areas (complete with barbecue pits) are underutilized and especially recommended.

500 Ninos Dr. *C* **805/962-5339,** or 805/962-6310 for a recording. www.santabarbarazoo.org. Admission $7 adults, $5 seniors and children 2–12, free for children under 2. Daily 10am–5pm; last admission is 1 hr. prior to closing. Closed Thanksgiving, Christmas.

Stearns Wharf California's oldest working wharf attracts visitors for strolling, shopping, and snacking. There's also a Sea Center with aquariums, an outdoor touch-tank, and other exhibits. Although the wharf no longer functions for passenger and freight shipping as it did when built in 1872 by local lumberman John C. Stearns, you might still see local fishing boats unload their daily catch. You could also take a narrated sunset harbor cruise aboard the *Harbour Queen* at **Captain Don's** (*C* **805/969-5217**). Public parking is available on the wharf; it's free with merchant validation.

At the end of State St.

BEACHES

East Beach is Santa Barbara's favorite beach, stretching from the Zoological Gardens to Chase Palm Park and the wharf. Nearer the pier you can enjoy manicured lawns, tall palms, and abundant facilities; to the east are many volleyball courts, plus the Cabrillo Pavilion, a recreational center, bathhouse, and architectural landmark dating from 1925. Picnic areas with BBQ grills, showers, and clean, well-patrolled sands make this beach a good choice for everyone.

On the other side of Santa Barbara Harbor is **Leadbetter Beach,** which is less sheltered than those to the south, and thus popular with surfers. It's reached by following Cabrillo Boulevard after it turns into Shoreline Drive. This beach is also a great place to watch pleasure boats entering or leaving the harbor. Leadbetter has basic facilities, including restrooms, picnic areas, and a metered parking lot. Two miles west of Leadbetter is the secluded but popular **Arroyo Burro**

Beach County Park, also known as "Hendry's Beach." This gem has a grassy park beneath the cliffs and a white crescent beach with great waves for surfing and bodysurfing. There are volleyball nets, picnic areas, restrooms, and a free parking lot.

OUTDOOR ACTIVITIES

BIKING & SURREY CYCLING   A relatively flat, palm-lined 2-mile coastal pathway, perfect for biking, runs along the beach. More adventurous riders can pedal through town (where painted bike lanes line many major routes, including one up to the mission). These routes and many more are outlined in the Santa Barbara County Bike Map, a free and comprehensive resource available at the Visitor Center (see above)or by calling ℭ **805/963-7283.**

Beach Rentals, 22 State St. (ℭ **805/966-6733**), rents well-maintained six-speed cruisers for $6 an hour or $15 all day. It also has tandem bikes and surrey cycles that can hold as many as four adults and two children; rates vary. The place is open daily from 8am to dusk. Several other operations on the same block rent similar equipment at similar prices.

BOATING   The **Santa Barbara Sailing Center,** in Santa Barbara Harbor (ℭ **800/350-9090** or 805/962-2826; www.sbsailctr.com), rents sailboats from 21 to 50 feet in length. Both skippered and bareboat charters are available by the day or hour. Sailing instruction for all levels of experience is also available. Coastal, island, whale-watching, dinner-cruise, and adventure tours are offered on the 50-foot sailing catamaran *Double Dolphin.*

GOLF   At the **Santa Barbara Golf Club,** 3500 McCaw Ave., at Las Positas Road (ℭ **805/687-7087**), there are a great 6,009-yard, 18-hole course and a driving range. Unlike many municipal courses, the Santa Barbara Golf Course is well maintained and presents a moderate challenge for the average golfer. Greens fees are $25 Monday to Friday and $35 on weekends ($30 for seniors). Optional carts rent for $24 for 18 holes, $14 for 9.

The 18-hole, 7,000-yard course **Sandpiper,** at 7925 Hollister Ave. (ℭ **805/ 968-1541**), a breathtakingly scenic oceanside course, has a pro shop and driving range. Greens fees are $68 Monday to Thursday and $108 Friday to Sunday. Carts cost $24.

HIKING   The foothill trails in the Santa Ynez Mountains above Santa Barbara are perfect for day hikes. In general, they aren't overly strenuous. Trail maps are available at **Pacific Travelers Supply,** 12 W. Anapamu St. (ℭ **805/963-4438**), at the visitor center (see "Visitor Information," earlier in this chapter), and from **Traffic Solutions** (ℭ **805/963-7283**).

One of the most popular hikes is the **Seven Falls/Inspiration Point Trail,** an easy trek that begins on Tunnel Road, past the mission, and skirts the edge of Santa Barbara's Botanic Garden (which contains some pleasant hiking trails itself).

SKATING   The paved beach path that runs along Santa Barbara's waterfront is perfect for skating. **Beach Rentals,** 22 State St. (ℭ **805/966-6733**), located near the path, rents both inline and conventional roller skates. The $5-per-hour fee includes wrist and knee pads.

WHALE-WATCHING   Whale-watching cruises are offered between late December and late March, when Pacific gray whales pass by on migratory journeys between their breeding lagoons in Baja California, Mexico, and their Alaskan feeding grounds. **Shoreline Park,** west of the harbor, has high bluffs ideal for land-based whale spotting. Sea excursions are offered by both **Captain**

Don's Harbor Tours (© 805/969-5217), on Stearns Wharf, and **The Condor** (© 888/77-WHALE or 805/963-3564), located on Cabrillo Boulevard at Bath Street.

SHOPPING

State Street from the beach to Victoria Street is the city's main thoroughfare and has the largest concentration of shops. Many specialize in T-shirts and postcards, but there are a number of boutiques as well. If you get tired of strolling, hop on one of the electric shuttle buses (25¢ fare) that run up and down State Street.

Also check out **Brinkerhoff Avenue** (off Cota Street, between Chapala and De La Vina Streets), Santa Barbara's "antique alley." Most shops here are open Tuesday to Sunday from 11am to 5pm. **El Paseo** (814 State St.) is a picturesque shopping arcade reminiscent of an old Spanish street. It was built around an 1827 adobe home and is lined with charming shops and art galleries. **Paseo Nuevo**, on the other side of State Street, is an equally charming modern outdoor mall, featuring familiar chain stores, inviting cafes, and anchored by an elegant branch of Nordstrom department store.

WHERE TO STAY

Before you even begin calling around for reservations, keep in mind that Santa Barbara's accommodations are expensive—especially in summer. Then decide whether you'd like to stay beachside (even more expensive) or downtown. Santa Barbara is small, but not small enough to happily stroll between the two areas.

The Convention and Visitors Bureau's one-stop reservations service, **Hot Spots** (© 800/793-7666 or 805/564-1637), keeps an updated list of availability for about 90% of the area's hotels, motels, inns, and B&Bs. The service will have the latest information on who might be looking to fill last-minute vacancies at reduced rates. Reservationists are available Monday to Saturday 9am to 9pm and Sunday 9am to 4pm. There's no charge for using the service.

VERY EXPENSIVE

Four Seasons Biltmore ★★★   This gem of the "American Riviera" manages to adhere to the most elegant standards of hospitality without making anyone feel unwelcome. It's easy to sense the ghosts of Golden Age Hollywood celebs like Greta Garbo, Errol Flynn, and Bing Crosby, who used to play croquet or practice putting on the hotel's perfectly manicured lawns and then head over to the private Coral Casino Beach & Cabana Club—because that's exactly what today's privileged guests are *still* doing! In 1987, the Four Seasons company acquired this Spanish-style hacienda (circa-1927) and tastefully restored the property without spoiling a bit of its historic charm. Rooms have an airy feel, heightened by white plantation shutters, light wood furnishings, and full marble bathrooms with all the modern amenities. Guests can amuse themselves with a putting green, plus shuffleboard and croquet courts. In addition to two acclaimed dining rooms, the Biltmore offers a no-holds-barred Sunday brunch that draws folks from 100 miles away. Afternoon tea and evening cocktails are served in a comfortable lounge; there's live jazz on Wednesday and Friday nights.

1260 Channel Dr. (at the end of Olive Mill Rd.), Santa Barbara, CA 93108. © 800/332-3442 or 805/969-2261. Fax 805/565-8323. 217 units. $295–$620 double; suites from $1,050. Extra person $35. Free for children age 18 and under. Special midweek and package rates available. AE, DC, MC, V. Valet parking $17; free self-parking. **Amenities:** 2 dining rooms, lounge; 2 outdoor heated pools; 3 lit tennis courts; health club; spa; Jacuzzi; complimentary bicycles; salon; 24-hour room service; dry cleaning/laundry service. *In room:* A/C, TV w/ pay movies, dataport, minibar, hair dryer, iron.

EXPENSIVE

El Encanto Hotel & Garden Villas ✦   This romantic hillside retreat, whose very name means "enchantment," was built in 1915 and is made up of charming Craftsman cottages and Spanish bungalows. Uphill from the mission and surrounded by an exclusive older residential community, El Encanto features a spectacular view, secluded nooks, peaceful gardens and lily ponds, and lush landscaping. The hotel's discreetly attentive service has made it a favorite among privacy-minded celebs. The spacious rooms are tastefully decorated in a European country style; many have fireplaces, balconies, or patios.

1900 Lasuen Rd., Santa Barbara, CA 93103. 🕾 **800/346-7039** or 805/687-5000. Fax 805/687-3903. www. elencantohotel.com. 83 units. $229–$269 double; suites from $379. AE, DC, MC, V. **Amenities:** Restaurant, lounge; outdoor heated pool; tennis courts; access to nearby health club; concierge; business center; room service (6am–10pm); in-room massage; babysitting; dry cleaning/laundry service. *In room:* TV, dataport, minibar, coffeemaker, hair dryer, iron.

Simpson House Inn Bed & Breakfast ✦✦   Simpson House is truly something special. Rooms within the 1874 Historic Landmark main house are decorated to Victorian perfection, with extras ranging from a clawfoot tub and antique brass shower to skylight and French doors opening to the masterfully manicured gardens; romantic cottages are nestled throughout the grounds. The rooms have everything you could possibly need, but most impressive are the extras: the gourmet Mediterranean hors d'oeuvres and Santa Barbara wines served every evening; the enormous video library; and the heavenly full gourmet breakfast (delivered, for detached cottages, on delicate china). Fact is, the Simpson House goes the distance—and then some—to create the perfect stay. Although this property is packed into a relatively small space, it still manages an ambiance of country elegance and exclusivity—especially if you book one of the cottages. *Note:* Some rooms don't come with a TV/VCR, but you can have one by request.

121 E. Arrellaga St. (between Santa Barbara and Anacapa Sts.), Santa Barbara, CA 93101. 🕾 **800/676-1280** or 805/963-7067. Fax 805/564-4811. www.simpsonhouseinn.com. 14 units. $215–$435 double; $500–$550 suite/cottage. 2-night minimum on weekends. Rates include full gourmet breakfast, evening wine and hors d'oeuvres. AE, DISC, MC, V. **Amenities:** Complimentary bicycles; concierge; in-room massage; dry cleaning/laundry service. *In room:* A/C, TV w/ VCR, dataport, coffeemaker, minibar, hair dryer, iron.

MODERATE

Casa del Mar Inn at the Beach   A half block from the beach (sorry, no views), Casa del Mar is an excellent-value Spanish architecture motel, Spanish architecture motel with one- and two-room suites. The largish rooms have relatively new furnishings, with plenty of pastels. The flower-sprinkled grounds are well maintained, with an attractive spa sundeck (but no swimming pool), and the staff is eager to please. Many rooms have kitchenettes, fridges, and stoves; a dozen different room configurations guarantee something to suit your needs (especially families). Guests get discounts at a nearby day spa, and golf packages can be arranged. *Tip:* Despite the hotel's dizzying rate structure, rooms can often be an unexpected bargain. Also check its website for frequent Internet-only specials.

18 Bath St., Santa Barbara, CA 93101. 🕾 **800/433-3097** or 805/963-4418. Fax 805/966-4240. www. casadelmar.com. 21 units. Memorial Day–Labor Day $159–$224 double, $209–$254 suite; Sept–Oct and Mar–May $154–$194 double, $194–$224 suite; Nov–Feb $139–$179 double, $179–$209 suite. Rates include continental breakfast and wine-and-cheese social. Extra person $10. AE, DC, DISC, MC, V. From northbound U.S. 101, exit at Cabrillo, turn left onto Cabrillo, and head toward the beach; Bath is the second street on the right after the wharf. From southbound U.S. 101, take the Castillo exit and turn right on Castillo, left on Cabrillo, and left on Bath. Pets accepted with $10 fee. **Amenities:** Jacuzzi; in-room massage; dry cleaning/laundry service. *In room:* TV, coffeemaker, hair dryer, iron; some units with kitchen or kitchenette.

The Upham Victorian Hotel and Garden Cottages   This conveniently located inn combines the intimacy of a B&B with the service of a small hotel. Built in 1871, the Upham is the oldest continuously operating hostelry in southern California. Somewhere the management made time for upgrades, though, because guest accommodations are complete with all the other modern comforts. The hotel is constructed of redwood, with sweeping verandas and a Victorian cupola on top. It has a warm lobby, a cozy restaurant, and a resident cat named Henry.

1404 De La Vina St. (at Sola St.), Santa Barbara, CA 93101. ℂ **800/727-0876** or 805/962-0058. Fax 805/963-2825. www.uphamhotel.com. 50 units. $155–$405 double; suites from $290. Rates include continental breakfast and afternoon wine and cheese. AE, DC, MC, V. **Amenities:** Restaurant; dry cleaning/laundry service. *In room:* TV.

INEXPENSIVE

All the best buys fill up fast in the summer months, so be sure to reserve your room—even if you're just planning to stay at the decent, reliable **Motel 6** (ℂ **800/466-8356** or 805/564-1392) near the beach.

Franciscan Inn *Value*   The Franciscan is nestled in a quiet neighborhood just a block from the beach, near Stearns Wharf. This privately owned and meticulously maintained hotel is an affordable retreat with enough frills that you'll still feel pampered. The small but comfy rooms feature a country-tinged decor and finely tiled bathrooms. Services include morning newspaper and free local calls. Most second-floor rooms have unobstructed mountain views, and some suites feature fully equipped kitchenettes. All in all, the inn stacks up as a great family choice that's classy enough for a romantic weekend too.

109 Bath St. (at Mason St.), Santa Barbara, CA 93101. ℂ **805/963-8845.** Fax 805/564-3295. 53 units. Summer (mid-May to mid-Sept) $95–$134 double; $145–$250 suite; winter $75–$120 double, $110–$200 suite. Extra person $8. Rates include continental breakfast and afternoon refreshments. AE, DC, MC, V. Free parking. **Amenities:** Heated outdoor pool; Jacuzzi; coin-op laundry; dry cleaning/laundry service. *In room:* A/C, TV w/ VCR, dataport, coffeemaker, hair dryer, iron; some with kitchenette.

WHERE TO DINE
EXPENSIVE

bouchon santa barbara ✸✸ CALIFORNIA   You can tell this warm and inviting restaurant is passionate about wine just from the name—*bouchon* is the French word for "wine cork". And not just any wines, but those of the surrounding Santa Barbara County. In fact, there are 50 different Central Coast wines available by the glass; have some fun by enhancing each course with a glass (or half-glass) of wine—knowledgeable servers stand by to help make the perfect match. Chef Charles Fredericks's seasonally composed—and regionally inspired—menu has included dishes such as smoked Santa Barbara albacore "carpaccio," deliciously arranged with a tangy vinaigrette and shaved imported Parmesan; luscious sweetbread and chanterelle ragout cradled in a potato-leek basket; local venison sliced and laid atop cumin spaetzle in a shallow pond of green peppercorn-Madeira demi-glace; or monkfish saddle fragrant with fresh herbs and accompanied by a creamy fennel-Gruyère gratin. Request a table on the romantic patio, and don't miss the mouthwatering signature chocolate soufflé for dessert.

9 West Victoria St. ℂ **805/730-1160.** www.bouchon.net. Reservations recommended. Main courses $18–$29. AE, DC, MC, V. Daily 5:30–10pm.

Wine Cask ✸✸ CALIFORNIA/ITALIAN   Take an 18-year-old wine shop, a large 1920s landmark dining room with a big stone fireplace, and outstanding

Italian fare, and mix them with an attractive staff and clientele, and you've got the Wine Cask—the most popular upscale dining spot in Santa Barbara. Here you'll be treated to such heavenly creations as lamb sirloin with twice-baked au gratin potatoes. Other options include potato and prosciutto-wrapped local halibut in cioppino sauce, or grilled marinated chicken breast in a red-wine reduction with prosciutto, wild mushrooms, fresh rosemary, and sage. The wine list reads like a novel, with more than 1,000 wines (ranging from $14 to $1,400), and has deservedly received the *Wine Spectator* award for excellence. There's also a happy hour at the beautiful maple bar from 4 to 6pm daily.

In El Paseo Center, 813 Anacapa, Santa Barbara. © 805/966-9463. Reservations recommended. Main courses lunch $8–$12; dinner $18–$29. AE, DC, MC, V. Mon–Thurs 11:30am–9pm; Fri 11:30am–10pm; Sat 5:30–10pm; Sun 5:30–9pm.

MODERATE

Brophy Bros. Clam Bar & Restaurant ⭐⭐ SEAFOOD   This place is most known for its unbeatable view of the marina, but the dependable fresh seafood keeps tourists and locals coming back. Dress is casual, portions are huge, and favorites include New England clam chowder, cioppino, and any one of an assortment of seafood salads. The scampi is consistently good, as is all the fresh fish, which comes with soup or salad, coleslaw, and pilaf or french fries. A nice assortment of beers and wines is available. *Be forewarned:* The wait at this small place can be up to 2 hours on a weekend night.

119 Harbor Way (off Cabrillo Blvd. in the Waterfront Center). © **805/966-4418.** Reservations not accepted. Main courses $9–$16. AE, MC, V. Sun–Thurs 11am–10pm; Fri–Sat 11am–11pm.

Palace Grill CAJUN/CREOLE   Strolling by this restaurant, just a stone's throw from State Street, you'll easily see why descriptions like "rollicking" and "atmosphere as hot as the food" are regularly applied to the Palace Grill. The scene extends to the sidewalk, where waiting diners thirst after Mason jar Cajun martinis and Caribbean rum punch. Once inside, you'll find yourself part of the loud and fun atmosphere; this is not the place for meaningful dinner conversation. Try a platter of spicy blackened steak and seafood, a rich crawfish étouffée, or Creole jambalaya pasta. Be sure to save room for the renowned Southern desserts, including sweet potato-pecan pie, Florida key lime pie, and the superstar Louisiana bread pudding soufflé, laced with Grand Marnier and accompanied by whiskey cream sauce.

8 E. Cota St., Santa Barbara. © **805/963-5000.** www.palacegrill.com. Reservations suggested; not accepted Fri–Sat. Main courses $5–$13 lunch; $9–$25 dinner. AE, MC, V. Daily 11am–3pm and 5:30–10pm (until 11pm Fri–Sat).

Pan e Vino ⭐ ITALIAN   The perfect Italian trattoria, Pan e Vino offers food as authentic as you'd find in Rome. The simplest dish, spaghetti topped with basil-tomato sauce, is so delicious it's hard to understand why diners would want to occupy their taste buds with more complicated concoctions. But this kitchen is capable of almost anything. Pasta puttanesca, with tomatoes, anchovies, black olives, and capers, is always tops. Pan e Vino also gets high marks for its reasonable prices, attentive service, and casual atmosphere. Although many diners prefer to eat outside on the intimate patio, some of the best tables are in the charming, cluttered dining room.

1482 E. Valley Rd., Montecito. © **805/969-9274.** Reservations required. Pastas $8–$10; meat and fish dishes $11–$18. AE, MC, V. Mon–Sat 11am–10pm; Sun 5–9pm.

INEXPENSIVE

La Super-Rica Taqueria 🏵🏵 MEXICAN   Looking at this street-corner shack, you'd never guess it's blessed with the Nobel Prize of cuisine—an endorsement by Julia Child. The tacos here are no-nonsense, generous portions of filling piled onto fresh, grainy corn tortillas. Try *bistec* (steak), *adobado* (marinated pork), or *gorditas* (thick corn *masa* pockets filled with spicy beans). A dollop of homemade salsa is the only adornment required. You might catch Julia lining up for Sunday's special, *pozole,* a stew of pork and hominy in red chile sauce. On Friday and Saturday, the specialty is freshly made tamales.

622 N. Milpas St. (between Cota and Ortega Sts.), Santa Barbara. (C) **805/963-4940.** Most menu items $3–$6. No credit cards. Sun–Thurs 11am–9pm; Fri–Sat 11am–9:30pm.

Stacky's Seaside *Value* SANDWICHES   Stacky's is an ivy-covered shack filled with fishnets, surfboards, and local memorabilia. The menu of sandwiches is enormous, as most of their pita pockets, hoagies, and club sandwiches. A sign proudly proclaims HALF OF ANY SANDWICH, HALF PRICE—NO PROBLEM, and Stacky's has made a lot of friends because of it. Choices include the Santa Barbaran (roasted tri-tip and melted jack cheese on sourdough), the Rincon pita (jack and cheddar cheeses, green Ortega chiles, onions, and ranch dressing), and a hot pastrami hoagie with Swiss cheese, mustard, and onions. Stacky's also serves breakfast, featuring scrambled egg sandwiches and south-of-the-border egg dishes. An order of crispy french fries is enough for two.

2315 Lillie Ave., Summerland (5 min. on the freeway from Santa Barbara). (C) **805/969-9908.** Most menu items under $6. AE, DISC, MC, V. Mon–Fri 6:30am–7:30pm; Sat–Sun 7am–7:30pm.

SANTA BARBARA AFTER DARK

To find out what's going on while you're in town, check the free weekly the *Independent,* or call the following venues: the **Center Stage Theater,** upstairs at the Paseo Nuevo Shopping Center, Chapala and De La Guerra Streets ((C) 805/963-0408); the **Lobero Theater,** 33 E. Canon Perdido St. ((C) 805/963-0761); the **Arlington Theater,** 1317 State St. ((C) 805/963-4408); and the **Earl Warren Showgrounds,** at Las Positas Road and U.S. 101 ((C) 805/687-0766).

At night, a young crowd spills out of the bars on lower State Street. Unless you're aching to relive your college days, it isn't likely to be your bag.

7 The Ojai Valley

35 miles E of Santa Barbara, 88 miles NW of Los Angeles

In a crescent-shaped valley between Santa Barbara and Ventura, surrounded by mountain peaks, lies Ojai (pronounced *o*-hi). It's a magical place, selected by Frank Capra as Shangri-La, the legendary utopia of his 1936 classic *Lost Horizon.* The spectacularly tranquil setting has made Ojai a mecca for artists and a particularly large population of New Age spiritualists, both drawn by the area's mystical beauty.

Life is low-key in the peaceful Ojai Valley. Perhaps the most excitement generated all year happens during the first week of June, when the **Ojai Music Festival** draws world-renowned contemporary jazz artists to perform in the Libbey Bowl amphitheater.

While in Ojai, you're bound to hear folks wax poetically about something called the "pink moment." It's a phenomenon first noticed by the earliest Native American valley dwellers, when the brilliant sunset over the nearby Pacific is reflected onto the mountainside, creating an eerie and beautiful pink glow.

ESSENTIALS

GETTING THERE   The 45-minute drive south from Santa Barbara to Ojai is along two-lane Calif. 150, a beautiful road that's as curvaceous as it is stunning. From Los Angeles, take U.S. 101 north to Calif. 33, which winds through eucalyptus groves to meet Calif. 150—the trip takes about 90 minutes. Calif. 150 is called Ojai Avenue in the town center and is the village's primary thoroughfare.

VISITOR INFORMATION   The **Ojai Valley Chamber of Commerce,** 150 W. Ojai Ave., Ojai, CA 93023 (© **805/646-8126;** www.the-ojai.org), distributes free area maps, brochures, and a *Visitor's Guide to the Ojai Valley,* which lists galleries and current events. It's open Monday through Friday from 9:30am to 4:30pm, Saturday and Sunday from 10am to 4pm. For information on the **Ojai Music Festival,** call © **805/646-2094.**

EXPLORING THE TOWN & VALLEY

Small Ojai is home to more than 35 artists working in a variety of media; most have home studios and are represented in one of several galleries in town. The best for jewelry and smaller pieces is **HumanArts,** 310 E. Ojai Ave. (© **805/ 646-1525**). It also has a home-accessories annex, **HumanArts Home,** 246 E. Ojai Ave. (© **805/646-8245**). Artisans band together each October for an organized **Artists' Studio Tour** (© **805/646-8126** for information). It's fun to drive from studio to studio at your own pace, meeting various artists and perhaps purchasing some of their work. Ojai's most famous resident is world-renowned Beatrice Wood, who worked up until her death in 1998 at 104 years of age. Her whimsical sculpture and luminous pottery are internationally acclaimed, and her spirit is still a driving force in Ojai.

Strolling the Spanish arcade shops downtown and the surrounding area will yield a treasure trove, including open-air **Bart's Books,** Matilija Street at Canada Street (© **805/646-3755**), an Ojai fixture for many years. Antiques hounds head for **The Antique Collection,** 236 W. Ojai Ave. (© **805/646-6688**), an indoor antiques mall packed to the rafters with treasures, trash, and everything in between.

Residents of the Ojai Valley *love* their equine companions—miles of bridle paths are painstakingly maintained, and horse-crossing signs are everywhere. If you'd like to explore the equestrian way, call the **Ojai Valley Inn's Ranch & Stables** (© **805/646-5511**).

Ojai has long been a haven for several esoteric sects of metaphysical and philosophical beliefs. The **Krotona Institute and School of Theosophy,** Calif. 33 and Calif. 150 at Hermosa Road (© **805/646-2653**), has been in the valley since moving from Hollywood in 1926, and visitors are welcome at their library and bookstore.

In the **Lake Casitas Recreation Area** (© **805/649-2233** for visitor information), the incredibly beautiful Lake Casitas boasts nearly 32 miles of shoreline and was the site of the 1984 Olympic canoeing and rowing events. You can rent rowboats and small powerboats year-round from the **boathouse** (© **805/ 649-2043**) or enjoy picnicking and camping by the lakeside. Because the lake serves as a domestic water supply, swimming is not allowed. From Calif. 150, turn left onto Santa Ana Road, and then follow the signs to the recreation area.

When Ronald Coleman saw Shangri-La in *Lost Horizon,* he was really admiring the Ojai Valley. To visit the breathtakingly beautiful spot where Coleman stood for his view of **Shangri-La,** drive east on Ojai Avenue, up the hill, and stop at the stone bench near the top; the view is spectacular.

WHERE TO STAY

The Moon's Nest Inn ⊛   Conveniently located a block off Ojai Avenue, this comfortable clapboard B&B was built as a schoolhouse in 1874 and is Ojai's oldest building, newly reborn as a charming bed-and-breakfast. Innkeepers Rich and Joan Assenberg have carefully preserved, replaced, or complemented the inn's historic details, and the building now boasts every modern comfort, including four private balconies. Throughout the house, from a cozy fireplace parlor to the sunny breakfast room, architectural features like crown moulding are highlighted by dramatically painted walls, and the entire inn is furnished with a mix of carefully chosen antiques and high-quality contemporary pieces. A once-neglected side lawn has been transformed into a restful, tree-shaded garden retreat, complete with rock-lined pond and large trellised veranda (where breakfast is served on pleasant days). A cottage on the grounds houses a friendly beauty-and-massage salon (in-room massage is available), and guests enjoy full privileges at the Ojai Valley Athletic Club for a nominal day-use fee.

210 E. Matilija, Ojai, CA 93023. (*) **805/646-6635.** Fax 805/646-5665. www.moonsnestinn.com. 7 units, 5 with bathroom. $95–$145 double. Rates include breakfast and evening wine and spirits. AE, DC, DISC, MC, V. Small pets accepted with $25 per night fee. **Amenities:** Nearby health club; bicycle rental; in-room massage. *In room:* A/C; no phone.

Ojai Valley Inn and Spa ⊛⊛   In 1923, famous Hollywood architect Wallace Neff designed the clubhouse that's now the focal point of this quintessentially Californian, colonial Spanish–style resort. The inn has carefully kept a sprawling ranch ambiance while providing gracious, elegant service and amenities, along with a beautifully oak-studded Senior PGA Tour golf course. Next to the golf course, the jewel of the resort is pampering Spa Ojai, where stylish spa treatments—many modeled after Native American traditions—are administered inside a beautifully designed and exquisitely tiled Spanish-Moorish complex. Mind and body fitness classes, art classes, nifty workout machines, and a sparkling outdoor pool complete the relaxation choices. Many guest rooms have fireplaces; most have sofas, writing desks, and secluded terraces or balconies that open onto expansive views of the valley and the magnificent Sierra Madre. Take advantage of the scenery with wooded jogging trails and available horseback riding. This chic country inn is worth the trip. (At press time, it was even offering a midweek, AAA-member rate of $129.)

905 Country Club Rd. (off Calif. 33), Ojai, CA 93023. (*) **800/422-OJAI** or 805/646-5511. Fax 805/646-7969. www.ojairesort.com. 206 units. $275–$390 double; from $390 suite. Golf and spa discount packages available. AE, DC, DISC, MC, V. Free self or valet parking. Pets permitted for $35 per night, with advance notice. **Amenities:** 2 restaurants (formal Maravilla dining room, and casual terrace grill overlooking the golf course), 2 lounges; 2 outdoor heated pools (including a 60-foot lap pool); Jacuzzi; championship golf course; 8 tennis courts (4 night-lit); fitness center; full-service spa; complimentary bicycles; "Camp Ojai" (children's programs); concierge; business center; room service (6am–11pm); in-room massage; babysitting; dry cleaning/laundry service. *In room:* A/C, TV w/ pay movies and Nintendo, fax machine, dataport, minibar, coffeemaker, hair dryer, iron, safe.

Rose Garden Inn   This classic ranch-style motel has been well maintained and presents an attractively low-key alternative to the pricey country club around the corner. Situated a few blocks from the heart of town, with rose-filled gardens that border the Ojai equestrian and walking trail, this inn has a lazy, nostalgic feel. Rooms are small but have kitchen alcoves and brand-new beds; a mismatch of functional furniture reflects this place's rustic and inexpensive nature. The Rose Garden's best feature is hidden behind mature hedges: an enormous heated swimming pool (and Jacuzzi) next to a tree-shaded yard complete with hammock. There's even a 2-person redwood sauna in a mini-spa facility! Always check for seasonal specials or the "Ghost Stalking" tour package. *Note:* The rooms and cottages in back tend to be quieter than the front rooms near the street.

615 W. Ojai Ave. (at Country Club Dr.), Ojai, CA 93023. ℂ **800/799-1881** or 805/646-1434. Fax 805/640-8455. www.rosegardeninnofojai.com. 18 units. $69–$119 double; $149–$195 cottage. Extra person $10. Rate includes continental breakfast and afternoon snacks. Off-season and other discounts available. AE, DISC, MC, V. **Amenities:** Heated outdoor pool; Jacuzzi. *In room:* A/C, TV, fridge, hair dryer.

WHERE TO DINE
EXPENSIVE

L'Auberge ✦✦ FRENCH/BELGIAN   Possibly the most romantic restaurant in the Ojai Valley, L'Auberge is located in a 1910 mansion with a fireplace, chandeliers, and a charming terrace with an excellent view of Ojai's famous sunset "pink moment." The dinner menu is traditional, featuring scampi, frog legs, poached sole, tournedos of beef, sweetbreads, and duckling à l'orange. The weekend brunch menu offers a selection of crepes. Service is expert and friendly, and this elegant house is an easy walk from downtown.

314 El Paseo (at Rincon St.). ℂ **805/646-2288.** Reservations recommended. Main courses $15–$20. AE, MC, V. Sat–Sun 11am–2:30pm; daily 5:30–9pm.

The Ranch House ✦✦✦ CALIFORNIA   This restaurant has been placing an emphasis on the freshest vegetables, fruits, and herbs since opening its doors in 1965, long before this practice became a national craze. Freshly snipped sprigs from the restaurant's lush herb garden will aromatically transform your simple meat, fish, or game dish into a work of art. From an appetizer of cognac-laced liver paté served with its own chewy rye bread to leave-room-for desserts such as fresh raspberries with sweet Chambord cream, the ingredients always shine through. And you'll dine in a magical setting, for the Ranch House offers alfresco dining year-round on the wooden porch facing the scenic valley, as well as in the romantic garden amid twinkling lights and stone fountains.

S. Lomita Ave. ℂ **805/646-2360.** www.TheRanchHouse.com. Reservations recommended. Main courses $20–$29. AE, DC, DISC, MC, V. Wed–Sat 5:30–8:30pm; Sun 11am–7:30pm. From downtown Ojai, take Hwy. 33 north to El Roblar Dr. Turn left, then left again at Lomita Ave.

MODERATE

Here's another choice for you: At press time the buzz was all about **Deer Lodge,** 2261 Maricopa Hwy. (ℂ **805/646-4256;** www.ojaideerlodge.com), the latest incarnation of Ojai's favorite hippie-biker hangout on Highway 33 a few minutes north of Ojai. Nestled in the valley's gorgeous foothills, the building dates back to the Depression, when it served as a country store with bait and hunting supplies for local sportsmen, but new owners have been busy sprucing the place up and expanding to include a live stage in the bar, enclosed outdoor dining, and a hearty lodge menu with enough contemporary touches to bring in an upscale—yet adventuresome—clientele.

Suzanne's Cuisine ✦✦ CONTEMPORARY EUROPEAN   Enjoy a great meal in a comfortably sophisticated setting at this local fave, where every little touch bespeaks a preoccupation with quality details. Ask for a table on the covered outdoor patio, where lush greenery frames a casual setting warmed by a fireplace; when it rains, a plastic curtain descends to keep water out without losing that airy garden feel. Favorites from a seasonally changing menu include the lunch-only Southwest salad (wild, brown, and jasmine rice tossed with smoked turkey, feta cheese, veggies, and green chilies) and pepper-and-sesame-crusted ahi, served at dinner either sautéed or seared (your choice). From seafood specialties to Italian recipes from chef and owner Suzanne Roll's family, everything is fresh and natural; veggies are crisply al dente, and even the occasional cream sauce tastes light and healthy. Don't skip dessert.

502 W. Ojai Ave. ☎ 805/640-1961. www.suzannescuisine.com. Reservations recommended. Main courses $7–$15 lunch; $14–$28 dinner. MC, V. Wed–Mon 11:30am–3pm and 5:30–8:30pm.

INEXPENSIVE

Boccali's ★ ITALIAN This small, wood-frame restaurant, set among citrus groves, is a pastoral pleasure spot where patrons eat outside at picnic tables under umbrellas and twisted oak trees, or inside at tables covered with red-and-white-checked oilcloths. Pizza is the main dish served here, topped California-style with the likes of crab, garlic, shrimp, and chicken. We think Boccali's lasagna (served piping hot *en casserole*) would win a statewide contest hands down. Fresh lemonade, squeezed from fruit plucked from local trees, is the usual drink of choice. Come hungry, and plan on sharing.

3277 Ojai –Santa Paula Rd. ☎ 805/646-6116. Reservations recommended for dinner. Pizza $9–$19; pasta $6–$12. No credit cards. Mon–Tues 4–9pm; Wed–Sun noon–9pm.

Oak Pit BBQ (Kids) BARBECUE This stick-to-your-ribs joint on the road between Ojai and Ventura is worth building up an appetite for. The rust-colored shack doesn't have much going for it—just some gingham curtains, a few tables indoors and out, and stacks of wood for firing up the BBQ—but generous portions of slowly oak-smoked meats will have dedicated carnivores coming back for more. BBQ tri-tip brisket, ham, pork, Cajun sausage, and chicken—they're all served up in sandwiches or full dinners, with available sides of coleslaw, potato salad, French fries, baked beans, and corn-on-the-cob.

820 N. Ventura Ave. (Calif. 33), Oak View. ☎ 805/649-9903. Reservations not accepted. Sandwiches $5; main courses $8–$12. AE, DISC, MC, V. Tues–Thurs and Sun 11:30am–8:30pm; Fri–Sat 11am–9pm.

8 En Route to Los Angeles: Ventura

15 miles SW of Ojai, 74 miles NW of Los Angeles

Nestled between gently rolling foothills and the sparkling blue Pacific Ocean, Ventura may not have the cultural and gastronomic appeal of Los Angeles or even nearby Santa Barbara, but it does boast the picturesque setting and clean sea breezes typical of California coastal towns. Southland antiques hounds know about Ventura's quirky collectible shops, and time-pressed vacationers zip up to charming bed-and-breakfasts just an hour from Los Angeles. Ventura is also the headquarters and main point of embarkation for Channel Islands National Park (see the following section).

Most travelers don't bother exiting U.S. 101 for a closer look. But think about stopping to wile away a couple of hours around lunchtime; sleepy Ventura's charm might even convince you to spend a night.

ESSENTIALS

GETTING THERE If you're traveling northbound on U.S. 101, exit at California Street; southbound, take the Main Street exit. If you're coming west on Calif. 33 from Ojai, there's also a convenient Main Street exit. By the way, don't let the directions throw you off; because of the curve of the coastline, the ocean is not always to the west, but often southward.

VISITOR INFORMATION For a visitor's guide and genial answers to any questions you might have, stop in at the **Ventura Visitors & Convention Bureau,** 89-C S. California St., Ventura, CA 93001 (© **800/333-2989** or 805/ 648-2075; www.ventura-usa.com).

EXPLORING THE TOWN

Much of Ventura's recent development has taken place inland and to the south, so many folks overlook the charming seaside **Main Street,** the town's historic center, which grew outward from the Spanish mission of San Buenaventura (see below). The best section for strolling is between the mission (to the north) and Fir Street (to the south). Both sides of the street are lined almost entirely with antiques stores, used-book stores, and charity thrift stores, making it perfect for browsing.

Although Ventura stretches south to one of California's most picturesque little harbors (the jumping-off point for the Channel Islands; see section 9), the town has its own simple **pier** at the end of California Street. Exceptionally well maintained and favored by area fishers, the charming wooden pier is the longest of its kind in California.

Mission San Buenaventura Founded in 1782 (current buildings date from 1815) and still in use for daily services, this whitewashed and red-tile church lent its style to the contemporary civic buildings across the street. Step back in time by touring the mission's inside garden, where you can examine the antique water pump and olive press once essential to daily life here. Good for a quick history fix, the mission is small and near the rest of Ventura's action. Pick up a self-guided tour brochure in the adjacent gift shop for the modest donation of $1 per adult, 50¢ per child.

225 E. Main St. © **805/643-4318.** Free admission; donations appreciated. Mon–Sat 10am–5pm; Sun 10am–4pm.

San Buenaventura City Hall This majestic neoclassical building was constructed in 1912 to serve as the Ventura County Courthouse. It sits on the hill-side, regally overlooking old downtown and the ocean. To either side on Poli Street are some of Ventura's best-preserved and most ornate late-19th- and early-20th-century houses. Full of architectural detail (like the carved heads of Franciscan friars adorning the facade) inside and out, City Hall can be fully explored by escorted tour.

501 Poli St. © **805/658-4726.** Guided tours $7 adults, free for children 6 and under. 1-hr. tours given May–Sept Sat 11am–1pm.

Ventura County Museum of History & Art This museum is worth visiting for its rich Native American Room, filled with Chumash treasures, and its Pioneer Room, which contains a collection of artifacts from the Mexican-American War (1846 to 1848). The art gallery features revolving exhibits of local painters and photographers, and the museum has an enormous archive (20,000 and counting) of photos depicting Ventura County from its origins to the present. There is also a small archaeological museum across Main Street from the main building.

100 E. Main St. © **805/653-0323.** www.vcmha.org. Admission $4 adults, $3 seniors 62+ and AAA members, $1 kids 6–17, free for children under 6. Tues–Sun 10am–5pm.

WHERE TO STAY

Bella Maggiore Inn The Bella Maggiore is an intimate Italian-style small hotel whose simply furnished rooms (some with fireplaces, balconies, or bay window seats) overlook a romantic courtyard or roof garden. The style is Mediterranean casual, with shuttered windows, ceiling fans, and fresh flowers in every room. An open-air center courtyard is the inn's focal point, with stone fountains and flowering trees. Complimentary breakfast is served downstairs at Nona's Courtyard Cafe, which also offers dinner and weekday lunches. A kind of European elegance pervades all but the reasonable rates here.

67 S. California St. (half a block south of Main St.), Ventura, CA 93001. ⓒ 800/523-8479 or 805/652-0277. www.bellamaggioreinn.com. 24 units. $75–$175 double; $105–$150 suite. Extra person $10. Rates include full breakfast and afternoon refreshments and appetizers. Ask about midweek specials. AE, DISC, MC, V. **Amenities:** Restaurant; dry cleaning/laundry service. *In room:* TV.

Holiday Inn Beach Resort *(Kids*   One of the nicer Holiday Inns we've seen, this waterfront high-rise enjoys some spectacular views courtesy of its 12 stories. Because there's little else around as tall, nearly every room has a panoramic view of the sea or Ventura's pretty foothills—or both! Situated on the boardwalk that runs between the pier and the fairgrounds, the hotel is also within easy walking distance of historic downtown Ventura. There's excellent beach access, a heated outdoor pool facing the ocean, a couple of nearby restaurants in addition to the hotel's coffee shop, plus bike and surrey rentals right outside the front door. Ride up to the top floor and check out the hotel's circular ballroom; its adjacent cocktail lounge is oh-so-perfect for sunset gazing. Guest rooms are decent and thoroughly renovated, but otherwise unremarkable.

450 E. Harbor Blvd. (at California St.), Ventura, CA 93001. ⓒ 800-HOLIDAY or 805/648-7731. Fax 805/653-6202. 260 units. $100–$110 double. AE, DC, DISC, MC, V. **Amenities:** Restaurant, 3 lounges; heated outdoor pool; 24-hour exercise room; bicycle rentals; game room; business center; room service; self-service laundromat; dry cleaning/laundry service. *In room:* A/C, TV w/ pay movies, dataport, hair dryer, iron.

La Mer European Bed & Breakfast ⋆   Perfect for a romantic getaway, La Mer is an 1890 Cape Cod–style home with a spectacular view of the ocean from the parlor and two of the five guest rooms, each of which is furnished in a different international style. Whether you choose the "Madame Pompadour" French chamber with wood-burning stove, the "Vienna Woods" Austrian hideaway with sunken bathtub, or one of three other rooms, you'll love this cozy little cottage. It offers generous activity packages for couples, which can include gourmet candlelit dinners, cruises to Anacapa Island, country carriage rides, therapeutic massages . . . or all of the above.

411 Poli St. (west of City Hall), Ventura, CA 93001. ⓒ 805/643-3600. Fax 805/653-7329. www.lamerbnb.com. 5 units (4 with private entrance). $115–$185 double. Rates include full breakfast and complimentary wine in room. MC, V. No children accepted. **Amenities:** In-room massage. *In room:* No phone.

WHERE TO DINE

Eric Ericsson's SEAFOOD/AMERICAN   Having already established a reputation in Ventura for crowd-pleasing seafood, Ericsson's moved to the pier-top spot in 1997. Here scruffy beachgoers mingle with suited business folk at lunch, sports fans and 20-somethings scarf down appetizers at cocktail hour, families come early for generous dinners, and couples on dates linger at window tables until closing. The staggering array of seafood includes clams, oysters, mussels, shrimp, scallops, cod, halibut, lobster, and calamari. Add specialties like Mexican cioppino or traditional clambake, plus plenty of non-fish and vegetarian dishes, and it's impossible to imagine anyone being stumped by this menu.

668 Harbor Blvd. (on the Ventura Pier). ⓒ 805/643-4783. Reservations suggested on weekends. Main courses $7–$15 lunch; most full dinners $12–$28. AE, MC, V. Sun–Thurs 11am–10pm; Fri–Sat 11am–11pm.

Rosarito Beach Cafe ✴ MEXICAN   The Rosarito Beach Cafe really packs them into this 1938 Aztec Revival Moderne building and its welcoming outdoor patio. In-the-know diners bring their palates for superb Baja-style cuisine (whose tangy elements are borrowed from the Caribbean), delicious handmade tortillas, and a culinary sophistication rare in modest Ventura.

692 E. Main St. (at Fir St.). ℭ 805/653-7343. Main courses $10–$19. AE, DISC, MC, V. Tues–Sat 11:30am–2pm; Tues–Thurs and Sun 5:30–9pm; Fri–Sat 5–10pm.

71 Palm Restaurant COUNTRY FRENCH   Situated in a charmingly restored 1905 Craftsman, this ambitious little restaurant is still working out some of the details, but its country French menu is a pleasant change of pace in town. Upstairs tables have an ocean view, while downstairs diners are warmed by a crackling fire. Stick with bistro basics like steak au poivre with crispy pommes frites, Provençal lamb stew, or country paté served with crusty bread and tangy cornichons; and don't miss the antique-filled original restrooms.

71 N. Palm St. (between Main and Poli Sts.). ℭ **805/653-7222.** www.71palm.com. Reservations recommended. Main courses $11–$19. AE, DISC, MC, V. Mon–Fri 11:30am–2pm; Mon–Sat 5–9pm.

9 Channel Islands National Park

Approximately 40 miles W (offshore) of Ventura

There's nothing like a visit to the Channel Islands for discovering the sense of awe explorers must have felt more than 400 years ago. It's miraculous what 25 miles of ocean can do; for compared to the mainland, this is wild and empty land. Whether you approach the islands by sea or air, you'll be bowled over by how untrammeled they remain despite neighboring southern California's teeming masses.

Channel Islands National Park encompasses the five northernmost islands of the eight-island chain: Santa Barbara, Anacapa, Santa Cruz, Santa Rosa, and San Miguel. The park also protects the ocean 1 nautical mile offshore from each island, thereby prohibiting oil drilling, shipping, and other industrial uses.

The islands are the meeting point of two distinct marine ecosystems: The cold waters of northern California and the warmer currents of southern California swirl together here, creating an awesome array of marine life. On land, the relative isolation from mainland influences has allowed distinct species, like the island fox and the night lizard, to develop and survive here. The islands are also the most important seabird nesting area in California and home to the biggest seal and sea lion breeding colony in the United States.

ESSENTIALS

VISITOR INFORMATION   Each of the five islands is relatively distinct and difficult to reach. Odds are, you're only going to visit one island on a given trip, so it's a good idea to study your options before going. Visit the **Channel Islands National Park Headquarters and Visitor Center,** 1901 Spinnaker Dr., Ventura, CA 93001 (ℭ **805/658-5700;** www.nps.gov/chis), to get acquainted with the various programs and individual personalities of the islands through maps and displays. Rangers run interpretive programs both on the islands and at the center year-round.

GETTING THERE   **Island Packers,** next door to the visitor center at 1867 Spinnaker Dr. (ℭ **805/642-7688** for recorded information, 805/642-1393 for reservations; www.islandpackers.com), is the park's concessionaire for boat transportation to and from the islands.

If you want to get to Santa Rosa in a hurry, **Channel Islands Aviation,** 305 Durley Ave., Camarillo (© **805/987-1678**), will fly you there in one of its small, fixed-wing aircraft. If you just want a quick overflight and maybe a picnic stop with a short hike, **Heli-Tours, Inc.,** at the Santa Barbara Airport (© **805/964-0684**), offers 3- to 4-hour excursions to Santa Cruz Island.

There are no park fees, but getting to the islands is expensive—anywhere from $32 to $120 per person—since you must go by boat or plane. Island Packers will take you on a range of regularly scheduled boat excursions, from 3½-hour non-landing tours of the islands ($24 per person) or full-day tours of individual islands led by naturalists ($32–$49 per person) to 2-day excursions to two islands ($245). Private yachts and commercial dive and tour boats from all over southern California also visit the park on a regular basis.

THE WEATHER   While the climate is mild, with little variation in temperature year-round, the weather in the islands is always unpredictable. Thirty-mile-per-hour winds can blow for days, or sometimes a fog bank will settle in and smother the islands for weeks at a time. Winter rains can turn island trails into mud baths. In general, plan on wind, lots of sun (bring sunscreen), cool nights, and the possibility of hot days. Water temperatures are in the 50s and 60s year-round. If you're camping, bring a good tent—if you don't know the difference between a good and a bad tent, the island wind will gladly demonstrate it for you.

CAMPING   Camping is permitted on all the park-owned islands, but is limited to a certain number of campers per night, depending on the island. Fires and pets are prohibited on all the islands. You must bring everything you'll need; there are no supplies on any of the islands. To reserve free camping permits for any of the islands, call © **800/365-CAMP.**

EXPLORING THE ISLANDS

SANTA BARBARA   As you come upon Santa Barbara Island after a typical 3-hour crossing, you'll think that someone took a single, medium-sized, grassy hill, ringed it with cliffs, and plunked it down in the middle of the ocean. When you drop anchor, you'll realize that your initial perception is basically on target. Landwise, there's just not a lot here. But the upside is that, of all the islands, Santa Barbara gives you the best sense of what it's like to be stranded on a desert isle. Being on Santa Barbara, far enough out to sea that the mainland is almost invisible, gives you an idea of just how immense the Pacific really is.

Other than the landing cove, there's no access to the water's edge. The snorkeling in the chilly cove is great. You can hike the entire 640-acre island in a few hours; then it's time to stare out to sea. You won't be let down. The cliffs and rocks are home to elephant seals, sea lions, and swarms of seabirds such as you'll never see on the mainland. There's also a small campground, pit toilets, and a tiny museum chronicling island history. Camping is available year-round, but Island Packers only schedules boats to Santa Barbara in summer and fall (see "Getting There," above).

ANACAPA   Most people who visit the park come to Anacapa. It's only 14½ nautical miles from Ventura, an easy half-day trip. At only 1.1 square miles, Anacapa—actually three small islets divided by narrow stretches of ocean—is only marginally larger than Santa Barbara and, consequently, not a place for those who need a lot of space to roam around. Only East Anacapa is open to visitors, as the other two islets are important brown-pelican breeding areas. Several trails on the island will take you to beautiful overlooks of clear-watered coves and wild ocean. **Arch Rock,** a natural land bridge, is visible from the landing cove, where you'll clamber up 154 stairs to the island's flat top.

Camping is allowed on East Anacapa year-round, but don't bring more than you can carry the half mile from the landing cove. Bring earplugs and steer clear of the foghorn, which can cause permanent hearing damage. Most of the waters around the island, including the landing cove, are protected as a National Marine Preserve, where divers can look but not take anything. Pack a good wet suit, mask, fins, and snorkel; you can dive right off the landing cove dock.

SANTA CRUZ   By far the biggest of the islands—nearly 100 square miles— Santa Cruz is also the most diverse. It has huge canyons, year-round streams, beaches, cliffs, the highest mountain in the Channel Islands (2,400 feet), now-defunct early cattle and sheep ranches, and Native American Chumash village sites—2,000 Chumash were probably living on the island when Cabrillo first visited in 1542. The island also hosts seemingly endless displays of flora and fauna, including 650 species of plants, nine of which are endemic; 140 land-bird species; and a small group of other land animals, including the island fox.

Most of the island is still privately owned: The Nature Conservancy holds the western nine tenths. When the park service took over the eastern end from the Gherini family, who had owned a sheep ranch here, it eliminated the island's for-merly exorbitant landing and camping fees, but also eliminated the Channel Islands' only non-camping overnight options—lodges that are being converted into interpretive centers.

Valdez Cave (also known as Painted Cave for its colorful rock types, lichens, and algae) is the largest and deepest known sea cave in the world. The huge cave stretches nearly a quarter of a mile into the island and is nearly 100 feet wide. The entrance ceiling rises 160 feet, and in the spring, a waterfall tumbles over the opening. Located on the northwest end of the island, the cave can only be entered via dinghy or kayak.

SANTA ROSA   Windy Santa Rosa also has a strong ranching past—one that ended in 1998 in a storm of controversy that pitted the National Park Service against both environmental groups and the 97-year-old Vail & Vickers cattle ranch. The cows are all gone now, taking with them a slice of history and leav-ing uncertainty that nature's balance can ever be restored on Santa Rosa. Santa Rosa is home to a large concentration of endangered plant species, 34 of which occur only on the islands. And like Santa Cruz, Santa Rosa is home to the diminutive island fox, a tiny cousin of the gray fox that has become nearly fear-less as it has evolved in the predator-free island environment. They'll walk right through your camp if you let them. Santa Rosa also has great beaches, a benefit somewhat outweighed by the nearly constant winds.

SAN MIGUEL   People often argue about what's the wildest place left in the lower 48 states. They bat around names like Montana, Colorado, and Idaho. Curiously, no one ever thinks to consider San Miguel. They should, for this 9,500-acre island is a wild, wild place. The wind blows constantly, and the island can be shrouded in fog for days at a time. Human presence is definitely not the status quo here.

Visitors land at Cuyler Harbor, a half-moon-shaped cove on the island's east end. Arriving here is like arriving on earth the day it was made: perfect water, perfect sand, outrageously blue water. Seals bask on the offshore rocks. The island's two most interesting features are the **Caliche Forest,** a sort of petrified forest left when the wind exposed sandstone casts of a forest that once stood on the island, and **Point Bennett,** the outrageous-sounding (and smelling) breeding ground of six separate species of seals and sea lions. In winter, thousands carpet the beach; their barking is deafening.

The waters around San Miguel are the richest and most dangerous of all the islands. The island is exposed to wave action from all sides. Many ships have sunk here. A 3-foot-tall stone cross stands in memory of Juan Rodríguez Cabrillo, the Spanish explorer credited with discovering the Channel Islands in 1542. Although his grave has never been found, Cabrillo is believed to be buried on the island.

Island Packers's schedule to San Miguel is sporadic in summer and almost nonexistent in winter, so call ahead. Primitive camping is allowed near the ranger's residence, but no potable water is available, and fires are prohibited.

THE EXTRA MILE: EXPLORING THE COASTLINE & WATERS OFF THE CHANNEL ISLANDS

DIVING   A good portion of Channel Islands National Park is underwater. In fact, twice as many visitors come annually to dive the waters than ever set foot on the islands. Scuba divers come here from all over the globe for the chance to explore stunning kelp forests, shipwrecks, and underwater caves, all with the best visibility in California. Everything from sea snails and urchins to orcas and great white sharks call these waters home.

Truth Aquatics, in Santa Barbara (© 805/962-1127; www.truthaquatics. com), is the best provider of single- and multi-day dive trips to all the islands. **Ventura Dive & Sport** (© 805/650-6500) also leads trips, including a "Discover Program" that allows novice and uncertified divers to explore the waters accompanied by an instructor. **Channel Islands Scuba** (© 805/644-3483) and **Pacific Scuba** (© 805/984-2566) also lead regular trips, as do boats from San Pedro and other southern California ports.

SEA KAYAKING   One of the best ways to explore the fascinating coastline of the islands is by kayak. Warren Glaser of **OAARS** (Outdoor and Aquatic Recreation Specialist), based in Ventura (© 805/642-2912), leads small group tours by sea kayak to all five Channel Islands. The trips allow you to explore sea caves and rock gardens. Channel crossing by charter boat, brief lessons, and lunch are included. Fares generally run $125 per person. Three-day adventures to Santa Rosa, with meals, campsite, and guide included are offered for $295. **Aqua Sports** (© 805/968-7231) and **Paddle Sports** (© 805/899-4925) also lead similar excursions, or trips can be arranged through **Island Packers** (© 805/ 642-7688 for recorded information, 805/642-1393 for reservations; www. islandpackers.com).

13

Los Angeles

by Stephanie Avnet Yates

The entire world knows what Los Angeles looks like. It's a real-life version of one of those souvenir postcard folders, which spills out images accordion style: tall palm trees sweeping an azure sky, the gleaming white HOLLYWOOD sign, freeways flowing like concrete rivers, a lone surfer riding the day's last wave silhouetted against the sunset's glow. These seductive images are just a few of many that bring to mind the city that everyone loves to hate—and to experience, at least once in a lifetime.

Los Angelenos know their city will never have the sophisticated style of Paris or the historical riches of London—but we cheerfully lay claim to being the most fun city in the United States, maybe even the world. Home to the planet's first amusement park, L.A. kind of feels like one, as the line between fantasy and reality is so often obscured. The colors of the city seem just a little bit brighter—and

more surreal—than in other cities, the angles just a little sharper. Everything seems larger than life. Drive down Sunset Boulevard, and you'll see what we mean: The billboards are just a little bit taller, the wacky folks just a touch wackier.

Part of the spontaneity and excitement of L.A. comes from the fact that the city is constantly redefining itself. Just like the movies and TV shows that come to life here, the physical landscape, social doctrines, and popular pastimes of the city itself are fluid and unreliable. L.A. gleefully embraces individuality, weirdness, and change. Collectively, the city is like a theatrical actor projecting to the very back row: We want everyone else to sit up and take notice—and we're constantly reinventing ourselves so they will. We'd never want our city to be Paris or London for all the *Mona Lisa*s in the world.

1 Orientation

ARRIVING

BY PLANE

LOS ANGELES INTERNATIONAL AIRPORT (LAX)   Most visitors to the area fly into Los Angeles International Airport, better known as LAX (© 310/646-5252). Situated oceanside just off I-405, between Santa Monica and Manhattan Beach, LAX is a convenient place to land; it's minutes away from all the city's beach communities, and about a half-hour drive from the Westside, Hollywood, or downtown. The airport's website (**www.lawa.org**) offers a bounty of information, including transportation contacts, nearby lodging, a map of the airport and surrounding streets, and links to related sites.

You'll probably be renting a **car** from LAX; you'll need one (see "Getting Around," later in this chapter). All the major car rental firms provide shuttles from the terminals to their off-site branches. To reach Santa Monica and other northern beach communities, exit the airport, take Sepulveda Boulevard north, and then follow the signs to Calif. 1 (Pacific Coast Highway, or PCH) north. To reach the southern beach communities, take Sepulveda Boulevard south, and then follow the signs to Calif. 1 (PCH) south. To reach Beverly Hills or Hollywood, exit the airport via Century Boulevard, then take I-405 north to Santa Monica Boulevard east. To reach downtown, exit the airport, turn right onto Sepulveda Boulevard south, then take I-105 east to I-110 north. To reach Pasadena, drive through downtown (following the directions above), and continue north on Calif. 110 (the Pasadena Freeway).

Many city hotels provide free **shuttles** for their guests; ask about transportation when you make reservations. You can also catch a taxi from your terminal. **Taxis** line up outside each terminal, and rides are metered. Expect to pay about $30 to Hollywood and downtown, $26 to Beverly Hills, $20 to Santa Monica, and $48 to Pasadena, including a $2.50 service charge for rides originating at LAX.

SuperShuttle (© **800/BLUE-VAN;** www.supershuttle.com) offers regularly scheduled minivans from LAX to any location in the city. The set fare can range from about $15 to $35 per person, depending on your destination. It's cheaper to cab it to most destinations if you're a group of three or more, but the vans are infinitely more comfortable; however, you might have to stop at other passengers' destinations before you reach your own. When you arrive at LAX, you can call SuperShuttle from a pay phone in baggage claim at the toll-free number above or at the courtesy phones at the services information board. If you call during a very busy time, however, expect a wait. Reservations are unnecessary for arrivals, but required for your return to the airport.

City **buses** also go between LAX and many parts of the city; phone **MTA Information** (© **213/626-4455;** www.mta.net) for schedules and fares.

OTHER AREA AIRPORTS   One of the area's smaller airports might be more convenient for you, landing you closer to your destination and allowing you to avoid the traffic and bustle of LAX. **Burbank-Glendale-Pasadena Airport** (© **818/840-8840;** www.burbankairport.com) is the best place to land if you're going to Hollywood or the Valleys. This small airport has especially good links to Las Vegas and other Southwestern cities. **Long Beach Municipal Airport** (© **562/570-2678;** www.lgb.org), south of LAX, is the best place to land if you're visiting Long Beach or northern Orange County, and want to avoid L.A. entirely. **John Wayne Airport,** in Orange County (© **949/252-5200;** www. ocair.com), is closest to Disneyland, Knott's Berry Farm, and other Anaheim-area attractions. For more information, see chapter 14, "Side Trips from Los Angeles."

BY CAR

If you're driving in **from the north,** you have two choices: the quick route, along I-5 through the middle of the state, or the scenic route along the coast.

Heading south along I-5, you'll pass a small town called Grapevine. This marks the start of a mountain pass known as the Grapevine. Once you've reached the southern end of the mountain pass, you'll be in the San Fernando Valley, and will have arrived in Los Angeles County. To reach the beach communities and L.A.'s Westside, take I-405 south; to get to Hollywood, take Calif. 170 south to U.S. 101 south (this route is called the Hollywood Freeway the entire way); I-5 will take you through downtown and into Orange County.

Southern California at a Glance

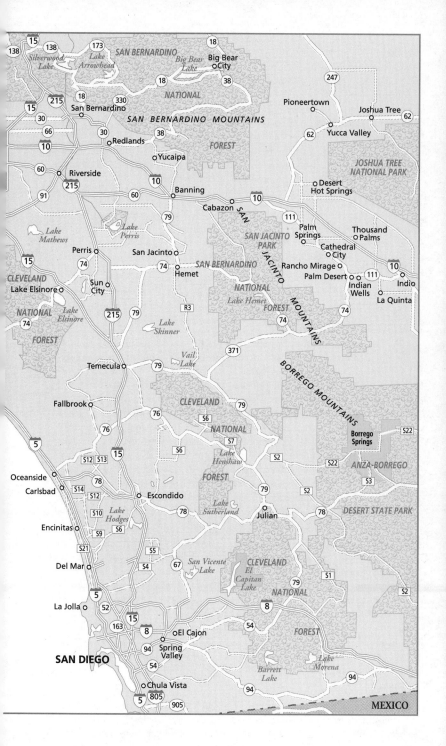

SAN BERNARDINO
Silverwood Lake
15
138
138
173
Lake Arrowhead
Big Bear Lake
18
Big Bear City
18
38
247
NATIONAL
Pioneertown
Joshua Tree
62
215
15
18
330
San Bernardino
SAN BERNARDINO MOUNTAINS
62
Yucca Valley
30
66
30
38
FOREST
JOSHUA TREE NATIONAL PARK
10
Redlands
60
Yucaipa
Riverside
10
Desert Hot Springs
215
60
Banning
91
Cabazon
SAN
10
111
Palm Springs
Thousand Palms
Lake Mathews
79
SAN JACINTO PARK
JACINTO
Cathedral City
Perris
Lake Perris
San Jacinto
SAN BERNARDINO
Rancho Mirage
111
10
15
74
74
Hemet
NATIONAL
Palm Desert
Indian Wells
Indio
CLEVELAND
Sun City
R3
FOREST
74
La Quinta
Lake Elsinore
MOUNTAINS
74
NATIONAL
215
79
Lake Elsinore
Lake Skinner
Lake Hemet
74
74
FOREST
371
Vail Lake
Temecula
79
BORREGO MOUNTAINS
CLEVELAND
79
Fallbrook
76
S6
S22
NATIONAL
Borrego Springs
76
S7
S2
S22
ANZA-BORREGO
5
15
S12 S13
S6
Lake Henshaw
S2
S3
Oceanside
78
FOREST
79
DESERT STATE PARK
Carlsbad
S14
S12
Escondido
S10
Lake Hodges
78
Lake Sutherland
Encinitas
S9
S6
Julian
78
S21
S5
CLEVELAND
S1
Del Mar
S4
67
San Vicente Lake
El Capitan Lake
79
S2
5
La Jolla
52
NATIONAL
163
15
8
54
FOREST
8
El Cajon
94
Spring Valley
SAN DIEGO
54
Barrett Lake
Lake Morena
94
Chula Vista
5
805
94
905
MEXICO

If you're taking the scenic coastal route in from the north, take U.S. 101 to I-405 or I-5, or stay on U.S. 101, following the instructions as listed above to your final destination.

If you're approaching **from the east,** you'll be driving in on I-10. For Orange County, take Calif. 57 south. I-10 continues through downtown and terminates at the beach. If you're heading to Hollywood, take U.S. 101 north; if you're heading to the Westside, take I-405 north. To get to the beaches, take Calif. 1 (PCH) north or south, depending on your destination.

If you're coming in **from the south,** head north on I-5. At the southern end of Orange County, I-405 splits off to the west; take this road to the Westside and beach communities. Stay on I-5 to reach downtown.

BY TRAIN

Passengers arriving via **Amtrak** (© 800/USA-RAIL; www.amtrak.com) will disembark at Union Station, on downtown's northern edge. From the station, you can take one of the many taxis that line up outside the station.

BY BUS

The main Los Angeles bus station for arriving **Greyhound** (© 800/231-2222; www.greyhound.com) buses is downtown at 1716 E. Seventh St., east of Alameda. For additional area terminal locations, call the toll-free number above.

VISITOR INFORMATION

The **Los Angeles Convention and Visitors Bureau** © 800/366-6166; events hotline 213/689-8822; www.lacvb.com), is the city's main source for information. In addition to maintaining an informative website and answering telephone inquiries, the bureau provides two **walk-in visitor centers:** 685 S. Figueroa St., downtown (open Monday through Friday from 8am to 5pm, and Saturday from 8:30am to 5pm); and in Hollywood, at the historic Janes House, 6541 Hollywood Blvd. (open Monday through Saturday from 9am to5 pm).

Many Los Angeles–area communities also have their own tourist offices: **Beverly Hills Visitors Bureau** (© 800/345-2210 or 310/271-8174; www.bhvb.org), **Pasadena Convention and Visitors Bureau** (© 626/795-9311; www.pasadenavisitor.org), **Santa Monica Convention and Visitors Bureau** (© 310/393-7593; www.santamonica.com), and **West Hollywood Convention and Visitors Bureau** (© 800/368-6020 or 310/289-2525; www.visitwesthollywood.acom). Call for information, hours, and locations.

OTHER INFORMATION SOURCES Several city-oriented newspapers and magazines offer up-to-date information on current happenings. The *L.A. Weekly* (www.laweekly.com), a free weekly listings magazine, is packed with information on current events around town. It's available from sidewalk news racks and in many stores and restaurants around the city. The *Los Angeles Times* "**Calendar**" section of the Sunday paper is an excellent guide to the world of entertainment in and around L.A., and includes listings of what's doing and where to do it. *Los Angeles* magazine (www.lamag.com) is a city-based monthly full of news, information, and previews of L.A.'s art, music, and food scenes. It's available at newsstands around town.

CITY LAYOUT

Los Angeles is not a single compact city, but a sprawling suburbia comprising dozens of disparate communities. Most of the city's communities are located between mountains and ocean, on the flatlands of a huge basin. Even if you've never visited L.A. before, you'll recognize the names of many of these areas: Hollywood, Beverly Hills, Santa Monica, and Malibu. Ocean breezes push the city's infamous smog inland, toward dozens of less well-known residential communities, and through mountain passes into the suburban sprawl of the San Fernando and San Gabriel Valleys.

Downtown Los Angeles—which isn't where most tourists will stay—is in the center of the basin, about 12 miles east of the Pacific Ocean. Most visitors will spend the bulk of their time either on the coast or on the city's Westside. (See "Neighborhoods in Brief," below, for details on all the city's sectors, as well as the map on p. 444 for an overview of the Los Angeles area's neighborhoods and freeway system.)

MAIN ARTERIES & STREETS   L.A.'s extensive freeway system connects the city's patchwork of communities; they work well together to get you where you need to be, although rush-hour traffic can sometimes be bumper to bumper. You might only drive on a couple of L.A.'s freeways, but here's an overview of the entire system:

U.S. 101, called the "Ventura Freeway" in the San Fernando Valley and the "Hollywood Freeway" in the city, runs across L.A. in a roughly northwest-southeast direction, from the San Fernando Valley to the center of downtown.

Calif. 134 continues as the Ventura Freeway after U.S. 101 turns into the city and becomes the Hollywood Freeway. The Calif. 134 branch of the Ventura Freeway continues directly east, through the valley towns of Burbank and Glendale, to I-210 (the "Foothill Freeway"), which will take you through Pasadena and out toward the eastern edge of Los Angeles County.

I-5, otherwise known as the "Golden State Freeway" north of I-10 and the "Santa Ana Freeway" south of I-10, bisects downtown on its way from San Francisco to San Diego.

I-10, labeled the "Santa Monica Freeway" west of I-5 and the "San Bernardino Freeway" east of I-5, is the city's major east-west freeway, connecting the San Gabriel Valley to downtown and Santa Monica.

I-405, also known as the "San Diego Freeway," runs north-south through L.A.'s Westside, connecting the San Fernando Valley with LAX and the southern beach areas.

I-105, Los Angeles' newest freeway—called the "Century Freeway"—extends from LAX east to I-605.

I-110, commonly known as the "Harbor Freeway," starts in Pasadena as **Calif. 110** (the "Pasadena Freeway"); it turns into the Interstate in downtown Los Angeles and runs directly south, where it dead-ends in San Pedro. The section that's now the Pasadena Freeway is Los Angeles' historic first freeway, known as the Arroyo Seco when it opened in 1940.

I-710, also called the "Long Beach Freeway," runs in a north-south direction through East Los Angeles and dead-ends at Long Beach.

I-605, the "San Gabriel River Freeway," runs roughly parallel to I-710 farther east, through the cities of Hawthorne and Lynwood and into the San Gabriel Valley.

Calif. 1—called "Highway 1," the "Pacific Coast Highway," or simply "PCH"—skirts the ocean, linking all of L.A.'s beach communities, from Malibu to the Orange Coast.

The freeways are complemented by a complex web of surface streets. The major east-west thoroughfares connecting downtown to the beaches (listed from north to south) are Sunset Boulevard, Santa Monica Boulevard, Wilshire Boulevard, and Olympic, Pico, and Venice Boulevards. The section of Sunset Boulevard that runs between Crescent Heights Boulevard and Doheny Drive is the famed Sunset Strip.

STREET MAPS   Because Los Angeles is so spread out, a good map of the area is essential. Foldout maps are available at gas stations, hotels, bookstores, and tourist-oriented shops around the city. Members of **ACCOMMODATIONS** should stock up on L.A. maps before they arrive; they're free to members and are the most precise and helpful area maps we've seen. For locations, call ☎ **800/ 922-8228;** the Hollywood-Wilshire branch is at 5550 Wilshire Blvd., Suite 101 (☎ **323/525-0018**). There's also an overview of the L.A. area included on the four-color sheet map in the back of this book.

NEIGHBORHOODS IN BRIEF

Los Angeles is a very confusing city, with fluid neighborhood lines and equally elastic labels. We've found that the best way to grasp the city is to break it into six regions—Santa Monica & the Beaches, Westside L.A. & Beverly Hills, Hollywood, Downtown, the San Fernando Valley, and Pasadena & Environs—each of which encompasses a more-or-less distinctive patchwork of city neighborhoods and independently incorporated communities.

Santa Monica & the Beaches

These are our favorite L.A. communities. The 60-mile beachfront stretching southward from Malibu to the Palos Verdes Peninsula has milder weather and less smog than the inland communities, and traffic is nominally lighter—except on summer weekends, of course. The towns along the coast each have their own mood and charm. We've listed them below from north to south:

Malibu, at the northern border of Los Angeles County, is 25 miles from downtown. Its particularly wide beaches, sparsely populated hills, and relative remoteness from the inner city make it extremely popular with rich recluses. With plenty of green space and dramatic rocky outcroppings, Malibu's rural beauty is unsurpassed in L.A.

Pretty **Santa Monica,** Los Angeles' premier beach community, is known for its long ocean pier, artsy atmosphere, and somewhat wacky residents. The Third Street Promenade, a pedestrians-only thoroughfare lined with great shops and restaurants, is one of the country's most successful revitalization projects.

Venice, a planned community in the spirit of its Italian forebear, was constructed with a series of narrow canals connected by quaint one-lane bridges. The area has been infested with grime and crime, but gentrification is in full swing. Some of L.A.'s most innovative and interesting architecture lines funky Main Street. Without question, Venice is best known for its Ocean Front Walk, a nonstop circus of skaters, sellers, and poseurs of all ages, colors, and sizes.

Marina del Rey, just south of Venice, is a somewhat quieter, more upscale community best known for its small-craft harbor, one of the largest of its kind in the world.

Manhattan, Hermosa & Redondo beaches are relatively sleepy residential neighborhoods with modest homes, mild weather, and easy parking. These communities have excellent beaches for volleyballers, surfers, and sun worshippers, but there's not much else about these South Bay suburbs for visitors to get very excited about—when it comes to good restaurants or cultural activities, pickings are slim.

L.A.'s Westside & Beverly Hills

The Westside, an imprecise, misshapen L sandwiched between Hollywood and the city's coastal communities, includes some of Los Angeles' most prestigious neighborhoods:

Beverly Hills is roughly bounded by Olympic Boulevard on the south, Robertson Boulevard on the east, and Westwood and Century City on the west; it extends into the hills to the north. Politically distinct from the rest of Los Angeles, this famous enclave is best known for its palm tree–lined streets of palatial homes and high-priced shops (does Rodeo Drive ring a bell?), but it's the healthy mix of the filthy rich, tourists, and wannabes that creates a unique—and sometimes bizarre—atmosphere.

West Hollywood is a key-shaped community (go ahead, look at your map) whose epicenter is the intersection of Santa Monica and La Cienega Boulevards. It's bounded on the west by Doheny Drive and on the south roughly by Melrose Avenue; the tip of the key extends east for several blocks north and south of Santa Monica Boulevard as far as La Brea Avenue, but it's primarily located to the west of Fairfax Avenue. Nestled between Beverly Hills and Hollywood, this politically independent town can feel either tony or tawdry, depending on which end of it you're in. In addition to being home to the city's best restaurants, shops, and art galleries, West Hollywood is the center of L.A.'s gay community.

Bel Air and **Holmby Hills,** located in the hills north of Westwood and west of the Beverly Hills city limits, comprise a wealthy residential area and feature prominently on most maps to the stars' homes.

Brentwood, once world-famous backdrop of the O. J. Simpson melodrama, is really just a tiny, quiet, relatively upscale neighborhood with the typical L.A. mixture of homes, restaurants, and strip malls. It lies west of I-405 and north of Santa Monica and West Los Angeles.

Westwood, an urban village that the University of California, Los Angeles (UCLA), calls home, is bounded by I-405, Santa Monica Boulevard, Sunset Boulevard, and Beverly Hills. The village used to be a hot destination for a night on the town, and still boasts some destination dining and a high concentration of movie theaters; but we're all waiting for Westwood to regain the charm it once had.

Century City is a compact, busy, high-rise district sandwiched between West Los Angeles and Beverly Hills. Once the back lot of 20th Century Fox studios, Century City is home to the Shubert Theater, the outdoor Century City Marketplace, and a couple of chic business and industry hotels. It's bounded by Century Park East, Century Park West, and Santa Monica and Pico Boulevards.

West Los Angeles is a label that basically applies to everything that isn't one of the other Westside neighborhoods. It's generally the area south of Santa Monica Boulevard, north of Venice Boulevard, east of the communities of Santa Monica and Venice, and west and south of Century City.

Hollywood

Yes, they still come. Young aspirants are attracted to this town like moths fluttering in the glare of neon lights. But Hollywood is now much more a state of mind than a glamour center. Many of the neighborhood's former movie studios have moved to less-expensive, more spacious venues. For our purposes, the label "Hollywood" extends to surrounding neighborhoods. It generally encompasses everything between Western Avenue to the east and Fairfax Avenue to the west and from the Hollywood Hills (with its dazzling homes and million-dollar views) south.

Hollywood itself, which centers around Hollywood and Sunset Boulevards (between La Brea and Vine), is the historic heart of L.A.'s movie industry. Visitors have always flocked to see landmark attractions like the star-studded Walk of Fame and Mann's Chinese Theatre. Hollywood Boulevard is, for the first time in decades, showing signs of rising out of a seedy slump, with refurbished movie houses and stylish restaurants creeping back to the 'hood. By the time you visit, the centerpiece "Hollywood & Vine" complex will anchor the neighborhood, with shopping, entertainment, and a luxury hotel built around a glamorous new theater designed to host the Academy Awards.

Melrose Avenue, a scruffy but fun neighborhood, is the city's funkiest shopping district.

The stretch of Wilshire Boulevard that runs through the southern part of Hollywood is known as the **Mid-Wilshire District,** or Miracle Mile. It's lined with contemporary apartment houses and office buildings; the stretch just east of Fairfax Avenue, now known as **Museum Row,** is home to almost a dozen museums, including the Los Angeles County Museum of Art, the La Brea Tar Pits, and that shrine to L.A. car culture, the Petersen Automotive Museum.

Griffith Park, up Western Avenue in the northernmost reaches of Hollywood, is one of the country's largest urban parks and home to the Los Angeles Zoo and the famous Griffith Observatory.

Downtown

Roughly bounded by U.S. 101, I-110, I-10, and I-5 freeways, L.A.'s downtown is home to a tight cluster of high-rise offices, El Pueblo de Los Angeles Historic District, and the neighborhoods of **Koreatown, Chinatown,** and **Little Tokyo.** For our purposes, the residential neighborhoods of **Los Feliz, Silver Lake** (a grungy burgeoning artistic community that has been called the "West Coast SoHo"), **Exposition Park** (home to Los Angeles Memorial Coliseum, several downtown museums, and USC), and **East and South-Central L.A.,** the city's famous barrios, all fall under the downtown umbrella.

The construction of skyscrapers—facilitated by earthquake-proofing technology—transformed downtown Los Angeles into the business center of the city. Despite the relatively recent construction of numerous cultural centers—including the Performing Arts Center and the Museum of Contemporary Art—and a few smart restaurants, downtown is not the hub it would be in most cities; the Westside, Hollywood, and the beach communities are all more popular.

San Fernando Valley

The San Fernando Valley, known locally as "the Valley," was nationally popularized in the 1980s by the notorious, mall-loving "Valley Girl" stereotype. Snuggled between the Santa Monica and the San Gabriel mountain ranges, most of the Valley is residential and commercial, and off the beaten tourist track. But there are some attractions bound to draw you over the hill: **Universal City,** located west of Griffith Park between U.S. 101 and Calif. 134, is home to Universal Studios Hollywood and CityWalk, a vast shopping and entertainment complex.

And you may want to make a trip to **Burbank,** just north of Universal City, to see one of your favorite TV shows being filmed at the NBC or Warner Bros. studios. There are also many good restaurants and shops along Ventura Boulevard in and around **Studio City.**

Pasadena & Environs

Best known to the world as the site of the Tournament of Roses Parade each New Year's Day, **Pasadena** was mercifully spared from the tear-down epidemic that swept L.A., so it has a refreshing old-time feel. Once upon a time, Pasadena was every Angeleno's best-kept secret—a quiet community whose slow and careful regentrification meant excellent, unique restaurants and boutique shopping without the crowds, in a revitalized downtown respectful of its old brick and stone commercial buildings. Although the area's natural and architectural beauty still

shines through—so much so that Pasadena remains Hollywood's favorite backyard location for count-less movies and TV shows—Old Town has become a pedestrian mall similar to Santa Monica's Third Street Promenade, complete with huge crowds, predictable mid-range chain eateries, and standard mall-issue stores. It still gets our vote as a scenic alternative to the congestion of central L.A., but it has lost much of its small-town charm.

The residential neighborhoods in Pasadena and its adjacent communities—Arcadia, La Cañada, San Marino, and South Pasadena—are renowned for well-preserved his-toric homes, ranging from humble bungalows to lavish mansions. Some present-day uses include pub-lic gardens, designated historic neighborhoods, house museums, and bed-and-breakfasts.

2 Getting Around

BY CAR

Despite its hassles, driving is the way to get around L.A. The golden rule is this: Always allow more time to get to your destination than you reasonably think it will take, especially during morning and evening rush hours.

RENTALS   Los Angeles is one of the cheapest places in the United States to rent a car. Among the national firms operating in L.A. are **Alamo** (© 800/327-9633), **Avis** (© 800/331-1212), **Budget** (© 800/527-0700), **Dollar** (© 800/800-3665), **Hertz** (© 800/654-3131), **National** (© 800/227-7368), and **Thrifty** (© 800/367-2277).

PARKING   Parking in L.A. is usually ample, but in some sections—most notably downtown and in Santa Monica, West Hollywood, and Hollywood—finding a space can be fraught with frustration. In most places, though, you'll be able to find metered street parking—be sure to carry plenty of quarters. When you can't, expect to valet or garage your car for somewhere between $4 and $10. Many restaurants and nightclubs, and even some shopping centers, offer valet parking; they usually charge about $3 to $6. Most of the hotels listed in this book offer off-street parking; it's often complimentary, but can cost as much as $23 per day in high-density areas.

BY PUBLIC TRANSPORTATION

There are visitors who successfully tour Los Angeles entirely by public trans-portation, but we can't honestly recommend that plan for most readers. L.A. is a metropolis that's grown up around—and made possible by—the automobile, and many areas are inaccessible without one. As a result, an overwhelming number of visitors rent a car when for their stay. Still, if you're in the city for only a short time, are on a very tight budget, or don't expect to be moving around a lot, public transport might be for you. The city's trains and buses are operated by the **Los Angeles County Metropolitan Transit Authority (MTA)** (© 213/626-4455; www.mta.net), and MTA brochures and schedules are available at area visitor centers.

LOCAL SHUTTLES Some of L.A.'s more popular (read: more congested) neighborhoods offer the opportunity to park once and take advantage of shuttle service. These include **downtown,** where Downtown Area Short Hop **(DASH)** buses run every 5 to 15 minutes and cost only 25¢. DASH also runs shuttles in **Hollywood** (along Sunset and Hollywood Boulevards) and between **Fairfax Avenue** and the **Beverly Center** (via Melrose Ave. and Third St.). Contact the Dept. of Transportation (© **808-2273** [all city area codes]; www.ladottransit.com) for schedules and route information.

In **Pasadena,** free **Arts Buses** run between Old Town and the Lake Avenue shopping district. Shuttles come every 20 minutes (12 minutes during lunchtime) between 11am and 8pm Monday through Saturday; stops are marked with ARTS BUS signs. The visitor center can provide additional information, including route maps.

 ***FAST FACTS:* Los Angeles**

American Express In addition to those at 327 N. Beverly Dr., Beverly Hills (© **310/274-8277**), and at 8493 W. Third St., Los Angeles (© **310/659-1682**), offices are located throughout the city. To locate one nearest you, call © **800/221-7282.**

Area Codes Within the past 20 years, L.A. has gone from having a single (213) area code to having a whopping seven. Even residents can't keep up with the changes. As of press time, here's the basic layout: Those areas west of La Cienega Boulevard, including Beverly Hills and the city's beach communities, use the **310** area code. Portions of Los Angeles County east and south of the city, including Long Beach, are in the **562** area code. The San Fernando Valley has the **818** area code, while points east—including parts of Burbank, Glendale, and Pasadena—use the newly created **626** code. What happened to 213, you ask? Only the downtown business area still uses **213.** All other numbers, including Griffith Park, Hollywood, and parts of West Hollywood (east of La Cienega Blvd.) now use the new area code **323.** If it's all too much to remember, just call directory assistance at © **411.**

Babysitters If you're staying at one of the larger hotels, the concierge can usually recommend a reliable baby sitter. If not, contact the **Baby-Sitters Guild** in Glendale (© **323/658-8792** or 818/552-2229), L.A.'s oldest and largest babysitting service.

Dentist For a recommendation in the area, call the **Dental Referral Service** (© **800/422-8338**).

Doctor Contact the **Uni-Health Information and Referral Hotline** (© **800/922-0000**) for a free, confidential physician referral.

Emergencies Dial (✆) **911** for police, fire, or highway patrol, or in case of life-threatening medical emergencies. No coins are required.

Hospital The centrally located **Cedars-Sinai Medical Center,** 8700 Beverly Boulevard, Los Angeles ((✆) **310/855-5000**), has a 24-hour emergency room staffed by some of the country's finest MDs.

Police For non-emergency police matters, phone (✆) **213/485-2121,** or 310/550-4951 in Beverly Hills.

Post Office Call (✆) **800/ASK-USPS** to find the one closest to you.

Taxes The combined Los Angeles County and California state sales taxes amount to 8%; hotel taxes range from 12% to 17%, depending on the municipality you're in.

Taxis You can call a taxi in advance from **Checker Cab** ((✆) 213/221-2355), **L.A. Taxi** ((✆) 213/627-7000), or **United Independent Taxi** ((✆) 213/483-7604).

Useful Telephone Numbers For the correct **time,** call (✆) 853-1212 (good for all local area codes). Call **Los Angeles Weather Information** ((✆) 213/554-1212) for the daily forecast. For beach conditions, call the **Zuma Beach Lifeguard** for recorded information ((✆) 310/457-9701).

3 Accommodations

by Cheryl Farr Leas

Due to space considerations, we've had to limit the number of hotels included here. If you'd like a larger selection, check out *Frommer's Los Angeles,* which has dozens of other options.

CHOOSING A LOCATION In sprawling Los Angeles, location is everything. Choosing the right neighborhood as a base can make or break your vacation; if you plan to while away a few days at the beach but base yourself downtown, for example, you're going to lose a lot of valuable relaxation time on the freeway. Take into consideration where you'll want to spend your time before you commit yourself to a base. But wherever you stay, count on doing a good deal of driving—no hotel in Los Angeles is convenient to everything.

In general, **downtown** hotels are business-oriented; they're sometimes popular with groups, but are largely ignored by independent tourists. The top hotels here are very good, but cheaper ones can be downright nasty. If you're on a budget, locate elsewhere.

Hollywood, which is centrally located between downtown and Beverly Hills and within easy reach of Santa Monica, makes a great base if you're planning to do a lot of touring—but there are fewer hotels here than you'd expect. The accommodations in Hollywood are usually moderately priced and generally well maintained, but otherwise unspectacular.

Most visitors stay on the city's **Westside,** a short drive from the beach and close to many of L.A.'s most colorful sights. The city's most elegant—and expensive—accommodations are in Beverly Hills and Bel Air. You'll find the city's best hotel values in West Hollywood, an exciting and convenient place to settle in.

Trendy, relatively smogless **Santa Monica** and its coastal neighbors are home to lots of hotels; book ahead because they fill up quickly in the summer, when everyone wants to be by the water. Santa Monica also enjoys convenient freeway

Los Angeles Area Accommodations

PACIFIC OCEAN

①	Lincoln Blvd. / Sepulveda Blvd. / Pacific Coast Hwy.	�91	Artesia Blvd. & Fwy. / Gardena Fwy. / Riverside Fwy.
②	Santa Monica Blvd. / Glendale Fwy.	⟨101⟩	Ventura Fwy. / Hollywood Fwy.
⑤	Golden State Fwy. / Santa Ana Fwy.	⟨105⟩	Century Fwy.
⑦⑤	Santa Monica Fwy. / San Bernardino Fwy.	⟨110⟩	Pasadena Fwy.
㉒	Garden Grove Fwy.	⟨110⟩	Harbor Fwy.
㉗	Topanga Canyon Blvd.	⟨134⟩	Ventura Fwy.
㉟	Beach Blvd. / San Gabriel Canyon Rd.	⟨170⟩	Hollywood Fwy.
㊼	Terminal Fwy. / Ocean Blvd.	⟨210⟩	Foothill Fwy.
㊵	Newport Fwy. & Blvd.	⟨405⟩	San Diego Fwy.
㊼	Orange Fwy.	⟨605⟩	San Gabriel River Fwy.
㉠	Pomona Fwy.	⟨710⟩	Long Beach Fwy.
㉙	Marina Fwy.		

LEGEND

㉒	State Highway
⟨101⟩	U.S. Highway
⟨210⟩	Interstate Highway

access to the popular tourist sights inland. Malibu and the South Bay communities (Manhattan, Hermosa, and Redondo Beaches) are more out of the way, and hence quieter.

Families might want to head to the **San Fernando Valley** to be near Universal Studios, or straight to Anaheim or Buena Park for easy access to Disneyland and Knott's Berry Farm (see chapter 14). **Pasadena** is a charming community with some unique accommodations, but it's not a good choice if you'll need to get back and forth across town.

RATES & RESERVATIONS   The hotels listed below are categorized first by area, then by price. Rates given are the rack rates for a standard room for two with private bathroom (unless otherwise noted); you can often do better. Ask about weekend packages and discounts, ACCOMMODATIONS or AARP discounts, corporate rates, family plans, and any other special rates that might be available. The prices given do not include state and city hotel taxes, which run from 12% to a whopping 17%, depending on which community you're in. Be aware that many hotels charge extra for parking (with in-and-out privileges, except where noted), and some levy heavy surcharges for telephone use.

Reservations services usually work as consolidators, sometimes garnering special deals that range from 10% to 50% off rack rates. You can still be better off speaking to the hotel directly, but these services are particularly helpful for last-minute reservations, when rooms are often scarce—or discounted. Two reputable companies serving the L.A. area (and offering online booking for some or all of their properties) are **California Reservations** (𝒞 **800/576-0003;** www. cal-res.com), which has a well-managed database of classy L.A. properties and offers 10% to 40% discounts on unsold rooms; and **Quikbook** (𝒞 **800/ 789-9887,** includes a fax on demand service; www.quikbook.com), which has access to discounted rooms at a select list of L.A. hotels in every price range, each one recommendable.

SANTA MONICA & THE BEACHES
VERY EXPENSIVE

Hotel Oceana 𝒜𝒜 *(Kids)*   Excellently located right across the street from the ocean, this all-suite hotel sits alongside low-rise, high-rent condos on a gorgeous stretch of Ocean Avenue, several blocks north of the Santa Monica hubbub. With their bright Matisse-style interiors and cushy IKEA-ish furniture, the wonderful apartment-style suites are colorful, modern, and amenity laden: Goodies run the gamut from comfy robes, multiple TVs, and CD players to full gourmet kitchens stocked with Wolfgang Puck microwavable pizzas, Häagen Dazs pints, and bottles of California merlot. The enormous size of the suites—even the studios are huge—makes the Oceana terrific for families or shares. Oceanview suites feature balconies and two-person whirlpool tubs in the mammoth baths, but don't feel the need to stretch your budget for a view, as all units sit garden style around the darling courtyard, with its cushiony chaises and cute boomerang-shaped pool. Everything is fresh, welcoming, and noninstitutional—the primary colors and playful modern style suits the beachy location perfectly, and service is excellent—so it's no wonder advertising execs and others who could stay anywhere make the Oceana their choice for long-term stays.

849 Ocean Ave. (south of Montana Ave.), Santa Monica, CA 90403. 𝒞 **800/777-0758** or 310/393-0486. Fax 310/309-2762 (reservations) or 310/458-1182. www.hoteloceana.com. 63 units. $340 studio suite; $360–$500 1-bedroom suite; $600–$700 2-bedroom suite. Rates include continental breakfast. AE, DC, DISC, MC, V. Valet parking $19. **Amenities:** Outdoor heated pool; exercise room; access to nearby health club; water-sports equipment; concierge; business center; room service from Wolfgang Puck Cafe (7am–10pm);

in-room massage; babysitting; dry-cleaning/laundry service. *In room:* A/C; TV/VCR w/ pay movies, video games, on-screen Internet access, CD players, dataport; full kitchen with minibar, fridge, coffeemaker, hair dryer, iron, safe.

Shutters on the Beach ★★★   Light and luxurious Shutters enjoys one of the city's most prized locations: directly on the beach, a block from Santa Monica Pier. Only relative newcomer Casa del Mar (directly above) can compete, but Shutters bests the Casa by attaching alfresco balconies to every guest room. The beach-cottage rooms overlooking the sand are more desirable and no more expensive than those in the towers. The views and sounds of the ocean are the most outstanding qualities of the spacious, luxuriously outfitted, Cape Cod–inspired rooms, some of which have fireplaces and/or whirlpool tubs; all have floor-to-ceiling windows that open. The elegant marble baths come with generous counter space and welcome whimsies that include waterproof radios, and toy duckies. A relaxed and elegant ambiance pervades the contemporary art–filled public spaces, which feel like the common areas of a deluxe Montauk beach house. The small swimming pool and the sunny lobby lounge overlooking the sand are two great perches for spotting the celebrities who swear by Shutters as an alternative hangout to smoggy Hollywood. One Pico, the hotel's premier restaurant, is very well regarded; the best meals at the more casual Pedals Cafe come from the wood-burning grill. Service is everything you'd expect it to be.

1 Pico Blvd., Santa Monica, CA 90405. © **800/334-9000** or 310/458-0030. Fax 310/458-4589. www. shuttersonthebeach.com. 198 units. $355–$595 double; from $750 suite. AE, DC, DISC, MC, V. Valet parking $22. **Amenities:** Well-regarded restaurant, charming upscale cafe, lobby lounge; outdoor heated pool; Jacuzzi; health club with spa services; sauna; extensive beach equipment rentals; concierge; activities desk; courtesy car; business center with secretarial services; 24-hour room service; babysitting; dry cleaning/laundry service; video library. *In room:* A/C, TV/VCR, CD player, dataport, minibar, hair dryer, iron, safe.

EXPENSIVE

Beach House at Hermosa Beach ★★ *(Finds)*   Your every need will be met at this luxurious and romantic inn—for a lot less than you'll pay at Shutters or Casa del Mar, 20 minutes to the north in Santa Monica. Sporting a cottage-y Cape Cod style that suits the on-the-sand location perfectly, the complex is comprised of beautifully designed and outfitted split-level studio suites. Every luxury unit boasts a fully outfitted, plushly furnished living room with woodburning fireplace (Duraflame logs provided) and complete entertainment center; an ultramodern microkitchen with china and flatware for four; an elevated sleeping niche area with a luxurious down-dressed king bed, a second TV, and a generous work area; an extra-large bathroom that's a study in relaxation, with extra-deep soaking tub, a separate shower, cotton robes, and Aveda products; and a furnished balcony, many of which overlook the beach. (While sofas do convert into second beds, the unit configuration is best suited to couples rather than families; more than three is too many.) Despite the summertime carnival atmosphere of the Strand, the Beach House keeps serene with double-paned windows and noise-insulated walls. The attentive staff has an easygoing attitude that suits the property perfectly. While L.A.'s city center is an easy half-hour's drive away, charming Hermosa is airport-convenient and ideal for a beachy getaway.

1300 The Strand, Hermosa Beach, CA 90254. © **888/895-4559** or 310/374-3001. Fax 310/372-2115. www. beach-house.com. 102 units. $209–$349 double. Rates include continental breakfast. Ask about midweek rates and packages. AE, DC, DISC, MC, V. Valet parking $17. **Amenities:** Full menu of in-room spa services; concierge; limited room service from nearby restaurant; dry cleaning/laundry service. *In room:* A/C, 2 TVs, stereo with 5-disc CD changer, dataport, kitchen, hair dryer, iron.

Georgian Hotel ★ *Finds*   This eight-story Art Deco delight boasts luxury comforts, loads of historic charm, and a terrific oceanview location, just across the street from Santa Monica's beach and pier, with prime Ocean Avenue dining just steps away. Established in 1933, the former Lady Windermere was popular among Hollywood's Golden Age elite; it even had its own speakeasy, rumored to have been established by Bugsy Siegel (guests now enjoy breakfast in the historic room). Today, the elegant Classical Revival architecture is beautifully, beachily accented with a well-chosen palette of bold pastels (à la Miami Beach's hotels of the same era). A wonderful veranda with cushy wicker chaises and unobstructed ocean views opens onto a light and airy lobby with comfortable seating nooks. An attended elevator leads to beautifully designed guest rooms that are an ideal blend of nostalgic style and modern-day amenities. Fittings include furnishings upholstered in gorgeous nubby textiles, all-new mattresses dressed in goose-down comforters, ceiling fans, terry robes, two-line cordless phones, fax machines, and desk-level inputs for laptop toters; suites have sleeper sofas and CD players as well. The hotel has an unobstructed coastal vista, so most rooms have at least a partial or full ocean view; the best views are above the third floor. Front rooms can be a bit noisy, so ask for a Malibu view for the best of both worlds. Back-facing rooms have city views that are more attractive than you'd expect, so nobody loses; these rooms are best for light sleepers.

1415 Ocean Ave. (between Santa Monica Blvd. and Broadway), Santa Monica, CA 90401. © **800/538-8147** or 310/395-9945. Fax 310/656-0904. www.georgianhotel.com. 84 units. $235–$310 double; from $350 suite. Rates include continental breakfast. Inquire about packages. AE, DISC, MC, V. Valet parking $16. **Amenities:** Speakeasy restaurant for breakfast, lobby bar; exercise room; concierge; activities desk; room service (6:30am–10:30pm); dry cleaning/laundry service. *In room:* TV w/ pay movies and Nintendo, dataport, fax, minibar, coffeemaker, hair dryer, iron, safe.

MODERATE

Casa Malibu ★★ *Finds*   Sitting right on its very own beach, this leftover jewel from Malibu's Golden Age doesn't try to play the sleek resort game—and we're delighted! Instead, the modest, low-rise motel sports a traditional California-beach-cottage look that's cozy and timeless.

Wrapped around a palm-studded inner courtyard brightened with well-tended flowerbeds and climbing cuppa d'oro vines, the 21 rooms are comfortable, charming, and thoughtfully outfitted. Many have been recently upgraded with Mexican-tile baths, air-conditioning (almost never needed on the cool coast), and VCRs, but even the unrenovated ones are in great shape and boast top-quality bedding and bathrobes. Depending on which one you choose, you might also find a fireplace, a kitchenette (in a half dozen or so), a CD player (in suites), a tub (instead of shower only), and/or a private deck over the sand. The upstairs Catalina Suite (Lana Turner's old hideout) has the best view, while the gorgeous Malibu Suite—the best room in the house—offers state-of-the-art pampering. More than half have ocean views, but even those facing the courtyard are quiet and offer easy beach access via wooden stairs to the private stretch of beach, which is raked smooth each morning. There's also a handsome, wind-shielded brick sundeck, which extends directly over the sand, allowing everyone to enjoy the blue Pacific even in cool months. Additional plusses include continental breakfast—fresh-brewed Starbuck's coffee and pastries from Wolfgang Puck's nearby Granita restaurant—plus the friendliest innkeepers in Los Angeles (really). Book well ahead for summer—this one's a favorite of locals and visitors alike.

22752 Pacific Coast Hwy. (about ¼ mile south of Malibu Pier), Malibu, CA 90265. © **800/831-0858** or 310/456-2219. Fax 310/456-5418. www.casamalibu.com. 21 units. $99–$169 garden- or oceanview double;

$199–$229 beachfront double; $229–$349 suite. Rates include continental breakfast. Extra person $15. AE, MC, V. Free parking. **Amenities:** Private beach; access to nearby health club; in-room massage; dry cleaning/ laundry service. *In room:* TV, dataport, fridge, coffeemaker, hair dryer, iron.

Hotel California ⭐ *Finds*   New management has completely remade this former backpackers' flophouse into a clean and welcoming hacienda-style beachfront motel, one that reflects the owner's love of surfing and California beach nostalgia. Boasting an enviable location on Ocean Avenue—right next door to the behemoth Loews—this place embodies the ocean ambience we all want from Santa Monica. The well-tended complex sits above and across an alley from the beach, but it offers excellent views and direct access to the sand via a 5-minute walk along pretty stepped path. Fully renovated in 2000, the inn offers small but comfortable rooms with brand-new furnishings, including beds with down comforters; freshly refinished woodwork on doors, floors, and decks; retiled bathrooms with all-new fixtures; and lovingly tended landscaping. Five 1-bedroom suites also have kitchenettes and pullout sofas that make them great for families or longer stays; all rooms have mini-fridges and ceiling fans. The suites and some rooms have a partially obstructed ocean view. A handful of rooms have showers only in the bathrooms, so be sure to request a room with a tub from the friendly front-desk staff if it matters to you. *Tip:* Pay a few bucks extra for a courtyard view, as the cheapest rooms face the parking lot and noisy Ocean Avenue.

1670 Ocean Ave. (south of Colorado Ave.), Santa Monica, CA 90401. �C **866/571-0000** or 310/393-2363. Fax 310/393-1063. www.hotelca.com. 26 units. $135–$295 double or suite. AE, DISC, MC, V. Self-parking $9. **Amenities:** Jacuzzi; activities desk; discount car-rental desk; dry cleaning/laundry service; high-speed Internet access, fax/copier, and coffeemaker in front office. *In room:* TV/VCR, dataport, fridge, hair dryer, iron, safe.

Hotel Shangri-La   Perched right on Ocean Avenue overlooking the Pacific, in a high-rent residential neighborhood just 2 blocks from Third Street Promenade shopping and dining, the seven-story Shangri-La has a great location. Built in 1939, the hotel sports an ultra-Moderne exterior and Art Deco interiors to match. The laminated furnishings are downright ugly and the hotel is decidedly low-tech, but considering the location, size, and comfort of these rooms—not to mention the free parking—the Shangri-La is a very good deal. The management is constantly making improvements; on my last visit, the exterior hallways that overlook the large rear courtyard and lead to the rooms had been freshly retiled. Guest rooms, which are mostly studio suites (most with kitchenettes, all with fridges), are extremely spacious, and most offer unencumbered ocean views. Bathrooms are small and simple but clean. The 2-bedroom/2-bath suites are spectacular bargain for large families. Just across the street is a gorgeous stretch of Palisades Park, which overlooks the beach and offers the coast's finest sunset views.

1301 Ocean Ave. (at Arizona Ave.), Santa Monica, CA 90401. ℂ **800/345-STAY** or 310/394-2791. Fax 310/ 451-3351. www.shangrila-hotel.com. 55 units. $160–$170 studio; from $205 1-bedroom suite; from $330 2-bedroom suite. Rates include continental breakfast and afternoon tea. Inquire about 10% discount for AAA members. AE, DC, DISC, MC, V. Free parking. **Amenities:** Small oceanview exercise room; dry cleaning/ laundry service; coin-op laundry. *In room:* A/C, TV, dataport, fridge, hair dryer, safe.

Marina del Rey Hotel   Beautifully situated on a pier jutting into the harbor, this modest low-rise hotel is bounded on three sides by the world's largest manmade marina; in fact, location is its best feature. The property is peaceful and quiet—the only noise you're likely to hear is the soothing metallic clang of sailboat rigging. Guest rooms are motel-basic but perfectly fine, with contemporary furnishings and a nautical nods here and there; a renovation, in the works at press time, should up the ante a bit. Most units have balconies or patios as well as harbor views; ask for one overlooking the main channel for the best view of the constant parade of boats. As long as you snare a rate below $170 or so, you're in good-value territory; otherwise, book elsewhere.

13534 Bali Way (west of Lincoln Blvd.), Marina del Rey, CA 90292. ✆ 800/882-4000 or 310/301-1000. Fax 310/301-8167. www.marinadelreyhotel.com. 157 units. $130–$220 double; from $300 suite. Check for seasonal specials and packages (as low as $119 at press time). AE, DC, MC, V. Free parking. **Amenities:** Bar and grill with marina views and alfresco seating; small heated outdoor pool; access to nearby health club; watersports equipment rentals; concierge; activities desk; car-rental desk; room service (6am–10:30pm); coin-op laundry. *In room:* A/C, TV w/ pay movies and video games, dataport, hair dryer, iron.

INEXPENSIVE

Best Western Marina Pacific Hotel & Suites ✷ 𝑲𝒊𝒅𝒔   This bright, fresh, newly renovated 4-story motel is a haven of smart value just off the rollicking Venice Boardwalk. A simple, contemporary lobby and new elevator lead to spacious rooms brightened with beachy colors and brand-new everything, including chain-standard furnishings, fridges, and two-line phones. The suites are absolutely terrific for families; they boast fully outfitted kitchens with microwave and dishwasher, dining areas, pullout sofas, and fireplaces, plus a connecting door that can form a well-priced two-bedroom, two-bath suite. Photos of local scenes and rock-'n'-roll legends, plus works by local artists, lend the public spaces a wonderful local vibe, and many rooms have at least partial ocean views. Additional incentives include a complimentary coffee-and-danish continental breakfast, free local shuttle service, and secured parking. Stay elsewhere, though, if you need a lot in the way of service or if you won't relish the party-hearty human carnival of Venice Beach (Santa Monica is generally quieter and more refined). Check both the Best Western reservations line and the direct number for the best rates.

1697 Pacific Ave. (at 17th Ave.), Venice, CA 90291. ✆ 800/780-7234 (Best Western reservations), 800/421-8151 (direct), or 310/452-1111. Fax 310/452-5479. www.mphotel.com or www.bestwestern.com. 88 units. $119–$159 double; $169–$249 suite. Rates include continental breakfast. Children 12 and under stay free in parents' room. Ask about AAA, senior, and other discounts; weekly and monthly rates also available. Extra person $10. AE, DC, DIS, MC, V. Self-parking $5–$10 (depending on season). **Amenities:** Free shuttle to Santa Monica and Marina del Rey; dry cleaning/laundry service. *In room:* A/C, TV, dataport, fridge, coffeemaker, hair dryer.

Cal Mar Hotel Suites ✷ 𝑽𝒂𝒍𝒖𝒆   Tucked away in a beautiful residential neighborhood just 2 blocks from the ocean, this garden apartment complex is lovingly cared for and delivers a lot of bang for your vacation buck. Each unit is an apartment-style suite with a living room with a pullout sofa, a full-size kitchen, and a separate bedroom; most are spacious enough to accommodate four in comfort. The building was constructed in the 1950s with an eye for quality (attractive tilework, large closets). While the furnishings aren't luxurious—they may remind you of a college-era dorm or apartment—and fixtures are from a couple of decades past, everything is well-kept and every need is provided for. It's easy to be comfortable here for stays of a week or more. The staff is attentive and courteous, which helps account for the high rate of repeat guests. The garden courtyard boasts a nice swimming pool and plenty of chaises for lounging. If you can afford it, pay a bit extra for one of the master suites, since the handful of efficiencies don't offer the same value, and the standard suites tend to be noisy.

220 California Ave., Santa Monica, CA 90403. ✆ 800/776-6007 or 310/395-5555. Fax 310/451-1111. www.calmarhotel.com. 36 units. $109–$169 suite. Extra person $10. Children under 10 stay free in parents' room. AE, DC, DISC, MC, V. Free parking. **Amenities:** Heated outdoor pool; coin-op laundry. *In room:* TV, full kitchen, fridge, coffeemaker, hair dryer, iron.

Sea Shore Motel ★★ *Value* Located in the heart of Santa Monica's best dining and shopping action, this small, friendly, family-run motel is the bargain of the beach. The Sea Shore is such a well-kept secret that most denizens of stylish Main Street are unaware of the incredible accommodations value in their midst. A recent total upgrade of the property—furnishings, fixtures, exterior—has made the entire place feel fresh and new. Arranged around a parking courtyard, rooms are small and unremarkable; but the conscientious management has done a nice job with them, installing attractive terra-cotta floor tiles, granite countertops, and conveniences like voice mail. Boasting a sitting room and microwave, the suite is a phenomenal deal; book it as far in advance as possible. With a full slate of restaurants out the front door and the Santa Monica Pier and beach just a couple of blocks away, the a terrific bargain base for exploring the sandy side of the city. A cute deli is attached, selling morning muffins and sandwiches and homemade soup at lunchtime, and a laundromat is next door. A real find!

2637 Main St. (south of Ocean Park Blvd.), Santa Monica, CA 90405. ☎ 310/392-2787. Fax 310/392-5167. www.seashoremotel.com. 20 units. $75–$95 double; $100–$120 suite. Children under 12 stay free in parents' room. Midweek discounts available. Extra person $5. AE, DISC, MC, V. Free parking. Pets accepted for $10-per-night fee. **Amenities:** Deli; coin-op laundry. *In room:* TV, dataport, fridge.

NEAR LAX

If you have an early-morning flight and you need an airport hotel, the **Westin Los Angeles Airport**, 5400 W. Century Blvd. (☎ **800/WESTIN-1** or 310/ 216-5858) is a cut above the rest with patented Westin "Heavenly Beds." Two good, moderately priced choices are **Sheraton Gateway Hotel**, 6101 W. Century Blvd., near Sepulveda Boulevard (☎ **800/325-3535** or 310/642-1111), a comfortable, California-style hotel that literally overlooks the runway; and the **Marriott Los Angeles Airport**, 5855 Century Blvd. (☎ **800/228-9290** or 310/ 641-5700), a reliable choice for travelers on-the-fly.

If you're looking for an inexpensive option, try the **Travelodge at LAX**, 5547 W. Century Blvd. (☎ **800/421-3939** or 310/649-4000), an otherwise standard member of the reliable chain with a surprisingly beautiful tropical garden surrounding the pool area.

L.A.'S WESTSIDE & BEVERLY HILLS
VERY EXPENSIVE

Beverly Hills Hotel & Bungalows ★★★ Behind this famous facade (pictured on the Eagles' *Hotel California*) lies the star-studded haven where legends are made, and many were: The "Pink Palace" was center stage for both deal- and star-making in Hollywood's golden days. Today, current stars and industry hotshots can still be found lazing around the Olympic-size pool, which Katharine Hepburn once dove into fully clothed, and digging into Dutch apple pancakes in the iconic Polo Lounge. Following a $100 million restoration a few years back, the hotel's grand lobby and impeccably landscaped grounds still retain their over-the-top glory, while the lavish guest rooms boast every state-of-the-art luxury, including two-line phones, CD players, and extra-large bathrooms with double Grecian marble sinks and TVs. The best original touches have been retained as well, like butler service at the touch of a button. Many rooms feature secluded private patios, whirlpool tubs, kitchens, and/or dining rooms. The bungalows are more luxurious than ever—and who knows whom you'll have as a neighbor?

9641 Sunset Blvd. (at Rodeo Dr.), Beverly Hills, CA 90210. ☎ 800/283-8885 or 310/276-2251. Fax 310/ 281-2905. www.beverlyhillshotel.com. 203 units. $335–$395 double; from $725 suite or bungalow. AE, DC, MC, V. Parking $23. Pets accepted in bungalows only. **Amenities:** 3 restaurants (Polo Lounge, Fountain Coffee Shop, alfresco Cabana Club Cafe), 2 lounges (Sunset Lounge for high tea and cocktails, bar in Polo

L.A.'s Westside & Beverly Hills

DINING ◆
The Apple Pan **7**
Bombay Cafe **5**
Chaya Brasserie **11**
Four Oaks **3**
Hard Rock Cafe **12**
Jozu **20**

Kate Mantilini **10**
La Serenata Gourmet **6**
Lawry's The Prime Rib **15**
Lucques **21**
Matsuhisa **16**
Maui Beach Cafe **4**

Mimosa **19**
Nyala **14**
Spago **9**
Versailles **13**

ATTRACTIONS ●

The Getty Center **2**
Los Angeles County Museum of Art **18**
Museum of Tolerance **8**
Pacific Design Center **23**

Peterson Automotive Museum **17**
Rudolph M. Schindler House **22**
Skirball Cultural Center **1**

Lounge); Olympic-size outdoor heated pool, fitness center; Jacuzzi; concierge; car-rental desk; courtesy limo; business center with computers; salon; 24-hour room service; in-room or poolside massage; babysitting; dry cleaning/laundry service; video rentals. *In room:* A/C, TV/VCR, CD player, dataport, fax/copier/scanner, minibar, hair dryer, safe.

Century Plaza Hotel & Spa ☆☆

This mammoth Westin hotel sits in the heart of Century City, on ten of L.A.'s most centrally located acres. It's so close to film and TV's nerve center that it has become the de facto home-away-from-home for countless rank-and-file industry execs and creative types. The hotel is also a natural for conventions and meetings, so there's always something going on here.

Despite the almost-foreboding scale, I love this place. The recently renovated guest rooms are much more beautiful than you'd expect, with designer furnishings, gorgeous warm-hued textiles, attractive contemporary prints, big closets with terry robes, and almost universally impressive views. The beautiful Italian-tile-and-glass bathrooms are some of L.A.'s best. Westin's celestial Heavenly Bed—touted as "ten layers of heaven"—really is the best hotel bed in the business, and these add cushioned headboards as an inspired finishing touch. Guest Office rooms add a fax/printer/copier, an ergonomic desk chair, glare-free task lighting, a coffee maker, late checkout, and continental breakfast for a few extra dollars.

Opening in mid-2001, the 30,000-square-foot, Asian-inspired Spa Mystique is set to L.A.'s finest spa, without peer in any sector. Its unparalleled features include an epic menu of traditional and Eastern treatments, impressive hydrotherapy features (including two Japanese *furo* pools), salon services, and a 21st-century fitness center with cardio machines that let you surf the web as you pump, plus a meditation garden and alfresco spa cafe. Also on its way is Breeze, the brand-new restaurant and raw bar designed by architect-of-the-moment Stephen Jacobs.

2025 Ave. of the Stars (south of Santa Monica Blvd.), Century City, CA 90067. ☎ **800/WESTIN-1** or 310/277-2000. Fax 310/551-3355. www.westin.com. 724 units. $350–$415 double; from $500 suite. Weekend, off-season, and other discounts available (from $279 at press time). AE, DC, DISC, MC, V. Valet parking $23, self-parking $15. Pets accepted with $50 deposit. **Amenities:** Brand-new California-style restaurant and lounge, spa cafe, lobby bar; outdoor heated pool; brand-new 30,000-square-foot Spa Mystique with state-of-the-art health club; Jacuzzi; sauna; Westin Kids Club; concierge; Hertz car-rental desk; business center; salon; 24-hour room service; in-room massage; dry cleaning/laundry service. *In room:* A/C, TV w/ pay movies, dataport, stocked minibar, coffeemaker, hair dryer, iron, safe.

Four Seasons Hotel Los Angeles at Beverly Hills ☆☆

This intimate-feeling 16-story hotel attracts a mix of A-list jet-setters justifiably loyal to the Four Seasons brand and an L.A. showbiz crowd who cherish the hotel as an après-event gathering place. The small marbled lobby is anchored by an always-stunning floral extravaganza, and lovely gardens will help you forget you're in the heart of the city. Four Seasons operates terrific hotels, with a concierge that's famously well connected and impeccable service that really goes the distance. Guest rooms are sumptuously furnished in traditional style and pastel hues. Luxuries include custom extra-stuffed Sealy mattresses with heavenly linens and pillows (which many guests fall so in love with that they order one for home), VCRs and CD players (suites have DVD players as well), desk-level inputs with high-speed connectivity for laptop toters, elegant marble baths with vanity TV, and French doors leading to private balconies. Room rates rise with the elevator, so bargain hunters sacrifice the view; ask for a corner room to get extra space at no additional cost.

In 2000, the hotel added a petite but first-rate full-service spa. The wonderful, view-endowed fourth-floor deck features a very nice lap pool, a poolside grill, and a fabulous glass-walled fitness center. Gardens is a terrific California-French restaurant that's often overlooked by locals.

300 S. Doheny Dr. (at Burton Way), Los Angeles, CA 90048. © 800/819-5053, 800/332-3442, or 310/273-2222. Fax 310/859-3824. www.fourseasons.com. 285 units. $370–$470 double; from $600 suite. AE, DC, DISC, MC, V. Valet parking $21, free self-parking. Pets under 15 lbs. welcomed (no charge). **Amenities:** Highly regarded restaurant, lounge, poolside grill; lovely rooftop heated pool; glass-enclosed exercise room; new full-service spa; Jacuzzi; children's program; concierge; courtesy limo within 5-mile radius; business center; 24-hour room service; in-room massage; dry cleaning/laundry service. *In room:* A/C, TV/VCR w/ pay movies, CD player, dataport and high-speed connectivity, minibar, hair dryer, iron, safe.

EXPENSIVE

Avalon Hotel ★★ *(Finds)*   The first style-conscious boutique hotel on the L.A. scene, this marvelous mid-century–inspired gem in the heart of Beverly Hills still leads the pack. Boasting a soothing sherbet-hued palette and classic Atomic Age furnishings—Eames cabinets, Heywood-Wakefield chairs, Nelson bubble lamps—mixed with smart custom designs, every room looks as if it could star in a *Metropolitan Home* photo spread. But fashion doesn't forsake function at this beautifully designed hotel, which boasts enough luxury comforts and amenities to please design-blind travelers, too.

The property is comprised of the former Beverly-Carlton (seen on *I Love Lucy* and once home to Marilyn Monroe and Mae West) as well as two neighboring 1950s-era apartment houses. The main building is the hub of a chic but low-key scene, but I prefer the quieter Canon building, where many of the units have kitchenettes and/or furnished terraces. No matter which one you end up in, you'll find a restful cocoon with extras that include a well-stocked fridge, terry bathrobes, and top-of-the-line bedding that includes a cozy, nubby throw. You'll also have easy access to the sunny courtyard with its retro-hip amoeba-shaped pool, the fitness room, and the groovy *Jetsons*-style restaurant and bar, which shakes a terrific green apple martini. Service is friendlier than you'll find in other style-minded hotels.

9400 W. Olympic Blvd. (at Beverly Dr.), Beverly Hills, CA 90212. © 800/535-4715 or 310/277-5221. Fax 310/277-4928. www.avalon-hotel.com. 88 units. $199–$289 double; from $249 junior or 1-bedroom suite. Extra person $25. AE, DC, MC, V. Valet parking $17. **Amenities:** Hip restaurant and lounge; courtyard pool; concierge; 24-hour room service; in-room massage; dry cleaning/laundry service. *In room:* A/C, TV/VCR w/ pay movies and video games, CD player, dataport, fax, minibar, coffeemaker, hair dryer, iron, safe.

Hyatt West Hollywood   An extensive renovation of this legendary 13-story Sunset Strip hotel erased any last remnants of its former debauched life as the rock 'n' roll "Riot Hyatt." It doesn't even look like other Hyatts, since the management eschewed the standard corporate decor and contracted locally; the end result is a stylish cross between the clean black-and-white geometrics of a 1930s movie set and a Scandinavian birch-and-ebony aesthetic. While not as fancy as the Mondrian across the street, it's not as expensive or snobbish either. Rooms have beautiful city or hillside views (about half have balconies), but stay away from front-facing rooms on the lower floors—too close to noisy Sunset Boulevard. Beyond the smart decor, the standard rooms bear generic but just-fine comforts. Some rooms have coffeemakers (in the works for all rooms at press time), and fridges are available upon request. Suites have VCRs, CD players, wetbars, and fridges, plus a groovy tropical aquarium built into the wall stocked with colorful temporary pets, which make the suites worth the extra bucks all by themselves. The rooftop pool is a real plus, offering cushy lounge chairs and a killer perch for peeping into the luxury homes that dot the hill behind the hotel; other brand-new features include a well-equipped exercise room and a new Italian bistro and bar.

8401 Sunset Blvd. (at Kings Rd., 2 blocks east of La Cienega Blvd.), West Hollywood, CA 90069. ℂ **800/ 233-1234** or 323/656-1234. Fax 323/650-7024. 262 units. $210–$240 double; from $325 suite. Check for discounted weekend, AAA, and senior rates (as low as $155 at press time). Children stay free in parents' room. Extra person $25. AE, DC, DISC, MC, V. Valet parking $20, self-parking $10–$15. **Amenities:** Indoor/outdoor Italian bistro, stylish bar, coffee/pastry kiosk in lobby; rooftop heated pool with chaises and terrific views; brand-new, state-of-the-art exercise room; concierge; business center; room service (from 6am–midnight); dry cleaning/laundry service; executive-level rooms. *In room:* A/C, TV w/ pay movies, dataport, hair dryer, iron, safe.

Le Montrose Suite Hotel ✦ *Value*   Nobody pays rack at this terrific all-suite hotel, which offers money-saving specials of every stripe for travelers who want more than a standard room for their accommodations dollars. Nestled on a quiet residential street just 2 blocks from the red-hot Sunset Strip, remarkably cozy Le Montrose features large split-level studio and one-bedroom apartments that feel more like comfortable, upscale condos than hotel rooms. Each contemporary-styled suite has a sizable living room with gas fireplace, a dining area, a comfortable sleeping nook (or dedicated bedroom), and a very nice bathroom. Executive and 1-bedroom suites have unstocked kitchenettes (better suited to takeout than actually cooking for yourself). The 2-bedrooms are a great deal for families or sharing friends. You have to go up to the roof for anything resembling a view, but once you're up there, you can swim in the pool, soak in the Jacuzzi, or brush up on your tennis game. This place is a favorite for long-term stays among the music and TV crowd, so don't be surprised if you spot a famous face in the pleasant Library restaurant during the breakfast hour. A $4 million renovation, spiffing up the already very nice digs, should be complete by the time you arrive.

900 Hammond St., West Hollywood, CA 90069. ℂ **800/776-0666** or 310/855-1115. Fax 310/657-9192. www.lemontrose.com. 132 units. $295–$575 suite. Money-saving deals abound; AAA, AARP, seasonal, and weekend rates as low as $159 at press time; breakfast (from $199), car, and Disneyland and Universal Studios–inclusive packages also available. AE, DC, DISC, MC, V. Valet and self-parking $18. Pets accepted with a $100-per-pet nonrefundable fee. **Amenities:** Continental restaurant; outdoor heated pool with Jacuzzi; lighted tennis court, exercise room with sauna; complimentary bicycles; concierge; Budget car-rental desk; business center; secretarial services; 24-hour room service; dry cleaning/laundry service; coin-op laundry; executive-level rooms; DVD and CD libraries. *In room:* A/C, TV/VCR w/ pay movies, Nintendo, Internet access, DVD, CD player, fax/copier/scanner, dataport and high-speed connectivity, minibar, coffeemaker, hair dryer, iron, safe.

Wyndham Bel Age Hotel ✦✦ *Kids*   This high-rise all-suite hotel is one of West Hollywood's best. The Bel Age has it all: huge, amenity-laden suites, excellent service, a terrific rooftop sundeck with pool and whirlpool, and an A-1 location just 1½ blocks off the Sunset Strip, but removed from the congestion and noise. What's more, thanks to an excellent art collection (assembled by the hotel's original owners) that fills both the public spaces and guest rooms, the hotel has significantly more personality than your average chain hotel.

Accommodations hardly get better for the money. The monster-size suites boast brand-new contemporary decor with a few classic touches and a serious, soothing palette of navy, burgundy, and gray. Selected to suit every need— including those of families and business travelers—luxuries include brand-new pillowtop mattresses with cushioned headboards and plush bedding, a sleeper sofa in the living area that opens into a second king bed, a wet bar, and an excellent workdesk with an ergonomically correct Herman Miller desk chair. The big bathrooms boast generous counter space and robes. The best rooms face south; on a clear day, you can see all the way to the Pacific. Make reservations before you leave home for a special meal at the Franco-Russian Diaghilev. The pretty Brasserie offers good Cal-Tuscan cuisine and top-flight jazz in the adjoining bar.

1020 N. San Vicente Blvd. (between Sunset and Santa Monica Blvds.), West Hollywood, CA 90069. © **800-WYNDHAM** or 310/854-1111. Fax 310/854-0926. www.wyndham.com. 200 units. $199–$339 suite (accommodates up to 4 at no extra charge). Ask about weekend rates, holiday specials, and discounts on longer stays. AE, DC, DISC, MC, V. Valet parking $18. **Amenities:** 2 restaurants (1 elegant Russian, 1 bar and grill with live entertainment); rooftop outdoor heated pool and Jacuzzi; exercise room; concierge; salon; room service (6am–2am); dry cleaning/laundry service. In room: A/C, TV/VCR w/ pay movies, Sony PlayStation, on-screen Internet access, CD player, dataport and high-speed connectivity, minibar, coffeemaker, hair dryer, iron.

MODERATE

Beverly Hills Inn   This value-conscious hotel is a real coup for those who want a gold-plated address at a moderate price. The A-1 location—just south of prime Beverly Hills shopping territory—premium comforts, and across-the-board quality add up to one of Beverly Hills' best values. The 46-room hotel is attractively done in a contemporary English garden style and boasts extras that usually cost more, like a good fitness room with dry sauna, an eager-to-please staff, and a small but well-tended pool. Freebies galore—covered parking, a generous continental breakfast spread, evening fruit and cheese—all add up to a very good deal in a high-rent neighborhood. A 2001 renovation should be complete by the time you arrive, and should increase the good value even more.

125 S. Spalding Dr., Beverly Hills, CA 90212. © **800/463-4466** or 310/278-0303. Fax 310/278-1728. www.innatbeverlyhills.com. 46 units. $179–$259 double; from $259 suite. Rates include full breakfast, plus afternoon fruit and cheese. AE, DC, MC, V. Free parking. **Amenities:** Heated outdoor pool; exercise room with sauna; tour desk; dry cleaning/laundry service. In room: A/C, TV, dataport, fridge, hair dryer, iron.

Carlyle Inn ★★ *Value*   Tucked away on an uneventful stretch of Robertson Boulevard just south of Beverly Hills, this four-story inn is one of L.A.'s best mid-priced finds. Making the most of a small lot, architects have created an attractive interior courtyard, which almost every room faces, that gives the property a feeling of openness and serenity that most others in this price range lack—not to mention good outdoor space for enjoying the free breakfast or afternoon munchies at umbrella-covered cafe tables on nice days. The well-planned, contemporary guest rooms are fitted with recessed lighting, Art Deco–inspired furnishings, new firm bedding, and well-framed architectural monoprints. Suites have a pullout sofa but are only slightly larger than standard rooms, so families may be better off in a double-double or connecting rooms. The conscientious manager keeps everything in racing form. The hotel's primary drawback is that it lacks views; curtains must remain drawn at all times to maintain any sense of privacy. Still, it doesn't seem to bother the 90% repeat clientele, who know good value when they find it.

1119 S. Robertson Blvd. (between Pico and Olympic Blvds.), Los Angeles, CA 90035. © **800/322-7595** or 310/275-4445. Fax 310/859-0496. www.carlyle-inn.com. 32 units. $120–$209 double; from $140 suite. Rates include full buffet breakfast and weekday afternoon hors d'oeuvres. Management will deal, so ask for discounts. AE, DC, DISC, MC, V. Parking $10. **Amenities:** Exercise room; Jacuzzi; dry cleaning/laundry service. In room: A/C, TV/VCR, minibar, coffeemaker, iron, safe.

Holiday Inn Brentwood/Bel-Air   This L.A. landmark is the last of a vanishing breed of circular hotels from the 1960s and 1970s. It's perched beside the city's busiest freeway a short hop from the popular Getty Center and centrally located between the beaches, Beverly Hills, and the San Fernando Valley. Completely refurbished in 2000, each pie-shaped room boasts a private balcony and double-paned glass to keep the freeway noise out; little extras like Nintendo games, in-room bottled water, and great views add panache to otherwise-unre-markable chain-style accommodations. You'll also enjoy a million-dollar 360° view from the hotel's top-floor Brentwood Terrace restaurant, which serves a casual, please-all cuisine; the adjoining cocktail lounge features live piano nightly. Popular with older travelers and museum groups, the hotel provides complimentary pick-up and drop-off service to the Getty Center and Westwood.

170 N. Church Lane (at intersection of Sunset Blvd. and I-405), Los Angeles, CA 90049. ⓒ **800/HOLIDAY** or 310/476-6411. Fax 310/472-1157. www.holiday-inn.com/brentwood-bel. 211 units. $149–$189 double; from $275 suite. Inquire about AAA and AARP discounts, breakfast packages, and "Great Rates," often as low as $119. AE, DC, DISC, MC, V. Valet parking $10, self-parking $8. Small pets accepted for $50-per-pet nonrefundable fee. **Amenities:** Rooftop restaurant and lounge, heated outdoor pool and Jacuzzi; exercise room; concierge; activities desk; free shuttle to Getty Center and within a 3-mile radius; room service (6am–10pm); dry cleaning/laundry service; coin-op laundry. *In room:* A/C, TV w/ pay movies and Nintendo, dataport, coffeemaker, hair dryer, iron.

Maison 140 𝒜𝒜 *(Finds)* Tucked away on an unassuming block just behind the Peninsula, this darling new hotel is the place to stay for *Wallpaper*-reading style hounds with edgy tastes and mid-range budgets. By breaking just about every design rule in the book, designer Kelly Wearstler has created a dazzling East-meets-West-meets-mod *pied à terre* that's so audacious in its surprises that it bursts with brazen sexuality. Think you didn't like hot pink and orange? Think again—because you'll love it here.

Narrow black-on-black hallways and a miniscule mirrored elevator with a zebra-print rug lead to the guest rooms, which come in a your choice of rule-busting palettes. Autumn ochres and soothing grays is the most sedate choice, the aforementioned pinks and oranges the wildest (and, I think, the most pleasing). The decor is a striking blend of Franco-Chinese-patterned textiles and wallpapers, original 1930s details juxtaposed with 1960s-modern touches (including generous use of Lucite), and individual accent pieces that are likely to be from Wearstler's fabulous collection of silk-shaded Asian figure lamps. Luxuries that surpass the price category include Frette linens, two-line phones, VCRs, CD players, and cotton robes. Unfortunately, many of the rooms are frighteningly small. The space is designed for maximum advantage—platform beds have drawers below, TVs are wall-mounted—but those who like to spread out will not be soothed. Some bathrooms are tiny and have showers only, but all have been beautifully renovated. If you want the high style without the squeeze, book a roomy Grande King, which even have space for a good-sized worktable.

140 S Lasky Dr. (just south of Wilshire Blvd.), Beverly Hills, CA 90212. ⓒ **800/432-5444** or 310/281-4000. Fax 310/281-4001. www.maison140.com. 45 units. $140–$215 double. Rates include continental breakfast. AE, DC, MC, V. Parking $15. **Amenities:** Sexy cocktail lounge; pool and fitness privileges at Avalon Hotel; concierge; in-room massage; dry cleaning/laundry service. *In room:* A/C, TV/VCR, CD player, dataport and high-speed connectivity, minibar, hair dryer, iron, safe.

The Standard 𝒜𝒜 If Andy Warhol had gone into the hotel business (which he no doubt would have, if he had arrived on the scene a few decades later), the Standard would've been the end result. Designed to appeal to the under-35 "It crowd," Andre Balazs's swank West Hollywood neo-motel is sometimes silly, sometimes brilliant, and always provocative (not to mention crowded!). It's a scene worthy of its Sunset Strip location: Shag carpeting on the lobby ceiling, blue Astroturf around the swimming pool, a DJ spinning ambient sounds while a performance artist showing more skin than talent poses in a display case behind the check-in desk—this place is definitely left of center.

The good news is that that Standard is more than just a pretty (wild) face. Constructed from the fine bones of a vintage 1962 motel, it boasts comfortably sized rooms outfitted with cobalt-blue indoor-outdoor carpeting, silver beanbag chairs, safety-orange tiles in the bathrooms, and Warhol's Poppy-print curtains, plus private balconies and minibars whose contents include goodies like sake, condoms, and animal crackers. Look past the retro clutter and often-raucous party scene, and you'll find a level of service more often associated with hotels costing twice as much. On the downside, the cheapest rooms face noisy Sunset Boulevard, no rooms are set aside for non-smokers, and the relentless scene can get tiring if you're not into it.

Set to open in late 2001 is **Downtown Standard,** 550 S. Flower St. (© **213/ 892-8080**), which will bring a similar dose of Generation Y-targeted cheap-cool style and tattoo-wearing, convention-busting attitude to suit-jacketed downtown L.A.

8300 Sunset Blvd. (at Sweetzer Ave.), West Hollywood, CA 90069. © **323/650-9090.** Fax 323/650-2820. www.standardhotel.com. 140 units. $95–$225 double; from $650 suite. AE, DC, DISC, MC, V. Valet parking $18. Pets under 30 lbs. accepted for $100-per-pet fee. **Amenities:** 24-hour hipster coffee shop, poolside cafe, bar/lounge; outdoor heated pool; access to nearby health club; concierge; barbershop; 24-hour room service; in-room massage; dry cleaning/laundry service. *In room:* A/C, TV/VCR w/ pay movies, CD player, dataport and high-speed connectivity, minibar.

INEXPENSIVE

Beverly Laurel Motor Hotel *(Value)*   The Beverly Laurel is a great choice for wallet-watching travelers who want a central-to-everything location and a room with a dash more style than your average cheap motel. Overlooking the parking lot, the budget-basic but well-kept rooms are smartened up with diamond-print spreads and eye-catching artwork; other nice features include a minifridge, microwave, and ample closet space, and you can have a large kitchenette for an extra tenspot. The postage-stamp-sized outdoor pool is a little public for care-free sunbathing, but does the job on hot summer days. Best of all is the motel's own excellent hipster coffee shop, Swingers (nobody serves burgers and malts better); you may even spot your favorite alt-rocker tucking into a 3pm breakfast in the vinyl booth next to yours.

8018 Beverly Blvd. (between La Cienega Blvd. and Fairfax Ave.), Los Angeles, CA 90048. © **800/962-3824** or 323/651-2441. Fax 323/651-5225. 52 units. $79–$84 double; $89 double with kitchen. AAA and senior discounts may be available. AE, DC, MC, V. Free parking. **Amenities:** Heated outdoor pool. *In room:* A/C, TV, dataport, fridge, hair dryer.

Hotel Del Capri *(Finds) (Kids)*   This well-located and well-kept Westwood hotel/motel is hugely popular with returning guests, thanks to spacious rooms, a helpful staff, and retro pricing. There are two parts to the Eisenhower-era property: a four-story tower and a charming two-story motel with white louver shutters and delightful flowering vines, whose units surround a pleasant pool. All guest rooms are clean and well cared for, but the decidedly discount decor won't be winning any style awards, and the basic bathrooms could use some upgrading (not to mention quieter fans). Still, every one is comfortable and well worth the money; free continental breakfast (delivered to your room) and free parking make a good value even better. The most notable room feature is electrically adjustable beds, a novel touch; you'll have to request hair dryers and irons if you want them. More than half of the units are 1- or 2-bedroom suites with kitchenettes, some of which have whirlpool tubs. Nothing is within walking distance of the ritzy high-rise neighborhood, but it's hard to be more freeway-convenient or centrally located. No room service, but nearly 50 restaurants will deliver.

10587 Wilshire Blvd. (at Westholme Ave.), Los Angeles, CA 90024. ✆ **800/44-HOTEL** or 310/474-3511. Fax 310/470-9999. www.hoteldelcapri.com. 77 units. $110–$125 double; from $135 suite. Rates include continental breakfast ($1 gratuity). Price breaks for almost everybody—AAA members, seniors, UCLA grads, military members, and more—so be sure to ask. Extra person $10. AE, DC, MC, V. Free parking. **Amenities:** Nice pool with deck chairs; tour desk; free shuttle service to UCLA, Westwood, Beverly Hills, and Century City with advance notice; dry cleaning/laundry service; coin-op laundry. *In room:* A/C, TV, adjustable beds.

HOLLYWOOD
MODERATE

Hollywood Roosevelt ✿ *Kids*   This 12-story movie-city landmark is located on an unabashedly touristy but no longer seedy section of Hollywood Boulevard, across from Mann's Chinese Theatre and just down the street from the Walk of Fame. This Tinseltown legend—host to the first Academy Awards, not to mention a few famous-name ghosts—is a great value because you get an A-1 location and buckets of Hollywood history, plus comforts and services that usually cost twice the price. The rooms are typical of chain hotels, and far less appealing than the exquisitely restored public areas; still, they're perfectly comfortable, and double-doubles suit small families just fine. Those on the upper floors have unbeatable skyline views, while cabana rooms have a balcony or patio overlooking the Olympic-size pool (whose mural was painted by David Hockney) and poolside bar. The specialty suites are named after stars who stayed in them during the glory days; some have grand verandas. The Cinegrill supper club draws locals with live jazz and top-notch cabaret entertainment.

7000 Hollywood Blvd., Hollywood, CA 90028. ✆ **800/950-7667** or 323/466-7000. Fax 323/462-8056. www.hollywoodroosevelt.com. 330 units. $149–$219 double; from $239 suite. Children under 18 stay free. Ask about AAA, senior, business, government, and other discounted rates (as low as $89 at press time). AE, DC, DISC, MC, V. Valet parking $12. **Amenities:** California/Continental restaurant, cocktail lounge, legendary Cinegrill cabaret and nightclub, coffee bar, poolside bar; outdoor pool and Jacuzzi; exercise room; concierge; activities desk; Thrifty car-rental desk; business center; room service (6am–11pm); babysitting; dry cleaning/laundry service; executive-level rooms. *In room:* A/C; TV w/ pay movies, video games, and on-screen Internet access; dataport; minibar; coffeemaker; hair dryer; iron; safe.

INEXPENSIVE

Best Western Hollywood Hills Hotel ✿   Location is a big selling point for this family-owned (since 1948) member of the reliable Best Western chain: It's just off U.S. 101 (the Hollywood Freeway), a Metro Line stop just 3 blocks away means easy car-free access to Universal Studios, and the famed Hollywood and Vine intersection is just a walk away. The walls showcase images from the golden age of movies, and the front desk offers an endless variety of arranged tours. Rooms are plain and clean but lack warmth—outer walls are painted cinder block, and closets are hidden behind institutional metal accordion doors. Still, management is constantly striving to improve the hotel, and all rooms have a refrigerator, a coffeemaker, a microwave, and free movies. Rooms in the back building are my favorites, as they sit well back from busy Franklin Avenue, face the gleaming blue-tiled, heated outdoor pool, and have an attractive view of the neighboring hillside. The newish bathrooms are jazzier in the front building, though. A huge plus: the Hollywood Hills Coffee Shop, a favorite among hipsters and celebs for its truly terrific fare.

6141 Franklin Ave. (between Vine and Gower Sts.), Hollywood, CA 90028. ✆ **800/287-1700** in CA only, or 323/464-5181. Fax 323/962-0536. www.bestwestern.com/hollywoodhillshotel. 82 units. $79–$129 double. AAA and AARP discounts available. AE, DISC, MC, V. Free covered parking. Small pets accepted with $25-per-night fee. **Amenities:** Excellent coffee shop; lovely heated outdoor pool; access to nearby health club; tour desk; coin-op laundry. *In room:* A/C, TV, fridge, coffeemaker, hair dryer, iron.

⌒ *Kids* Kid-Friendly Hotels

Best Western Marina Pacific Hotel & Suites *(p. 450)*   This hotel gives families a place to stay just off the carnival-like Venice Boardwalk. The suites are a terrific choice for the brood because each features a full kitchen, a dining area, a pullout sofa, and a connecting door to an adjoining room that lets you form an affordable two-bedroom, two-bath suite.

Beverly Garland's Holiday Inn *(p. 465)*   This hotel is a terrific choice for wallet-watching families because rates are low, the North Hollywood location is close to Universal Studios (a free shuttle is even on hand), and kids stay and eat free.

Hollywood Roosevelt Hotel *(p. 460)*   Kids under 18 stay free with their parents in this landmark hotel, which is home to lots of old Hollywood lore (plus a few benevolent ghosts). The heart-of-gentrified-Hollywood location makes an excellent base for families who want easy access to the touristy but fun Walk of Fame.

Hotel del Capri *(p. 459)*   This hotel offers spacious, retro-priced rooms and suites to families with kids—and anybody who wants a big bang for their buck. You and the kids can even hop a free shuttle to Westwood to stroll, shop, and maybe even watch a few celebs walk the red carpet into their latest movie premiere.

Hotel Oceana *(p. 446)*   Here you'll find big apartment-style suites outfitted with all the conveniences of home. Kids will love the bright colors, the cushy furniture, the video games on the TV, and the location—across the street from the beach.

Magic Hotel *(p. 462)*   This is a good budget choice, with roomy apartment-style suites and a location close to Hollywood Boulevard's family-friendly attractions.

Sheraton Universal Hotel *(p. 466)*   This Sheraton enjoys a terrifically kid-friendly location, adjacent to Universal Studios and the fun City-Walk mall. Babysitting services are available, and there's even a game room on the premises.

Wyndham Bel Age Hotel *(p. 456)*   This terrific all-suite hotel's mega-size suites feature everything a family requires, including a sleeper sofa in the living area that opens into a second king bed, VCR and Sony Playstation on the TV, and a wet bar with fridge that allows for easy prep of morning cereal. There's no extra-person charge for kids (rates include up to four per unit), which improves the value-for-dollar ratio even more.

Days Inn Hollywood/Universal Studios   While it's well east of the prime Sunset Strip action, this freshly renovated motel is safe and freeway convenient, and extras like free underground parking and continental breakfast make it an especially good value. Double-doubles are large enough for families to share. Some rooms already have microwaves, fridges and coffeemakers; if yours doesn't have a hair dryer or an iron, they're available for lending at the front desk. It's usually easy to snare an under-$100 rate; for maximum bang for your buck, ask for a room overlooking the pool.

7023 Sunset Blvd. (between Highland and La Brea Aves.), Hollywood, CA 90028. 🕻 **800-544-8313**, 800/346-7723, or 323/464-8344. Fax 323/962-9748. www.daysinn.com. 72 units. $82–$160 double; $125–$200 whirlpool suite. Rates include continental breakfast. Ask about AAA, AARP, and other discounted rates (as low as $73 at press time). AE, DC, DISC, MC, V. Free secured parking. **Amenities:** Heated outdoor pool; dry cleaning/laundry service. *In room:* A/C, TV.

Magic Hotel ★ *Kids*   Located a stone's throw Hollywood Boulevard's attractions, this garden-style hotel/motel at the base of the Hollywood Hills offers L.A.'s best cheap sleeps. You won't see the Magic Hotel in a shelter mag spread anytime soon—the rooms are done in high Levitz style—but the units are spacious, comfortable, and extremely well kept. Named for the Magic Castle, the landmark illusionist club just uphill, the hotel was once an apartment building; it still feels nicely private and insulated from Franklin Avenue's constant stream of traffic. The units are situated around a pretty swimming-pool courtyard. Most are full, extra-large apartments, with kitchens with microwave and coffeemaker. Several units also have balconies overlooking the large heated pool. Ideal for wallet-watching families or long-term stays.

7025 Franklin Ave. (between La Brea and Highland), Hollywood, CA 90028. 🕻 **800/741-4915** or 323/851-0800. Fax 323/851-4926. www.magichotel.com. 49 units. $79 double; $99–$179 suite. Off-season and other discounts available. Extra person $10. AE, DC, DISC, MC, V. Free secured parking. **Amenities:** Pool, coin-op laundry. *In room:* A/C, TV, dataport coffeemaker, hair dryer, iron, safe.

DOWNTOWN
EXPENSIVE/MODERATE

How much you'll pay at any of the following hotels largely depends on when you come. All become quite affordable once the business travelers go home; more often than not, rooms go for a relative song over holidays and weekends. Some even offer good-value weekday rates to leisure travelers during periods when rooms would otherwise sit open.

Millennium Biltmore Hotel Los Angeles ★★   Built in 1923 and encompassing an entire square block, this opulent Italian-Spanish Rennaissance landmark is the grande dame of L.A.'s hotels. You've seen the Biltmore in many movies, including *The Fabulous Baker Boys, Beverly Hills Cop,* and Barbra Streisand's *A Star Is Born;* the Crystal Ballroom appeared upside-down in *The Poseidon Adventure.* Always in fine shape and host to world leaders and luminaries, the former Regal Biltmore is now under the guiding hand of the excellent Millennium Hotels group, and the sense of refinement and graciousness endures. The generally large guest rooms aren't quite as eye-popping, but they've recently undergone a sumptuous redecorating that suits the hotel's vibe beautifully; bathrooms are on the small side, but peach-toned marble and plush robes add a luxurious edge.

A range of dining and cocktail outlets includes classic Bernard's for high-quality continental cuisine, plus pretty, casual Smeraldi's serves homemade pastas and lighter California fare. Off the lobby is the stunning Gallery Bar, named by *Los Angeles* magazine as one of the sexiest cocktail lounges in L.A. Afternoon tea and cocktails are served in the Rendezvous Court (the hotel's original lobby). Spend the few bucks it takes to appreciate the Art Deco Health Club, with its gorgeous Roman-style pool.

506 S. Grand Ave. (between Fifth and Sixth Sts.), Los Angeles, CA 90071. 🕻 **800/245-8673** or 213/624-1011. Fax 213/612-1545. www.millennium-hotels.com. 683 units. $225–$245 double; from $370 suite. Super breakfast and weekend discount packages available. AE, DC, DISC, MC, V. Parking $22. **Amenities:** 4 restaurants

(Bernard's Bistro for Continental fine dining, Sai Sai for elegant Japanese, Smeraldi's for Cal-Italian and espresso, the casual Grand Ave. Sports Bar) and 2 lounges (the terrific Gallery Bar and intimate Cognac Room, and Rendezvous Court for afternoon tea and evening cocktails); health club with original 1923 inlaid pool; Jacuzzi; steam; sauna; concierge; Enterprise car-rental desk; courtesy car; business center; salon; 24-hour room service; in-room massage; babysitting; dry cleaning/laundry service; executive-level rooms. *In room:* A/C, TV w/ pay movies, dataport, minibar, hair dryer, safe.

Omni Los Angeles ✶✶

The Omni chain forsook their old location (now the Wilshire Grand, below) to assume this elegant tower (the former Inter-Continental Los Angeles). Its lovely, view-endowed situation as the centerpiece of California Plaza elevates the hotel above the noise and traffic of downtown. And now that it's adjacent to the Museum of Contemporary Art and within walking distance of the Music Center, the Omni is downtown's best base for culture buffs. Recognizing the geographical appeal, the hotel caters to theatergoers more than any of its peers with complimentary car service until 11:30pm (great for dinner and show evenings) and good-value theater packages.

The property is beautifully run by an eager-to-please staff, and public areas enjoy a graceful air thanks to elegant Asian accents and artworks from the likes of Jim Dine and David Hockney (on loan from the Museum of Contemporary Art). Conservatively styled, amenity-packed rooms boast floor-to-ceiling views and oversized bathrooms with separate dressing areas; larger rooms also have a chaise, and business rooms feature an extra-large work desk with halogen task lighting and desk-level inputs (most also have a fax/copier/printer). A soft goods upgrade (bedding, towels, curtains) was in the works at press time, so comforts will only improve. At $35 extra for 2, club-level rooms are a great value considering the accompanying freebies: continental breakfast, all-day beverages and pastries, and evening cocktails and appetizers. The Grand Cafe specializes in sumptuous buffets, while the gorgeous Angel's Flight is one of downtown's best lounges, with stellar views and a pianist tickling the ivories nightly.

251 S. Olive St., Los Angeles, CA 90012. ✆ **213/617-3300.** Fax 213/617-3399. www.omnihotels.com. 439 units. $265–$315 double; from $450 suite. Inquire about weekend rates and packages (as low as $119 at press time), which may include breakfast or dinner. AE, DC, DISC, MC, V. Valet parking $22. Pets accepted for $100 non-refundable fee. **Amenities:** Restaurant, lounge; outdoor heated lap pool; exercise room with sauna and steam; access to nearby health club; Omni Kids program; concierge; courtesy car within 3-mile radius; business center with secretarial services; 24-hour room service; babysitting; dry cleaning/laundry service; executive-level rooms; 24-hour on-call physician. *In room:* A/C; TV w/ pay movies, Nintendo, and Internet access; dataport; minibar; hair dryer; iron.

Westin Bonaventure Hotel & Suites ✶✶

This 35-story, 1,300-plus-room monolith is the hotel that locals love to hate. The truth of the matter, though, is that the Bonaventure is a terrific hotel. It's certainly not for travelers who want intimacy or personality in their accommodations—but with more than 20 restaurants and bars, a full-service spa, a monster health club, a Kinko's-sized business center, and much more on hand, you'll be hard-pressed to want for anything here (except maybe some individualized attention). And with a $35 million renovation just complete, this convention favorite has never looked better or felt fresher.

The hotel's five gleaming glass silos encompass an entire square block and form one of downtown's most distinctive landmarks (in fact, you may recognize them from such films as *In the Line of Fire* and *Rain Man*). The 6-story lobby houses fountains and trees (and, most importantly, a Starbuck's). A tangle of concrete ramps and 12 high-speed glass elevators lead to the extensive array of shops and services. Among the highlights are the rooftop L.A. Prime steakhouse and revolving BonaVista lounge, both offering unparalleled views; the Bonaventure Brewing Co. for notable microbrews and California cuisine; and the rave-worthy Bonaventure Chowder Bar.

The pie-shaped guest rooms are on the small side, but a wall of windows offering great views, nice contemporary furnishings, and Westin's unparalleled Heavenly Bed—the ultimate in hotel-bed comfort—make for a very comfortable cocoon. With an executive workstation, fax, and wet bar, guest office suites are great for business travelers, while tower suites—with a living room, an extra half bath, minifridge, microwave, and two TVs—are ideal for families.

404 S. Figueroa St. (between Fourth and Fifth Sts.), Los Angeles, CA 90071. ✆ 800/WESTIN-1 or 213/624-1000. Fax 213/612-4800. 1,354 units. $227–$279 double; from $287 suite. Ask about theater packages. AE, DC, DISC, MC, V. Valet parking $19. **Amenities:** 17 restaurants and fast-food outlets, 5 bars and lounges; outdoor heated lap pool; 15,000-square-foot full-service spa with exercise room, running track, and access to adjacent 85,000-square-foot health club; Westin Kids Club; concierge; tour desk; Dollar Rent-a-Car desk; full-service business and copy center; shops; salon; 24-hour room service; babysitting; dry cleaning/laundry service; Executive Club level. *In room:* A/C, TV w/ pay movies and video games, dataport, coffeemaker, hair dryer, iron, safe.

Wyndham Checkers Hotel ★★   The atmosphere at this boutique version of the Biltmore is as removed from "Hollywood" as a top L.A. hotel can get. Built in 1927, the hotel is protected by the City Cultural Heritage Commission as a Historic Cultural Monument. Plenty of polished brass complements the neutral sand-colored decor; both conspire to accentuate the splendid architectural features that remain intact, despite a complete update over the past couple of years (which included a total guest room overhaul in 2001). Your room is a pristine temple, warmly radiant and immaculately outfitted. Checkers is a European-styled hotel, without a lot of flashy amenities—but first-class all the way. Spacious marble bathrooms feature bathrobes. Public areas include a wood-paneled library, a classy bar stocked with fine cigars and an impressive collection of single-malt scotches and cognacs, and serene corridors punctuated with Asian antiques. Checkers Restaurant is one of downtown's finest dining rooms, with a weekend brunch worth planning for in advance.

535 S. Grand Ave., Los Angeles, CA 90071. ✆ 800/996-3426, 800/423-5798, or 213/624-0000. Fax 213/626-9906. www.checkershotel.com or www.wyndham.com. 188 units. $199–$289 double; from $500 suite. Weekend specials, often as low as $109. AE, DC, DISC, MC, V. Valet parking $23, self-parking (off-site) $20. **Amenities:** Highly regarded restaurant and lounge; rooftop heated lap pool and Jacuzzi; exercise room with men's and women's saunas and massage services; concierge; courtesy car; secretarial services; 24-hour room service; in-room massage; babysitting; dry cleaning/laundry service. *In room:* A/C, TV w/ pay movies, dataport and high-speed connectivity, minibar, coffeemaker, hair dryer, iron.

INEXPENSIVE

Hotel Figueroa ★★ *(Finds)*   With an artistic eye and a heartfelt commitment to budget travelers, owner Uno Thimansson has transformed a 1925-vintage former YMCA into L.A.'s best budget hotel. This enchanting 12-story property sits in a nicely gentrified corner of downtown, within shouting distance of the Staples Center and a block from the Original Pantry Cafe, the landmark 24-hour breakfast house.

The big, airy lobby exudes a romantic Spanish Colonial–Gothic vibe with beamed ceilings and soaring columns, Mexican chandeliers, medievalish furnishings, oversized Balinese pots with towering palms, Navajo prints, and an artistic paint job in muted Southwest colors. Elevators lead to equally artistic guest rooms. Even the smallest ones are good-sized and extremely comfortable. Each boasts terra cotta–sponged walls, a firm, well-made bed with a wrought-iron headboard or canopy and a Georgia O'Keeffe–reminiscent spread, a lovely

Mexican-tiled bath, Indian saris that double as blackout drapes, and an old TV hidden in an armoire; most have unstocked fridges. My favorite is no. 1130, a large double-double with a Navajo-print chaise, but you can't go wrong with any room. The Casa Blanca Suite is a Moroccan pleasure den, ideal for romance-seeking couples in search of something different. Out back is a gorgeous desert-garden deck with mosaic-tiled pool and whirlpool. A minor complaint is that the professional staff allows the heavily European and Japanese clientele to smoke in the public spaces, but it's not usually intrusive.

939 S Figueroa St. (at Olympic Blvd.), Los Angeles, CA 90015. © 800/421-9092 or 213/627-8971. Fax 213/689-0305. www.figueroahotel.com. 285 units. $88–$114 double; $175 Casa Blanca suite. AE, DC, MC, V. Parking $8. **Amenities:** Lobby Cafe for breakfast/lunch; Music Room for American-style steaks, chicken, and chops, and indoor/outdoor Veranda Bar; gorgeous outdoor pool area with lounge chairs and Jacuzzi; business center. *In room:* A/C, TV, dataport.

Hotel Stillwell   The Stillwell is far from fancy, but its modestly priced rooms are a good option in a generally pricey neighborhood. Built in 1906, this once-elegant 250-room hotel is conveniently located, close to Staples Center, the Civic Center, and the Museum of Contemporary Art. Rooms are clean, basic, and simply decorated with decent furnishings; much-needed new paint and carpeting were installed in 2000, but the ancient TVs still look like something from great-uncle Horace's rumpus room. The hotel is quiet, though, and hallways feature East Indian artwork; I much prefer the Hotel Figueroa, but this is a less eccentric and perfectly reasonable choice. The lobby-level Indian restaurant is a popular lunch spot for downtown office workers; other options include a casual Mexican restaurant and so-old-it's-retro Hank's Bar for cocktails.

838 S. Grand Ave. (between 8th and 9th Sts.), Los Angeles, CA 90017. © 800/553-4774 or 213/627-1151. Fax 213/622-8940. www.stillwell-la.com. 250 units. $59 double; $75–$95 suite. AE, DC, MC, V. Parking $4. **Amenities:** 2 restaurants, lounge; activities desk; business center; dry cleaning/laundry service; coin-op laundry. *In room:* A/C, TV, fridge, iron.

SAN FERNANDO VALLEY
EXPENSIVE

Hilton Universal City & Towers   Although this shiny 24-story hotel sits right outside Universal Studios, there's more of a conservative–business-traveler feel here than the raucous family-with-young-children vibe you might expect. Still, free tram service to the theme park and adjacent Universal CityWalk for shopping and dining means that it's hard for families to be better situated. The polished brass and upscale attitude set the business-like tone, and a light-filled glass lobby leads to a seemingly endless series of conference and banquet rooms, the hotel's bread and butter. The oversized guest rooms are tastefully decorated and constantly refurbished, and have exceptional views (even if the modern, mirror-surfaced windows don't actually open). I prefer the adjacent Sheraton (below) for leisure stays, but go here for the best rate.

555 Universal Terrace Pkwy., Universal City, CA 91608. © 800/HILTONS or 818/506-2500. Fax 818/509-2031. www.universalcity.hilton.com. 483 units. $225–$260 double; from $350 suite. Weekend and other discounts often available. AE, DC, DISC, MC, V. Valet parking $16, self-parking $11. **Amenities:** Cafe-style restaurant; outdoor heated pool and Jacuzzi; exercise room; concierge; activities desk; car-rental desk; business center; 24-hour room service; babysitting; dry cleaning/laundry service; executive-level rooms. *In room:* A/C, TV w/ pay movies and video games, dataport, minibar, coffeemaker, hair dryer, iron, safe.

MODERATE

Beverly Garland's Holiday Inn *(Kids)*   The "Beverly Garland" in this 258-room hotel's name is the actress who played Fred MacMurray's wife on the later Technicolor episodes of *My Three Sons*. Grassy areas and greenery abound at this

North Hollywood Holiday Inn, a virtual oasis in the concrete jungle that is most of L.A. The mission-influenced buildings are a bit dated, but if you grew up with *Brady Bunch* reruns, this only adds to the charm—the spread looks like something Mike Brady would have designed. Southwestern-themed fabrics complement the natural-pine furnishings in the spacious and recently renovated guest rooms, attracting your attention away from the somewhat unfortunate painted cinder-block walls. On the upside, all of the well-outfitted rooms have balconies overlooking the pleasant grounds; a nice pool and two lighted tennis courts are also on hand. With Universal Studios just down the street and a free shuttle to the park, the location can't be beat for families. Since proximity to the 101 and 134 freeways also means the constant buzz of traffic, ask for a room facing Vineland Avenue for maximum quiet.

4222 Vineland Ave., North Hollywood, CA 91602. (©) **800/BEVERLY**, 800/HOLIDAY, or 818/980-8000. Fax 818/766-5230. www.beverlygarland.com or www.holiday-inn.com. 267 units. $149–$179 double; from $209 suite. Ask about AAA, AARP, corporate, military, Great Rates, weekend, and other discounted rates (from $109 at press time). Kids 12 and under stay and eat free. AE, DC, DISC, MC, V. Free parking. **Amenities:** Restaurant; heated outdoor pool; lighted tennis courts; sauna; car-rental desk; complimentary shuttle to Universal Studios. *In room:* A/C, TV, coffeemaker, hair dryer, iron.

Sheraton Universal Hotel 𝄞 *(Kids)*   Despite the addition of the sleekly modern Hilton just uphill, the 21-story Sheraton is still considered "the" Universal City hotel of choice for tourists, businesspeople, and industry folks visiting the studios' production offices. It has a spacious 1960s feel, with updated styling and amenities; although the Sheraton does its share of convention and event business, the hotel feels more leisure-oriented than the Hilton next door (an outdoor elevator connects the two properties). Choose a Lanai room for balconies that overlook the lushly planted pool area, or a Tower room for stunning views and solitudes. The hotel is very close to the Hollywood Bowl, and you can practically roll out of bed and into the theme park (via a continuous shuttle). An extra $35 per night buys a Club Level room—worth the money for the extra in-room amenities, plus free continental breakfast and afternoon hors d'oeuvres; business rooms also feature a moveable workstation and a fax/copier/printer.

333 Universal Terrace Pkwy., Universal City, CA 91608. (©) **800/325-3535** or 818/980-1212. Fax 818/985-4980. www.sheraton.com. 442 units. $149–$219 double; from $350 suite. Children stay free in parents' room. Ask about AAA, AARP, and corporate discounts; also inquire about packages that include theme-park admission. AE, DC, DISC, MC, V. Valet parking $16; self-parking $11. **Amenities:** Casual indoor/outdoor restaurant, lobby lounge with pianist, Starbucks coffee cart in lobby; outdoor pool and Jacuzzi; health club; game room; concierge; free shuttle to Universal Studios every 15 minutes; business center; room service (from 6am–midnight); babysitting; dry cleaning/laundry service; executive-level rooms. *In room:* A/C, TV w/ pay movies and video games, dataport, minibar, safe; hair dryer and iron in club-level rooms.

Sportsmen's Lodge   It's been a long time since this part of Studio City was wilderness enough to justify the lodge's name. This sprawling motel has been enlarged and upgraded since, but the lovely garden-like grounds still conjure up images of those days. Done in a country-ish style, guest rooms are large and comfortable but not luxurious; all have balconies or patios. L-shaped studio suites, which can sleep a maximum of five, and new executive king rooms boast two-line phones, a big work desk with a fax machine, a free welcome cocktail, and a coffeemaker and a hair dryer (amenities that should—and usually do—come standard in all categories these days). Those in standard rooms have to request goodies like hair dryers; fridges are also available. You might take advantage of the lovely pool and patio cafe and bar, which will let you forget all about busy Ventura Boulevard just out the front door; don't miss the beautiful black and white swans frolicking out back in the koi-filled ponds. The neighborhood is pleasant and offers easy canyon and freeway access to L.A., but those of you heading to Universal Studios can usually hop a free shuttle. *Money-saving tip:* Ask about discount tickets to Universal, which are usually available at the front desk.

12825 Ventura Blvd. (east of Coldwater Canyon), Studio City, CA 91604. ✆ **800/821-8511** or 818/769-4700. Fax 818/769-4798. www.slhotel.com. 191 units. $122–$172 double; from $180 suite. Ask about discounted AAA and AARP rates; Internet specials as low as $99 at press time. AE, DC, DISC, MC, V. Free parking. **Amenities:** Cafe-style restaurant, bar and grill, pub-like bar; outdoor heated Olympic-size pool and Jacuzzi; well-equipped exercise room; activities desk; Avis car-rental desk; courtesy shuttle to Burbank Airport and Universal Studios; salon; room service (6:45am–8:45pm); dry cleaning/laundry service; coin-op laundry. *In room:* A/C, TV.

INEXPENSIVE

Best Western Mikado Hotel   This nice Asian-flavored garden hotel has been a Valley fixture for 40-plus years. A complete 1999 renovation muted but didn't obliterate the kitsch value, which extends from the pagoda-style exterior to the sushi bar (the Valley's oldest) across the driveway. Two-story motel buildings face two well-maintained courtyards, one with a koi pond and wooden footbridge, the other with a shimmering blue-tiled pool and Jacuzzi. The facelift stripped most of the Asian vibe from guest rooms, which are fresh-feeling, comfortable, and well outfitted. Furnished in 1970s-era chic (leather sofas, earth tones), the one-bedroom apartment is a steal, with enormous rooms and a full-size kitchen.

12600 Riverside Dr. (between Whitsett and Coldwater Canyon), North Hollywood, CA 91607. ✆ **800/ 826-2759,** 800/433-2239 in CA, or 818/763-9141. Fax 818/752-1045. www.bestwestern.com/mikadohotel. 58 units. $129–$139 double; $175 1-bedroom apartment. Rates include full American breakfast. Children under 12 stay free. Ask about AAA, senior, and other discounted rates (as low as $98 at press time). Extra person $10. AE, DC, DISC, MC, V. Free parking. **Amenities:** Japanese restaurant and sushi bar, cocktail lounge; outdoor pool and Jacuzzi; fax and copying services at front desk. *In room:* A/C, TV, dataport, coffeemaker, hair dryer, iron.

Safari Inn ⊛ *Finds*   This 1957-vintage motel is so deliciously retro that it— and its landmark neon sign—have starred in such films as *Apollo 13* and *True Romance.* The exterior is still gloriously intact, while the interiors have been beautifully upgraded with a smart, colorful SoCal look and all the modern comforts. Everything within is 21st-century new, including attractive IKEA-style furniture, bright contemporary textiles and wallprints, and sparkling modern bathrooms; about 10 rooms also have microkitchens (basically wet bars) with a microwave. Everything is clean, fresh, and pleasing. Attention families: Book now to snare one of the two in-demand suites, which have pullout sofas, huge closets, full kitchens, and a second TV.

Located just down the street from the movie studios, the neighborhood is modest but quiet and nice, and convenient for those interested in studio tours, TV-show tapings, and easy freeway access to Universal Studios. In classic motor lodge–style, a petite pool sits in a gated corner of the parking lot, but it's surprisingly attractive and inviting on hot Valley days.

1911 W Olive Ave., Burbank, CA 91506. ✆ **818/845-8586.** Fax 818/845-0054. 55 units. $109–$139 double; $168 suite. AAA and corporate rate $95. Extra person $10. AE, DC, DISC, MC, V. Free parking. Pets accepted with $100 deposit. **Amenities:** Restaurant and martini bar (in sister hotel next door); heated outdoor pool; exercise room; limited room service; dry cleaning/laundry service; coin-op laundry. *In room:* TV w/ pay movies, dataport, coffeemaker, fridge, iron, hair dryer.

PASADENA & ENVIRONS
VERY EXPENSIVE

Ritz-Carlton, Huntington Hotel & Spa ⊛⊛⊛   Built in 1906, the opulent Huntington Hotel was one of America's grandest hotels—but not earthquake-proof! No matter—it was meticulously re-created on the same spot in the 1980s, and the astonishing authenticity (including reinstallation of many decorative features) even fools patrons from the resort's early days. This Spanish-Mediterranean beauty sits on 23 spectacularly landscaped acres that seem a world apart from L.A., though downtown is only 20 minutes away. Each oversized guest room is dressed in conservatively elegant Ritz-Carlton style, softened by ultra-pretty English garden textiles and a lovely palette of celadon, cream, and butter yellow. Luxuries include beds dressed in Frette, marble bathrooms, thick carpets, and terry robes. You might consider spending a few extra valuewise dollars on club-level rooms, which also feature featherbeds, CD players, morning coffee delivered with your wake-up call, and access to the club lounge with dedicated concierge and complimentary gourmet spreads all day (including breakfast).

A relatively new addition is the state-of-the-art 12,000-square-foot spa, salon, and fitness center, which makes the Huntington an ideal place for a pampering getaway. Local seniors love to celebrate in the continental-elegant Georgian Room, but I prefer the more casual California-style Cafe, which also serves at umbrella-covered tables by the Olympic-size pool (southern California's first). High tea is served in the Lobby Lounge.

1401 S. Oak Knoll Ave., Pasadena, CA 91109. ℭ 800/241-3333 or 626/568-3900. Fax 626/568-3700. www.ritzcarlton.com. 392 units. $310–$420 double; from $415 suite. Discount packages always available. AE, DC, MC, V. Valet parking $20. Pets accepted. **Amenities:** 2 restaurants (formal Grill, poolside Terrace), 2 lounges (elegant bar, Lobby Lounge for high tea and evening cocktails); Olympic-size heated outdoor pool and Jacuzzi; lighted tennis courts; full-service spa with Jacuzzi, sauna, and steam; concierge; business center; 24-hour room service; salon; in-room massage; babysitting; dry cleaning/laundry service. *In room:* A/C, TV w/ pay movies, CD player, dataport and high-speed connectivity, minibar, hair dryer, iron, safe.

MODERATE

Artists' Inn & Cottage Bed & Breakfast
Pleasantly unpretentious and furnished with wicker throughout, this yellow-shingled Victorian-style inn was built in 1895 as a farmhouse, and recently expanded to include a neighboring 1909 home. Each of the nine rooms is creatively decorated to reflect the style of a particular artist or period. Among the artistically inspired choices are the country-cozy New England–style Grandma Moses room; the soft, pastel-hued Degas suite; and the bold-lined, primary-hued Expressionist suite, a nod to such artists as Picasso and Dufy. Every room is thoughtfully arranged and features a private bath (many with period fixtures, three with whirlpool tubs), fresh roses from the front garden, port wine, and chocolates. Most rooms have TVs; if yours doesn't, friendly innkeeper Janet Marangi will provide one if you want it. She's constantly improving the home—a 30-foot Seurat-inspired mural was added in 2000—so you can expect everything to be in tip-top shape. The quiet residential location is just 5 minutes from the heart of Old Town Pasadena.

1038 Magnolia St., South Pasadena, CA 91030. ℭ 888/799-5668 or 626/799-5668. Fax 626/799-3678. www.artistsinns.com. 10 units. $110–$205 double. Rates include full breakfast and afternoon tea. Check for midweek specials. Extra person $20. AE, MC, V. Free parking. *In room:* A/C, dataport, hair dryer.

Bissell House Bed & Breakfast
Hidden behind tall hedges that carefully isolate it from busy Orange Grove Avenue, this antique-filled 1887 gingerbread Victorian—the former home of the Bissell vacuums heiress—offers a delightful taste of life on what was once Pasadena's "Millionaire's Row." Outfitted in a traditional chintz-and-cabbage roses style, all rooms have private bathrooms (one with an antique clawfoot, one with a whirlpool tub, one with shower only). The modern world doesn't interfere with the mood in these romantic sanctuaries, but the downstairs library features a TV with VCR, a telephone, and a fax machine

for guests' use. The beautifully landscaped grounds boast a petite pool and a whirlpool.

201 Orange Grove Ave. (at Columbia St.), South Pasadena, CA 91030. © 800/441-3530 or 626/441-3535. Fax 626/441-3671. www.bissellhouse.com. 5 units. $125–$185 double. Rates include full breakfast, plus afternoon snacks and all-day beverages. AE, MC, V. Free parking. **Amenities:** Outdoor pool and Jacuzzi; CD and video libraries. *In room:* A/C, hair dryer, iron; no phone.

INEXPENSIVE

Saga Motor Hotel *Value* This 1950s relic of old Route 66 has far more character than most other motels in its price range. The rooms are small, clean, and simply furnished with just the basics. The double-doubles are spacious enough for shares, but budget-minded families will prefer the extra-large configuration dedicated to them, which has a king and two doubles. The best rooms are in the front building surrounding the gated swimming pool, which is shielded from the street and inviting in warm weather. The grounds are attractive and surprisingly well kept, if you don't count the Astroturf "lawn" on the pool deck. The location is very quiet and very good, just off the Foothill (I-210) Freeway about a mile from the Huntington Library and within 10 minutes of both the Rose Bowl and Old Pasadena.

1633 E. Colorado Blvd. (between Allen and Sierra Bonita Aves.), Pasadena, CA 91106. © 800/793-7242 or 626/795-0431. Fax 626/792-0559. www.thesagamotorhotel.com. 70 units. $63–$89 double; $92–$98 family suite. Rates include continental breakfast. AE, DC, DISC, MC, V. Free parking. **Amenities:** Outdoor heated pool; dry cleaning/laundry service; free self-serve laundromat. *In room:* A/C, TV, dataport.

4 Dining

Since the advent of California cuisine, now a staple across the country, trend-watchers have looked to L.A. restaurants for culinary fashion tips. L.A. gourmands have lately embraced New American fare, where the meat-and-potatoes appear both *haute* and humble. But jazzed-up comfort food is only part of the story. The 2000 Census painted a multi-ethnic portrait of a Los Angeles with more minorities than majorities, a diversity reflected in a rainbow of Argentinean, Armenian, Cajun/Creole, Caribbean, Cuban, Ethiopian, Indian, Korean, Lebanese, Oaxacan, Peruvian, Spanish, Thai, and Vietnamese dining choices.

The restaurants below are categorized first by geographic area, then by price. Keep in mind that many of the restaurants listed as "Expensive" are moderately priced at lunch. Reservations are recommended almost everywhere, particularly on weekends and during peak lunch (noon to 1:30pm) and dinner (7 to 8:30pm) hours.

If you're looking for the **Hard Rock Cafe** (www.hardrockcafe.com), the city has two locations: the Beverly Center, 8600 Beverly Blvd. (at San Vicente Boulevard), Los Angeles (© 310/276-7605); and Universal CityWalk, Universal Center Drive exit off U.S. 101 (© 818/622-7625).

Limited space forced us to make tough choices; for a greater selection of reviews, see *Frommer's Los Angeles.* For additional late-night dining options, see "Late-Night Bites" under "Los Angeles After Dark," later in this chapter.

SANTA MONICA & THE BEACHES
EXPENSIVE

The Lobster ✦ SEAFOOD There's been a seafood shack called The Lobster on the Santa Monica Pier since 1923—almost as long as the pier's been standing—but 2000's revival brings a new sophistication to the old favorite. The interior was completely rebuilt, but still accentuates a bright seaside ambiance and million-dollar ocean view. The menu has been revamped by chef Allyson Thurber, who brings an impressive culinary pedigree (including downtown's Water Grill) to the kitchen. Ultra-fresh fish and thoughtful preparation are the hallmarks here, with choices that range from a namesake steamed live Maine lobster or spicy Louisiana prawns to sautéed North Carolina black bass luxuriating in white truffle sauce and accompanied by lobster salad. Creative appetizers include ahi carpaccio with tangy tobiko wasabi, steamed mussels and Manila clams with applewood bacon, and oysters plain or fancy. The menu offers a couple of fine steaks for landlubbers, and there's a practiced bar for dedicated imbibers.

1602 Ocean Ave. (at Colorado) (℃) 310/458-9294. www.thelobster.com. Reservations recommended. Main courses $15–$32. AE, MC, V. Daily 11:30am[nd3pm and 5–10pm.

Michael's ★★★ CALIFORNIA   Owner Michael McCarty, L.A.'s answer to Alice Waters, is considered by many to be the father of California cuisine. Since the opening of Michael's in 1979 (when McCarty was only 25), several top L.A. restaurants have caught up to it, but this fetching Santa Monica restaurant remains one of the city's best, though Michael has handed executive chef responsibilities to Sam Yoon, whose impressive pedigree includes stints at L.A.'s and San Francisco's most renowned restaurants. The dining room is filled with contemporary art by Michael's wife, Kim McCarty, and the restaurant's beloved garden is a relaxed setting for always-inventive menu choices like Baqueta sea bass with a chanterelle mushroom ragout and fresh Provençal herbs, seared Hawaiian ahi accented with braised enoki mushrooms and earthy-tangy sesame wasabi ponzu sauce, or grilled pork chop sweetened with sweet potato purée and anise-pinot noir sauce. Don't miss Michael's famous warm mushroom salad, tossed with crumbled goat cheese, watercress, caramelized onion, and mustard-sage vinaigrette. *Note:* Michael's automatically adds a 15% service charge to the check.

1147 Third St. (north of Wilshire Blvd.), Santa Monica. (℃) 310/451-0843. Reservations recommended. Main courses $13–$23 lunch; $27–$34 dinner. AE, DC, DISC, MC, V. Mon–Fri 11:30am–2:30pm and 6–10:30pm; Sat 6–10:30pm. Valet parking $4.50.

Röckenwagner ★★ CALIFORNIA   Set in Frank Gehry's starkly modern Edgemar complex (itself a work of art), chef Hans Röckenwagner's eponymous restaurant continues the motif by presenting edible sculpture amid a gallery-like decor. Although it sits in the midst of a popular shopping area, the space manages to be refreshingly quiet. Röckenwagner takes his art—and his food—very seriously, once orchestrating an entire menu around German white asparagus at the height of its short season. The delightfully unpretentious staff serves deliciously pretentious dishes fusing Pacific Rim ingredients with traditional European preparations; a good example is the langoustine ravioli with mangoes in port-wine reduction and curry oil. The menu tastes as good as it reads, and desserts are to die for. Don't overlook the lunch bargains here, or the unique European-style breakfast of bread and cheese.

2435 Main St. (north of Ocean Park Blvd.), Santa Monica. (℃) 310/399-6504. Reservations recommended. Main courses $22–$31 dinner. AE, DC, MC, V. Mon–Fri 6–10pm; Sat 10am–2:30pm and 5:30–11pm; Sun 10am–2:30pm and 5:30–10pm. Valet parking $4.

Valentino ★★ NORTHERN ITALIAN   Valentino is a good choice if you're splurging on just one special dinner. Charming owner Piero Selvaggio oversees two other restaurants, but his distinctive touch still pervades this 26-year-old flagship. This elegant spot continues to maintain its position as *Wine Spectator*

The Wolfgang Puck Experience

For the quintessential L.A. dining experience, be sure to try at least one of Wolfgang Puck's L.A. restaurants. Of course, there's **Spago** (see p. 476), the original and reigning temple of California Cuisine. Puck also has two terrific restaurants near the beach. **Chinois on Main,** 2709 Main St., Santa Monica (© 310/392-9025), serves terrifically quirky East-meets-West Franco-Chinese cuisine. At **Granita,** 23725 W. Malibu Rd. (in the Malibu Colony Mall), Malibu (© 310/456-0488), Puck applies his signature California style to seafood—very successfully, of course. If you're dining on a budget, try one of the several **Wolfgang Puck Cafe** branches around town, where Puck's cuisine is interpreted in an affordable style and served up in colorful surroundings. There's one in West Hollywood, at 8000 Sunset Blvd. (© 323/ 650-7300); one in Santa Monica, at 1323 Montana Ave. (© 310/393-0290); and one at Universal CityWalk (© 818/985-9653). You can visit them all online at **www.wolfgangpuck.com.**

magazine's top wine cellar, and former *New York Times* food critic Ruth Reichl calls this the best Italian restaurant in the U.S. The creations of Selvaggio and his brilliant young chef, Angelo Auriana, make dinners here lengthy multicourse affairs (often involving several bottles of wine). You might begin with a crisp pinot grigio paired with caviar-filled cannolli, or crespelle, thin little pancakes with fresh porcini mushrooms and a rich melt of fontina cheese. A rich Barolo is the perfect accompaniment to rosemary-infused roasted rabbit; the fantastically fragrant risotto with white truffles is one of the most magnificent dishes we've ever had. Jackets are all but required in the elegant dining room.

3115 Pico Blvd. (west of Bundy Dr.), Santa Monica. © 310/829-4313. www.welovewine.com. Reservations required. Main courses $22–$32. AE, DC, MC, V. Mon–Thurs 5:30–10:30pm; Fri 11:30am–2:30pm and 5:30–11pm; Sat 5:30–11pm. Valet parking $4.

MODERATE

Border Grill ★★★ MEXICAN   Before Mary Sue Milliken and Susan Feniger spiced up cable TV as "Too Hot Tamales," they started this restaurant over in West Hollywood. Now Border Grill has moved to a boldly painted, cavernous (read: loud) space in Santa Monica, and the gals aren't in the kitchen here very much at all (though cookbooks and paraphernalia from their Food Network show are displayed prominently for sale). But their influence on the inspired menu is enough to maintain the cantina's enormous popularity with folks who swear by the authentic flavor of Yucatán fish tacos, rock shrimp with ancho chilies, and meaty *ropa vieja,* the traditional Latin stew. The best meatless dish is *mulitas de hongos,* a layering of portobello mushrooms, poblano chilies, black beans, cheese, and guacamole, spiced up with roasted garlic and seared red chard. Distracting desserts are displayed prominently near the entrance, so you may spend the meal fantasizing about the yummy coconut flan or Key lime pie.

1445 Fourth St. (between Broadway and Santa Monica Blvd.), Santa Monica. © 310/451-1655. www.millikenandfeniger.com. Reservations recommended. Main courses $10–$21. AE, DC, DISC, MC, V. Mon 5–10pm; Tues–Thurs and Sun 11:30am–10pm; Fri–Sat 11:30am–11pm.

Chez Melange ★★ CALIFORNIA   Located inside the modest Palos Verdes Inn, this well-regarded brasserie has been presenting artful California cuisine so long it's become a South Bay institution. Though the menu is no longer cutting-edge, it does seem to get more and more eclectic, moving seamlessly from Japanese to Cajun, Italian to Chinese, and keeping up-to-date with premium vodkas and a mouthwatering oyster-and-seafood bar. The decor has a dated, late-1980s feel, but the conservative, moneyed crowd here doesn't mind a bit. Each meal begins with a basket of irresistible breads before moving on to dizzyingly international dishes like shrimp and chicken in orange vindaloo curry over basmati rice with sweet, chunky chutney; rosemary laced pork tenderloin and shallot-sherry cream sauce; Parmesan-crusted albacore with Greek feta salad and tabouleh; or spicy blackened halibut sauced with horseradish and served with seafood gumbo. Spa cuisine selections are available at every meal.

1716 Pacific Coast Hwy. (between Palos Verdes Blvd. and Prospect Ave.), Redondo Beach. ℂ 310/540-1222. www.chezmelange.com. Reservations recommended. Main courses $13–$19 dinner; $8–$13 lunch. AE, DISC, MC, V. Mon–Thurs and Sun 8am–10pm; Fri–Sat 8am–11pm. Free parking.

Joe's 🏵 AMERICAN ECLECTIC   This is one of West L.A.'s best dining bargains. Chef and owner Joe Miller excels in simple New American cuisine, particularly grilled fish and roasted meats accented with piquant herbs. Set in a tiny, quirky storefront, the humble room is a blank palette that belies Joe's popularity. The best tables are tucked away on the enclosed back patio. Lunch is a hidden treasure for those with a champagne palate but a seltzer pocketbook. Topping out at $15, all lunches include salad, one of Miller's exquisite soups, and especially prompt service. Beer and wine are served, except during weekday lunchtime (regulation, due to the elementary school across the street).

1023 Abbot Kinney Blvd., Venice. ℂ 310/399-5811. www.joesrestaurant.com. Reservations required. Main courses $8–$15 lunch; $18–$25 dinner. AE, MC, V. Tues–Fri 11:30am–2:30pm and 6–10pm; Sat–Sun 11am–2:30pm and 6–11pm. Free street parking.

INEXPENSIVE

Bread & Porridge 🏵 INTERNATIONAL/BREAKFAST   A dozen tables are all that compose this neighborhood cafe, but steady streams of locals mill outside, reading their newspapers and waiting for a vacant seat. Once inside, surrounded by the vintage fruit-crate labels adorning the walls and tabletops, you can sample the delicious breakfasts, fresh salads and sandwiches, and superaffordable entrees. There's a vaguely international twist to the menu, which leaps from breakfast quesadillas and omelets—all served with black beans and salsa—to the Southern comfort of Cajun crab cakes and coleslaw to typical Italian pastas adorned with Roma tomatoes and plenty of garlic. All menu items are cheap—truck stop cheap—but with an inventive elegance that truly makes this a best-kept secret. Get a short stack of one of five varieties of pancakes with any meal; this place thoughtfully serves breakfast all day.

2315 Wilshire Blvd. (3 blocks west of 26th St.), Santa Monica. ℂ 310/453-4941. Main courses $6–$9. AE, MC, V. Daily 7am–2pm. Metered street parking.

Good Stuff ⟨Value⟩ AMERICAN/INTERNATIONAL   A mainstay of local casual dining, this popular crowd-pleaser suits beachgoers, lunch-breakers, families, couples, and more—there's something for everyone. Inside the gray clapboard corner restaurant you'll find brightly painted marine-themed murals, lifeguard memorabilia, and picture windows to let in the sunshine. On nice days the outdoor patio fills first; its glass railings ensure a good view of bustling downtown MB's human parade. Cheerful servers positively bounce through the restaurant, clad in casual sport togs, and ferry generous platters of food that's fresh, carefully prepared, and very affordable. The mile-long menu runs the gamut, featuring standouts like Santa Fe chicken omelet, cinnamon swirl French toast, a superb homemade veggie burger, burritos and Mexican favorites, enormous main-course salads, steaming hot pastas, and a selection of dinner-only entrees. Nightly bargain "get stuffed" dinners are sized for satisfaction—the seafood stew, for example, is guaranteed to be filling or your second bowl's on the house.

Other South Bay locations include Hermosa Beach, 1286 The Strand (© 310/374-2334), and Redondo Beach's Riviera Village, 1617 Pacific Coast Hwy. (© 310/316-0262).

1300 Highland Ave. (at 13th St.), Manhattan Beach. © 310/545-4775. www.eatgoodstuff.com. Reservations accepted only for parties of 5 or more. Most menu items under $10. AE, DC, DISC, MC, V. Daily 7am–10pm. Free parking.

Jody Maroni's Sausage Kingdom *Finds* SANDWICHES/SAUSAGES Your cardiologist might not approve, but Jody Maroni's all-natural, preservative-free "haut dogs" are some of the best wieners served anywhere. The grungy walk-up (or inline skate-up) counter looks fairly foreboding—you wouldn't know there was gourmet fare behind that aging hot-dog–stand facade, from which at least 14 different grilled-sausage sandwiches are served up. Bypass the traditional hot Italian and try the Toulouse garlic, Bombay curried lamb, all-chicken apple, or orange-garlic-cumin. Each is served on a freshly baked onion roll and smothered with onions and peppers. Burgers, BLTs, and rotisserie chicken are also served, but why bother?

Other locations include the Valley's Universal CityWalk (© 818/622-JODY), and inside LAX Terminals 3, 4, and 6, where you can pick up some last-minute vacuum-packed sausages for home. Having elevated sausage-worship to an art form, Jody's now boasts a helpful and humorous cookbook, plus its own website.

2011 Ocean Front Walk (north of Venice Blvd.), Venice. © 310/822-5639. www.maroni.com. Sandwiches $4–$6. No credit cards. Daily 10am–sunset.

Kay 'n Dave's Cantina HEALTHY MEXICAN A beach community favorite for "really big portions of really good food at really low prices," Kay 'n Dave's cooks with no lard and has a vegetarian-friendly menu with plenty of meat items too. Come early (and be prepared to wait) for breakfast, as local devotees line up for five kinds of fluffy pancakes, zesty omelets, or one of the best breakfast burritos in town. Grilled tuna Veracruz, spinach and chicken enchiladas in tomatillo salsa, seafood fajitas tostada, vegetable-filled corn tamales, and other Mexican specialties really are served in huge portions, making this mostly locals minichain a great choice to energize for (or reenergize after) an action-packed day of beach sightseeing. Bring the family—there are a kids' menu and crayons on every table.

262 26th St. (south of San Vicente Blvd.), Santa Monica. © 310/260-1355. Reservations not accepted. Main courses $5–$10. AE, MC, V. Mon–Thurs 11am–9:30pm; Fri 11am–10pm; Sat 8:30am–10pm; Sun 8:30am–9:30pm. Metered street parking

L.A.'S WESTSIDE & BEVERLY HILLS
EXPENSIVE

Four Oaks ★★★ CALIFORNIA Just looking at the menu here makes us swoon. The country-cottage ambience and chef Peter Roelant's superlative blend of fresh ingredients with luxurious continental flourishes make a meal at the Four Oaks one of our favorite luxuries. Dinner is served beneath trees festooned with twinkling lights. Appetizers like lavender-smoked salmon with crisp potatoes

Sea Breezes & Sunsets: Oceanview Dining in Malibu

Despite fires, mud slides, and high rents, Malibu residents remain enamoured of their precious parcel of beachfront paradise. There really is a beautifully calm, on-vacation vibe to this upscale stretch of coast. One of the best ways to sample a slice of this happiness pie is to (literally) turn your back on the frenzy of L.A. and gaze upon the sparkling Pacific—at least for the duration of a meal. From south to north, numerous restaurants dot the coastline, all exploiting as much ocean view as their property line allows. Here are three of our favorites:

Gladstone's 4 Fish, 17300 Pacific Coast Hwy., at Sunset Boulevard (℡ 310/454-3474), shares a parking lot with a public beach, so its wood deck has a constant view of surfers, bikini-clad sunbathers, and other frolicking beachgoers. At busy times, Gladstone's even sets up picnic-style tables right out on the sand. The moderately priced menu boasts several pages of fresh fish and seafood, augmented by a few salads and other meals for landlubbers. Gladstone's is popular for afternoon and evening drinks, its nearly 20 seafood appetizer platters, and its decadent chocolate-y desserts. Open Monday through Thursday from 11am to 11pm, Friday from 11am to midnight, Saturday from 7am to midnight, and Sunday from 7am to 11pm. Parking $3.50.

The Malibu branch of the surf-and-turf **Chart House** chain, at 18412 Pacific Coast Hwy., south of Topanga Canyon (℡ 310/454-9321), lets its dramatic location steal the show. Built on a rocky point, suspended over the sand, and often perilously close to the breaking surf, the Chart House's dark, woody dining room is terraced, affording every table a great view. The menu, though predictable (prime rib, steaks, lobster, seafood), is first class. Prices are moderate to expensive. Open Monday and Tuesday from 5 to 9:30pm, Wednesday and Thursday from 11:30am to 9:30pm, Friday and Saturday from 11:30am to 10:30pm, and Sunday from 11am to 9:30pm. Free valet parking.

Duke's Malibu, 21150 Pacific Coast Hwy., at Las Flores Canyon (℡ 310/317-0777), is worth a visit for the impressive memorabilia alone. Named for Hawaiian surf legend "Duke" Kahanamoku, Duke's offers up decent food at inflated, but not outrageous, prices. You'll find good-quality fresh fish prepared in the Hawaiian regional style, hearty surf-and-turf, a smattering of chicken and pasta dishes, and plenty of finger-lickin' appetizers to accompany the Day-Glo tropical cocktails. Open Monday through Thursday from 11:30am to 10pm, Friday and Saturday from 11:30am to 10:30pm, Sunday from 10am to 10pm. Valet parking $2 (dinner and weekends only, otherwise free self-parking).

and horseradish crème fraîche complement mouth-watering dishes like roasted chicken with sage, Oregon forest mushrooms, artichoke hearts, and port-balsamic sauce. If you're looking for someplace special, head to this canyon hideaway—you won't be disappointed.

2181 N. Beverly Glen Blvd., Los Angeles. (310/470-2265. www.fouroaksrestaurant.com. Reservations required. Main courses $22–$29. AE, DISC, MC, V. Tues–Sat 11:30am–2pm and 6–10pm; Sun 10:30am–2pm and 6–10pm. Valet parking $4.

Jozu ✺✺ PACIFIC RIM/CALIFORNIA   *Jozu* means "excellent" in Japanese, and the word perfectly describes everything about this tranquil restaurant. All meals begin with complimentary sake from Jozu's premium sake list. Chef Hisashi Yoshiara's menu presents Asian flavors interpreted with an international inventiveness. Outstanding dishes include delicately roasted sea bass on a bed of crunchy cabbage, accented with tangy *ponzu* sauce; albacore tuna wrapped in a crispy potato nest and bathed in soy butter; and rack of lamb perfectly char-broiled and presented over a warm bell-pepper and arugula ragout. Appetizers range from shrimp sui-mai in rich lobster sauce to spicy halibut sashimi. The dessert of choice is Asian pear tart, lightly caramelized fruit in a buttery crust. The restaurant's interior is warmly comfortable and subtly lit; plenty of beautiful Hollywood types dine here, but it's quiet enough for real dinner conversation.

8360 Melrose Ave. (at Kings Rd.), West Hollywood. (323/655-5600. www.jozu.com. Reservations recommended. Main courses $16–$25. AE, MC, V. Thurs–Fri 12noon–2pm and 5:30–10:30pm; Sat–Wed 5:30–10:30pm. Valet parking $3.50.

Lawry's The Prime Rib ✺ STEAKS/SEAFOOD   Most Americans know Lawry's only as a brand of seasoned salt (which was invented here). Going to this family-run institution is an Old World event, where the main menu offerings are four cuts of prime rib that vary in thickness from two fingers to an entire hand. Every standing rib roast is dry-aged for 2 to 3 weeks, sprinkled with Lawry's famous seasoning, and then roasted on a bed of rock salt. A carver wheels the cooked beef tableside, then slices it properly, rare to well done. All dinners come with creamy whipped horseradish, Yorkshire pudding, and the Original Spinning Bowl Salad (drenched in Lawry's signature sherry French dressing). Lawry's moved across the street from its original location a few years ago but retained its throwback-to-the-1930s clubroom atmosphere, complete with Persian-carpeted oak floors, high-backed chairs, and European oil paintings.

100 N. La Cienega Blvd. (north of Wilshire Blvd.), Beverly Hills. (310/652-2827. Reservations recommended. Main courses $20–$30. AE, DC, DISC, MC, V. Mon–Thurs 5–10pm; Fri 5–11pm; Sat 4:30–11pm; Sun 4–10pm. Valet parking $3.50.

Lucques ✺✺ FRANCO-MEDITERRANEAN   Once Los Angeles became accustomed to this restaurant's unusual name—"Lucques" is a variety of French olive, pronounced "Luke"—local foodies fell hard for this quietly and comfort-ably sophisticated new home of former Campanile chef Suzanne Goin. The old brick building, once silent star Harold Lloyd's carriage house, is decorated in mute, clubby colors with subdued lighting that extends to the handsome enclosed patio behind. Goin cooks with bold flavors, fresh-from-the-farm pro-duce, and an instinctive feel for the food of the Mediterranean. The short and oft-changed menu makes the most of unusual ingredients like salt cod and oxtails. Standout dishes include Tuscan bean soup with tangy greens and pistou, grilled chicken served alongside spinach sautéed with pancetta and shallots, rus-tic mascarpone polenta topped with wild mushroom ragout and wilted greens, and perfect vanilla *pôt de crème* for dessert. Lucques's bar menu, featuring steak frites bearnaise, omelets, and tantalizing hors d'oeuvres (including olives, warm almonds, sea salt, and chewy bread), is a godsend for late-night diners.

8474 Melrose Ave. (east of La Cienega), West Hollywood. (323/655-6277. Reservations recommended. Main courses $18–$30. AE, MC, V. Tues–Sat noon–2:30pm and 6pm–1:30am; Sun 5:30pm–midnight. Metered street parking or valet ($3.50).

Matsuhisa ✿✿✿ JAPANESE/PERUVIAN Japanese chef and owner Nobuyuki Matsuhisa arrived in Los Angeles via Peru and opened what may be the most creative restaurant in the entire city. A true master of fish cookery, Matsuhisa creates fantastic, unusual dishes by combining Japanese flavors with South American spices and salsas. Broiled sea bass with black truffles, sautéed squid with garlic and soy, and Dungeness crab tossed with chilies and cream are good examples of the masterfully prepared delicacies that are available in addition to thickly sliced nigiri and creative sushi rolls. Matsuhisa is perennially popular with celebrities and hard-core foodies, so reserve early for those hard-to-get tables. The small, crowded main dining room suffers from poor lighting and precious lack of privacy; many big names are ushered through to private dining rooms. If you dare, ask for omakase, and the chef will personally compose a selection of eccentric dishes.

129 N. La Cienega Blvd. (north of Wilshire Blvd.), Beverly Hills. ✆ 310/659-9639. Reservations recommended. Main courses $14–$26; sushi $4–$13 per order; full omakase dinner from $65. AE, DC, MC, V. Mon–Fri 11:45am–2:15pm; daily 5:45–10:15pm. Valet parking $3.50.

Mimosa ✿ FRENCH PROVENÇAL It takes seasoned maitre d' Silvio de Mori to fend off the throngs clamoring to get into chef Jean-Pierre Bosc's country French bistro, still the finest of the Provençal culinary invasion a few years ago. Decked out in traditional bistro garb (butter-yellow walls, artistic photos, and French posters), Mimosa also attracts plenty of French expatriates and Euro-style denizens with a truly authentic menu. You won't get the classic French of caviar and truffles, but rather regional peasant specialties like rich veal daube, tripe sausage (*andouillette*), perfect steak fries, and a slow-cooked pork roast with horseradish lentils. The appetizer list usually includes a splendid terrine, and bowls of house-cured *cornichons* and spicy Dijon mustard accompany bread to every table. Despite the occasional tinge of trendy attitude—usually precipitated by the presence of habitues like Tom Cruise, Jennifer Aniston, and Brad Pitt—Mimosa should be appreciated for its casual, comforting bistro fare.

8009 Beverly Blvd. (west of Fairfax), Los Angeles. ✆ 323/655-8895. Reservations recommended. Main courses $13–$24. AE, MC, V. Mon–Fri 11:30am–3pm; daily 5:30pm–midnight. Metered street parking.

Spago ✿✿✿ CALIFORNIA Wolfgang Puck is more than a great chef, he's also a masterful businessman and publicist who has made Spago one of the best-known restaurants in the United States. Despite all the hoopla—and almost 20 years of service—Spago remains one of L.A.'s top-rated restaurants. Talented Puck henchman Lee Hefter presides over the kitchen, delivering the culinary sophistication demanded by an upscale Beverly Hills crowd. This high-style indoor-outdoor space glows with the aura of big bucks, celebrity, and the perfectly honed California cuisine that can honestly take credit for setting the standard. Spago is also one of the last places in L.A. where men will feel most comfortable in jacket and tie (suggested, but not required). All eyes may be on the romantically twinkle-lit outdoor patio (the most coveted tables), but the food takes center stage. You simply can't choose wrong—highlights include the appetizer of foie gras "three ways"; savory duck either honey-lacquered and topped with foie gras, or Cantonese-style with a citrus tang; and rich Austrian dishes from "Wolfie's" childhood, like spicy beef goulash or perfect veal schnitzel.

176 N. Canon Dr. (north of Wilshire). ✆ 310/385-0880. www.wolfgangpuck.com. Reservations required. Main courses $18–$34; tasting menu $85. AE, DC, DISC, MC, V. Sun and Tues–Thurs 6–10pm; Fri–Sat 5:30–11pm.

MODERATE

Bombay Cafe 🦋🦋 INDIAN   This friendly sleeper may well be L.A.'s best Indian spot, serving excellent curries and kurmas typical of South Indian street food. Once seated, immediately order *sev puri* for the table; these crispy little chips topped with chopped potatoes, onions, cilantro, and chutneys are the perfect accompaniment to what's sure to be an extended menu-reading session. Also recommended are the burrito-like "frankies," juicy little bread rolls stuffed with lamb, chicken, or cauliflower. The best dishes come from the tandoor and include spicy yogurt-marinated swordfish, lamb, and chicken. While some dishes are authentically spicy, plenty of others have a mellow flavor for less incendiary palates. This restaurant is phenomenally popular and gets its share of celebrities: Meg Ryan and Dennis Quaid once hired the Bombay Cafe to cater an affair at their Montana ranch.

12021 W. Pico Blvd. (at Bundy). ⓒ 310/473-3388. Reservations recommended for dinner. Main courses $9–$17. AE, MC, V. Mon–Thurs 11:30am–3pm and 5–10pm; Fri 11:30am–3pm and 5–11pm; Sat 5–11pm; Sun 5–10pm. Metered street parking (lunch); valet parking $3.50 (dinner).

Chaya Brasserie 🦋🦋 FRANCO-JAPANESE   Now open for nearly 20 years, Chaya has become well ensconced as one of Los Angeles's finest restaurants. This continental bistro with Asian overtones is popular with film agents during lunch and a particularly beautiful assembly of stars at night (spotted recently: George Clooney, Mark Walberg, and the Baldwin brothers). The place is loved for its exceptionally good food and refreshingly unpretentious atmosphere. Despite a high noise level, the stage-lit dining room feels sensuous and swoony. On warm afternoons and evenings, the best tables are on the outside terrace, overlooking the busy street. Chaya is best known for superb grilled fish and meats, like seared soy-marinated Hawaiian tuna and Long Island duckling. Chef Shigefumi Tachibe's lobster ravioli with pesto-cream sauce is both stylish and delicious, as is tangy grilled chicken Dijon, a house specialty. Chaya is also a hot late-night rendezvous, with a short but choice supper menu served until 12:15am Tuesday through Saturday.

8741 Alden Dr. (east of Robertson Blvd.). ⓒ 310/859-8833. Reservations recommended on weekends. Main courses $10–$16 lunch; $15–$27 dinner. AE, DC, MC, V. Mon–Fri 11am–2:30pm; Mon–Thurs 6–10:30pm; Fri–Sat 6–11pm; Sun 6–10pm. Valet parking $3.50.

Kate Mantilini AMERICAN   It's rare to find a restaurant that feels comfortably familiar yet cutting-edge trendy at the same time—and also happens to be one of L.A.'s few late-night eateries. Kate Mantilini fits the bill perfectly. One of the first to bring meat loaf back into fashion, Kate's offers a huge menu of upscale truck-stop favorites like "white" chili (made with chicken, white beans, and Monterey Jack cheese), grilled steaks and fish, a few token pastas, and just about anything you might crave. At 2am, nothing quite beats a steaming bowl of lentil-vegetable soup and some garlic-cheese toast, unless your taste runs to fresh oysters and a dry martini—Kate has it all. The huge mural of the Hagler-Hearns boxing match that dominates the stark, open interior provides the only clue to the namesake's identity: Mantilini was an early female boxing promoter, around 1947.

9101 Wilshire Blvd. (at Doheny Dr.), Beverly Hills. ⓒ 310/278-3699. Reservations accepted only for parties of 6 or more. Main courses $7–$16. AE, MC, V. Mon–Thurs 7:30am–1am; Fri 7:30am–2am; Sat 11am–2am; Sun 10am–midnight. Validated valet parking.

La Serenata Gourmet ✹✹ MEXICAN Westsiders rejoiced when this branch of Boyle Heights's award-winning La Serenata de Girabaldi began serving its authentic, but innovative, Mexican cuisine just a block away from the Westside Pavilion shopping center. This place is casual, fun, and intensely delicious. Specialties like shrimp enchiladas, fish tacos, and pork *gorditas* are all accented with hand-patted corn tortillas, fresh chips dusted with añejo cheese, and flavorful fresh salsas. Always packed to capacity, the restaurant finally expanded in 1998, but try to avoid the prime lunch and dinner hours nevertheless.

Adventurous diners head to the original La Serenata de Girabaldi, 1842 First St. (between Boyle and State Streets; ℂ **213/265-2887**), reopened in 2000 after an extensive remodeling. The menu is more formal, the ambiance is more authentic, and secured valet parking is provided for those worried about the sketchy neighborhood.

10924 W. Pico Blvd., West L.A. ℂ 310/441-9667. Main courses $8–$13. AE, MC, V. Daily 11am–3:30pm and 5–10pm (Fri–Sat until 10:30pm). Metered street parking.

Maui Beach Cafe PACIFIC RIM/HAWAIIAN Enormously popular with both students from nearby UCLA and foodies from throughout the Westside, this casual and noisy island party zone features looming interior palm trees and wavy walls that glow tropical-wave blue. The menu is refreshingly different, offering a true sampling of Hawaiian Regional Cuisine, an amalgam of influences from Japan, China, Thailand, Korea, and Portugal—all composed using fresh Hawaiian fish, lush fruits, and tropical produce. Island-born chef Mako Segawa-Gonzales trained on Maui with HRC guru Roy Yamaguchi, and he tosses a few Latin elements into the mix, in honor of his new L.A. home. You can feast on Asian tapas like baby back ribs glazed with guava-hoisin; slurp up pastas such as thick Shanghai noodles tossed with crispy vegetables and roasted garlic; or dig your chopsticks into "Da Maui Bowls," nicely composed one-bowl meals atop rice (white or brown) or noodles (udon or soba).

1019 Westwood Blvd. (at Le Conte), Westwood. ℂ 310/209-0494. www.mauibeachcafe.com. Reservations suggested for dinner. Main courses $6–$12 lunch; $8–$22 dinner. AE, DC, MC, V. Mon–Thurs 11:30am–3pm and 5–10pm; Fri 11:30am–3pm and 5–11pm; Sat 11:30am–11pm; Sun 11:30am–10pm. Metered street or lot parking.

Nyala ✹ ETHIOPIAN There are no fewer than four Ethiopan eateries along two compact blocks of Fairfax, but our favorite is Nyala; it's one of the larger ones, and probably the most popular. In a mellow setting—all earthen colors, tribal prints, and African music—an ethnically mixed crowd finds common ground in the expertly spiced (smouldering, rather than fiery) cuisine. For the uninitiated, Ethiopian food is a mosaic of chopped salads, chunky stews, and saucy vegetables, all served on a colorful enamel platter for communal enjoyment. There are no utensils, merely a basket of *injera*, the thick, tangy crepe used to scoop and enfold everything else. Choices range from hearty chicken or lamb chunks stewed with tomatoes and onions to a parade of vegetarian choices (lentils, chick-peas, greens), each with a distinctive marinade. African beers and honey wine are perfect accompaniments.

1076 S. Fairfax Ave. (south of Olympic). ℂ 323/936-5918. Reservations suggested. Main courses $8–$15. AE, DISC, MC, V. Daily 11:30am–11pm. Street parking.

INEXPENSIVE

The Apple Pan ✹✹ SANDWICHES/AMERICAN There are no tables, just a U-shaped counter, at this classic American burger shack and L.A. landmark. Open since 1947, the Apple Pan is a diner that looks—and acts—the part. It's famous for juicy burgers, bullet-speed service, and an authentic frills-free atmosphere. The hickory burger is best, though the tuna sandwich also has its huge share of fans. Ham, egg salad, and Swiss cheese sandwiches round out the menu. Definitely order fries and, if you're in the mood, the home-baked apple pie, too.

10801 Pico Blvd. (east of Westwood Blvd.). ☎ 310/475-3585. Most menu items under $5. No credit cards. Tues–Thurs and Sun 11am–midnight; Fri–Sat 11am–1am.

Versailles *Value* CUBAN Outfitted with Formica tabletops and looking something like an ethnic IHOP, Versailles feels very much like any number of Miami restaurants that cater to the Cuban community. The menu reads like a veritable survey of Havana-style cookery and includes specialties like "Moors and Christians" (flavorful black beans with white rice), *ropa vieja* (a stringy beef stew), *eastin lechón* (suckling pig with sliced onions), and fried whole fish (usually sea bass). Shredded roast pork is particularly recommendable, especially when tossed with the restaurant's trademark garlic-citrus sauce. But what everyone comes for is the chicken—succulent, slow roasted, smothered in onions and either garlic-citrus sauce or barbecue sauce. Almost everything is served with black beans and rice; wine and beer are available. Because meals are good, bountiful, and cheap, there's often a wait.

Another Versailles restaurant is located in Culver City at 10319 Venice Blvd. (☎ **310/558-3168**).

1415 S. La Cienega Blvd. (south of Pico Blvd.). ☎ **310/289-0392**. Main courses $5–$11. AE, MC, V. Daily 11am–10pm. Free parking.

HOLLYWOOD
EXPENSIVE
Campanile ★★ CALIFORNIA/MEDITERRANEAN Built as Charlie Chaplin's private offices in 1928, this lovely building has a multilevel layout with flower-bedecked interior balconies, a bubbling fountain, and a skylight through which diners can see the *campanile* (bell tower). The kitchen, headed by Spago alumnus and chef-owner Mark Peel, gets a giant leg up from baker (and wife) Nancy Silverton, who runs the now-legendary La Brea Bakery next door. Meals here might begin with fried zucchini flowers drizzled with melted mozzarella or lamb carpaccio surrounded by artichoke leaves—a dish that arrives looking like one of van Gogh's sunflowers. Chef Peel is particularly known for his grills and roasts; try the grilled prime rib smeared with black-olive tapenade or pappardelle with braised rabbit, roasted tomato, and collard greens. And don't skip dessert—the restaurant's many enthusiastic sweets fans have turned Nancy's dessert book into a bestseller. Breakfast is a surprising crowd-pleaser and a terrific way to appreciate this beautiful space on a budget.

624 S. La Brea Ave. (north of Wilshire Blvd.). ☎ **323/938-1447**. www.campanilerestaurant.com. Reservations required. Main courses $24–$37. AE, MC, V. Mon–Thurs 11:30am–2:30pm and 6–10pm; Fri 11:30am–2:30pm and 5:30–11pm; Sat 9:30am–1:30pm and 5:30–11pm; Sun 9:30am–1:30pm. Valet parking $3.50.

Patina ★★★ CALIFORNIA/FRENCH Joachim Splichal, arguably L.A.'s very best chef, is also a genius at choosing and training top chefs to cook in his kitchens while he jets around the world. Patina routinely wins the highest praise from demanding gourmands, who are happy to empty their bank accounts for unbeatable meals that almost never miss their intended mark. The dining room is straightforwardly attractive, low key, well lit, and professional, without the slightest hint of stuffiness. The menu is equally disarming: "Mallard Duck with Portobello Mushrooms" gives little hint of the brilliant colors and flavors that appear on the plate. The seasonal menu features partridge, pheasant, venison, and other game in winter and spotlights exotic local vegetables in warmer months. Seafood is always available; if Maine lobster cannelloni or asparagus-wrapped John Dory is on the menu, order it. Patina is justifiably famous for its mashed potatoes and potato-truffle chips; be sure to include one (or both) with your meal.

5955 Melrose Ave. (west of Cahuenga Blvd.). ℭ **323/467-1108.** Reservations required. Main courses $18–$30. AE, DC, DISC, MC, V. Sun–Thurs 6–9:30pm (Tues also noon–2pm); Fri 6–10:30pm; Sat 5:30–10:30pm.

MODERATE

Authentic Cafe SOUTHWESTERN/ECLECTIC   True to its name, this restaurant serves authentic Southwestern food in a casual atmosphere. It's a winning combination that quickly made this place an L.A. favorite, although popularity has dropped off recently due to the decline of Southwestern cuisine and the rush for the next big thing. But Authentic Cafe still has a loyal following of locals who appreciate generous portions and lively flavor combinations. You'll sometimes find an Asian flair to chef Roger Hayot's dishes. Look for Brie, papaya, and chili quesadillas; other worthwhile dishes are the chicken casserole with a cornbread crust, fresh corn and red peppers in chili-cream sauce, and meat loaf with caramelized onions.

7605 Beverly Blvd. (at Curson Ave.). ℭ **323/939-4626.** Reservations accepted only for parties of 8 or more. Main courses $9–$19. AE, MC, V. Mon–Thurs 11:30am–10pm; Fri 11:30am–11pm; Sat 10:30am–11pm; Sun 10:30am–10pm.

Ca' Brea ⚑⚑ NORTHERN ITALIAN   When Ca' Brea opened in 1991, its talented chef and owner Antonio Tommasi was catapulted into a public spotlight shared by only a handful of L.A. chefs—Wolfgang Puck, Michel Richard, and Joachim Splichal. Since then, Tommasi has opened two other celebrated restaurants, Locanda Veneta in Hollywood and Ca' Del Sole in the Valley, but, for many, Ca' Brea remains tops. The restaurant's refreshingly bright two-story dining room is a happy place, hung with colorful, oversize contemporary paintings and backed by an open prep-kitchen where you can watch as your seafood cakes are sautéed and your Napa cabbage braised. Booths are the most coveted seats; but with only 20 tables in all, be thankful you're sitting anywhere. Detractors might complain that Ca' Brea isn't what it used to be since Tommasi began splitting his time between three restaurants, but Tommasi stops in daily and keeps a very close watch over his handpicked staff. Consistently excellent dishes include the roasted pork sausage, the butter squash-stuffed ravioli, and a different risotto each day—always rich, creamy, and delightfully indulgent.

346 S. La Brea Ave. (north of Wilshire Blvd.). ℭ **323/938-2863.** Reservations recommended. Main courses $9–$21; lunch $7–$20. AE, DC, MC, V. Mon–Fri 11:30am–2:30pm; Mon–Thurs 5:30–10:30pm; Fri–Sat 5:30–11pm. Valet parking $3.50.

Musso & Frank Grill ⚑ AMERICAN/CONTINENTAL   A survey of Hollywood restaurants that leaves out Musso & Frank is like a study of Las Vegas singers that fails to mention Wayne Newton. As L.A's oldest eatery (since 1919), Musso & Frank is the paragon of Old Hollywood grillrooms. This is where Faulkner and Hemingway drank during their screenwriting days and where Orson Welles used to hold court. The restaurant is still known for its bone-dry martinis and perfectly seasoned Bloody Marys. The setting is what you'd expect: oak-beamed ceilings, red-leather booths and banquettes, mahogany room dividers, and chandeliers with tiny shades. The extensive menu is a veritable survey of American/Continental cookery. Hearty dinners include veal scaloppine Marsala, roast spring lamb with mint jelly, and broiled lobster. Grilled meats are a specialty, as is the Thursday-only chicken potpie. Regulars also flock in for Musso's trademark "flannel cakes," crepe-thin pancakes flipped to order.

6667 Hollywood Blvd. (at Cherokee Ave.). ℂ 323/467-7788. Reservations recommended. Main courses $13–$32. AE, DC, MC, V. Tues–Sat 11am–11pm. Self parking $2.25 with validation

Sofi *(Finds* GREEK   Look for the simple black awning over the narrow passageway that leads from the street to this hidden Aegean treasure. Be sure to ask for a table on the romantic patio amid twinkling lights, and immediately order a plate of their thick, satisfying *tsatziki* (yogurt-cucumber-garlic spread) accompanied by a basket of warm pitas for dipping. Other specialties (recipes courtesy of Sofi's old-world grandmother) include herbed rack of lamb with rice, fried calamari salad, *saganaki* (kasseri cheese flamed with ouzo), and other hearty taverna favorites. Sofi's odd, off-street setting, near the Farmers Market in a popular part of town, has made it an insiders' secret.

8030³/₄ W. Third St. (between Fairfax Ave. and Crescent Heights Blvd.). ℂ 323/651-0346. Reservations recommended. Main courses $7–$14. AE, DC, MC, V. Mon–Sat noon–3pm; daily 5:30–11pm. Metered street parking or valet parking $3.

Tahiti ✯ WORLD CUISINE   Tahiti has a rapidly growing fan base of showbiz types and artists who inhabit the eclectic surrounding neighborhood. Chef and owner Tony DiLembo's distinctive "world cuisine" is a provocative mix of zesty influences that produces diverse specialties like rare ahi tuna drizzled with lime-ginger butter, sprinkled with toasted sesame seeds, and served with wasabi horseradish and papaya garnish; Argentinean-style T-bone with chimichurri dipping sauce; sherry-sautéed chicken and spinach potstickers accented with mint; and perennial standout rosemary chicken strips with fettuccine in sun-dried tomato-cream sauce. The relaxing decor is sophisticated South Seas with a modern twist, incorporating thatch, batik, rattan, and palm fronds. In the adjacent Tiki Lounge, tropical concoctions contribute to the island ambiance. If the weather is nice, try to get a table on the patio. And don't forget to save room for Tahiti's tropical-tinged desserts.

7910 W. Third St. (at Fairfax), Los Angeles. ℂ 323/651-1213. Reservations recommended. Main courses $11–$17. AE, MC, V. Mon–Fri 11:30am–2:30pm; Mon–Thurs 6–10pm; Fri–Sat 6–11pm; Sun 5–9pm. Valet parking $3.75.

INEXPENSIVE

El Cholo ✯ MEXICAN   There's authentic Mexican and then there's traditional Mexican—El Cholo is comfort food of the latter variety, south-of-the-border cuisine regularly craved by Angelenos. They've been serving it up in this pink adobe hacienda since 1927, even though the once-outlying mid-Wilshire neighborhood around them has turned into Koreatown. El Cholo's expertly blended margaritas, invitingly messy nachos, and classic combination dinners don't break new culinary ground, but the kitchen has perfected these standards over 70 years. We wish they bottled their rich enchilada sauce! Other specialties include seasonally available green-corn tamales and creative sizzling vegetarian fajitas that go way beyond just eliminating the meat. The atmosphere is festive, as people from all parts of town dine happily in the many rambling rooms that compose the restaurant. There's valet parking as well as a free self-park lot directly across the street.

Westsiders head to El Cholo's Santa Monica branch at 1025 Wilshire Blvd. (📞 **310/899-1106**).

1121 S. Western Ave. (south of Olympic Blvd.). 📞 **323/734-2773**. www.elcholo.com. Reservations suggested. Main courses $8–$14. AE, DC, MC, V. Mon–Thurs 11am–10pm; Fri–Sat 11am–11pm; Sun 11am–9pm. Free self-parking or valet parking $3.

Hollywood Hills Coffee Shop DINER   Having for years served as the run-of-the-mill coffee shop for the attached freeway-side Best Western, this place took on a life of its own when chef Susan Fine commandeered the kitchen and spiked the menu with quirky Mexican and Asian touches. Hotel guests spill in from the lobby to rub noses with the actors, screenwriters, and other artistic types who converge from nearby canyons while awaiting that sitcom casting call or feature-film deal—a community immortalized in the 1996 film *Swingers,* which was filmed in the restaurant. Prices have gone up (to pay for the industrial-strength cappuccino maker visible behind the counter?), and the dinner menu features surprisingly sophisticated entrees. But breakfast and lunch are still bargains, and the comfy Americana atmosphere is a nice break from the bright lights of nearby Hollywood Boulevard.

6145 Franklin Ave. (between Gower and Vine Sts.). 📞 **323/467-7678**. Most items less than $10. AE, DISC, MC, V. Daily 7am–10pm. Free parking.

Pink's Hot Dogs *Kids* HOT DOGS   Pink's isn't your usual guidebook recommendation, but then again, this crusty corner stand isn't your usual doggery either. The heartburn-inducing chili dogs are craved by even the most upstanding, health-conscious Angelenos. Bruce Willis reportedly proposed to Demi Moore at the 59-year-old shack that grew around the late Paul Pink's 10¢ wiener cart. Pray the bulldozers stay away from this little nugget of a place.

709 N. La Brea Ave. (at Melrose Ave.). 📞 **323/931-4223**. www.pinkshollywood.com. Hot dogs $2.10. No credit cards. Sun–Thurs 9:30am–2am; Fri–Sat 9:30am–3am.

Roscoe's House of Chicken 'n' Waffles SOUTHERN/BREAKFAST   It sounds like a bad joke: Only chicken and waffle dishes are served here, a rubric that also encompasses eggs and chicken livers. Its close proximity to CBS Television City has turned this simple restaurant into a kind of de facto commissary for the network. A chicken-and-cheese omelet isn't everyone's ideal way to begin the day, but it's de rigueur at Roscoe's. At lunch, few calorie-unconscious diners can resist the chicken smothered in gravy and onions, a house specialty that's served with waffles or grits and biscuits. Large chicken-salad bowls and chicken sandwiches also provide plenty of cluck for the buck. Homemade corn bread, sweet-potato pie, homemade potato salad, and corn on the cob are available as side orders, and wine and beer are sold.

Roscoe's can also be found at 4907 W. Washington Blvd., La Brea Avenue (📞 **323/936-3730**), and 5006 W. Pico Blvd. (📞 **323/934-4405**).

1514 N. Gower St. (at Sunset Blvd.). 📞 **323/466-7453**. Main courses $4–$11. No credit cards. Sun–Thurs 9am–midnight; Fri–Sat 9am–4am. Metered street parking

Swingers 🔦 DINER/AMERICAN   Resurrected from a motel coffee shop so dismal we can't even remember it, Swingers was transformed by a couple of L.A. hipster nightclub owners into a 1990s version of comfy Americana. The interior seems like a slice of the 1950s until you notice the plaid upholstery and Warholesque graphics, which contrast nicely with the retro red-white-and-blue "Swingers" logo adorning *everything.* Guests at the attached Beverly Laurel Motor Hotel chow down alongside body-pierced industry hounds from nearby record companies, while a soundtrack that runs the gamut from punk rock to "Schoolhouse Rock" plays in the background. It's not all attitude here, though—you'll enjoy a menu of high-quality diner favorites spiked with trendy crowd-pleasers: Steel-cut Irish oatmeal, challah French toast, grilled Jamaican jerk chicken, and a nice selection of tofu-enhanced vegetarian dishes are just a few of the eclectic offerings. Sometimes we just "swing" by for a malt or milkshake to go—they're among the best in town.

8020 Beverly Blvd. (west of Fairfax Ave.). (C) 323/653-5858. Most items less than $8. AE, DISC, MC, V. Sun–Thurs 6am–2am; Fri–Sat 9am–4am. Metered street parking.

Toi on Sunset ★ (Value THAI   Because they're open *really* late, Toi has become an instant fave of Hollywood hipsters like Sean Penn and Woody Harrelson, who make post-clubbing excursions to this rock-and-roll eatery a few blocks from the Sunset Strip. After all the hype, we were surprised to find possibly L.A.'s best bargain Thai food, authentically prepared and served in portions so generous the word *enormous* seems inadequate. Menu highlights include hot-and-sour chicken, coconut soup, and the house specialty: chicken curry somen, a spicy dish with green curry and mint sauce spooned over thin Japanese rice noodles. Vegetarians will be pleased with the vast selection of meat-free items like *pad kee mao,* rice noodles served spicy with tofu, mint, onions, peppers, and chili. The interior is a noisy amalgam of cultish movie posters, rock-and-roll memorabilia, and haphazardly placed industrial-issue dinette sets; and the plates, flatware, and drinking glasses are cheap coffee-shop issue. In other words, it's all about the food and the scene—neither will disappoint.

Westsiders can opt for **Toi on Wilshire,** 1120 Wilshire Blvd., Santa Monica (© **310/394-7804**), open daily from 11am to 3am.

7505 ½ Sunset Blvd. (at Gardner). (C) 323/874-8062. Reservations accepted only for parties of 6 or more. Main courses $6–$11. AE, DISC, MC, V. Daily 11am–4am.

DOWNTOWN
EXPENSIVE
Water Grill ★★★ SEAFOOD   This restaurant is popular with the suit-and-tie crowd at lunch and with concertgoers en route to the Music Center at night. The dining room is a stylish and sophisticated fusion of wood, leather, and brass, but it gets a lighthearted lift from cavorting papier-mâché fish that play against an aquamarine ceiling painted with bubbles. Water Grill, considered by many to be L.A.'s best seafood house, is best known for its shellfish; among the appetizers are a dozen different oysters. Main courses are imaginative dishes influenced by the cuisines of Hawaii, the Pacific Northwest, New Orleans, and New England. Try the appetizer seafood platter, a mouthwatering assortment served with well-made aïoli; bluefin tuna tartare; Santa Barbara spot prawns paired with fingerling potato salad; Maine lobster stuffed with Dungeness crab; perfectly pan-roasted Alaskan halibut; and simple desserts like mascarpone with figs and cherries.

544 S. Grand Ave. (between 5th and 6th Sts.). (C) 213/891-0900. Reservations recommended. Main courses $19–$31. AE, DC, DISC, MC, V. Mon–Tues 11:30am–9pm; Wed–Fri 11:30am–10pm; Sat 5–10pm; Sun 4:30–9pm. Valet parking $4.

MODERATE
Cha Cha Cha ★★ CARIBBEAN   Cha Cha Cha serves the West Coast's best Caribbean food in a fun and funky space on the seedy fringe of downtown. The restaurant is a festival of flavors and colors that are both upbeat and offbeat. It's

impossible to feel down when you're part of this eclectic hodgepodge of pulsating Caribbean music, wild decor, and kaleidoscopic clutter; still, the intimate dining rooms cater to lively romantics, not obnoxious frat boys. Claustrophobes should choose seats in the airy covered courtyard. The very spicy black-pepper jumbo shrimp gets top marks, as does the paella, a generous mixture of chicken, sausage, and seafood blended with saffron rice. Other Jamaican-, Haitian-, Cuban-, and Puerto Rican–inspired recommendations include jerk pork and mambo gumbo, a zesty soup of okra, shredded chicken, and spices. Hard-core Caribbeanites might visit for breakfast, when the fare ranges from plantain, yucca, onion, and herb omelets to scrambled eggs with fresh tomatillos served on hot grilled tortillas.

656 N. Virgil Ave. (at Melrose Ave.), Silver Lake. ✆ 323/664-7723. Reservations recommended. Main courses $8–$15. AE, DC, DISC, MC, V. Sun–Thurs 8am–10:30pm; Fri–Sat 8am–11:30pm. Valet parking $3.50.

Ciudad ✷✷ LATIN   The latest venture of TV's *Too Hot Tamales*—Susan Feniger and Mary Sue Milliken—is this intriguingly conceived restaurant in the heart of downtown's high-rises. The name, Ciudad, means "city" in Spanish and is a nod to the partners' long-ago venture City Restaurant. Here, amidst juicy sherbet pastel walls and 1950s geometric abstract designs, exuberant crowds gather to revel in a menu that brings together cuisines from the world's great Latin urban centers: Havana, Rio de Janeiro, Barcelona, and so on. Standout dishes include Honduran ceviche presented in a martini glass and accented with tropical coconut and pineapple, Argentine rib eye stuffed with jalapeño chilies and whole garlic cloves, and citrus-roasted Cuban-style chicken served with Puerto Rican rice and fried plantains. Between 3 and 7pm on weekdays, Ciudad presents *cuchifrito,* traditional Latin snacks served at the bar; it's easy to make a meal of several, choosing from sweet-savory pork-stuffed green tamales, *papas rellenos* (mashed potato fritters stuffed with oxtail stew), plantain gnocchi in tomatillo sauce, and more. As with the pair's Border Grill, desserts are worth saving room for, and large enough to share.

445 S. Figueroa St. ✆ 213/486-5171. www.millikenandfeniger.com. Reservations recommended. Main courses $12–$23; *cuchifrito* $5–$8. AE, MC, V. Mon–Fri 11:30am–10pm; Sat–Sun 5–10pm. Free parking days; valet parking (after 5pm) $3.50.

R23 ✷✷ JAPANESE/SUSHI   This gallery-like space in downtown's out-of-the-way warehouse/artist loft district has been the secret of sushi connoisseurs since 1991. At the back of R23's single, large dining room, the 12-seat sushi bar shines like a beacon; what appear at first to be ceramic wall ornaments are really stylish sushi platters hanging in wait for large orders. More functional art reveals itself in the corrugated cardboard chairs—they're funky, yet far more comfortable than wood! Genial sushi wizards stand in wait, cases of the finest fish before them. Salmon, yellowtail, shrimp, tuna, and scallops are among the always-fresh selections; an excellent and unusual offering is seared *toro,* where the rich belly tuna absorbs a faint and delectable smoky flavor from the grill. Though R23's sublimely perfect sushi is the star, the short but inventive menu also includes pungent red miso soup, creamy baked scallops, finely sliced beef "sashimi," and several other choices.

923 E. Third St. (between Alameda St. and Santa Fe Ave.). ✆ 213/687-7178. Reservations recommended. Main courses $12–$20; sushi $4–$8. AE, MC, V. Mon–Fri noon–2pm and 6–10pm; Sat 6–10pm. Free parking.

Traxx ✷ *(Finds* CALIFORNIA   There's always been a restaurant—of some sort—inside the Union Station passenger concourse, but Traxx is the first to do justice to its grand, historic setting. Boasting just the right mix of retro-evocative art deco character with sleek contemporary touches, the interior blends seamlessly with the station's architecture, a unique fusion of Spanish Colonial Revival and Streamline Moderne. Elegant enough for a low-lit romantic dinner, yet welcoming to the casual commuter in search of a stylish lunch or sit-down snack, Traxx features a menu designed by executive chef Tara Thomas to have the same cosmopolitan flavor as the station itself. Samples range from "small plates" of ahi tuna Napoleon with crispy wonton or "Really Good" (and they are) crab cakes with a chipotle kick to main dishes like grilled salmon with a Mediterranean flair or the much-talked-about Gorgonzola-crusted beef tenderloin presented atop crispy mashed potatoes surrounded by a pool of demi-glace/herb reduction.

In Union Station, 800 N. Alameda St. (at Cesar E. Chavez Ave.). ✆ 213/625-1999. Reservations suggested for dinner. Main courses $10–$15 lunch; $10–$25 dinner. AE, MC, V. Mon–Fri 11am–10pm; Sat 6–10pm. Free valet parking with validation.

Yang Chow Restaurant ★★ CHINESE   Open for more than 30 years, family-operated Yang Chow is one of downtown's more popular Chinese restaurants. It's not the dining room's bland and functional decor that accrues accolades, however; what makes Yang Chow so popular is an interesting menu of seafood specialties complementing well-done Chinese standards. After covering the Mandarin and Szechuan basics—sweet-and-sour pork, shrimp with broccoli, moo shu chicken—the kitchen leaps into high gear, concocting dishes like spicy Dungeness crab, a tangy and hot sautéed squid, and sautéed shellfish with a pungent hoisin-based dipping sauce. The key to having a terrific meal is to first order the house specialty—plump steamed pork dumplings presented on a bed of fresh spinach—then respectfully ask for recommendations from your server.

819 N. Broadway (at Alpine St.), Chinatown. ✆ 213/625-0811. Reservations recommended on weekends. Main courses $8–$14. AE, MC, V. Daily 11:30am–2:30pm; Sun–Thurs 5–9:30pm; Fri–Sat 5–10:30pm. Free parking.

INEXPENSIVE

The Original Pantry Cafe *Value* AMERICAN/BREAKFAST   An L.A. institution if there ever was one, this place has been serving huge portions of comfort food around the clock for more than 60 years. In fact, there isn't even a key to the front door. Owned by former L.A. Mayor Richard Riordan, the Pantry is especially popular with politicos, who come here for weekday lunches, and with conferencegoers en route to the nearby L.A. Convention Center. The well-worn restaurant is also a welcoming beacon to clubbers after hours, when downtown becomes a virtual ghost town. A bowl of celery stalks, carrot sticks, and whole radishes greets you at your Formica table, and creamy coleslaw and sourdough bread come free with every meal. Famous for quantity rather than quality, the Pantry serves huge T-bone steaks, densely packed meat loaf, macaroni and cheese, and other American favorites. A typical breakfast (served all day) might consist of a huge stack of hotcakes, a big slab of sweet cured ham, home fries, and coffee.

877 S. Figueroa St. (at 9th street). ✆ 213/972-9279. Main courses $6–$11. No credit cards. Daily 24 hr. Free parking with validation.

Philippe the Original SANDWICHES   Good old-fashioned value is what this legendary landmark cafeteria is all about. Popular with both south-central project dwellers and Beverly Hills elite, Philippe's decidedly unspectacular dining room is one of the few places in L.A. where everyone can get along. Philippe's claims to have invented the French-dipped sandwich at this location in 1908; it remains the most popular menu item. Patrons push trays along the counter and watch while their choice of beef, pork, ham, turkey, or lamb is sliced and layered onto crusty French bread that's been dipped in meat juices. Other menu items include homemade beef stew, chili, and pickled pigs' feet. A hearty breakfast, served daily until 10:30am, is worthwhile if only for Philippe's uncommonly good cinnamon-dipped French toast. Beer and wine are available.

1001 N. Alameda St. (at Ord St.). © **213/628-3781.** www.philippes.com. Most menu items under $7. No credit cards. Daily 6am–10pm. Free parking.

THE SAN FERNANDO VALLEY
EXPENSIVE
Pinot Bistro ⊀⊀ CALIFORNIA/FRENCH   When the Valley crowd doesn't want to make the drive to Patina, they pack into Pinot Bistro, one of Joachim Splichal's other hugely successful restaurants. The Valley's only great bistro is designed with dark woods, etched glass, and cream-colored walls that scream "trendy French" almost as loudly as the rich, straightforward cooking. The menu, a symphony of California and continental elements, includes a beautiful warm potato tart with smoked whitefish, and baby lobster tails with creamy polenta—both studies in culinary perfection. The most popular dish here is chef Octavio Becerra's French-ified Tuscan bean soup, infused with oven-dried tomatoes and roasted garlic and served over crusty ciabatta bread. The generously portioned main dishes continue the gourmet theme: baby lobster risotto, braised oxtail with parsley gnocchi, and puff pastry stuffed with bay scallops, Manila clams, and roast duck. The service is good, attentive, and unobtrusive. Many regulars prefer Pinot Bistro at lunch, when a less expensive menu is served to a more easygoing crowd.

12969 Ventura Blvd. (west of Coldwater Canyon Ave.), Studio City. © **818/990-0500.** Reservations required. Main courses $7–$13 lunch; $16–$22 dinner. AE, DC, DISC, MC, V. Mon–Fri 11:30am–2:30pm; Mon–Thurs 6–10pm; Fri 6–10:30pm; Sat 5:30–10:30pm; Sun 5:30–9:30pm. Valet parking $3.50.

MODERATE
Jerry's Famous Deli ⊀ (Kids) DELI   Here's a simple yet sizable deli where all the Valley's hipsters go to relieve their late-night munchies. This place probably has one of the largest menus in America—a tome that spans cultures and continents, from Central America to China to New York. From salads to sandwiches to steak-and-seafood platters, everything—including breakfast—is served all day. Jerry's is consistently good at lox and eggs, pastrami sandwiches, potato pancakes, and all the deli staples. It's also an integral part of L.A.'s cultural landscape and a favorite of the show-business types who populate the adjacent foothill neighborhoods. It even has a full bar.

12655 Ventura Blvd. (just east of Coldwater Canyon Ave.), Studio City. © **818/980-4245.** Dinner main courses $9–$14; breakfast $2–$11; sandwiches and salads $4–$12. AE, MC, V. Daily 24 hr. Free parking.

Katsu ⊀⊀⊀ JAPANESE   The latest entry onto Studio City's unofficial "Sushi Row" is no newcomer: Katsu Michite has been teaching Angelenos to love fine sushi for years, and many of the city's star sushi masters at places like R23 and the Hump are veterans of Katsu's much-missed Los Feliz flagship. Katsu's new venue is this stark, contemporary space accented with rough-cut wood and bamboo; in addition to the main dining room and intimate sushi counter, there's an even smaller, hidden bar where Katsu-san delivers his unequaled *omakase* (chef's choice). Masterful touches distinguish Katsu's fare from its neighbors, little things such as fresh-grated wasabi, or respectfully decanted chilled sake. The sushi is always perfect and never fancy (better look elsewhere for those trendy "inside-out" rolls), and there's a long menu of cooked delicacies like meltingly good grilled butterfish, satisfying tofu steak piled high with flaky bonito and shredded scallions, and outstanding crisp salmon skin salad.

On the other side of the hill, **Katsu 3rd** (8636 W. Third St.; (*C* **310/ 273-3605**) sits across the street from Cedars-Sinai and attracts a trendy, less food-serious crowd.

11920 Ventura Blvd. (east of Laurel Canyon), Studio City. *C* 818/760-4585. Reservations recommended. Main courses $9–$20; sushi $3–$7; *omakase* from $70 up. AE, MC, V. Mon–Fri 11:30am–2:30pm; daily 5–10:30pm. Valet parking $3.

Miceli's *(Kids* ITALIAN   Mostaccioli marinara, lasagna, thin-crust pizza, and eggplant parmigiana are indicative of the Sicilian-style fare at this cavernous, stained-glass windowed Italian restaurant adjacent to Universal City. The wait-staff sings show tunes or opera favorites in between serving dinner (and some-times instead of); make sure you have enough Chianti to get into the spirit of it all. This is a great place for kids, but way too rollicking for romance.

If you're near Hollywood Boulevard, visit the original (since 1949) Miceli's at 1646 N. Las Palmas (*C* **323/466-3438**).

3655 Cahuenga Blvd. (east of Lankershim), Los Angeles. *C* 818/508-1221. Main courses $7–$12; pizza $9–$15. AE, DC, MC, V. Mon–Thurs 5pm–midnight; Fri 5pm–1am; Sat 4pm–1am; Sun 4–11pm. Parking $2.50.

Paul's Cafe *☆☆* CALIFORNIA/FRENCH   One of the Valley's hardest reser-vations (hint: call early, dine early, or both) is at this midsize neighborhood bistro, where a quietly elegant setting belies the friendly prices that have made Paul's a big success. Expect the seasonal menu to include plenty of seafood (roasted sea bass laid atop spinach with a mushroom vinaigrette and sautéed sea scallops with saffron risotto and lobster sauce), hearty meats (filet mignon with port sauce accompanied by a creamy sweet potato–Gorgonzola gratin and garlic-rubbed rack of lamb sweetened with mint), and appetizers that ought to be main courses (pepper crusted seared ahi drizzled with scallion vinaigrette and crab cakes with lobster aïoli). Soup or a small salad is only $1 with any dinner, and locals love the mere $2 corkage fee. Paul's manages to be intimate enough for lovers yet also welcoming for families—its success is no surprise.

13456 Ventura Blvd. (between Dixie Canyon and Woodman Ave.), Sherman Oaks. *C* 818/789-3575. Main courses $12–$17 dinner; $8–$11 lunch. AE, MC, V. Mon–Thurs 11:30am–2:30pm and 5:30–10pm; Fri 11:30am–2:30pm and 5:30–11pm; Sat 5–11pm; Sun 5–9:30pm. Metered street parking or valet parking $4.

INEXPENSIVE

Du-par's Restaurant & Bakery *☆*AMERICAN/DINER   It's been called a "culinary wax museum," the last of a dying breed, the kind of coffee shop Donna Reed took the family to for blue-plate specials. This isn't a trendy new theme place, it's the real deal—and that motherly waitress who calls everyone under 60 "hon" has probably been slinging hash here for 20 or 30 years. Du-par's is popular among old-timers who made it part of their daily routine decades ago, show-business denizens who eschew the industry watering holes, a new genera-tion that appreciates a tasty, cheap meal . . . well, everyone, really. It's common knowledge that Du-par's makes the best buttermilk pancakes in town, though some prefer the eggy, perfect French toast (extra-crispy around the edges, please). Mouth-watering pies (blueberry cream cheese, coconut cream, and more) line the front display case and can be had for a song.

West Hollywood denizens can visit the branch of Du-par's in the Ramada Hotel, 8571 Santa Monica Blvd., west of La Cienega (*C* **310/659-7009**);

they're open until 3am on weekends *and* have a full bar. There's another Du-par's in Los Angeles at the Farmers Market, 6333 W. 3rd St. (© **323/933-8446**), but it doesn't stay open as late.

12036 Ventura Blvd. (1 block east of Laurel Canyon Blvd.), Studio City. © 818/766-4437. www.Dupars.com. All items under $11. AE, DC, DISC, MC, V. Sun–Thurs 6am–1am; Fri–Sat 6am–4am. Free parking.

PASADENA & ENVIRONS

During the past decade or so, Pasadena has grown into one of the premier dining destinations for Angelenos in the know. It's now packed with restaurants ranging from elegant art-food dining to casual sidewalk cafes, and Pasadena is no longer anybody's secret.

EXPENSIVE

Bistro 45 ✸✸✸ CALIFORNIA/FRENCH   All class, yet never stuffy, Bistro 45 is a favorite among Pasadena's Old Guard and nouvelle riche. The restaurant's warm, light, ambiance, and gallery-like decor are an unexpected surprise after the ornately historic Art Deco exterior (the building is a former bank), but provide a perfect backdrop for owner Robert Simon's lilting, refreshing cuisine. The seasonally inspired menu changes frequently; sample dishes include salmon and tuna tartares flavored with cilantro, rock shrimp risotto with saffron, pan-roasted monkfish with garlic polenta, roasted veal loin filled with Roquefort, Fanny Bay oyster salad, and Nebraska pork with figs. For dessert, try the "chocolate soup," a creamy soufflé served with chocolate-kirsch sauce and vanilla ice cream. The practiced knowledgeable waitstaff can answer any questions about the excellent wine list; Bistro 45 appears regularly on *Wine Spectator*'s "Best of" lists, and hosts special-event wine dinners.

45 Mentor Ave. (between Colorado and Green), Pasadena. © 626/795-2478. Reservations recommended. Main courses $11–$16 lunch; $17–$27 dinner. AE, MC, V. Tues–Thurs 11:30am–2:30pm and 6–10pm; Fri 11:30am–2:30pm and 6–11pm; Sat 6–11pm; Sun 5–9pm. Valet parking $4.

Parkway Grill ✸ CALIFORNIA ECLECTIC   This vibrant, quintessentially southern California restaurant has been one of the L.A. area's top-rated spots since it opened in 1985, quickly gaining a reputation for avant-garde flavor combinations and gourmet pizzas to rival Spago's. Although some critics find many dishes too fussy, others thrill to appetizer innovations like lobster-stuffed cocoa crepes or Dungeness crab cakes with ginger cream and two salsas. The stars of the menu are meat and game from the iron mesquite grill, followed by richly sweet (and substantial) desserts. Located where the old Arroyo Seco Parkway glides into an ordinary city street, the Parkway Grill is within a couple of minutes' drive from Old Pasadena and thoughtfully offers free valet parking.

510 S. Arroyo Pkwy. (at California Blvd.), Pasadena. © 626/795-1001. Reservations recommended. Main courses $8–$27. AE, DC, MC, V. Mon–Thurs 11:30am–2:30pm and 5:30–11pm; Fri 11:30am–2:30pm and 5pm–midnight; Sat 5pm–midnight; Sun 5–11pm. Free valet parking.

The Raymond ✸✸ NEW AMERICAN/CONTINENTAL   With its easy-to-miss setting in a sleepy part of Pasadena, the Raymond is a jewel even few locals know about. This Craftsman cottage was once the caretaker's house for a grand Victorian hotel called The Raymond. Though the city has grown to surround it, the place maintains an enchanting air of seclusion and serenity. Chef and owner Suzanne Bourg brings a romantic sensibility and impeccable culinary instincts to dishes that are mostly haute American—with an occasional European flair. The menu changes weekly. One night a grilled rack of lamb is sauced with orange, Grand Marnier, and peppercorns; another night it comes with a creamy white wine and chèvre sauce punctuated with dried cherries. Bourg's soups are always heavenly (the restaurant gladly gives out the recipes), and desserts are inspired. Tables are scattered throughout the house and in the lush English garden, and there's plenty of free, non-valet parking. (You wouldn't find *that* on the Westside!)

1250 S. Fair Oaks Ave. (at Columbia St.), Pasadena. (C) 626/441-3136. Reservations required. Main courses lunch $12–$19, dinner $29–$33, 4-course dinner $43–$47, prix fixe 3-course dinner $33 (including wine). AE, DC, DISC, MC, V. Tues–Thurs 11:30am–2:30pm and 6–9:30pm; Fri 11:30am–2:30pm and 5:45–10pm; Sat 11am–2:30pm and 5:45–10pm; Sun 10am–2:30pm and 4:30–8pm; afternoon tea Tues–Sun noon–4pm. Free parking.

MODERATE

Cafe Santorini ✿ MEDITERRANEAN Located at ground zero of Pasadena's crowded Old Town shopping mecca, this second-story gem has a secluded Mediterranean ambience, due in part to its historic brick building with splendid patio tables overlooking, but insulated from, the busy plaza below. In the evening, lighting is subdued and romantic, but the ambience is casual; many diners are coming from or going to an adjacent movie-theater complex. The food is outstanding and affordable, featuring expertly grilled meats and kebobs, pizzas, fresh and tangy hummus, plenty of warm pitas, and other staples of Greek cuisine. The menu includes regional flavors like lamb, feta cheese, spinach, or Armenian sausage; the vegetarian baked butternut squash is filled with fluffy rice and smoky roast vegetables.

64 W. Union St. (main entrance at the shopping plaza at the corner of Fair Oaks and Colorado), Pasadena. (C) 626/564-4200. www.cafesantorini.com. Reservations recommended on weekends. Main courses $9–$22. AE, DC, DISC, MC, V. Daily 11am–11pm (until midnight Fri–Sat). Valet or self parking $4.

Yujean Kang's Gourmet Chinese Cuisine ✿✿ CONTEMPORARY CHINESE Many Chinese restaurants put the word *gourmet* in their name, but few really mean it—or deserve it. Not so at Yujean Kang's, where Chinese cuisine is taken to an entirely new level. A master of "fusion" cuisine, the eponymous chef and owner snatches bits of techniques and flavors from both China and the West, co-mingling them in an entirely fresh way. Can you resist such provocative dishes as "Ants on Tree" (beef sautéed with glass noodles in chili and black sesame seeds), lobster with caviar and fava beans, or Chilean sea bass in passion-fruit sauce? Kang is also a wine aficionado and has assembled a magnificent cellar of California, French, and particularly German wines. Try pairing a German Spätlese with tea-smoked duck salad. The red-wrapped dining room is less subtle than the food, but just as elegant.

There's a second Yujean Kang's in West Hollywood, at 8826 Melrose Ave. ((C) 310/288-0806). Even though Kang consulted with a feng shui master on the location and layout of the new space, some Angelenos grumble about the less adventurous menu and higher prices. Others are just grateful they don't have to trek to Pasadena anymore.

67 N. Raymond Ave. (between Walnut St. and Colorado Blvd.), Pasadena. (C) 626/585-0855. Reservations recommended. Main courses $8–$19. AE, MC, V. Daily 11:30am–2:30pm and 5–10pm. Street parking.

INEXPENSIVE

Crocodile Cafe CASUAL ECLECTIC Casual and colorful, this offshoot of Pasadena's groundbreaking Parkway Grill builds a menu around simple crowd-pleasers (pizza, pasta, burgers, and salads) prepared with nice, fresh ingredients and jazzed up with creative marinades, vinaigrettes, and salsas. It's a formula that works; this Lake Ave. branch is the original location, but siblings have sprung up throughout the San Fernando and San Gabriel Valleys—even as far away as Santa Monica! Favorite selections include the oakwood-grilled burger with curly French fries, the Croc's signature blue corn chicken tostada with warm black beans and fresh guacamole, wood-grilled gourmet pizzas in the California Pizza Kitchen style, zesty tortilla soup, and ooey gooey desserts.

Other branches include Old Town Pasadena, 88 W. Colorado Blvd. (© **626/ 568-9310**); Glendale, 626 N. Central Ave (© **818/241-1114**); and Santa Monica, 101 Santa Monica Blvd. (© **310/394-4783**).

140 So. Lake Ave., Pasadena. © 626/449-9900. www.crocodilecafe.com. Main courses 8[nd15. AE, MC, V. Daily 11am–10pm (till midnight Fri–Sat). Free self-parking.

Old Town Bakery & Restaurant CALIFORNIA/BAKERY Set back from the street in a quaint fountain courtyard, this cheery bakery is an especially popular place to read the morning paper over a tasty breakfast such as pumpkin pancakes or zesty omelets. The display counters are packed with cakes, muffins, scones, and other confections, all baked expressly for this shop. The rest of the menu is a mishmash of pastas, salads, and the like, borrowing heavily from Latin and Mediterranean cuisines. This is a great place to spy on local Pasadenans in their natural habitat.

166 W. Colorado Blvd. (at Pasadena Ave.), Pasadena. © 626/792-7943. Main courses $5–$11. DISC, MC, V. Sun–Thurs 7:30am–10pm; Fri–Sat 7:30am–midnight. Metered street parking.

5 The Top Attractions

SANTA MONICA & THE BEACHES

Venice Ocean Front Walk ★★ This has long been one of L.A.'s most colorful areas. Founded at the turn of the century, the town of Venice was a theme development inspired by its Italian namesake. Authentic Venetian gondolas plied miles of inland waterways lined with rococo palaces. In the 1950s, Venice became the celebrated stomping grounds of Jack Kerouac, Allen Ginsberg, William S. Burroughs, and other beats. In the 1960s, this was the epicenter of L.A.'s hippie scene.

Today, Venice is still one of the world's most engaging bohemias. It's not an exaggeration to say that no visit to L.A. would be complete without a stroll along the famous beach path, an almost-surreal assemblage of every L.A. stereotype— and then some. Among stalls and stands selling cheap sunglasses, Mexican blankets, and "herbal ecstasy" pills swirls a carnival of humanity that includes bikini-clad in-line skaters, tattooed bikers, muscle-bound pretty boys, panhandling vets, beautiful wanna-bes, and plenty of tourists and gawkers. On any given day you're bound to come across all kinds of performers: mimes, breakdancers, buskers, chain-saw jugglers, talking parrots, or an occasional apocalyptic evangelist.

On the beach, between Venice Blvd. and Rose Ave.

L.A.'S WESTSIDE & BEVERLY HILLS

J. Paul Getty Museum at the Getty Center ★★ Since opening in 1997, the Richard Meier–designed Getty Center has quickly assumed its place in the L.A. landscape (literally and figuratively) as a cultural cornerstone and international mecca. Headquarters for the Getty Trust's research, education, and conservation concerns, the complex is most frequently visited for the museum galleries displaying collector J. Paul Getty's enormous collection of important art. Always known for antiquities, expanded galleries now allow the display of impressionist paintings, French decorative arts, fine illuminated manuscripts, and contemporary photography and graphic arts that were previously overlooked. A sophisticated system of programmable window louvers allows many outstanding works to be displayed in natural light for the first time in the modern era. One of these is van Gogh's *Irises,* one of the museum's finest holdings. Trivia buffs will enjoy knowing that the museum spent $53.9 million to acquire this painting; it's displayed in a complex that cost roughly $1 billion to construct.

Visitors to the center park their cars at the base of the hill and ascend via a cable-driven electric tram. On clear days, the sensation is of being in the clouds, gazing across Los Angeles and the Pacific Ocean (and into a few chic Brentwood backyards). In addition to a casual cafe and several espresso-snack carts, the complex even has a bona fide restaurant on-site, complete with a panoramic view.

Parking reservations are required weekday. College students with current ID and those arriving by public transportation, motorcycle, or bicycle do not require reservations. Reservations are not required after 4pm, or all day Saturday and Sunday. *Insider tip:* Avoid the crowds by visiting in the late afternoon or evening; the center is open until 9pm Friday and Saturday, the nighttime view is breathtaking, and you can finish with a late dinner on the Westside.

1200 Getty Center Dr., Los Angeles. ✆ 310/440-7300. www.getty.edu. Free admission. Tues–Thurs and Sun 10am–6pm, Fri–Sat 10am–9pm. Closed major holidays. Parking $5; reservations required weekdays (see above).

Rancho La Brea Tar Pits/George C. Page Museum ✮✮ Kids   An odorous, murky swamp of congealed oil continuously oozes to the earth's surface in the middle of Los Angeles. No, it's not a low-budget horror movie set—it's the La Brea Tar Pits, an awesome, primal pool right on Museum Row, where hot tar has been bubbling from the earth for over 40,000 years. The glistening pools, which look like murky water, have enticed thirsty animals throughout history. Thousands of mammals, birds, amphibians, and insects—many of which are now extinct—mistakenly crawled into the sticky sludge and stayed forever. In 1906 scientists began a systematic removal and classification of entombed specimens, including ground sloths, giant vultures, mastodons, camels, bears, lizards, even prehistoric relatives of today's beloved super rats. The best finds are on display in the adjacent George C. Page Museum of La Brea Discoveries, where an excellent 15-minute film documenting the recoveries is also shown. Archaeological work is ongoing; you can watch as scientists clean, identify, and catalog new finds in the Paleontology Laboratory.

5801 Wilshire Blvd. (east of Fairfax Ave.), Los Angeles. ✆ 323/934-PAGE. www.tarpits.org. Admission $6 adults, $3.50 seniors 62 and older and students with ID, $2 children ages 5–12, free for kids age under 5; free for everyone the 1st Tues of every month. Daily 10am–5pm (museum).

HOLLYWOOD

Farmers Market ✮✮   The original market was little more than a field clustered with stands set up by farmers during the Depression so they could sell directly to city dwellers. Eventually, permanent buildings grew up, including the trademark shingled 10-story clock tower. Today the place has evolved into a sprawling food marketplace with a carnival atmosphere, a kind of "turf" version of San Francisco's surfy Fisherman's Wharf. About 100 restaurants, shops, and grocers cater to a mix of workers from the adjacent CBS Television City complex, locals, and tourists, who are brought here by the busload. Retailers sell greeting cards, kitchen implements, candles, and souvenirs; but everyone comes

here for the food stands, which offer oysters, Cajun gumbo, fresh-squeezed orange juice, roast-beef sandwiches, fresh-pressed peanut butter, and all kinds of international fast foods. You can still buy produce here—it's no longer a farm-fresh bargain, but the selection's better than at the grocery stores. Don't miss **Kokomo,** a "gourmet" outdoor coffee shop that has become a power breakfast spot for showbiz types. Red turkey hash and sweet-potato fries are the dishes that keep them coming back.

At press time, Farmers Market was still in the construction phase of a massive improvement that will bring a Nordstrom-anchored shopping plaza to one end of the complex. Parking is limited during the project, so be prepared.

6333 W. 3rd St. (corner of Fairfax Ave.). ☏ **323/933-9211.** www.farmersmarketla.com. Mon–Sat 9am–6:30pm; Sun 10am–5pm.

Griffith Observatory ★★   Made world-famous in the film *Rebel Without a Cause,* Griffith Observatory's bronze domes have been Hollywood Hills landmarks since 1935. Most visitors never actually go inside; they come to this spot on the south slope of Mount Hollywood for unparalleled city views. On warm nights, with the lights twinkling below, this is one of the most romantic places in L.A.

The main dome houses a **planetarium,** where narrated projection shows reveal the stars and planets that are hidden from the naked eye by the city's lights and smog. Other shows take you on excursions into space to search for extra-terrestrial life, or examine the causes of earthquakes, moonquakes, and star-quakes. Presentations last about an hour. Show times vary, so call for information.

The adjacent **Hall of Science** holds exhibits on galaxies, meteorites, and other cosmic objects, including a telescope trained on the sun, a Foucault pen-dulum, and earth and moon globes 6 feet in diameter. On clear nights you can gaze at the heavens through the powerful 12-inch telescope.

2800 E. Observatory Rd. (in Griffith Park, at the end of Vermont Ave.). ☏ **323/664-1191,** or 323/663-8171 for the Sky Report, a recorded message on current planet positions and celestial events. www.griffith observatory.org. Free admission; planetarium show tickets $4 adults, $3 seniors, $2 children ages 5–12. June–Aug daily 12:30–10pm; Sept–May Tues–Fri 2–10pm, Sat–Sun 12:30–10pm.

Hollywood Sign ★   These 50-foot-high white sheet-metal letters have come to symbolize both the movie industry and the city itself. The sign was erected in 1923 as an advertisement for a fledgling real-estate development. The full text originally read HOLLYWOODLAND. Actress Peg Entwistle leapt to her death from the "H" in 1932. An earthquake-monitoring seismograph is now buried near its base. The installation of motion detectors around the sign just made this graffiti tagger's coup a target even more worth boasting about. A thorny hiking trail leads toward the sign from Durand Drive near Beachwood Drive, but the best view is from down below, at the corner of Sunset Boulevard and Bronson Avenue.

At the top of Beachwood Dr., Hollywood.

Hollywood Walk of Fame ★★   More than 2,500 celebrities are honored along the world's most famous sidewalk. Each bronze medallion, set into the center of a granite star, pays homage to a famous television, film, radio, theater, or recording personality. Although about a third of them are just about as obscure as Andromeda—their fame simply hasn't withstood the test of time—millions of visitors are thrilled by the sight of famous names like **James Dean** (1719 Vine St.), **John Lennon** (1750 Vine St.), **Marlon Brando** (1765 Vine St.), **Rudolph Valentino** (6164 Hollywood Blvd.), **Marilyn Monroe** (6744 Hollywood Blvd.), **Elvis Presley** (6777 Hollywood Blvd.), **Greta Garbo** (6901

Stargazing in L.A.: Top Spots About Town for Sighting Celebrities

Celebrities pop up everywhere in L.A. If you spend enough time here, you'll surely bump into a few of them. If you're only in the city for a short time, however, it's best to go on the offensive.

Restaurants are your surest bet. Dining out is such a popular recreation amongst Hollywood's elite that you sometimes wonder whether frequently sighted folks like Johnny Depp, Nicole Kidman, Bridget Fonda, Nicolas Cage, Brad Pitt, or Cindy Crawford ever actually eat at home. **Matsuhisa, Spago, Mimosa, Jozu, Lucques,** and **Maple Drive** can almost guarantee sightings any night of the week. The city's stylish hotels can also be good bets—the **Mondrian** draws stars galore to its dining room Asia de Cuba, as well as the elite Sky Bar; and **Shutters'** lobby lounge is the rendezvous of choice for famous faces heading to dinner at the hotel's **One Pico** restaurant. The trendiest clubs and bars—**House of Blues, Viper Room,** and **Sky Bar**—are second-best for star sighting, but cover charges can be astronomical and the velvet ropes oppressive.

Often, the best places to see members of the A-list aren't as obvious as a back-alley stage door or the front room of Spago. Shops along Sunset Boulevard, like **Tower Records** and the **Virgin Megastore,** are often star-heavy. **Book Soup,** that browser's paradise across the street from Tower, is usually good for a star or two. A midafternoon stroll along **Melrose Avenue** might also produce a familiar face; likewise the chic European-style shops of **Sunset Plaza** or casual boutiques of **Montana Avenue.**

Or you can even seek out the celebrities on the job. It's not uncommon for star-studded movie productions to use L.A.'s diverse cultural landscape for **location shots;** for the inside track on where the action is, check out the Internet **"Shoot Sheet"** site (www.eidc.com/EIDC_and_Community/Shoot_Sheet/shoot_sheet.html). Don't worry—you're not logging onto some unreliable word-of-mouth groupie posting. This is a strictly legit online listing of every filming permit applied for within the city limits, listing production hours and exact street addresses.

Keep your eyes peeled for celebrities—everyone does in L.A.—and you'll more than likely be rewarded.

Hollywood Blvd.), **Louis Armstrong** (7000 Hollywood Blvd.), and **Barbra Streisand** (6925 Hollywood Blvd).

The sight of bikers, metalheads, druggies, hookers, and hordes of disoriented tourists all treading on memorials to Hollywood's greats makes for quite a bizarre tribute indeed. But the Hollywood Chamber of Commerce has been doing a terrific job sprucing up the pedestrian experience with filmstrip crosswalks, swaying palms, and more. And at least one weekend a month, a privately organized group of fans calling themselves Star Polishers busy themselves scrubbing tarnished medallions.

The legendary sidewalk is continually adding new names. The public is invited to attend dedication ceremonies; the honoree is usually in attendance. Contact the **Hollywood Chamber of Commerce,** 6255 Sunset Blvd., Suite 911, Hollywood, CA 90028 (© **323/469-8311**), for information on who's being honored this week.

Hollywood Blvd., between Gower St. and La Brea Ave.; and Vine St., between Yucca St. and Sunset Blvd. © 323/469-8311.

Mann's Chinese Theatre   This is one of the world's great movie palaces and one of Hollywood's finest landmarks. The Chinese Theatre was opened in 1927 by entertainment impresario Sid Grauman, a brilliant promoter who's credited with originating the idea of the paparazzi-packed movie "premiere." Outrageously conceived, with both authentic and simulated Chinese embellishments, gaudy Grauman's theater was designed to impress. Original Chinese heavenly doves top the facade, and two of the theater's exterior columns once propped up a Ming Dynasty temple.

Visitors flock to the theater by the millions for its world-famous entry court, where stars like Elizabeth Taylor, Paul Newman, Ginger Rogers, Humphrey Bogart, Frank Sinatra, Marilyn Monroe, and about 160 others set their signatures and hand- and footprints in concrete. It's not always hands and feet, though: Betty Grable made an impression with her shapely leg; Gene Autry with the hoofprints of his horse, Champion; and Jimmy Durante and Bob Hope with their trademark noses.

6925 Hollywood Blvd. (1 block west of Highland Ave.). © 323/464-MANN or 323/461-3331. Movie tickets $9. Call for show times.

DOWNTOWN

El Pueblo de Los Angeles Historic Monument ★ *Kids*   This historic district was built in the 1930s, on the site where the city was founded, as an alternative to the wholesale razing of a particularly unsightly slum. The result is a contrived, nostalgic fantasy of the city's beginnings, a kitschy theme park portraying Latino culture in a Disneyesque fashion. Nevertheless, El Pueblo has proven wildly successful, as L.A.'s Latinos have adopted it as an important cultural monument.

El Pueblo is not entirely without authenticity. Some of L.A.'s oldest buildings are located here, and the area really does exude the ambience of Old Mexico. At its core is a Mexican-style marketplace on old Olvera Street. The carnival of sights and sounds is heightened by mariachis, colorful piñatas, and more-than-occasional folkloric dancing. Olvera Street, the district's primary pedestrian thoroughfare, and adjacent Main Street are home to about two dozen 19th-century buildings; one houses an authentic Mexican restaurant, **La Golondrina.** Stop in at the **visitor center,** 622 N. Main St. (© **213/628-1274;** open Mon to Sat from 10am to 3pm). Don't miss the **Avila Adobe,** at E-10 Olvera St. (open Mon to Sat from 10am to 5pm); built in 1818, it's the oldest building in the city.

Enter on Alameda St. across from Union Station. © 213/628-1274. www.cityofla.org/elp.

THE SAN FERNANDO VALLEY

Universal Studios Hollywood ★★★ *Kids*   Believing that filmmaking itself was a bona fide attraction, Universal Studios began offering tours to the public in 1964. The concept worked. Today Universal is more than just one of the largest movie studios in the world—it's one of the biggest amusement parks.

The main attraction continues to be the **Studio Tour,** a 1-hour guided tram ride around the company's 420 acres. En route you pass stars' dressing rooms and production offices before visiting famous back-lot sets that include an eerily familiar Old West town, a clean New York City street, and the famous town square from the *Back to the Future* films. Along the way the tram encounters several staged "disasters," which we won't divulge here lest we ruin the surprise.

Other attractions are more typical of high-tech theme-park fare, but all have a film-oriented slant. On **Back to the Future—The Ride,** you're seated in a mock time-traveling DeLorean and thrust into a fantastic multimedia roller-coasting extravaganza— it's far and away Universal's best ride. The **Waterworld** live-action stunt show is thrilling to watch (and probably more successful than the film that inspired it), while the special-effects showcase, **Jurassic Park—The Ride,** is short in duration but long on dinosaur illusions and computer magic lifted from the Universal blockbuster. The latest thrill is **Terminator 2 3-D,** a virtual adventure utilizing triple-screen technology to impact all the senses. **Totally Nickelodeon** is an interactive live show from the kids' TV network, providing adventure and gallons of green slime.

Universal Studios is a really fun place. But just as in any theme park, lines can be long; the wait for a 5-minute ride can sometimes last more than an hour. In summer, the stifling Valley heat can dog you all day. To avoid the crowds, skip weekends, school vacations, and Japanese holidays.

Hollywood Fwy. (Universal Center Dr. or Lankershim Blvd. exits), Universal City. © **818/662-3801.** www. universalstudios.com. Admission $41 adults, $36 seniors 60 and over, $31 children ages 3–11, free for kids under 3. Parking $7. Summer daily 8am–10pm; the rest of the year daily 9am–7pm.

PASADENA & ENVIRONS

Huntington Library, Art Collections & Botanical Gardens ⊛   The Huntington Library is the jewel in Pasadena's crown. The 207-acre hilltop estate was once home to industrialist and railroad magnate Henry E. Huntington (1850 to 1927), who bought books on the same massive scale on which he acquired businesses. The continually expanding collection includes dozens of Shakespeare's original works, Benjamin Franklin's handwritten autobiography, a Gutenberg Bible from the 1450s, and the earliest known manuscript of Chaucer's *Canterbury Tales.* Although some rare works are available only to visiting scholars, the library has a regularly changing (and always excellent) exhibit showcasing different items in the collection.

If you prefer canvas to parchment, Huntington also put together a terrific 18th-century British and French **art collection.** The most celebrated paintings are Gainsborough's *The Blue Boy,* and *Pinkie,* a companion piece by Sir Thomas Lawrence depicting the youthful aunt of Elizabeth Barrett Browning. These and other works are displayed in the stately Italianate mansion on the crest of this hillside estate, so you can also get a glimpse of its splendid furnishings.

But it's the **botanical gardens** that draw most locals to the Huntington. The Japanese Garden comes complete with a traditional open-air Japanese house, koi-filled stream, and serene Zen garden. The cactus garden is exotic, the jungle garden is intriguing, the lily ponds are soothing—and there are many benches scattered about so you can sit and enjoy the surroundings.

Because the Huntington surprises many with its size and wealth of activities to choose from, first-timers might want to start by attending one of the regularly scheduled 12-minute introductory slide shows; you can also take the more in-depth 1-hour garden tour, given each day at 1pm. We also recommend that you tailor your visit to include the popular English high tea served Tuesday through Sunday from 1:30 to 3:30pm. The charming tearoom overlooks the Rose Garden (home to 1,000 varieties displayed in chronological order of their breeding), and because the finger sandwiches and desserts are served buffet style, it's a genteel bargain (even for hearty appetites) at $11 per person. Call ✆ **626/ 683-8131** for reservations.

1151 Oxford Rd., San Marino. ✆ **626/405-2141.** www.huntington.org. Admission $8.50 adults, $8 seniors 65 and over, $6 students and children age 12 and over, free to children under 12; free to all the 1st Thurs of each month. Sept–May Tues–Fri noon–4:30pm, Sat–Sun 10:30am–4:30pm; June–Aug Tues–Sun 10:30am–4:30pm. Closed major holidays.

6 Exploring the City

ARCHITECTURAL HIGHLIGHTS

Los Angeles is a veritable Disneyland of architecture. The city is home to an amalgam of distinctive styles, from art deco to Spanish revival to coffee-shop kitsch to suburban ranch to postmodern—and much more. Cutting-edge, over-the-top styles that would be out of place in other cities, from the oversize hot dog that is Tail o' the Pup to the mansions lining the streets of Beverly Hills, are perfectly at home in movie city.

SANTA MONICA & THE BEACHES

When you're strolling the historic canals and streets of Venice, be sure to check out **Chiat/Day** offices at 340 Main St. What would otherwise be an unspectacular contemporary office building is made fantastic by a three-story pair of binoculars that frames the entrance to this advertising agency. The sculpture is modeled after a design created by Claes Oldenburg and Coosje van Bruggen.

When you're flying in or out of LAX, be sure to stop for a moment to admire the **Control Tower and Theme Building** ✯. The spacey *Jetsons*-style "Theme Building," which has always loomed over LAX, has been joined by a brand-new silhouette. The main control tower, designed by local architect Kate Diamond to evoke a stylized palm tree, is tailored to present southern California in its best light. You can go inside to enjoy the view from the Theme Building's observation deck, or have a space-age cocktail at the Technicolor bachelor pad that is Encounter restaurant.

L.A.'S WESTSIDE & BEVERLY HILLS

Winding your way through the streets of Beverly Hills off Sunset Boulevard, you'll see everything the overactive, deep-pocketed imagination can conjure up, from faux Merry-Olde-England hunting lodges to turreted Sleeping Beauty castles.

The **Rudolph M. Schindler House,** 835 N. Kings Rd. (✆ **310/651-1510**; www.makcenter.com), is distinguished by the intermingling of indoors and out, daring modern (1921 to 1922) design, and technological innovations. A protégé of Frank Lloyd Wright and contemporary of Richard Neutra, the Austrian architect was very active in Los Angeles; little survives of his work, and his own home barely escaped the wrecking ball. But Austria's Museum of Applied Arts (MAK) now maintains the restored house as a mini-MAK, and also offers guided tours on weekends.

Postmodern-architecture lovers should check out the **Pacific Design Center** at 8687 Melrose Ave. (✆ **310/657-0800**). Designed by Argentinean Cesar Pelli, the bold architecture and overwhelming scale of the center aroused plenty of controversy when it was erected in 1975. Sheathed in gently curving cobalt-blue glass, the seven-story building, housing over 750,000 square feet of wholesale interior-design showrooms, is known to locals as "the blue whale." Nearby on San Vicente Boulevard—on a totally different scale—is the iconic **Tail o' the Pup** ✦. This is roadside art—and the wiener at its best.

HOLLYWOOD

In addition to the **Griffith Observatory** and **Mann's Chinese Theatre** (see "The Top Attractions," earlier in this chapter), and the **Hollywood Roosevelt Hotel** (see "Accommodations," earlier in this chapter), check out the old **Egyptian Theatre,** 6712 Hollywood Blvd. Conceived by grandiose Sid Grauman, it's just down the street from Grauman's better-known Chinese Theatre, but remains less altered from its 1922 design based on the then-headline news discovery of hidden treasures in Pharaohs' tombs. It has just undergone a sensitive restoration by American Cinematheque, which now screens rare, classic, and independent films (see "Los Angeles After Dark," later in this chapter, for details).

Farther east is the **Capitol Records Building.** This 12-story tower just north of the legendary intersection of Hollywood and Vine is one of the city's most recognizable buildings. Often, but incorrectly, rumored to have been made to resemble a stack of 45s on a turntable (it kinda does, really), this circular tower is nevertheless unmistakable. Nat "King" Cole, songwriter Johnny Mercer, and other 1950s Capitol artists populate a giant exterior mural.

DOWNTOWN

Built in 1928, the 27-story **City Hall,** at 200 N. Spring St., remained the tallest building in the city for more than 30 years. The structure's distinctive ziggurat roof was featured in the film *War of the Worlds,* but is probably best known as the headquarters of the *Daily Planet* in the *Superman* TV series. On a clear day, the top-floor observation deck (open Monday through Friday from 10am to 4pm) offers views of Mount Wilson, 15 miles away.

On West Fifth Street, between Flower Street and Grand Avenue, is one of L.A.'s early architectural achievements, the carefully restored **Central Library** ✦ (the majestic main entrance is actually on Flower St.). Working in the 1920s, architect Bertram G. Goodhue played on the Egyptian motifs and materials popularized by the discovery of King Tut's tomb, combining them with modern concrete block to great effect.

The 1893 **Bradbury Building,** at South Broadway and Third Street, is Los Angeles' oldest commercial building, and one of the city's most revered architectural landmarks. You've got to go inside to appreciate it. The glass-topped atrium is often used as a movie and TV set; you've seen it in *Chinatown* and *Blade Runner.*

Union Station, at Macy and Alameda Streets, is one of the finest examples of California mission–style architecture, built with the opulence and attention to detail that characterize 1930s WPA projects. The cathedral-size, richly paneled ticket lobby and waiting area of this fantastic cream-colored structure stand sadly empty most of the time, but the MTA does use Union Station for Blue Line commuter trains; and adventuresome diners flock to the retro-flavored **Traxx** restaurant on the concourse (see "Dining" earlier in this chapter).

For a taste of what downtown's Bunker Hill was like before the bulldozers tore through, visit the residential neighborhood of **Angelino Heights,** near Echo Park. Entire streets are still filled with stately gingerbread Victorian homes; most still enjoy the splendid views that led early L.A.'s elite to build here. The 1300 block of Carroll Avenue is the best preserved. Don't be surprised if a film crew

Stargazing, Part II: The Less-than-Lively Set

Almost everybody who visits L.A. hopes to see a celebrity—they are, after all, our most common export item. But celebrities usually don't cooperate, failing to gather in readily viewable herds. There's a much, much better alternative, an absolutely guaranteed method of being within 6 feet of your favorite star—cemeteries. What follows is a guide to the most fruitful cemeteries, listed in order (more or less) of their friendliness to stargazers.

Weathered Victorian and Deco memorials add to the decaying charm of **Hollywood Forever** (formerly Hollywood Memorial Park), 6000 Santa Monica Blvd., Hollywood (✆ **323/469-1181**). Fittingly, there's a terrific view of the HOLLYWOOD sign over the graves, as many of the founders of the community rest here. The most notable tenant is Rudolph Valentino, who rests in an interior crypt. Outside are Tyrone Power, Jr.; Douglas Fairbanks, Sr.; Cecil B. DeMille (facing Paramount, his old studio); Alfalfa from *The Little Rascals* (contrary to what you might think, the dog on his grave is not Petey); Hearst mistress Marion Davies; John Huston; and a headstone for Jayne Mansfield (she's really buried in Pennsylvania with her family). In 2000, Douglas Fairbanks, Jr. joined his dad at Hollywood Forever.

Catholic **Holy Cross Cemetery,** 5835 W. Slauson Ave., Culver City (✆ **310/670-7697**), hands out maps to the stars' graves. In one area, within mere feet of each other, lie Bing Crosby, Bela Lugosi (buried in his Dracula cape), and Sharon Tate; not far away are Rita Hayworth and Jimmy Durante. Also here are "Tin Man" Jack Haley and "Scarecrow" Ray Bolger, Mary Astor, John Ford, and Gloria Morgan Vanderbilt. More recent arrivals include John Candy and Audrey Meadows.

The front office at **Hillside Memorial Park,** 6001 Centinela Ave., Baldwin Hills (✆ **310/641-0707**), can provide a guide to this Jewish cemetery, which has an L.A. landmark: the behemoth tomb of Al Jolson, another humble star. His rotunda, complete with a bronze reproduction of Jolson and cascading fountain, is visible from I-405. Also on hand are Jack Benny, Eddie Cantor, Vic Morrow, and Michael Landon.

is scouting locations while you're there—these blocks appear often on the silver screen.

The **Watts Towers,** at 1765 E. 107th St. (✆ **323/847-4646**; www.culturela. org), are more than a bit off the beaten track, but they warrant a visit. The fantastically colorful, 99-foot-tall concrete-and-steel sculptures are ornamented with mosaics of bottles, seashells, cups, plates, generic pottery, and ceramic tiles. They were completed in 1954 by folk artist Simon Rodia, an immigrant Italian tile setter who worked on them for 33 years. Call for a tour schedule.

PASADENA & ENVIRONS
For a quick but profound architectural fix, stroll past Pasadena's grandiose and baroque **City Hall,** 100 N. Garfield Ave., 2 blocks north of Colorado; closer

You just know developers get stomach aches looking at **Westwood Memorial Park,** 1218 Glendon Ave., Westwood (℗ **310/474-1579;** the staff can direct you around), smack-dab in the middle of some of L.A.'s priciest real estate. But it's not going anywhere. Especially when you consider its most famous resident: Marilyn Monroe. It's also got Truman Capote, John Cassavetes, Armand Hammer, Donna Reed, and Natalie Wood. Walter Matthau was buried here in 2000.

Forest Lawn Glendale, 1712 S. Glendale Ave. (℗ **323/254-3131**), likes to pretend it has no celebrities. The most prominent of L.A. cemeteries, it's also the most humorless. The place is full of bad art, all part of the continuing vision of founder Hubert Eaton, who thought cemeteries should be happy places. So he banished all those gloomy upright tombstones and monuments in favor of flat, pleasant, character-free, flush-to-the-ground slabs.

Contrary to what you've heard, Walt Disney was *not* frozen and placed under Cinderella's castle at Disneyland. His cremated remains are in a little garden to the left of the Freedom Mausoleum. Turn around, and just behind you are Errol Flynn and Spencer Tracy. In the Freedom Mausoleum are Nat "King" Cole, Chico Marx, Gummo Marx, and Gracie Allen—finally joined by George Burns. In a columbarium near the Mystery of Life is Humphrey Bogart. Unfortunately, some of the best celebs—such as Clark Gable, Carole Lombard, and Jean Harlow—are in the Great Mausoleum, which you often can't get into unless you're visiting a relative.

Forest Lawn Hollywood Hills, 6300 Forest Lawn Dr. (℗ **800/ 204-3131**), is slightly less anal than the Glendale branch, but the same basic attitude prevails. On the right lawn, beside the wall near the statue of George Washington, is Buster Keaton. In the Courts of Remembrance are Lucille Ball, Charles Laughton, and the not-quite-gaudy-enough tomb of Liberace. Outside, in a vault on the Ascension Road side, is Andy Gibb. Bette Davis' sarcophagus is in front of the wall, to the left of the entrance to the Courts. Gene Autry was also buried here, almost within earshot of the museum that bears his name.

—Mary Herczog

inspection will reveal its classical colonnaded courtyard, formal gardens, and spectacular tiled dome.

Architects Charles and Henry Greene built prolifically in Pasadena's Arroyo Seco area (overlooking the Rose Bowl) in the early 1900s, their masterpiece being the **Gamble House** ✿, 4 Westmoreland Place (off Orange Grove, north of the Ventura Freeway). Intricately crafted teakwood interiors, custom furnishings, and California-specific features like a sleeping porch make this a one-stop primer in Craftsman design. One-hour tours are given Thursday through Sunday afternoons; call ℗ **626/793-3334** for more information. Additional elegant Greene & Greene creations (still privately owned) abound 2 blocks away along **Arroyo Terrace,** including address nos. **368, 370, 400, 408, 424,** and **440;** the Gamble House bookshop can give you a walking-tour map and conducts guided neighborhood tours by appointment.

Downtown Los Angeles

W. Temple St.

S. Virgil Ave.
Commonwealth Ave.
Hoover St.
Benton Way
Rampart Blvd.

LAFAYETTE PARK

MACARTHUR PARK

Westmoreland Ave.
S. Hoover St.
San Marino St.
W. 8th St.
W. 9th St.

Westlake Ave.
S. Burlington Ave.
Bonnie Brae St.
S. Union Ave.

W. 11th St.

W. 12th St.
W. Pico Blvd

Magnolia Ave.

W. Venice Blvd

W. Washington Blvd

W. 20th St.
Santa Monica Freeway
10

W. 23rd St.
110

Information ⓘ
Parking Ⓟ

0   1/2 mi
0   .5 km

27

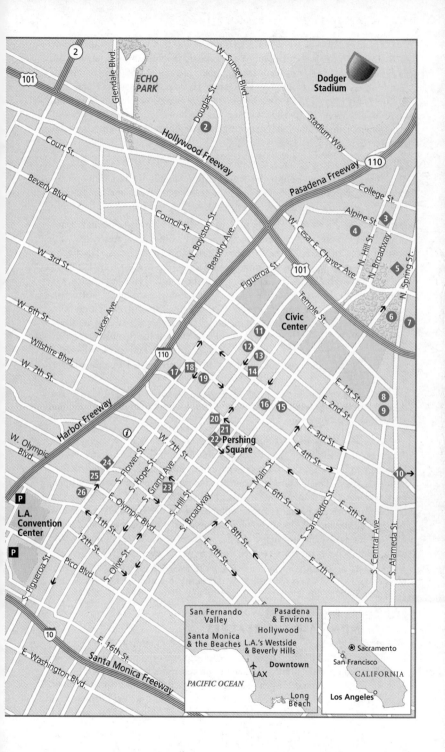

While the Greenes were building retreats for the wealthy, scaled-down Craftsman bungalows were becoming the standard in affordable housing nearby. An exceptionally well-preserved neighborhood of around 900 pre-Depression homes is the Landmark District **Bungalow Heaven,** between Lake and Hill Avenues north of Orange Grove Boulevard. The Bungalow Heaven Neighborhood Association (✆ **626/585-2172**) conducts a house tour each April, and can give you information on taking a self-guided walking tour of this charming enclave.

MISSIONS

Two of the 21 missions built by Franciscan missionaries in the late 18th century along the California coast from San Diego to Sonoma are in the Los Angeles area. The valleys in which they're nestled eventually took their names.

Mission San Fernando   Established in 1797, Mission San Fernando once controlled more than 1½ million acres, employed 1,500 Native Americans, and boasted more than 22,000 head of cattle and extensive orchards. The fragile adobe mission complex was destroyed several times, but it was always faithfully rebuilt with low buildings surrounding grassy courtyards. The aging church was replaced in the 1940s, and again in the 1970s after a particularly destructive earthquake. The Convento, a 250-foot-long colonnaded structure dating from 1810, is the compound's oldest remaining building. Some of the mission's rooms, including the old library and the private salon of the first bishop of California, have been restored to their late–18th-century appearance. A half-dozen padres and many hundreds of Shoshone Indians are buried in the adjacent cemetery.

15151 San Fernando Mission Blvd., Mission Hills. ✆ **818/361-0186.** Admission $4 adults, $3 seniors and children ages 7–15, free for kids under 7. Daily 9am–5pm. From I-5, exit at San Fernando Mission Blvd. east and drive 5 blocks to the mission.

Mission San Gabriel Arcangel   Founded in 1771, Mission San Gabriel Arcangel still retains its original facade, notable for its high oblong windows and large capped buttresses that are said to have been influenced by the cathedral in Cordova, Spain. The mission's self-contained compound encompasses an aqueduct, a cemetery, a tannery, and a working winery. Within the church stands a copper font with the dubious distinction of being the first one used to baptize a Native Californian. The most notable contents of the mission's museum are Native American paintings depicting the Stations of the Cross, done on sailcloth, with colors made from crushed desert flower petals.

428 S. Mission Dr., San Gabriel (15 min. south of Pasadena). ✆ **626/457-3035.** www.sangabrielmission.org. Admission $5 adults, $4 seniors and students, $2 children ages 6–12, free for kids under 6. Daily 9am–4:30pm. Closed holidays.

MUSEUMS & GALLERIES
SANTA MONICA & THE BEACHES

Museum of Flying ✪   Once headquarters of the McDonnell Douglas corporation, the Santa Monica Airport is the birthplace of the DC-3 and other pioneers of commercial aviation. The museum celebrates this bit of local history with 24 authentic aircraft displays and some interactive exhibits. In addition to antique Spitfires and Sopwith Camels, there's a new kid-oriented learning area, where hands-on exhibits detail airplane parts, pilot procedures, and the properties

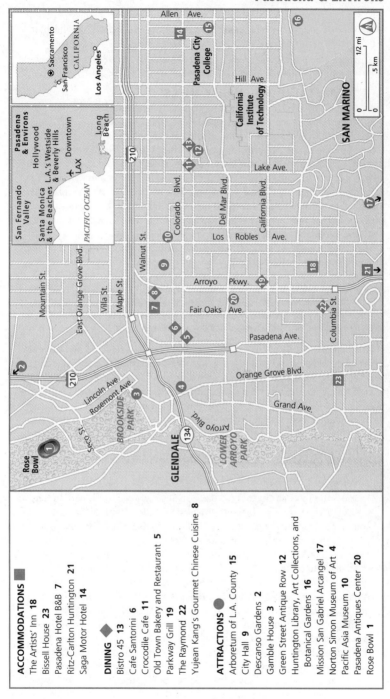

Pasadena & Environs

ACCOMMODATIONS ■

The Artists' Inn **18**
Bissell House **23**
Pasadena Hotel B&B **7**
Ritz-Carlton Huntington **21**
Saga Motor Hotel **14**

DINING ◆

Bistro 45 **13**
Cafe Santorini **6**
Crocodile Cafe **11**
Old Town Bakery and Restaurant **5**
Parkway Grill **19**
The Raymond **22**
Yujean Kang's Gourmet Chinese Cuisine **8**

ATTRACTIONS ●

Arboretum of L.A. County **15**
City Hall **9**
Descanso Gardens **2**
Gamble House **3**
Green Street Antique Row **12**
Huntington Library, Art Collections, and Botanical Gardens **16**
Mission San Gabriel Arcangel **17**
Norton Simon Museum of Art **4**
Pacific Asia Museum **10**
Pasadena Antiques Center **20**
Rose Bowl **1**

of air and aircraft design. The museum shop is full of scale models of World War II birds; the coffee-table book *The Best of the Past* beautifully illustrates 50 years of aviation history.

At Santa Monica Airport, 2772 Donald Douglas Loop N., Santa Monica. ℂ 310/392-8822. www.museumof flying.com. Admission $7 adults, $5 seniors, $3 children under 17. Wed–Sun 10am–5pm.

L.A.'S WESTSIDE & BEVERLY HILLS

Museum of Tolerance ✦   The Museum of Tolerance is designed to expose prejudices and to teach racial and cultural tolerance. It's located in the Simon Wiesenthal Center, an institute founded by the legendary Nazi-hunter. While the Holocaust figures prominently here, this is not just a Jewish museum—it's an academy that broadly campaigns for a live-and-let-live world. Tolerance is an abstract idea that's hard to display, so most of this $50 million museum's exhibits are high-tech and conceptual in nature. Fast-paced interactive displays are designed to touch the heart as well as the mind, and engage both serious investigators and the MTV crowd. One of two major museums in America that deal with the Holocaust, the Museum of Tolerance is considered by many to be inferior to its Washington, D.C., counterpart. Visitors might be frustrated by the museum's policy of insisting that you follow a prescribed 2½-hour route through the exhibits.

9786 W. Pico Blvd. (at Roxbury Dr.). ℂ 310/553-8403. www.wiesenthal.com/mot. Admission $8.50 adults, $6.50 seniors, $5.50 students, $3.50 children ages 3–12, free for children under 3. Advance purchase recommended. Mon–Thurs 10am–4pm; Fri 10am–3pm (to 1pm Nov–Mar); Sun 11am–5pm (closing hours represent last entry time). Closed many Jewish and secular holidays; call for schedule.

Skirball Cultural Center ✦   This strikingly modern museum and cultural center is quick to remind us that Jewish history is about more than the Holocaust. Nestled in the Sepulveda Pass uphill from the Getty Center, the Skirball explores American Jewish life, American democratic values, and the pursuit of the American Dream—a theme shared by many immigrant groups. The Skirball's core exhibits chronicle the journey of the Jewish people through the ages, with particular emphasis on American Jewry. Related events are held here throughout the

---

Value **The "Hollywood" CityPass**

In 2000, the folks at **CityPass** (ℂ **888/330-5008**; www.citypass.net) added Los Angeles to their nationwide list of destinations with money-saving combination attraction passes. The CityPass booklet includes tickets to six popular attractions, a 2-hour bus tour of Beverly Hills and celebrity homes from **Starline Tours,** and savings coupons for Beverly Center shopping. The main draw, and the primary reason to purchase CityPass, is **Universal Studios Hollywood;** the rest are the **Hollywood Entertainment Museum, American Cinemateque at the Egyptian Theatre, Museum of Television and Radio, Petersen Automotive Museum,** and **Autry Museum of Western Heritage.** Purchase the pass at any of the seven attractions, or visit their website to buy advance passes online, find links to the attraction websites, and peruse hotel packages that include CityPass. The pass costs $59 for adults ($39 for kids ages 3 to 11) and will expire 30 days from the first use. Is it a good deal? If you use all the tickets, you'll end up saving 45% over individual, full-price admissions (adult prices).

year; one recent highlight was a rollicking festival of klezmer music (a traditional Jewish folk style).

2701 N. Sepulveda Blvd. (at Mulholland Dr.). ℂ 310/440-4500. www.skirball.org. Admission $8 adults, $6 students and seniors 65 and over, free for kids under 12. Tues–Sat noon–5pm; Sun 11am–5pm. Free parking. From I-405, exit at Skirball Center Dr./Mulholland Dr.

HOLLYWOOD

Autry Museum of Western Heritage 𝒢𝒢   If you're under the age of 45, you might not be familiar with Gene Autry, a Texas-born actor who starred in 82 westerns and became known as the "Singing Cowboy." Located north of Downtown in Griffith Park, his eponymous museum is one of California's best, a collection of art and artifacts of the European conquest of the West, remarkably comprehensive and intelligently displayed. Evocative exhibits illustrate the everyday lives of early pioneers, not only with antique firearms, tools, saddles, and the like, but with many hands-on displays that successfully stir the imagination and the heart. You'll find footage from Buffalo Bill's Wild West Show, movie clips from the silent days, contemporary films, the works of Wild West artists, and plenty of memorabilia from Autry's own film and TV projects. The "Hall of Merchandising" displays Roy Rogers bedspreads, Hopalong Cassidy radios, and other items from the collective consciousness—and material collections—of baby boomers. Provocative visiting exhibits (whose banners are visible from Interstate 5) usually focus on cultural or domestic regional history.

4700 Western Heritage Way (in Griffith Park). ℂ 323/667-2000. www.autry-museum.org. Admission $7.50 adults, $5 seniors 60 and over and students ages 13–18, $3 children 2–12, free for kids under 2; free to all 2nd Tues each month. Tues–Sun 10am–5pm (Thurs until 8pm).

Craft & Folk Art Museum   This gallery, housed in a prominent Museum Row building, has grown into one of the city's largest. "Craft and folk art" is a large rubric that encompasses everything from clothing, tools, religious artifacts, and other everyday objects to wood carvings, papier-mâché, weaving, and metalwork. The museum displays folk objects from around the world, but its strongest collection is masks from India, America, Mexico, Japan, and China. The museum is also well known for its annual International Festival of Masks, a colorful celebration held each October in Hancock Park, across the street.

5814 Wilshire Blvd. (at Curson Ave.). ℂ 323/937-4230. Admission $3.50 adults, $2.50 seniors and students, free for children under 12; free to all the 1st Wednesday each month. Tues–Sun 11am–5pm.

Los Angeles County Museum of Art 𝒢𝒢   This is one of the finest art museums around. The huge complex was designed by three very different architects over a span of 30 years. The architectural fusion can be migraine inducing, but this city landmark is well worth delving into.

The newest wing is the **Japanese Pavilion,** which has exterior walls made of Kalwall, a translucent material that, like shoji screens, permits the entry of soft natural light. Inside is a collection of Japanese Edo paintings that's rivaled only by the holdings of the emperor of Japan. The **Anderson Building,** the museum's contemporary wing, is home to 20th-century painting and sculpture. Here you'll find works by Matisse, Magritte, and a good number of Dada artists. The **Ahmanson Building** houses the rest of the museum's permanent collections. Here you'll find everything from 2,000-year-old pre-Columbian Mexican ceramics to 19th-century portraiture to a unique glass collection spanning the centuries. Other displays include one of the nation's largest holdings of costumes and textiles, and an important Indian and Southeast Asian art collection. The

Hammer Building is primarily used for major special-loan exhibitions. Free guided tours covering the museum's highlights depart on a regular basis from here.

The museum recently took over the former May Company department store one block away, converting the historic Art Deco building into gallery space.

5905 Wilshire Blvd. ⓒ **323/857-6000.** www.lacma.org. Admission $7 adults, $5 students and seniors age 62 and over, $1 children ages 6–17, free for kids under 6; regular exhibitions free for everyone the 2nd Tues of each month. Mon–Tues and Thurs noon–8pm; Fri noon–9pm; Sat–Sun 11am–8pm.

Petersen Automotive Museum 🖈 When the Petersen opened in 1994, many locals were surprised that it had taken this long for the City of Freeways to salute its most important shaper. Indeed, this museum says more about the city than probably any other in L.A. Named for Robert Petersen, the publisher responsible for *Hot Rod* and *Motor Trend* magazines, the four-story museum displays more than 200 cars and motorcycles, from the historic to the futuristic. Cars on the first floor are exhibited chronologically, in period settings. Other floors are devoted to frequently changing shows of race cars, early motorcycles, and famous movie vehicles. Past shows have included a comprehensive exhibit of "woodies" and surf culture, and displays of the Flintstones' fiberglass-and-cotton movie car and of a three-wheeled scooter that folds into a Samsonite briefcase (created in a competition by a Mazda engineer).

6060 Wilshire Blvd. (at Fairfax Ave.). ⓒ **323/930-CARS.** www.petersen.org. Admission $7 adults, $5 seniors and students, $3 children ages 5–12, free for kids under 5. Parking $6. Tues–Sun 10am–6pm.

DOWNTOWN

California ScienCenter 🖈🖈 *(Kids)* A $130 million remodel—reinvention, actually—has turned the former Museum of Science and Industry into Exposition Park's newest attraction. Using high-tech sleight-of-hand, the center stimulates kids of all ages with questions, answers, and lessons about the world. One of the museum's educational highlights is Tess, a 50-foot animatronic woman whose muscles, bones, organs, and blood vessels are revealed, demonstrating how the body reacts to a variety of external conditions and activities. (Appropriate for children of all ages, Tess doesn't possess reproductive organs.)

There are nominal fees to enjoy the science center's more thrilling attractions. You can pedal a bicycle across a high-wire suspended 43 feet above the ground (demonstrating the principle of gravity and counterweights) or get strapped into the Space Docking Simulator for a virtual-reality taste of zero gravity. There's plenty more, and plans for expansion are already in the works. The newly expanded IMAX theater now boasts a screen seven stories high and 90 feet wide, with state-of-the-art surround sound and 3-D technology. Films are screened throughout the day until 9pm and are nearly always breathtaking, even the ones in 2-D.

700 State Dr., Exposition Park. ⓒ **213/SCI-ENCE,** or 213/744-7400; IMAX theater ⓒ **213/744-2014.** www. casciencectr.org. Free admission to the museum; IMAX theater $7 adults, $4.75 ages 18–21, $4 seniors and children. Multishow discounts available. Parking $5. Daily 10am–5pm. Closed Thanksgiving, Christmas, and New Year's Day.

Japanese American National Museum 🖈 Located in an architecturally acclaimed modern building in Little Tokyo, this museum is a private nonprofit institute created to document and celebrate the history of the Japanese in America. Its fantastic permanent exhibition chronicles Japanese life in the United

States, while temporary exhibits highlight distinctive aspects of Japanese-American culture, from the internment-camp experience to the lives of Japanese-Americans in Hawaii. Don't miss the museum store, which carries everything from hand-fired sake sets to mini Zen gardening kits.

369 E. First St. (at Central Ave.). ⓒ **213/625-0414.** www.janm.org. Admission $6 adults, $5 seniors, $3 students and kids 6–17, free for kids under 6; free to all the 3rd Thurs of each month, and every Thurs after 5pm. Tues–Sun 10am–5pm (Thurs till 8pm).

Museum of Contemporary Art & Geffen Contemporary at MOCA 🟊🟊

MOCA is Los Angeles's only institution exclusively devoted to art from 1940 to the present. Displaying works in a variety of media, it's particularly strong in works by Cy Twombly, Jasper Johns, and Mark Rothko, and shows are often superb. For many experts, MOCA's collections are too spotty to be considered world-class, and the conservative museum board blushes when offered controversial shows. (They passed on a Whitney exhibit that included photographs by Robert Mapplethorpe.) Nevertheless, we've seen some excellent exhibitions here.

MOCA is one museum housed in two buildings that are close to one another but not within walking distance. The Grand Avenue main building is a contemporary red sandstone structure by renowned Japanese architect Arata Isozaki. The museum restaurant, **Patinette** (ⓒ **213/626-1178**), located here, is the casual-dining creation of celebrity chef Joachim Splichal (see Patina in section 4, "Dining," earlier in this chapter).

The museum's second space, on Central Avenue in Little Tokyo, was the "temporary" Contemporary while the Grand structure was being built, and it now houses a superior permanent collection in a fittingly neutral, warehouse-type space recently renamed for entertainment mogul and passionate art collector David Geffen. An added feature here is a detailed timeline corresponding to the progression of works. Unless there's a visiting exhibit of great interest at the main museum, we recommend that you start at the Geffen building—where it's also easier to park.

250 S. Grand Ave. and 152 N. Central Ave. ⓒ **213/626-6222** or 213/621-2766. www.moca-la.org. Admission $6 adults, $4 seniors and students, free for children age under 12. Tues–Wed and Fri–Sun 11am–5pm; Thurs 11am–8pm.

Natural History Museum of Los Angeles County (Kids) The "Fighting

Dinosaurs" are not a high-school football team but the trademark symbol of this massive museum: *Tyrannosaurus rex* and *Triceratops* skeletons are poised in a stance so realistic that every kid feels inspired to imitate their Jurassic Park bellows. Opened in 1913 in a beautiful domed Spanish Renaissance building, this museum is a 35-hall warehouse of Earth's history, chronicling the planet and its inhabitants from 600 million years ago to the present day. There's a mind-numbing number of exhibits of prehistoric fossils, bird and marine life, rocks and minerals, and North American mammals. The best permanent displays include the world's rarest shark, a walk-through vault of priceless gems, and an Insect Zoo.

The Dinosaur Shop sells ant farms and exploding volcano and model kits. The Ethnic Arts Shop has one-of-a-kind folk art and jewelry from around the world. The bookstore has an extensive selection of scientific titles and hobbyists' field guides.

900 Exposition Blvd., Exposition Park. ⓒ **213/763-3466.** www.nhm.org. Admission $8 adults; $5.50 children ages 13–17, seniors, and students with ID; $2 children 5–12; free for kids under 5; free for everyone the 1st Tues of each month. Daily 10am–5pm.

PASADENA & ENVIRONS

Norton Simon Museum of Art ★★   Named for a food-packing king and financier who reorganized the failing Pasadena Museum of Modern Art, this has become one of California's most important museums. Comprehensive collections of masterpieces by Degas, Picasso, Rembrandt, and Goya are augmented by sculptures by Henry Moore and Auguste Rodin, including *The Burghers of Calais,* which greets you at the gates. The "Blue Four" collection of works by Kandinsky, Jawlensky, Klee, and Feininger is particularly impressive, as is a superb collection of Southeast Asian sculpture. *Still Life with Lemons, Oranges, and a Rose* (1633), an oil by Francisco de Zurbarán, is one of the museum's most important holdings. One of the most popular pieces is *The Flower Vendor/Girl with Lilies* by Mexican artist Diego Riveras. Architect Frank Gehry recently helped remodel the galleries.

411 W. Colorado Blvd., Pasadena. ✆ **626/449-6840.** www.nortonsimon.org. Admission $6 adults, $3 seniors, free for students and kids under 13. Free parking. Wed–Mon noon–6pm (Friday till 9pm).

Pacific Asia Museum   The most striking aspect of this museum is the building itself. Designed in the 1920s in Chinese Imperial Palace style, it's rivaled in flamboyance only by Mann's Chinese Theatre in Hollywood (see "The Top Attractions," earlier in this chapter). Rotating exhibits of Asian art span the centuries, from 100 B.C. to the current day. This manageably sized museum is usually worth a peek.

46 N. Los Robles Ave., Pasadena. ✆ **626/449-2742.** www.pacasiamuseum.org. Admission $5 adults, $3 students and seniors, free for children under 12; free for everyone the 3rd Sat of each month. Wed–Fri noon–5pm (Thurs till 8pm); Sat–Sun 11am–5pm.

PARKS

Griffith Park ★★   Mining tycoon Griffith J. Griffith donated these 4,000 acres of Hollywood parkland to the city in 1896. Today, Griffith Park is one of the largest city parks in the United States. There's a lot to do here, including hiking, horseback riding, golfing, swimming, biking, and picnicking (see "Outdoor Pursuits," later in this chapter). For a general overview, drive the mountainous loop road that winds from the top of Western Avenue, past Griffith Observatory, and down to Vermont Avenue. For a more extensive foray, turn north at the loop road's midsection onto Mt. Hollywood Drive. To reach the golf courses or Los Angeles Zoo, take Los Feliz Boulevard to Riverside Drive, which runs along the park's western edge. Near the zoo, in a particularly dusty corner of the park, you'll find the **Travel Town Museum,** 5200 Zoo Dr. (✆ **323/662-5874**), a little-known outdoor museum with a small collection of vintage locomotives and old airplanes. Kids love it.

Entrances along Los Feliz Blvd. at Riverside Dr., Vermont Ave., and Western Ave. ✆ **323/913-4688.** www.cityofla.org/RAP/grifmet/gp. Park admission free.

Will Rogers State Historic Park   Will Rogers State Historic Park was once Will Rogers's private ranch and grounds. Willed to the state of California in 1944, the 168-acre estate is now both a park and a historic site, supervised by the Department of Parks and Recreation. Visitors may explore the grounds, the former stables, and the 31-room house filled with the original furnishings, including a porch swing in the living room and many Native American rugs and baskets. Charles Lindbergh and his wife, Anne Morrow Lindbergh, hid out here in the 1930s during part of the craze that followed the kidnap and murder of their first son. There are picnic tables, but no food is sold.

Will Rogers (1879 to 1935) was born in Oklahoma and became a cowboy in the Texas Panhandle before drifting into a Wild West show as a folksy, speechifying roper. The "cracker-barrel philosopher" performed lariat tricks while carrying on a humorous deadpan monologue on current events. The showman moved to Los Angeles in 1919, where he become a movie actor as well as the author of numerous books detailing his down-home "cowboy philosophy."

1501 Will Rogers State Park Rd., Pacific Palisades (between Santa Monica and Malibu). ℰ 310/454-8212. Park entrance $6 per vehicle. Daily 8am–sunset. House opens daily at 10am; guided tours can be arranged for groups of 10 or more. From Santa Monica, take the Pacific Coast Hwy. (Calif. 1) north, turn right onto Sunset Blvd., and continue to the park entrance.

PIERS

Santa Monica Pier ✮   This famous pier is doing a pretty good job of recapturing the glory days of southern California piers. Built in 1909 for passenger and cargo ships, the wooden wharf is now home to seafood restaurants and snack shacks, a touristy Mexican cantina at the far end, and a gaily colored turn-of-the-century indoor wooden carousel (which Paul Newman operated in *The Sting*). Summer evening concerts, which are free and range from big band to Miami-style Latin, draw huge crowds, as does the new fun-zone perched halfway down. Its name, **Pacific Park** (ℰ **310/260-8744;** www.pacpark.com), hearkens back to the granddaddy pier amusement park in California, Pacific Ocean Park; this new version has a roller coaster and other rides, plus a high-tech arcade shoot-out. But fishermen still head to the end to angle, and nostalgia buffs to view the photographic display of the pier's history. This is the last of the great pleasure piers, offering rides, romance, and perfect panoramic views of the bay and mountains.

The pier is about a mile up Ocean Front Walk from Venice; it's a great round-trip stroll. For information on twilight concerts (generally held Thurs between mid-June and the end of Aug), call ℰ **310/458-8900** or visit www. twilightdance.org.

Ocean Ave. at the end of Colorado Blvd., Santa Monica. www.santamonicapier.org.

THEME PARKS

You'll find L.A.'s most famous theme park, **Universal Studios Hollywood,** under "The Top Attractions," earlier in this chapter.

Six Flags California (Magic Mountain & Hurricane Harbor) ✮✮   What started as a countrified little amusement park with a couple of relatively tame roller coasters in 1971 has since been transformed by Six Flags into a thrill-a-minute daredevil's paradise. Located about 20 to 30 minutes north of Universal Studios, **Magic Mountain** is the lesser known of the two Six Flags parks, but it is enormously popular with teenagers and young adults—height-based ride restrictions make the place a big bore for little kids who haven't yet sprouted over 48 inches tall. Bring an iron constitution; rides with names like Ninja, Viper, Colossus, and Psyclone will have your cheeks flapping with the G-force, and queasy expressions are common at the exit. But where else can you experience zero-gravity weightlessness, careen down vertical tracks into relentless hairpin turns, or "race" another train on a side-by-side wooden roller coaster? Some rides are themed to action-film characters (like Superman—The Escape and Batman—The Ride); others are loosely tied to their themed surroundings, like a Far East pagoda or gold rush mining town. Arcade games and summer-only entertainment (stunt shows, zany carnivals, and parades) round out the park's attractions.

Hurricane Harbor is Six Flags's over-the-top water park. While it's advertised as a companion to Magic Mountain, you really can't see both in one day—combo tickets allow you to return within a year's time. Bring your own swimsuit; the park has changing rooms with showers and lockers. Like Magic Mountain, areas have themes like a tropical lagoon or an African river (complete with ancient temple ruins). The primary activities are swimming, water slides, rafting, volleyball, and lounging; many areas are designed especially for the "little buccaneer."

Magic Mountain Pkwy. (off Golden State Fwy. [I-5] north), Valencia. © **661/255-4100** or 818/367-5965. www.sixflags.com. Magic Mountain $40.99 adults, $20.50 seniors 55+ and children age 2 to 48 in. high, free for kids under 2; Hurricane Harbor $19 adults, $12 seniors, $12 children; adult combo ticket $52.99. Magic Mountain open daily April–Sept; weekends and holidays only rest of year. Hurricane Harbor open daily Memorial Day–Labor Day; weekends May and Sept; closed Oct–Apr. Both parks open 10am, closing hours vary between 6pm and midnight. Parking $7. Take the San Diego Fwy. (I-405) or the Hollywood Fwy. (U.S. 101/170) north; both will eventually merge with I-5; from I-5, take the Magic Mountain Pkwy. exit.

THE ZOO

Los Angeles Zoo (Kids)   The L.A. Zoo, which shares its parking lot with the Autry Museum, has been welcoming visitors and busloads of schoolkids since 1966. In 1982, the zoo inaugurated a display of cuddly koalas, still one of its biggest attractions. While mature shade trees now help cool the once-barren grounds, and new habitats are light-years ahead of the cruel concrete round-houses originally used to exhibit animals, there are still some depressing remnants of the humble old zoo—like a polar bear whose enclosure looks much more like a suburban swimming pool than the Arctic. Stick with the newer, more humane exhibits, like the interactive and educational Adventure Island (though promoted as the Children's Zoo, it's actually just as cool for grown-ups too), and the brand-new Chimpanzees of the Mahale Mountains habitat, where visitors can see plenty of primate activity. The year 2000 saw the opening of Red Ape Rain Forest, a natural orangutan habitat. The facility is renowned in zoological circles for the successful breeding and releasing of California condors, and occasionally it has some of these majestic and endangered birds on exhibit.

5333 Zoo Dr., Griffith Park. © **323/644-6400**. www.lazoo.org. Admission $8.25 adults, $5.25 seniors 65 and over, $3.25 kids ages 2–12, free to children under 2. Daily 10am–5pm. Closed Christmas Day. Free parking.

ORGANIZED TOURS
STUDIO TOURS

NBC Studios (★)   According to a security guard, John Wayne and Redd Foxx once got into a fight here after Wayne refused to ride in the same limousine as Foxx, who called the movie star a "redneck." Well, your NBC tour will probably be a bit more docile than that. The guided 1-hour tour includes a behind-the-scenes look at *The Tonight Show with Jay Leno* set; wardrobe, makeup, and set-building departments; and several sound studios. The tour also includes some cool video demonstrations of high-tech special effects.

3000 W. Alameda Ave., Burbank. © **818/840-3537**. Tours $6 adults, $5.50 seniors, $3.75 children ages 6–12. Children under 6 are not admitted. Mon–Fri 9am–3pm.

Paramount Pictures (★)   Paramount's 2-hour walking tour around its Hollywood headquarters is both a historical ode to filmmaking and a real-life look at a working studio. Tours depart hourly; the itinerary varies, depending on what productions are in progress. Visits might include a walk through the soundstages of TV shows or feature films, though you can't enter while taping is taking place. Cameras, recording equipment, and children under 10 are not allowed.

5555 Melrose Ave. © **323/956-1777**. www.paramount.com. Tours $15 per person. Mon–Fri 9am–2pm.

Warner Brothers Studios ★★

Warner Brothers offers the most comprehensive—and the least theme park–like—of the studio tours. The tour takes visitors on a 2-hour informational drive-and-walk jaunt around the studio's faux streets. After a brief introductory film, you'll pile into glorified golf carts and cruise past parking spaces marked "Clint Eastwood," "Michael Douglas," and "Sharon Stone," then walk through active film and television sets. Whether it's an orchestra scoring a film or a TV show being taped or edited, you'll get a glimpse of how it's done. Stops may include the wardrobe department or the mills where sets are made. Whenever possible, you can also visit working sets to watch actors filming actual productions. Reservations are required; children under 8 are not admitted.

Olive Ave. (at Hollywood Way), Burbank. © 818/972-TOUR; www.studio-tour.com. Advance reservations recommended. Tours $32 per person. Mon–Fri 9am–4pm.

SIGHTSEEING TOURS

L.A. Tours (© **800/881-7715** or 323/937-3361; www.la-tours.com) operates regularly scheduled tours of the city. Plush shuttle buses (27 passengers maximum) pick up riders from major hotels for morning or afternoon tours of Sunset Strip, the movie studios, Farmers Market, Hollywood, homes of the stars, and other attractions. Different itineraries are available, if you're interested in downtown and the Music Center, for example, or want to spend your time exploring the beaches and shopping in Santa Monica. Tours vary in length from a half day to a full day and cost $42 to $58 for adults. There are discounts for kids; book online for a $4-per-person discount. Advance reservations are required.

Next Stage Tour Company offers a unique Insomniacs' Tour of L.A. (© **213/939-2688**), a 3am tour of the predawn city that usually includes trips to the *Los Angeles Times;* the flower, produce, and fish markets; and the top of a skyscraper to watch the sun rise over the city. The fact-filled tour lasts about 6½ hours and includes breakfast. Tours depart twice monthly and cost $47 per person. Phone for information and reservations.

The **L.A. Conservancy** (© **213/623-2489;** www.laconservancy.org) conducts a dozen fascinating, information-packed walking tours of historic downtown L.A., the seed of today's sprawling metropolis. The most popular is "Broadway Theaters," a loving look at movie palaces. Other intriguing ones include "Marble Masterpieces," "Art Deco," "Mecca for Merchants," "Terra-Cotta," and tours of the landmark Biltmore Hotel and City Hall. They're usually held on Saturday mornings and cost $8. Call Monday through Friday between 9am and 5pm for the exact schedule and information.

In Pasadena, various tours spotlighting architecture or neighborhoods are lots of fun, given this area's history of wealthy estates and ardent preservation. Call **Pasadena Heritage** (© **626/793-0617;** www.pasadenaheritage.org) for a schedule of guided tours, or pick up "Ten Tours of Pasadena," self-guided walking or driving maps available at the **Pasadena Convention and Visitors Bureau,** 171 S. Los Robles Ave. (© **626/795-9311**).

7 TV Tapings

Being part of the audience for the taping of a television show might be the quintessential L.A. experience. This is a great way to see Hollywood at work, to find out how your favorite sitcom or talk show is made, and to catch a glimpse of your favorite TV personalities. Timing is important here—remember that most series productions go on hiatus between March and July. And tickets to the top shows, like *Friends* and *Everybody Loves Raymond,* are in greater demand than others, so getting your hands on them usually takes advance planning—and possibly some time waiting in line. Request tickets as far in advance as possible. More likely, however, you'll be given a list of shows that are currently filming, and you won't recognize many of the titles. Tickets are always free, usually limited to two per person, and are distributed on a first-come, first-served basis. Many shows don't admit children under the age of 10; in some cases no one under the age of 18 is admitted.

Tickets are sometimes given away to the public outside popular tourist sites like Mann's Chinese Theatre in Hollywood and Universal Studios in the Valley; L.A.'s visitor information centers in downtown and Hollywood often have tickets as well (see "Orientation," earlier in this chapter). But if you're determined to see a particular show, contact the following suppliers:

Audiences Unlimited (© **818/506-0043** or 818/506-0067; www.tvtickets. com) is a good place to start. It distributes tickets for most of the top sitcoms, including *Friends, That '70s Show, Will & Grace, The Drew Carey Show, Everybody Loves Raymond,* and many more. This service is organized and informative, and fully sanctioned by production companies and networks. ABC, for example, no longer handles ticket distribution directly, but refers all inquiries to Audiences Unlimited. **Television Tickets** (© **323/467-4697**) distributes tickets for talk and game shows, including the popular *Jeopardy!* show.

You also may want to contact the networks directly for information on a specific show, including some whose tickets are not available at the above agencies. At **ABC**, all ticket inquiries are referred to Audiences Unlimited (see above), but you may want to check out ABC's website at **www.abc.com** for a colorful look at their lineup and links to specific shows' sites. For tickets to *Politically Incorrect with Bill Maher,* call the show's ticket line at ⓒ **323/852-2655** to make a reservation (taken on a first-come, first-served basis), or order online at **www.abc.com/pi**.

For **CBS**, 7800 Beverly Blvd., Los Angeles, CA 90036 (ⓒ **323/852-2458**), call to see what's being filmed while you're in town. Tickets for CBS tapings are distributed on a first-come, first-served basis; you can write in advance to reserve them or pick them up directly at the studio up to an hour before taping. Tickets for many CBS sitcoms, including *Everybody Loves Raymond,* are also available from Audiences Unlimited (see above). Tickets for *The Price Is Right* must be requested by mail; allow 4 to 6 weeks. For a virtual visit to CBS's shows, log onto **www.cbs.com**.

For **NBC**, 3000 W. Alameda Ave., Burbank, CA 91523 (ⓒ **818/840-4444** or 818/840-3537), call to see what's on while you're in L.A. Tickets for NBC tapings, including *The Tonight Show with Jay Leno,* can be obtained in two ways: either pick them up at the NBC ticket counter on the day of the show you want to see (they're distributed on a first-come, first-served basis at the ticket counter off California Avenue), or, at least 3 weeks before your visit, send a self-addressed, stamped envelope with your ticket request to the address above. All the NBC shows are represented online at **www.nbc.com**.

8 Beaches

Los Angeles County's 72-mile coastline sports over 30 miles of beaches, most of which are operated by the **Department of Beaches & Harbors,** 13837 Fiji Way, Marina del Rey (ⓒ **310/305-9503**). County-run beaches usually charge for parking ($4 to $8). Alcohol, bonfires, and pets are prohibited, so you'll have to leave Fido at home. For recorded surf conditions (and coastal weather forecast), call ⓒ **310/457-9701.** The following are the county's best beaches, listed from north to south.

EL PESCADOR, LA PIEDRA & EL MATADOR BEACHES *(Finds)* These relatively rugged and isolated beaches front a 2-mile stretch of the Pacific Coast Highway (Calif. 1) between Broad Beach and Decker Canyon Roads, about a 10-minute drive from the Malibu Pier. Picturesque coves with unusual rock formations are perfect for sunbathing and picnicking, but swim with caution as there are no lifeguards or other facilities. These beaches can be difficult to find; they're marked only by small signs on the highway. Visitors are limited by the small number of parking spots atop the bluffs. Descend to the beach via stairs that cling to the cliffs.

ZUMA BEACH COUNTY PARK *(R)* Jam-packed on warm weekends, L.A. County's largest beach park is located off the Pacific Coast Highway (Calif. 1), a mile past Kanan Dume Road. While it can't claim to be the loveliest beach in the Southland, Zuma has the most comprehensive facilities: plenty of restrooms, lifeguards, playgrounds, volleyball courts, and snack bars. The southern stretch, toward Point Dume, is Westward Beach, separated from the noisy highway by sandstone cliffs. A trail leads over the point's headlands to Pirate's Cove, once a popular nude beach.

Los Angeles Beaches & Coastal Attractions

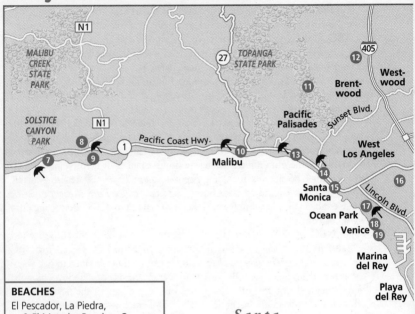

BEACHES
El Pescador, La Piedra,
 & El Matador Beaches **3**
Hermosa City Beach **21**
Leo Carrillo Beach **2**
Malibu Lagoon State Beach **7**
Manhattan State Beach **20**
North County Line Beach **1**
Paradise Cove **6**
Point Dume Beach **5**
Redondo State Beach **22**
Santa Monica State Beach **14**
Surfrider Beach **9**
Topanga State Beach **10**
Venice Beach **18**
Will Rogers State Beach **13**
Zuma Beach County Park **4**

SIGHTS & ATTRACTIONS
Aquarium of the Pacific **23**
Chiat/Day Headquarters **17**
Getty Center **12**
Long Beach Museum of Art **25**
Museum of Flying **16**
Pepperdine University **8**
Queen Mary **24**
Venice Ocean Front Walk **19**
Will Rogers State Historic Park **11**
Santa Monica Pier **15**

PARADISE COVE   This private beach in the 28000 block of the Pacific Coast Highway (Calif. 1) charges $15 to park and $5 per person if you walk in. Changing rooms and showers are included in the price. The beach is often full by noon on weekends.

MALIBU LAGOON STATE BEACH 🎔🎔   Not just a pretty white-sand beach but an estuary and wetlands area as well, Malibu Lagoon is the historic home of the Chumash Indians. The entrance is on the Pacific Coast Highway (Calif. 1) south of Cross Creek Road, and there's a small admission charge. Marine life and shorebirds teem where the creek empties into the sea, and the waves are always mild. The historic Adamson House is here, a showplace of Malibu tile now operating as a museum.

SURFRIDER BEACH   Without a doubt, L.A.'s best waves roll ashore here. One of the city's most popular surfing spots, this beach is located between the Malibu Pier and the lagoon. In surf lingo, few "locals-only" wave wars are ever fought here—surfing is not as territorial here as it can be in other areas, where out-of-towners can be made to feel unwelcome. Surfrider is surrounded by all of Malibu's hustle and bustle; don't come here for peace and quiet.

TOPANGA STATE BEACH   Noise from the highway prevents solitude at this short, narrow strip of sand located where Topanga Canyon Boulevard emerges from the mountains. Why go? Ask the surfers who wait in line to catch Topanga's excellent breaks. There are restrooms and lifeguard services here, but little else.

WILL ROGERS STATE BEACH   Three miles along the Pacific Coast Highway (Calif. 1), between Sunset Boulevard and the Santa Monica border, are named for the American humorist whose ranch-turned-state-historic-park (see "Parks," earlier in this chapter) is nestled above the palisades that provide the striking backdrop for this popular beach. A pay parking lot extends the entire length of Will Rogers, and facilities include restrooms, lifeguards, and a snack hut in season. While the surfing is only so-so, the waves are friendly for swimmers of all ages.

SANTA MONICA STATE BEACH _Kids_   The beaches on either side of the Santa Monica Pier (see "Piers," earlier in this chapter) are popular for their white sands and easy accessibility. There are big parking lots, eateries, and lots of well-maintained restrooms. A paved beach path runs along here, allowing you to walk, bike, or skate to Venice and points south. Colorado Boulevard leads to the pier; turn north on the Pacific Coast Highway (Calif. 1) below the coastline's striking bluffs, or south along Ocean Avenue; you'll find parking in both directions.

VENICE BEACH 🎔🎔   Moving south from the city of Santa Monica, the paved pedestrian Promenade becomes Ocean Front Walk and gets progressively weirder until it reaches an apex at Washington Boulevard and the Venice fishing pier. Although there are people who swim and sunbathe, Venice Beach's character is defined by the sea of humanity on the Ocean Front Walk, plus the bevy of boardwalk vendors and old-fashioned pedestrian streets a block away (see "The Top Attractions," earlier in this chapter). Park on the side streets or in the plentiful lots west of Pacific Avenue.

MANHATTAN STATE BEACH   The Beach Boys used to hang out at this wide, friendly beach backed by beautiful ocean-view homes. Plenty of parking on 36 blocks of side streets (between Rosecrans Avenue and the Hermosa Beach border) draws weekend crowds from the L.A. area. Manhattan has some of the best surfing around, along with restrooms, lifeguards, and volleyball courts. Manhattan Beach Boulevard leads west to the fishing pier and adjacent seafood restaurants.

HERMOSA CITY BEACH ✦   A very, very wide, white-sand beach with tons to recommend it, Hermosa extends to either side of the pier and includes "The Strand," a pedestrian lane that runs its entire length. Main access is at the foot of Pier Avenue, which itself is lined with interesting shops. There are plenty of street parking, restrooms, lifeguards, volleyball courts, a fishing pier, playgrounds, and good surfing.

REDONDO STATE BEACH   Popular with surfers, bicyclists, and joggers, Redondo's white-sand and ice plant–carpeted dunes are just south of tiny King Harbor, along "The Esplanade" (South Esplanade Drive). Get there via the Pacific Coast Highway (Calif. 1) or Torrance Boulevard. Facilities include restrooms, lifeguards, and volleyball courts.

9 Outdoor Pursuits

BICYCLING   L.A. is great for biking. If you're into distance pedaling, you can't do better than the flat, 22-mile paved **Ocean Front Walk** that runs along the sand from Pacific Palisades in the north to Torrance in the south. The path attracts all levels of riders, so it gets pretty busy on weekends. For information on this and other city bike routes, phone the **Los Angeles Dept. of Transportation** (© 213/485-9957).

The best place to mountain-bike is along the trails of **Malibu Creek State Park** (© 800/533-7275 or 818/880-0350), in the Santa Monica Mountains between Malibu and the San Fernando Valley. Fifteen miles of trails rise to a maximum of 3,000 feet and are appropriate for intermediate to advanced bikers. Pick up a trail map at the park entrance, 4 miles south of U.S. 101 off Las Virgenes Road, just north of Mulholland Highway. Park admission is $5 per car.

Spokes 'n Stuff Bike Rental has two locations: 4175 Admiralty Way, Marina del Rey (© 310/306-3332), and 1715 Oceanfront Walk, behind Loews Hotel, Santa Monica (© 310/395-4748). They'll rent 10-speed cruisers for $7 per hour and $16 per day; 15-speed mountain bikes rent for $8 per hour and $20 per day.

FISHING   **Del Rey Sport Fishing,** 13759 Fiji Way (© 310/822-3625) has four deep-sea boats departing daily on half- and full-day ocean fishing trips. Of course, it depends on what's running when you're out, but bass, barracuda, halibut, and yellowtail tuna are the most common catches on these party boats. Excursions cost $22 to $30; tackle rental is available. Phone for reservations. No permit is required to cast from shore or to drop a line from a pier.

GOLF   Most of the city's public courses are administered by the Department of Parks and Recreation, which follows a complicated registration/reservation system for tee times. While visitors cannot reserve start times in advance, you're welcome to play any of the courses by showing up and getting on the call sheet. Expect to wait for the most popular tee times, but try to use your flexible vacationer status to your advantage by avoiding the early-morning rush.

Of the city's seven 18-hole and three 9-hole courses, you can't get more central than the **Rancho Park Golf Course,** 10460 W. Pico Blvd. (© 310/838-7373), located smack-dab in the middle of L.A.'s Westside. The par-71 course has lots of tall trees, but not enough to blot out the towering Century City buildings next door. Rancho also has a nine-hole, par-three course.

For a genuinely woodsy experience, try one of the three courses inside Griffith Park, northeast of Hollywood (see "Parks," earlier in this chapter). All named for presidents, the courses are extremely well maintained, challenging without being frustrating, and (despite some holes alongside I-5) a great way to leave the city behind. Bucolic pleasures abound, particularly on nine-hole **Roosevelt,** on Vermont Avenue across from the Greek Theatre; early-morning wildlife often includes deer, rabbits, skunks, and raccoons (fore!). **Wilson** and **Harding** are each 18 holes and start from the main clubhouse off Riverside Drive, the park's main entrance.

Greens fees on all city courses are $18 Monday through Friday, $25 Saturday, Sunday, and holidays; nine-hole courses charge $11 weekdays, $14 on weekends and holidays. For details on other city courses, or to contact the starter directly by phone, call the **Department of Parks and Recreation** (© 213/485-5566).

HIKING The Santa Monica Mountains, a small range that runs only 50 miles from Griffith Park to Point Mugu, on the coast north of Malibu, makes Los Angeles a great place for day hikes. The mountains peak at 3,111 feet and are part of the **Santa Monica Mountains National Recreation Area,** a contiguous conglomeration of 350 public parks and 65,000 acres. Many animals make their homes in this area, including deer, coyote, rabbit, skunk, rattlesnake, fox, hawk, and quail. The hills are also home to almost 1,000 drought-resistant plant species, including live oak and coastal sage.

Santa Ynez Canyon, in Pacific Palisades, is a long and difficult climb that rises steadily for about 3 miles. At the top, hikers are rewarded with fantastic views over the Pacific. Also at the top is Trippet Ranch, a public facility providing water, restrooms, and picnic tables. From Santa Monica, take the Pacific Coast Highway (Calif. 1) north. Turn right onto Sunset Boulevard, then left onto Palisades Drive. Continue for 2½ miles, turn left onto Verenda de la Montura, and park at the cul-de-sac at the end of the street, where you'll find the trailhead.

Temescal Canyon, in Pacific Palisades, is far easier than the Santa Ynez Trail and, predictably, far more popular with locals. It's one of the quickest routes into the wilderness. Hikes here are anywhere from 1 to 5 miles. From Santa Monica,

Spectator Sports

The **Los Angeles Dodgers** (© 213/224-1500) play at Dodger Stadium, 1000 Elysian Park, near Sunset Boulevard. The team's slick, interactive website (**www.dodgers.com**) offers everything from game schedules to souvenir merchandise online.

Los Angeles has two NBA franchises, the **L.A. Lakers** (© 310/419-3100; www.nba.com/lakers) and the **L.A. Clippers** (© 213/745-0400; www.nba.com/clippers). Both teams play in the new $300 million **STAPLES Center** in downtown L.A., 1111 S. Figueroa St. (© 877/673-6799; www.staplescenterla.com). Celebrity fans like Jack Nicholson and Dyan Cannon have the best tickets, but this 20,000-seater should have room for you too.

Los Angeles suffers from an absence of major-league football, but is blessed with two popular college teams. The college ball season runs from September to November; if you're interested in checking out a game, contact **UCLA Bruins Football** (© 310/825-2106) or **USC Trojan Football** (© 213/740-2311; www.usctrojans.com).

take the Pacific Coast Highway (Calif. 1) north; turn right onto Temescal Canyon Road and follow it to the end. Sign in with the gatekeeper, who can also answer your questions.

Will Rogers State Historic Park, Pacific Palisades, is a terrific place for hiking. An intermediate-level hike from the park's entrance ends at Inspiration Point, a plateau from which you can see a good portion of L.A.'s Westside. See "Parks" under "Exploring the City," earlier in this chapter, for complete information.

Griffith Park (also discussed in "Parks," earlier in this chapter) is an urban hiker's paradise. This 100-year-old park used to have dozens of paved roads popular for weekend motorists, but cuts in funding over the years have forced the park to stop maintenance and close them to car traffic. The good news is that they make great hiking routes—they're safe, easy to follow, and lead to some of the most spectacular city vistas in L.A. The park also has dozens of dirt trails at every endurance level; you can get a map of both paved roads and hiking trails at the ranger center 1 mile inside the Riverside Drive main entrance.

HORSEBACK RIDING The **Griffith Park Livery Stable,** 480 Riverside Dr. (in the Los Angeles Equestrian Center), Burbank (© **818/840-8401**), rents horses by the hour for western or English riding through Griffith Park's hills. There's a 200-pound weight limit, and children under 12 are not permitted to ride. Horse rental costs $15 per hour; maximum rental is 2 hours. You can also arrange for private 1-hour lessons ($35). The stables are open daily from 8am to 5pm, and cash is required for payment.

SKATING The 22-mile-long **Ocean Front Walk** that runs from Pacific Palisades to Torrance is one of the premier skating spots in the country. In-line skating is especially popular, but conventionals are often seen here, too. Rollerskating is allowed just about everywhere bicycling is, but be aware that cyclists have the right-of-way. **Spokes 'n Stuff,** 4175 Admiralty Way, Marina del Rey (© **310/306-3332**), is just one of many places to rent wheels near the Venice portion of Ocean Front Walk. Skates cost $5 per hour; kneepads and wrist guards come with every rental. In the South Bay, in-line skate rentals are available 1 block from the Strand at **Hermosa Cyclery,** 20 13th Street (© **310/374-7816**). Skates cost around $6 per hour; kneepads and wrist guards come with every rental.

SURFING If you're a first-timer eager to learn the sport, contact **Pure Surfing Experience** (© **310/546-4451**; www.campsurf.com) in Manhattan Beach. This highly respected school features a team of experienced instructors and will supply all necessary equipment. Single lessons are $100, but subsequent followups are deeply discounted. Call for reservations (also available online).

Boards are available for rent at shops near all top surfing beaches in the L.A. area. **Zuma Jay Surfboards,** 22775 Pacific Coast Hwy., Malibu (© **310/456-8044**), is about a quarter mile south of Malibu Pier. Rentals are $20 per day, plus $8 to $10 for wet suits in winter.

TENNIS You'll find mostly hard-surface courts in California. If your hotel doesn't have a court, try the well-maintained, well-lit **Griffith Park Tennis Courts,** on Commonwealth Road just east of Vermont Avenue. Or call the **City of Los Angeles Department of Parks and Recreation** (© **213/485-5555**) to make a reservation at a municipal court near you.

10 Shopping

Here's a rundown of the primary shopping areas, along with descriptions of a few of their best stores. The sales tax in Los Angeles is 8%, but savvy out-of-state shoppers know how to have more expensive items shipped directly home, thereby avoiding the tax.

SANTA MONICA & THE BEACHES

Third Street Promenade   Packed with chain stores and boutiques as well as dozens of restaurants and a large movie theater, Santa Monica's pedestrians-only section of Third Street is one of the most popular shopping areas in the city. The Promenade bustles on into the evening with a seemingly endless assortment of street performers and shoppers. Stores stay open late (often until 1 or 2am on the weekends) for the movie-going crowds. There's plenty of metered parking in structures on the adjacent streets, so bring lots of quarters!

Highlights include **Hennessey & Ingalls,** 1254 Third Street Promenade (© 310/ 458-9074), a bookstore devoted to art and architecture, from magnificent coffee-table photography books to graphic-arts titles and obscure biographies of artists and art movements; **Midnight Special Bookstore,** 1318 Third Street Promenade (© 310/393-2923), a medium-size general bookshop known for its good small-press selection and regular poetry readings; **Restoration Hardware,** 1221 Third Street Promenade (© 310/458-7992), the retro-current source for reproduction home furnishings and accessories; and **Puzzle Zoo,** 1413 Third Street Promenade (© 310/393-9201), where you'll find the double-sided World's Most Difficult Puzzle, the Puzzle in a Bottle, and many other brain-teasing challenges. Puzzle Zoo was voted "Best in L.A." by *Los Angeles* magazine. Book lovers may also want to stop by the local **Barnes & Noble,** 1201 Third Street Promenade (© 310/260-9110), which carries thousands of titles; or **Borders Books & Music,** which has a branch across town at 330 S. La Cienega Blvd., at Third Street (© 310/659-4045). Third St., from Broadway to Wilshire Blvd., Santa Monica. www.thirdst.com.

Main Street   Another good strip for strolling, Main Street boasts a healthy combination of mall standards as well as upscale, left-of-center individual boutiques. You'll also find plenty of casually hip cafes and restaurants. The primary strip connecting Santa Monica and Venice, Main Street has a relaxed, beach-community vibe that sets it apart from similar strips. The stores here straddle the fashion fence between upscale trendy and beach-bum edgy.

Highlights include **C. P. Shades,** 2925 Main St. (© 310/392-0949), a San Francisco women's clothier whose loose and comfy cotton and linen line is carried by many department stores and boutiques. **Horizons West,** 2011 Main St., south of Pico Blvd. (© 310/392-1122), sells brand-name surfboards, wet suits, leashes, magazines, waxes, lotions, and everything else you need to catch the perfect wave. Stop in and say hi to Randy, and pick up a free tide table. If you're looking for some truly sophisticated, finely crafted eyewear, friendly **Pepper's Eyeware,** 2904 Main St., between Ashland and Pier Streets (© 310/392-0633), is for you. Ask for frames by cutting-edge L.A. designers Bada and Koh Sakai. If you're lucky enough to have perfect vision, consider some stylish shades. Outdoors types will get lost in 5,600-square-foot **Patagonia,** 2936 Main St. (© 310/ 314-1776), where climbers, surfers, skiers, and hikers can gear up in the functional, colorful duds that put this environmentally friendly firm on the map. Between Pico Blvd. and Rose Ave., in Santa Monica & Venice.

Montana Avenue   This breezy stretch of slow-traffic Montana is one of our favorite regentrified parts of the city. Okay, so it's gotten a lot more pricey than in the late 1970s, when tailors and Laundromats ruled the roost, but we're just happy the specialty shops still outnumber the chains. Look around and you'll see upscale Moms with strollers and cell phones shopping for designer fashions, country-home decor, and gourmet takeout.

Montana's biggest selling point is that it's still original enough for residents from across town to make a special trip to shop here, seeking out distinctive shops like **Shabby Chic,** 1013 Montana Ave. (© 310/394-1975), a much-copied purveyor of slipcovered sofas and flea-market furnishings. Clotheshorses shop for designer wear at minimalist **Savannah,** 706 Montana Ave. (© 310/458-2095); ultra-hip **Jill Roberts,** 920 Montana Ave. (© 310/260-1966); and sleekly professional **Weathervane,** 1209 Montana Ave. (© 310/393-5344). Upscale Moms can find tiny fashions at **Real Threads,** 1527 Montana Ave. (© 310/393-3175), and kid-sized bedroom furnishings at **Little Folk Art,** 1120 Montana Ave. (© 310/576-0909). For more grown-up style, head to **Ponte Vecchio,** 702 Montana Ave. (© 310/394-0989), for Italian hand-painted dishes and urns, or to **Cinzia,** 1129 Montana Ave. (© 310/393-7751), which features a smattering of both Tuscan and English home accessories. If Valentine's Day is approaching, duck into **Only Hearts,** 1407 Montana Ave. (© 310/393-3088) for heart-themed gifts and seductively comfortable intimate apparel. The stylish choice for lunch is **Wolfgang Puck Cafe,** 1323 Montana Ave. (© 310/ 393-0290). Between Seventh and 17th Sts., in Santa Monica.

Bergamot Station *(Finds)*   Once a station for the Red Car trolley line, this industrial space is now home to the **Santa Monica Museum of Art,** plus two dozen art galleries, a cafe, a bookstore, and offices. Most of the galleries are closed Monday. The train yard is located at the terminus of Michigan Avenue, west of Cloverfield Boulevard.

Exhibits change often and vary widely, ranging from a Julius Shulman black-and-white photo retrospective of L.A.'s Case Study Houses, to a provocative exhibit of Vietnam War propaganda posters from the United States and Vietnam, to whimsical furniture constructed entirely of corrugated cardboard. A sampling of offerings includes the **Gallery of Functional Art** (© 310/829-6990), which features one-of-a-kind and limited-edition furniture, lighting, bathroom fixtures, and other functional art pieces, as well as smaller items like jewelry, flatware, ceramics, and glass. **The Rosamund Felson Gallery** (© 310/828-8488) is well known for showcasing L.A.-based contemporary artists; this is a good place to get a taste of current trends. **Track 16 Gallery** (© 310/264-4678) has exhibitions that range from pop art to avant-garde inventiveness—try to see what's going on here. 2525 Michigan Ave. (east of Cloverfield Blvd.), Santa Monica. © 310/829-5854.

L.A.'S WESTSIDE & BEVERLY HILLS

West Third Street   You can shop till you drop on this trendy strip, anchored on the east end by the Farmers Market (see "The Top Attractions," earlier in this chapter). Many of Melrose Avenue's shops have relocated here, alongside some terrific up-and-comers and several cafes. "Fun" is more the catchword here than "funky," and the shops (including the vintage-clothing stores) tend a bit more to the refined than do those along Melrose.

The **Cook's Library,** 8373 W. Third St. (© 323/655-3141; www.cookslibrary.com), is where the city's top chefs find both classic and deliciously offbeat cookbooks and other food-oriented tomes. Browsing is welcomed, even encouraged, with tea, tasty treats, and rocking chairs. **Traveler's Bookcase,** 8375 W. Third St. (✆ 323/655-0575; www.travelbooks.com), is truly one of the best travel-book shops in the West, stocking a huge selection of guidebooks and travel literature, as well as maps and travel accessories. A quarterly newsletter chronicles the travel adventures of the genial owners, who know firsthand the most helpful items to carry.

There's a lot more to see along this always-growing street, enough to take up several hours. Refuel at **Chado Tea Room** ☆, 8422 W. Third St. (✆ 323/ 655-2056), a temple for tea lovers. Chado is designed with a nod to Paris's renowned Mariage Frères tea purveyor; one wall is lined with nooks whose recognizable brown tins are filled with over 250 different varieties of tea from around the world. Among the choices are 15 kinds of Darjeeling, Indian teas blended with rose petals, and ceremonial Chinese and Japanese blends. You can also get tea meals here, featuring delightful sandwiches and individual pots of any loose tea in the store. Between Fairfax Ave. and Robertson Blvd.

Sunset Strip   The monster-size billboards advertising the latest rock god make it clear that this is rock-'n'-roll territory. So it makes sense that you'll find legendary **Tower Records,** 8801 W. Sunset Blvd. (✆ 310/657-7300; www. towerrecords.com), in the heart of the action. Tower insists that it has L.A.'s largest selection of CDs—over 125,000 titles—despite the Virgin Megastore's contrary claim. Even if Virgin has more, Tower's collection tends to be more interesting and browser friendly. And the shop's enormous blues, jazz, and classical selections are definitely better than the competition's. It's open 365 days a year. At the east end of the strip sits the gigantic **Virgin Megastore,** 8000 Sunset Blvd., at Crescent Heights (✆ 323/650-8666). Some 100 CD listening posts and an in-store radio station make this megastore a music lover's paradise. Virgin claims to stock 150,000 titles, including an extensive collection of hard-to-find artists.

The "Strip" is lined with trendy restaurants, industry-oriented hotels, and dozens of shops offering outrageous fashions and chunky stage accessories. One anomaly is **Sunset Plaza,** an upscale cluster of Georgian-style shops resembling Beverly Hills at its snootiest. Here's where you'll find **Billy Martin's,** 8605 Sunset Blvd. (✆ 310/289-5000), which was founded by the legendary Yankee manager in 1978. This chic men's Western shop—complete with fireplace and leather sofa—stocks hand-forged silver and gold belt buckles, Lucchese and Liberty boots, and stable staples like flannel shirts. **Book Soup,** 8818 Sunset Blvd. (✆ 310/659-3110; www.booksoup.com), has long been one of L.A.'s most celebrated bookshops, selling both mainstream and small-press books and hosting regular book signings and author nights. A great browsing shop, it has a large selection of show-biz books and an extensive outdoor news- and magazine stand on one side. Between La Cienega Blvd. and Doheny Dr., West Hollywood.

La Brea Avenue   This is L.A.'s artsiest shopping strip. Anchored by the giant **American Rag, Cie.** alterna-complex, 150 S. La Brea Ave. (✆ 323/935-3157), La Brea is home to lots of great urban antiques stores dealing in Deco, Arts and Crafts, 1950s modern, and the like. You'll also find vintage clothiers, furniture galleries, and other warehouse-size stores, as well as some of the city's hippest restaurants, such as Campanile.

Bargain hunters find flea-market furnishings at **Nick Metropolis,** 100 S. La Brea Ave. (✆ 323/934-3700), while more upscale seekers of home decor head to **Mortise & Tenon,** 446 S. La Brea Ave. (© **323/937-7654**), where hand-crafted heavy wood pieces sit next to overstuffed velvet-upholstered sofas and even vintage steel desks. Stuffed to the rafters with hardware and fixtures of the last 100 years, **Liz's Antique Hardware,** 453 S. La Brea Ave. (© **323/ 939-4403**), thoughtfully keeps a canister of wet-wipes at the register—believe us, you'll need one after sifting through bags and crates of doorknobs, latches, finials, and any other home hardware you can imagine needing. Perfect sets of Bakelite drawer pulls and antique ceramic bathroom fixtures are some of the more intriguing items. Be prepared to browse for hours, whether you're redecorating or not!

Although the art of millinery often seems to have gone the way of white afternoon gloves for ladies, inventive **Drea Kadilak** ✦, 463 S. La Brea Ave., at Sixth Street (© **323/931-2051**), charms us with her tiny hat shop. Designing in straw, cotton duck, wool felt, and a number of more unusual fabrics, she does her own blocking, will cheerfully take measurements for custom ladies' headwear, is reasonably priced, and gives away signature hatboxes with your purchase.

The best place for a snack is Nancy Silverton's **La Brea Bakery,** 624 S. La Brea Ave. (© **323/939-6813**), which foodies know from gourmet markets and the attached Campanile restaurant (see "Dining," earlier in this chapter). Hipsters also head up the street to **Yellowstone,** 712 N. La Brea Ave. (© **323/931-6616**) for vintage duds, and souvenir seekers know to visit **Moletown,** 900 N. La Brea Ave. (© **800/851-7221**) for studio merchandise featuring logo graphics from the hottest new movies. North of Wilshire Blvd.

Rodeo Drive & Beverly Hills' Golden Triangle Everyone knows about Rodeo Drive, the city's most famous shopping street. Couture shops from high fashion's Old Guard are located along these three hallowed blocks, along with plenty of newer high-end labels. And there are two examples of the Beverly Hills version of mini-malls, albeit more insular and attractive—the **Rodeo Collection,** 421 N. Rodeo Dr., and **Two Rodeo,** at Wilshire Boulevard. The 16-square-block area surrounding Rodeo Drive is known as the "Golden Triangle." Shops off Rodeo are generally not as name-conscious as those on the strip (you might actually be able to buy something!), but they're nevertheless plenty upscale. Little Santa Monica Boulevard has a particularly colorful line of specialty stores, and Brighton Way is as young and hip as relatively staid Beverly Hills gets.

The big names to look for here are **Giorgio Beverly Hills,** 327 N. Rodeo Dr. (© 800/GIORGIO or 310/274-0200); **Gucci,** 347 N. Rodeo Dr. (© 310/278-3451); **Hermès,** 343 N. Rodeo Dr. (© 310/278-6440); **Louis Vuitton,** 307 N. Rodeo Dr. (© 310/859-0457); **Polo/Ralph Lauren,** 444 N. Rodeo Dr. (© 310/281-7200); and **Tiffany & Co.,** 210 N. Rodeo Dr. (© 310/273-8880). The newest arrival is **Niketown,** at the corner of Wilshire Boulevard and Rodeo Drive (© 310/275-9998), a behemoth shrine to the reigning athletic-gear king. Wilshire Boulevard is also home to New York–style department stores (each in spectacular, architectural landmark buildings) like **Saks Fifth Avenue,** 9600 Wilshire Blvd. (© 310/275-4211), **Barney's New York,** 9570 Wilshire Blvd. (© 310/276-4400), and **Neiman Marcus,** 9700 Wilshire Blvd. (© 310/ 550-5900). Between Santa Monica Blvd., Wilshire Blvd., and Crescent Dr.

HOLLYWOOD

Melrose Avenue Melrose is showing some wear—some stretches have become downright ugly—but this is still one of the most exciting shopping streets in the country for cutting-edge fashions—and some eye-popping people

Dressing the Part: Where to Find Hollywood's Hand-Me-Downs

Admit it: You've dreamed of being a glamorous movie or TV star—everyone has. Well, you shouldn't expect to be "discovered" during your L.A. vacation, but you can live out your fantasy by dressing the part. Costumes from famous movies, TV show wardrobes, castoffs from celebrity closets—they're easier to find (and more affordable to own) than you might think.

A good place to start is **Studio Wardrobe/Reel Clothes,** 5525 N Cahuenga Blvd., North Hollywood (© **818/508-7762;** www.reel-clothes.com). You may recognize some of the clothes here from movies and TV shows; most of the items were worn by stars or extras before being turned over for public sale. Prices range from $10 to $1,000. New shipments arrive every few days, and often include props and accessories from sets. Open daily noon to 6pm.

At **The Place & Co.,** 8820 S. Sepulveda Blvd., Westchester (© **310/ 645-1539**), the anonymity of the well-heeled clientele (sellers and buyers) is strictly honored. Here you'll find men's and women's haute couture—always the latest fashions, gently worn—at a fraction of the Rodeo Drive prices. All the designers are here: Ungaro, Bill Blass, Krizia, and Donna Karan. You may have even seen that Armani suit or Sonia Rykiel gown you found in the racks on an Academy Awards attendee last year! Open Monday to Saturday 10am to 6pm.

For sheer volume, you can't beat **It's A Wrap,** 3315 W. Magnolia Blvd., Burbank (© **818/567-7366;** www.movieclothes.com). Every item here is marked with its place of origin, and the list is staggering: *Beverly Hills, 90210, Melrose Place, Seinfeld, Baywatch, Seventh Heaven, Sabrina the*

watching to boot. There are scores of shops selling the latest in clothes, gifts, jewelry, and accessories. Melrose is a playful stroll, dotted with plenty of hip restaurants and funky shops that are sure to shock. Where else could you find green patent-leather cowboy boots, a working 19th-century pocket watch, an inflatable girlfriend, and glow-in-the-dark condoms in the same shopping spree? From east to west, here are some highlights.

l.a. Eyeworks, 7407 Melrose Ave. (© **323/653-8255**), revolutionized eyeglass designs from medical supply to stylish accessory, and now their brand is sold nationwide. **Retail Slut,** 7308 Melrose Ave. (© **323/934-1339**), is a famous rock-'n'-roll shop carrying new clothing and accessories for men and women. The unique designs are for a select crowd (the name says it all), so don't expect to find anything for your next PTA meeting here. **Betsey Johnson Boutique,** 7311 Melrose Ave. (© **323/931-4490**), is a favorite among the young and pencil-thin; the New York–based designer has brought her brand of fashion—trendy, cutesy, body-conscious women's wear in colorful prints and faddish fabrics—to L.A. It's also in Santa Monica at 2929 Main St. (© **310/ 452-7911**).

Across the street, **Off the Wall,** 7325 Melrose Ave. (© **323/930-1185**), is filled with neon-flashing, bells-and-whistles kitsch collectibles, from vintage

Teenage Witch, American Beauty, The Truman Show, and so on. Many of these wardrobes (which include shoes and accessories) aren't outstanding but for their Hollywood origins: Jerry Seinfeld's trademark polo shirts, for instance, are standard mall-issue. Some collectible pieces, like Sylvester Stallone's *Rocky* stars-and-stripes boxers, are framed and on display. Open Monday to Saturday 11am to 6pm, Sunday 11am to 4pm.

The grande dame of all wardrobe and costume outlets is **Western Costume,** 11041 Vanowen St., North Hollywood (© **818/760-0900;** www.westerncostume.com). In business since 1912, Western Costume still designs and executes entire wardrobes for major motion pictures; when filming is finished, the garments are added to their staggering rental inventory. This place is perhaps best known for outfitting Vivien Leigh in *Gone With the Wind.* Several of Scarlett O'Hara's memorable gowns were even available for rent until they were recently auctioned off at a charity event. Western also maintains an outlet store on the premises, where damaged garments are sold at rock-bottom (nothing over $15) prices. If you're willing to do some rescue work, there are definitely hidden treasures here. Open for rentals Monday to Friday 8am to 5:30pm, for sales Tuesday to Friday 10am to 5pm.

Finally, don't miss **Golyester,** 136 S. La Brea Ave. (© **323/931-1339**). This shop is almost a museum of finely preserved (but reasonably priced) vintage clothing and fabrics. The staff will gladly flip through stacks of Vogue magazines from the 1930s, 1940s, and 1950s with you, pointing out the lavish, star-studded original advertisements for various outfits in their stock. Open Monday to Saturday 11am to 6pm.

Wurlitzer jukeboxes to life-size fiberglass cows. The L.A. branch of a Bay Area hipster hangout, **Wasteland,** 7428 Melrose Ave. (© **323/653-3028**), has an enormous steel-sculpted facade. There's a lot of leather, denim, and some classic vintage—but mostly funky 1970s garb, both vintage and contemporary. This ultra-trendy store is packed with the flamboyantly colorful polyester halters and bell-bottoms from the decade some of us would rather forget. More racks of vintage treasures (and trash) are found at **Aardvark's Odd Ark,** 7579 Melrose Ave. (© **323/655-6769**), which stocks everything from suits and dresses to neckties, hats, handbags, and jewelry. This place also manages to anticipate some of the hottest new street fashions. There's another Aardvark's at 85 Market St., Venice (© **310/392-2996**). Between Fairfax and La Brea Aves.

Hollywood Boulevard   One of Los Angeles's most famous streets is, for the most part, a sleazy strip. But along the Walk of Fame, between the T-shirt shops and greasy pizza parlors, you'll find some excellent poster shops, souvenir stores, and Hollywood-memorabilia dealers that are worth getting out of your car for—especially if there's a chance of getting your hands on that long-sought-after Ethel Merman autograph or 200 Motels poster.

Some longstanding purveyors of memorabilia include **Book City Collectibles,** 6631 Hollywood Blvd. (© **323/466-0120**), which has more than

70,000 color prints of past and present stars available, along with a good selection of autographs from the likes of Lucille Ball ($175), Anthony Hopkins ($35), and Grace Kelly ($750). **Hollywood Book and Poster Company,** 6349 Hollywood Blvd. (℃ **323/465-8764**), has an excellent collection of movie posters (from about $15 each), particularly strong in horror and exploitation flicks. Photocopies of about 5,000 movie and television scripts are also sold for $10 to $15 each, and the store carries music posters and photos, too. **Collectors Book Store,** 6225 Hollywood Blvd., at Gower Street (℃ **323/467-3296**), sells movie-related merchandise of all kinds, including vintage fan mags like *Photoplay* and *Screen Stars,* reproduction lobby cards, black-and-white 8×10s (like the classic Betty Grable pinup shot), and an eclectic array of collector's card series. Between Gower St. and La Brea Ave.

SILVER LAKE & LOS FELIZ
Located at the eastern end of Hollywood, and technically part of just plain Los Angeles, these two communities have been steadily rising on the hipness meter. Silver Lake, named for the man-made Silver Lake Reservoir at its center, is a bohemian community of artists and ethnic families that's popular for night-clubbing and barhopping. Los Feliz is northwest of Silver Lake, centered on Vermont and Hillhurst Avenues between Sunset Boulevard and Los Feliz Boulevard; it's slightly tamer, and filled with 1920s and 1930s buildings. You'll find tons of unique businesses of all sorts, including artsy boutiques, music stores, and furniture dealers that have inspired some to compare the area to New York's SoHo.

Because so many alternative bands call Silver Lake home, it's not surprising to find cutting-edge music stores around every corner. A neighborhood mainstay is **Rockaway Records,** 2395 Glendale Blvd., south of Silver Lake Boulevard (℃ **323/664-3232;** www.rockaway.com), with tons of used CDs, collectible discs, and new releases. Platter collectors head to the local branch of Melrose's **Vinyl Fetish,** 1750 N. Vermont Ave. (℃ **323/660-4500**) for new and used vinyl records. (Yes, it carries CDs too.)

Vintage clothing is another big draw in these parts: The most reliable yet eclectic selections to browse through are at **Ozzie Dots,** 4637 Hollywood Blvd., west of Hillhurst (℃ **323/663-2867**); **Pull My Daisy,** 3908 Sunset Blvd., at Griffith Park Boulevard (℃ **323/663-0608**); and **Squaresville,** 1800 N. Vermont Ave., south of Franklin (℃ **323/669-8464**).

Hollywood set designers know to prowl the vintage furniture stores of Silver Lake. The best for mid-century modern gems are **Edna Hart,** 2945 Rowena Ave., south of Hyperion (℃ **323/661-4070**); and **Rubbish,** 1630 Silver Lake Blvd., north of Sunset (℃ **323/661-5575**). Plastic decorative items, from the 1950s on, reign at the aptly named **Plastica,** 4685 Hollywood Blvd., east of Hillhurst (℃ **323/644-1212**). One not-to-be-missed neighborhood highlight is the wacky and eclectic **Soap Plant/Wacko/La Luz de Jesus Art Gallery,** 4633 Hollywood Blvd., west of Hillhurst (℃ **323/663-0122**), a three-in-one business with candles, art books, erotic toys, soap and bath items, and a large selection of lava lamps. Local fixture **Y-Que,** 1770 N. Vermont Ave. (℃ **323/664-0021**), almost defies description, selling a variety of wacky stuff ranging from a knock-off *Austin Powers* penis pump to psychedelic lava lamps. Truly left-of-center bibliophiles head to the R-rated **Koma Bookstore,** 1764 N. Vermont Ave. (℃ **323/ 665-0956;** www.komabookstore.com), still called Amok by the faithful legions who come for hard-to-find volumes on Satanic rituals, radical political tracts, and lurid 1940s pulp erotica.

DOWNTOWN

Since the late, lamented grande dame department store Bullock's closed in 1993 (its deco masterpiece salons were rescued to house the Southwestern Law School's library), downtown has become even less of a shopping destination than ever. But although many of the once-splendid streets are lined with cut-rate luggage and cheap electronics storefronts, shopping downtown can be a rewarding if gritty experience for the adventuresome.

Savvy Angelenos still go for bargains in the garment and fabric districts, florists and bargain hunters arrive at the vast Flower Mart before dawn for the city's best selection of fresh blooms, and families of all ethnicities stroll the **Grand Central Market** ⋆, 317 S. Broadway, between Third and Fourth Streets (**℗ 213/624-2378**). Opened in 1917, this bustling market has watched the face of downtown L.A. change while changing little itself. Today, it serves Latino families, enterprising restaurateurs, and home cooks in search of unusual ingredients and bargain-priced fruits and vegetables. On weekends, you'll be greeted by a lively mariachi band at the Hill Street entrance, near our favorite market feature—the fruit juice counter, which dispenses 20 fresh varieties from wall spigots and blends up the tastiest, healthiest "shakes" in town. Farther into the market, you'll find produce sellers and prepared-food counters, plus spice vendors who seem straight out of a Turkish alley, and a grain-and-bean seller who will scoop out dozens of exotic rices and dried legumes.

THE SAN FERNANDO VALLEY

Technically an outdoor mall rather than a shopping area, **Universal CityWalk** (**℗ 818/622-4455**) gets mention here because it's so utterly unique. A pedestrian promenade next door to Universal Studios, CityWalk is dominated by brightly colored, outrageously surreal, oversize storefronts. The heavily touristed faux street is home to an inordinate number of restaurants, including B. B. King's Blues Club, the newest Hard Rock Cafe, and a branch of the Hollywood Athletic Club featuring a restaurant and pool hall. This is consumer culture gone haywire, an egotistical eyesore not worth a special visit, unless you have the kids in tow—they'll love it.

PASADENA & ENVIRONS

Compared to L.A.'s behemoth shopping malls, the streets of pretty, compact Pasadena are a true pleasure to stroll. As a general rule, stores are open daily from about 10am, and while some close at the standard 5 or 6pm, many stay open until 8 or 9pm to accommodate the before- and after-dinner/movie crowd.

In our opinion, historic **Old Pasadena** (centered around the intersection of Colorado Boulevard and Fair Oaks Avenue) has some of the best shopping in L.A., but we hope it retains more of the mom-and-pop businesses currently being pushed out by the likes of Banana Republic and Crate & Barrel. As you move eastward, the mix begins to include more eclectic shops and galleries commingling with dusty, pre-yuppie relics.

In addition to Old Town Pasadena, there are numerous good hunting grounds in the surrounding area. Antiques hounds might want to head to the **Green Street Antique Row,** 985–1005 E. Green St., east of Lake Avenue; or the **Pasadena Antiques Center,** on South Fair Oaks Boulevard south of Del Mar. Each has a rich concentration of collectibles that can captivate for hours.

You never know what you'll find at the **Rose Bowl Flea Market,** at the Rose Bowl, 991 Rosemont Ave., Pasadena (**℗ 626/577-3100**). Built in 1922, the horseshoe-shaped Rose Bowl is one of the world's most famous stadiums, home to the UCLA's Bruins, the annual Rose Bowl Game, and an occasional Super Bowl. California's largest monthly swap meet, on the second Sunday of every month from 9am to 3pm, is a favorite of Los Angeles antiques hounds (who know to arrive as early as 6am for the best finds). Antique furnishings, clothing, jewelry, and other collectibles are assembled in the parking area to the left of the entrance, while the rest of the flea market surrounds the exterior of the Bowl. Expect everything from used surfboards and car stereos to one-of-a-kind lawn statuary and bargain athletic shoes. Admission is $5 after 9am (early-bird admission is $10 to $15).

11 Los Angeles After Dark

The *L.A. Weekly* (www.laweekly.com), a free weekly paper available at sidewalk stands, shops, and restaurants, is the best place to find up-to-date news on what's happening in Los Angeles' playhouses, cinemas, museums, and live-music venues. The "Calendar" section of the *Los Angeles Times* (www.calendarlive.com) is also a good place to see what's going on after dark.

Ticketmaster (© 213/480-3232; www.ticketmaster.com) is the major charge-by-phone ticket agency in the city, selling tickets to concerts, sporting events, plays, and special events.

THEATER

Tickets for most plays usually cost $10 to $35, though performances of big-name shows at the major theaters can fetch up to $75 for the best seats. **Theatre League Alliance** (© 213/688-2787; www.TheatreLA.org), an association of live theaters and producers in Los Angeles (and the organization that puts on the yearly Ovation Awards, L.A.'s answer to Broadway's Tonys), offers same-day, half-price tickets via **Web Tix,** an Internet-only service at **www.TheatreLA.org**. Tickets are available Tuesday through Saturday from 4am to 11pm; purchase them online with a credit card and they'll be waiting for you at the box office. The site features a frequently updated list of shows and availability, and you can also sign up for e-mail alerts. In town without your computer? You can log on at any public library, Internet cafe, or office service store (like Kinko's).

MAJOR THEATERS & COMPANIES

The **Ahmanson Theater** and **Mark Taper Forum,** the city's top two playhouses and home to the Center Theater Group (www.taperahmanson.com), are both part of the all-purpose **Performing Arts Center of Los Angeles County** (formerly the Music Center), 135 N. Grand Ave., downtown. The **Ahmanson Theater** (© 213/972-7401) is active year-round, either with shows produced by the in-house Center Theater Group or with traveling productions, often Broadway or London bred. Each season has guaranteed a handful of high-profile shows, such as Andrew Lloyd Webber's *Phantom of the Opera,* the Royal National Theatre's production of Ibsen's *Enemy of the People,* starring Sir Ian McKellan, and ballet impresario Matthew Bourne's *Cinderella.* The Ahmanson is so huge that you'll want seats in the front third or half of the theater.

The **Mark Taper Forum** (© 213/972-0700) is a more intimate, circular theater staging contemporary works by international and local playwrights. Neil Simon's humorous and poignant *The Dinner Party* and Tom Stoppard's witty and eclectic *Arcadia* are two recent productions, each ideally suited to this intimate setting. Ticket prices vary depending on the performance. *Insider tip:* 2 hours prior to curtain time, the Mark Taper Forum offers specially priced $12 tickets, which must be purchased in person with cash.

Big-time traveling troupes and Broadway-bound musicals that don't go to the Ahmanson head instead for the **Shubert Theater,** in the ABC Entertainment Center, 2020 Avenue of the Stars, Century City (✆ **800/233-3123**). This plush playhouse presents major musicals on the scale of *Cats, Sunset Boulevard,* and *Les Misérables.*

Across town, the moderately sized **Geffen Playhouse,** 10886 Le Conte Ave., Westwood (✆ **310/208-5454;** www.geffenplayhouse.com), presents dramatic and comedic productions by prominent and cutting-edge writers. UCLA purchased the theater—which was originally built as a Masonic temple in 1929, and later served as the Westwood Playhouse—back in 1995 with a little help from L.A.'s philanthropic entertainment mogul David Geffen. This charming playhouse is often the West Coast choice of many acclaimed off-Broadway shows, and it also attracts locally based TV and movie actors eager for the immediacy of stage work. One recent highlight featured Annette Bening in Ibsen's *Hedda Gabler.* Always audience friendly, the Playhouse prices tickets in the $25 to $38 range.

One of the most highly acclaimed professional theaters in L.A., the **Pasadena Playhouse,** 39 S. El Molino Ave., near Colorado Boulevard, Pasadena (✆ **626/ 356-7529;** www.pasadenaplayhouse.org), is a registered historic landmark that has served as the training ground for many theatrical, film, and TV stars, including William Holden and Gene Hackman. Productions are staged on the main theater's elaborate Spanish Colonial revival.

SMALLER PLAYHOUSES & COMPANIES

It's a little-known fact that on any given night, there's more live theater to choose from in Los Angeles than in New York, due, in part, to the surfeit of ready actors and writers just chomping at the bit to make it in Tinseltown. The city is home to nearly 200 small- and medium-sized theaters and theater companies. With so many options, navigating the scene can be a monumental undertaking. Your safest bet is to choose one of the theaters listed below, which have each established excellent reputations for their consistently high-quality productions; otherwise, consult the *L.A. Weekly,* which advertises most current productions, or call **Theatre LA** (✆ **213/688-2787**) for up-to-date performance listings.

The **Colony Studio Theatre,** 555 N. Third St., Burbank (✆ **818/558-7000;** www.colonytheatre.org) was formed in 1975 and has developed from a part-time ensemble of TV actors longing for their theatrical roots into a nationally recognized resident company. Recently relocated from its longtime former home, a converted silent-movie house, the company now produces plays in all genres at the 276-seat Burbank Center Stage, which is shared with other performing arts groups.

Founded in 1965, **East-West Players,** 120 N. Judge John Aiso St., Los Angeles (✆ **323/625-7000;** www.eastwestplayers.com), is now the oldest Asian-American theater company in the United States. It's been so successful that the company moved from a 99-seat venue to the 200-seat David Henry Huang theater in downtown L.A. in March 1998. To commemorate the massacre in Tiananmen Square, EWP presented the musical *Beijing Spring* in 1999, and in 2001 revived Frank Chin's Asian-American classic, *Year of the Dragon.*

The 25-year-old **L.A. Theatre Works** (© 310/827-0889) is renowned for its marriage of media and theater and has performed more than 200 plays and logged over 350 hours of on-air programming. Performances are held at the delightful Skirball Cultural Center (see "Exploring the City" earlier in this chapter for a full listing), nestled in the Sepulveda Pass near the Getty Center. In the past, personalities such as Richard Dreyfuss, Julia Louis-Dreyfuss, Jason Robards, Annette Bening, and John Lithgow have given award-winning performances of plays by Arthur Miller, Neil Simon, Joyce Carol Oates, and more. For 7 years now, the group has performed simultaneously for viewing and listening audiences in its radio theater series. In 2001, L.A. Theatre Works presented Checkhov's *The Cherry Orchard,* starring veteran actress Marsha Mason. Tickets are usually around $35; a full performance schedule can be found online at **www.skirball.org**.

CLASSICAL MUSIC & OPERA

Beyond the pop realms, music in Los Angeles generally falls short of that found in other cities. For the most part, Angelenos rely on visiting orchestras and companies to fulfill their classical music appetites; scan the papers to find out who's performing while you're in the city.

The **Los Angeles Philharmonic** (© 323/850-2000; www.laphil.org) isn't just the city's top symphony; it's the only major classical music company in Los Angeles. Finnish-born music director Esa-Pekka Salonen concentrates on contemporary compositions; despite complaints from traditionalists, he does an excellent job attracting younger audiences. Tickets can be hard to come by when celebrity musicians like Itzhak Perlman, Isaac Stern, Emanuel Ax, and Yo-Yo Ma are in town. In addition to regular performances at the Music Center's **Dorothy Chandler Pavilion,** 135 N. Grand Ave., downtown, the Philharmonic also plays a popular summer season at the **Hollywood Bowl** (see "Concerts Under the Stars," below).

Slowly but surely, the **L.A. Opera** (© 213/972-8001; www.laopera.org) is gaining both respect and popularity with inventive stagings of classic operas, usually with guest divas. The Opera also calls the Dorothy Chandler Pavilion home.

CONCERTS UNDER THE STARS

Hollywood Bowl   Built in the early 1920s, the Hollywood Bowl is an elegant Greek-style natural outdoor amphitheater cradled in a small mountain canyon. This is the summer home of the Los Angeles Philharmonic Orchestra. Internationally known conductors and soloists often sit in on Tuesday and Thursday nights. Friday and Saturday concerts often feature orchestral swing or pops concerts. The summer season also includes a jazz series; past performers have included Natalie Cole, Dionne Warwick, and Chick Corea. Other events, from Garrison Keillor programs and summer fireworks galas, to an annual Mariachi Festival, are often on the season's schedule.

To round out an evening at the Bowl, many concertgoers use the occasion to enjoy a picnic dinner and a bottle of wine—it's one of L.A.'s grandest traditions. You can prepare your own, or order a picnic basket with a choice of hot and cold dishes and a selection of wines and desserts from Patina's on-site catering department, who also provide delivery to box seats. Call © **323/850-1885** by 4pm the day before you go to place y our food order. 2301 N. Highland Ave. (at Pat Moore Way), Hollywood. © **323/850-2000**. www.hollywoodbowl.org.

THE CLUB & MUSIC SCENE

Let's face it: Los Angeles is more or less the center of the entertainment industry. So, on any given night, finding something to satisfy any musical fancy can be a snap. From acoustic rock to jazz fusion, from Judas Priest cover bands to Latin funk, from the up-and-coming to the already gone, L.A.'s got something for everyone. For a listing of shows closer to the date of your arrival, remember that both the *LA Weekly* and the *Los Angeles Times* "Calendar" section have websites (see above). We also recommend logging onto **www.localmusic.com**, which provides 2 weeks' worth of show schedules conveniently organized by neighborhood and/or style.

B. B. King's Blues Club   Nestled away in CityWalk's brightly lit commercial plaza, this three-level club and restaurant—the ribs alone are worth the trip—hosts plenty of great local and touring national blues acts and is a testament to the establishment's venerable namesake. There's no shortage of good seating, but if you find yourself on the top two levels, it's best to grab a table adjacent to the railing to get an ideal view of the stage. CityWalk, Universal City. ✆ 818/622-5464. Cover varies.

Dragonfly   Not one to miss a trend, Dragonfly went from being a dance club that offered live music to becoming a live stage that offers dancing. From "surprise" shows by top-notch local acts such as Rage Against the Machine and Porno for Pyros to national acts like Run-D.M.C., Dragonfly is soaring. Overheated guests and smokers also enjoy its cool outdoor patio. 6510 Santa Monica Blvd., Hollywood. ✆ 323/466-6111. www.dragonfly.com. Cover varies.

House of Blues   In spite of its frequently ridiculed, cartoonish "Country Bear Jamboree" facade, there are plenty of reasons music fans and industry types keep coming back to House of Blues. Night after night, audiences are dazzled by performances from nationally and internationally acclaimed acts as diverse as Duran Duran, Eric Clapton, and the Fugees. The food in the upstairs restaurant can be great (reservations are a must), and the Sunday gospel brunch, though a bit pricey, promises a rollicking time. 8430 Sunset Blvd., West Hollywood. ✆ 323/ 848-5100. www.hob.com. Ticket prices vary.

Jazz Bakery *(Finds*   Ruth Price's nonprofit venue is renowned for attracting some of the most important names in jazz—and for the restored Helms bakery factory that houses the club and inspires its name. Hers is a no-frills, all-about-the-music affair, and the place is pretty much BYO in the drinks department. Drummer Jimmy Cobb, the last remaining member of Miles Davis's "Kind of Blue" band, had a 4-night stint at JB recently. 3233 Helms Ave., Culver City. ✆ 310/ 271-9039. www.thejazzbakery.com. All ages. Cover $10–$25.

The Knitting Factory   Straight from the New York City legend, a West Coast branch of the famous Knitting Factory has arrived in the redeveloping Hollywood Boulevard nightlife district. The Main Stage was inaugurated by a Posies performance, and sees such diverse bookings as Kristin Hersh, Pere Ubu, and Jonathan Richman; a secondary AlterKnit stage has sporadic shows. The new Factory is totally wired for digital, including interactive online computer stations throughout the club. 7021 Hollywood Blvd., Hollywood. ✆ 323/463-0204. www. theknittingfactory.com/KFLA. Cover varies.

The Mint   Once a shotgun shack serving fried chicken and blues in a beer-only bar, the Mint has re-emerged as a gloriously lounge-y hangout for rock, pop, and blues devotees. The clientele—ranging from youthful scenesters to middle-aged moms—packs the place to catch regular performances by such diverse artists as G. Love & Special Sauce, Gwen Stefani, the Rembrandts, and Duke Robillard. 6010 W. Pico Blvd., Los Angeles. ℂ **323/954-9630.** Cover $5–$10.

Moomba   This branch of New York's West Village hot spot promises serious New American cuisine, hip supper club entertainment, and several satellite bars for lounging. The nightclub, in the former LunaPark space in WeHo's congested club zone, has been completely overhauled with "cruelty free" and environmentally chic interiors. Proprietor Jeff Gossett is ensuring that, like its NYC edition, Moomba will be as much a restaurant destination as nightspot—he's garnered a heavy-hitting San Francisco chef de cuisine and former Spago manager. 665 N. Robertson Blvd., West Hollywood. ℂ **310/652-6364.** Cover varies.

Roxy   Veteran record producer and executive Lou Adler opened this Sunset Strip club in the mid-1970s with concerts by Neil Young and a lengthy run of the pre-movie *Rocky Horror Show.* Since then, it's remained among the top showcase venues in Hollywood—although its pre-eminence among cozy clubs is now challenged by the revitalized Troubadour and such new entries as the House of Blues. 9009 Sunset Blvd. ℂ **310/276-2222.** Cover varies.

Spaceland   The wall-to-wall mirrors and shiny brass posts decorating the interior create the feeling that, in a past life, Spaceland must've been a seedy strip joint, but the club's current personality offers something entirely different. Having hosted countless performances by cutting-edge artists, such as Pavement, Mary Lou Lord, Grant Lee Buffalo, Elliot Smith, and the Eels, this hot spot on the fringe of east Hollywood has become one of the most important clubs on the LA circuit. 1717 Silver Lake Blvd., Silver Lake. ℂ **323/661-4380.** Cover varies.

The Troubadour   This famous West Hollywood mainstay radiates rock history—from the 1960s to the 1990s; the Troub really has seen 'em all. Audiences are consistently treated to memorable shows from the many already-established or young-and-promising acts that take the Troubadour's stage. But bring your earplugs—this beer- and sweat-soaked club likes it loud. 9081 Santa Monica Blvd., West Hollywood. ℂ **310/276-6168.** www.troubadour.com. All ages. Cover varies.

Viper Room   This world-famous club on the Strip has been king of the hill since it was first opened by actor Johnny Depp and co-owner Sal Jenco back in 1993. With an intensely electric and often star-filled scene, the intimate club is also known for unforgettable, late-night, surprise performances from such power-houses as Johnny Cash, Iggy Pop, Tom Petty, Nancy Sinatra, and Everclear (to name but a few on the long and impressive list) after headline gigs elsewhere in town. 8852 Sunset Blvd., West Hollywood. ℂ **310/358-1880.** www.viperroom.com. Cover varies.

DANCE CLUBS

The Coconut Club   Master of entertainment Merv Griffin, remembering the legendary Coconut Grove ballroom in the now-abandoned Ambassador Hotel, has lavishly re-created its classy swank atmosphere with this A-list dine-and-dance club in the Beverly Hilton. It offers some of the city's very best in Latin and swing dance on Fridays and Saturdays. This is a wonderful place to bring your guy or doll to reenact the romantic splendor of Hollywood past. Entrance to Chimps Cigar Club is also included in the cover charge. 9876 Wilshire Blvd., Beverly Hills. ℂ **310/285-1358.** Cover $10.

The Conga Room   Attracting such Latin-music luminaries as Tito Puente and Pucho & The Latin Soul Brothers, this one-time Jack LaLanne health club on the Miracle Mile has quickly become *the* night spot for live salsa and merengue. Break up the evening of heart-melting, sexy Latin dancing with a trip to the dining room, where the chef serves up savory Cuban fare in a setting that conjures the romance of pre-Castro Cuba, or indulge yourself in the Conga Room's stylish cigar lounge. 5364 Wilshire Blvd., Los Angeles. © 323/938-1696. www.congaroom.com. Cover varies.

The Derby   This class-A east-of-Hollywood club has been at ground zero of the swing revival since the very beginning. Located at a former Brown Derby site, the club was restored to its original luster and detailed with a heavy 1940s edge. With Big Bad Voodoo Daddy as the onetime house band and regular visits from Royal Crown Revue, hip guys and dolls knew that the Derby was money even before *Swingers* transformed it into one of the city's most happenin' hangs. But if you come on the weekends, expect a wait to get in, and once you're inside, dance space is at a premium. 4500 Los Feliz Blvd., Los Feliz. © 323/663-8979. www.the-derby.com. Cover $7–$10.

El Floridita   This tiny Cuban restaurant-and-salsa club is hot, hot, hot. Despite its modest strip-lot locale, it draws the likes of Jennifer Lopez, Sandra Bullock, Jimmy Smits, and Jack Nicholson, in addition to a festive crowd of Latin-dance devotees who groove well into the night. The hippest nights continue to be Mondays, when Johnny Polanco and his swinging New York–flavored salsa band get the dance floor jumpin'. 1253 N. Vine St., Hollywood. © 323/871-8612. Cover $10.

Hollywood Athletic Club   Built in 1924, this pool hall, restaurant, and nightclub is home to some groovin' dance clubs. Saturdays feature a lively mix of progressive house music spun by DJs Drew Down and Dave Audé. On Sundays, the sounds of Latin house, merengue, hip-hop, and salsa fill the air. Hollywood Athletic Club also hosts concerts from internationally known DJs and bands as diverse as Mono and the Wu-Tang Clan. 6525 Sunset Blvd., Hollywood. © 323/962-6600. Cover $10–$20.

The Palace   Weekend nights this Hollywood landmark music hall turns the power of its 20,000-watt sound system on the dancing set. Fridays feature DJ's upstairs and down, plus a cash-reward dance contest. Hip-hop, house, and pop are the order of the day on Saturdays, when Klub KIIS takes control of the turntables while also broadcasting live from the club. 1735 N. Vine Ave., Hollywood. © 323/462-3000. www.hollywoodpalace.com. 18 and over. Cover $10–$12.

Vynyl   This big open room, located on a Hollywood side street in the former home of a divey rock 'n' roll club, has theatrical—almost gothic—overtones. A trendy dance club with DJs (including occasional big-name guests) spinning house and electronica, it also feature concerts by local and visiting bands. Though the crowd naturally varies according to what's on the night's schedule, Vynyl is more upscale than trashy, with a look-like-you-mean-it dress code. 1650 Schrader Blvd., Hollywood. © 323/465-7449. Cover varies.

BARS & COCKTAIL LOUNGES

Beauty Bar   It's a concept proven to work in New York and San Francisco; a combination cocktail lounge and beauty salon. Decorated with vintage salon gear and sporting a hip-retro vibe, the Beauty Bar is campy, fun, and trendy all at the same time. Where else can you actually get a manicure while sipping cocktails with names like Blue Rinse (made with Blue Curacao) or Prell (their version of a grasshopper)? 1638 N Cahuenga Blvd., Hollywood. © 323/464-7676. www. beautybar.com. No cover.

Cat N' Fiddle Pub and Restaurant   Nothing to be snooty about here: no A-list crowd, no red velvet ropes, no gimmicky cocktails. This is simply Hollywood's home for lovers of the basic British pub. Sit next to the fountain in the spacious courtyard while sipping tasty pints of Boddingtons, Bass, Guinness, Harp, or Newcastle; or head inside to toss some darts and plunk those extra dollars into the jukebox. 6530 W. Sunset Blvd., Hollywood. © 323/468-3800. No cover.

Good Luck Bar   Until they installed a flashing neon sign outside, only locals and hipsters knew about this Kung Fu–themed room in the Los Feliz–Silver Lake area. The dark red windowless interior boasts Oriental ceiling tiles, fringed Chinese paper lanterns, sweet-but-deadly drinks like the "Yee Mee Loo" (translated as "blue drink"), and a jukebox with selections ranging from Thelonius Monk to Cher's "Half Breed." The spacious sitting room, furnished with mismatched sofas, armchairs, and banquettes, provides a great atmosphere for conversation or romance. Arrive early to avoid the throngs of L.A. scenesters. 1514 Hillhurst Ave. (between Hollywood and Sunset Boulevards), Los Angeles. © 323/666-3524. No cover.

Skybar, at Mondrian Hotel   Since its opening in hotelier Ian Schraeger's refurbished Sunset Strip hotel, Skybar has been a favorite among L.A.'s most fashionable of the fashionable set. This place is so hot that even the agents to the stars need agents to get in. (Rumor has it that one agent was so desperate to get in he promised one of the servers a contract.) Nevertheless, a little image consulting—affect the right look, strike the right pose, and look properly disinterested—might get you in to rub elbows with some of the faces that regularly appear on the cover of *People*. (But please don't stare.) 8440 W. Sunset Blvd., West Hollywood. © 323/848-6025.

360   This 19th-story, penthouse-perched restaurant and lounge is a perfect place to romance your special someone. It's all about the view here—all 360° of it. The understated and softly lit sleek interior emphasizes the scene outside the plentiful windows, including a spectacular vista of the famed HOLLYWOOD sign. 6290 Sunset Blvd., Hollywood. © 323/871-2995. www.360hollywood.com. No cover.

GAY AND LESBIAN BARS & CLUBS

Although West Hollywood, often affectionately referred to as "Boys Town," has the densest gay population in Los Angeles, there are several other noteworthy enclaves. Silver Lake, in particular, has a longstanding gay community; Santa Monica and Venice also have a strong gay and lesbian presence.

If you're looking for more specific info on gay culture in L.A., beyond what we've included below, check out one of these resources: *4-Front Magazine* (© 323/650-7772), *Edge Magazine* (© 323/962-6994), or *Frontiers* (© 323/848-2222). Women might want to pick up a copy of *Female FYI* (© 323/938-5969), *LA Girl Guide* (© 310/391-8877), or *Lesbian News* (© 310/392-8224). *Edge* and *Frontiers* are the most prominently featured free biweekly gay mags and are readily available in coffeehouses and newsstands citywide. If you're having a difficult time locating any of these magazines, give the good people at **A Different Light Bookstore,** 8853 Santa Monica, West Hollywood

(📞 **310/854-6601**), a call, or visit for in-person assistance. The *L.A. Weekly* and *New Times Los Angeles* also contain lesbian and gay articles and listings.

The Abbey   This is *the* gay coffee bar. You can sit inside or out, drink a latte, and watch the passing parade of WeHo boys in muscle shirts. Most of West Hollywood seems to end up here on Saturday nights; k.d. lang occasionally makes an appearance. 692 N. Robertson Blvd., West Hollywood. 📞 **310/289-8410**. No cover.

Club 7969   Fashionable of late, Club 7969 features male and female strippers baring it all while mingling with the gay, lesbian, and straight crowd. Each night has a different theme, ranging from drag burlesques to techno parties. On Tuesdays, Michelle's CC revue—with its legion of topless female dancers—attracts a largely lesbian crowd. 7969 Santa Monica Blvd., West Hollywood. 📞 **323/654-0280**. Cover varies.

Dragstrip 66   Note the cover disparity: If you ain't in drag, prepare to pay for it (and wait in line a wee bit longer than the more fashionably hip). This all-time great drag club, located in a Mexican restaurant, switches themes each month ("Chicks with Dicks" was a standout), and it offers up every type of music—except disco and Liza. That's entertainment. The second Saturday of each month at Rudolpho's, 2500 Riverside Dr., Silver Lake. 📞 **323/969-2596**. Cover $10–$20.

Micky's   A diverse, outgoing, and mostly older crowd cruises back and forth between the front-room bar and the dance floor in back. More women—probably looking to party with the friendly crowd and enjoy the great drink specials—are drawn to Micky's than to some of the neighboring bars. 8857 Santa Monica Blvd., West Hollywood. 📞 **310/657-1176**. www.mickys.com. Cover varies.

Rage   For almost 20 years this high-energy, high-attitude disco has been the preferred mainstay on WeHo's gay dance club circuit. Between turns around the dance floor, shirtless muscle boys self-consciously strut about—like peacocks flashing their plumes—looking to exchange vital statistics. 8911 Santa Monica Blvd., West Hollywood. 📞 **310/652-7055**. Cover varies.

COMEDY & CABARET

The Cinegrill   The Cinegrill, located in one of L.A.'s most historic hotels, draws locals with a zany cabaret show and guest chanteuses ranging from Eartha Kitt to Cybill Shepherd. Some of the country's best cabaret singers pop up here regularly. 7000 Hollywood Blvd., in the Hollywood Roosevelt Hotel, Hollywood. 📞 **323/466-7000**. www.cinegrill.com. Cover varies.

Comedy Store   You can't go wrong here: New comics develop their material, and established ones work out their kinks, at this landmark venue owned by Mitzi Shore (Pauly's mom). The **Best of the Comedy Store Room,** which seats 400, features professional stand-ups continuously on Friday and Saturday nights. Several comedians are always featured, each doing about a 15-minute stint. The talent here is always first-rate and includes comics who regularly appear on the *Tonight Show* and other shows. The **Original Room** features a dozen or so comedians back-to-back nightly. Sunday night is amateur night: Anyone with enough guts can take the stage for 3 minutes, so who knows what you'll get. 8433 Sunset Blvd., West Hollywood. 📞 **323/656-6225**. www.comedystore.com. Cover varies.

Groundling Theater   L.A.'s answer to Chicago's Second City has been around for over 25 years, yet it remains the most innovative and funny group in town. The skits change every year or so; but they take new improvisational twists every night, and the satire is often savage. The Groundlings were the springboard to fame for Pee-Wee Herman, Elvira, and former *Saturday Night Live* stars Jon Lovitz, Phil Hartman, and Julia "It's Pat" Sweeney. Trust me—you haven't laughed this hard in ages. Phone for show times and reservations. 7307 Melrose Ave., Los Angeles. ⓒ 323/934-9700. www.groundlings.com. Tickets $10–$20.

The Improv   A showcase for top stand-ups since 1975, the Improv offers something different each night. Although it used to have a fairly active music schedule, the place is now mostly doing what it does best—showcasing comedy. Owner Budd Freedman's buddies—like Jay Leno, Billy Crystal, and Robin Williams—hone their skills here more often than you would expect. But even if the comedians on the bill the night you go are all unknowns, they won't be for long. Shows are at 8pm Sunday and Thursday, at 8:30 and 10:30pm Friday and Saturday. 8162 Melrose Ave., West Hollywood. ⓒ 323/651-2583. Cover varies.

COFFEEHOUSES

Anastasia's Asylum   Stop by for a cup of joe to go or stick around and while away the hours at this top-notch coffeehouse. Anastasia's boasts an eclectic clientele, diverse live music ranging from jazz and folk to acoustic and plugged-in rock, vintage furniture in a classy decor, constantly changing art exhibits, and a great menu, making it a favorite draw for folks from around the city. 1028 Wilshire Blvd., Santa Monica. ⓒ 310/394-7113.

Bourgeois Pig   With its positively gothic aversion to natural lighting (the only street-front window is covered with a blood-red tint), this dark cavern has more of a bar atmosphere than the usual coffeehouse. In fact, Bourgeois Pig is to Starbucks what Marilyn Manson is to Celine Dion. This veteran, located on a hot business strip at the Hollywood–Los Feliz border, is a favorite among youths and showbiz drones, who enjoy losing themselves on couches tucked into shadowed corners, shooting a game of pool, or perusing something from the terrific newsstand next door. 5931 Franklin Ave., Hollywood. ⓒ 323/962-6366.

Equator   Airy and comfy, this brick room, on a busy alleyway in the heart of resurgent Old Town Pasadena, has withstood the challenge of a Starbucks that moved in a block away. The menu—with smoothies, soup, and desserts, in addition to a wide variety of coffee drinks—and the friendly service keep people coming back. The post-Haring art on the walls contributes to the distinctive character of the place, which has been used for scenes in *A Very Brady Sequel* and *Beverly Hills, 90210.* 22 Mills Place, Pasadena. ⓒ 626/564-8656.

Highland Grounds   Predating the coffeehouse explosion, this comfortable, relatively unpretentious place set the L.A. standard with a vast assortment of food and drink—not just coffee—and often first-rate live music, ranging from nationally known locals, such as Victoria Williams, to open-mike Wednesdays for all-comers. The ample patio is often used for readings and record-release parties. 742 N. Highland Ave., Hollywood. ⓒ 323/466-1507.

LATE-NIGHT BITES

Canter's Fairfax Restaurant, Delicatessen & Bakery   This 24-hour Jewish deli has been a winner with late-nighters since it opened more than 65 years ago. If you show up after the clubs close, you're sure to spot a bleary-eyed celebrity or two alongside the rest of the after-hours crowd, chowing down on a giant pastrami sandwich, matzoh-ball soup, potato pancakes, or other deli favorites. Try a potato knish with a side of brown gravy—trust me, you'll love it. 419 N. Fairfax Ave. (C) **323/651-2030.**

Du-par's Restaurant & Bakery   During the week, this popular Valley coffee shop serves up blue-plate specials until 1am; come the weekend, they're slingin' hash until 4am. The new West Hollywood location, in the Ramada Hotel at 8571 Santa Monica Blvd., west of La Cienega ((C) **310/659-7009**), is open till 3am on the weekends. 12036 Blvd. (1 block east of Laurel Canyon), Studio City. (C) **818/766-4437.**

Fred 62   Silver Lake–Los Feliz hipsters hankering for a slightly demented take on classic American comfort grub skulk into Fred around the clock. Local chef Fred Eric remodeled the formerly tiny corner diner with spiffy 1950s car-culture icons, including hood-ornament sconces and blue service-station smocks for the waitstaff; named the place after himself (and his birth year); and peppered the menu with puns and inside jokes. There's a daily "cream of what Fred wants" soup, plus salads, burgers, sandwiches, and a handful of Asian noodle bowls. 1850 N. Vermont, Los Angeles. (C) **323/667-0662.**

Jerry's Famous Deli   Valley hipsters head to 24-hour Jerry's to satiate the late-night munchies. See "Dining" earlier in this chapter for a full restaurant listing. 12655 Ventura Blvd. (east of Coldwater Canyon Ave.), Studio City. (C) **818/980-4245.**

Mel's Drive-in   Straight from an episode of *Happy Days,* this 24-hour 1950s diner on the Sunset Strip attracts customers ranging from chic shoppers during the day to rock-and-rollers at night. The fries and shakes here are among the best in town. 8585 Sunset Blvd. (west of La Cienega), West Hollywood. (C) **310/854-7200.**

Original Pantry Cafe   Owned by former Los Angeles mayor Richard Riordan, this downtown diner has been serving huge portions of comfort food around the clock for more than 60 years; in fact, they don't even have a key to the front door. See "Dining" for a full restaurant listing. 877 S. Figueroa St. (at 9th St.), downtown. (C) **213/972-9279.**

Pink's Hot Dogs   Many a woozy hipster has awakened with the telltale and unrecalled signs of a post-cocktailing trip to this greasy streetside hot-dog stand—the oniony morning-after breath and chili stains on your shirt are dead giveaways. Open Friday and Saturday until 3am, all other nights until 2am. See "Dining" earlier in this chapter for a full restaurant listing. 709 N. La Brea Ave., Los Angeles. (C) **323/931-4223.**

Swingers   This hip coffee shop keeps L.A. scene-stealers happy with its retro comfort food. Open Friday and Saturday until 2am, all other nights until 1am. See "Dining" earlier in this chapter for a full restaurant listing. 8020 Beverly Blvd. (west of Fairfax Ave.), Los Angeles. (C) **323/653-5858.**

Toi on Sunset   Those requiring a little more *oomph* from their late-night snack should come here. At this colorful and *loud* hangout, garbled pop culture metaphors mingle with the tastes and aromas of "rockin' Thai" cuisine in delicious ways, until 3am nightly. See "Dining" earlier in this chapter for a full restaurant listing. 7505 Sunset Blvd. (at Gardner), Hollywood. (C) **323/874-8062.**

MOVIES

Promoting moving pictures as this country's great art form, **The American Cinematheque** (Hollywood; (C) **323/466-3456;** www.egyptiantheatre.com), presents not-readily-seen videos and films, ranging from the wildly arty to the old classics. Since relocating to the historic and beautifully refurbished 1923 **Egyptian Theater** (6712 Hollywood Blvd., Hollywood), American Cinematheque has hosted several film events, including a celebration of contemporary flicks from Spain, a tribute to the femme fatales of film noir, and a retrospective of the films of William Friedkin.

The **Bing Theater,** at the **L.A. County Museum of Art,** 5905 Wilshire Blvd., Los Angeles (✆ **323/857-6010**), presents a specially themed film series each month. Past subjects have ranged from 1930s blonde-bombshell films to thinly veiled Cold War–propaganda flicks to a three-day Monty Python's Flying Circus marathon.

Fans of silent-movie classics might already know about the renowned **Silent Movie Theatre,** 611 N. Fairfax Ave. (½ block south of Melrose), near the Miracle Mile (✆ **323/655-2520** for recorded program information, 323/655-2510 for main office; www.silentmovietheatre.com), where Charlie Chaplin's appeal, Clara Bow's sexuality, and Edward G. Robinson's menace are once again bigger than life. Live music accompanies the silents (classic "talkies" are shown Tues nights); the theater is open Tuesday through Sunday, and tickets are $8 ($6 for kids and seniors).

The **Nuart Theater,** 11272 Santa Monica Blvd., Los Angeles (✆ **310/478-6379**), digs deep into the archives for some real classics, from campy to cool. One recent Nuart highlight was "Francois Truffaut: A Celebration," in which new 35mm prints of the French director's works were shown during a 2-week retrospective.

14

Side Trips from Los Angeles

by Stephanie Avnet Yates

The area within a 100-mile radius of Los Angeles is one of the most diverse regions in the world: There are arid deserts, rugged mountains, industrial cities, historic towns, alpine lakes, rolling hillsides, and sophisticated seaside resorts. You'll also find an off-shore island that's been transformed into the ultimate city-dweller's hide-away, not to mention the Happiest Place on Earth.

1 Long Beach & the *Queen Mary*

21 miles S of downtown Los Angeles

The fifth-largest incorporated city in California, Long Beach is best known as the permanent home of the former cruise liner Queen Mary, and in mid-April for the annual Long Beach Grand Prix, whose star-studded warm-up race sends the likes of young hipster Jason Priestley and perennial racer Paul Newman burning rubber through the streets of the city. A sleek new aquarium is the cornerstone of Long Beach's waterfront attractions.

ESSENTIALS

GETTING THERE From Los Angeles, take either I-5 or I-405 to I-710 south; it follows the Los Angeles River on its path to the ocean and leads directly to both downtown Long Beach and the *Queen Mary* Seaport.

VISITOR INFORMATION Contact the **Long Beach Area Convention & Visitors Bureau,** One World Trade Center, Suite 300 (© **800/4LB-STAY** or 562/436-3645; www.golongbeach.org). For further information on the **Long Beach Grand Prix,** call © **562/981-2600** or check out www.longbeachgp.com.

ORIENTATION Downtown Long Beach is at the eastern end of the vast Port of Los Angeles; Pine Avenue is the central restaurant and shopping street, which extends south to Shoreline Park and the Aquarium. The *Queen Mary* is docked just across the waterway, gazing south toward tiny Long Beach marina and Naples Island.

THE MAJOR ATTRACTIONS

Queen Mary ✸✸✸ It's easy to dismiss this old cruise ship/museum as a barnacle-laden tourist trap, but it's the only surviving example of this particular kind of 20th-century elegance and excess. From the staterooms paneled lavishly in now-extinct tropical hardwoods to the perfectly preserved crew quarters and the miles of hallway handrails made of once-pedestrian Bakelite, wonders never cease aboard this Deco luxury liner. Stroll the teakwood decks with just a bit of imagination and you're back in 1936 on the maiden voyage from Southampton, England. Don't miss the Streamline Moderne observation lounge, featured often in period motion pictures. Kiosk displays of photographs and memorabilia are everywhere—following the success of the movie *Titanic*, the *Queen Mary* even hosted an exhibit of artifacts from its less fortunate cousin. The Cold War–era Soviet submarine *Scorpion* resides alongside; separate admission is required to tour the sub. Buy both tickets and you'll also get a behind-the-scenes guided tour, peppered with worthwhile anecdotes and details.

1126 Queen's Hwy. (end of I-710), Long Beach. © 562/435-3511. www.queenmary.com. Admission $15 adults, $13 seniors age 55 and over and military, $9 children ages 4–11, free for kids under 4. Daily 10am–6pm (last entry at 5:30pm), with extended summer hours. Parking $8.

Aquarium of the Pacific ★★ *Kids*   This enormous aquarium is the cornerstone of Long Beach's new waterfront destination. Figuring that what stimulated flagging economies in Monterey and Baltimore would work in Long Beach, planners gave their all to this project, creating a crowd-pleasing attraction just across the harbor from Long Beach's other mainstay, the *Queen Mary.* The vast facility—it has enough exhibit space to fill three football fields—re-creates three areas of the Pacific: the warm Baja and southern California regions, the Bering Sea and chilly northern Pacific, and faraway tropical climes, including stunning re-creations of a lagoon and barrier reef. There are more than 12,000 animals in all, from sharks and sea lions to delicate sea horses and moon jellies. Learn little-known aquatic facts at the many educational exhibits, or come nose-to-nose with sea lions, eels, sharks, and other inhabitants of giant, three-story-high tanks.

100 Aquarium Way, off Shoreline Dr., Long Beach. © 562/590-3100. www.aquariumofpacific.org. Admission $14.95 adults, $11.95 seniors age 60 and over, $7.95 children 3–11, free to kids under 3. Daily 9:30am–6pm. Closed Christmas Day and Toyota Grand Prix weekend (mid-Apr). Parking $7 maximum.

OTHER WATERFRONT DIVERSIONS

Situated on a prime waterfront knoll, the **Long Beach Museum of Art,** 2300 E. Ocean Ave. (© **562/439-2119;** www.lbma.org), was built in 1912 as the summer home of New York philanthropist Elizabeth Milbank Anderson. The grand mansion functioned as a private social club and WWII officers' club before becoming the museum's home in 1957. In 2000, an ambitious expansion project was completed that restored the home to its original state and built a complementary gallery annex on the property. The Museum is not only a historic site but also notable for its collection of 20th-century European modernists, postwar art from California, and decorative arts from the past 300 years. Open Tuesday through Sunday from 11am to 7pm. Admission $5 adults, $4 students and seniors, free for kids under 12.

Take to the waterways Italian-style at nearby Naples Island with **Gondola Getaway,** 5437 E. Ocean Blvd. (© **562/433-9595;** www.gondolagetawayinc. com). Since 1982, these authentic Venetian gondolas have been snaking around the man-made canals of Naples Island, under gracefully arched bridges and past the gardens of resort cottages. Perhaps your traditionally clad oarsman will sing an Italian aria or relate the many tales of marriage proposals (some not so successful!) made by romance-minded passengers. You'll also get a nice basket of bread, cheese, and salami, plus wineglasses and a full ice bucket; feel free to bring your beverage of choice. Gondola Getaway operates daily between 11am and 11pm; a 1-hour cruise for two is $60.

WHERE TO STAY

Hotel Queen Mary ★ *Finds*   The *Queen Mary* isn't only a piece of maritime history; it's also a hotel. But although the historic ocean liner is considered the most luxurious vessel ever to sail the Atlantic, with the largest rooms ever built aboard a ship, the quarters aren't exceptional when compared to those on terra firma today, nor are the amenities. The idea is to enjoy the novelty and charm of features such as the original bathtub watercocks ("cold salt," "cold fresh," "hot salt," "hot fresh"). The beautifully carved interior is a feast for the eye and fun to explore, and the weekday rates are hard to beat. Three onboard restaurants are overpriced but convenient, and the shopping arcade has a decidedly British feel (one shop sells great *Queen Mary* souvenirs). An elegant Sunday champagne brunch—complete with ice sculpture and harpist—is served in the ship's Grand Salon, and it's always worth having a cocktail in the Art Deco Observation Bar. If you're too young or too poor to have traveled on the old luxury liners, this is the perfect opportunity to experience the romance of an Atlantic crossing— and with no seasickness, cabin fever, or week of formal dinners.

1126 Queen's Hwy. (end of I-710), Long Beach, CA 90802-6390. (C) 800/437-2934 or 562/435-3511. Fax 562/437-4531. www.queenmary.com. 365 units. $105–$275 double; from $350 suite. Many packages available. AE, DC, MC, V. Valet parking $5; self-parking included in rate. **Amenities:** 3 restaurants; shopping arcade. *In room:* A/C, TV.

Lord Mayor's Inn   Situated in a formerly elite residential neighborhood downtown, this elegant and impeccably restored Edwardian home was built in 1904 and belonged to Long Beach's first mayor, Charles H. Windham. The main house offers five charming guest rooms, each furnished with impeccably chosen antiques, luxurious high-quality linens, and heirloom bedspreads and accessories. All boast private bathrooms cleverly re-created with vintage fixtures and painstakingly matched materials (the original home had only one bathroom). Seven more rooms—four with private bathrooms—are available in two less-formal adjacent cottages, also dating from the early 20th century; they offer a private option for families or those seeking seclusion and independence. All guests gather at their leisure in the main-house dining room for innkeeper Laura Brasser's lavish breakfasts, which include specialties like Old World pancakes with fried apples, delicate asparagus eggs, and hearty stuffed French toast.

435 Cedar Ave., Long Beach, CA 90802. (C) 562/436-0324. www.lordmayors.com. 12 units. $85–$140 double. Rate includes full breakfast. AE, DISC, MC, V. *In room:* No phone.

WHERE TO DINE

The Madison Restaurant & Bar ✯ STEAKS/SEAFOOD   This elegant 1920s-style supper club offers fine dining reminiscent of majestic ocean-liner dining salons. A beautifully restored historic bank building (and dinner music from the 1940s) provides the grand backdrop for service that's deferential without being stuffy. The Madison serves exceptional dry-aged beef, broiled and accompanied by à la carte sides like buttery garlic potatoes or perfectly seasoned creamed spinach. The menu also includes seafood dishes like grilled salmon atop mussels and clams with a creamy ginger-citrus sauce, or oyster-stuffed sole breaded and drizzled with *buerre blanc* and fragrant fresh dill. Desserts are artistic renditions of reliable favorites—a s'mores sundae or sugary apple crumble.

102 Pine Ave., Long Beach. (C) 562/628-8866. www.madisonsteakhouse.com. Reservations recommended. Main courses $10–$22 lunch, $18–$29 dinner. AE, MC, V. Mon–Thurs 11am–11pm; Fri 11am–midnight; Sat 5pm–midnight; Sun 5–11pm. Valet parking $3.

Papadakis Taverna GREEK   The food here rates higher than the ambience— even genial host John Papadakis's hand-kissing greeting doesn't soften the blunt lines and bright lights of this banquet room–like space decorated with equal parts Aegean murals and football art (in deference to Papadakis's glory days as a University of Southern California football legend). The waiters dance and sing loudly when they're not bringing plates of *spanikopita* (spinach-filled phyllo pastries) or thick, satisfying *tsatziki* (garlic-laced cucumber-and-yogurt spread) to your table. Servings are very generous, and the wine list has something for everyone.

301 W. Sixth St. (at Centre St.), San Pedro. ℂ **310/548-1186.** Reservations recommended. Main courses $12–$35. AE, DC, MC, V. Daily 5–10pm.

Shenandoah Cafe 🅰🅰 AMERICAN/SOUTHERN   Here's a place where "American" food means regional home-style cuisines served in a high-ceilinged parlor that's equal parts New Orleans mansion and Grandma's house. Definitely not for vegetarians or light eaters; even fresh fish specialties are given rich and heavy Southern treatments, and meats take up most of the menu. Start by nibbling on irresistible, fresh-from-the-oven apple fritters, and prepare for an enormous meal that also includes soup or salad and sides. Recommended specialties include Texas-sized chicken-fried steak with country gravy, Santa Fe–style baby back ribs glazed with smoky chipotle, Cajun blackened fresh catch-of-the-day, and Granny's deep-fried chicken.

4722 E. Second St. (at Park Ave.), Long Beach (Belmont Shore). ℂ **562/434-3469.** www. shenandoahcafe.com. Reservations recommended. Main courses $13–$25. AE, DC, MC, V. Mon–Thurs 5–10pm; Fri 5–11pm; Sat 4:30–11pm; Sun 10am–2pm and 4:30–10pm.

2 Santa Catalina Island

22 miles W of mainland Los Angeles

Santa Catalina—which everyone calls simply Catalina—is a small, cove-fringed island famous for its laid-back inns, largely unspoiled landscape, and crystal-clear waters. Many devotees consider it southern California's alternative to Capri or Malta. Because of its relative isolation, out-of-state tourists tend to ignore it, but those who do show up have plenty of elbow room to boat, fish, swim, scuba, and snorkel. There are miles of hiking and biking trails, plus golf, tennis, and horseback riding.

Catalina is so different from the mainland that it almost seems like a different country, remote and unspoiled. In 1915, the island was purchased by William Wrigley, Jr., the chewing-gum manufacturer, who had plans to develop it into a fashionable pleasure resort. To publicize the new vacation land, Wrigley brought big-name bands to the Avalon Ballroom and moved the Chicago Cubs, which he owned, to the island for spring training. His marketing efforts succeeded, and this charming and tranquil retreat became what it still is: a favorite vacation resort for mainlanders.

Today, about 86% of the island remains undeveloped, owned and preserved by the Santa Catalina Island Conservancy. Some of the spectacular outlying areas can only be reached by arranged tour (see "Exploring the Island," below).

ESSENTIALS

GETTING THERE   The most common way to get to and from the island is via the **Catalina Express** (ℂ **800/481-3470** or 562/519-1212; www.catalina express.com), which operates up to 30 daily departures year-round from San Pedro and Long Beach. The trip takes about an hour. Round-trip fares are $40 for adults, $36.50 for seniors 55 and over, $30.50 for children ages 2 to 11, and $2 for infants. In San Pedro, the Catalina Express departs from the **Sea/Air**

Terminal, Berth 95; take the Harbor Freeway (I-110) south to the Harbor Boulevard exit, then follow signs to the terminal. In Long Beach, boats leave from the **Queen Mary Landing;** take the Long Beach Freeway (I-710) south, following the QUEEN MARY signs to the Catalina Express port. Call ahead for reservations. *Note:* Luggage is limited to 50 pounds per person; reservations are necessary for bicycles, surfboards, and dive tanks; and there are restrictions on transporting pets. You can leave your car at designated lots at each departure terminal; the parking fee is around $8 per 24-hour period.

   Island Express Helicopter Service, 900 Queens Way Dr., Long Beach (© **800/2-AVALON** or 310/510-2525; www.islandexpress.com), flies from Long Beach or San Pedro to Avalon in about 15 minutes. It flies on demand between 8am and sunset year-round, charging $67 each way. It also offers brief air tours over the island; prices vary. Island Express shares terminals with Catalina Express.

VISITOR INFORMATION   The **Catalina Island Chamber of Commerce and Visitors Bureau,** P.O. Box 217, Avalon, CA 90704 (© **310/510-1520;** fax 310/510-7606), located on the Green Pleasure Pier, distributes brochures and information on island activities, hotels, and transportation. Call for a free 100-page visitors' guide. Its colorful website, **www.catalina.com**, offers current news from the *Catalina Islander* newspaper in addition to updated activities, events, and general information.

ORIENTATION   The picturesque town of **Avalon** is both the port of entry for the island and the island's only city. From the ferry dock, you can wander along Crescent Avenue, the main road along the beachfront, and easily explore adjacent side streets.

   Northwest of Avalon is the village of **Two Harbors,** accessible by boat or shuttle bus. Its twin bays are favored by pleasure yachts from L.A.'s various marinas, so there's more camaraderie and a less touristy ambiance overall.

GETTING AROUND   Only a limited number of cars are permitted on the island; visitors are not allowed to drive cars on the island, and most residents, in fact, motor around in golf carts (many of the homes only have golf-cart–size driveways). Don't worry, though—you'll be able to get everywhere you want to go by renting a cart yourself or just hoofing it, which is what most visitors do.

   If you want to explore the area around Avalon beyond where your feet can comfortably carry you, try renting a mountain bike or tandem from **Brown's Bikes,** 107 Pebbly Beach Rd. (© **310/510-0986**), or even a gas-powered golf cart from **Cartopia,** on Crescent Avenue at Pebbly Beach Road (© **310/510-2493**), where rates are about $30 per hour.

EXPLORING THE ISLAND

ORGANIZED TOURS   The Santa Catalina Island Company's **Discovery Tours** (© **800/626-7489** or 310/510-TOUR; www.scico.com) has a ticket and information office on Crescent Avenue across from the pier. It offers the greatest variety of excursions from Avalon; many last just a couple of hours, so you don't have to tie up your whole day. In addition to day and night scenic tram tours of Avalon, glass-bottomed boat cruises, and bus trips along Skyline Drive to the Airport in the Sky, Discover conducts some very worthwhile outings none of the other operators offer. Tours are available in money-saving combo packs; inquire when you call.

Noteworthy excursions include the **Undersea Tour,** a slow 1-hour cruise of Lover's Cove Marine Preserve in a semi-submerged boat ($21 for adults and $13 for kids); the **Casino Tour,** a fascinating 1-hour look at the style and inventive engineering of this elegant ballroom ($8.50 adults, $4.25 kids); nighttime **Flying Fish Boat Trips,** a 70-minute Catalina tradition in searchlight-equipped open boats ($8.50 adults, $4.25 kids); and the **Inland Motor Tour,** a half-day (4-hour) jaunt through the island's rugged interior, including an Arabian-horse show and refreshments at Wrigley's Rancho Escondido ($30 adults, $15 kids).

VISITING TWO HARBORS   If you want to get a better look at the rugged natural beauty of Catalina and escape the throngs of beachgoers, head over to Two Harbors, the quarter-mile "neck" at the island's northwest end that gets its name from the "twin harbors" on each side, known as the Isthmus and Cat Harbors. An excellent starting point for campers and hikers, Two Harbors also offers just enough civilization for the less-intrepid traveler.

The **Banning House Lodge** (℃ 310/510-2800) is an 11-room bed-and-breakfast overlooking the Isthmus. The clapboard house was built in 1910 for Catalina's pre-Wrigley owners, and has seen duty as on-location lodging for movie stars like Errol Flynn and Dorothy Lamour. Peaceful and isolated, the simply furnished but comfortable lodge has spectacular views of both Isthmus harbors. Rates range from $77 to $201 (April through October), and they'll even give you a lift from the pier.

Everyone eats at **Doug's Harbor Reef** (℃ 310/510-7265), down on the beach. This nautical- and tropical-themed saloon/restaurant serves breakfast, lunch, and dinner, the latter consisting of hearty steaks, ribs, swordfish, chicken teriyaki, and buffalo burgers in summer. The house drink is sweet "buffalo milk," a potent concoction of vodka, crème de cacao, banana liqueur, milk, and whipped cream.

WHAT TO SEE & DO IN AVALON   Walk along horseshoe-shaped Crescent Avenue, past private yachting and fishing clubs, toward the landmark **Casino** building. You can see the Art Deco **theater** for the price of a movie ticket any night. Also on the ground floor is the **Catalina Island Museum** (℃ 310/510-2414), which features exhibits on island history, archaeology, and natural history. The museum has a contour relief map of the island that's helpful to hikers. Admission is $1.50 for adults, 50¢ for kids; it's included in the price of Discovery's Casino Tour (see above).

Around the point from the Casino lies **Descanso Beach Club** (℃ 310/510-7410), a mini–Club Med in a private cove. While you can get on the beach year-round, the club's facilities (including showers, restaurant/bar, volleyball lawns, and thatched beach umbrellas) are only open from Easter to September 30. Admission is $1.50.

About 1½ miles from downtown Avalon is the **Wrigley Memorial and Botanical Garden** (℃ 310/510-2288), an invigorating walk or short taxi ride. The specialized gardens, a project of Ada Wrigley, showcase plants endemic to California's coastal islands. Open daily from 8am to 5pm; admission is $1.

SNORKELING, DIVING & KAYAKING

Snorkeling, scuba diving, and sea kayaking are among the main reasons mainlanders head to Catalina. Purists will prefer the less-spoiled waters of Two Harbors, but Avalon's many coves have plenty to offer as well, especially the protected marine life in Casino Point Underwater Park. **Catalina Snorkeling Adventures,** at Lover's Cove (℃ 877/SNORKEL), offers snorkel gear rental. **Scuba Luv**

(✆ **800/262-DIVE** or 310/510-2350) offers guided half-day to 2-day snorkel and scuba tours with certified instructors. **Descanso Beach Ocean Sports** (✆ **310/510-1226**) offers sea kayak and snorkel rentals with instruction, plus specialty expeditions and kids' programs.

At Two Harbors, stop by **West End Dive Center** (✆ **310/510-2800**). Excursions range from half-day introductory dives to complete certification courses to multi-day dive packages. It also rents snorkel gear and offers kayak rental, instruction, and excursions.

WHERE TO STAY

If you plan to stay overnight, be sure to reserve a room in advance, because most places fill up pretty quickly during the summer and holiday seasons. **Catalina Island Accommodations** (✆ **310/510-3000**) might be able to help you out in a pinch; it's a reservations service with updated information on the whole island.

Hotel Metropole ✦   Named for Avalon's historic grande dame hotel, today's Metropole is the cornerstone of a shopping plaza that looks like Disneyland's New Orleans Square. Built in the early 1990s, this sleek and well-appointed replacement has the ambiance of a boutique inn, affording nice views from almost every room on its three floors. There's a wind-shielded rooftop deck and whirlpool overlooking the harbor, and some rooms have luxurious touches like fireplaces, whirlpool tubs, and balconies. Furnishings throughout public areas and guest rooms alike are contemporary with a tropical air, reminiscent of a Florida plantation. Just outside the front door is all of Avalon Bay's activity, starting with the theme-y Metropole Market Place in the ground-floor courtyard. It may look touristy from the outside, but the Metropole shapes up as a classy, comfortable retreat that's equally suitable for romantic interludes or family getaways.

205 Crescent Ave. (PO Box 1900), Avalon, CA 90704. ✆ **800/300-8528** or 310/510-1884. Fax 310/510-2534. www.hotel-metropole.com. 48 units. May–Oct $135–$259 double, from $335 suite; winter $109–$229 double, from $249 suite. Rates include continental breakfast. AE, MC, V. **Amenities:** Adjacent restaurant; charming massage/spa studio; Jacuzzi; room service (11am–8pm); in-room massage; babysitting; self-service laundromat. *In room:* A/C, TV w/ DVD, dataport, minibar, hair dryer.

The Inn on Mt. Ada ✦✦   When William Wrigley, Jr. purchased Catalina Island in 1921, he built this ornate hilltop Georgian colonial mansion as his summer vacation home; it's now one of the finest small hotels in California. The opulent inn has several ground-floor salons, a club room with fireplace, a deep-seated formal library, and a wickered sunroom where tea, cookies, and fruit are always available. The best guest room is the Grand Suite, fitted with a fireplace and a large private patio. Amenities include bathrobes and the use of a golf cart during your stay. TVs are available on request, but there are no phones in the rooms. A hearty full breakfast, a light deli-style lunch, and a beautiful multicourse dinner complemented by a limited wine selection are included in the tariff.

398 Wrigley Rd. (P.O. Box 2560), Avalon, CA 90704. ✆ **800/608-7669** or 310/510-2030. Fax 310/510-2237. www.catalina.com/mtada. 6 units. Nov–May Mon–Thurs $280–$350 double, $350–$455 suite; June–Oct and Fri–Sun year-round $300–$475 double, $475–$620 suite. Rates include 3 meals daily. DC, MC, V. **Amenities:** Courtesy car. *In room:* TV, hair dryer, iron; no phone.

Zane Grey Pueblo Hotel   Author and avid fisherman Zane Grey spent his later years in Avalon and wrote many books here, including *Tales of Swordfish and Tuna,* which tells of his local fishing adventures. Perched atop a steep road overlooking the bay, this unfancy house still sports many of the ethnic touches (Tahitian teak, Hopi elements) Grey enjoyed. The simply furnished guest rooms have private bathrooms and ceiling fans; a comfortable living room features a fireplace, grand piano, and TV. The house is one of only two Avalon hotels with its own pool; shuttle service is offered to and from town.

Off Chimes Tower Rd., north of Hill St. (P.O. Box 216), Avalon, CA 90704. ℂ **800/3-PUEBLO** or 310/510-0966. www.zanegreyhotel.com. 16 units. June–Sept $135–$165 double; Oct–May $80–$125 double. Winter discounts available. Rates include continental breakfast. AE, MC, V. **Amenities:** Outdoor pool. *In room:* No phone.

WHERE TO DINE

Other than the choices below, recommended Avalon options include **The Busy Bee,** 306 Crescent Ave. (ℂ **310/510-1983**), an always-crowded waterfront diner with a heated and wind-protected patio. On the Two Harbors side of the island, **Doug's Harbor Reef** is the place to eat; see "Exploring the Island," above.

The Channel House CONTINENTAL   With a secluded outdoor patio that's generally agreed to be the most romantic dining spot in Avalon, this very traditional restaurant manages to attract as many jeans-clad vacationers as dressed-up islanders. Dinner always begins with an enormous platter of fresh crudités and creamy dip, whose bounty often dispels any thought of a first course. The menu is enticing, with local seafood offerings like mako shark, fresh Catalina lobster, or grilled island sand dabs. Meat and poultry are invariably served sauced; you'll find plenty of rich touches like goose liver, béarnaise, and butter galore. Surprisingly, the restaurant offers just a couple of perfunctory desserts, hardly the lavish selection of mousses and rich cakes you might expect.

205 Crescent Ave. (at Sumner Ave.). ℂ 310/510-1617. Reservations recommended. Main courses $12–$25. AE, DISC, MC, V. Daily 11am–3pm (July–Oct only) and 5–10pm year-round (subject to Mon–Tues closure in winter).

Clubhouse Bar & Grille ✸ CALIFORNIA   Find some of Avalon's most elegant meals here, at the landmark Catalina Country Club, whose stylish Spanish-Mediterranean clubhouse was built by William Wrigley, Jr. during the 1920s. Recently restored, it exudes a chic and historic atmosphere; the menu is peppered with archival photos and vintage celebrity anecdotes. Sit outdoors in an elegant tiled courtyard, or inside the intimate, clubby dining room. Much of the menu is served throughout the afternoon, including gourmet pizzas, international appetizer samplers, and soups (fisherman's bisque or French onion, both available in a sourdough bowl). Dinner offerings follow a fusion style, such as New Zealand lamb accented with a piquant mango-mint chutney; cioppino and pad thai both appear on the menu. The club is a few blocks uphill, so shuttle service is available from Island Plaza (on Sumner Ave.) on weekends.

1 Country Club Dr. (above Sumner Ave.). ℂ 310/510-7404. Reservations recommended. Main courses $10–$30. AE, DISC, MC, V. Daily 11:30am–2:30pm and 5–9pm (closing hours will vary seasonally).

El Galleon AMERICAN   Here at Catalina's answer to Disney's *Pirates of the Caribbean,* step from the busy bayside promenade into a fantastic collage of brass portholes, ship's rigging, ample red-leather booths, and wrought-iron conquistador decor. This setting feels just right for the hearty menu of steaks and seafood, featuring enormous cuts of Midwest aged beef (petite filets and smaller cuts are available) and fresh local and regional fish (Catalina swordfish, Hawaiian mahi-mahi, Alaskan halibut). You can also make a respectable repast from the many appetizer selections, each of which is like a meal. Our favorites are zesty BBQ pork ribs, Cajun crab cakes with Creole sauce, and warm spinach-artichoke dip with chewy sourdough bread.

411 Crescent Ave. (between Catalina and Claressa Aves.). ℂ 310/510-1188. Reservations recommended on weekends. Main courses $6–$12 lunch; $11–$25 dinner. AE, MC, V. Daily 11am–10pm. Bar daily 11am–2am.

3 Big Bear Lake & Lake Arrowhead

100 miles NE of Los Angeles

These two deep-blue lakes lie close to each other in the San Bernardino Mountains and have long been a favorite year-round alpine playground for city-weary Angelenos.

Big Bear Lake has always been popular with skiers as well as avid boaters (it's much larger than Arrowhead, and equipment rentals abound), and in the past decade the area has been given a much-needed face-lift. Big Bear Boulevard was substantially widened to handle high-season traffic, and downtown Big Bear Lake (the "Village") was spiffed up without losing its woodsy charm. In addition to two excellent ski slopes less than 5 minutes from town (see "Winter Fun," below), you can enjoy the comforts of a real supermarket (there's even a Kmart now) and several video-rental shops, all especially convenient if you're staying in a cabin. Most people choose Big Bear over Arrowhead because there's so much more to do, from boating, fishing, and hiking to snow sports, mountain biking, and horseback riding. The weather is nearly always perfect at this 7,000-foot-plus elevation: If you want proof, ask Caltech, which operates a solar observatory here to take advantage of nearly 300 days of sunshine per year.

Lake Arrowhead has always been privately owned, as is immediately apparent from the affluence of the surrounding homes, many of which are gated estates rather than rustic mountain cabins. The lake and the private docks lining its shores are reserved for the exclusive use of homeowners, but visitors can enjoy Lake Arrowhead by boat tour (see "Organized Tours," below) or use of the summer-season beach clubs, a privilege included in nearly all private-home rentals (see "Where to Stay," later in this chapter). Reasons to choose a vacation at Lake Arrowhead? The roads up are less grueling than the winding ascent to Big Bear Lake and, being at a lower elevation, Arrowhead gets little snow (you can forget those pesky tire chains). It's very easy and cost effective to rent a luxurious house from which to enjoy the spectacular scenery, crisp mountain air, and relaxed resort atmosphere—and if you do ski, the slopes are only a half hour away.

ESSENTIALS

GETTING THERE   Lake Arrowhead is reached by taking Calif. 18 from San Bernardino. The last segment of this route takes you along the aptly named **Rim of the World Highway,** offering a breathtaking panoramic view out over the valley below on clear days. Calif. 18 then continues east to Big Bear Lake, but to get to Big Bear Lake it's quicker to bypass Arrowhead by taking Calif. 330 from Redlands, which meets Calif. 18 in Running Springs. During heavy-traffic periods, it can be worthwhile to take scenic Calif. 38, which winds up from Redlands through mountain passes and valleys to approach Big Bear from the other side.

Note: Nostalgia lovers can revisit legendary **Route 66** on the way from Los Angeles to the mountain resorts, substituting scenic motor courts and other relics of the "Mother Road" in place of impersonal I-10. See chapter 15, "The Southern California Desert," for a complete driving tour.

VISITOR INFORMATION   National ski tours, mountain-bike races, and one of southern California's largest Oktoberfest gatherings are just some of the many events held here year-round—which may either entice or discourage you from visiting when they're on. Contact the **Big Bear Lake Resort Association,**

630 Bartlett Rd., Big Bear Lake Village (© **909/866-7000;** www.bigbearinfo. com), for schedules and information. It also provides information on sight-seeing and lodging and will send you a free visitors' guide.

In Lake Arrowhead, contact the **Lake Arrowhead Communities Chamber of Commerce** (© **800/337-3716** for the Lodging Information Line, or 909/ 337-3715; fax 909/336-1548; www.lakearrowhead.net). The visitor center is located in the Lake Arrowhead Village lower shopping center.

ORIENTATION   The south shore of Big Bear Lake was the first resort area to be developed and remains the most densely populated. Calif. 18 passes first through the city of Big Bear Lake and its downtown village; then, as Big Bear Boulevard, it continues east to Big Bear City, which is more residential and sub-urban. Calif. 38 traverses the north shore, home to pristine national forest and great hiking trails, as well as a couple of small marinas (see "Watersports," below) and a lakefront bed-and-breakfast inn (see Windy Point in "Where to Stay," later in this chapter).

Arrowhead's main town is Lake Arrowhead Village, located on the south shore at the end of Calif. 173. The village's commercial center is home to factory-outlet stores, about 40 chain and specialty shops, and the Lake Arrowhead Resort Hotel. Minutes away is the town of Blue Jay (along Calif. 189), where the Ice Castle Skating Rink is located (see "Winter Fun," below).

ENJOYING THE OUTDOORS

In addition to the activities below, there's a great recreation spot for families near the heart of Big Bear Lake: **Magic Mountain,** on Calif. 18/Big Bear Boulevard (© **909/866-4626**), has a year-round bobsled-style Alpine Slide, a splashy dou-ble water slide open from mid-June to mid-September, and bunny slopes for snow tubing from November to Easter. The dry Alpine Slide is $3 a ride, the water slide is $1 (or $10 for a day-pass), and snow play costs $10 per day includ-ing tube and rope tow.

The **Moonridge Animal Park** (© **909/866-0183;** www.moonridgezoo.com), located at the base of the Bear Mountain Ski Resort, offers an opportunity to roam around and get an up-close look at mountain lions, raccoons, hawks, tim-ber wolves, grazing deer, owls, bobcats, and more. The zoo is a sanctuary for orphaned and injured animals unable to be released into the wild, including grizzly bears. It's open May through October, daily from 10am to 5pm; Novem-ber through April, daily from 10am to 4pm. Admission is $2.50 for adults, $1.50 for kids ages 3 to 11, and free for kids under 3.

WATERSPORTS

BOATING   You can rent all kinds of boats—including speedboats, rowboats, paddleboats, pontoons, sailboats, and canoes—at a number of Big Bear Lake marinas. Rates vary only slightly from place to place: A 14-foot dinghy with an outboard runs around $10 per hour or $30 for a half day; pontoon (patio) boats that can hold large groups range in size and price from $25 to $45 per hour or $80 to $150 for a half day. **Pine Knot Landing** (© **909/866-BOAT**) is the most centrally located marina, behind the post office at the foot of Pine Knot Boulevard in Big Bear Lake. **Gray's Landing** (© **909/866-2443**) is just across the dam on the north shore and offers the best prices and the least attitude. **Big Bear Marina,** Paine Road at Lakeview (© **909/ 866-3218**), is also close to Big Bear Lake Village and provides take-along chicken dinners when you rent a pontoon boat for a sunset cruise ($75 for 3 hours).

FISHING   Big Bear Lake brims with rainbow trout, bass, and catfish in spring and summer, the best fishing seasons. Phone ℭ **310/590-5020** for recorded stocking information. A fishing license is required and costs $8.95 per day, $24.95 per year. Pine Knot Landing, Gray's Landing, and Big Bear Marina (see "Boating," above) all rent fishing boats and have bait and tackle shops that sell licenses.

JET-SKIING   Personal Water Craft (PWCs) are available for rent at **Big Bear Marina** (see "Boating," above) and **Pleasure Point Landing,** 603 Landlock Landing Rd. (ℭ **909/866-2455**), where you can rent a single-rider SeaDoo for $35 an hour, or opt for a two-seat WaveRunner at $55 per hour. **North Shore Landing,** on Calif. 38, 2 miles west of Fawnskin (ℭ **909/868-4386**), rents jet skis and two- and three-person WaveRunners at rates ranging from $55 to $65 per hour. Call ahead to reserve your craft and check age and deposit requirements.

WATER-SKIING   Big Bear Lake, Pine Knot Landing, North Shore Landing, and Big Bear Marina (see "Boating," above) all offer water-ski lessons and speed-boat rentals. Lake Arrowhead is home to the McKenzie Water Ski School, dock-side in Lake Arrowhead Village (ℭ **909/337-3814**), famous for teaching Kirk Douglas, George Hamilton, and other Hollywood stars to ski. It's open from Memorial Day to the end of September and offers group lessons for $115 per hour, short refresher lessons for $35, and boat charters (including driver) for $95 an hour.

OTHER WARM-WEATHER ACTIVITIES

GOLF   The **Bear Mountain Golf Course,** Goldmine Drive, Big Bear Lake (ℭ **909/585-8002**), is a nine-hole, par-35, links-style course that winds through a gently sloping meadow at the base of the Bear Mountain Ski Resort. The course is open daily from April through November. Greens fees are $22 and $32 for nine and 18 holes, respectively. Both riding carts and pull carts are available. Phone for tee times.

HIKING   Hikers will love the San Bernardino National Forest. The gray squirrel is a popular native so you may see them scurrying around gathering acorns or material for their nests. You can sometimes spot deer, coyotes, and American bald eagles, which come here with their young in winter. The black-crowned Steller's jay and the talkative red, white, and black acorn woodpecker are the most common of the great variety of birds in this pine forest.

Stop in at the **Big Bear Discovery Center** (ℭ **909/866-3437;** www.bigbeardiscoverycenter.org) on Calif. 38, 3 miles east of Fawnskin (and about ¼ mile west of the Big Bear Ranger Station) on Big Bear Lake's north shore. Here you can pick up free trail maps as well as other information on the area's plants, animals, and geology. The best choice for a short mountain hike is the **Woodland Trail,** which begins near the ranger station. The best long hike is a section of the **Pacific Crest Trail,** which travels 39 miles through the mountains above Big Bear and Arrowhead Lakes. The most convenient trailhead is located at Cougar Crest, half a mile west of the Big Bear Ranger Station.

The best place to begin a hike in Lake Arrowhead is at the **Arrowhead Ranger Station** (ℭ **909/337-2444**), located in the town of Skyforest on Calif. 18 a quarter mile east of the Lake Arrowhead turnoff (Calif. 173). The staff will provide you with maps and information on the best area trails, which range from easy to difficult. The **Enchanted Loop Trail,** near the town of Blue Jay, is an easy half-hour hike. The **Heaps Peak Arboretum Trail** winds through a grove of redwoods; the trailhead is on the north side of Calif. 18, at an auxiliary ranger kiosk west of Running Springs.

The area is home to a **National Children's Forest,** a 20-acre area developed so that children, the wheelchair-bound, and the visually impaired could enjoy nature. To get to the Children's Forest from Lake Arrowhead, take Calif. 330 to Calif. 18 east, past Deer Lick Station; when you reach a road marked IN96 (open only in summer), turn right and go 3 miles.

HORSEBACK RIDING   Horses are permitted on all the mountain trails through the national forest. **Bear Mountain Stables,** at Bear Mountain Ski Resort, City of Big Bear Lake (✆ **909/878-HORSE**), offers 1- and 2-hour guided rides for $20 per hour, and sunset hay rides for $45. The stables are open daily from May through December; phone for reservations. **Baldwin Lake Stables,** southeast of Big Bear City (✆ **909/585-6482;** www.baldwinlakestables. com), conducts hourly, lunch, and sunset rides in addition to offering lessons.

MOUNTAIN BIKING   Big Bear Lake has become a mountain-biking center, with most of the action around the Snow Summit Ski Area (see "Winter Fun," below), where a $7 lift ticket will take you and your bike to a scenic web of trails, fire roads, and meadows at about 8,000 feet. Call its **Summer Activities Hotline** (✆ **909/866-4621**). The lake's north shore is also a popular biking destination; the forest service ranger stations (see "Hiking," above) have maps to the historic gold rush–era Holcomb Valley and the 2-mile Alpine Pedal Path (an easy lakeside ride).

Big Bear Bikes, 41810 Big Bear Blvd. (✆ **909/866-4565**), rents mountain bikes for $6 an hour or $21 for 4 hours. **Bear Valley Bikes,** 40298 Big Bear Blvd. (✆ **909/866-8000**), rents bikes and offers free lessons on Sundays. **Team Big Bear** is located at the base of Snow Summit (✆ **909/866-4565**); it rents bicycles and provides detailed maps and guides for all Big Bear–area trails.

At Lake Arrowhead, bikes are permitted on all hiking trails and backroads except the Pacific Crest Trail. See the local ranger station for an area map. Gear can be rented from the **Lake Arrowhead Resort** (✆ **909/336-1511**) or **Above & Beyond Sports,** 32877 Calif. 18, Running Springs (✆ **909/867-5517**).

WINTER FUN

SKIING & SNOWBOARDING   When the L.A. basin gets wintertime rain, skiers everywhere rejoice, for they know snow is falling up in the mountains. The last few seasons have seen abundant natural snowfall at Big Bear, augmented by sophisticated snowmaking equipment. While the slopes can't compare with those in Utah or Colorado, they do offer diversity, difficulty, and convenience.

Snow Summit at Big Bear Lake (✆ **909/866-5766;** www.snowsummit.com) is the skier's choice, especially because it installed its second high-speed quad express from the 7,000-foot base to the 8,200-foot summit. Another nice feature is green (easy) runs even from the summit, so beginners can also enjoy the Summit Haus lodge and breathtaking lake views from the top. Advanced risktakers will appreciate three double black-diamond runs. Lift tickets range from $32 to $45. The resort offers midweek, beginner, half-day, night, and family specials, as well as ski and snowboard instruction. Hey, you can even ski free on your birthday here! Other helpful Snow Summit phone numbers include advance lift-ticket sales (✆ **909/866-5841**), the ski school (✆ **909/866-4546**), and a snow report (✆ **310/390-1498** in L.A. County).

The **Bear Mountain Resort** at Big Bear Lake (© **800/BEAR-MTN** or 909/585-2519; www.bearmtn.com) has the largest beginner area, but experts flock to the double-black-diamond "Geronimo" run from the 8,805-foot Bear Peak. Natural-terrain skiers and snowboarders will enjoy legal access to off-trail canyons, but the limited beginner slopes and kids' areas get pretty crowded in season. One of two high-speed quad expresses rises from the 7,140-foot base to 8,440-foot Goldmine Mountain; most runs from here are intermediate. Bear Mountain has a ski-and-snowboard school, abundant dining facilities, and a well-stocked ski shop.

The **Snow Valley Ski Resort** in Arrowbear, midway between Arrowhead and Big Bear (© **800/680-SNOW** or 909/867-2751; www.snow-valley.com), has improved its snowmaking and facilities to be competitive with the other two major ski areas, and is the primary choice of skiers staying at Arrowhead. From a base elevation of 6,800 feet, Snow Valley's 13 chairlifts (including five triples) can take you from the beginner runs all the way up to black-diamond challenges at the 7,898-foot peak. Lift tickets cost $35 to $40 for adults; children's programs, night skiing, and lesson packages are available.

ICE-SKATING The **Blue Jay Ice Castle,** at North Bay Road and Calif. 189 (© **909/33-SKATE;** www.ice-castle.com), near Lake Arrowhead Village, is a training site for world champion Michelle Kwan and boasts Olympic gold medalist Robin Cousins on its staff. Several public sessions each day—as well as hockey, broomball, group lessons, and book-in-advance private parties—give non-pros a chance to enjoy this impeccably groomed "outdoor" rink (it's open on three sides to the scenery and fresh air).

ORGANIZED TOURS

LAKE TOURS The *Big Bear Queen* (© **909/866-3218;** www.bigbearmarina. com), a midget Mississippi-style paddle wheeler, cruises Big Bear Lake on 90-minute tours daily from late April through November. The boat departs from Big Bear Marina (at the end of Paine Avenue). Tours are $10 for adults, $8 for seniors 65 and older, $5 for children ages 3 to 12, and free for kids under 3. Call for reservations and information on the special Sunday brunch, champagne sunset, and dinner cruises.

Fifty-minute tours of Lake Arrowhead are offered year-round on the *Arrowhead Queen* (© **909/336-6992**), a sister ship that departs hourly each day between 10am and 6pm from Lake Arrowhead Village. Tours are $10 for adults, $8.50 for seniors, $6.50 for children 2 to 12, and free for kids under 2. It's about the only way to really see this alpine jewel, unless you know a resident with a boat.

FOREST TOURS Big Bear Jeep Tours (© **909/878-JEEP;** www.bigbear jeeptours.com) journeys into Big Bear Lake's backcountry, including historic Holcomb Valley, relic of the gold rush, plus the panoramic viewpoint Butler Peak. These off-road adventures range in length from 2 to 4½ hours, and cost from $40 to $85 per person. Bring your own snack, though, because although the guide carries ample water, the longer excursions include short but appetite-building hikes. Phone for reservations, particularly on weekends and holidays (no tours offered in winter).

WHERE TO STAY
BIG BEAR LAKE
Vacation rentals are plentiful in the area, from cabins to condos to private homes. Some can accommodate up to 20 people and can be rented on a weekly

or monthly basis. For a wide range of rental properties, all pictured in detail online, contact **Big Bear Mountain Rentals** (© **909/878-2233;** www.bigbear mountainrentals.com). The **Village Reservation Service** (© **909/866-8583;** www.bigbear.com/villageres) can arrange for everything from condos to lakefront homes, or call the **Big Bear Lake Resort Association** (© **909/866-7000**) for information and referrals on all types of lodgings.

Besides the places below, other choices we recommend are **Apples Bed & Breakfast Inn,** 42430 Moonridge Rd. (© **909/866-0903;** www.applesbedand breakfast.com), a crabapple-red New England–style clapboard that blends hotel-like professionalism with B&B amenities (and lots of cute, frilly touches); and **Gold Mountain Manor,** 1117 Anita Ave. (© **909/585-6997;** www. bigbear.com/goldmtn), a woodsy 1920s lodge that's now an ultra-cozy (and affordable) B&B.

Grey Squirrel Resort *Kids*   This is the most attractive of the many cabin-cluster–type motels near the city of Big Bear Lake, offering a wide range of rustic cabins, most with fireplace and kitchen. They're adequately, if not attractively, furnished—the appeal here is the flexibility and privacy afforded large or long-term parties. Facilities include a heated pool that's enclosed in winter, an indoor spa, a fire pit and barbecues, volleyball and basketball courts, laundry facilities, and completely equipped kitchens.

39372 Big Bear Blvd., Big Bear Lake, CA 92315. © 800/381-5569 or 909/866-4335. Fax 909/866-6271. www.greysquirrel.com. 18 cabins. $75–$95 1-bedroom cabin; $99–$125 2-bedroom cabin; $125–$275 3-bedroom cabin. Value rates available. Higher rates on holidays. AE, DISC, MC, V. Pets welcome for extra $10 fee per day. **Amenities:** Heated indoor/outdoor pool; indoor Jacuzzi; self-service laundromat. *In room:* TV w/ VCR.

Holiday Inn Big Bear Chateau   One of only two traditional full-service hotels in Big Bear, this European-flavored property underwent a complete renovation in 1997. Its highly visible location—just off Big Bear Boulevard, at the base of the road to Bear Mountain—makes the Chateau a popular choice for skiers and families. The rooms are modern but more charming than your average Holiday Inn, with tapestries, brass beds, antique furniture, gas fireplaces, and lavish marble bathrooms, all with heated towel racks and many with whirlpool tubs. The entire compound is surrounded by tall forest. The restaurant (which also provides room service) is advertised as "casually elegant," which means you can enjoy upscale continental/American cuisine even in après-ski duds.

42200 Moonridge Rd. (P.O. Box 1814), Big Bear Lake, CA 92315. © 800/BEAR-INN or 909/866-6666. Fax 909/866-8988. www.bigbearinn.com. 80 units. Winter $99–$180 double; summer $79–$160 double. Children under 18 free; extra person $10. Winter ski and summer-fun packages available. AE, DISC, MC, V. **Amenities:** Restaurant, lounge; heated outdoor pool; Jacuzzi; children's activities; room service (limited hours). *In room:* A/C, TV, dataport, coffeemaker, hair dryer, iron.

Knickerbocker Mansion Country Inn ✦   Innkeepers Thomas Bicanic and Stan Miller faced quite a task reviving this landmark log house; when they moved in, it was empty of all furnishings and suffered from years of neglect at the hands of the former B&B owners. But Knickerbocker Mansion has risen to become the most charming and sophisticated inn on the lake's south side; chef Bicanic, who honed his craft in L.A.'s culinary temple Patina restaurant, even has plans to begin serving intimate gourmet dinners. The pair scoured antiques stores in Big Bear and Los Angeles for vintage furnishings, creating a warm and relaxing ambiance in the grand-yet-quirky, hand-built house of legendary local character Bill Knickerbocker, who assembled it by hand almost 90 years ago. Today's guest rooms are a cedar-paneled dream, with luxury bed linens, cozy bathrobes, modern marble bathrooms with deluxe Australian showerheads, and refreshing mountain views. After Bicanic's stunning breakfast, you can spend the day relaxing on veranda rockers or garden hammocks; Big Bear's village is also an easy walk away.

869 Knickerbocker Rd. (P.O. Box 1907), Big Bear Lake, CA 92315. ℂ **800/388-4179** or 909/878-9190. Fax 909/878-4248. www.knickerbockermansion.com. 11 units. $110–$155 double; $200–$225 suite. Rates include full gourmet breakfast and all-day refreshments and snacks. AE, DISC, MC, V. *In room:* TV w/ VCR, dataport, refrigerator, coffeemaker, hair dryer.

Windy Point Inn ✫✫   A contemporary architectural showpiece on the scenic north shore, the Windy Point is the only shorefront B&B in Big Bear; most rooms have spectacular sunrise and sunset views. Hosts Val and Kent Kessler's attention to detail is impeccable—if you're tired of knotty pine and Victorian frills, here's a grown-up place for you, with plenty of romance and all the pampering you can stand. Every room has a wood-burning fireplace, feather bed, private deck, and VCR (borrow tapes from the inn's plentiful video library); some also feature whirlpool tubs, CD players, and luxurious state-of-the-art bathrooms. The welcoming Great Room features a casual sunken fireplace nook with floor-to-ceiling windows overlooking the lake, a telescope for stargazing, a baby grand, and up-to-date menus for every local eatery. You might not want to leave the cocoon of your room after Kent's custom gourmet breakfast, but if you do, you'll find a wintertime bald-eagle habitat is just up the road, and the city of Big Bear Lake is only a 10-minute drive around the lake.

39015 North Shore Dr., Fawnskin, CA 92333. ℂ **909/866-2746.** Fax 909/866-1593. www. windypointinn.com. 5 units. $135–$255 double. Rates include welcome cookies, lavish full breakfast, and afternoon hors d'oeuvres. Midweek discounts available. AE, DISC, MC, V. *In room:* Coffeemaker, refrigerator, hair dryer; no phone.

LAKE ARROWHEAD

There are far more private homes than tourist accommodations in Arrowhead, but rental properties abound, from cozy cottages to palatial mansions; many can be surprisingly economical for families or other groups. Two of the largest agencies are **Arrowhead Cabin Rentals** (ℂ **800/244-5138** or 909/337-2403) and **Arrowhead Mountain Resorts Rentals** (ℂ **800/743-0865** or 909/337-4413). Overnight guests in rental properties enjoy some resident lake privileges—be sure to ask when you reserve.

Two other options are **Chateau du Lac,** 911 Hospital Rd. (ℂ **800/601-8722** or 909/337-6488; www.lakearrowhead.com/chateaudulac), an elegant and contemporary five-room B&B with stunning views of the lake; and the **Saddleback Inn,** 300 S. Calif. 173 (ℂ **800/858-3334** or 909/336-3571; www.lakearrowhead. com/saddleback), an inn and restaurant that still boasts historic charm while offering up-to-date amenities, all at a prime location in the center of the village.

Bracken Fern Manor ✫ *Finds*   Billing itself as a "House of Now Fine Repute," this off-the-beaten-path inn boasts a registered historical marker as well as a checkered past. The present owners work hard at evoking its 1930s heyday: They've preserved the downstairs public rooms, along with many well-maintained antiques, and named each guest room for one of the "girls." There are many quiet corners for relaxing, including a games room, hidden library, whirlpool gazebo, and wood-lined sauna. Rooms are decorated in a fresh country style and have private bathrooms, a feature not originally included in the house. A detached cottage sleeps four and rents for $425/2 nights (includes $50 cleaning fee).

815 Arrowhead Villas Rd. (P.O. Box 1006), Lake Arrowhead, CA 92352. © **909/337-8557.** Fax 909/337-3323. www.brackenfernmanor.com. 10 units. $80–$185 double. Rates include full breakfast. MC, V. Located half a mile north of Calif. 18. **Amenities:** Jacuzzi; sauna. *In room:* No phone.

Lake Arrowhead Resort *(Kids)*   This sprawling resort has been upgraded somewhat since it was part of the Hilton chain, but location is still its most outstanding feature, coupled with unparalleled (for the mountains) service and facilities. Situated on the lakeshore adjacent to Lake Arrowhead Village, the hotel has its own beach, plus docks that are ideal for fishing. The rooms are fitted with good-quality, bulk-purchased contemporary furnishings, and most have balconies, king-size beds, and fireplaces. The suites, some in private cottages, are equipped with full kitchens and whirlpool tubs.

The hotel caters primarily to groups, and sports a business-like ambiance during the week. A full program of supervised children's activities, ranging from nature hikes to T-shirt painting, is offered on weekends year-round.

27984 Hwy. 189, Lake Arrowhead, CA 92352. © **800/800-6792** or 909/336-1511. Fax 909/336-1378. www.lakearrowheadresort.com. 177 units. $119–$229 double; $299–$399 suite. Inquire about auto-club discounts. AE, DC, DISC, MC, V. **Amenities:** 2 restaurants (1 year-round casual, 1 fancy and seasonal); outdoor pool (heated summer only); tennis courts; health club; Jacuzzi; children's programs; video arcade; business center; salon; babysitting; laundry/dry-cleaning service. *In room:* A/C, TV w/ pay movies, dataport, minibar, coffeemaker, hair dryer.

Pine Rose Cabins *(Kids)*   The only place of its kind in Lake Arrowhead, Pine Rose Cabins is a good choice for families. Situated on five forested acres about 3 miles from the lake, the wonderful freestanding cabins offer lots of privacy. Innkeepers Tricia and David Dufour have 15 cabins, ranging in size from romantic studios to a large five-bedroom lodge, each decorated in a different theme: The Indian cabin has a teepee-like bed; the bed in Wild Bill's cabin is covered like a wagon. Multi-bedroom units have fully stocked kitchens and separate living areas; for all cottages, daily maid service is available at an additional charge. There are plenty of fun-and-games on the premises, including swing sets, croquet, tetherball, and Ping-Pong.

25994 Calif. 189 (P.O. Box 31), Twin Peaks, CA 92391. © **800/429-PINE** or 909/337-2341. Fax 909/ 337-0258. www.lakearrowheadcabins.com. 17 units. $79–$179 studio for 2; $75–$169 1-, 2-, and 3-bedroom cabins for up to 10 people; $375–$450 large group lodges. Ski packages available. AE, DISC, MC, V. Pets accepted with $5 fee per night and $100 refundable deposit. **Amenities:** Outdoor heated pool; Jacuzzi. *In room:* TV/VCR; kitchen in multi-bedroom units.

WHERE TO DINE
BIG BEAR LAKE
Another very reliable option for all-day dining is **Stillwell's,** 40650 Village Dr. (© **909/866-3121,** ext. 7885). You might otherwise pass right by, because Stillwell's is the dining room for convention-friendly Northwoods Resort at the edge of the village; despite the unmistakable hotel feel, though, its something-for-everyone American/Continental menu is surprisingly good, with noted attention to detail and fair prices (rare in this mountain resort town).

The Captain's Anchorage STEAK/SEAFOOD   Historic and rustic, this knotty-pine restaurant has been serving fine steaks, prime rib, seafood, and lobster since 1947. Inside, the dark, nautical decor and fire-warmed bar are just right on blustery winter nights. It's got one of those mile-long soup-and-salad bars, plus some great early-bird and weeknight specials.

Moonridge Way at Big Bear Blvd., Big Bear Lake. ℂ **909/866-3997.** Reservations recommended. Full dinners $15–$29. AE, MC, V. Sun–Thurs 4:30–9pm; Fri–Sat 4:30–10pm.

Madlon's AMERICAN/CONTINENTAL   One of the few non-retro–fare dining rooms at the mountain resorts, Madlon's brings a bit of European flair to this fairy-tale cottage. A variety of creative croissant sandwiches at lunch are complemented by dinner selections like black-pepper filet mignon with mushroom-and-brandy sauce, and lemon-pepper-marinated chicken breast over pasta, all of which are prepared with a sophisticated touch.

829 W. Big Bear Blvd., Big Bear City. ℂ **909/585-3762.** Reservations recommended. Main courses $12–$25. DC, DISC, MC, V. Sat–Sun 8am–2pm; Tues–Fri 11am–2pm; Tues–Sun 5–9pm.

Mozart's Bistro CALIFORNIA   At last, a trendy Big Bear restaurant (the regular weekenders from L.A. must have been complaining). Mozart's isn't perfect—at these prices, the service could be more polished, the bar better stocked, and some grouse about seriously "off" nights—but its immediate surge in popularity shows how starved the community was for a sophisticated menu incorporating American-based fusion and Pacific Rim cuisine. The house specialty is rack of pork glazed with hard-cider molasses sauce served with chayote squash and garlic mashed potatoes; other seasonal choices include mahi-mahi in a macadamia-coconut crust on a pool of honey-lime beurre blanc, and breaded veal schnitzel with lingonberry port-wine sauce—a nod to the Bavarian flavor of the building (which was formerly Hansel's Cottage).

40701 Village Dr., Big Bear Lake. ℂ **909/866-9497.** Main courses $7–$10 lunch; $14–$25 dinner. AE, DISC, MC, V. Tues–Sun 11:30am–3pm; Tues–Thurs and Sun 5:30–9pm; Fri–Sat 5:30–10pm.

Old Country Inn DINER/GERMAN   The Old Country Inn has long been a favorite for hearty pre-ski breakfasts and stick-to-your-ribs old-world dinners. The restaurant is casual and welcoming, and the adjacent cocktail lounge is raucous on weekends. At breakfast, enjoy German apple pancakes or colossal omelets, while lunch choices include salads, sandwiches, and burgers. At lunch or dinner, feast on Wiener schnitzel, sauerbraten, and other gravy-topped German standards, along with grilled steaks and chicken.

41126 Big Bear Blvd., Big Bear Lake. ℂ **909/866-5600.** Main courses $5–$20. AE, DC, DISC, MC, V. Sun–Thurs 8am–9pm; Fri–Sat 8am–10pm.

LAKE ARROWHEAD

For an affluent residential community, there are surprisingly few dining options around Lake Arrowhead. But not surprisingly, what there is tends to run toward pricey elegance—elegant for a rustic mountain resort, that is. Although there are both a California/continental restaurant and a casual family eatery in the Lake Arrowhead Resort (see "Where to Stay," above), you might want to venture out to some of the locals' choices. These include the **Chef's Inn & Tavern,** 29020 Oak Terrace, Cedar Glen (ℂ **909/336-4488**), a moderate to expensive continental restaurant in a turn-of-the-century former bordello; the **Antler's Inn,** 26125 Calif. 189, Twin Peaks (ℂ **909/337-4020**), serving prime rib, seafood, and buffalo in a historic log lodge; the **Royal Oak,** 27187 Calif. 189, Blue Jay Village (ℂ **909/337-6018**), an expensive American/continental steak house with a pub; and **Belgian Waffle Works,** dockside at Lake Arrowhead Village (ℂ **909/337-5222**), an inexpensive coffee shop with Victorian decor, known for its generous, crispy waffles with tasty toppings.

4 Disneyland & Other Anaheim-Area Attractions

30 miles SE of downtown Los Angeles

The sleepy Orange County town of Anaheim grew up around Disneyland, the West's most famous theme park. Now, even beyond the park that bills itself the Happiest Place on Earth, the city and its neighboring communities are kid-central. Otherwise unspectacular, sprawling suburbs have become a playground of family hotels and restaurants, and unabashedly tourist-oriented attractions. Among the nearby draws are Knott's Berry Farm, another family-oriented theme park, in nearby Buena Park. At the other end of the scale is the Richard Nixon Library and Birthplace, a surprisingly compelling presidential library and museum, just 7 miles northeast of Disneyland in Yorba Linda.

ESSENTIALS

GETTING THERE   From Los Angeles, take I-5 south till you see signs for Disneyland; dedicated off-ramps from both directions lead to into the attractions' parking lots and surrounding streets. The drive from downtown L.A. takes approximately 45 minutes. If Anaheim is your first—or only—destination, and you want to avoid L.A. altogether, try flying directly into **John Wayne Airport** in Santa Ana (✆ **949/252-5200;** www.ocair.com), Orange County's largest airport. It's about 15 miles from Disneyland. Check to see if your hotel has a free shuttle to and from either airport (some will pick you up at LAX, 30 minutes away), or call one of the following commercial shuttle services (fares are generally $10 one way from John Wayne): **L.A. Xpress** (✆ 800/I-ARRIVE), **Prime Time** (✆ 800/262-7433), or **SuperShuttle** (✆ 714/517-6600). Car-rental agencies located at the John Wayne Airport include **Budget** (✆ 800/221-1203) and **Hertz** (✆ 800/654-3131).

VISITOR INFORMATION   The **Anaheim/Orange County Visitor and Convention Bureau,** 800 W. Katella Ave. (✆ **714/765-8888;** www.anaheimoc. org), can fill you in on area activities and shopping shuttles. It's across the street from Disneyland inside the Convention Center, next to the dramatic cantilevered arena. It's open Monday to Friday from 8:30am to 5:30pm. The **Buena Park Convention and Visitors Office,** 6280 Manchester Blvd., Suite 103 (✆ **800/541-3953** or 714/562-3560; www.buenapark.com/cvo), provides specialized information on the area, including Knott's Berry Farm.

THE DISNEYLAND RESORT 👹👹👹

It's not called "The Happiest Place on Earth" for nothing, you know . . . Disneyland sister parks have sprung up in Florida, Tokyo, and even France, but there's still nothing to compare with the original. Smaller than Walt Disney World, Disneyland has always capitalized on being the world's first family-oriented mega–theme park. Nostalgia is a big part of the appeal, and despite many advancements, changes, and expansions over the years, Disneyland remains true to the original vision of founder Walt Disney.

In 2001, Disney unveiled a brand-new theme park (California Adventure), a new shopping, dining, and entertainment district (Downtown Disney), and a third on-site hotel (Disney's California Adventure). They also revamped their own name to "The Disneyland Resort," reflecting a greatly expanded array of entertainment options. What does this all mean for you? Well, first of all, you'll probably want to think seriously about budgeting more time (and yes, more money) for your Disney visit—you'll need at least three full days to see it all. If you have limited time, plan carefully so you don't skip what's important to you; in the pages ahead we'll describe what to expect throughout the new resort. And, most of all, get ready to have fun—there's lots of great new stuff to check out!

ADMISSION, HOURS & INFORMATION   Admission to *either* Disneyland or California Adventure, including unlimited rides and all festivities and entertainment, is $43 for adults and children over 11, $41 for seniors 60 and over, $33 for children 3 to 11, and free for children under 3. Parking is $7. Three- and four-day "Park Hopper" passports are available, allowing you unlimited in-and-out privileges at *both* parks every day. Prices for adults/children are $111/$87 (3-day) and $137/$107 (4-day). In addition, some area accommodations offer lodging packages that include admission for one or more days.

Disneyland and California Adventure are open every day of the year, but operating hours vary, so we recommend that you call for information that applies to the specific day(s) of your visit (© 714/781-4565). The same information, including ride closures and show schedules, can also be found online at **www.disneyland.com**. Generally speaking, the parks are open from 9 or 10am to 6 or 7pm on weekdays, fall to spring; and from 8 or 9am to midnight or 1am on weekends, holidays, and during winter, spring, or summer vacation periods.

If you plan on arriving during a busy time (when the gates open in the morning, or between 11am and 2pm), purchase your tickets in advance and get a jump on the crowds at the ticket counters. Advance tickets may be purchased through Disneyland's website (www.disneyland.com), at Disney stores in the United States, or by calling the ticket mail order line (© 714/781-4043).

DISNEY TIPS   Disneyland is busiest from mid-June to mid-September and on weekends and school holidays year-round. Peak hours are from noon to 5pm; visit the most popular rides before and after these hours, and you'll cut your waiting times substantially. If you plan to arrive during a busy time, buy your tickets in advance and get a jump on the crowds at the ticket counters. Advance tickets may be purchased through Disneyland's website at www.disneyland.com, at Disney stores in the United States, or by calling the ticket mail-order line (© 714/781-4043).

Many visitors tackle Disneyland (or California Adventure) systematically, beginning at the entrance and working their way clockwise around the park. But a better plan of attack is to arrive early and run to the most popular rides— Rocket Rods, the Indiana Jones Adventure, Star Tours, Space Mountain, Big Thunder Mountain Railroad, Splash Mountain, the Haunted Mansion, and Pirates of the Caribbean in Disneyland; and Soarin' Over California, Grizzly River Run, and It's Tough to be a Bug in California Adventure. Lines for these rides can last an hour or more in the middle of the day. This time-honored plan of attack may eventually become obsolete, however, thanks to the new **FastPass** system. Here's how it works: Say you want to ride Space Mountain, but the line is long—*so* long the wait sign indicates a 75-minute standstill! Now you can head to the Automated FastPass ticket dispensers allow you to swipe the magnetic strip of your Disneyland entrance ticket, get a FastPass for later that day, and return to use the reduced-wait FastPass entrance. At press time, about a half dozen Disneyland rides were equipped with FastPass; several more will be added by the time you read this. The hottest features at California Adventure had FastPass built in from the start; for a complete list for each park, check your official map and guide when you enter.

Anaheim Area & Orange Coast Attractions

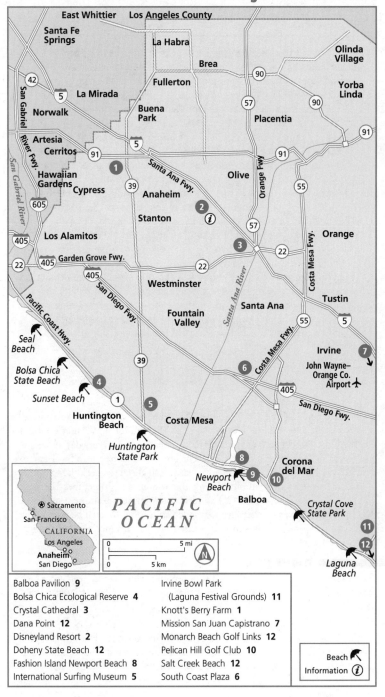

Balboa Pavilion **9**
Bolsa Chica Ecological Reserve **4**
Crystal Cathedral **3**
Dana Point **12**
Disneyland Resort **2**
Doheny State Beach **12**
Fashion Island Newport Beach **8**
International Surfing Museum **5**

Irvine Bowl Park
(Laguna Festival Grounds) **11**
Knott's Berry Farm **1**
Mission San Juan Capistrano **7**
Monarch Beach Golf Links **12**
Pelican Hill Golf Club **10**
Salt Creek Beach **12**
South Coast Plaza **6**

Beach
Information (i)

(Value The Art of the (Package) Deal

If you intend to spend 2 or more nights in Disney territory, it pays to investigate the bevy of packaged vacation options available. Start by contacting your hotel (even those in Los Angeles or San Diego), to see whether they have Disneyland admission packages. Many vacation packagers include Disneyland and/or California Adventure (and other attractions) with their inclusive packages; see p. ### in chapter 2, "Planning Your Trip to California," for information. And put a call in to the official Disney agency, **Walt Disney Travel Co. (©️ 800/225-2024** or 714/520-5050). You can request a glossy catalog by mail, or log onto **www.disneyland.com** and click on "Book Your Vacation" to peruse package details, take a virtual tour of participating hotel properties, and get online price quotes for customized, date-specific packages. Their packages are value-packed time-savers with abundant flexibility. Hotel choices range from the official Disney hotels to one of 35 "neighbor hotel" in every price range (economy to superior) and category (from motel to all-suite); a wide range of available extras includes admission to other southern California attractions and tours (like Universal Studios, or a Tijuana shopping spree), and behind-the-scenes Disneyland tours, all in limitless combinations. Every time we check, rates are highly competitive, considering each package includes multi-day admission, early park entry, free parking (at the Disney hotels), plus keepsake souvenirs and southern California coupon books.

If you're going to spend the night in Anaheim, you might want to consider staying at the **Disneyland Hotel, Paradise Pier Hotel,** or **Disney's Grand Californian.** Hotel guests get to enter the park early almost every day and enjoy the major rides before the lines form. The amount of time varies from day to day, but usually you can enter 1½ hours early. Call ahead to check the schedule.

Attendance falls dramatically during the winter, and sometimes the park offers discounted (about 25% off) admission to Southern California residents, who may buy up to six tickets per ZIP code verification. If you'll be visiting the park with someone who lives here, be sure to check in advance whether the special prices are in effect.

TOURING DISNEYLAND

The Disneyland complex is divided into several theme "lands," each of which has a number of rides and attractions that are, more or less, related to that land's theme.

MAIN STREET U.S.A.   At the park's entrance, Main Street U.S.A. is a cinematic version of turn-of-the-century small-town America. The whitewashed Rockwellian fantasy is lined with gift shops, candy stores, a soda fountain, and a silent theater that continuously runs early Mickey Mouse films. Here you'll find the practical things you might need, such as stroller rentals and storage lockers.

Because there are no rides, it's best to tour Main Street during the middle of the afternoon, when lines for rides are longest, and in the evening, when you can rest your feet in the theater that features "Great Moments with Mr. Lincoln," a patriotic (and audio-animatronic) look at America's 16th president. There's always something happening on Main Street; stop in at the information booth to the left of the main entrance for a schedule of the day's events.

ADVENTURELAND   Inspired by the most exotic regions of Asia, Africa, India, and the South Pacific, Adventureland is home to several popular rides. Here's where you can cavort inside **Tarzan's Treehouse,** a climb-around attraction based on the animated film. Its African-themed neighbor is the **Jungle Cruise,** where passengers board a large authentic-looking Mississippi River paddleboat and float along an Amazon-like river; a spear's throw away is the **Enchanted Tiki Room,** one of the most sedate attractions in Adventureland. Inside, you can sit down and watch a 20-minute musical comedy featuring electronically animated tropical birds, flowers, and "tiki gods."

The **Indiana Jones Adventure** is Adventureland's star ride. Based on the Steven Spielberg films, this ride takes adventurers into the Temple of the Forbidden Eye, in joltingly realistic all-terrain vehicles. Riders follow Indy and experience the perils of bubbling lava pits, whizzing arrows, fire-breathing serpents, collapsing bridges, and the familiar cinematic tumbling boulder (an effect that's very realistic in the front seats!).

NEW ORLEANS SQUARE   A large, grassy green dotted with gas lamps, New Orleans Square is home to the **Haunted Mansion,** the most high-tech ghost house we've ever seen; the clever events inside are as funny as they are scary.

Even more fanciful is **Pirates of the Caribbean,** one of Disneyland's most popular rides. Visitors float on boats through mock underground caves, entering an enchanting world of swashbuckling, rum-running, and buried treasure. Even in the middle of the afternoon you can dine by the cool moonlight and to the sound of crickets in the **Blue Bayou** restaurant, situated in the middle of the ride itself.

CRITTER COUNTRY   An ode to the backwoods, Critter Country is a sort of Frontierland without those pesky settlers. Little kids like to sing along with the audio-animatronic critters in the musical **Country Bear Jamboree** show. Older kids and grown-ups head straight for **Splash Mountain,** one of the largest water flume rides in the world. Loosely based on the Disney movie *Song of the South,* the ride is lined with about 100 characters that won't stop singing "Zip-A-Dee-Doo-Dah." Be prepared to get wet, especially if someone sizable is in the front seat of your log-shaped boat.

FRONTIERLAND   Inspired by 19th-century America, Frontierland features a raft to **Tom Sawyer's Island** and a do-it-yourself play area with balancing rocks, caves, and a rope bridge; board the **Big Thunder Mountain Railroad,** a runaway roller coaster that races through a deserted 1870s gold mine. You'll also find a petting zoo and an Abe Lincoln–style log cabin here; both are great for exploring with the little ones.

On Saturdays, Sundays, and holidays, and during vacation periods, head to Frontierland's **Rivers of America** after dark to see the FANTASMIC! show. It mixes magic, music, live performers, and sensational special effects. Just as he did in *The Sorcerer's Apprentice,* Mickey Mouse appears and uses his magical powers to create giant water fountains, enormous flowers, and fantasy creatures.

There's plenty of pyrotechnics, lasers, and fog, as well as a 45-foot-tall dragon that breathes fire and sets the water of the Rivers of America aflame.

MICKEY'S TOONTOWN   This is a colorful, whimsical world inspired by the "Roger Rabbit" films—a wacky, gag-filled land populated by 'toons. There are several rides, including **Roger Rabbit's CarToonSpin,** but they take a back seat to Toontown itself—a trippy, smile-inducing world without a straight line or right angle in sight.

FANTASYLAND   With a storybook theme, this is the catch-all "land" for stuff that doesn't quite fit anywhere else. Most of the rides are geared to the under-6 set, including the **King Arthur Carousel,** the **Dumbo the Flying Elephant ride,** and the **Casey Jr. Circus Train.** Some, like **Mr. Toad's Wild Ride** and **Peter Pan's Flight,** appeal to grown-ups as well. You'll also find Alice in Wonderland, Snow White's Scary Adventures, Pinocchio's Daring Journey, and more.

The most lauded attraction is **It's a Small World,** a slow-moving indoor river ride through a saccharine nightmare of all the world's children singing the song everybody loves to hate. For a different kind of thrill, try the **Matterhorn Bobsleds,** a zippy roller coaster through chilled caverns and drifting fog banks. It's one of the park's most popular rides.

TOMORROWLAND   Conceived as an optimistic look at the future, Tomorrowland employs an angular, metallic look popularized by futurists like Jules Verne.

Thrilling long-time Tomorrowland favorites **are Space Mountain** (a pitch-black indoor roller coaster that assaults your equilibrium and ears), and **Star Tours** (the original Disney–George Lucas joint venture; it's a 40-passenger Star-Speeder that encounters a space-load of misadventures on the way to the Moon of Endor, achieved with wired seats and video effects—not for the queasy).

TOURING CALIFORNIA ADVENTURE 🎡🎡

With a grand entrance designed to resemble one of those "Wish you were here" scenic postcards, California Adventure starts out with a bang. Beneath a scale model of the Golden Gate Bridge (watch carefully, the monorail passes overhead), handmade tiles of across-the-state scenes glimmer on either side. Just inside, an enormous gold titanium "sun" shines all day, illuminated by computerized heliostats that follow the real sun's path. From this point, visitors can head into three distinct themed areas, each containing rides, interactive attractions, live-action shows, and plenty of dining, snacking, and shopping opportunities. Two parades wind through the park, including the resurrected—and renamed—Disney's Electrical Parade.

THE GOLDEN STATE   This multi-dimensional area represents California's history, heritage, and physical attributes. Sound boring? Actually, the park's splashiest attractions are here. "Condor Flats" is a tribute to daring aviators; inside a weathered corrugated test-pilots' hangar is **Soarin' Over California,** the ride that immediately rose to the top on everyone's run-to-get-in-line-first list (it's equipped with FastPass, but often sells out by mid-day anyway). It uses cool cutting-edge technology to combine suspended seats with a spectacular IMAX-style surround-movie—so riders literally "soar" over California's scenic wonders.

Nearby, California Adventure's iconic "Grizzly Peak" towers over the **Grizzly River Run,** a splashy gold-country ride through caverns, mineshafts, and waterslides; it culminates with a wet plunge into a spouting geyser. Kids can cavort nearby on the **Redwood Creek Challenge Trail,** a forest playground with smokejumper cable slides, net climbing, and swaying bridges.

Pacific Wharf was inspired by Monterey's Cannery Row and features mouth-watering demonstration attractions by **Boudin Sourdough Bakery, Mission Tortillas,** and **Lucky Fortune Cookies.** If you get hungry, each has a food counter where you can enjoy soup-in-a-sourdough-bowl; tacos, burritos, and enchiladas; and teriyaki bowls, egg rolls, and wonton soup.

Straight from the imagination of Disney CEO Michael Eisner comes the "Bountiful Farm," constructed to pay tribute to California's rich agriculture. The Robert Mondavi **Golden Vine Winery** boasts a demonstration vineyard, Mission-style "aging room" (with a back-to-basics presentation on the art of winemaking), wine bars, and the park's most upscale eatery, **Vineyard Room** (see "Where to Dine," later in this chapter). Next to a demonstration produce garden lies another California Adventure "E ticket," the interactive film **"It's Tough To Be A Bug."** Using next-generation 3-D technology, *A Bug's Life* characters Flik and Hopper lead the audience on a slap-happy underground romp with bees, termites, grasshoppers, stink bugs, spiders, and a few surprises that keep everyone hopping, ducking, and laughing along.

PARADISE PIER   Journey back into the glory days of California's beachfront amusement piers—remember Santa Monica, Santa Cruz, Belmont Park?—on this fantasy boardwalk. Highlights include **California Screamin',** a classic roller coaster that replicates the whitewashed wooden white-knucklers of the past—but with state-of-the-art steel construction and a smooth, computerized ride. There's also the **Maliboomer,** a trio of towers (giant strongman sledgehammer tests) that catapult riders to the tip-top bell, then lets them down bungee-style with dangling feet; the **Orange Stinger,** a whooshing swing ride inside an enormous orange, complete with orange scent piped in; **Mulholland Madness,** a wacky wild-trip along L.A.'s precarious hilltop street; and the **Sun Wheel Carousel,** featuring unique zig-zagging cars that bring new meaning to the familiar ride.

There are all the familiar boardwalk games (complete with stuffed prizes), guilty-pleasure fast foods like pizza, corn dogs, and burritos.

HOLLYWOOD PICTURES BACKLOT   If you've visited Disney in Florida, you'll recognize many elements of this *trompe l'oeil* recreation of a Hollywood movie studio lot. Pass through a classic studio archway flanked by gigantic golden elephants, and you'll find yourself on a surprisingly realistic "Hollywood Boulevard." In the **Disney Animation** building, visitors can participate in several different interactive galleries: Learn how stories become animated features; watch Robin Williams become an animated character; listen to a Disney illustrator invent "Mushu" from *Mulan;* and even take a computerized personality test to see which Disney character *you* resemble most.

At the end of the street, the replica movie palace **Hyperion Theater** presents a live-action tribute to classic Disney films, and the **"Get A Grip"** stunt show pays tribute to stagehands and reveals some of the simple tricks behind movie illusion. Across the way, step aboard the **Superstar Limo,** where you're cast as a hot new star being chauffeured around Hollywood to sign a big movie deal; the wacky but tame ride winds through Malibu, Rodeo Drive, Beverly Hills, and the Sunset Strip.

The Backlot's main attraction is **Jim Henson's MuppetVision 3D,** an on-screen blast from the past featuring Kermit, Miss Piggy, Gonzo, Fozzie Bear—and even hecklers Waldorf and Statler. A bevy of dining options is led by the **ABC Soap Opera Bistro,** where you can dine in replica sets from your favorite soap operas.

TOURING DOWNTOWN DISNEY 🍂🍂

Borrowing a page from Central Florida's successful Disney compound, **Downtown Disney** is a district filled with restaurants, shops, and entertainment for all ages. Whether you want to stroll with kids in tow, have an upscale dinner-for-two, or party into the night, this colorful and sanitized "street scene" fills the bill.

The promenade begins at the amusement park gates and stretches toward the Disneyland Hotel; there are nearly 20 shops and boutiques, and a dozen-plus restaurants, live music venues, and entertainment options.

Highlights include **House of Blues,** the blues/jazz restaurant and club that features Delta-inspired cuisine and big-name music; **Ralph Brennan's Jazz Kitchen,** a spicy mix of New Orleans traditional foods and live jazz; **ESPN Zone,** the ultimate sports dining and entertainment experience, including an interactive game room; **Y Arriba! Y Arriba!,** where Latin cuisine combines with spicy entertainment and dancing; and **World of Disney,** one of the biggest Disney shopping experiences anywhere, with a vast and diverse range of toys, souvenirs, and collectibles. There is also a 12-screen multiplex, LEGO Imagination Center, Sephora cosmetics store, and much more.

Even if you're not staying at one of the Disney hotels, Downtown Disney is worth a visit. Locals and day-shoppers take advantage of the no-gate free entry and validated Downtown Disney parking lots (3 hours free, 5 hours free with restaurant or theater validation).

KNOTT'S BERRY FARM 🍂

Cynics say that Knott's Berry Farm is for people who aren't smart enough to find Disneyland. The reality is that Knott's simply can't compete with the Disney allure, and focuses on newer and faster thrill rides that target southern California youths and families instead.

Like Disneyland, Knott's Berry Farm is not without historical merit. Rudolph Boysen crossed a loganberry with a raspberry, calling the resulting hybrid the boysenberry. In 1933, Buena Park farmer Walter Knott planted the boysenberry and launched Knott's berry farm on 10 acres of leased land. When things got tough during the Depression, Mrs. Knott set up a roadside stand, selling pies, preserves, and home-cooked chicken dinners. Within a year she was selling 90 meals a day. Lines became so long that Walter decided to create an Old West Ghost Town as a diversion for waiting customers.

Locals flock to Knott's Berry Farm in the second half of October, when the entire park is revamped as "Knott's *Scary* Farm." The ordinary attractions are made spooky and haunted, every grassy area is transformed into a graveyard or gallows, and even the already-scary rides get special surprise extras, like costumed ghouls who grab your arm in the middle of a roller-coaster ride!

GETTING THERE   Knott's Berry Farm is at 8039 Beach Blvd. in Buena Park. It's about a 5-minute ride north on I-5 from Disneyland. From I-5 or Calif. 91, exit south onto Beach Boulevard. The park is about half a mile south of Calif. 91.

ADMISSION, HOURS & INFORMATION Admission to the park, including unlimited access to all rides, shows, and attractions, is $40 for adults and children 12 and over, and $30 for 60+seniors, kids 3 to 11, non-ambulatory visitors, and expectant mothers; children under 3 are admitted free. Admission is $16.95 for everyone after 4pm. Parking is $7. Like Disneyland, Knott's offers discounted admission for southern California residents during the off-season, so if you're bringing local friends or family members along, be sure to take advantage of the bargain. Also like Disneyland, Knott's Berry Farm's hours vary from week to week, so call ahead. The park generally is open during the summer daily from 9am to midnight. The rest of the year, it opens at 10am and closes at 6 or 8pm, except Saturday, when it stays open until 10pm. Knott's is closed December 25. Special hours and prices are in effect during Knott's Scary Farm in late October. Stage shows and special activities are scheduled throughout the day. Pick up a schedule at the ticket booth.

For more information, call ℂ 714/220-5200 or log onto **www.knotts.com**.

TOURING THE PARK
Knott's Berry Farm maintains much of its original Old West motif, and is divided into seven "Old Time Adventures" areas. The newest attraction—the one you'll see pictured on those freeway billboards—is the Perilous Plunge. True to the name, it's the world's tallest, steepest, wettest water ride. If that sounds good to you, climb aboard!

OLD WEST GHOST TOWN The park's original attraction is a collection of refurbished 19th-century buildings that have been relocated from deserted Old West towns. You can pan for gold, ride an authentic stagecoach, take rickety train cars through the Calico Mine, get held up aboard the Denver and Rio Grande Calico Railroad, and hiss at the villain during a melodrama in the Birdcage Theater.

FIESTA VILLAGE Here you'll find a south-of-the-border theme. That means festive markets, strolling mariachis, and wild rides like Montezooma's Revenge and Jaguar!, a roller coaster that includes two heart-in-the-mouth drops and a loop that turns you upside down.

THE ROARING '20s AMUSEMENT AREA This area contains Sky Tower, a parachute jump and drop with a 20-story free-fall. Other white-knuckle rides include XK-1, an excellent flight simulator "piloted" by the riders; and Boomerang, a state-of-the-art roller coaster that turns riders upside down six times in less than a minute. Kingdom of the Dinosaurs features extremely realistic *Jurassic Park*–like creatures. It's quite a thrill, but it may scare the little kids.

WILD WATER WILDERNESS This is a $10 million, 3½-acre attraction styled like a turn-of-the-century California wilderness park. The top ride is a white-water adventure called Bigfoot Rapids, with a long stretch of artificial rapids; it's the longest ride of its kind in the world.

CAMP SNOOPY This will probably be the youngsters' favorite area. It's meant to re-create a wilderness camp in the picturesque High Sierra. Its six rustic acres are the playgrounds of Charles Schulz's beloved beagle and his pals, Charlie Brown and Lucy, who greet guests and pose for pictures. The rides here, including Beary Tales Playhouse, are tailor-made for the 6-and-under set.

THUNDER FALLS Here you can look Mystery Lodge right in the eye. It's a truly amazing high-tech, trick-of-the-eye attraction based on the legends of local Native Americans. Don't miss this wonderful theater piece.

THE BOARDWALK   The park's newest theme area is a salute to southern California's beach culture. The main attraction is Windjammer, a dual roller coaster originally intended to evoke the flips and glides of windsurfing, but often advertised as a twister tornado.

WHERE TO STAY IN THE DISNEYLAND AREA
EXPENSIVE

The Disneyland Hotel ☆☆ *(Kids*   The holy grail of Disneygoers has always been this, the "Official Hotel of the Magic Kingdom." A direct monorail connection to Disneyland (and California Adventure) means you'll be able to return to your room anytime, whether to take a much-needed nap or to change your soaked shorts after your Splash Mountain or Grizzly Peak adventure. The theme hotel is a wild attraction unto itself, and the very best choice for families with small children. The rooms aren't fancy, but they're comfortably and attractively furnished, like a good-quality business hotel, and all have balconies. In-room amenities include movie channels (with free Disney Channel, naturally) and cute-as-a-button Disney-themed toiletries and accessories. This all-inclusive resort offers over 10 combined restaurants, snack bars, and cocktail lounges; every kind of service desk imaginable; a fantasy swimming lagoon with white-sand beach; and video game center. The complex includes the adjoining Paradise Pier Hotel, which offers a Disney version of Asian tranquility; adults and older kids looking to escape the frenetically colorful Disney atmosphere will appreciate this option.

Best of all, hotel guests get to enter the park early almost every day and enjoy the major rides before the lines form. The amount of time varies from day to day, but usually you can enter 1½ hours early. Call ahead to check the schedule.

When you're planning your trip, inquire about multiple-day packages that allow you to take on the park at your own pace and usually include free parking.

1150 Magic Way, Anaheim, CA 92802. (℃ **714/956-MICKEY** (central reservations) or 714/778-6600 (Disneyland Hotel) or 714/999-0990 (Paradise Pier Hotel). Reservations fax 714/956-6582. www.disneyland.com. 1,198 units. $170–$285 double; from $275 suite. AE, MC, V. Parking $10. **Amenities:** 10 restaurants, 3 lounges; 3 outdoor pools; health club; Jacuzzi; children's programs; game room; concierge; shopping arcade; salon; 24-hour room service; babysitting; laundry/dry cleaning service. *In room:* A/C, TV w/ pay movies, dataport, minibar, coffeemaker, hair dryer, safe.

Disney's Grand Californian Hotel ☆☆ *(Kids*   Disney spared no details when constructing this enormous version of an Arts and Crafts–era lodge (think Yosemite's Awhanee, Pasadena's Gamble House), hiring craftspeople throughout the state to contribute one-of-a-kind tiles, furniture, sculptures, and artwork. Taking inspiration from California's redwood forests, mission pioneers, and plein-air painters, designers managed to create a nostalgic yet state-of-the-art high-rise hotel.

Enter through subtle (where's the door?) stained-glass sliding panels to the hotel's centerpiece, a six-story "living room" with a William Morris–designed marble "carpet," an angled skylight which can be seen through exposed support beams, display cases of Craftsman treasures, and a 3-story walk-in "hearth" whose fire warms Stickley-style rockers and plush leather armchairs.

Guest rooms are spacious and smartly designed, carrying through the Arts-and- Crafts theme surprisingly well considering the hotel's grand scale. The best ones overlook the park (but you'll pay for that view). Despite the sophisticated, luxurious air of the Grand Californian, this is a hotel that truly caters to families, with a bevy of room configurations including one with a double bed plus bunk-beds-with-trundle. Because the hotel provides sleeping bags (rather than rollaways) for kids, this standard-size room will sleep a family of six—but you have to share the bathroom.

1600 So. Disneyland Dr., Anaheim, CA 92802. ✆ **714/956-MICKEY** (central reservations) or 714/635-2300. Fax 714/956-6099. www.disneyland.com. 751 units. $205–$335 double; from $345 suite. AE, DC, DISC, MC, V. Free self parking; valet $6. **Amenities:** 3 restaurants, lounge; 2 outdoor pools; health club and spa; Jacuzzi; children's center; game room/arcade; concierge; business center; 24-hour room service; laundry/ dry cleaning service; concierge-level rooms. *In room:* A/C, TV w/ pay movies, dataport, minibar, coffeemaker, hair dryer, iron, safe, portable crib.

Sheraton Anaheim Hotel ✦

This hotel rises to the festive theme-park occasion with its fanciful English Tudor architecture; it's a castle that lures business conventions, Disney-bound families, and local high school proms. The public areas are quiet and elegant—intimate gardens with fountains and koi ponds, plush lobby and lounges—which can be a pleasing touch after a frantic day at the amusement park. The rooms are modern and unusually spacious, but otherwise not distinctive. A large swimming pool sits in the center of the complex, surrounded by attractive landscaping. Don't be put off by the high rack rates; rooms commonly go for $100 to $130, even on busy summer weekends.

1015 W. Ball Rd. (at I-5), Anaheim, CA 92802. ✆ **800/325-3535** or 714/778-1700. Fax 714/535-3889. 489 units. $190–$225 double; $290–$360 suite. AE, DC, MC, V. Parking $10; free Disneyland shuttle. **Amenities:** 2 restaurants, lounge; outdoor pool; fitness center; Jacuzzi; concierge; 24-hour room service; laundry/ dry cleaning service; coin-op laundry. *In room:* A/C, TV w/ pay movies, dataport, minibar, coffeemaker, hair dryer, iron.

WestCoast Anaheim Hotel ✦

Although this hotel, in the Anaheim Convention Center complex (across the street from Disneyland), draws primarily a business crowd, it has much to appeal to the leisure traveler. The contemporary, comfortable rooms in the 12-story tower all have balconies overlooking either Disneyland or the hotel's luxurious pool area, which includes an attractive sundeck, and snack and cocktail bar gazebo. The front desk can provide fax machines and refrigerators upon request. The Old West frontier-themed restaurant serves steak and seafood along with a few colorful game selections.

1855 S. Harbor Blvd. (south of Katella Ave.), Anaheim, CA 92802. ✆ **800/426-0670** or 714/750-1811. Fax 714/971-2485. www.westcoastanaheimhotel.com. 500 units. $195 double. Disneyland package available. AE, DC, DISC, MC, V. Self-parking $10, valet $13; free Disneyland shuttle. **Amenities:** 2 restaurants, 2 lounges; outdoor pool; fitness center; deluxe Jacuzzi; activities desk; car-rental desk; 24-hour business center; room service (6am–11pm); laundry/dry cleaning service. *In room:* A/C, TV w/ pay movies and Sony PlayStation, dataport, coffeemaker, hair dryer, iron.

MODERATE

Anaheim Plaza Hotel ✦ *Value*

You can easily cross the street to Disneyland's main gate, or take the Anaheim Plaza's free shuttle. Once you return, you'll appreciate the way this 32-year-old hotel's clever design shuts out the noisy world. In fact, the seven two-story garden buildings remind me more of 1960s Waikiki than busy Anaheim. The Olympic-size heated outdoor pool and whirlpool are surrounded (unfortunately) by Astroturf, and the plain motel-style furnishings are beginning to look a little tired. On the plus side, nothing's changed about the light-filled modern lobby or the friendly rates, which often drop as low as $49.

1700 S. Harbor Blvd., Anaheim, CA 92802. ✆ **800/228-1357** or 714/772-5900. Fax 714/772-8386. 300 units. $79–$150 double; from $185 suite. Rates include continental breakfast. AE, DC, DISC, MC, V. Free parking and Disneyland shuttle. **Amenities:** Restaurant, lounge; outdoor pool; Jacuzzi; room service (8am–11pm); laundry/dry cleaning service; coin-op laundry. *In room:* A/C, TV, coffeemaker.

Candy Cane Inn ✶✶ *Value*   Take your standard U-shaped motel court with outdoor corridors, spruce it up with cobblestone drives and walkways, old-time street lamps, and flowering vines engulfing the balconies of attractively painted rooms, and you have the Candy Cane. The face-lift worked, making this gem near Disneyland's main gate a treat for the stylish bargain hunter. The guest rooms are decorated in bright floral motifs with comfortable furnishings, including queen beds and a separate dressing and vanity area. Breakfast is served in the courtyard, where you can also splash around in a heated pool, spa, or kids' wading pool.

1747 S. Harbor Blvd., Anaheim, CA 92802. ✆ **800/345-7057** or 714/774-5284. Fax 714/772-5462. 173 units. $84–$129 double. Rates include expanded continental breakfast. AAA discount available. AE, DC, DISC, MC, V. Free parking and Disneyland shuttle. **Amenities:** Outdoor pool; Jacuzzi; laundry/dry cleaning service; coin-op laundry. *In room:* A/C, TV, coffeemaker, hair dryer.

Howard Johnson Hotel ✶   This hotel occupies an enviable location, directly opposite Disneyland, and a cute San Francisco trolley car runs to and from the park every 30 minutes. Guest rooms were renovated in 1999. They're divided among several low-profile buildings, all with balconies opening onto a central garden with two heated pools for adults and one for children. Garden paths lead under eucalyptus and olive trees to a splashing circular fountain. During the summer you can see the nightly fireworks display at Disneyland from the upper balconies of the park-side rooms. Try to avoid the rooms in the back buildings, which get some freeway noise. Services and facilities include room service from the attached Coco's Restaurant, airport shuttle, and family lodging/Disney admission packages. We think it's pretty classy for a HoJo's.

1380 S. Harbor Blvd., Anaheim, CA 92802. ✆ **800/422-4228** or 714/776-6120. Fax 714/533-3578. www.hojoanaheim.com. 320 units. $74–$109 double. AE, DC, DISC, MC, V. Free parking and Disneyland trolley. **Amenities:** Restaurant; 3 outdoor pools; Jacuzzi; concierge; game room; room service (7am–11pm); laundry/dry cleaning service; coin-op laundry. *In room:* A/C, TV w/ pay movies, dataport, fridge, coffeemaker.

Radisson Resort Knott's Berry Farm ✶ *Kids*   Within easy walking distance of Knott's Berry Farm, this spit-shined Radisson (the former Buena Park Hotel) also offers a free shuttle to Disneyland, 7 miles away. The pristine lobby has the look of a business-oriented hotel, and that it is. But vacationers can also benefit from the elevated level of service. Be sure to ask about "Super Saver" rates (as low as $99—with breakfast—at press time), plus Knott's or Disneyland package deals. The rooms in the nine-story tower were tastefully redecorated when Radisson took over. Doting parents can even treat their kids to a Snoopy-themed room!

7675 Crescent Ave. (at Grand), Buena Park, CA 90620. ✆ **800/333-3333** or 714/995-1111. Fax 714/828-8590. www.radisson.com/buenaparkca. 320 units. $129–$139 double; $159–$299 suite. Discounts and packages available. AE, DC, DISC, MC, V. Free parking and Disneyland shuttle. **Amenities:** 2 restaurants, lounge; outdoor pool; night-lit tennis courts; fitness center; Jacuzzi; video arcade; concierge; 24-hour room service; laundry/dry cleaning service; self-service laundry. *In room:* A/C, TV w/ pay movies, fax, dataport, coffeemaker, hair dryer, iron, safe.

INEXPENSIVE

Best Western Anaheim Stardust   Located on the back side of Disneyland, this modest hotel will appeal to the budget-conscious traveler who isn't willing to sacrifice everything. All rooms have a refrigerator and microwave, breakfast is served in a refurbished train dining car, and you can relax by the large outdoor heated pool and spa while using the laundry room. The extra-large family rooms accommodate virtually any brood, and shuttles run regularly to the park.

1057 W. Ball Rd., Anaheim, CA 92802. © **800/222-3639** or 714/774-7600. Fax 714/535-6953. www. bestwestern.com. 121 units. $64–$89 double; $105 family room. Rates include full breakfast. AE, DC, DISC, MC, V. Free parking and Disneyland shuttle. **Amenities:** Restaurant; outdoor heated pool; Jacuzzi; self-service laundry. *In room:* A/C, TV, fridge.

WHERE TO DINE IN THE DISNEYLAND AREA

If you're visiting the Disneyland Resort, chances are you'll probably eat at one of the many choices either inside the theme parks or at Downtown Disney; there are plenty of restaurants to choose from for all tastes and budgets. At Disneyland, in the Creole-themed **Blue Bayou,** you can sit under the stars inside the Pirates of the Caribbean ride—no matter what time of day it is. California Adventure features two bonified sit-down options: **Avalon Cove** is a Wolfgang Puck seafood restaurant overlooking a boardwalk amusement zone, and the Robert Mondavi-backed **Vineyard Room** offers upscale prix-fixe wine country cuisine matched to Mondavi wines (the more casual Golden Vine Terrace is downstairs). Make reservations early in the day for dinner, as they all fill up pretty quickly.

And at Knott's Berry Farm, try the fried-chicken dinners and boysenberry pies at Mrs. Knott's historic **Chicken Dinner Restaurant** (see below for full listing). We've also listed some of the best bests in the surrounding area, including nearby **Orange,** whose charming historic downtown is home to several of the region's best dining options, if you're willing to drive 10 to 15 minutes.

Citrus City Grille ✦✦ CALIFORNIAN Though housed in Orange's second-oldest brick building, this sophisticated crowd-pleaser is furnished without an antique in sight, paying homage to the town's agricultural (citrus) legacy with a bold industrial chic. World-inspired appetizers range from Hawaiian-style ahi poke to southeast Asian coconut shrimp tempura accented with spiced apricots. Main courses come from the Mediterranean (pasta and risotto), Mexico (carne asada with avocado-corn relish), the American south (authentic Louisiana gumbo), and your Mom's kitchen (meatloaf smothered in gravy and fried onions). Gleaming bar shelves house myriad bottles for the extensive Martini menu, and outdoor foyer tables are nicely protected from the street.

122 No. Glassell St. (½ block north of Chapman), Orange. © **714/639-9600.** Reservations recommended. Main courses $8–$13 lunch; $12–$24 dinner. AE, DC, MC, V. Tues–Sat 11:30am–3pm and 5–10pm.

Felix Continental Cafe ✦ CUBAN/SPANISH If you like the re-created Main Street in the Magic Kingdom, you'll love the historic 1886 town square in the city of Orange, on view from the cozy sidewalk tables outside the Felix Continental Cafe. Dining on traditional Cuban specialties (such as citrus-marinated chicken, black beans and rice, and fried plantains) and watching traffic spin around the magnificent fountain and rose bushes of the plaza evokes old Havana or Madrid rather than the cookie-cutter Orange County communities just blocks away. The food receives praise from restaurant reviewers and loyal locals alike.

36 Plaza Sq. (at the corner of Chapman and Glassell), Orange. © **714/633-5842.** Reservations recommended for dinner. Main courses $6–$14. AE, DC, MC, V. Mon–Thurs 7am–9pm; Fri 7am–10pm; Sat 8am–10pm; Sun 8am–9pm.

Mrs. Knott's Chicken Dinner Restaurant ✦ *Kids* AMERICAN Knott's Berry Farm got its start as a down-home diner, and you can still get a hearty all-American meal without even entering the theme park. The restaurant that started it all, descended from Cordelia Knott's humble Depression-era farmland tea room, stands just outside the park's entrance, with plenty of free parking for patrons. Looking just as you'd expect—country cute, with window shutters and paisley a'plenty —the restaurant's featured attraction is the original fried chicken dinner, complete with soup, salad, buttermilk biscuits, mashed potatoes and gravy, and a slice of famous pie. Country fried steak, pot roast, roast turkey, and pork ribs are options, as well as sandwiches, salads, and a terrific chicken pot pie. Boysenberries abound (of course!), from breakfast jam to traditional double-crust pies, and there's even an adjacent take-out shop that's always crowded.

8039 Beach Blvd. (near La Palma), Buena Park. © **714/220-5080.** Reservations not accepted. Main courses $5–$7; complete dinners $10.95. AE, DC, DISC, MC, V. Sun–Thu 7am– 8:30pm; Fri 7am– 9pm; Sat 7am–9:30pm.

The White House 🏨🏨 NORTHERN ITALIAN/FRENCH   Once surrounded by nothing but orange groves, this stately 1909 Colonial-style mansion now sits on a wide industrial street just 5 minutes from Disneyland. It's set nicely back, though, framed by lovely lawns and gardens, and exudes gentility and nostalgia. The huge home is nicely restored inside and out; the restaurant opened in 1981, when it was named after its stylistic cousin in Washington— *the* White House. Owner Bruno Serato maintains this architectural treasure, serving northern Italian cuisine—with a French accent—in elegant white-on-white rooms on the main and second floors. Dinner courses are whimsically named for fashion giants (Versace whitefish, Prada rack of lamb), and sometimes arrive on oddly shaped platters that work better as artwork than dishware. But chef David Libby knows what he's doing, applying just the right amount of sauce to pastas both formal (gnocchi in velvety Gorgonzola sauce) and rustic (linguini with chunky garlic, roasted peppers, and olives). Prices tend to reflect the suited-expense-account and well-heeled-retiree crowd, but lunch prices (including a terrific prix-fixe bargain) deliver the same bang for fewer bucks.

887 Anaheim Blvd. (north of Ball Rd.), Anaheim. © **714/772-1381.** www.anaheimwhitehouse.com. Reservations recommended at dinner. Main courses $10–$16 lunch; $18–$28 dinner. AE, MC, V. Mon–Fri 11:30am–2pm and 5–10pm; Sat–Sun 5–10pm.

5 The Orange Coast

Huntington Beach is 39 miles S of Los Angeles; Newport Beach, 49 miles; Dana Point, 65 miles

Whatever you do, don't say "Orange County" here. The mere name evokes images of smoggy industrial parks, cookie-cutter housing developments, and the staunch Republicanism that prevails behind the so-called "orange curtain." We're talking instead about the Orange Coast, one of southern California's best-kept secrets, a string of seaside jewels that have been compared with the French Riviera or the Costa del Sol. Here, 42 miles of beaches offer pristine stretches of sand, tide pools teeming with marine life, ecological preserves, charming secluded coves, quaint pleasure-boat harbors, and legendary surfers atop breaking waves. Whether your bare feet want to stroll a funky wooden boardwalk or your gold card gravitates toward a yacht club, you've come to the right place.

ESSENTIALS
GETTING THERE   See "Orientation," in chapter 13, "Los Angeles," for airport and airline information. By car from Los Angeles, take I-5 or I-405 south. The scenic, shore-hugging Pacific Coast Highway (Calif. 1, or just PCH to the locals) links the Orange Coast communities from Seal Beach in the north to Capistrano Beach just south of Dana Point, where it merges with I-5. To reach

A Special Arts Festival

A tradition for 60-plus years in arts-friendly Laguna, the **Festival of Arts and Pageant of the Masters** is held each summer throughout July and August. Festivities include a fantastic performance-art production in which live actors re-create famous Old Masters paintings, live music, crafts sales, art demonstrations and workshops, and the grass-roots Sawdust Festival across the street. Grounds admission is $3; pageant tickets range from $15 to $40. Call ℂ **800/487-FEST** or 949/494-1145, or check out www.foapom.com.

---

the beach communities directly, take the following freeway exits: **Seal Beach,** Seal Beach Boulevard from I-405; **Huntington Beach,** Beach Boulevard/Calif. 39 from either I-405 or I-5; **Newport Beach,** Calif. 55 from either I-405 or I-5; **Laguna Beach,** Calif. 133 from I-5; **San Juan Capistrano,** Ortega Highway/ Calif. 74 from I-5; and **Dana Point,** Pacific Coast Highway/Calif. 1 from I-5.

VISITOR INFORMATION   The **Huntington Beach Conference & Visitors Bureau,** 417 Main St., Suite A-2 (ℂ **800/SAY-OCEAN** or 714/969-3492; www.hbvisit.com), genially offers tons of information, enthusiasm, and personal anecdotes. Open Monday through Friday from 9am to 5pm.

The **Newport Beach Conference & Visitors Bureau,** 3300 W. Coast Hwy. (ℂ **800/94-COAST** or 949/722-1611; www.newportbeach-cvb.com), distributes brochures, sample menus, a calendar of events, and its free and helpful *Visitor's Guide.* Call or stop in Monday through Friday from 8am to 5pm (plus weekends in summer).

The **Laguna Beach Visitors Bureau,** 252 Broadway (ℂ **800/877-1115** or 949/497-9229; www.lagunabeachinfo.org), is in the heart of town and distributes lodging, dining, and art-gallery guides. It's open Monday through Friday from 9am to 5pm and on Saturday from 10am to 4pm (plus Sundays in summer).

The **San Juan Capistrano Chamber of Commerce,** Franciscan Plaza, 31781 Camino Capistrano, Suite 306 (ℂ **949/493-4700;** www.sanjuancapistrano. com), is within walking distance of the mission and offers a walking-tour guide to historic sites. Open Monday through Friday from 8:30am to 4pm.

The **Dana Point Chamber of Commerce,** 24681 La Plaza, Suite 120 (ℂ **800/ 290-DANA** or 949/496-1555; www.danapoint-chamber.com), is open Monday through Friday from 9am to 4:30pm and carries some restaurant and lodging information as well as a comprehensive recreation brochure.

DRIVING THE ORANGE COAST

You'll most likely be exploring the coast by car, so we cover the beach communities in order, from north to south. Keep in mind, however, that if you're traveling between Los Angeles and San Diego, the Pacific Coast Highway (Calif. 1) is a splendidly scenic detour that adds less than an hour to the commute—so pick out a couple of destinations and go for it.

Huntington Beach is probably the largest Orange Coast city; it stretches quite a ways inland and has seen the most urbanization. To some extent, this has changed the old boardwalk and pier into a modern outdoor mall where cliques of kids coexist with families and the surfers who continue to flock here, drawn by Huntington's legendary place in surf lore. Hawaiian surfer Duke Kahanamoku brought the sport here in the 1920s, and some say the breaks around the pier and Bolsa Chica are the best in California. The world's top wave-riders flock to Huntington each August for the rowdy but professional **U.S. Open of Surfing** (call ℭ **949/885-8200** for information).

The name **Newport Beach** conjures comparisons to Rhode Island's Newport, where the well-to-do enjoy seaside living with all the creature comforts. That's the way it is here, too, but on a less grandiose scale. From the million-dollar Cape Cod–style cottages on sunny Balboa Island in the bay to elegant shopping complexes like Fashion Island and South Coast Plaza (an über-mall with valet parking, car detailing, limo service, and concierge), this is where fashionable socialites, right-wing celebrities, and business mavens can all be found. Alternatively, you could explore **Balboa Peninsula's** historic Pavilion and old-fashioned pier or board a passenger ferry to Catalina Island.

Laguna Beach, whose breathtaking geography is marked by bold elevated headlands, coastal bluffs, and pocket coves, is known as an artists' enclave, but the truth is that Laguna has became so *in* (read: expensive) that it's driven most of the true Bohemians *out.* Their legacy remains with the annual **Festival of Arts and Pageant of the Masters** (see "A Special Arts Festival," above), as well as a proliferation of art galleries intermingling with high-priced boutiques along the town's cozy streets. In warm weather, Laguna Beach has an overwhelming Mediterranean-island ambiance, which makes *everyone* feel beautifully, idly rich.

San Juan Capistrano, nestled in the verdant headlands just inland of Dana Point, is defined by Spanish missions and its loyal flock of swallows. The mission architecture is authentic, and history abounds. Consider San Juan Capistrano a compact, life-size diorama illustrating the evolution of a small western town from Spanish-mission era to secular rancho period, into statehood and the 20th century. Ironically, Mission San Juan Capistrano (see "Seeing the Sights," below) is once again the center of the community, just as the founding friars intended 200 years ago.

Dana Point, the last town south, has been called a "marina development in search of a soul." Overlooking the harbor stands a monument to 19th-century author Richard Henry Dana, who gave his name to the area and described it in *Two Years Before the Mast.* Activities generally center around yachting and Dana Point's jewel of a harbor; nautical themes are everywhere. Bordering the harbor is Doheny State Beach (see "Beaches & Nature Preserves," below), with seaside park and camping facilities.

ENJOYING THE OUTDOORS

BEACHES & NATURE PRESERVES The **Bolsa Chica Ecological Reserve,** in Huntington Beach (ℭ **714/897-7003**), is a 300-acre restored urban salt marsh that's a haven to more than 200 bird species as well as a wide variety of protected plants and animals. Naturalists come to spot herons and egrets as well as California horn snails, jackknife clams, sea sponges, common jellyfish, and shore crabs. An easy $1\frac{1}{2}$-mile loop trail begins from a parking lot on the Pacific Coast Highway (Calif. 1) a mile south of Warner Boulevard; docents lead a narrated walk the first Saturday of every month. The Bolsa Chica Conservancy has been working since 1978 on reclaiming the wetlands from oil companies that began drilling here 70 years ago. It's an ongoing process, and you can still see those "seesaw" drills dotting the outer areas of the reserve.

Huntington City Beach, adjacent to Huntington Pier, is a haven for volleyball players and surfers; dense crowds abound, but at least so do amenities like outdoor showers, beach rentals, and restrooms. Just south of the city beach is 3-mile-long **Huntington State Beach.** Both popular beaches have lifeguards and concession stands seasonally. The state beach also has restrooms, showers, barbecue pits, and a waterfront bike path. The main entrance is on Beach Boulevard, and there are access points all along the Pacific Coast Highway (Calif. 1).

Newport Beach runs for about 5 miles and includes both Newport and Balboa Piers. There are outdoor showers, restrooms, volleyball nets, and a vintage boardwalk that just may make you feel as though you've stepped 50 years back in time. **Balboa Bike and Beach Stuff** (✆ **949/723-1516**), at the corner of Balboa and Palm near the pier, rents a variety of items, from pier fishing poles to bikes, beach umbrellas, and body boards. The **Southwind Kayak Center,** 2801 W. Pacific Coast Hwy. (✆ **800/768-8494** or 949/261-0200; www.southwindkayaks.com), rents sea kayaks for use in the bay or open ocean at rates of $10 to $14 per hour; instructional classes are available on weekends, with some midweek classes in summer. It also conducts bird-watching kayak expeditions into the Upper Newport Bay Ecological Reserve at rates of $40 to $65.

Crystal Cove State Park, which covers 3 miles of coastline between Corona del Mar and Laguna Beach and then extends up into the hills around El Moro Canyon, is a good alternative to the more popular beaches for you seekers of solitude. (There are, however, lifeguards and restrooms.) The beach is a winding, sandy strip, backed with grassy terraces; high tide sometimes sections it into coves. The entire area offshore is an underwater nature preserve. There are four entrances, including Pelican Point and El Moro Canyon. For more information, call ✆ **949/494-3539.**

Salt Creek Beach Park lies below the palatial Ritz-Carlton Laguna Niguel; guests who tire of the pristine swimming pool venture down the staircase on Ritz-Carlton Drive to wiggle their toes in the sand. The setting is marvelous, with wide white-sand beaches looking out toward Catalina Island. (Why do you think the Ritz-Carlton built here?) There are lifeguards, restrooms, a snack bar, and convenient parking near the hotel.

Doheny State Beach in Dana Point has long been known as a premier surfing spot and camping site. Just south of lovely Dana Point Marina (enter off Del Abispo Street), Doheny has the friendly vibe of beach parties in days gone by: Tree-shaded lawns give way to wide beaches, and picnicking and beach camping are encouraged. There are 121 sites for both tents and RVs, plus a state-run visitor center featuring several small aquariums of sea and tide-pool life. For more information and camping availability, call ✆ **949/492-0802.**

BICYCLING Biking is the most popular beach activity up and down the coast. A slower-paced alternative to driving, it allows you to enjoy the clean, fresh air and notice smaller details of these laid-back beach towns and harbors. The Newport Beach Visitor Center (see "Visitor Information," above) offers a free Bike Ways map of trails throughout the city and harbor. Bikes and equipment can be rented at **Balboa Bike & Beach Stuff,** 601 Balboa Blvd., Newport Beach (✆ 949/723-1516); **Laguna Beach Cyclery,** 240 Thalia St. (✆ 949/494-1522); and **Dana Point Bicycle,** 34155 Pacific Coast Hwy. (✆ 949/661-8356).

GOLF Many golf-course architects have used the geography of the Orange Coast to its full advantage, molding challenging and scenic courses from the rolling bluffs. Most courses are private, but two outstanding ones are open to the public. **The Links at Monarch Beach,** 33033 Niguel Rd., Dana Point (✆ **949/ 240-8247**), is particularly impressive, a hilly and challenging course designed by Robert Trent Jones, Jr. Most holes offer great ocean views, but afternoon winds can sneak up, so accuracy is essential. Weekend greens fees are $145 ($115 weekdays).

Another challenge is the **Pelican Hill Golf Club,** 22651 Pelican Hill Rd. S., Newport Beach (© **949/760-0707** starter; 949/640-0238 pro shop; www. pelicanhill.com), with two Tom Fazio–designed courses. The Ocean North course is heavily bunkered, while the Ocean South course features canyons and rocky ravines; both have difficult, large, multi-tier greens. Weekend greens fees are $250, weekdays $175. And remember, when putting near the ocean, the break is always toward the water!

SEEING THE SIGHTS

The charm of the pretty little neighborhood of **Balboa Island** isn't diminished by knowing that the island was man-made—and it certainly hasn't affected the price of real estate. Tiny clapboard cottages in the island's center and modern houses with two-story windows and private docks along the perimeter make a colorful and romantic picture. You can drive onto the island on Jamboree Road to the north or take the three-car ferry from Balboa Peninsula (about $1.50 per vehicle). It's generally more fun to park and take the ferry as a pedestrian, because the tiny alleys they call streets are more suitable for strolling, there are usually crowds, and parking spaces are scarce. **Marine Avenue,** the main commercial street, is lined with small shops and cafes that evoke a New England fishing village. Refreshing shaved ices sold by sidewalk vendors will relieve the heat of summer.

International Surfing Museum   Nostalgic Gidgets and Moondoggies shouldn't miss this monument to the laid-back sport that has become synonymous with California beaches. You'll find gargantuan long boards from the sport's early days, memorabilia of Duke Kahanamoku and the other surfing greats represented on the "Walk of Fame" near Huntington Pier, and a gift shop where a copy of the *Surfin'ary* can help you bone up on your surfer slang even if you can't "Hang 10."

411 Olive Ave., Huntington Beach. © **714/960-3483.** www.surfingmuseum.org. Admission $2 adults, $1 students, free for kids under 7. Mid-June to late Sept daily noon–5pm; rest of the year Wed–Sun noon–5pm.

Balboa Pavilion ★ (Kids)   This historic cupola-topped structure, a California Historical Landmark, was built in 1905 as a bathhouse for swimmers in their ankle-length bathing costumes. Later, during the Big Band era, dancers rocked the Pavilion doing the "Balboa Hop." Now it serves as the terminal for Catalina Island passenger service, harbor and whale-watching cruises, and fishing charters. The surrounding boardwalk is the Balboa Fun Zone, a collection of carnival rides, game arcades, and vendors of hot dogs and cotton candy. For Newport Harbor or Catalina cruise information, call © **949/673-5245;** for sportfishing and whale-watching, call © **949/673-1434.**

400 Main St., Balboa, Newport Beach. © **949/673-5245.** From Calif. 1, turn south onto Newport Blvd. (which becomes Balboa Blvd. on the peninsula); turn left at Main St.

Laguna Art Museum   This beloved local institution is working hard to position itself as the artistic cornerstone of the community. In addition to a small but interesting permanent collection, the museum presents installations of regional works definitely worth a detour. Past examples include a display of surf photography from the coast's 1930s and '40s golden era, and dozens of plein-air impressionist paintings (ca. 1900 to 1930) by the founding artists of the original colony. The museum is also open during Laguna Beach Artwalk, the first Thursday each month, when all are admitted free.

307 Cliff Dr., Laguna Beach. © **949/494-8971.** www.lagunaartmuseum.org. Admission $5 adults, $4 students and seniors, free for kids under 12. Tues–Sun 11am–5pm.

Mission San Juan Capistrano   The 7th of the 21 California coastal missions, Mission San Juan Capistrano is continually being restored. The mix of old ruins and working buildings is home to small museum collections and various adobe rooms that are as quaint as they are interesting. The intimate mission chapel with its ornate baroque altar is still regularly used for religious services, and the mission complex is the center of the community, hosting performing arts, children's programs, and other cultural events year-round.

This mission is best known for its **swallows,** which are said to return to nest each year at their favorite sanctuary. According to legend, the birds wing their way back to the mission annually on March 19, St. Joseph's Day, arriving here at dawn; they are said to take flight again on October 23, after bidding the mission farewell. In reality, however, you can probably see the well-fed birds here any day of the week, winter or summer.

Ortega Hwy. (Calif. 74), San Juan Capistrano. ℂ 949/234-1300. www.missionsjc.com. Admission $6 adults, $5 seniors, $4 children. Daily 8:30am–5pm.

 ## Artistic Laguna: A Guide to Gallery-Hopping

Within moments of entering town, you'll realize you can't turn a corner without encountering one of Laguna's more than 100 galleries. I've highlighted some of the best below. You can also pick up an expanded gallery guide at the Laguna Beach Visitors Bureau (see "Visitor Information," above). *Local Arts* is a slick, colorful, free quarterly that covers all of Orange County, with a particularly good emphasis on the Laguna galleries.

Most of the area's galleries line Coast Highway; they're easy to spot, clustered together throughout town. At the northern end of town lies historic **Gallery Row** (where you'll also find the Laguna Art Museum; see "Seeing the Sights," above), dating back to the founding of Laguna's original artists' colony. **Laguna North Gallery,** 376 N. Coast Hwy. (ℂ 949/494-4324; open Wed to Fri 11am to 5pm), showcases 12 local artists, with an emphasis on watercolorists. Many of these originals are quite affordable, and the artists often hang around this friendly gallery and will discuss their work with visitors. Down the street is **California Art Gallery,** 305 N. Coast Hwy., Suite A (ℂ 949/494-7270; open Wed to Sat 11am to 5pm, Sun noon to 5pm), which showcases early California oil and watercolor artists, plus the work of eight contemporary plein-air painters; it also offers Arts and Crafts furniture and pottery.

Farther south along Coast Highway, across the street from the Surf & Sand Hotel, is the **Art Center,** a collection of around a dozen galleries. While quality (and prices) vary widely, even casual browsers should stop into the **Redfern Gallery,** 1540 S. Coast Hwy. (ℂ 949/497-3356; open Wed to Sun 10am to 5pm), which has specialized for more than 20 years in the California Impressionist School. This school, active from the 1890s to the 1940s, was the primary focus of Laguna's founding artists. Many of the gallery's pieces are museum quality, and they often carry fascinating stories of former owners.

SHOPPING

Shoppers from all over the Southland flock to the two excellent malls listed below. If that isn't to your taste, a drive along the Pacific Coast Highway will yield many other opportunities for browsing and souvenir purchases.

Fashion Island Newport Beach   It's actually *not* an island, unless you count the nearly impenetrable sea of skyscrapers that border this posh mall, which is designed to resemble an open-air Mediterranean village. Anchored by Neiman-Marcus, Bloomingdale's, and Macy's, the mall is lined with outdoor artwork, upscale shops, and specialty boutiques including Allen Allen women's casual wear and the trendy Optical Shop of Aspen; 12 different restaurants offer something for everyone. 401 Newport Center Dr., Newport Beach. © **949/721-2000**. www. fashionisland-nb.com.

South Coast Plaza ★★   South Coast Plaza, one of the most upscale shopping complexes in the world, is so big that it's a day's adventure unto itself. This beautifully designed center is home to some of fashion's most prominent boutiques, including Emporio Armani, Chanel, Alfred Dunhill, and Coach; beautiful branches of the nation's top department stores such as Saks Fifth Avenue and Nordstrom; and outposts of the best high-end specialty shops like Williams Sonoma, L.A. Eyeworks, and Rizzoli Booksellers. The multidimensional mall is also home to many impressive works of modern art, and snacking and dining options are a cut above as well—you won't find Hot-Dog-on-a-Stick among the 40 or so restaurants scattered throughout. Wolfgang Puck Cafe, Morton's of Chicago, Ghirardelli Soda Fountain, Planet Hollywood, and Scott's Seafood Grill lure the hungry away from Del Taco and McDonald's. 3333 Bristol St. (at I-405), Costa Mesa. © **800/782-8888** or 714/435-2000. www.southcoastplaza.com.

WHERE TO STAY
VERY EXPENSIVE

Ritz-Carlton Laguna Niguel ★★★   The Old World meets the Pacific Rim at this glorious hotel, majestically set among terraces and fountained gardens on a 150-foot-high bluff above a 2-mile-long beach. There's a beautiful limestone fireplace in the elegant, silk-lined lobby, and lush foliage abounds throughout the interior. A ravishingly arched lounge is perfect for watching the sun set over the Pacific. The service, in Ritz-Carlton style, is unassuming and impeccable. Some guests, however, might find the hotel's palatial airs out of keeping with the beachy location. The spacious rooms are outfitted with sumptuous furnishings and fabrics; despite their generous size, some are overfurnished to the point of being cramped. All come with a terrace; an Italian marble bathroom equipped with double vanity; three phones (with voice mail); and a shoe polisher. Some rooms even have fireplaces.

1 Ritz-Carlton Dr., Dana Point, CA 92629. © **800/241-3333** or 949/240-2000. Fax 949/240-0829. 393 units. $375–$645 double; from $515 suite. Children under 18 stay free in parents' room. Midweek and special packages available. AE, DC, DISC, MC, V. Parking $25. **Amenities:** 4 restaurants, 6 bars; tennis courts; health club; Jacuzzi; sauna; children's programs; concierge; regular shuttle service to/from the beach and the golf course; business center; 24-hour room service; in-room massage; babysitting; dry cleaning/laundry service; executive-level rooms. *In room:* A/C, TV w/ pay movies, minibar, hair dryer, iron, safe.

Surf and Sand Resort ★★   The fanciest hotel in Laguna Beach has come a long way since it started life in 1937 as a modest little inn with just 13 units. Still occupying the same fantastic oceanside location, it now features dozens of top-of-the-line luxurious rooms that, despite their standard size, feel enormously decadent. They're very bright and beachy; every one is done entirely in white and has a private balcony with an ocean view, a marble bathroom, and plush robes. Some have whirlpool tubs. Try to get a deluxe corner room. Stunning Splashes restaurant serves three meals daily in a beautiful oceanfront setting; the Mediterranean cuisine is perfect against a backdrop of sunlight and crashing waves.

1555 S. Coast Hwy. (south of Laguna Canyon Rd.), Laguna Beach, CA 92651. ⓒ **800/524-8621** or 949/497-4477. Fax 949/494-2897. www.surfandsandresort.com. 164 units. Apr–Oct $290–$440 double, from $475 suite; Nov–Mar $275–$350 double, from $450 suite. AE, DC, DISC, MC, V. **Amenities:** Restaurant, bar; outdoor heated pool; spa; Jacuzzi; summer children's programs; concierge; business center; room service (6:30am–10pm); in-room massage; babysitting; dry cleaning/laundry service; concierge-level rooms. *In room:* TV w/ pay movies, minibar, hair dryer, iron, safe.

EXPENSIVE

Portofino Beach Hotel   This oceanfront inn, built in a former seaside rail station, is located just steps away from the Newport Pier, along a stretch of beachy bars and equipment-rental shacks; the beach is across the parking lot. The place maintains a calm, European air even in the face of the midsummer beach frenzy. Although it can get noisy in summer, there are advantages to being at the center of the action. The hotel has its own enclosed parking, and sunsets are spectacular when viewed from a plush armchair in the upstairs parlor. Guest rooms, furnished with old-world antique reproductions, are on the second floor—the first is occupied by a guests-only bar and several cozy sitting rooms—and most have luxurious skylit bathrooms.

2306 W. Ocean Front, Newport Beach, CA 92663. ⓒ **949/673-7030.** Fax 949/723-4370. www.portofinobeachhotel.com. 20 units. $159–$279 double. Rates include continental breakfast. Free parking. AE, DC, DISC, MC, V. **Amenities:** Jacuzzi; dry-cleaning/laundry service; coin-op laundry. *In room:* A/C, TV.

MODERATE

Blue Lantern Inn ✦   A newly constructed three-story New England–style gray clapboard inn, the Blue Lantern is a pleasant cross between romantic B&B and sophisticated small hotel. Almost all the rooms, which are decorated with reproduction traditional furniture and plush bedding, have a balcony or deck overlooking the harbor. All have a fireplace and whirlpool tub. You can have your breakfast here in private (clad perhaps in the fluffy robe provided), or go downstairs to the sunny dining room that also serves complimentary afternoon tea. There is an exercise room and a cozy lounge with menus for many area restaurants. The friendly staff welcomes you with home-baked cookies at the front desk.

34343 St. of the Blue Lantern, Dana Point, CA 92629. ⓒ **800/950-1236** or 949/661-1304. Fax 949/496-1483. www.foursisters.com. 29 units. $150–$500 double. Rates include full breakfast and afternoon wine and hors d'oeuvres. AE, DC, MC, V. **Amenities:** Jacuzzi; exercise room; complimentary bicycles; dry cleaning/laundry service. *In room:* A/C, TV w/ VCR., minibar, coffeemaker, hair dryer.

Casa Laguna ✦   Once you see this romantic terraced complex of Spanish-style cottages amid impossibly lush gardens and secluded patios, which offers all the amenities of a B&B *and* affordable prices, you might wonder: What's the catch? Well, the noise of busy PCH wafts easily into Casa Laguna, a background hum that might prove disturbing to sensitive ears and light sleepers. Still, the Casa has been a favorite hideaway since Laguna's early days, and now glows under the watchful eye of a terrific new owner, who's been upping the comfort ante. Some rooms—especially the suites—are downright luxurious, with fireplace, kitchen, bathrobes, CD player, VCR, and other in-room goodies.

Throughout the property, Catalina tile adorns fountains and bougainvillea spills into paths; each room has an individual charm. Breakfast is served in the sunny morning room of the Crafstman-style Mission House, where a cozy living room also invites relaxation and conversation.

2510 S. Coast Hwy., Laguna Beach, CA 92651. ⒸⓇ 800/233-0449 or 949/494-2996. Fax 949/494-5009. 21 units. $120–$195 double; $195–$295 suite. Rates include breakfast and afternoon wine and hors d'oeuvres. Off-season and midweek discounts available. AE, DISC, MC, V. **Amenities:** Heated outdoor pool; Jacuzzi. *In room:* TV.

WHERE TO DINE

Crab Cooker SEAFOOD   Since 1951, folks in search of fresh, well-prepared seafood have headed to this bright-red former bank building. Also a fish market, the Crab Cooker has a casual atmosphere of humble wooden tables, uncomplicated smoked and grilled preparations, and meticulously selected fresh fare. The place is especially proud of its Maryland crab cakes and recently added clams and oysters to its repertoire.

2200 Newport Blvd., Newport Beach. ⒸⓇ 949/673-0100. Main courses $8–$19 lunch; $10–$25 dinner. AE, MC, V. Sun–Thurs 11am–9pm; Fri–Sat 11am–10pm.

5′0″ (Five Feet) ⋆⋆ CALIFORNIA/ASIAN   While 5′0″ may no longer break culinary ground, chef and proprietor Michael Kang still combines the best in California cuisine with Asian technique and ingredients. The restaurant has a minimalist, almost-industrial decor that's brightened by a friendly staff and splendid cuisine. Menu selections run the gamut from tea-smoked filet mignon topped with Roquefort cheese and candied walnuts to a hot Thai-style mixed grill of veal, beef, lamb, and chicken stir-fried with sweet peppers, onions, and mushrooms in curry-mint sauce. The menu changes daily, but you can always find the house specialty, whole braised catfish. And controversy continues on the origin of this restaurant's funny name; some believe it refers to its elevation (5 feet above sea level), while others insist it's the height of diminutive Kang!

328 Glenneyre, Laguna Beach. ⒸⓇ 949/497-4955. Reservations recommended. Main courses $18–$30. AE, DC, DISC, MC, V. Sun–Thurs 5–10pm; Fri–Sat 5–11pm.

Las Brisas *Moments*   MEXICAN SEAFOOD   Las Brisas is popular for its breathtaking view of the Pacific, sunset drinks, and alfresco appetizers—so popular that it can get pretty crowded during the summer months. Affordable during lunch but pricey at dinner, the menu consists mostly of seafood recipes from the Mexican Riviera. Even the standard enchiladas and tacos get a zesty update with crab or lobster meat and fresh herbs. Calamari steak is sautéed with bell peppers, capers, and herbs in a garlic-butter sauce, and king salmon is mesquite broiled and served with a creamy lime sauce. Although a bit on the touristy side, Las Brisas can be a fun part of the Laguna Beach experience.

361 Cliff Dr. (off the PCH north of Laguna Canyon), Laguna Beach. ⒸⓇ 949/497-5434. Reservations recommended. Main courses $10–$24. AE, DC, DISC, MC, V. Mon–Sat 8am–10:30pm; Sun 9am–10:30pm.

Ramos House Cafe ⋆⋆ REGIONAL AMERICAN   Hidden away in the historic Rios district next to the train tracks, this converted 1881 cottage brings the flavor of a simpler time to busy Orange County. The small seasonal menu of regional American favorites utilizes garden-grown herbs, house-baked breads, and hand-turned ice cream. The all-purpose breakfast-lunch menu (dinner only for special events) features warmly satisfying cinnamon-apple beignets, wild mushroom and sun-dried-tomato omelets, fried green tomatoes sauced with goat cheese, southern fried chicken salad bathed in pumpkin seed–buttermilk dressing, shrimp and sourdough bread pudding, an always-changing but always superb fresh soup, and more comfort food faves with a Southern flair. Seating is outside, on a tree-shaded brick garden patio that invites leisure.

31752 Los Rios St. (off Del Obispo St.), San Juan Capistrano. ℂ 949/443-1342. Main courses $5–$10. AE, DC, DISC, MC, V. Tues–Sun 8am–3pm.

Roy's of Newport Beach ✫ HAWAIIAN REGIONAL/PACIFIC RIM   Any foodie who's been to Hawaii in the past decade knows the name of Roy Yamaguchi, father of Hawaiian Regional Cuisine (HRC) and the islands' answer to Wolfgang Puck. Roy's empire expanded to southern California in 1999, with the opening of this immediately successful dinner-only restaurant on the fringe of Fashion Island shopping center. Yamaguchi developed a menu that faithfully represents his groundbreaking East/West/Polynesian cuisine but can be reliably executed by chefs in far-flung kitchens. Most of each night's specials are fresh Pacific fish, given the patented HRC touch with Japanese, Thai, and even Latin accents. Signature dishes include island-style ahi poke, spicy Mongolian-glazed rack of lamb, and blackened yellowfin tuna in soy-mustard-butter sauce. The bar whips up "vacation" cocktails in tropical colors, and there's a to-die-for chocolate soufflé dessert.

453 Newport Center Dr., Fashion Island. ℂ 949/640-ROYS. Reservations suggested. Main courses $16–$29. AE, DC, DISC, MC, V. Mon–Thurs 5–10pm; Fri–Sat 5–11pm.

15

The Southern California Desert

by Stephanie Avnet Yates

To the casual observer, southern California's desert seems desolate—nothing but vast landscapes baking under a relentless sun. Its splendor is subtle, though; you have to discover its beauty in your own time. For some travelers it will be the surprising lushness of trees, flowering cacti, fragrant shrubs, and other plants—many of them unique to the region—that have adapted ingeniously to the harsh climate. The unique Joshua tree, which some deem majestic and others call ugly, thrives in the upper Mojave Desert. Each spring, the ground throughout the Lancaster area is carpeted with brilliant golds and oranges of the poppy, California's state flower. Like the autumn leaves in New England, the poppies draw seasonal tourists in droves.

If it looks as though nothing except insects could survive here, look again: You're bound to see a speedy roadrunner or a tiny gecko dart across your path. Close your eyes and listen for the cry of a hawk or an owl. Check the ground for coyote or bobcat tracks. Notice the sparkle of fish in the streams running through flourishing palm oases. Check the road signs, which warn of desert tortoise crossings. The tortoise is just one of the many endangered species found only here; fortunately, most of the southern California desert's flora and fauna is protected by the federal government in a wildlife sanctuary.

Perhaps the beauty you seek is that of personal renewal in the spectacular desert landscape. Whether it's in the shadow of purple-tinged mountains, amid otherworldly rock formations, or beside a sparkling swimming pool, you'll find as much or as little to occupy your time as you desire. Destinations range from gloriously untouched national parks to ultra-luxurious resorts—and it's a rare day when the sun doesn't shine out here.

1 En Route to the Palm Springs Resorts

If you're making the drive from Los Angeles via I-10, your first hour or so will be spent just, well, getting out of the L.A. metropolitan sprawl. Soon you'll leave the Inland Empire auto plazas behind, sail past the last of the bedroom-community shopping malls, and edge ever closer to the snowcapped (if you're lucky) San Bernardino and San Jacinto mountain ranges. (Coming from San Diego via I-15, the area discussed below is east of the junction with I-10.)

For frequent travelers on this stretch of highway, there are certain unmistakable signposts. Roadside attractions are part of what makes every moment of the vacation enjoyable. Below are three of our favorites.

Desert Hills Premium Outlets Factory-outlet malls are all the rage among bargain-hunters, and this one is truly a cut above the rest—or maybe it's just so massive, the schlock gets lost in the shuffle. Pick up a map to help navigate this

---

(Fun Fact   Jurassic Park in the Desert

As the cities give way to pale, dry desert, keep your eyes peeled for the dinosaurs that stand guard over the **Wheel Inn Restaurant** (② **760/ 849-7012**), in Cabazon. That's right, a four-story-tall brontosaurus and his Tyrannosaurus rex pal. You can even climb into the belly of the larger one, where you'll find a remarkably spacious gift shop.

---

two-part behemoth, or you may find yourself browsing Timberland when you'd rather be shopping the Gap. Some of our faves: Kenneth Cole, J. Crew, Eddie Bauer, Coach, Barney's New York, A/X Armani Exchange, Banana Republic, Donna Karan DKNY, Max Studio, Nike, and Quiksilver. The list goes on; there are 15 shoe stores alone here.

48400 Seminole Dr. (off I-10), Cabazon. ② **909/849-6641.** Sun–Thurs 10am–8pm; Fri 10am–9pm; Sat 9am–9pm.

Hadley's Fruit Orchards   This friendly emporium has been a fixture here since 1931, long before the outlet mall went up down the road. It's always packed with folks shopping for dates, dried fruits, nuts, honey, preserves, and other regional products. A snack bar serves the beloved date shake; there are also plenty of gift-packed treats to carry (or ship) home. (For more about the date mystique, see "Sweet Treat of the Desert: The Coachella Valley Date Gardens," later in this chapter.)

48190 Seminole Dr. (off I-10), Cabazon. ② **800/854-5655** or 909/849-5255. www.hadleys.com. Mon–Thurs 8am–8pm; Fri–Sun 8am–9pm.

Windmill Tours   Travelers through the San Gorgonio Pass have, for years, been struck by an awesome and otherworldly sight: never-ending windmill fields that harness the powerful force of the wind gusting through this passage and convert it to electricity to power air-conditioners throughout the Coachella Valley. If you really get a charge from them, consider a unique guided tour offering a look into this alternative energy source. Learn how designers have improved the efficiency of wind turbines (technically they're not windmills, which are used in the production of grain) over the years, and measure those long rotors against the average human height (about 10 people could lie along one span).

Interstate 10, Indian Ave. exit, Palm Springs. ② **877/449-WIND** or 760/251-1997. www.windmilltours.com. Admission $23 adults, $20 seniors, $15 students, $10 kids under 14. Tours Mon–Sat at 9am, 11am, 1pm, and 3pm (varies seasonally).

2 Get Your Kicks on Historic Route 66

There's a way for nostalgia buffs to take a detour down memory lane on their way to desert destinations: Just eschew the fast-paced, faceless I-10 for a very special interstate highway—Route 66.

It's been immortalized in film, song, literature, memory, and the popular imagination. But is anything really left of this great snaking highway, this dependable, comforting spirit John Steinbeck called "the Mother Road?" What of the path to adventure traveled by Tod and Buz in their trademark red Corvette on the namesake 1960s TV series?

The answer is, yes, it's still there: You just have to be willing to look for it.

Until the final triumph of the multi-lane superslab in the early 1960s, Route 66 was the only automobile route between the windy Chicago shores of Lake Michigan and L.A.'s golden Pacific beaches. "America's Main Street" rambled through eight states, and today, in each one, there are enthusiastic organizations dedicated to preserving its remnants. California is fortunate to have a lengthy stretch of the original highway, many miles of which still proudly wear the designation "California State Highway 66." It's not just weed-split abandoned blacktop, either. These are active streets, often the main commercial drag of the community. Many stretches have become clusters of new home developments, stucco shopping centers, and fast-food chains. Pretty mundane—until you round a curve and unexpectedly see a vintage wood-frame house, perhaps from a pre–Great Depression ranch. There's poignancy here: That house was probably set way back from the road, amidst a shady grove, before highway workers buried the front yard under asphalt.

Other picturesque relics of that bygone era—single-story motels, friendly two-pump gas stations—exist beside their modern neighbors, inviting nostalgia for a slower, simpler time, a time when the vacation began the moment you backed out of the driveway.

ESSENTIALS

THE ROUTE Our drive begins in Pasadena and ends in downtown San Bernardino, 56 miles west of Palm Springs. In San Bernardino, I-215 intersects Route 66; take it 4 miles south to rejoin I-10 and continue east.

Note: This detour works equally well if your destination is Lake Arrowhead or Big Bear Lake; take I-215 north 3 miles to Calif. 30 and continue into the mountains. For more information, see chapter 14, "Side Trips from Los Angeles." The drive will add anywhere from 30 minutes to 3 hours to your trip, depending on how many relics and photo opportunities you stop to enjoy. Some suitably retro meal suggestions are included in case you want to incorporate lunch into your drive.

VISITOR INFORMATION For more information, contact the **National Historic Route 66 Federation,** headquartered in the Los Angeles area (© 818/ 352-7232; www.national66.com). There's also a quarterly *Route 66 Magazine;* for information, call © 520/635-4322 (www.route66magazine.com).

LET'S HIT THE ROAD!

Although Route 66 officially ended at the picturesque Pacific, there are very few reminders left in the heart of L.A. Besides, we assume you've already seen the city, so Pasadena is the best point to begin your time-warp experience.

One of our favorite places is the **Fair Oaks Pharmacy,** Fair Oaks Avenue and Mission Street, 1.6 miles south of Colorado Boulevard (© 626/799-1414; open Mon through Sat from 9am to 6pm, Sun from 11am to 6pm), a fixture on this street corner since 1915. If you're in the mood for a treat, try an authentic ice-cream soda, a sparkling phosphate, a "Route 66" sundae, or an old-fashioned malt (complete with the frosty mixing can), all served by today's fresh-faced soda jerks from behind the marble counter. They also serve soup, sandwiches, and other snacks. The Fair Oaks is still a dispensing pharmacy and offers a variety of charming gifts, including an abundance of Route 66–themed items.

Perhaps you'd like some appropriate driving music, or a souvenir to help you reminisce about your Route 66 experience later. If so, there's no better place than **Canterbury Records,** 805 E. Colorado Blvd., a block west of Lake Avenue (© 626/792-7184), open Monday through Friday from 9am to 8pm, Saturday from 9am to 6pm, and Sunday from 10am to 5pm. It has L.A.'s finest selection of big bands and pop vocalists on CD and cassette; perhaps you'll choose one of the many renditions of Bobby Troup's homage, "(Get Your Kicks on) Route 66."

As you continue east on Colorado Boulevard, keep your eyes peeled for **motels** like the Saga Motor Hotel, Swiss Lodge, Siesta Inn, Astro (fabulous *Jetsons*-style architecture), and Hi-Way Host. In fact, lodgings have proven the hardiest post-66 survivors, and you'll be seeing many unique frozen-in-time motor courts along the way.

Turn left on Rosemead Boulevard, passing under the freeway (boo, hiss) to Foothill Boulevard. Turning right, you'll soon be among the tree-lined residential streets of **Arcadia,** home to the Santa Anita Racetrack and the Los Angeles Arboretum, the picturesque former estate of "Lucky" Baldwin, whose Queen Anne cottage has been the setting for many movies and TV shows. Passing into Monrovia, look for the life-size plastic cow on the southeast corner of Mayflower. It marks the drive-thru called **Mike's Dairy**—a splendid example of this auto-age phenomenon. If you're observant, you'll see many drive-thru dairies along our route (mostly Alta-Dena brand). Mike's has all the typical features, including the refrigerated island display case still bearing a vintage DRIFTWOOD DAIRY PRODUCTS price sign.

Next, look for Magnolia Avenue and the outrageous **Aztec Hotel** on the northwest corner. Opened in 1925, the Aztec was a local showplace, awing guests with its overscale, dark, Native American–themed lobby; garish Mayan murals; and exotic Brass Elephant bar. An arcade of shops once held the city's most prominent barbershop, beauty salon, and pharmacy. Little has changed about the interior, and a glance behind the front desk will reveal the original cord-and-plug telephone switchboard still in use. If you care to wet your whistle, stop into the bar before continuing on.

Leaving the Aztec, you'll pass some splendid Craftsman bungalows and other historic homes. The street dead-ends at Mountain Avenue; turn right to catch up with the 1930s alignment of Route 66. Make a left turn on Huntington Drive, and look out for **The Trails,** a prime example of the "wagon wheel–Wild West" theme restaurants. Its super-tall DINING sign will let you know when you're getting close. Now you're in **Duarte,** where Huntington Drive is lit by graceful and ornate double street lamps on the center median. This stretch also has many fabulous old motor courts; see if you can spot the Filly, Ranch Inn, Evergreen, and Capri.

Crossing over the wide but nearly dry San Gabriel River, glance right from the bridge to see cars streaming along the interstate that supplanted Route 66. In Irwindale—which smells just like the industrial area it is, with manufacturing plants ranging from a Miller brewery to Health Valley Foods—the street resumes the Foothill Boulevard name, and you'll pass into Azusa. Look for the elegant 1932 **Azusa City Hall and Auditorium,** whose vintage lampposts and Moorish fountain enhance a charming courtyard.

Our route swerves right onto Alosta Avenue at the **Foothill Drive-In Theater,** southern California's last single-screen drive-in. As you cruise by, think of the days when our cars were an extension of our living rooms (with the great snacks Mom wouldn't allow at home), and the outdoor theaters were filled every summer evening by dusk.

Continuing on Alosta, you'll enter Glendora, named in 1887 by founder George Whitcomb for his wife, Ledora. Look for the **Palm Tropics,** one of the best-maintained old motels along the route. On the northeast corner of Grand

Avenue stands the "world-famous" **Derby East** restaurant. It's not affiliated with the legendary Hollywood watering hole, but was clearly built in the 1940s to capitalize on both its famous namesake and the nearby Santa Anita Racetrack. Farther along on the left-hand side is the **Golden Spur,** which began 70 years ago as a ride-up hamburger stand for the equestrian crowd. Unfortunately, the restaurant has been remodeled in boring stucco, leaving only the original sign, with its neon cowboy boot, as a reminder of its colorful past. In a block or two, you'll pass briefly through San Dimas, a ranch-like community where you must pay attention to the HORSE CROSSING street signs. At the corner of Cataract Avenue, a covered wagon announces the **Pinnacle Peak** restaurant, guarded by a giant steer atop the roof.

Don't blink, because almost immediately the street rejoins Foothill Boulevard, passing underneath the ramps to I-210 (boo, hiss); now you're in La Verne, home of **La Paloma** Mexican cafe, a fixture on the route for many years. Continue on to the community of Claremont, known these days for the highly respected group of **Claremont Colleges.** You'll pass several of them along this eucalyptus-lined boulevard. In days gone by, drivers would cruise along this route for mile upon mile, through orchards and open fields, the scenery punctuated only by ambling livestock or a rustic wood fence.

At Benson Avenue in Upland, a classic **1950s-style McDonald's** stands on the southeast corner, its golden arches flanking a low, white, walk-up counter with outdoor stools. The fast-food chain has its roots in this region: Richard and

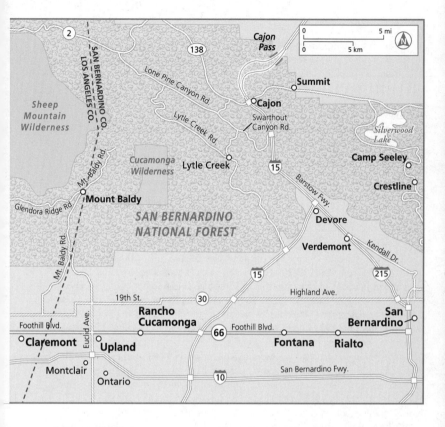

Maurice McDonald opened their first burger joint in San Bernardino in 1939. The successful brothers expanded their business, opening locations throughout southern California, until entrepreneur Ray Kroc purchased the chain in 1955 and franchised McDonald's nationwide. Farther along, look north at the intersection of Euclid Avenue for the regal **monument to pioneer women.**

Pretty soon you'll be cruising through Rancho Cucamonga, whose fertile soil still yields a reliable harvest. You might see impromptu **produce stands** springing up by the side of the road; stop and pick up a fresh snack. If you're blessed with clear weather, gaze north at the gentle slope of the **San Gabriel Mountains** and you'll understand how Foothill Boulevard got its name. The construction codes in this community are among the most stringent in California, designed to respect the region's heritage and restrict runaway development. All new buildings are Spanish-Mediterranean in style and amply landscaped. At the corner of San Bernardino Road, the playful architectural bones of a wonderful old service station can't be obscured by the flashy car-stereo/cellular-phone store that inhabits it now. Across the street is the **Sycamore Inn,** nestled in a grove of trees and looking very much like an old-style stagecoach stop. This reddish-brown wooden house, dating from 1848, has been a private home and gracious inn; today, it serves the community of Cucamonga as a restaurant and civic hall.

Rancho Cucamonga has earnestly preserved two historic wineries. First you'll see the **Thomas Vineyards,** at the northeast corner of Vineyard Avenue, established in 1839. Legend holds that the first owner mysteriously disappeared,

Take a Break

If all this driving has made you hungry, consider the **Magic Lamp Inn**, 8189 Foothill Blvd. ((*℃* 909/981-8659), open for lunch and dinner Tuesday through Friday and dinner only on Saturday and Sunday. Built in 1957, the Magic Lamp offers excellent continental cuisine (nothing nouvelle about Route 66!) in a setting that's part manor house and part *Aladdin* theme park. Dark, stately dining rooms lurk behind a funky banquette cocktail lounge punctuated by a psychedelic fountain/fire pit and a panoramic view. The genie-bottle theme is everywhere, from the restaurant's dinnerware to the plush carpeting, which would be right at home in a Las Vegas casino. Lovers of kitsch and hearty retro fare shouldn't pass this one up.

leaving hidden treasure still undiscovered on the property. The winery's preserved structures now hold two eateries, a country crafts store, and a bookstore housed in the former brandy still. Take a minute to stop into the shopping mall behind the Thomas Winery to tour the **Route 66 Territory Museum and Visitor's Bureau** (*℃* 909/592-2090), a minimuseum and gift shop. You'll see lovingly tended exhibits of old gas pumps, road signs, and other relics, plus an array of books, maps, glassware, garments, jewelry, and other souvenirs. Many items bear the original black-on-white Route 66 shield, the ubiquitous highway marker purged from the old route by state transportation officials in 1984. The brown markers you see today were subsequently placed by the historical associations.

Continuing on to Hellman Avenue, look for the **New Kansan Motel** (on the northeast corner). With that name, it must have seemed welcoming to Dust Bowl refugees. Near the northwest corner of Archibald Avenue, you'll find lonely remnants of a **1920s–era gas station.** Empty now, those service bays have seen many a Ford, Studebaker, and Packard in need of a helping hand. Next you'll pass the **Virginia Dare Winery,** at the northwest corner of Haven Avenue, whose structures now house part of a large business park/shopping mall, but retain the flourish of the original (1830s) winery logo.

Soon you'll pass the I-15 junction and be driving through Fontana, whose name in Italian means "fountain city." There isn't too much worth stopping for along this stretch, but definitely slow down to have a look at the **motor-court hotels** lining both sides of the road. They're of various vintages, all built to cater to the once-vigorous stream of travelers passing through. Although today they're dingy, the melody of their names conjures up those glory days: Ken-Tuck-U-Inn, Rose Motel, Moana, Dragon, Sand & Sage, Sunset, 40 Winks, and Redwing.

After entering Rialto, be on the lookout for Meriden Avenue, site of the fanciful **Wigwam Motel.** Built in the 1950s (along with an identical twin motor court in Holbrook, Arizona), the whimsy of these stucco tepees lured many a road-weary traveler in for the night. Its catchy slogan, "Sleep in a wigwam, get more for your wampum," has been supplanted today by the more to-the-point "Do it in a teepee." But, as with many of the motor courts we'll pass on this drive, you need only picture a few large, shiny Buicks, T-bird convertibles, and "woodie" station wagons pulling in for the night and your imagination will drift back to days gone by.

Soon Foothill Boulevard will become Fifth Street, a sign that you're nearing **San Bernardino,** which must have been a welcome sight for hot and weary westbound travelers emerging from the Mojave Desert. Route 66 wriggled through the steep Cajon Pass into a land fragrant with orange groves, where agricultural prosperity had quickly earned this region a lasting sobriquet: "the Inland Empire."

The year 1928 saw the grand opening of an elegant movie palace, the **California Theater,** 562 W. Fourth St., only a block from Route 66. From Fifth Street east, turn right at E Street, then make a right on Fourth Street, where you can pull over to view the theater. Lovingly restored and still popular for nostalgic live entertainment and the rich tones of its original Wurlitzer pipe organ, the California was a frequent site of Hollywood "sneak previews." Humorist Will Rogers made his last public appearance here, in 1935. (Following his death, the highway was renamed the "Will Rogers Memorial Highway" in his honor, but it remained popularly known as Route 66.) Notice the intricate relief of the theater's stone facade, and peek into the lobby to see the red velvet draperies, rich carpeting, and gold-banistered double staircase leading up to the balcony.

The theater is the last stop on your time-warp driving tour. Continue west on Fourth Street to the superslab highway only 2½ blocks away—that's I-215, your entry back to the present (see "Essentials," above).

3 The Palm Springs Desert Resorts

120 miles E of Los Angeles, 135 miles NE of San Diego

Palm Springs had been known for years as a golf-course-studded retirement mecca that's invaded annually by raucous hordes of libidinous college kids on spring break. Well, the city of Palm Springs has been quietly changing its image and attracting a whole new crowd. Former mayor (later U.S. congressman) Sonny Bono's revolutionary "anti-thong" ordinance in 1991 put a lightning-quick halt to the spring-break migration by eliminating public display of the bare coed derrière, and the upscale fairway-condo crowd has decided to congregate in the tony outlying resort cities of Rancho Mirage, Palm Desert, Indian Wells, and La Quinta.

These days, there are no billboards allowed in Palm Springs itself, all the palm trees in the center of town are appealingly back-lit at night, and you won't see the word "motel" on any establishment. Senior citizens are everywhere, dressed to the nines in brightly colored leisure suits and keeping alive the retro-kitsch establishments from the days when Elvis, Liberace, and Sinatra made the balmy desert a swingin' place. But they're not alone: Baby boomers and yuppies nostalgic for the kidney-shaped swimming pools and backyard luaus of the Eisenhower/Kennedy glory years are buying ranch-style vacation homes and restoring them to their 1950s splendor. Hollywood's young glitterati are returning, too. Today, the city fancies itself a European-style resort with a dash of good ol' American small town thrown in for good measure—think *Jetsons* architecture and the crushed-velvet vibe of piano bars with the colors and attitude of a laid-back Aegean island village. One thing hasn't changed: Swimming, sunbathing, golfing, and playing tennis are still the primary pastimes in this convenient little oasis.

Another important presence in Palm Springs has little to do with socialites and Americana. The Agua Caliente band of **Cahuilla Indians** settled in this area 1,000 years before the first golf ball was ever teed up. Recognizing the beauty and spirituality of this wide-open space, they lived a simple life around the natural mineral springs on the desert floor, migrating into the cool canyons during the hot summer months. Under a treaty with the railroad companies and the

U.S. government, the tribe owns half the land on which Palm Springs is built and actively works to preserve Native American heritage. It's easy to learn about the American Indians during your visit, and it will definitely add to your appreciation of this part of California.

ESSENTIALS

GETTING THERE   Several airlines service the **Palm Springs Regional Airport,** 3400 E. Tahquitz Canyon Way (© **760/323-8161**), including **Alaska Airlines** (© **800/426-0333;** www.alaskaair.com), **America West** (© **800/235-9292;** www.americawest.com), **Delta/Skywest** (© **800/453-9417;** www.delta-air.com), **United Express** (© **800/241-6522;** www.ual.com), and **US Airways Express** (© **800/428-4322;** www.usairways.com). Flights from Los Angeles International Airport take about 40 minutes. For more information, see "Orientation," in chapter 13, "Los Angeles."

If you're driving from Los Angeles, take I-10 east to the Calif. 111 turnoff to Palm Springs. You'll breeze into town on North Palm Canyon Drive, the main thoroughfare. The trip from downtown Los Angeles takes about 2 hours. If you're driving from San Diego, take I-15 north to I-10 east; it's a little more than 2 hours.

VISITOR INFORMATION   Be sure to pick up *Palm Springs Life* magazine's free monthly **"Desert Guide."** It contains tons of visitor information, including a comprehensive calendar of events. Copies are distributed in hotels and newsstands and by the **Palm Springs Desert Resorts Convention & Visitors Bureau,** in the Atrium Design Centre, 69930 Calif. 111, Suite 201, Rancho Mirage, CA 92270 (© **800/41-RELAX** or 760/770-9000). The bureau's office staff can help with maps, brochures, and advice Monday through Friday from 8:30am to 5pm. They also operate a 24-hour information line (© **760/770-1992**) and a website (www.PalmSpringsUSA.com).

Another website worth browsing is **www.inpalmsprings.com**, which contains a wealth of information designed for locals as well as visitors.

The **Palm Springs Visitors Information Center,** 2781 N. Palm Canyon Dr. (© **800/34-SPRINGS;** fax 760/323-3021; www.palm-springs.org), offers maps, brochures, advice, souvenirs, and a free hotel reservation service. The office is open Monday through Saturday from 9am to 5pm and on Sunday from 8am to 4pm.

ORIENTATION   The commercial downtown area of Palm Springs stretches about half a mile along North Palm Canyon Drive between Alejo and Ramon Streets. The street is one-way through the heart of town, but its other-way counterpart is Indian Canyon Drive, 1 block east. The mountains lie directly west and south, while the rest of Palm Springs is laid out in a grid to the southeast. Palm Canyon forks into South Palm Canyon (leading to the Indian Canyons) and East Palm Canyon (the continuation of Calif. 111) traversing the resort towns of Cathedral City, Rancho Mirage, Palm Desert, Indian Wells, and La Quinta before looping up to rejoin I-10 at Indio. Desert Hot Springs is north of Palm Springs, straight up Gene Autry Trail. Tahquitz Canyon Way creates North Palm Canyon's primary intersection, tracking a straight line between the airport and the heart of town.

GREAT GOLF COURSES

The Palm Springs desert resorts are world-famous meccas for golfers (see "Fairways & Five-Irons, Desert Style," below). There are nearly 100 public, semiprivate, and private courses in the area. If you're the kind who starts polishing

Palm Springs Desert Resorts

ACCOMMODATIONS ■
Ballantine's Movie Colony **4**
Casa Cody **7**
Estrella Inn **7**
Holiday Inn Palm Mountain **7**
Korakia Pensione **7**
La Mancha Resort Village **3**
La Quinta Resort & Club **19**
Marriott's Desert Springs **16**
Marriott's Rancho Las Palmas **15**
The Orbit In **7**
Orchid Tree Inn **7**
Spa Hotel & Casino **5**
Villa Royale **9**
Westin Mission Hills Resort **13**

ATTRACTIONS ●
Coachella Valley Preserve **14**
El Paseo **17**
Indian Canyons **12**
The Living Desert
   Wildlife and Botanical Park **18**
Palm Springs Aerial Tramway **2**
Palm Springs Desert Museum **6**
Palm Springs Oasis Waterpark **10**
Shields Date Gardens **20**
Smoke Tree Stables **11**
Tahquitz Canyon **8**
Windmill Tours **1**

Fairways & Five-Irons, Desert Style

Two hours outside of Los Angeles in the Coachella Valley, strung like ripe dates from I-10, lie the resort cities of Palm Springs, Rancho Mirage, Palm Desert, Indian Wells, and La Quinta. This all-season golfer's paradise boasts close to 100 courses, their lush fairways and velvety greens incongruously carved from the arid desert scruff. Both public and resort/semiprivate courses range in difficulty to accommodate low-handicappers and weekend duffers alike, and every imaginable service is available nearby.

If you'd like to sharpen your game, all the principal clubs have resident pros, and there are several schools and clinics, including the **Indian Wells Golf School** at Indian Wells Resort (© 800/241-5782 or 760/346-4653), the **Golf Center at Palm Desert** (© 760/779-1877), and the **Leadbetter Golf Academy** at PGA West in La Quinta (© 800/424-3542 or 760/564-0777). If you're looking to pick up new equipment or some stylish attire, try **Nevada Bob's Discount Golf** in Palm Springs (© 760/324-0196) and Indian Wells (© 760/346-6166), the **Roger Dunn Golf Shop** in Palm Desert (© 760/345-3133) and Cathedral City (© 760/324-1160), and **Lady Golf** in Rancho Mirage (© 760/773-4949).

Many fine resorts offer generous golf packages, among them **Marriott's Desert Springs Spa & Resort** in Palm Desert (© 760/341-2211), **Marriott's Rancho Las Palmas Resort & Spa** in Rancho Mirage (© 760/568-2727), the **Hyatt Grand Champions** in Indian Wells (© 760/341-1000), **La Quinta Resort & Club** in La Quinta (© 760/346-2904), and the **Estrella Inn** (© 800/237-3687 or 760/320-4417).

Tee times at many courses cannot be booked more than a few days in advance for non-guests, but **Golf à la Carte** (© 877/887-6900 or

your irons the moment you begin planning your vacation, you're best off staying at one of the valley's many golf resorts, where you can enjoy the proximity of your hotel's facilities as well as smart package deals that can give you a taste of country-club membership. If, on the other hand, you'd like to fit a round of golf into an otherwise varied trip and you aren't staying at a hotel with its own links, there are courses at all levels open to the general public, mostly in Palm Springs. Call ahead to see which will rent clubs or other equipment to the spontaneous player.

Beginners will enjoy **Tommy Jacobs' Bel-Air Greens,** 1001 El Cielo, Palm Springs (© **760/322-6062**), a scenic nine-hole, par-32 executive course that has some water- and sand-trap challenges but also allows for a few confidence-boosting successes. Generally flat fairways and mature trees characterize the relatively short (3,350-yard) course. The complex also offers an 18-hole miniature golf course. Greens fees range from $17 to $19.

Slightly more intermediate amateurs will want to check out the **Tahquitz Creek Golf Resort,** 1885 Golf Club Dr., Palm Springs (© **760/328-1005**), whose two diverse courses both appeal to mid-handicappers. The "Legend's" wide, water-free holes will appeal to anyone frustrated by the "target" courses popular with many architects, while the new Ted Robinson–designed "Resort"

760-320-8713; www.palmspringsgolf.com) is able to make arrangements several months earlier and even construct a custom package for you with accommodations, golf, meals, and other extras. A valuable service for the budget traveler is **Stand-By Golf** (© **866/244-2665** or 760/ 321-2665; www.stand-bygolf.com), which helps more than 35 area courses—including prestigious semi-private and resort courses—fill their bookings by offering players a last-minute discount of up to 50%. Most tee times are for same or next day; call between 7am and 9pm daily.

For the non-playing spectator (or anyone longing to see the pros make it look *so* easy), there are dozens of golf tournaments year-round, including many celebrity and pro-am events in addition to regular PGA, LPGA, and Senior Tour stops. February brings the PGA Tour's **Bob Hope Chrysler Classic** at the Bermuda Dunes Country Club and the **Frank Sinatra Celebrity Invitational** at Marriott's Desert Springs Resort & Spa. In March, catch the LPGA Tour's **Nabisco Dinah Shore** at the Mission Hills Country Club; in April, the Senior PGA's **Liberty Mutual Legends of Golf** comes to PGA West. November brings two of the desert's longest-running charity events: the **24th Annual Frostig Center/Chris Korman Celebrity Tournament,** at the Westin Mission Hills; and the **Billy Barty/ 7-Up Celebrity Golf Classic,** at the Mesquite Country Club in Palm Springs. Also in November, check out the wacky **Palm Desert Golf Cart Parade** along El Paseo.

For more information, you can call the Palm Springs Desert Resorts Convention and Visitors Bureau (© **800/41-RELAX** or 760/770-9000; www.PalmSpringsUSA.com). The bureau also maintains an activities hotline (© **760/770-1992**).

course offers all those accuracy-testing bells and whistles more common to lavish private clubs. Greens fees, including cart, range from $55 to $100 depending on the day of the week.

The **Palm Springs Country Club,** 2500 Whitewater Club Dr. (© **760/ 323-8625**), is the oldest public-access golf course within the city of Palm Springs, and is especially popular with budget-conscious golfers, as greens fees are only $35 to $60, including the required cart. The challenge of bunkers and rough can be amplified by the oft-blowing wind along the 5,885 yards of this unusually laid-out course.

The **Westin Mission Hills Resort Course,** Dinah Shore and Bob Hope Drives, Rancho Mirage (© **760/328-3198**), is somewhat more forgiving than most of legendary architect Pete Dye's courses, but don't play the back tees unless you've got a consistent 220-yard drive and won't be fazed by the Dye-trademark giant sand bunkers and elevated greens. Water only comes into play on four holes, and the scenery is an exquisite reward for low-handicappers. |Non-guest greens fees are $150 to $175, including cart.

One of our favorite desert courses is the **PGA West TPC Stadium Course,** La Quinta Resort & Club, 49499 Eisenhower Dr., La Quinta (© **760/ 564-4111**), which received *Golf* magazine's 1994 Gold Medal Award for the total golf-resort experience. The par-three 17th has a picturesque island green where Lee Trevino made Skins Game history with a spectacular hole-in-one. The rest of Pete Dye's 7,261-yard design is flat, with huge bunkers, lots of water, and severe mounding throughout. Also open for semiprivate play is the **Mountain Course at La Quinta,** another Dye design that regularly appears on U.S. top-100 lists. It's set dramatically against the rocky mountains, which thrust into fairways to create tricky doglegs, and its small Bermuda greens are well guarded by boulders and deep bunkers. Greens fees for non-guests vary seasonally, from $85 to $225, at both La Quinta courses.

A complete **golfer's guide** is available from the Palm Springs Desert Resorts Convention & Visitors Bureau (see "Visitor Information," above).

MORE OUTDOOR FUN

The Coachella Valley Desert is truly a playground, and what follows is but a sampling of the opportunities to enjoy the abundant sunshine during your vacation here. But the strong sun and dry air that are so appealing can also sneak up on you in the form of sunburn and heat exhaustion. Especially during the summer, but even in milder times, always carry and drink plenty of water.

A FAMILY WATER PARK   Palm Springs Oasis Waterpark, off I-10 south on Gene Autry Trail between Ramon Road and East Palm Canyon Drive (© 760/325-7873; www.oasiswaterresort.com), is a water playground with 12 water slides, body- and board surfing, an inner-tube ride, and more. Dressing rooms, lockers, and private beach cabanas (with food service) are available. Admission is $19 for visitors over 5 feet tall, $12 for kids 3 to 5 feet, and free for kids under 3 feet ($11 for seniors). The park is open mid-March through Labor Day, daily from 11am to 6pm, plus weekends through all of October.

BALLOONING   This is perhaps the most memorable way to see the desert: floating above the landscape in a colorful hot-air balloon. Choose from specialty themes like sunrise, sunset, or romantic champagne flights. Rides are offered by **Dream Flights** (© 800/933-5628 or 760/321-5154; www.dreamflights.com), and **Fantasy Balloon Flights** (© 800/GO-ABOVE or 760/568-0997). Rates range from $145 to $160 per person.

BICYCLING   The clean, dry air just cries out to be enjoyed—what could be better than to pedal your way around town or into the desert? **Adventure Bike Tours** (© 760/328-0282) will outfit you with a bike, helmet, souvenir water bottle, and certified guide. Tours, which meet at local hotels, start at about $40, and bike rentals are $10 per hour or $28 for the day. If you're just looking to rent some wheels and a helmet, **Mac's Bicycle Rental,** 79953 Calif. 111, between Country Club and Frank Sinatra Drives (© 760/321-9444), rents bikes for the hour ($7), the day ($19), or the week ($65), and offers children's and mountain models. The **Bighorn Bicycle Rental & Tour Company,** 302 N. Palm Canyon (© 760/325-3367) has hourly ($7) and daily ($27) rental rates in addition to guided bike treks (a 4-hour guided ride/hike is $45 per person including all equipment and snacks).

GUIDED JEEP & WAGON EXCURSIONS   Desert Adventures (© 888/440-JEEP or 760/324-JEEP; www.red-jeep.com) offers four-wheel-drive eco-tours led by experienced naturalist guides. Your off-road adventure may take you to a replica of an ancient Cahuilla village, the rugged Santa Rosa Mountain roads overlooking the Coachella Valley, or picturesque ravines on the way to the San Andreas Fault. Tours range in duration from 2 to 4 hours and in price from

$79 to $129. Advance reservations are required. The company's trademark red Jeeps depart from the Desert Adventures Ranch on South Palm Canyon near the entrance to the Indian Canyons, but most of the longer excursions include hotel pickup and return.

Covered Wagon Tours (© 800/367-2161 or 760/347-2161; www.covered wagontours.com) embraces the pioneer spirit with a 2-hour ride through the Coachella Valley Nature Preserve followed by a good old-fashioned barbecue and live country music. The tours take place seven days a week from October to mid-May; the cost is $55 for adults, $27.50 for children ages 7 to 16, and free for kids age under 7. Without the "grub," the charge is $40 per adult and $20 per child. Advance reservations are required.

HIKING   The most popular spot for hiking is the nearby **Indian Canyons** (© 760/325-5673 for information). The Agua Caliente tribe made their home here centuries ago, and remnants of their simple lifestyle can be seen among the streams, waterfalls, and astounding palm groves in Andreas, Murray, and Palm Canyons. Striking rock formations and herds of bighorn sheep and wild ponies will probably be more appealing than the "Trading Post" in Palm Canyon, but it does sell detailed trail maps. This is Indian land, and the Tribal Council charges admission of $6 per adult, with discounts for seniors, children, students, and military. The canyons are closed to visitors from late June to early September.

Here's the Rub: Two Bunch Palms Desert Spa

Since the time of the Native American Cahuilla, who knew how great it felt to soak in the Coachella Valley's natural hot springs, this desert has drawn stressed-out masses seeking relaxation, rejuvenation, and the pure sigh-inducing pleasure only a health spa can deliver. Our number-one, we-can't-recommend-it-enough choice is heavenly **Two Bunch Palms,** annually voted one of the world's "Top Ten" by *Travel & Leisure* magazine. Posh yet intimate, this spiritual sanctuary in Desert Hot Springs (about 20 minutes north of Palm Springs) has been drawing weary city dwellers since Chicago mobster Al Capone hid out here in the 1930s. Two Bunch Palms later became a playground for the movie community, but today it's a friendly and informal haven offering renowned spa services, quiet bungalows nestled on lush grounds, and trademark lagoons of steaming mineral water. Service is famously—and excellently—discreet; and legions of return guests will attest that the outstanding spa treatments (nine varieties of massage, mud baths, body wraps, facials, salt rubs, and more) and therapeutic waters are what make the luxury of Two Bunch Palms irresistible. Room rates start at $175 (including breakfast) in the high season, with midweek and substantial seasonal discounts available. Spa treatments average between $75 to $100 per hour, and money-saving room/meal/spa packages are always offered. Don't want to stay over? Then book one of Two Bunch's new six-hour Day Spa packages. The resort is located off Palm Drive (Gene Autry Trail) at 67425 Two Bunch Palms Trail (© 800/472-4334 or 760/329-8791; www.twobunchpalms.com).

Don't miss the opportunity to explore the newly re-opened **Tahquitz Canyon** (500 W. Mesquite, west of Palm Canyon Drive), also an Agua Caliente territory. This incredibly scenic canyon, which features the waterfall filmed for the classic *Lost Horizon,* was closed to the public for nearly 30 years after it became an all-night party zone for hippies, who vandalized land considered sacred—serious injuries also plagued careless canyon squatters. But now the vegetation is renewed and decades' worth of dumping cleaned up, and in 2001 the tribe began offering 2-hour ranger-led hikes into their most spiritual and beautiful place. The canyon is open daily from 8am to 5pm, with hikes departing every hour until 3pm. The fee is $10 for adults and $5 for kids under 12; call © **760/ 416-7044** for information and reservations.

Ten miles east of Palm Springs is the 13,000-acre **Coachella Valley Preserve** (© **760/343-1234**), which is open daily from sunrise to sunset. There are springs, mesas, both hiking and riding trails, the Thousand Palms Oasis, a visitor center, and picnic areas.

If you're heading up to Joshua Tree National Park (see "Joshua Tree National Park," below), consider stopping at the **Big Morongo Canyon Preserve** (© **760/ 363-7190**), which was once an Indian village and later a cattle ranch. It's open to visitors Wednesday through Sunday from 7:30am to sundown. The park's high water table makes it a magnet for birds and other wildlife; the lush springs and streams are an unexpected desert treat.

HORSEBACK RIDING   Equestrians from novice to advanced can experience the natural solitude and quiet of the desert on horseback at **Smoke Tree Stables** (© **760/327-1372**). Located south of downtown and ideal for exploring the nearby Indian Canyon trails, Smoke Tree offers guided rides for $25 per hour. But don't expect your posse leader to be primed with facts on the nature you'll encounter—this is strictly a do-it-yourself experience.

TENNIS   Virtually all the larger hotels and resorts have tennis courts; but if you're staying at a B&B, you might want to play at the **Tennis Center,** 1300 Baristo Rd., Palm Springs (© **760/320-0020**), which has nine courts and offers day and evening clinics for adults, juniors, and seniors, as well as ball machines for solo practice. USPTA pros are on hand.

If you'd like to play for free, the night-lit courts at **Palm Springs High School,** 2248 E. Ramon Rd., are open to the public on weekends, on holidays, and in summer. There are also eight free night-lit courts in beautiful **Ruth Hardy Park** at Tamarisk and Caballero Streets.

EXPLORING THE AREA

The Living Desert Wildlife and Botanical Park 👁   This 1,200-acre desert reserve, museum, zoo, and educational center is designed to acquaint visitors with the unique habitats that make up the southern California deserts. You can walk or take a tram tour through sectors that re-create life in several distinctive desert zones. See and learn about a dizzying variety of plants, insects, and wildlife, including bighorn sheep, mountain lions, rattlesnakes, lizards, owls, golden eagles, and the ubiquitous roadrunner.

47900 Portola Ave., Palm Desert. © **760/346-5694.** www.livingdesert.org. Admission $8.50 adults, $7.50 seniors age 62 and over, $4.25 children 3–12, free for kids under 3. Daily 9am–5pm (last entrance 4:30pm); summer (June 16–Aug) 8am–1pm. Closed Christmas Day.

Palm Springs Aerial Tramway 👁👁   To gain a bird's-eye perspective on the Coachella Valley, take this 14-minute ascent up 2½ miles to the top of Mount San Jacinto. While the Albert Frey–designed boarding stations retain their 1960s

Sweet Treat of the Desert: The Coachella Valley Date Gardens

In a splendid display of both wishful thinking and clever engineering, the Coachella Valley has grown into a rich agricultural region, known internationally for grapefruit, figs, and grapes—but mostly for dates. Turn-of-the-century entrepreneurs, fascinated with Arabian lore and fueled by the Sahara-like conditions of the desert around Indio, planted the area's date palm groves in the 1920s. Launched with just a few parent trees imported from the Middle East, the groves now produce 95% of the world's date crop.

Farmers hand-pollinate the trees, and the resulting precious fruit is bundled in wind-protective paper while still on the tree, which makes an odd sight indeed. You'll see them along Calif. 111 through Indio, where the road is sometimes referred to as the "Date Highway."

For decades, **Shields Date Gardens,** 80225 Calif. 111 (© **760/347-0996;** www.shieldsdates.com), has been enticing visitors into its splendid 1930s Moderne building with banners proclaiming free admission to the continuously running film *The Romance and Sex Life of the Date.* (Fair warning: Its racy title is the best part.) Even if you're not interested in the flick, stop by the lunch counter (date shake, anyone?) and store (which sells an endless variety of dates and related goodies) and sample some date ice cream or date crystals, a mysterious sweet product that seems to have many practical uses—until you actually get it home. But the quality and selection of fresh-harvested dates is superb; we guarantee you'll find yourself snacking on them before long. Open daily from 8am to 6pm.

There's no more picturesque place in the valley to sample dates than **Oasis Date Gardens,** 59111 Calif. 111 (© **800/827-8017** or 760/399-5665), started in 1912 with nine Moroccan trees and now one of the largest commercial date groves in the United States. It's a drive—about 40 minutes from downtown Palm Springs—but there's a lot to do here. Picnic tables dot an inviting lawn, videos illustrate the history and art of date cultivation, and there's a cool palm arboretum and cactus exhibit, plus a petting zoo for impatient youngsters. Many varieties of dates are laid out for free tasting; Oasis also sells date shakes, ice cream, chewy date pie by the slice, homemade chili and sandwiches, and gourmet food gifts from all over the Southwest. Open daily (except Christmas) from 6am to 5:30pm.

ski-lodge feel, newly installed Swiss funicular cars are sleekly modern and rotate during the trip to allow each passenger a panoramic view. There's a whole other world once you arrive: alpine scenery, a ski-lodge–flavored restaurant and gift shop, and temperatures typically 40° cooler than the desert floor. The most dramatic contrast is during the winter, when the mountaintop is a snowy wonderland, irresistible to hikers and bundled-up kids with saucers. The excursion might not be worth the expense during the rest of the year. Guided mule rides and cross-country ski equipment are available at the top.

Tramway Rd. off Hwy. 111, Palm Springs. © 888/515-TRAM or 760/325-1391. www.pstramway.com. Tickets $19.65 adults, $17.65 seniors, $12.50 children ages 3–12, free for kids under 3; Ride 'n' Dine combination (available after 2:30pm, dinner served after 4pm) $23.65 adults, $15.50 children. Mon–Fri 10am–8pm; Sat–Sun 8am–8pm. Free parking.

Palm Springs Desert Museum ⚔   Unlikely though it may sound, this well-endowed museum is a must-see. Exhibits include world-class Western and Native American art collections, the natural history of the desert, and an outstanding anthropology department, primarily representing the local Cahuilla tribe. Traditional Indian life as it was lived for centuries before the white presence is illustrated by tools, baskets, and other relics. Check local schedules to find out about visiting exhibits (which are usually excellent). Plays, lectures, and other events are presented in the museum's Annenberg Theater.

101 Museum Dr. (just west of the Palm Canyon/Tahquitz intersection), Palm Springs. © 760/325-7186. www.psmuseum.org. Admission $7.50 adults, $6.50 seniors age 62 and over, $3.50 military and children 6–17, free for children under 6, free for everyone the 1st Fri of each month. Tues–Sat 10am–5pm; Sun noon–5pm.

SHOPPING

Downtown Palm Springs revolves around **North Palm Canyon Drive;** many art galleries, souvenir shops, and restaurants are located here, along with a couple of large-scale hotels and shopping centers. This wide, one-way boulevard is designed for pedestrians, with many businesses set back from the street itself—don't be shy about poking around the little courtyards you'll encounter. On Thursday night from 6 to 10pm, the blocks between Amado and Baristo Roads are transformed into **VillageFest,** a street fair tradition celebrating its sixth anniversary. Handmade-crafts vendors and aromatic food booths compete for your attention with wacky street performers and even wackier locals shopping at the mouthwatering fresh-produce stalls.

The northern section of Palm Canyon is becoming known for vintage collectibles and is being touted as the **Antique and Heritage Gallery District.** Check out **John's Resale Furnishings,** 891 N. Palm Canyon Dr. (© 760/416-8876), for a glorious collection of mid-century modern furnishings; **Bandini Johnson Gallery,** 895 N. Palm Canyon Dr. (© 760/323-7805), a cramped warren of eclectic treasures; and the **Antiques Center,** 798 N. Palm Canyon Dr. (© 760/323-4443), a discriminating mall-style store whose 35 dealers display wares ranging from vintage linens to handmade African crafts to prized Bakelite jewelry.

Down in Palm Desert lies the delicious excess of **El Paseo,** a glitzy cornucopia of high-rent boutiques, salons, and upscale eateries reminiscent of Rodeo Drive in Beverly Hills, along with a dozen or more major shopping malls just like back home.

Factory-outlet shopping is 20 minutes away in Cabazon (see section 1, "En Route to the Palm Springs Resorts," earlier in this chapter).

GAY LIFE IN PALM SPRINGS

Don't think the local chamber of commerce doesn't recognize that the Palm Springs area is among the current top-three American destinations for gay travelers. After just a short while in town, it's easy to see how the gay tourism dollar is courted as aggressively as straight spending. Real-estate agents cater to gay shoppers for vacation properties, while entire condo communities are marketed toward the gay resident. Advertisements for these and scores of other gay-owned businesses can be found in *The Bottom Line,* the desert's free biweekly magazine of articles, events, and community guides for the gay reader, which is available at hotels, at newsstands, and from select merchants.

Throughout the year, events are held that transcend the gay community to include everyone. In March, the **Desert AIDS Walk** benefits the Desert AIDS Project, while the world's largest organized gathering of lesbians coincides with the **Nabisco Dinah Shore Golf Tournament.**

Be sure to visit **Village Pride,** 214 E. Arenas Rd. (℃ **760/323-9120**), a coffee-house and local gathering place. Besides offering a selection of gay- and lesbian-oriented reading material, Village Pride also serves as the lobby for the **Top Hat Playhouse.** This short block of Arenas is home to a score of gay establishments, including **Streetbar** (℃ **760/320-1266**), a neighborhood gathering spot for tourists and locals alike.

Just a few blocks away is a cozy neighborhood of modest homes and small hotels, concentrated on Warm Sands Drive south of Ramon. Known simply as **"Warm Sands,"** this area holds the very nicest "private resorts"—mostly discreet and gated B&B-style inns. Locals recommend the co-ed **El Mirasol,** 525 Warm Sands Dr. (℃ **800/327-2985** or 760/326-5913), a charming historic resort; or **Sago Palms,** 595 Thornhill Rd. (℃ **800/626-7246** or 760/323-0224), which is small, quiet, and affordable. The **Bee Charmer,** 1600 E. Palm Canyon Dr. (℃ **888/321-5699;** www.beecharmer.com), is one of the few all-women resorts in town.

Gay nightlife is everywhere in the valley, and especially raucous on holiday weekends. Pick up *The Bottom Line* for the latest restaurant, nightclub, theater, and special-events listings.

WHERE TO STAY

The city of Palm Springs offers a wide range of accommodations, but we particularly like the inns that have opened as new owners renovate the many fabulous 40- to 60-year-old cottage complexes in the wind-shielded "Tennis Club" area west of Palm Canyon Drive. The other desert-resort cities offer mostly sprawling resort complexes, many boasting world-class golf, tennis, or spa facilities and multiple on-site restaurants. Most are destinations in and of themselves, offering activities for the whole family (including a whole lot of relaxing and being pampered). So if you're looking for a good base from which to shop or sightsee, Palm Springs is your best bet.

Regardless of your choice, remember that the rates given below are for high season (winter, generally October through May). During the hotter summer months, it's common to find $300 rooms going for $99 or less as part of off-season packages. Even in high season, midweek and golf packages are common, so always ask when making your reservation.

PALM SPRINGS
Expensive

La Mancha Resort Village ✦   The security-gated entry makes La Mancha look like a private community, and it was designed that way. Once you're inside, though, a warmly respectful staff will pamper you, just the way they've coddled the countless celebs who've lent their names to the brochure. What distinguishes La Mancha from other resorts is its quiet elegance and service, not its modern but unoriginal furnishings. Most units are suites with TV/VCRs and phones in every room. (They'll even provide Nintendo for the kids.) Many guests opt for the villas, which have private pools, fireplaces, and wet bars. Fruit baskets welcome guests on arrival. A private fleet of rental cars stand ready should you want to venture the half mile into town, or you can simply relax the days away—how about a massage on your personal patio?

444 Avenida Caballeros, Palm Springs, CA 92262. ℂ **888/PRIVACY** or 760/323-1773. www.la-mancha.com. 66 units. $150–$245 double; villas from $295. AE, DC, DISC, MC, V. Free parking. Dogs allowed with $200 fee. **Amenities:** Restaurant, lounge; outdoor heated pool; tennis courts; fitness center with spa; Jacuzzi; in-room massage; complimentary bicycles; room service (7am–11pm). *In room:* A/C, TV w/ VCR, fridge, coffeemaker, hair dryer, iron, safe.

Spa Hotel & Casino This is one of the more unusual choices in town. It's located on the Indian-owned parcel of land containing the original mineral springs for which Palm Springs was named. The Cahuilla claimed that the springs had magical powers to cure illness. Today's travelers still come here to pamper both body and soul by "taking the waters," though now the facility is sleekly modern. There are three pools on the premises: One is a conventional outdoor swimming pool; the other two are filled from the underground natural springs brimming with revitalizing minerals. Inside the hotel's extensive spa are private sunken marble swirlpools fed by the springs. After your bath, you can avail yourself of the many other pampering treatments offered. The hotel recently opened the adjoining Vegas-style casino, featuring the familiar hush of card gaming tables and clanging of video poker and slot machines. Despite that contemporary addition, the Cahuilla have truly managed to integrate modern hotel comforts with the ancient healing and Indian spirit this land represents.

100 N. Indian Canyon Dr., Palm Springs, CA 92263. ℂ **800/854-1279** or 760/325-1461. Fax 760/325-3344. www.spahotelandcasino.com. 230 units. $159–$239 double; $219–$279 suite. AE, DC, MC, V. Free parking. **Amenities:** 2 restaurants, 2 bars; 3 outdoor heated pools; full-service spa; fitness center; concierge; car-rental desk; 24-hour room service. *In room:* A/C, TV, minibar, hair dryer, iron.

Moderate

Ballantine's Movie Colony ✿✿ Take one classic 1930s hotel designed by prolific and renowned area architect Albert Frey, add a warehouse's worth of barely-used, mid-century furnishings and repro classics—cleverly grouped to create mini-theme rooms, sprinkle generously with stylish vacationers and flavor-of-the-month celebs, and you've got Palm Springs's grooviest new digs. Situated off the town's main drag in a neighborhood once favored by Golden-Age celebs (hence the name), Ballantine's offers a quietly hip, highly personalized experience in a setting marked by scrupulous detail and tantalizing colors; the swimming pool is edged in brilliant lime, the "Sinatra" room is boldly orange (Frank's favorite color), and the made-to-look-old rotary(!) phones are jelly-bean bright.

The same brilliant owners have a similarly outfitted property a few blocks away; **Ballantine's Original,** 1420 N. Indian Canyon Dr. (ℂ **760/320-2449**), has fewer rooms and a more discreet facade (is there a hotel here?), while still boasting the same fabulous amenities, including a pool with fire pit and outdoor bar, meticulous mid-century furnishings, and personal service.

726 N. Indian Canyon Dr., Palm Springs. ℂ **800/780-3464** or 760/320-1178. Fax 760/320-5308. www. ballantineshotels.com. 18 units. High season $139–$260 double. Rates include continental breakfast and evening cocktail. Midweek and summer discounts available (as low as $79). AE, MC, V. Free parking. **Amenities:** Outdoor heated pool; Jacuzzi. *In room:* A/C, TV, fridge, hair dryer, iron.

Estrella Inn ✿ Once the choice of Hollywood celebrities, this outstanding historic hotel is quiet and secluded, yet wonderfully close to the action. It's composed of three distinct properties from three different eras, all united by a peachy desert color scheme and uniformly lavish landscaping. Guest rooms vary widely according to location, but all include pampering touches—some have fireplaces and/or full kitchens, others have wet bars or private balconies. The real deals are the studio bungalows, even though they have tiny 1930s bathrooms. The Estrella has an outdoor barbecue, plus a lawn with games equipment. Ask about attractive golf packages that include play at one of several nearby courses.

415 S. Belardo Rd. (south of Tahquitz Way), Palm Springs, CA 92262. ℭ **800/237-3687** or 760/320-4117. Fax 760/323-3303. www.estrella.com. 63 units. $150 double; $225–$275 1- or 2-bedroom suite; $250–$350 1- or 2-bedroom bungalow. Rates include continental breakfast. Monthly rates available. AE, DC, MC, V. Free parking. Pets allowed in tile-floored units for $20 fee. **Amenities:** 3 outdoor heated pools (including 1 children's pool); 2 Jacuzzi; coin-op laundry. *In room:* A/C, TV, fridge, coffeemaker, hair dryer.

Korakia Pensione 🏵🏵   If you can work within the Korakia's rigid deposit-cancellation policy, you're in for a special stay at this Greek-Moroccan oasis just a few blocks from Palm Canyon Drive. This former artist's villa from the 1920s draws a hip international crowd of artists, writers, and musicians. The simply furnished rooms and unbelievably spacious suites are peaceful and private, surrounded by flagstone courtyards and flowering gardens. Rooms are divided between the main house, a second restored villa across the street, and surrounding guest bungalows. Most have kitchens; many have fireplaces. All beds are blessed with thick feather duvets, and the windows are shaded by flowing white canvas, Mediterranean style draperies. You also get a sumptuous breakfast served in your room or poolside. *Korakia* is Greek for "crow," and a tile mosaic example graces the pool bottom.

257 S. Patencio Rd., Palm Springs, CA 92262. ℭ **760/864-6411.** Fax 760/864-4147. www.korakia.com. 22 units. $119–$279 double. Rates include breakfast. MC, V. Free parking. **Amenities:** 2 outdoor heated pools; in-room massage. *In room:* A/C, fridge, coffeemaker, safe.

The Orbit In 🏵🏵   This much-hyped renovation of a classic 1950s motel gets our vote as grooviest digs in town, exceeding everyone's expectations with a mix of streamlined mid-century style, cocktails-by-the-pool Rat Pack aesthetic, and almost scholarly appreciation of the architects and designers responsible for Palm Springs's reign as a mecca of vintage modernism. Serious connoisseurs of interior design will find a museum's worth of furnishings in these rooms, each of which adheres to its theme (Martini Room, Bertoia's Den, Atomic Paradise, and so on) right down to customized lounge-music CDs for your in-room listening pleasure. The rest of us just enjoy tripping down memory lane with amoeba-shaped coffee tables, glowing rocket-ship lamps, Eames recliners, kitschy Melmac dishware, and strappy vintage chaises on each room's private patio. Contemporary comforts are impeccably provided, from cushy double pillow-top mattresses to poolside misters that create an oasis of cool even during mid-summer scorchers. Kitchenettes all boast charming restored fixtures, as do the candy-pink-tiled original bathrooms, which have only stall showers, but make up for the lack of tubs by being surprisingly spacious—and naturally sunlit. Guests gather at the poolside "boomerang" bar, or in the Albert Frey lounge (homage to the late, great architect whose unique home sits midway up the mountain backdrop); a central "movies, books, and games" closet encourages old-fashioned camaraderie amidst this chic atmosphere.

562 W. Arenas Rd., Palm Springs, CA 92262. ℭ **877/99-ORBIT** or 760/323-3585. Fax 760/323-3599. www.orbitin.com. 10 units. $209–$249 double. Midweek and off-season discounts as low as $149. Rates include deluxe continental breakfast and evening hors d'oeuvres. AE, DISC, MC, V. Free parking. **Amenities:** Outdoor heated pool with adjacent honor bar; Jacuzzi with adjacent fire pit; complimentary Schwinn cruiser bicycles. *In room:* A/C, TV/VCR, dataport, Internet access, CD player, fridge, coffeemaker, hair dryer, iron, safe, finest-quality bathrobes.

Villa Royale ✿   This charming inn, 5 minutes from the hustle and bustle of
downtown Palm Springs, evokes a European cluster of villas, complete with
climbing bougainvillea and rooms filled with international antiques and artwork.
The main building was once home to Olympic and silver-screen ice skater Sonya
Henie. Villa Royale's reputation had been suffering due to indifferent management, but new ownership has brought renovation and a renewed dedication to
service. Uniform luxuries (down comforters and other pampering touches)
appear throughout. Rooms vary widely in size and ambience; large isn't always
better, as some of the inn's most appealing rooms are in the smaller, more affordable range. Many rooms have fireplaces, private patios with whirlpools, full
kitchens, and a variety of other amenities. A continental breakfast is served in an
intimate garden setting surrounding the main pool. The hotel's romantic restaurant, Europa, is a sleeper, offering some of Palm Springs's very best meals (see
"Where to Dine," below).

1620 Indian Trail (off East Palm Canyon), Palm Springs, CA 92264. ✆ **800/245-2314** or 760/327-2314.
Fax 760/322-3794. www.villaroyale.com. 31 units. High season (Oct–May) $125–$175 double, $230–$275
suite; summer $87–$125 double, $165–$195 suite. Rates include full breakfast. Extra person $25. AE, DC,
DISC, MC, V. Free parking. Small pets accepted with $50 deposit. **Amenities:** Restaurant; outdoor heated
pool; Jacuzzi; concierge; in-room massage. *In room:* A/C, TV, hair dryer, iron.

Inexpensive

Casa Cody ✿   Once owned by "Wild" Bill Cody's niece, this 1920s casa with a
double courtyard (each with swimming pool) has been restored to fine condition.
It now sports a vaguely Southwestern decor and peaceful grounds marked by
large lawns and mature, blossoming fruit trees. You'll feel more like a houseguest
than a hotel client at the Casa Cody. It's located in the primarily residential
"Tennis Club" area of town, a couple of easy blocks from Palm Canyon Drive.
Many units here have fireplaces and full-size kitchens. Breakfast is served poolside, as are complimentary wine and cheese on Saturday afternoons.

175 S. Cahuilla Rd. (between Tahquitz Way and Arenas Rd.), Palm Springs, CA 92262. ✆ **760/320-9346.**
Fax 760/325-8610. www.palmsprings.com/hotels/casacody. 23 units. $79–$99 double; $99–$159 studio;
$149–$259 suite; 2-bedroom adobe $299–$359. Rates include expanded continental breakfast. AE, DC, DISC,
MC, V. Pets accepted for $10 fee per night. **Amenities:** 2 outdoor heated pools; Jacuzzi; in-room massage.
In room: A/C, TV, fridge.

Holiday Inn Palm Mountain Resort (Kids)   Within easy walking distance of
Palm Springs's main drag, this Holiday Inn (like most in the chain) welcomes
kids under 18 free in their parents' room, making it a terrific choice for families.
The rooms are in the two- or the three-story wing, and many have a patio or balcony, with a view of the mountains or the large Astroturf courtyard. Midweek
and summer rates can be as low as $59. For the best rates, book online or ask
for "Great Rates."

155 S. Belardo Rd., Palm Springs, CA 92262. ✆ **800/622-9451** or 760/325-1301. Fax 760/323-8937.
www.palmmountainresort.com. 122 units. High season $89–$169 double. Children under 18 stay free in parents' room. AE, DC, DISC, MC, V. Free parking. **Amenities:** Restaurant, lounge, poolside bar; heated outdoor
pool. *In room:* A/C, TV, fridge, coffeemaker.

Orchid Tree Inn   Billed as a "1930s desert garden retreat," the Orchid Tree is
a sprawling complex of buildings from the 1920s to 1950s, located just a block
from Palm Canyon Drive in the historic "Tennis Club" district. Dedicated family ownership ensures that the place is impeccably maintained. The inn truly
feels like a retreat. The grounds are rich with flowering shrubs, mature citrus
trees, and multitudes of twittering hummingbirds, sparrows, and quail drawn by

bird feeders and birdbaths. The rooms are nicer than you'd expect at this price, in keeping with the overall grace and excellence of the entire neighborhood. Room types range from simple, hotel-style doubles to charming bungalows to pool-front studios with sliding-glass doors.

261 S. Belardo Rd. (at Baristo Rd.), Palm Springs, CA 92262. (C) **800/733-3435** or 760/325-2791. Fax 760/ 325-3855. www.orchidtree.com. 40 units. Nov–May $110–$185 double; $150–$395 suite. Summer $65–$125 double, $105–$285 suite. Extra person $15. Rates include expanded continental breakfast (Nov–May only). AE, DC, DISC, MC, V. **Amenities:** 3 swimming pools; 2 Jacuzzis. *In room:* A/C, TV, hair dryer.

RANCHO MIRAGE

Marriott's Rancho Las Palmas Resort & Spa   The early California charm of this relaxing Spanish hacienda makes Rancho Las Palmas one of the less pretentious luxury resorts in the desert. Dedicated golfers come to play on the adjoining country club's 27 holes of golf; tennis buffs flock to the 25 hotel courts (three of them red clay); everybody enjoys the brand-new, world-class health spa with pampering treatments plus a separate pool with water slide. Guest rooms are arranged in a complex of low-rise, tile-roofed structures, and the public areas have an easygoing elegance, filled with flower-laden stone fountains, smooth terra-cotta tile floors, and rough-hewn wood trim. All rooms have a balcony or patio.

41000 Bob Hope Dr., Rancho Mirage, CA 92270. (C) **800/I-LUV-SUN** or 760/568-2727. Fax 760/568-5845. www.rancholaspalmas.com. 450 units. Sept–May $250–$425 double; Memorial Day–Labor Day $$160–$255 double. Children under 18 stay free in parents' room. Packages and off-season discounts available. AE, DC, DISC, MC, V. Free valet and self-parking. **Amenities:** 5 restaurants (ranging from casual patio dining to dressy dinner fare), cocktail lounge; 2 outdoor heated pools; 2 Jacuzzis; night-lit outdoor tennis courts; health club; full-service spa; children's programs; concierge; activities desk; business center; room service (6:30am–11pm); babysitting; laundry/dry cleaning service. *In room:* A/C, TV w/ pay movies, dataport, Internet access, minibar, coffeemaker, hair dryer, iron, safe.

Westin Mission Hills Resort   Designed to resemble a Moroccan palace surrounded by pools, waterfalls, and lush gardens, this self-contained resort stands on 360 acres. It's an excellent choice for families and for travelers who take their golf game seriously. (Regular desert visitors will note the Westin is ideally situated so Palm Springs and Palm Desert are equally accessible without driving on congested Hwy. 101.) Rooms are arranged around the grounds in a series of two-story buildings, with accommodations that range from basic to palatial. All have terraces and come with an array of creature comforts befitting this price range—including the Westin trademark "Heavenly Bed," an ultra-comfy white confection so popular many guests order one for home.

Though the Westin has the business demeanor of a practiced group-and-meeting hotel, it offers a multitude of recreation options for leisure travelers, gamblers attracted to the nearby Agua Caliente Casino, or professionals after the day's business is concluded. In addition to their championship golf course, you'll find a running track, bike trails, lawn games, and the freshly expanded Spa at Mission Hills, a stylishly boutique-like oasis whose treatments range from sports massage to pampering Hawaiian body treatments.

71-333 Dinah Shore Dr. (at Bob Hope Dr.), Rancho Mirage, CA 92270. (C) **800/WESTIN-1** or 760/328-5955. Fax 760/321-2955. 512 units. Jan–Apr $470–$515 double; May and Sept–Dec $360–$415 double; Memorial Day–Labor Day $219–$249 double. Extra person $35. Children under 18 stay free in parents' room. Golf, spa, and family packages available. AE, DC, DISC, MC, V. Free valet and self-parking. **Amenities:** Excellent all-day restaurant; 2 lounges, 3 poolside cabana bars; multiple outdoor heated pools and Jacuzzis; night-lit outdoor tennis courts; health club; full-service spa; bicycle rental; children's activity center; concierge; business center; 24-hour room service; in-room massage; babysitting; dry cleaning/laundry service. *In room:* A/C, TV w/ pay movies, dataport, minibar, coffeemaker, hair dryer, iron, safe.

PALM DESERT

Marriott's Desert Springs Spa & Resort   A tourist attraction in its own right, Marriott's Desert Springs Resort is worth a peek even if you're not lucky enough to stay here. Most of the guests are attracted by the excellent golf and tennis facilities, and the huge, luxurious, full-service spa is an added perk, offering massages, facials, aerobics classes, and supervised weight training. Visitors enter this artificial desert oasis via a sweeping palm-tree-lined road wending its way past a small pond that's home to a gaggle of pink flamingos. Once inside, guests are greeted by a shaded marble lobby "rain forest" replete with interior moat and the squawk of tropical birds; gondolas even ply the lobby's waterways.

While the rooms here are not as fancy as the lobby would lead you to believe, they're exceedingly comfortable, decorated with muted pastels and contemporary furnishings. All have terraces with views of the golf course and the San Jacinto Mountains. Recreational options like a jogging trail, 36 holes of golf, driving range, unique 18-hole putting range, basketball courts, lawn croquet, and a sunbathing "beach" with volleyball court—we guarantee you don't have to ever leave the perimeter if you don't want to.

74855 Country Club Dr., Palm Desert, CA 92260. ✆ **800/331-3112** or 760/341-2211. Fax 760/341-1872. www.desertspringsresort.com. 884 units. Sept–May $290–$550 double; Memorial Day–Labor Day $195–$385 double. Children under 18 stay free in parents' room. Packages and off-season discounts available. AE, DC, DISC, MC, V. **Amenities:** 6 restaurants, 4 snack bars, 2 lounges (one with live entertainment); 4 heated outdoor pools; 3 outdoor Jacuzzis; 20 tennis courts (hard, clay, and grass; 7 lit); full-service spa and health club; bicycle rental; children's programs; game room; concierge; tour desk; car-rental desk; business center; 24-hour room service; in-room massage; shopping arcade; salon; babysitting; dry cleaning/laundry service. *In room:* A/C, TV w/ pay movies, dataport, minibar, coffeemaker, hair dryer, iron, safe.

LA QUINTA

La Quinta Resort & Club   A luxury resort set amid citrus trees, towering palms, cacti, and desert flowers at the base of the rocky Santa Rosa Mountains, La Quinta is *the* place to be if you're serious about your golf or tennis game. The resort includes Spa La Quinta, a deluxe mission-style complex with 35 treatment rooms for every pampering luxury. All guest rooms are in comfortable single-story, Spanish-style buildings scattered throughout the grounds. Each has a private patio and access to one of several dozen small pools, enhancing the feeling of privacy at this retreat. All units come with two phones and the resort's trademark discreet service; some have a fireplace or private Jacuzzi. The tranquil lounge and library in the unaltered original hacienda hearkens back to the early

---

A La Quinta Bed & Breakfast Hideaway

Devotees of bed-and-breakfasts or boutique inns might find the La Quinta Resort's 900-plus rooms a little daunting, but there's a way to enjoy this quiet, affluent end of the valley with a little more intimacy. Check out the hidden-secret **Lake La Quinta Inn**, 78-120 Caleo Bay, La Quinta, CA 92253 (✆ **888/226-4546** or 760/564-7332; www.lakelaquintainn.com), a 12-room Norman-style bed-and-breakfast on the shores of a man-made lake (surrounded by equally luxurious homes) just blocks from the famous resort. Exquisitely outfitted rooms, delightful knowledgeable hosts, on-site massage, and 24-hour pool and Jacuzzi complete the fantasy. Rates range from $189 to $329 in season, with off-season discounts as low as $99; golf, romance, and dinner packages are available.

days of the resort, when Clark Gable, Greta Garbo, Frank Capra, and other luminaries chose La Quinta as their hideaway. The resort is renowned for its five championship golf courses—including one of California's best, Pete Dye's PGA West TPC Stadium Course.

49499 Eisenhower Dr., La Quinta, CA 92253. ℂ **800/598-3828** or 760/564-4111. Fax 760/564-7656. www.laquintaresort.com. 919 units. High-season $340–$460 double; mid-June through Sept $170–$290 double. Extra person $15. Children under 18 stay free in parents' room. Packages available. AE, MC, V. Free self parking; valet $3 ($12 overnight). Pets allowed with $250 refundable deposit. **Amenities:** 5 restaurants (including Montanas, with outstanding Mediterranean fare); 3 bars (two with entertainment); 42 outdoor pools with Jacuzzis; 23 outdoor tennis courts (10 night-lit); full-service spa; bicycle rental; children's programs; concierge; business center; 24-hour room service; in-room massage; babysitting; laundry service. *In room:* A/C, TV/VCR w/ pay movies, dataport, minibar, coffeemaker, hair dryer, iron, safe.

WHERE TO DINE
PALM SPRINGS
Expensive

Europa Restaurant 🐸🐸 CALIFORNIA/CONTINENTAL   Long advertised as the "most romantic dining in the desert," Europa is a sentimental favorite of many regulars among an equally gay and straight clientele. This European-style hideaway exudes charm and ambience. Whether you sit under the stars on Europa's garden patio, or in subdued candlelight indoors, you'll surely savor dinner prepared by one of Palm Springs's most dedicated kitchens and served by a discreetly attentive staff. Standout dishes include deviled crab fritters on mango-papaya chutney, filet mignon on a bed of crispy onions with garlic butter, and a show-stopping salmon baked in parchment with crème fraîche and dill. For dessert, don't miss the signature chocolate mousse—smooth, grainy, and addictive.

1620 Indian Trail (at the Villa Royale). ℂ **760/327-2314.** Reservations recommended. Main courses $18–$32. AE, DC, DISC, MC, V. Tues–Sat 5:30–10pm; Sun 11:30am–2pm and 5:30–10pm (also open Tues–Sat noon–2:30pm Oct–May only).

Palmie 🐸 CLASSIC FRENCH   You can't see Palmie from the street, and once you're seated inside its softly lit, lattice-enclosed dining patio, you won't see the bustle outside anymore, either. Martine and Alain Clerc's cozy bistro is filled with Art Deco posters of French seaside resorts. Chef Alain sends out masterful traditional French dishes such as bubbling cheese soufflé, green lentil salad dotted with pancetta, steak au poivre rich with cognac sauce, and lobster raviolis garnished with caviar; in fact, every carefully garnished plate is a work of art. To the charming background strains of French chanteuses, hostess and manager Martine circulates between tables, determined that visitors should enjoy their meals as much as do the loyal regulars she greets by name. Forget your cardiologist for one night and don't leave without sampling dessert. Our favorite is the trio of petite crème brûlées, flavored with ginger, vanilla, and Kahlúa.

276 N. Palm Canyon Dr. (across from the Hyatt). ℂ **760/320-3375.** Reservations recommended. Main courses $12–$26. AE, DC, MC, V. Mon–Sat 5:30–9:30pm.

Moderate

La Provence 🐸🐸 COUNTRY FRENCH   The casually elegant La Provence is a favorite of locals and often gets recommended by knowledgeable innkeepers. This restaurant eschews heavy traditional French cream sauces in favor of carefully combined herbs and spices. The second-story terrace filled with tables sets a lovely mood on balmy desert evenings. The menu offers some expected items (escargots in mushroom caps, bouillabaisse, steak au poivre) as well as inventive pastas, like wild-mushroom raviolis in a sun-dried tomato and sweet-onion sauce. Foodies will note with pleasure that executive chef Clay Arkless comes by way of New York City's River Cafe.

254 N. Palm Canyon Dr. (upstairs). ⓒ **760/416-4418**. Reservations recommended. Main courses $14–$29. AE, DC, DISC, MC, V. Tues–Sun 5–10:30pm.

Las Casuelas Terraza CLASSIC MEXICAN   The original Las Casuelas, a tiny storefront several blocks away, is still open, but the bougainvillea-draped front patio here is a much better place to people-watch. You can order Mexican standards like quesadillas, enchiladas, and mountainous nachos, as well as equally super-sized margaritas. Inside, the action heats up with live music and raucous happy-hour crowds. During hot weather, the patio and even sidewalk passersby are cooled by the restaurant's well-placed misters, making this a perfect late-afternoon or early-evening choice.

222 S. Palm Canyon Dr. ⓒ **760/325-2794**. Reservations recommended on weekends. Main courses $7–$13. AE, DC, DISC, MC, V. Mon–Thurs 11am–10pm; Fri–Sat 11am–11pm; Sun 10am–10pm.

Inexpensive

Edgardo's Café Veracruz ⓕ *Value* MEXICAN   The pleasant but humble ambience at Edgardo's is a welcome change from touristy Palm Springs. The expert menu features authentic Mayan, Huasteco, and Aztec cuisine. The dark interior boasts an array of colorful masks and artwork from Central and South America, but the postage-stamp–sized front patio with a trickling fountain is the best place to sample Edgardo's tangy quesadillas, desert cactus salad, and traditional poblano chiles rellenos—and perhaps even an oyster-tequila shooter from the oyster bar!

494 N. Palm Canyon (at W. Alejo Rd.). ⓒ **760/320-3558**. Reservations recommended for weekend dinner. Main courses $3.50–$15. DISC, MC, V. Mon–Fri 11am–3pm and 5:30–9:30pm; Sat–Sun 8am–10pm (sometimes later). Free parking.

Mykonos GREEK   Locals have been enjoying authentic Greek specialties at this family-run spot for 10 years. Mykonos is supercasual, offering simple, candle-lit tables (with vinyl tablecloths and the like) in an off-street brick courtyard, but it's a pleasant treat. Traditional lamb shanks over rice, dolmades (stuffed grape leaves), tangy salads with crumbled feta cheese, and sweet, sticky baklava are among the best items.

139 Andreas (just off Palm Canyon). ⓒ **760/322-0223**. Most items under $10. MC, V. Wed–Mon 11am–10pm.

PALM DESERT

Doug Arango's ⓕ NORTHERN ITALIAN   With so many Italian restaurants that are either old-world lasagna joints or pricey resort trattorias, it's no wonder Doug's is always packed with locals thankful for an affordable, stylish choice offering northern Italian fare without pretension. Expect a friendly, noisy clatter when it's full, and beware: The kitchen can be heavy-handed with the garlic. Crispy, thin-crust individual pizzas are one specialty, and everyone raves about the appetizer of zucchini pancakes with scallion sour cream. The decor is understated, with black-and-white tiles, glass urns of marinating delicacies, and an open kitchen you can gaze into from the large, oval bar.

73520 El Paseo. ⓒ **760/341-4120**. www.dougarangos.com. Reservations recommended. Main courses $12–$28. AE, MC, V. Tues–Sat 11:30am–2:30pm (Oct–May); Tues–Sun 5:30–10pm (year-round).

Louise's Pantry ⓕ COFFEE SHOP/DINER   A real old-fashioned diner, Louise's was a fixture in Palm Springs since opening as a drugstore lunch counter in 1945. The original location on Palm Canyon Drive fell victim to skyrocketing property values, but not before establishing this welcome offshoot decorated with vintage photos of Louise's heyday. Devoted patrons—young and old—still flock in for premium quality comfort foods such as Cobb salad, Reuben and French dip sandwiches, chicken and dumplings, hearty breakfasts with biscuits and gravy, and tasty fresh-baked pies. Breakfast and lunch only.

44491 Town Center Way (at Fred Waring Dr. north of Hwy. 111). ℂ 760/346-9320. Reservations not accepted. Most menu items under $10. MC, V. Daily 7am–3pm.

Palomino CALIFORNIA/MEDITERRANEAN Opened by the Seattle team responsible for other upscale "chains" like Kincaid's, this local branch of their "Euro Bistro" seems to have hit a nerve with Palm Desert locals, providing just the right blend of casual, trendy, and good value. The menu reads better than it eats, because the assembly-line kitchen is better-suited for pared-down dishes than some of the more complex or delicate preparations; stick with the creative pizzas, daily fresh seafood (like cedar-plank salmon from the Northwest), and meats from the Italian spit-roaster. Portions are enormous, the atmosphere is divided between the high-style designer setting and the low-key, and chatty service is provided by a youthful staff. This place is a happening scene most nights in season, so prepare for a buzz of noise from other diners—and the attached bar. Forego valet parking for a space in the lot behind Palomino.

73101 Hwy. 111 (at Monterey Ave.). ℂ 760/773-9091. Reservations recommended in season. Main courses $14–$27. AE, MC, V. Sun–Thurs 5–10pm; Fri–Sat 5–11pm.

Tommy Bahama's Tropical Cafe CARIBBEAN If all this desert makes you long for de islands, mon, step upstairs from fashionable Tommy Bahama's boutique for a dose of Caribbean relaxation. The decor alone is worth a visit— a fantasy port-of-call, around 1940, with ceiling fans, plenty of rattan and palms, and upholstery in TB's signature tropical prints. Enormous umbrellas shade patio seating with valley views, and spacious indoor booths make for easy relaxing over a series of sweet umbrella drinks. The food is a delicious change of pace, its Caribbean zing not overly spiced; check out coconut shrimp with mango dip, conch fritters, mango shrimp salad, Boca Chica chicken, Jamaican jerk pork, and Key lime pie for dessert. Because the store and cafe anchor Palm Desert's hottest new upscale shopping mall, diners are an entertaining mix of fresh-from-the-courts socialites, always-on-vacation retirees, and well-heeled shoppers.

73595 El Paseo (at Larkspur Ave.). ℂ 760/836-0188. Reservations recommended in season. Main courses $8–$15. AE, MC, V. Daily 11am–10pm.

THE DESERT RESORTS AFTER DARK

Every month a different club or disco is the hot spot in the Springs, and the best way to tap into the trend is by consulting *The Desert Guide, The Bottom Line* (see "Gay Life in Palm Springs," earlier in this chapter), or one of the many other free newsletters available from area hotels and merchants. **VillageFest** (see "Shopping," earlier in this chapter) turns Palm Canyon Drive into an outdoor party every Thursday night. Below, we've described a couple of the enduring arts and entertainment attractions around the desert resorts.

The **Fabulous Palm Springs Follies,** at the Plaza Theatre, 128 S. Palm Canyon Dr., Palm Springs (ℂ 760/327-0225; www.psfollies.com), a vaudeville-style show filled with lively production numbers, is celebrating its 11th year in the historic Plaza Theatre in the heart of town. With a cast of energetic retired showgirls, singers, dancers, and comedians, the revue has been enormously popular around town. Call for show schedule. Tickets range from $35 to $65.

The **McCallum Theatre for the Performing Arts,** 73000 Fred Waring Dr., Palm Desert (© **760/340-ARTS**), offers the only cultural high road around. Frequent symphony performances with visiting virtuosos such as conductor Sciji Ozawa or violinist Itzhak Perlman, musicals like Tommy Tune's *Grease* or *A Chorus Line* revival, and pop performers like the Captain and Tennille or the Ink Spots are among the theater's recent offerings. Call for upcoming event information.

4 Joshua Tree National Park

40 miles NE of Palm Springs, 128 miles E of Los Angeles

The trees themselves are merely a jumping-off point for exploring this seemingly barren desert. Viewed from the roadside, the dry land only hints at hidden vitality, but closer examination reveals a giant mosaic of intense beauty and complexity. From lush oases teeming with life to rusted-out relics of man's attempts to tame the wilderness, from low plains of tufted cacti to mountains of exposed, twisted rock, the park is much more than a tableau of the curious tree for which it is named.

The Joshua tree is said to have been given its name by early Mormon settlers traveling west, for its upraised limbs and bearded appearance reminded them of the prophet Joshua leading them to the promised land.

Other observers were not so kind. Explorer John C. Frémont called it "the most repulsive tree in the vegetable kingdom." Nature writer Charles Francis Saunders opined: "The trees themselves were as grotesque as the creations of a bad dream; the shaggy trunks and limbs were twisted and seemed writhing as though in pain, and dagger-pointed leaves were clenched in bristling fists of inhospitality."

Harsh criticism for this hardy desert dweller, which is really not a tree, but a variety of yucca and member of the lily family. The relationship is apparent when pale yellow, lily-like flowers festoon the limbs of the Joshuas when they bloom in March, April, or May (depending on rainfall). When Mother Nature cooperates, the park also puts on quite a wildflower display, and you can get an updated report on prime viewing sites by calling the park ranger (see below).

> **Traveler's Tip**
> No restaurants, lodging, gas stations, or stores are found within Joshua Tree National Park. In fact, water is only available at four park locations: Cottonwood Springs, the Black Rock Canyon Campground, the Indian Cove Ranger Station, and the Oasis Visitor Center. Twentynine Palms and Yucca Valley have lots of restaurants, markets, motels, and B&Bs.

The park, which reaches the southernmost boundary of this special tree's range, straddles two desert environments. There's the mountainous, Joshua tree–studded Mojave Desert forming the northwestern part of the park, while the Colorado Desert—hotter, drier, lower, and characterized by a wide variety of desert flora including cacti, cottonwood, and native California fan palms—comprises the southern and eastern sections of the park. Between them runs the "transition zone," displaying characteristics of each.

The area's geological timeline is fascinating, stretching back eight million years to a time when the Mojave landscape was one of rolling hills and flourishing grasslands; horses, camels, and mastodons abounded, preyed upon by saber-toothed tigers and wild dogs.

Displays at the Oasis Visitor Center show how resulting climatic, volcanic, and tectonic activity have created the park's signature cliffs and boulders and turned Joshua Tree into the arid desert you see today.

Human presence has been traced back nearly 10,000 years with the discovery of Pinto Man, and evidence of more recent habitation can be seen in the form of Native American pictographs carved into rock faces throughout the park. Miners and ranchers began coming in the 1860s, but the boom went bust by the turn of the century. Then a Pasadena doctor, treating World War I veterans suffering from respiratory and heart ailments caused by mustard gas, prescribed the desert's clean, dry air—and the modern town of Twentynine Palms was (re)born.

In the 1920s, a worldwide fascination with the desert emerged, and cactus gardens were very much in vogue. Entrepreneurs hauled truckloads of desert plants into Los Angeles for quick sale or export, and souvenir hunters removed archaeological treasures. Incensed that the beautiful Mojave was in danger of being picked clean, Los Angeles socialite Minerva Hoyt organized a desert conservation movement and successfully lobbied for the establishment of Joshua Tree National Monument in 1936.

In 1994, under provisions of the federal California Desert Protection Act, Joshua Tree was "upgraded" to national park status and expanded to nearly 800,000 acres.

ESSENTIALS

GETTING THERE   From metropolitan Los Angeles, the usual route to the Oasis Visitor Center in Joshua Tree National Park is via I-10 to its intersection with Calif. 62 (some 92 miles east of downtown). Calif. 62 (the Twentynine Palms Highway) leads northeast for about 43 miles to the town of Twentynine Palms. Total driving time is around 2½ hours. In town, follow the signs at National Park Drive or Utah Trail to the visitor center and ranger station. Admission to the park is $10 per car (good for 7 days).

VISITOR CENTERS & INFORMATION   In addition to the main **Oasis Visitor Center** at the Twentynine Palms entrance, **Cottonwood Visitor Center** is at the south entrance, and the privately operated **Park Center** is located in the town of Joshua Tree.

The Oasis Visitor Center is open daily (except Christmas) from 8am to 4:30pm. Check here for a detailed map of park roads, plus schedules of ranger-guided walks and interpretive programs. Ask about the weekend tours of the Desert Queen Ranch, once a working homestead and now part of the park.

For information before you go, contact the **Park Superintendent's Office,** 74485 National Park Dr., Twentynine Palms, CA 92277 (© **760/367-5500;** www.nps.gov/jotr). Another terrific website on the park and surrounding communities is **www.desertgold.com.**

EXPLORING THE PARK

An excellent first stop, outside the park's north entrance, is the main **Oasis Visitor Center,** located alongside the Oasis of Mara, also known as the Twentynine Palms Oasis. For many generations, the native Serrano tribe lived at this "place of little springs and much grass." Get maps, books, and the latest in road, trail, and weather conditions before beginning your tour.

From the Oasis Center, drive south to **Jumbo Rocks,** which captures the complete essence of the park: a vast array of rock formations, a Joshua tree forest, and the yucca-dotted desert, open and wide. Check out Skull Rock (one of the many rocks in the area that appear to resemble humans, dinosaurs, monsters,

cathedrals, and castles) via a 1½-mile-long nature trail that provides an introduction to the park's flora, wildlife, and geology.

At Cap Rock Junction, the main park road swings north toward the
Wonderland of Rocks, 12 square miles of massive jumbled granite. This
curious maze of stone hides groves of Joshua trees, trackless washes, and several
small pools of water. To the south is Keys View Road, which dead-ends at mile-
high **Keys View.** From the crest of the Little San Bernardino Mountains, enjoy
grand desert views that encompass both the highest (Mount San Gorgonio) and
lowest (Salton Sea) points in southern California.

Don't miss the contrasting Colorado Desert terrain found along Pinto Basin
Road—to conserve time, you might plan to exit the park via this route, which
ends up at I-10. You'll pass both the **Cholla Cactus Garden** and spindly
Ocotillo Patch on your way to vast, flat **Pinto Basin,** a barren lowland surrounded by austere mountains and punctuated by trackless sand dunes. The
dunes are an easy 2-mile (round-trip) hike from the backcountry camping board
(one of the few man-made markers along this road and one of the only designated parking areas), or simply continue to **Cottonwood Springs,** near the
southern park entrance. Besides a small ranger station and well-developed campground, Cottonwood has a cool, palm-shaded oasis that is the trailhead for a
tough hike to Lost Palms Oasis.

HIKING, BIKING & CLIMBING

HIKING & NATURE WALKS   The national park holds a variety of nature
trails ranging in difficulty from strenuous challenges to kid-friendly interpretive
walks—two of these (**Oasis of Mara** and **Cap Rock**) are paved and wheelchair-
accessible. Our favorite of the 11 short interpretive trails is **Cholla Cactus
Garden,** smack-dab in the middle of the park, where you stroll through dense
clusters of the deceptively fluffy-looking "teddy bear cactus."

For the more adventurous, **Barker Dam** is an easy 1.1-mile loop accessible by
a graded dirt road east of Hidden Valley. A small, man-made lake is framed by
the majestic Wonderland of Rocks. In addition to scrambling atop the old dam,
it's fun to search out Native American petroglyphs carved into the base of cliffs
lining your return to the trailhead.

The moderately challenging **Lost Horse Mine Trail** near Keys View leads
through rolling hills to the ruins of a successful gold-mining operation; once
here, a short, steep hike leads uphill behind the ruins for a fine view into the
heart of the park.

When you're ready for a strenuous hike, try the **Fortynine Palms Oasis Trail,**
accessible from Canyon Road in Twentynine Palms. After a steep, harsh ascent
to a cactus-fringed ridge, the rocky canyon trail leads to a spectacular oasis, complete with palm-shaded pools of green water and abundant birds and other
wildlife. Allow 2 to 3 hours for the 3-mile (round-trip) hike.

Another lush oasis lies at the end of **Lost Palms Oasis Trail** at Cottonwood
Springs. The first section of the 7½-mile trail is moderately difficult, climbing
slowly to the oasis overlook; from here, a treacherous path continues to the
canyon bottom, a remote spot that the elusive bighorn sheep find attractive.

MOUNTAIN BIKING   Much of the park is designated wilderness, meaning
that bicycles are limited to roads (they'll damage the fragile ecosystem if you venture off the beaten track). None of the paved roads have bike lanes, but rugged
mountain bikes are a great tool to explore the park via unpaved roads, where dis-
traction from autos is light.

Try the 18-mile **Geology Tour Road,** which begins west of Jumbo Rocks; dry lake beds contrast with towering boulders along this sandy downhill road, and you'll also encounter abandoned mines.

A shorter but still rewarding ride begins at the **Covington Flats** picnic area; a steep 4-mile road climbs through Joshua trees, junipers, and piñon pines to Eureka Peak, where you'll be rewarded by a panoramic view.

For other bike-friendly unpaved and four-wheel-drive roads, consult the official park map.

ROCK CLIMBING From Hidden Valley to the Wonderland of Rocks, the park has emerged as one of the world's premier rock-climbing destinations. The park offers some 4,000 climbing routes, ranging from the easiest of bouldering to some of the sport's most difficult technical climbs. November through May is the prime season to watch lizard-like humans scale sheer rock faces with impossible grace. Even beginners can get into the act: At **First Ascent** (✆ **800/ 325-5462**), certified guides start the day with detailed instruction, then stay with you, providing guidance as you learn the ropes. All equipment is provided, and prices start at $75.

ACCOMMODATIONS & CAMPING

If you're staying in the Palm Springs area, it's entirely possible to make a day-trip to the national park. But if you'd like to stay close by and spend more time here, Twentynine Palms, just outside the north boundary of the national park on Calif. 62, offers budget to moderate lodging.

Near the visitor center in the Oasis of Mara is the rustic **29 Palms Inn** (✆ **760/367-3505;** www.29palmsinn.com), a cluster of adobe cottages and old cabins dating from the 1920s; its garden-fresh restaurant is the best in town. There's also the 100-room **Best Western Garden Inn** (✆ **760/367-9141;** www. bestwestern.com), a comfortable base from which to maximize your outdoor time.

For a complete listing of Twentynine Palms lodging, contact the **29 Palms Chamber of Commerce,** 5672 Historic Plaza, Twentynine Palms, CA 92277 (✆ **760/367-3445;** fax 760/367-3366; www.29chamber.com).

Nine **campgrounds** scattered throughout the park offer pleasant though often spartan accommodations, with just picnic tables and pit toilets for the most part. Only two—**Black Rock Canyon** and **Cottonwood Springs**—have potable water and flush toilets, plus a $10 overnight fee. You can make campground reservations online at http://reservations.nps.gov or by calling ✆ **800/365-2267.**

5 Mojave National Preserve

180 miles E of Los Angeles, 75 miles SW of Las Vegas

Two decades of park politicking finally ended in 1994 when President Clinton signed into law the California Desert Protection Act, which created the new Mojave National Preserve. Thus far, the Mojave's elevated status has not attracted hordes of sightseers, and devoted visitors are happy to keep it that way. Unlike a fully protected national park, the "national preserve" designation allows certain commercial land uses, and the continued grazing and mining within the preserve's boundaries are a sore spot for ardent environmentalists.

To most Americans, the East Mojave is that vast, bleak, interminable stretch of desert to be crossed as quickly as possible while leaving California via I-15 or I-40. Few realize that these highways are the boundaries of what some have long considered the crown jewel of the California desert.

This land is a hard one to get to know—unlike more developed desert parks, it has no lodgings or concessions, few campgrounds, and only a handful of roads suitable for the average passenger vehicle. But hidden within this natural fortress are some true gems—the preserve's 1.4 million acres include the world's largest Joshua tree forest; abundant wildlife; spectacular canyons, caverns, and volcanic formations; nationally honored scenic back roads and footpaths to historic mining sites; tabletop mesas; and a dozen mountain ranges.

ESSENTIALS

GETTING THERE   I-15, the major route taken between the southern California metropolis and the state line by Las Vegas–bound travelers, extends along the northern boundary of Mojave National Preserve. I-40 is the southern access route to the East Mojave.

WHEN TO GO   Spring is a splendid time to visit this desert (autumn is another). From March to May, the temperatures are mild, the Joshua trees are in bloom, and the lower Kelso Dunes are bedecked with yellow and white desert primrose and pink sand verbena.

VISITOR CENTERS & INFORMATION   The best source for up-to-date weather conditions and a free topographical map is the **Mojave Desert Information Center,** 72157 Baker Blvd. (under the "World's Tallest Thermometer"), Baker, CA 92309 (✆ **760/733-4040**), which is open daily from 9am to 5pm and also has a superior selection of books for sale.

Those coming in on I-40 should stop in **Needles,** where the **Needles Information Center,** 707 W. Broadway, Needles, CA 92363 (✆ **760/326-6322**) is open Tuesday through Sunday 8am to 4pm.

Additional information and maps are available inside the preserve at the **Hole-in-the-Wall Campground's Visitor Center** ✆ **760/928-2572,** which is open seasonally (as staffing allows).

There's also the **California Desert Information Center,** 831 Barstow Rd., Barstow, CA 92311 (✆ **760/255-8760**), which has a minimuseum and educational displays on the history and characteristics of the desert. It's open daily from 9am to 5pm. You can visit the preserve online at **www.nps.gov/moja**.

EXPLORING THE PARK

One of the preserve's spectacular sights is the **Kelso Dunes,** the most extensive dune field in the West. The 45-square-mile formation of magnificently sculpted sand is famous for "booming": Visitors' footsteps cause mini-avalanches and make the dunes go "sha-boom-sha-boom-sha-boom." Geologists speculate that the extreme dryness of the East Mojave Desert, combined with the wind-polished, rounded nature of the individual sand grains, has something to do with their musicality. Sometimes the low rumbling sound resembles a Tibetan gong; other times, it sounds like a 1950s doo-wop musical group.

A 10-mile drive from the Kelso Dunes is **Kelso Depot,** built by the Union Pacific in 1924. The Spanish revival–style structure was designed with a red-tile roof, graceful arches, and a brick platform. The depot continued to be open for freight-train crew use through the mid–1980s, although it ceased to be a railroad stop for passengers after World War II. The National Park Service is considering refurbishing the building for use as the preserve's visitor center.

On and around **Cima Dome,** a rare geological anomaly, grows the world's largest and densest Joshua tree forest. Botanists say Cima's Joshuas are more symmetrical than their cousins elsewhere in the Mojave. The dramatic colors of the sky at sunset provide a breathtaking backdrop for Cima's Joshua trees, some more than 25 feet tall and several hundred years old.

Tucked into the Providence Mountains, in the southern portion of the preserve, is a treat everyone should try to see. The **Mitchell Caverns,** contained in a State Recreation Area within the National Preserve, are a geological oddity exploited for tourism but still quite fascinating. Regular tours are conducted of these cool rock "rooms"; in addition to showcasing marvelous stalactites, stalagmites, and other limestone formations, the caves have proven to be rich in Native American archaeological finds.

Hole-in-the-Wall and Mid Hills are the centerpieces of Mojave National Preserve. Both locales offer diverse desert scenery, fine campgrounds, and the feeling of being in the middle of nowhere—because you are.

The preserve's best drive links the two sites. In 1989, **Wildhorse Canyon Road,** which loops from Mid Hills Campground to Hole-in-the-Wall Campground, was declared the nation's first official "Back Country Byway," an honor federal agencies bestow upon America's most scenic back roads. The 11-mile, horseshoe-shaped road crosses wide-open country dotted with cholla and, in season, delicate purple, yellow, and red wildflowers. Dramatic volcanic slopes and flat-top mesas tower over the low desert.

Mile-high **Mid Hills,** so named because of its location halfway between the Providence and New York mountains, recalls the Great Basin Desert topography of Nevada and Utah. Mid Hills Campground offers a grand observation point from which to gaze out at the creamy, coffee-colored Pinto Mountains to the north and the rolling Kelso Dunes shining on the western horizon.

Hole-in-the-Wall is the kind of place Butch Cassidy and the Sundance Kid would have chosen as a hideout. This twisted maze of rhyolite rocks is a form of crystallized red-lava rock. A series of iron rings aids descent into Hole-in-the-Wall; they're not particularly difficult for those who are reasonably agile and take their time.

Kelso Dunes, Mitchell Caverns, Cima Dome, and Hole-in-the-Wall—these highlights of the preserve can be viewed in a weekend. But you'll need a week just to see all the major sights, and maybe a lifetime to really get to know the East Mojave. And right now, without much in the way of services, the traveler to this desert must be well prepared and self-reliant. For many, this is what makes a trip to the East Mojave an adventure.

If Mojave National Preserve attracts you, you'll want to return again and again to see the wonders of this desert, including **Caruthers Canyon,** a "botanical island" of piñon pine and juniper woodland, and **Ivanpah Valley,** which supports the largest desert tortoise population in the California desert.

HIKING & BIKING

HIKING   The free-form ambling climb to the top of the **Kelso Dunes** is 3 miles round-trip. A cool, inviting piñon pine/juniper woodland is explored by the **Caruthers Canyon Trail** (3 miles round-trip). The longest pathway is the 8-mile (one-way) **Mid Hills to Hole-in-the-Wall Trail,** a grand tour of basin and range tabletop mesas, large piñon trees, and colorful cacti. If you're not up for a long day hike, the 1-mile trip from **Hole-in-the-Wall Campground** to **Banshee Canyon** and the 5-mile jaunt to **Wildhorse Canyon** offer some easier alternatives. Be sure to pick up trail maps at one of the visitor centers.

MOUNTAIN BIKING   Opportunities are as extensive as the preserve's hundreds of miles of lonesome dirt roads. The 140-mile-long historic **Mojave Road,** a rough four-wheel-drive route, visits many of the most scenic areas in the East Mojave; sections of this road make excellent bike tours. Prepare well: The Mojave Road and other dirt roads are rugged routes through desert wilderness.

CAMPING

The **Mid Hills Campground** is located in a piñon pine/juniper woodland and offers outstanding views. This mile-high camp is the coolest in the East Mojave. Nearby **Hole-in-the-Wall Campground** is perched above two dramatic canyons. *Warning:* The washboard dirt road between the two might be too jarring for many two-wheel-drive passenger cars.

There are also some sites at **Providence Mountain State Recreation Area** (Mitchell Caverns, see "Exploring the Park," above).

One of the highlights of the East Mojave Desert is camping in the open desert all by your lonesome, but certain rules apply. Call the Mojave Desert Information Center for suggestions.

NEARBY TOWNS WITH TOURIST SERVICES

BARSTOW   This sizable town has a great many restaurants and motels, and is roughly a 1-hour drive from the center of the preserve. Of the dozen motels in town, the most reliable are the **Best Western Desert Villa,** 1984 E. Main St., Barstow, CA 92311 (© **760/256-1781**), and the **Holiday Inn,** 1511 E. Main St., Barstow, CA 92311 (© **760/256-5673**).

BAKER   Accommodations and food are available in this small desert town, which is a good place to fill up your gas tank and purchase supplies before entering Mojave National Preserve. Inexpensive lodging can be secured at the **Bun Boy Motel,** P.O. Box 130, Baker, CA 92309 (© **760/733-4363**). The Bun Boy Coffee Shop is open 24 hours. For a tasty surprise, stop at the **Mad Greek** (© **760/733-4354**). Order a Greek salad, a souvlaki, or baklava, and marvel at your good fortune—imagine finding such tasty food and pleasant surroundings in the middle of nowhere.

NIPTON   This tiny, charming town boasts a "trading post" that stocks snacks, maps, ice, and native jewelry; and the **Hotel Nipton** (© **760/856-2335**), a B&B with a sitting room, two bathrooms down the hall, and four guest rooms, each going for $60 a night. Jerry Freeman, a former hard-rock miner who purchased the entire town in 1984, says hotel occupancy is up 80% since the East Mojave became a national preserve. He and his wife, Roxanne, moved from the famous sands of Malibu to the abandoned ghost town and have gradually brought it back to life. Nipton is located on Nipton Road, a few miles from I-15 near the Nevada state line.

PRIMM (FORMERLY STATELINE)   This privately owned town on the California–Nevada border features three hotel/casinos—Whiskey Pete's, Buffalo Bill's, and Primadonna—each as large and garish as an amusement park and all managed by the same company. Rooms here are pretty nice, really cheap, and (if you have a twisted sense of humor) an ironic counterpoint to the wilderness you came for. With a dozen restaurants, including those low-cost Vegas-style buffets, Primm might also be your best dining bet. For reservations, call © **800/ FUNSTOP** or browse through **www.vegas.com**.

6 Death Valley National Park

115 miles N of Baker, 290 miles NE of Los Angeles

Park? Death Valley National Park? The Forty-niners, whose suffering gave the valley its name, would have howled at the notion. To them, other four-letter words would have been more appropriate: gold, mine, heat, lost, dead. And the four-letter words shouted by teamsters who drove the 20-mule-team borax wagons need not be repeated.

Americans looking for gold in California's mountains in 1849 were forced to cross the burning sands to avoid severe snowstorms in the nearby Sierra Nevada. Some perished along the way, and the land became known as Death Valley.

Mountains stand naked, unadorned. The bitter waters of saline lakes evaporate into bizarre, razor-sharp crystal formations. Jagged canyons jab deep into the earth. Oven-like heat, frigid cold, and the driest air imaginable combine to make this one of the most inhospitable locations in the world.

But, human nature being what it is, it's not surprising that people have long been drawn to challenge the power of Mother Nature, even in this, her home court. Man's first foray into tourism began in 1925, a scant 76 years after the Forty-niners' harrowing experiences (which would discourage most sane folks from ever returning!). It probably would have begun sooner, but the valley had been consumed with lucrative borax mining since the late 1880s.

Death Valley is raw, bare earth, the way it must have looked before life began. Here, forces of the earth are exposed to view with dramatic clarity; just looking out on the landscape, it's impossible to know what year—or what century—it is. It's no coincidence that many of Death Valley's topographical features are associated with hellish images—the Funeral Mountains, Furnace Creek, Dante's View, Coffin Peak, and the Devil's Golf Course. But it can be a place of serenity.

In one of his last official acts, President Herbert Hoover signed a proclamation designating Death Valley a national monument on February 11, 1933. With the stroke of a pen, he not only authorized the protection of a vast and wondrous land, but also helped to transform one of the earth's least hospitable spots into a popular tourist destination.

The naming of Death Valley National Monument came at a time when Americans began to discover the romance of the desert. Land that had previously been considered hideously devoid of life was now celebrated for its spare beauty; places that had once been feared for their harshness were now admired for their uniqueness.

In 1994, when President Clinton signed the California Desert Protection Act, Death Valley National Park became the largest national park outside Alaska, with over 3.3 million acres. Though remote, it's one of the most heavily visited, and you're likely to hear less English spoken than German, French, and Japanese.

Today's visitor to Death Valley drives in air-conditioned comfort, stays in comfortable hotel rooms or at well-maintained campgrounds, orders meals and provisions at park concessions, even quaffs a cold beer at the local saloon. You can take a swim in the Olympic-size pool, tour a Moorish castle, shop for souvenirs, and enjoy the desert landscape while hiking along a nature trail with a park ranger.

ESSENTIALS

GETTING THERE   There are several routes into the park, all of which involve crossing one of the steep mountain ranges that isolate Death Valley from, well, everything. Perhaps the most scenic entry to the park is via Calif. 190, east of Calif. 178 from Ridgecrest. Another scenic drive to the park is by way of Calif. 127 and Calif. 190 from Baker. You'll be required to pay a $10-per-car entrance fee, valid for 7 days.

VISITOR CENTER & INFORMATION   The **Death Valley Visitor Center** at Furnace Creek, 15 miles inside the eastern park boundary on Calif. 190 (© **760/786-2331**), offers interpretive exhibits and an hourly slide program. Ask at the information desk for ranger-led nature walks and evening naturalist programs. Hours are daily from 8am to 7pm in winter (to 5pm in summer). For information before you go, contact the Superintendent, Death Valley National Park, Death Valley, CA 92328 (© **760/786-2331;** www.nps.gov/deva).

EXPLORING THE PARK

A good first stop after checking in at the main park visitor center in Furnace Creek is the **Harmony Borax Works**—a rock-salt landscape as tortured as you'll ever find. Death Valley prospectors called borax "white gold," and though it wasn't exactly a glamorous substance, it was a profitable one. From 1883 to 1888, more than 20 million pounds of borax were transported from the Harmony Borax Works, and borax mining continued in Death Valley until 1928. A short trail with interpretive signs leads past the ruins of the old borax refinery and some outlying buildings.

Transport of the borax was the stuff of legends, too. The famous 20-mule teams hauled the huge loaded wagons 165 miles to the rail station at Mojave. (To learn more about this colorful era, visit the Borax Museum at Furnace Creek Ranch and the park visitor center, also located in Furnace Creek.)

Badwater—at 282 feet below sea level, the lowest point in the Western Hemisphere—is also one of the hottest places in the world, with regularly recorded summer temperatures of 120°F.

Salt Creek is the home of the **Salt Creek pupfish,** found nowhere else on earth. This little fish, which has made some amazing adaptations to survive in this arid land, can be glimpsed from a wooden-boardwalk nature trail. In spring, a million pupfish might be wriggling in the creek, but by summer's end only a few thousand remain.

Before sunrise, photographers set up their tripods at **Zabriskie Point** and aim their cameras down at the magnificent panoramic view of Golden Canyon's pale mudstone hills and the great valley beyond. For another spectacular vista, check out **Dante's View,** a 5,475-foot viewpoint looking out over the shimmering Death Valley floor, backed by the high Panamint Mountains.

Just south of Furnace Creek is the 9-mile loop of **Artists Drive,** an easy must-see for visitors (except those in RVs, which can't negotiate the sharp, rock-bordered curves in the road). From the highway, you can't see the splendid palette of colors splashed on the rocks behind the foothills; once inside, though, stop and climb a low hill that offers an overhead view, then continue through to aptly named **Artists Palette,** where an interpretive sign explains the source of nature's rainbow.

Scotty's Castle, the Mediterranean hacienda in the northern part of the park, is unabashedly Death Valley's premier tourist attraction. Visitors are wowed by the elaborate Spanish tiles, well-crafted furnishings, and innovative construction that included solar water heating. Even more compelling is the colorful history of this villa in remote Grapevine Canyon, brought to life by park rangers dressed in 1930s period clothing. Don't be surprised if the castle cook or a friend of Scotty's gives you a special insight into castle life.

Construction of the "castle"—more officially, Death Valley Ranch—began in 1924. It was to be a winter retreat for eccentric Chicago millionaire Albert Johnson. The insurance tycoon's unlikely friendship with prospector, cowboy,/ and spinner-of-tall-tales Walter Scott put the $2.3-million structure on the map and captured the public's imagination. Scotty greeted visitors and told them fanciful stories from the early hard-rock mining days of Death Valley.

The 1-hour walking tour of Scotty's Castle is excellent, both for its inside look at the mansion and for what it reveals about the eccentricities of Johnson and Scotty. Tours fill up quickly; arrive early for the first available spots (there's an $8 fee). A snack bar and gift shop make the wait more comfortable. To learn more about the castle grounds, pick up the pamphlet *A Walking Tour of Scotty's Castle,* which leads you on an exploration from stable to swimming pool, from bunkhouse to powerhouse.

Near Scotty's Castle is **Ubehebe Crater.** It's known as an explosion crater—one look and you'll know why. When hot magma rose from the depths of the earth to meet the groundwater, the resultant steam blasted out a crater and scattered cinders.

BIKING & HIKING

BIKING   Because most (94%) of the park is federally designated wilderness, cycling is allowed only on roads used by cars. Cycling is not allowed on hiking trails.

Good routes for bikers include Racetrack (28 miles, mainly level), Greenwater Valley (30 miles, mostly level), Cottonwood Canyon (20 miles), and West Side Road (40 miles, fairly level with some washboard sections). Artists Drive is 8 miles long and paved, with some steep uphills. A favorite is Titus Canyon (28 miles on a hilly road—it's highly recommended that you make this a one-way descent).

HIKING   The trails in Death Valley range from the half-mile **Salt Creek Nature Trail,** an easy boardwalk path suitable for everyone in the family, to the grueling **Telescope Peak Trail** (14 miles round-trip), an all-day challenge. Telescope Peak is a strenuous, 3,000-foot climb to the 11,049-foot summit, where you'll be rewarded by the view described by one pioneer: "You can see so far, it's just like looking through a telescope." Snow-covered during the winter, the peak is best climbed between May and November.

But there are lots of levels in between. We like the trail into **Mosaic Canyon,** near Stovepipe Wells, where water has polished the marble rock into white, gray, and black mosaics. It's a relatively easy 2½-mile scramble through long, narrow walls that seem quite "gallery-like"—and provide welcome shade at every turn.

Romping among the **Sand Dunes** on the way to Stovepipe Wells is also fun, particularly for kids. It's a free-form adventure, and the dunes aren't particularly high—but the sun can be merciless. The sand in the dunes is actually tiny pieces of rock, most of them quartz fragments. As with all desert activities, your water supply is crucial.

Near the park's eastern border, two trails lead from the **Keane Wonder Mill,** site of a successful gold mine. The first is a steep and strenuous 2-mile challenge leading to the mine itself, passing along the way the solid, efficient wooden tramway that carried ore out of the mountain.

If that's beyond your fitness level, try the **Keane Wonder Spring Trail,** leading in another direction. This 2-mile walk is much easier, and the spring that supplied water for the Keane Wonder operation will announce itself with a sulfur smell and piping birdcalls.

If you're visiting **Ubehebe Crater,** there's a steep but plain trail leading from the parking area up to the crater's lip and around some of the contours. Fierce winds can hamper your progress, but you'll get the exhilarating feeling that you're truly on another planet.

Park rangers can provide topographical maps and detailed directions to these and a dozen other hiking trails within the national park.

CAMPING & ACCOMMODATIONS

The park's nine campgrounds are located at elevations ranging from below sea level to 8,000 feet. In Furnace Creek, **Sunset** offers 1,000 spaces with water and flush toilets. **Furnace Creek Campground** has 200 similarly appointed spaces. **Stovepipe Wells** has 200 spaces with water and flush toilets. Camping reservations may be made online at **http://reservations.nps.gov** or by calling ✆ **800/365-2267.**

The **Furnace Creek Ranch** (✆ **760/786-2345;** www.furnacecreekresort. com) has 224 no-frills cottage units with air-conditioning and showers. The swimming pool is a popular hangout for tired lodgers. Nearby are a coffee shop, saloon, steak house, and general store.

Stove Pipe Wells Village (✆ **760/786-2387**) has 74 modest rooms with air-conditioning and showers, plus a casual dining room that closes between meals.

The only lodging within the park not operated by the official concessionaire is the **Panamint Springs Resort** (✆ **702/482-7680;** www.deathvalley.com), a truly charming rustic motel, cafe, and snack shop about an hour east of Furnace Creek.

Because accommodations in Death Valley are both limited and expensive, you might consider the money-saving (but inconvenient) option of spending a night at one of the two gateway towns: **Lone Pine,** on the west side of the park, or **Baker,** on the south. **Beatty, Nevada,** which has inexpensive lodging, is an hour's drive from the park's center. The restored **Amargosa Hotel** (✆ **760/ 852-4441**) in Death Valley Junction offers 14 rooms in a historic, out-of-the-way place, 40 minutes from Furnace Creek.

Helpful hint: Meals and groceries are exceptionally costly due to the remoteness of the park. If possible, consider bringing a cooler with some snacks, sandwiches, and beverages to last the duration of your visit. Ice is easily obtainable, and you'll also be able to keep water chilled.

Furnace Creek Inn   Like an oasis in the middle of stark Death Valley, the inn's red-tiled roofs and sparkling blue mineral-spring-fed swimming pool hint at the elegance within. The hotel has equipped its 66 deluxe rooms and suites with every modern amenity while successfully preserving the charm of this 1930s resort. Stroll the lush, palm-shaded gardens before sitting down to a meal in the elegant Dining Room, where the food is excellent but the formality a bit out of place. Don tennis whites for a match in the mid-winter sunshine, enjoy 18 holes of golf nearby, take an excursion on horseback—there's even a shuttle from the Furnace Creek private airstrip for well-heeled clientele. Reserve early: The inn is booked solid year-round with American and European guests who appreciate a little pampering after a day spent in the park.

Hwy. 190 (P.O. Box 1), Death Valley, CA 92328. ✆ **800/236-7916** or 760/786-2345. Fax 760/786-2307. www.furnacecreekresort.com. 66 units. Oct–May $230–$335 double; $325–$350 suite; off-season $155–$200 double, $225 suite. Extra person $15. AE, DC, DISC, MC, V. **Amenities:** Restaurant, lounge; naturally heated outdoor swimming pool; night-lit tennis courts; nearby golf course; room service (7am–10pm); in-room massage. *In room:* A/C, TV, fridge, hair dryer, iron.

16

San Diego & Environs

by Stephanie Avnet Yates

San Diego is best known for its benign climate and fabulous beaches, attributes that make the city one big outdoor playground on sunny days. With 70 miles of sandy coastline—plus pretty, sheltered Mission Bay—you can choose from swimming, snorkeling, windsurfing, kayaking, bicycling, skating, and tons of other fun in or near the water. The city is also home to top-notch attractions, including three world-famous animal parks and splendid Balboa Park, a cultural and recreational jewel that's one of the finest urban parks in the country. Once dismissed as a slow-growth, conservative Navy town, San Diego has been expanding steadily over the past decade or two, and now boasts an almost Los Angeles–like diversity of neighborhoods and residents. A heightened sensitivity to historical preservation means formerly seedy downtown neighborhoods and architecturally rich suburbs are being carefully restored; they draw a stylish young crowd that's updating the face of San Diego dining, shopping, and entertainment. California's first city, San Diego reflects its Spanish-Mexican heritage in every corner—in fact, bustling Tijuana is just across the border, less than 30 minutes away. So pack a laid-back attitude along with your sandals and swimsuit, and welcome to California's grown-up beach town.

1 Orientation

ARRIVING

BY PLANE

San Diego International Airport, 3707 N. Harbor Dr. (© **619/231-2100;** www.portofsandiego.org/sandiego_airport/index.html), locally known as Lindbergh Field, is just 3 miles from downtown. Most of the major carriers fly here. Lindbergh Field consists of three adjacent passenger buildings: Terminal 1, Terminal 2, and the Terminal 2 Expansion. Short local flights use the Commuter Terminal, which is a half mile away and can be reached from the main airport by the free "red bus" shuttle.

TRANSPORTATION FROM THE AIRPORT All the major car rental agencies have offices at the airport, including **Avis** (© 800/331-1212), **Budget** (© 800/527-0700), **Dollar** (© 800/800-3665), and **Hertz** (© 800/654-3131). If you're driving to downtown from the airport, take Harbor Drive south to Broadway, the main east-west thoroughfare, and turn left. To reach Hillcrest or Balboa Park, exit the airport toward I-5, and follow the signs for Laurel Street. To reach Mission Bay (home of SeaWorld), take I-5 north to I-8 west. To reach La Jolla, take I-5 north to the Ardath Road exit, turning onto Torrey Pines Road.

    Metropolitan Transit System (MTS) (© **619/233-3004;** www.sdcommute. com/sdmts) bus route no. 992 provides service between the airport and downtown San Diego. Route no. 992 bus stops are located at each of the three terminals.

The one-way fare is $2.25. Request a transfer if you're connecting to another bus or the San Diego Trolley route downtown. Downtown, route no. 992 stops on Broadway. The ride takes about 15 minutes; buses come at 10- to 15-minute intervals. At Broadway and First Avenue is the **Transit Store** (© **619/234-1060**), where the staff can answer your transit questions and provide free route maps to help you get where you're going.

Several **shuttles** run regularly from the airport to downtown hotels. They charge around $5 to $9 per person, and you'll see designated areas outside each terminal. The shuttles are a good deal for single travelers; two or more people traveling together might as well take a taxi.

Taxis line up outside both terminals and charge around $8 to $10 to take you to a downtown location.

BY CAR

From Los Angeles, you'll enter San Diego via coastal route I-5. From points northeast of the city, you'll come down on I-15 (link up with I-8 west and Calif. 163 south to drive into downtown). From the east, you'll come in on I-8, connecting with Calif. 163 south (Calif. 163 turns into 10th Avenue). From the south, take I-5. The freeways are well marked, pointing the way to downtown streets.

BY TRAIN

Amtrak (© **800/USA-RAIL;** www.amtrak.com) trains connect San Diego to Los Angeles and the rest of the country. Trains pull into San Diego's pretty mission-style **Santa Fe Station,** 1850 Kettner Blvd. (at Broadway), within walking distance of many downtown hotels and 1½ blocks from the Embarcadero. Expect to pay about $23 one-way from Los Angeles.

BY BUS

Greyhound (© **800/231-2222;** www.greyhound.com) serves San Diego; the bus terminal is downtown, on Broadway between Front Street and First Avenue.

VISITOR INFORMATION

The official **International Visitor Information Center** (© **619/236-1212;** www.sandiego.org) is on First Avenue at F Street, street level at Horton Plaza. The glossy *San Diego Visitors Planning Guide* includes information on accommodations, dining, activities, attractions, tours, and transportation. Ask for the *Super Savings Coupon Book,* which is full of money-saving coupons. The center is open Monday through Saturday from 8:30am to 5pm year-round and Sunday from 11am to 5pm June through August; it's closed Thanksgiving, Christmas, and New Year's Day.

Traveler's Aid (© 619/231-7361) has booths at Terminals 1 and 2 and the train station. Volunteers answer questions and provide helpful brochures and maps.

Specialized visitor information outlets include the **Balboa Park Visitors Center,** located at 1549 El Prado (© 619/239-0512); **Coronado Visitors Bureau,** 1047 B Ave., Coronado (© 800/622-8300 or 619/437-8788; www.coronadovisitors.com); and **La Jolla Town Council,** 7734 Herschel Ave., La Jolla, CA 92038 (© 858/454-1444). The **Mission Bay Visitor Information Center,** 2688 E. Mission Bay Dr., San Diego (© 619/276-8200; www.infosandiego.com), is conveniently located on Mission Bay next to I-5 (exit Clairemont Drive/Mission Bay Drive and head toward the water). The **San**

The San Diego Area at a Glance

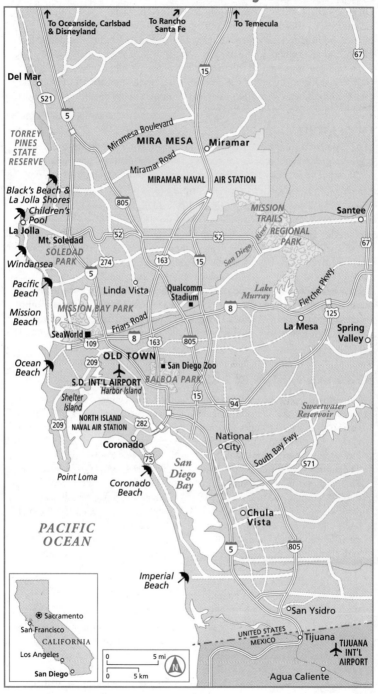

To Oceanside, Carlsbad & Disneyland

To Rancho Santa Fe

To Temecula

67

15

Del Mar

S21

5

TORREY PINES STATE RESERVE

Miramesa Boulevard

MIRA MESA

Miramar

Miramar Road

MIRAMAR NAVAL AIR STATION

Santee

Black's Beach & La Jolla Shores

Children's Pool

La Jolla

805

MISSION TRAILS REGIONAL PARK

San Diego River

67

Mt. Soledad

SOLEDAD PARK

52

52

Windansea

274

163

15

San Diego River

125

Pacific Beach

5

Linda Vista

Qualcomm Stadium

Lake Murray

Fletcher Pkwy.

Mission Beach

MISSION BAY PARK

Friars Road

8

La Mesa

Spring Valley

SeaWorld

109

8

163

805

OLD TOWN

209

San Diego Zoo

Ocean Beach

S.D. INT'L AIRPORT

Harbor Island

BALBOA PARK

15

94

Sweetwater Reservoir

Shelter Island

209

NORTH ISLAND NAVAL AIR STATION

282

National City

South Bay Fwy.

S71

Point Loma

Coronado

75

San Diego Bay

Coronado Beach

Chula Vista

5

805

PACIFIC OCEAN

Imperial Beach

San Ysidro

UNITED STATES
MEXICO

Tijuana

TIJUANA INT'L AIRPORT

CALIFORNIA

Sacramento

San Francisco

CALIFORNIA

Los Angeles

San Diego

0   5 mi

0   5 km

N

Agua Caliente

619

Diego North County Convention & Visitors Bureau, 720 N. Broadway, Escondido (© 800/848-3336 or 760/745-4741; www.sandiegonorth.com), can provide information on excursion areas in San Diego County, including Del Mar, Carlsbad, Escondido, Julian, and Anza-Borrego Desert State Park.

To find out what's on at the theater and who's playing in the clubs during your visit, pick up a copy of the *Reader,* a free weekly newspaper available all over the city. There's also a Thursday entertainment supplement called **"Night & Day"** in the *San Diego Union-Tribune.*

CITY LAYOUT

San Diego has a clearly defined downtown, which is surrounded by a dozen or more separate neighborhoods—each with its own personality, but all legally part of the city. The street system is straightforward, so getting around is fairly easy.

MAIN ARTERIES & STREETS   I-5 runs south to the United States–Mexico border and north to Old Town, Mission Bay, La Jolla, and beyond. It's the most important thoroughfare in San Diego, connecting the city's divergent parts with one another and the entire region with the rest of the state. Access to the Coronado Bay Bridge is via I-5. Balboa Park is most easily accessible via 12th Avenue, which becomes Park Boulevard. Fifth Avenue leads to the Hillcrest/Uptown area.

Downtown, Broadway is the main street. Located in the heart of the central business district, it's intersected by Fourth and Fifth Avenues (running south and north, respectively). Harbor Drive, hugging the waterfront (Embarcadero), connects downtown with the airport to the northwest and the Convention Center to the south.

NEIGHBORHOODS IN BRIEF

Downtown   The business, shopping, dining, and entertainment heart of the city, it includes Horton Plaza, the Gaslamp Quarter, the Embarcadero (waterfront), and the distinctive Convention Center. Visitors with business to conduct in the city center would be wise to stay downtown. The **Gaslamp Quarter** is the center of a massive redevelopment kicked off in the mid-1980s with the opening of **Horton Plaza,** a colorful multi-level six-block shopping mall that's a major attraction in itself. Now the once-seedy area is filled with trendy boutiques, chic restaurants, and swingin' nightspots.

Hillcrest/Uptown   Despite the cachet of being adjacent to **Balboa Park**—home to the **San Diego Zoo** and numerous splendid museums—this once-elite suburban area

north of downtown fell into neglect during the 1960s and 1970s. However, Hillcrest's charms have been restored by legions of preservation-minded residents—including a very active and fashionable gay community—and is the local equivalent of L.A.'s West Hollywood or New York's SoHo. Centrally located and packed with the latest in stylish restaurants and avant-garde boutiques, Hillcrest also offers less expensive and more personalized accommodations than anywhere else in the city.

Old Town & Mission Valley   This area encompasses the Old Town State Historic Park, Presidio Park, Heritage Park, and numerous museums harking back to the turn of the century and the city's beginnings. There's shopping and dining here, too, all aimed at tourists. Not far from Old Town lies the vast suburban sprawl of Mission Valley, home to San Diego's gigantic shopping centers. Between them is **Hotel Circle,** adjacent to I-8, where a string of mid-price and budget hotel options offer an alternative to more desirable neighborhoods.

Mission Bay & the Beaches Mission Bay is a watery playground perfect for water-skiing, sailing, and windsurfing. The adjacent communities of Ocean Beach, Mission Beach, and Pacific Beach are known for their wide stretches of sand fronting the Pacific, active nightlife, and California-casual dining. The **boardwalk,** which runs from South Mission Beach through North Mission Beach to Pacific Beach, is a popular place for in-line skating, bike riding, and watching sunsets.

La Jolla With an atmosphere that's a cross between Rodeo Drive and a Mediterranean village, this seaside community is home to an inordinate number of wealthy folks who could live anywhere, but choose to live here, surrounded by the beach, the University of California at San Diego, outstanding restaurants, pricey and traditional shops, and some of the world's best medical facilities. The name is a compromise between Spanish and American Indian, as is the pronunciation—la *hoy*-ya—and it has come to mean "the jewel."

Coronado The "island" of Coronado is actually a peninsula, home to the U.S. Naval Air Station and a town filled with charming cottages, quaint shops along Orange Avenue (the main street), and ritzy hotels and resorts that include the landmark Hotel del Coronado. Coronado has a lovely duned beach; it's also home to more retired admirals than any other community in the country.

2 Getting Around

BY CAR

San Diego has its fair share of traffic, concentrated in the downtown area, and heaviest during the morning and evening commuting hours. Aside from that, it's a very car-friendly town and easy to navigate.

Driving downtown, many streets run one way, and finding a parking space can be tricky—but some reasonably priced parking lots are centrally located.

RENTALS   All the large, national car -rental firms have rental outlets at the airport (see "Arriving," above), in the major hotels, and at other locations around the city. **Avis** (© **800/331-1212**), like several other companies, will allow its cars into Mexico as far as Ensenada, providing that you stop before crossing the border and buy Mexican auto insurance. You would also be wise to buy insurance if you drive your own car south of the border.

PARKING   Parking meters are plentiful in most San Diego areas: Posted signs indicate operating hours—generally between 8am and 6pm, even on weekends—and most meters accept only quarters. In the popular Gaslamp Quarter, consider parking in Horton Plaza's garage (G Street and Fourth Avenue), which is free to shoppers for the first 3 hours, $1 for every additional half hour.

BY PUBLIC TRANSPORTATION

Both city buses and the **San Diego Trolley**—which runs to the Mexican border, Old Town, and East County—are operated by the **San Diego Metropolitan Transit System (MTS)** (© **619/233-3004;** www.sdcommute.com/sdmts). The system's **Transit Store,** 102 Broadway at First Avenue (© **619/234-1060**), is a complete public transportation information center, supplying travelers with passes, tokens, timetables, maps, and brochures. It's open Monday through Friday from 8:30am to 5:30pm, Saturday and Sunday from 10am to 4pm. Request a copy of the useful brochure, *Your Open Door to San Diego,* which details the city's most popular tourist attractions and the buses that take you to them. For **bus route information** (and other transit FAQ), you can also call ✆ **619/ 685-4900** 24 hours a day.

The $5 **Day-Tripper pass** allows for 1 day of unlimited rides on the public transit system; you can also get a 4-day pass for $12. Passes are available from the Transit Store and at all Trolley Station automatic ticket vending machines.

BY BUS   Bus stops are marked by rectangular blue signs, every other block or so on local routes. More than 20 bus routes traverse downtown. Most fares range from $1.75 to $2.25, depending on the distance and type of service (local or express). Buses accept dollar bills, but the driver can't give change. Most buses run every half hour. Transfers should be obtained from the driver when boarding.

The **Coronado Shuttle,** route no. 904, runs between the Coronado Island Marriott and the Old Ferry Landing along Orange Avenue to the Hotel del Coronado, Glorietta Bay, Loews Coronado Bay Resort, and back again. It costs only $1 per person. Route no. 901 goes to Coronado from downtown San Diego; the fare is $2 for adults, $1 for seniors and children. Call ✆ **619/ 233-3004** for information.

BY TROLLEY   The San Diego Trolley system runs south to the Mexican border (a 40-minute trip), north to Old Town, and east to the city of Santee. Within the city, trolleys stop at many popular locations; fares range from $1.25 to $2.50. Children under 5 ride free; seniors and riders with disabilities pay only 75¢. For **recorded trolley information,** call ✆ **619/685-4900.** To talk to a real person, you can call ✆ **619/233-3004** from 5:30am to 8:30pm Monday to Friday.

Trolleys operate on a self-service fare-collection system; riders purchase tickets from machines in stations before boarding, and fare inspectors board trains at random to check tickets. The bright-red trains run every 15 minutes during the day (every half hour at night) and stop for only 30 seconds at each stop. To board, push the lighted green button beside the doors; to exit the car, push the lighted white button.

Trolleys generally operate daily from 5am to about 12:30am, although the Blue Line, which goes to the border, runs around the clock on Saturday.

BY TRAIN   Within the San Diego area, **Amtrak** (✆ **800/USA-RAIL**) stops downtown, in Solana Beach, and in Oceanside. Fares range from $3 to $3.75 each way, depending on how far you go. You can also get to Disneyland in Anaheim (see chapter 14, "Side Trips from Los Angeles") via the train; call for details.

San Diego's express rail commuter service, **The Coaster** (✆ **800/COASTER**), travels between downtown and Oceanside with stops en route at Old Town, Sorrento Valley, Solana Beach, Encinitas, and Carlsbad.

BY FERRY & WATER TAXI   There's regularly scheduled **ferry service** (✆ **619/234-4111**) between San Diego and Coronado. Ferries leave from the Broadway Pier on the hour from 9am to 9pm daily (until 10pm Friday and Saturday), and return from the Old Ferry Landing in Coronado to the Broadway Pier every hour on the 42-minute mark from 9:42am to 9:42pm daily (until 10:42pm Friday and Saturday). Ferries also run from the Fifth Avenue Landing near the Convention Center to the Old Ferry Landing at 1-hour intervals during roughly the same time period. The fare is $2 for each leg of the journey (50¢ extra if you bring your bike). Purchase tickets in advance at the Harbor Excursion kiosk on the Broadway Pier, at the Fifth Avenue Landing in San Diego, or at the Old Ferry Landing in Coronado.

Water taxis (© 619/235-TAXI) will take you around most of San Diego Bay for $5. If you want to go to the southern part of the bay (to Loews Coronado Bay Resort, for example), you'll be charged a flat fee of $25.

BY TAXI

Cab companies don't have standardized rates, except from the airport into town, which costs about $8.50 with tip. It's uncommon to find taxis cruising for passengers; phone for a guaranteed pickup. Companies include **Orange Cab** (© 619/291-3333), **San Diego Cab** (© 619/226-TAXI), and **Yellow Cab** (© 619/234-6161). The **Coronado Cab Company** (© 619/435-6211) serves Coronado. In La Jolla, call **La Jolla Cab** (© 858/453-4222).

BY ORGANIZED TOUR

The **Old Town Trolley Tours** (© 619/298-TOUR; www.trolleytours.com) isn't a trolley at all; rather, it's a privately operated open-air tour bus that travels in a continuous loop around the city, stopping at sightseeing highlights. It stops at more than a dozen places around the city, and you can hop on and off as many times as you please during one entire loop (but once you've completed the circuit, you can't go around again). A nonstop tour takes 90 minutes and is accompanied by a fast-moving live commentary on city history and sights. Major stops include Old Town, Presidio Park, Bazaar del Mundo, Balboa Park, the San Diego Zoo, the Embarcadero, Seaport Village, and the Gaslamp Quarter. Tours operate daily from 9am to 5pm; they cost $24 for adults and $12 for children ages 4 to 12; kids under 4 ride free.

Gray Line San Diego (© 800/331-5077 or 619/491-0011; www.grayline. com) offers city sightseeing, including tours of Cabrillo National Monument, SeaWorld, and La Jolla. Other trips go farther afield, to the Wild Animal Park, Wine Country, and Tijuana and Ensenada, Mexico. Prices range from $24 to $56 for adults and $10 to $35 for children. **Contact Tours** (© 800/235-5393 or 619/477-8687; www.contactours.com) offers city sightseeing tours, including a "Grand Tour" that covers San Diego, Tijuana, and a 1-hour harbor cruise. It also runs trips to the San Diego Zoo, SeaWorld, Disneyland, Universal Studios, Tijuana, Rosarito Beach, and Ensenada. Prices range from $26 to $62 for adults, $14 to $44 for children under 12, and include admissions.

BY BICYCLE

San Diego is great for bikers; it's relatively flat and many roads have designated bike lanes. If you didn't bring your own wheels, you can rent from **Bike Tours San Diego,** 509 Fifth Ave. (© 619/238-2444), or **Hamel's Action Sports Center,** 704 Ventura Place, off Mission Boulevard in Mission Beach (© 619/ 488-8889). In Coronado, there's **Bikes & Beyond** at the Old Ferry Landing (© 619/435-7180). Expect to pay $5 to $6 per hour for bicycles, $15 to $25 for surreys (pedal-powered carriages).

The **San Diego Region Bike Map** is available at visitor centers; to receive a copy in advance, call © 619/231-BIKE.

If a bus stop has a bike-route sign attached (not all of them do), you can place your bike on the bus's bike rack for free while you ride. The San Diego Trolley

FAST FACTS: **San Diego**

American Express A full-service office is located downtown at 258 Broadway, at Third Avenue ((C) **619/234-4455**).

Area Codes In the past couple of years, San Diego County's area code layout has become more complicated—much like the rest of California! The main area code, 619, is now used primarily by the core city, including downtown, uptown, Mission Valley, and Point Loma. Northern and coastal areas, including Mission Beach, Pacific Beach, La Jolla, Del Mar, Rancho Sante Fe, and Rancho Bernardo, use the area code 858. The vast southeastern portion of the city, primarily bedroom communities like El Cajon, La Mesa, National City, and Chula Vista, now use 935. Use 760 to reach the remainder of San Diego County, including Encinitas, Carlsbad, Oceanside, Escondido, Ramona, Julian, and Anza–Borrego.

Babysitters **Marion's Childcare** ((C) **619/582-5029**), has bonded baby sitters available to come to your hotel room.

Dentist/Doctor For dental referrals, contact the **San Diego County Dental Society** at (C) **800/201-0244** or 800/DENTIST. **Hotel Docs** ((C) **800/468-3537** or 619/275-2663) is a 24-hour network of physicians, dentists, and chiropractors who claim they'll come to your hotel room within 35 minutes of your call. They accept credit cards, and their services are covered by most insurance policies.

Emergencies For police, fire, highway patrol, or life-threatening medical emergencies, dial (C) **911** from any phone. No coins are required.

Hospitals The most conveniently located emergency room is at **UCSD Medical Center–Hillcrest,** 200 W. Arbor Dr. ((C) 619/543-6400). In Coronado, head to **Coronado Hospital,** 250 Prospect Place ((C) 619/435-6251). In La Jolla, **Thornton Hospital,** 9300 Campus Point Dr. ((C) 858/657-7600), has a good emergency room.

Police For non-emergency matters, contact the downtown precinct, 1401 Broadway ((C) **619/531-2000**).

Post Office Post offices are located downtown, at 815 E St.; at 51 Horton Plaza, beside the Westin Hotel; and toward Point Loma, at 2535 Midway Dr. They are generally open Monday through Friday during regular business hours, plus Saturday mornings; for specific branch information, call (C) **800/ASK-USPS** or log onto www.usps.gov.

Safety As cities go, San Diego is pretty safe. But use particular caution on beaches after dark, and stay on designated walkways and away from secluded areas in Balboa Park—night or day. In the Gaslamp Quarter, try to stay west of Fifth Avenue. Take particular care to lock your car and park in well-lit areas; San Diego's proximity to the border contributes to its high rate of auto theft.

Taxes A 7.5% sales tax is added at the register for all goods and services purchased in San Diego. The city hotel tax is 10.5%.

Useful Telephone Numbers For the correct time, call (C) **853-1212** (works in all area codes). For local **weather,** call (C) **619/289-1212.**

also allows bikes onboard for free. You just need a bike permit, which is available for $4 from the Transit Store, 102 Broadway at First Avenue (© 619/234-1060). Bikes can also be brought aboard the San Diego–Coronado ferry.

3 Accommodations

The rates listed below are all "rack," or official rates—you can often do better. Rates tend to be highest in summer (especially true of beach hotels) and when there's a big convention in town. Remember to factor in the city's 10.5% hotel tax.

For good prices in all accommodation categories, contact **San Diego Hotel Reservations** (© 800/SAVE-CASH or 619/627-9300; www.sandiegohotelres.com). Bed-and-breakfasts are growing in popularity, and several are listed below; for additional choices, contact the **San Diego Bed & Breakfast Guild** (© 619/523-1300; www.bandbguildsandiego.org).

DOWNTOWN

The downtown area is very convenient for business travelers, but also includes hotels in the stylish Gaslamp Quarter, as well as those located near the harbor and other leisure attractions.

EXPENSIVE

Embassy Suites ★★   What might seem like an impersonal business hotel is actually one of the better deals in town. It provides modern accommodations with lots of room for families or claustrophobes. Built in 1988, this neoclassical high-rise is topped with a distinctive neon bull's-eye that's visible from far away. Every room is a suite, with sofa beds in the living-dining areas and convenient touches like microwaves in the kitchenette. All rooms open onto a 12-story atrium filled with palm trees, koi ponds, and a bubbling fountain; each also has a city or bay view. One block from Seaport Village and 5 blocks from downtown, the Embassy Suites is the second choice of Convention Center groups (after the pricier Hyatt Regency) and as a result it can be fully booked at unexpected times.

601 Pacific Hwy. (at N. Harbor Dr.), San Diego, CA 92101. © 800/EMBASSY or 619/239-2400. Fax 619/239-1520. 337 suites. $189–$300 suite. Rates include full breakfast and afternoon cocktail. Children under 18 stay free in parents' room. AE, DC, DISC, MC, V. Valet parking $14; indoor self-parking $11. Bus: 7. Trolley: Seaport Village. **Amenities:** 2 restaurants; indoor pool; tennis court; exercise room; Jacuzzi; concierge; car-rental desk; babysitting; laundry service; self-service laundry; VIP rooms. *In room:* A/C, TV w/ pay movies, dataport, kitchenette, fridge, coffeemaker, hair dryer, iron.

Holiday Inn on the Bay ★★ *(Kids)*   With a location and list of services that make it ideal for business gatherings, vacationing families, and airport stopovers, this better-than-average Holiday Inn is reliable and nearly always offers great deals. The multi-building high-rise complex is located on the Embarcadero across from the harbor and the Maritime Museum—this scenic spot is only 1½ miles from the airport (you can watch planes landing and taking off), and 2 blocks from the train station and trolley. Rooms, while basic, always seem to sport clean new furnishings and plenty of thoughtful comforts. Choose your room carefully; while the bay views are astounding, city views can be depressing. In either case, request the highest floor possible.

1355 N. Harbor Dr. (at Ash St.), San Diego, CA 92101-3385. © 800/HOLIDAY or 619/232-3861. Fax 619/232-4924. 600 units. $189–$209 double; from $400 suite. Children under 18 stay free in parents' room. Terrific packages are available, as well as AARP and AAA rates as low as $99–$139. AE, DC, MC, V. Parking $13 (self) or $18 (valet). Bus: 22, 23, 992. Pets accepted with $25 fee and $75 deposit. **Amenities:** 4 restaurants,

San Diego Area Accommodations

Downtown

See La Jolla map

PACIFIC OCEAN

La Jolla Cove

LA JOLLA

UCSD

La Jolla Village Square

University Towne Center

Miramar Naval Air Staion

MISSION BAY PARK

MISSION BAY

PACIFIC BEACH

SDSU

Qualcomm Stadium

Balboa Park Inn **25**
The Beach Cottages **13**
Beach Haven Inn **14**
Best Western Bayside Inn **3**
Best Western Blue Sea Lodge **15**
Catamaran Resort Hotel **16**
Clarion Hotel Bay View **9**
Comfort Inn–Downtown **4**
Coronado Inn **28**
Coronado Island
  Marriott Resort **29**
The Cottage **23**
Crone's Cobblestone Cottage **22**
Crystal Pier Hotel **11**
El Cordova Hotel **30**
Elsbree House **18**
Embassy Suites **7**
Gaslamp Plaza Suites **5**
Glorietta Bay Inn **32**
Heritage Park
  Bed & Breakfast Inn **21**
Holiday Inn on the Bay **2**
Horton Grand **8**
Hotel del Coronado **33**
Keating House **27**
La Pensione Hotel **1**
Loews Coronado Bay Resort **34**
Ocean Park Inn **12**
Pacific Terrace Hotel **10**
Paradise Point Resort **17**
Park Manor Suites **26**
Red Lion Hanalei Hotel **20**
Sommerset Suites Hotel **24**
US Grant Hotel **6**
Vacation Inn **19**
Village Inn **31**

lounge; outdoor heated pool; exercise room; concierge; business center; room service (6–11am and 5–11pm); babysitting; laundry service; self-service laundry. *In room:* A/C, TV w/ pay movies, dataport, coffeemaker, hair dryer, iron.

U.S. Grant Hotel ★★★

In 1910, Ulysses S. Grant, Jr. opened this stately hotel, now on the National Register of Historic Places, in honor of his father. Famous guests have included Albert Einstein, Charles Lindbergh, FDR, and JFK. Resembling an Italianate palace, the hotel is of a style more often found on the East Coast. An elegant atmosphere prevails, with age-smoothed marble, wood paneling, crystal chandeliers, and formal room decor that verges on stuffy. Guest rooms are quite spacious, as are the richly outfitted bathrooms. Extras in the suites make them worth the splurge; each has a fireplace and whirlpool tub, and suite rates include continental breakfast and afternoon cocktails and hors d'oeuvres. Afternoon tea is served in the lobby Tuesday through Saturday with soft piano music as a backdrop. While the hotel has preserved a nostalgic formality, the surrounding neighborhood has become a hodgepodge of chic bistros, wandering panhandlers, and the visually loud Horton Plaza shopping center. (Planet Hollywood looms large right across the street.)

326 Broadway (between Third and Fourth Aves.), San Diego, CA 92101. ✆ **800/237-5029** or 619/232-3121. Fax 619/232-3626. www.grandheritage.com. 340 units. $195–$215 double; from $275 suite. Children under 12 stay free in parents' room. AAA, off-season, and weekend rates ($139–$179 double) available; off-season packages available. AE, DC, MC, V. Parking $17. Bus: 2. Trolley: Civic Center (C St. and Third Ave.). Pets welcomed. **Amenities:** Restaurant, jazz lounge; 24-hour fitness center; in-room exercise bike/rowing machine rental; concierge; courtesy airport shuttle; business center; 24-hour room service; babysitting; laundry and dry cleaning service. *In room:* A/C, TV w/ pay movies, dataport, minibar, hair dryer.

MODERATE

Other reliable choices include the **Clarion Hotel Bay View San Diego,** 660 K St., at Sixth Avenue (✆ **800/766-0234** or 619/696-0234; www.clarionbayview.com), adjacent to downtown and the Gaslamp Quarter. The **Best Western Bayside Inn,** 555 W. Ash St., at Columbia Street (✆ **800/341-1818** or 619/233-7500; www.baysideinn.com), is popular with business travelers and boasts magnificent views.

Gaslamp Plaza Suites ★★ Value

You can't get closer to the center of the vibrant Gaslamp Quarter than this impeccably restored late Victorian. At 11 stories, it was San Diego's first skyscraper in 1913. Built (at great expense) of Australian gumwood, marble, brass, and exquisite etched glass, this splendid building originally housed San Diego Trust & Savings. Various other businesses (jewelers, lawyers, doctors, photographers) set up shop here until 1988, when the elegant structure was placed on the National Register of Historic Places and reopened as a boutique hotel.

You'll be surprised at the timeless elegance, from the dramatic lobby and wide corridors to guest rooms furnished with European flair. Each bears the name of a writer (Emerson, Swift, Zola, Shelley, Fitzgerald, and so on). Most rooms are spacious and offer luxuries rare in this price range, like pillow-top mattresses and premium toiletries; microwave ovens and dinnerware; and impressive luxury bathrooms. Beware of the few cheapest rooms, however; they are uncomfortably small (although they do have regular-size bathrooms).

Do remember where you are, though, and expect to hear some traffic and street noise, even in your room.

520 E St. (corner of 5th Ave.), San Diego, CA 92101. ✆ **619/232-9500.** Fax 619/238-9945. 64 units. $93–$139 double; $139–$179 suite. Rates include continental breakfast. AE, DC, DISC, MC, V. Valet parking $11. Bus: 1, 3, 25. Trolley: Fifth Ave. **Amenities:** Restaurant; access to nearby health club; rooftop Jacuzzi. *In room:* A/C, TV/VCR, dataport, fridge, coffeemaker, hair dryer, iron.

Horton Grand ★★   A cross between an elegant hotel and a charming inn, the Horton Grand combines two hotels that date from 1886—the Horton Grand (once an infamous red-light establishment) and the Brooklyn Hotel (which for a time was the Kahle Saddlery Shop). Both were saved from demolition, moved to this spot, and connected by an airy atrium lobby filled with white wicker. The facade, with its graceful bay windows, is original.

Each room is utterly unique; all were renovated in 2000 with vintage furnishings, gas fireplaces, and business-savvy features; bathrooms are resplendent with reproduction floor tiles, fine brass fixtures, and genteel appointments. Rooms overlook either the city or the fig tree–filled courtyard—they're divided between the clubby and darker "saddlery" side and the pastel-toned and Victorian "brothel" side. The suites (really just large studio-style rooms) are located in a newer wing; choosing one means sacrificing historic character for a sitting area/sofa bed and minibar with microwave oven. With all these offerings, there's a room that's right for everyone, so query your reservationist on the different features.

The Palace Bar serves afternoon tea Tuesday through Saturday from 2:30 to 5pm; there's live music Thursday through Saturday evenings and Sunday afternoons.

311 Island Ave. (at Fourth Ave.), San Diego, CA 92101. ℂ 800/542-1886 or 619/544-1886. Fax 619/544-0058. www.hortongrand.com. 132 units. $139–$169 double; $249 suite. Children under 18 stay free in parents' room. Packages available. AE, DC, MC, V. Valet parking $10. Bus: 1. Pets accepted with $50 fee. **Amenities:** Restaurant, lounge. *In room:* A/C, TV.

INEXPENSIVE

Another budget-conscious choice is **Comfort Inn–Downtown,** 719 Ash St., at Seventh Avenue (ℂ **800/228-5150** or 619/232-2525; www.comfortinnsandiego. com), offering clean and safe accommodations in a quieter corner of downtown. Or try **Keating House,** 2331 Second Ave. (ℂ **800/995-8644** or 619/239-8585; www.keatinghouse.com), a bed-and-breakfast set in a restored mansion between downtown and Hillcrest.

La Pensione Hotel ★ *Value*   This place has a lot going for it: modern amenities, remarkable value, a convenient location within walking distance of the central business district, a friendly staff, and parking (a premium for small hotels in San Diego). The three-story La Pensione is built around a courtyard and feels like a small European hotel; in fact, it's the number one choice of foreign students attending the downtown Language Institute. The decor throughout is modern and streamlined, with plenty of sleek black and metallic surfaces, crisp white walls, and minimal furniture. Guest rooms, while not overly large, make the most of their space and leave you with room to move around. Each room offers a tub-shower combination, ceiling fan, and microwave oven; try for a bay or city view rather than the concrete courtyard view. La Pensione is in San Diego's Little Italy and within walking distance of eateries (mostly Italian) and nightspots; there are two restaurants directly downstairs.

606 W. Date St. (at India St.), San Diego, CA 92101. ℂ 800/232-4683 or 619/236-8000. Fax 619/236-8088. www.lapensionehotel.com. 80 units. $60–$80 double. AE, DC, DISC, MC, V. Limited free underground parking. Trolley: County Center/Little Italy. **Amenities:** Access to nearby health club; bike rental; self-service laundry. *In room:* TV, dataport, fridge.

HILLCREST/UPTOWN

The regentrified historic neighborhoods north of downtown are something of a bargain: Well located to take advantage of Balboa Park (yet providing easy access to the rest of town), they're also filled with chic casual restaurants, eclectic shops and movie theaters, and sizzling nightlife. An additional park-side choice is the **Balboa Park Inn,** 3402 Park Blvd., at Upas Street (© **800/938-8181** or 619/298-0823; www.balboaparkinn.com).

MODERATE

Park Manor Suites *(Value)*   Popular with actors appearing at the Old Globe Theatre in neighboring Balboa Park, this eight-floor Italianate masterpiece was built as a full-service luxury hotel in 1926 on a prime corner overlooking the park. One of the original investors was the family of child actor Jackie Coogan. The Hollywood connection continued—the hotel became a popular stopping-off point for celebrities headed for Mexican vacations in the 1920s and '30s. Guest rooms are spacious and comfortable, featuring full kitchens, dining rooms, living rooms, and bedrooms with a separate dressing area. A few have glassed-in terraces; request one when you book. The overall feeling is that of a pre-war East Coast apartment building, complete with steam heat and lavish moldings. Park Manor Suites does have its weaknesses: Bathrooms have mostly original fixtures and could use some renovation; and the rooftop banquet room, where a simple continental breakfast buffet is served, suffers from bad '80s decor (though the view is spectacular). But prices are quite reasonable for the trendy Hillcrest neighborhood; there's a darkly Old World restaurant on the ground floor, and laundry service is available.

525 Spruce St. (between Fifth and Sixth Aves.), San Diego, CA 92103. © **800/874-2649** or 619/291-0999. Fax 619/291-8844. www.parkmanorsuites.com. 80 units. $99–$129 studio; $139–$179 1-bedroom suite; $199–$239 2-bedroom suite. Rates include continental breakfast. Children under 12 stay free in parents' room. Extra person $15. Weekly rates available. AE, DC, DISC, MC, V. Free parking. Bus: 1, 3, 25. **Amenities:** Restaurant and bar; access to nearby health club; bike rental; laundry/dry cleaning service; self-service laundry. *In room:* TV, dataport, kitchen, coffeemaker, hair dryer, iron.

Sommerset Suites Hotel *(★★)*   This all-suite hotel on a busy street was originally built as apartment housing for interns at the hospital nearby. It retains a residential ambiance and unexpected amenities such as huge closets, medicine cabinets, and fully equipped kitchens in all rooms (executive suites even have dishwashers). Poolside barbecue facilities encourage warm-weather mingling. The hotel has a personal, welcoming feel, from the friendly, helpful staff to the snacks, soda, beer, and wine served each afternoon. You'll even get a welcome basket with cookies and microwave popcorn. Rooms are comfortably furnished, and each has a private balcony. Be prepared for noise from the busy thoroughfare below, though. Several blocks of Hillcrest's chic restaurants and shops (plus a movie multiplex) are within easy walking distance. Guest services include a courtesy van to the airport, SeaWorld, the zoo, and other attractions within a 5-mile radius.

606 Washington St. (at Fifth Ave.), San Diego, CA 92103. © **800/962-9665** or 619/692-5200. Fax 619/692-5299. www.sommersetsuites.com. 80 units. $109–$195 double. Rates include continental breakfast and afternoon refreshments. Children under 12 stay free in parents' room. AE, DC, DISC, MC, V. Free covered parking. Take Washington St. exit off I-5. Bus: 16 or 25. **Amenities:** Outdoor pool; Jacuzzi; coin-op laundry. *In room:* A/C, TV, dataport, coffeemaker, hair dryer, iron.

INEXPENSIVE

Two extremely cozy and welcoming bed-and-breakfasts under $100 are **The Cottage,** 3829 Albatross St., off Robinson (© **619/299-1564**), and **Crone's Cobblestone Cottage,** 1302 Washington Place, 2½ blocks west of Washington Street at Ingalls Street (© **619/295-4765**).

OLD TOWN & MISSION VALLEY

Old Town is a popular area for families because of its proximity to Old Town State Historic Park and other attractions within walking distance. Hotel Circle, on the way to Mission Valley, offers easy freeway access to a bevy of mostly chain hotels convenient for sports fans or bargain seekers.

MODERATE

Heritage Park Bed & Breakfast Inn 🏃🏃   This exquisite 1889 Queen Anne mansion is set in a Victorian park—an artfully arranged cobblestone cul-de-sac lined with historic buildings saved from the wrecking ball and assembled here, near Old Town, as a tourist attraction. Most of the Inn's rooms are in the main house, with a handful of equally appealing choices in an adjacent 1887 Italianate companion. Owner Nancy Helsper is an amiable and energetic innkeeper with an eye for every necessary detail; she's always eager to share tales of these homes' fascinating history and how they crossed paths with Nancy and her husband Charles. A stay here is about surrendering to the pampering of afternoon tea, candlelight breakfast, and a number of romantic extras (champagne and chocolates, private in-room dinner) available for special celebrations. Like the gracious parlors and porches, each room is outfitted with meticulous period antiques and luxurious fabrics; the practiced staff provides turn-down service and virtually anything else you might require. Although the fireplaces are all ornamental, some rooms have whirlpool baths. In the evenings, vintage films are shown in the Victorian parlor.

2470 Heritage Park Row, San Diego, CA 92110. © **800/995-2470** or 619/299-6832. Fax 619/299-9465. www.heritageparkinn.com. 12 units. $100–$235 double. Rates include full breakfast and afternoon tea. Extra person $20. AE, DC, DISC, MC, V. Free parking. Take I-5 to Old Town Ave., turn left onto San Diego Ave., then turn right onto Harney St. *In room:* A/C, hair dryer, iron.

Red Lion Hanalei Hotel 🏃   Our favorite hotel on Hotel Circle has a Polynesian theme and comfort-conscious sophistication that sets it apart from the rest of the pack. Rooms are split between two high-rise towers, set far away from the freeway and cleverly positioned so that the balconies open onto the tropically landscaped pool courtyard or the luxurious links of a formerly private golf club on the Mission Valley floor. The heated outdoor pool is large enough for any luau, as is the oversized whirlpool beside it. The hotel boasts an unmistakable 1960s vibe and Hawaiian ambiance—the restaurant and bar have over-the-top kitschy decor, with waterfalls, outrigger canoes, and more. But guest rooms sport contemporary furnishings and conveniences; some have microwaves and refrigerators. Services include a free shuttle to Old Town and other attractions, plus extensive and meeting facilities.

2270 Hotel Circle North, San Diego, CA 92108. © **800/RED-LION** or 619/297-1101. Fax 619/297-6049. www.redlion.com. 416 units. $109–$159 double; $275–$375 suite. Off-season, AARP, and AAA discounts and golf packages available. Extra person $10. AE, DISC, MC, V. Parking $8. From I-8, take Hotel Circle exit, follow signs for Hotel Circle N. Bus: 6. Pets accepted with $25 fee. **Amenities:** 2 restaurants, lounge; outdoor pool; nearby golf; fitness center; Jacuzzi; game room; activities desk; 24-hour business center; room service (6am–10pm); laundry/dry cleaning service; self-service laundry. *In room:* A/C, TV w/ pay movies, dataport, coffeemaker, hair dryer, iron.

Vacation Inn 🏃   Just a couple of easy walking blocks from the heart of Old Town, the Vacation Inn has a Colonial Spanish exterior that suits the neighborhood's theme. Inside you'll find better-than-they-have-to-be contemporary furnishings and surprising small touches that make this hotel an affordable option favored by business travelers and families alike. There's nothing scenic on the adjacent streets, so the hotel is smartly oriented toward the inside; request a room whose patio or balcony opens onto the pleasant courtyard. Rooms are thoughtfully and practically appointed, with extras like microwave ovens and writing tables. The lobby, surrounded by French doors, features a large fireplace, several sitting areas, and a TV. The hotel entrance, on Jefferson Street, is hard to find but definitely worth the search.

3900 Old Town Ave., San Diego, CA 92110. © **800/451-9846** or 619/299-7400. Fax 619/299-1619. 124 units. June–Sept $119–$129 double, $130–$175 suite; Oct–May $89–$109 double, $99–$165 suite. Rates include continental breakfast and afternoon refreshments. Children under 18 stay free in parents' room. Extra person $10. AE, DC, DISC, MC, V. Free parking. Bus: 5, 5A. **Amenities:** Outdoor pool; whirlpool; laundry/dry cleaning service. *In room:* A/C, TV, fridge, coffeemaker.

INEXPENSIVE

Room rates at properties on Hotel Circle are significantly cheaper than those in many other parts of the city. You'll find a cluster of inexpensive chain hotels and motels, including **Best Western Seven Seas** (© **800/421-6662** or 619/291-1300), **Comfort Inn & Suites** (© **800/647-1903** or 619/291-7700), **Mission Valley Center Travelodge** (© **800/255-3050** or 619/297-2271), **Ramada Inn** (© **800/532-4241** or 619/291-6500), and **Vagabond Inn** (© **800/522-1555** or 619/297-1691).

MISSION BAY & THE BEACHES

If you plan to enjoy the beach and aquatic activities during your visit (including SeaWorld), staying in this part of town will set you up in the right spot.

VERY EXPENSIVE

Pacific Terrace Hotel 🕸🕸 The best modern hotel on the boardwalk recently emerged from a multi-million-dollar renovation sporting a soothing South Seas ambiance—rattan fans caress the lobby and hint at the sunny Indonesian-inspired decor in guest rooms. Hands-on owners kicked the luxury factor (and prices) up a notch, resulting in an upscale atmosphere and relaxed ambiance that stand apart from the casual beach pads in the area.

Large, comfortable guest rooms each come with balconies or terraces and fancy wall safes; bathrooms—newly redesigned with warm-toned marble and natural woods—have a separate sink and vanity area. About half the rooms have kitchenettes, and top-floor rooms in this three-story hotel enjoy particularly nice views—you'll find yourself mesmerized by the rhythmic waves and determined surfers below. Management keeps popcorn, coffee, and lemonade at the ready throughout the day; the lushly landscaped pool and Jacuzzi face a relatively quiet stretch of beach with fire rings for bonfires or barbecues. Several local restaurants allow meals to be billed to the hotel but there's no restaurant on the premises.

610 Diamond St., San Diego, CA 92109. © **800/344-3370** or 858/581-3500. Fax 858/274-3341. www.pacificterrace.com. 75 units. $269 standard double; $369 oceanfront double; from $395 suite. Rates include continental breakfast. 10% AAA discount June 15–Sept 15 (25% Sept 16–June 14). AE, DC, DISC, MC, V. Parking $5. Take I-5 to Grand/Garnet exit and follow Grand or Garnet west to Mission Blvd., turn right (north), then left (west) onto Diamond; hotel is at the end of the street on the right. Bus: 34 or 34A. **Amenities:** Oceanview outdoor pool; access to nearby health club; Jacuzzi; bike rental nearby; activities desk; room service (7am–midnight); in-room massage; laundry/dry cleaning service; coin-op laundry. *In room:* A/C, TV w/ pay movies, dataport, minibar, coffeemaker, hair dryer, iron.

Paradise Point Resort 🕸🕸🕸 *(Kids)* Smack dab in the middle of Mission Bay, this hotel complex is as much a theme park as its closest neighbor, SeaWorld (a 3-minute drive). Single-story accommodations are spread across 44 acres of duck-filled lagoons, tropical gardens, and swim-friendly beaches; all rooms have private lanais (patios) and plenty of thoughtful conveniences. Recently updated to keep its low-tech 1960s charm but lose tacky holdovers—for example, rooms now sport a refreshingly colorful beach cottage-y decor—the resort offers so much fun and recreation you may never want to leave! And despite daunting high-season rack rates, there's usually a deal to be had here. In 2000, the resort unveiled its upscale waterfront Baleen restaurant (excellent fine dining in a contemporary, fun space), and started work on a massive on-site spa that should be in prime pampering form by the time you visit.

1404 W. Vacation Rd. (off Ingraham St.), San Diego, CA 92109. © 800/344-2626 or 858/274-4630. Fax 858/581-5977. www.paradisepoint.com. 462 units. Memorial Day thru Labor Day $220–$350 double, from $325 suite; off-season $175–$325 double, from $300 suite. Children 17 and under stay free in parents' room. Discounts and packages frequently available. Extra person $20. AE, DC, DISC, MC, V. Free parking. Follow I-8 west to Mission Bay Dr. exit; take Ingraham St. north to Vacation Rd. **Amenities:** 3 restaurants, lounge, pool bar; 6 outdoor pools; 18-hole putting course; tennis courts; croquet; sand volleyball; fitness center; full-service spa; Jacuzzi; bike rental; shuttle to area shopping; room service (7am–10pm); laundry/dry cleaning service. *In room:* A/C, TV w/ pay movies, dataport, fridge, coffeemaker, hair dryer, iron.

EXPENSIVE

Catamaran Resort Hotel 🌟🌟 *(Kids)*   Ideally situated right on Mission Bay, the Catamaran has its own bay and ocean beaches, with water-sports facilities. Built in the 1950s, the hotel has been fully renovated to modern standards without losing its trademark Polynesian theme; the atrium lobby holds a 15-foot waterfall and full-size dugout canoe, and koi-filled lagoons meander through the property. After dark, torches blaze throughout the grounds, with numerous varieties of bamboo and palms sprouting; during the day, the resident tropical birds chirp away. Guest rooms—in a 13-story building or one of the six two-story buildings—have subdued South Pacific decor, and each has a balcony or patio. Tower rooms have commanding views of the bay, the San Diego skyline, La Jolla, and Point Loma. Studios and suites have the added convenience of kitchenettes. The Catamaran is within walking distance of Pacific Beach's restaurant and nightlife. It's also steps away from the bay's exceptional jogging and biking path; runners with tots-in-tow can rent jogging strollers at the hotel.

3999 Mission Blvd. (4 blocks south of Grand Ave.), San Diego, CA 92109. © 800/422-8386 or 858/488-1081. Fax 858/488-1619. www.catamaranresort.com. 315 units. $195–$265 double; from $400 suite. Children under 12 stay free in parents' room. Off-season discounts and packages available. AE, DC, DISC, MC, V. Valet parking $10; self-parking $8. Take Grand/Garnet exit off I-5 and go west on Grand Ave., then south on Mission Blvd. Bus: 34, 34A/B. **Amenities:** Restaurant, nightclub, piano bar; outdoor pool; tennis courts; health club; whirlpool; water-sport equipment rental; bike rental; children's programs; concierge; activities desk; car-rental desk; room service (5am–11pm); in-room massage; babysitting; laundry/dry cleaning service. *In room:* A/C, TV w/ pay movies, dataport, fridge, coffeemaker, hair dryer, iron.

Crystal Pier Hotel 🌟🌟 *(Finds)*   When historic charm is higher on your wish list than hotel-style service, head to this utterly unique cluster of cottages sitting literally over the surf on the vintage Crystal Pier. Like renting your own self-contained hideaway, you'll get a separate living room and bedroom, fully equipped kitchen, and private patio with breathtaking ocean views—all within the whitewashed walls of blue-shuttered cottages that date from 1936 but have been meticulously renovated. The sound of waves is soothing, but the boardwalk action is only a few steps (and worlds) away, and the pier is a great place for watching sunsets and surfers. Guests drive right out and park beside their cottages, a real boon on crowded weekends. There are vending machines and movie rentals; boogie boards, fishing poles, beach chairs, and umbrellas are also available, but it's strictly BYOBT (beach towels!). The office is open daily from 8am to 8pm. These accommodations book up fast, especially with long-term repeat guests, so reserve for summer at least 4 months in advance.

4500 Ocean Blvd. (at Garnet Ave.), San Diego, CA 92109. (℃ **800/748-5894** or 858/483-6983. Fax 858/483-6811. www.crystalpier.com. 26 units. Cottages for 2–6 people $135–$335 mid-June to mid-Sept; $105–$275 mid-Sept to mid-June. 3-night minimum in summer. DISC, MC, V. Free parking. Take I-5 to Grand/Garnet exit; follow Garnet to the pier. Bus: 34 or 34A. **Amenities:** Beach equipment rental. *In room:* TV, kitchen.

MODERATE

Another beachfront choice in this price range is the **Best Western Blue Sea Lodge,** 707 Pacific Beach Dr. (℃ **800/BLUE-SEA** or 858/488-4700; www.bestwestern-bluesea.com).

The Beach Cottages *(Kids* This family-owned operation has a variety of guest quarters (most geared to the long-term visitor), but the cute little detached cottages steps from the sand give it real appeal. Most other units are perfectly adequate, especially for budget-minded families who want to log major hours on the beach, but stay away from the plain motel rooms—they're just dingy. All accommodations except the motel rooms have fully equipped kitchens. The Beach Cottages are within walking distance of shops and restaurants—look both ways for speeding cyclists before crossing the boardwalk—and enjoy shared barbecue grills, shuffleboard courts, and table tennis. The cottages themselves aren't pristine, but have a rustic charm that makes them popular with young honeymooners and those nostalgic for the golden age of laid-back California beach culture. With one or two bedrooms, each cottage sleeps up to six; each has a patio with tables and chairs.

To make a reservation, call between 9am and 9pm, when the office is open. Reserve the most popular cottages well in advance.

Kids Family-Friendly Hotels

Holiday Inn on the Bay *(see p. 625)* Kids under 18 stay free, and so does the family pet. The hotel is well priced for strained family budgets, and even offers babysitting services for strained parents.

Catamaran Resort Hotel *(see p. 633)* Myriad sports facilities and a safe swimming beach make this resort an ideal place for families. Accommodations are comfortable, but not so posh that Mom and Dad need to worry.

Paradise Point Resort *(see p. 632)* This self-contained property in the middle of Mission Bay has plenty of space for kids to safely explore, and is just up the street from SeaWorld.

The Beach Cottages *(see p. 634)* Kids enjoy the informal atmosphere and the location near the beach.

The Sea Lodge *(see p. 636)* Right smack on the beach, kids can choose between the pool and the ocean. They can even eat in their swimsuits on the patio.

Loews Coronado Bay Resort *(see p. 639)* In the summer, the Commodore Kids Club, for children ages 4 to 12, provides supervised indoor and outdoor activities during the day and some evenings, too. Programs for older kids keep them out of harm's way without making them feel baby-sat.

4255 Ocean Blvd. (1 block south of Grand Ave.), San Diego, CA 92109-3995. ℂ **858/483-7440.** Fax 858/ 273-9365. www.beachcottages.com. 61 units, 17 cottages. July 1–Labor Day $95–$115 double; $130 studio for up to 4; $150–$195 apt for up to 6; $150–$185 cottage for up to 6; $225–$245 2-bedroom suite for up to 6. Off-season discounts and off-season weekly rates available. AE, DC, DISC, MC, V. Free parking. Take I-5 to Grand/Garnet exit, go west on Grand Ave. and right on Mission Blvd. Bus: 34 or 34A. **Amenities:** Self-service laundry. *In room:* TV, fridge, coffeemaker.

Ocean Park Inn ⭐ This modern oceanfront motor hotel offers attractive, spacious rooms with well-coordinated contemporary furnishings. Although the inn has a level of sophistication uncommon in this casual, surfer-populated area, you won't find solitude and quiet. The cool marble lobby and plushly carpeted hallways will help you feel a little insulated from the raucous scene outside, though. You can't beat the location (directly on the beach) and the view (ditto). Rates vary according to view, but most rooms have at least a partial ocean view; all have a private balcony or patio. Units in front are most desirable, but it can get noisy directly above the boardwalk; try for the second or third floor. The Ocean Park Inn doesn't have its own restaurant, but the casual Firehouse Beach Cafe (see "Dining" later in this chapter for full review) is outside the front door.

710 Grand Ave., San Diego, CA 92109. ℂ **800/231-7735** or 858/483-5858. Fax 858/274-0823. www. oceanparkinn.com. 73 units. Mid-May to mid-Sept $104–$239 double, $169–$304 suite; winter $89–$214 double, $124–$274 suite. Rates include continental breakfast. AE, DC, DISC, MC, V. Free indoor parking. Take Grand/Garnet exit off I-5; follow Grand Ave. to ocean. Bus: 34, 34A/B. **Amenities:** Outdoor pool; Jacuzzi; laundry/dry cleaning service. *In room:* A/C, TV, dataport, fridge, coffeemaker, hair dryer.

INEXPENSIVE

Other inexpensive options in the beach area include an immaculate, comfortable, and contemporary bed-and-breakfast near Ocean Beach's "Antique Row": **Elsbree House,** 5054 Narragansett Ave. (ℂ **619/226-4133;** www.oceanbeach-online.com/b&b).

Beach Haven Inn ⭐ A great spot for beach lovers, this motel is about half a block from the sand. Rooms face an inner courtyard, where guests enjoy a secluded ambiance for relaxing by the pool. On the street side it looks kind of marginal, but once on the property we found all quarters well-maintained and sporting clean modern furnishings—nearly all units have eat-in kitchens. The friendly staff provides free coffee in the lobby and rents VCRs and movies.

4740 Mission Blvd. (at Missouri St.), San Diego (Pacific Beach), CA 92109. ℂ **800/831-6323** or 858/272-3812. Fax 858/272-3532. www.beachhaveninn.com. 23 units. Summer (June through mid-Sept) $99–$140 double; winter $79–$115. Rates include continental breakfast. Children under 12 stay free in parents' room. Extra person $5. AE, DC, DISC, MC, V. Free parking. Bus: 30 or 34. **Amenities:** Outdoor pool; Jacuzzi. *In room:* A/C, TV; kitchenette in most units.

LA JOLLA

While you'll have a hard time finding bargain accommodations in this upscale, conservative community, it's not to be missed for the sheer physical beauty of its coastline, as well as a compact downtown village that makes for delightful strolling. An additional choice worth checking out is the **Bed & Breakfast Inn at La Jolla,** 7753 Draper Ave., near Prospect (ℂ **800/582-2466** or 858/456-2066; www.InnLaJolla.com), set in an Irving Gill–designed house near the museum; rates range from inexpensive to expensive.

VERY EXPENSIVE

La Valencia Hotel ⭐⭐⭐ Within its bougainvillea-draped walls and wrought-iron garden gates, this gracious bastion of gentility does a fine job of resurrecting its golden-age elegance, when celebrities like Greta Garbo and

Charlie Chaplin vacationed alongside the world's moneyed elite. The cliff-top hotel has been the centerpiece of La Jolla since opening in 1926. Today, brides pose in front of the lobby's picture window (against a backdrop of La Jolla Cove and the Pacific), well-coifed ladies lunch in the dappled shade of the garden patio, and neighborhood cronies quaff libations in the clubby Whaling Bar, once a western Algonquin for literary inebriates. One chooses La Valencia for its history and unbeatably scenic location, but you won't be disappointed by the old-world standards of service and style. Rooms are comfortably and traditionally furnished, each boasting an individual decor, lavish appointments, and all-marble bathrooms with signature toiletries. Because rates vary wildly according to view, our advice is to get a cheaper room and enjoy the view from one of the many cozy lounges or serene garden terraces. Room decor and layouts vary wildly too—a few extra minutes spent with the reservationist will ensure a custom match for you.

1132 Prospect St. (at Herschel Ave.), La Jolla, CA 92037. ℂ 800/451-0772 or 858/454-0771. Fax 858/456-3921. www.lavalencia.com. 132 units. $250–$500 double; from $550 suite. Extra person $15. AE, DC, DISC, MC, V. Valet parking $14. Take Torrey Pines Rd. to Prospect Place and turn right. Prospect Place becomes Prospect St. **Amenities:** 3 restaurants, bar; outdoor pool; exercise room w/ spa treatments; Jacuzzi; sauna; concierge; secretarial services; 24-hour room service; babysitting; laundry/dry cleaning service. *In room:* A/C, TV w/ VCR, dataport, minibar, coffeemaker, hair dryer.

EXPENSIVE

You may also want to consider the La Jolla Beach & Tennis Club's sister property **The Sea Lodge,** 8110 Camino del Oro, at Avenida de la Playa (ℂ **800/237-5211** or 858/459-8271), also located on the beach. Or, for a B&B ambiance, try **Scripps Inn,** 555 Coast Blvd. S., at Cuvier (ℂ **858/454-3391**).

La Jolla Beach & Tennis Club 🏵🏵   Pack your best tennis whites for a stay at La Jolla's private "B&T" (as it's locally known), where CEOs and MDs come to relax and recreate. Surprisingly, rates for the club's overnight accommodations aren't that much higher than at the sister hotel next door, but the exclusive atmosphere and extensive amenities are far superior. Guest rooms are unexpectedly plain and frill-free, though they are equipped with the basic amenities you'll need. Most have well-stocked full kitchens that are ideal for families or longer stays. This historic property was founded in the 1920s, when original plans included constructing a private yacht harbor. Today it's known primarily for tennis. The beach is popular here; the staff sets up comfy sand chairs and umbrellas, and races to supply club members and guests with fluffy towels, beverages, and snacks. Kayaks and water-sport equipment can be rented; there's even a sand croquet court. Surprisingly, there's no room service; besides the on-site dining options, several cozy neighborhood trattorias are 2 blocks away. Take a peek into the hotel's distinctive Marine Room restaurant, where waves literally smash against the windows inches away from well-coifed diners. The menu is pricey, but for the price of a cocktail you can enjoy the same astounding view.

2000 Spindrift Dr., La Jolla, CA 92037. ℂ 800/624-CLUB or 858/454-7126. Fax 858/456-3805. www.ljbtc.com. 90 units. June–Sept $170–$349 double, from $275 suite; off-season $139–$239 double, from $215 suite. Children under 12 stay free in parents' room. Extra person $20. AE, DC, MC, V. Take La Jolla Shores Dr., turn left on Paseo Dorado, and follow to Spindrift Dr. **Amenities:** 2 restaurants; seasonal beach hut; elegant Olympic-size pool; 9-hole pitch-and-putt course that winds around a lagoon along the stately entry drive; 12 championship tennis courts and a tennis shop; fitness room; playground; massage; babysitting; laundry/dry cleaning service; coin-op laundry. *In room:* TV w/ pay movies, dataport, coffeemaker, hair dryer, iron.

MODERATE

Best Western Inn by the Sea 🏵   Occupying an enviable location at the heart of La Jolla's charming village, this independently managed property puts guests just a short walk from the cliffs and beach. The low-rise tops out at five stories, with the upper floors enjoying ocean views (and the highest room rates). The Best Western (and the more formal Empress, a block away), offer a terrific alternative to pricier digs nearby. Rooms here are Best Western standard issue—freshly maintained, but nothing special. All rooms do have balconies, though, and refrigerators are available at no extra charge; the hotel offers plenty of welcome amenities.

7830 Fay Ave. (between Prospect and Silverado Sts.), La Jolla, CA 92037. ℂ 800/462-9732, 800/526-4545 in California and Canada, or 858/459-4461. Fax 858/456-2578. 132 units. $129–$199 double; $175–$450 suite. Rates include continental breakfast. Off-season discounts available. AE, DC, DISC, MC, V. Parking $5. Take Torrey Pines Rd. to Prospect Place and turn right. Prospect Place becomes Prospect St.; proceed to Fay Ave. and turn left. **Amenities:** Outdoor pool; car-rental desk; room service; laundry/dry cleaning service. *In room:* A/C, TV w/ pay movies, dataport, hair dryer, iron.

Empress Hotel of La Jolla ★★
The Empress Hotel offers spacious quarters with traditional furnishings a block or two from La Jolla's main drag and the ocean. It's quieter here than at the premium clifftop properties, and you'll sacrifice little other than direct ocean views. (Many rooms on the top floors afford a partial view.) If you're planning to explore La Jolla on foot, the Empress is a good base, and it exudes a classiness many comparably priced chains lack. Rooms are tastefully decorated (and frequently renovated), and well equipped. Bathrooms are of average size but exceptionally well appointed, and four "Empress" rooms have sitting areas with full-size sleeper sofas. On nice days, breakfast is set up on a serene sundeck.

7766 Fay Ave. (at Silverado), La Jolla, CA 92037. ℂ 888/369-9900 or 858/454-3001. Fax 858/454-6387. www.empress-hotel.com. 73 units. $149–$229 double; $349 suite. Rates include continental breakfast. Children under 18 stay free in parents' room. Off-season and long-stay discounts available. Extra person $10. AE, DC, DISC, MC, V. Valet parking $7. Take Torrey Pines Rd. to Girard Ave., turn right, then left on Silverado St. **Amenities:** Fitness room and spa; room service. *In room:* A/C, TV, dataport, fridge, coffeemaker, hair dryer, iron.

La Jolla Cove Suites *(Value)*
Tucked in beside prime oceanview condos across from Ellen Browning Scripps Park, this family-run 1950s-era complex actually sits closer to the ocean than pricey uphill neighbors La Valencia and the Grande Colonial. The to-die-for ocean view is completely unobstructed, and La Jolla Cove—one of California's prettiest swimming spots—is steps away from the hotel. The property is peaceful at night, but Village dining and shopping are only a short walk away. You'll pay more depending on the quality of your view; about 80% of guest quarters gaze upon the ocean. On the plus side, rooms are wonderfully spacious, each featuring a fully equipped kitchen, plus private balcony or patio. On the minus side, their functional but almost institutional furnishings could use a touch of Martha Stewart. An oceanview rooftop deck offers lounge chairs and cafe tables; breakfast is served up here each morning, indoors or outdoors depending on the weather.

1155 Coast Blvd. (across from the cove), La Jolla, CA 92037. ℂ 888/LA-JOLLA or 858/459-2621. Fax 858/ 551-3405. www.lajollacove.com. 90 units. Summer (Memorial Day thru Labor Day) $135–$175 double; $190–$280 suite; winter $110–$135 double, $145–$225 suite. Rates include continental breakfast. Midweek, AAA, and weekly discounts available. Extra person $15. AE, DC, DISC, MC, V. Free parking. Take Torrey Pines Rd. to Prospect Place and turn right. When the road forks, veer right (downhill) onto Coast Blvd. **Amenities:** Outdoor (non-view) pool; Jacuzzi; car-rental desk; coin-op laundry. *In room:* TV, kitchen, safe.

INEXPENSIVE

Wealthy, image-conscious La Jolla is *really* not the best place for deep bargains, but if you're determined to stay here as cheaply as possible, you won't do better than the **La Jolla Cove Travelodge,** 1141 Silverado St., at Herschel Avenue

(© **800/578-7878** or 858/454-0791). Despite its name, it sits in the Village several blocks from the cove. This 30-room motel is standard Americana, arranged around a small parking lot with cinder-block construction and small, basic rooms. The surrounding La Jolla glamour and bargain rates of $59 to $98 make it an acceptable option.

CORONADO

The "island" (really a peninsula) of Coronado offers a great escape with its quiet, architecturally rich streets; a small-town, Navy-oriented atmosphere; and laid-back vacationing on one of the state's most beautiful and welcoming beaches. Choose a hotel on the ocean side for a view of Point Loma and the Pacific, or stay facing the city for a spectacular skyline vista (especially at night). You may feel pleasantly isolated here, so it isn't your best choice if you're planning to spend lots of time in more central parts of the city.

A note on driving directions: To reach the places listed here, take I-5 to the Coronado Bridge, and then follow individual directions. If you're two or more in a car, stay in the far right lanes to avoid paying the bridge toll.

VERY EXPENSIVE

Another upscale destination is **Coronado Island Marriott Resort,** 2000 Second St., at Glorietta Boulevard (© **800/228-9290** or 619/435-3000; http://marriotthotels.com/SANCI). Boasting a spa and vast recreational facilities, the Marriott has a low-key elegance and excellent service. Or consider the **Glorietta Bay Inn,** 1630 Glorietta Blvd., near Orange Avenue (© **800/283-9383** or 619/435-3101; www.gloriettabayinn.com), across the street from the "Del" in a 1908 mansion.

Hotel del Coronado ✦✦✦   Opened in 1888 and designated a National Historic Landmark in 1977, the "Hotel Del," as it's affectionately known, is the last of California's grand old seaside hotels. Legend has it that the Duke of Windsor met his American duchess here, and Marilyn Monroe frolicked around the hotel in *Some Like It Hot.* This monument to Victorian grandeur boasts tall cupolas, red turrets, and gingerbread trim, all spread out over 26 acres. Rooms run the gamut from compact to extravagant, and all are packed with antique charm; most have custom-made furnishings. The best rooms have balconies fronting the ocean and large windows that take in one of the city's finest white-sand beaches. If you're a stickler for detail, ask to stay in the original building rather than in the contemporary tower additions.

In 2000, the hotel completed a painstaking, multimillion-dollar, 3-year restoration. Purists will rejoice to hear that historical accuracy was paramount, resulting in this priceless *grande dame* being returned to its turn-of-the-19th-century splendor. Even if you don't stay here, don't miss a stroll through the grand, wood-paneled lobby or along the pristine wide beach. Accolades have been awarded to the Prince of Wales Grill, recently remodeled from a dark, clubby room to an airy, elegant salon with oceanfront dining; cocktails and afternoon tea are served in the wood-paneled lobby and adjoining conservatory lounge.

1500 Orange Ave., Coronado, CA 92118. © **800/468-3533** or 619/435-8000. Fax 619/522-8238. www. hoteldel.com. 700 units. $215–$340 double (garden or city view), $360–$640 double (ocean view); suites from $700. Children under 18 stay free in parents' room. Sport, spa, and romance packages available. AE, DC, DISC, MC, V. Valet parking $16, self-parking $12. From Coronado Bridge, turn left onto Orange Ave. Bus: 901. Ferry: from Broadway Pier. **Amenities:** 9 restaurants/lounges; 2 outdoor pools; 3 tennis courts; health club and spa; 2 Jacuzzis; bike rental; children's activities; concierge; car-rental desk; shopping arcade; 24-hour room service; babysitting; laundry/dry cleaning service. *In room:* A/C, TV w/ pay movies, dataport, minibar, hair dryer, iron, safe.

Loews Coronado Bay Resort ★★ (Kids)   This luxury resort opened in 1991 on a secluded 15-acre peninsula, slightly removed from downtown Coronado and San Diego. It's perfect for those who prefer a self-contained resort in a get-away-from-it-all location, and is surprisingly successful in appealing to business travelers, convention groups, vacationing families, and romance-minded couples. All units offer terraces that look onto the hotel's private 80-slip marina, the Coronado Bay Bridge, or San Diego Bay. A private pedestrian underpass leads to nearby Silver Strand Beach. Rooms boast finely appointed marble bathrooms; VCRs come standard in suites, and are available free upon request to any room. Video rentals are available. A highlight here is the **Gondola Company** (© 619/429-6317), which offers romantic and fun gondola cruises through the canals of tony Coronado Cays. The seasonal Commodore Kids Club, for children ages 4 to 12, offers supervised half-day, full-day, and evening programs with meals.

4000 Coronado Bay Rd., Coronado, CA 92118. © 800/81-LOEWS or 619/424-4000. Fax 619/424-4400. 437 units. $235–$325 double; from $450 suite. Children under 18 stay free in parents' room. Packages available. AE, DC, DISC, MC, V. Valet parking $16; covered self-parking $12. From Coronado Bridge, go left onto Orange Ave, continue 8 miles down Silver Strand Hwy. Turn left at Coronado Bay Rd., entrance to the resort. Pets under 25 lbs. accepted. **Amenities:** 3 restaurants (including acclaimed Azzura Point), lounge; 3 outdoor pools; tennis courts; fitness center; spa; Jacuzzi; water-sports equipment rental; bike/skate rental; children's programs; concierge; car-rental desk; business center; salon; 24-hour room service; in-room massage; babysitting; laundry/dry cleaning service. In room: A/C, TV, dataport, minibar, coffeemaker, hair dryer, iron, safe.

MODERATE

El Cordova Hotel ★   This Spanish hacienda across the street from the Hotel del Coronado began life as a private mansion in 1902. By the 1930s it had become a hotel, the original building augmented by a series of attachments housing retail shops along the ground-floor arcade. Shaped like a baseball diamond and surrounding a courtyard with meandering tiled pathways, flowering shrubs, a swimming pool, and patio seating for Miguel's Cocina Mexican restaurant, El Cordova hums pleasantly with activity.

Each room is a little different from the next—some sport a Mexican colonial ambiance, while others evoke a comfy beach cottage. All feature ceiling fans and brightly tiled bathrooms, but lack the frills that would command exorbitant rates. El Cordova has a particularly inviting aura, and its prime location makes it a popular option; we advise reserving several months in advance, especially for the summer. Facilities include a barbecue area with picnic table.

1351 Orange Ave. (at Adella Ave.), Coronado, CA 92118. © 800/229-2032 or 619/435-4131. Fax 619/435-0632. www.elcordovahotel.com. 40 units. Mid-Apr thru Sept $119–$167 double, $203–$306 suite; winter $114–$155 double, $179–$246 suite. Children under 12 stay free in parents' room. Weekly and monthly rates available in winter. AE, DC, DISC, MC, V. No off-street parking. From Coronado Bridge, turn left onto Orange Ave. Parking available on street. **Amenities:** Restaurant; outdoor pool; shopping arcade; coin-op laundry. In room: A/C, TV.

INEXPENSIVE

Also in this price range is the ideally located **Village Inn,** 1017 Park Place, at Orange Avenue (© 619/435-9318), a modest, breakfast-included, European-style small hotel with charming rooms but teensy bathrooms.

Coronado Inn ★   Well-located and terrifically priced, this renovated 1940s courtyard motel has such a friendly ambiance; it's like staying with old friends. Iced tea, lemonade, and fresh fruit are even provided poolside on summer days. It's still a motel, though—albeit with brand-new paint and fresh tropical floral decor—so rooms are pretty basic. The six rooms with bathtubs also have small kitchens; microwaves are available for the rest, along with hair dryers and irons (just ask up front). Rooms close to the street are noisiest, so ask for one toward the back. The Coronado shuttle stops a block away; it serves the shopping areas and Hotel Del.

266 Orange Ave. (corner of 3rd St.), Coronado, CA 92118. (Ⓒ 800/598-6624 or 619/435-4121. www. coronadoinn.com. 30 units (most with shower only). Memorial Day through Labor Day $110–$175 up to 4 people; winter $90–$120. Rates include continental breakfast. Discounts available. AE, DISC, MC, V. Free parking. From Coronado Bridge, stay on 3rd St. Pets accepted; $10 per night. **Amenities:** Outdoor pool; coin-op laundry. *In room:* A/C, TV, dataport, fridge.

4 Dining

What follows is only a sampling of San Diego's dining scene. For a greater selection of reviews, see *Frommer's San Diego.*

DOWNTOWN
EXPENSIVE

Another well-regarded bayfront seafooder is **Star of the Sea,** 1380 N. Harbor Dr., at Ash St. (Ⓒ **619/232-7408;** www.starofthesea.com), a venerable oldie with a new look, new chef, and sophisticated menu.

Croce's Restaurant & Nightclubs ✦ AMERICAN/ECLECTIC Ingrid Croce, widow of singer-songwriter Jim, was instrumental in the resurgence of the once-decayed Gaslamp Quarter, and her establishment has expanded to fill every corner of this 1890 Romanesque building. Croce's features a menu that fuses Southern soul food and Southwestern spice with Asian flavors and Continental standards. Add the raucous Top Hat Bar & Grille and the intimate Jazz Bar, and the complex is the hottest ticket in town, with crowds lining up for dinner tables and nightclub shows.

An evening in the Gaslamp Quarter isn't complete without at least strolling by the Croce's corner; expect a festive good time any night of the week. Those who dine in either of the restaurant's side-by-side seating areas can enter the two nightspots without paying the cover charge.

802 Fifth Ave. (at F St.). (Ⓒ 619/233-4355. www.croces.com. Reservations not accepted; call for same-day "priority seating" (before walk-ins). Main courses $14–$23. AE, DC, DISC, MC, V. Daily 5pm–midnight. Valet parking $7 with validation. Bus: 3, 5, 16, or 25. Trolley: Gaslamp Quarter.

Fio's ✦✦✦ NORTHERN ITALIAN Fio's has been *the* spot to see and be seen in the Gaslamp Quarter since it opened, and it's the granddaddy of the new wave of trendy Italian restaurants. Set in an 1881 Italianate Victorian that once housed chic Marston's department store, Fio's has a sophisticated ambiance and is *always* crowded. Once cutting-edge, the upscale trattoria menu is now practiced and consistently superior. It features jet-black linguini tossed with the freshest seafood, delicate angel hair pasta perfectly balanced with basil and pine nuts, and gourmet pizzas served at regular tables and the special pizza bar. The menu pleases both light eaters (with antipasti and pastas) and heartier palates—the impressive list of meat entrees includes mustard-rosemary rack of lamb, veal shank on saffron risotto, and delicately sweet hazelnut-crusted pork loin with Frangelico and peaches. If you stop by without a reservation, you can sit at the elegant cocktail bar and order from the complete menu.

801 Fifth Ave. (at F St.). (Ⓒ 619/234-3467. Reservations recommended. Main courses $11–$25. AE, DC, DISC, MC, V. Mon–Thurs 5–10:30pm; Fri–Sat 5–11pm; Sun 5–10pm. Valet parking $6 with validation. Bus: 3, 5, 16, or 25. Trolley: Gaslamp Quarter.

The Fish Market ★★ SEAFOOD   Ask any San Diegan where to go for the biggest selection of the freshest fish, and they'll send you to the bustling Fish Market on the end of the G Street Pier on the Embarcadero. Chalkboards announce the day's catches—be it Mississippi catfish, Maine lobster, Canadian salmon, or Mexican yellowtail—sold by the pound or available in a number of classic, simple preparations in the casual restaurant. Upstairs, the related Top of the Market offers similar fare at jacked-up prices; we recommend having a cocktail in Top's posh clubby atmosphere with stupendous panoramic bay views, then head downstairs for affordable fare and/or treats from the sushi and oyster bars.

There is another Fish Market Restaurant in Del Mar at 640 Via de la Valle (© **858/755-2277**).

750 N. Harbor Dr. © **619/232-FISH.** www.thefishmarket.com. Reservations not accepted. Main courses $9–$25. AE, DC, DISC, MC, V. Daily 11am–10pm. Valet parking $4. Bus: 7/7B. Trolley: Seaport Village.

MODERATE

Other recommended choices in this price range include **Dakota Grill and Spirits,** 901 Fifth Ave., at E Street (© **619/595-7959**), a downtown lunch favorite whose raucous atmosphere suits the spicy Southwestern cuisine; and **Panda Inn,** Horton Plaza (© **619/233-7800**), a surprisingly upscale Chinese restaurant tucked away on the top floor of the Gaslamp Quarter's premier shopping mall.

Osteria Panevino ★ ITALIAN   Expertly prepared, intricate dishes set Osteria Panevino apart from the Gaslamp Quarter's ubiquitous trattorias. The setting is welcoming, a New York–like space with bare brick walls and a small sidewalk-seating area. The unselfconscious atmosphere belies the sophistication of the menu, which peaks with homemade pastas in rich, complex sauces. Antipasti are so satisfying that they are almost mini-meals; we recommend mozzarella wrapped in prosciutto and baked over sautéed spinach, or filet mignon carpaccio topped with hearts of palm, avocado, goat cheese, and olive oil. Fish and meat entrees are equally enticing, bathed in rich reduction sauces and accented with inventive flavors. A good wine list is made better with special themed trios of 2-ounce tastings. Sometimes the hostess, clad in evening gown and heels, warmly greets passersby from the doorway like a high-class circus barker. The atmosphere is cozy or crowded, depending on how close you like to be to your fellow diners.

722 Fifth Ave. (between F and G Sts.). © **619/595-7959.** Reservations recommended. Main courses $11–$23. AE, DC, DISC, MC, V. Sun–Thurs 11:30am–10pm; Fri–Sat 11:30am–11:30pm. Valet parking $6. Bus: 3, 5, 16, or 25. Trolley: Gaslamp Quarter.

INEXPENSIVE

Café Lulu ★ COFFEEHOUSE/VEGETARIAN   Smack-dab in the heart of the Gaslamp Quarter, Café Lulu aims for a hip, bohemian mood despite its location half a block from commercial Horton Plaza. Ostensibly a coffee bar, the cafe makes a terrific choice for casual dining; if the stylishly metallic interior is too harsh for you, watch the street action from a sidewalk table. The food is health conscious, prepared with organic ingredients and no meat. Soups, salads, cheese melts, and veggie lasagna are on the menu; breads come from the incomparable Bread & Cie., 350 University Ave. (© **619/683-9322**). Eggs, granola, and waffles are served in the morning, but anytime is the right time to try one of the inventive coffee drinks, like cafe Bohème (mocha with almond syrup) or cafe L'amour (iced latte with a hazelnut tinge). Beer and wine are also served.

419 F St. (near Fourth Ave.). © **619/238-0114.** Main courses $3–$7. No credit cards. Sun–Thurs 10am–1am; Fri–Sat 9:30am–3am. Bus: 3, 5, 16, or 25. Trolley: Gaslamp Quarter.

Filippi's Pizza Grotto ★★ *(Value* ITALIAN   Think Little Italy, and this is the picture that comes to mind. To get to the dining area, decorated with Chianti bottles and red-checked tablecloths, you walk through an Italian grocery store and deli strewn with cheeses, pastas, wines, bottles of olive oil, and salamis. You might even end up eating behind shelves of canned olives, but don't feel bad— this has been a tradition since 1950. The intoxicating smell of pizza wafts into the street; Filippi's has more than 15 varieties (including vegetarian), plus Old World spaghetti, lasagna, and other pasta. Children's portions are available, and kids will feel right at home.

The original of a dozen branches, this Filippi's has free parking; other locations include 962 Garnet Ave., Pacific Beach (© **858/483-6222**); Kearny Mesa; East Mission Valley; and Escondido.

1747 India St. (between Date and Fir Sts.), Little Italy. © 619/232-5095. Main courses $5–$13. AE, DC, DISC, MC, V. Sun–Thurs 11am–10pm; Fri–Sat 11am–11pm. Free parking. Bus: 5. Trolley: County Center/Little Italy.

Kansas City Barbecue AMERICAN   Kansas City Barbecue's honky-tonk mystique was fueled by its appearance as the fly-boy hangout in the movie *Top Gun*. Posters from the film share wall space with county-fair memorabilia, old Kansas car tags, and a photograph of official "bar wench" Carry Nation. This homey dive is right next to the railroad tracks and across from the tony Hyatt Regency. The spicy barbecue ribs, chicken, and hot links are slow-cooked over an open fire and served with sliced white bread and your choice of coleslaw, beans, fries, onion rings, potato salad, or corn on the cob. The food is okay, but the atmosphere is the real draw.

610 W. Market St. © 619/231-9680. Reservations accepted only for parties of 8 or more. Main courses $9–$12. MC, V. Daily 11am–1am. Trolley: Seaport Village.

HILLCREST/UPTOWN

Other choices in this fashionable neighborhood include **Cafe Eleven,** 1440 University Ave. (© **619/260-8023**), a dinner-only country French restaurant with charm and good value; **Ichiban,** 1449 University Ave. (© **619/299-7203**), where locals on the run stop in for a fix of sushi, teriyaki bowls, or yakisoba noodles; and **Hob Nob Hill,** 2271 First Ave., at Juniper (© **619/239-8176**), a 1940s-era diner that's a favorite neighborhood hangout.

EXPENSIVE

California Cuisine ★★ CALIFORNIA   While this excellent restaurant's name is no longer as cutting-edge as when it opened in the early 1980s, the always-creative menu keeps up with contemporary trends. A quiet, understated

---

⟨*Tips* **Where to Find the Famous Theme Restaurants**

San Diego's branch of **Planet Hollywood** (© **619/702-STAR;** www. planethollywood.com) can be found downtown at 197 Horton Plaza (corner of Broadway and Fifth Avenue), in the heart of the Gaslamp Quarter. There's nearly always a line of folks waiting to eat here and ogle the movie memorabilia; the wait staff regularly pacifies diners with free movie posters and theater passes.

You'll find the **Hard Rock Cafe's** rock-'n'-roll memorabilia—and great burgers—in the Gaslamp Quarter, 801 Fourth Ave. (© **619/615-7625;** www.hardrock.com), and in La Jolla at 909 Prospect St., La Jolla (© **858/454-5101**).

dining room and delightfully romantic patio set the stage as the smoothly professional and respectful staff proffers fine dining at moderate prices to a casual crowd.

The menu changes daily and contains mouth-watering appetizers like sesame-seared ahi with hot-and-sour raspberry sauce, or caramelized onion and Gruyère tart on balsamic baby greens. Main courses are, more often than not, stacked in trendy towers, and their flavors are composed with equal care: Blackened beef tenderloin sits atop sun-dried mashed potatoes surrounded by bright tomato puree, and Chilean sea bass is poached in saffron broth with tangy capers and buttery Yukon gold potatoes. Early birds and bargain seekers will appreciate the theater menu, which is a great deal. Parking can be scarce along this busy stretch of University. You'll spot the light-strewn bushes in front of the restaurant.

1027 University Ave. (east of 10th St.). © **619/543-0790.** Reservations recommended for dinner. Main courses $13–$20; 3-course theater menu (daily 5–7pm) $22. AE, DISC, MC, V. Tues–Fri 11am–10pm; Sat–Sun 5–10pm. Bus: 8, 11, 16, or 25.

Laurel ★★★ FRENCH/MEDITERRANEAN   Given its sophisticated decor, pedigreed chefs, prime Balboa Park location, and well-composed menu of country French dishes with a Mediterranean accent, it's no wonder this relatively new restaurant was an instant success. It's also popular with theatergoers, offering shuttle service to the Old Globe. Live piano music adds to the glamour of dining in this swank room on the ground floor of a new office building. Start by choosing from an extensive selection of tantalizing appetizers, including saffron-tinged red pepper–and–shellfish soup, veal sweetbreads with portobello mushrooms and grainy mustard sauce, and warm caramelized onion and Roquefort tart. Main courses include crisp Muscovy duck confit, roasted salmon with tangy red-beet vinaigrette, and venison in a rich shallot–port wine sauce. One of the most stylish choices near often-funky Hillcrest, Laurel has an almost New York ambiance coupled with moderate prices.

505 Laurel St. (at Fifth Ave.). © **619/239-2222.** www.winesellar.com. Reservations recommended. Main courses $15–$26. AE, DC, DISC, MC, V. Sun–Thurs 5–10pm; Fri–Sat 5–11pm. Valet parking $6. Bus: 1, 3, or 25.

MODERATE

Mixx ★★ *Finds* CALIFORNIA/INTERNATIONAL   Aptly named for its subtle global fusion fare, Mixx embodies everything good about Hillcrest dining: an attractive, relaxing room; a sophisticated crowd; thoughtfully composed dinners; and polished, friendly service. It's easy to see why hip locals gravitate to Mixx's wood-paneled street-level cocktail lounge and the often-jovial dining room above. Menu standouts include a starter of pepper-seared ahi over ginger-jicama slaw, duck and wild mushroom ravioli, and pepper filet mignon on truffle mashed potatoes with an armagnac, cream, and port wine reduction. Even carnivores should check out chef Josh McGinnis's surprisingly inventive nightly vegetarian special. Prepared, plated, and presented with finesse, one meal here will quickly convince you that Mixx cares about style, substance, *and* value. Allow time to search for that elusive Hillcrest parking space!

3671 Fifth Ave. (at Pennsylvania Ave.). © **619/299-6499.** Reservations recommended, especially on weekends. Main courses $12–$24. AE, DC, DISC, MC, V. Sun–Thurs 5–10pm; Fri–Sat 5–11pm. Bus: 1, 3, or 25.

Parallel 33 ★★ INTERNATIONAL FUSION   Inspired by a theory that all locales along the 33rd parallel of the globe might share the rich culinary traditions of the Tigris-Euphrates Valley (birthplace of civilization), chef Amiko Gubbins presents a cuisine that beautifully combines flavors from Morocco,

Lebanon, India, China, and Japan. Even if you find the concept befuddling, you're sure to savor the creativity displayed in a menu that leaps happily from fragrant Moroccan chicken *b'stilla* to soft shell crab crusted with *panko* (wispy Japanese bread crumbs) and black sesame seeds, then enthusiastically back to grilled duck with fiery Chinese five-spice sauce alongside crisp spring rolls. The ahi poke appetizer fuses a Hawaiian mainstay with sweet mango and Japanese wasabi—it's a winner! The restaurant is nice but not fancy, just an upscale neighborhood joint (in the most stylish section of town). A multi-ethnic Indian-African-Asian decor throws soft shadows throughout, inviting conversation and leisurely dining. This place was instantly popular after opening in 1999, and devout fans show no signs of waning—so reserve a table in advance.

741 W. Washington St. (at Falcon), Mission Hills. © 619/260-0033. Reservations recommended. Main courses $10–$14 lunch; $15–$22 dinner. AE, DISC, MC, V. Mon–Thurs 5:30–10pm; Fri–Sat 5:30–11pm. Bus: 3, 8 or 16.

INEXPENSIVE
Also consider Hillcrest's nostalgic crowd-pleaser, the 1950s flashback **Corvette Diner** is located at 3946 Fifth Ave., between Washington Street and University Avenue (© **619/542-1001**).

San Diego Chicken Pie Shop ✸ *Value* AMERICAN Visitors might think this throwback diner is hidden away in a nondescript neighborhood northeast of Balboa Park, but residents and regulars know it well. Whether you're looking for a quick-but-hearty lunch, need a square meal on a Skid Row budget, desire a freezer-full of easy-bake dinners, or simply want to experience a genuine 1940s moment, this humble institution fits the bill. Decorated with 60+ years' worth of chicken (and turkey) *tchotchkes* sent by grateful patrons, the dining room is welcoming enough for solo diners, and casual enough for the kids' soccer team. The eponymous pies (fresh-from-the-oven), are so good, we've never even wanted to try the baked ham, roast sirloin, chicken-fried steak, or sautéed chicken livers on the dinner menu. But they're there for dissenters, and a full dinner—including soup, potatoes, vegetable, coleslaw, bread, and dessert—clocks in at under $5! Order a $2 pie a-la-carte and you can still get a slice of apple pie for just 85¢. Ridiculous, huh? At lunchtime, sandwiches round out the menu.

2633 El Cajon Blvd. (at Oregon), North Park. © **619/295-0156**. Most menu items under $5. No credit cards. Daily 10am–8pm (till 8:30pm Fri–Sat). Bus: 1.

The Vegetarian Zone ✸✸ VEGETARIAN San Diego's only strictly vegetarian restaurant is a real treat, and word has gotten around—it's nearly always crowded, and everyone knows about it. Even if you're wary of tempeh, tofu, and meat substitutes, there are plenty of veggie ethnic selections on the menu. Greek spinach-and-feta pie has crispy edges and buttery phyllo layers; Indian turnovers are sweet and savory, flavored with pumpkin and curry; and the Mediterranean roasted-vegetable sandwich is accented with smoky mozzarella cheese. If you're ordering salad, don't miss the tangy miso-ginger dressing. In business since 1975, the Vegetarian Zone has opened a deli next door. There's seating indoors and on a casual patio; soothing music creates a pleasant ambiance enjoyed by trendy Hillcrest types, business lunchers, and the health-conscious from all walks of life. Wine is served by the glass. In case you feel deserving of a treat after such a healthful meal, the heavenly Extraordinary Desserts is next door.

2949 Fifth Ave. (between Palm and Quince Sts.). © **619/298-7302**, or 619/298-9232 for deli and takeout. Reservations accepted only for parties of 6 or more. Main courses $5–$10. AE, DC, DISC, MC, V. Mon–Thurs 11:30am–9pm; Fri 11:30am–10pm; Sat 10:30am–10pm; Sun 10:30am–9pm. Free parking. Bus: 1, 3, or 25.

OLD TOWN & MISSION VALLEY
EXPENSIVE

Cafe Pacifica ★★ CALIFORNIA   You can't judge a book by its cover: Inside this cozy Old Town *casita,* the decor is cleanly contemporary (but still romantic) and the food anything but Mexican. Established in 1980 by the now revered duo of Kipp Downing and Deacon Brown, Cafe Pacifica serves upscale, imaginative seafood and produces kitchen alumni who go on to enjoy local fame. Among the temptations on the menu are crab-stuffed portobello mushroom topped with grilled asparagus; anise-scented bouillabaisse; and daily fresh-fish selections served grilled with your choice of five sauces. Signature items include Hawaiian ahi with shiitake mushrooms and ginger butter, griddled mustard catfish, and the "Pomerita," a pomegranate margarita. Patrons tend to dress up, though it's not required. To avoid the crowds, arrive in the early evening.

2414 San Diego Ave. © **619/291-6666.** www.cafepacifica.com. Reservations recommended. Main courses $12–$22. AE, DC, DISC, MC, V. Mon–Sat 5:30–10pm; Sun 5–9:30pm. Valet parking $4. Bus: 5/5A. Trolley: Old Town.

MODERATE

Berta's Latin American Restaurant ★★ *Finds* LATIN AMERICAN Berta's is a welcome change from the nacho-and-fajita joints that dominate Old Town dining, though it can attract as large a crowd on weekends. Housed in a charming, basic cottage tucked away on a side street, Berta's faithfully re-creates the sunny flavors of Central America, where slow cooking mellows the heat of chilies and other spices. Everyone starts with a basket of fresh flour tortillas and mild salsa verde, which usually vanishes before you're done contemplating such mouthwatering dishes as Guatemalan *chilimal,* a rich pork-and-vegetable casserole with chiles, tomatoes, cornmeal *masa,* coriander, and cloves. Try the Salvadoran *pupusas* (at lunch only)—dense corn-mash turnovers with melted cheese and black beans, their texture perfectly offset with crunchy cabbage salad and one of Berta's special salsas. Or opt for a table full of Spanish-style *tapas,* grazing alternately on crispy empanadas (filled turnovers), strong Spanish olives, or *Pincho Moruno,* skewered lamb and onion redolent of spices and red saffron.

3928 Twiggs St. (at Congress St.). © **619/295-2343.** Main courses $5–$7 lunch; $11–$13 dinner. AE, MC, V. Tues–Sun 11am–10pm (lunch menu till 3pm). Bus: 5/5A. Trolley: Old Town.

INEXPENSIVE

Casa de Bandini ★ MEXICAN   As much an Old Town tradition as the mariachi music that's played here on weekends, Casa de Bandini is the most picturesque of several Mexican restaurants with predictable food and birdbath-size margaritas. It fills the nooks and crannies of an adobe hacienda built in 1823 for Juan Bandini, a local merchant and politician. The superbly renovated enclosed patio has iron gates, flowers blooming around a bubbling fountain, and umbrella-shaded tables for year-round alfresco dining. Some of the dishes are gourmet Mexican, others simple south-of-the-border fare. The crowd consists mainly of out-of-towners, but the ambiance and towering tostada salads draw a lunchtime crowd. The setting makes this restaurant extra-special, and makes the less-than-remarkable meal worthwhile.

2754 Calhoun St. (opposite Old Town Plaza). © **619/297-8211.** Reservations not accepted. Main courses $6–$16. AE, DC, DISC, MC, V. Daily 11am–9pm (till 10pm in summer). Free parking. Bus: 5/5A. Trolley: Old Town.

Old Town Mexican Café ★ MEXICAN   This place is so popular that it's become an Old Town tourist attraction in its own right. It keeps expanding into additional colorful dining rooms and outdoor patios, but the wait for a table is still often 30 to 60 minutes. Pass the time gazing in from the sidewalk as tor-tillas are hand-patted the old-fashioned way, soon to be a hot-off-the-grill treat accompanying every meal. Once inside, order what some consider the best mar-garita in town, followed by one of the cafe's two specialties: *carnitas,* the tradi-tional Mexican dish of deep-fried pork served with tortillas, guacamole, sour cream, beans, and rice; or rotisserie chicken with the same trimmings. It's loud and crowded and the *cerveza* flows like, well, beer . . . but this Old Town main-stay is the best in the city for traditional Mexican.

2489 San Diego Ave. (℆ 619/297-4330. Reservations accepted only for parties of 10 or more. Main courses $7.50–$11.50. AE, DISC, MC, V. Sun–Thurs 7am–11pm; Fri–Sat 7am–midnight; bar service daily until 2am. Bus: 5/5A. Trolley: Old Town.

MISSION BAY & THE BEACHES

Another noteworthy beach spot is **Kono's Surf Club Cafe,** 704 Garnet Ave. (℆ **858/483-1669**), a Hawaiian-themed boardwalk breakfast shack that's cheap and delicious—a plump Kono's breakfast burrito provides enough fuel for an entire day of surfing or sightseeing, while a side order of savory "Kono Potatoes" is a meal in itself. And sushi lovers will want to head straight for **Sushi Ota,** 4529 Mission Bay Dr., at Bunker Hill (℆ **858/270-5670**), where the minimal-ist decor is a perfect backdrop for artful bundles of the best fresh seafood, plus a full menu of Japanese specialties.

EXPENSIVE

Baleen 🏵🏵🏵 SEAFOOD/CALIFORNIA Crowning the multi-million-dollar transformation of the former Vacation Village into the contemporary playground Paradise Point Resort, this fine waterfront eatery is exactly the touch-of-class planners hoped for when they lured celebrity restaurateur Robbin Haas (creator of Baleens in Coconut Grove and Naples, Florida). With a spec-tacular bayfront view (and dining deck for pleasant weather), it's easy to miss the design details indoors—from a monkey motif that includes simians hanging off chandeliers to specialized serving platters for many of Baleen's artistically arranged dishes. Start with chilled lobster in a martini glass, a warm salad of roasted mushrooms and asparagus, or fresh oysters delivered in a small cart and shucked tableside. Then savor a selection of seafood simply grilled, wood-roasted, or sautéed, with hummus crust, honey wasabi glaze, or ginger sauce. Wood-roasted meats include Roquefort-crusted filet mignon and veal T-bone marinated in olive oil, rosemary, and roasted garlic. Should you have appetite—and credit—left over, indulge in an intricately rich dessert like chocolate fondue, or the quartet of fruit-infused custards.

In Paradise Point Resort, 1404 Vacation Rd., Mission Bay. (℆ 858/490-6363. www.baleensandiego.com. Reservations recommended. Main courses$10–$21 lunch; $18–$30 dinner. AE, DC, DISC, MC, V. Daily 7am–11pm. Follow I-8 west to Mission Bay Dr. exit; take Ingraham St. north to Vacation Rd.

MODERATE

Caffe Bella Italia 🏵🏵 NORTHERN ITALIAN You'd think passersby might flock to this excellent family-run Garnet Avenue newcomer, but most just look . . . and keep on walking or driving. They're discouraged by Bella Italia's—the kindest word I can think of is *underwhelming*—street presence, housed in a former plain-Jane stucco dry cleaner. Trust me on this one, it's lovely inside, and the food will knock your socks off. Romantic lighting, sheer draperies, and warmly earthy walls create an unexpected ambiance, assisted by the lilting Milan accents of the staff. Each and every item on the menu bears the unmistakable flavor of freshness and homemade care—even the simplest curled-edge ravioli stuffed with ricotta, spinach, and pine nuts is elevated to culinary nirvana. Indulge in the traditional *tartufo* ice cream dessert (bathed in a shot of espresso), and you'll leave wishing you could be adopted by this delicious family.

1525 Garnet Ave. (between Ingraham and Haines), Pacific Beach. (C) 858/273-1224. Reservations suggested for dinner. Main courses $7–$11 lunch; $9–$18 dinner. AE, MC, V. Tue–Thurs 11am–2:30pm and 5–10pm; Fri–Sat 11am–2:30pm and 5–11pm; Sun 5–10pm. Free parking lot. Bus: 27.

The Green Flash 🦀 AMERICAN   Known throughout Pacific Beach for its location and hip, local clientele, the Green Flash serves reasonably good (and typically beachy) food at decent prices. The menu includes plenty of grilled and deep-fried seafood, straightforward steaks, and giant main-course salads. You'll also find platters of shellfish (oysters, clams, shrimp) and ethnic appetizers. On the glassed-in patio, locals congregate every evening to catch a glimpse of the optical phenomenon for which this boardwalk hangout is named. It has something to do with the color spectrum at the moment the sun disappears below the horizon, but the scientific explanation becomes less important—and the decibel level rises—with every round of drinks.

701 Thomas Ave. (at Mission Blvd.), Pacific Beach. (C) **858/270-7715.** Reservations not accepted. Main courses $10–$20; sunset specials Sun–Thurs 4:30–7pm. AE, DC, DISC, MC, V. Daily 8am–10pm. Bus: 34/34A.

INEXPENSIVE

For all-day breakfast, light lunch, or a soup bowl–sized *caffe latte,* follow the locals to **The Mission,** 3795 Mission Blvd., at San Jose ((C) **858/488-9060**), a funky and casual coffeehouse at the heart of the Mission Beach scene.

Firehouse Beach Café AMERICAN   Ceiling fans stir the air in this cheerful, comfortably crowded place, and there's pleasant rooftop dining with an ocean view if you're lucky enough to snag a seat. Just off the Pacific Beach boardwalk, the cafe sees a lot of foot traffic and socializing locals. Those in the know go for great breakfasts—choices include Mexican-style eggs and breakfast burritos, French toast, and omelets. During happy hour (4 to 6pm), you'll find bargain prices on drinks and finger-lickin' appetizers. The rest of the menu is adequate, running the gamut from fish tacos to Tex-Mex fajitas to lasagna and all-American burgers.

722 Grand Ave., Pacific Beach. (C) **858/272-1999.** Reservations recommended on weekends. Main courses $6–$13. AE, DISC, MC, V. Sun–Thurs 7am–9pm; Fri–Sat 7am–10pm. Free parking. Bus: 34/34A.

LA JOLLA
EXPENSIVE

Cafe Japengo ⭐⭐ PACIFIC RIM/SUSHI   Despite being contrived and self-conscious, Cafe Japengo is worth a trip for the food alone. With subdued lighting and a highly stylized Asian atmosphere, this restaurant is the best of several attached to the Golden Triangle's behemoth Hyatt Regency Hotel. The beautiful people know they look even more so among the warm woods and leafy shadows here, so there's lots of posing and people-watching. It's always packed; patrons come from all over the county for Japengo's Pacific Rim fusion cuisine, which incorporates South American and even European touches.

Some offerings, like the pot-stickers in tangy coriander-mint sauce or lemongrass-marinated swordfish, are superb; others, like the seared ahi "Napoleon," suffer from extra ingredients that just make the dish fussy. Sushi here is the same way; Japengo features the finest and freshest fish, but churns out enormously popular specialty rolls (combinations wrapped in even more ingredients, often drenched in sauce and garnished even further). The dramatic, colorfully presented inventions are enormously popular, but sushi purists will be happiest sticking to the basics.

At the Hyatt Regency La Jolla, 8960 University Center Lane. © **858/450-3355.** Reservations recommended. Main courses $14–$28. AE, DC, DISC, MC, V. Mon–Fri 11:30am–2:30pm; Sun–Thurs 5–10pm; Fri–Sat 5–10:30pm (sushi bar open till 11pm Mon–Thurs, midnight Fri–Sat). Valet parking $3, validated self-parking free. From I-5, take La Jolla Village Dr. E.

George's at the Cove ✦✦✦ CALIFORNIA You'll find host and namesake George Hauer at his restaurant's door most nights; he greets loyal regulars by name, and his confidence assures newcomers that they'll leave impressed with this beloved La Jolla tradition. Voted most popular in the *Zagat* restaurant survey, George's wins consistent praise for impeccable service, gorgeous views of the cove, and outstanding California cuisine.

The menu, in typical San Diego fashion, presents many inventive seafood options, filtered through the myriad influences of chef Trey Foshee. Classical culinary training, Hawaiian ingenuity, and a stint at Robert Redford's Utah Sundance resort are among his many accomplishments. Dishes combine many flavors with practiced artistry, ranging from the Asian-tinged grilled swordfish atop gingered vegetables accented with Thai coconut sauce to a Provençal-inspired rack of lamb in aromatic spices with Foshee's version of ratatouille. George's signature smoked chicken, broccoli, and black-bean soup is still a mainstay; they'll even give out the recipe for this local legend. As an alternative to dinner's pricey main courses, try the tasting menu, which offers a seasonally composed five-course sampling for around $49 per person; or try the more reasonably priced lunch menu. The informal Ocean Terrace Cafe is upstairs.

1250 Prospect St. © **858/454-4244.** www.georgesatthecove.com. Reservations recommended. Main courses $13–$17 lunch; $25–$35 dinner. AE, DC, DISC, MC, V. Mon–Fri 11:30am–2:30pm; Sat–Sun 11:30am–3pm; Mon–Thurs 5:30–10pm; Fri–Sat 5–10:30pm; Sun 5–10pm. Valet parking $5–$6.

Trattoria Acqua ✦✦ ITALIAN/MEDITERRANEAN Nestled on tiled terraces close enough to catch ocean breezes, this excellent Northern Italian spot has a more relaxed ambiance than similarly sophisticated Gaslamp Quarter trattorias. Rustic walls and outdoor seating shaded by flowering vines evoke a romantic Tuscan villa. A mixed crowd of suits and well-heeled couples gather to enjoy expertly prepared seasonal dishes; every table starts with bread served with an indescribably pungent Mediterranean spread. Acqua's pastas (all available as appetizers or main courses) are as good as it gets—rich, heady flavor combinations like spinach, chard, and four-cheese gnocchi, or veal-and-mortadella tortellini in fennel cream sauce. Other specialties include *saltimbocca con funghi* (veal scaloppini with sage, prosciutto, and forest-mushroom sauce), *cassoulet* (traditional Toulouse-style duck confit, sausage, and braised lamb baked with white beans, tomato, and fresh thyme), and *salmone al pepe* (roasted peppercorn-crusted Atlantic salmon served over lentils with sherry-and-shallot vinaigrette). The well-chosen wine list has received *Wine Spectator* accolades several years in a row.

1298 Prospect St. (on Coast Walk). © **858/454-0709.** www.trattoriaacqua.com. Reservations recommended. Main courses $13–$27. AE, MC, V. Daily 11:30am–2:30pm; Sun–Thurs 5–9:30pm; Fri–Sat 5–10:30pm. Validated self-parking.

MODERATE

Don't forget about the **Ocean Terrace** at George's at the Cove (see above), where many of the same dishes come with a fresh-air ocean view—and a slimmer bill than the downstairs dining room.

Brockton Villa ★★ *Finds* BREAKFAST/CALIFORNIA   In a restored 1894 beach bungalow, this charming cafe has a history as intriguing as its varied, eclectic menu. Named for an early resident's hometown (Brockton, MA), the cottage is imbued with the spirit of artistic souls drawn to this breathtaking perch overlooking La Jolla Cove. Rescued by the trailblazing Pannikin Coffee Company in the 1960s, the restaurant is now independently run by a Pannikin alum.

The biggest buzz is at breakfast, when you can enjoy inventive dishes such as soufflé-like "Coast Toast" (the house take on French toast) and Greek "steamers" (eggs scrambled with an espresso steamer, then mixed with feta cheese, tomato, and basil). The dozens of coffee drinks include the "Keith Richards"—four shots of espresso topped with Mexican hot chocolate. (Mother's Little Helper indeed!) Lunch stars include homemade soups and salads, plus unusual sandwiches like turkey meat loaf on toasted sourdough bread with spicy tomato-mint chutney. The constantly expanding dinner menu includes salmon *en croute* (wrapped in prosciutto, Gruyère, and sage, with a grainy mustard sauce), plus pastas, stews, and grilled meats. Steep stairs from the street limit access for wheelchair users.

1235 Coast Blvd. (across from La Jolla Cove). (C) **858/454-7393.** Reservations recommended (call by Thurs for Sun brunch). Breakfast $4–$8; dinner main courses $12–$21. AE, DISC, MC, V. Mon 8am–5pm, Tues–Sun 8am–9pm.

Spice & Rice Thai Kitchen ★ THAI   This stylish Thai restaurant is a couple of blocks from the village's tourist crush—far enough to ensure effortless parking. The lunch crowd consists of shoppers and curious tourists, while dinner is quieter; all the local businesses have shut down and many diners are going to the old-fashioned Cove movie theater next door. The food is excellent, with polished presentations and expert renditions of the classics like pad Thai, satay, curry, and glazed duck. The starters often sound as good as the entrees—consider making a grazing meal of house specialties like "gold bags" (minced pork, vegetables, and herbs wrapped in crispy rice paper and served with earthy plum sauce) or minced roast duck spiced with chiles and lime juice; spicy calamari is flavored with ginger, cilantro, lime, and chili sauce. The romantically lit covered front patio has a secluded garden feel, and inside tables also have indirect lighting. Despite the passage of time, this all-around satisfier remains something of an insider's secret.

7734 Girard Ave. (C) **858/456-0466.** Reservations recommended. Main courses $8–$13. AE, MC, V. Mon–Thurs 11am–3pm and 5–10pm; Fri–Sat 11am–3pm and 5–11pm; Sun 5–10pm.

INEXPENSIVE

The Cottage ★ BREAKFAST/CALIFORNIA   La Jolla's best—and friendliest—breakfast is served at this turn-of-the-century bungalow on a sunny village corner. Newly modernized, the cottage is light and airy, but most diners opt for tables outside, where a charming white picket fence encloses the trellis-shaded brick patio. Omelets and egg dishes feature Mediterranean, Asian, or classic American touches; my favorite has creamy mashed potatoes, bacon, and melted cheese folded inside. The Cottage bakes its own muffins, breakfast breads, and—you can quote me on this—the best brownies in San Diego. While breakfast dishes are served all day, toward lunch the kitchen begins turning out freshly made, healthful soups, light meals, and sandwiches. Summer dinners (never heavy, always tasty) are a delight, particularly when you're seated before dark on a balmy seaside night.

7702 Fay Ave. (at Kline St.). (C) **858/454-8409.** www.cottagelajolla.com. Reservations accepted for dinner only. Breakfast and lunch $5–$7; dinner main courses $8–$18. AE, DISC, MC, V. Daily year-round 7:30am–3pm; May 15–Sept 30 Tues–Sat 5–9:30pm.

CORONADO

If you're in the mood for a special-occasion meal that'll knock your socks off, consider **Azzura Point** (© 619/424-4000), in Loews Coronado Bay Resort. With its plushly upholstered, gilded, and view-endowed setting, this stylish dining room wins continual raves from deep-pocketed San Diego foodies willing to cross the bay for inventive and artistic California-Mediterranean creations.

EXPENSIVE

Chez Loma ☆☆ FRENCH   You'd be hard pressed to find a more romantic dining spot than this intimate Victorian cottage filled with antiques and subdued candlelight. The house dates from 1889, the French-Continental restaurant from 1975. Tables are scattered throughout the house and on the enclosed garden terrace; an upstairs wine salon, reminiscent of a Victorian parlor, is a cozy spot for coffee or conversation.

Among the creative entrees are salmon with smoked-tomato vinaigrette, and roast duckling with green-peppercorn sauce. All main courses are served with soup or salad, rice or potatoes, and fresh vegetables. California wines and American microbrews are available. Follow dinner with a creamy crème caramel or Kahlúa crème brûlée. Chez Loma's service is attentive, the herb rolls addictive, and early birds enjoy specially priced meals.

1132 Loma (off Orange Ave.). © 619/435-0661. www.chezloma.com. Reservations recommended. Main courses $17–$25. AE, DC, MC, V. Daily 5–10pm; Sun 10am–2pm. Bus: 901.

Peohe's ☆ PACIFIC RIM/SEAFOOD   With over-the-top Polynesian decor of which Disneyland would be proud, Peohe's is definitely touristy and definitely overpriced—but there's no denying the awesome view across the bay or the excellent Hawaiian-style seafood and Pacific Rim–accented cuisine. Every table in the giant, light- and plant-filled atrium has a view; there are even better tables on the wooden deck at the water's edge. Dinner main courses include acclaimed crunchy coconut shrimp; island-style halibut sautéed with banana, macadamia nuts, and Frangelico liqueur; and rack of New Zealand lamb with Hunan barbecue sauce. Lunchtime options include more casual sandwiches and salads, and the tropical fantasy desserts are delectably rich. For those who love theme restaurants and Polynesian kitsch, Peohe's is a worthwhile splurge.

1201 First St. (Ferry Landing Marketplace). © 619/437-4474. www.peohes.com. Reservations recommended. Main courses $9–$16 lunch; $19–$30 dinner. AE, DC, DISC, MC, V. Mon–Sat 11:30am–2:30pm; Sun 10:30am–2:30pm; Mon–Thurs 5:30–9pm; Fri 5:30–10pm; Sat 5–10pm; Sun 4:30–9pm. Bus: 901 or 904.

MODERATE

Bay Beach Cafe AMERICAN/SEAFOOD   This loud, friendly gathering place isn't on the beach at all, but enjoys a prime perch on San Diego Bay. Seated indoors or on a glassed-in patio, diners gaze endlessly at the city skyline, which is dramatic by day and breathtaking at night. The cafe is quite popular at happy hour, when the setting sun glimmers on downtown's mirrored high-rises. The ferry docks at a wooden pier a few steps away, discharging passengers into the complex of gift shops and restaurants with a New England fishing-village theme. At the Bay Beach Cafe, the food takes a back seat to the view, but the pub menu of burgers, sandwiches, salads, and appetizers is inexpensive and satisfying. Dinner entrees aren't quite good enough for the price.

1201 First St. (Ferry Landing Marketplace). © 619/435-4900. Reservations recommended for dinner on weekends. Main courses $9–$18; pub menu $6–$10. AE, DISC, MC, V. Mon–Fri 7–10:30am and 11am–4pm; Sat–Sun 7–11:30am and noon–4pm; daily 5–10:30pm. Free parking. Bus: 901 or 904.

Tips **Coronado's Wide World of Hors D'Oeuvres**

If you're longing for some great appetizers—more sophisticated than popcorn shrimp and potato skins—then the **Chameleon Cafe & Lizard Lounge,** 1301 Orange Ave., Coronado (📞 **619/437-6677**), is your answer. The latest venture of chef Ken Irvine (the local superstar of Chez Loma fame), this casual and eclectic eatery is half cocktail lounge; fitting, because the menu is half appetizers. The "first plates" range in price from $4 to $9, and are generously sized and suitable for sharing. Relax—and watch the activity along Orange Avenue—while nibbling on Asian delicacies (lobster/crab potstickers, smoked salmon and avocado sushi), Southwestern spice (goat-cheese tamale, pork empanada), or Mediterranean standards (grilled pizzas with smoked chicken and fontina cheese or portobello mushrooms). The bar features premium vodkas and aged tequilas; we recommend eschewing the restaurant's pricier main courses and having a "grazing" meal in the bar, which stays open from lunchtime until closing. The eatery is open Sunday through Thursday from 11:30am to 10pm, Friday and Saturday from 11:30am to 11pm.

INEXPENSIVE

Primavera Pastry Caffé ⭐ *Value* SANDWICHES/LIGHT FARE   If the name sounds familiar, it's because this fantastic little cafe—the best of its kind on the island—is part of the family that includes Primavera Ristorante, up the street. In addition to fresh-roasted coffee and espresso drinks, it serves omelets and other breakfast treats (till 1:30pm), burgers and deli sandwiches on the delicious house bread, and a daily fresh soup. It's the kind of spot where half the customers are greeted by name. Locals rave about the "Yacht Club" sandwich, a croissant filled with yellowfin tuna, and the breakfast croissant, topped with scrambled ham and eggs and cheddar cheese. We can't resist Primavera's fat, gooey cinnamon buns.

956 Orange Ave. 📞 **619/435-4191.** Main courses $4–$6. No credit cards. Daily 6:30am–6pm. Bus: 901.

5 The Main Attractions: The Zoo, SeaWorld & the Wild Animal Park

San Diego Zoo ⭐⭐⭐ *Kids*   More than 4,000 animals reside at this world-famous zoo, which was founded in 1916 with a handful of animals originally brought here for the 1915–16 Panama–California International Exposition. Many of the buildings you see in surrounding Balboa Park were built for the exposition. The zoo's founder, Dr. Harry Wegeforth, a local physician and life-long animal lover, once braved the fury of an injured tiger to toss medicine into its roaring mouth.

In the early days of the zoo, "Dr. Harry" traveled around the world and bartered native Southwestern animals such as rattlesnakes and sea lions for more exotic species. The loan of two giant pandas from the People's Republic of China was a twist on the long-standing tradition—instead of exchanging exotic species, the San Diego Zoo agreed to pay $1 million for each year that the pandas are here, to aid the conservation effort in China. The lovable pandas, which arrived in 1996, were an instant hit with zoo-goers, but their keepers' behind-the-scenes mission was to scientifically encourage the breeding of this near-extinct animal.

In August of 1999, their efforts were rewarded with the birth of Hua Mei, a healthy and perfect female cub. To ensure a glimpse of the panda family, call the zoo's panda-viewing hotline at ☎ **888/MY-PANDA** before visiting.

The zoo is also an accredited botanical garden, representing more than 6,000 species of flora from many climate zones, all installed to help simulate the animals' native environments.

The giant pandas may be the big attention-getters, but the zoo has many other rare and exotic species: cuddly koalas from Australia, long-billed kiwis from New Zealand, wild Przewalski horses from Mongolia, lowland gorillas from Africa, and giant tortoises from the Galapagos. Of course, the zoo's regulars—lions, elephants, giraffes, tigers, and bears—prowl around as well, and the zoo is home to a great number of tropical birds. Most of the animals are housed in barless, moated enclosures that resemble their natural habitats.

The zoo offers two types of bus tours. Both provide a narrated overview and allow you to see 75% of the park. On the **35-minute guided bus tour,** you get on the bus and complete a circuit around the zoo. It costs $4 for adults, $3 for children ages 3 to 11, and is included in the deluxe package. The **Kangaroo Bus Tour** allows you to get on and off the bus as many times as you want at any of the eight stops—you can even go around more than once. It costs $8 for adults and $5 for children. In general, it's better to take the tour early in the morning or later in the afternoon, when the animals are more active. Call the **Bus Tour Hot Line** (☎ **619/685-3264**) for information about these tours, as well as Spanish-language tours, a comedy tour, and signed tours for the hearing impaired.

You can also get an aerial perspective from the **Skyfari,** which costs $1 per person each way. The ride lasts about 5 minutes—but, because it doesn't get particularly close to the animals, it's better for a bird's-eye view of Balboa Park and a survey of the zoo.

The **Children's Zoo** is scaled to a youngster's viewpoint. There's a nursery with baby animals and a petting area where kids can cuddle up to sheep, goats, and the like. The resident wombat is a special favorite here.

2920 Zoo Dr., Balboa Park. ☎ 619/234-3153. www.sandiegozoo.com. Admission $18 adult, $8 children 3–11, military in uniform free. Deluxe package (admission, guided bus tour, round-trip Skyfari aerial tram) $27 adults, $24.30 seniors 60 and over, $15 children. Combination Zoo and Wild Animal Park package (deluxe zoo package, Wild Animal Park admission) $40.75 adults, $25.55 children; valid for 5 days from date of purchase. DISC, MC, V. Daily year-round 9am–4pm (grounds close at 5pm); summer 9am–9pm (grounds close at 10pm). Bus: 7/7B.

San Diego Wild Animal Park ★★★ *Kids*   Just 30 miles north of San Diego, outside of Escondido, the Wild Animal Park transports you to the African plains and other landscapes. Originally begun as a breeding facility for the San Diego Zoo, the WAP now holds around 3,200 animals—many endangered species— roaming freely over the park's 1,800 acres. Approximately 650 baby animals are born every year in the park.

The simplest way to see the animals is by riding the 5-mile **monorail** (included in the price of admission); for the best views, sit on the right-hand side. During the 50-minute ride, you'll pass through areas resembling Africa and Asia, past waterholes and swaying grasses. Trains leave every 20 minutes from the station in Nairobi Village, the commercial hub of the park with more traditional animal exhibits, souvenir stores, and refreshment vendors. (It may sound persnickety, but the food inside the park is mediocre and overpriced . . . think about smuggling in your own snacks!)

Nairobi Village isn't much more than a small zoo whose best feature is the nursery area, where irresistible young 'uns can be seen, frolicking, being bottle-fed, and sleeping. If you want to experience the vast landscape and large animals that make the Wild Animal Park unique, you can take one of two self-guided walking trails: the 1¾-mile **Kilimanjaro safari walk,** which visits the Australian rain forest and East Africa, or the **Heart of Africa,** a ¾-mile trail that winds through dense forest, flourishing wetlands, sprawling savannas, and open plains.

The surest way to get up-close-and-personal, though, is to take a **photo car-avan tour** ($65–$95 per person, park admission included). In our experience, the photos are secondary to the enjoyment. (How many of us point-and-shoot shutterbugs can really hope to top the professional shots gracing the official sou-venir postcards, anyway?) What matters is crossing the fence to meet the rhinos, ostriches, zebras, deer, and giraffes on their home turf, even feeding giraffes along the way.

15500 San Pasqual Valley Rd., Escondido. ✆ 760/747-8702. www.wildanimalpark.com. Admission $23.95 adults, $21.55 seniors 60 and over, $16.95 children 3–11, free for children under 3 and military in uniform. Combination Zoo and Wild Animal Park package (includes deluxe zoo package) $40.75 adults, $25.55 chil-dren; valid for 5 days from date of purchase. DISC, MC, V. Daily 9am–4pm (grounds close at 5pm); extended hours during summer and Festival of Lights in December. Parking $6 per car. Take I-15 to Via Rancho Pkwy.; follow signs for about 3 miles.

SeaWorld ★★★ *(Kids)*   One of the best-promoted attractions in California, SeaWorld may be your main reason for coming to San Diego. The 165-acre, multimillion-dollar aquatic playground is a showplace for marine life, made politically correct with a nominally educational atmosphere. Several successive 4-ton black-and-white killer whales have functioned as the park's mascot, Shamu. At its heart, SeaWorld is a family entertainment center where the performers are dolphins, otters, sea lions, walruses, and seals. Shows run continuously through-out the day, while visitors can rotate through the various theaters.

The 2-acre hands-on area called **Shamu's Happy Harbor** encourages kids to handle things—and features everything from a pretend pirate ship, with plenty of netted towers, to tube crawls, slides, and chances to get wet. The newest attraction is **Shipwreck Rapids,** a wet adventure ride on raft-like inner tubes through caverns, waterfalls, and wild rivers. Other draws include **Wild Arctic,** a virtual-reality trip to the frozen North, complete with polar bears, beluga

---

(Value Now That's What I Call a Deal!

Always aware of what side their tourism bread is buttered on, San Diego's three main family attractions have joined forces with combo ticket deals that reward you with big savings for visitors with recreational stamina. Here's how it works: If you plan to visit both the zoo and Wild Animal Park, a two-park ticket (deluxe zoo package, Wild Animal Park admission) is $40.75 for adults and $25.55 for children ages 3 to 11. You get one visit to each attraction, to be used within 5 days of purchase.

What's that you say, you want *more?* OK, then—add SeaWorld to your plans with a three-park ticket (deluxe zoo package, Wild Animal Park admission, and SeaWorld admission) for $73.95 adults, $50.95 children 3 to 11. You get *unlimited* use at all three parks for 5 days from date of purchase!

San Diego Attractions

654

PACIFIC
OCEAN

MISSION BEACH

OCEAN BEACH

Point Loma

Cabrillo National Monument **16**

Fiesta Island

SeaWorld **9**

San Diego Sports Arena

OLD TOWN

Shelter Island

Harbor Island

San Diego International Airport

Point Loma

San Diego Bay

U.S. Naval Air Station

UPTOWN/HILLCREST

Area of Inset

Embarcadero

Seaport Village

San Diego Convention Center

CORONADO

Ferry Landing Market Place

San Diego–Coronado Bridge

Silver Strand

BALBOA PARK

54th St

El Cajon Blvd.

University Ave.

Robinson Ave.

El Prado

1st Ave.
4th Ave.
5th Ave.

Ash St.
Broadway
F St.

Date St.

Market St.

Imperial Ave.

Pershing Dr.

Ocean-View Blvd.

National Ave.

Harbor Dr.

2nd St.
3rd St.
4th St.
6th St.

Orange Ave.

Adella Ave.

Friars Rd.

Hotel Circle   Hotel Circle

Fort Stockton Dr.

Washington St.

Goldfinch St.

India St.

Harney St.

Pacific Highway

San Diego Ave.

Barnett Ave.

Rosecrans

Nimitz Blvd.

West Point Loma Blvd.

Sunset Cliffs Blvd.

Catalina Blvd.

Hill St.

Narragansett Ave.

Voltaire St.

Chatsworth

Cabrillo Memorial Dr.

Mission Bay Dr.

SeaWorld Dr.

Sea World Fwy.

Ocean Beach Fwy.

Midway Dr.

N

0   1 mi
0   1 km

Balboa Park Museums **14**
Belmont Park **8**
Cabrillo National Monument **16**
Children's Museum of San Diego **4**
Horton Plaza **5**
Hotel del Coronado **15**
Maritime Museum **2**
Marston House **12**
Mission Basilica San Diego de Alcala **11**
Museum of Contemporary Art, Downtown **3**
San Diego Zoo **13**
Sea World **9**
Serra Museum **10**
Villa Montezuma **7**
Wild Animal Park **1**
William Heath Davis House Museum **6**

CALIFORNIA
⊛ Sacramento
San Francisco
Los Angeles
San Diego

whales, walruses, and harbor seals; and the 4-D interactive movie *Pirates*, a comic adventure written by *Monty Python's* Eric Idle and starring the deadpan Leslie Nielsen.

The **Dolphin Interaction Program** creates an opportunity for people to meet bottlenose dolphins. Although the program stops short of allowing you to swim with the dolphins, it does offer the opportunity to wade waist-deep, and plenty of time to stroke the mammals and give commands like the trainers. This 1-hour program includes some classroom time before you wriggle into a wetsuit and climb into the water; it costs $125 per person, not including admission to the rest of the adventure park. Space is limited, so advance reservations are required (© **877/4-DOLPHIN**). Participants must be 6 or older.

Although SeaWorld is best known as Shamu's home, the facility also plays an important role in rescuing and rehabilitating beached animals found along the West Coast—including more than 300 seals, sea lions, marine birds, and dolphins in an average year. Following the successful rescue and 1998 release of a young California gray whale, SeaWorld turned its attention to the manatee, an unusual aquatic mammal rarely seen outside Florida's tropical waters—several permanent residents are on display in the **Manatee Rescue** exhibit area.

500 Sea World Dr., Mission Bay. © **619/226-3901**. www.seaworld.com. Admission $39 adults, $35 seniors 55 and over, $30 children 3–11, free for children under 3. AE, DISC, MC, V. Parking $7. Guided 90-min. walking tours $8 adults, $7 children. Memorial Day–Labor Day daily 9am–11pm or 12midnight; Sept–May daily 10am–5pm. Bus: 9. By car from I-5, take Sea World Dr. exit; from I-8, take W. Mission Bay Dr. exit to Sea World Dr.

6 Beaches

San Diego County is blessed with 70 miles of sandy coastline and more than 30 beaches that attract surfers, snorkelers, swimmers, and sunbathers. In summer, the beaches teem with locals and visitors alike. The rest of the year, they are popular places to walk and jog, and surfers don wet suits to pursue their passion. The following are some of our favorite San Diego beaches, arranged geographically from south to north.

IMPERIAL BEACH   Half an hour south of San Diego by car or trolley, and only a few minutes from the Mexican border, lies Imperial Beach. It's popular with surfers and local youth, who can be somewhat territorial about "their" sands in summer. Imperial plays host to the annual U.S. Open Sandcastle Competition each August, with world-class sand creations ranging from sea scenes to dragons to dinosaurs.

CORONADO BEACH   Lovely, wide, and sparkling white, this beach is conducive to strolling and lingering, especially in the late afternoon. It fronts Ocean Boulevard and is especially pretty in front of the Hotel del Coronado. The islands visible from here, but 18 miles away, are named "Los Coronados," and they belong to Mexico.

OCEAN BEACH   The northern end of Ocean Beach Park is officially known as **Dog Beach,** and is one of only two in San Diego where your pooch can roam freely on the sand (and frolic with several dozen other people's pooches). Surfers generally congregate around the Ocean Beach Pier, where rip currents are strong and discourage most swimmers from venturing out beyond waist-depth. Facilities at the beach include restrooms, showers, picnic tables, and plenty of metered parking lots.

MISSION BAY PARK   In this 4,600-acre aquatic playground, you'll discover 27 miles of bay front, 17 miles of oceanfront beaches, picnic areas, children's playgrounds, and paths for biking, roller skating, and jogging. The bay lends itself to windsurfing, sailing, jet-skiing, water-skiing, and fishing. There are dozens of access points; one of the most popular is off I-5 at Clairemont Drive, where there's a visitor information center.

MISSION BEACH   While Mission Bay Park is a body of salt water surrounded by land and bridges, Mission Beach is actually a beach on the Pacific Ocean. Surfing is popular year-round here. The long beach and boardwalk extend from Pacific Beach Drive south to Belmont Park and beyond to the jetty.

PACIFIC BEACH   Pacific Beach is the home of **Tourmaline Surfing Park,** where the sport's old guard gather to surf waters where swimmers are prohibited; and there's always some action at Mission Beach, particularly along **Ocean Front Walk,** a paved promenade featuring a human parade akin to that at L.A.'s Venice Beach boardwalk. It runs along Ocean Boulevard (just west of Mission Boulevard), north of Pacific Beach Drive.

WINDANSEA   The fabled locale of Tom Wolfe's *Pump House Gang,* Windansea is legendary to this day among California's surf elite. Reached via Bonair Street (at Neptune Place), Windansea has no facilities, and street parking is first-come, first-served. Come to surf, watch surfers, or soak in the camaraderie and party atmosphere of Windansea locals.

CHILDREN'S POOL BEACH   Much of the sand near the point of La Jolla's peninsula is cordoned off for the resident sea-lion population; the rest is inhabited by curious shutterbugs and families taking advantage of the same calm conditions that keep the sea lions around. The beach is located at Coast Boulevard and Jenner Street; there's limited free street parking.

LA JOLLA COVE   The protected, calm waters—praised as the clearest along the California coast—attract swimmers, snorkelers, scuba divers, and families. There's a small sandy beach, and on the cliffs above, the Ellen Browning Scripps Park. The cove's "look but don't touch" policy protects the colorful marine life in this Underwater Park. La Jolla Cove can be accessed from Coast Boulevard.

LA JOLLA SHORES BEACH   The wide, flat mile of sand at La Jolla Shores is popular with joggers, swimmers, and beginning body and board surfers, as well as with families. Weekend crowds can be enormous, though, quickly occupying both the sand and the metered parking spaces in the beach's lot. Facilities include restrooms, showers, and picnic areas.

BLACK'S BEACH   The area's unofficial (and illegal) nude beach, it lies north of La Jolla Shores Beach, below some steep cliffs. Black's isn't easy to reach—take North Torrey Pines Road, park at the Glider Port, and walk down from there. *Note:* Although the water is shallow and pleasant for wading, this area is known for its rip currents.

7 Exploring the Area

BALBOA PARK

Balboa Park is one of the nation's largest, loveliest, and most important municipal greenbelts. This is no simple city park; it boasts walkways, gardens, historical buildings, a restaurant, an ornate pavilion with one of the world's largest outdoor organ, and the world-famous San Diego Zoo (see "The Main Attractions," above). Stroll along El Prado, the park's main street, and admire the distinctive Spanish-Mediterranean buildings, which house an amazing array of museums.

Tips Balboa Park Money-Savers

Many Balboa Park attractions are open free-of-charge one Tuesday each month; there's a rotating schedule so three or more participate each Tuesday. (Call ☎ **619/239-0512** or log on to www.balboapark.org for a complete schedule.) If you plan to visit more than three of the park's museums, buy the Passport to Balboa Park, a coupon booklet that allows one entrance to each of 11 museums (the rest are always free) and is valid for 1 week. The $21 passport can be purchased at any participating museum or the visitor center.

Filled on weekends with locals, El Prado is also popular with musicians and other performers who provide an entertaining backdrop.

Entry to the park is free, but most of its museums have admission charges and varying open hours. A free tram will transport you around the park. Get details from the **Balboa Park Visitors Center,** located in the House of Hospitality (☎ **619/239-0512;** www.balboapark.org). Below are the highlights:

San Diego Aerospace Museum ★★, 2001 Pan American Plaza (☎ **619/234-8291;** www.aerospacemuseum.org). Great achievers and achievements in the history of aviation and aerospace are celebrated by this superb collection of historical aircraft and related artifacts, including art, models, dioramas, and films.

Museum of Art ★, 1450 El Prado (☎ **619/232-7931;** www.sdmart.com). With one of the grandest entrances along El Prado, the museum is known in the art world for outstanding collections of Italian Renaissance and Dutch and Spanish baroque art, along with an impressive collection of Toulouse-Lautrec. Prestigious traveling exhibits are often shown here, and the museum's high-tech touch is an interactive computer image system that allows visitors to locate museum highlights and custom-design a tour.

Museum of Photographic Arts, 1649 El Prado (☎ **619/238-7559;** www.mopa.org). If the names of Ansel Adams, Margaret Bourke-White, Imogen Cunningham, Edward Weston, and Henri Cartier-Bresson stimulate your interest, then don't miss the 3,600+ image collection of this museum—one of few in the United States devoted exclusively to the photographic arts.

Natural History Museum, 1788 El Prado (☎ **619/232-3821;** www.sdnhm.org). The museum focuses on the flora, fauna, and mineralogy of the Southwest. Kids marvel at the animals they find here and enjoy exploring the Desert Lab, home to live snakes and tarantulas. Call or check the museum's website for a current schedule of special visiting exhibits.

Reuben H. Fleet Science Center ★★, 1875 El Prado (☎ **619/238-1233;** www.rhfleet.org). Easily the park's busiest museum, the Science Center features five galleries with hands-on exhibits as intriguing for grown-ups as for kids, including SciTours, a simulator ride that voyages into space and the worlds of science and biology. Equally popular is the OMNIMAX movie theater, surrounding viewers with breathtaking adventure travelogues. You can avoid waiting in line by buying tickets in advance.

Museum of Man, 1350 El Prado (☎ **619/239-2001;** www.museumofman.org). This museum is devoted to the sociology and anthropology of the peoples of North and South America, and includes life-size replicas of a dozen varieties of Homo sapiens.

Balboa Park

San Diego Automotive Museum ✪, 2080 Pan American Plaza (𝄞 **619/ 231-2886;** www.sdautomuseum.org). Even if you don't know a distributor from a dipstick, you're bound to ooh-and-aah over the classic, antique, and exotic cars here. Every one is so pristine you'd swear it just rolled off the line; some days you can take a peek at the ongoing restoration program.

Botanical Building, El Prado. More than a thousand varieties of tropical and flowering plants are sheltered within this graceful structure, and the lily pond out front attracts the occasional street performer.

Hall of Champions, 2133 Pan American Plaza (𝄞 **619/234-2544;** www. sandiegosports.org). Sports fans will want to check out this museum, which highlights dozens of different professional and amateur sports and athletes.

Japanese Friendship Garden ✪, 2216 Pan America Rd. (𝄞 **619/232-2721;** www.niwa.org). Although parts of the garden are still being developed, visitors can sample the tranquility of traditional elements like a koi-filled stream, pastoral meadow, and ancient *sekitei* (sand-and-stone garden). Visit the Japanese tea room and snack bar for udon soup, sushi, or Pokémon candies.

Marston House Museum, 3525 Seventh Ave. at Upas Street, in the northwest corner of the park (𝄞 **619/298-3142**). Designed by local architect Irving Gill, this fine example of Craftsman-style architecture exhibits antique and reproduction period furniture.

Model Railroad Museum ✪, 1649 El Prado (𝄞 **619/696-0199;** www. sdmodelrailroadm.com). Four scale-model railroads depict southern California's transportation history and terrain. There's a terrific gift shop, plus multimedia exhibits and hands-on Lionel trains for kids.

San Diego Historical Society Museum, 1649 El Prado (𝄞 **619/232-6203**). Photographs and other changing exhibits tell the city's story.

Spreckels Organ Pavilion (𝄞 **619/226-0819**). The ornate pavilion houses a fantastic organ with more than 4,000 individual pipes. Free concerts are given Sundays at 2pm year-round and on summer evenings.

Mingei International Museum ✪, 1439 El Prado (𝄞 **619/239-0003;** www. mingei.org). Its name means "art of the people" in Japanese, and it offers changing exhibitions celebrating human creativity with textiles, costumes, jewelry, toys, pottery, paintings, and sculpture, all employing natural materials. This is one of only two major museums in the United States devoted to crafts on a worldwide scale (the other is in Santa Fe).

Christmas on the Prado takes place in Balboa Park from 5 to 9pm on the first Friday and Saturday nights in December. This popular event features free entry to all museums, carol singing in the Spreckels Organ Pavilion, holiday decorations, and various food booths.

MORE ATTRACTIONS IN & AROUND SAN DIEGO
DOWNTOWN

Cabrillo National Monument ✪ Enjoy stunning views while you learn about California history at this monument commemorating Juan Rodríguez Cabrillo, the European discoverer of America's West Coast. At the restored Old Point Loma Lighthouse, you'll be treated to a sweeping vista of the ocean, bays, islands, mountains, valleys, and plains that make up San Diego. Visit between mid-December and mid-March and you can see the annual California gray-whale migration from a glassed-in observatory; films and other educational exhibits on the whales are offered as well. A road leads to tide pools that beg for exploration.

1800 Cabrillo Memorial Dr., Point Loma. © 619/557-5450. www.nps.gov/cabr. Admission $5 per vehicle, $2 for walk-ins, free for children under 17 and seniors age 62 and over (with a National Parks Service Golden Age Passport). Daily 9am–5:15pm. Take I-5 or I-8 to Highway 209/Rosecrans St. and follow signs. Bus: 26.

Children's Museum of San Diego *Kids*   This interactive attraction, which encourages participation, is a home away from home for kids. It provides ongoing supervised activities, as well as a monthly special celebration, recognizing important issues such as earth awareness or African-American history. The indoor-outdoor art studio is a big draw for kids ages 2 to 10. There is also a theater with costumes for budding actors to don, plus an observation walk above the exhibits that kids climb on and exit by way of a spiral slide. The museum shop is filled with toys, games, crafts, and books. School groups come in the morning, so you might want to schedule your visit for the afternoon.

200 W. Island Ave. © 619/233-KIDS. www.sandiegochildren.com. Admission $6 adults and children, $3 seniors, free for children under 2. Tues–Sun 10am–4pm. Trolley: Convention Center; museum is a block away. All-day parking (across the street) about $3.

Maritime Museum ★★ *Kids*   This unique museum consists of a trio of fine ships: the full-rigged merchant vessel *Star of India* (1863), whose impressive masts are an integral part of the San Diego cityscape; the gleaming white San Francisco–Oakland steam-powered ferry *Berkeley* (1898), which worked round-the-clock to carry people to safety following the 1906 San Francisco earthquake; and the sleek *Medea* (1904), one of the world's few remaining large steam yachts. You can board and explore each vessel, and from April through October you can watch movies on deck (see "San Diego After Dark," later in this chapter).

1306 N. Harbor Dr. © 619/234-9153. www.sdmaritime.com. Admission $6 adults, $4 seniors over 62 and youths 13–17, $2 children 6–12, free for children under 6. Daily 9am–8pm. Bus: 2. Trolley: America Plaza.

Museum of Contemporary Art, Downtown (MCA)   MCA Downtown is the second location of the Museum of Contemporary Art—the first is in La Jolla. Two large galleries and two smaller ones present changing exhibitions of distinguished contemporary artists. Lectures and tours for adults and children are offered.

1001 Kettner Blvd. (at Broadway). © 619/234-1001. www.mcasandiego.org. Free admission. Thurs–Tue 11am–5pm. Parking $2 with validation at America Plaza Complex. Trolley: America Plaza.

Villa Montezuma ★ *Finds*   Just east of downtown, this stunning mansion was built in 1887 for then internationally acclaimed musician and author Jesse Shepard. Lush with Victoriana, it features stained-glass windows depicting Mozart, Beethoven, Sappho, Rubens, St. Cecilia (patron saint of musicians), and other notables. The San Diego Historical Society painstakingly restored the house, which is on the National Register of Historic Places, and furnished it with period pieces. If you love Victorian houses, don't miss this one for its quirkiness.

1925 K St. (at 20th Ave.). © 619/239-2211. Admission $5 adults, $4 seniors and students, $2 kids 6–17, free for children under 6. Fri–Sun 10am–4:30pm. Bus: 3, 3A, 4, 5, 16, or 105 to Market and Imperial Sts. By car, follow K St.

William Heath Davis House Museum   Shipped by boat to San Diego in 1850 from Portland, Maine, this is the oldest structure in the Gaslamp Quarter. It is a well-preserved example of a prefabricated "saltbox" family home and has remained structurally unchanged for more than 120 years. A museum on the first and second floors is open to the public, as is the small park adjacent to the house. The house is also home to the Gaslamp Quarter Historical Foundation, which sponsors walking tours of the quarter for about $8 (the fee includes museum admission). At least one tour is conducted each day; call ahead for specific schedule.

410 Island Ave. (at Fourth Ave.). © **619/233-4692.** Suggested donation $3. Tue–Sun 11am–3pm. Call ahead to verify hours. Bus: 1, 3, or 3A. Trolley: Gaslamp Quarter/Convention Center W.

OLD TOWN & BEYOND: A LOOK AT CALIFORNIA'S BEGINNINGS

The birthplace of San Diego is Old Town, the hillside where the Spanish Presidio and Father Junípero Serra's mission (the first in California) were built. By protecting the remaining adobes and historic buildings, **Old Town State Historic Park** brings to life Mexican California, which existed here until the mid-1800s. Much of the surrounding area, however, has become a mini–Mexican theme park. You can get to Old Town on the trolley or Coaster (see "Getting Around," earlier in this chapter), and free walking tours leave daily at 10:30am and 2pm from **Seeley Stables Visitor Center** (© **619/220-5422**). Other nearby sites of interest are listed below.

Heritage Park   This 7.8-acre county park contains seven original 19th-century houses moved here from other places and given new uses. Among them are a bed-and-breakfast, a doll shop, and a gift shop. The most recent addition is the small synagogue, placed near the park's entrance in 1989. A glorious coral tree crowns the top of the hill.

2455 Heritage Park Row (corner of Juan and Harney Sts.), Old Town. For information, call the Parks Department at © **619/694-3049.** Free admission. Daily 9:30am–3pm. Bus: 4, 5, or 105.

Mission Basilica San Diego de Alcala ✪   Established in 1769, this was the first link in a chain of 21 missions founded by Spanish missionary Junípero Serra. In 1774, the mission was moved to its present site for agricultural reasons, and to separate Native American converts from the fortress that included the original building. A few bricks belonging to the original mission can be seen in Presidio Park in Old Town. Mass is said daily in this active Catholic parish. Other missions in the San Diego area include Mission San Luis Rey de Francia in Oceanside, Mission San Antonia de Pala near Mount Palomar, and Mission Santa Ysabel near Julian.

10818 San Diego Mission Rd., Mission Valley. © **619/281-8449.** Admission $3 adults, $2 seniors and students, $1 children under 13. Free Sun and for daily masses. Daily 9am–5pm; mass daily 7am and 5:30pm. Take I-8 to Mission Gorge Rd. to Twain Ave. Bus: 6, 16, 25, 43, or 81.

Serra Museum   Perched on a hill above Old Town, the stately mission-style building overlooks the hillside where, in 1769, the first mission and first non-native settlement on the west coast of the United States and Canada were founded. The museum's exhibits introduce visitors to the Native American, Spanish, and Mexican people who first called this place home. On display are their belongings, from cannons to cookware; a Spanish furniture collection; and one of the first paintings brought to California, which survived being damaged in an Indian attack. The mission remained San Diego's only settlement until the 1820s, when families began to move down the hill into what is now Old Town. You can also watch an ongoing archaeological dig uncovering more of the items used by early settlers. From the 70-foot tower, visitors can compare the spectacular view with historic photos to see how this land has changed over time.

2727 Presidio Dr., Presidio Park. © **619/297-3258.** www.sandiegohistory.org. Admission $5 adults, $4 seniors and students, $2 children 6–17, free for children under 6. Fri–Sun 10am–4:30pm. Take I-8 to the Taylor St. exit. Turn right on Taylor, then left on Presidio Dr.

Whaley House   In 1856, this striking two-story house (the first one in these parts) just outside Old Town State Historic Park was built for Thomas Whaley and his family. Whaley was a New Yorker who arrived here via San Francisco, where he had been lured by the gold rush. The house is one of only two authenticated haunted houses in California, and 10,000 schoolchildren come here each year to see for themselves. Exhibits include a life mask of Abraham Lincoln, one of only six made; the spinet piano used in the movie *Gone with the Wind;* and the concert piano that accompanied Swedish soprano Jenny Lind on her final U.S. tour in 1852.

2482 San Diego Ave. ☎ 619/298-2482. Admission $4 adults, $3 seniors over 60, $2 children 5–18, free for children under 5. June–Sept daily 10am–5pm; Oct–May Wed–Mon 10am–5pm. Closed on major holidays.

MISSION BAY & THE BEACHES
This area is great for walking, jogging, in-line skating, biking, and boating; for details, see "Outdoor Pursuits," below.

Giant Dipper Roller Coaster   A local landmark for 70 years, the Giant Dipper is one of two surviving fixtures from the original Belmont Amusement Park (the other is the Plunge swimming pool). After sitting dormant for 15 years, the vintage wooden roller coaster, with more than 2,600 feet of track and 13 hills, underwent extensive restoration and reopened in 1991. If you're in the neighborhood (especially with older kids), it's worth a stop. You must be 50 inches tall to ride the roller coaster. You can also ride on the Giant Dipper's neighbor, the Liberty Carousel ($1).

3190 Mission Blvd. ☎ 858/488-1549. www.giantdipper.com. Ride on the Giant Dipper $3.50. MC, V. Sun–Thurs 11am–10pm; Fri–Sat 11am–11pm. Take I-5 to the SeaWorld exit, and follow W. Mission Bay Dr. to Belmont Park.

LA JOLLA
Some folks just enjoy driving around La Jolla, taking in the sea views and the 360° vista from the top of **Mount Soledad.** However, La Jolla also offers other attractions, including **Torrey Pines State Reserve** (☎ 858/755-2063), which has an interpretive center, hiking trails with wonderful ocean views, and a chance to see the rare Torrey pine. Admission is free, as are the guided walks on Saturdays and Sundays. Access is via North Torrey Pines Road; parking costs $4 per car, $3 for seniors.

Birch Aquarium at Scripps ✸✸   The aquarium offers close-up views of the Pacific Ocean in 33 marine-life tanks. The giant kelp forest is particularly

---

Finds Hidden La Jolla

While droves of folks stroll the sidewalks adjacent to the San Diego–La Jolla Underwater Park and La Jolla Cove, only a few know about **Coast Walk.** Starting behind the **Cave Store,** 1325 Coast Blvd. (☎ 858/459-0746), it meanders along the wooded cliffs and affords a wonderful view of the beach and beyond. The shop also serves as entry for **Sunny Jim Cave,** a large and naturally occurring sea cave reached by a steep and narrow staircase through the rock. The tunnel was hand-carved in 1903—it lets out on a wood-plank observation deck from which you can gaze out at the sea. It's a cool treat, particularly on a hot summer day, and costs only $2 per person ($1 for kids). Hold the handrail and your little ones' hands tightly.

La Jolla

To Del Mar ↑ (3 miles)

↑ To Los Angeles ↑ (110 miles) **5**

Boomer Beach **1**

Shell Beach

2

Coast **Blvd** **4**

3

Prospect St.

Fay Ave.

Girard

Herschel Ave.

Ivanhoe Ave.

Wall St.

CALIFORNIA

⊕ Sacramento

San Francisco

Los Angeles

San Diego ○

0 ———— 2 mi
0 ———— 2 km
N

Post Office ✉

6

N. Torrey Pines Rd.

Miramar

Genesee Ave.

UCSD

La Jolla

Village Dr.

Villa La Jolla Dr.

Gilman Dr.

Nobel Ave.

Scripps Pier

La Jolla Shores Dr.

La Jolla Scenic Dr. N.

Torrey Pines Rd.

Regents Rd.

La Jolla Shores Beach

7

see inset above

La Jolla Cove

8 *Av. de la Playa*

La Jolla Caves

Children's Pool Beach

Coast Blvd.

Prospect St.

Jenner

Wall St.

Cave St.

Exchange Place

Ardath Rd.

Via Capri

PACIFIC OCEAN

Casa Beach **9**

10 11

Silverado St.

14

Ivanhoe Ave.

Herschel Ave.

Torrey Pines Ave.

52

Wipeout Beach

12

13

Kline St.

Girard Ave.

Fay Ave.

Pearl St.

Eads Ave.

5

Coast Blvd. South

Draper Ave.

La Jolla Blvd.

Marine Street Beach

High Ave.

La Jolla Country Club

15

Center St.

West Muirlands Dr.

La Jolla Scenic Dr. S.

To Windansea Beach ↓

ACCOMMODATIONS ■

Bed & Breakfast Inn at La Jolla **12**
Best Western Inn by the Sea **11**
Empress Hotel of La Jolla **13**
La Jolla Beach & Tennis Club **8**
La Jolla Cove Suites **4**
La Jolla Cove Travelodge **14**
La Valencia Hotel **3**
Scripps Inn **9**
The Sea Lodge **7**

ATTRACTIONS ●

Birch Aquarium at Scripps **6**
Coast Walk **2**
Ellen Browning Scripps Park **1**
Mount Soledad **15**
Museum of Contemporary Art,
    San Diego **10**
Torrey Pine State Reserve **5**

impressive. World renowned for its oceanic research, Scripps offers visitors a chance to view its marine aquarium and artificial outdoor tide pools. The museum has interpretive exhibits on the current and historical research done at the institution, which has been in existence since 1903.

2300 Expedition Way. © 858/534-FISH. www.aquarium.ucsd.edu. Admission $8.50 adults, $7.50 seniors, $5 children 3–17, free for children under 3. Parking $3. AE, MC, V. Daily 9am–5pm. Take I-5 to La Jolla Village Dr. exit, go west 1 mile, and turn left at Expedition Way. Bus: 34.

Museum of Contemporary Art, San Diego (MCA)✦✦   Museum holdings include works from every major art movement of the past half century, with a strong representation of California artists and particularly noteworthy examples of minimalism, light and space work, conceptualism, installation, and site-specific art (including outdoor sculptures). The museum's facade incorporates the original Irving Gill architecture, and the rear galleries feature outstanding ocean views.

700 Prospect St. © 858/454-3541. www.mcasandiego.org. Admission $4 adults, $2 students and seniors, free for children under 12; free 1st Tues and Sun of each month. Summer (Memorial Day–Labor Day) Thurs–Fri and Mon–Tue 11am–8pm, Sat–Sun 11am–5pm; rest of year Fri–Tue 11am–5pm, Thurs 11am–8pm. Take the Ardath Rd. exit off I-5 north or the La Jolla Village Dr. west exit off I-5 south. Take Torrey Pines Rd. to Prospect Place and turn right. Prospect Place becomes Prospect St.

8 Outdoor Pursuits

For coverage of San Diego's best beaches, see section 6, earlier in this chapter.

BALLOONING   For a bird's-eye view of the area at sunrise or sunset, followed by champagne and hors d'oeuvres, contact **Skysurfer Balloon Company** (© **800/660-6809** or 858/481-7500) or **California Dreamin'** (© **800/373-3359** or 760/438-3344; www.californiadreamin.com). From aloft, you'll enjoy sweeping views of the entire southern California coast.

BICYCLING & MOUNTAIN BIKING   Mission Bay and Coronado are especially good for leisurely bike rides. The boardwalks in Pacific Beach and Mission Beach can get very crowded, especially on weekends. Most major thoroughfares offer bike lanes. Just remember to wear a helmet; it's the law. For information on bike rentals, see "Getting Around," earlier in this chapter.

   Adventure Bike Tours, in the San Diego Marriott (© **619/234-1500,** ext. 6514), offers guided bicycle tours, bike rentals, and in-line skate rentals. The "Bay to Breakers" ride starts in downtown San Diego and includes Coronado; $40 covers bikes, helmets, and the ferry.

BOATING   **Club Nautico,** at the San Diego Marriott Marina, 333 W. Harbor Dr. (© **619/233-9311**), provides an exhilarating way to see the bay by the hour, half day, or full day in 20- to 27-foot offshore powerboats. Rentals start at $89 per hour. It also rents WaveRunners and allows its boats to be taken into the ocean, and provides diving, water-skiing, and fishing packages as well.

   Seaforth Boat Rental, 1641 Quivira Rd., Mission Bay (© **888/834-2628;** www.seaforth-boat-rental.com/seaforth), has a wide variety of fishing boats for the bay and ocean, powerboats for $55 to $95 per hour, and 14- to 30-foot sailboats for $20 to $45 per hour; inquire about half- and full-day rates. Canoes, pedal boats, kayaks, and rowboats are available for those who prefer a slower pace, as are bicycles and equipment with which you can fish off the Municipal Pier (see "Fishing," below).

Mission Bay Sportcenter, 1010 Santa Clara Place (☏ **858/488-1004;** www.missionbaysports.com), rents sailboats, catamarans, sailboards, kayaks, personal watercrafts, and motorboats. Prices range from $12 to $72 an hour, with discounts for 4-hour and full-day rentals. Instruction is available.

Coronado Boat Rental, 1715 Strand Way, Coronado (☏ **619/437-1514**), has powerboats renting from $65 to $90 per hour, with half- and full-day rates available; 14- to 30-foot sailboats from $25 to $40 per hour; plus jet skis, ski boats, canoes, pedal boats, kayaks, fishing skiffs, and charter boats.

FISHING   Public fishing piers are at Shelter Island (where there's a statue dedicated to anglers), Ocean Beach, and Imperial Beach. Anglers of any age can fish free of charge without a license off any municipal pier in California. Call the **City Fish Line** (☏ **619/465-3474**) for information on fishing.

For **sportfishing,** you can go out on a large boat for about $25 for a half day, or $40 to $100 for three-quarters to a full day. To charter a boat for up to six people, the rates run about $550 for a half day and $1,000 for an entire day, more in summer; call around and compare prices. Summer and fall are excellent times for excursions. Locally, the waters around Point Loma are filled with bass, bonita, and barracuda; the Coronado Islands, which belong to Mexico but are only about 18 miles from San Diego, are popular for abalone, yellowtail, yellowfin, and big-eyed tuna. Some outfitters will take you farther into Baja California waters.

Fishing charters depart from Harbor and Shelter Islands, Point Loma, the Imperial Beach Pier, and Quivira Basin in Mission Bay (near the Hyatt Islandia Hotel). The following outfitters offer short or extended outings with daily departures: **H&M Landing** (☏ 619/222-1144), **Islandia Sportfishing** (☏ 619/222-1164), **Lee Palm Sportfishers** (☏ 619/224-3857), **Point Loma Sportfishing** (☏ 619/223-1627), and **Seaforth Boat Rentals** (☏ 888/834-2628). Participants over the age of 16 need a California fishing license.

GOLF   With nearly 80 courses, 50 of them open to the public, San Diego County has much to offer the golf enthusiast. Courses are diverse, some with vistas of the Pacific, others with views of country hillsides or of desert. **M&M Tee Times** (☏ **800/867-7397** or 858/456-8366; www.torreypines.com) can arrange tee times for you at most golf courses.

And where else but San Diego can you practice your golf swing in the middle of the central business district? The **Metro Golf Harborside,** 801 W. Ash St., at Pacific Highway (☏ **619/239-GOLF**), is open Monday through Friday from 7am to 10pm, Saturday from 8am to 10pm, and Sunday from 9am to 9pm. Here you'll find 80 tees, a USGA putting and chipping area, a pro shop, and a golf school. It's lit for after-dark play. Club rental is available at $1 each; a large bucket of balls costs $6 and a small bucket, $3.

Balboa Park Municipal Golf Course ⍟, 2600 Golf Course Dr., San Diego (☏ **619/570-1234** for automated tee times, or 619/239-1660 for pro shop), is a wooded 18-hole course with skyline views nestled in the southeast corner of Balboa Park. Convenient and affordable, it might remind you of your muni course back home, down to the bare-bones 1940s clubhouse where old guys hold down lunch counter stools for hours after the game. Non-resident greens fees are $32 Monday through Friday and $37 Saturday and Sunday; cart rentals are $20, pull carts $5. Reservations are suggested at least a week in advance.

Coronado Municipal Golf Course, 2000 Visalia Row, Coronado (☏ **619/435-3121**), is the first sight that welcomes you as you cross the Coronado Bay Bridge (the course is off to the left). It's an 18-hole, par-72 course overlooking

Glorietta Bay, and there's a coffee shop, pro shop, and driving range. Two-day prior reservations are strongly recommended; call any time after 7am. Greens fees are $20 to walk and $34 to ride for 18 holes; $10 to walk and $18 to ride after 4pm. Club rental is $15, and pull-cart rental is $4.

Riverwalk Golf Club, 1150 Fashion Valley Rd., Mission Valley (© 619/698-GOLF), is a Ted Robinson/Ted Robinson, Jr.–designed course meandering along the Mission Valley floor. It features four lakes with waterfalls (in play on 13 of the 27 holes); open, undulating fairways; and the red San Diego Trolley speeding through the middle now and then. Non-resident greens fees—including cart—are $75 Monday through Thursday, $85 Friday and Sunday, and $95 Saturday (fees for residents are $30 less).

Torrey Pines Golf Course, 11480 Torrey Pines Rd., La Jolla (© 858/552-1784 for information, 858/570-1234 for tee times, or 858/452-3226 for the pro shop; www.torreypinesgc.com), is actually two gorgeous 18-hole championship clifftop courses overlooking the ocean; the north course is more picturesque, the south course more challenging. Tee times are taken by computer, starting at 5am, up to 7 days in advance by telephone only. *Insider tip:* Single golfers stand a good chance of getting on the course if they just turn up and wait for a threesome. Greens fees for out-of-towners are $55 during the week and $60 on Saturday, Sunday, and holidays for 18 holes; $30 for nine holes. Cart rental is $30.

San Diego hosts some of the country's most important golf tournaments, including the **Buick Invitational of California,** held every February at Torrey Pines Golf Course in La Jolla (© **800/888-BUICK** or 619/281-4653).

HIKING & WALKING   The **Sierra Club** sponsors regular hikes in the San Diego area, and nonmembers are welcome to participate; there are both day and evening hikes, most free. For a recorded schedule, call © **619/299-1744,** or call the office at © **619/299-1743** Monday through Friday from noon to 5pm and Saturday from 10am to 4pm.

The Bayside Trail near **Cabrillo National Monument** is popular because it affords great views. Drive to the Monument and follow signs to the trail. Parking costs $4 per car. **Mission Trails Regional Park,** 8 miles northeast of downtown, offers a glimpse of what San Diego looked like before development. Located between Calif. 52 and I-8 and east of I-15, its rugged hills, valleys, and open areas provide a quick escape from urban hustle-bustle. A visitor and interpretive center (© **619/668-3275**) is open daily from 9am to 5pm. Access is via Mission Gorge Road from either Calif. 52 or I-8.

The best beaches for walking are La Jolla Shores, Mission Beach, and Coronado. You can also walk around **Mission Bay** on a series of connected footpaths. If a four-legged friend is your walking companion, head for **Dog Beach** in Ocean Beach or **Fiesta Island** in Mission Bay, two of the few areas where dogs can legally go unleashed.

IN-LINE SKATING   Gliding around San Diego, especially the Mission Bay area, on in-line skates is as much a southern California experience as sailing or surfing. Skate rentals along with necessary protective gear are available at **Skates Plus,** 3830 Mission Blvd. (© 858/488-PLUS) or **Hamel's Action Sports Center,** 704 Ventura Place, off Mission Boulevard at Ocean Front Walk (© 858/488-8889). In Pacific Beach, try **Pacific Beach Sun and Sea,** 4539 Ocean Blvd. (© 858/483-6613). In Coronado, go to **Mike's Bikes,** 1343 Orange Ave. (© 619/435-7744), or **Bikes and Beyond,** 1201 First St. and at the Ferry Landing (© 619/435-7180). Be sure to ask for protective gear.

SURFING   Get where-to-go info from section 6 above, and rent a board (if you didn't BYO) from **La Jolla Surf Systems,** 2132 Avenida de la Playa, La Jolla Shores (© 858/456-2777), or **Emerald Surf & Sport,** 1118 Orange Ave., Coronado (© 619/435-6677).

For surfing lessons, with all equipment provided, check with **Kahuna Bob's Surf School** (© 800/KAHUNAS or 760/721-7700; www.kahunabob.com) or **San Diego Surfing Academy** (© 800/447-SURF or 858/565-6892; www.surfSDSA.com).

TENNIS   There are 1,200 public and private tennis courts in San Diego. Public courts are located throughout the city, including the **La Jolla Recreation Center** (© **858/459-9950),** **Morley Field** (© 619/295-9278) in Balboa Park, and the brand-new **Barnes Tennis Center,** 4490 W. Point Loma Blvd., near Ocean Beach and SeaWorld (© 619/221-9000; www.tennissandiego.com).

9 Shopping

All-American San Diego has embraced the suburban shopping mall with vigor—several massive complexes in Mission Valley are where many residents do the bulk of their shopping, and every possible need can be met here. Local neighborhoods also offer individualized specialty shopping that meets the needs—and mirrors the personality—of those parts of town. For example, hip and trendy Hillcrest is the place to go for cutting-edge boutiques, while conservative La Jolla offers many upscale traditional shops, especially jewelers.

Sales tax in San Diego is 7.5%, and savvy out-of-state shoppers know to have larger items shipped directly home at the point of purchase, thereby avoiding the tax.

DOWNTOWN & GASLAMP QUARTER

Horton Plaza, 324 Horton Plaza (© **619/238-1596;** www.hortonplaza.com), the Disneyland of shopping malls, is at the heart of the revitalized city center, bounded by Broadway, First and Fourth Avenues, and G Street. This multilevel shopping center has 140 specialty shops, including art galleries, clothing and shoe stores, several fun shops for kids, bookstores, a 14-screen cinema, three major department stores, and a variety of restaurants and short-order eateries. With a rambling and confusing series of paths and bridges, the complex was supposedly inspired by European shopping districts. Parking is free the first 3 hours with validation (4 hours at the movie theater and the Lyceum Theatre), $1 per half hour thereafter; parking levels are confusing, and temporarily losing your car is part of the Horton Plaza experience. Take bus no. 2, 7, 9, 29, 34, or 35, or the trolley to City Center.

Other downtown shopping opportunities include **Seaport Village,** on Harbor Drive at Kettner Boulevard (© **619/235-4014),** a Cape Cod–style "village" of cutesy shops snuggled alongside San Diego Bay; it's worth a visit for the 1890 carousel imported from Coney Island, New York.

Seekers of serious art might want to head to Little Italy's burgeoning **Studio Arts Complex,** north of downtown. Among the galleries housed at 2400 Kettner Blvd. is **David Zapf Gallery** (no. 104, © **619/232-5004),** which can feature painting, sculpture, drawings, or furniture; they also distribute the *Arts Down Town* guide. Photographer **Steve McClelland** (no. 213, © **619/582-9812)** divides his time between traveling (his images bring the colors, textures, and emotions of the world vividly to life) and commissioned architectural photography in color and black & white. Artist **Charlotte Bird** (no. 224, ✆ **619/239-9353**) works in fiber arts, producing fine quilts, dolls, and one-of-a-kind women's clothing. The **Pratt Gallery** (✆ **619/236-0211**) has a changing display space, often featuring innovative paintings, photography, or other highly individual work.

HILLCREST/UPTOWN

Compact Hillcrest is an ideal shopping destination for browsing unique and often wacky shops, but also for buying things at the area's vintage-clothing stores, memorabilia shops, recognizable chains, and snack-friendly bakeries and cafes. Start at the neighborhood's hub, the intersection of University and Fifth Avenues. Street parking is available; most meters allow 2-hour parking and devour quarters at a rate of one per 15 minutes, so be armed with plenty of change. You can also park in an area parking lot—rates vary, but you'll come out ahead if you're planning to stroll for several hours.

San Diego's self-proclaimed **Antique Row** is located north of Balboa Park, along Park Boulevard (beginning at University Avenue in Hillcrest) and Adams Avenue (extending to around 40th Street in Normal Heights). For more information and an area brochure with map, contact the **Adams Avenue Business Association** (✆ **619/282-7329;** www.GoThere.com/AdamsAve).

OLD TOWN & MISSION VALLEY

Old Town Historic Park is a restoration of some of San Diego's historic sites and adobe structures, a number of which now house shops that cater to tourists. Many have a "general-store" theme, and carry gourmet treats and inexpensive Mexican crafts alongside the obligatory T-shirts, baseball caps, and other San Diego–emblazoned souvenirs. More shops are concentrated in colorful **Bazaar del Mundo,** 2754 Calhoun St. (✆ **619/296-3161;** www.bazaardelmundo.com), arranged around a fountain courtyard.

Mission Valley is home to two giant malls (**Fashion Valley** and **Mission Valley**), with more than enough stores to satisfy any shopper. Here book lovers will find the local outposts of **Barnes & Noble,** 7610 Hazard Center Dr. (✆ **619/220-0175**), and **Borders,** 1072 Camino del Rio N. (✆ **619/295-2201**).

MISSION BAY & THE BEACHES

The beach communities all offer laid-back shopping in typical California fashion: plenty of surf shops, recreational gear, casual garb, and youth-oriented music stores. If you're in need of a new bikini, the best selection is at **Pilar's,** 3745 Mission Blvd., Pacific Beach (✆ **858/488-3056**), where dozens of racks are meticulously organized and choices range from chic designer suits to hot trends inspired by surf- and skate-wear. Some of San Diego's best **antiquing** can be found in Ocean Beach, along a single block of Newport Avenue, the town's main drag.

LA JOLLA

It's clear from the look of La Jolla's village that shopping is a major pastime in this upscale community of moneyed professionals and retirees. Women's-clothing boutiques tend toward conservative and costly, like those lining Girard and Prospect Streets (Ann Taylor, Armani Exchange, Polo/Ralph Lauren, Talbots, and Sigi's Boutique).

Even if you're not in the market for furnishings and accessories, the many home-decor boutiques make for great window shopping, as do La Jolla's ubiquitous jewelers: Swiss watches, tennis bracelets, precious gems, and pearl necklaces sparkle at you from windows along every street. No visit to La Jolla is complete without seeing **John Cole's Bookshop,** 780 Prospect St. (© **858/454-4766**), an eclectic, family-run local favorite set in a charming old cottage.

CORONADO

This rather insular, conservative Navy community doesn't have a great many shopping opportunities; what there is lines Orange Avenue at the western end of the island. In addition to some scattered housewares and home-decor boutiques, as well as several small women's boutiques, there are gift shops at Coronado's major resorts. The **Ferry Landing Marketplace,** 1201 First St., at B Avenue (© **619/435-8895**), is a faux-seaport with shops, restaurants, and a sweeping view of the bay and the downtown skyline.

FARMERS MARKETS

Throughout San Diego County, there are no fewer than two dozen regularly occurring street markets featuring fresh fruits and vegetables from southern California farms and augmented by crafts, ethnic-food vendors, flower stands, and other surprises. Below is a sampling.

In **Hillcrest,** the market sets up Sundays from 9am to noon at the corner of Normal Street and Lincoln Avenue, several blocks north of Balboa Park. The atmosphere is festive, and exotic culinary delights reflect Hillcrest's eclectic ambiance. For more information, call the **Hillcrest Association** (© **619/299-3330**).

In **Ocean Beach,** there's a fun-filled market Wednesday evenings between 4 and 8pm (until 7pm in fall and winter) in the 4900 block of Newport Avenue. In addition to fresh-cut flowers, produce, and exotic fruits and foods laid out for sampling, the market features llama rides and other entertainment. For more information, call the **Ocean Beach Business Improvement District** (© **619/224-4906**).

Or head to **Pacific Beach** on Saturday from 8am to noon, when Mission Boulevard between Reed Avenue and Pacific Beach Drive is transformed into a bustling morning marketplace, as locals stock up for the week and visitors begin to enjoy the beach communities on vacation.

And on **Coronado** on Tuesday afternoons, the Ferry Landing Marketplace (corner of First and B Streets) hosts a produce and crafts market from 2:30 to 6pm.

10 San Diego After Dark

San Diego is hardly the wild 'n' crazy nightlife capital of America, but pockets of lively after-dark entertainment do exist around the city. On the more sedate side of things, the city offers wonderful and varied live theater experiences— both the Old Globe and La Jolla Playhouse have won Tony Awards for Best Regional Theater.

For a rundown of the latest performances, gallery openings, and other events in the city, check the listings in "Night and Day," the Thursday entertainment section of the *San Diego Union-Tribune,* or the *Reader,* San Diego's free alternative newspaper, published every Thursday. For what's happening in the gay scene, get the weekly *San Diego Gay & Lesbian Times.* The *San Diego Performing Arts Guide,* produced every 2 months by the San Diego Theatre Foundation, is also very helpful; you can pick one up at the Arts Tix booth.

THE PERFORMING ARTS

Half-price tickets to theater, music, and dance events are available at the **ARTS TIX** booth, in Horton Plaza Park, at Broadway and Third Avenue (park in the Horton Plaza parking garage and have your parking validated, or pause at the curb nearby). The kiosk is open Tuesday through Saturday from 10am to 7pm. Half-price tickets are available only the day of the show except for Sunday and Monday performances, sold on Saturday. Only cash payments are accepted. For a daily listing of half-price offerings, call © **619/497-5000.** Full-price advance tickets are also sold; the kiosk doubles as a Ticketmaster outlet, selling tickets to concerts throughout California.

THEATER & OPERA

The **San Diego Repertory Theatre** offers professional, culturally diverse productions of contemporary and classic dramas, comedies, and musicals at the Lyceum Theatre, 79 Broadway Circle, in Horton Plaza (© **619/544-1000;** www.SanDiegoRep.com). Ticket prices are $21 to $32.

In Coronado, **Lamb's Players Theatre,** at 1142 Orange Ave. (© **619/437-0600;** www.lambsplayers.org), is a professional repertory company whose season runs from February through December. Shows are staged in its 340-seat theater in Coronado's historic Spreckels Building, where no seat is more than seven rows from the stage. Tickets range from $18 to $40.

The **San Diego Opera** performs at the Civic Theater, 202 C St. (© **619/232-7636;** www.sdopera.com), and often showcases international stars. The season runs from January through May; call for schedule. The box office is located across the plaza from the theater and is open Monday through Friday from 9am to 5pm. Tickets range from $31 to $112. Ask about standing room or student and senior discounts.

The Globe Theatres   This complex of three performance venues sits just inside Balboa Park, behind the Museum of Man; though best known for the 581-seat Old Globe (fashioned after Shakespeare's), it also includes the 245-seat Cassius Carter Centre Stage and the 620-seat open-air Lowell Davies Festival Theatre. Between them, they mount 14 plays a year between January and October, from world premieres of such Broadway hits as *Into the Woods,* or the live production of *The Full Monty,* to the excellent Shakespeare San Diegans have come to expect from "their" Globe. Leading performers regularly grace the stage, including Marsha Mason, John Goodman, Hal Holbrook, Jon Voight, and Christopher Walken. Tours are offered year-round, Saturday and Sunday at 11am and cost $3 for adults, $1 for students, seniors, and military. The box office is open Tuesday through Sunday from noon to 8:30pm. Balboa Park. © 619/239-2255, or 619/23-GLOBE (24-hr. hot line). Fax 619/231-5879. www.theglobetheatres.org. Tickets $23–$39. Senior and student discounts. Bus: 7 or 25. Free parking.

La Jolla Playhouse   Boasting a Hollywood pedigree (founded in 1947 by Gregory Peck, Dorothy McGuire, and Mel Ferrer), and a 1993 Tony Award for outstanding American regional theater, the Playhouse stages six productions each year (April or May through November) at two fine theaters on the UCSD campus. It seems like each one has something outstanding to recommend it; a nationally acclaimed director, for example, or highly touted revival (such as when Matthew Broderick starred in *How to Succeed in Business Without Really Trying* before it went on to Broadway). The box office is open daily from noon to 6pm. For each show, one Saturday matinee is a "pay-what-you-can" performance.

Each night, any unsold tickets are available for $10 each in a "public rush" sale 10 minutes before curtain. 2910 La Jolla Village Dr. (at Torrey Pines Rd.). ✆ **858/550-1010.** Fax 858/550-1025. www.lajollaplayhouse.com. Tickets $21–$52. Bus: 30, 34, or 34A.

MOVIES, SAN DIEGO STYLE

Many multiscreen complexes around the city show first-run films. More avant-garde and artistic current releases play at **Hillcrest Cinema,** 3965 Fifth Ave., Hillcrest, which offers 3 hours' free parking (✆ **619/299-2100**); the **Ken Cinema,** 4061 Adams Ave., Kensington near Hillcrest (✆ **619/283-5909**); and the **Cove,** 7730 Girard Ave., La Jolla (✆ **858/459-5404**). The irrepressible *Rocky Horror Picture Show* is resurrected every Friday and Saturday at midnight at the Ken. The **OMNIMAX** theater at the Reuben H. Fleet Science Center (✆ **619/238-1233**), in Balboa Park, features movies and three-dimensional laser shows projected onto the 76-foot tilted dome screen. A truly unique movie venue is **Movies Before the Mast** (✆ **619/234-9153**), aboard the *Star of India* at the Maritime Museum. Movies of the nautical genre (such as *Captain Blood, Hook,* or *The Muppets' Treasure Island*) are shown on a special "screensail" from approximately March through October.

THE CLUB & MUSIC SCENE

A note on smoking: In January 1998, California enacted controversial legislation banning smoking in all restaurants and bars. While opponents immediately began lobbying to repeal the law, it's a good idea to check before you light up in nightclubs, lounges, and so on.

ROCK, POP, FOLK, JAZZ & BLUES

The Casbah, 2501 Kettner Blvd., near the airport (✆ 619/232-4355; www.casbahmusic.com), is a divey joint with a rep for breakthrough alternative and rock bands. **Croce's Nightclubs,** 802 Fifth Ave., at F St. (✆ 619/233-4355; www.croces.com), are attached to one of the Gaslamp Quarter's most popular restaurants, and feature jazz and rhythm and blues. **4th & B,** 345 B St., downtown (✆ 619/231-4343; www.4thandB.com), is a quality venue with perform-ances ranging from rock-'n'-roll to chamber music. **Humphrey's,** 2241 Shelter Island Dr. (✆ 619/523-1010; www.humphreysconcerts.com), is a 900-seat out-door venue set on the water, and has a seasonal (May through October) lineup that ranges from rock to folk to international. **Belly Up Tavern,** 143 Cedros Ave., Solana Beach (✆ 760/481-9022; www.bellyup.com), is a recycled Quon-set hut worth the 20-minute drive from downtown for an eclectic mix of acclaimed artists.

DANCE CLUBS & DISCOS

The Gaslamp Quarter is ground zero for the city's hottest dance clubs—the most popular at the moment are **Olé Madrid,** 751 Fifth Ave. (✆ 619/557-0146), a loud, energetic club with tapas and sangria from the adjoining Spanish restaurant; **Sevilla,** 555 Fourth Ave. (✆ 619/233-5979), where you can salsa and merengue to Brazilian dance music; and **Supper Club A-Go-Go,** 322 Fifth Ave. (✆ 619/235-4646), where postmodern hipsters swing to 1940s tunes or recline with a martini.

GAY & LESBIAN CLUBS & BARS

Bourbon Street, 4612 Park Blvd., University Heights (✆ 619/291-0173), is a jazzy and elegant piano bar with a New Orleans–esque patio. **The Brass Rail,** 3796 Fifth Ave., Hillcrest (✆ 619/298-2233), is loud and proud, with energetic dancing, bright lights, and go-go boys. **The Flame,** 3780 Park Blvd. (© 619/ 295-4163), is the city's top lesbian dance club. **Kickers,** 308 University Ave., at Third Avenue, Hillcrest (© 619/491-0400), is a country-western dance hall that attracts both sexes for two-stepping, line-dancing, and the adjacent Hamburger Mary's restaurant. Finally, **Rich's,** 1051 University Ave., between 10th and 11th Avenues (© 619/295-2195, or 619/497-4588 for upcoming events; www.richs-sandiego.com), is a high-energy, high-image dance club, with house music and a video bar.

BARS & COCKTAIL LOUNGES

Cannibal Bar, inside the Catamaran Hotel at 3999 Mission Blvd., Mission Beach (© 858/539-8650), features a tropical theme, Polynesian cocktails, DJ dancing, and occasional live bands. **The Bitter End,** 770 Fifth Ave., Gaslamp Quarter (© 619/338-9300; www.thebitterend.com), has three levels for its martini bar, late-night dance club, and relaxing cocktail lounge. **Martini Ranch,** 528 F St., Gaslamp Quarter (© 619/235-6100), is a split-level bar boasting 30 kinds of martinis and microrooms from video bars to conversation pits. **Top O' The Cove,** 1216 Prospect Ave., La Jolla (© 858/454-7779), offers an intimate setting for mellow piano music.

11 North County Beach Towns

Picturesque beach towns, each poised over their own stretch of sand, dot the coast of San Diego County from Del Mar to Oceanside. These make great day-trip destinations for sun worshipers and surfers.

ESSENTIALS

Getting there is easy: Del Mar is only 18 miles north of downtown San Diego; Carlsbad, about 33; and Oceanside, 36. If you're driving, follow I-5 north: You'll find freeway exits for Del Mar, Solana Beach, Cardiff by the Sea, Encinitas, Leucadia, Carlsbad, and Oceanside.

Check with **Amtrak** (© 800/USA-RAIL) or the **Coaster** (© 800/COASTER) for transit information.

The **San Diego North County Convention and Visitors Bureau** (© 800/ 848-3336; www.sandiegonorth.com) is also a good information source.

DEL MAR

Less than 20 miles up the coast lies Del Mar, a small community with just over 5,000 inhabitants in a 2-square-mile municipality. The town has adamantly maintained its independence, eschewing incorporation into the city of San Diego. Sometimes known as "the people's republic of Del Mar," this community was one of the nation's first to ban smoking. Come summer, the town explodes as visitors flock in for the thoroughbred horseracing season and the county's Del Mar Fair. The history and current popularity of Del Mar is, in fact, inextricably linked to the **Del Mar Race Track & Fairgrounds,** 2260 Jimmy Durante Blvd. (© 858/753-5555; www.delmarfair.com), which, in turn, still glows with the aura of Hollywood celebrity. Established in the 1930s by crooner and actor Bing Crosby, the track still begins each season by playing "Where the Surf Meets the Turf."

Del Mar City Beach is a wide, well-patrolled beach popular for sunbathing, swimming, and bodysurfing. Get there by taking 15th Street west to Seagrove Park, where college kids can always be found playing volleyball and other lawn games while older folks snooze in the shade. There are **free concerts** in the park during July and August; for information, contact the City of Del Mar (© **858/755-9313**).

For more information about Del Mar, contact or visit the **Del Mar Chamber of Commerce Visitor Information Center**, 1104 Camino del Mar #101, Del Mar, CA 92014 (© **858/755-4844**; www.delmar.ca.us), which also provides a folding, detailed map of the area. Open hours vary according to volunteer staffing, but usually mimic weekday business hours.

WHERE TO STAY

Del Mar Motel on the Beach   The only property in Del Mar right on the beach, this simply furnished little white-stucco motel has been here since 1946. Upstairs rooms have one king-size bed; downstairs units have two double beds. Half are reserved for non-smokers, and only oceanview rooms have bathtubs. This is a good choice for beach lovers, because you can walk along the shore for miles, and the popular seaside restaurants Poseidon and Jake's are right next door. The motel has a barbecue and picnic table for guests' use.

1702 Coast Blvd. (at 17th St.), Del Mar, CA 92014. © **800/223-8449** for reservations, or 858/755-1534. 45 units (some with shower only). $130–$180 double. Substantial off-season discounts available. AE, DC, DISC, MC, V. Take I-5 to Via de la Valle exit. Go west, then south on Hwy. 101 (Pacific Coast Hwy.); veer west onto Coast Blvd. *In room:* A/C, TV, fridge, coffeemaker.

L'Auberge Del Mar Resort and Spa 🌟🌟🌟   Because Del Mar strives to keep a low profile, most lodgings here feel like an afterthought . . . except for prominent L'Auberge, the town's centerpiece. Sitting on the site of the historic Hotel Del Mar (1909 to 69), this luxurious yet intimate inn manages to attract casual weekenders as easily as the rich-and-famous horsey set, who flock here during summer racing season. Always improving itself, the resort has recently enhanced the lower-level full-service spa, polished up the poolside ambiance, and completely revamped the dining room. The result is an atmosphere of complete relaxation and welcome. Guest rooms exude the elegance of a European country house, complete with marble bathrooms, architectural accents, well-placed casual seating, and the finest bed linens and appointments. Many boast romantic fireplaces; all have a private balcony or terrace (several with an unadvertised view to the ocean). The hotel is across the street from Del Mar's main shopping and dining scene, and a short jog from the sand. Redesigned in 2000, the hotel's Mediterranean dining room easily stands alone as one of Del Mar's fine restaurants; at the very least, don't miss its legendary breakfast *huevos rancheros*.

1540 Camino del Mar (at 15th St.), P.O. Box 2889, Del Mar, CA 92014. © **800/553-1336** or 858/259-1515. Fax 858/755-4940. www.laubergedelmar.com. 120 units. $225–$380 double; from $650 suite. Ask about off-season and midweek discounts; spa, romance, and other packages available. AE, DC, MC, V. Valet parking $12. Take I-5 to Del Mar Heights Rd. west, then turn right onto Camino del Mar Rd. **Amenities:** Restaurant; lounge; 2 swimming pools; tennis courts; indoor/outdoor fitness center; full-service spa; Jacuzzi; concierge; courtesy van; room service (6:30am–10pm); laundry/dry cleaning service. *In room:* A/C, TV w/ pay movies, dataport, minibar, coffeemaker, hair dryer, iron.

Wave Crest 🌟🌟   On a bluff overlooking the Pacific, these gray-shingled bungalow condominiums are beautifully maintained and wonderfully private . . . from the street it looks nothing like a hotel, because a good portion of these condos are owner-occupied year-round. The studios and suites surround a landscaped courtyard; each has a queen-size bed, sofa bed, artwork by local artists, VCR, stereo, full bathroom, and fully equipped kitchen with dishwasher. The studios sleep one or two people; the one-bedroom accommodates up to four. It's a 5-minute walk to the beach, and shopping and dining spots are a few blocks away. There is an extra fee for maid service. Amenities include a common lounge with a fireplace, TV, and newspapers; pool and whirlpool tub overlooking the ocean; irons, ironing boards, and laundry facilities.

1400 Ocean Ave., Del Mar, CA 92014. © **858/755-0100**. 31 units. Summer (mid-June to mid-Sept) $180–$205 studio, $240–$330 suite; winter $145–$165 studio, $170–$225 suite. Weekly rates available. MC, V. **Amenities:** Outdoor pool; Jacuzzi; self-service laundry. *In room:* TV/VCR, kitchen, iron.

WHERE TO DINE

Head to the upper level of the centrally located Del Mar Plaza, at Camino del Mar and 15th Street. You'll find **Il Fornaio Cucina Italiana** (© 858/755-8876), for excellent Italian cuisine; **Epazote** (© 858/259-9966), for Mexican, Tex-Mex, and Southwestern fare; and **Pacifica Del Mar** (© 858/792-0476), which serves outstanding seafood. Kids like **Johnny Rockets** (© 858/755-1954), an old-fashioned diner on the lower level. On the beach, **Jake's Del Mar,** 1660 Coast Blvd. (© 858/755-2002), and **Poseidon Restaurant on the Beach,** 1670 Coast Blvd. (© 858/755-9345), are both good for California cuisine and sunset views. If you want to eat at either of these popular spots, reserve early. The racetrack crowd congregates at **Bully's Restaurant,** 1404 Camino del Mar (© 858/755-1660), for burgers, prime rib, and crab legs; the gold-card crowd heads for special occasion meals at acclaimed **Pamplemousse Grill,** 514 Via de la Valle (© 858/792-9090). And if you're looking for fresh seafood—and lots of it—head to the Del Mar branch of San Diego's popular **Fish Market,** 640 Via de la Valle (© 858/755-2277), near the racetrack.

CARLSBAD & ENCINITAS

Fifteen miles north of Del Mar and around 30 miles from downtown San Diego (a 45-minute drive), the pretty communities of Carlsbad and Encinitas provide many reasons to linger on the California coast: good swimming and surfing beaches, small-town atmosphere, an abundance of antiques and gift shops, and a seasonal display of the region's most beautiful flowers.

Carlsbad was named for Karlsbad, Czechoslovakia, because of the similar mineral (some say curative) waters they both produced, but the town's once-famous artesian well has long been plugged up. Carlsbad is also a noted commercial flower–growing region, along with its neighbor **Encinitas.** A colorful display can be seen at **Carlsbad Ranch** (© 760/431-0352) each spring, when 45 acres of solid ranunculus fields bloom into a breathtaking rainbow visible even from the freeway. In December, the nurseries are alive with holiday poinsettias. You can also stroll through 30 acres of California native plants, exotic tropicals, palms, cacti, and more at **Quail Botanical Gardens** in Encinitas (© 760/436-3036).

The **Carlsbad Visitor Information Center,** 400 Carlsbad Village Dr. (in the old Santa Fe Depot), Carlsbad, CA 92008 (© 800/227-5722 or 760/434-6093), has lots of additional information on flower fields and nursery touring.

Carlsbad State Beach runs alongside downtown. It's a great place to stroll along a wide concrete walkway, surrounded by like-minded outdoor types walking, jogging, and in-line skating, even at night (thanks to good lighting). Enter on Ocean Boulevard at Tamarack Avenue; there's a $4 fee per vehicle.

Four miles south of town is **South Carlsbad State Beach,** almost 3 miles of cobblestone-strewn sand. A state-run campground at the north end is immensely popular year-round, and the southern portion is favored by area surfers. There's a $4 fee at the beach's entrance, along Carlsbad Boulevard at Poinsettia Lane.

Down in Encinitas, everyone flocks to **Moonlight Beach,** the city's sandy playground with plenty of facilities, including free parking, volleyball nets, restrooms, showers, picnic tables and fire grates, and the company of fellow sunbathers. The beach is accessed at the end of B Street (Encinitas Boulevard).

LEGOLAND 👶👶 *Kids* The ultimate monument to the world's most famous plastic building blocks, LEGOLAND (opened in 1999) is the third such theme park; the branches in Denmark and Britain have proven enormously successful. Attractions include hands-on interactive displays; a life-size menagerie of tigers, giraffes, and other animals; scale models of international landmarks (the Eiffel Tower, Sydney Opera House, and so on)—all constructed of real LEGO bricks! "MiniLand" is a 1:20 scale representation of American achievement, from a New England Pilgrim village to Mount Rushmore. There's a gravity coaster ride (don't worry, it's built from steel) through a LEGO castle, a DUPLO building area to keep smaller children occupied, and a brand-new ride where older kids can compete in LEGO TECHNIC car races.

While the park's official guidelines imply its attraction is geared toward children of all ages, we think the average MTV- and PlayStation-seasoned kid over 10 will find it kind of a snooze. Don't be afraid your toddler is too young, though . . . there'll be plenty for them to do. One last note on age—it may be "a country just for kids," but the sheer artistry of construction (especially Mini-Land) can be enthralling for adults, too.

1 Lego Drive. ℭ **877/534-6526** or 760/918-LEGO. www.legolandca.com. $38 adults, $32 seniors and kids 3–16, free to children under 3. AE, DISC, MC, V. Daily 10am–dusk; extended summer and holiday hours. Parking $7. From I-5 take the Cannon Rd. exit east, following signs for Lego Dr.

WHERE TO STAY

For the ultimate pampering golf, tennis, or spa vacation in Carlsbad, head to the **Four Seasons Resort Aviara,** 7100 Four Seasons Point (ℭ **800/332-3442** or 760/603-6800; www.fourseasons.com/aviara), or **La Costa Resort and Spa,** Costa del Mar Rd. (ℭ **800/854-5000** or 760/438-9111; www.lacosta.com).

Beach Terrace Inn At Carlsbad's only beachside hostelry (others are across the road or a little farther away), the rooms and the swimming pool and whirlpool all have ocean views. This downtown Best Western property also has a helpful staff. Rooms, although not elegant, are extra large, and some have balconies, fireplaces, and kitchenettes. Suites have separate living rooms and bedrooms. VCRs and films are available at the front desk. This is a good place for families. You can walk everywhere from here—except LEGOLAND, which is a 5-minute drive away.

2775 Ocean St., Carlsbad, CA 92003. ℭ **800/433-5415** outside CA, 800/622-3224 in CA, or 760/729-5951. Fax 760/729-1078. www.beachterraceinn.com. 49 units. Summer $129–$299 double; from $154 suite. Off-season $119–$209 double; from $134 suite. Rates include continental breakfast. Extra person $20. AE, DC, DISC, MC, V. Free parking. **Amenities:** Outdoor pool; Jacuzzi; dry cleaning service; self-service laundry. *In room:* A/C, TV w/ pay movies, dataport, fridge, coffeemaker, hair dryer, iron, safe.

Pelican Cove Inn 👶 Located 2 blocks from the beach, this Cape Cod–style hideaway combines romance with luxury. Hosts Kris and Nancy Nayudu see to your every need, from furnishing guest rooms with soft feather beds and down comforters to providing beach chairs and towels or preparing a picnic basket (with 24 hours' notice). Each room features a fireplace and private entrance; some have private spa tubs. The airy, spacious La Jolla room is loveliest, with bay windows and a cupola ceiling. Breakfast can be enjoyed in the garden if weather permits. Courtesy transportation from the Oceanside train station is available.

320 Walnut Ave., Carlsbad, CA 92008. © **888/PEL-COVE** or 760/434-5995. www.pelican-cove.com. 8 units. $90–$180 double. Rates include full breakfast. Midweek and seasonal discounts available. Extra person $15. AE, MC, V. Free parking. From downtown Carlsbad, follow Carlsbad Blvd. south to Walnut Ave.; turn left and drive 2½ blocks. *In room:* TV, no phone.

Tamarack Beach Resort ☆   This resort property's rooms, in the village across the street from the beach, are restfully decorated with beachy wicker furniture. Fully equipped suites have stereos, full kitchens, washers, and dryers. The pretty Tamarack has a pleasant lobby and a sunny pool courtyard with barbecue grills. Dini's by the Sea is a good restaurant that is popular with locals.

3200 Carlsbad Blvd., Carlsbad, CA 92008. © **800/334-2199** or 760/729-3500. Fax 760/434-5942. www.tamarackresort.com. 77 units. $140–$215 double; $210–$340 suite. Rates include continental breakfast. Children 12 and under stay free in parents' room. Off season discounts and weekly rates available. AE, MC, V. Free underground parking. **Amenities:** Restaurant; outdoor pool; 2 Jacuzzi; exercise room. *In room:* A/C, TV/VCR w/complimentary movie library, fridge, coffeemaker.

WHERE TO DINE

Local favorites include **Neiman's,** 2978 Carlsbad Blvd., Carlsbad (© **760/ 729-4131**), serving American fare in a restored Victorian mansion, and the **Potato Shack,** 120 W. I St., Encinitas (© **760/436-1282**), a spuds-intensive diner open for breakfast and lunch only.

Bellefleur Winery & Restaurant ☆☆ CALIFORNIA/MEDITERRANEAN This popular restaurant boasts the "complete wine country experience" although there's no wine country evident among the surrounding outlet mall and car dealerships. But their cavernous semi-industrial dining room, coupled with the wood-fired and wine-enhanced aromas emanating from Bellefleur's clanging open kitchen, do somehow evoke the casual yet sophisticated ambiance of California wine-producing regions like Santa Barbara and Napa. This multifunctional space includes a stylish tasting bar and open-air dining patio in addition to the main seating area and a glassed-in barrel aging room. The place can be noisy and spirited, drawing both exhausted shoppers and savvy San Diegans for a cuisine that incorporates North County's abundant produce with fresh fish and meats. Lunchtime sandwiches and salads surpass the shopping-mall standard, while dinner choices feature oak-grilled beef tenderloin or Colorado rack of lamb, mashed potatoes enhanced with garlic, horseradish, or olive tapenade, and rich reduction sauces of premium balsamic vinegar, wild mushroom demiglace, or sweet-tart tamarind.

5610 Paseo del Norte, Carlsbad. © **760/603-1919.** www.bellefleur.com. Reservations recommended for Fri–Sat dinner. Main courses $7–$15 lunch; $14–$23 dinner. AE, DISC, MC, V. Daily 11am–3pm and 5–9pm (till 10pm Fri–Sat).

OCEANSIDE

The most northerly town in San Diego County (36 miles north of San Diego), Oceanside claims almost 4 miles of beaches and one of the West Coast's longest over-the-water wooden piers, where a tram does nothing but transport people from the street to the end of the 1,954-foot-long pier and back for 25¢ each way. The wide, sandy beach, pier, and well-tended recreational area with playground equipment and an outdoor amphitheater are within easy walking distance of the train station.

One of the nicest things to do in Oceanside is to take a stroll around the city's upscale **harbor;** it's bustling with pleasure craft, lined with condominiums, and boasts a Cape Cod–themed shopping village. A launch ramp, visitor boat slips, charter fishing, boat rentals, and the village of shops are found here; several restaurants, including **Chart House,** offer harborside dining. The **Marina Inn,** at 2008 Harbor Dr. N., Oceanside, CA 92054 (© **800/252-2033** or 760/ 722-1561; fax 760/439-9758), has comfortable rooms and suites that offer harbor and ocean views.

The **Harbor Days Festival** in mid-September typically attracts 100,000 visitors to its crafts fair, entertainment, and food booths.

Oceanside is home to the **California Surf Museum,** 223 North Coast Hwy. (© **760/721-6876;** www.surfmuseum.org). Founded in 1985, the museum has an unbelievably extensive collection. Boards and other relics chronicle the development of the sport—many belonged to the names revered by local surfers, including Hawaiian Duke Kahanamoku and local daredevil Bob Simmons. Vintage photographs, beach attire, 1960s beach graffiti, and surf music all lovingly bring surfing to life—there's even a photo display of the real-life Gidget.

The area's biggest attraction is **Mission San Luis Rey** (© **760/757-3651**), a few miles inland. Founded in 1798, it's the largest of California's 21 missions. There is a small charge to tour the mission, its impressive church, exhibits, grounds, and cemetery. You might recognize it as the backdrop for one of the Zorro movies.

The **Oceanside Beach** runs all the way from just outside Oceanside Harbor, where routine harbor dredging makes for a pretty substantial amount of clean white sand, continuing almost 4 miles south at the Carlsbad border. Along the way you can enjoy the **Strand,** a grassy park stretching alongside the beach between Fifth Street and Wisconsin Avenue. Around the pier are restrooms, showers, picnic areas, and volleyball nets.

Oceanside's world-famous surfing spots attract numerous competitions, including the **Longboard Surf Contest** and **World Bodysurfing Championships,** both in August.

For an information packet about Oceanside and its attractions, contact the **Oceanside Visitor & Tourism Center,** 928 North Coast Hwy., Oceanside, CA 92054 (© **800/350-7873** or 760/721-1101; www.oceansidechamber.com).

12 Julian: Apples, Pies & a Slice of Small-Town California

60 miles NE of San Diego, 35 miles W of Anza-Borrego Desert State Park

A trip to Julian (population 1,500) is a trip back in time. The old gold-mining town, now best known for its apples, has some good eateries and a handful of cute B&Bs, but its popularity is based on the fact that it provides a chance for city-weary folks to get away from it all.

ESSENTIALS

GETTING THERE   The 90-minute drive can be made via Calif. 78 or I-8 to Calif. 79. We suggest taking one route going and the other coming back. Calif. 79 winds through scenic Rancho Cuyamaca State Park, while Calif. 78 traverses open country and farmland.

VISITOR INFORMATION   Town maps and fliers for accommodations are available from the Town Hall, on Main Street at Washington Street. The town has a 24-hour hot line (© **760/765-0707**) that provides information on lodging, dining, shopping, activities, upcoming events, weather, and road conditions. For a brochure on what to see and do, contact the **Julian Chamber of Commerce** (© **760/765-1857;** www.julianca.com).

SPECIAL EVENTS   Julian's popular fall apple harvest starts in mid-September and continues for an entire month. The annual wildflower show lasts for a week in early May; there's also a Spring Fine Arts Show in May. And the annual weed show, a tradition since 1961, is usually held the last few weeks in August or the beginning of September. Contact the Julian Chamber of Commerce (see above) for details on all of these events.

EXPLORING THE TOWN

This 1880s gold-mining town has managed to retain a rustic, woodsy sense of its historic origins. Radiating the dusty aura of the Old West, Julian offers an abundance of early California history, quaint Victorian streets filled with apple pie shops and antiques stores, crisp fresh air, and friendly people. Be forewarned, however: Julian's charming downtown can become exceedingly crowded during the fall harvest season, so consider making your trip during another time in order to enjoy this unspoiled relic with a little privacy. (Rest assured, apple pies are being baked year-round.) At around 4,500 feet elevation, the autumn air is crisp and bracing, and Julian sees a dusting (and often more) of snow during the winter months.

The best way to experience tiny Julian is on foot. After stopping in at the **Chamber of Commerce** in the old Town Hall—check out the vintage photos of Julian's yesteryear—cross the street to the **Julian Drug Store,** 2134 Main St. (*℃* **760/765-0332**), an old-style soda fountain serving sparkling sarsaparilla, conjuring images of boys in buckskin and girls in bonnets. The **Eagle and High Peak Mines** (built around 1870) at the end of C Street (*℃* **760/765-0036**), although seemingly a tourist trap, offers an interesting and educational look at the town's one-time economic mainstay.

While in Julian, consider a ride in horse-drawn carriage by **Country Carriages** (*℃* **760/765-1471**). A rambling drive down country roads and through town is $20 per couple, or you can choose an abbreviated spin around town for $5 per adult, $2 per child. The town's **Pioneer Cemetery** is a must-see for graveyard buffs; contemporary graves belie the haphazard, overgrown look of this hilly burial ground, and eroded older tombstones tell the intriguing story of Julian's rough pioneer history. You can drive in via the A Street entrance, or climb the steep stairway leading up from Main Street; until 1924 this ascent was the only point of entry, even for processionals.

Apple pie is the town's mainstay, and the **Julian Pie Company,** 2225 Main St. (*℃* **760/765-2449**), is the most charming pie shop of them all. It serves original, Dutch, apple–mountain berry, and no-sugar-added pies as well as other baked goodies. Another great bakery is the aptly named **Mom's Pies,** 2119 Main St. (*℃* **760/765-2472**), whose special attraction is a sidewalk plate-glass window through which you can observe the Mom-on-duty rolling crust, filling pies, and crimping edges. Nearby is the **Julian Cider Mill,** 2103 Main St. (*℃* **760/ 765-1430**), where you can see cider presses at work from October through March; it offers free tastes of the fresh nectar and sells jugs to take home.

There are dozens of **roadside fruit stands and orchards** in the Julian hills; during autumn they're open all day, every day, but in the off-season some might open only on weekends or close entirely. Most stands sell, depending on the season, apples, pears, peaches, cider, jams, jellies, and other homemade foodstuffs. Many are along Highway 78 between Julian and Wynola (3 miles away); there are also stands along Farmers Road, a scenic country lane leading north from downtown Julian. Happy hunting!

Ask any of the San Diegans who regularly make excursions to Julian: No trip would be complete without a stop at **Dudley's Bakery,** Calif. 78, Santa Ysabel (© **800/225-3348** or 760/765-0488), for a loaf or three of its popular bread. Loaves are stacked high, and folks are often three deep at the counter, clamoring for the 20(!) varieties of bread baked fresh daily—varieties range from raisin-date-nut to jalapeño, with some garden-variety sourdough and multigrain in between. Dudley's is a local tradition, built in 1963 and has expanded several times to accommodate an ever-growing business. It's open Wednesday through Sunday from 8am to 5pm (subject to early closure on Sunday).

OUTDOOR PURSUITS

Within 10 miles of Julian are numerous hiking trails traversing rolling meadows, high chaparral, and thick pine forests. The most spectacular hike is at **Volcan Mountain Preserve,** north of town along Farmers Road; the trail to the top is a moderately challenging hike of around 3½ miles round-trip with a 1,400-foot elevation gain. From the top, hikers have a panoramic view of the desert, mountains, and sea. Docent-led hikes are offered year-round at no charge (usually on one Saturday per month). For a hike schedule, call © **760/765-0650.**

In **William Heise County Park,** off Frisius Drive outside of Pine Hills, the whole family can enjoy hikes ranging from a self-guided nature trail to a cedar-scented forest trail, plus moderate to vigorous trails into the mountains. A ranger kiosk at the entrance can provide trail maps.

Cuyamaca Rancho State Park covers 30,000 acres along Calif. 79 southeast of Julian, the centerpiece of which is **Cuyamaca Lake.** In addition to lake recreation (© **760/765-0515** or 760/447-8123; www.lakecuyamaca.org), there are several wooded picnic areas, three campgrounds, and 110 miles of hiking trails through the Cleveland National Forest. Activities at the lake include fishing (trout, bass, catfish, bluegill, and crappie) and boating; there's a general store and restaurant at lake's edge. The fishing fee (license required) is $4.75 per day for adults and $2.50 per day for kids ages 8 to 15; rowboats are $12 per day, and outboard motors an additional $13. Canoes and paddleboats can be rented by the hour for $4 to $7. For a trail map and further information about park recreation, stop in at **park headquarters,** on Calif. 79 (© **760/765-0755**), Monday through Friday between the hours of 8am and 5pm. An adjacent park museum is open Monday through Friday from 10am to 5pm and Saturday and Sunday from 10am to 4pm.

For a different way to tour, try **Llama Trek,** P.O. Box 2363, Julian, CA 92036 (© **800/LAMAPAK** or 760/765-1890; www.wikiupbnb.com). Trips include rural neighborhoods, a historic gold mine, mountain and lake views, and apple orchards. Rates run from $75 to $85 per person and include lunch; overnight wilderness treks are also available.

WHERE TO STAY

For a list and description of more than 20 B&Bs, contact the **Julian Bed & Breakfast Guild** (© **760/765-1555**; www.julianbnbguild.com). Noteworthy member inns are the **Artists' Loft** (© **760/765-0765**), a peaceful hilltop retreat offering two artistically decorated rooms and a cozy cabin with a wood-burning stove; the **Julian White House** (© **800/WHT-HOUS** or 760/765-1764), a lovely faux-antebellum mansion, 4 miles from Julian in Pine Hills, with four frilly Victorian-style guest rooms; and the romantic **Random Oaks Ranch** (© **800/BNB-4344** or 760/765-1094), which features two themed cottages, each with its own wood-burning fireplace and outdoor Jacuzzi.

A word of caution: Reservations for the fall harvest season must be made several months in advance.

Julian Hotel ✦   Built in 1897 by freed slave Albert Robinson, this frontier-style hotel is a living monument to the area's gold boom days. Centrally located at the crossroads of downtown, the Julian Hotel isn't as secluded or plush as the many B&Bs in town, but if you seek historically accurate lodgings to complete your weekend time warp, this is the place. The 13 rooms and 2 cottages have been authentically restored (with nicely designed private baths added where necessary) and boast antique furnishings; some rooms are also authentically tiny so claustrophobes should inquire when reserving! An inviting private lobby is stocked with books, games, literature on local activities, and a wood-burning stove.

Main St. and B St., P.O. Box 1856, Julian, CA 92036. © 800/734-5854 or 760/765-0201. Fax 760/765-0327. www.julianhotel.com. 15 units. $72–$125 double; $110–$175 cottage. Rates include full breakfast and afternoon tea. AE, MC, V. *In room:* No phone.

Orchard Hill Country Inn ✦✦   Hosts Darrell and Pat Straube offer the most upscale lodging in Julian, a two-story lodge and four Craftsman cottages on a hill overlooking the town. Ten guest rooms, a guests-only dining room, and a great room with a massive stone fireplace are in the lodge. Twelve suites are in cottages spread over 3 acres of grounds. All units feature contemporary, unfrilly country furnishings and snacks. While rooms in the main lodge feel somewhat hotel-ish, the cottage suites are secluded and luxurious, with private porches, fireplaces, whirlpool tubs, and robes. Several hiking trails lead from the lodge into adjacent woods.

2502 Washington St., at Second St., P.O. Box 2410, Julian, CA 92036. © 800/71-ORCHARD or 760/765-1700. Fax 760/765-0290. www.orchardhill.com. 22 units. $185–$285 double. Rates include breakfast and hors d'oeuvres. Extra person $25. 2-night minimum stay if including Sat. AE, MC, V. From Calif. 79, turn left on Main St., then right on Washington St. *In room:* A/C, TV/VCR (complimentary tape library).

WHERE TO DINE

Julian Grille ✦ AMERICAN   Set in a cozy cottage festooned with lacy draperies, flickering candles, and a warm hearth, the Grille is the nicest eatery in town. Lunch here is an anything-goes affair, ranging from soups, sandwiches, and large salads to charbroiled burgers and hearty omelets. Dinner features grilled and broiled meats, seafood, and prime rib. I'm partial to delectable appetizers like baked Brie with apples and mustard sauce, Baja-style shrimp cocktail, and "Prime tickler" (chunks of prime rib served cocktail-style *au jus* with horseradish sauce). Dinners include soup or salad, hot rolls, potatoes, and a vegetable.

2224 Main St. (at A St.). © 760/765-0173. Reservations required Fri–Sun. Main courses $13–$21. AE, MC, V. Daily 11am–3pm; Tues–Sun 5–9pm.

Romano's Dodge House ✦ ITALIAN   Occupying a historic home just off Main Street (vintage photos illustrate the little farmhouse's past), Romano's is proudly the only restaurant in town not serving apple pie. It's a home-style Italian spot, with red-checked tablecloths and straw-clad Chianti bottles. Romano's offers individual lunch pizzas, pastas bathed in rich marinara sauce, veal parmigiana, chicken cacciatore, and the signature dish, pork Juliana (loin chops in a whisky–apple cider sauce). There's seating on a narrow shaded porch, in the wood-plank dining room, and in a little saloon in back.

2718 B St. (just off Main). © 760/765-1003. www.romanosjulian.com. Reservations required for dinner Fri–Sat, recommended other nights. Main courses $8–$16. No credit cards. Wed–Mon 11am–8:30pm.

13 Anza-Borrego Desert State Park

35 miles E of Julian, 90 miles NE of San Diego

The sweeping 600,000-acre Anza-Borrego Desert State Park is home to fossils and rocks dating from 540 million years ago; human beings arrived only 10,000 years ago. The terrain ranges in elevation from 15 feet to more than 6,000 feet above sea level, and incorporates dry lake beds, sandstone canyons, granite mountains, palm groves fed by year-round springs, and more than 600 kinds of desert plants. After the spring rains, thousands of wildflowers burst into bloom, transforming the desert into a brilliant palette of pink, lavender, red, orange, and yellow. The rare bighorn sheep can often be spotted navigating rocky hillsides, and an occasional migratory bird stops off on the way to the Salton Sea. A sense of timelessness pervades this landscape; travelers tend to slow down and take a long look around.

When planning a trip here, keep in mind that temperatures rise to as high as 115°F in summer.

ESSENTIALS

VISITOR INFORMATION   The **Anza-Borrego Desert State Park Visitor Center** lies just west of the town of Borrego Springs. You can contact park headquarters at ✆ **760/767-4205** (www.anzaborrego.statepark.org); the visitor center is open October through May daily from 9am to 5pm, and June through September weekends from 10am to 5pm.

For other local information, contact the **Borrego Springs Chamber of Commerce,** 622 Palm Canyon Dr., Borrego Springs, CA 92004 (✆ **800/559-5524** or 760/767-5555; www.borregosprings.com).

SPECIAL EVENT   From mid-March to the beginning of April, the desert wildflowers and cacti are usually in bloom, a hands-down, all-out natural special event that's not to be missed. The wildflower hot line is ✆ **760/767-4684.**

EXPLORING THE DESERT

When you're touring in this area, remember that hydration is of paramount importance. Whether you're walking, cycling, or driving, always have a bottle of water at your side.

You can explore the desert's stark terrain via one of its trails or a self-guided driving tour; the visitor center can supply maps. For starters, the **Borrego Palm Canyon** self-guided hike (1½ miles each way), which starts at the campgrounds near the visitor center, is beautiful, easy to get to, and easy to do. Within about half an hour you'll come to a waterfall and massive fan palms.

You can also take a guided off-road tour of the desert with **Desert Jeep Tours** (✆ **888/BY-JEEPS;** www.desertjeeptours.com). View spectacular canyons, fossil beds, ancient Native American sites, caves, and more in excursions by desert denizen Paul Ford ("Borrego Paul"). Tours go to the awesome viewpoint at Font's Point, where you can look out on the Badlands—named by the early settlers because it was an impossible area for moving or grazing cattle. Along the way, you'll learn about the history and geology of the area. Tours include drinks, snacks, and pickup at any Borrego Springs lodgings; prices range from $59 to $99 per person.

Call **Carrizo Bikes** (✆ **760/767-3872**) and talk with Dan Cain (a true desert rat) about bike rentals and tours in the area. For a thrilling 12-mile bicycle ride down Montezuma Valley Grade, try the Desert Descent offered by **Gravity Activated Sports** (✆ **800/985-4427** or 760/742-2294).

WHERE TO STAY

Borrego Springs is small, but there are enough accommodations to suit all travel styles and budgets. Other decent options include **Palm Canyon Resort,** 221 Palm Canyon Dr. (© **800/242-0044** or 760/767-5341), a large complex that includes a moderately priced hotel, RV park, restaurant, and recreational facilities; and **Borrego Valley Inn,** 405 Palm Canyon Dr. (© **760/767-0311,** www. borregovalleyinn.com), a newly built Southwestern complex featuring sand-colored pueblo-style rooms and upscale bed-and-breakfast amenities. Camping in the desert is a meditative experience, to be sure; but if you truly want to splurge, you can do that too.

La Casa del Zorro Desert Resort 🀫🀫   This pocket of heaven on earth was built in 1937, and the tamarind trees that were planted then have grown up around it. Accommodations are scattered around the lushly landscaped grounds; guests can choose from standard hotel rooms, suites, or one-, two-, or three-bedroom adobe casitas with tile roofs. Each casita has a mini-fridge and microwave, some have a fireplace or pool, and each bedroom has a separate bathroom. Outdoor diversions include horseshoes, Ping-Pong, volleyball, jogging trails, basketball, shuffleboard, and a life-size chess set. If you come to this desert oasis during the week, you'll benefit from lower room rates.

3845 Yaqui Pass Rd., Borrego Springs, CA 92004. © **800/824-1884** or 760/767-5323. Fax 760/767-5963. www.lacasadelzorro.com. 77 units. Jan 15–Apr 30 $295 double weekends, $225 weekdays; from $295 casitas weekends, $225 weekdays. May 1–Jun 30 and Oct 1–Jan 15 $225 double weekends, $175 weekdays; from $240 casitas weekends, $175 weekdays. July 1–Sept 30 $155 double or casita weekends, $135 weekdays. Weekday rates do not apply on holidays Tennis, jazz, holiday, and other packages available. Extra person $10. AE, DC, DISC, MC, V. **Amenities:** Restaurant (men are required to wear a jacket and a collared shirt at dinner October through May), lounge; 3 outdoor pools; 9-hole putting green; 6 tennis courts; health club and spa; 2 Jacuzzis; bike rental; activities desk; courtesy car to golf; business center; salon; room service (7am–11pm); in-room massage; babysitting. *In room:* A/C, TV/VCR w/ pay movies, dataport, minibar, coffee-maker, hair dryer, iron.

The Palms at Indian Head 🀫🀫 *Finds*   It takes a sense of nostalgia and an active imagination for most visitors to truly appreciate Borrego Springs's only bed-and-breakfast. The once-chic resort is slowly being renovated by its fervent owners, David and Cynthia Leibert. Originally opened in 1947, then rebuilt after a fire in 1958, the Art Deco–style hilltop lodge was a favorite hideaway for San Diego's and Hollywood's elite. It played host to movie stars like Bing Crosby, Clark Gable, and Marilyn Monroe. The Leiberts rescued it from extreme disrepair in 1993, clearing away some dilapidated guest bungalows and uncovering original wallpaper, light fixtures, and priceless memorabilia. As soon as they'd restored several rooms in luxurious Southwestern style, they began taking in guests to help finance the ongoing restoration.

Now up to 10 rooms, the inn also boasts a restaurant, the Krazy Coyote (see "Where to Dine," below), that's a culinary breath of fresh air in town. Also completely restored is the 42-by-109-foot pool, soon to be joined by the original subterranean grotto bar behind viewing windows at the deep end. The inn occupies the most envied site in the valley—shaded by palms and adjacent to the state park with a panoramic view across the entire Anza-Borrego region. A hiking trail begins just steps from the hotel. If you don't mind getting an insider's view of this work-in-progress, the Palms at Indian Head rewards you with charm, comfort, and convenience.

2220 Hoberg Rd., P.O. Box 525, Borrego Springs, CA 92004. © **800/519-2624** or 760/767-7788. Fax 760/767-9717. www.thepalmsatindianhead.com. 10 units. Nov–May $105–$159 double; June–Oct $95 double.

Midweek discounts available. Extra person $20. DC, DISC, MC, V. Take S22 into Borrego Springs; at Palm Canyon Dr., S22 becomes Hoberg Rd. Continue north ½ mile. **Amenities:** Restaurant, bar; fantastic outdoor pool; room service (8am–8pm); in-room massage; laundry service. *In room:* A/C, TV, fridge, coffeemaker.

CAMPING

The park has two developed campgrounds. **Borrego Palm Canyon,** with 117 sites, is 2½ miles west of Borrego Springs and near the visitor center. Full hookups are available, and there's an easy hiking trail. **Tamarisk Grove,** at Calif. 78 and county road S3, has 27 sites. Both have campfire programs and restrooms with showers; reservations are a good idea. The park allows open camping along all the trail routes. For more information, check with the visitor center (© 760/767-4205).

WHERE TO DINE

There's also a high-priced (but admittedly excellent) dining room at La Casa del Zorro (see above). For light fare and coffee drinks amidst a small but well-stocked bookstore, head to the **Coffee & Book Store,** 590 Palm Canyon Dr. (© 760/767-5080).

Bailey's Cafe COFFEE SHOP   Here's an economical little spot to grab a quick bite. Emu burgers from the local emu and ostrich farm are the specialty of the house. Buffalo burgers and Mexican dishes are also popular. Dinner choices include pork chops and chicken-fried steak. The cafe claims its apple pies are better than Julian's. Anything can be packed to go if you'd rather dine overlooking the desert.

In the Mall, Borrego Springs. © 760/767-3491. Main courses $3.50–$7.95 lunch; $5.95–$10.95 dinner. MC, V. Sept–May daily 6am–8pm; June–Aug Thurs–Mon 6am–8pm.

Krazy Coyote Saloon & Grille ⭐ ECLECTIC MENU   The same style and perfectionism that pervades David and Cynthia Leibert's bed-and-breakfast is evident in this casual restaurant, which overlooks the inn's swimming pool and the vast desert beyond. An eclectic menu encompasses quesadillas, club sandwiches, burgers, grilled meats and fish, and individual gourmet pizzas. The Krazy Coyote also offers breakfast (rich and hearty for an active day, or light and healthy for diet-watchers). The evening ambiance is welcoming and romantic, as the sparse lights of tiny Borrego Springs twinkle on the desert floor below.

In the Palms at Indian Head, 2220 Hoberg Rd. © 760/767-7788. Main courses $7.50–$12 lunch; $10–$22 dinner. AE, MC, V. Open daily; call for seasonal hours.

Appendix: California in Depth

by Matthew R. Poole & Mary Anne Moore

The more you know about California, the more you're likely to enjoy and appreciate everything the state has to offer. The pages that follow include a brief yet enlightening tale of how California came to be the most plentiful and powerful state in the nation, a wide-ranging list of highly recommended books, and more.

1 California Today

A recent survey of the most popular name given to California's newborns says a lot about the direction the Golden State is headed. You probably didn't guess José, but then again, you may not have known that California is the most racially diverse state in the nation, playing host to every race, ethnic heritage, language group, and religion in the *world*. So if you're prone to xenophobia, you might want to spend your vacation elsewhere, because California will soon be the mother of all melting pots, where no single race or ethnic group will constitute a majority of the state's population.

The numbers are already bewildering: 34 million people, a whopping one third of whom live in the Los Angeles Basin. California already receives the highest numbers of immigrants each year—more than 200,000 annually. Whether this is a potential boon or time bomb for California's future, is impossible to predict, but in the meantime it makes for a very interesting place to live and visit. (Heck, why bother traveling all the way to Europe or Asia when you can visit immigrant communities in Los Angeles and San Francisco that are uncanny replicas of the societies they've left behind?)

Much of California's prosperity and popularity can be attributed to deft restructuring of the economy during the post–Cold War era. A classic example is the numerous Air Force and Naval bases that were shut down, leaving thousands of civilians unemployed. Yet, thanks to an unprecedented collaboration between government and private enterprise, many of the former bases were reopened as computer manufacturing plants, tourist attractions, and, in some cases, even movie studios. California high-tech industries, once employed to build better bombs, have retooled their trade toward computer and information-based enterprises. Meanwhile, the industries that have always bolstered California's economy—agriculture, tourism, entertainment, and manufacturing—continue to thrive.

And don't let those energy-crisis tales deter you. The lights may occasionally be romantically dim, but the party is still in full swing.

2 History 101

EUROPEAN DISCOVERY & COLONIZATION Although very little remains to mark the existence of West Coast Native Americans, anthropologists estimate that as many as half

Dateline

- 1542 Juan Cabrillo enters San Diego Bay and sails up California's coast in first documented European visit.

continues

a million aborigines flourished on this naturally abundant land for thousands of years before the arrival of Europeans in the mid–16th century. Sailing from a small colony, established 10 years before, on the southern tip of Baja (Lower) California, Portuguese explorer Juan Rodrígues Cabrillo is credited with being the first European to "discover" California, in 1542. Over the next 200 years, dozens of sailors mapped the coast, including British explorer Sir Francis Drake, who sailed his *Golden Hind* into what is now called Drake's Bay in 1579, and Spanish explorer Sebastian Vizcano, who, in 1602, bestowed most of the place-names that survive today, including San Diego, Santa Barbara, and Carmel.

European colonial competition and Catholic missionary zeal prompted Spain to establish settlements along the Alta (Upper) California coast and claim the lands as its own. In 1769, Father Junípero Serra, accompanied by 300 soldiers and clergy, began forging a path from Mexico to Monterey. A small mission and presidio (fort) were established that year at San Diego, and by 1804, a chain of 21 missions, each a day's walk from the next along a dirt road called *Camino Real* (Royal Road), stretched all the way to Sonoma. Most of the solidly built missions still remain—Mission Delores, Mission San Juan Bautista, Mission San Diego de Alcala, to name just a few—and offer public tours.

During that time, thousands of Native Americans were converted to Christianity and coerced into labor. Many others died from imported diseases. Because not all the natives welcomed their conquerors with open arms, many missions and pueblos (small towns) suffered repeated attacks, leading to the construction of California's now ubiquitous—and fireproof—red-tile roofs.

- 1579 Sir Francis Drake drops anchor in the San Francisco Bay area and claims the land for England's Queen Elizabeth I.
- 1602 Spanish explorer and merchant Sebastian Vizcano sails up the coast, naming many regions along the way.
- 1769 Mission San Diego de Alcala is founded by Franciscan monk Father Junípero Serra.
- 1775 Juan Manuel de Ayala maps San Francisco Bay.
- 1777 Monterey is made capital of Spain's California territory.
- 1781 Los Angeles is founded.
- 1804 Spain divides its California territory into Baja (Lower) California and Alta (Upper) California; Jose Joaquin de Arrillaga becomes the first governor of Alta California.
- 1808 Connecticut sea captain William Shaler publishes his *Journal,* the first extensive account of California.
- 1821 Mexico wins independence from Spain and annexes California.
- 1836 Governor Juan Batista Alvarado declares California a "free and sovereign state."
- 1846 John C. Fremont leads the Bear Flag Revolt; California is drawn into the Mexican-American War; the U.S flag is raised in Yerba Buena (San Francisco) and Los Angeles.
- 1847 Yerba Buena is renamed San Francisco; the Donner Party is trapped by heavy Sierra Nevada snows.
- 1848 James Wilson Marshall discovers gold in Coloma; California is officially made a U.S. Territory.
- 1849 The gold rush is in full swing, bringing more than 300,000 men and women; a constitutional convention meets in Monterey; and San Jose becomes the state capital.
- 1850 California becomes the 31st state.
- 1853 Levi Strauss sells his first pair of canvas trousers.
- 1854 Sacramento becomes the permanent state capital.
- 1857 Hungarian Agoston Haraszthy establishes the state's first winery, Buena Vista.

continues

No settlement had more than 100 inhabitants when Spain's sovereignty was compromised by an 1812 Russian outpost called Fort Ross, 60 miles north of San Francisco (which, remarkably enough, still stands and is open to the public). But the biggest threat came from the British—who had strengthened their own claims to America with the Hudson's Bay Company trading firm—and their short-lived, last-ditch effort to win back their territories in the War of 1812.

Embattled at home as well as abroad, the Spanish finally relinquished their claim to Mexico and California in 1821. Under Mexican rule, Alta California's Spanish missionaries fell out of favor and lost much of their land to the increasingly wealthy *Californios*—Mexican immigrants who had been granted vast tracts of land.

AMERICAN EXPANSION Beginning in the late 1820s, Americans from the East began to make their way to California, via a 3-month sail around Cape Horn. Most of them settled in the territorial capital of Monterey and in northern California.

From the 1830s on, inspired by the doctrine of Manifest Destiny—an almost religious belief that the United States was destined to cover the continent from coast to coast—more and more settlers headed west. Along with them came daring explorers. In 1843, Marcus Whitman, a missionary seeking to prove that settlers could travel overland through the Oregon Territory's Blue Mountains, helped blaze the Oregon Trail; the first covered-wagon train made the 4-month crossing in 1844. Over the next few years, several hundred Americans made the trek to California over the Sierra Nevada range via Truckee Pass, just north of Lake Tahoe. A memorial to the Donner Party—the most famous tragedy in the history of westward

- 1859 Prospector James Finney discovers silver ore, the Comstock Load.
- 1861 California swears allegiance to the Union.
- 1862 The first telegraph line is established between San Francisco and New York.
- 1867 Anti-Chinese demonstrations take place in San Francisco in the wake of rising immigration.
- 1869 The transcontinental railroad is completed.
- 1873 The University of California opens its campus at Berkeley; the first cable car appears in San Francisco.
- 1879 The University of Southern California is founded.
- 1881 The *Los Angeles Times* begins publication.
- 1888 Lick Observatory is established.
- 1890 Yosemite gains National Park status.
- 1906 San Francisco is decimated by an earthquake and fire, leaving 300,000 people homeless.
- 1911 Hollywood's first film studio is established.
- 1915 The first transcontinental telephone call is made from San Francisco to New York.
- 1919 William Randolph Hearst begins construction of his castle at San Simeon.
- 1922 The Hollywood Bowl and amphitheater opens.
- 1924 The first transcontinental airmail flight is made from San Francisco to New York.
- 1928 Walt Disney creates Mickey Mouse.
- 1929 Hollywood hosts the first Academy Awards presentation.
- 1934 Alcatraz Island is converted to a maximum security penitentiary.
- 1935 Statewide irrigation system begins.
- 1936 The San Francisco–Oakland Bay Bridge opens.
- 1937 The Golden Gate Bridge opens.
- 1945 The United Nations is founded in San Francisco.
- 1955 Disneyland opens in Anaheim; actor James Dean dies in a car accident near Paso Robles at age 24.

continues

migration—marks the site of the ill-fated travelers.

As the drive to the west increased, the U.S. Government sought to extend its control over Mexican territory north of the Rio Grande, the river that now divides the United States and Mexico. In 1846, President James Polk offered Mexico $40 million for California and New Mexico. The offer might have been accepted, but America's simultaneous annexation of Texas, to which Mexico still laid claim, resulted in a war between the two countries. Within months, the United States overcame Mexico and took possession of the entire West Coast.

GOLD & STATEHOOD   In 1848, California's non–Native American population was around 7,000. That same year, flakes of gold were discovered by workers building a sawmill along the American River. Word of the find spread quickly, bringing more than 300,000 men and women into California between 1849 and 1851, one of the largest mass migrations in American history. Of course, very few prospectors unearthed a gold mine, and within 15 years the gold had dissipated, though many of the new residents remained. In fact, much of the mining equipment and gold rush–era buildings remain today, and are on display throughout the Gold Country.

In 1850, California was admitted to the Union as the 31st state. The state constitution on which California applied for admission included several noteworthy features. To protect the miners, slavery was prohibited. To attract women from the East Coast, legal recognition was given to the separate property of a married woman (California was the first state to offer such recognition). By 1870, almost 90% of the state's Native American population had been wiped out, and the bulk of the rest were removed to undesirable inland reservations.

- 1958 California acquires its first major-league baseball team, the San Francisco Giants.
- 1960 San Francisco's Candlestick Park opens.
- 1962 California becomes the most populous state in the Union.
- 1964 Mario Savio speaks before Free Speech Movement demonstrators at UC Berkeley.
- 1967 San Francisco's Haight-Ashbury experiences the "Summer of Love."
- 1968 Robert Kennedy is assassinated at L.A.'s Ambassador Hotel.
- 1972 The BART system opens in San Francisco.
- 1978 Steve Wozniak and Steve Jobs revolutionize personal computing with the launch of Apple Computers; San Francisco Mayor George Moscone and Supervisor Harvey Milk are assassinated at City Hall.
- 1984 Los Angeles hosts the Summer Olympic Games.
- 1989 An earthquake registering 7.1 on the Richter scale hits San Francisco, causing 63 deaths and $10 billion in damage.
- 1991 AIDS becomes San Francisco's number-one killer of men.
- 1992 Fire rages through the Berkeley/Oakland hills, destroying 2,800 homes.
- 1992 Los Angeles experiences the worst race riots in American history: 50 dead, hundreds injured; California becomes first state in the Union to send two female senators to Washington.
- 1993 Firestorms sweep through Los Angeles area; an earthquake registering 6.2 on the Richter scale strikes.
- 1994 An earthquake measuring 6.8 on the Richter scale hits L.A., killing more than 60 people and injuring thousands.
- 1996 Former Assembly Speaker Willie Brown is elected mayor of San Francisco.
- 1997 El Niño floods cause billions in damage throughout California.
- 1998 Gray Davis is elected governor, the first Democrat to hold the office since 1986.

continues

Mexican and Chinese laborers were brought in to help local farmers and to work on the transcontinental railroad, which was completed in 1869. The new rail line transported Easterners to California in just 5 days, marking a turning point in the settlement of the West. Many of those same steam engines are on display at the California State Railroad Museum in Sacramento.

- **2000** The sale of the *Los Angeles Times* to the Chicago-based *Tribune* is announced.
- **2001** Dot-coms falter; energy crisis results in rolling blackouts.

GROWTH & INDUSTRY   In 1875, when the Santa Fe Railroad reached Los Angeles, southern California's population of just 10,000 was divided equally between Los Angeles and San Diego. Los Angeles, however, began to grow rapidly in 1911, when the film industry moved here from the East Coast to take advantage of cheap land and a warm climate that enabled movies to be shot outdoors year-round. The movies' glamorous, idyllic portrayal of California boosted the region's popularity and population, especially during the Great Depression of the 1930s, when thousands of families (like the Joads in John Steinbeck's novel *The Grapes of Wrath*) packed up their belongings and headed west in search of a better life.

World War II brought heavy industry to California, in the form of munitions factories, shipyards, and airplane manufacturing. Freeways were built, military bases were opened, and suburbs were developed. In the 1950s, California in general, and San Francisco in particular, became popular with artists and intellectuals. The so-called Beat Generation appeared, later to inspire alternative-culture groups, most notably the "flower children" of the 1960s, in San Francisco's Haight-Ashbury district. During the "Summer of Love" in 1967, as the war in Vietnam escalated, student protests increased at Berkeley and elsewhere in California, as they did across the country. A year later, amid rising racial tensions, Martin Luther King, Jr., was killed, setting off riots in the Watts section of Los Angeles and in other cities. Soon thereafter, Robert F. Kennedy was fatally shot in Los Angeles after winning the California Democratic Party presidential primary. Antiwar protests continued into the 1970s.

Perhaps in response to an increasingly violent society, the 1970s also gave rise to several exotic religions and cults, which found eager adherents in California. The spiritual "New Age" continued into the 1980s, along with a growing population, environmental pollution, and escalating social ills, especially in Los Angeles. California also became very rich. Real estate values soared, the computer industry—centered in "Silicon Valley" south of San Francisco—boomed, and banks and businesses prospered.

RECESSION & REDEMPTION   The late 1980s and early 1990s, however, brought a devastating recession to the state. Californians, like many other Americans, became increasingly more conservative. Though they remained concerned about the nation's problems—economic competition from abroad, the environment, drugs, and the blight of homelessness afflicting cities large and small—their fascination with alternative lifestyles ebbed as the former campus rebels among them settled into comfortable positions in industry and politics. In short, the baby boomers were growing up and settling down.

The plight of AIDS also became a major issue of the 1990s, particularly in San Francisco, where it quickly became the number-one killer of young men. Los Angeles had its problems as well, most notably the race riots spurred by a videotaping (and subsequent acquittal) of four white police officers beating a

A Tale of Two States

It doesn't take a psychiatrist to figure out that California suffers from an acute case of bipolar schizophrenia. We Californians may, on the surface, appear to be one big *Happy Days* family, but in reality we've divided our state into separate factions worthy of Montague and Capulet. That is, you're either a northern Californian or a southern Californian, two opposing tribes that have little in common. In fact, which side you even choose to visit may reveal something about yourself.

All the California glamour, wealth, fame, fast cars, surf scenes, and buxom blondes you see on television is pure southern invention. If this is the California you're looking for, head due south—assuming you're not terribly interested in intellectual stimulation, you won't be disappointed. In fact, it's nearly impossible not to be immediately swept up by the energy and excitement that places like West Hollywood and Venice Beach exude. It's a narcotic effect, the allure of flashy wealth, gorgeous bodies, and celebrity status. Even watching it all as a bystander imparts a heady mixture of thrill and envy.

Northern California may be frightfully demure in comparison, but in the long run, its subdued charms and natural beauty prevail. Wealth is certainly in abundance, but rarely displayed. The few hard bodies that exist are usually swathed in loose jeans and shirts. The few celebrities who live here keep very low profiles, and are more likely to be on their ranches than Rodeo Drive. Ostentation in any form is looked down upon (of course, it's okay to own a BMW, as long as it's slightly dirty), and unlike Los Angeles, you can actually explore smog-free San Francisco on foot.

Ironically, it's the northern Californians who think of themselves as superior for having prudently eschewed the trappings of wealth and status (L.A.-bashing is a popular pastime). Southern Californians, on the other hand, couldn't care less what the northerners think of them; it's all sour grapes as they bask poolside 300 sunny days of the year. In fact, most southern Californians would be perfectly content as their own state were it not for one key factor: water. Northern California holds two-thirds of the state's watershed, and without the incredibly complex system of aqueducts, reservoirs, and dams that keep huge flows going southward, southern California's 13 million citizens would be in a world of hurt.

Will Californians ever agree to a legally mutual breakup? The idea has been bandied about the state capital for years, but it consistently meets its Waterloo when it comes to water rights, always a hotly contested issue in California politics. But regardless of our polarized views and lifestyles, most Californians do agree on one thing: We're still the best damn dysfunctional state in America.

black motorist, Rodney King. Two years later, a major earthquake would cause billions of dollars in damage to L.A.'s buildings and freeways, and leave thousands injured and homeless, while Oakland's hills became a raging inferno, killing 26 people and destroying 3,000 homes.

Midway through the 1990s, America's economy slowly yet surely began to improve, a welcome relief to recession-battered Californians. Crime and unemployment began to drop, while public schools received millions for much-needed improvements. Computer- and Internet-related industries flourished in the Bay Area, with entrepreneurialism fueling much of the explosive growth. As the stock market continued its record-setting pace through the end of the decade, no state reaped more benefits than California, which was gaining new millionaires by the day. At the millennium, optimism in the state's economy and quality of life was at an all-time high.

Today, although the economy is still strong, the unemployment rate still low, and property rates still rising, the state is struggling to deal with an energy deregulation scheme gone awry, leaving irate residents with periodic rolling blackouts and escalating energy bills. If the cloud has a silver lining, it's that never have so many taken such a sudden, intense interest in ways to save and create energy. State-of-the-art windmills may yet replace the golden bear as the state icon. The other blip on the economic screen is the rapid demise of many, if not most, of the baby dot-coms in the stock market decline. Not to be deterred, however, new websites gleefully chronicling the death throes of the fledgling enterprises popped up to amuse the formerly envious. Oh, California. If life hands us a lemon, we'll slice it into our imported water.

Index

FROMMER'S® COMPLETE TRAVEL GUIDES

Alaska
Amsterdam
Argentina & Chile
Arizona
Atlanta
Australia
Austria
Bahamas
Barcelona, Madrid & Seville
Beijing
Belgium, Holland & Luxembourg
Bermuda
Boston
British Columbia & the Canadian
    Rockies
Budapest & the Best of Hungary
California
Canada
Cancún, Cozumel & the Yucatán
Cape Cod, Nantucket &
    Martha's Vineyard
Caribbean
Caribbean Cruises & Ports of Call
Caribbean Ports of Call
Carolinas & Georgia
Chicago
China
Colorado
Costa Rica
Denmark
Denver, Boulder & Colorado Springs
England
Europe
European Cruises & Ports of Call
Florida
France

Germany
Great Britain
Greece
Greek Islands
Hawaii
Hong Kong
Honolulu, Waikiki & Oahu
Ireland
Israel
Italy
Jamaica
Japan
Las Vegas
London
Los Angeles
Maryland & Delaware
Maui
Mexico
Montana & Wyoming
Montréal & Québec City
Munich & the Bavarian Alps
Nashville & Memphis
Nepal
New England
New Mexico
New Orleans
New York City
New Zealand
Nova Scotia, New Brunswick &
    Prince Edward Island
Oregon
Paris
Philadelphia & the Amish Country
Portugal
Prague & the Best of the Czech
    Republic

Provence & the Riviera
Puerto Rico
Rome
San Antonio & Austin
San Diego
San Francisco
Santa Fe, Taos & Albuquerque
Scandinavia
Scotland
Seattle & Portland
Shanghai
Singapore & Malaysia
South Africa
South America
Southeast Asia
South Florida
South Pacific
Spain
Sweden
Switzerland
Texas
Thailand
Tokyo
Toronto
Tuscany & Umbria
USA
Utah
Vancouver & Victoria
Vermont, New Hampshire
    & Maine
Vienna & the Danube Valley
Virgin Islands
Virginia
Walt Disney World & Orlando
Washington, D.C.
Washington State

FROMMER'S® DOLLAR-A-DAY GUIDES

Australia from $50 a Day
California from $70 a Day
Caribbean from $70 a Day
England from $70 a Day
Europe from $70 a Day

Florida from $70 a Day
Hawaii from $80 a Day
Ireland from $60 a Day
Italy from $70 a Day
London from $85 a Day

New York from $90 a Day
Paris from $80 a Day
San Francisco from $70 a Day
Washington, D.C., from $70
    a Day

FROMMER'S® PORTABLE GUIDES

Acapulco, Ixtapa & Zihuatanejo
Alaska Cruises & Ports of Call
Amsterdam
Aruba
Australia's Great Barrier Reef
Bahamas
Baja & Los Cabos
Berlin
Big Island of Hawaii
Boston
California Wine Country
Cancún
Charleston & Savannah
Chicago
Disneyland

Dublin
Florence
Frankfurt
Hong Kong
Houston
Las Vegas
London
Los Angeles
Maine Coast
Maui
Miami
New Orleans
New York City
Paris

Phoenix & Scottsdale
Portland
Puerto Rico
Puerto Vallarta, Manzanillo &
    Guadalajara
San Diego
San Francisco
Seattle
Sydney
Tampa & St. Petersburg
Vancouver
Venice
Virgin Islands
Washington, D.C.

FROMMER'S® NATIONAL PARK GUIDES

Family Vacations in the National
    Parks
Grand Canyon

National Parks of the American
    West
Rocky Mountain
Yellowstone & Grand Teton

Yosemite & Sequoia/
    Kings Canyon
Zion & Bryce Canyon

FROMMER'S® MEMORABLE WALKS

Chicago
London

New York
Paris

San Francisco

FROMMER'S® GREAT OUTDOOR GUIDES

Arizona & New Mexico
New England

Northern California
Southern New England

Vermont & New Hampshire

SUZY GERSHMAN'S BORN TO SHOP GUIDES

Born to Shop: France
Born to Shop: Hong Kong,
  Shanghai & Beijing

Born to Shop: Italy
Born to Shop: London

Born to Shop: New York
Born to Shop: Paris

FROMMER'S® IRREVERENT GUIDES

Amsterdam
Boston
Chicago
Las Vegas
London

Los Angeles
Manhattan
New Orleans
Paris
Rome

San Francisco
Seattle & Portland
Vancouver
Walt Disney World
Washington, D.C.

FROMMER'S® BEST-LOVED DRIVING TOURS

Britain
California
Florida
France

Germany
Ireland
Italy

New England
Scotland
Spain

HANGING OUT™ GUIDES

Hanging Out in England
Hanging Out in Europe

Hanging Out in France
Hanging Out in Ireland

Hanging Out in Italy
Hanging Out in Spain

THE UNOFFICIAL GUIDES®

Bed & Breakfasts and Country
  Inns in:
    California
    New England
    Northwest
    Rockies
    Southeast
Beyond Disney
Branson, Missouri
California with Kids
Chicago
Cruises
Disneyland

Florida with Kids
Golf Vacations in the
  Eastern U.S.
The Great Smokey &
  Blue Ridge Mountains
Inside Disney
Hawaii
Las Vegas
London
Mid-Atlantic with Kids
Mini Las Vegas
Mini-Mickey
New England & New York
  with Kids

New Orleans
New York City
Paris
San Francisco
Skiing in the West
Southeast with Kids
Walt Disney World
Walt Disney World for
  Grown-ups
Walt Disney World for Kids
Washington, D.C.
World's Best Diving Vacations

SPECIAL-INTEREST TITLES

Frommer's Adventure Guide to Australia & New
  Zealand
Frommer's Adventure Guide to Central America
Frommer's Adventure Guide to India & Pakistan
Frommer's Adventure Guide to South America
Frommer's Adventure Guide to Southeast Asia
Frommer's Adventure Guide to Southern Africa
Frommer's Britain's Best Bed & Breakfasts and
  Country Inns
Frommer's France's Best Bed & Breakfasts and
  Country Inns
Frommer's Italy's Best Bed & Breakfasts and Country
  Inns
Frommer's Caribbean Hideaways

Frommer's Exploring America by RV
Frommer's Gay & Lesbian Europe
Frommer's The Moon
Frommer's New York City with Kids
Frommer's Road Atlas Britain
Frommer's Road Atlas Europe
Frommer's Washington, D.C., with Kids
Frommer's What the Airlines Never Tell You
Israel Past & Present
The New York Times' Guide to Unforgettable
  Weekends
Places Rated Almanac
Retirement Places Rated

Let Us Hear From You!

Dear Frommer's Reader,

You are our greatest resource in keeping our guides relevant, timely, and lively. We'd love to hear from you about your travel experiences—good or bad. Want to recommend a great restaurant or a hotel off the beaten path—or register a complaint? Any thoughts on how to improve the guide itself?

Please use this page to share your thoughts with me and mail it to the address below. Or if you like, send a FAX or e-mail me at frommersfeedback@hungryminds.com. And so that we can thank you—and keep you up on the latest developments in travel—we invite you to sign up for a free daily Frommer's e-mail travel update. Just write your e-mail address on the back of this page. Also, if you'd like to take a moment to answer a few questions about yourself to help us improve our guides, please complete the following quick survey. (We'll keep that information confidential.)

Thanks for your insights.

Yours sincerely,

Michael Spring

Michael Spring, *Publisher*

Name (Optional) ————————————————————————

Address ———————————————————————————

————————————————————————————————

City—————————————————————— **State**——— **ZIP** ———

Name of Frommer's Travel Guide ————————————————

Comments———————————————————————————

————————————————————————————————

————————————————————————————————

————————————————————————————————

————————————————————————————————

————————————————————————————————

————————————————————————————————

————————————————————————————————

————————————————————————————————

Please tell us a little about yourself so that we can serve you and the Frommer's community better. We will keep this information confidential.

Age: ( )18-24; ( )25-39; ( )40-49; ( )50-55; ( )Over 55

Income: ( )Under $25,000; ( )$25,000-$50,000; ( )$50,000-$100,000; ( )Over $100,000

I am: ( )Single, never married; ( )Married, with children; ( )Married, without children; ( )Divorced; ( )Widowed

Number of people in my household: ( )1; ( )2; ( )3; ( )4; ( )5 or more

Number of people in my household under 18: ( )1; ( )2; ( )3; ( )4; ( )5 or more

I am ( )a student; ( )employed full-time; ( )employed part-time; ( )not employed at this time; ( )retired; ( )other

I took ( )0; ( )1; ( )2; ( )3; ( )4 or more leisure trips in the past 12 months

My last vacation was ( )a weekend; ( )1 week; ( )2 weeks; ( )3 or more weeks

My last vacation was to ( )the U.S.; ( )Canada; ( )Mexico; ( )Europe; ( )Asia; ( )South America; ( )Central America; ( )the Caribbean; ( )Africa; ( )Middle East; ( )Australia/New Zealand

( )I would; ( )would not buy a Frommer's Travel Guide for business travel

I access the Internet ( )at home; ( )at work; ( )both; ( )I do not use the Internet

I used the Internet to do research for my last trip. ( )Yes; ( )No

I used the Internet to book accommodations or air travel on my last trip. ( )Yes; ( )No

My favorite travel site is ( )frommers.com; ( )travelocity.com; ( )expedia.com;

other _____

I use Frommer's Travel Guides ( )always; ( )sometimes; ( )seldom

I usually buy ( )1; ( )2; ( )more than 2 guides when I travel

Other guides I use include _____

What's the most important thing we could do to improve Frommer's Travel Guides?

_____

_____

_____

_____

Yes, please send me a daily e-mail travel update. My e-mail address is

_____

Mail to: Michael Spring, Publisher and Vice President, Frommer's Travel Guides
909 Third Ave., New York, NY 10022 Fax: 212.884.5432

You can't get any closer to the real Hollywood.

So close, you can feel his breath! At Universal Studios Hollywood, you'll splash through the past or blast into the future...in a boat, on a bike, in a show or in 3D! You'll see what the real Hollywood is all about, and there's plenty of Hollywood magic for even your littlest celebrities. Finish your day with a visit to Universal CityWalk, featuring 65 of L.A.'s hottest restaurants, nightclubs and shops.

UNIVERSAL STUDIOS
HOLLYWOOD

WORLD'S LARGEST MOVIE STUDIO AND THEME PARK